DICTIONARY OF THE POLITICAL THOUGHT OF THE PEOPLE'S REPUBLIC OF CHINA

Dictionary of the Political Thought of the People's Republic of China

中华人民共和国
政治文化用语大典

Henry Yuhuai He

An East Gate Book

M.E.Sharpe
Armonk, New York
London, England

An East Gate Book

Library of Congress Cataloging-in-Publication Data

He, Henry Yuhuai, 1941–
Dictionary of the political thought of the People's Republic of China / Henry Yuhuai He.
p. cm.
ISBN 0-7656-0569-4 (alk. paper)
1. China—Politics and government—1976—Dictionaries. 2. China—Economic conditions—1976—Dictionaries. 3. China—Civilization—1949—Dictionaries. I. Title.

JQ1501.A25 H4 2000
320.951′03—dc21 99-050216

Printed in the United States of America

The paper used in this publication meets the minimum requirements of
American National Standard for Information Sciences
Permanence of Paper for Printed Library Materials,
ANSI Z 39.48-1984.

BM (c) 10 9 8 7 6 5 4 3 2 1

Contents

ACKNOWLEDGEMENTS

While acknowledging full responsibility for my work, which definitely could not be free from shortcomings or mistakes, I would like to thank many people for their generous help: Professor Chen Peng-hsiang, Chair, English Department, Shih Hsin University, Taipei, Taiwan; Dr. Jocelyn Chey, Visiting Professor, Asian Studies, University of Sydney, Australia; Mr. C. C. Chin, Vice Chairman, National Book Development Council of Singapore and Advisor, Singapore Society of Asian Studies, Singapore; Professor Paul Clark, Head, Department of Asian Languages and Literatures, University of Auckland, New Zealand; Dr. Feng Chongyi, Head, China Session, Institute for International Studies, University of Technology, Sydney; Professor Edmund S. K. Fung, Director, Asian Studies, Faculty of Humanities & Social Sciences, University of Western Sydney, Sydney; Mr. Gong Lulin, Sydney Chinese Writers Association; Professor David S. G. Goodman, Director, Institute for International Studies, University of Technology, Sydney; Associate Professor Hans Hendrischke, Head, Department of Chinese and Indonesian, University of New South Wales, Sydney; Dr. Bion T. Hung, President, New Zealand Chinese Cultural Centre and the *Asian Times,* Auckland; Mr. Willing Hwang, President, Sydney Chinese Writers Association; Professor Daniel Kane, Head, Department of Chinese Studies, Macquarie University, Sydney; Dr. Jon Eugene Von Kowallis, Department of Chinese and Indonesian, University of New South Wales, Sydney; Mr. Francis Lee, President, Sydney Ethnic Media Association; Associate Professor Mabel Lee, former Associate Dean, Faculty of Arts, University of Sydney; Ms. Stella Li, President, New Zealand Yiyan Association, Auckland; Dr. Min Lin, Department of East Asian Studies, University of Waikato, Hamilton, New Zealand; Professor Kam Louie, Head, Department of Asian Languages and Studies, University of Queensland, Brisbane, Australia; Mr. K. H. Lun, University of Auckland Library; Ms. Patricia Loo, Assistant Editor, Asian Studies, M. E. Sharpe; Professor Helmut Martin (deceased), former Head, Department of East Asian Studies, Ruhr University, Bochum, Germany; Mr. Doug Merwin, Vice President, M. E. Sharpe; Professor John Minford, former Director, Centre of Translation Studies, Hong Kong Polytechnic University, Hong Kong; Mr. Ng Sai Tung, Vice Secretary-General, International Chinese Poets Pen Club; Ms. Angela Piliouras, Production Editor, M. E. Sharpe; Professor William Tay, Department of Comparative Literature, University of California, San Diego, USA; Professor Fred Teiwes, Department of Government & Public Administration, University of Sydney; Professor Wang Gungwu, Chairman, Institute of East Asian Political Economy, Singapore; Mr. Kenneth X. Wang, New Zealand Zhonghua Association; Professor Wong Tak-wai, Department of Comparative Literature, University of Hong Kong; Mr. Vincent Wong, former President, New Zealand Chinese Writers Association; Professor Wong Yoon Wah, Department of Chinese Studies, National University of Singapore; and Dr. You Ji, School of Political Science, University of New South Wales, Sydney.

INTRODUCTION

It is said that China is too complicated to understand. No doubt, in the case of China, wise heads avoid firm prediction. People still remember that a whole generation of starry-eyed China hands had to apologize for their failure to grasp the dark truth of the Cultural Revolution. There was a similar misunderstanding of the ill-conceived Great Leap Forward of 1958. But it is difficult to avoid talking about the future. Nowadays, China's rise seems to be on everyone's mind. William Overholt's book, *The Rise of China: How Economic Reform Is Creating a New Superpower*, has become a very timely best-seller. U.S. President Clinton also became an adept prophet. In a speech in November 1996, he said that people would agree that one of the five big questions that will determine the shape of the world fifty years from now will surely be: How will the Chinese define their greatness in the twenty-first century? He was of course very careful. In fact, he merely raised another question: "Will they define their greatness in terms of the incredible potential of their people to learn, to produce, to succeed economically, culturally, and politically? Or, will they define their greatness in terms of their ability to dominate their neighbors and others, perhaps against their will, or take other actions which could destabilize the march towards democracy and prosperity of other people?" (*Sydney Morning Herald*, 29 Nov. 1996)

The implications of these questions are not only domestic but international. There is a saying that the twenty-first century will be a Chinese century. It is predicted that China will be the biggest economy in the world before 2020, even if its growth slows from the average of 9 percent since 1979 to 7 percent, as forecast for the years ahead. What is more, following Hong Kong and Macao, Taiwan will be peacefully reunified with the mainland. Against this background the term "Greater China" is used. It is argued that "Greater China" is not simply an abstract concept, it is a rapidly growing cultural and economic reality and is becoming a political one (Samuel P. Huntington, *The Clash of Civilizations and the Remaking of World Order*, NY, Simon & Schuster, 1996, p. 169).

Another term, both conspicuous and controversial, is "Chinese hegemony". According to Samuel Huntington, China's history, culture, traditions, size, economic dynamism, and self-image all impel it to assume a hegemonic position in East Asia. This position will be a natural result of its rapid economic development (ibid., p. 229). Some analysts have compared the emergence of China to the rise of Wilhelmine Germany as the dominant power in Europe in the late nineteenth century, and Lee Kuan Yew observed in 1994 that China is "the biggest player in the history of man". Echoing these observations, Huntington sent out a warning to the world: "If Chinese economic development continues for another decade, as seems possible, and if China maintains its unity during the succession period, as seems probable, East Asian countries and the world will have to respond to the increasingly assertive role of this biggest player in human history" (ibid., p. 231).

These statements may seem exaggerated somewhat, or misleading, or simply untenable. There is no doubt, however, that China is in rapid transition. For a better perspective, one should review the past few decades, during which the country has undergone great turbulence and change. Indeed, it is impossible to ignore such events as these: the 1957 Anti-Rightist Struggle, as a result of which half a million Chinese intellectuals and other persons were persecuted; the 1958 Great Leap Forward, which should be held at least partly responsible for the horrific famine in the early 1960s (possibly the worst in human history); the polemic between the CCP and the CPSU during the 1960s; the Great Proletarian Cultural Revolution (1966-1976), which lasted a long ten years; Mao's death on 9 September 1976 and the ensuing arrest of the so-called Gang of Four; the 1978 short-lived Beijing Spring period; the 1978 Third Plenum of the Eleventh Central Committee of the CCP at which Deng Xiaoping's policy was established; the 1989 pro-democracy movement as a natural end result of the "rampant bourgeois liberalization" in the so-called "new period"; the resignations of Hua Guofeng, Hu Yaobang and Zhao Ziyang from their top Party position in 1981, 1987, and 1989 respectively; the shocking June 4th Incident of 1989; Deng's Southern Tour in early 1992 to reactivate his reform and open door policies; Deng's death on 19 February 1997; Hong Kong's return to China on 1 July of the same year; the establishment of the Jiang Zemin era at the fifteenth CCP National Congress; the exchange of visits between PRC President Jiang Zemin in October 1997 and U.S. President Clinton in June 1998; the 7 May 1999 bombing of the Chinese Embassy in Belgrade and the following upsurge of anti-U.S. sentiment spread throughout the country; Lee Teng-hui raising his "two states" theory on 9 July 1999; and Chen Shui-bian of the Democratic Progressive Party, which is pro-Taiwan independence, was elected Taiwan's tenth president on 18 March 2000. Each of these events and many others not mentioned here helped make China what it is today.

Indisputably, the most outstanding feature of China in the last two decades or so must be the implementation of Deng's policies, which focus on economic construction under the reform and open door program, that is, on building "socialism with Chinese characteristics". Deng's unique efforts can be described in his own words: "Reform is China's second revolution", with a term coined in the West: "Great Leap Outward". He put tremendous changes in motion for the 1.2 billion people; changes from the crushing, dogmatic isolation of Maoism into a quasicapitalist economic miracle. Though now Deng has passed into history, those sympathizing with his policies are still sanguine about the future of the regime.

Within his Party, however, not everyone appreciates the "second revolution". Some CCP figures have attacked it as a reaction to Mao's "first revolution". Among many others who consider the attack ridiculous, some defend Deng, some do not. One may ignore this political debate, but something quite ironic has apparently resulted from the interrelation and interaction of these revolutions. As China critics have said, the Chinese leadership, while insisting that the outside world observe a one-China policy, has split the country into two Chinas at home: it created the first China during thirty years of central planning and the second since the late Deng launched his market reforms.

Deng and his comrades wanted to save the Party by economic reform while maintaining the one-party dictatorship. To the CCP, however, reform is a double-edged sword. The economy in mainland China has undergone reform for so many years that it may be difficult to pull it off the track of "liberalization". Now a problem for the central authorities is the rising influence or even centrifugal force of the provincial economy, which has weakened the central authorities' hold, and will probably continue to do so. Even worse is the universal corruption in the Party. In the official wording, this has become a "life-and-death matter" to the Party and the state. Possibly the outcome will be, as China critics predict: either the destruction of the Party by even worsening corruption or the destruction of the present politico-social system, as the price of successful anticorruption measures.

Deng, a pragmatic patriarch, tended to emphasize the national creation of wealth over both politics and social concerns. Admittedly an economic miracle is taking place, but breakneck growth is socially destabilizing. A direct consequence of this growth is the increasing disparity between the rich and the poor, which is accompanied by rampant money worship, hedonism, widespread corruption, rising crime, and large floating populations of unemployed in big cities. Any serious attempt to rationalize the sprawling state-sector industries, which serve also as mammoth welfare agencies for hundreds of millions, may spark even more instability. Besides, some issues that are often ignored will much affect coming generations: waste of natural resources, ecological imbalance, and environmental pollution.

To the current CCP leadership with Jiang Zemin as its core, now is the crucial time to solve the many hard-to-tackle issues accumulated during the years of reform. The host of challenges range from consolidating their political positions to meeting the ever-expanding needs of a rapidly changing nation. These needs include not only material and cultural life but also political rights. Like Deng, Jiang emphasizes that China's political reform (that is, democratization) must be instituted under the strong leadership of the CCP. No challenge to the Party's monopoly on political power is to be tolerated. Yet, China critics maintain that democracy is not simply a dead destination; first of all it is a live process. The odds against achieving full modernization without losing political control are daunting. Logically, then, the more the Party wins in its reform drive, the more it loses in maintaining its power. How Jiang and his colleagues deal with these challenges will certainly be interesting to watch.

With a broader historico-philosophical perspective, one would also ask this question: Whither Chinese culture (essentially, whither China)? The difficulty of this question is that in mainland China today three major cultures—traditional Chinese culture, Marxist-Leninist culture (or revolutionary culture), and modern Western culture—coexist, coalesce, and clash. In the early 1980s, humanism (or Marxist humanism) and the theory of socialist alienation were once very popular. Then there was the ideological trend of Westernization, to go with the anti-tradition sentiment. During the 1990s, neo-conservatism replaced the radicalism of the 1980s. Various doctrines, such as nationalism, neo-Confucianism, neo-Maoism, and liberalism, strongly expressed themselves. Today, officially, Marxism is still the guiding ideology of the CCP, but it has been reinterpreted with Deng Xiaoping Theory as the reference frame. When discussing issues like globalization, modernization, freedom, democracy, the market economy, and social justice, people try to find answers with a much wider perspective. One can also find that it is modernization that constitutes a real threat to tradition. The old Chinese civilization is now being pounded by many new phenomena emerging with reform, such as commodity economy, marketing consciousness, and the trend toward commercial activities. A subtle but profound change has taken place in the way people think, in their sense of value, and in the economy, culture, and social life at large. This is clear: the multiplicity of economic sectors is bringing about the multiplicity of politics and culture. This, however, has not answered the whole question. Indeed, no matter what kind of attitude or opinion one has about China, its culture, and its politico-social system, one must find that there are too many Chinese puzzles, deriving mostly from the need to reconcile the conflict between its ancient cultural tradition and its modern politics.

It is against this background that this book has been written and compiled. There are about 2,200 entries. Each of the majority of the entries occupies about half a page. Key terms and theses need several pages each. Presented in the order of the Chinese phonetic alphabet (hanyu pinyin), each entry consists of four parts: (a) the term or thesis written in its original Chinese characters; (b) the term or thesis written in its Chinese phonetic alphabet; (c) an English translation; and (d) an explanation or discussion in English. This is not a monograph discussing a single subject in the usual systematic and comprehensive way. As shown by its title, it is a reference book of PRC political thought since its founding fifty years ago, especially since the downfall of the Gang of Four in 1976, up to the present. A large number of terms and theses emerged throughout the period as part of Chinese political and cultural life (many of them came from the CCP lexicon). Those most important and most commonly used have been collected in this book. Occasionally, a description of an event is presented. Some entries are literary or politico-literary. In view of the long Chinese tradition of literature as a vehicle for conveying principles, this is understandable. It occurred to the author that knowledge of these terms, theses, and events expresses a specific aspect of contemporary Chinese issues.

One characteristic of this book is its collection not only of terms but also of theses. They are explained in the context of how they were first used and have been treated in the course of time. Each entry provides a specific message, as succinctly and clearly as possible. Another characteristic, perhaps more attractive, is the huge academic potentials contained in many of the entries, which those interested could develop in their own studies. Some items may be controversial, though the author intends to provide a true historical picture. It is hoped that this book, up to date and complete, could become something like a first-aid kit for those who come across an unfamiliar term or thesis. It could also be general reading for those who wish to better understand contemporary Chinese cultural, academic, and political issues and to form a basis for judging a country with an area of 9.8 million square kilometers and a population of one-fifth of mankind, a country with the world's biggest momentum of economic development and a deeply held cultural conviction that it must regain its ranking in world history.

ABBREVIATIONS

ACF	All-China Federation of Literary and Art Circles
BR	Beijing Review, Beijing
CASS	Chinese Academy of Social Sciences
CCP	Chinese Communist Party
CL	Chinese Literature, Beijing
CMC	Central Military Commission
CPPCC	Chinese People's Political Consultative Conference
CPSU	Communist Party of Soviet Union
CWA	Chinese Writers Association
DD	Dangdai (Contemporary, Beijing)
DS	Dushu (Reading, Beijing)
FLP	Foreign Languages Press, Beijing
FLW	Fang Lizhi, Liu Binyan, Wang Ruowang Yanlun Zhaibian (Excerpts from Remarks of Fang Lizhi, Liu Binyan and Wang Ruowang; Hong Kong, Shuguang Tushu, 1988)
GMRB	Guangming Ribao (Guangming Daily, Beijing)
GPCR	Great Proletarian Cultural Revolution
HKSAR	Hong Kong Special Administrative Region
HQ	Hongqi (Red Flag, Beijing)
JFJB	Jiefangjun Bao (Liberation Army Daily, Beijing)
JFRB	Jiefang Ribao (Liberation Daily, Shanghai)
JN	Jiushi Niandai (The Nineties, Hong Kong)
KMT	Kuomintang
LBY	Liu Binyan Lun Wenxue Yu Shenghuo (Wu Jishi, ed., Liu
Binyan	on Literature and Life; Beijing, Renmin Wenxue, 1985)
MZXJ	Mao Zedong Xuanji (Selected Works of Mao Zedong; 1, 2, 3, 4, & 5; Beijing, Renmin, 1951, 1952, 1953, 1960, & 1977)
NPC	Chinese National People's Congress
PCC	Party Central Committee (the Central Committee of the CCP)
PLA	People's Liberation Army
PRC	People's Republic of China
QN	Qishi Niandai (The Seventies, Hong Kong)
RMRB	Renmin Ribao (People's Daily, Beijing)
RMRB, HWB	Renmin Ribao, Haiwaiban (People's Daily, Overseas Edition, Beijing)
RMWX	Renmin Wenxue (People's Literature, Beijing)
SHWX	Shanghai Wenxue (Shanghai Literature, Shanghai)
SK	Shikan (Poetry, Beijing)
SWD	Selected Works of Deng Xiaoping, 1975-1982 (Beijing, FLP, 1984)
SWM	Selected Works of Mao Zedong (Beijing, FLP; 1-3, 1965; 4, 1961)
SY	Shiyue (October, Beijing)
WHB	Wenhui Bao (Wenhui Daily, Shanghai)

WRB	Wei Rendaozhuyi Bianhu (Wang Ruoshui, In Defence of Humanism; Beijing, Sanlian, 1986)
WXPL	Wenxue Pinglun (Literary Review, Beijing)
WXZTX	Dangqian Wenxue Zhutixing Wenti Lunzheng (He Huoren, ed., The Current Debate over Problems Concerning the Subjectivity of Literature; Fuzhou, Haixia Wenyi, 1986)
WYB	Wenyi Bao (Literary Gazette, Beijing)
WYLZJ	Wenyi Lunzheng Ji, 1979-1983 (Shen Taihui, Chen Quanrong, and Yang Zhijie, eds., Essays of Literary Debates; Zhengzhou, Huanghe Wenyi, 1985)
XHWZ	Xinhua Wenzhai (New China Literary Digest, Beijing)
XHYB, WZB	Xinhua Yuebao, Wenzhaiban (New China Monthly, Literary Supplement, Beijing)
XWX	Zhongguo Xinwenxue Daxi, 1927-1937 (Ding Jingtang et al., eds., Anthology of Modern Chinese Literature, 1927-1937; Shanghai, Shanghai Wenyi, 1986)
XWY	Zhongguo Xinwenyi Daxi, 1976-1982 (Chen Huangmei et al., eds., Anthology of Modern Chinese Literature and Art, 1976-1982; Beijing, Zhongguo Wenlian, 1985-1987)
XXWY	Zhongguo Xin Xieshizhuyi Wenyi Zuopin Xuan (Bi Hua and Yang Ling, eds., Selected Works of China's New Realism, v. 1, etc.; Hong Kong, Dangdai Wenxue Yanjiushe, 1980, etc.)

DICTIONARY OF THE POLITICAL THOUGHT OF THE PEOPLE'S REPUBLIC OF CHINA

爱国统一战线
aiguo tongyi zhanxian
(patriotic united front)

See "tongzhan" (united front).

爱国主义
aiguozhuyi
(patriotism)

According to Mao Zedong (1893-1976), the two kinds of patriotism are "parochial patriotism" (xia'ai aiguozhuyi) and "proletarian patriotism" (wuchanjieji aiguozhuyi). The CCP upholds proletarian patriotism, which is synonymous with "proletarian internationalism" (wuchanjieji guojizhuyi) or its concrete embodiment; hence, a "unity of patriotism and internationalism" (aiguozhuyi yu guojizhuyide tongyi)—Communists are at once internationalists and patriots. The specific content of patriotism, Mao said, is determined by historical conditions. Thus, during wars of national liberation patriotism is "applied internationalism" (*SWM*, 2, p. 196). In recent years, the two terms, proletarian internationalism and proletarian patriotism, have almost disappeared in official documents. According to the CCP, however, patriotism is still a cardinal virtue. It is even used in reference to secret societies. In 1992, Public Security Minister Tao Siju (b. 1935) is believed to have met with leaders of the Sun Yee On, Hong Kong's—and perhaps the world's—most powerful triad, in Beijing. Tao echoed a famous remark attributed some years ago to the paramount leader Deng Xiaoping (1904-1997): "There are patriots even among the triads."

In China's recent political education drives, patriotism has been a central theme; for example, during the 6th Plenum of the 14th PCC held in Beijing from 7 to 10 October 1996. In his closing speech to the Plenum, CCP General Secretary Jiang Zemin (b. 1926) emphasized the need for patriotic education (aiguozhuyi jiaoyu) for the building of a "spiritual civilization" (jingshen wenming). According to Jiang, such an education must be stressed throughout the entire process of socialist modernization. The Party should beware of the reappearance of what he called the remnant dregs of a "colonial culture" (zhimin wenhua).

Accordingly, the Plenum adopted a seven-part "Decision of the PCC Regarding Important Issues on Promoting Socialist Ethical and Cultural Progress". It acknowledged that ideological education and ethical and cultural progress had been neglected by the leadership in some sectors, resulting in serious problems. The Plenum called for the cultivation of "socialist citizens" with lofty ideals, moral integrity, good education, and a strong sense of discipline ("siyou": you lixiang, you daode, you jiaoyu, you jilü, as first formulated at the CCP's 12th National Congress in 1982). Efforts should be intensified to strike a balance between material and spiritual progress. Patriotic education must be resolutely carried out, in a deep and protracted way. The purpose is to help the people see "the truth that only socialism can save and develop China", and to foster a national spirit of "self-esteem, self-confidence, and self-reliance" (zizun, zixin, zizhu), whereby devotion to building and defending the socialist motherland is the greatest glory, and damage to national interests and dignity is the greatest shame.

The patriotic education movement drew reproach from some people in the West, including, for example, James Lilley, former U.S. ambassador to China. Since the appeal of communism no longer exists in China, Lilley wrote in an article in the *New York Times*, xenophobia is being fomented to fill the vacuum, thus diverting public attention from the regional decentralization and income disparities. The logic at work here was seen by the Chinese authorities as much the same as that invoked by the "China threat" theory (Zhongguo weixie lun). The authorities tried to elucidate what they called the "unity of patriotism and socialism" (aiguozhuyi yu shehuizhuyide tongyi) and the essential difference between the patriotism that they meant to uphold and the "parochial nationalism" (xia'ai minzuzhuyi) or, even worse, the xenophobia, that they were accused of upholding. See also "wujiang, simei, sanre'ai" (five stresses, four points of beauty, and three loves), "minzuzhuyi" (nationalism), "shijie geming" (world revolution), and "Zhongguo keyi shuo bu" (China can say no).

爱国主义教育
aiguozhuyi jiaoyu
(patriotic education)

See "aiguozhuyi" (patriotism).

爱国主义与国际主义的统一
aiguozhuyi yu guojizhuyide tongyi
(unity of patriotism and internationalism)

See "aiguozhuyi" (patriotism).

爱国主义与社会主义的统一
aiguozhuyi yu shehuizhuyide tongyi
(unity of patriotism and socialism)

See "aiguozhuyi" (patriotism).

爱情至上
aiqing zhishang
(love is supreme)

During the "seventeen years" (from the founding of the PRC in 1949 to the start of the GPCR in 1966), because of the repeated attacks on humanism, all heroes and heroines in literature did not seem to care about personal happiness, and they were merely tools of class struggle. A writer of love stories could be charged with preaching the belief that "love is supreme". During the first large-scale criticism of humanism (1957-1960), works about love produced in the latter half of 1956 and the first half of 1957, known as the "hundred flowers" period (baihua shiqi), were invariably subjected to criticism. For instance, Deng Youmei's "On the Precipice" ("Zai xuanya shang", *Wenxue yuekan,* Sept. 1956; reprinted in *Wenyi xuexi,* 1:29-39, 1957, and *Deng Youmei Duanpian Xiaoshuo Xuan—Selected Short Stories of Deng Youmei,* Beijing, Beijing, 1981, pp. 197-236), one of the first love stories about intellectuals to be published since the founding of the PRC, was accused of being in bad taste for describing a kind of love that stands "on the precipice".

During the GPCR the charge of "love is supreme" was less common because it was too weak. A more serious label—"decadent bourgeois outlook on life"—took its place. After the GPCR the label was referred to even less frequently, but for the opposite reason: "love" had re-found a place in life. See also "renxing lun" (theory of human nature).

安定团结
anding tuanjie
(stability and unity)

In a 1974 directive, Mao Zedong asked for "stability and unity" in the Party and the country. He hoped that with his authority he could bring about an end to the long-drawn-out and devastating inner-Party strife and chaos that existed everywhere in the society.

However, less than two years later a fierce political struggle erupted over this directive. Deng Xiaoping, having returned to power as CCP vice-chairman and PRC first vice-premier, was a central figure in this struggle. Eventually, Deng was overthrown once again in Mao's last campaign of his life, a campaign called "criticize Deng Xiaoping and counter the Right deviationist trend to reverse correct verdicts". In the 1976 New Year's Day joint editorial in the *People's Daily*, *Red Flag*, and the *Liberation Army Daily*, a new directive by Mao was issued: "Stability and unity does not mean giving up class struggle. Class struggle is the key link, and everything else hinges on it" *(RMRB,* 1 Jan. 1976).

In July 1977, at the 3rd Plenum of the 10th PCC, Deng was restored to all his former posts. And, at the December 1978 3rd Plenum of the 11th PCC, Deng's rehabilitation was formally announced. In fact, at that time Deng became the paramount leader of the CCP. As to the concept of "stability and unity", it is always invoked by the CCP leadership, and is considered to be the underlying premise for carrying out all Party tasks, particularly, the program of the "four modernizations" (si ge xiandaihua). In 1989, Deng announced a new slogan: "The need for stability overwhelms everything else" (wending yadao yiqie). See also "pi Deng, fanji youqing fan'anfeng" (campaign to criticize Deng Xiaoping and counter the Right deviationist trend to reverse correct verdicts) and "wending yadao yiqie" (the need for stability overwhelms everything else).

安定团结不是不要阶级斗争
anding tuanjie bushi buyao jieji douzheng
(stability and unity is not to give up class struggle)

See "anding tuanjie" (stability and unity), and "pi Deng, fanji youqing fan'anfeng" (campaign to criticize Deng Xiaoping and counter the Right deviationist trend to reverse correct verdicts).

安全系数
anquan xishu
(safety coefficient)

During the Mao period, the role of literature and art was often exaggerated to an absurd degree. Consequently, writers had to keep in mind the "safety coefficient" when writing, fearing that they would be held responsible if their works were to be accused of causing any bad social effects. Even after Mao's death, such fear lingered, because the painful memories of the past were still fresh in their minds. For instance, because the three scripts criticized at the 1980 Script Writing Forum all tried to tackle current social problems, when they were later banned, authors of similar works began to panic. After the Forum, in fact, few playwrights dared to write about similar subject matters and many turned to subjects with greater "safety coefficients". As a result, much of the drama lacked poignancy and involvement in life—essential characteristics of the genre.

Besides "lingering fears" (yuji), there were also "premonitions" (yuji) in the depths of writers and artists' hearts. They had a panic psychology of "doubtful prognosis" (yuhoubuliang). This was the case when in 1980 Zhong Dianfei, a well-known film critic and director, wanted to film "A Woman Thief" (Nü zei), one of the three scripts criticized at the 1980 Script Writing Forum. In his opinion, there was a certain "plasticity" in the script. The crux of the matter was how the director handled the story. He knew that the filming might be a very difficult and even a dangerous job, but it seemed to him to be an interesting and unprecedented opportunity. To his disappointment, the script was finally rejected. Both he and the author of the script were hurt. They were victims of some people's panic psychology of "doubtful prognosis". As Zhong said, this was a unique psychological attitude that had existed in China for thirty years (Zhong Dianfei, "Lun ruhe shiji duidai xianshizhuyide pianpo he buzu"—"How to Treat *A Woman Thief*", *WYB*, 8, 1980, extracted and reprinted in *XHYB, WZB*, 11:151, 1980).

The three scripts criticized at the 1980 Script Writing Forum were: "What If I Really Were" (Sha Yexin, Li Shoucheng, and Yao Mingde, "Jiaru wo shi zhende", also entitled "Pianzi"—"Impostor", in the special issue of *Xiju yishu* and *Shanghai xiju*, 1979, trans. in Perry Link, ed., *Stubborn Weeds: Popular and Controversial Chinese Literature after the Cultural Revolution,* Bloomington, Indiana University Press, 1983, pp. 198-250; in Lee Yee, ed., *The New Realism: Writings from China after the Cultural Revolution,* N.Y., Hippocrene Books, 1983, pp. 261-322; and in *Renditions*, 19 & 20:333-69, Spring & Autumn 1983, with an introduction by Geremie Barmé, pp. 319-32); "In the Unwritten Records" (Wang Jing, "Zai shehuide dang'an li", in *Wotu,* 2:19-59, 1979, reprinted in *Dianying chuangzuo,* 10:22-43, 1979; trans. in Lee Yee, ed., *The New Realism,* pp. 102-41), and "A Woman Thief" (Li Kewei, "Nü zei", in *Dianying chuangzuo,* 11, 1979). See also "shehui xiaoguo lun" (social effect theory).

"鞍钢宪法"
"An'gang xianfa"
("Charter of the Anshan Iron and Steel Company")

The Anshan Iron and Steel Company is a large state-run enterprise in Anshan city, Liaoning province. The "Charter of the Anshan Iron and Steel Company" was originally a written comment by Mao on 22 March 1960 on a report presented by the Anshan City CCP Committee about current technical innovation and revolution in industry. Later regarded as the "basic principle for running socialist enterprises", it consisted of five key points: 1. keep politics firmly in command, 2. strengthen Party leadership, 3. launch vigorous mass movements, 4. practice "two participations, one change, and three combinations" ("liang can yi gai san jiehe", that is, workers participate in management while cadres participate in labor; reform irrational and outdated rules and regulations; and maintain close cooperation among cadres, workers, and technicians), and 5. go all out with technical reform.

The "Charter of the Anshan Iron and Steel Company", having been forgotten for almost two decades, reappeared favorably, in discussions in the 1990s, by those dubbed "neo-Leftists" (xinzuopai) or "neo-Maoists" (xin Mao Zedong zhuyizhe), such as Cui Zhiyuan, a Chinese scholar now teaching in America. Interpreted in light of neo-Marxism, the "Charter" was seen by Cui to be a Chinese version of post-Fordism that advocated economic democracy (Cui Zhiyuan, "An'gang xianfa yu hou Futezhuyi"—"The Charter of the Anshan Iron and Steel Company and post-Fordism", *Zhongguo yu shijie*, Jan. 1997). According to this school, which emerged in the 1990s, only the legacy of Mao can save China. See also "xinzuopai" (neo-Leftists) and "jingji gaige" (economic reform).

按既定方针办
an jiding fangzhen ban
(act according to principles laid down)

"Act according to principles laid down" was first made public as Mao Zedong's deathbed instruction in "Chairman Mao Will Live in Our Hearts Forever" ("Mao zhuxi yongyuan huo zai women xinzhong"), a joint editorial in the *People's Daily, Red Flag,* and the *Liberation Army Daily* on 16 September 1976. Reportedly, Mao did utter these several words to Zhang Chunqiao, then a member of the PCC Politburo Standing Committee, on 5 September 1976, four days before his death. Obviously, with the publication of this instruction, those later known as the "Gang of Four" (sirenbang)—Jiang Qing (1913-1991), Zhang Chunqiao (b. 1917), Wang Hongwen (1935-1992), and Yao Wenyuan (b. 1931)—were posed to be Mao's orthodox successors.

For Hua Guofeng (b. 1921), then CCP first vice-chairman and PRC premier, this was a signal that the Gang of Four was attempting to seize from him supreme Party and state power. Hua counterattacked on 2 October, when he deleted this instruction from the text of a speech Foreign Minister Qiao Guanhua was to deliver at the General Assembly of the United Nations. "Act according to principles laid down", Hua pointed out, was a corrupted alteration of "follow the principles of the past" (zhao guoqu fangzhen ban), one of the three instructions Mao had written for him on 30 April 1976.

Two days later, the Gang published an article entitled "Forever Act According to Principles Laid Down" (Liang Xiao, "Yongyuan an jiding fangzhen ban", *GMRB*, 4 Oct. 1976), which claimed: "Distorting the principles laid down by Chairman Mao means betraying Marxism, socialism, and the great doctrine of continuing the revolution under the dictatorship of the proletariat". It also stated: "Any revisionist chieftain who dares to distort the principles laid down by Chairman Mao will definitely come to no good end." This was nothing less than a mobilization order to usurp power. Realizing this, Hua decided to act. On 6 October 1976, with the help of Ye Jianying (1897-1986), CCP vice-chairman, Wang Dongxing (b. 1916), CCP Politburo member, and Li Xiannian (1909-1992), CCP Politburo member and PRC vice-premier, Hua had the Gang of Four arrested in the name of the PCC Politburo.

Several years later, when Hua's own position was declining, the authorities attached less importance to this event. Deng Xiaoping simply attributed it to Hua's alleged "two-whatevers" mistakes. In a talk with leading figures of the PCC (on 27 June 1980), Deng said: "According to the 'two-whatevers' viewpoint, we should adhere, without the slightest change, to Comrade Mao's erroneous views in his later years. The slogan 'Act according to principles laid down' meant to act in accordance with the erroneous principles Comrade Mao laid down in the evening of his life" (*SWD*, p. 283). See also "sirenbang" (Gang of Four), "liang ge fanshi" (two-whatevers), and "yingming lingxiu" (wise leader).

八德八念
bade banian
(eight virtues and eight calls)

See "Kylin wenhua" (Kylin Culture).

八九民运
bajiu minyun
(1989 pro-democracy movement)

The 1989 pro-democracy movement is an important and controversial event in contemporary China. It proceeded as follows:

With the failure of price reform in the summer of 1988, a series of problems, such as the return of a high birth rate, cultural and educational crises, agricultural collapse, and industrial imbalance, became conspicuous. The economic reform slowed down, and in some fields there were reversals. A number of reformists inside and outside the CCP lost their power or influence, and political reform was much less likely. Such an unprecedented setback was strongly felt throughout the country. At the same time, corruption in CCP organizations and government departments became more and more serious. Social inequalities led to resentment among the people, and complaints were widespread. A cloud of depression and loss loomed over the country.

A number of intellectuals and others who were worried about the future of the reform, tried to find a way to solve these problems. Some of these people felt it was vital to promote freedom and democracy. Under their influence and participation, a pro-democracy movement erupted in the first half of 1989, for the first time in the history of contemporary China. During the first stage of the movement, a number of open letters appealed to the CCP authorities. On 6 January 1989, Fang Lizhi, a leading astrophysicist, wrote an open letter to Deng Xiaoping, proposing that Wei Jingsheng and other political prisoners be released in a general amnesty. Following Fang's letter, on 13 February 1989, an open letter signed by 33 intellectuals within China was sent to the NPC Standing Committee and the PCC. This was the first time that Chinese intellectuals under the Communist régime had taken direct and joint action after so many years of persecution.

Thereafter, there was a wave of appeals. Hundreds of Chinese scholars, writers, artists, and students abroad also participated. There was also international support.

The second stage began with Hu Yaobang's death and ended with the "May Tempest" (wuyue fengbao). During this stage, students demonstrated in Tiananmen Square, calling for democratization and an end to corruption.

On 15 April, Hu Yaobang, the disgraced former CCP general secretary, died. The unexpected death intensified the situation. After 17 April, the largest student demonstrations to occur since 1976 took place in Tiananmen Square.

On the evening of 21 April, about sixty thousand students, at an all-night peaceful sit-in in Tiananmen Square, mourned Hu Yaobang's death. Hu was highly praised as "the soul of China".

On 23 April, the "Autonomous Alliance of Beijing Students of Higher Education" (Gaozilian) was established.

On 24 April, the PCC Politburo held a meeting, during which Li Ximing and Chen Xitong, two Beijing Party leaders, presented a report about the current situation. On 26 April, a *People's Daily* editorial alleged that the student movement was a "turmoil" (dongluan) and should be opposed with "a clear-cut stand". This provoked a series of further protests.

On 4 May, taking advantage of the annual meeting of the Asian Development Bank, Zhao Ziyang (b.1919), CCP general secretary, let it be known that he felt that the problem in the Tiananmen Square should be solved "on the track of democracy and legality". However, his opinion was not heeded.

On the same day, over five hundred editors and reporters from Beijing media circles took to the streets, shouting that they wanted to speak the truth.

On 13 May, students from institutions of higher education in Beijing began a hunger strike. By 16 May, the protests had spread all over the country, involving people from all walks of life.

On 16 May, Beijing intellectuals issued the "Statement of 16 May", strongly protesting the CCP leadership's characterization of the student patriotic movement as a "turmoil".

On the afternoon of 16 May, when Mikhail Gorbachev, general secretary of the CPSU, was visiting China, Zhao Ziyang told his guest that the 1st Plenum of the 13th PCC had resolved that Deng Xiaoping would be at the helm for any problems of vital importance.

A turning point occurred on 17 May. In the early hours, Zhao Ziyang, on behalf of the PCC Politburo Standing Committee, made public a written statement in which he confirmed the students' patriotic enthusiasm and appealed to them to stop their hunger strike. But the students, a number of whom seemed to be not so reasonable and to be out of control, rejected Zhao's appeal. In the afternoon, a meeting was held at Deng Xiaoping's home, where Yao Yilin (b. 1917), member of the PCC Politburo Standing Committee, and Li Peng (b. 1928), PRC premier, favored enforcing martial law.

During the day, more than one million Beijing people took to the streets in support of the hunger-striking students. As a follow-up to the "Statement of 16 May", Yan Jiaqi, Bao Zunxin, Xu Gang, and ten other intellectuals issued a "Manifesto of 17 May". It asserted that the recent development of events fully revealed China's problems, which were caused by the fact that, as a result of unlimited power being held in the hands of a dictator, the Chinese government had lost all feeling of humanity and all sense of responsibility. The manifesto proclaimed that it was already seventy-six years since the fall of the Qing dynasty, and yet China was still ruled by an emperor, even though he did not bear that title, a dictator who was long past his time. It announced that the Chinese people could not wait any longer for a dictator to admit his mistakes. There was no other choice but to overthrow China's last emperor Deng Xiaoping and give a final burial to the emperor system in China.

In the early morning of 19 May, Zhao Ziyang appeared in Tiananmen Square, making a last effort to urge the students to stop the hunger strike. As before, the students refused to retreat.

In the evening, in Zhao's absence, Li Peng delivered a stern speech to a large meeting of high-ranking cadres in Beijing, in which he asserted that a "turmoil" had been taking place in Beijing and that he was about to take vigorous measures to bring it to an end. Then, on the next morning, the State Council promulgated a decree proclaiming that, as of ten o'clock on that date, martial law was to be put into effect in a number of major districts of Beijing. A bloodbath was in the making—this marked the beginning of the third stage.

Quite unexpectedly to the authorities, people still stood firm at this dangerous time. On 23 May, Beijing intellectuals and cadres in government posts carried out the most massive demonstrations to occur in Beijing since the imposition of martial law. About one million people marched in the streets. Massive demonstrations also took place in Shanghai, Chengdu, Guizhou, Guangzhou, Hong Kong, and other cities. On the next day, the Association of Beijing Academic Circles was established. In its "Statement to All Chinese Countrymen", it called on all Chinese people to take action to save their country. Its six demands included the lifting of martial law and the dismissal of Li Peng.

On the evening of 3 June, the "University of Democracy" was founded in Tiananmen Square. Yan Jiaqi, director of the Politics Institute, CASS, was appointed honorary president. In his speech at the opening ceremony, Yan talked about democracy, freedom, rule of law, human rights, and the possibility that people would build democracy with their blood and life. While people were listening to his speech, more and more troops were entering the city. Under strict orders issued by the CCP hardliners, the army began its slaughter. The "Beijing Massacre" ("Beijing can'an", also called the "Tiananmen Massacre"—"Tiananmen can'an"), during which several hundred people lost their lives, took place on 4 June. The brutality shocked the entire world.

Thereafter, a number of student leaders, and the so-called "black hands" (heishou), were arrested. Others succeeded in fleeing abroad. The movement was thus suppressed with the use of guns and tanks.

On 9 June 1989, Deng Xiaoping, the only person who had the power to order the PLA to shoot student demonstrators, reappeared, receiving cadres of army level and above from the Beijing martial law troops. Deng congratulated them for "quelling a counter-revolutionary rebellion". Referring to the "rebellion", Deng said: "The storm was bound to break out sooner or later. This was a matter that had been determined by the international macro-climate and the micro-climate in China. It was bound to happen and was independent of man's will" ("Deng Xiaoping liuyue jiuri dui Beijing jieyan budui jun yishang ganbude jianghua"—"Deng Xiaoping's 9 June Speech to Cadres of Army Level and Above from the Beijing Martial Law Troops", *RMRB*, *HWB*, 28 June 1989).

At the 4th Plenum of the 13th PCC, which was concluded on 24 June 1989, Li Peng's report on Zhao Ziyang's "mistakes during the anti-Party and anti-socialist agitation" was approved. Zhao was said to have made grave errors in supporting the 1989 "turmoil" and in his attempts to split the Party, while "the Party and the nation were at a life and death juncture" ("Communiqué of the 4th Plenum of the 13th PCC", *RMRB, HWB*, 25 June 1989).

In his report on the "June 4th counter-revolutionary rebellion" (liusi fan'geming baoluan) presented to the NPC in July 1989, Chen Xitong emphasized that "political forces in the West" had supported the student demonstrators as part of a larger strategy to make China give up the socialist road. The PLA's suppression was thus justified. The justification was later further strengthened by the fact that within two years all Marxist-Leninist parties in the East European bloc and the Soviet Union were actually overthrown. The CCP claimed that a similar fate would have befallen itself and China would have been in a chaotic, disastrous state were it not for Deng's wise and resolute decision to end the rebellion.

The brand of "June 4th counter-revolutionary rebellion" stood conspicuously for a few years. When meeting Dr. Mahathir, the visiting Malaysian prime minister on 12 May 1994, Jiang Zemin used the phrase "the June 4th political disturbance" (liusi zhengzhi fengbo) to describe the incident for the first time. Since then, the terms "the June 4th political disturbance" or "the June 4th disturbance" (liusi fengbo) have been officially used, obviously with a political implication. But up to the present, more than ten years since the movement, the official verdict has not been overturned, though official policy seems more low-keyed. It is hoped by the authorities that the current economic boom will make ordinary people forget the brutality. Some analysts, particularly in the Western business community, believe that the Chinese government acted wisely to avoid chaos. Moreover, they believe that this "historical episode" should be laid to rest now that Wang Dan, the No. 1 student leader of the 1989 movement, has been released and sent into exile to the U.S. (on 19 April 1998).

Many Chinese, however, find it hard to forget the event, which they call the "June 4th massacre" (liusi can'an), "Beijing massacre" (Beijing can'an), or "Tiananmen massacre" (Tiananmen can'an), because on that day several hundred people were killed. They insist on pressuring for a reversal of the official verdict. As many forcefully argue, Deng's statement about the 1976 Tiananmen incident can also well be applied to the 1989 incident—Deng said on 19 September 1977: "In view of the very large numbers of people involved in the Tiananmen Incident, it definitely cannot be labeled counter-revolutionary" ("Setting Things Right in Education", *SWD*, p. 80). It is hoped that the movement participants will be hailed as patriots who sought to improve their country and who will become a crucial political force in the post-Deng era (Deng hou shidai). Cases in point are, for instance, the alleged letter of 12 September 1997 by Zhao Ziyang to the CCP 15th National Congress, or the document of 15 May 1999 signed by 105 family members of victims of the massacre, calling for a criminal inquiry into Li Peng's actions. Indeed, there are people, both at home and abroad, who are waiting, and preparing, for the day when a reversal of the verdict is made. What is called a "June 4th complex" (liusi qingjie) continues to exist.

Because of the 1989 pro-democracy movement and the following suppression with guns and tanks on 4 June, Tiananmen of Beijing is very well-known in the world. In America, the word Tiananmen symbolizes an amalgamation of Chinese human-rights violations, including the continued detention of dissidents and the subjugation of Tibet. "The image of China that is frozen in the American consciousness," said Robert Manning, Asia fellow at the Council on Foreign Relations in Washington, "is that of a lone man standing in front of a tank" (*Far Eastern Economic Review*, 30 Oct. 1997, p. 25).

The American obsession with Tiananmen often frustrates Chinese officials. This can be seen during Jiang Zemin's October 1997 state visit to the U.S. To the surprise of many, the Chinese president's press conference with U.S. President Bill Clinton devolved into an odd public debate. After Jiang defended his government's 1989 actions, Clinton countered: "On this issue, we believe the policy of the government is on the wrong side of history." As international observers agree, this was the most blunt criticism any world leader standing with Jiang had publicly made. See also "siwu yundong" (April 5th Movement), "ziyouhua" (liberalization), "fan fubai" (anti-corruption), and "zhengzhi gaige" (political reform).

八十年代三件大事
bashiniandai sanjian dashi
(three major tasks for the 1980s)

On 16 January 1980, in a speech (entitled "The Present Situation and the Tasks before Us"—"Muqiande xingshi he renwu"; trans. in *SWD*, pp. 224-58) delivered on behalf of the PCC at a high-ranking cadre meeting, Deng Xiaoping listed three major tasks for the 1980s: 1. to oppose hegemonism and to safeguard world peace in dealing with international affairs; 2. to accomplish the return of Taiwan to China and the reunification of the country; and 3. to speed up the building of the "four modernizations", which should be core of the three tasks. Apparently, at that time Deng did not fully understand the complexity of the Taiwan issue. See also "shijie geming" (world revolution), "Taiwan wenti" (Taiwan issue), and "si ge xiandaihua" (four modernizations).

八亿人民八出戏
bayi renmin ba chu xi
(eight dramas for 800 million people)

See "wen'ge wenyi" (GPCR literature and art).

巴黎公社
Bali gongshe
(Paris Commune)

See "daminzhu" (extensive democracy) and "yiyue geming" (January Revolution).

拔白旗，插红旗
ba baiqi, cha hongqi
(pull up the white flag and hoist the red flag)

See "dayuejin" (Great Leap Forward).

把党的工作重心转移到四个现代化上
ba angde gongzuo zhongxin zhuanyidao "si ge xiandaihua" shang
(shift the focus of all Party work to the "four modernizations")

See "si ge xiandaihua" (four modernizations).

把方便让给别人，把困难留给自己
ba fangbian ranggei bieren, ba kunnan liugei ziji
(take difficulties on oneself and make things easy for others)

This was said to be a slogan raised by the workers of the Daqing oil enterprise in the early 1960s. See "gongye xue Daqing" (in industry, learn from Daqing).

把关
baguan
(guard a pass)

Originally an old military tactical term, "baguan" is now used to mean to "check on". Hence the following phrases: "cengceng baguan"—to make checks at all levels;

"bahao zhengzhi guan"—to ensure political soundness; and "bahao zhiliang guan"—to guarantee the quality (of products). Furthermore, "baguan" can mean to "have the final say" or to "be at the helm" (baduo). A famous example of the later is found in the resolution at the 1st Plenum of the 13th PCC—Deng Xiaoping would be at the helm and have the final say in case any problems of vital importance were to erupt.

霸权主义
baquanzhuyi
(hegemonism)

See "shijie geming zhongxin" (center of world revolution), "bashiniandai sanjian dashi" (three major tasks for the 1980s), and "minzuzhuyi" (nationalism).

百花齐放，百家争鸣
baihuaqifang, baijiazhengming
(let a hundred flowers bloom and a hundred schools of thought contend)

See "shuangbai fangzhen" (Double Hundred policy).

百花齐放，推陈出新
baihuaqifang, tuichenchuxin
(let a hundred flowers bloom and weed through the old to bring forth the new)

See "tuichenchuxin" (weeding through the old to bring forth the new) and "shuangbai fangzhen" (Double Hundred policy).

百花时期
baihua shiqi
("hundred flowers" period)

See "shuangbai fangzhen" (Double Hundred policy).

白桦事件
Bai Hua shijian
(Bai Hua Incident)

In early 1981, some Party and army leaders regarded the current politico-cultural situation as being marked by so-called bourgeois liberalization (zichanjieji ziyouhua). This concern finally found expression in an open and fierce attack upon the army writer Bai Hua and his film script (coauthored with Peng Ning) "Unrequited Love" (Bai Hua and Peng Ning, "Kulian", *SY*, 3:140-71, 248, Sept. 1979, reprinted in *Shidaide baogao*, 23 Apr. 1981, pp. 5-8, *Cheng Ming*, 44:82-98, June 1981, and in *Kulian*, Taipei, Youshi Wenhua, 1982, pp. 1-87; trans. in T. C. Chang, S. Y. Chen, and Y. T. Lin, eds., *Unrequited Love: With Related Introductory Materials*, Taipei, Institute of Current China Studies, 1981, pp. 21-95; adapted into a film under the title of *Sun and Man* by the Changchun Film Studio in 1980 and by the Sanyi Yule Company in Taiwan in 1982, with Wang Tong as director. For an analysis of the work, see, for instance, Michael S. Duke, "Resurgent Humanism in Bai Hua's *Bitter love*", in his *Blooming and Contending,* Bloomington, Indiana University Press, 1985, pp. 123-48).

"Unrequited Love", described as a film-poem (the film, *Sun and Man,* has never been allowed to show to the public), is a tragedy about a painter by the name of Ling Chenguang who returns home from abroad after the New China is founded, but he is subjected to all kinds of humiliation during the GPCR, and he finally dies a hunted criminal. As a eulogy to human dignity, the work is full of sentiments of de-Maoification. Bai Hua also declared that the theme of this work is love—the protagonist's love towards his motherland was similar to Bai Hua's love of the motherland. Unfortunately, it was a kind of "unrequited" love. The work was accused of expressing hatred towards the Party, its leader, and socialist China, and of violating Deng Xiaoping's "four cardinal principles" (sixiang jiben yuanze), as emphasized in the first article of criticism, "The Four Cardinal Principles Must Not Be Violated" ("Sixiang jiben yuanze burong weifan"), published on 20 April 1981 in the *Liberation Army Daily* under the authoritative name "Special Guest Commentator" of the paper.

The surprise attack, however, turned out to be a failure; many people throughout the country voiced their support for Bai Hua. By mid-June 1981, the storm seemed to have subsided—the Bai Hua Incident "began as a tragedy and ended in a comedy".

But later developments showed the complexity of political-literary affairs in China. In early August 1981, seeing some serious problems arising from (or revealed by) the attack, the CCP authorities convened a national meeting to tackle them, and announced a call to counter "bourgeois liberalization" (zichanjieji ziyouhua). With the purpose of strengthening Party leadership, the campaign found its main target—the idea of "governing by doing nothing that goes against nature" (wuweierzhi). Finally, Bai Hua wrote his self-criticism on 25 November 1981, in the form of an open letter to the editorial boards of the *Liberation Army Daily* and *Literary Gazette*, admitting that there were "contradictions" in his world outlook.

In Bai Hua's "Unrequited Love" and in many other Chinese writers' works, one can feel the "bitter love complex of Chinese intellectuals" (Zhongguo zhishifenzide kulian qingjie). The love of Chinese intellectuals towards their motherland is unquestionable, no matter whether they are at home or abroad, or whether their love is requited or unrequited. The last scene in "Unrequited Love" is a powerful symbol: as a hunted "criminal", the protagonist dies on a snowy landscape in his country which he loved so much, his frozen body leaving an imprint in the shape of a huge question mark.

Such love is based on traditional Chinese culture. The script begins with a famous line from *Li Sao*, an important work by Qu Yuan (340-278 B.C.), the great patriotic poet of ancient China who ultimately committed suicide because of his unrequited love to his motherland: "Long, long is the road and far, far the journey: / I shall seek high and low in my steadfast quest." This is similar to the indomitable quest of Ling Chenguang. The pointed question the protagonist's daughter (who was born under the flag of the newly-founded PRC) asks her father is all the more sad and stirring: "You love our country... but does this country love you?"

But Deng Xiaoping thought otherwise. Referring to this controversial work, Deng stated: "Someone has said that not loving socialism isn't equivalent to not loving one's motherland. Is the motherland something abstract? If you don't love socialist New China led by the Communist Party, what motherland do you love?" *(SWD,* pp. 369-70). Indeed, it was because of Deng's support that the attacks on "Unrequited Love" were so fierce. On 27 March 1981, Deng told leaders of the PLA General Political Department that it was necessary to criticize "Unrequited Love" because the issue involved was the upholding of the "four cardinal principles" *(SWD,*

p. 359). On 17 July 1981, Deng returned to this issue again, cheering up the *Liberation Army Daily*, which had been condemned by the public for its publication of "The Four Cardinal Principles Must Not Be Violated" and other articles. Deng admitted the problems of these articles, saying that they "were not always entirely reasonable, and some of their tactics and arguments were not carefully thought out", but he insisted that it was right for this army newspaper to launch the attack *(SWD*, p. 369). In the talk with leaders of the central propaganda departments, Deng asked *Literary Gazette*, the most prestigious national literary magazine, to continue the attack by publishing several "first-class articles", which should be reprinted in the *People's Daily (SWD*, 371). See also "wenyide wuweierzhi" ("governing by doing nothing that goes against nature" in literature and art), "sixiang jiben yuanze" (four cardinal principles), and "ziyouhua" (liberalization).

百日文革
bairi wen'ge
(one hundred day Cultural Revolution)

See "qingwu yundong" (campaign to eliminate spiritual pollution) and "wen'ge" (Cultural Revolution).

白
bai
(white)

See "hong" (red).

白人优越论
bairen youyue lun
(theory of White superiority)

See "weidu Zhongguo" (containment against China).

白色恐怖
baise kongbu
(white terror)

In the CCP lexicon, the "white terror" usually refers to brutality against and persecution of the revolutionaries by their enemies (for example, to the Communists by the KMT during the civil war periods).

But Mao once used this term in a surprising way. On 1 June 1966, Liu Shaoqi (1898-1969), PRC president and CCP vice-chairman, on behalf of the PCC, sent out "work teams" (gongzuo dui) to various universities and middle schools in Beijing. Their task was to give guidance in the GPCR, as before in the numerous political movements the Party had carried out. On 28 July 1966, however, they were disbanded and Liu was fiercely attacked. In his 5 August 1966 big-character poster "Bombard the Headquarters" ("Paoda silingbu"), Mao stated: "In the last 50 days or so some leading comrades from the central down to the local levels have acted in a diametrically opposite way. Adopting the reactionary stand of the bourgeoisie, they have enforced a bourgeois dictatorship and struck down the surging movement of the GPCR. They have stood facts on their head and juggled black and white, encircled and suppressed revolutionaries, stifled opinions differing from their own, and imposed a white terror...."

Imposing a "white terror" was certainly a very serious charge. Mao's poster, indeed, foresaw the downfall of the PRC president. See also "hong" (red) and "wen'ge" (Cultural Revolution).

白专
baizhuan
(white and expert)

The term "baizhuan" ("white and expert" or "apolitical specialization") is virtually no longer used today, but it was a frightening political label for many Chinese intellectuals and students during the Mao period. Liu Binyan, a famous writer of reportage literature (now living in exile in the U.S.) provided the following description. When speaking of the consequences of the 1957 anti-Rightist campaign, he found the path open to youth and intellectuals had become "extraordinarily narrow." "If you aspired to be an upstanding and honest man politically," this former convicted Rightist said, "then you would inevitably end up as a counter-revolutionary, so there was no way out. If, on the other hand, you felt you had some talent, in science or technology, and you were hopeful about making some contribution to the country, then it wouldn't be long before you would be attacked for 'apolitical specialization' and 'bourgeois individualism' (zichanjieji gerenzhuyi). That would provide no way out either... So what was left for China's intellectuals? Really only one path, or only one that was relatively safe and comfortable: that was to become a political opportunist. This was how limited the possibilities had become. Group after group of intellectuals took this way out, quite a number of them becaming the power base of the Cultural Revolution, and it is these people who are the obstacles in our way today...." (Liu Binyan, "Zai Nankai Daxuede jianghua"—"Speech at Nankai University", 21 Nov. 1986, excerpts in *FLW*, pp. 111-20). See also "dangde jiaoyu fangzhen" (the Party's educational policy).

半边天
banbiantian
(other half of the sky)

During the more than two thousand years of the feudal system, a number of rules of conduct were formed for Chinese women, as summed up in the "three obediences" and the "four virtues" (sancong side). The "three obediences" mean that a woman should obey father before marriage, obey husband after marriage, and obey son after the death of husband. The "four virtues" are morality, proper speech, modest manner, and diligent work. In the "three cardinal guides" and the "five constant virtues" (san'gang wuchang), which were specified as the feudal ethical code, one of the cardinal guides is that husband guides wife. (The other two are that ruler guides subject and father guides son. The "five constant virtues" are benevolence, righteousness, propriety, wisdom, and fidelity.) So while a man in China was usually subjected to domination by three systems of authorities—political authority (zhengquan), clan authority (zuquan), and religious authority (shenquan), a woman, in addition to these, was also dominated by masculine authority (fuquan—the authority of the husband). The four authorities (siquan), the embodiment of the feudal-patriarchal ideology and system, were four thick ropes binding Chinese women. Symbolically, for one thousand years, they had to follow the "footbinding" practice. (Hu Shi, one of the most influential intellectuals in China in the first half of the twentieth century, ridiculed footbinding and opium-smoking as China's "national essence".)

Since the May 4th Movement of 1919, women liberation was always a slogan in various revolutionary struggles. In the "Common Program" ("Gongtong gangling") adopted at the first plenum of the CPPCC on 21 September 1949, the principle of equality of men and women was stipulated. Both the Marriage Laws promulgated on 1 May 1950 and 10 September 1980 represented major efforts by the PRC government to improve women's status. In 1992, gender equality was reaffirmed in the Law on the Protection of the Rights and Interests of Women. Today, the Chinese female force of 600 million certainly cannot be ignored, as expressed in the well-known metaphor "the other half of the sky", which implies that women are as important as men. Mao's slogan was: "Women hold up half the sky" (funü neng ding banbiantian).

But as noted by many, legal requirements for gender equality are not always fulfilled. Chinese women today participate in most occupations, but they are usually clustered in low-status, lower-paid, and gender-specific jobs. In fields such as politics, as Beijing's Federation of Chinese Women summarized, there is a "yidi sanshao" ("one low and three fews") situation: a low proportion of women engage in politics and few women at higher levels, in top positions, and in key sectors. In 1995, 27.3 percent of women in the country were illiterate (while 10.1 percent of men were illiterate). In some rural areas, the sale of women and female infanticide still exist. Prostitution, which was eliminated in the Mao period, is thriving in some urban areas (especially in special economic zones) and has become a serious social problem, as mockingly described by a phrase: "fanrong chang sheng"—"The more prosperous the economy is, the more prostitution will thrive."

搬起石头砸自己的脚
banqi shitou za zijide jiao
(lifting a rock only to drop it on one's own feet)

The phrase refers to the stupidity of making an effort to do something, only to end up hurting oneself. In his speech at the Meeting of the Supreme Soviet of the U.S.S.R. in Celebration of the 40th Anniversary of the Great October Socialist Revolution on 6 November 1957, Mao said: "'Lifting a rock only to drop it on one's own feet' is a Chinese folk saying to describe the behavior of certain fools. The reactionaries in all countries are fools of this kind. In the final analysis, their persecution of the revolutionary people only serves to accelerate the people's revolutions on a broader and more intense scale. Did not the persecution of the revolutionary people by the tsar of Russia and by Chiang Kai-shek perform this function in the great Russian and Chinese revolutions?"

Mao used this phrase on quite a number of occasions, the objects of his taunts ranging from "U.S. imperialists" to "bourgeois Rightists" (zichanjieji youpaifenzi).

保持革命晚节
baochi geming wanjie
(maintain one's revolutionary integrity in one's later years)

See "zhanhao zuihou yi ban gang" (continue working well until the last minute).

保皇派
baohuangpai

(royalist faction)

See "zaofan youli" (it is right to rebel).

报告文学热

baogao wenxue re

(reportage literature craze)

See "yi wenti wei zhongxinde baogao wenxue" (problem-centered reportage literature).

暴露文学

baolu wenxue

(exposure literature)

In his 1942 *Talks at the Yan'an Forum on Literature and Art,* Mao Zedong said: "Many petty-bourgeois writers have never discovered the bright side. Their works only expose the dark. This is what is known as 'exposure literature'. Some of these works simply specialize in preaching pessimism and world-weariness."

A target of the attack on "exposure literature" in the Yan'an rectification movement was Wang Shiwei's 1942 essay "The Wild Lily" ("Ye baihehua", *JFRB,* 13 & 23 Mar. 1942, reprinted in *Cheng Ming,* 41:37-38, 84, Mar. 1981, and in Robert Tung, ed., *Proscribed Chinese Writing,* London, Curzon Press, 1976, pp. 1-10; trans. in Gregory Benton, ed., *Wild Lilies, Poisonous Weeds: Dissident Voices from People's China,* London, Pluto Press, 1982, pp. 179-86). Also subject to attack were the writers Ding Ling, Xiao Jun, Ai Qing, and Luo Feng, all of whom were allegedly involved in producing "exposure literature". Wang Shiwei, a literary critic, was executed in March 1947 as a "secret agent". Ding Ling and others were attacked again as "bourgeois Rightists" in the 1957-58 anti-Rightist campaign, for their old and new "anti-Party and anti-socialist poisonous weeds" (ducao).

After the downfall of the Gang of Four in 1976, almost all "bourgeois Rightists" were rehabilitated. But, Wang Shiwei's case was more difficult. Many people in cultural circles claimed that Wang was definitely wronged, one of whom was Dai Qing, who published "Wang Shiwei and 'The Wild Lily'", a piece of reportage literature, in 1988 ("Wang Shiwei he 'Ye baihehua'", *Wenhui yuekan,* 5:22-41, 1988, reprinted in her *Liang Shuming, Wang Shiwei, Chu Anping,* Nanjing, Jiangsu Wenyi, 1989, pp. 37-107). In 1991, the CCP finally approved Wang Shiwei's rehabilitation.

Since the term "exposure literature" has frightening overtones, China's writers had to be very cautious about it. One such case was that of the "scar literature" (shanghen wenxue), a genre that appeared after the downfall of the Gang of Four in 1976. For some people, especially those in powerful positions, such works violated the long-established principles of socialist literature and art, thus constituting a kind of threat. Initially, they were also labeled as "exposure literature". See also "shanghen wenxue" (scar literature), "wenyi wei zhengzhi fuwu" (literature and art serve politics), and "fan youpai yundong" (anti-Rightist campaign).

暴露与歌颂

baolu yu gesong

(exposure and eulogy)

See "shehuizhuyi beiji" (socialist tragedy) and "xie zhenshi" (writing about reality).

爆炸性作品
baozhaxing zuopin
("explosive" writings)

See "xinshiqi wenxuede duoyuan fazhan" (pluralistic development of the literature of the new period).

北伐
beifa
(Northern Expedition)

See "tongzhan" (united front).

北京惨案
Beijing can'an
(Beijing massacre)

See "ziyouhua" (liberalization) and "bajiu minyun" (1989 pro-democracy movement).

北京之春
Beijing zhi chun
(Beijing Spring)

In the spirit of the April 5th Movement of 1976—which, to a great extent, was responsible for the downfall of the Gang of Four—a pro-democracy and human rights movement spontaneously erupted in Beijing in September 1978.

In the struggle at that time against the "whateverists" (fanshipai) headed by Party Chairman Hua Guofeng, Deng Xiaoping's faction encouraged people to express opinions and grievances against earlier miscarriages of justice. (See, for instance, the *People's Daily* of 28 November 1978.) In Beijing such grievances were posted on a wall in Xidan district, which soon became known as "Xidan Democracy Wall" (Xidan minzhuqiang) or "Democracy Wall". During the exciting period of what was later called the "Beijing Spring", the movement rapidly expanded and spread to other cities as a result of the official policy of "relaxation". In return, during its early stage, the movement greatly helped Deng's faction to consolidate its power. According to Ruan Ming, a former Hu Yaobang adviser, Democracy Wall changed the originally scheduled orientation of the Central Work Conference held from 10 November to 15 December 1978, which made preparations for the 3rd Plenum of the 11th PCC, thus guaranteeing Deng's victory at the Plenum. (Ruan Ming helped draft Deng's closing speech at the Central Work Conference and the communiqué of the Plenum. For a description of all this, see his *Lishi Zhuanzhedianshangde Hu Yaobang—Hu Yaobang on the Historical Turning Point,* Global Publishing, pp. 27-31.) Deng praised this movement. He even said: "What a revolutionary political party should fear is that it does not hear the people's voice. Most dreadful is 'not even a crow or sparrow can be heard'," quoting a Chinese idiom to make his statement more emphatic (see *Deng Xiaoping Wenxuan—Selected Works of Deng Xiaoping,* Beijing, Renmin, 1983, p, 134). Ye Jianying commented that the 3rd Plenum of the 11th PCC was a fine example of inner Party democracy, and Xidan Democracy Wall was an example of people's democracy. It is thus not surprising that the *People's Daily* hailed the movement with the slogan "Long live the people!" *(RMRB,* 21 Dec. 1978).

However, as it turned out, the movement became increasingly radical, ultimately alienating its original supporters. Towards the end of 1978 some of the poster-writers and democracy activists, in Beijing and in other cities, cooperated in publishing quite a number of unofficial magazines and journals. Famous among these in Beijing included *April 5th Tribune (Siwu Luntan,* edited by Xu Wenli and Liu Qing), *Exploration (Tansuo,* edited by Wei Jingsheng), *Beijing Spring (Beijing Zhi Chun,* edited by Wang Juntao), and *Today (Jintian,* edited by Bei Dao). The more radical activists were not only against a few "bad" Party and state leaders, as those in the April 5th Movement of 1976 had been, but also against the entire Communist regime in China. They demanded emancipation of individuality, human rights, and democratic reform of the political structure. Wei Jingsheng, editor of *Exploration*, even asked the people to beware of the possibility that Deng Xiaoping could become a dictator, at a time just when Deng was hailed by many as a new savior.

An alarm was sounded by the so-called "restoration faction within the establishment" (tizhineide huanyuanpai)—those devoting themselves mainly to a restoration of the damaged Communist order, such as Chen Yun, Deng Liqun, and Hu Qiaomu: Things could get out of control if left unchecked. As a result, Deng abruptly changed his attitude. This, China critics said, was very natural for him. When he needed the movement in his fight against the remnants of the Gang of Four and the "whateverists", he supported it; but once he found that his position was secure and that the movement not only was of little value to him but also constituted a threat to his regime, he suppressed it ruthlessly. On 29 March 1979, Wei Jingsheng was arrested. (Later, a few other activists were also arrested.) On 30 March 1979, Deng Xiaoping delivered a speech drafted by Hu Qiaomu, in which he put forth the "four cardinal principles". On 16 October 1979, Wei was sentenced to fifteen years' imprisonment. On 6 December 1979, the Beijing Municipal Revolutionary Committee issued a notice banning big-character posters on Xidan wall. Wall-posters and unofficial publications were regarded as anti-socialism and against the CCP leadership. The Beijing Spring thus came to an end. In Party politics, this can be said to have been a struggle in which the influence of the "restoration faction" became dominant after the "reformists within the establishment" (tizhineide gaigepai) defeated the "whateverists" with the help of the "radical democrats outside the system" (tizhiwaide jijin minzhupai) and then the reformists discarded and suppressed the radical democrats.

Despite the ban and the arrests in Beijing, incredibly, some of those involved in the movement continued their activities in other parts of the country. During the 1979 to 1980 period, the number of their publications surpassed 130. Following warnings by the authorities that every publication had to be backed by a recognized organization which would be held responsible for it, the editors of twenty-nine unofficial journals even formed the "National Association of Democratic Journals", a group which was somewhat like a political opposition organization, in Guangzhou in autumn 1980.

In early 1981 two government documents were issued to deal with the situation. The first was the No. 7 document which enjoined writers and artists not to produce too many *exposé* works about the 1957 anti-Rightist campaign, the 1959 anti-Right deviation campaign, and the GPCR. The second was the No. 9 document which banned what was claimed to be "illegal publications" (such as self-published or unofficial journals) and "illegal organizations" (i.e., organizations not specifically recognized by and registered with the regime, including organizations which published unofficial journals). In April 1981, in an attempt to put an end to all these activities once and for all, the authorities arrested the twenty principal editors of the unofficial journals. Others were arrested later, during the spring and summer of 1981. Several were tried in closed trials in 1982 and 1983, and sentenced to long prison terms on "counter-revolutionary" charges. With the implementation of the CCP policy of repression, this pro-democracy movement of ordinary people, especially the young, was finally extinguished.

When China's dissidents use the term "the first thought-emancipation movement" (diyi ci sixiang jiefang yundong), they are referring to this pro-democracy movement, marked by the "Beijing Spring". Accordingly, to them it lasted only about ten months, from the publication of "Practice Is the Sole Criterion for Testing Truth" ("shijian shi jianyan zhenlide weiyi biaozhun") in the *Guangming Daily* on 11 May 1978 to Deng's pronouncement of the "four cardinal principles" on 30 March 1979. See also "siwu yundong" (April 5th Movement), "liang ge fanshi" (two whatevers), "si xiang jiben yuanze" (four cardinal principles), and "bajiu minyun" (1989 pro-democracy movement).

北京人什么都敢说，广州人什么都敢吃，上海人什么都敢做
Beijingren shenme dou gan shuo, Guangzhouren shenme dou gan chi, Shanghairen shenme dou gan zuo
(Beijingers can talk about anything, Cantonese can eat anything, Shanghainese can do anything)

To some extent, this saying reveals the different characteristics of residents in Beijing, Guangzhou, and Shanghai, three big cities in China's north, south, and east.

背靠背批判
bei kao bei pipan
("back-to-back" criticism)

See "douzhenghui" (public accusation meeting).

被管制分子
beiguanzhi fenzi
(persons under surveillance)

See "guanzhi" (surveillance).

本位主义
benweizhuyi
(departmentalism)

See "difangzhuyi" (localism).

本位主义是放大了的个人主义
benweizhuyi shi fangdalede gerenzhuyi
(departmentalism is magnified individualism)

See "difangzhuyi" (localism) and "ziyouzhuyi" (liberalism).

本质不等于主流
benzhi budengyu zhuliu
("essence" is not the same as "mainstream")

See "shehuizhuyi xianshizhuyi" (socialist realism).

闭关政策
biguan zhengce
(closed-door policy)

See "xiandaide shijie shi kaifangde shijie" (today's world is an open world).

闭关自守
biguan zi shou
(closing the country to international intercourse)

See "xiandaide shijie shi kaifangde shijie" (today's world is an open world).

必要的祸害
biyaode huohai
(necessary scourge)

See "xin quanweizhuyi lunzheng" (neo-authoritarianism debate).

变色
bianse
(change political color)

See "xiuzhengzhuyi" (revisionism).

辩证唯物主义
bianzheng weiwuzhuyi
(dialectical materialism)

According to CCP doctrine, dialectical materialism, the unity of materialism and dialectics, was established by Marx and Engels. It is a science of universal laws in nature, human society, and thought developments. It holds that the cause of all the motion and change in the world does not lie in any "higher" spiritual reality, but in the material world itself. For the world is by its very nature material. Ideology, as the outcome of material when highly developed, is the reflection of material. This reflection—an active, dialectical process based on practice—both relies on and serves practice. The unity of opposites is the fundamental law of the universe. Between the opposites in a contradiction there is at once unity and struggle, and it is this that impels things to move and change. Materialist dialectics (weiwu bianzhengfa) holds that external causes are the condition of change and internal causes are the basis of change, and that external causes become operative through internal causes (waiyin tongguo neiyin qi zuoyong).

When the principle of dialectical materialism is applied to studying social life, this is historical materialism (lishi weiwuzhuyi). Mao had a very straightforward explanation for historical materialism. He said: "In class struggle, some classes triumph, others are eliminated. Such is history, such is the history of civilization for thousands of years. To interpret history from this viewpoint is historical materialism; standing in opposition to this viewpoint is historical idealism" *(SWM,* 4, p.428).

Dialectical materialism and historical materialism constitute Marxist philosophy. They are said to be the world outlook (shijieguan) and the methodology (fangfalun) of the proletariat, with which the proletariat understands and remolds the world. As Mao said, "The Marxist philosophy of dialectical materialism has two outstanding characteristics. One is its class nature: it openly avows that dialectical materialism is in the service of the proletariat. The other is its practicality: it emphasizes the dependence of theory on practice, emphasizes that theory is based on practice and in turn serves practice" ("On Practice", *SWM,* 1, p. 297).

Interestingly, during their lifetimes Marx and Engels only used the term "historical materialism", but they never used the term "dialectical materialism". In the opinion of Wang Ruoshui, a famous philosopher (who lost his post as deputy editor-in-chief of the *People's Daily* in the 1983 campaign to eliminate "spiritual pollution"), the starting point of Marxism was neither "spirit" nor "material"; it was "man", man in reality (xianshide ren) or man in practice (shijiande ren). Essentially, therefore, Marxist philosophy is a philosophy about man. It can be called Marxist philosophical anthropology (zhexuede renxue), or, as Wang calls it, "shijiande weirenzhuyi"—"humanism in practice". Wang believes the Marxist philosophy about man to still have "vitality" and to be "most valuable" in the whole system of Marxism. It provides one with a value standard, with which one can criticize either capitalism or socialism in reality. It also enables one to maintain one's self, to have an independent character, and not to lose sight of human value in a society full of power alienation and money alienation (Wang Ruoshui, "Wode Makesizhuyi guan"—"My View on Marxism", *Beijing zhi chun,* Jan. 1996). See also "shijieguan" (world outlook) and "jieji douzheng" (class struggle).

表态
biaotai
(make known one's position)

As part of their political life, people in China, especially those holding public office, used to be asked to make known their position concerning a particular issue at a public meeting or before their superior (privately if necessary). Such a practice is no longer common.

表扬为主
biaoyang wei zhu
(praise is essential)

See "weitiao yishu" (art of "fine tuning").

拨乱反正
boluanfanzheng
(set wrong things right)

At the 1978 3rd Plenum of the 11th PCC, all the participants shared the following opinion: The Party must make great efforts to set right those things that had been thrown into disorder during the GPCR (that is, to go back to the "correct road" of the past). On 1 September 1982, in his report to the CCP's 12th National Congress, Hu Yaobang (1915-1989), as CCP general secretary, declared that a great victory had been achieved in bringing order out of chaos on all fronts ("Quanmian kaichuang shehuizhuyi xiandaihua jianshede xin jumian"—"Open Up All-sidedly a New Phase of Socialist Modern Construction", *HQ*, 18:6-30, 1982; trans. and published in book form, Beijing, FLP, 1982).

In 1987, Party ideologue Deng Liqun, making use of the current campaign against so-called "bourgeois liberalization" (see "ziyouhua"), went so far as to advocate another "setting right things that had been thrown into disorder". At the Tianjin Forum for Ideological Work in Trade Unions held in mid-April, Deng Liqun stated that "those advocating capitalism have been criticized but not those engaging in it". He was pointing his spearhead at the 1978 3rd Plenum of the 11th PCC, which implemented Deng Xiaoping's political line; he thus ambitiously intended to change the direction of policy to be more in accord with his own ideas. With the support of some Party elders, Deng Liqun was casting his greedy eyes on the post of Party General Secretary, which was held at that time by Zhao Ziyang. But Deng Xiaoping opposed any attacks on the achievements of the 3rd Plenum. On 30 April 1987, even while the anti-bourgeois liberalization campaign was still going on, Deng Xiaoping suddenly announced that the greatest danger was still from the "Left"—he saw the threat embodied in Deng Liqun's remarks.

不点名批判
bu dianming pipan
(criticize somebody without naming)

See "dapipan" (mass criticism).

不独，不统，不对抗
bu du, bu tong, bu duikang
(no independence, no reunification, and no confrontation)

See "Taiwan wenti" (Taiwan issue).

不反腐败，亡国；而彻底反腐败，亡党
bu fan fubai, wang guo; er chedi fan fubai, wang dang
(destruction of the country will occur without anti-corruption, whereas thorough anti-corruption will lead to the destruction of the Party)

See "fan fubai" (anti-corruption).

不合理的时代的合理婴儿
bu helide shidaide heli ying'er
(a reasonable child of an unreasonable era)

See "menglongshi" (misty poetry) and "menglongshi lilunde san ci jueqi" ("three rises" in the theory of misty poetry).

不接触，不谈判，不妥协
bu jiechu, bu tanpan, bu tuoxie

(no contact, no negotiation, no compromise)

See "santong siliu" (three opening-ups and four exchanges).

不破不立

bu po bu li

(without destruction there is no construction)

At the beginning the GPCR, an editorial in the *People's Daily* said: "Without destruction there is no construction. Destruction here means criticism, means revolution. Destruction necessarily calls for reasoning, and reasoning is construction; destruction comes first, and in the course of it there is construction (pozi dangtou, li za qizhong)" *(RMRB,* 8 June 1966). The sentence "Without destruction there is no construction", which later became a frequently quoted slogan during the GPCR, came from Mao's article entitled "On New Democracy" (Xin minzhuzhuyi lun), published in January 1940. Mao asserted in that article that if the old Chinese culture was not swept away, no new culture of any kind could be built up. This view is responsible for the destructive outcome of the Cultural Revolution. See also "wen'ge" (Cultural Revolution).

"不争论"论

bu zhenglun lun

("no debate" theory)

On 15 February, 2 March, 22 March, and 22 April 1991, the *Liberation Daily,* the mouthpiece of the CCP Shanghai Municipal Committee, carried a series of comments written under the pen name of Huang Fu Ping. They vigorously defended Deng's line of reform and the open door. Most eye-catching was the 22 March article "An Opening-up Consciousness Should Be Strengthened" ("Kuoda kaifangde yishi yao gengqiangxie"). It said that some Shanghai leaders were not brave enough, thus hindering the city from achieving greater success in the 1980s. It appealed that in the 1990s Shanghai should take a bigger step, and not be obstructed by the "socialism or capitalism" question.

Very soon thereafter an attack was launched on Huang Fu Ping, lasting for more than half a year (which is called the "Huang Fu Ping Incident"). Most active were those magazines reportedly associated with Deng Liqun, former member of the CCP Secretariat: *Seeking Truth (Qiushi), Ideological Trends of the Contemporary Age (Dangdai Sichao), In Quest of the Truth (Zhenlide Zhuiqiu),* and *On the Theoretical Front of Tertiary Education (Gaoxiao Lilun Zhanxian).* The two important newspapers, the *People's Daily* and the *Guangming Daily,* also joined in the attack. It was repeated again and again: when dealing with a certain matter, one must first make clear whether it is of a capitalist or a socialist nature; otherwise, the reform and open door will lead to capitalism and China's socialist cause will be ruined. For a time, many powerful people felt that the line of reform and the open door was rife with problems.

This should not be considered strange. After the June 4th Incident of 1989, what the Party was most concerned about were "peaceful evolution" (heping yanbian)—peaceful evolution from socialism back to capitalism, as was taking place in the Soviet Union and the East European bloc, and "bourgeois liberalization" (zichanjieji ziyouhua)—which had led to the 1989 pro-democracy movement. The view that "peaceful evolution" and "bourgeois liberalization" constituted an "immediate threat" to China's independence and sovereignty, and to its construction, reform, and the open-door program was dominant. It was said that the Leftist forces were especially encouraged by the message in General Secretary Jiang Zemin's speech of 1 July 1991 marking the 70th anniversary of the founding of the Party. They hailed the speech as a new "Manifesto of the Communist Party" (xin "Gongchandang Xuanyan"), for its alleged "keynote" was to oppose "peaceful evolution", what they considered to be the most serious problem facing the CCP. Taking advantage of the message in Jiang's speech, they seemed to have gotten the upper hand in the "capitalism or socialism" debate (xing "zi" xing "she" zhi zheng).

As a result, Deng Xiaoping made a tour in early 1992 to China's southern provinces, where he gave a series of talks calling for a more vigorous open-door and active economic policy. He told the people: "Watch out for the Right, but mainly defend against the 'Left'." With regard to the issue of whether things are of a capitalist or a socialist nature, there are three criteria, that is, it depends on whether or not they accord with the "three favorables" (san ge youliyu)—favorable to developing the productive forces in the socialist society, to consolidating China's comprehensive national strength, and to raising the people's living standards. He called for an end to the capitalism or socialism debate. To carry out such debates, Deng explained, would make things complicated and waste time. There were so many things to be done, and no time should be wasted. The "no debate" theory was his own invention, Deng added.

Those describing themselves as true Marxists simply found the no-debate theory untenable. They attacked it whenever they had a chance (without mentioning Deng's name, though). They accused the theory of contributing to the "vicious trend" of "bourgeois liberalization". As for the reformers, they warmly welcomed this theory, for it meant that they could speed up reform and make greater changes without fear of being questioned. Later, in the propaganda drive of July to August 1997 in the lead-up to the 15th CCP National Congress, the reformers declared that the "no debate" proposal had been merely an expedient measure, and that now a debate was called for, in which they could well justify what they had been doing. Of course, this must need a "new socialist view". See also "xin shehuizhuyi guan" (new socialist view) and "Deng Xiaoping lilun" (Deng Xiaoping Theory).

不管白猫黑猫，抓着老鼠就是好猫
buguan baimao heimao, zhuazhao laoshu jiushi haomao (no matter whether it is white or black, it is a good cat that catches mice)

As a pragmatist, Deng Xiaoping was willing to employ a temporary expedient whenever necessary, which was most vividly expressed by his well-known saying: "No matter whether it is white or black, it is a good cat that catches mice."

Originally, this was a saying among locals in his native Sichuan province (in which the "white cat" was "yellow"). In speeches at two meetings held on 2 and 7 June 1962, Deng, CCP general secretary, used this quote to support Liu Shaoqi's new policy for the rural economy. He later repeated it on several occasions. In an article entitled "Only Socialism Can Save China" ("Zhiyou shehuizhuyi caineng jiu Zhongguo") published in the *People's Daily* on 3 December 1967, Deng's "cat" theory (in which the "yellow" cat had become "white") was attacked as a "reactionary fallacy". In 1968, when confronted with this charge, Deng had to admit in his self-criticism that the idea was "extremely erroneous" (see "Wode zishu"—"An Account of My Understanding of Some Issues" written 20 June to 5 July 1968). Perhaps Deng had no choice in order to survive. After he resumed office, he never mentioned the saying again. Nor was it regarded as official policy by the authorities. When questioned, the authorities would say that the "mice" refers to productivity and the "cat" is the form of production relations, not the social system.

Nevertheless, the saying is generally accepted as symbolic of Deng's open-door and reform policy. Deng said that he was building socialism with Chinese characteristics; but, as many China observers have pointed out, to do this he resorted to a number of capitalist measures. See also "xin shehuizhuyi guan" (new socialist view) and "Deng Xiaoping lilun" (Deng Xiaoping Theory).

不管白鼠黑鼠，猫逮不着就是好老鼠
buguan bai shu hei shu, mao dai buzhe jiushi hao laoshu
(no matter whether it is white or black, it is a good mouse if it can escape from the cat)

This is a corruption of Deng Xiaoping's most famous aphorism: "No matter whether it is white or black, it is a good cat that catches mice." On the anniversary of the death of this paramount pragmatist, while the official media published pages of hyperbole to commemorate his role in modernizing China, many urban Chinese poked fun at this quote and found an expression for their cynicism—the implication of the saying is: No matter what illegal means one resorts to, as long as one is capable of making money and is not caught by the law, one will be highly respected in the society. See also "buguan heimao baimao, zhuazhao laoshu jiushi haomao" (no matter whether it is white or black, it is a good cat that catches mice).

不管黄猫黑猫，抓得住老鼠就是好猫
buguan huangmao heimao, zhuadezhu laoshu jiushi haomao
(no matter whether it is yellow or black, it is a good cat if it catches mice)

See "buguan heimao baimao, zhuazhao laoshu jiushi haomao" (no matter whether it is white or black, it is a good cat that catches mice).

不断革命
buduan geming
(uninterrupted revolution)

According to "dialectical materialism" (bianzheng weiwuzhuyi), all things are invariably in a process of continuous change and development. In order to reach the final goal of the revolution, the proletariat must push the revolution forward in an uninterrupted way. The CCP also sees itself as a supporter of the theory of "the development of revolution by stages" ("geming fazhan jieduan lun", that is, revolution must be launched in stages). It is opposed to the theory of "a single revolution" ("yici geming lun") which denies that each phase of the revolution is distinct from the others and embodies a different character and task.

The theory of "uninterrupted revolution" may help explain why Mao launched so many political campaigns even after the founding of the regime. During the GPCR, Mao developed the theory of "uninterrupted revolution" into the theory of "continuing the revolution under the dictatorship of the proletariat". See also "wuchanjieji zhuanzheng" (dictatorship of the proletariat).

不正之风
buzheng zhi feng
(unhealthy tendencies)

See "zou houmen" (get in through the back door) and "fan fubai" (anti-corruption).

补课
buke
(supplementary lessons; to make up for missed lessons)

If a certain campaign or task is not launched in a deep probing and meticulous manner, the work may be unsatisfactory. Thus, "supplementary lessons" must be conducted to solve the problems.

"Buke", which also means "to make up for missed lessons", was frequently mentioned by China's intellectuals in the first few years after the end of the GPCR. The "missed lesson" referred to "democracy", which was found to be terribly lacking in China. Later, it referred to "capitalism". It was said that capitalism, which had never been fully developed in China, should be practiced in light of the Marxist theory of the impossibility of skipping over any necessary stage of historical development. See also "ren shi mudi, ren shi zhongxin" (man is the aim, man is the center).

补课队
buke dui
(remedial teaching team)

In the eyes of some critics and writers, particularly the younger ones, during the 1980s Liu Zaifu (Director of the Literature Institute of CASS before the June 4th Incident of 1989) and others had been advocating something that ought to have existed earlier, something commonplace and not worthy of mention. As members of the "second wave," they had to be very careful; hence, the nickname "remedial teaching team". But the young people, for example Huang Ziping, a young critic who was the co-author of the widely noted article, "A Discussion on 'Chinese Literature of the Twentieth Century'" (Huang Ziping, Chen Pingyuan, and Qian Liqun, "Lun 'Ershi shiji Zhongguo wenxue'", *WXPL,* 5:3-13, 1985; abridged trans. in *CL,* 2:186-93, summer 1988) wanted to promote a "third wave." Liu Xiaobo, another critic, went even further. He used the term "intercomplementary thinking" (hubu siwei) to bluntly criticize Liu Zaifu's principle of dual combination in characterization (erchong zuhe yuanli) and his theory of the subjectivity of literature (wenxue zhutixing). Traditionally, Liu Xiaobo explains, influenced by the "doctrine of the mean" (zhongyong) characteristic of Confucianism and the "integral grasping" (zhengti ba'e) as expressed in the *Book of Changes,* the Chinese were brought up to emphasize intercomplementarity, reconciliation, and balance. The fatal weakness of "intercomplementary thinking" is that, when it rejects the ability to grasp things in the movement of conflict, negation, and opposition, it strangles initiative in practice. This leads people's thoughts and actions, rather than aiming at destroying the old entity and promoting the birth of a new one, to attempt by all means to maintain the old entity so that it will last steadily for a long time or even without end (see Liu Xiaobo, "Zai lun xinshiqi wenxue mianlin weiji"—"More on the Crisis of the New Period Literature", *Bai jia,* 1:12-26, Jan. 1988).

参政党
canzheng dang
(parties participating in government affairs)

See "minzhu dangpai" (democratic parties).

忏悔意识
chanhui yishi
(consciousness of repentance)

See "shehuizhuyi beiji" (socialist tragedy).

唱对台戏
chang duitaixi
(put on a rival show)

In his 1980 "Speech at the Forum on Script Writing" ("Zai juben chuangzuo zuotanhuishangde jianghua", *WYB,* 1:2-20, 1981; *XHWZ,* 3:126-37, 1981; *HQ,* 20:7-25, 1981; and *WYLZJ*, pp. 1-38; trans. in *Issues and Studies* 2:67-106, 1982), Hu Yaobang, director of the Propaganda Department of the PCC, voiced his views about "being involved in life" (ganyu shenghuo), a literary slogan first put forth by the famous journalist Liu Binyan. The crux of the matter, as Hu saw it, was not the slogan itself but its interpretation and application. If it meant that literature and art should reflect reality more actively, if it required writers to take a correct stance, analyse life correctly, criticize the old, and encourage the new, so as to inspire, educate, and guide the broad masses of the people in their struggle for a better future, this was very good. But, if it meant deviating from a Marxist world outlook and the guidance of the Party's correct line, principles, and policies, and exaggerating the dark side of society so as to make people lose confidence in life, that was simply an incorrect way of using literature and art to "be involved in" life. It was even more incorrect if it meant using literary and art creation to "put on a rival show" against the Party.

Here, as pointed out by some critics, Hu Yaobang betrayed a fear that had haunted the peasant Chinese Communist Party. Always suspecting writers and intellectuals of "putting on a rival show" against them, the CCP demanded that all works be produced in light of the principles of the Party spirit (dangxing), and they should have the social effect of helping to fulfill the Party's tasks. This obsession tended to confuse the Party's conception about the nature of the arts. For instance, the Party always found tragedies to be unacceptable.

长城
changcheng
(Great Wall, i.e., the PLA)

A metaphor for the Chinese People's Liberation Army (PLA).

In August 1967, the GPCR rebels further intensified their counter-attack on the "adverse February current" (eryue niliu). They thus raised a new slogan: "Ferret out a handful of capitalist-roaders in the army" (jiu junnei yixiaocuo). The slogan became official when it was adopted as the title of an editorial of the Party magazine *Red Flag*. Mao read it and was enraged. He wrote four Chinese characters: "huan wo changcheng" (Give me back my Great Wall), warning the rebels not to make trouble in the army and cause the situation to spin out of control. This event led to the stepdown and arrest of Wang Li and Guan Feng, both members of the Central GPCR Group (Zhongyang Wen'ge Xiaozu), and Lin Jie, who drafted the editorial. (Reportedly, Mao had approved the formulation of "ferretting out a handful of capitalist-roaders in the army" before the 25 July 1967 Beijing mass rally where the slogan was publicized.)

In recent years, corruption has run rampant in the PLA. Smuggling is commonplace, reportedly defrauding the PLA of some 20 billion Chinese dollars per year. In July 1998, at a national anti-smuggling conference, Jiang Zemin ordered the military to end all its commercial activities. On this occasion, Jiang quoted from an instruction by Deng Xiaoping about the danger of "self-destruction of the Great Wall" (zihui changcheng). See also "eryue niliu" (adverse February current) and "fan fubai" (anti-corruption).

长期共存，互相监督
changqi gongcun, huxiang jiandu
(long-term co-existence and mutual supervision)

See "minzhu dangpai" (democratic parties).

超阶级的人性
chao jiejide renxing
(human nature transcending class)

See "gongtong renxing" (common human nature) and "renxing lun" (theory of human nature).

超常性
chaochangxing
(transcending the norm)

See "zuojia zhutixing" (writer's subjectivity).

超级大国
chaoji daguo
(superpower)

For several decades, Beijing used this term in reference to the United States and the Soviet Union. After the Soviet Union disintegrated (it ceased to exist on 26 December 1991), the United States was the only superpower in the world. Beijing declares that China will never be a superpower. See also "lengzhanhou shidaide xin diguozhuyi" (neo-imperialism in the post-Cold War era) and "weidu Zhongguo" (containment against China).

超级三大件
chaoji san da jian
(three super articles)

See "lao san jian" (former three most sought-after articles).

超前性
chaoqianxing
(transcending precedents)

See "zuojia zhutixing" (writer's subjectivity).

超我性
chaowoxing
(self-transcending)

See "zuojia zhutixing" (writer's subjectivity).

扯後腿
che houtui
(pull back the leg)

See "la houtui" (pull back the leg).

彻底否定文革
chedi fouding wen'ge
(complete negation of the GPCR)

In his last years, Mao must have been aware of the increasingly disastrous consequences of the GPCR which he had personally initiated. On 30 April 1974, in a conversation with Hua Guofeng, Wang Hongwen, Zhang Chunqiao, Jiang Qing, Yao Wenyuan, and Wang Hairong, Mao admitted, as a result of his self-reflection, that the GPCR should be assessed as "70 percent achievements and 30 percent mistakes". He said that in his lifetime, he had embarked on only two major undertakings: one was to overthrow Chiang Kai-shek, the other was the GPCR. In a sentimental tone, he said that it seemed that he would be unable to conclude either of these in his lifetime.

Mao must have thought his "70-30 ratio assessment" (sanqikai pingjia) would be accepted by his Party. It could hardly have occurred to him at that time that the Cultural Revolution, his unique brain-child, would be negated only a few years after his death.

For the Chinese people, the GPCR was a ten-year nightmare, and of course should be negated. Many CCP veteran cadres shared this view with the ordinary people, for they too had also suffered during the GPCR. For example, on 25 October 1980, Deng Xiaoping, in referring to the GPCR, said: "He (Mao) said that its mistakes amounted to only 30 percent and its achievements to 70 percent. And when he referred to the 30 percent of mistakes, he meant 'overthrowing all' and waging a 'full-scale civil war'. How can anyone reconcile this with the idea of 70 percent achievements?" *(SWD*, p. 287).

Under Deng's personal guidance, the 6th Plenum of the 11th PCC adopted on 27 June 1981 the important document "Resolution on Certain Questions in the History of Our Party since the Founding of the PRC" ("Zhongguo Gongchandang Zhongyang Weiyuanhui guanyu jian guo yilai dangde ruogan lishi wentide jueyi", *HQ,* 13:3-27, 1981; trans. in *BR,* 27:10-39, 6 July 1981). This document re-assessed many of the inner Party struggles over the past three decades, and it negated the achievements of the GPCR.

But this assessment was quite complicated. Notably, as early as 1980-81 when the draft of this document was in the process of being written, Deng Xiaoping gave instructions that the GPCR, though "an error of particular gravity, one affecting the overall situation", should only be written about in "broad outline" (cuxiantiao). Deng is said to have preferred leaving a thorough study of the GPCR to future generations. The new Party authorities faced a dilemma: On the one hand, they had to negate the GPCR, whose destructive and disastrous consequences had affected the whole country. Without such a negation, many Party leaders, including Deng himself, would not be able to find grounds for rehabilitation, still less, for carrying out the new reform policies. However, such a negation was not an easy task and there were many obstacles. This is why as late as 1984 the leaders still had to appeal to the whole Party for a "complete negation" of the GPCR (see the 23 April 1984 *People's Daily* commentary, "The Cultural Revolution Must Be Totally Negated"—"Jiushiyao chedi fouding wen'ge"). A nationwide education movement was carried out in 1984 for that precise purpose.

On the other hand, the Party authorities had to emphasize that during the GPCR years, neither Chinese socialist society nor the CCP had changed its nature, and that Mao's "mistakes" were those of "a great revolutionary, a great Marxist". The authorities were fully aware of the danger that one step further and the "Gang of Four" would become a "Gang of Five", thus questioning all the Party doctrines and even the legitimacy of the Party itself. It was quite understandable, therefore, that, although the Party wanted the GPCR to be negated or even "totally negated", it still banned any attempt to study the GPCR comprehensively. An example was the suppression of the 1986 book, *Turbulent Decade: A History of the Cultural Revolution (Zhongguo "wen'ge" shinian shi,* Tianjin, Tianjin Renmin, 1986, and Hong Kong, Ta-kung Pao, 1986; trans. and ed. by D. W. Kwok, Honolulu, Univ. of Hawaii Press, 1997), the first book of its kind, by Yan Jiaqi and his wife Gao Gao. Another example was the cold reception to Ba Jin's suggestion that a "Cultural Revolution Museum" be built. In particular, the world's academic circles were shocked by the arrest of Song Yongyi, a librarian-scholar at Dickinson College, U.S., in Beijing on 24 December 1999 because he collected GPCR documents during his visit to China.

The CCP's treatment of the GPCR is controversial. Some scholars agree that it is beneficial to national stability. Others, however, find the so-called "total negation" to be a Party shield, with which it can stop dissident voices that will refresh and question the memory of the ten-year nightmare. Others ask for a once-and-for-all repudiation of anything like the 70-30 assessment. Mao also gave Stalin a 70-30 assessment *(MZXJ,* 5, p. 286), but few Russians accepted it. The fundamental error of this assessment, they point out, is that it violates modern legal principles. Contribution is contribution, while crime is crime; one's crime should not be offset by one's contribution (if any). See also "wen'ge" (Cultural Revolution), "quanmian neizhan" (full-scale civil war), "huaiyi yiqie, dadao yiqie" (suspect all, overthrow all), and "xinzuopai" (neo-Leftists).

彻底的人道主义只有在文学艺术中才能实现
chedide rendaozhuyi zhiyou zai wenxue yishuzhong caineng shixian (thoroughgoing humanism can only be realized in literature and art)

See "yishu jieshouzhede zhutixing" (subjectivity of art receptor).

陈希同事件
Chen Xitong shijian
(Chen Xitong Incident)

On the afternoon of 27 April 1995, it was announced that at a just concluded enlarged meeting of the CCP Beijing Municipal Committee, CCP Politburo member Chen Xitong had resigned his position as Beijing Party secretary (which was taken over by Wei Jianxing, another Politburo member, who entered the Politburo Standing Committee at the 1997 CCP's 15th National Congress). Chen was held responsible for the case of Wang Baosen, Beijing deputy Major in charge of day-to-day business who had committed suicide early in the month due to alleged economic crimes. Several months later, at the 5th Plenum of the 14th PCC (held in Beijing from 25 to 28 September 1995), the former Beijing boss was expelled from both the CCP Central Committee and its Politburo. On 29 August 1997, Chen was also expelled from the Party, following the decision of the PCC Commission for Discipline Inspection. On 31 July 1998, he was sentenced to 16 years' imprisonment by the Beijing Higher People's Court for his alleged crimes in economic and other fields.

A power struggle was believed to be another reason for the fall of Chen Xitong. A Sichuan native at the age of sixty-five, Chen had been in Beijing officialdom for forty years, gradually rising from an obscure deputy head of a street police substation to the revered position as the Party boss of the PRC capital city. After the June 4th Incident of 1989, contrary to many people's expectations, and also to Chen's own expectations, he (at that time Beijing Major) and Li Ximing (at that time Beijing Party secretary) were not promoted, even though both of them had performed outstanding service as hardliners in the suppression of the pro-democracy movement. Instead, Jiang Zemin was recruited from Shanghai to replace Zhao Ziyang as CCP general secretary. Thereafter, there were frequent clashes between Chen and Jiang. As a most powerful and most recalcitrant "duke", Chen Xitong was reported to have gone so far as to accuse Jiang of organizing a "Shanghai gang" (Shanghai bang). Chen's downfall, undoubtedly, was a great victory for Jiang Zemin, who, at a crucial time when Deng Xiaoping had no more influence in the CCP and government policymaking, showed to the world that he was ready for the post-Deng era.

The serious corruption within the CCP was also an issue in the Chen Xitong case. It is said that a number of high-ranking Party and government officials and their families may have been involved. After the case was revealed to the public, a poignant, though perhaps somewhat exaggerated, saying circulated in Beijing: "A thorough investigation of the case will lead to the destruction of the Party; if it is covered up, the destruction of the country will occur" (cha qing wang dang, cha bu qing wang guo). The Chen Xitong case came to light neither by the Party or government procuratorial organs nor by public informers. Instead, it was incidentally revealed in relation to the Wang Baosen case. This shows that neither the official departments nor the public had an effective means to check curruption. See also "fan fubai" (anti-corruption).

惩前毖後，治病救人
cheng qian bi hou, zhi bing jiu ren
(learning from past mistakes to avoid future mistakes and curing the sickness to save the patient)

See "tuanjie—piping—tuanjie" (unity—criticism—unity).

成分
chengfen
(an individual's class status)

See "jiating chengfen" (family origin; class status of one's family).

城市人民公社
chengshi renmin gongshe
(urban people's communes)

See "dayuejin" (Great Leap Forward).

吃二遍苦
chi erbianku
(suffer once again)

See "yi ku si tian" (recalling past sufferings and thinking about present happiness).

吃小亏占大便宜
chi xiao kui, zhan da pianyi
(take small losses for the sake of big gains)

See "hei liu lun" (six sinister theories).

吃忆苦饭
chi yikufan
(have a poor meal especially prepared to recall past sufferings)

See "yi ku si tian" (recalling past sufferings and thinking about present happiness).

吃饭不要钱
chifan buyao qian
(free meals for all)

See "dayuejin" (Great Leap Forward).

持不同政见者
chi butong zhengjianzhe
(dissidents)

The awkward-sounding phrase "chi butong zhengjianzhe", obviously a translation of a foreign term (which does derive from the former socialist countries of Eastern Europe), began to be used by the public only a few years ago.

The PRC Constitution guarantees political and civil freedoms. Even in the Mao period, political dissidence was not a crime in the penal laws. But political offenders, or "dissidents" as termed today, could be charged with "counter-revolution" or other crimes, and were treated severely and cruelly. Among the 552,877 "bourgeois Rightists"—Mao called them "bourgeois reactionaries who oppose the Communist Party, oppose the people, and oppose socialism" *(MZXJ,* 5, p. 438)—many were certainly dissidents, even though they were not aware of this or dared not to think so in the political atmosphere where everyone claimed that he/she was at one with the Party (gen dang yitiaoxin). During the GPCR, as known to all, numerous political offenders were imprisoned; many were executed or persecuted to death. After Mao, dissidents were active during the Beijing Spring period. Wei Jingsheng was one of them.

The 1989 pro-democracy movement was obviously promoted by a number of dissidents. But even then "dissident" was still a derogatory term, and few would openly call themselves dissidents. An example was Liu Binyan. He had long cherished what he called the "second type of loyalty" (di'erzhong zhongcheng). After the June 4th Incident, which broke his last illusion about the CCP, he confessed: "I thought I was not a dissident, but the development of the situation inside China has more and more made a dissident of me; I did not want to live in exile, now it seems, however, that the increasing possibility is that I will be banished" (Lee Yee, "Zhongguo Faxisi jiao riben geng canku—fang Liu Binyan"—"Chinese Fascists Are More Cruel than Japanese: An Interview with Liu Binyan", *JN*, 234:30, July 1989).

After the June 4th Incident of 1989, some of the Tiananmen protesters fled China. On 24 September 1989, sponsored by Yan Jiaqi, Wuer Kaixi, Wan Runnan, Liu Binyan, and Su Shaozhi, a dissident organization, "Minzhu Zhongguo Zhenxian" (the Alliance for Chinese Democracy), was established in Paris (Yan Jiaqi was elected the Alliance's first chairman while Liu Binyan and Su Shaozhi did not join it when it was founded). Its program can be summed up in four points: 1. to safeguard basic human rights; 2. to defend social justice; 3. to develop a private economy; and 4. to put an end to one-party tyranny (See "Minzhu Zhongguo Zhenxian chengli xuanyan"—"Manifesto of the Alliance for Chinese Democracy", *Xinwen ziyou daobao*, 30 Sept. 1989).

Besides the Alliance for Chinese Democracy, there are several overseas Chinese dissident organizations, including "Zhongguo Minzhu Tuanjie Lianmeng" (the Chinese Alliance for Democracy), the first of its kind, established in 1982 by Wang Bingzhang and his comrades. Important dissident magazines and newspapers include: *Beijing Zhi Chun (Beijing Spring), Zhongguo Zhi Chun (China Spring), Minzhu Zhongguo (China Monthly), Xinwen Ziyou Daobao (Press Freedom Guardian), Xin Shiji (New Century), Huaxia Wenzhai (China News Digest), Xiaocankao (Reference News),* and *Dacankao (VIP Reference Online Magazine).*

Among dissidents living overseas in exile, some were famous when in China, such as Fang Lizhi, Liu Binyan, Yan Jiaqi, Su Shaozhi, Wang Ruowang, Wei Jingshen, Su Xiaokang, Ruan Ming, Guo Luoji, Li Honglin, Zheng Yi, Chen Yizi, Wan Runnan, Cai Ling, Wuer Kaixi, Wang Dan, Wang Juntao, Hu Ping, Wang Xizhe, Zhang Weiguo, and Bei Dao. But now it seems that their influences in China are much smaller than before, weakened, for instance, by isolation from their social milieu. Efforts of dissidents and their organizations are sometimes also damaged by their disunity.

Domestically, an important event of the dissident movement occurred in 1998. Wang Youcai, a Zhejiang-based pro-democracy activist, and his comrades announced on 25 June 1998 that preparations was being made for the founding of what they named "Zhongguo Minzhudang" (the China Democracy Party). Taking advantage of U.S. President Clinton's China visit (on occasions such as this, the Chinese authorities usually act somewhat carefully), they attempted to register this first opposition party under the Chinese Communist regime. This put the CCP leadership to a crucial test. As it turned out, the Party was not yet ready for this landmark action. In an interview with the German daily *Handelsblatt* on 23 November 1998, Li Peng, NPC chairman, ruled out any new political parties or organizations. In an apparent reference to the embryonic China Democracy Party, he said: "If it is designed to establish a multiparty system and to try to negate the leadership of the Communist Party, then it will not be allowed to exist" *(RMRB,* 1 Dec. 1998).

Political dissidence from religious circles, especially from those of national minorities, also constitutes a threat to the CCP rule. Since Marxism (which includes dialectical materialism, atheism, etc.) is stipulated as the guiding thought for the country, potential conflicts over beliefs are always there, though for most of the time not intensified. When religious beliefs are involved in political struggles, things are much more complicated. A long-standing problem, for example, is the Tibet independence movement promoted by the Dalai Lama and his followers. Recent cases were Falun Gong and Zhong Gong, two popular spiritual groups. The authorities were shocked by the 25 April 1999 protest from more than ten thousand Falun Gong practitioners gathering outside the compound at Zhongnanhai in Beijing, where the PCC and PRC central government offices are located. Following the event, Falun Gong was banned as an "illegal organization" on 22 July 1999 and announced to be an "evil religion" (xiejiao) on 25 October 1999. On 30 October 1999, the 12th Session of the NPC Standing Committee adopted a resolution concerning the banning of heretic cult organizations, prevention measures against them, and punishment for cult activities. In light of this resolution, Zhong Gong, together with other spiritual groups similar to the already banned Falun Gong, was suppressed.

Like Falun Gong, Zhong Gong is popular, reportedly having several million learners in 20 provinces; but it has a longer history and more elaborate organizational structure, and seems more politically conscious—it is guided by what is called the "Kylin Culture" (Kylin wenhua), or "Kylin philosophy" created by Zhang Hongbao, Zhong Gong's founder. Zhang totally negates Marxist philosophy (dialectical materialism and historical materialism), Marxist political economy, and scientific socialism, the three components of Marxism. On the basis of traditional Chinese philosophies and his criticism and repudiation of Marxism, he provides a set of philosophical-political-religious beliefs for his disciples. Zhang not only attacks the Communist ultimate goal but also the "irrationality" of China's current power structure, while openly praising U.S. government structure of tripartite division of legislature, administration, and judiciary. The CCP authorities have reason to believe that this organization, if unchecked, will probably develop to become an opposition party.

"Dissidents within the Party" (dangnei chi butong zhengjianzhe) is an interesting subject. In CCP history, the Party leader launched numerous purge campaigns or inner Party struggles to suppress dissidents (his opponents) and to maintain what he deemed to be the Party's correct guiding ideology. For Stalin and his Chinese agent, Mao Zedong was a dissident within the Party; for Mao, Liu Shaoqi and Deng Xiaoping were dissidents; and for Deng, Hu Yaobang and Zhao Ziyang could also be said to be such people. In most cases, dissident intellectuals within the Party were major victims of the numerous purge campaigns, which was true not only in the Mao period but also in the Deng period. For example, at the beginning of the 1987 anti-bourgeois liberalization campaign, leading astrophysicist Fang Lizhi, famous journalist Liu Binyan, and veteran writer Wang Ruowang were expelled from the Party. In the summer of 1987, as a repercussion of the campaign (which had already been checked in May 1987), there was a so-called "five gentlemen incident" (wu junzi shijian). Five well-known intellectuals—Wang Ruoshui, Wu Zuguang, Su Shaozhi, Zhang Xianyang, and Sun Changjiang—were punished by the Party. (Before punishment, Su Shaozhi had been director of the Institute of Marxism-Leninism-Mao Zedong Thought, CASS; Zhang Xianyang, director of the Research Center of Lenin and Stalin, Institute of Marxism-Leninism-Mao Zedong Thought, CASS; Sun

Changjiang, deputy editor-in-chief of *Zhongguo Keji Bao—China's Science and Technology;* Wang Ruoshui, a controversial philosopher and former deputy editor-in-chief of the *People's Daily;* and Wu Zuguang, a famous dramatist.) It is noted that many other dissidents within the Party are not so barefaced as those mentioned above. They usually do what the Protestants did during the Reformation of the Roman Catholic Church: changing course while using the same *Bible*. As a Chinese saying goes, "Gua yangtou, mai gourou"—in front of the shop the sheep's head dangles, but inside the shop one sells dog's meat.

Political dissidence is also from old-line Leftists and neo-Leftists. They assert that the present CCP leaders are precisely those who "sell dog's meat" in the shop in front of which the sheep's head dangles, already having abandoned the basic principles of Marxism-Leninism-Mao Zedong Thought and thus causing "peaceful evolution" (heping yanbian) in China. Party leaders respond with an argument that they uphold Deng Xiaoping Theory, which is "Marxism in modern China" and should be taken as the "reference frame" (canzhaoxi) in guiding Party ideology. But in the eyes of today's Leftists, Deng was the very "China's Khrushchev" Mao had asked people to be watchful against. Their Marxist or Maoist argumentation, though unpopular in the country, may embarrass Party leaders, who still claim to be Marxists.

The CCP authorities punish dissidents outside the Party much more severely than those inside. (Obviously, the two groups are different in nature.) The Party policy is clear, that is, nip in the bud. Wei Jingsheng's case was well-known. He was arrested on 29 March 1979 and sentenced to 15 years' imprisonment on 16 October 1979, on grounds of selling state secrets to foreigners and engaging in counter-revolutionary activities. Having been released on parole on 14 September 1993, he was detained in April 1994 and sentenced to a further 14 years' imprisonment on 13 December 1995, charged with subversion. A recent example was the treatment of the leaders of the banned China Democracy Party. Within a year and a half since December 1998, about 23 of them were arrested and some given heavy sentences (11 years' imprisonment to Wang Youcai, 12 years to Qin Yongmin of Wuhan city, 13 years to Xu Wenli of Beijing city, and 10 years to Zhu Zhengming of Hangzhou city). Since at the 5th Session of the 8th NPC held in March 1997 the "counter-revolutionary" penal code was deleted from the revised Criminal Law and replaced by the crime of "jeopardizing national security", their charges were made accordingly.

The authorities also find it a good measure to exile noted dissidents from China. Among those the authorities released and allowed to fly to the United States for medical treatment (baowai jiuyi) in the past 10 years were Fang Lizhi and his wife Li Shuxian (on 25 June 1990), Wang Juntao (on 23 April 1994), Wei Jingsheng (on 16 November 1997), and Wang Dan (on 19 April 1998). Human rights groups were grateful for their freedom, but they rejected any suggestion that these moves showed an improvement in China's treatment of political or religious prisoners. Sidney Jones, executive director of Human Rights Watch Asia, called Wei Jingsheng's release "hostage politik" (renzhi zhengzhi), a strategy the Chinese leadership has used since 1989. "When they need to offer a concession for political reasons," said Jones, "they release someone they never should have arrested in the first place. When the political climate permits, they arrest a few more as bargaining chips for the next time around" *(Sydney Morning Herald,* 18 Nov. 1997). Wei was released for a short time in 1993 because at that time China was bidding for the 2000 Olympics. When Beijing lost the Games to Sydney—and Wei continued to speak out against the government—he was soon back in jail. Then Beijing bartered Wei's freedom in return for the success of President Jiang Zemin's October 1997 state visit to Washington and to win trade concessions for China.

So far in mainland China there is no powerful and visible dissident influence that can really shake the CCP rule. In addition to what has been discussed above, there are also other reasons for the feeble state of Chinese dissidence. As a tradition, Chinese are not good at striving for, and exercising, their democratic rights. Very often, they resign themselves to adversity, especially when facing the power of a police state. Instead of changing China's present institutional structure itself from outside, many sincerely hope that a gradual reform within the institutional structure can succeed. The rapid economic development, while attracting many former political activists into business, also seems to justify the official slogan, "The need for stability overwhelms everything else" (wending yadao yiqie).

China's present political system cannot tolerate the existence of any dissidence (even in its broad sense, as discussed above). But so long as such a system remains unchanged, dissidents will certainly keep active. As is pointed out by many, there is a confrontation between the trend of so-called "bourgeois liberalization" (zichanjieji ziyouhua) and Deng's "four cardinal principles" (si xiang jiben yuanze). Such a trend, the formation of which to a great extent can be ascribed to the efforts by dissidents, also serves as an environment in which political dissidence works. See also "fan youpai yundong" (anti-Rightist campaign), "yao minzhu haishi yao xinde ducai" (democracy or neo-dictatorship), "bajiu minyun" (1989 pro-democracy movement) "wuchanjieji zhuanzheng" (dictatorship of the proletariat), "si xiang jiben yuanze" (four cardinal principles), "ziyouhua" (liberalization), "Kylin wenhua" (Kylin Culture), and "renquan wenti" (human rights issue).

充分的爱学
chongfende ai xue
(study of sufficient love)

See "ren ji tianxia" (benevolence for the people of the world).

充分主体性和充分超越性
chongfen zhutixing he chongfen chaoyuexing
(sufficiency in subjectivity and in transcendence)

See "wenxue zhutixing" (subjectivity of literature).

冲破论
chongpo lun
(theory of breakthrough)

Hu Qili (b. 1929) was a prominent figure before the June 4th Incident of 1989. A member of the CCP's Politburo Standing Committee, Hu was considered to be a potential successor to CCP General Secretary Hu Yanbang.

In a speech to the 3rd Session of the 4th NPC in March 1986, Hu suggested the creation of a comparatively loose economic environment and a better socio-political and socio-psychological environment. In addition, he proposed that, in order to quicken the process of reform, the CCP "must make preparations not only in the economic field, but also in the fields of theory, ideology, and psychology". After the close of the Congress, Hu made an inspection tour of Shanghai, where he established wide contacts with the city's literary, theoretical, scientific, and technological circles. In his talks in Shanghai, he perfected his theory of "relaxation" (kuansong). He appealed for an atmosphere created by a joint effort, whereby a relationship of unity, harmony, mutual trust, and mutual understanding existed between the Party and intellectuals, such that a comparatively relaxed environment beneficial to reform and construction could be set up. He reiterated the principle of "creative freedom" (chuangzuo ziyou) he had set forth at the 4th Congress of the CWA (held 29 December 1984 to 5 January 1985), promising that the Party would adopt "an attitude of democracy and tolerance towards literature and art", letting writers and artists carry out their creative activities according to artistic laws. On the issue of humanism, Hu expressed the opinion that the right to use such slogans as democracy, freedom, humanism, and human rights should not be regarded as belonging exclusively to capitalist countries. He asked: 'If that right were to be abandoned, what then would be left for socialism? Should socialism only have dictatorship, suppression, and struggle?"

Later, on 1 May, at a meeting at the Great Hall of the People celebrating the centenary of International Labor Day, Hu Qili, on behalf of the PCC, delivered a long speech, "The Historical Mission of the Contemporary Chinese Working Class" ("Dangdai Zhongguo gongrenjiejide lishi shiming", *RMRB*, 1 May 1986), in which he elaborated on what is described by China observers as the "theory of breakthrough". He called on the people to break through outdated Marxist viewpoints that conflicted with present-day reality and to build up a new theory to justify the reforms.

Like Hu Yaobang, Hu Qili was regarded as an enlightened Party leader. Because of his association with Hu Yaobang, Hu Qili had to make a serious self-criticism when the former was dismissed in January 1987. His further set-back occurred in 1989 when he was deprived of political power because of his siding with Zhao Ziyang in opposing Deng's confrontational policy toward the students' pro-democracy movement. See also "fandui zichanjieji ziyouhua yundong" (anti-bourgeois liberalization campaign) and "bajiu minyun" (1989 pro-democracy movement).

重放的鲜花
chongfangde xianhua
(reblooming flowers)

In the favorable situation following the "Double Hundred" (shuangbai) policy put forth by Mao in May 1956, a number of fine literary works emerged, boldly exposing the dark side of social life, or truthfully presenting the characters' inner selves, or both. However, only one year later, almost all of these works were attacked as "anti-Party, anti-people, and anti-socialist poisonous weeds", and their authors were cruelly persecuted. It was not until the end of the GPCR that these writers were rehabilitated, and their works were again highly appreciated. Compared to "reblooming flowers", they were reprinted in the 1979 anthology *Reblooming Flowers (Chongfangde xianhua,* Shanghai, Shanghai Wenyi, 1979; nine works from the book are trans. by Geremie Barmé and Bennett Lee in William Jenner, ed., *Fragrant Weeds—Chinese Short Stories Once Labeled as "Poisonous Weeds",* Hong Kong, Joint Publishing Co., 1983). See also "shuangbai fangzhen" (Double Hundred policy).

重庆诗歌会议
Chongqing shige huiyi
(Chongqing Forum on Poetry)

See "menglongshi" (misty poetry), "menglongshi lilunde san ci jueqi" ("three rises" in the theory of misty poetry), and "ziwo biaoxian" (expression of the subjective ego).

重写文学史
chongxie wenxueshi
(re-writing the literary history)

After the Beijing forum on innovating the study of modern Chinese literature held in early 1985, especially after the publication of the article "A Discussion on 'Chinese Literature of the 20th Century'" by Huang Ziping, Chen Pingyuan, and Qian Liqun in September 1985, many literary critics reflected upon previous studies of modern Chinese literature. A number of earlier conclusions, long regarded as authoritative, were found to be problematic. Discussions in 1985 and 1986, however, were still vague and general. Later, in 1988, a big step was taken when two Shanghai critics, Chen Sihe and Wang Xiaoming, began directing a special column "Re-writing the Literary History" in the April 1988 issue of the journal *Shanghai Literature*. For several months, a number of incisive articles came out one after another in this Shanghai-based major literary magazine. Similar discussions also soon took place in some other magazines. For instance, the *Literary Gazette* initiated a column under the name of "The Past Road and the Present Situation of Chinese Writers" ("Zhongguo zuojiade lishi daolu he xianzhuang yanjiu"), and the journal *Series of Study of Modern Chinese Literature* created a new column entitled "Famous Works Revisited" ("mingzhu chongdu"). During these discussions, more and more critics began to accept the view that the history of modern Chinese literature (from the May 4th Movement of 1919 to the start of the GPCR in 1966) should be re-examined and re-written. This new view shocked those who adhered to the ossified literary theory, many of whose judgements on events and issues in the period were considered out-dated and untenable. After the June 4th Incident of 1989, such discussions resumed outside of China, for example, in the re-published magazine *Jintian (Today)*. Within China, it took a few years before such discussions were resumed. One of the early articles was Chen Sihe's "A Tentative Explanation of the Literary History from the Anti-Japanese War Period to the Cultural Revolution", published in *Shanghai Literature* at the beginning of 1994 ("Minjiande chenfu—dui kangzhan zhi wen'ge wenxueshide yige changshixing jieshi", *SHWX*, 1, 1994). In September of the same year, ten authors discussed this "re-writing" in the "Critics' Club" column in the same magazine. In 1998, significantly, a four-volume work, *Essays on Chinese Literature of the 20th Century (Ershi Shiji Zhongguo Wenxue Shilun,* Shanghai, Dongfang, Nov. 1997, Feb. 1998) was published. Edited by Wang Xiaoming, Luo Gang, Ni Wei, Ni Wenjian, and Xue Yi, it includes more than eighty articles written by scholars at home and abroad in the past fifteen years. The effort to re-write literary history does not seem to have dissipated.

臭老九
choulaojiu
(stinking number nine)

During the GPCR, intellectuals were slandered as the "stinking number nine"—the ninth category after landlords, rich peasants, counter-revolutionaries, bad elements, Rightists, renegades, enemy agents, and capitalist roaders. Mao found that he had to oppose such slander. In his talk on 3 May 1975 with members of the Politburo who were then in Beijing, Mao quoted from an actor's line in the Beijing opera *Taking Tiger Mountain by Strategy*: "We can't do without number nine" (laojiu buneng zou). See also "hong" (red), "sileifenzi" (four kinds of elements), "geming yangbanxi" (model revolutionary dramas), and "zhishifenzi wenti" (issue of intellectuals).

抽象人性论的唯心史观
chouxiang renxinglunde weixin shiguan
(historical idealism of the theory of abstract human nature)

See "rendaozhuyide liang ge hanyi" (two meanings of humanism).

抽象的人性
chouxiangde renxing
(human nature in the abstract)

A label often employed in political-literary campaigns during the Mao period. See "gongtong renxing" (common human nature).

出口加工区
chukou jiagong qu
(zones where goods are processed for export)

See "jingji tequ" (special economic zone).

出土文物
chutu wenwu
(unearthed cultural relic)

As a result of political persecutions, quite a number of writers and other intellectuals disappeared for a very long time. After the 1976 downfall of the Gang of Four, many were rehabilitated and reappeared. One such case was that of Xiao Jun, author of the novel *Village in August (Bayuede xiangcun,* Shanghai, Nudi, 1935, trans., New York, Smith & Durrell, Inc., 1942). Since the early 1940s, this veteran writer had been attacked again and again, and he virtually disappeared for some thirty years. When he reappeared in 1979, his old friends jokingly referred to him as an "unearthed cultural relic".

出身
chushen
(family origin)

See "jiating chengfen" (family origin; class status of one's family).

除七害
chu qihai
(eliminate the seven pests)

See "chu sihai" (eliminate the four pests).

除四害
chu sihai
(eliminate the four pests)

There was a campaign in the mid-1950s in the whole of China which sought to eliminate "four pests"—rats, sparrows, flies, and mosquitoes. This was written into a

Party document called "The National Program for the 1956-1967 Development of Agriculture (Draft)" ("1956 nian dao 1967 nian quanguo nongye fazhan gangyao cao'an"). Its Article 27 reads: "The elimination of the four pests: within five, seven or twelve years starting from 1956, rats, sparrows, flies and mosquitoes should in the main be eliminated in all possible places" *(RMRB,* 13 Feb. 1956). In 1958, the campaign reached its climax. Shanghai Party boss Ke Qingshi (1900-1965) further raised the demand that in three years Shanghai urban and suburban areas would strive to eliminate basically mosquitoes, flies, rats, sparrows, bugs, grasshoppers, and snails. He predicted that this task would be thoroughly carried out in five years so that there would be no opportunity for pests to breed *(RMRB,* 25 Jan. 1958).

Sparrows were later found to be beneficial, so they were replaced by bed-bugs.

传宗接代
chuan zong jie dai
(perpetuating the family name)

See "yitaihua" (single-child policy).

创作典型人物
chuangzuo dianxing renwu
(creation of typical characters)

See "fanyinglun shi wenxue yanjiude zhexue jichu" (the theory of reflection is the philosophical basis for literary study).

创作自由
chuangzuo ziyou
(creative freedom)

"Creative freedom", a seemingly unquestionable concept, became a concern of China's cultural circles in the mid-1980s.

It began with Hu Qili's opening ceremony speech delivered on behalf of the PCC Secretariat at the 4th Congress of the CWA on 29 December 1984. In his speech, Hu significantly declared that "creation must be free" *(RMRB,* 30 Dec. 1984). He admitted frankly that "shortcomings really do still exist with regard to the Party's leadership in literature and art" (ibid.). He cited the following most important shortcomings. First, there were certain 'Left' deviations. For a considerable period of time, there had been too much interference, too many political labels, and too many administrative orders. Second, the Party had appointed to cultural organizations a number of cadres who knew little about literature and art, and this had affected the relationship between the Party and writers and artists. Third, the relationships between cultural workers, between writers, between Party members, between Party and non-Party members, and between regions were still irregular and excessively sensitive. There was still too much mutual recrimination and too many bad feelings.

It was of course good news to Chinese writers that the Party could now admit such a crucial fact—that a "Left" deviation still existed with regard to its leadership over literature and art. The Congress, indeed, was marked by the slogan "creative freedom". Zhang Guangnian, CWA vice-chairman, devoted much of his work report to elucidating the idea newly endorsed by the Party authorities. He said: "As a consequence of the long-term influence of 'Left' ideas, many comrades have avoided talking about creative freedom, as though the very mention of it would result in the unchecked spreading of corrosive bourgeois ideologies. In fact, creative freedom is an essential aspect of Marxist aesthetics and socialist literary theory, and we should expound upon it in a bold and scientific manner" (ibid.). Xia Yan, a prominent writer and senior cultural leader, compared the Congress to the 1935 historic "Zunyi Conference" (Zunyi Huiyi) held at a crucial period during the Long March.

However, Xia Yan, and many others, proved to be too optimistic. Not long after its close, Party documents accused the Congress of promoting "bourgeois liberalization". Under pressure from conservative Party elders, Hu Yaobang had to pour cold water on any high hopes for intellectual freedom. In his 8 February 1985 speech at a CCP Secretariat meeting, Hu emphasized that journalism should be "the mouthpiece of the Party and the government". He reiterated the demand he had made of writers at the 1980 Script Forum, that social reality should be gripped from "an overall perspective". In his talk to cultural leaders on 11 April 1985, Hu Yaobang had to deny any special significance to the slogan "creative freedom", asserting that there was nothing new in it. Around the time of the September 1985 CCP National Conference, under the pretext of building a "socialist spiritual civilization", some powerful people endeavoured once more to suppress what seemed to them to be a "heretical development".

During the course of these changes, there was a debate on freedom within China's intellectual circles. It was aroused by Hu Qiaomu's attack on the slogan of "creative freedom" in his February 1985 article "Creative Freedom and the Sense of Social Responsibility of Literary Workers" ("Chuangzuo ziyou he wenyi gongzuozhede shehui zerengan", *WYB*, 6, Feb. 1985). In the article, which he asked the *Literary Gazette* to publish under the name of a "*WYB* staff commentator", Hu made China's intellectuals once again face the often deliberate confusion of the two meanings of freedom—one as a philosophical category (the opposite of "necessity") and the other as a social-political term. Among those who felt it necessary to expose the untenability of Hu's view was Wang Ruoshui. He pointed out that no matter whether one judged "creative freedom" by the Constitution, or by a series of Party policies, what was meant by the term was freedom in a political sense. Wang said that it was simply pointless for Hu to repeat the platitude that "there is no absolute, unconditioned, and abstract freedom", because no writer or scholar was demanding such an absolute. The crux of the matter, Wang pointed out, was not whether there was a limit to freedom, but where the line was to be drawn, and who was to draw it—the law of the state, or the will of an individual official (Wang Ruoshui, "Wenxuede ziyou he ziyoude wenxue"—"The Freedom of Literature and Free Literature", *JFRB*, 4 June 1986). For the same reason, Yu Haocheng, director of the Masses Publishing House in Beijing, also opposed "A Reflection on the Question of Freedom" ("Guanyu ziyoude 'fansi'", *HQ*, 17, 1986, reprinted in *XHWZ*, 12:19-22, 1986), an officially praised article by Wu Jianguo, an editor of *Red Flag*. As a legal expert, Yu Haocheng found Wu's "reflection" to be a regrettable retrogression (Yu Haocheng, "Ziyoude liang zhong gainian buneng hunxiao"—"The Two Concepts of Freedom Must Not Be Confused", *WHB*, 7 Nov. 1986, reprinted in *XHWZ*, 12:23-24, 1986).

There were two points which were particularly objectionable about the issue of freedom. One was that there would be ideological chaos in the society as a whole if creative freedom and academic freedom were to be approved and advocated; the other was that no one could have creative or academic freedom if they did not possess a Marxist world outlook and had not mastered a Marxist method. As He Kuang, another scholar, saw it, this "actually amounts to abolishing creative and academic freedom". He called this simply a "ziyou kongjuzheng"—"freedom-fearing disease" (He Kuang, "Chuangzuo ziyou, xueshu ziyou yu shuangbai fangzhen"—"Creative Freedom, Academic Freedom, and the Double Hundred Principle", *RMRB*, 20 June 1986). Among those refuting the "freedom-fearing disease", the most noted person was perhaps Hu Deping, the son of Hu Yaobang. When this scholar-turned-official was working in Hubei province in the mid-1980s, he appealed to people not to treat the word "freedom" as a taboo (Hu Deping, "Wei ziyou ming pao"—"In Defense of Freedom", *Qingnian Luntan*, inaugural issue, 1986).

Liu Binyan was one who studied the issue of freedom most fervently. According to Liu, "freedom has been reduced instead of being expanded since Liberation" (*Shenzhen qingnian bao*, 12 Sept. 1986). After the CCP victory on the mainland (which is described by the CCP, ironically, as "liberation"), the word "freedom" (and later also the word "happiness") disappeared from popular vocabulary, except when used in attacks upon "liberalism", "bourgeois ideas about freedom and democracy", or the "bourgeois slogan of freedom, equality, and fraternity". Liu reported that what was always on his mind, and on the minds of many other writers and artists, was the question: What is "bourgeois liberalization"? It was Liu's opinion that literature would not flourish in China as long as it was not clearly (and strictly of course) circumscribed (Liu Binyan, "My Diary", in *XXWY*, 5, p. 440).

Liu Binyan described his theory of "freedom exploitation". Quoting the saying, "If you don't use your power when you have it, you will be sorry when it expires" ("you quan bu yong, guoqi zuo fei", which satirizes those bureaucrats of various ranks who scramble for power and profit), Liu made the following comment: "Does the same not hold true for creative freedom? Now that you have 70 percent of freedom, why do you begrudge using it and spend only 30 percent of it? It should be understood that freedom cannot be saved. It is not like money, but rather somewhat like air; it is no good if you save it. Perhaps the more you employ your freedom, the more of it you possess" (Liu Binyan, "Wode zizhuan"—"My Autobiography", in *LBY*, p. 351). Liu himself was an example of one who practiced this theory, exploiting to the fullest extent the freedom he was allowed to have in a situation where Party policies often oscillated. Of course, at the same time, he was running a great risk, which, eventually, led to his being expelled from the CCP in the 1987 campaign against "bourgeois liberalization" and to his having to live in exile after the June 4th Incident of 1989.

For many Chinese writers and artists, this may be too great a price to pay. They have long hoped that there would be legislation protecting literature and art (wenyi lifa). As early as February 1979, Ba Jin (b. 1904) had said that writers must have courage, acting as spokesmen for the people; but, on the other hand, there must be "sound legislation" to protect them (Ba Jin, "Zuojia yao you yongqi, wenyi yao you fazhi"—"Writers Should Have Courage and the Arts Should Be Protected by a Legal System", *SHWX*, 2, 1979).

On this point, Wang Ruoshui had a somewhat different, more sophisticated, view. In a sober-minded fashion, he warned that, in a country like China that lacks a tradition of democracy, legislation is of little use. Wang found it abnormal that there was such heart-felt enthusiasm for the "creative freedom" promise made by Party leaders at the 4th CWA Congress, whereas there was little reaction when it was adopted in the 1982 PRC Constitution. In fact, "creative freedom" had been stipulated as early as the 1954 first PRC Constitution. However, as Wang continued: "A constitution often sinks into the limbo of oblivion, whereas a leader's words play a far greater role. That is where the problem lies" (Wang Ruoshui, "Shuangbai fangzhen he gongmin quanli"—"The Double Hundred Principle and the Rights of a Citizen", *Hua sheng bao*, 8 Aug. 1986).

Another example was the Double Hundred policy. When people enthusiastically marked the anniversary of Mao's promulgation of the policy, Wang pointed out, very poignantly, it was perhaps because the date was so excessively endowed with significance that it was difficult to carry it out, there having been so many twists and turns in the past three decades. Wang Ruoshui advised people that it was not right to treat the Double Hundred only as Party policy. If it were, then people would think of it as a favor—and a favor could be taken away at any time just as arbitrarily as it was bestowed. In fact, as a Party policy, the Double Hundred was discarded by Mao himself the very year after it was published. Wang raised a very important issue: the CCP should establish a legal system and conscientiously change the practice of an arbitrary "one voice chamber" (yiyantang); and writers and intellectuals should set up the concept of law in their minds and they should never yield to the practice of "rule by individuals" (renzhi), nor praise for this feudal tradition (Wang, ibid.).

But "creative freedom" as freedom in the depth of a writer's heart could be a very interesting topic for research, and a number of literary theorists did devote themselves to it. One of them was Sun Shaozhen. In his 1985 article "On 'Three-dimensional' Images and Freedom in the Depth of a Writer's Heart" ("Xingxiangde sanwei jiegou he zuojiade neizai ziyou", *WXPL,* 4:10-25, 1985), Sun questions the thesis of "the unity of life and art" (shenghuo yu yishude tongyi), which had long been held as an unquestionable Marxist theoretical explanation for all literary phenomena in history—from the flourishing of the poetry in the Tang dynasty to the rise of modern literature. Sun argues that artistic creation is so called precisely because it does away with a passive dependence on life. Only by paying attention to the "contradiction between life and art" (shenghuo yu yishude maodun), and ridding oneself of a passive state, can a writer obtain the "interior freedom" (neizai ziyou) required for creativity. This should be a logical starting point for the study of artistic images.

Indeed, as Sun says, a writer's freedom does not lie in selecting, adjusting, and reforming life, which can all be done at will. Freedom is primarily interior; it exists in one's emotions. The most basic psychological quality for a writer, according to Sun, is "a unique and free emotion", which can, by assimilation, change even outmoded traits of life into novel artistic images (ibid., p. 14). A writer's creativity depends on the extent to which his emotions are unique and free.

Sun Shaozhen asserts that the crisis of losing one's subjective ego (ziwo) exists universally. Only a small number of people can rediscover their subjective egos, and this means that they can gain their inner freedom. When a writer's emotion is substantiated by his reason, he will obtain more inner freedom to understand life and master his emotions.

As Sun points out, it is an eternal law that the form and its norm always lag behind the content. Facing the challenge of the content to the form, a writer should obtain his freedom at the lowest level by experiencing and understanding; at the middle level, he should obtain the freedom to exert his imagination and master the norm of the form; and at the highest level, he should obtain the freedom to break through the form and set up new norms, new styles, new schools, and new artistic methods. Through the three levels, the "three-dimensional" images will develop into maturity. Having discussed all this, Sun tells his readers: "To a genuine writer, the lack of interior freedom is much more disastrous than the lack of exterior freedom (waizai ziyou). The latter is frightening because it suppresses the conscientious pursuit of freedom. Very often, however, a writer who truly obtains his interior freedom cannot be conquered by the pressures and interference of exterior restrictions" (ibid., p. 25).

What Sun Shaozhen attempted was a purely theoretical exploration. While he correctly claimed that interior freedom is much more important than exterior freedom to a genuine writer, he failed to point out that in a strict sense, as a member of society, a writer's interior freedom does not exist independently. It is always conditioned by various social factors. There is something beyond the problem of whether a person is capable of rediscovering his subjective ego and making a breakthrough in artistic form. See also "ziwo biaoxian" (expression of the subjective ego).

创作力消退现象
chuangzuoli xiaotui xianxiang
(phenomenon of diminishing creativity)

Many "pre-Liberation" writers underwent personal experiences of diminishing creativity during the Communist regime. Examples include those famous masters such as Shen Congwen, Cao Yu, Ba Jin, and Lao She. At the age of twenty-three, Cao Yu wrote *Thunderstorm* and within a few years finished four other important plays, laying a foundation for modern Chinese spoken drama. (The five plays written by Cao Yu during the period are *Lei yu—Thunderstorm*, 1934; *Richu—Sunrise*, 1936; *Yuanye—Savage Land*, 1937; *Tuibian—Degeneration*, 1939; and *Beijingren—Beijing Man*, 1941.) But in the thirty years after 1949 this pioneer only wrote three plays and they were for the most part written to fulfill some particular political mission. With his practical experience and talent, he could certainly have written many more good plays. This also holds true for Xia Yan, who was also a cultural leader. In his speech to the 2nd Congress of Chinese Film Artists (held during the 4th Congress of Chinese Writers and Artists), Xia Yan complained, quite bluntly: "I have written only one play since Liberation. This was the worst piece I ever created because I worried over each sentence, wondering whether or not it would conflict with Party policy. Many playwrights assembled here have even more experience of this than I" ("Wode xiwang"—"My Hope", *Renmin xiju*, 12:17-20, 1979). As for Shen Congwen, he simply had to stop all literary activities after the Communist takeover. Obviously, literature was severely damaged by political interference not only during the GPCR but also in the earlier period. A consensus on the part of writers and artists was that it was difficult to engage in genuine creation after Liberation.

吹风
chuifeng
(advise in advance)

See "Lin Biao shijian" (Lin Biao Incident).

春天里的一股冷风
chuntianlide yigu lengfeng
(a blast of cold wind in spring)

See "gedepai" (virtue-eulogists).

纯文学
chun wenxue
(pure literature)

See "jingji duoyanghua xuyao wenhua duoyanghua" (the multiplicity of economic sectors requires the multiplicity of culture).

从群众中来，到群众中去
cong qunzhongzhong lai, dao qunzhongzhong qu
(from the masses, to the masses)

See "qunzhong luxian" (mass line).

错位
cuowei
(malposition)

In the academic discussions in the 1990s in China, the medical term "malposition", or a term from soccer competition, "offside" ("yuewei"), often appeared. Scholars find "malposition" in understanding, or "offside application" (yuewei yingyong) of concepts, often takes place, resulting in confusion and mistakes. For instance, when speaking of "anti-tradition", one must be clear about what kind of tradition. There is the tradition of the Confucian civilization of over two thousand years, which can be called the "old tradition" or the "grand tradition". But there is also a tradition formed on the basis of the "anti-feudalism" victory and characteristic of CCP doctrine. This is a "new tradition", or a "revolutionary tradition". "Malposition" in understanding can occur because of different cultural, social, or political positions. Take Hu Shi (Hu Shih, 1891-1962) for example. He was radical in his opposition to traditional Chinese culture and promotion of a new cultural movement. However, judging from his political reformism, especially from the stand he took in the CCP-KMT struggle, he was conservative. Neo-conservatism is another example. In the West, it upholds liberalism (classical liberal principles), but in China, neo-conservatism attacks liberalism, though the latter has only re-emerged recently and has not yet become a substantial ideological trend.

What can be called an "offside application" of concepts has become a problem in today's China. In this respect, scholars often mention "post-modernism" (hou xiandaizhuyi). In the West, they say, post-modernism is relevant to the drawbacks and evils in society, which has undergone the course of modernization for several centuries. But when it is indiscriminately applied in today's China, a large "malposition" in space and time will take place. Instead of critically reflecting upon the old ideology, its spearhead may be directed to the ideals of democracy and freedom, which the Chinese people have pursued unsuccessfully for several generations. Corruption and social injustice are two serious problems in China today, and their real roots lie deep in China's old politico-social system but not in so-called Western modernity.

"Resisting the cultural hegemony of the West" (fandui xifang wenhua baquan) is another example. This thesis was raised in the mid-1990s as part of the upsurge of nationalism. Many scholars found it untenable against the background of China's current social-cultural situation. There is no need, they argued, to follow blindly those post-modernist theorists in the West, for, at least at the present, resistance to the so-called "cultural hegemony" of the developed Western capitalist countries does not constitute a task of primary importance in Chinese ideological-cultural circles. In addition, if China's intellectuals, living in an oppressive cultural environment, are seeking freedom of thought, they should be very clear about where their spiritual pressure comes from and what kinds of cultural hegemony they face. See also "xin baoshouzhuyi" (neo-conservatism), "minzuzhuyi" (nationalism), "xinzuopai" (neo-Leftists), and "ziyouzhuyi" (liberalism).

打苍蝇
da cangying
(to swat flies)
See "da laohu" (big tigers) and "fan fubai" (anti-corruption).

打歼灭战
da jianmiezhan
(fighting a battle of annihilation)
See "dapipan" (mass criticism).

打老虎
da laohu
(to hunt tigers)
See "da laohu" (big tigers) and "fan fubai" (anti-corruption).

打砸抢
da za qiang
(beating, smashing, and looting)
See "hongweibing" (Red Guards) and "sanzhongren" (three kinds of people).

打棍子
dagunzi
(to bludgeon)
Here it means to adopt organizational measures. See "sanbu zhengce" ("three don'ts" policy).

打击一大片，保护一小撮
daji yidapian, baohu yixiaocuo
(hitting hard at many to protect a handful)
In 1967, when PRC President Liu Shaoqi was attacked by Mao's followers, "hitting hard at many to protect a handful" was said to be a component part of the so-called "Liu Shaoqi bourgeois reactionary line". It meant "hitting hard at the broad revolutionary masses and large numbers of good or comparatively good cadres in order to protect their own handful—a handful of Party persons in power taking the capitalist road (dangnei zou zibenzhuyi daolu dangquanpai)". So the line was "'Left' in form but Right in substance", and it ran counter to the chief target of Mao's attack in the GPCR.

打招呼
dazhaohu
(give previous notice)
See "Lin Biao shijian" (Lin Biao Incident).

打着红旗反红旗
dazhe hongqi fan hongqi
(waving the "red flag" to oppose the red flag)

A term frequently used in the GPCR. People who wave the "red flag" to oppose the red flag were "representatives of the bourgeoisie" who had sneaked into the Party. Many of them were alleged "capitalist-roaders". They were accused of wantonly spreading poison and deceiving people, dressing themselves up as authorities to clarify the Party's policies.

大饥荒
da jihuang
(the worst famine)

See "dayuejin" (Great Leap Forward).

大老虎
da laohu
(big tigers)

The term "da laohu" (or "laohu"), first used in the "three-anti" campaign (sanfan yundong) in 1952, refers figuratively to high-ranking officials who committed serious corrupt offenses. Correspondingly, low-ranking officials committing light corrupt offenses are called "flies" (cangying). As is often the case, the authorities hesitated to deal with the "tigers". As a result, the following complaint was often heard: "(They) only swat flies but they don't hunt tigers" (zhi da cangying, bu da laohu). See also "fan fubai" (anti-corruption).

大炼钢铁
dalian gangtie
(make steel in a big way)

See "dayuejin" (Great Leap Forward).

大中华
da Zhonghua
(Greater China)

According to Samuel P. Huntington, professor of Government at Harvard University, "Greater China" is not simply an abstract concept. It is already a rapidly growing cultural and economic reality and it is also beginning to be a political reality. Huntington further asserts that the emergence of the greater China co-prosperity sphere (da Zhonghua gongrongquan) was greatly facilitated by a "bamboo network" of family and personal relationships and a common culture (*The Clash of Civilizations and the Remaking of World Order*, NY, Simon & Schuster, 1996, pp. 169, 170).

"Greater China" is indeed a popular contemporary term that has accompanied the economic boom in China and its increasing political, economic, and cultural influence. The term can be understood in an economic sense, a political sense, or a cultural sense. Thus, there are also three derivatives: the "Greater China economic circle" (da Zhonghua jingjiquan), the "Greater China political circle" (da Zhonghua zhengzhiquan), and the "Greater China cultural circle" (da Zhonghua wenhuaquan).

The "Greater China cultural circle" can also be expressed by another term, "Cultural China" (wenhua Zhongguo), which is often employed by those trying to find a foundation for the reunification of the two sides of the Taiwan Straits. It also is related to "Confucianism in its third stage of development" (ruxue disanqi) and the theory of the "superiority of Chinese culture" (Zhongguo wenhua youyue lun).

The term "Greater China economic circle", or "economic China" (jingji Zhongguo), suggests that Chinese mainland, Taiwan, and Hong Kong, together with Chinese entrepreneurs throughout the world, can unite to establish a "Greater China economic circle". Some Chinese business circles have been promoting this concept vigorously, but it seems that the CCP authorities handle it with due care. In May 1995, at a forum held by the Asia-Pacific Studies Center, International Studies Institute, Stanford University, Wu Xueqian, China's former foreign minister and NPC vice-chairman, made it clear that China rejects the idea of a "Greater China economic circle", even though overseas Chinese play an important role in China's economic development. Wu emphasized that his country had a vast domestic market, and it would never resort to economic expansionism or be involved in dividing the world. Many other Chinese leaders agree with this view, wishing to put to rest the worry that China's rapid economic development may lead to economic expansionism and to political and military expansionism (the former usually requires the support of the latter). According to Zheng Zhuyuan, a professor of Economics who first put forth the term "Greater China economic circle", CCP leaders do not like the term also because they do not want to see Chinese mainland and Taiwan on an equal footing (He Pin, *Deng Xiaoping zhihoude Zhongguo—China After Deng*, Taipei, Xin Xinwen Wenhua, 1994, pp. 333-34).

The "Greater China political circle", or "political China" (zhengzhi Zhongguo), is less often discussed. Perhaps this is because the time has not yet come; there are a number of difficult and sensitive issues. One such issue is "political identification" (zhengzhi rentong), a long-standing issue caused by past and current CCP-KMT struggles. A more complicated situation followed Taiwan's second direct presidential election on 18 March 2000. Chen Shui-bian of the Democratic Progressive Party, which is pro-Taiwan independence, was elected and became Taiwan's tenth president on 20 May 2000.

Many find the term "Greater China" itself problematic, even expansionist and imperialist-sounding. Wang Gungwu, former vice-chancellor of the University of Hong Kong and current chairman of the Institute of East Asian Political Economy in Singapore, is of this view. In an interview in April 1996, he said: "I have strong views about using the term Greater China. I think the term should never be applied to the Chinese overseas. Greater China is in fact a myth, in my view.... If you extend it beyond the Hong Kong-Taiwan-mainland China triangle, it begins to have a political significance that is quite misleading and, I would say, wrong" *(Free China Review*, June 1996, p. 49). See also "ershiyishiji shi Zhongguorende shiji" (the twenty-first century will be the Chinese century), "Taiwan wenti" (Taiwan issue), "weidu Zhongguo" (containment against China), "minzuzhuyi" (nationalism), and "wenhua Zhongguo" (cultural China).

大中华共荣圈
da Zhonghua gongrongquan
(Greater China co-prosperity sphere)

See "da Zhonghua" (Greater China).

大中华经济圈
da Zhonghua jingjiquan
(Greater China economic circle)

See "da Zhonghua" (Greater China).

大中华文化圈
da Zhonghua wenhuaquan
(Greater China cultural circle)

See "da Zhonghua" (Greater China).

大中华政治圈
da Zhonghua zhengzhiquan
(Greater China political circle)

See "da Zhonghua" (Greater China).

大中华主义
da Zhonghuazhuyi
("Greater China" doctrine)

See "Taiwan wenti" (Taiwan issue) and "da Zhonghua" (Greater China).

大办民兵师
daban minbingshi
(organize contingents of the people's militia on a big scale)

See "renmin zhanzheng" (people's war) and "renmin gongshe" (People's Commune).

大报
dabao
(big-sized newspaper)

See "xinwen ziyou wenti" (issue of press freedom).

大兵团作战
dabingtuan zuozhan
(large formation warfare)

See "dapipan" (mass criticism).

大传统
dachuantong
(grand tradition)

See "fan chuantong" (anti-tradition) and "sixiang gaizao" (ideological remolding).

大串联
dachuanlian
(massive exchange of revolutionary experiences)

See "geming dachuanlian" (massive exchange of revolutionary experiences).

大胆干预生活，严肃探讨人生
dadan ganyu shenghuo, yansu tantao rensheng
(be bravely involved in life and seriously probe into it)

See "ganyu shenghuo" (be involved in life).

大鼓劲、大团结、大繁荣
dagujing, datuanjie, dafanrong
(great enthusiasm, great unity, and great prosperity)

During a forum held in September 1984 to discuss the Party's current work in literature and art and to make preparations for the forthcoming 5th National Congress of Chinese Writers and Artists, Hu Yaobang, CCP general secretary, became the chief architect of a dramatic turn of events. The forum, initiated by Hu Qiaomu and Deng Liqun in the name ot the PCC Propaganda Department, began with a very strong anti-Rightist tone. But half-way into the forum Hu Yaobang interfered, sending Hu Qili to control the course of events. The forum concluded with the following announcement: "At present, as far as the leadership is concerned, stress should be laid on overcoming and preventing 'Left' influence in the implementation of literary and art policies" (*RMRB*, 18 Sept. 1984).

Now Hu Yaobang's strategy in the literary field was, as embodied in a slogan he brought forth for Chinese writers and artists, to strive for "great enthusiasm, great unity, and great prosperity". That was why he felt it vital to check the "Left" forces. As a result, writers who had been attacked in the past few years were now "rehabilitated" in one form or another. Ye Wenfu, the young army poet who had written the famous poem "General, You Just Can't Do Such Things!" ("Jiangjun, buneng zheyang zuo", *SK,* 8:50-55, 1979; trans. in Helen F. Siu and Zelda Stern eds., *Mao's Harvest: Voices from China's New Generation,* New York, Oxford Univ. Press, 1983, pp. 158-65, and Lee Yee, ed., *The New Realism,* pp. 86-91) and who had been attacked by Deng Xiaoping personally, was allowed to publish again. Others, such as Zhang Xiaotian and Zhang Xinxin, were among the delegates to the 4th Congress of the CWA (held from 29 December 1984 to 5 January 1985).

As it turned out, an anti-Left atmosphere prevailed during the 4th CWA Congress (after several postponements, the 5th National Congress of Chinese Writers and Artists was held from 8 to 11 November 1988). At the opening ceremony, writers publicly defied the authority of Hu Qiaomu and Deng Liqun by not responding to their congratulations, while Zhou Yang's message was received with thunderous applause lasting two minutes. (See "qingwu yundong"—campaign to eliminate spiritual pollution—and other relevant entries.) As Liu Binyan commented in his diary that night, "Everyone understood the multiple meanings of the applause"—a conspicuous demonstration of Chinese writers' support for Zhou Yang, one of the major victims of the 1983 campaign to eliminate "spiritual pollution". The Congress, in effect, was an occasion to examine the consequences of that unpopular campaign. One of the most emotional speeches was made by Wu Zuguang, a veteran playwright, who strongly condemned the recent "Left" policy, those who had implemented it, and the political persecution he had suffered. The Congress ended with a landslide electoral victory for the liberalizers and their sympathizers. Second to Ba Jin who was elected chairman of the association with the highest number of votes, the controversial Liu Binyan was elected vice-chairman. Bai Hua, Xie Mian, and Shu Ting were all elected council members, though originally none of them had been nominated because of their political problems—their names were only added to the list of candidates at the last minute. Wang Ruowang, the Shanghai veteran writer who had been accused of opposing the Party leadership, was also elected to the council. In contrast, many high-ranking cultural conservatives lost their posts, including, for example, He Jingzhi, deputy head of the PCC Propaganda Department, and Liu Baiyu, head of the Cultural Department in the General Political Department of the PLA.

When Hu Yaobang was forced to step down from the top CCP post in January 1987, the liberal atmosphere at the 4th CWA Congress was alleged to be one of his political mistakes. A PCC document (No. 8, 1997) accused the congress of being a "demonstration of bourgeois liberalization, characterized by opposing and breaking away from Party leadership". See also "fandui zichanjieji ziyouhua yundong" (anti-bourgeois liberalization campaign) and "ziyouhua" (liberalization).

大锅饭
daguofan
(big cauldron canteen food)

This is a colloquial reference to the egalitarian practices during the Mao period. It implies that there is not much difference in reward whether or not the people work hard. Hence "tiefanwan" (iron rice bowl), which means that once one has a job, it will remain secure, and the person will enjoy pay similar to that of others, no matter what kind of job it is and whether or not it is done well. This practice, however, began to change in the Deng Xiaoping period with the carrying out of his policies of reform and the open door.

Today, jobs-for-life are a thing of the past. But this is not good for everyone. Further economic reforms will leave innumerable money-losing state enterprises unable to care for millions of workers. As China speeds up reform of the state sector, it needs to establish a new welfare safety net. See also "xinzuopai" (neo-Leftists), "jingji gaige" (economic reform), and "xiagang" (leaving one's post).

大国沙文主义
daguo shawenzhuyi
(big-nation chauvinism)

See "minzuzhuyi" (nationalism).

大汉族主义
da Hanzuzhuyi
(Han chauvinism)

See "minzuzhuyi" (nationalism).

大节
dajie
(political integrity)

The term was frequently used during the GPCR in judging, selecting, and promoting cadres. Attention was paid to the essentials, i.e., the political integrity, of the candidate. Small matters (xiaojie), such as matters concerning personal life, were also noted, but the main thing was to judge by political integrity. At that time, political integrity meant loyalty to Chairman Mao; today it requires, first of all, being in keeping with the Party Center with Jiang Zemin as its core.

大救星
dajiuxing
(the great saviour)

Young Chinese today may not know the meaning of the "great saviour". For several decades after Mao was described as "the great saviour of the Chinese people" in the folk song "The East Is Red" ("dongfang hong") of the early 1940s, this saying was repeated again and again throughout the country, and no one dared to doubt it. This became a major topic in a 1979 controversy caused by an article written by a young and obscure critic Li Jian, "'Praising Virtue' and 'Lacking Virtue'" ("'Gede' yu 'quede'", *Hebei wenyi*, 6:5-6, 1979). For the first time, it was necessary to criticize and repudiate the saying.

One such critical article was written by Yan Xiu (the pen name of Zeng Yanxiu) in his article "On 'Virtue-Eulogists'" ("Lun 'gede pai'", *Dushu*, 7, 1979, reprinted with slight revisions in *XHYB, WZB*, 12:168-75, 1979). As Yan Xiu pointed out, it was very wrong to call Mao Zedong "the great saviour of the Chinese people" and to insist that praise of Mao should be the eternal, universal, and most important content of Chinese literary and art creations. Even in the Soviet Union, where from the 1930s the personality cult of Stalin existed for a long period of time, no similar demand was formally put forward, or, at least, propagated with as much emphasis as that in China. Yan Xiu sarcastically said that calling Mao the "great saviour" was by no means Li Jian's invention. The mistake of this young critic, who did not necessarily have the loyalty which was characteristic of a "feudal man of letters", was not to realize that he was too late in reiterating this cliché. See also "gedepai" (virtue-eulogists) and "geren chongbai" (personality cult).

大款
dakuan
(upstarts)

The term "dakuan" ("da" means "big" in terms of number, strength, etc.; "kuan" here can mean "money" or "style") was coined in the 1980s to refer to "baofahu"—upstarts or nouveaux riches, those self-employed businessmen who made money quickly and easily, taking advantage of imperfections in the laws and regulations during the wave of economic reform. Another term of the same meaning is "dawan" ("wan" means "arm"). Both terms also, perhaps jokingly, refer to those (not necessarily businessmen) who made a fortune and had certain influence in their circles. Coined together with these two terms was also the term "xiaomi". "Xiao" means "little" or "young", while "mi", according to its pronunciation, can either mean "honey" or "secretary" (in this case, "mi" is short for "mishu"). In fact, "xiaomi" refers to those beautiful young girls who are the mistresses or secretaries of the dakuan, considered to be one of the four "belongings", or status symbols, of the dakuan in the 1990s. (The other three are: a villa, a limousine, and a pet dog.) In the eyes of many people, these upstarts are no more than "barbarians cloaked in modern materials".

In recent years, quite a number of dakuan found themselves getting into real trouble. For example, Mou Qizhong, China's richest upstart who headed the Nande Economic Group of Tianjin, was sentenced to imprisonment for life for economic crimes by Wuhan Intermediate People's Court on 30 May 2000. See also "xinsheng zichanjieji" (newborn bourgeoisie) and "jingji gaige" (economic reform).

大款四大件
dakuan si da jian
(four "belongings" of the upstarts)

See "dakuan" (upstarts).

大民主
daminzhu
(extensive democracy)

On 15 November 1956, at the 2nd Plenum of the 8th PCC, Mao talked about "extensive democracy", in view of recent disturbances at home and in Poland and Hungary. Mao said he opposed "bourgeois extensive democracy". What he wanted was "extensive democracy under the leadership of the proletariat", which, he said, could be used to deal with subjectivism, sectarianism, and bureaucratism *(MZXJ,* 5, pp. 323 & 327).

Mao carried out his ideas in the GPCR. On 3 November 1966, CCP Vice-chairman Lin Biao (1907-1971), who became the Party's No. 2 boss following the 11th Plenum of the 8th PCC, called on Red Gards and other revolutionary people to exercise "extensive democracy". He told his listeners at a Red Guard rally in Beijing: "By the use of 'extensive democracy', the Party is fearlessly permitting the broad masses to criticize and supervise the Party and government leading institutions and leaders at all levels by airing views freely, putting up big-character posters, holding great debates, and carrying out massive exchanges of revolutionary experience. At the same time, the people's democratic rights are being fully realized in accordance with the principles of the Paris Commune" *(RMRB,* 4 Nov. 1966). In December 1966, the concept of "extensive democracy" was further explained in a *Red Flag* article, entitled "The Dictatorship and the Great Proletarian Cultural Revolution" (Wang Li et al., "Wuchanjieji zhuanzheng he wuchanjieji wenhua dageming").

According to Cui Zhiyuan, Mao tried to solve the series of inner contradictions in the structure of China's "state socialism" (guojia shehuizhuyi) by "extensive democracy", thus making a great contribution to the Marxist doctrine about socialism and state (see Cui Zhiyuan, "Mao Zedong 'wen'ge' lilunde deshi yu 'xiandaixing'de chongjian"—"The Success and Failure of Mao Zedong's Cultural Revolution Theory and the Rebuilding of Modernity", *Xianggang shehui kexue xuebao,* 7:49-74, Spring 1996). In John King Fairbank's *China: A New History* (Cambridge, Harvard University Press, 1992), what Mao thought he was doing in launching the GPCR is summed up as an effort to make "democratic centralism" (minzhu jizhongzhi) more democratic and less centralist (p. 386).

Many scholars, however, find it difficult to speak favorably of Mao's "extensive democracy" (if this term could be used in this case). In the first place, Mao and his colleagues stressed that only "the people" (a political term) could enjoy "extensive democracy", and "the people" certainly did not include the so-called "nine kinds of black elements" (heijiulei). During the GPCR, moreover, anyone at any time could be suddenly singled out for attack and become an enemy of the people. Second, it was for the purpose of overthrowing alleged "capitalist-roaders" that the people were "permitted" (as used by Lin Biao) to practice "extensive democracy". This was not at all democracy or freedom of speech in the modern legal sense. In fact, when "Chairman Mao's revolutionary line had achieved an all-around victory over Liu Shaoqi's counter-revolutionary revisionist line", as announced at the 1969 9th CCP National Congress, the right of "extensive democracy" was considered to be not only no longer necessary but also harmful to the newly established leadership system. Finally, Mao's "extensive democracy" led to the horrifying "dictatorship of the masses" (qunzhong zhuanzheng). In the frenzied and lawless mass movement of the GPCR, "mass organizations" throughout the country became tools by Mao and his followers for massive political persecutions. During the GPCR, according to official statistics, 20 million people were killed and 100 million people persecuted (Ma Licheng and Ling Zhijun, *Jiaofeng: Dangdai San Ci Sixiang Jiefang Shilu—Crossing Swords: Three Thought Emancipations in Contemporary China,* Beijing, Jinri Zhongguo, Jan. 1998, p. 9). The "dictatorship of the masses" certainly had much to do with these killings and persecutions. All those with the GPCR experience can confirm that the most horrifying of it was that almost everyone was involved in Mao's autocracy and became its "accomplice", thus forming a nationwide mass violence similar to that in the Nazi movement. See also "wuchanjieji zhuanzheng" (dictatorship of the proletariat) and "minzhu jizhongzhi" (democratic centralism).

大民族主义
daminzuzhuyi
(big nationality chauvinism)

See "minzuzhuyi" (nationalism).

大鸣大放大字报大辩论
daming, dafang, dazibao, dabianlun
(speaking out freely, airing one's views fully, writing big-character posters, and holding great debates)

See "sida" (four bigs).

大批判
dapipan
(mass criticism)

During past political campaigns, especially during the GPCR, it was common to set someone (or some people) as the target of "mass criticism". With exaggeration, threats, and the attaching of political labels, "mass criticism", or "revolutionary mass criticism" (geming dapipan), aimed at overthrowing and discrediting the target (pi dao pi chou). The target would be openly assailed by name (gongkai dianming pipan), or without naming (budianming pipan), depending on the seriousness of the matter, the background of the target, or whether or not the opportune moment had already arrived (very often, there would be a process from being attacked without naming to being openly attacked by name).

"Mass criticism" is Party's "mass line" (qunzhong luxian) applied in political-cultural fields. The Party demands that everybody be a critic in the "mass criticism" movement. In fact, "everyone is a critic" (renren doushi pipanjia) was a slogan during Mao's period. At that time, interestingly, many people demonstrated a high degree of political enthusiasm and moral courage when attacking others or criticizing the so-called "bourgeois ideology" or the "four olds" ("sijiu"—old ideas, old culture, old customs, and old habits), supposedly meeting the demand in light of Mao Zedong Thought. When they were attacked in the name of the Party or the masses, however, their resistance was very weak. Almost without exception, they would come to admit their alleged problems, or even worse, crimes (so-called crimes were usually the "three-anti's"—anti-Party, anti-people, and anti-socialism). "Mass criticism" certainly makes one feel the pressure of a "denunciation by the whole nation" (quanmin gongtaozhi). It embodies a combination of state dictatorship and the "dictatorship of the masses" (qunzhong zhuanzheng) and a combination of an "ideological-cultural hegemony" (sixiang wenhua baquan) and a "political hegemony" (zhengzhi baquan).

"Mass criticism" is a major manifestation of "Party culture" (dangwenhua). That is why this practice cannot be easily abandoned, even though many Party leaders also denounced it when recalling their sufferings during the GPCR. Take the 1981 Bai Hua Incident for example. When the film script "Unrequited Love" was attacked by the critique "The Four Cardinal Principles Must Not Be Violated" in the 20 April 1981 issue of the authoritative newspaper *Liberation Army Daily*, and when on the same day this article was also broadcast to the whole country as an important program by the Central People's Broadcasting Station, it brought to mind the frightening articles of "mass criticism" during the GPCR. In the accusation movement following the June 4th Incident of 1989, similar practice appeared again.

One can trace the practice of "mass criticism" to Mao's belief, and the nationwide influence of his belief, in the strength of cultural criticism, ideological struggle, and revolution in the superstructure. The allegedly effective practice of "beginning with a mass criticism" (dapipan kailu) is an illustration. When there was a certain Party task to be fulfilled, Mao would first carry out a mass criticism and repudiation, so as to create a political situation in which the people's thinking would be consistent with that of Mao and his Party, thus helping to fulfill the task with greater enthusiasm. In addition, Mao tended to make an example of literary and art circles before launching a political campaign. As early as the Yan'an period, for instance, Mao believed that, for the 1941-42 Rectification Movement to succeed, it was absolutely necessary to bring Wang Shiwei, and several other recalcitrant writers, to heel. After the founding of the PRC, this became a regular practice. Hence, so many cultural mass criticism movements. All of them were essentially political, and, as history has proved, they were all records of failure.

Military expressions were common in "mass criticism", which mirrored Mao's belief in his war-time experience. For instance, in 1954 when praising the two articles by Li Xifan and Lan Ling concerning study of *A Dream of Red Mansions*, Mao used a military phrase "kaihuo" (open fire), saying that they were "the first serious fire in over thirty years on the erroneous views of a so-called authoritative writer". On 5 August 1966, Mao put up a "big-character poster" under the eye-catching title "Bombard the Headquarters" ("Paoda silingbu"), accusing Liu Shaoqi, then PRC president and CCP vice-chairman, of suppressing the GPCR. "Mass criticism" adopts war strategy and tactics, such as "surprise attack", "people's war" (renmin zhanzheng), "fighting a battle of annihilation (da jianmiezhan), "encircling and suppressing" (weijiao), and "large formation warfare" (dabingtuan zuozhan), as one can see in the 1957 anti-Rightist campaign and in the GPCR. Interestingly, in 1999, the last year of the twentieth century, the method of "people's war" was resorted to again in the nationwide "three-refutation movement" (sanpi yundong) conducted by the Party Center, which aimed to refute Falun Gong and its founder Li Hongzhi, refute Lee Teng-hui's "two states" theory, and refute U.S. hegemonism. See also "Bai Hua shijian" (Bai Hua incident), "Falun Gong" (Law Wheel Cultivation), "Taiwan wenti" (Taiwan issue), and "lengzhanhou shidaide xin diguozhuyi" (neo-imperialism in the post-Cold War era)

大批判开路
dapipan kailu
(to begin with a mass criticism)

See "dapipan" (mass criticism).

大气候
daqihou
(macro-climate)

See "xiaoqihou" (micro-climate).

大是大非问题
dashidafei wenti
(major issues of principle)

In 1957 when accusing the bourgeois Rightists, Mao raised the following questions about what he deemed were major issues of principle: issues involving the socialist system, the dictatorship of the proletariat, the leadership of the Party, and solidarity inside and outside the country:

"Ours is a people's revolution, a revolution by 600 million people under the leadership of the proletariat; it is the people's cause. The democratic revolution was the people's cause, the socialist revolution is the people's cause, and so is socialist construction. Then, are the socialist revolution and construction good or not? Have there been achievements? Which is primary, achievements or mistakes?" (Mao Zedong, "Beat Back the Attacks of the Bourgeois Rightists", in *Selected Works of Mao Zedong,* v. 5, Beijing, FLP, 1977, p. 459).

Later, Mao invented a metaphor of "nine fingers and one finger" (jiu ge zhitou he yi ge zhitou), with which he emphasized that in China's socialist revolution and socialist construction achievement is the important thing and shortcomings are only secondary. In the "Sixty Articles of Working Methods (Draft)" ("Gongzuo fangfa liushi tiao cao'an") which he presented to the PCC on 31 January 1958, Mao asked people to be adept in distinguishing between the nine fingers, i.e., achievements, and one finger, i.e., shortcomings. "This is the difference between the general situation and the local situation, between the general and the individual, and between the main trend and the side issue," he said *(RMRB,* 21 Mar. 1958).

For many years, all Chinese had to answer these questions and understand this metaphor, and many were persecuted to various degrees because their answers or understandings were considered to be not what the Party thought correct.

大同
datong
(Great Harmony)

See "quanqiuhua" (globalization) and "ruxue disanqi" (Confucianism in its third stage of development).

大同王国
datong wangguo
(Kingdom of Great Harmony)

See "quanqiuhua" (globalization) and "renmin gongshe" (People's Commune).

大腕
dawan
(upstarts)

See "dakuan" (upstarts).

大写十三年
daxie shisannian
(go all out to write about the "thirteen years")

In a speech on 4 January 1963, Ke Qingshi, first secretary of the CCP Shanghai Municipal Committee, advanced the slogan "Go all out to write about the "'thirteen years'" (or "Write about the "'thirteen years'"). He asked writers to make great efforts to reflect chiefly on the socialist revolution and construction during the thirteen years since the founding of the PRC. According to Ke, this was to be a "core subject-matter" (hexin ticai). Zhang Chunqiao, a member of the Secretariat of the CCP Shanghai Municipal Committee, asserted that there were "ten advantages" to writing about the "thirteen years".

Post-Mao critics have blamed this slogan for leading to the theory of "subject-matter as the decisive factor" ("ticai jueding" lun) and for doing great harm to contemporary Chinese literature and art.

大跃进
dayuejin
(Great Leap Forward)

During his stay in Moscow in November 1957, Mao declared that China would catch up with and surpass Great Britain within 15 years. On 13 November 1957, a *People's Daily* editorial called for a "Great Leap Forward" movement. This was the first time the term "Great Leap Forward" was used openly in a newspaper. Mao spoke highly of this editorial. At the 2nd Plenum of the 8th PCC (held from 5 to 22 May 1958), following Mao's proposal, a "General Line for Socialist Construction" was confirmed, which was marked by the slogan "Go all out, aim high, and achieve greater, faster, better, and more economical results in building socialism". Mao officially called for a great leap. He wanted to beat Stalin at his own collective game. The great leap was expected to carry China into the new Marxist millennium where the "Communist principle" would be put into practice: from each according to his ability, to each according to his needs (ge jin suo neng, ge qu suo xu). To persuade the entire nation to plunge into the great leap, Mao thus described China's good prospects: "Apart from their other characteristics, the outstanding thing about China's 600 million people is that they are 'poor and blank'. This may seem a bad thing, but in reality it is a good thing. Poverty gives rise to the desire for change (Qiong ze si bian), the desire for action and for revolution. On a blank sheet of paper free from any mark, the freshest and most beautiful characters can be written, the freshest and most beauful pictures can be painted" (Mao Zedong, "Jieshao yi ge hezuoshe"—"Introducing a Co-operative", *RMRB*, 27 May 1958).

Thus the "Great Leap Forward" took place throughout the country. Unfortunately, it turned out to be an ill-conceived mass movement, during which a number of wrong slogans were raised and a number of unscientific and harmful practices were adopted, causing a great disaster. For instance, there was a movement called "making steel in a big way" (dalian gangtie) or "making steel by the whole people" (quanmin liangang). The entire nation was mobilized to make steel (with 90 million people directly involved) and all methods—indigenous or foreign, small-scale or of a mass nature—were used, in order to fulfill an untenable plan made by the first secretaries of the CCP provincial committees at the Beidaihe meeting (an enlarged PCC Politburo meeting held at Beidaihe in August 1958). For the planned 1958 steel output of 10.7 million tons, which was a 100 percent increase from the 5.35 million tons of 1957, ironically, 5 billion Chinese dollars (amounting to 75 billion Chinese dollars today) were wasted. In agriculture, there was a movement to make the fields turn out exceptionally high yields (gao'e fengchantian yundong)—guided by an absurd slogan: "The bolder the man is, the higher yields the fields will turn out" (ren you duo da dan, di you duo da chan). The high-yield experimental fields were called "satellite fields" (weixing tian); villagers' record-breaking efforts for high grain yields were described as "launching satellites" (fang weixing). During the "Great Leap Forward" days, "launching satellites" became a most frequently used term to describe the achieving of new records not only in agriculture but also in industry, commerce and other undertakings. (The term was coined in honor of the first sputnik ever launched by the USSR).

During the period, the most important event was the establishment of the People's Communes, as part of Mao's "Three Red Banners" (san mian hongqi) campaign. Within two months after the August 1958 Beidaihe meeting, over 99 percent of farm households in over 740,000 cooperatives throughout the country were reorganized into 26,000 People's Communes. In the autumn of 1958, what is called "the Communist wind" (gongchan feng) occurred. Major manifestations were: first, equality among rich and poor production teams in a commune; second, accumulation of collective assets and excessive voluntary labor; and third, "sharing" of private property. "Free meals for all" (chifan buyao qian), a practice in the People's Communes, was highly praised in the resolution of the 6th Plenum of the 8th PCC adopted on 10 December 1958 *(RMRB,* 19 Dec. 1958). In addition, after August 1958, following the model of the "Red Flag People's Commune" set up in Jiaozuo city, Henan province, urban people's communes (chengshi renmin gongshe) were promoted in the country. At that time many CCP leaders thought communism was just around the corner. Therefore the Party also carried out an education movement in 1958, in which Chinese people were asked to "pull up the white flag and hoist the red flag" (ba baiqi, cha hongqi)—socialist and Communist thinking was praised as the "red flag", while individualism and various so-called "unhealthy ideas" were criticized as the "white flag," or the "grey flag". Unfortunately, accompanying "the Communist wind", those erroneous practices also became a trend, such as "arbitrary and impractical directions" (xia zhihui) and "proneness to boasting and exaggeration" (fukua feng). Even worse, when problems in the "Great Leap" became so clear and Mao's policies were questioned, Mao reacted by attacking the alleged "Peng Dehuai anti-Party clique" at the 8th Plenum of the 8th PCC (held in Lushan in August 1959) and by unfolding an "anti-Right-deviation" campaign (fan youqing yundong) throughout the country. During the campaign, a large number of people, many of them Party cadres at various levels, were attacked and labeled as "Right opportunists".

One of the disastrous consequences of the "Great Leap" was the occurrence of the worst famine in Chinese history, possibly the worst famine in human history. In the three years from 1959 to 1961, according to government records and scholarly investigations, about 40 million people died in the famine. At the "7,000-person meeting" (the PCC enlarged work conference) held in Beijing from 11 January to 7 February 1962, Liu Shaoqi admitted that the famine was probably 70 percent man-made and 30 percent the result of natural causes (sanfen tianzai, qifen renhuo). Liu Shaoqi showed great courage in admitting this, and in the end he paid dearly for such an admission. Nevertheless, even he did not give the full picture. In fact, there was no serious natural disaster in those years. There never would have been a famine on such a scale if it had not been for Mao's arrogance, wishful thinking, and disregard of science. (See, for instance, Jin Hui, "Sannian ziran zaihai beiwanglu"—"Three Years' Natural Disaster: A Memorandum", Shanghai, *Shehui,* May 1993; and Jasper Becker, *Hungry Ghosts,* London, John Murray, 1996.)

Because of its disastrous consequences the "Great Leap Forward" is often called sarcastically the "Great Leap Backward". But it still has been a model for other regimes. Once in power in 1975, Pol Pot, as the leader of the Khmer Rouge, sought to emulate Mao's idea, trying to introduce socialism into Cambodia faster than the Chinese, who had been trying to do it faster than the Soviets. And again, a devastating disaster occurred in Cambodia.

Perhaps inspired by the two above phrases, there is another term, "Great Leap Outward", coined in the West to describe the tremendous changes Deng Xiaoping put into effect for one-fifth of mankind, changes from the crushing, dogmatic isolation of Maoism to a quasi-capitalist economic miracle. See also "san mian hongqi" (Three Red Banners) and "qiqianren dahui" (7,000-person meeting).

大治之年
dazhi zhi nian
(year of great order)

See "yingming lingxiu" (wise leader).

大众文化
dazhong wenhua
(popular culture)

See "guoxue" (Chinese traditional learning), "renwen jingshen lunzheng" ("humanistic spirit" debate), and "xin baoshouzhuyi" (neo-conservatism).

大众化
dazhonghua
(popularization)

"Popularization" and "nationalization" (minzuhua) were considered by Mao and his literary theorists as two requirements for China's Communist literature and art, so as to enable them to better serve the generally less educated workers, peasants, and soldiers and proletarian politics. In his *Yan'an Talks,* Mao suggested a raising of standards on the basis of popularization (zai pujide jichushang tigao) and a combination of the two (puji yu tigao xiangjiehe). Mao encouraged writers and artists to be good at using Chinese national forms in their creative activities. Currently, popularization is no longer required, but nationalization is still promoted by many theorists. They find the formula first initiated by Stalin about "socialist content and national forms" to still be valid. Zheng Bonong and He Jingzhi, for example, even assert that socialist literature and art must follow nationalization. (See Zheng Bonong, "Minzuhua: shehuizhuyi wenyide bi you zhi lu"—"Nationalization Is the Only Road for Socialist Literature and Art", *GMRB*, 13 Jan. 1983; and He Jingzhi, "Xinshiqide wenyi yao jinchi minzuxing"—"The Literature and Art of the New Period Must Uphold Nationalization", *GMRB*, 6 Jan. 1983.)

In the history of China's New Poetry, "nationalization" and "popularization" were two areas of particularly long-standing controversy. According to Xie Mian, a poetry critic and professor at Beijing University, the road the New Poetry took during the sixty years after it was born did not grow broader; rather it became narrower. Under the control of the "Left" ideology, the three debates in the area of poetry—one on "popularization" in the 1930s, one on "nationalization" in the 1940s, and one on "learning from new folk songs" in the 1950s—resulted in little more than driving the New Poetry from this world. Xie Mian also observed that all three debates uniformly neglected the issue of the New Poetry learning from foreign poetry—as if by prior agreement. This one-sided emphasis on nationalization and popularization, in Xie's view, inevitably lead to a "cultural xenophobia" (Xie Mian, "Zai xinde jueqi mianqian"—"Before the New Rise", *GMRB*, 7 May 1980). See also "menglongshi" (misty poetry) and "menglongshi lilunde san ci jueqi" ("three rises" in the theory of misty poetry).

戴帽子
daimaozi
(stick on ideological/political labels)

See "sanbu zhengce" ("three don'ts" policy).

代替说
daiti shuo
("replacement" theory)

See "wenxue guilu lunzheng" (1986 debate on the law of literature).

带着问题学
daizhe wenti xue
(have specific problems in mind when studying Mao's works)

See "tuchu zhengzhi" (giving prominence to politics).

带着枷锁的舞蹈
daizhe jiasuode wudao
(dance in fetters)

From October 1976 until the end of 1978, in tandem with the nationwide political movement orchestrated by the top Party authorities against the remaining forces and influence of Lin Biao and the Gang of Four, Chinese literary and art circles were engaged in exposing and criticizing what they believed to be the crimes of Lin Biao and the Gang of Four in the fields of literature and art. This was a political rather than a literary undertaking, carried out strictly according to political demands, a typical case-study demonstrating how contemporary Chinese literature and literary criticism are an integral part of political struggle. Figuratively, this was a "dance in fetters", as so dubbed by Chinese writers and artists. See also "sirenbang" (Gang of Four).

带着阶级性的人性
daizhe jiejixingde renxing
(human nature bearing a class character)

See "gongtong renxing" (common human nature).

单位
danwei
(unit)

"Danwei" or "gongzuo danwei" refers to workplace—an organization, department, division, section, etc., where one works. Hence these terms: "xingzheng danwei" (administrative unit), "shengchan danwei" (production unit), and "jiceng danwei" (basic or grass-roots unit).

After the establishment of the Communist regime in 1949, Party and government power quickly expanded to every corner of society. Civil society ("minjian shehui" or "gongmin shehui"), or society in its original sense, which is relatively independent of state power, no longer existed. Chinese society became a "society of units" (danwei shehui)—all people belonged to, and lived in, a certain unit. In theory, they were masters of the country, but in actual fact they were employees of the state; without this employer, they could not even survive. The units thus constituted the foundation of state power; everyone was like a cog or a screw fixed in a machine.

Today, with the carrying out of the reform and open-door program since 1978, this "danwei" system has begun to change. In rural areas, the most significant change took place when the People's Communes disintegrated. Further changes occurred when private business emerged in both the countryside and cities. But up to the present, "danwei" is still important for most urban people, where they settle down and get on with their pursuits. Only after a mature market economy has been established and the present political system completely reformed will this "danwei" system come to an end.

China's "danwei" system is an important subject in the study of contemporary Chinese issues. One of the fruits in this field is a 1999 book entitle *China's Danwei System* (Yang Xiaomin and Zhou Yihu, *Zhongguo Danwei Zhidu*, Beijing, Zhongguo Jingji, 1999). See also "jigou gaige" (reform of administrative structures), "jingji gaige" (economic reform), and "zhengzhi gaige" (political reform).

单位社会
danwei shehui
(society of units)

See "danwei" (unit).

当官作老爷
dang guan zuo laoye
(act as overlords)

As a description of those officials who stand above the masses and blindly order them about, this phrase is often used in the practice of criticism and self-criticism. For instance, in an instruction written on 27 June 1964, Mao accused cultural leaders of having acted as high and mighty bureaucrats, not going to the workers, peasants, and soldiers, and not reflecting the socialist revolution and socialist construction.

Government and Party officials, who should be "public servants of the people" (gongpu), had become lords and masters (laoye)—this was a form of "socialist alienation", and a major danger to a socialist society, according to the "alienation critics" in the early 1980s. See also "dui wenyijiede liang ge zhiming daji" (two telling blows to literary and art circles) and "shehuizhuyi tiaojianxia rende yihua" (man's alienation under the condition of socialism).

当代论争备忘录
dangdai lunzheng beiwanglu
(a memorandum on a contemporary debate)

With great courage, Gao Ertai, an aesthete, in 1986 published a long article entitled "Humanism: A Memorandum on a Contemporary Debate" ("Rendaozhuyi—dangdai zhenglunde beiwanglu", *Sichuan shida xuebao,* 4, 1986, extracted and reprinted in *XHWZ,* 10:25-33, 1986). Rather than a summary or a memorandum of the humanism debate of the early 1980s, it voiced support for Zhou Yang, Wang Ruoshui, and other so-called "humanistic Marxists", who were fiercely attacked in the 1983 campaign to eliminate "spiritual pollution". Though Gao Ertai did not directly mention Hu Qiaomu by name, he impressively refuted Hu's views and methodology, as in his article "On Problems Concerning Humanism and Alienation" ("Guanyu rendaozhuyi he yihua wenti", *RMRB*, 27 Jan. 1984; reprinted in *HQ,* 2:2-28, 1984; in book form by Beijing, Renmin, Jan. 1984; revised in *WYLZJ,* pp. 50-102).

Gao Ertai called his essay a "memorandum", recording in it some shabby tricks adopted by Hu Qiaomu and his like in the debate, such as "attacking at random" (wu di fang shi) and "framing a target to attack" (wei shi zao di). For instance, Hu and his followers kept repeating self-evident things, ABCs of historical materialism and ethics, as if their opponents had not understood and opposed them. They argued as if their opponents had been advocating all the evils in society. Indignantly, Gao declared that the purpose of his memorandum was to point out solemnly that it was the adherents of "Marxist humanism", and not those against humanism, who first exposed malpractices in the society and subjected them to serious, theoretical criticism. Gao went on to say that in the 1983 campaign such an arbitrary attitude eventually led to the lumping together of such irrelevant things as the theory of humanism with feudal superstition and pornographic video tapes. Moreover, some articles, regardless of the plain fact that the adherents of humanism aimed at criticizing Lin Biao and the Gang of Four and at thoroughly negating the GPCR, unscrupulously accused them of impressing upon the people the idea that to realize the "four modernizations" was "not to increase the interests of the masses of the people, but to damage their interests" (Hu Qiaomu, *WYLZJ,* p. 74). Gao Ertai said that such a brazen distortion was really "shocking". He continued: "Since the issue has been distorted to such a serious degree, we should like to ask: who are those who are really opposing the four modernizations, in the name of Marxism?" (Gao Ertai, *XHWZ,* 10:27, 1986).

Since Deng Xiaoping had made known his view on the alienation problem—and "from an overall strategic consideration"—at the October 1983 2nd Plenum of the 12th PCC, for a time no one in China's intellectual circles dared to touch upon it again openly. This included even Gao Ertai, whose defiance, in his notable article

"Memorandum", went no further than to criticize Hu Qiaomu and was confined only to the problem of humanism. Of course, Gao had hoped to lessen the potential obstacles to its publication. He had, as he said, avoided the discussion of alienation even at the expense of "many ideas not yet more clearly expounded" (Gao Ertai, *XHWZ,* 10:33, 1986). Even so, the article, completed in February 1985, could not be published until August 1986 "for reasons known to all" (ibid.). (In early 1989, Gao published his views on the concept of alienation in an article entitled "On the Concept of Alienation"—"Lun yihua gainian", which Wang Ruoshui regarded as the most profound and comprehensive elucidation in China on the issue of alienation at that time.) See also "rendaozhuyi lunzheng" (humanism debate).

当代中国文学
dangdai Zhongguo wenxue
(contemporary Chinese literature)

As accepted at present by literary theorists in mainland China, contemporary Chinese literature begins with the founding of the PRC in 1949. Many others, however, hold that it begins with the end of the GPCR, that is, with the "new period literature" (xinshiqi wenxue) starting in 1976. See "xinshiqi wenxue" (literature of the new period) and "xinshiqi wenxuede duoyuan fazhan" (pluralistic development of the literature of the new period).

当代中国知识分子道德勇气的沦丧
dangdai Zhongguo zhishifenzi daode yongqide lunsan
(the loss of moral courage of contemporary Chinese intellectuals)

See "sixiang gaizao" (ideological remolding).

当代中国知识分子的心声
dangdai Zhongguo zhishifenzide xinsheng
(the heartfelt wishes and aspirations of contemporary Chinese intellectuals)

See "Zhou Yang beiju" (tragedy of Zhou Yang).

当代中国知识分子的原罪意识
dangdai Zhongguo zhishifenzide yuanzui yishi
(consciousness of the "original sin" of contemporary Chinese intellectuals)

See "sixiang gaizao" (ideological remolding).

当今世界的两大主题
dangjin shijiede liang da zhuti
(two themes of today's world)

See "heping yu fazhan shi dangjin shijiede liang da zhuti" (peace and development are the two themes of today's world).

当前文化领域的主要矛盾是文明与愚昧的矛盾
dangqian wenhua lingyude zhuyao maodun shi wenming yu yumeide maodun
(the current principal contradiction in the cultural field is between civilization and ignorance)

See "shehuizhuyi chuji jieduande shehui zhuyao maodun" (the principal contradiction in the primary stage of socialism).

当然的革命接班人
dangrande geming jiebanren
(natural revolutionary successors)

See "hongweibing" (Red Guards).

党八股
dang bagu
(stereotyped Party writing; Party jargon)

"Bagu" here refers to "baguwen", that is, "stereotyped writing", or, literally, the "eight-legged essay" that was the prescribed form of the imperial competitive examinations in feudal China from the 15th to the 19th centuries in which the main body of the essay was made up of eight parts.

Mao raised the slogan of "opposing stereotyped Party writing" during the 1942 rectification movement. He maintained that subjectivist and sectarian tendencies—the two targets for attack in the movement—found expression in stereotyped Party writing. Since then, the term "dang bagu" has been used as a metaphor to ridicule CCP dogmatism. See also "xiuzhengzhuyi" (revisionism).

党和国家领导体制改革
dang he guojia lingdao tizhi gaige
(reform of the system of Party and state leadership)

See "dangde lingdao" (Party leadership) and "zhengzhi gaige" (political reform).

党要管党
dang yao guan dang
(the Party should supervise itself)

See "dangde lingdao" (Party leadership) and "zhengzhi gaige" (political reform).

党在社会主义初级阶段的基本纲领
dang zai shehuizhuyi chuji jieduande jiben gangling
(the basic program of the Party for the primary stage of socialism)

See "shehuizhuyi chuji jieduan lun" (theory of the primary stage of socialism).

党在整个社会主义历史阶段的基本路线

dang zai zhengge shehuizhuyi lishi jieduande jiben luxian (the Party's basic line for the entire historical period of socialism)

See "dangde jiben luxian" (the Party's basic line).

党政不分
dang zheng bu fen (no distinction between the functions of the Party and the government)

See "dangde lingdao" (Party leadership) and "zhengzhi gaige" (political reform).

党政分家
dang zheng fen jia (to make a distinction between the functions of the Party and the government)

See "dangde lingdao" (Party leadership) and "zhengzhi gaige" (political reform).

党指挥笔
dang zhihui bi (the Party commands the pen)

See "qiangganzi he biganzi" (the gun and the pen).

党指挥枪
dang zhihui qiang (the Party commands the gun)

See "qiangganzi he biganzi" (the gun and the pen).

党报
dang bao (Party newspaper)

See "xinwen ziyou wenti" (issue of press freedom).

党的喉舌
dangde houshe (the Party's mouthpiece)

See "xinwen ziyou wenti" (issue of press freedom).

党的基本路线
dangde jiben luxian (the Party's basic line)

At the Beidaihe PCC Work Conference held in August 1962 and at the 10th Plenum of the 8th PCC one month later, Mao Zedong formulated a basic line for his

Party. It read as follows: "Socialist society covers a considerably long historical period. In the historical period of socialism, there are still classes, class contradictions, and class struggle; there is a struggle between the socialist road and the capitalist road, and there is a danger of capitalist restoration. We must recognize the protracted and complex nature of this struggle. We must heighten our vigilance. We must conduct socialist education. We must correctly understand and handle class contradictions and class struggle, distinguish the contradictions between ourselves and the enemy from those among the people and handle them correctly. Otherwise a socialist country like ours will turn into its opposite and degenerate, and a capitalist restoration will take place" *(RMRB,* 28 Apr. 1969).

As Mao envisaged, this basic line was for "the entire historical period of socialism". He emphasized: "From now on we must remind ourselves of this every year, every month, and every day, so that we can retain a sober understanding of the problem and keep a Marxist-Leninist line" (ibid.). But this formulation has long been outdated. At the 13th National Congress of the CCP held in October 1987, the Party decided that the current period is the "primary stage of socialism" (shehuizhuyi chuji jieduan), and the phrase "one center, two basic points" (yi ge zhongxin, liang ge jibendian), which is Deng Xiaoping's line, is stipulated as the Party's basic line during this stage. Deng declared in his talks during the 1992 Southern tour that the Party must unwaveringly adhere to this basic line for one hundred years (jiben luxian yibainian budongyao). See also "jieji douzheng" (class struggle) and "shehuizhuyi chuji jieduan lun" (theory of the primary stage of socialism).

党的教育方针
dangde jiaoyu fangzhen
(the Party's educational policy)

Mao long held grievances against China's established educational system. In his speech "On the Correct Handling of Contradictions among the People", delivered on 27 February 1957 at the 11th meeting (enlarged) of the Supreme State Council, he stated his education policy as follows: "to enable everyone who receives an education to develop morally, intellectually, and physically and to become a worker with both socialist consciousness and culture" ("Guanyu zhengque chuli renmin neibu maodunde wenti", *MZXJ,* 5, p. 385). In the "Sixty Articles of Working Methods (Draft)", a document Mao presented to the PCC on 31 January 1958, he asked students and intellectuals to be "both red and expert" ("you hong you zhuan", i.e., "both socialist-minded and professionally proficient"). During an inspection tour of Tianjin University, Tianjin city, on 13 August 1958, he noted that "Productive labor must be combined with education". Thereafter, a more clear orientation for the Party's educational work was put forth in a 1958 directive jointly promulgated by the PCC and the State Council: "Education must serve proletarian politics and be combined with productive labor" (Jiaoyu bixu wei wuchanjieji zhengzhi fuwu, bixu tong shengchan laodong xiang jiehe). In order to actualize this, the directive demanded an even more powerful Party leadership. In a series of political campaigns, many teachers and students were convicted as "bourgeois Rightists", or vilified as "white and expert" (baizhuan), "only expert and not red" (zhi zhuan bu hong), or "shoots of revisionism" (xiuzhengzhuyi miaozi).

Two documents, "Fourteen Articles on Scientific Work" ("Kexue Gongzuo Shisitiao") and "Sixty Articles on Work in Institutions of Higher Learning" ("Gaojiao Liushitiao"), were issued in 1961. They were expected to check Mao's Leftist tendency, which some leaders in the Party regarded as harmful to China's educational cause. But this did not result in many changes. On 13 February 1964,

Mao made known some of his extreme views about education at the Spring Festival symposium. Later, he even gave the following instructions: "The period of schooling must be shortened. A Revolution must be carried out in education. The phenomenon of the bourgeois intellectuals ruling our schools must not be allowed to continue any longer." During the GPCR, intellectuals were slandered as the "stinking number nine" (chou laojiu). There was a saying that "the more a person knows, the more reactionary he will become" (zhishi yueduo yue fandong). Many young people were influenced by a "futility of education" theory (dushu wuyong lun).

Furthermore, with Mao's approval, what was called the "two appraisals" (liang ge guji) was put forward on 13 August 1971 in the "Summary" of the National Conference on Educational Work which was held in Beijing from April to July 1971. The first appraisal was: During the seventeen years prior to the start of the GPCR (1949 to 1966), the bourgeoisie exercised dictatorship over the proletariat in the educational sphere, that is, there was a "dictatorship by the proponents of a sinister line". The second appraisal was that the world outlook of the vast majority of intellectuals was basically bourgeois, that is, they were bourgeois intellectuals.

The "two appraisals" served as a good excuse to persecute China's intellectuals. After the downfall of the Gang of Four, intellectuals strongly expressed their opposition to these two appraisals. Deng Xiaoping supported this, because he too had been a victim of the GPCR. He rectified a number of problems, asserting that it was the "red line" ("hongxian", i.e., Chairman Mao's revolutionary line) that had been dominant in China's educational work in the first seventeen years since the founding of the People's Republic (at that time this was an argument in favor of China's intellectuals). Deng explained what was meant by "both red and expert" and what "reasonable standards" should be set for intellectuals. He rehabilitated most of those who had been persecuted in the various movements during Mao's regime. Instead of continuing Mao's "uniting with, educating, and remolding intellectuals" policy, Deng announced that China's intellectuals were already part of the working class. Under his auspices, the "two appraisals" were finally rescinded in a written directive by the PCC on 19 March 1979.

On 10 September 1983, Deng Xiaoping wrote an inscription for the Jingshan School of Beijing, which says: "Education must be modernization-oriented, world-oriented, and future-oriented" (Jiaoyu yao mianxiang xiandaihua, mianxiang shijie, mianxiang weilai). The "three orientations" were later accepted by the Party as the "strategic orientation" for China's "socialist education" and the "guiding principle" for its reform and development.

In 1985, a new organ, the State Education Commission, was established. In 1995, the PRC Education Law was promulgated. In 1996, a long-range development program toward the year 2010 was released. The Party is now promoting the slogan "ke jiao xing guo" (revitalize China through science and education). See also "ke jiao xing guo" (revitalize China through science and education).

党的领导
dangde lingdao
(Party leadership)

After the founding of the PRC, a slogan was continually and most frequently repeated, that is, "Strengthen Party leadership".

"Party leadership" refers to CCP leadership. "Were it not for the Communist Party there would be no New China." Therefore, it cannot be questioned (and is specially stipulated in the PRC Constitution) that the CCP provides leadership in every field, including government departments, the army, other parties and social organizations, education, science, technology, economic development, mass media, and commercial and cultural activities. A major characteristic of the Chinese Communist regime ever since it was set up has been: "no distinction between the functions of the Party and the government" (dang zheng bu fen).

During the GPCR there was a slogan "The working class must exercise leadership in everything" (gongrenjieji bixu lingdao yiqie). This was of course only another expression of Party leadership (since "the Communist Party is the vanguard of the working class"). In rebuilding Party organizations in the later years of the GPCR, the authorities emphatically asked for a "centralized Party leadership" (dangde yiyuanhua lingdao). The personality cult of Mao affected all aspects of life. This was a natural development. As many have pointed out, a one-class dictatorship will inevitably lead to a one-party dictatorship (yidangzhuanzheng) and then to a dictatorship by the individual. The CCP leadership system can be said to be a Leninist model plus Chinese feudal autocracy. There is a tight power net: the whole country is subject to the Party's absolute rule and the whole Party is subject to the rule of a few leaders, and very often one leader at the very top.

As early as 1956, after Stalin was exposed for having committed serious crimes and having gravely damaged legality in the Soviet Union, Mao Zedong pointed out, correctly, that the things Stalin did would have been impossible in Western countries like Britain, France, and the United States. Unfortunately, Mao did not, and could not, solve the problems in the Chinese system of leadership. Instead, his Leftist policies became increasingly rampant, bringing terrible disasters to the Chinese people.

The vital problem of the Party leadership system was fully revealed during the GPCR. After its end, even CCP leaders themselves came to the conclusion that the existing system of Party leadership was devastating and needed to be reformed. In fact, reform of the system of Party and state leadership was the major item on the political reform agenda that Deng planned to carry out in 1980.

In his speech "On the Reform of the System of Party and State Leadership", delivered on 18 August 1980 to an enlarged meeting of the PCC Politburo, Deng said that past Party errors were attributable partially to the way of thinking and style of work of some leaders, and even more to the problems in the Party's organizational and working systems. The major problems, Deng admitted, included "bureaucracy, over-concentration of power, patriarchal methods, life tenure in leading posts, and privileges of various kinds" (*SWD*, p. 309). He stated, most correctly: "If these systems are sound, they can place restraints on the actions of bad people; if they are unsound, they may hamper the efforts of good people or indeed, in certain cases, may push them in the wrong direction" (*SWD*, p. 316). Mao, Deng said, was "influenced to a serious degree by certain unsound systems and institutions" (ibid.).

It is remarkable that Deng, a victim of the GPCR, as early as 1980 brought up the issue of the system of Party and state leadership. It is a pity, however, that he failed to further promote political reform. Moreover, as noted by China critics, it is ironic that Deng himself also became a "victim" of the "unsound" system. At the 13th National Congress of the CCP held in October 1987, Deng "stepped down" from the Party's Politburo and its Standing Committee, and even from the PCC (only retaining his post as CMC chairman as a makeshift measure until Jiang Zemin could take over in November 1989). However, a resolution passed at the 1st Plenum of the 13th PCC declared that Deng Xiaoping would be at the helm and have the final say if any problems of vital importance were to emerge. Extraordinarily, he had reached the culmination of his power. The new "invisible" power structure enabled Deng to bring his views and will into full play, with virtually no threat of challenges from within the Party. This led to his tragedy—in his treatment of the 1989 pro-democracy movement. If the system had been sound, the use of force and the tragic loss of life could have been avoided.

There was a deep inherent contradiction. When Deng discussed improving Party leadership (his idea of political reform), he meant how to uphold and strengthen it (*SWD*, p. 256). He put forth his "four cardinal principles", the core of which was to uphold CCP leadership. He wished to have the reform carried out under the Party's strong leadership. In his opinion, the stronger the Party leadership, the more successful the reform would be. But a serious political reform, including more radical measures such as democratic elections and practicing a multiparty system (if possible), would certainly weaken the power of CCP leaders at various levels and damage their vested interests. This was also true of separating the functions of the Party and the government—the CCP is a colossal body of 61 million members in 3.5 million units and all its activities, from central to local, big or small, are mostly financed by the government. (A new law was adopted in 1998: "Zhongguo gongchandang he guojia jiguan jiceng zuzhi gongzuo tiaoli"—"Regulations for Primary Organizations of the Chinese Communist Party and the Chinese Government". According to this document, CCP officials are "full-time working personnel for Party affairs"—"zhuanzhi dangwu gongzuo renyuan", and their outlay is treated as government's administrative expenditure.) Thus, it logically follows: the more successful the reform is, the weaker Party leadership will be. Therefore, one can detect a danger: the stronger Party leadership is, the greater the obstacles to reform. This helps explain why to date political reform has achieved so little.

There is another dilemma. The CCP declares itself to be leading the Chinese people in building "socialism with Chinese characteristics". It is the Party that defines the basic line of Deng's blueprint for reform: in order to build a powerful, prosperous China, economic liberalization is necessary, but such a liberalization must not jeopardize the CCP's monopoly on power. Jiang Zemin seems certain to continue this line. Yet, as China critics maintain, "the odds against achieving full modernization without losing political control are daunting" ("The Next China", *Time*, 3 Mar. 1997). The Party's claim to legitimacy rests on its pledge to carry out reform and the open-door program, on its ability to deliver sustained economic growth and rising incomes. Once the people are better off, they will demand a say in their own governance. China will not be able to continue its long-term economic advances without modifying—or being forced to modify—its repressive political system. A "reverse law" is at work here: the more the Party wins (in its reform drive), the more it loses (in maintaining its power).

Another legacy of Deng concerning Party leadership was his emphasis of the importance of establishing a correct and strong "core" of the Party leadership. He found Jiang Zemin to be such a core.

Soon after the June 4th Incident of 1989, Jiang Zemin was confirmed as CCP general secretary. On 16 June 1989, Deng gave a talk on "the core of Party leadership" to the two senior statesmen, Yang Shangkun (b. 1907) and Wan Li (b. 1916), and the six newly elected members of the Politburo's Standing Committee: Jiang Zemin (b. 1926), Li Peng (b. 1928), Qiao Shi, (b. 1924), Yao Yilin (b. 1917), Song Ping (b. 1917), and Li Ruihuan (b. 1934). According to Deng, there were three generations of CCP leadership. Mao Zedong was the core of the first generation and Deng was the core of the second generation. Now the third generation of the Party's collective leadership had been established, with Jiang Zemin at the core. There must be a core of the leadership, Deng said, for without a core the leadership is not reliable. In Deng's opinion, it was because there was a Mao Zedong that the GPCR could not overthrow the Communist Party. In Deng's generation, even though a change of leaders occurred twice (Hu Yaobang and Zhao Ziyang) in 1987 and 1989 respectively, the Party leadership was not much affected, and this was also because there was a core (that is, Deng himself). Now Jiang Zemin, who had been selected from Shanghai by Deng himself, was the core. Deng asked all present to support and safeguard Jiang as the new core of the Party leadership (Jiang hexin) with a high degree of consciousness.

Speaking of the generations of CCP leadership, some observers argue that Deng Xiaoping, together with other Party elders, still should be classified in the first generation, while Hua Guofeng, Hu Yaobang, Zhao Ziyang, and Jiang Zemin should be considered part of the second generation. Hua Guofeng's succession was aborted because of his failure to overcome the obstacle of Deng, which Hua felt sharply at the 1978 3rd Plenum of the 11th PCC. The contradiction between the first and the second generations also found expression in the downfall of Hu Yaobang and Zhao Ziyang. Neither of them obviously could win favor with the Party elders. When they finally lost Deng's support—their appointment to the position of Party's general secretary was derived precisely from Deng's support—it meant the end of their political life. In this regard, Jiang Zemin has been lucky. No matter whether he is of the second or the third generation, he is very well positioned to take all power into his hands because he is the formal head of the Party (PCC general secretary), the state (PRC president), and the armed forces (CMC chairman). Neither Mao or Deng enjoyed such a position. Some others argue that Deng could be regarded as the leader of the second generation because he initiated the reform and open door after the end of the GPCR and thus opened up a new era in the CCP history. Jiang Zemin, however, should not be counted as the leader of a new generation, at least at this stage, because he only inherits Deng's legacies and does not have a theory or a new orientation of his own.

Some people fundamentally refuse to accept that an individual should be the core of the leadership. They argue that even Mao did not accept this idea. Instead, Mao had said: "The force at the core leading our cause forward is the Chinese Communist Party" (1954) or "The Chinese Communist Party is the core of the leadership of the whole Chinese people" (1957). They also point out that the concept of "the core of the first, second, or third generation of the CCP leadership" violates the Party Constitution, which stipulates a five-year tenure of office for a Party leader and an election to be held every five years. This concept precisely comes from the practice of imperial power inheriting in the feudal age.

Today, the vital problem affecting Party leadership is the universal corruption in the Party. Deng was aware of this. He warned: "If there are to be any serious problems arising in China, they are very likely to occur within the Communist Party". (*People's Daily* commentator, "Dang yao guan dang"—"The Party Should Supervise Itself", *RMRB*, 22 Oct. 1994). Deng told his followers that "the Party should supervise itself" (ibid.). This thesis is praised as an important point in Deng's theory of CCP building. But Deng failed to solve the corruption problem.

In his report at the CCP's 15th National Congress on 12 September 1997, Jiang Zemin said, with a stern tone: "The fight against corruption is a grave political struggle vital to the very existence of the Party and the state." He pledged to carry out his anti-corruption campaign in a serious and regularized way. While reiterating his loyalty to Deng Xiaoping Theory, the new core of the Party leadership stressed an ethical dimension to economic growth (which somewhat set Jiang apart from Deng). He pledged to pay close attention to the handling of the relationship between material progress and cultural and ethical progress. While confirming that economic backwardness is not socialism, Jiang added that spiritual deficiency also is not socialism. On 14 January 2000 at the 4th Plenum of the CCP Central Commission for Discipline Inspection, Jiang announced that the Party must strictly discipline itself before it can run the country well (zhi guo bi xian zhi dang, zhi dang wubi cong yan).

Jiang did adopt some strict anti-corruption measures. But it is still doubtful that the third generation "core" of leadership can fundamentally solve this problem without reforming the present politico-social system. As observers point out, corruption in today's China is a structural problem. It is a "political cancer" with Chinese characteristics.

On 24 February 2000, at a forum on Party building held in Guangzhou city, Jiang expressed his wish that his Party always earnestly represent the development requirements of China's advanced social productive forces, the progressive course of China's advanced culture, and the fundamental interests of the Chinese people. Jiang's thought about the "three represents" (san ge daibiao) was hailed by his supporters as the "great program for an all-round strengthening of Party building" (*People's Daily* editorial, "Quanmian jiaqiang dangde jianshede weida gangling"—'The Great Program for an All-Round Strengthening of Party Building", *RMRB*, 22 May 2000). Jiang's is no doubt an inspiring wish, but the people still have to ask how the Party solves its own problems, in particular, corruption. See also "zhengzhi gaige" (political reform), "fan fubai" (anti-corruption), and "ziyouhua" (liberalization).

党的领导核心
dangde lingdao hexin
(the core of Party leadership)

See "dangde lingdao" (Party leadership).

党的三大作风
dangde san da zuofeng
(the Party's three important styles of work)

See "san da zuofeng" (three important styles of work).

党的一元化领导
dangde yiyuanhua lingdao
(centralized Party leadership)

See "dangde lingdao" (Party leadership) and "zhengzhi gaige" (political reform).

党内持不同政见者
dangnei chi butong zhengjianzhe
(dissidents within the Party)

See "chi butong zhengjianzhe" (dissidents).

党内和平论
dangnei heping lun
(theory of "inner-Party peace")

See "hei liu lun" (six sinister theories).

党内走资本主义道路当权派
dangnei zou zibenzhuyi daolu dangquanpai

(people in power within the
Party taking the capitalist road)

See "zou zibenzhuyi daolu dangquanpai" (those in power taking the capitalist road).

党天下
dangtianxia
(the Party is the entire world)

The term "dangtianxia" was first used in 1957 by Chu Anping, deputy director of the Propaganda Department of the September 3rd Academy (Jiu San Xueshe) and editor-in-chief of *Guangming Daily*. It figuratively describes the Western term "party-state".

At a meeting on 1 June 1957 summoned by the PCC United Front Department, Chu tried to explain his point that "the Party leadership of the nation is not equivalent to the whole nation belonging to the Party". The current situation was, he said, within the the bounds of the nation, all units, large and small, even a section or a group, were headed by a Party member. And all matters, important or trivial, were carried out based on the whims of the Party members. Chu hoped that such a situation, which he described as "the Party is the entire world", could be changed. At the time, he recalled Mao's 1945 promise about organizing a "coalition government" (lianhe zhengfu). When the PRC was founded in 1949, there were three non-Party personages (dangwai renshi) among the six vice-chairmen of the PRC Central Government, and two non-Party personages among the four vice-premiers. "That was something like a coalition government," Chu said. But later things greatly changed after a government reshuffling. The three non-Party personages became vice-chairmen of the NPC, and among the twelve vice-premiers, there were no non-Party personages at all *(RMRB*, 2 June 1957).

Before "counter-attacking the bourgeois Rightists", Mao asked the people to air their views freely and to help the Party in its rectification drive. Many doing so fell victim to Mao's "overt trick" (yangmou) and were later cruelly persecuted as bourgeois Rightists. Chu Anping's remark that "the Party is the entire world", together with Luo Longji's "rehabilitation committee" (pingfan weiyuanhui) and Zhang Bojun's "political design academy" (zhengzhi shejiyuan), were condemned as the "three major reactionary theories" of China's Rightists. See also "fan youpai yundong" (anti-Rightist campaign) and "dangde lingdao" (Party leadership).

党外人士
dangwai renshi
(non-Party personages)

In mainland China, the Chinese character "dang" (party) is habitually used as the equivalent of "Zhongguo Gongchandang" (the CCP), that is, "the Party" refers to the Chinese Communist Party. So "dangwai renshi" means "personages outside the CCP". It can also be translated as "non-Party personages", referring to all those who are not CCP members, no matter whether they belong to a "democratic party" or not. See also "dangtianxia" (the Party is the entire world).

党文化
dangwenhua

(Party culture)

See "sixiang gaizao" (ideological remolding) and "xinwen ziyou wenti" (issue of press freedom).

党中央
dangzhongyang
(Party Center)

See "zhongyang" (Party Center) and "xiangpi tuzhang" (rubber stamp).

党中央编戏，国务院演戏，人大评戏，政协看戏
dangzhongyang bianxi, guowuyuan yanxi, renda pingxi, zhengxie kanxi
(the Party Center writes plays, whereas the State Council puts them on, the NPC makes comments, and the CPPCC functions as an audience)

See "xiangpi tuzhang" (rubber stamp).

道德滑坡
daode huapo
(decline of morality)

See "fazhan caishi ying daoli" (development is the most essential criterion).

道德复苏
daode fusu
(morality resuscitation)

See "fazhan caishi ying daoli" (development is the most essential criterion).

德才兼备
de cai jian bei
(equal stress on political integrity and professional competence)

See "disan tidui" (third echelon).

邓後时代
Deng hou shidai
(post-Deng era)

Deng Xiaoping died on 19 February 1997. This marked the end of the Deng Xiaoping era and the beginning of the post-Deng era.

A number of books on the "uncertainties" about the new era had been published before Deng's death, such as *China after Deng (Deng Xiaoping Zhihoude Zhongguo—Jiexi Shi Ge Shengsiyouguande Wenti,* Taipei, Shijie Shuju, 1995) by Wu Guoguang and Wang Zhaojun, and *Challenges Faced by Jiang Zemin (Jiang Zemin Mianlinde Tiaozhan,* New York, Mirror Books, July 1996) by Wang Shaoguang, Ho Pin, Wu

Guoguang, Gao Xin, and Qin Qi. These were questions people usually asked: Who will finally be Deng's heir as the supreme power holder? Is there any possibility that the CCP regime will come to an end? Will the economy in mainland China keep flourishing? What are the chances for a revolt by the people? Is it likely that a separatist regime will be set up by a local force and a war between local warlords will break out? Will national issues lead to the disintegration of China? Will there be a war between the two sides of the Taiwan Straits? Will any political or economic earthquakes occur in Hong Kong? And, finally, will China bring a "yellow peril" to the world? For the present CCP leadership with Jiang Zemin as its core, this is certainly a crucial period to solve the many hard-to-tackle issues which have accumulated over the years of reform. The host of challenges faced by Jiang range from consolidating his political position to meeting the ever-expanding needs of a rapidly changing nation. It is vitally important to maintain stability. Turmoil of any sort must be avoided, whether in society or in the leadership. Jiang himself, of course, wishes to achieve some successes, in what can be called the "Jiang Zemin era" (Jiang Zemin shidai). And it seems that he would be lucky enough to have his wish fulfilled. Whatever the case, optimistically, the Chinese people look forward to a new system in the new era.

Both the Mao Zedong and Deng Xiaoping eras, led by the so-called first and second generations, are said to be eras of political "strong men". After Deng, in Jiang Zemin's own words, there will be no "strong man" in the CCP leadership. Admittedly, Jiang is definitely not an equel of Mao or Deng, and he most likely realizes this. But, as many scholars argue, the Chinese nation has not yet got over its "great leader complex". It tends to worship imperial power (huangquan). Throughout history, following the fall of one strong man there always would be the rise of another strong man. Only those who do not really understand China's "national characteristics" (guoqing) dare say that the death of Deng will usher in a new era in which there is no more strongman politics. Very likely, Jiang will become a new strong man, first by his supporters within the Party. For instance, in all official propaganda celebrating the 50th anniversary of the founding of the PRC, Jiang was conspicuously feature along with Mao and Deng. The same treatment was also seen in a number of newly published books, one of them being *Mao Zedong, Deng Xiaoping, and Jiang Zemin on Ideological-Political Work* (PCC Propaganda Department, ed., *Mao Zedong, Deng Xiaoping, and Jiang Zemin Lun Sixiang Zhengzhi Gongzuo,* Beijing, Xuexi, Feb. 2000).

At a luncheon with the visiting Japanese Prime Minister Keizo Obuchi on 9 July 1999, as observers noted, Jiang mentioned that the CCP Constitution stipulates no tenure limit for the general secretary. On several other occasions, Jiang also suggested letting his younger assistants take up more duties. It was predicted that at the next (that is, the 16th) CCP National Congress to be held in 2002, Jiang probably would still keep one or two key positions. He may adopt the Deng mode as Party's paramount leader. See also "zhengzhi gaige" (political reform).

邓後时代第一篇政治宣言
Deng hou shidai diyi pian zhengzhi xuanyan
(the first political manifesto of the post-Deng era)

See "Deng Xiaoping lilun" (Deng Xiaoping Theory).

邓六条
Deng liutiao

(Deng Xiaoping's six principles)

On 26 June 1983, when meeting with Yang Liyu, an American professor, Deng presented his tentative plan for the peaceful reunification of Taiwan and Chinese mainland, which was made up of "six principles". Deng made it clear that he opposed the idea of a "complete autonomy" (wanquan zizhi) for Taiwan. He envisaged a "one country, two systems", though the term—"yiguo liangzhi" in Chinese—was not yet used. See also "Taiwan wenti" (Taiwan issue).

邓小平理论
Deng Xiaoping lilun
(Deng Xiaoping Theory)

Deng Xiaoping Theory mainly refers to Deng's theory of "building socialism with Chinese characteristics" (jianshe you Zhongguo tese shehuizhuyi).

This term first appeared in Deng Xiaoping's opening speech to the CCP's 12th National Congress on 1 September 1982, when he called for "integrating the universal truth of Marxism with the concrete realities of China, blazing a path of our own, and building a socialism with Chinese characteristics" (*SWD,* p. 395).

In his review of *Building Socialism with Chinese Characteristics (Jianshe you Zhongguo tesede shehuizhuyi),* a collection of Deng's relevant remarks which was published at the end of 1984 (enlarged edition in 1987), Ma Hong, then CASS president, stated that the spirit of the book could be summed up by four points: 1. taking our own path and realizing the great goal of socialist modernization; 2. upholding activation of the economy as a domestic policy and the open door as a foreign policy; 3. respecting knowledge and talented personnel; and 4. reforming the system of economic administration (Ma Hong, "Tan jianshe you Zhongguo tesede shehuizhuyi"—"On Building Socialism with Chinese Characteristics", *HQ,* 2, 1985). These can be regarded as the key points of Deng's early idea in building socialism with Chinese characteristics.

The maturity of Deng Xiaoping Theory was marked by Deng's talks during his tour to China's southern provinces from 18 January to 21 February 1992. At that time, Deng was eighty-eight years of age, nearly deaf, and without any positions in the Party. Sensing that his reform and open-door program might be undermined by conservative forces, he emerged from seclusion to rout his opponents. On his "Southern tour", where he gave a series of talks calling for a more vigorous reform and open-door policy, Deng abandoned his long-standing ambivalence about what he believed was more dangerous to China—threats from the political left or right. He said in Shenzhen: "Watch out for the Right, but mainly defend against the 'Left'" (yao jingti you, dan zhuyao shi fangzhi "zuo"). This thesis was regarded by many as a significant summation of CCP experience, both positive and negative, in the long history of Chinese revolution and construction. With this statement, Deng made an explicit, final break with China's Maoist past.

With regard to the issue of whether things are of a capitalist or a socialist nature, Deng raised three criteria, that is, it depends on whether or not they accord with the "three favorables" (san ge youliyu)—favorable to developing the productive forces in the socialist society, to consolidating China's comprehensive national strength, and to raising the people's living standards. Deng promoted his "no debate" theory (bu zhenglun lun), calling for an end to the capitalism or socialism debate, which had been provoked by the Leftists. He explained: More planning or more market—this does not tell the essential distinction between socialism and capitalism. The planned economy does not amount to socialism; capitalism also needs planning. Similarly, the market economy does not mean capitalism; there is also a market in socialism. Planning and market are both economic measures.

Deng further advanced the following thesis: "Development is the most essential criterion" (fazhan caishi ying daoli). This thesis has since often been cited by China's reformists.

On 28 February 1992, Deng's talks were issued to the whole Party in the form of PCC document under the file of "Zhong Fa (1992) No. 2". They were later compiled in the new three-volume *Selected Works of Deng Xiaoping* as the last article of the third volume. China observers compare these talks to Deng's 13 December 1978 speech at the closing session of the Central Work Conference ("Emancipate the Mind, Seek Truth from Facts and Unite as One in Looking to the Future"—"Jiefang sixiang, shishiqiushi, tuanjie yizhi xiangqiankan", *SWD*, pp. 151-65, which served as the keynote address for the epoch-making 3rd Plenum of the 11th PCC). While Deng's 13 December 1978 speech was a thought-emancipation declaration marking the beginning of the "new period", Deng's talks during his 1992 "Southern tour" were a thought-emancipation declaration marking the new stage of China's historical development. In fact, an immediate effect of these talks can be seen in the approval of a socialist market economy (shehuizhuyi shichang jingji) at the 1992 14th CCP National Congress.

As Jiang Zemin pointed out in his eulogy to Deng in Beijing's Great Hall of the People on 25 February 1997 (Deng died on 19 February 1997), Deng Xiaoping Theory took shape and developed gradually over the years. It came into being "under the historical conditions of peace and development being the theme of the times, through the practice of China's reform, opening-up, and socialist modernization drive, and on the basis of summing up the historical experiences of the triumphs and setbacks of China's socialist cause and the ups and downs of other socialist countries" (*BR*, 10-16 Mar. 1997, p.19). Most contemporary CCP theorists agree that the establishment of Deng Xiaoping Theory was one of the "two historic leaps" (the other being that of Mao Zedong Thought) in the CCP history of Sinicized Marxism (Makesizhuyi Zhongguohua).

It was generally accepted that Jiang Zemin, in the interests of the Party and also in his, would carry out a Deng Xiaoping line without Deng Xiaoping (meiyou Deng Xiaopingde Deng Xiaoping luxian), waving the banner of Deng Xiaoping Theory whenever necessary. In his hour-long speech—which was seen as the first political manifesto of the post-Deng era—he told his listeners that Deng's theory of building socialism with Chinese characteristics and the Party's basic line for the primary stage of socialism, which was formulated under the guidance of Deng's theory, were Deng's most precious legacy to China. In Jiang's opinion, the theory scientifically grasped the essence of socialism, and, for the first time, provided a systematic and initial answer to a series of basic questions, such as how to build socialism in an economically and culturally underdeveloped country like China, and how to consolidate and develop socialism. Jiang called this "Marxism of contemporary China" (ibid.).

On 29 May 1997, Deng Xiaoping Theory about building socialism with Chinese characteristics became the "guiding ideology" (zhidao sixiang) of the CCP. This was advanced by Jiang Zemin in a notable speech at the Central Party School, which was arguably the most liberal and unequivocally reformist oration Jiang had ever made. As Deng's successor, Jiang Zemin's eulogy to the late patriarch was all-inclusive. He called on the whole Party, the whole army, and all the Chinese people to hold high the banner of Deng's theory in their "new Long March" (xin changzheng) into the twenty-first century.

On 12 September 1997, in his report at the CCP's 15th National Congress, Jiang Zemin reiterated his loyalty to Deng Xiaoping Theory. At the Congress, Deng Xiaoping Theory, with the theory of the primary stage of socialism as its core, was written into the Party Constitution as its "guiding ideology", juxtaposed with Marxism-Leninism and Mao Zedong Thought. In celebrating the 50th anniversary of the founding of the PRC, Deng Xiaoping Theory was the theme of three official slogans. One of them was: "Long live great Marxism-Leninism, Mao Zedong Thought and Deng Xiaoping Theory!"

But, as many have pointed out, Deng was not a theoretician. As the "general architect of China's reform and open-door program" (Zhongguo gaige kaifangde zong shejishi), Deng initiated and led China's reform and open-door program in the last twenty years of his life and this was his greatest contribution to the Chinese people. As a result, he was one of the great leaders not only in Chinese history but also in world history. But Deng did not believe the supremacy of ideology. In 1984 he pointed out that there had been confusion in the past in the understanding of the question of what was Marxism and what was socialism ("Deng Xiaoping on Socialism with Chinese Characteristics", *Liaowang,* 34, 1984). Deng's disdain for traditional socialist concepts found expression in his advice he offered to visiting Mozambique President Joachim Chissano in May 1988 about being careful of socialism. It was reported that Deng warned his visitor not to carry out socialism, at least not socialism in a general sense, according to Chinese experience. "If you really want to," Deng said, "you may carry out socialism with the characteristics of your country" *(JN,* 222:47, July 1988). Deng did make some statements about the meaning of socialism (such as "The fundamental task of socialism is to develop productivity") or what it is not (such as "Socialism is not equal to poverty"). Nevertheless, he never completely and comprehensively defined socialism. Some regard this as an indication of Deng's remarkable wisdom. Others, however, argue that this was his shortcoming. Whatever the case, this was certainly characteristic of Deng's style, and, as a result, he did not leave a dogmatic formula to his successor.

As a pragmatist, Deng Xiaoping was willing to employ a temporary expedient whenever necessary, which was most vividly expressed by his well-known saying: "No matter whether it is white or black, it is a good cat that catches mice" (buguan heimao baimao, zhuazhao laoshu jiushi haomao). Deng promoted the idea of "crossing the river by feeling the stones" (mozhe shitou guo he)—in carrying out reform and the open-door policies in building socialism with Chinese characteristics, there is no reliable model to go by, and people have to advance step-by-step by summing up the situation from their experience, both positive and negative. Like his "cat" theory (mao lun) and "no debate" theory, the theory of "feeling the stones" is also of great significance. Deng did not seem to trust any ready-made blueprint or "guiding principles". While Mao ruled the country with a set of doctrines, Deng believed practice was the sole criterion for testing truth. This was regarded as Deng's best contribution.

In the eyes of Maoists, Deng might be a Rightist. But China's dissidents point out that Deng had a dual nature. He was radical in his economic reform but conservative when facing demands for political reform. While a dove when he declared that China's intellectuals were already part of the working class, he was a hawk when he ordered the army to gun down the demonstrating students in the June 4th Incident of 1989. He promoted economic liberalization marked by a market economy, while opposing "bourgeois liberalization" politically and emphasizing a one-party autocracy. One may remember the "two basic points" in Party line. Deng opposed "Left" ideology in the economic field with his reform and the open-door policy, while he opposed "Right" ideology in the political field with his "four cardinal principles". Many agree that Deng's reform and open-door program is pushing China on a track of de-Maoism. But they also point out that as its "general architect", Deng was hurt by his own self-contradictions. One can find a number of "complexes" (qingjie) in Deng, caused by his difficult treatment of Mao's legacy, his GPCR experience, the collapse of the Deng Xiaoping-Hu Yaobang-Zhao Ziyang leadership system, the Tiananmen Incident, and the sharp contrast in his two different kinds of devotion before and after the GPCR. See also "zhengzhi gaige" (political reform), "jingji gaige" (economic reform), and other relevant entries.

敌我矛盾
di wo maodun
(contradictions between the people and their enemy)

See "zhengque chuli renmin neibu maodun" (correctly handling contradictions among the people).

帝修反
di xiu fan
(imperialism, modern revisionism, and reactionaries)

A popular slogan during the GPCR was "Down with imperialism, modern revisionism, and reactionaries of various countries!" Imperialism mainly referred to the United States, and modern revisionism referred to the Soviet Union. See "shijie geming zhongxin" (center of world revolution).

第二次革命
di'er ci geming
(second revolution)

On 28 March 1985, when meeting Japanese visitors, Deng pointed out: "Reform is China's second revolution" (gaige shi Zhongguode di'er ci geming). The "second revolution" refers to the establishment of Deng Xiaoping's line at the 1978 3rd Plenum of the 11th PCC (which was said to be "the Zunyi Conference of the socialist period") and its implementation thereafter, which focuses on economic construction under the reform and open-door program. As its chief architect, Deng was recognized by many, both at home and abroad, for having created the miracle of rapid economic development in contemporary China.

Deng's "second revolution" has been attacked by some CCP figures as a reaction to the "first revolution" under the leadership of Mao Zedong. Others, however, argue that this is precisely Deng's contribution to the Chinese people, and thus it should be praised. To many others, the thesis that Deng's "second revolution" is a reaction to Mao's "first revolution" is simply untenable. Some argue in defense of Deng, and others are opposed to Deng. See also "zhengzhi gaige" (political reform), "jingji gaige" (economic reform), and "Deng Xiaoping lilun" (Deng Xiaoping Theory).

第二次冷战
di'er ci lengzhan
(second Cold War)

See "lengzhanhou shidaide xin diguozhuyi" (neo-imperialism in the post-Cold War era) and "weidu Zhongguo" (containment against China).

第二次农村革命
di'er ci nongcun geming
(second rural revolution)

See "renmin gongshe" (People's Commune).

第二次新文化运动
di'er ci xinwenhua yundong
(second New Culture Movement)

See "wenhua re" (culture craze).

第二次原始积累
di'er ci yuanshi jilei
(second previous accumulation)

See "yuanshi jilei" (previous accumulation).

第二世界
di'er shijie
(second world)

See "san ge shijie lun" ("three worlds" theory).

第二梯队
di'er tidui
(second echelon)

See "disan tidui" (third echelon).

第二种忠诚
di'erzhong zhongcheng
(second type of loyalty)

See "Liu Binyan xianxiang" (Liu Binyan phenomenon) and "chi buting zhengjianzhe" (dissidents).

第三代领导的政治宣言和行动纲领
disan dai lingdaode zhengzhi xuanyan he xingdong gangling
(political declaration and program of action of the third generation leadership)

On 12 September 1997, in his report at the CCP's 15th National Congress, Jiang Zemin reiterated his loyalty to Deng Xiaoping Theory.

Jiang's report, more than 30,000 words, was regarded as a "political declaration and program of action of the third generation leadership" which would lead the Chinese people into the twenty-first century.

Jiang Zemin was expected to carry out a Deng Xiaoping line without Deng Xiaoping. What set the new core of the Party leadership somewhat apart from Deng was its stress on an ethical dimension to economic growth. It paid close attention to the handling of the relationship between material progress and cultural and ethical progress. While confirming that economic backwardness is not socialism, Jiang added that spiritual deficiency also is not socialism. Jiang carried out his anti-corruption campaign in a proper way. Echoing Deng's view about social stability as a basic prerequisite, Jiang stressed the need to balance reform, development, and stability (gaige, fazhan he wendingde pingheng). He formulated his basic principle as follows: "seizing the current opportunity to deepen reforms and open China wider to the outside world, promoting development and maintaining stability".

Mao united China. Deng took China from a period of class struggle to one of reform. Jiang's goal is to keep the whole situation stable and growing smoothly. According to China observers, if he is able to do this, Jiang's historical legacy will rank with that of China's political titans. See also "xin shehuizhuyi guan" (new socialist view), "zhengzhi gaige" (political reform), and "jingji gaige" (economic reform).

第三代作家
disan dai zuojia
(writers of the third generation)

See "xinshiqi wenxue" (literature of the new period).

第三力量
disan liliang
(third force)

During the prolonged struggle between the CCP and the KMT in the so-called "new democratic revolution" (xin minzhuzhuyi geming) from the May 4th Movement of 1919 up to the founding of the PRC in 1949, the third force attempted to take a "third road" (disantiao daolu) or a "middle road" (zhongjian luxian), so as to distinguish itself from both the CCP and the KMT, the two major parties in China. The third force was most active during the few years after the end of the Second World War, when all the Chinese confronted a crucial question: what kind of China was to be built.

The CCP did not believe there could be an independent third force that could take a "third road" in China. In his 30 June 1949 article "On the People's Democratic Dictatorship" ("Lun renmin minzhu zhuanzheng", in *MZXJ*, 4, pp. 1473-86) and in other articles, Mao warned that "the third road", essentially a road of "bourgeois dictatorship of the British and American type", would definitely lead to a dead end. Due to the success of the CCP's "united front" work, the left wing of the third force, such as Zhang Bojun and Luo Longji, two leaders of the Chinese Democracy Alliance (Zhongguo Minzhu Tongmeng), became anti-KMT and greatly helped the CCP to seize state power. During the 1957 anti-Rightist campaign, unfortunately, many of these former Leftists were convicted as "bourgeois Rightists". See also "yibiandao" (lean to one side) and "minzhu dangpai" (democratic parties).

第三世界
disan shijie
(third world)

See "san ge shijie lun" ("three worlds" theory).

第三梯队
disan tidui
(third echelon)

According to the CCP, the "first echelon" is made up of those Party elders who have retired but who, from time to time, especially on important occasions, give their opinions about how to handle the situation. The "second echelon" refers to members of the "leading group" (lingdao banzi) currently working in their positions. The "third echelon" are those selected to be future leaders of the Party-state departments.

After the GPCR, as a "lesson" drawn from what it called the "civil strife", the CCP leadership deemed the building of the "third echelon" to be an urgent task. On 2 November 1979, at a meeting of cadres of the rank of vice-minister and above from the central Party, government, and army organizations, Deng urged that leaders make earnest efforts to select successors and to regard this as a "veteran cadres' responsibility" *(SWD,* p. 214). On 18 August 1980, when speaking to an enlarged meeting of the PCC Politburo on the reform of the system of Party and state leadership, Deng further elucidated his view about selecting cadres. He advocated an "equal stress on political integrity and professional competence" (de cai jian bei). By political integrity he meant principally keeping to the socialist road and upholding the leadership of the Party. With this as a prerequitite, Deng hoped to recruit younger cadres who were better educated, and better qualified professionally. Moreover, Deng said, the employment and promotion of such cadres should be institutionalized (*SWD*, pp. 308-9). Then, in his opening speech at the September 1982 CCP 12th National Congress, Deng raised "four standards" for selecting cadres (ganbu si hua)—"more revolutionary, younger average age, better educated, and professionally more competent" *(SWD,* p. 396). At the Congress, the "four standards" were written into the Party Constitution.

At a meeting called a "democratic consultation" (minzhu xieshang hui) held in Beijing from 31 May to 16 June 1983, Hu Yaobang, CCP general secretary, announced for the first time that the PCC was busy building the "third echelon" in accordance with the "four standards" *(RMRB,* 3 June 1983). For two years after this meeting, the country was involved in a cadre-selection drive and nearly one thousand people were chosen.

In building the "third echelon", Deng and his colleagues especially emphasized that "three kinds of people" should not be selected in any case. And if any of these people already held certain positions, they should be singled out as targets for purging. This was an important part of Deng Xiaoping's organizational line since the 1978 3rd Plenum of the 11th PCC. The "three kinds of people" referred to those who established themselves by following the rebellion conducted by the "Lin Biao and Jiang Qing counter-revolutionary cliques", those with serious factional leanings, and those committing serious crimes of "beating, smashing, and looting" (da za qiang) during the GPCR. In 1984, Chen Yun (1905-1995), chairman of the CCP's Central Commission for Inspecting Discipline, announced that "veteran Red Guards" did not fall into any category of the "three kinds of people" and outstanding veteran Red Guards should be selected for the "third echelon".

In the past 15 years or more, many "third echelon" members have become leaders of various Party-state departments. Unfortunately, quite a number of them eventually proved to be unqualified. Some were even convicted for criminal activities. The practice of building the "third echelon" quietly came to an end, but the "four standards" for selecting cadres continue to be valid. See also "geming jiebanren" (revolutionary successors) and "hongweibing" (Red Guards).

第三条道路
disantiao daolu
(the third road)

See "disan liliang" (third force), "yibiandao" (lean to one side), and "fansi" (reflection).

第三只眼睛
disanzhi yanjing
(the third "eye")

In March 1994, a book under the conspicuous title *Viewing China with the Third Eye (Disanzhi yanjing kan Zhongguo)* was published by Shanxi People's Publishing House. Pretending to be a translation (from German to English and from English to Chinese) of a work by a German China hand, it claimed to discuss issues of vital importance to China, such as the present economic situation, the peasantry, the intellectuals, and future leaders, from a new "objective", "historical" perspective. It was soon discovered that the "third" eye did not belong to a foreigner but rather to a Chinese named Wang Shan. More interesting was the immediate reaction to the book. It was banned soon after publication. Then, suddenly, some top leaders highly praised it. And soon thereafter, it was banned again.

The book shocked intellectual circles because of its alleged disguised political ambitions. Wang Meng, former minister of culture, opined that the book was full of the "bloody smell of fascism". Outwardly, he said, it seemed to praise reform and the open door but in essence it opposed them. Wang Meng also doubted the authenticity of Wang Shan's authorship, believing that there must have been some people behind the "second pretended author". Some Beijing analysts even went so far as to say that *The Third Eye* was a product of the resurgence of an ultra-Leftist force. By discussing the mistakes in Deng's reform and its negative social consequences, the book tried to "lay a theoretical foundation" for the possible reemergence of Leftist policies in the coming post-Deng era.

In early 1995, Wang Shan finished another book, entitled *Viewing China with the Fourth Eye*, which mainly offered advice to top CCP leaders about how to solve the problems presented in *The Third Eye*. (See Wang Shan, "Cong 'disanzhi yanjing' dao 'disizhi yanjing'"—"From the 'Third Eye' to the 'Fourth Eye'", *Mingbao yuekan,* 11:30-33, Nov. 1994). With these two books, Wang Shan came to be regarded as a representive of the "neo-conservative" trend. See also "xin baoshouzhuyi" (neo-conservatism).

第五代导演
diwu dai daoyan
(directors of the fifth generation)

At the 9th Hong Kong International Film Festival held in March 1985, *Yellow Earth (Huangtudi,* 1984), a feature film directed by Chen Kaige, attracted great attention. Over 230 articles commented on it, the majority of which were favorable. It was noted for its profound philosophy and its rebellious message against traditional film. Plots and characters, which were vital in traditional film, no longer played a leading role. It was at this time that the term "directors of the fifth generation" was first used, and positively, to refer to Chen Kaige and some other young film directors of his generation, such as Zhang Yimou and Tian Zhuangzhuang. For ten years, these directors, many of whom were classmates who had graduated from the Beijing Film Institute in 1982, once and again shocked film circles both home and abroad with a number of unique films, such as *Yellow Earth, Red Sorghum (Hong gaoliang,* dir. Zhang Yimou, 1987), *Blue Kite (Lan fengzheng,* dir. Tian Zhuangzhuang, 1993), *Farewell My Concubine (Bawang bieju,* dir. Chen Kaige, 1993) and *To Live (Huozhe,* dir. Zhang Yimou, 1994).

The term "directors of the fifth generation" was controversial. In fact, at the September 1988 forum on China's neo-film held by the editorial board of the magazine *Film Art,* they were referred to as makers of "neo-film" ("xin dianying"). Although now the term "directors of the fifth generation" seems to have been generally accepted, it is still considered to be inaccurate by those who do not like it. Admittedly, the artistic creations by these directors have been a dynamic process. Take Zhang Yimou for example. A change in style can be seen if one compares his recent works, such as *Not a Single Drop-out (Yi ge dou buneng shao,* dir. Zhang Yimou, 1998) with his early works, such as *Red Sorghum.*

These directors have often caused problems for the authorities. From time to time, there is news about their works being banned (*Blue Kite* and *To Live,* for instance). In 1995, at the centenary celebration of the birth of the film industry, Zhang Yimou was selected by international film circles as one of the ten most prominent directors in the world. In China, however, his name was not included on the list of the fifteen "best film workers", a list prepared for the Chinese Film Century Prize for the 90th anniversary of the birth of Chinese film sponsored by the Ministry of Broadcast, Film, and Television, the Chinese Film Association, and several other organizations.

第五个现代化
diwu ge xiandaihua
(the fifth modernization)

On 5 December 1978, Wei Jingsheng, editor of *Exploration*, put up a big-character poster entitled "The Fifth Modernization: Democracy and Other Things" ("Diwu ge xiandaihua: minzhu ji qita"). This most radical activist of the Beijing Spring period asserted that if the Chinese people want to realize the "four modernizations", that is, the modernization of agriculture, industry, science and technology, and national defense, they must first practice democracy, and they must first modernize China's social system. Wei thus regarded democracy as the fifth modernization, as a necessary condition for the "four modernizations". See also "si ge xiandaihua" (four modernizations) and "yao minzhu haishi yao xinde ducai" (democracy or neo-dictatorship).

第一世界
diyi shijie
(the first world)

See "san ge shijie lun" ("three worlds" theory).

第一梯队
diyi tidui
(first echelon)

See "disan tidui" (third echelon).

地富反坏右
di fu fan huai you
(landlords, rich peasants, counter-revolutionaries, bad elements, and Rightists)

See "hong" (red).

地方霸权主义
difang baquanzhuyi
(local hegemonism)

See "shijie geming" (world revolution).

地方民族主义
difang minzuzhuyi
(local nationalism)

See "minzuzhuyi" (nationalism).

地方主义
difangzhuyi
(localism)

The Party Center always emphasizes the need to oppose localism. In the past, localism often displayed itself in the form of an inner-party struggle. A standard accusation was: Localism is the product of extreme individualism and feudal-sectarianism. It appears to be representing the interests of the locality, but in fact, it only stands for the interests and the demands of a few careerists. In order to maintain their honor, position, and authority in a certain place, such careerists run counter to the political and organizational lines of the Party Center. In CCP history, there were cases of those practising localism being accused of "setting up an independent kingdom" (gao duli wangguo) or organizing an anti-Party clique.

Currently, localism is found to be more of an economic problem. A new definition reads as follows: Localism aims at pursuing local economic and political interests, usually presenting itself as a formal or informal institutional arrangement by the local governments. It emphasizes internal integration and external expansion, and inevitably leads to a clash of interests between the central government and the local governments, and among local governments of various regions. If unchecked, it can develop into protecting illegal market behavior and other criminal activities. Since it is impossible to eliminate localism completely, the only practical solution is to legislate an integration of interests between the central and local governments and among the local governments of various regions.

Related to localism is the term "the 'mountain-stronghold' mentality" (shantouzhuyi), which is derived from the guerrilla war period. During the long years of guerrilla war, the various CCP-led rural base areas were cut off from one another by the enemy. As these areas were, for the most part, established in mountainous regions, each functioned like an autonomous mountain stronghold. If it was unavoidable historically, it became increasingly harmful to the central Party authority. As early as the 1941-42 Yan'an rectification movement, Mao called on his followers to combat sectarianism and to solve the problem of the "mountain-stronghold" mentality in all Party organizations in different places, especially in the army (Mao later systematized his idea in this April 1944 article "Our Study and the

Current Situation"—"Xuexi yu shiju"). After the founding of the PRC, this term—standing for cliquism—was used to criticize those leaders in army or civilian units who exercised power in their own ways and did not carry out the policies of the "Party Center".

A related term is "sectarianism" (zongpaizhuyi), another problem existing within the CCP. During the Yan'an rectification movement, Mao targeted for attack subjectivist and sectarian tendencies. Sectarianism was regarded as another form of feudalism.

Wrong tendencies also include "departmentalism" (benweizhuyi), but it is not loaded with as much political seriousness and it is usually found in people's daily lives. The attitude of caring only for one's own interests to the exclusion of others, or of being concerned only for one's own part of the work at the expense of the entire work, is called "departmentalism" (or, "selfish departmentalism" or "departmental selfishness"). Departmentalism, described as magnified individualism (fangdalede gerenzhuyi), is considered very harmful and must be opposed.

As opposed to "departmentalism", "localism", "sectarianism", and "the 'mountain-stronghold' mentality", the Party Center asks all cadres to adopt an overall point of view (quanju guandian), or, figuratively, to coordinate all the activities of the nation as in a chess game (quanguo yipanqi). Mao said: "Communists must grasp the principle of subordinating the needs of the part to the needs of the whole. If a proposal appears feasible for a partial situation but not for the situation as a whole, then the part must give way to the whole. Conversely, if the proposal is not feasible for the part but is feasible in light of the situation as a whole, again the part must give way to the whole. This is what is meant by considering the situation as a whole" (*SWM*, 2, p. 201). See also "zhuhou jingji" (duchy economy) and "jingji gaige" (economic reform).

地理环境决定论
dili huanjing jueding lun
(theory of "geographical environments as a decisive factor")

See "huangtu wenming" (yellow earth civilization) and "*Heshang* shijian" (*River Elegy* Incident).

地域文化小说
diyu wenhua xiaoshuo
(regional culture fiction)

See "xungen re" (intense search for "roots").

典型环境中的典型人物
dianxing huanjingzhongde dianxing renwu
(typical characters in typical circumstances)

See "xianshizhuyide yuanze" (principle of realism).

典型环境不等于整个社会生活的缩影
dianxing huanjing bu dengyu
zhengge shehui shenghuode suoying

(typical circumstances are not the "epitome" of an entire social life)

see "shehuizhuyi xianshizhuyi" (socialist realism).

定框框
ding kuangkuang
(set a frame)

Refers to a common practice by the "Leftist" critics. See "sanbu zhengce" ("three don'ts" policy).

顶峰论
dingfeng lun
("pinnacle" theory)

At the March 1958 Chengdu Conference, a PCC work conference held in Chengdu city, Sichuan province, Mao made known his idea about the "two different kinds of personality cult", which implied that his personality cult should not be questioned (see "geren chongbai"). Thereafter, Kang Sheng (1898-1975), a member of the CCP Politburo Standing Committee, looked for every chance to flatter Mao. In the summer of that year, at a meeting of political teachers of the Beijing Conservatory of Music, Kang Sheng asserted that Mao Zedong Thought was the pinnacle of Marxism-Leninism. This was the first mention of the "pinnacle" theory. Admittedly, however, it was Lin Biao who was its biggest advocate. Lin regarded it as the most important theme for the PLA high-ranking officers' conference held from September to October 1960 and for the conference on the army's political work held from the end of December 1965 to 18 January 1966. By the eve of the GPCR, Lin had succeeded in making the "pinnacle" theory accepted in the whole army, the whole Party, and the whole country.

The "pinnacle" theory was regarded as ridiculous by post-Mao critics. Deng also joined in the attack, as in his speech of 18 August 1980 entitled "On the Reform of the System of Party and State Leadership" *(SWD*, pp. 312-13). See also "shehuizhuyi yihua lun" (theory of socialist alienation).

东西文明冲突论
dong xi wenming chongtu lun
(theory of the clash between the Eastern and the Western civilizations)

The theory of the clash between the Eastern and the Western civilizations has been a hot and controversial topic among international scholars in recent years.

It is derived from an article entitled "The Clash of Civilizations?" published in the distinguished American journal *Foreign Affairs* in the summer of 1993. Its author is Samuel P. Huntington, a Harvard professor of Government. The article, according to the editors, stirred up more discussion than any other article they had published since George Kennan's "X" article on containment in the 1940s. The responses and comments on it came from every continent and from scores of countries.

In 1996 Huntington published *The Clash of Civilizations and the Remaking of World Order* (New York, Simon & Schuster). The book is intended to provide a fuller, deeper, and more thoroughly documented answer to his previous article's question. Huntington explains how the population explosion in Muslim countries and the economic rise of East Asia are changing global politics. These developments challenge Western dominance, promote opposition to supposedly "universal" Western ideals, and intensify conflict between civilizations over such issues as nuclear proliferation, immigration, human rights, and democracy.

Samuel P. Huntington struck a nerve in people of every civilization. As early as when he published his article "The Clash of Civilizations?" in 1993, a debate was ignited. And the debate still continues. The title of the article had a question mark, but it was generally ignored. As described by Huntington, people were "variously impressed, intrigued, outraged, frightened, and perplexed" by the argument that the central and most dangerous dimension of the emerging global politics would be a conflict between groups from differing civilizations. To some, Huntington's thesis can be seen as a remedy for the decline of Western hegemonism. They also argue that Huntington only contributes his analysis on the basis of facts. Furthermore, events over the past few years have confirmed his judgments. If one still doubts whether world politics today is being reconfigured along cultural lines, they say, one can see for certain that new patterns of conflict and cooperation are replacing those of the Cold War. But others do not share this argument, for example, Robert G. Sutter and Seong Eun Choi, as seen in their book, *Shaping China's Future in World Affairs: The Role of the United States* (Boulder, Colorado, Westview Press, 1996).

Scholars influenced by Confucian are more interested in the theory of the coalescence of Eastern and Western civilizations (dong xi wenming ronghe lun), and thus any barefaced discussion about a "clash" is considered suspect. It is difficult for them to share Huntington's view. Typical are two groups of articles published in 1993 in the 19th and 20th issues of the *21st Century*, a prestigious journal sponsored by the Chinese University of Hong Kong. These articles tend to see culture more as a starting point of coalescence than as a source of conflict (Ho Hsin-chuan, "Wenhua: Shijie chongtude laiyuan yihuo ronghede qidian?"—"Culture: Source of Conflict or Starting Point of Coalescence?" *ES*, 7-10, Dec. 1993). Or they may argue that self-interests will outweigh civilization (Liu Xiao-feng, "Liyi zhongyu wenhua"—"The Exaltation of Self-Interests above Civilization", *ES*, 26-27, Oct. 1993). They believe they better understand Chinese nationalism (F. C. Chen, "Lun Zhongguo minzuzhuyi yu shijie yishi"—"On Chinese Nationalism and the Global Perspective", *ES*, 28-35, Oct. 1993). For them, Confucianism is relevant to the twenty-first century (Liu Shu-hsien, "Rujia sixiang yu weilai shijiede xiangganxing"—"The Relevance of Confucianism to the Next Century", *ES*, 11-15, Dec. 1993). They envisage a course towards an "integrated world" (Hsu Cho-yuen, "Zouxiang zhenghede shijie"—"Towards an Integrated World", *ES*, 4-6, Dec. 1993). If Huntington's article makes any contributions, one such article observes sarcastically, the most important is that it marks the end of Western-Centrism (Jin Guan-tao, "Xifang zhongxin lunde pomie: Ping quanqiu wenhua chongtulun"—"The End of Western-Centrism: On the Theory of the Clash of Civilizations", *ES*, 22-25, Oct. 1993).

Even stronger was the response from a political point of view. For some time there was a fear that if China were to initiate the political reform promoted by the West, it would share a fate similar to that of the Russians. Coincidentally, from 1994 to 1995, arguments supporting a policy to "contain China" were popular in America. This lent credence to this fear. After Huntington's book was published, suspicion of the West grew even stronger. It is no wonder that his argument faced vociferous attacks not only from Chinese-Americans and Hong Kong academics, but also from intellectuals in mainland China. In 1995, for instance, ten negative pieces were published, some by the so-called "liberals", who were all especially outspoken in their opposition to Huntington's theory. Huntington aims, they pointed out, at setting forth a strategy for the West to preserve its hegemony (including cultural hegemony), although he also talks about the need for people everywhere to learn to coexist in a complex, multipolar, multicivilizational world. It may be true that the Muslim population surge has resulted in many small wars throughout Eurasia, but one should not jump to the conclusion that the rise of China would lead to a global war of civilizations. People should watch out for the theory of a "yellow peril" (huanghuo lun), they emphasized.

A study of how Huntington has been treated in mainland China is of significance. At the end of 1980s and the beginning of 1990s, his book, *Political Order in Changing Societies* (Yale University Press, 1968), was highly praised first by neo-authoritarianism proponents and then by neo-conservatism proponents. A few years later, his *Clash of Civilizations* was fiercely attacked, in particular, by those who maintain that the Eastern culture (Chinese culture or Confucian culture, to be more exact) can save the world. It is argued that though the neo-authoritarianism and neo-conservatism proponents identify themselves with Huntington, they are actually different in terms of value, conception of history, and political attitude. In contrast, those "Eastern Savior" proponents who totally reject Huntington actually see eye to eye with him in terms of international politics (see Bian Wu, "Zhen jia Hengtingdun yu dong xi Hengtingdun"—"The False Huntington and the Huntington of the East", *Kaifang shidai*, 5:36-40, 1998). See also "ruxue disanqi" (Confucianism in its third stage of development), "minzuzhuyi" (nationalism), "ershiyishiji shi Zhongguorende shiji" (the twenty-first century will be the Chinese century), and "weidu Zhongguo" (containment against China).

东西文明融合论
dong xi wenming ronghe lun
(theory of the coalescence of Eastern and Western civilizations)

See "dong xi wenming chongtu lun" (theory of the clash between the Eastern and the Western civilizations) and "quanqiuhua" (globalization).

东方文化优越论
dongfang wenhua youyue lun
(theory of the superiority of Eastern culture)

See "quanqiuhua" (globalization) and "minzuzhuyi" (nationalism).

东方之珠
dongfang zhi zhu
(pearl of the Orient)

It is generally agreed that Hong Kong has a unique position in the world's trading and financial business. To China, it is the goose that lays the golden eggs, so only fools would try to kill it. According to 1996 statistics, Hong Kong contributes about one-third of China's foreign exchange earnings, and accounts for 62 percent of foreign investment in China, while 92 percent of its re-exports either originated in China or were destined for China. No wonder the Chinese call Hong Kong "the pearl of the Orient". Deng Xiaoping even declared that China should "build" several Hong Kongs in its interior.

The "pearl of the Orient" also refers to Shanghai, a new rapidly developing center of business and culture in East China.

东风压倒西风
dongfeng yadao xifeng
(the East wind prevails over the West wind)

From 2 to 21 November 1957, Mao was in Moscow for the celebration of the 40th anniversary of the October Revolution at the invitation of Khrushchev (1894-1971), first secretary of the Central Committee of the Communist Party of the Soviet Union (CPSU). Mao was very happy about the hospitality of his host, especially about the "Moscow Statement" passed at the conference of the sixty-four Communist parties held in Moscow concurrently with the celebration. On 17 November, at a meeting with Chinese students and trainees in the city, Mao talked about the current international situation. He said: "The October Revolution produced a new world. After forty years, the strength of the new world has exceeded that of the old" *(RMRB,* 19 Nov. 1957). What Mao had meant was that the "socialist camp" headed by the USSR had overpowered the "capitalist camp" headed by the U.S. Quoting a famous saying from *Dream of the Red Mansions (Honglou Meng),* a classical Chinese novel, he described such a situation as "not the West wind prevailing over the East wind, but the East wind prevailing over the West wind". Mao repeated this at the Moscow Meeting of Communist and Workers' Parties on the next day. "It is my opinion," he said, "that the international situation has now reached a new turning point. There are two winds in the world today, the East wind and the West wind. There is a Chinese saying, 'Either the East wind prevails over the West wind, or the West wind prevails over the East wind.' I believe it is characteristic of the situation today that the East wind is prevailing over the West wind. That is to say, the forces of socialism have become overwhelmingly superior to the forces of imperialism." See also "zhilaohu" (paper tiger), "yibiandao" (lean to one side), and "shijie geming" (world revolution).

动乱精英
dongluan jingying
(*élite* of the turmoil)

See "wenhua re" (culture craze) and "ziyouhua" (liberalization).

斗批改
dou pi gai
(struggle, criticism, and reform)

These refer to the main purposes and targets of the GPCR as stipulated in the "PCC Decision on the GPCR" passed at the 11th Plenum of the 8th PCC on 8 August 1966. They are also dubbed "one struggle, two criticisms, and three reforms" (yi dou er pi san gai). "One struggle" referred to the struggle against those in power within the Party taking the capitalist road. The "two criticisms" were: criticizing reactionary bourgeois academic authorities (zichanjieji fandong xueshu quanwei) and criticizing the ideologies of the bourgeois and all other exploiting classes. The "three reforms" referred to reforms in (1) education, (2) literature and art, and (3) all superstructures (shangcengjianzhu) not adapted to the socialist economic base (jingjijichu).

By the end of 1966, Mao and his followers had hoped, as can be seen in the joint editorial of the *People's Daily* and *Red Flag* on the 1967 New Year's Day, "Carry the

Great Proletarian Cultural Revolution through to the End" (Ba wuchanjieji wenhua dageming jinxing daodi"), that 1967 would see a decisive victory for the "struggle, criticism, and reform". As it turned out, however, 1967 instead saw an "all-round civil war" (quanmian neizhan) breaking out in China. The GPCR did not end until after Mao's death on 9 September 1976. See also "wen'ge" (Cultural Revolution) and "xinzuopai" (neo-Leftists).

斗私批修
dousi pixiu
(fighting one's self, criticizing and repudiating revisionism)

According to a *People's Daily* editorial of 6 October 1967, "fighting one's self" meant making great efforts to restrain and further get rid of selfishness in one's thinking, and "criticizing and repudiating revisionism" meant combating revisionism and waging a struggle against those in power within the Party who take the capitalist road. Both should be done in light of Marxism-Leninism-Mao Zedong Thought, so that a revolution will break out in the depths of the soul (linghun shenchu baofa geming).

During the GPCR, people had to practice "fighting one's self, criticizing and repudiating revisionism" with great reverence and solemnity, because it was Mao's "great militant call" to all Chinese people. If it is remembered in today's China, it refers only to a ridiculous story. See also "wen'ge" (Cultural Revolution).

斗争会
douzhenghui
(public accusation meeting)

Public accusation meetings were typically held during the numerous mass movements of the Mao era. People were encouraged to make "face-to-face" criticism (mian dui mian pipan). If the target for public accusation was absent, it was called a "back-to-back" criticism (bei kao bei pipan). Targets were usually called "niuguisheshen", that is, class enemies of all descriptions. Landlords, for instance, were the targets in the land reform movement of 1950; "anti-Party, anti-people, and anti-socialism" bourgeois Rightists in the 1957 anti-Rightist campaign; and persons in authority taking the capitalist road in the GPCR. Those targets in the public accusation meetings suffered tremendously from public humiliation. Many reached breaking points and some ended up taking their lives after these meetings. See also "wuchanjieji zhuanzheng" (dictatorship of the proletariat), "douzheng chongbai" (struggle worship), and "jieji douzheng" (class struggle).

斗争崇拜
douzheng chongbai
(struggle worship)

"The philosophy of the Communist Party is that of struggle" (Gongchandangde zhexue jiushi douzhengde zhexue), one of Mao's theses most often cited during the GPCR, succinctly and powerfully encapsulates his whole system of political philosophy. From this is derived the concept of "struggle philosophy" (douzheng zhexue), which is said to be first advanced by Lin Biao to sum up Mao's idea. Mao was, indeed, the supreme representative of those obsessed with "struggle worship".

There were five characteristics that distinguished him from other Marxists, according to Liu Xiaogan, a scholar of Chinese philosophy. First, Mao not only resorted to struggle as a means one had to employ for a certain historical mission, but also regarded it as a value which would endow one with "endless happiness". Second, Mao, during his whole life, even after he had become a ruler, upheld struggle from the perspective of the oppressed and rebellious. Third, he specifically emphasized prolonged, repeated, and all-around struggles, large-scale struggles that the whole nation would be involved in. Fourth, Mao succeeded in developing a unique theoretical system for "struggle worship", his *On Contradiction (Maodun lun)* providing a philosophical foundation for it, and his attacks upon the "theory of human nature", such as those in his 1942 *Yan'an Talks,* clearing away what might be his theoretical and psychological obstacles. Fifth, Mao's "struggle worship" functioned for the longest time with a far and wide influence, so much so that many Chinese, instead of being forced to follow the struggle worship, simply took it of their own free will as a noble value and a magic weapon to reform society and history (See Liu Xiaogan, *Liangjihua yu fencungang: jindai Zhongguo jingying xicaode bingtai fenxi—The Extreme Approach and the Sense of Propriety: An Analysis of the Morbid Psychology in the Ideological Trend of Modern Chinese Elite,* Taipei, Dongda, 1994).

During those years, examples of Mao's "struggle worship" were abundant. The "struggle philosophy" was applied in a most preposterous way. Take literary creation as an example. In order to avoid the label of "bourgeois humanism", writers had to praise class struggle, describing it in their works as existing everyday and everywhere in the country. Such examples include Hao Ran's novels *Bright Sunny Days (Yanyangtian)* and *The Golden Highway (Jinguang dadao)*, two of the few "approved" literary works in the GPCR. More illustrative, perhaps, were the revisions of the Beijing opera *On the Docks (Haigang)* and the modern opera *Sons and Daughters on the Prairie (Caoyuan ernü)*. Originally, these two works did not discuss class struggle. During the GPCR, they underwent repeated revisions, and each time they were revised, more plots of class struggle were added and underlined until their themes were completely changed, resulting in stories that were ridiculous and unbelievable.

斗争哲学
douzheng zhexue
(struggle philosophy)

See "douzheng chongbai" (struggle worship) and "jieji douzheng" (class struggle).

都市百相小说
dushi baixiang xiaoshuo
(fiction of the multiple features of urban life)

In 1985, there appeared a new genre of fiction that described the multiple features of urban life. In works such as "You Have No Other Choice" ("Ni bie wu xuanze", *RMWX,* 3:4-29, 1985) by Liu Suola, "Themeless Variation" ("Wuzhuti bianzou", *RMWX,* 7, 1985) by Xu Xing, and "Curly Locks" ("Quanmao", *SY,* 3, 1986; trans. in *CL,* 2:47-128, 1988) by Chen Jiangong, one can feel the perplexities, confusion, and the sense of estrangement and solitude in urban life, and how the younger generation tries some other ways of life so as to express their rebellious consciousness and their new values. Later, in 1988, Cui Jian's rock 'n' roll music and Wang Shuo's "riffraff literature" (pizi wenxue), which were all the rage for a few years among the young people in mainland China, evolved from this approach. See also "xinshiqi wenxue" (literature of the new period) and "xinshiqi wenxuede duoyuan fazhan" (pluralistic development of the literature of the new period).

毒草
ducao
(poisonous weed)

This term, meaning something bad, reactionary, and considered to be "anti-Party, anti-people, and anti-socialism" was added to the speech Mao delivered at the 11th meeting (enlarged) of the Supreme State Council on 27 February 1957, when it was formally published on 19 May 1957. In the speech, entitled "On the Correct Handling of Contradictions among the People", Mao Zedong put forth six criteria by which to judge what is a "xianghua" (fragrant flower, i.e., good, revolutionary work) and what is a "ducao". See "zhengque chuli renmin neibu maodun" (correctly handling contradictions among the people) and "si xiang jiben yuanze" (four cardinal principles).

独台
du Tai
(independent Taiwan)

See "Taiwan wenti" (Taiwan issue).

独立王国
duli wangguo
(independent kingdom)

"Duli wangguo", a figure of speech, was often used in an exaggerated sense. For instance, in a self-criticism, one would describe oneself as having a realm (duli wangguo) of bourgeois ideology in one's mind. When used in political struggle, however, it had substantial political significance. "Gao duli wangguo" (setting up an independent kingdom) refers to local leaders administering their departments and areas for their own interests and resisting the Party Center. One early such case was that of Gao Gang (1905-1954), who was in charge of northeast China and concurrently held the post of PRC vice-president. He was accused of setting up an independent kingdom at the February 1954 4th Plenum of the 7th PCC. In March 1955, after Gao Gang committing suicide in prison, the CCP convened a national conference to expel him from the Party. Another such case was that of Peng Zhen, who was accused of setting up an impenetrable independent kingdom in Beijing at the beginning of the GPCR. At that time, Peng was a member of the PCC Politburo, member of the PCC Secretariat, first secretary of the CCP Beijing Municipal Committee, vice-chairman of the NPC Standing Committee, and mayor of Beijing. See also "difangzhuyi" (localism).

独立自主
duli zizhu
(maintain independence and keep the initiative in our own hands)

See "zili gengsheng" (self-reliance) and "minzuzhuyi" (nationalism).

独立自主，自力更生
duli zizhu, zili gengsheng
(independence and self-reliance)

See "zili gengsheng" (self-reliance) and "minzuzhuyi" (nationalism).

读书无用论
dushu wuyong lun
("futility of education" theory)

During the GPCR, the cruel persecution of intellectuals led many Chinese to believe that it was of no use for one to receive an education and, even worse, that being an intellectual was a curse. This served as proof of the success of the GPCR in destroying the "sijiu" (the four olds). As is well known, there is a saying in China: "The noblest is to be a scholar, whereas everything else is inferior" (Wanban jie xiapin, weiyou dushu gao). This was a common belief in traditional Chinese society. See also "dangde jiaoyu fangzhen" (the Party's educational policy).

对机械反映论一次密集的批判
dui jixie fanying lun yici mijide pipan
(an extensive criticism of the theory of mechanical reflection)

The center of Liu Zaifu's entire theory of subjectivity is man. He first discusses man's subjective position as the object of literature, and then goes further into man's subjective position in the totality of literary activities—creation, reading, and criticism. The creative subject and the subject of reception embody man's dynamic role in understanding, mastering, and transcending reality, and in sublimating works of literature and art. Judged on a theoretical level, to achieve man's subjective position as creator and receptor is more intrinsic, complicated, and difficult than to restore man's subjective position as the object of literature.

Liu Zaifu stresses subjectivity in the hope of ridding literary concepts of the influence of the theory of mechanical reflection, which is deep-rooted in Marxist literary theory in contemporary China. Liu does not deny the historical and theoretical grounds of the theory of reflection; he is, however, opposed to approaching the literary theory of realism in a static and one-sided way, as if realism is merely something based on the theory of mechanical reflection. He criticizes the theory of mechanical reflection extensively, accusing it of a series of defects:

First, the theory of mechanical reflection, when explaining literature as reflecting the objective world, often only emphasizes reflection and does not deal with the various ways of reflecting. The same is true of the interior mechanism of creation which makes dynamic reflection possible. In other words, it only pays attention to objective entities while ignoring man's psychological structure of subjective aesthetics that dynamically reflects them. Each structure, however, is a unique world full of changes and wonders and with initiative and creativity. To ignore this will lead to a weakening of the brilliance of literature.

Second, the theory of mechanical reflection fails to determine the multiple possibilities of dynamic reflection, and it is only concerned with whether the reflection is correct or erroneous. In actuality, all reflections, correct ones included, are relative, often capable of only showing a certain facet of a thing and not capable of mastering it as a whole. On the other hand, those sorts of reflection regarded as erroneous, such as illusion, exaggeration, weirdness, distortion, and abnormality, can probably reflect the partial essence of a thing. Indeed, very often, they do so even more profoundly. It is out of such "errors" that literature and art build their charming colorful world of beauty.

Third, while aware of the inherent attributes with which the object (the actual world) is endowed by nature, the theory of mechanical reflection often pays no attention to the attribute of value man gives to it. It often separates the cognition, reflection, and appraisal of the object by the subject, thereby ignoring the relationship between the object and man. Literature and art, however, are not merely representation, imitation, and reflection of objects, and not merely an activity of cognition; they are a projection of a subjective spirit, a kind of need, and an activity of appraisal.

Fourth, the theory of mechanical reflection, while emphasizing the objectivity of the object, ignores its subjectivity; and when explaining man, it only notes the subjectivity of the subject and pays no attention to its objectivity. The theory often forgets that man is the object as well as the subject and that, particularly, man's spiritual world is also an objective existence. The reflection of the objective world given in literature and art, therefore, should include two aspects—the pure objective world and man's subjective world.

As Liu Zaifu says, the modern sciences have forced people to shift the focus in epistemological research from issues concerning the objectivity of knowledge to issues concerning the dynamic role of the subject, from the theory of mechanical reflection to the theory of man as the subject. If the concept of reflection in the past concentrated on elucidating the conformity and identity between cognition and its object, then the new science of thinking today places more emphasis on revealing the mechanism of man in understanding reality dynamically, on illustrating the selectivity and creativity of man's cognition. The transfer from the theory of reflection to that of man as the subject does not mean discarding fundamentally the principle of the theory of reflection, but certainly this principle should be transcended and complemented. As Liu Zaifu confidently states: "The change has enabled the current scientific system to be characterized by subjective traits as never seen before. All those who respect science cannot but acknowledge this great trend" ("On the Subjectivity of Literature", *WXPL,* 1:18, 1986). See also "wenxue zhutixing" (subjectivity of literature).

对四人帮三次沉重的打击
dui sirenbang san ci chenzhongde daji
(three heavy blows to the Gang of Four)

See "sirenbang" (Gang of Four).

对文艺界的两个致命打击
dui wenyijiede liang ge zhiming daji
(two telling blows to literary and art circles)

After the 1962 10th Plenum of the 8th PCC, Mao gave a series of talks and instructions concerning Party work in literature and art. Two of these dealt the most telling blows to China's literary and art circles. The first was his written instruction of 12 December 1963 to Peng Zhen and Liu Ren, Party leaders in Beijing (at that time, Peng Zhen was a CCP Politburo member, Beijing mayor, and first secretary of the CCP Beijing Municipal Committee, and Liu Ren was a secretary of the Committee) on "problems" in the arts, in which he said:

"Problems abound in all forms of art such as drama, ballads, music, the fine arts, dance, cinema, poetry, and literature, and the people involved are numerous; in many departments very little has been achieved so far in socialist transformation. The 'dead' still dominate in many departments. What has been achieved in cinema, new poetry, folk songs, the fine arts, and novels should not be underestimated, but there, too, there are quite a few problems. As for such departments as drama the problems are even more serious. The social and economic base has changed, but the arts as part of the superstructure, which serve this base, still remain a serious problem. Hence we should proceed with investigation and earnestly study and attend to this matter.

Isn't it absurd that many Communists are enthusiastic about promoting feudal and capitalist art, but not socialist art?"

The second was the instruction Mao wrote on 27 June 1964 on the "Report on the Rectification Campaign in the ACF and in Its Various National Associations (Draft)" prepared by the PCC Propaganda Department, which reads as follows:

"In the last fifteen years these associations, most of their publications (it is said that a few are good), and by and large the people in them (that is, not everybody) have not carried out the policies of the Party. They have acted as high and mighty bureaucrats, have not gone to the workers, peasants, and soldiers, and have not reflected on the socialist revolution and socialist construction. In recent years, they have slid right down to the brink of revisionism. Unless they remold themselves in earnest, at some future date they are bound to become groups like the Hungarian Petofi Club."

After its 3rd Plenum in December 1978, the 11th PCC formally declared that the criticisms contained in Mao's two written instructions of 1963 and 1964 did not tally with the actual situation, and that these criticisms were later used in Jiang Qing's February 1966 "Summary of the Forum" in such a way as to have the most serious consequences.

对资产阶级实行全面专政
dui zichanjieji shixing quanmian zhuanzheng
(exercise an all-round dictatorship over the bourgeoisie)

See "wuchanjieji zhuanzheng" (dictatorship of the proletariat).

对立统一规律是宇宙的根本规律
duili tongyi guilü shi yuzhoude genben guilü
(the law of the unity of opposites is the fundamental law of the universe)

See "yi fen wei er" (one divides into two).

对内搞活，对外开放
duinei gao huo, duiwai kaifang
(upholding activation of the economy as a domestic policy and the open door as a foreign policy)

See "zhengzhi gaige" (political reform), "jingji gaige" (economic reform), and "Deng Xiaoping lilun" (Deng Xiaoping Theory).

对内开放
duinei kaifang
(domestic opening)

See "zhengzhi gaige" (political reform).

对外开放
duiwai kaifang
(opening to the outside world)

See "zhengzhi gaige" (political reform) and "jingji gaige" (economic reform).

对象的人化
duixiangde renhua
(humanization of the object)

See "shehuizhuyi yihualun" (theory of socialist alienation) and "rendaozhuyi lunzheng" (humanism debate).

蹲点
dundian
(squat at point)

See "zhong shiyantian" (cultivating experimental farming plots).

多快好省
duo kuai hao sheng
(achieve greater, faster, better, and more economical results)

See "shehuizhuyi jianshe zongluxian" (General Line for Socialist Construction).

多党合作制
duodang hezuo zhi
(multi-party cooperative system)

See "minzhu dangpai" (democratic parties) and "wuchanjieji zhuanzheng" (dictatorship of the proletariat).

多党制
duodangzhi
(multi-party system)

See "minzhu dangpai" (democratic parties) and "wuchanjieji zhuanzheng" (dictatorship of the proletariat).

多极论
duojilun
(theory of "multipolarity")

See "san ge shijie lun" ("three worlds" theory).

恶性循环
exing xunhuan
(vicious circle)

See "shiqinian" (seventeen years).

二重组合原理
erchong zuhe yuanli
(principle of the dual combination in characterization)

When Liu Zaifu finished the postscript to *The Aesthetic Thought of Lu Xun* in 1980, it occurred to him that the study of one of Lu Xun's aesthetic concepts—that literary creation should not treat good characters as entirely good and bad characters as entirely bad—should be developed into a complete theory. So in early 1983 he started a new work entitled *A Theory of Combination in Characterization (Xingge Zuhe Lun,* Shanghai, Shanghai Wenyi, July 1986). The central idea of this book of nearly 360,000 Chinese characters, which was listed as one of the ten top best-sellers among books in the social sciences in China in 1986, is the "principle of the dual combination in characterization". As Liu opines, the human personality is extremely complex and consists of two opposites. In literature there are two common examples of this. One is that the dual components, positive and negative, co-exist in a personality in an explicitly antagonistic state, and thereby different types of behavior occur at different times—sometimes displaying a personality's positive factors and sometimes its negative factors. The other is that both positive and negative factors in a personality merge with each other so that a definite type of behavior at a definite time and place will consist of both good and bad, beauty and ugliness—the same factor in a personality displaying dual, or even multiple significances, to different visions.

At that time this was a startling view in China, sharply contrasting with the idea of "typical", one-dimensional characters, as advocated by the orthodox theorists. In fact, after Liu made known his basic view in an article published in May 1984—the first of a series of articles elucidating his view before the book *A Theory of Combination in Characterization* came out in 1986—a controversy ensued. Du Shuying, a critic, argued that a complex character could be achieved not necessarily by presenting its characteristics as consisting of two extreme opposites (Du Shuying, "'Fuza xingge' yu dianxing chuangzao"—"'Complex Personality' and the Creation of a Typical Character", *WYB,* 10:36-37, 1984). Chen Jin, another critic, tried to accuse Liu of advocating a "theory of human nature". Echoing the attack in the 1983 campaign, Chen jumped to the conclusion that "people had already tasted the bitter fruit of those characters created according to the combination of the two opposites—good and bad, beauty and ugliness" (Chen Jin, "'Renwu xingge erchong zuhe yuanli' yiyi"—"An Objection to the 'Principle of Dual Combination in Characterization'", *WYB,* 10:38, 1984). But it seemed that more people supported Liu Zaifu. He Xilai, for instance, held that Liu's principle constituted a step forward, offering a deeply-structured theoretical analysis of the contradictions within a character. He praised Liu for bringing a historical perspective to bear on the question of artistic characterization, and for adopting new research methods from the natural sciences. Zhuang Jiyu, another critic, went so far as to suggest that Liu Zaifu had achieved two breakthroughs in contemporary Chinese literature, one being an exploration of the law governing the development of literature and art itself; the other being endowing the study of the social sciences, literature and art included, with the precision of the natural sciences (see Bi Hua, "Yong renxue daiti shenxue he moxue: Liu Zaifu de 'xingge erchong zuhe lun' shuping"—"On Liu Zaifu's 'Theory of Dual Combination in Characterization'", in his *Zhongguo Xinxieshuzhuyi Wenyi Lungao, erji—Essays on China's New Realistic Literature,* v. 2, Hong Kong, Dangdai Wenxue Yanjiushe, 1987, pp. 229-30).

二律背反现象
erlü beifan xianxiang
(reverse law)

See "wenxue duixiang zhutixing" (subjectivity of the object of literature).

二十年来最具影响力的十个口号
ershinianlai zuiju yingxianglide shi ge kouhao
(ten most influential slogans in the past two decades)

In the past two decades since the 1978 Third Plenum of the 11th PCC, according to Shanghai's prestigious *Wenhui Daily,* there have been ten most influential slogans. They are: 1. "Practice is the sole criterion for testing truth" (Shijian shi jianyan zhenlide weiyi biaozhun). 2. "Allow a proportion of the people to get rich first" (Rang yibufen ren xian fu qilai). 3. "Single-child families are fine" (Zhi sheng yi ge hao). 4. "Time is money" (Shijian jiushi jinqian), which is said to have first appeared in Shenzhen, the first special economic zone in Guangdong province. This is accompanied by another slogan: "Efficiency is life" (Xiaolü jiushi shengming). 5. "Long live understanding" (Lijie wansui), which is said to give expression to the yearning for mutual respect and tolerance towards multiple choices. 6. "Socialism is not equal to poverty" (Pinqiong bushi shehuizhuyi). 7. "Science and technology are the first important productive forces" (Kexue jishu shi diyi shengchanli). 8. "Development is the most essential criterion" (Fazhan caishi ying daoli). 9. "Be articulate with international norms" (Yu guoji jiegui), which is said to be a natural and inevitable choice of a nation constantly striving to become stronger in an age of economic globalization. 10. "Revitalize China through science and education" (Ke jiao xing guo). See also relevant entries.

二十三条
ershisan tiao
(Twenty-three Articles)

See "shejiao" (socialist education movement).

二十世纪八十年代资产阶级人道主义宣言
ershishiji bashiniandai zichanjieji rendaozhuyi xuanyan
(the declaration of bourgeois humanism in the 1980s)

In 1980, Dai Houying, a Shanghai woman writer, published her first novel *Humanity!* (*Ren a, ren!*, Guangzhou, Huacheng, 1980; trans. by Frances Wood under the title *Stones of the Wall,* London, Michael Joseph, 1985). The novel immediately became controversial. To its supporters, it was a record of the resuscitation of human nature, a work calling for a summing up of historical lessons with a "correct attitude" that gives no thought to old scores or personal gains or losses, so that alienated human nature can be resuscitated and people can love one another and start a new life. The significance of the novel, favorable critics asserted, was that, through several middle-aged intellectuals' differing life-paths, full of zigzags and frustrations, it probes the external causes that bring about the "alienated disposition" (xingge yihua) of its protagonists. Powerfully reflected in their mental distortion (their internal contradictions) are various external contradictions, the various crises of the social environment in which they live. The "invisible injury" (neishang) of society has thus been put into words. Almost every character in the work, as those critics put it, is a "flaw detector", with which the degree of society's injury can be measured. In short, like other similar works, *Humanity!* strives to discover the causes of man's alienation and expresses a wish to eliminate alienation and to resuscitate human nature.

In her postscript, Dai Houying describes how she changed in her thinking, which led to her writing of the novel. She writes that she had been a person already deprived of the freedom to think but still believed herself to be free, a person happy at showing off her spiritual shackles as a beautiful necklace. Eventually, she woke up. She came to realize that she had been playing a tragic role in the form of a comedy. She said: "I have escaped from the role I have been playing, and have discovered myself. It has turned out that I am a real person, with love and hatred and all other human emotions and desires and capable of thinking. I should have my own human value and not be belittled as, or willingly degenerate into, a 'tame tool'". Since Dai Houying felt that she had awakened, she decided to announce her awakening publicly. It seemed to her that human nature, human feelings, and humanism were a song long abandoned and forgotten but now tripping off of her tongue. Indeed, she regarded her novel as a record of the "resuscitation of human nature".

In the 1983 campaign to "eliminate spiritual pollution", the novel *Humanity!* and its "Postscript" were under fierce attack. They were described as "a declaration of bourgeois humanism in the 1980s". Tragically, Dai, a much distressed humanist, was murdered in her home by a thief in 1996. See also "rendaozhuyi lunzheng" (humanism debate) and "renxing lun" (theory of human nature).

二十世纪九十年代的圈地运动
ershishiji jiushiniandaide quandi yundong
(the enclosure of the 1990s)

See "kaifaqu re" ("development zone" craze).

二十世纪六十年代北京公社宣言
ershishiji liushiniandai Beijing Gongshe xuanyan
(declaration of the Beijing Commune of the 1960s)

See "quanguo diyizhang Maliezhuyi dazibao" (the first Marxist-Leninist big-character poster in the whole country).

二十世纪人类的两个遗产
ershishiji renleide liang ge yichan
(two legacies of the human race in the twentieth century)

See "xin shehuizhuyi guan" (new socialist view).

二十一世纪是中国人的世纪
ershiyishiji shi Zhongguorende shiji
(the twenty-first century will be the Chinese century)

The rise of China (Zhongguode jueqi) is currently a popular topic. William Overholt's book, *The Rise of China: How Economic Reform Is Creating a New Superpower,* New York, W. W. Norton, 1993, very quickly became a best-seller. U.S. President Clinton also turned out to be a perceptive prophet. In a speech to a Canberra audience in November 1996, he said that one of the five big questions that will determine the shape of the world fifty years from now will surely be: how the Chinese define their greatness in the twenty-first century. "Will they define their greatness in terms of the incredible potential of their people to learn, to produce, to succeed economically, culturally, and politically? Or, will they define their greatness in terms of their ability to dominate their neighbors and others, perhaps against their will, or take other actions which could destabilize the march towards democracy and prosperity of other people?" *(Sydney Morning Herald,* 29 Nov. 1996).

These questions have both domestic and international implications. There is a saying that the twenty-first century will be a Chinese century. It is predicted that, even if growth slows from the average of 9 percent since 1979 to the 7 percent now forecast for the years ahead, China still will be the largest economy in the world before the year 2020. In addition, following Hong Kong and Macao, Taiwan will also be peacefully reunified with the mainland. Against this background the term "Greater China" (da Zhonghua) evolved. It is argued that "Greater China" is not simply an abstract concept. It is a rapidly growing cultural and economic reality, and it has even begun to become a political reality (Samuel P. Huntington, *The Clash of Civilizations and the Remaking of World Order*, p. 169).

The term "Chinese hegemony" (Zhongguo baquan) is also frequently used. China's history, culture, traditions, size, economic dynamism, and self-image, Huntington opined, all impel it to assume a hegemonic position in East Asia. This goal is a natural result of its rapid economic development (ibid., p. 229). Echoing some analysts' comparison of the emergence of China to the rise of Germany as the dominant power in Europe in the late nineteenth century and Lee Kuan Yew's 1994 observation of China as "the biggest player in the history of man", Huntington issued a warning. He said: "If Chinese economic development continues for another decade, as seems possible, and if China maintains its unity during the succession period, as seems probable, East Asian countries and the world will have to respond to the increasingly assertive role of this biggest player in human history" (ibid., p. 231).

In the upsurge of nationalism in China in the 1990s, some Chinese began to talk about the "Chinese century". They claimed that they had to resist "Western-centrism" (xifang zhongxinzhuyi), or, as it has been more recently termed, "the cultural hegemony of Western imperialism" (xifang diguozhuyi wenhua baquan). Criticism and repudiation of so-called "Western values" (xifang jiazhi) became popular. On the other hand, "Asian values", "the superiority of Chinese culture", or "the superiority of Eastern culture" were promoted. Intoxicated with self-satisfaction, they believed that the rejuvenation of Chinese culture (in the sense of world history) was just around the corner.

Some circumspect and farsighted individuals simply reject the thesis of "a Chinese century". For one thing, it is a mere supposition. For another, it can be misleading and can give rise to racial hatreds and conflicts. A logic may be at work here: the rise of China will lead to a Chinese century in the twenty-first century; this constitutes a China threat; and this is why it is necessary to contain China. Such an inference may not only be politically biased but also very dangerous. If there was a "Chinese century", the eighteenth century might have been such a century. But all these were something of the past—the Chinese century, the British century, or the American century. The twenty-first century should be a new century, in which no hegemony should be allowed. For the benefit of the entire world, China should take the initiative to join in the world's mainstream civilization, play an active role, and help create a new century of peace, democracy, and common prosperity. In the new century, all nations should be equal, enjoy multi-development, and share what can be called "global values" (quanqiu jiazhi), while each civilization should fully display its own merits. See also "weidu Zhongguo" (containment against China) and "minzuzhuyi" (nationalism).

二线
erxian
(second line)

At the end of 1953, according to Deng Xiaoping, Mao first proposed that the work of the PCC be divided into a "front line" (yixian) and a "second line" *(SWD,* p. 278).

In the CCP's lexicon, among the top Party leaders, those working at central Party, government, and army organizations are on the "front line". Those on the "second line" do not exercise direct leadership but function as advisers and influence policymaking from behind the scenes. After the GPCR, because many living leaders were senile, Deng found this practice to be of immediate significance. In 1980, when talking about reform of the system of Party and state leadership, Deng said: "It is of great strategic importance for us to ensure the continuity and stability of the correct leadership of our Party and state by having younger comrades take the 'front-line' posts while the older comrades give them the necessary advice and supports" *(SWD,* p. 303). See also "quanli douzheng lun" ("power struggle" theory) and "wen'ge" (Cultural Revolution).

二月逆流
eryue niliu
(adverse February current)

In February 1967, at briefings of the PCC Politburo (the Huairentang meetings—so called because they were held in the Huairentang hall inside the compound at Zhongnanhai in Beijing) and CMC meetings, several Party and army leaders who were losing power—Tan Zhenlin, Chen Yi, Ye Jianying, Li Fuchun, Li Xiannian, Xu Xiangqian, and Nie Rongzhen—strongly criticized what they considered to be the mistaken methods of the GPCR (one of the Huairentang meetings was held on 16 February, during which one of the most serious clashes between them and the GPCR faction took place). This led to their being accused of having churned up an adverse current—the "adverse February current". Zhu De (1886-1976) and Chen Yun, two major leaders, were also attacked. After the 1971 Lin Biao Incident, Mao said that the "February adverse current" should not be brought up again. Following the "October 6 coup" of 1976, the PCC formally announced the reversal of the verdict on the "adverse current".

Another account of the current is as follows: In January 1967, seeing that Party and government organs at various levels had been smashed by the rebels in their "January Revolution", Mao asked the PLA to reorganize local power and maintain social order (he issued the call: "The PLA should support the broad masses of the

Left"). This led to a new conflict—a conflict between the PLA and the radical rebels. In February and March 1967, the military carried out a large-scale suppression. Many rebel organizations collapsed, and their leaders and key members were arrested.

Then Mao made another change, when he saw that the GPCR might thus be aborted. He agreed to strike back at what was termed by the rebels as the "adverse February current". In the Communiqué of the Enlarged 12th Plenum of the 8th PCC, the nature of the current was described as follows: "The Plenum seriously criticized and repudiated the 'adverse February current' of 1967 which was directed against the decision of the 11th Plenum of the 8th PCC, against the GPCR, and against the proletarian headquarters...."

To the rebels, to counter-attack the "adverse February current" meant to counter-attack persecution. That was why they went all out and intensified their struggle to "ferret out a handful of capitalist-roaders in the army" (jiu junnei yixiaocuo). See also "changcheng" (Great Wall, i.e., the PLA).

二月提纲
eryue tigang
("February Outline Report")

Dubbed the "February Outline Report" because it was made in February, the full title of the document is the "Outline Report on the Current Academic Discussion by the Group of Five in Charge of the Cultural Revolution" ("Wenhua geming wuren xiaozu guanyu dangqian xueshu taolun huibao tigang"). Mao's fierce attack on this "Outline Report" marked the beginning of the GPCR.

On 3 February 1966, the "Group in Charge of the Cultural Revolution" (that is, the "Group of Five", with Peng Zhen as its leader and Lu Dingyi as its deputy leader) held an enlarged meeting to discuss problems arising from the current academic criticism. The "Outline Report" was drafted after the meeting on the basis of the results of the discussion. In the current academic criticism, the document held, the policy of "fang"—letting people air views—must be adopted. Debates should be conducted based on reason and facts, and everyone should be treated as equal before the truth (zhenli mianqian renren pingdeng). There should be construction as well as destruction (you po you li). Furthermore, those who make mistakes should be allowed to correct them by themselves. The document asked for a prudent policy with regard to carrying out an open criticism by name in magazines and newspapers.

Two days later, the "Outline Report" was passed at a meeting presided over by Liu Shaoqi and attended by the Politburo Standing Committee members who were in Beijing at the time. On 8 February, Peng Zhen, Lu Dingyi, and Xu Liqun (one of the group members) made a special trip to Wuchang, Hubei province, where Mao was staying temporarily at the time, to give Mao an account of the document. Mao asked a few questions, but he did not say anything against it. Then, on 12 February, the PCC promulgated the "Outline Report" to the whole Party.

Thereafter, Mao began to make known his negative views of the "Outline Report", first to Jiang Qing, Kang Sheng, and others. In his three talks with them from 28 to 30 March 1966, he fiercely criticized the CCP Beijing Municipal Committee and the PCC Propaganda Department, and the "Party lord" behind them (i.e., Peng Zhen, as Mao had implied). On 1 April, directed by Zhang Chunqiao, a document entitled "A Few Opinions on the 'Outline Report on the Current Academic Discussion by the Group of Five in Charge of the Cultural Revolution'" ("Dui 'Wenhua geming wuren xiaozu guanyu dangqian xueshu taolun huibao tigang' de jidian yijian") was written. Finally, the "May 16th Circular" of 1966 ("wuyiliu tongzhi"), which was drafted under the supervision of Chen Boda (1904-1989) and revised seven times by Mao, was passed at an enlarged meeting of the CCP Politburo on 16 May 1966. Accordingly, the "Group of Five" was dismissed and the "February Outline Report" became a target for attack. See also "wuyiliu tongzhi" (May 16th Circular).

法轮大法
Falun Dafa
(System of Law Wheel)

See "Falun Gong" (Law Wheel Cultivation).

法轮功
Falun Gong
(Law Wheel Cultivation)

On 25 April 1999, more than ten thousand practitioners of what is called "Falun Gong" (or "Falun Dafa") gathered outside the compound at Zhongnanhai in Beijing, where the PCC and PRC central government offices are located, protesting against their being discredited and treated unfairly. The quiet and orderly gathering, the largest demonstration since the 1989 pro-democracy movement, shocked the world.

Since Falun Gong was introduced by its founder Li Hongzhi in 1992, it has reportedly attracted several million people in mainland China and throughout the world. Li and his disciples describe Falun Gong as an advanced system of cultivation and practice. Its foundation consists of a body of fundamental knowledge essential for the task of undertaking proper cultivation towards higher stages of attainment. It comprises Master Li's teachings collected in a number of books, the most important of which is *Zhuan Falun (Revolving the Law Wheel,* an edition of which was published in Beijing, in December 1994 by China Radio & Television Publishing House). Many of the teachings are said to be highly classified knowledge that have been imparted exclusively from master to trusted disciples since antiquity in China.

According to these teachings, Falun Gong is characterized by the cultivation of a Falun (Law Wheel), located at the "dantian" (lower abdomen). The Taoist Yin-Yang and the Buddha's Dharma-wheel are both reflected in the Falun. As an intelligent spinning body of high-energy substance, the Falun automatically absorbs energy from the universe, while relieving the body of bad elements. A miniature universe, it shares the same characteristics as the universe. Its rotation synchronizes with the universe's rotation. Falun is constantly rotating, putting the practitioner in a state of cultivation for twenty-four hours a day. Of all the "qigong" or cultivation systems known to the public, Falun Gong is described as the first and only one that solves the conflicting time-requirements for practicing and work or study. Moreover, in addition to being a powerful mechanism for healing, stress relief, and health improvements, it is said to be different from other "qigong" techniques in its higher objective of cultivation and practice towards enlightenment. It is complete with its own system of principles and empirical techniques.

In the past two decades, "qigong" has developed quickly and widely in mainland China. But it was quite unexpected that Falun Gong would become so popular. Its popularity, according to Li Hongzhi and his disciples, is due to the fact that it not only helps practitioners cure their illnesses but it also enables them to reach higher realms of the mind. Falun Gong gives top priority to the cultivation of "xinxing" (mind nature) and its assimilation of "zhen" (truth, truthfulness), "shan" (compassion, kindness, benevolence) and "ren" (tolerance, forbearance). "Xinxing" is the key to the growth of cultivation energy and the level of "xinxing" determines the level of cultivation energy. "Zhen-shan-ren" are regarded as "the supreme nature of the universe" (yuzhou zuigao texing), and people should conduct themselves according to these guiding principles.

However, many people cannot bring themselves to believe Li's teachings and accept the alleged miracle of Falun Gong. The series of theories Li has devised are found to go against science and civilized society, claiming that, while scientific reasoning and common sense are foolish, the Falun Dafa alone offers the right law and super science. The Chinese authorities, particularly, find it necessary to suppress this belief system. On 22 July 1999, they issued a ban against it, labeling it as an "illegal organization". On 29 July, through the Interpol, the PRC Public Security Ministry issued an order for arrest of Li Hongzhi (who left China for the U.S. in 1995 and became a U.S. citizen in 1998). At the same time, arrests of its key and/or loyal practitioners were carried out. On 25 October, the Chinese government announced that Falun Gong is an "evil religion" (xiejiao). On 30 October 1999, the 12th Session of the NPC Standing Committee adopted a resolution concerning the banning of heretic cult organizations, prevention measures against them, and punishment for cult activities. (In light of this resolution, other organizations similar to the already banned Falun Gong would be treated likewise. For example, Zhong Gong, a spiritual group founded in 1987 by Zhang Hongbao with his "Kylin" philosophy, was outlawed.)

According to the *People's Daily* editorial of 23 July 1999, opposing Falun Gong is "a grave ideological-political struggle that has a bearing on the fate of the Party and the country". In the nationwide condemnation movement, every Chinese must understand clearly that Falun Gong is not Buddhism or Taoism, nor a kind of normal qigong, but a cult, an evil organization. It is, in the official language, an anti-scientific, anti-human, anti-social, anti-government and illegal organization with all the characteristics of an evil religion. It was accused of competing with the CCP for the masses of the Chinese people and even trying to overthrow the Party's leadership. China's religious leaders also joined in the condemnation. Zhao Puchu (1907-2000), chairman of the Buddhist Association of China, declared: "It is very necessary for the Party to rid itself of this big disaster for the people and remove this big cancer from society" (*BR*, 23 Aug. 1999).

China critics regarded the suppression, which brought about an anti-persecution mentality (fan pohai yishi) among Falun Gong practitioners, as violating the United Nations' Universal Declaration of Human Rights, the Declaration on the Elimination of All Forms of Intolerance and of Discrimination Based on Religion or Belief, and the International Covenant on Civil and Political Rights. The Party leaders, however, came to the conclusion that they had no other choice. Politically, the popularity of Falun Gong certainly made them uneasy. What would happen if things were to spin out of control? Falun Gong does not fit into the category of Communist theory, thus constituting a real threat to the ideological monopoly which the authorities wish to conserve. (Ironically, many CCP members were also Falun Gong practitioners.)

Several key questions remain unanswered: why did so many people practice Falun Gong in mainland China? What were the superficial and inner reasons for the "Falun Gong phenomenon"? Will labeling Falun Gong as an "evil religion" and banning it be successful—which pushed so many people to oppose the government? Or has the Falun Gong phenomenon simply been exaggerated? See also "Kylin wenhua" (Kylin Culture), "renquan wenti" (human rights issue), and "chi butong zhengjianzhe" (dissidents).

法轮功现象
Falun Gong xianxiang
("Falun Gong" phenomenon)

See "Falun Gong" (Law Wheel Cultivation).

发财光荣
facai guangrong
(to get rich is glorious)

On 13 December 1978, in his speech at the closing session of the **Central Work** Conference, which prepared for the epoch-making 3rd Plenum of the 11th PCC, Deng Xiaoping announced a new Party policy: a proportion of the people would be allowed to get rich first (rang yibufen ren xian fu qilai). This led to the spread of the following slogan: To get rich is glorious. With these words, Deng had ignited China's boom.

As some China observers have pointed out, Deng, a pragmatic patriarch, wanted to promote a nationwide creation of wealth over both politics and social concerns. But breakneck growth can be socially destabilizing. A direct consequence of this has been the increasing disparities between the rich and the poor. This has been accompanied by rampant money worship, hedonism, widespread corruption, rising crime, and huge floating populations of unemployed in the big cities. Any serious attempt to rationalize the sprawling state-sector industries, which serve also as mammoth welfare agencies for hundreds of millions of workers, may spark even more instability.

Jiang Zemin's plan is to carry out a Deng Xiaoping line without Deng Xiaoping, as he vowed at the September 1997 CCP 15th National Congress. What sets the new core of Party leadership somewhat apart from Deng is Jiang's stress on an ethical dimension to economic growth.

In fact, among China's thinking public, some of Deng's views began to be questioned, such as "allowing a proportion of the people to get rich first". In the first place, they said, this implies that distribution will be affected by power, by the will and decision of Party leaders. Moreover, very often, those in power will "allow" themselves, and their children, relatives, and subordinates, to get rich first. As a result, social inequities are a serious problem that must be addressed. See also "ershinianlai zuiju yingxianglide shi ge kouhao" (ten most influential slogans in the past two decades) and "jingji gaige" (economic reform).

发展才是硬道理
fazhan caishi ying daoli
(development is the most essential criterion)

During his tour in early 1992 to China's southern provinces, Deng issued a loud and clear statement: "Development is the most essential criterion." Since then, this phrase has frequently been cited by China's reformists. (Also often cited is another phrase which is derived from it, "Without development there will no true stability"—"Meiyou fazhan bian meiyou zhenzhengde wending", which was reported to have been created by Jiang Chunyun, who was then secretary of the CCP Shandong Provincial Committee and was later promoted by Deng to vice premier.)

Deng's view about "development"is considered to be the core of his strategic thought. On 25 February 1997, in his eulogy to Deng in Beijing's Great Hall of the People, Jiang Zemin reminded his listeners of Deng's instructions. He pledged to continue with the patriarch's platform of economic reforms. "We must take the deepening of reform (shenhua gaige) as the key to eliminating barriers to the development of productive forces and further advancing our entire cause," he said.

Significantly, in the second half of the 1990s, in view of the serious corruption in the Party and government and the universal "decline of morality" (daode huapo) in society, many farsighted scholars found themselves sharing the view that man should be at the center of development (fazhan shi yi ren wei zhongxinde fazhan). As they said, science and technology do not produce ethics and morality; money cannot replace values. Chinese should not become "political animals" (zhengzhi dongwu), nor should they become "economic animals" (jingji dongwu). Development, as the international standard defines, is the sum total of various factors, including economic growth, political democracy, the development of science and technology, changes in cultural values, transition of the social mode, and ecological balance and protection. These scholars appealed for the setting up of a political economy for China during the "mode transition" period, for a fight against a "power economy" (quanli jingji), for "morality resuscitation" (daode fusu), and social justice. Compared with "development", they asserted that "Justice is the more essential criterion" (gongzheng gengshi ying daoli). See also "ershinianlai zuiju yingxianglide shi ge kouhao" (ten most influential slogans in the past two decades) and "jingji gaige" (economic reform).

发展是以人为中心的发展
fazhan shi yi ren wei zhongxinde fazhan
(man should be at the center of development)

See "fazhan caishi ying daoli" (development is the most essential criterion).

发展中的马克思主义
fazhanzhongde Makesizhuyi
(Marxism in development)

See "zhengtong Makesizhuyi zhengzai zou xiang siwang" (orthodox Marxism is heading for death) and "rendaozhuyide Makesizhuyi" (humanistic Marxism).

法，术，势
fa, shu, shi
(Han Fei's theoretical system of "rule by law")

See "yi fa zhi guo" (ruling the nation by law).

法律至上
falü zhishang
(law is supreme)

See "yi fa zhi guo" (ruling the nation by law).

法治
fazhi
(rule by law)

See "yi fa zhi guo" (ruling the nation by law).

法制
fazhi
(system of law)

See "yi fa zhi guo" (ruling the nation by law).

凡有人群的地方，都有左中右
fanyou renqunde difang, douyou zuo, zhong, you
(wherever there are masses of people, they are invariably divided into the Left, the middle, and the Right)

In May 1957, when sensing the political situation developing not so much on the track that he had expected for his ongoing rectification movement, Mao warned, in a secret document for high-ranking officials: "Except in deserts, wherever there are masses of people, they are invariably divided into the Left, the middle, and the Right. The same will remain true even in ten thousand years" ("Things Are Beginning to Change"—"Shiqing zhengzai qi bianhua", *MZXJ,* 5, p. 428). He mentioned the term "youpai" (Rightists) and alleged that "Rightists" were attempting to exterminate the Communist Party. This marked the beginning of the 1957 anti-Rightist campaign.

Mao's idea can be traced back to his March 1926 article "Analysis of the Classes in Chinese Society" ("Zhongguo shehui gejieji fenxi", *MZXJ,* 1, pp. 13-21). In this important work, Mao raised what he insisted was "a question of first importance for the revolution"—to distinguish real friends from real enemies in order to unite with real friends and to attack real enemies. Indeed, class analysis was a basic method Mao employed for half a century to make his revolution. He asked his Party to adhere strictly to class line (jieji luxian). Therefore, when a political campaign was carried out, there would be "queuing up" (paidui)—political comparisons and classifications of people, especially of cadres and working personnel of leading bodies at various levels. In accordance with their different political attitudes and activities, they were classified as left, middle right, extreme-right or, core elements. They were also classified as activists, middle-of-the-roaders, politically reliable personnel, politically-doubtful personnel, or targets of political campaign. See also "jieji luxian" (class line) and "fan youpai yundong" (anti-Rightist campaign).

繁体字
fantizi
(traditional Chinese characters)

Traditional Chinese characters are Chinese characters in their original complex form. See "wenzi gaige" (reform of written Chinese).

反潮流
fan chaoliu
(go against the tide)

In the summer of 1973, Mao put forth the slogan: "Go against the tide." He further explained that "Going against the tide is a Marxist principle" (fan chaoliu shi Makesizhuyide yi ge yuanze).

In view of Mao's unique and consistent style of thinking, it was not unusual for him to raise such a slogan. Thereafter, those in charge of Party propaganda lost no time in telling the public that by going against the tide Mao meant going against the adverse tide of revisionism, splitism, and conspiracy. As advocated in Marxism, they said, one must oppose all reactionary and backward currents, and oppose different forms of adverse currents. They pointed out that at the moment when there was a current of Rightist reversion in the country's educational field, everyone must participate to oppose it. This led to the creation of several model heroes. One such hero was Zhang Tiesheng, a rusticated educated youth who, when sitting for a university entrance exam, handed in a blank examination paper as a protest against what he asserted to be the Rightist reversion. This act was hailed as "a spirit of going against the tide" (fan chaoliu jingshen), in a *People's Daily* article of 16 August 1973 (Yang Pu, "Fan chaoliu jingshen"—"The Spirit of Going Against the Tide").

Not long after the downfall of the Gang of Four, Zhang Tiesheng was arrested and later sentenced to seventeen years' imprisonment, branded as the Gang of Four's hatchet man and tool, an active counter-revolutionary. "Going against the tide" was then described as an "evil torrent against the proletarian revolutionary cause".

反潮流精神
fan chaoliu jingshen
(spirit of going against the tide)

See "fan chaoliu" (go against the tide).

反潮流是马克思主义的一个原则
fan chaoliu shi Makesizhuyide yi ge yuanze
(going against the tide is a Marxist principle)

See "fan chaoliu" (go against the tide).

反传统
fan chuantong
(anti-tradition)

The term "anti-tradition" is based on the following series of terms. The term "new tradition" (xinchuantong), also known as the "petit tradition" (xiaochuantong), is used as distinct from the "grand tradition" (dachuantong), which refers to the over two thousand years' tradition of Chinese culture and society. The term "new tradition", when employed in the Communist regime, in effect means "orthodoxy" (zhengtong) or the "mainstream ideology" (zhuliu yishixingtai) in the regime, as expressed by terms such as the "revolutionary tradition" (geming chuantong), the "May 4th tradition" (wusi chuantong), and the "Yan'an tradition" (Yan'an chuantong).

Generally speaking, the Communist "new tradition" is anti-tradition, or, to be exact, anti-grand tradition. But this is not so quite simple. According to Jin Guantao and Liu Qingfeng, the two coauthors of *New Decameron (Xin Shiritan,* Hong Kong, Cosmos Books, 1990), the deep structure of Confucian culture influences contemporary Chinese culture, including Marxism in China. In other words, the deep structure of the new tradition is still the same as the grand tradition. Hence the terms "Sinicized Marxism" (Zhongguohuade Makesizhuyi or Makesizhuyi Zhongguohua) and "Confucianized Marxism" (Rujiahuade Makesizhuyi or Makesizhuyi rujiahua).

The anti-tradition trend in mainland China finds expression on the one hand in the destruction of tradition (that is, the grand tradition) by communism, and on the other in the sublation (yangqi) of communism by the new culture. The cause for this unique phenomenon can be traced back to the May 4th Movement of 1919 with the introduction into China of the two ideological trends of Westernization and communism, which contradicted each other but at the same time shared a common enemy—tradition. Therefore, when cultural change (wenhua bianqian) occurs, evoking the spirit of the May 4th Movement, anti-tradition is natural and inevitable. Another reason, which is easily ignored but worth probing, can be found in the fact that since 1949 the thirty years' politico-cultural reality in the mainland was characterized by the elimination of the liberal spirit (which was brought about by the May 4th Movement) by communism, with the help of the tradition it had absorbed.

As some scholars suggest, the present-day cultural clash (wenhua chongtu) in mainland China is no longer simply a clash between Western culture and Chinese culture, or between Westernization and anti-Westernization. While such a clash between the two cultures exists and can be felt in the people's daily life, of more significance is the interpenetration and interaction (of both their merits and defects) of the two cultures. In describing the cultural clash in China today, one may say, more accurately, that there is a clash between the new civil culture (minjian wenhua), as marked by pluralistic openness, human rights, and democracy, and the old official culture (guanfang wenhua) which is characterized by closed-doorism, conservatism, centralization of state power, and inhumanity.

The "anti-tradition" signboard is very often a cloak under which the Communist ideology is the real target. When talking of the evils of the traditional autocracy, one may be criticizing the present politico-cultural reality. Just as criticism of tradition instead of the Communist system is not to the point, a discussion of tradition will achieve nothing if it ignores the present Communist system. According to Su Xiaokang, a dissident writer (living in exile in the U.S. since the June 4th Incident of 1989), traditional Chinese culture now faces two challenges: how to survive the Communist shambles and how to co-exist with modernization. (No matter how strong the anti-tradition force is, tradition will not completely vanish in a pre-modern society; it is modernization that constitutes a real threat to tradition.) Su predicted that a cultural tension (wenhua jinzhang), deriving from the two challenges, will therefore continue into the twenty-first century. (See Su Xiaokang, "Dangdai Zhongguode wenhua jinzhang"—"The Cultural Tension in Contemporary China", in Chen Kuide, ed., *Changes in Contemporary Culture in Mainland China—Zhongguo dalu dangdai wenhua bianqian,* Taipei, Guiguan, 1991, pp. 21-35.) See also "wenhua re" (culture craze) and "sixiang gaizao" (ideological remolding).

反腐败
fan fubai
(anti-corruption)

Currently in China there are three organizations responsible for anti-corruption activities at three different levels. First, the PCC Commission for Discipline Inspection is responsible for investigating violations of discipline within the Party; second, the government supervision department is responsible for investigating violations of discipline within administrative departments and cases involving government functionaries; and, finally, the people's procuratorate handles corruption and bribery cases of public officials found criminally responsible. It has established a nationwide offense-reporting system.

With regard to anti-corruption legislation, China has enacted numerous special laws and regulations, such as the Supplementary Stipulations to the Criminal Law Concerning Punishment for Acts of Corruption and Bribery and the Provisional Stipulations on Disciplinary Sanctions Against Government Functionaries Involved in Acts of Corruption and Bribery. Other new laws include the Anti-Corruption Law, the Administrative Supervision Law, the Reporting System for Major Issues of Leading Cadres, and the Law on the Declaration of the Property and Incomes of Government Functionaries.

After being formally appointed as Deng's successor at the 1994 4th Plenum of the 14th PCC, Jiang Zemin wisely chose "anti-corruption" as the goal of his new administration. Two major cases were exposed, apparently aiming to reduce the people's complaints (as expressed in the often heard saying: "Only swat flies but not hunt tigers"—"zhi da cangying, bu da laohu"). One was the case of Chen Xitong, former CCP Politburo member and Beijing Party secretary. (On 29 August 1997 Chen was expelled from the Party following the decision of the PCC Commission for Discipline Inspection, and on 31 July 1998 he was sentenced to 16 years' imprisonment by the Beijing Higher People's Court.) The other was the case of Zhou Beifang, former Hong Kong chief executive of the Capital Iron and Steel Company. (Zhou was arrested in Beijing on 13 February 1995, and sentenced to death with two years' reprieve in November 1996.) Moreover, after many years of preparation, the Anti-Corruption and Bribery Administration of the Supreme People's Procuratorate was founded in November 1995. At its founding it was declared that China's anti-corruption effort had embarked "on a specialized and regularized track".

Jiang further pledged to carry out his anti-corruption campaign in a serious and regularized way at the CCP's 15th National Congress. In his report of 12 September 1997, while reiterating his loyalty to Deng Xiaoping Theory, the new core of the Party leadership stressed an ethical dimension to economic growth. He pledged to pay close attention to the handling of the relationship between material progress and cultural and ethical progress. While confirming that economic backwardness is not socialism, Jiang added that spiritual deficiency also is not socialism. He said, with a stern tone: "The fight against corruption is a grave political struggle vital to the very existence of the Party and the state."

With Jiang focusing on his anti-corruption campaign, the two legal bodies, the PRC Supreme People's Court and the PRC Supreme People's Procuratorate, were found to be problematic. A working group headed by Wei Jianxing, member of the PCC Politburo Standing Committee, was established, following a Politburo decision announced on 10 May 1998 at a meeting jointly convened by the PCC, the State Council, and the PCC Commission for Discipline Inspection. Luo Ji, the first director of the new Anti-Corruption and Bribery Administration, and his three deputies were reportedly arrested on 12 May. Unprecedentedly, the Chinese central authorities launched a nationwide probe into its anti-corruption efforts in 3,700 localities, focusing on about 2,000 chief prosecutors and bureau heads. Then, in July 1998, at a national anti-smuggling conference, Jiang ordered the military to end all commercial activities. (This was a new policy different from Deng's.) After the conference, the military, and all the legal bodies—courts, procuratorates, and public security departments—had to pledge obedience. Jiang's anti-corruption campaign continued. Li Jizhou, deputy minister of public security, was detained on 17 December 1998 and formally arrested in April 2000. On 8 March 2000, Hu Changqing, former Jiangxi province deputy governor, was executed after a quick trial. On 31 July 2000, Cheng Kejie, former NPC vice-chairman and Guangxi autonomous region governor, was sentenced to death (so far the highest-ranking official under sentence of death). Jiang announced on 14 January 2000 at the 4th Plenum of the CCP Central

Commission for Discipline Inspection that the Party must strictly discipline itself before it can run the country well (zhi guo bi xian zhi dang, zhi dang wubi cong yan).

All of these events show the determination of the Chinese central authorities to check the corruption problem. But these facts also confirm that corruption in China, especially within the CCP, has indeed become universal and very serious. As the saying goes: "If you don't use your power when you have it, you will be sorry when it expires" (you quan buyong, guoqi zuofei), bureaucrats of various ranks scramble for power and profit by every means. For a number of years, China has been listed as one of the world's most corrupt countries. It has been suggested that: "The speed of corruption has surpassed the growth of the GNP" (fubai sudu chaoguo guomin shengchan zongzhi zengzhanglu), by Hu An'gang, a key research fellow at the State Situation Analysis Group, CASS. According to Hu, no other country has more official organizations in charge of anti-corruption than China (in both the CCP and in the government). However, because of the lack of a "sound system": the harder the people try to check corruption, the more serious it will become (Hu An'gang, "Zhidu chuangxinde shidai"—"An Era for System Innovation", *Lianhe zaobao,* Singapore, 11 June 1995). Many fear that corruption in China, if unchecked, will lead to a national disaster. Hu An'gang warns that it is likely that something like the June 4th Incident of 1989 could take place (ibid.).

While admitting the existence of corruption, some still maintain "corruption is reasonable" (fubai youli) and "corruption is favorable" (fubai youli). They regard corruption as a necessary social cost of the reform program, and a small cost at that. Corruption, they argue, involves buying institutional power with outside economic resources. It forces those in power to peacefully accept a transfer of economic resources. When the already dead resources within the institution are appropriated, they are revived, and they re-enter the process of expanded reproduction. As a result, new things replace the old; and the old institutions are replaced.

Many are opposed to this argument. On the basis of her experience and investigation, He Qinglian, an outstanding economist, points out that corruption heavily consumes social resources, accounting for 70 percent of the loss of state assets and capital. Moreover, the remaining 30 percent is not necessarily used as capital for domestic production (see He Qinglian, *Zhongguode Xianjing—The Pitfalls of China,* Hong Kong, Mirror, Sept. 1997). According to May 1998 statistics provided by the State Statistical Bureau, in the five years from 1993 to 1997, over 355 billion Chinese dollars of state assets and capital disappeared, of which over 250 billion were siphoned abroad. Other sources report that the rate of China's state-property losses totals about 30 billion U.S. dollars per year. This is consistent with the views of He Qinglian and other economists.

As pointed out by many, what corruption will possibly dispel is not the old institutions but the law, the new rules and regulations which have been made and brought into effect with great efforts. The ultimate result of the rampant corruption is that a "civil society ruled by law" (gongmin fazhi shehui), which many are enthusiastically talking about, will not be realized. Instead, it will lead to vicious money-power politics (jin quan zhengzhi), in the Italian mode where the government and the Mafia both rule the society. Indeed, as far as China is concerned, corruption is a "political cancer" (zhengzhi zhi ai). It simply cannot be explained in the realm of morality. It is a structural problem deriving from China's present institutional structure and the strategy for the reform program. In turn, it greatly sabotages the reform itself.

Officially, anti-corruption has become a "life-and-death matter" to the Party and the state. Party leaders have come to see it as a "self-revolution" (ziwo geming) of the CCP. However, thus far Jiang Zemin has found it difficult to solve the fundamental problem, even though it has enhanced his personal prestige for a time. The crux of the matter, China critics claim, lies in the one-party autocracy whereby there are no independent judicial organs and no sufficient supervision by a free media. If there is no change in the one-party autocracy, corruption will only become worse in the future. There is a poignant, though perhaps somewhat exaggerated, saying circulating in the country: "The destruction of the country will occur without anti-corruption, whereas a thorough anti-corruption drive will lead to the destruction of the Party" (bu fan fubai, wang guo; er chedi fan fubai, wang dang). A possible outcome may be: either the destruction of the Party by the worsening corruption or the success of the anti-corruption drive but the destruction of the present politico-social system. See also "Chen Xitong shijian" (Chen Xitong Incident), "jingji gaige" (economic reform), and "zhengzhi gaige" (political reform).

反腐败是关系党和国家生死存亡的严重政治斗争
fan fubai shi guanxi dang he guojia shengsi cunwangde yanzhong zhengzhi douzheng
(the fight against corruption is a grave political struggle vital to the life and death of the Party and the state)

See "fan fubai" (anti-corruption).

反火药味论
fan "huoyao wei" lun
(theory of opposition to the "smell of gunpowder")

This was one of the "eight sinister theories" singled out for attack in the 1966 Party document the "Summary". Qu Baiyin, a well-known film critic, can be considered responsible for this theory. In 1962, he published an article, opposing dogmatism in literature and art. Today, the article, entitled "A Monolog on Blazing a New Path in Film", is regarded as an important milestone in the history of Chinese modern film ("Guanyu dianying chuangxin wentide dubai", *Dianying yishu*, 3, 1962, reprinted in *XHYB*, 1:163-168, 1980). See also "jiyao" ("Summary") and "fan 'ticai jueding' lun" (theory of opposition to "subject-matter as the decisive factor").

反激进主义
fan jijinzhuyi
(anti-radicalism)

See "xin baoshouzhuyi" (neo-conservatism).

反极左
fan jizuo
(anti-ultra-Left)

See "you" (Right).

反理性
fan lixing
(anti-rationalism)

Another term for "feilixing" (irrational). See "menglongshi lilunde san ci jueqi" ("three rises" in the theory of misty poetry) and "gei feilixing zai yishu chuangzuozhong yige yingyoude diwei" (give the irrational due place in artistic creation).

反理性神秘主义
fan lixing shenmizhuyi
(anti-rational mysticism)

A term appearing in the 1987 campaign against "bourgeois liberalization", "anti-rational mysticism" was used to attack certain literary experiments in China at that time. To people like Xiong Fu, then editor-in-chief of *Red Flag,* the situation in the previous few years of the campaign had been very bad. Xiong felt as if he had been living "in a nightmare", shocked and isolated, where he could hardly hear anything that was derived from Marxism. As he said, "various modernist rubbish" filled all the journals and other publications. A number of works came out which were "full of pornography and other vulgar interests, with absurd plots which transcend time and space and mix up human beings, animals, and gods". There were also works "devoted to anti-rational mysticism, with the result that present-day life was distorted and ugliness was eulogized as beauty". See "An Internal Speech by Xiong Fu" ("Xiong Fu neibu jianghua", *JN,* 209:31, June 1987; extracts trans. in Geremie Barmé and John Minford, eds., *Seeds of Fire*, 1988, pp. 403-6). See also "gei feilixing zai yishu chuangzuozhong yige yingyoude diwei" (give the irrational due place in artistic creation).

反冒进
fan maojin
(opposing rash advance)

See "xiaojiao nuren" (women with bound feet).

反美反蒋统一战线
fan Mei fan Chiang tongyi zhanxian
(anti-U.S. and anti-Chiang Kai-shek united front)

See "tongzhan" (united front).

反迫害意识
fan pohai yishi
(anti-persecution mentality)

See "Falun Gong" (Law Wheel Cultivation).

反题材决定论
fan "ticai jueding" lun
(theory of opposition to "subject-matter as the decisive factor")

As agreed by post-Mao critics, no one was explicitely responsible for the theory of opposition to "subject-matter as the decisive factor", one of the "eight sinister theories" singled out for attack in the 1966 Party document the "Summary". To break out from the many restrictions on subject-matter in "socialist literature and art", however, was a long-cherished wish of many writers and critics. In March 1961, for instance, the *Literary Gazette* published Zhang Guangnian's treatise "Problems of Subject-Matter" ("Ticai wenti"). A few months later, a discussion was carried in the sixth and seventh issues, with Xia Yan, Tian Han, Lao She, and others taking part. As early as May 1966 Zhang's article had been attacked as an "anti-Party and anti-socialist poisonous weed".

But the argument in favor of greater variety in subject-matter was so strong that the 1978 critics could easily rehabilitate it. Zhou Ke, a pseudonym used by the editorial board of the *Literary Review* at the time, simply stated that no such theory existed and that it only had been invented by the Gang of Four (Zhou Ke, "Bo luan fan zheng, kaizhan chuangzaoxingde wenxue yanjiu pinglun gongzuo"—"Bring Order out of Chaos and Carry Out Creative Literary Studies and Criticism", *WXPL,* 3:3-9, 1978). Luo Xiaozhou, a critic, further asserted that the Gang fabricated the theory of "opposition to 'subject-matter as the decisive factor'" because they advocated the theory of "subject-matter as the decisive factor", which was "one of the theoretical foundations for their conspiratorial literature and art" (Luo Xiaozhou, "'Ticai jueding' lun yu yinmou wenyi"—"The Theory of 'Subject-Matter as the Decisive Factor' and the 'Conspiratorial Literature and Art'", *RMWX,* 2:18-22, 1978). The two so-called theories of "opposition to 'the smell of gunpowder'" and of "discarding the classics and rebelling against orthodoxy" were also claimed to be mere exaggerations based on some individuals' fragmentary remarks. See also "jiyao" ("Summary").

反修防修
fan xiu fang xiu
(combating and preventing revisionism)

See "Mao Zedong lixiangzhuyi waihua lun" (theory of the exteriorization of Mao's idealism), "xiuzhengzhuyi" (revisionism), and "wen'ge" (Cultural Revolution).

反右派斗争
fan youpai douzheng
(struggle against Rightists)

See "fan youpai yundong" (anti-Rightist campaign).

反右派斗争扩大化
fan youpai douzheng kuodahua
(undue broadening of the scope of the anti-Rightist struggle)

See "fan youpai yundong" (anti-Rightist campaign).

反右派运动
fan youpai yundong
(anti-Rightist campaign)

In 1957, Mao and his colleagues launched a campaign to beat off the so-called "reckless attack by bourgeois Rightists". It is called the "campaign against bourgeois Rightists", or "anti-Rightist campaign" ("fan youpai yundong", "fanyou yundong", or "fanyou") for short. The CCP authorities would also call it the "struggle against bourgeois Rightists" (fandui zichanjieji youpai fenzide douzheng), or "anti-Rightist struggle" ("fan youpai douzheng", "fanyou douzheng", or "fanyou") for short.

At first, in the spring of 1956, Mao Zedong advanced the Double Hundred principle for China's academic, literary, and art circles and the policy of "long-term co-existence and mutual supervision" (changqi gongcun, huxiang jiandu) as the basic guideline for the relationship between the CCP and China's eight "democratic parties" (minzhu dangpai). After the Hungarian Incident (which took place on 23 October 1956), Mao put forth the concept of "contradictions among the people". Then, on 27 April, the PCC promulgated the "Instructions Regarding the Rectification Movement" ("Guanyu zhengfeng yundongde zhishi"). A Party-wide rectification movement was launched against "bureaucratism", "sectarianism", and "subjectivism"—what was called the "three evils" (sanhai). Mao personally asked nonparty personages and members of the democratic parties to criticize CCP cadres and organizations at various levels. Many people, especially intellectuals and university students, were aroused and actively threw themselves into the movement, becoming involved in the "sida" practice, i.e., to "speak out freely, air one's views fully, write big-character posters, and hold great debates", so as to expose and attack the bureaucrats in Party and government departments.

Before long, however, the situation changed abruptly, and tragically. On 15 May 1957, seeing that his Communist regime might be damaged by the unexpected fierce attacks, Mao wrote a secret document for high-ranking officials, entitled "Things Are Beginning to Change" ("Shiqing zhengzai qi bianhua", *MZXJ*, 5, pp. 423-29). He alleged that "Rightists" were attempting to exterminate the Communist Party. On 8 June, the *People's Daily* published an editorial (written by Mao), entitled "What Is This For? ("Zhe shi wei shenme?"), accusing "certain people" of making use of the Party's rectification movement to unfold an acute class struggle. On the same day, the PCC issued the "Instructions on Organizing Forces in Preparation for Counterattacking Rightists", in which Mao personally called for beating off the "attack by bourgeois Rightists" ("Guanyu zuzhi liliang zhunbei fanji youpai jingongde zhishi", *MZXJ*, 5, pp. 431-33). Mao declared that bourgeois Rightists were "bourgeois reactionaries who oppose the Communist Party, oppose the people, and oppose socialism" *(MZXJ*, 5, p. 438). The rectification movement then became an anti-Rightist campaign.

During the campaign, which lasted almost one year, 552,877 "bourgeois Rightists" were named. (This is a post-Mao official figure, which some scholars still consider to be on the low side, or at least incomplete. According to the July 1995 issue of *Reading* magazine, the total number of "Rightists" may be as high as 1.02 million.) Overnight, they became "contemptible wretches" (jianmin), forced to face lives of misery. Among those most "notorious" were some leaders of the democratic parties. For instance, Zhang Bojun and Luo Longji, two vice-chairmen of the Chinese Democracy Alliance (Zhongguo Minzhu Tongmeng), were accused of forming an anti-CCP political alliance. Chu Anping's remark about "the Party being the entire world" (dangtianxia), Luo Longji's "rehabilitation committee" (pingfan weiyuanhui), and Zhang Bojun's "political design academy" (zhengzhi shejiyuan), were condemned as the "three major reactionary theories" of China's Rightists. Mao later argued that his was an "overt trick" (yangmou) and not a "conspiracy" (yinmou), with which to discover "Rightists" who, making use of the rectification movement, engaged in "anti-Party, anti-people, and anti-socialism" activities. The methods included "luring the snake out of the pit—so as to make the target fully exposed" (yin she chu dong), "drawing fire against oneself—making self-criticism to encourage criticism from others" (yin huo shao shen), "following the vine to get the melon—tracking down the suspect by following clues" (shun teng mo gua), and "shooting the outstanding bird—attacking the most active first" (qiang da chutouniao).

By 1980 almost all of the "Rightists" had been rehabilitated (in the end, verdicts on ninety-six cases were considered "correct" and they were not rehabilitated). However, after twenty-two years, there were limits to their sense of satisfaction. There were simply too many victims; the period of their suffering had been too long; and the whole event seemed all the more like an absurd nightmare. Furthermore, the 1957 anti-Rightist campaign is still officially considered "correct"; the only problem is that its scope was "unduly broadened". This was chiefly decided by Deng Xiaoping, who played an instrumental role in the campaign, as general secretary of the CCP and director of the Office in Charge of the Anti-Rightist Struggle. Deng repeatedly emphasized the correctness of his decision (see, for instance, relevant articles in *Selected Works of Deng Xiaoping, 1975-1982,* Beijing, FLP, 1984). After so many years, Deng still remembered "how aggressive some Rightists were" ("Concerning Problems on the Ideological Front, July 17, 1981", in *SWD*, p. 368). But the campaign experienced by most Chinese writers and intellectuals was certainly not what Deng was referring to. Some Rightists might have seemed "aggressive" to him. But who were these people? And how many were there in all? And how were they aggressive? If any of them had committed crimes, they should have been punished by law, and not otherwise. When more than 99.9 percent of the convicted Rightists were proved innocent, how can one still insist that the campaign was correct?

Naturally, many Chinese disagree with Deng's conclusion. This is most clearly revealed in a great number of literary works. An early example is *A Legend of the Tianyun Mountains*. An important work awarded a national prize in 1981, it describes how the "Rightists" were wronged. (In this regard, ironically, those attacking the novella were quite correct in pointing out its political potentials.) In 1986, many writers and intellectuals wished to push even further, taking advantage of the then relatively relaxed political atmosphere. For instance, in an effort to break down the prohibited zone, Liu Binyan intended to compile a book providing some historical truth about the 1957 tragedy. He joined Fang Lizhi, a leading astrophysicist, and Xu Liangying, a veteran scholar, in trying to sponsor what they called an "Academic Forum on the History of the Anti-Rightist Campaign". But this, in part, led to the 1987 campaign against "bourgeois liberalization". In his 30 December 1986 talk, Deng once again reaffirmed his judgment on the 1957 tragedy.

Many Chinese intellectuals of the older generation worry that the young people do not fully understand the historical truth. In his speech on 13 September 1986 to Heilongjiang University students, Liu Binyan spoke of his worry:

"Ours is a forgetful nation, and this is not something we should feel proud of. I would like to ask you students present here.... How much do you know about the 1957 anti-Rightist campaign? Do you know how many Rightists were convicted in China? By what means were they convicted? What were the consequences of the campaign? What is its relationship with the Cultural Revolution? No one has told you. And this is a prohibited zone" ("Liu Binyan's Speech at Heilongjiang University", in *FLW,* pp. 83-84).

Many believe that the 1957 anti-Rightist campaign will be completely negated someday in the future. Not only will Mao's "overt trick" be openly condemned, but the root of this disaster will be attributed to the social system, where the entire country is subject to the CCP's absolute rule and the entire Party is subject to the rule of one leader at the very top. See also "you" (Right), "Deng Xiaoping lilun" (Deng Xiaoping Theory), "zhishifenzi wenti" (issue of intellectuals), and "wuchanjieji zhuanzheng" (dictatorship of the proletariat).

反右倾
fan youqing
(anti-Right-deviation)

See "you" (Right) and "fan youqing yundong" (anti-Right-deviation campaign).

反右倾运动
fan youqing yundong
(anti-Right-deviation campaign)

The "anti-Right deviation", or "anti-Right", was a substantial part of Mao's political life. The anti-Right-deviation campaign usually refers to the 1959-60 campaign following the 1959 "Peng Dehuai Incident".

At the 8th Plenum of the 8th PCC held in Lushan, a summer resort, in August 1959, a resolution was passed on the alleged "anti-Party clique" headed by Peng Dehuai (1898-1974), who was disgraced and lost his job as defense minister at the Plenum. Thereafter, an "anti-Right-deviation" campaign was carried out throughout the country. During the campaign, a large number of people, many of them Party cadres at various levels, were attacked and labeled as "Right opportunists".

At the expanded work conference (the "7000-person meeting") convened by the CCP's Central Committee in Beijing from 11 January to 7 February 1962, at a time when the Party faced serious economic setbacks, it was promised that those who had been wrongly treated in the 1959-60 "anti-Right-deviation" campaign would be rehabilitated. However, Peng Dehuai, the convicted number one Right opportunist, was excluded. His case was not redressed until after the 1978 3rd Plenum of the 11th PCC—four years after his death (Peng was persecuted to death during the GPCR). See also "dayuejin" (Great Leap Forward) and "Peng Dehuai shijian" (Peng Dehuai Incident).

反动人道主义
fandong rendaozhuyi
(reactionary humanism)

A label often used in the political-literary campaigns during the Mao period. According to the Leftist critics, it was absolutely impossible that genuine love or sympathy could occur between members of the exploiting classes on the one hand and the laboring people on the other. In a literary work, for instance, if any love or sympathy of this kind was described, it would be attacked as "reactionary humanism attempting to lull and deceive people so that they will not rise in rebellion". The more realistic and believable the description was, the more reactionary it would be, because it would be more harmful to the people. This charge applied particularly to theatrical works about honest and upright officials in feudal times (qingguan xi). See "renxing lun" (theory of human nature).

反对本本主义
fandui benbenzhuyi
(opposing book worship)

See "xiuzhengzhuyi" (revisionism).

反对党八股
fandui dang bagu
(opposing stereotyped Party writing)

See "xiuzhengzhuyi" (revisionism).

反对官僚主义是社会主义文学的重要使命
fandui guanliaozhuyi shi shehuizhuyi wenxuede zhongyao shiming
(opposing bureaucracy is an important mission of socialist literature)

In 1979, somewhat out of tune with the call issued at the 3rd Plenum of the 11th PCC that one should "look forward", there seemed to be "competition" among some writers as to who could recount the most shocking crimes and ugliness in contemporary China and provoke the most critical incisiveness and political-social furor. Symbolically, two favorite topics were: juvenile delinquency and the special privileges enjoyed by leading cadres and their bureaucratism. Produced mostly by obscure young authors, these works, attracting mass appeal, were very often written in satirical and/or tragic tones. People seemed to agree with this thesis: "Opposing bureaucracy is an important mission of socialist literature." (See Peng Yunqian and Yang Zhijie, "Fandui guanliaozhuyi shi shehuizhuyi wenxuede zhongyao shiming"—"Opposing Bureaucracy Is an Important Mission of Socialist Literature", *SHWX*, 9, 1979, reprinted in *XHYB, WZB*, 1, 1980.) See also "wenyi wei zhengzhi fuwu" (literature and art serve politics) and "ganyu shenghuo" (be involved in live).

反对西方文化霸权
fandui xifang wenhua baquan
(resisting the cultural hegemony of the West)

See "cuowei" (malposition) and "xin baoshouzhuyi" (neo-conservatism).

反对资产阶级右派分子的斗争
fandui zichanjieji youpai fenzide douzheng
(struggle against bourgeois Rightists)

See "fan youpai yundong" (anti-Rightist campaign).

反对资产阶级自由化
fandui zichanjieji ziyouhua
(opposing bourgeois liberalization)

Politically, "opposing bourgeois liberalization" was first issued at the Central Work Conference held from 16 to 25 December 1980. In his speech delivered on the last day of the conference, Deng Xiaoping called for "criticizing and opposing the tendency to worship capitalism and to advocate bourgeois liberalization" (*SWD*, p. 350). Deng's speech, entitled "Implement the Policy of Readjustment, Ensure Stability and Unity", was drafted by Hu Qiaomu and Deng Liqun, two conservative Party ideologues, who enjoyed the support of the Party elder Chen Yun.

According to China critics, this conference witnessed a great setback in China's political reform. See also "ziyouhua" (liberalization) and "fandui zichanjieji ziyouhua yundong" (anti-bourgeois liberalization campaign).

反对资产阶级自由化运动
fandui zichanjieji ziyouhua yundong
(anti-bourgeois liberalization campaign)

This mainly refers to the 1987 anti-bourgeois liberalization campaign, though both before and after there were several similar campaigns.

On 28 September 1986, Deng Xiaoping told the participants of the 6th Plenum of the 12th PCC that the idea of "opposing bourgeois liberalization" must be written into the Plenum's "Resolution Concerning the Guiding Principle in Building Socialist Spiritual Civilization". He said: "Liberalization is only of a bourgeois nature. There is no proletarian, socialist liberalization." As it turned out, contrary to the expectations of the people, the Plenum failed to achieve anything with respect to reform of the political structure. In December 1986, disappointed with the situation, demonstrations by university students, on a scale unprecedented since the founding of the PRC, erupted in a number of cities throughout the country. With this as an excuse, the top level of the Party made the decision to oppose what was called "bourgeois liberalization". The following is a chronicle of the major events in the first few weeks of the campaign.

On 27 December 1986, by deliberate arrangement, several top Party leaders, Wang Zhen (b. 1908), Bo Yibo, (b. 1908), Song Renqiong, Hu Qiaomu, and Deng Liqun, together received Yuan Runcheng, a story-telling performer. Taking advantage of the opportunity, they attacked what they called "national nihilism" and "bourgeois liberalization" (*RMRB,* 28 Dec. 1986).

On 30 December 1986, Deng Xiaoping gave a talk to Hu Yaobang, Zhao Ziyang, Wan Li, Hu Qili, Li Peng, and He Dongchang, which was promulgated in early January 1987 as the PCC Document No. 1 (1987). The main points were as follows:

1. The sedition of the students is of a serious nature, a result of the ambiguous, infirm attitude adopted by Hu Yaobang and other Party leaders in the last few years towards opposition to "bourgeois liberalization".

2. No bourgeois democracy, such as the tripartite division of the legislature, the executive, and the judiciary (san quan fen li), should be allowed.

3. The open-door policy, which is merely a complement of socialist construction, should not deviate from the socialist road.

4. The means of the dictatorship should not only be referred to but should be exercised when necessary. It is essential.

5. Party members who are against socialism and the Party must be disciplined. Fang Lizhi, Wang Ruowang, and Liu Binyan should be resolutely expelled from the Party.

6. Opposition to "bourgeois liberalization" must be carried out, at least for the next twenty years. (See Deng Xiaoping, "Qizhi xianmingde fandui zichanjieji ziyouhua"—"Take a Clear-cut Stand against Bourgeois Liberalization" in his *Jianshe you Zhongguo tesede shehuizhuyi—Building Socialism with Chinese Characteristics,* enlarged edition, 1987; trans. in *Fundamental Issues in Present-day China,* Beijing, FLP, 1987, pp. 161-6.)

On 2 January 1987, Hu Yaobang tendered his resignation to Deng.

On 4 January, Deng invited Peng Zhen, Wang Zhen, Zhao Ziyang, Bo Yibo, and Yang Shangkun to his place, where they decided to dismiss Hu Yaobang from office.

On 6 January, the *People's Daily* carried an editorial ("Qizhi xianmingde fandui zichanjieji ziyouhua"—"Take a Clear-cut Stand against Bourgeois Liberalization") calling for opposition to bourgeois liberalization "with a clear-cut stand", which was based on Deng's 30 December 1986 talk.

On 14 January, Wang Ruowang was expelled from the CCP. His "mistakes" included "preaching bourgeois liberalization", "opposing the four cardinal principles", and "refusing to mend his ways despite repeated admonition" (*RMRB*, 15 Jan. 1987).

On 16 January, Hu Yaobang lost his position as general secretary at an enlarged meeting of the Politburo of the CCP (*RMRB*, 17 Jan. 1987). Bo Yibo delivered a speech at the meeting in regard to the alleged mistakes of Hu Yaobang (which was printed as "PCC Document No. 3 (1987)"; trans. in *Inside China Mainland*, 5:1-3, May 1987).

On 17 January, Fang Lizhi was expelled from the Party, accused of "committing five serious mistakes", including advocating "wholesale Westernization" (quanpan xihua) and the "outdatedness of Marxism" (*RMRB*, 20 Jan. 1987).

On 23 January, Liu Binyan was expelled from the Party. Two days later, the *People's Daily* carried a front page commentary attacking Liu, who was said to have "violated the Party Constitution and the Party disciplines and resolutions". Liu's problems included "negating the four cardinal principles", "preaching bourgeois liberalization", and "vilifying and opposing Party leadership" (*RMRB*, 25 Jan. 1987).

On 28 January, the PCC issued a document entitled "Notice Regarding Issues of the Current Opposition to Bourgeois Liberalization" ("Guanyu dangqian fandui zichanjieji ziyouhua ruogan wentide tongzhi").

On 31 January, *Red Flag* fiercely attacked Fang Lizhi, Liu Binyan, and Wang Ruowang, describing them as "elements taking the capitalist road" (*HQ*, 3:2, 1987).

On 4 February, a spokesman for the Ministry of Foreign Affairs confirmed that Zhu Houze's directorship of the PCC Propaganda Department had been taken over by Wang Renzhi, former deputy editor-in-chief of *Red Flag*.

On 10 February, the *Shenzhen Youth Herald* was ordered to stop publication, followed by a number of other newspapers and journals which were in trouble in varying degrees.

On 18 February, Liu Xinwu, the famous Beijing fiction writer, was ordered temporarily relieved of his chief editorship of *People's Literature* for "self-examination" (*RMRB*, 21 Feb. 1987).

The campaign started with such a momentum that many China-watchers were reminded of the GPCR or of the 1957 anti-Rightist purge. Significantly, however, times had changed. The campaign, in the main, had been checked by May 1987 (though in the summer there was the "five gentlemen incident"—see "wu junzi shijian"). One of the reasons for the change was the positive role played by Zhao Ziyang, the successor to Hu Yaobang as CCP acting general secretary, who realized that the reform would be greatly damaged if the campaign were allowed to continue. A more compelling factor, however, was the resistance on the part of Chinese intellectuals. Facing grim political pressure, they did not retreat. Unexpectedly, reform was the keynote at the 13th CCP National Congress held in October 1987, and a number of younger people were promoted to key positions. By the beginning of 1988, Xiong Fu, editor-in-chief of *Red Flag*, Deng Liqun, a PCC member, and He Jingzhi, deputy director of the PCC Propaganda Department, had lost their posts, as well as many other conservatives. As Liu Binyan commented in March 1988, on the eve of his departure for America, the social and political atmosphere in the entire country had become "more liberal"—it was "like a yeast in the air that made things expand" (see "A Cigarette Pack, Not a Matchbox", *Time*, 13:23, 28 Mar. 1988). See also "ziyouhua" (liberalization) and "Deng Xiaoping lilun" (Deng Xiaoping Theory).

反革命
fan'geming
(counter-revolutionary)

The "counter-revolutionary" penal code was formulated in 1951. Accordingly, anyone trying by any way to overthrow CCP power or to shake the socialist system was regarded as a "counter-revolutionary", and the maximun penalty was a death sentence. Since then, almost all crimes were described as "counter-revolutionary", such as "counter-revolutionary rumor-mongering", "counter-revolutionary propaganda and inflammatory delusion", and "counter-revolutionary murder". Counter-revolutionaries were divided into active counter-revolutionaries and historical counter-revolutionaries. The latter referred to those who had carried out counter-revolutionary activities and had committed crimes, or had held certain posts, during the KMT regime.

In 1982 when the Criminal Law was revised, the "counter-revolutionary" penal code was not eliminated, disappointing many people. At the 5th Session of the 8th NPC held in March 1997, the offense was finally deleted from the revised Criminal Law. It was replaced by the crime of "jeopardizing national security". See also "wuchanjieji zhuanzheng" (dictatorship of the proletariat).

反攻大陆
fangong dalu
(launch a counterattack and recover the lost mainland)

See "Taiwan wenti" (Taiwan issue).

反击右倾翻案风
fanji youqing fan'anfeng
(campaign to counter the "Right deviationist trend to reverse correct verdicts")

See "pi Deng, fanji youqing fan'anfeng" (campaign to criticize Deng Xiaoping and counter the Right deviationist trend to reverse correct verdicts).

反面教材
fanmian jiaocai
(teaching material by negative example)

According to Mao, the revolutionary parties and the revolutionary people could temper themselves, reach maturity, and gain assurance of victory only through the process of repeated education by positive and negative examples (zhengmian jiaoyu he fanmian jiaoyu) and through the process of comparison and contrast. Mao listed Marx, Engels, Lenin, and Stalin as "positive teachers" (zhengmian jiaoyuan), whereas "teachers by negative example" (fanmian jiaoyuan) included Chiang Kai-shek, the Japanese imperialists, the U.S. imperialists, and those in the Party who adopted Left or Right opportunist lines. Mao said: "The Chinese revolution would not have won victory had there been only positive teachers and no teachers by negative example. Those who belittle the role of teachers by negative example are not thoroughgoing dialectical materialists" (*RMRB*, 26 Feb. 1965).

Significantly, as many have pointed out, China's intellectuals often became Mao's "teachers by negative example" or "teaching material by negative example"

Like many Chinese rulers in feudal times, Mao harbored a strong distrust of intellectuals. In particular, he could not bear to have his authority challenged by them. He tended to make an example of literary and art circles before launching a political campaign. As early as the Yan'an period, for instance, Mao believed that, for the 1941-42 Rectification Movement to succeed, it was absolutely necessary to bring Wang Shiwei, and several other recalcitrant writers, to heel. People were said to have been educated by these "negative examples".

反面教育
fanmian jiaoyu
(education by negative example)

See "fanmian jiaocai" (teaching material by negative example).

反面教员
fanmian jiaoyuan
(teacher by negative example)

See "fanmian jiaocai" (teaching material by negative example).

反思
fansi
(reflection)

"Fansi" is a frequently used term in contemporary China.

After the nightmare of the ten years of the GPCR, many Chinese, from Party leaders to ordinary people, tried to understand why all this could have happened. This conformed to the fact that by late 1978, as a result of the implementation of the PCC's No. 11, 1978 Document, not only had practically all those disgraced during the GPCR been rehabilitated, but nearly all the Rightists of earlier campaigns had had their labels removed. Clearly, neither the Gang of Four nor Lin Biao and his clique could be charged with causing the sufferings of so many people, since many of them had even been persecuted before the start of the Cultural Revolution in 1966. Sympathy for the persecuted was shared by all. Some considered the more fundamental problems, such as problems in the social system and the Party leadership (understandably, only very preliminarily). This was the so-called "political reflection" (zhengzhixing fansi). At that time, as a result of this reflection, "scar literature" (shanghen wenxue), "reflection literature" (fansi wenxue), and "reform literature" (gaige wenxue) appeared in literary fields. Later, for several years after the latter half of 1984, there was a great mass fervor for "cultural reflection" (wenhuaxing fansi), when a number of cultural issues, such as "tradition and modernization" and "China and the West", were hotly discussed. A theoretical-ideological reform (sixiang lilunde gaige) appeared, which was enthusiastically hailed by many as a major development since the May 4th period. In their opinion, this was another constructive adjustment in the course of the development of the "new culture" in China. It could even be considered a design of vital significance for the modern construction of Chinese culture.

An enthusiasm for reflection in literature overflowed into the realm of literary creation and literary research, in particular, literary criticism and literary theory. A re-examination was carried out of those basic theories, basic concepts, and basic ways of thinking which had dominated Chinese literature over the past several decades. As a result of reflection, Liu Zaiu thus described modern and contemporary

Chinese literary criticism: "From the 1930s up to now, our literary criticism has formed a set mode of thinking, which, in the main, is a mental inertia of linearity (xianshi siwei guanxing) based on the vulgar theory of class struggle and the theory of direct reflection. Political background becomes the major reference by which to observe things. We cannot exclude the system of political reference, and we also fully respect the theory of reflection (fanyinglun), but it is not enough for our thinking to have only these two as its foundation. Since this habitual way of thinking has been formed over a long period of time, to a great extent already becoming a type of collective unconscious (jiti wuyishi), it is very difficult to transcend it" (Liu Zaifu, "Wenxuede fansi he ziwo chaoyue"— "Reflections on Literature and the Transcendence of the Self", *WYB*, 31 Aug. 1985).

As Chen Yong, Liu's chief opponent, pointed out, here Liu Zaifu was actually saying that the history of Chinese literary and art thought from the 1930s up to the present was in the main "a history of mistakes" (Chen Yong, "Problems Concerning Methodology in the Study of Literature and Art", *WXZTX*, p. 146). This judgment meant that the whole history of modern and contemporary Chinese literature had to be re-written. This was of course "not a minor issue", towards which Chen was absolutely intolerant. Obviously, here lies the crux of the matter in the 1986 debate between Chen Yong and Liu Zaifu, and their respective supporters. For some authorities within the establishment, consequences of such reflections were certainly very serious and disastrous. This is why following the June 4th Incident of 1989 the ideological-literary mainstream of the 1980s characterized by these reflections was stopped.

In the 1990s reflections took place from various perspectives, presenting a complicated situation. Typically indicating the difference between China's thinking public in the 1980s and that in the 1990s was the change from the call for modernization (huhuan xiandaihua) to reflection on modernity (fansi xiandaixing). A number of new ideological trends came into being, such as "neo-conservatism" (xin baoshouzhuyi), "liberalism" (ziyouzhuyi), "nationalism" (minzuzhuyi), and the school of "neo-Leftists" (xinzuopai). They were all results of reflections—by different people from different perspectives and on different stands. For instance, neo-Leftists underlined problems generated during the twenty years of Deng's reform; they declared that only the legacy of Mao Zedong can save China. Liberal thinkers, however, advocated further and deepgoing reforms, not only in economic fields but also, and more importantly, in political fields. They opposed nationalism and favored globalization. The complicated situation can also be seen in the "three reflections" (san ge fansi) among China's politico-ideological circles in the last few years of the 1990s—it was claimed that reflections must be seriously carried out on the introduction of Marxism into China during the May 4th Movement of 1919, on the socialist road of the CCP after seizing state power in 1949, and on the reform and open-door program initiated by Deng at the 3rd Plenum of the 11th PCC in 1978. See also "wenhua re" (culture craze), "minzuzhuyi" (nationalism), "xin baoshouzhuyi" (neo-conservatism), "xinzuopai" (neo-Leftists), and "ziyouzhuyi" (liberalizm).

反思文学
fansi wenxue
(reflection literature)

After early 1979, quite a number of outstanding works—later dubbed "reflection literature"—emerged. Not satisfied with reflecting only on the GPCR, writers wanted to gain a wider historical perspective. They began to set their tragedies in the years prior to the GPCR, dealing with the tragic fate of those 1957 Rightists who were loyal sons and daughters of the motherland. This was a popular theme, but it could be controversial, involving such problems as the social system and the Party's leadership. One such case was Lu Yanzhou's novella "A Legend of the Tianyun Mountains" ("Tianyunshan chuanqi", *Qingming* 1, 1979, reprinted in *Zhongpian xiaoshuo xuan—Selected Novelettes*, Kunming, Yunnan Renmin, 1980, pp. 1-96, and *Shanghen—The Wounded*, Taipei, You Shi Wenhua Shiye Gongsi, 1982, pp. 187-279). The first important literary work, published at the beginning of 1979, to re-examine the 1957 anti-Rightist campaign, it admirably eulogizes "Rightist" Luo Qun, while mercilessly castigating Wu Yao, an anti-Rightist "hero" who is described as an extremely selfish and stubborn bureaucrat. Furthermore, not only does it represent the tragic fate of its characters in absurd reality, it also looks into the historical cause for those unjust charges. It investigates why the treatment of a comrade as an enemy could be repeated again and again. This theme was naturally intolerable to some people. When the film adaptation was released in 1981, it sparked a debate. In 1982 as the movement to oppose "bourgeois liberalization" continued, the attack on "A Legend of the Tianyun Mountains" escalated. Charges included "completely distorting the historical truth of the anti-Rightist struggle" and "damaging the image of the Party", being "a reflection of bourgeois liberalist trends in literature and art". The attack was so serious that even such people as Sun Zhifang, an eminent economist who had never before been involved in any literary debate, felt it necessary to stand up and defend the work (see his "Ye ping 'Tianyunshan chuanqi'"—"Also on 'A Legend of the Tianyun Mountains'", *WYB*, 6, 1982).

"Reflection literature", together with "scar literature" and "reform literature", was the product of the so-called "political reflection". But scholars and writers were dissatisfied with this reflection, which only focused on the GPCR, the anti-Rightist campaign, and other political movements during the Communist regime. They thus further widened their perspectives. Starting in the latter half of 1984, there appeared a great mass fervor in what was dubbed "cultural reflection" (wenhuaxing fansi). In the culture craze (wenhua re), a number of cultural issues with important significance were hotly discussed. In literary creation, a new genre, the "root-seeking" fiction, emerged, which contributed to the people's "cultural reflection". Other genres also made similar contributions.

An outstanding piece, for instance, was Wang Meng's 1985 novel, *Movable Parts* (*Huodong Bian Renxing,* Beijing, Renmin Wenxue, Mar. 1987; trans. in Wang Meng, *Selected Works of Wang Meng,* v. 2, Beijing, FLP, 1989, pp. 1-423). In this work, a tragedy about how a man, originally clever and vivacious, gradually loses his soul under absurd circumstances, Wang Meng probes both the traditional and contemporary Chinese cultural-psychological structure, touching on the "collective unconscious layer" (jiti wuyishi cengci) of the Chinese nation. In his long speech expounding on humanism as the mainstream of the literature of the new period, which was delivered at the September 1986 forum sponsored by the Literature Institute of CASS, Liu Zaifu pointed out that the appearance of *Movable Parts* marked a new profundity in the historical consciousness of Chinese writers. This novel could be regarded as a mirror of Chinese historical cultural psychology. It subjects to "a very sober and stern trial" those hard-to-change dark sides in the deep structure of Chinese history and culture, which Liu believed were "the very cultural foundation" of the ten years of the catastrophe. See also "fansi" (reflection) and "wenhua re" (culture craze).

反映典型环境的本质部分
fanying dianxing huanjingde benzhi bufen
(reflect the essential aspect of typical circumstances)

See "shehuizhuyi xianshizhuyi" (socialist realism) and "wenyi wei zhengzhi fuwu" (literature and art serve politics).

反映论是文学研究的哲学基础
fanyinglun shi wenxue yanjiude zhexue jichu (the theory of reflection is the philosophical basis for literary study)

This Marxist view was seriously questioned in the 1986 "subjectivity" debate. The target was the article, "Problems Concerning Methodology in the Study of Literature and Art" ("Wenyixue fangfalun wenti", *HQ*, 8, 1986, reprinted in He Huoren, ed., *WXZTX*, pp. 124-46), by Chen Yong, a former Rightist but then an adviser to the Policy Research Office under the PCC Secretariat.

Chen Yong asserts that "the creation of a typical character (dianxing) has more and more become the central issue of literature" (ibid.). His sociological appreciation of a typical character adheres to the principle that a typical character with aesthetic significance should represent the essence of a certain social force. His philosophical basis for literary study is the theory of reflection, which emphasizes that "a particular literature or art is the reflection of a particular system of politics and economy", a thesis not to be questioned during the Mao period. Furthermore, Chen regards the relationship between literature and art on the one hand and politics and the economy on the other as one between form and content. These arguments precisely confirmed the problem of the Marxist theory Chen and his like held, a theory that was introduced into China from the Soviet Union in the 1930s and became systematized in the 1950s and 1960s by mixing with some traditional Chinese literary thoughts (such as "wen yi zai dao"—literature as a vehicle for ideology). As Hong Yongping, a critic, pointed out, Chen Yong's ideas served as striking proof that the slogan "literature and art must serve politics" was still living in quite a number of people's hearts (Hong Yongping, "Makesizhuyi yu wenyi guilü wenti"—"Marxism and the Law of Literature and Art", *WXPL*, 4:4-11, July 1986).

The fundamental drawback of Chen Yong's literary view (and also of the literary theory he defends), according to the critic Yang Chunshi, is that it cuts off the flesh-and-blood tie between literature and the subject (zhuti), regarding literature as a passive reflection of reality. Even when Chen Yong acknowledges the existence of the subject of literature, the "subject" is merely a means of reflection without the essential force of man, and it is not the motivating force, essence, and purpose of literary creation. Chen's article, indeed, embodies in a concentrated form the serious defect of orthodox literary theory. Starting from the theory of passive reflection, it denies the subjectivity of literature. Since it denies the subjectivity of literature, it falls into the category of mechanical determinism, which naturally denies the transcendence of the subject. Accordingly, it holds that literature has no specific intrinsic law and that the essential law of literature is the decisive effect of politics and the economy upon literature. It further deduces the theory of linear causality (xianxing yinguo lun) which holds that literature, not having its own initiative, can simply be explained by economic relationships. Hence its absurd conclusion: Literature or art is not an independent entity; it is "a form of politics, with politics as its content" (Yang Chunshi, "Lun wenyide chongfen zhutixing he chaoyuexing"—"Sufficiency in Subjectivity and Transcendence for Literature and Art", *WXPL*, 4:19, July 1986). See also "shehuizhuyi xianshizhuyi" (socialist realism) and "wenyi wei zhengzhi fuwu" (literature and art serve politics).

反右
fanyou
(anti-Rightist campaign)

See "fan youpai yundong" (anti-Rightist campaign).

反右斗争
fanyou douzheng
(anti-Rightist struggle)

See "fan youpai yundong" (anti-Rightist campaign).

反右斗争扩大化
fanyou douzheng kuodahua
(undue broadening of the scope of the anti-Rightist struggle)

See "fan youpai yundong" (anti-Rightist campaign).

反右运动
fanyou yundong
(anti-Rightist campaign)

See "fan youpai yundong" (anti-Rightist campaign).

方法论年
fangfalun nian
(year of methodology)

It has been noted that 1985 was a "year of methodology" in mainland China, a year in which many new methods, including those in Western social and natural sciences, such as systems theory, information theory, and cybernetics (together the three theories are called "sanlun"—"xitonglun", "xinxilun", and "kongzhilun"), were introduced into China's literary and art circles and applied to the study of literature and art. (See Liu Zaifu, "Wenxue yanjiu siwei kongjiande tuozhan"—"Expanding the Scope of Thinking in Literary Research", *DS*, 2 & 3, 1985, reprinted in *WXZTX*, pp. 3-38.) Within just a few years, the whole process of one hundred years of development of Western literary theory and criticism appeared in China's literary and art circles. This occurred so rapidly that problems were inevitable because of insufficient preparations in theoretical knowledge or in cultural understanding. The impact, nevertheless, was far reaching. The new system of literary theory and criticism was very different from that of Mao which had not been questioned for more than half a century.

防扩散
fang kuosan
(prevent from spreading)

To "prevent from spreading" means preventing whatever documents harmful (or likely to be harmful) to Party leaders from spreading to the public. It has long been one of the measures, when necessary, to protect Party leaders from damage to their prestige. For instance, three days after the 1971 "September 13th Incident", Zhou

Enlai (1898-1976), PRC premier and CCP vice chairman, and Kang Sheng, CCP vice chairman, penned a letter to Mao, suggesting that all letters and conversation records between Mao and Lin Biao since 1965 be immediately sealed for safekeeping and that a group in charge of the matter be established, consisting of Kang Sheng (group leader), Jiang Qing, Wang Dongxing, Ji Dengkui, and Chen Xilian. Mao lost no time to fully agree to the suggested measures. Similarly, on 15 October 1976 Wang Dongxing wrote a report to Hua Guofeng about how to dispose of the letters and conversation records between Mao and the Gang of Four. Hua gave instructions to seal them up immediately so as to "protect the brilliant image of Chairman Mao". This was fully agreed to by Ye Jianying, Li Xiannian, Chen Xilian, Ji Dengkui, and Wu De. Because of such measures, a great quantity of state and Party documents have long been kept from the public as top secrets, thus causing difficulty in the study of historical truth.

放
fang
(loosening up)

As Mao himself explained, "loosening up" meant to let people express their opinions freely, so that they dare to speak, dare to criticize, and dare to debate; it meant not to be afraid of wrong views and anything poisonous; it meant to encourage arguments and criticism among people holding differing views, allowing freedom for both criticism and counter-criticism; it meant not to suppress even wrong views but to convince people by reasoning with them. In contrast, the policy of "tightening up" (shou) meant to forbid people from airing different opinions and from expressing wrong ideas, and to "finish them off with a single blow" (yigunzi dasi) if they do so. This was a way to aggravate rather than to resolve contradictions, as Mao had correctly said. At that time Mao had just raised his Double Hundred policy (shuangbai fangzhen)—"Let a hundred flowers bloom and a hundred schools of thought contend"—aimed at guiding and promoting science, culture, literature, and art. He was confident of his rule, so he asked for "loosening up". Mao declared: "We are prepared to use the 'loosening up' policy to unite with the several million intellectuals and change their present outlook" (*MZXJ,* 5, p. 415).

This was a typical expression of Mao's "rule by individuals" (renzhi) concept. In fact, he rejected the Double Hundred policy within less than two years. This led to the anti-Rightist campaign, large-scale persecution of intellectuals. Because of imperfections in the legal system and because leaders' words carried more weight than the law, the political situation often oscillated between "loosening up" and "tightening up". Cycles of relaxation and repression appeared to be built-in mechanisms of the Communist regime.

放收整三部曲
fang shou zheng sanbuqu
(trilogy of loosening up, tightening up, and punishing)

See "fang" (loosening up), "pingfan weiyuanhui" (rehabilitation committee), and "fan youpai yundong" (anti-Rightist campaign).

放卫星
fang weixing

(launch satellites)

See "dayuejin" (Great Leap Forward).

放下包袱
fangxia baofu
(get rid of baggage)

See "sixiang baofu" (mental burdens) and "sixiang gaizao" (ideological remolding).

非非主义
feifeizhuyi
(Not-Not-ism)

A poetic school emerging in mainland China in the mid-1980s, it denies the rational and seeks a turning back to a pre-cultural stage. According to this theory, genuine beauty can be obtained only by expressing indefinite self-intuition with indefinite language. (See Zhou Lunyou and Lan Ma, "Feifeizhuyi xuanyan, 1986 nian 5 yue 4 ri, Chengdu, Sichuan"—"The Not-Not-ism Manifesto, 4 May 1986, Chengdu, Sichuan", *Shenzhen qingnian bao*, 21 Oct. 1986; extracts trans. in Geremie Barmé and John Minford, eds., *Seeds of Fire,* 1988, p. 405.) In the 1987 campaign against "bourgeois liberalization", this school was attacked as "a monster growing in socialist China, suckling on the milk of various non-rationalisms and mysticisms of the West" ("An Internal Speech by Xiong Fu", *JN*, 209:31, June 1987). See also "xinshiqi wenxue" (literature of the new period) and "xinshiqi wenxuede duoyuan fazhan" (pluralistic development of the literature of the new period).

非理性
feilixing
(irrational)

See "menglongshi lilunde san ci jueqi" ("three rises" in the theory of misty poetry) and "gei feilixing zai yishu chuangzuozhong yige yingyoude diwei" (give the irrational due place in artistic creation).

非理性民族主义
feilixing minzuzhuyi
(irrational nationalism)

See "minzuzhuyi" (nationalism).

焚书坑儒
fen shu keng ru
(burning books and burying scholars alive)

The first large-scale suppression of intellectuals in Chinese history was the "burning books and burying scholars alive" events during the reign of Ying Zheng, the first emperor of the Qin dynasty. The burning of books took place in 213 B.C., and in the next year some 460 scholars were buried alive. When Mao Zedong quoted this historical event in his 8 May 1958 speech at the 2nd Plenum of the 8th PCC, he said that what he and his Party had done was almost the same, but on a hundredfold larger scale, and it was absolutely necessary for the consolidation of the new political power. In the 1973-74 campaign to criticize Confucius (551 BC-479 BC) and Lin Biao, the "burning books and burying scholars alive" events were a positive model, in the "struggle against counter-restoration, a form of dictatorship over the enemy, as well as a method of consolidating the nation's unity" *(HQ,* 10, 1973, p. 37).

According to some sources, during the Mao period, about 30 million people were killed. Today, a question raised by many Chinese is: Is it enough to criticize Mao only as being "Leftist" for his brutal ways of ruling the country, if compared with Ying Zheng who has been condemned by the Chinese people for two thousand years? See also "pi Lin pi Kong yundong" (campaign to criticize Lin Biao and Confucius), "ru fa douzheng" (struggle between the Confucian and Legalist schools), and "wuchanjieji zhuanzheng" (dictatorship of the proletariat).

风
feng
(wind)

See "guafeng" (to stir up a "wind").

风派
fengpai
(tune-changers)

After the downfall of the Gang of Four on 6 October 1976, the new CCP authorities began a ferreting-out of followers of the Lin Biao and the Jiang Qing cliques at various levels of the Party-state departments and in the mass organizations throughout the country. They were called tune-changers, shakers, movers, and members of a cover-up faction. Tune-changers referred to those who were shifty and fickle, and quick to follow trends. Shakers tried to create disorder, causing disturbances wherever they went and seizing power amidst the chaos. Movers were well aware that they had committed a great amount of atrocities with Lin Biao and the Gang of Four, but they acted as if they had been right all along. If an investigation into their responsibility was launched, they would try to slip away. The cover-up faction always pretended to be innocent and tried to cover up the truth of their crimes. They defended themselves by attacking and intimidating others, with an air of self-assumed authority.

封，资，修
feng, zi, xiu
(feudalism, bourgeois ideology, and revisionism)

See "san tuoli" (three divorced), "dangde jiaoyu fangzhen" (the Party's educational policy), and "xiuzhengzhuyi" (revisionism).

封闭就要落後，落後就要挨打
fengbi jiuyao luohou; luohou jiuyao aida
(a closed door leads to backwardness, and backwardness proves vulnerable to attack)

See "xiandaide shijie shi kaifangde shijie" (today's world is an open world) and "minzuzhuyi" (nationalism).

封建法西斯专政
fengjian faxisi zhuanzheng
(feudal-fascist dictatorship)

See "wuchanjieji zhuanzheng" (dictatorship of the proletariat).

浮夸风
fukua feng
(tendency for boasting and exaggeration)

See "dayuejin" (Great Leap Forward).

腐败速度超过国民生产总值增长率
fubai sudu chaoguo guomin
shengchan zongzhi zengzhanglu
(the speed of corruption has
surpassed the growth of the GNP)

See "fan fubai" (anti-corruption).

腐败有理
fubai youli
(corruption is reasonable)

See "fan fubai" (anti-corruption).

腐败有利
fubai youli
(corruption is favorable)

See "fan fubai" (anti-corruption).

复辟资本主义的温床
fubi zibenzhuyide wenchuang
(hotbed to restore capitalism)

See "qiangganzi he biganzi" (the gun and the pen) and "wenyi wei zhengzhi fuwu" (literature and art serve politics).

复杂的经历、思想、感情
和生活需要复杂的艺术形式
fuzade jingli, sixiang, ganqing he
shenghuo xuyao fuzade yishu xingshi
(complex experiences, thoughts, feelings,
and life require a complex artistic form)

See "yishiliude Zhongguo dailiren" (Chinese agent of the stream-of-consciousness) and "xinshiqi wenxue" (literature of the new period).

妇女能顶半边天
funü neng ding banbiantian
(women hold up half the sky)

See "banbiantian" (other half of the sky).

改革开放的十一个必须
gaige kaifangde shiyi ge bixu
(eleven musts in the reform and open-door program)

At a grand gathering held in Beijing on 18 December 1998 to mark the 20th anniversary of the 3rd Plenum of the 11th PCC, which kick started Deng's reform and open-door program, Jiang Zemin used eleven "musts" to expound the "historical experience" of this two-decade-long and still ongoing program:

1. The Party's Marxist ideological line must be upheld;
2. The Party's basic line in the primary stage of socialism must be implemented in a comprehensive, correct, and active way;
3. Top priority must be given to combining all forces to develop the social productive force;
4. Unswerving efforts must be made to push forward the reform and opening-up drive;
5. Economic system and structure that can meet the demand of the development of the productive force must be established and brought to perfection;
6. Continuous efforts must be made to build socialist democratic politics with Chinese characteristics;
7. While seeking material progress, painstaking efforts must be made to achieve ethical and cultural progress at the same time.
8. The social and political situation of stability and unity must be safeguarded and maintained;
9. An international environment of long-lasting peace must be earned for China's reform, opening-up, and socialist modernization drive;
10. Safeguarding and promoting the interests of the broad masses of the people must be regarded as the ultimate goal of reform and economic construction; and
11. Party leadership must be adhered to, strengthened, and further improved to provide a basic guarantee for the victory of China's socialist cause.

Jiang Zemin said that the most important historical experience is to combine the fundamental theories of Marxism with China's real situation, take a distinct path of development, and build socialism with Chinese characteristics. He stressed the important significance of Deng Xiaoping Theory, honoring the Theory as "Marxism in modern China", "inheritance and development of Mao Zedong Thought", and a "new stage of development for Marxism in China". See also "Deng Xiaoping lilun" (Deng Xiaoping Theory), "xin shehuizhuyi guan" (new socialist view), "zhengzhi gaige" (political reform), and "jingji gaige" (economic reform).

改革疲劳症
gaige pilaozheng
(reform fatigue symptoms)

See "xin quanweizhuyi lunzheng" (neo-authoritarianism debate).

改革是中国的第二次革命
gaige shi Zhongguode di'er ci geming

(reform is China's second revolution)

See "di'er ci geming" (second revolution).

改革文学
gaige wenxue
(reform literature)

After the 1978 3rd Plenum of the 11th PCC, which confirmed that economic construction was the focus of all Party work, the reform and open door became an irresistible trend in mainland China. This was reflected in a new genre: "reform literature". The first of its kind was Jiang Zilong's 1979 prize-winning short story, "Manager Qiao Assumes Office" ("Qiao changzhang shangren ji", *RMWX,* 7, 1979, reprinted in *XWY, Short Stories 1,* pp. 394-419; trans in *CL,* 2:25-62, 1980, and in Lee Yee, ed., *The New Realism,* pp. 56-85). Other important works appearing at the early stage include Shui Yunxian's 1981-82 prize-winning novelette, "Internal Strife Afoot" ("Huoqixiaoqiang", *Shouhuo,* 1, 1981), Zhang Jie's 1985 Mao Dun Literary Prize winning novel, *Heavy Wings (Chenzhongde chibang, SY,* 4 & 5, July & Sept. 1981, reprinted in book form in Beijing, Renmin Wenxue, 1st ed., 1981, 2nd ed., 1984; trans. with a preface by Gladys Yang, an afterword by Delia Davin, and published in London, Virago Press, 1987; also trans. by Howard Goldblatt and published in New York, Grove Weidenfeld, 1989), Deng Gang's 1983 prize-winning short story, "The Throe" ("Zhentong", *Yalujiang,* 4, 1983) and Lu Wenfu's 1983 prize-winning short story, "The Enclosing Wall" ("Weiqiang", *RMWX,* 2, 1983). "Reform literature", judged from its theme, can be considered to serve current politics in the "new period". See also "xinshiqi wenxue" (literature of the new period) and "wenyi wei zhengzhi fuwu" (literature and art serve politics).

改革的窗口
gaigede chuangkou
(window for reform)

See "jingji tequ" (special economic zone) and "tequ bu te" (special economic zones should enjoy no more preferential treatment).

改正右派
gaizheng youpai
(corrected Rightist)

See "tuomao youpai" (uncapped Rightist).

赶任务
gan renwu
(rush through the job)

As early as 1950, there was a discussion among literary and art circles about the issue of "rushing through the job", which was caused by the fact that writers and artists were often asked to dash off works in the service of Party policies during various mass movements. Naturally, it was questionable whether this conformed with the laws of art and whether great works could be produced in this way. The discussion, unfortunately, ended disappointingly. Mao Dun, despite his rich creative experience, could not say "no" to the demand. Instead, he had to say that to rush through one's job could bring a sort of "pleasant sensation" (kuaigan) (*RMWX,* v. 1, 5, 1951). Shao Quanlin (1906-1971), as a cultural leader and literary theoretician, tried to persuade China's writers and artists that the Party's policy could enable them to "achieve richer realistic content" in their works (Quanlin, "Lun wenyi chuangzuo yu zhengze he ren-wu xiangjiehe"—"Combining Literary Creation with Policies and Political Tasks", *WYB,* v. 3, 1:10, 1950). See also "wenyi wei zhengzhi fuwu" (literature and art serve politics).

干预灵魂
ganyu linghun
(be involved in the soul)

See "ganyu shenghuo" (be involved in life).

干预生活
ganyu shenghuo
(be involved in life)

Liu Binyan was the first advocate in China of the idea that literature should "be involved in life". In the mid-1950s, he not only introduced the so-called "involvement" works of the Soviet writer Valentin Ovechkin, but he also helped to transplant into China the new literary genre known as "reportage literature" (baogao wenxue) or "special feature" (texie). He wrote at this time his well-known works "At the Bridge Construction Site" ("Zai qiaoliang gongdi shang", *RMWX,* 4, Apr. 1956, reprinted in *Liu Binyan Zuopin Jingxuan—Selected Works of Liu Binyan,* Hong Kong, Wenxue Yanjiushe, pp. 3-38) and "The Confidential News of This Newspaper" ("Benbao neibu xiaoxi", *RMWX,* 6 & 10, 1956, reprinted in *Liu Binyan Zuopin Jingxuan,* pp. 39-98; trans. in Nieh Hualing, ed. and co-trans., *Literature of the Hundred Flowers,* v. 2, New York, Columbia University Press, 1981, pp. 411-64, and W. J. F. Jenner, ed., *Fragrant Weeds,* pp. 1-70), pungently exposing and criticizing the bureaucracy in China's daily life. Soon after publication, however, they were attacked as deviating from socialist realism and the principle of literature and art serving the workers, peasants, and soldiers and proletarian politics, and they were ultimately condemned as "anti-Party, anti-people, and anti-socialist big poisonous weeds". Consequently, Liu Binyan was labeled a "bourgeois Rightist", and cruelly persecuted.

In March 1979, just a month after his rehabilitation, Liu Binyan published "On 'Writing about the Dark Side' and 'Being Involved in Life'" ("Guanyu 'xie yin'an mian' he 'ganyu shenghuo'", *SHWX,* 3:49-57, 1979, reprinted in *LBY,* pp. 3-17). He significantly systematized his literary stand, a stand which he had stuck to for over two decades and for which he had paid very dearly.

As he explains, "writing about the dark side" and "being involved in life" were raised to oppose the then prevailing tendency in literature and art to evade or gloss over contradictions and conflicts in real life. Liu does not consider "writing about the dark side" as the whole or major task of literature, but he does hold that the truth should be displayed in an all-around way, reflecting and revealing all the contradictions and struggles in life, including those negative phenomena that hinder social progress. He does not understand why the arts should be expected to provide people with a false picture of life, since the task of the proletariat is to "reform the world on the basis of a correct understanding of it".

As for "being involved in life", Liu deems it first and foremost a standard by which to judge a man's conduct. Even in feudal society a man would be praised for speaking out from a sense of justice, and much more for sacrificing his own life to criticize an emperor's faults. It is, therefore, a monstrous absurdity that, in socialist society, a man should not be allowed to become involved in those major issues of principle that concern the people's interests and the future of the socialist cause. So, for a writer, according to Liu, "to be involved in life" means on the one hand to reveal new things and new issues in the depths of life, so as to arouse readers to support the new things and to solve the new issues; and, on the other, it means to expose and castigate those people, or phenomena, that sabotage or hinder the advance of socialism.

Liu Binyan had fellow travellers. In June 1957, Gao Xiaosheng, a young writer, and his fellow "pursuers" (tanqiuzhe) Lu Wenfu, Fang Zhi, and Ye Zhicheng put forward a similar slogan for their artistic creations: "Be bravely involved in life and seriously probe into it" (dadan ganyu shenghuo, yansu tantao rensheng). Gao also paid dearly for promoting this slogan. Like many others, he was convicted as a "Rightist" and forced to labor in the countryside for over twenty years (Gao was rehabilitated after the end of the GPCR. He died in July 1999).

As a definition of the purpose of literature, it should be pointed out, many Chinese writers and critics do not agree with Liu Binyan's vision, though they understand, sympathize with, and even admire this former Rightist. Zhu Zhai, for instance, doubted its accuracy, even though he highly appreciated Liu's motive ("Lishi zhuanzhezhongde wenxue piping"—"Literary Criticism at a Historical Turning-Point", *WXPL*, 4:19, July 1984). Lu Shuyuan, another critic, believed journalists were more suited for the job of being involved in life ("Yong xinlixuede yanguang kan wenxue"—"Looking at Literature from a Psychological Perspective", *WXPL*, 4:9, 1985). Many writers prefer to make literature "involved in the soul" (ganyu linghun). One such example is Wang Meng, another former Rightist who was elected vice-chairman of the CWA together with Liu Binyan in 1985 and who became minister of culture in 1986. (See his "Zai Aihehua di'er ci 'Zhongguo zhoumo' shang de fayan"—"Speech at the Second 'China Weekend' of Iowa", *QN*, 130:95, Nov. 1980.) Gao Xiaosheng also came to agree that "being involved in the soul" is a better literary slogan than "being involved in life". At a 1980 forum, when recalling his former slogan, he said he wanted it to be changed into: "Be loyal to life and involved in the soul" (Zhongyu shenghuo, ganyu linghun).

But the significance of Liu's stand should not be underestimated. For him, the "dark side" first of all referred to the three main dangers (which Lenin had warned socialism might face): 1. those careerists, adventurers, and swindlers who pretend to be Communists and have wormed themselves into the Party; 2. bureaucracy; 3. mistakes by the policymakers ("On 'Writing about the Dark Side' and 'Being Involved in Life'", in *LBY*, p. 14). "To be involved in life", therefore, for the most part means to be involved in politics (ganyu zhengzhi). According to Liu Binyan, despite the risk, writers should function as public procurators and judges. See also "Liu Binyan xianxiang" (Liu Binyan phenomenon) and "xinshiqi wenxuede duoyuan fazhan" (pluralistic development of the literature of the new period).

干预政治
ganyu zhengzhi
(be involved in politics)

See "ganyu shenghuo" (be involved in life) and "yi wenti wei zhongxinde baogao wenxue" (problem-centered reportage literature).

干部四化
ganbu sihua

(four standards for selecting cadres)

See "disan tidui" (third echelon).

干部下放
ganbu xiafang
(transferring cadres to the lower levels)

See "xiafang" (transfer to a lower level).

港人治港
gangren zhi gang
(Hong Kong residents governing Hong Kong)

When Margaret Thatcher, prime minister of the United Kingdom, visited Beijing in September 1982 to confirm the process of the return of Chinese sovereignty over Hong Kong, Deng Xiaoping spoke of "one country, two systems". With this as the guideline, the two countries reached a joint declaration, which was signed by Thatcher and Zhao Ziyang, PRC premier, on 19 December 1984. Then, on 4 April 1990, the 3rd Session of the 7th NPC passed the Basic Law (Jibenfa) for the future Special Administrative Region of Hong Kong. The idea of "one country, two systems" was thus legalized.

A key point embodying this idea is the principle of "Hong Kong residents governing Hong Kong", as stipulated in the Basic Law. According to this principle, on 11 December 1996, the 400 members of the Selection Committee for the first government of the Hong Kong Special Adminstrative Region voted in secret ballot in Hong Kong for the first chief executive. Tung Chee Hwa, a 59-year-old shipping magnate, won 320 votes, defeating two other candidates. Tung's election was hailed by the Chinese leadership as an expression of the principle of "Hong Kong residents governing Hong Kong". This implied that, over the past 156 years of British rule, there had been no democracy to speak of in Hong Kong—all twenty-eight governors had been appointed by the British monarch.

On 1 July 1997, sovereignty over Hong Kong returned to China. But there were still many questions about how Tung Chee Hwa and his colleagues would govern the Hong Kong Special Adminstrative Region of the People's Republic of China. See also "yiguo liangzhi" (one country, two systems).

高大全
gao da quan
(lofty, great, and perfect)

According to Jiang Qing and her supporters, the major heroic characters in a work of proletarian literature must be lofty, great, and perfect, as summed up in the principle of the "three prominences". See "wen'ge wenyi" (GPCR literature and art) and "yihua wenxue" (alienated literature; literature of alienation).

高额丰产田运动
gao'e fengchantian yundong
(movement to make the fields turn out exceptionally high yield)

See "dayuejin" (Great Leap Forward).

搞试点
gao shidian
(make a key-point experiment)

See "zhong shiyantian" (cultivating experimental farming plots).

告别革命
gaobie geming
(farewell to revolution)

The proposition "farewell to revolution" was put forward by Li Zehou, a well-known philosopher and aesthete, and Liu Zaifu, former director of the Literature Institute of CASS, in their 1995 book *Farewell to Revolution: Looking Back upon China of the Twentieth Century (Gaobie Geming: Huiwang Ershishiji Zhongguo,* Hong Kong, Tiandi, 1995).

In the form of a dialog, the book records conversations between the two cultural figures during almost three years from January 1992 during their exile in America. The theme of the book, as indicated by its title, is to say good-bye to revolutions, either of the Left or of the Right, which have tragically affected and determined the fate of China in the twentieth century. The entire century was consumed with ideology worship, dialectical materialism, the theory of class struggle, and the view that it is right to make violent revolution. Li and Liu criticize and repudiate all these ideas. They advocate: taking the economy as the basis, class compromise, class cooperation, pluralism, coexistence, reformism, gradual advance in due order, freedom of public opinion, dualism in the relationship between politics and literature, distinction between social and governmental functions, paying attention to the reverse law in historical development, and reconfirming human value. They suggest the following order of gradual reform (so as to bid farewell to revolution): 1. economic development; 2. individual freedom; 3. social justice; and 4. political democracy (jingji fazhan, geren ziyou, shehui zhengyi, zhengzhi minzhu). All of these presuppose social stability *(Farewell to Revolution,* p. 55).

Li and Liu appeal for an end to revolution in the twenty-first century. The Chinese people should no longer praise and worship revolution as something sacred. Moreover, China should not pretend to be the center of world revolution. The twenty-first century should be a century in which China will be self-adjusting, self-improving, and self-strengthening.

It was of symbolic significance that the proposition "farewell to revolution" was put forward after the failure of the 1989 pro-democracy movement. The book became controversial immediately after its publication. Some (such as Liu Xiaobo) regarded it as a work of "neo-conservatism". They even suspected the two authors of aiming to curry favor with the Chinese authorities. One of the controversial points is the thesis of the "four steps" of economic development, individual freedom, social justice, and political democracy. It was argued that in each phase economic reform and political reform should coordinate and promote each other. Democracy is not a spontaneous, natural end result; It cannot be obtained without people's joint efforts. In addition, in the striving for democracy, the economy also benefits. Li Zehou defended his views in an August 1999 article "Chinese Dialectics: The Art of 'Du'" (Zhongguode bianzhengfa: 'du'de yishu", *Mingbao yuekan,* 8:101-104, 1999). He wrote that the four items, while in order of importance and urgency, infiltrate one another. How to handle their complicated relations needs Chinese dialectics—the art of "du" (adequate proportion, relationship, and structure). In his opinion, both "populists" ("mincuipai", referring to those also dubbed "neo-Leftists") and "liberals" have lost "du" when the former exaggerated the injustice in today's China and advocated the relativity and particularity of post-modernism and the latter exaggerated the rationality of market economy and political democracy and advocated the objectivity and universality of the doctrine of enlightenment.

Interestingly, attacks came from Beijing too. Xing Bensi, editor-in-chief of *Seek Truth* and vice-president of the PCC Party School, accused Liu Zaifu and Li Zehou of trying to write off Marxism, China's mainstream ideology (Xing Bensi, "Jianchi Makesizhuyi budongyao"—"Unswervingly Adhering to Marxism", *RMRB*, 6 June 1996). In October 1996, Hu Sheng, CASS president, also joined in the attack *(Bainian Chao,* inaugural issue, Oct. 1996). The book has so far been banned in mainland China. Liu Zaifu asked: "'Farewell to revolution' means avoiding violent rebellion. Why is the CCP, a ruling party, afraid of this?" (Liu Zaifu, "Chong xie Zhongguo jindaishide qidai"—"Rewriting Modern Chinese History: An Expectation", *Mingbao yuekan*, 5:37, May 1998.) See also "xin baoshouzhuyi" (neo-conservatism).

告别革命四顺序
gaobie geming si shunxu
(four steps in bidding farewell to revolution)

See "gaobie geming" (farewell to revolution).

割资本主义尾巴
ge zibenzhuyi weiba
(cut off capitalist tails)

See "yidaoqie" (a single cut).

歌德文学
gede wenxue
(virtue-praising literature)

See "gedepai" (virtue-eulogists).

歌德与缺德
gede yu quede
(praising virtue and lacking virtue)

See "gedepai" (virtue-eulogists).

歌德派
gedepai
(virtue-eulogists)

In the summer of 1979, during the discussion of "forward-looking literature" and "backward-looking literature" (see "xianghoukan wenyi"—"backward-looking literature"), another controversy arose. This was provoked by the unknown writer Li Jian, who in June 1979 published an essay entitled "'Praising Virtue' and 'Lacking Virtue'". Li Jian preached that the fundamental task of socialist literature and art was "praising virtue"—the "virtue" of the Communist Party, its leader, and the workers, peasants, and soldiers, as well as the "virtue" of the socialist cause. At the same time, Li crudely attacked those who did not agree as "lacking virtue". Wang Ruowang, then a very active critic, was the first to severely criticize Li Jian, labelling his article "a blast of cold wind in spring" (chuntianlide yigu lengfeng) and asking people to beware of it.

Another notable article was Yan Xiu's "On 'Virtue-Eulogists'" ("Lun 'gedepai'", *DS,* 7, 1979). As Yan recalled, during the 1957 anti-Rightist campaign, to oppose "virtue-eulogists" was regarded as a crime, for which many Rightists were convicted. During the latter part of the GPCR when the Gang of Four felt confident about their position, their supporters, first in Shanghai, clamored that they were determined to be "virtue-eulogists" and that "virtue-praising" must be advocated and carried out in the fields of literature and art. They maintained that creation of "virtue-praising literature" (gede wenxue) was writers' "fundamental" task. Based on this, "conspiratorial literature" (yinmou wenxue), an example of which was the film *Counterattack* (*Fanji;* dir. Li Wenhua, Beijing Film Studio, 1976), was developed. In conformity with the "fundamental task", logically, the "three prominences" (santuchu) became the "fundamental" creative method. Furthermore, as an organizational measure to promote "virtue-praising literature" and "conspiratorial literature", the Gang also set out to build their own literary and art contingent. All this, according to Yan Xiu, was a summation of the Gang of Four's theory and practice in literature and art. He declared that he was simply astonished to see the "coincidence" in Li Jian's essay, which repeatedly preached that the fundamental task of socialist literature and art was "praising virtue" and crudely attacked those who did not agree as "lacking virtue". Even if Li Jian and his supporters knew nothing about the historical background of the term "praising virtue", Yan Xiu said, "Such a coincidence still provides food for thought. This, in philosophical terms, is called contingency in necessity, or, contingency that embodies necessity" (Yan Xiu, ibid.). See also "wenyi wei zhengzhi fuwu" (literature and art serve politics) and "wen'ge wenyi" (GPCR literature and art).

革命大串联
geming dachuanlian
(massive exchange of revolutionary experiences)

After the "May 16th Circular", the programmatic document with which Mao started the GPCR, was published on 17 May 1966 in the *People's Daily* and other newspapers and broadcast by all the radio stations throughout the country, many "big-character posters" were posted at schools and institutions of higher education in Beijing. Students outside of Beijing also became excited. They went to Beijing to "learn from others' experience" (qujing). But it was after Mao received the Red Guards for the first time on 18 August 1966 that there appeared the so-called massive exchange of revolutionary experiences on a nationwide scale. Red Guards poured into Beijing and other cities from all over the country. Greatly encouraged by Mao's call to bombard the "bourgeois headquarters" and carry on the GPCR through to the end, they engaged in what they thought to be revolutionary activities—to do away with the "four olds" and cultivate the "four news" and to struggle against alleged "capitalist-roaders" at various levels of Party and government organizations.

In his speech at a Beijing rally on 31 August 1966, Zhou Enlai agreed that the "massive exchange of revolutionary experiences" on a nationwide scale would certainly and potently deepen the GPCR (*RMRB,* 1 Sept. 1966). However, such "revolutionary travel", which was free of charge, resulted in serious consequences, increasing economic difficulties and creating nationwide chaos. On 3 February and 19

March 1967, the central authorities successively published two calls to stop it. However, it continued into 1968, though on a smaller scale. See also "hongweibing" (Red Guards) and "po sijiu, li sixin" (do away with the "four olds" and cultivate the "four news").

革命大批判
geming dapipan
(revolutionary mass criticism)

See "dapipan" (mass criticism).

革命发展阶段论
geming fazhan jieduan lun
(theory of the development of revolution by stages)

See "buduan geming" (uninterrupted revolution).

革命接班人
geming jiebanren
(revolutionary successors)

In the early 1960s, when Mao came to the conclusion that the Soviet Union had already changed its colors (bianse) and was under the rule of "modern revisionists" headed by Khrushchev (1894-1971), then the CPSU first secretary, he issued an urgent Party task to cultivate "successors to the proletarian revolutionary cause" (wuchanjieji geming shiye jiebanren). In a talk on 16 June 1964, Mao suggested five requirements for such successors: 1. to practice Marxism-Leninism and not revisionism; 2. to serve the majority of the people; 3. to be able to unite with the majority of the people; 4. to possess a democratic style; and 5. to conduct self-criticism when making a mistake. In the CCP's 9th critique, published on 14 July 1964, on the open letter of the CPSU Central Committee, Mao personally added a passage concerning the successor issue and finalized his "five requirements" (see "Guanyu Heluxiaofude jia gongchanzhuyi jiqi zai shijie lishishangde jiaoxun"—"On Khrushchev's Pseudo-Communism and Its Lesson in World History", *RMRB*, 14 June 1964). These five requirements were included in both the two versions of the CCP Constitution respectively passed at the Party's 1969 9th National Congress *(RMRB*, 29 Apr. 1969) and its 1973 10th National Congress *(RMRB*, 2 Sept. 1973).

According to these "five requirements", Mao began to suspect his selected successor Liu Shaoqi. He ruthlessly removed Liu, calling him "China's Khrushchev" and persecuting him to death on 12 November 1969. Then he selected Lin Biao. As it turned out, Lin was a "careerist" and "conspirator", who was killed on 13 September 1971 following an unsuccessful coup d'état in which he attempted to kill Mao. Mao's next choice was Wang Hongwen, a new political star who had risen during the GPCR. But during the successful coup d'état by Hua Guofeng, Ye Jianying, Wang Dongxing, and Li Xiannian on 6 October 1976, Wang was overthrown as a member of the Gang of Four and later sentenced to life imprisonment. (Wang died of hepatitis in prison on 3 August 1992.) In his final year, Mao had also put his hopes on Hua Guofeng to be his successor, or at least a transitional figure. On 21 and 28 January 1976 Mao twice proposed that Hua be acting premier in charge of daily activities. Then on 7 April of the same year, Mao further appointed him to the positions of CCP first vice-chairman and PRC premier. However, Hua eventually lost out to Deng Xiaoping, even though, after the "October 6 coup" of 1976, he had become CCP chairman, PRC premier and CMC chairman, and he was hailed as the "wise leader" who would lead the Chinese people into the twenty-first century in a so-called "new Long March".

Such cultivation of "revolutionary successors" is reminiscent of feudal hereditary traditions and the practice of "rule by man" (renzhi). See also "Lin Biao shijian" (Lin Biao Incident), "sirenbang" (Gang of Four), and "yingming lingxiu" (wise leader).

革命群众组织
geming qunzhong zuzhi
(revolutionary mass organizations)

In 1966, with Mao's approval, slogans such as "Revolution is no crime; it is right to rebel" (Geming wuzui, zaofan youli) and "Liberate yourself, educate yourself" (Ziji jiefang ziji, ziji jiaoyu ziji) were promoted in order to incite young students and other people to rise up and rebel, i.e., to topple the "capitalist-roaders" and to crush government organizations. The groups of Red Guards, workers, peasants, and "revolutionary intellectuals and cadres" that arose to carry out this rebellion were referred to as "revolutionary mass organizations". See also "wen'ge" (Cultural Revolution).

革命人道主义
geming rendaozhuyi
(revolutionary humanism)

"Heal the wounded, rescue the dying, practice revolutionary humanism" was a slogan put forth by Mao during the revolutionary war years. Obviously, here Mao treated humanism as an ethical principle that included some humanitarian practices, such as healing the wounded and rescuing the dying. In his January 1984 article "On Problems Concerning Humanism and Alienation", Hu Qiaomu adhered to Mao's view, and advocated propagating and practicing socialist humanism. But by socialist humanism, he meant "an ethical principle with a Marxist interpretation of the world and history as its basis". On the one hand, he explained, it is a development of revolutionary humanism. On the other, it is inferior to Communist morality, which is the highest moral standard for contemporary people.

As part of the 1980s humanism debate, Wang Ruoshui refuted the treatment of "revolutionary humanism" as only a kind of moral norm and not as a world outlook. In June 1985, with the help of Deng Pufang, Deng Xiaoping's son, Wang's view was published in the *Workers' Daily* ("Guanyu 'geming rendaozhuyi'"—"On 'Revolutionary Humanism'", reprinted in *WRB*, pp. 234-38). Adroitly, Wang made use of Deng Xiaoping's saying: "The basic question as regards world outlook is whom one is to serve", quoted from his March 1978 "Speech at the Opening Ceremony of the National Conference on Science" ("Zai quanguo kexue dahui kaimushishangde jianghua", *SWD*, p. 107). See also "rendaozhuyi lunzheng" (humanism debate) and "shehuizhuyi rendaozhuyi" (socialist humanism).

革命统一战线
geming tongyi zhanxian
(revolutionary united front)

See "tongzhan" (united front).

革命委员会
geming weiyuanhui
(revolutionary committee)

See "yiyue geming" (January Revolution) and "wen'ge" (Cultural Revolution).

革命无罪，造反有理
geming wuzui, zaofan youli
(revolution is no crime; it is right to rebel)

See "geming qunzhong zuzhi" (revolutionary mass organizations) and "zaofan youli" (it is right to rebel).

革命现代戏
geming xiandai xi
(revolutionary theatrical works on contemporary themes)

See "wen'ge wenyi" (GPCR literature and art).

革命现实主义
geming xianshizhuyi
(revolutionary realism)

See "shehuizhuyi xianshizhuyi" (socialist realism).

革命现实主义与革命浪漫主义相结合
geming xianshizhuyi yu geming langmanzhuyi xiangjiehe
(combination of revolutionary realism and revolutionary romanticism)

See "shehuizhuyi xianshizhuyi" (socialist realism).

革命样板戏
geming yangbanxi
(model revolutionary dramas)

See "wen'ge wenyi" (GPCR literature and art).

革命造反派
geming zaofanpai
(revolutionary rebels)

See "zaofan youli" (it is right to rebel).

革命的爱国主义
gemingde aiguozhuyi
(revolutionary patriotism)

See "shijie geming" (world revolution) and "aiguozhuyi" (patriotism).

革命的根本问题是政权问题
gemingde genben wenti shi zhengquan wenti
(the fundamental question of revolution is political power)

See "wuchanjieji zhuanzheng" (dictatorship of the proletariat) and "qiangganzi he biganzi" (the gun and the pen).

革命的两手
gemingde liangshou
(revolutionary dual tactics)

According to Mao's teaching, the CCP must deal with its enemies' "counter-revolutionary dual tactics" with its "revolutionary dual tactics", that is, the use of military force on the battlefield and diplomatic negotiations at the conference table, which is a method to gain and expose the enemy.

革命化，年轻化，知识化，专业化
geminghua, nianqinghua, zhishihua, zhuanyehua
(more revolutionary, younger in age, better educated, and professionally more competent)

See "disan tidui" (third echelon).

革委会
geweihui
(revolutionary committee)

An abbreviation for "geming weiyuanhui"—"revolutionary committee". See "yiyue geming" (January Revolution) and "wen'ge" (Cultural Revolution).

各尽所能，各取所需
ge jin suo neng, ge qu suo xu
(from each according to his ability, to each according to his needs)

See "dayuejin" (Great Leap Forward) and "ziwo shixian" (self-actualization).

个人成分
geren chengfen
(an individual's class status)

See "jiating chengfen" (family origin; class status of one's family).

个人崇拜
geren chongbai
(personality cult)

At the March 1958 Chengdu Conference, a PCC work conference held in Chengdu city, Sichuan province, Mao decided to respond to the personality cult issue raised by the 20th National Congress of the CPSU held in February 1956. At that time, as a result of the Congress, the Communist world condemned the personality cult of Stalin.

Mao expounded his idea about "two different kinds of personality cult": "geren mixin" ("mixin" can be translated as "superstition") and "geren chongbai" ("chongbai" can be translated as "worship"). Each had its own meaning—while the former should be opposed, the latter should be accepted, Mao emphasized. In fact, however, both "geren mixin" and "geren chongbai" refer to "personality cult". Mao also confused the two concepts of "personality cult" and "worship of truth" (chongbai zhenli). Obviously, he was juggling the words. His purpose was to imply that the personality cult of Mao should not be questioned.

The "personality cult" was a major target for attack after Mao's death. Deng also joined in this attack. In an important speech, entitled "On the Reform of the System of Party and State Leadership", delivered on 18 August 1980 to a Politburo enlarged meeting, Deng agreed that there should be less publicity about individuals (CCP leaders). He also said that he opposed an over-concentration of power in the hands of individuals (*SWD*, pp. 312-13). On 20 October 1980, the Party decided that photos of the present leader not be hanged in public places so as to help reduce the influence of personality cult.

In the above noted speech, Deng not only was referring to Mao but also to Hua Guofeng, then CCP chairman who was said to have also encouraged his own personality cult. But not long thereafter, Deng's decisions were also unassailable. Interestingly, after Deng's death, Jiang Zemin's turn came. Jiang is now juxtaposed with Mao and Deng as one of the three great leaders in CCP history. Because of its long tradition in the Chinese political culture, the personality cult is indeed not a simple issue. The truth is that Chinese leaders have traditionally enjoyed being worshipped, and many people have tried to benefit from this. See also "xiandai mixin" (modern superstition), "tuchu zhengzhi" (giving prominence to politics), "dangde lingdao" (Party leadership), and "shehuizhuyi yihua lun" (theory of socialist alienation).

个人服从集体，少数服从多数，下级服从上级，全党服从中央
geren fucong jiti, shaoshu fucong duoshu, xiaji fucong shangji, quandang fucong zhongyang (individuals are subordinate to the organizations they belong to, the minority is subordinate to the majority, lower authorities are subordinate to higher authorities, and the whole party is subordinate to the Party Center)

See "renminxing he dangxingde maodun" (contradiction between the party spirit and affinity to the people) and "minzhu jizhongzhi" (democratic centralism).

个人迷信
geren mixin (personality cult)

See "geren chongbai" (personality cult).

个人主义
gerenzhuyi
(individualism)

See "ziyouzhuyi" (liberalism).

个人主义是对抗专制的最佳方式
gerenzhuyi shi duikang zhuanzhide zuijia fangshi
(individualism is the best resistance to autocracy)

See "ziyouzhuyi" (liberalism).

给非理性在艺术创作中一个应有的地位
gei feilixing zai yishu chuangzuo-zhong yige yingyoude diwei
(give the irrational due place in artistic creation)

Irrationalism was rejected in the CCP's orthodox literary theory. In the debate of the early 1980s on "misty poetry", the concept of "the irrational" and the thesis of "giving the irrational due place in artistic creation" were controversial. See "xinde meixue yuanze zai jueqi" (a new aesthetic principle is rising) and "xinshiqi wenxuede duoyuan fazhan" (pluralistic development of the literature of the new period).

跟党一条心
gen dang yitiaoxin
(be at one with the Party)

See "chi butong zhengjianzhe" (dissidents) and "yu zhongyang baochi yizhi" (be in keeping with the Party Center).

公私溶化论
gong si ronghua lun
(theory of "merging private and public interests")

See "hei liu lun" (six sinister theories).

公共空间
gonggong kongjian
(public sphere)

See "wenhua re" (culture craze) and "danwei" (unit).

公开点名批判
gongkai dianming pipan
(criticize someone openly by name)

See "dapipan" (mass criticism).

公民法治社会
gongmin fazhi shehui

(civil society ruled by law)

See "fan fubai" (anti-corruption) and "danwei" (unit).

公民社会
gongmin shehui
(civil society)

See "danwei" (unit).

公仆变老爷
gongpu bian laoye
(change from public servants of the people to their lords and masters)

See "shehuizhuyi tiaojianxia rende yihua" (man's alienation under the condition of socialism).

公式化，概念化
gongshihua, gainianhua
(the tendency to be formulistic and abstract)

Among Chinese writers and artists during the Mao period, there was always a strong objection to the tendency to be formulistic and abstract, which produces monotonous, stiff, mechanical, and stereotyped works. But this was difficult because works had to be based on the "politics first and art second" criteria (zhengzhi diyi, yishu di'er) and they had to cater to the Party demand that literature and art serve politics. In his work report delivered at the 1979 4th National Congress of Chinese Writers and Artists, Zhou Yang touched on this problem. Zhou recalled how Chinese literary and art circles had come under the influence of the "Left" tendency, with the result that literary and artistic issues were dealt with in an oversimplified and even vulgarized manner; both theories and praxes (artistic creation) tended to follow formulas and deal in generalities, criticisms became harsh and arbitrary, and democracy in the arts was severely impaired. He told his listeners that all these should be changed (Zhou Yang, "Jiwangkailai, fanrong shehuizhuyi xinshiqide wenyi"—Be Both Successors and Pioneers, Bring Literature and Art into Flower in the New Period of Socialism", *WYB*, 11-12:8-26, 1979 and *RMRB*, 20 Nov. 1979). See also "wenyi wei zhengzhi fuwu" (literature and art serve politics).

公有制不等于国有制
gongyouzhi budengyu guoyouzhi
(public ownership does not amount to state ownership)

See "quanmin suoyouzhi" (ownership by the whole people), "jingji gaige" (economic reform), and "jiejue gongyouzhi xingshi shi you yici sixiang jiefang" (solving the issue of public ownership forms is another emancipation of the mind).

公有制实现形式可以而且应当多样化
gongyouzhi shixian xingshi keyi erqie yingdang duoyanghua

(public ownership can and
should take diversified forms)

See "quanmin suoyouzhi" (ownership by the whole people), "jingji gaige" (economic reform) and "jiejue gongyouzhi xingshi shi you yici sixiang jiefang" (solving the issue of public ownership forms is another emancipation of the mind).

公有制的控制经济
gongyouzhide kongzhi jingji
(the controlled economy of public ownership)

See "jingji gaige" (economic reform).

公正更是硬道理
gongzheng gengshi ying daoli
(justice is the more essential criterion)

See "fazhan caishi ying daoli" (development is the most essential criterion).

工农兵学员
gong nong bing xueyuan
(students selected from among
workers, peasants, and soldiers)

See "shang, guan, gai" (attendance, management, and reform).

工具说
gongju shuo
("tool" theory)

See "wenyi shi jieji douzhengde gongju" (literature and art are tools of class struggle).

工人无祖国
gongren wu zuguo
(the working men have no country)

See "shijie geming" (world revolution).

工人阶级必须领导一切
gongrenjieji bixu lingdao yiqie
(the working class must
exercise leadership in everything)

On 26 August 1968, Yao Wenyuan published an article in the *People's Daily*, entitled "The Working Class Must Exercise Leadership in Everything" ("Gongrenjieji bixu lingdao yiqie"), which was Mao's latest directive concerning sending workers (in the name of "Mao Zedong Thought Propaganda Teams") to Qinghua University in Beijing in view of the escalation of Red Guard factional fighting on the campus. During the rest of the GPCR, this directive by Mao was one of the most powerful slogans. No doubt there was still the Party leadership, but for a time workers did become leaders, even in such institutions as schools, hospitals, and academies of sciences, where they were sent (often together with PLA officers) to "propagate Mao Zedong Thought". Nowadays, people find this ridiculous and difficult to understand. See also "dangde lingdao" (Party leadership).

工业学大庆
gongye xue Daqing
(in industry, learn from Daqing)

In 1964, Mao issued the call: "In agriculture, learn from Dazhai! In industry, learn from Daqing!"

Daqing is an oil enterprise in northeastern China, whose construction began in 1960. On 20 April 1964, the *People's Daily* praised "the spirit of Daqing". As part of the spirit, it lauded the work style of "sanlao siyan" (three honests and four stricts), said to be characteristic of the Daqing workers. The "three honests" refer to being an honest person, honest in word, and honest in deed in relation to the revolutionary cause. The "four stricts" refer to strict standards, strict organization, a strict attitude, and strict discipline in relation to work. Wang Jinxi, the 1205 drilling team leader at Taqing, was dubbed the "iron man" for his bravery and persistent efforts to open the oil field in extremely difficult conditions. See also "tuchu zhengzhi" (giving prominence to politics).

工作单位
gongzuo danwei
(unit)

See "danwei" (unit).

共产党领导下的多党合作及政治协商制
gongchandang lingdaoxiade duo dang hezuo ji zhengzhi xieshang zhi
(the system of multiparty cooperation and political consultation led by the Communist Party)

See "minzhu dangpai" (democratic parties) and "wuchanjieji zhuanzheng" (dictatorship of the proletariat).

共产党是工人阶级的先锋队
gongchandang shi gongrenjiejide xianfengdui
(the Communist Party is the vanguard of the working class)

See "dangde lingdao" (Party leadership).

共产党的哲学就是斗争的哲学
gongchandangde zhexue jiushi douzhengde zhexue
(the philosophy of the Communist Party is the philosophy of struggle)

See "douzheng chongbai" (struggle worship).

共产风
gongchan feng
(Communist wind)

See "dayuejin" (Great Leap Forward).

共产主义新人
gongchanzhuyi xin ren
(new Communist man)

See "shehuizhuyi xin ren" (new socialist man).

共产主义思想是社会主义精神文明的核心
gongchanzhuyi sixiang shi shehuizhuyi jingshen wenmingde hexin
(Communist ideology is the core of socialist spiritual civilization)

In his report "Open Up All-sidedly a New Phase of Socialist Modern Construction" delivered at the September 1982 12th CCP National Congress, Hu Yaobang, who was to be elected Party general secretary at the Congress, emphasized that, while enhancing the socialist material civilization, a "socialist spiritual civilization" must also be built. Notably, on the eve of the Congress, a political incident occurred, when the *Liberation Army Daily* carried an eye-catching article, "Communist Ideology Is the Core of Socialist Spiritual Civilization" ("Gongchanzhuyi sixiang shi shehuizhuyi jingshen wenmingde hexin", *JFJB*, 28 Aug. 1982), written by its deputy editor-in-chief Zhao Yiya: this article advanced a number of views in opposition to Hu's political report. Zhao held the "ideological guidance" by the Party responsible for the spread of "bourgeois liberalization" in China in the past few years. This was an open challenge not only to Hu Yaobang, the future CCP general secretary, but also to the authority of Deng Xiaoping, at that time Hu's patron. In the end, Zhao Yiya lost his post, as did Wei Guoqing, director of the PLA General Political Department, who was considered Zhao's backer. See also "liang ge wenming" (two civilizations) and "shehuizhuyi chuji jieduan lun" (theory of the primary stage of socialism).

共产主义的基本原则是人的全面自由发展
gongchanzhuyide jiben yuanze shi rende quanmian ziyou fazhan
(the basic principle of communism is an all-around and free development of man)

See "ziwo shixian" (self-actualization).

共产主义的战歌
gongchanzhuyide zhan'ge
(a battle song of communism)

In 1965, Jin Jingmai, a young army writer in the Guangzhou Military Area, published a novel entitled *The Song of Ouyang Hai (Ouyang Hai Zhi Ge, Jiefangjun wenyi,* 6, 1965, reprinted in book form, Beijing, Jiefangjun Wenyi, 1965; excerpts trans. by Sidney Shapiro in *CL,* 7:71-132, 8:30-96, 9:88-141, 10:75-103, 11:61-104, 1966). The work, which is about a living soldier hero in the PLA, has little artistic value. However, because of its political value, it was praised all over the country immediately after its publication. Liu Baiyu, a top PLA cultural leader, called it a "battle song of communism" *("Ouyang Hai Zhi Ge* shi gongchanzhuyide zhan'ge"—"A Battle Song of Communism", *RMRB*, 26 Mar. 1966, reprinted in *WYB*, 4:18-26, 1966; trans. in *CL*, 7:142-155, 1966). Guo Moruo (1892-1978), a world-famous scholar, called the novel a "heroic epic in the era of Mao Zedong" ("Mao Zedong shidaide yingxiong shishi"—"A Heroic Epic in the Era of Mao Zedong", *WYB*, 4:13-17, 1966). This was a typical case of literary criticism at that time. See also "wenyi wei zhengzhi fuwu" (literature and art serve politics).

共同纲领
gongtong gangling
(Common Program)

See "zhengxie" (CPPCC).

共同美感
gongtong meigan
(common sense of beauty)

See "gongtong renxing" (common human nature).

共同人性
gongtong renxing
(common human nature)

By 1979, excessive accusations against the so-called theory of human nature and humanism, which ran rampant for a long time, had already duly been rejected by China's ideological-literary circles. Evidence can be found in the actual creative activities at the time. Nevertheless, people still wanted to see a theoretical solution. As they also understood, it was out of the question to have a comprehensive solution right away; a preliminary breakthrough was needed first.

Mao Zedong's alleged approval of a "common sense of beauty" (gongtong meigan) was first made known to the public in an article published in September 1977. The author He Qifang (1912-1977), a prominent poet and literary theorist, recalled a meeting with Mao in 1961, at which the late Party chairman said: "Each class has its own sense of beauty; all classes also share a common sense of beauty" (He Qifang, "Mao Zedong zhi ge"—"An Eulogy for Mao Zedong", *RMWX*, 9:87, 1977). Such an assertion, though quite commonplace, was cheered enthusiastically by the literary and art world. Indeed, since the principle of the "two whatevers" (see "liang ge fanshi") was still dominant at the time, the disclosure meant that a spiritual shackle had been removed. It later led to a nationwide discussion of a "common sense of beauty". The discussion further developed into the sphere of a "common human nature". It occurred to many that this could open a road that had before been blocked, and that the concept of a "common human nature" could probably be accepted if it was given due explanation. At any rate, no one could deny that the sense of beauty and human nature, though belonging to two different categories, were very closely related to each other. A number of critics, such as Gu Xiang, Huang Yaomian, Chen Jianyu, Wang Shuming, and Hu Yicheng, took the lead in probing this issue. Though they differed from one another, their joint efforts finally made the acknowledgment of a "common human nature" a *fait accompli* among China's ideological-cultural circles in the early 1980s.

First, they very carefully re-explained Mao's ideas in this regard. In his 1942 *Yan'an Talks*, Mao severely criticized what he considered "muddled" ideas, such as "human nature transcending class" and "human love", ideas which, he said, some people held because they lacked "basic political common knowledge". He said: "Is there such a thing as human nature? Of course there is. But there is only human nature in the concrete, no human nature in the abstract. In class society there is only human nature bearing a class character; there is no human nature above classes."

This assertion by Mao had long been regarded by China's critics as the "most powerful weapon" against the so-called "theory of human nature" (renxing lun) of the bourgeoisie and the landlord class. In 1980, critics such as Hu Yicheng and Wang Shuming found they could explain it thus: 1. By "human nature" Mao only means man's whole social relationships which are in a process of change throughout history, namely, man's social character; 2. Even so, no one can deny that here Mao still acknowledges that there exists such a thing as "human nature"; 3. Regarding the assertion that concrete human nature in class society bears (daizhe, in the Chinese original) class character, obviously, "to bear" does not mean "to be" or "to amount to"; 4. In addition, "no human nature above classes" can be explained as concrete human nature that displays itself only in an entity of both class and non-class characters (such an entity, naturally, at any time and under any circumstances in a class society, will include class character as one of its aspects); and 5. Mao's remarks also imply that human nature will not bear a class character in a non-class society—this is of "profound significance" to people living in the "transition period from a class society to a non-class society" (see Hu Yicheng, "Ren, renxing, renqing"—"Human Beings, Human Nature, and Human Feelings", *Shehuikexue,* 1, 1980; and Wang Shuming, "Renxing, wenxue ji qita"—"Human Nature, Literature, and Other Things", *WXPL,* 5, 1980).

Focusing on the phrase "human nature bearing a class character", the critic Zheng Zujie provided another interesting explanation. If the phrase is analyzed semantically, he said, there must be a "subject" that "bears" something and an "object" that is "borne". Human nature, discernibly, is the "subject" and class character the "object". In a class society, whether a person bears a class character or not, as far as his whole ideology is concerned, cannot be decided by his own subjective will. With regard to a specific, individual thought, however, there is a distinction of whether or not, or how much, it bears class character (Zheng Zujie, "Fa hu qing, zhi hu li yi—tan daizhe jiejixingde renxing"—"On Human Nature Bearing a Class Character", *Donghai,* 8, 1979).

Another statement in Mao's *Talks*—"We uphold the human nature of the proletariat and of the masses of the people"—also gave rise to many analyses. Human nature of "the masses of the people" and that of "the proletariat", as the critic Chen Jianyu pointed out, are two different concepts—"the people" (renmin) consists of the proletariat and other classes according to Mao himself. So Chen suggested that it might be right to interpret "human nature of the masses of the people" as "common human nature among the people". In light of his interpretation, Mao actually agreed: Different classes have a different human nature; different classes also share a common human nature (Chen Jianyu, "Dianyingzhongde renxing he renqing"—"Human Nature and Human Feelings As Represented in Films", *Dianying yishu,* 5, 1980, excerpted and reprinted in *XHYB, WZB,* 10:158, 1980).

According to these post-Mao critics' analyses, it appears that Mao had long acknowledged a "common human nature". This, though helpful at the time, was of course untenable. Very soon, when people felt more confident, they began to criticize Mao directly on this issue. Even Hu Qiaomu, the CCP theoretical authority, joined in. In a speech delivered at the 1981 Forum on Problems on the Ideological

Front convened by the PCC Propaganda Department, Hu admitted that Mao in his *Yan'an Talks* oversimplified human nature (which bears a social character) as class character, and that this was incorrect (Hu Qiaomu, "Dangqian sixiang zhanxiande ruogan wenti"—"Some Current Problems on the Ideological Front", *HQ*, 23:19, 1981). Nevertheless, one should sympathize with the 1980 critics in their attempt to prove that Mao himself was also an advocate of a "common human nature". After all, their efforts did lead to a significant breakthrough—though a preliminary one—that is, a general acknowledgment of a "common human nature", a taboo in the Mao period, among China's ideological-cultural circles.

In the 1979-81 discussion of the "common human nature" issue, critics suggested a number of theories. Some, for instance, maintained that a "common human nature" referred to man's innate nature plus the non-class parts of his social nature. The desire for eating and drinking, the enjoyment of good health, the anguish in suffering from illness, paying attention to hygiene and courtesy, the ability to use language, to think and to work, personality and temperament, a common sense of beauty, etc.—all these were said to be a "common human nature" which exists concretely in the social practice of human beings, and is compatible and shared by human beings of different classes. Hu Yicheng, who shared this view, further pointed out that human nature always merges innate nature, social nature, and class nature into an organic whole. He said that factors above classes always coexist with those of class nature, though he also noted that class nature is in a dominant position (Hu Yicheng, "Human Beings, Human Nature and Human Feelings").

Gu Xiang raised the theory of "common psychological phenomena" (gongtong xinli xianxiang). He admitted that human nature as a psychological phenomenon, either thinking, feeling, personality, or desire, was generally branded with a class character. However, he argued that the part of human nature branded with a class character does not amount to the whole of human nature. It cannot be denied, he said, that in a class society, there still exist similarities, compatibility and closeness of human feelings, wills, and habits. Otherwise, men cannot understand and interact with one another and a society cannot be established (Gu Xiang, "Renxing yu jiejixing"—"Human Nature and Class Character", *Wenyi yanjiu*, 3, 1980).

Wang Runsheng held that the relationship between common human nature and class character was not a relationship between opposites. Class character, in his view, originates from: 1. innate nature, which demonstrates itself in seeking its own interests; and 2. social character, which can be seen in people's attitudes towards a certain social being. Since a human being's innate nature, as the subject, is inevitably related to the social being the object, and since the object is always rich and colorful and full of changes, it is certain that, when the two integrate, the subject will present its diversity along with the change and development of the object. Human beings' class character is actually a specific manifestation of their innate nature under a given social and historical condition. Such a manifestation is a social as well as a natural process, with class character and innate nature related by "internal integration" (neizai jiehede) (Wang Runsheng, "Rende ziranxing, shehuixing he jiejixing"—"Human Beings' Innate Nature, Social Nature, and Class Nature", *Liaoning daxue xuebao*, 3, 1980).

In the discussion, Qian Gurong, a veteran critic, declared: Since literature takes human beings as its object, definitely it should be based on human nature. A literary work, if divorced from human nature, will not only hardly arouse the readers' interest, but also will fail to be understood. The very reason why masterpieces produced in different times by different nations and different classes are loved by the whole of mankind is that they all have a foundation of "universal human nature" (pubian renxing). Therefore, Qian suggested, if proletarian literature and art intends to influence and educate people, it should concentrate its efforts on developing and enhancing human nature.

It was significant that Qian Gurong, who had been attacked more than once in the Mao period, was now able to voice his view about "universal human nature". But of more significance, perhaps, was that this was not a new idea. More than fifty years earlier, Liang Shiqiu, a literary figure from the "Crescent School" (xinyue pai), had already pointed out that "Great literature is based on a fixed universal human nature" ("Wenxue yu geming"—"Literature and Revolution, *Xinyue,* 1, 4, 1928, reprinted in *XWX 2,* p. 209). History, indeed, was repeating itself—but on a new level, of course.

共同心理现象
gongtong xinli xianxiang
(common psychological phenomena)

See "gongtong renxing" (common human nature).

股份制改造
gufenzhi gaizao
(joint stock system reform)

The experimentation of a joint stock system occurred as early as 1983, at first only sporadically, and furtively, because at that time (and in fact even quite a few years later) this was regarded as violating the socialist principle of public ownership. The number of joint stock companies exploded after 1992 when Deng ended the debate on this issue. At the end of October 1993, there were more than 3,800 such companies. In 1995, as an extension of the joint stock system experiment, the government started the experiment with the "modern enterprise system" (xiandai qiye zhidu), the central objective being the corporatization of state-owned enterprises. At the 15th CCP National Congress of September 1997, the joint stock system was included as a form of public ownership.

The joint stock system is perceived by many as the most promising direction for the state-owned enterprise reform. It is widely believed that by letting workers and managers own shares, their personal interests will be closely linked to enterprise performance. Therefore, they will care about the long-term growth of the enterprise and have fewer incentives to demand excessive wage increases or in-kind benefits. In other words, the decade-long problem of the state-owned enterprise's "short-term behavior" will disappear. Unfortunately, things were not so simple, as evidence from the experimental joint stock companies suggested. It was unlikely that all the problems would be solved once the joint stock system was adopted (yi gu jiu ling). Many shareholders, the so-called masters of the company, were only concerned with how to sell their shares and make profits, and not with the company itself, and there were few opportunities for them to exercise their power to run the company. Various short-term behaviorial problems still remained. In many cases, the problems were exacerbated since the joint stock system provided a more discretionary environment than the old system. According to official statistics, only one-third of these companies made profits, while the rest suffered losses, overtly or covertly.

Why were so many local governments and state-owned enterprises keen on this joint stock system reform when the actual implementation deviated so significantly from what had been expected? As He Qinglian, the author of *The Pitfalls of China*, points out, the truth is that those in power benefited from this reform. In fact, as early as more than ten years ago when a great number of Chinese-foreign joint ventures were set up, He Qinglian writes, those with foresight had effectively made use of this form to begin "previous accumulation" (yuanshi jilei). They deliberately underestimated the assets of the state enterprises they represented and their foreign partners repaid them under the table. According to statistics provided by He Qinglian, up to 1992, such losses of state assets amounted to 46 billion Chinese dollars.

Poignantly, He Qinglian calls this a "socialist free lunch" (shehuizhuyi mianfei wucan), a "free lunch" provided by socialist public ownership to be enjoyed only by those in power. It was a large-scale plunder of state property carried out by "insiders" by the means of their power. There was a fear that the introduction of the joint stock system, which was approved at the 15th CCP National Congress, might end up as another round of plunder of state wealth.

This was really a warning: the joint stock system will not be successful unless the social environment does not allow power to affect distribution and unless the principle of "rule by law" (fazhi) is common place and respected and observed by all.

古为今用
gu wei jin yong
(make the past serve the present)

See "shuangbai fangzhen" (Double Hundred policy).

古怪诗
guguai shi
(eccentric school of poetry)

See "menglong shi" (misty poetry).

挂羊头，卖狗肉
gua yangtou, mai gourou
(in front of the shop the sheep's head dangles, but inside the shop one sells dog's meat)

See "chi butong zhengjianzhe" (dissidents) and "zhengtong Makesizhuyi zhengzai zou xiang siwang" (orthodox Marxism is heading for death).

刮风
guafeng
(to stir up a "wind")

As a political term, this refers to the vacillation of national policies, which results in a popular loss of confidence in the Party-state authorities.

官倒
guandao
(official profiteers)

With the carrying out of Deng's policy of reform and the open door in recent years, a business fever has spread throughout China. A new social stratum—"official profiteers"—has appeared. Quite a number of government officials (and also retirees) and/or their children, taking advantage of their power and/or their relationships, have engaged in commerical activities, directly or indirectly (one form of such business is "switch operations"—"zhuanshou jiaoyi"), and they have made huge profits. This, of course, has caused great resentment among the people. In the 1989 pro-democracy movement, one of the slogans was: "Down with official profiteers!" See also "taizidang" (princes' clique) and "jingji gaige" (economic reform).

官僚资本
guanliao ziben
(bureaucrat-capital)

A classic Marxist description of "capital" is: "Capital comes dripping from head to foot, from every pore, with blood and dirt." In traditional CCP doctrine, bureaucrat-capital refers to "capital that is closely tied up with imperialist and feudal forces in conducting activities to monopolize and control the people's livelihood and to undermine the national economy (minzu jingji)". In the past, when talking about bureaucrat-capital, people referred to the monopoly capital headed by the "four notorious clans" (si da jiazu) of Chiang Kai-shek, T. V. Soong, H. H. Kung, and Chen Li-fu. They were the representatives of "bureaucrat-bourgeoisie" (guanliao zichanjieji) in China in the 1930s and 1940s. Furthermore, bureaucrat-capitalism was considered to be one of the "three big mountains" (a metaphor for imperialism, feudalism, and bureaucrat-capitalism) weighing on the backs of the Chinese people before liberation.

With the current establishment of a market economy (shichang jingji) in China, the concept of "capital" is accepted as being very necessary. However, the twenty years of transformation from a planned economy to a market economy is characterized by "power capitalization" (quanli zibenhua). What can be called a "power economy" (quanli jingji) has quickly expanded. In an environment of a power economy, "power capital" (quanli ziben), the integration of power and capital, runs rampant. By taking advantage of the dual price system, the "development zone" craze of the early 1990s, the joint stock system reform, etc., those in power or close to power (such as the so-called princes' clique) unceasingly turned their power into capital, such that social wealth rapidly became their private capital. That was their "previous accumulation" (yuanshi jilei), as a result of which their capital amounted to not less than thirty thousand billion Chinese dollars (as provided in 1998 by Yang Fan, a research fellow at the Economics Institute, CASS. See his article in *Hong Kong Economic Journal Monthly,* July 1998). A privileged bureaucratic stratum has thus come into being.

A power economy is a bureaucrat economy; power capital is bureaucrat-capital. (In addition to bureaucrat-capitalsim, there is "nepotic capitalism"—"zufa zibenzhu-yi"—the bureaucrat himself does not engage in commercial activities but with his power arranges his family members and relatives to do so and make huge profits. This is also called "yijia liangzhi"—"one family, two systems".) Now the problem is, in some people's eyes, even bureaucrat-capital needs to be justified. There is a saying in its favor that "Bureaucrat-capital is the first stage rocket" (guanliao ziben shi diyi ji huojian). It means that bureaucrat-capital, or power capital, should be hailed because it plays an important role in pushing China's economy forward. This view was strongly criticized by many economists. In contrast, they pointed out that there had been disastrous effects due to the build-up of bureaucrat-capital, such as unbearable disparities between the rich and the poor, destruction of confidence in legal commercial activities and investment, degeneration of social morality, and subversion of laws and regulations. Some even predicted that, if there is no reform for democracy and rule by law, such that power must withdraw from the market, an economic-political crisis will break out within a few years, thus seriously affecting the global economy. Another solution suggested by neo-Leftists is to have another

GPCR in the economic fields. See also "jingji gaige" (economic reform) and "fan fubai" (anti-corruption).

官僚资本是第一级火箭
guanliao ziben shi diyi ji huojian
(bureaucrat-capital is the first stage rocket)

See "guanliao ziben" (bureaucrat-capital) and "jingji gaige" (economic reform).

官僚资本主义
guanliao zibenzhuyi
(bureaucrat-capitalism)

See "guanliao ziben" (bureaucrat-capital) and "jingji gaige" (economic reform).

观念年
guannian nian
(year of concepts)

1986 was said to be the "year of concepts", for in this year a great number of new literary concepts (some introduced from the West) were used and discussed in China's literary circles, something unseen for several decades. For instance, in this year, Liu Zaifu proposed his theory of the "subjectivity of literature", which was a preliminary but far-sighted effort that challenged the existing study of literary laws. Liu's argument provoked much controversy. See also "wenxue zhutixing" (subjectivity of literature) and "wenxue guilü lunzheng" (1986 debate on the law of literature).

关系
guanxi
(personal connections)

See "zou houmen" (get in through the back door).

关系是第一生产力
guanxi shi diyi shengchanli
("guanxi" is the first important productive force)

See "zou houmen" (get in through the back door).

管得太具体，文艺没希望
guande tai juti, wenyi mei xiwang
(watched too closely, literature and art have no hope)

See "Zhao Dan yizhu" (Zhao Dan testament).

管制
guanzhi
(surveillance)

Surveillance was a common form of legal sanction (or illegal sanction) in the past. The term was stipulated to be no more than three years but it could be extended when necessary. Persons under surveillance (called "guanzhi fenzi" or "beiguanzhi fenzi") were usually the "heiwulei"—landlords, rich peasants, counter-revolutionaries, bad elements, and Rightists. Such punishment was also given to those who committed a crime not so serious as to incur arrest and imprisonment. Persons under surveillance were not allowed to speak and act as others, and they were forced to labor under government surveillance or the supervision of the masses (guanzhi laodong).

More specifically, there were several different treatments to those under surveillance. Some could be allowed to remain in their respective organizations, but they were deprived of their political rights. This was "surveillance by the administrative organ" (jiguan guanzhi). Or they could lose their posts and be forced to stay home and receive "surveillance by the neighborhood committee" (jiedao guanzhi). Or, even worse, they could be sent back to their home villages under "surveillance by the village administration" (nongcun guanzhi).

管制分子
guanzhi fenzi
(persons under surveillance)

See "guanzhi" (surveillance).

管制劳动
guanzhi laodong
(labor under surveillance)

See "guanzhi" (surveillance).

广泛性，公平性，真实性
guangfanxing, gongpingxing, zhenshixing
(extensiveness, fairness, and authenticity)

See "renquan wenti" (human rights issue).

广州会议
Guangzhou huiyi
(Guangzhou conference)

See "Xinqiao huiyi" (Xinqiao conference).

过渡时期总路线
guodu shiqi zongluxian
(general line for the transitional period)

The CCP put forth a "general line" for the "transitional period" in 1953, which can be summed up as "gradually bringing about socialist industrialization and socialist transformation of agriculture, handicrafts, and capitalist industry and commerce".

The "socialist transformations" of agriculture, handicrafts, and capitalist industry and commerce is called "three great transformations" (san da gaizao). Their completion at the end of 1956, as the CCP announced, marked the beginning of the period of "socialist construction". See also "shehuizhuyi jianshe zongluxian" (General Line for Socialist Construction).

国兴科教
guo xing ke jiao
(revitalize national science and education)

See "ke jiao xing guo" (revitalize China through science and education).

国防文学
guofang wenxue
(national defense literature)

See "sanshiniandai wenyi yundong" (the literature and art movement of the 1930s) and "jiyao" ("Summary").

国际共产主义运动
guoji gongchanzhuyi yundong
(international Communist movement)

See "xiuzhengzhuyi" (revisionism) and "shijie geming" (world revolution).

国际共产主义运动总路线
guoji gongchanzhuyi yundong zongluxian
(general line of the international Communist movement)

See "xiuzhengzhuyi" (revisionism) and "shijie geming" (world revolution).

国际互联网将迎来中国下一个文化大革命
guoji hulianwang jiang yinglai Zhongguo xia yi ge wenhua dageming
(the Internet will lead to China's next Cultural Revolution)

See "xinwen ziyou wenti" (issue of press freedom).

国际社会主义运动
guoji shehuizhuyi yundong
(international socialist movement)

See "shijie geming" (world revolution) and "minzhu dangpai" (democratic parties).

国际主义
guojizhuyi
(internationalism)

See "shijie geming" (world revolution) and "xiuzhengzhuyi" (revisionism).

国家社会主义
guojia shehuizhuyi

(state socialism)

See "daminzhu" (extensive democracy).

国家所有制
guojia suoyouzhi
(state ownership)

See "quanmin suoyouzhi" (ownership by the whole people), "jingji gaige" (economic reform), and "jiejue gongyouzhi xingshi shi you yici sixiang jiefang" (solving the issue of public ownership forms is another emancipation of the mind).

国家调节市场，市场引导企业
guojia tiaojie shichang, shichang yindao qiye
(the state adjusts the market, and the market guides the enterprises)

See "jingji gaige" (economic reform).

国家至上
guojia zhishang
(supremacy of the state)

See "ziyouzhuyi" (liberalism) and "xin baoshouzhuyi" (neo-conservatism).

国情教育
guoqing jiaoyu
(education of national characteristics)

In order to make people (especially the young) understand the country's current situation and adopt an attitude acceptable to the Party, the authorities would from time to time carry out an "education of national characteristics" campaign. This is a kind of "patriotic education".

When such an education campaign is carried out, China critics observe, conservative forces are dominant. This was clearly seen in the education campaign carried out after the June 4th Incident of 1989. For a time, speeches and publications with ossified views were released. Some rigid and unpopular measures were adopted. In the literary and art fields, a new Party document was issued, which ran counter to the idea of "less interference, less involvement" (shao ganyu, shao jieru) in regard to Party leadership over literature and art (the latter idea had been put forward by Zhao Ziyang in the early 1989 document "Some Suggestions from the PCC on How to Promote the Further Enrichment of Literature and Art"). The purpose of the campaign was to prevent an outbreak of "peaceful evolution" (heping yanbian) in China. See also "xiuzhengzhuyi" (revisionism).

国体
guoti
(state system)

See "wuchanjieji zhuanzheng" (dictatorship of the proletariat).

国学
guoxue
(Chinese traditional learning)

The term "guoxue" (or "Zhongxue", as used in the late Qing dynasty) specifically refers to Chinese traditional learning, including studies of China's philosophy, history, archaeology, art, literature, and linguistics in a tradition of several thousand years. For several decades after the founding of the PRC, the term basically disappeared, officially regarded as a synonym for a decadent and moribund traditional culture. In the 1990s, however, such studies have been revived and have become a trend among academics, owing to various political and cultural reasons. One can understand this phenomenon against the background of the current upsurge of nationalism as a mainstream ideology, which supports the efforts by scholars of Chinese traditional learning to resist the "cultural radicalism" (wenhua jijinzhuyi) of the 1980s and the "popular culture" (dazhong wenhua) which gained momentum in the early 1990s. Interestingly, the trend started at Beijing University, a cradle of new, radical thoughts in modern times. On 16 August 1993, eye-catchingly, the *People's Daily* devoted a full page to an enthusiastic report of what it called the "Chinese traditional learning craze" (guoxue re) in the university. "Guoxue" was of course no longer a derogatory term. See also "xin baoshouzhuyi" (neo-conservatism).

国学热
guoxue re
(Chinese traditional learning craze)

See "guoxue" (Chinese traditional learning) and "xin baoshouzhuyi" (neo-conservatism).

"海瑞罢官"批判
Hai Rui Baguan pipan
(the attack on *Hai Rui Dismissed from Office*)

The theatrical work *Hai Rui Dismissed from Office* (*Hai Rui Baguan*, *Beijing wenyi*, 1, 1961; trans. in Edward M. Gunn, ed., *Twentieth-Century Chinese Drama: An Anthology*, Bloomington, Indiana University Press, 1983, pp. 381-99) was written in 1960 by Wu Han, a famous historian and deputy mayor of Beijing. The play was essentially a tribute to Hai Rui, an honest and upright Ming dynasty official, who was tragically dismissed from office because he performed benevolent deeds intolerable to the ruling class while serving as Grand Coordinator in the area of Yingtian. Such deeds included returning the land to the peasants, freeing the unjustly imprisoned, and executing corrupt officials and despots. After its first public performance in Beijing in early 1961, the play received rave reviews. Mao Zedong was an enthusiastic viewer. He praised Wu Han for the text and for achieving a great success in his first Beijing opera work. Mao had his own reasons to be satisfied. In fact, before the play, Wu had written a series of articles focusing on Hai Rui: "Hai Rui Scolds the Emperor" ("Hai Rui ma huangdi"), "Hai Rui" ("Hai Rui"), "Hai Rui: An Upright Official" ("Qingguan Hai Rui"), "The Story of Hai Rui" ("Hai Ruide gushi"), and "On Hai Rui" ("Lun Hai Rui"), and all of them were in response to Mao's call to promote what he considered "the spirit of Hai Rui" at a Party work meeting in Shanghai in early 1959.

However, in 1965, based on his political needs, Mao sacrificed this Beijing opera as part of the power struggle campaign which he intended to launch. On Mao's instructions, Jiang Qing arranged that Zhang Chunqiao and Yao Wenyuan issue an attack in Shanghai. On 10 November 1965, the article, "On the Rewritten Historical Play *Hai Rui Dismissed from Office*" ("Ping xin bian lishiju *Hai Rui baguan*"),was published in Shanghai's *Wenhui Daily*. This article had been concocted secretly eight months earlier, with Yao Wenyuan having written nine drafts, and Mao personally revising it three times. On 21 December 1965, in a talk with Chen Boda and others in Hangzhou, Mao confirmed that Yao's article was "very good" (see Yan Jiaqi and Gao Gao, *Zhongguo "wen'ge" shinian shi—Turbulent Decade: A History of the Cultural Revolution*, Hong Kong, Ta-kung Pao, 1986, p. 12).

Under great pressure, Wu Han had to admit his "mistake". His "Self-criticism Concerning *Hai Rui Dismissed from Office*" ("Guanyu *Hai Rui baguan* de ziwo piping") was published in *Beijing Daily* on 27 December 1965. But this did not help him. He and his wife were both persecuted to death during the GPCR. Their daughter became mentally deranged and died in prison.

The reason Mao chose to criticize the play was Marshal Peng Dehuai's professed identification with Hai Rui, expressed in his words at the 1959 Lushan Conference: "We must not keep silent, we must emulate Hai Rui." Mao singled out the theme of "dismissal from office" as the "crux" of the play. He said: "In the sixteenth century, Emperor Jiajing dismissed Hai Rui from office; in 1959, we dismissed Peng Dehuai from office. Peng is a Hai Rui." (That was why Mao, on the one hand, confirmed that Yao Wenyuan's article was "very good", and, on the other hand, he was not yet completely satisfied with it, for it had not explicitly pointed out what he asserted to be the "crux" of the play. See Yan Jiaqi and Gao Gao, *History*, p. 12.) More profoundly, Mao regarded the reference to the wrongful dismissal of Hai Rui in the play as an attempt not only by Wu Han but also by some powerful figures in the CCP to reverse the verdict on Peng Dehuai, as he could sense at the PCC expanded work conference held in Beijing from 11 January to 7 February 1962. As Mao himself said, if Peng were to be rehabilitated, it would mean that Mao had been wrong and that the "Three Red Banners" should be eliminated. Even worse, it would lead to Mao's stepping down and Liu Shaoqi's taking over his position. So Mao decided that a political movement with "far-reaching significance" should be initiated, and that the criticism of *Hai Rui Dismissed from Office* should be its breakthrough point (tupo kou). With the attack on Wu Han and his play, Mao targeted Peng Zhen and his "impenetrable independent kingdom" (Beijing CCP committee and government), and then Liu Shaoqi and his "bourgeois headquarters" within the Party, as Mao later dubbed it.

Few people expected at the time that the article, "On the Rewritten Historical Play *Hai Rui Dismissed from Office*", would serve as the prelude to the GPCR, an unprecedented nationwide disaster that lasted ten years. After the downfall of the Gang of Four in 1976, the article, because of the fact that it had been approved and revised by Mao personally, remained untouched until the last months of 1978—one of the earliest critiques was "On Yao Wenyuan's 'On the Rewritten Historical Play *Hai Rui Dismissed from Office*'" ("Ping Yao Wenyuan 'Ping xinbian lishi ju *Hai Rui ba guan*'", *GMRB*, 15 Nov. 1978) by the critic Su Shuangbi. The Play *Hai Rui Dismissed from Office* was not restaged until February 1979, when it was performed by the Beijing Opera Troupe of Beijing. See also "Peng Dehuai shijian" (Peng Dehuai Incident) and "qiqianren dahui" (7,000-person meeting).

海外华人
haiwai huaren
(overseas Chinese)

It is estimated that "haiwai huaren" in the world number 57 million, with assets of 2 to 3 thousand billion U.S. dollars. The term "overseas Chinese economic circle" (haiwai huaren jingjiquan) indicates their economic strength, which is said to rank third in the world. Some scholars, especially those in the PRC, find these estimates somewhat exaggerated. But there is no denying the fact that since China began its reform and open-door program in 1978, about 80 percent of the total direct investment in Chinese mainland (11.3 billion U.S. dollars in 1992, for example) came from "huaren" overseas, including Hong Kong, Macao, Taiwan, Singapore and, Thailand, and they have greatly helped promote China's economic development.

For Westerners, the role played by "haiwai huaren" is difficult to understand; first of all, the term itself is somewhat ambiguous. In the past, few used the term "huaren" or "haiwai huaren". Instead, the term "huaqiao" or "haiwai huaqiao" (as distinct from "gui guo huaqiao"—"returned overseas Chinese") was employed to include all Chinese or even part-Chinese outside of China. But grouping together all those of Chinese descent as "overseas Chinese" is ambiguous. Then there was a distinction between "huaqiao" and "huaren". The term "huaqiao" refers to Chinese nationals (including those from the PRC and Taiwan, and also Hong Kong and Macao residents without the right of abode elsewhere) who have left to live abroad, and "huaren" refers to ethnic Chinese with foreign nationalities or foreign permanent residence rights. Nevertheless, the problem has not yet been completely resolved. As Wang Gungwu, a famous scholar on the overseas Chinese, points out, there is often a difference between the terminology used in the sending country and that used in the receiving country. China uses the mixed term "huaqiao-huaren" as a kind of continuum, while the receiving countries often cannot decide what they think of their Chinese immigrants. They vacillate between using terms like "overseas Chinese" indiscriminately and employing national labels that show acceptance of those of Chinese descent (Wang Gungwu, "Upgrading the Migrant: Neither Huaqiao nor Huaren", paper presented at the ISSCO Conference, HKU, 19 Dec. 1994).

For whatever reason, all countries receiving migrants have similar expectations of their new citizens. Each in its own way recognizes the ethnic Chinese as their own nationals. They all hope that an upgrading of status will be rewarded with contributions to the national economy and to social and cultural life, and eventually with total political loyalty to the adopted country. In this context, Wang argues, there is no room for terms like "huaqiao" (except for those who remain citizens of China); even "huaren" is not appropriate, at least not for long, nor is the extended use of the combined "huaqiao-huaren" term. From the point of view of the receiving countries, if the Chinese migrants have been upgraded, they are neither "huaqiao" nor "huaren".

Placed together with the use of the term "overseas Chinese" to include all Chinese in the world outside of the PRC, Wang continues, "there is the alarming sense of outreach and extension of an unstoppable force" (ibid.).

In this regard, Professor Samuel Huntington is very critical of the Chinese government's policy concerning overseas Chinese affairs. In his controversial book *The Clash of Civilizations and the Remaking of World Order,* he states poignantly: "To the Chinese government, people of Chinese descent, even if citizens of another country, are members of the Chinese community and hence in some measure subject to the authority of the Chinese government" (p. 169).

Wang Gungwu's question is: If nationals of Chinese descent take an active part in politics as a matter of course, is it not anachronistic to retain terms such as "huaren"? He suggests from the evidence so far that the fuller the participation in national politics of the "huaren", the sooner the concept will be diluted and replaced. If the idea of "hua" is to remain, the term "huayi", foreign citizen of Chinese origin, will preserve the link. To justify himself, Wang raises the following cases for consideration: "If some new Chinese-Americans are less than loyal, they could find themselves acting as agents for a rejuvenated and expanding China. On the other hand, if the enthusiasm for the U.S. is real, those who share it might prefer to be bearers of the political culture of liberal democracy and human rights to the Chinese in China. The first kind of action would mean that they remain Chinese loyal to China, no matter what their nationality. The second would suggest that they are ready to be patriotic Americans who see the political reform of China as a legitimate American cause. In either case, these are serious problems for both China and the U.S. governments. It is doubtful, under such circumstances, if terms like 'huaqiao' and 'huaren' are adequate to describe what they stand for" (ibid.).

海外华人经济圈
haiwai huaren jingjiquan
(overseas Chinese economic circle)

See "haiwai huaren" (overseas Chinese).

海洋文明
haiyang wenming
(oceanic civilization)

See "huangtu wenming" (yellow earth civilization) and "*Heshang* shijian" (*River Elegy* Incident).

好人犯错误
haoren fan cuowu
(good persons making mistakes)

According to Mao's doctrine about class and class struggle, there should be a distinction between "good persons making mistakes" and "bad persons doing bad things". The criteria might vary. Usually, "good persons" referred to those with good family backgrounds (i.e., "hongwulei"—the five categories of revolutionary people) who enjoyed the trust of their superiors. When they did something wrong, it could be explained that their intentions were good, and they should be forgiven and given no or light punishment.

Whether one is a "good person making mistakes" or a "bad person doing bad things" can be decided by his/her superiors. In the 1983 campaign to "eliminate spiritual pollution", for instance, both Wang Ruoshui, then deputy editor-in-chief of the *People's Daily*, and Hu Jiwei, then its director, were criticized and lost their posts. But the charge against Wang was more serious than that against Hu, who at that time was regarded as a good person making a mistake.

合二而一
he er er yi
(two combine into one)

See "yi fen wei er" (one divides into two).

和而不独

he er budu
(peace but no independence)

See "Meiguo dui Tai sanbu zhengce" (U.S. "three-nos" Taiwan policy).

和而不统
he er butong
(peace but no reunification)

See "Meiguo dui Tai sanbu zhengce" (U.S. "three-nos" Taiwan policy).

和风细雨
hefeng xiyu
(a gentle breeze and a mild rain)

This means to carry out criticism in a gentle and mild way—like a gentle breeze and a mild rain. The practice was proposed by Mao Zedong in 1957 specifically to handle what he called "contradictions among the people" (renmin neibu maodun). However, because Mao himself tended to amplify class struggle and turn "contradictions among the people" into "contradictions between the people and their enemies" (diwo maodun), the practice was rarely used in actual life. Literary criticism, for example, usually turned out to be political denunciations. See also "zhengque chuli renmin neibu maodun" (correctly handling contradictions among the people).

和平共处
heping gongchu
(peaceful coexistence)

The policy of "peaceful coexistence" was first raised by Lenin after the October Revolution of 1917. The CCP accepted it as a foreign policy of the Chinese government. In 1954, for instance, the Chinese government put forth the "five principles of peaceful coexistence" (heping gongchu wuxiang yuanze).

During the 1960s open polemics between the CCP and the CPSU, the policy of "peaceful coexistence" became an issue of controversy. The CCP asserted that the CPSU leadership headed by Khrushchev advocated a modern revisionist line in the international Communist movement, and that part of the line was Khrushchev's theory of "peaceful coexistence". See also "xiuzhengzhuyi" (revisionism).

和平共处五项原则
heping gongchu wuxiang yuanze
(five principles of peaceful coexistence)

Zhou Enlai, former PRC premier, put forward a five-point foreign policy in the "Agreement on Commerce and Transportation between India and Tibet" signed in Beijing on 27 April 1954. The five points were: 1. mutual respect for each other's sovereignty and territorial integrity; 2. mutual non-aggression; 3. mutual non-interference in each other's internal affairs; 4. equality and mutual benefit; and 5. peaceful coexistence. Later called the "five principles of peaceful coexistence", they were announced by Zhou at the Bandung International Conference, held 18 to 24 April 1955. The "ten principles of the Bandung Conference" were established on the basis of the five principles. These principles have since been accepted by a number of countries as cardinal principles in dealing with international relations. See also "xiuzhengzhuyi" (revisionism).

和平过渡
heping guodu
(peaceful transition)

See "xiuzhengzhuyi" (revisionism).

和平竞赛
heping jingsai
(peaceful competition)

See "xiuzhengzhuyi" (revisionism).

和平演变
heping yanbian
(peaceful evolution)

See "xiuzhengzhuyi" (revisionism).

和平与发展是当今世界的两大主题
heping yu fazhan shi dangjin shijiede liang da zhuti
(peace and development are the two themes of today's world)

The assertion, "Peace and development are the two themes of today's world", was put forth by Deng Xiaoping on 4 March 1985 when meeting Japanese friends. More specifically, in the global strategy, peace is an East-West issue and development is a North-South issue.

Up to the early 1980s, CCP leaders were haunted by the view that a world war was unavoidable and China must prepare for an early outbreak of war, either a large-scale war or a nuclear war. But at the enlarged CMC meeting held in Beijing 23 May to 6 June 1985, Deng, then CMC chairman, announced that the size of the PLA would be reduced by one million. This policy change was made on the grounds that in today's world the forces of peace had increased over the forces for war and it was unlikely that a big war would occur within a fairly long period.

In light of this conclusion, Deng asked the people to seize firmly the "historical opportunity once in a century" (bainian buyude lishi jiyu) and do a good job in domestic construction. Later, during his early 1992 "Southern tour", Deng further advanced the following thesis: "Development is the most essential criterion" (fazhan caishi ying daoli). This thesis has since often been cited by China's reformists.

At the 15th CCP National Congress held in September 1997, Jiang Zemin echoed Deng's view about the current world situation. "The trend toward multipolarity has further developed globally or regionally in the political, economic and other fields. World forces are experiencing a new split and realignment," he noted, adding that the development of the trend toward multipolarity contributes to world peace, stability and prosperity. For a fairly long period of time to come, it will be possible to avert a new world war and secure a favorable, peaceful international environment.

Deng's assertion about the age of peace and development, though explained in only a few sentences, is generally considered to have great significance, even greater than the whole big book *On Imperialism*. Of course, many Leftists still do not find it convincing, especially when certain international problems come up. They believe today is still the age of imperialism, i.e., the age of world revolution of the proletariat. See also "Deng Xiaoping lilun" (Deng Xiaoping Theory).

和平长入社会主义
heping zhangru shehuizhuyi
(growing peacefully into socialism)

See "xiuzhengzhuyi" (revisionism).

和平主义
hepingzhuyi
(pacifism)

An often-employed label in political-literary campaigns during the Mao period. See "renxing lun" (theory of human nature).

"河殇"论争
Heshang lunzheng
(*River Elegy* debate)

See "*Heshang* shijian" (*River Elegy* Incident).

"河殇"热
Heshang re
(*River Elegy* craze)

See "*Heshang* shijian" (*River Elegy* Incident).

河殇事件
Heshang shijian
(*River Elegy* Incident)

On 11 June 1988, just in the middle of the "year of the dragon" (longnian), *River Elegy*, a television political commentary series, began to be broadcast on the Central Television Station in Beijing. Its general editors were Su Xiaokang and Wang Luxiang. Zhang Gang, Xie Xuanjun, and Yuan Zhiming also took part in the preparation of the material. The director was Xia Jun. The advisors were Jin Guantao and Li Yining. These were all people with considerable academic achievements. Some had already enjoyed fame both at home and abroad.

As a deliberate choice made by its originators, the ideological content of *River Elegy* was made the primary element, more important than the scenery, background music, dialog, etc. Consisting of six episodes—"In Quest of the Dream" ("Xun meng"), "Fate" ("Mingyun"), "Spiritual Enlightenment" ("Lingguang"), "The Opening of a New Era" ("Xin jiyuan"), "Worries and Anxieties" ("Youhuan"), and "Deep Blue" ("Weilinse")—the series centers around a political commentary that takes as its background the historical and poetic aspects revealed by a backward look over the whole course of Chinese history as it developed during several thousand years along the Yellow River. Using the river as its connecting thread, the series conveys some deep thoughts of contemporary scholars on Chinese history, culture, and society, in order to indicate the historical fate of the Sinitic civilization as examined from a large-scale view of the history of human civilization as a whole.

The work, a unique and ambitious TV project, provided much food for thought. It immediately elicited an enormous response that far exceeded expectations, from viewers of all walks of life. The Central Television Station received more than one thousand letters requesting that the series be re-run (it later re-ran the series in August of the same year). There were also several hundred requests for videotape copies. It was also broadcast on many local stations. The Shanghai Television Station carried it on six successive evenings at prime time. At the same time, at least eight newspapers printed the full text or part of the work. This led to a great deal of feedback, culminating in what was called the "*River Elegy* craze", which focused on another upsurge in the intense search for "culture", a great mass fervor emerging in the latter half of 1984 but suppressed in the 1987 anti-liberalization campaign.

The emergence of *River Elegy* was certainly of great significance. It might be something of an exaggeration to say that the series inaugurated the first "enlightenment movement" to occur since "May 4th" of 1919. But its supporters emphasized that the thought content underlying the work was drawn from intellectual circles throughout the country and was based upon the concern felt by the cultural *élite*. As He Xilai, a critic, said, *River Elegy* would not have been produced if Chinese intellectuals had not been pondering these issues over the past ten years (He Xilai, "Zhexue sixiang yu xingxiangde jiehe"—"A Combination of Philosophical Thinking and Artistic Image", *WYB*, 16 July 1988, reprinted in *XHWZ*, 9:120, 1988). They acclaimed the series as "not only demonstrating that a cultural *élite* with an independent scholarly awareness had already been formed, but also showing the achievements of their independent reflections on the fate of the nation" (quoted from Qi Fang, "Dui *Heshang* ji qi taolun zhi wo jian"—"My View on *River Elegy* and Its Discussion", *Qiushi*, 8, 1988, reprinted in *XHWZ*, 12:129, 1988). Tian Benxiang, another critic, suggested that, when appraising *River Elegy*, one should not concentrate on its arguments concerning specific academic issues (the series, in fact, does not intend to provide academic conclusions); but on the poetic passion and the critical, rational spirit it has manifested (Tian Benxiang, "*Heshang* lun"—"On *River Elegy*", *Qiushi*, 8:30, 1988).

However, as Li Zehou pointed out, the backwardness of China today should not simply be ascribed to its cultural problem. *River Elegy*'s treatment of traditional Chinese culture, which constituted an "intellectual backlash against the culture as a whole" and led to the conclusion that it had been "in decline", was intolerable to many other scholars, both at home and abroad. In the hot debate that followed, the series was accused of regarding Chinese civilization as a predestined backward and bad "yellow earth civilization" (huangtudi wenming), or a "Yellow River civilization" (Huanghe wenming), or a "yellow civilization" (huangse wenming), in contrast to the predestined advanced and good "oceanic civilization" (haiyang wenming), or the "blue civilization" (weilanse wenming), of the West. This was said to be an untenable theory of "geographical environments as a decisive factor" (dili huanjing jueding lun).

Even those who approved of the criticism of the "conservativeness" and "closeness" of the Chinese tradition had to point out that, academically, the work was problematic, damaged by its emotionality and oversimplification. People also observed that there was an inherent split of values: it advocated, on the one hand, strong nationalism and, on the other, a clear inclination to Westernization. This was precisely a characteristic of the long dominant ideological trend since the "May 4th" period of 1919.

But the *River Elegy* debate was also a political incident. What aroused the ire of the CCP's extreme conservatives, for instance, was the fact that the series ignored the "great achievements" of the revolution under the leadership of the CCP. Accordingly, it did not mention at all the 1941-42 Yan'an Rectification Movement, which is regarded by the CCP as the "second movement for the emancipation of thought" in modern Chinese history. (For the three movements to "emancipate thinking", see Zhou Yang, "San ci weidade sixiang jiefang yundong"—"Three Great Movements to Emancipate Thinking", *RMRB,* 7 May 1979, reprinted in *XHYB, WZB,* 1-9, 1979.) In fact, the series contains sequences that criticize some views about history and society advocated by "revolutionary leaders", and implies that what the CCP has done is questionable. For instance, it evokes Plekhanov (1856-1918), known as the "Father of Russian Marxism". Plekhanov firmly supported the Marxist theory of the impossibility of skipping over any necessary stage of historical development, which negates any premature seizure of political power. He felt that any undue haste in trying to bring about socialism would lead to the most serious kind of economic disaster. The work makes it clear that the doubts entertained by Plekhanov have been taken up by history. It is not history that has to give way; those who try to transcend history are ultimately unable to escape punishment, as can be seen from what has happened in the Soviet Union, China, and the East European bloc. Now, one by one, they all have had to embark upon the path of reform.

The series flatly rejects Mao's view of the role of peasant uprisings in history. According to Mao, "it was the class struggles of the peasants, the peasant uprisings and peasant wars that constituted the real motive force of historical development in Chinese feudal society" ("The Chinese Revolution and the Chinese Communist Party", *SWM,* 2, p. 308). The authors of *River Elegy,* however, find the reality very different from that represented by Mao. The result of peasant insurrections was not to strike a blow against the feudal regime of the time, and thereby, also to stimulate the development of the forces of production in society. On the contrary, their real historical significance was only to reveal the astounding destructive force and cruelty that they had caused. Since this theory of Mao is part of the basic core of Mao Zedong Thought, the criticism of it in the series is deadly. If this point were to be accepted by China's historical-ideological circles, as critics pointed out, all the current textbooks of Chinese history would have to be rewritten.

The authors of *River Elegy* show deep concern about the present reform in China (to a certain extent, the authors were encouraged by the current success of the reportage literature and tried to make use of television programs to promote economic-political reform, or, in other words, to be involved in politics). In view of the serious corruption in society and above all within the CCP, they remind their viewers that the monopoly of power by administrators and the power of the privileged classes to allocate products can arbitrarily destroy the socialist system of ownership and, moreover, poison the morale of the ruling Party and of society. They worry: anyone who holds any kind of power can easily transform the right of using or the right of administering into a right of owning, and thus can transform state property into that of a department or of an individual. This implies that a bureaucratic-capitalist class has emerged in today's China, and it is a great danger to the reform.

In fact, by the summer of 1988, China's reform, the focus of which at the time was price reform, had met with unprecedented difficulties and setbacks. Zhao Ziyang, CCP general secretary, had to obey orders from Deng Xiaoping and could not carry out his own ideas effectively. The theory of "the primary stage of socialism", which

Zhao enthusiastically advocated at the 1987 CCP 13th National Congress (see Zhao Ziyang, "Yanzhe you Zhongguo tesede shehuizhuyi daolu qianjin"—"Advancing Along the Road of Socialism with Chinese Characteristics", *HQ*, 21:3-27, 1987), did not seem to help much, either. Perhaps, even Zhao himself realized that his effort to promote a market economy would not succeed as long as property rights remained vague. In this regard, the authors of *River Elegy* tried to provide a solution. They pointed out that only with the development of healthy markets could the three elements of equality, opportunity, and competition be linked together. If competition did not have social equality as a precondition, the sort of price deregulation that conformed with the rules of a commodity economy would, instead, only bring about economic instability and chaos. It would also lead to panic, and might even result in social upheaval. They mentioned the failure of the reforms of Wang Anshi eight hundred years earlier and of Tan Sitong ninety years earlier, warning that these tragedies could be re-enacted *(Heshang*, Joint Publishing Co., 1988, p. 71).

The authors of the series wanted to see the reformists in the CCP develop and carry out more liberal policies. According to their view, up to the present, the reforms had done little more than "sprinkle a few drops of water from the deep blue-coloured oceanic civilization over the parched yellow earth". Indeed, the main message conveyed by this stirring and stimulating series was very clear: the need to reform, to discard what is outmoded and seek what is new, to break through and sweep away all the obstacles that block China's modernization, to select both material and spiritual things from all over the world that will be useful for the Chinese people. As the work concludes: Turn away from the old and concentrate on the new; any other course will lead to death and disaster.

Extreme conservatives feared these ideas. Indeed, if it was normal for a TV series like *River Elegy* to create controversy, the escalated attacks on it were certainly abnormal. The most fierce accusation came from Wang Zhen, then PRC vice-president. At a conference in Ningxia on 27 September 1988, he alleged that *River Elegy* insulted the Yellow River and the Great Wall and slandered the great Chinese people.

Significantly, a confrontation between two groups of top CCP leaders eventually developed, caused by divergences in opinion about *River Elegy*. Zhao Ziyang distinguished himself from the hardliners, such as Wang Zhen. He held that the series was worth watching (he even gave it as a present to Lee Kuan Yew, the visiting prime minister of Singapore). He vetoed the publication of an article critical of the series (see the editor's note preceding Yi Jiayan, "*Heshang* xuanyangle shenme?"—"What Does *River Elegy* Preach?", *RMRB, HWB,* 19 July 1989). Hu Qili, then a member of the Politburo Standing Committee, was of a similar opinion. In an interview with the *New Perspectives Quarterly,* an American publication, he made the following remark:

"Generally speaking, this TV series is a good one. It is conducive to reform. There are drawbacks, though. A film or work of art should take a more analytical attitude towards the heritage of a country. A more analytical attitude would discard the dross but not the essence of our inheritance. Of course, we cannot expect any TV series to be perfect. It is a good thing that people have different opinions on this film. I think the controversy over this TV series is itself the success" (quoted from Frederic Wakeman, Jr., "All the Rage in China", *The New York Review of Books*, 2 Mar. 1989, p. 19).

After the June 4th Incident of 1989, the series became the first work subjected to fierce attack; even videotapes of it were publicly destroyed by a steam roller. See also "wenhua re" (culture craze).

何新爱国宣言
He Xin aiguo xuanyan
(He Xin's patriotism declaration)

See "He Xin xuanfeng" (He Xin whirlwind).

何新现象
He Xin xianxiang
(He Xin phenomenon)

See "He Xin xuanfeng" (He Xin whirlwind).

何新旋风
He Xin xuanfeng
(He Xin whirlwind)

On 11 December 1990, eye-catchingly, the *People's Daily* devoted two and a quarter pages (beginning from its front page) to an article by He Xin entitled "The World Economic Situation and China's Economic Issues—A Dialog between He Xin and Economics Professor S of Japan" ("Shijie jingji xingshi yu Zhongguo jingji wenti—He Xin yu Riben jingjixue jiaoshou S de tanhualu"). After its publication, according to Sun Yongren, director of the Theory Department of the *People's Daily*, who was in charge of this matter, a "large-scale, multi-leveled, and long-lasting sensational effect" was aroused among the readership at home and abroad. Within a month or more, they received about a thousand letters, of which over 98 percent supported He's viewpoints. A "He Xin whirlwind" was strongly blowing (Sun Yongren, "He Xin xuanfeng: He Xin wenzhang fabiao jingguo ji qi yingxiang"—"The He Xin Whirlwind: The Publication and the Influence of He Xin's Article", in He Xin, *Zhi Zhongnanhai Miza/Wei Zhongguo Shengbian—Letters Eyes only for Zhongnanhai and an Argument to Justify the Chinese Cause*, HK, Mingjing, Feb. 1997, pp. 62-84).

He's article was favorably described by official departments as a "patriotism declaration" (aiguo xuanyan). The "He Xin whirlwind" was a "whirlwind of patriotism".

He Xin was born in Wenzhou, Zhejiang province in December 1949. He was sent to work in the countryside in 1968 when he was a secondary school graduate. In 1980, two years after returning to Beijing, he entered the prestigious CASS and began his scholarly career. He was promoted to assistant research fellow in 1985, associate research fellow in 1987, and research fellow in 1989. In the autumn of 1991, he became a full-time member of the CPPCC. The fields of his research were wide and various, and he could be said to be a productive, and often controversial, writer. In particular, he played a unique role in the transformation from neo-authoritarianism to neo-conservatism, which took place among China's thinking public in the early 1990s. Interestingly, He Xin not only disdained neo-authoritarianism, he also refused the title of neo-conservative. He preferred to be a spokesman of nationalism.

But his most conspicuous hallmark was that his reports promptly reached top Party leaders. As a scholar, admittedly, no one exerted more influence than He Xin on the Zhongnanhai rulers on economic-political issues in the few years following the June 4th Incident of 1989. He Xin was unique and at the same time typical of a certain group of Chinese intellectuals. This was called the "He Xin phenomenon" (He Xin xianxiang), itself also an interesting topic of study. See also "xin baoshouzhuyi" (neo-conservatism).

黑
hei
(black)

See "hong" (red).

黑八论
hei ba lun
(eight sinister theories)

See "jiyao" ("Summary") and "hong" (red).

黑六论
hei liu lun
(six sinister theories)

During the GPCR, Liu Shaoqi was accused of advocating "six sinister theories":

1. The theory of "the dying out of class struggle" (jieji douzheng ximie lun). After the mid-1950s, Liu had a view that major class struggle in China had been basically over or basically solved.

2. The theory of being "docile tools" (xunfu gongju lun). Liu was accused of advocating this theory in many of his works, including *On the Self-Cultivation of Communists (Lun Gongchandangyuande Xiuyang,* July 1939) and "Training in Organization and Discipline" ("Zuzhi jilü xunlian", 1941).

3. The theory that "the masses are backward" (qunzhong luohou lun). This was said to be found in Liu's works, such as "A Concise History of Workers Movement in China" ("Zhongguo gongren yundong jianshi", May 1939) and "The Class Character of Man" ("Rende jiejixing", June 1941). Liu was accused of opposing what Mao said were the two cardinal principles—to have faith in the masses and in the Party.

4. The theory of "entering the Party in order to be an official" (ru dang zuo guan lun). Liu's report to the 1st national organizational work conference in March 1951 was found to have advocated this theory, which was "a vain attempt to corrode the souls of our Communist Party members".

5. The theory of "inner-Party peace" (dangnei heping lun). This was chiefly found in Liu's speech, entitled "On Inner-Party Struggle" ("Lun dangnei douzheng"), on 2 and 3 July 1941 at the Party School of the CCP's Central China Bureau. In his speech, Liu declared that he opposed those inner-Party struggles that were mechanical, unprincipled, and intemperate. He opined that it was necessary to make all possible compromise. During the GPCR, the theory was said to "strangle the revolutionary nature of Party members".

6. The theory of "merging private and public interests" (gong si ronghua lun). This theory, also known as "taking small losses for the sake of big gains" (chi xiao kui, zhan da pianyi), was said to have been advocated by Liu in a talk in February 1960 with leaders of the Chinese Association for the Founding of a Democratic Nation (Zhongguo Minzhu Jianguohui) and the Chinese National Association of Industry and Commerce (Zhongguo Quanguo Gongshangye Lianhehui). Liu told his listeners to make small concessions so as to achieve large gains and avoid suffering great losses.

Liu Shaoqi's most important work is *On the Self-Cultivation of Communists.* Originally a speech of July 1939 at the Yan'an Marxism-Leninism Institute, its first revised edition was published by Beijing's People's Publishing House in August 1949. In September 1962, its second revised edition was published. At the same time, *Red Flag*, the PCC magazine, carried its full text in the combined issues of Nos. 15 and 16, 1962. Many of Liu's ideas, especially his so-called "docile tools" theory, can be found in this book. This is why this book was attacked during the GPCR as "sinister *Self-Cultivation*" (hei "xiuyang"). After Liu was officially rehabilitated at the 5th Plenum of the 11th PCC on 29 February 1980, his position and contributions in CCP history was reconfirmed. His articles were republished, many collected in *Liu Shaoqi on Party Building (Liu Shaoqi on Dangde Jianshe)* and *Selected Works of Liu Shaoqi (Liu Shaoqi Xuanji,* 1 & 2, Beijing, Renmin, Dec. 1981 & Dec. 1985). "On the Self-Cultivation of Communists" *(Liu Shaoqi Xuanji,* 1, pp. 97-167), in particular, was considered to be a "brilliant work" of important significance, especially against the background of the universal corruption in the Party today.

黑修养
hei xiuyang
(sinister book *Self-Cultivation)*

See "hei liu lun" (six sinister theories).

黑帮
heibang
(reactionary gang)

See "hong" (red).

黑材料
heicailiao
(black materials)

See "hong" (red).

黑会
heihui
(black meetings)

See "hong" (red).

黑九类
heijiulei
(nine kinds of black elements)

See "hong" (red) and "sileifenzi" (four kinds of elements).

黑幕文学
heimu wenxue
(sinister project literature)

China has witnessed breakneck growth with reform and open-door policies carried out for two decades. But breakneck growth is socially destabilizing. Today, money worship, hedonism, widespread corruption, rising crime, and huge floating populations of unemployed in the big cities are rampant. People are gravely concerned about social evils and problems. Sinister project literature is thus popular. One of the noted works of this new genre was *The Wrath of God: A Mayor's Severe Crime (Tiannu: Shizhang Yao'an)*, a novel by Fang Wen (the pen name of Chen Feng), a 53-year-old Beijing-based writer of fiction as well as film and TV scripts. Though published by an obscure "Yuanfang" (meaning "distant place") Publishing House of Inner Mongolia, the 5,000 copies of its first printing sold out immediately after its release in January 1997. It was soon banned by the authorities, but various pirated versions found their way to the market—reportedly 5 million copies were reprinted within two years. In August 1998, the author published a new and much enlarged version of this novel (together with its sequel running into more than 7 hundred thousand Chinese characters), under the title *The Wrath of God, the Resentment of the people (Tiannu Renyuan)*. Chen Feng had to have his new work published outside the mainland by the Pacific Century Press of Hong Kong. The reasons for its ban as well as for its popularity were the same: it is closely based on the recent corruption cases involving Wang Baosen, former Beijing deputy major in charge of day-to-day business who committed suicide in early April 1995 for his alleged economic crimes, and of Chen Xitong, former CCP Politburo member and Beijing Party secretary who was purged and arrested for his involvement in the Wang Baosen case and for his own alleged economic crimes (see "Chen Xitong shijian"—Chen Xitong Incident). In fact, the subtitle of *The Wrath of God, the Resentment of the people* is: Jiang Zemin vs Chen Xitong.

The attraction of this sort of story was justly felt in literary circles. Writing of this genre became increasingly popular. Many critics agreed: The vanguard literature and the riffraff literature have disappeared; now it is time for the "sinister project" literature. See also "fan fubai" (anti-corruption), "zhengzhi gaige" (political reform), and "jingji gaige" (economic reform).

黑手
heishou
(black hands)

See "hong" (red).

黑四类
heisilei
(four kinds of black elements)

See "hong" (red) and "sileifenzi" (four kinds of elements).

黑五类
heiwulei
(five kinds of black elements)

See "hong" (red) and "sileifenzi" (four kinds of elements).

黑线专政论
heixian zhuanzheng lun
("dictatorship of a sinister line" theory)

See "jiyao" ("Summary") and "wuchanjieji zhuanzheng" (dictatorship of the proletariat).

横扫一切牛鬼蛇神
hengsao yiqie niuguisheshen
(sweep away all monsters and demons)

The issuance of the 16 May 1966 Party document, "Circular of the Central Committee of the CCP" ("Zhongguo Gongchandang Zhongyang Weiyuanhui tongzhi"), to the whole Party marked the beginning of the GPCR. On 30 May, Liu Shaoqi, Zhou Enlai, and Deng Xiaoping suggested to Mao Zedong that Chen Boda, as the leader of the Central GPCR Group, be sent to supervise the *People's Daily* and all journalistic work. Mao approved immediately and Chen began his new job. The first of his accomplishments was the publication of a *People's Daily* editorial on 1 June 1966, under the eye-catching title: "Sweep Away All Monsters and Demons" ("Hengsao yiqie niuguisheshen").

Thereafter, in the early days of the GPCR, "sweep away all monsters and demons" was frequently used as a slogan. "Niuguisheshen", or "monsters and demons", referred to class enemies of all descriptions, that is, the "nine kinds of black elements" as they were later dubbed. See also "sileifenzi" (four kinds of elements) and "wen'ge" (Cultural Revolution).

轰动效应
hongdong xiaoying
(sensational effect)

During the "new period", along with the great changes in politico-social life, there appeared a number of literary works which reflected the changes and exerted a "sensational effect" on a large readership in the country. In its early stage, many of these works were in the genre of fiction, such as "The Class Teacher" (Liu Xinwu, "Ban zhuren", *RMWX,* 11, 1977, reprinted in *Quanguo Youxiu Duanpian Xiaoshuo Ji—A Collection of Chinese Best Short Stories;* Jiangsu, Renmin, 1979, pp. 1-27; trans. in *CL,* 1:15-35, 1979, and Geremie Barmé and Bennett Lee, eds., *The Wounded: New Stories of the Cultural Revolution 1977-1978*, Hong Kong, Joint Publishing Co., 1979, pp. 147-178), "The Scar" (Lu Xinhua, "Shanghen", *WHB,* 11 August 1978; trans. in *CL,* 1, 1979 and in Geremie Barmé and Bennett Lee, eds., *The Wounded*, pp. 9-24), "A Legend of the Tianyun Mountain", "Manager Qiao Assumes Office", "At Middle Age" (Shen Rong, ""Ren dao zhongnian", *Shouhuo,* 1, 1980, reprinted in *Shen Rong Ji—Works of Shen Rong,* Fuzhou, Haixia Wenyi, 1986, pp. 149-236, and in *XWY*, *Novelettes,* 1, pp. 136-88; trans. in *CL,* 10, 1980, in Lee Yee, ed., *The New Realism*, pp. 142-94, and in Perry Link, ed., *Roses and Thorns,* pp. 261-338), *Humanity!,* and "Wreaths at the Foot of the High Mountains" (Li Cunbao, "Gaoshanxiade huahuan", *SY,* 6, 1982)—just to mention a few on a long list. Later, in particular in 1988, which was dubbed the year of "reportage literature fever", more works of reportage literature aroused huge repercussions. Among them were, for example, "Going Abroad: A Great Trend" (Hu Ping and Zhang Shengyou, "Shijie dachuanlian", *DD,* 1, 1988), "Forest-destroyers, Wake Up!" (Xu Gang, "Famuzhe, xinglai", *Xin guancha,* 2, 1988), "Migrants in Western China" (Mai Tianshu, "Xibu zai yimin", *RMWX,* 5, 1988, reprinted in *XHWZ,* 10:98-119, 1988), "Wang Shiwei and 'The Wild Lily'" (Dai Qing, "Wang Shiwei he 'Ye baihehua'",

Wenhui yuekan, 5:22-41, 1988), *On the Altar of "Utopia"—1959 Summer in Lushan Mountain* (Su Xiaokang, Luo Shixu, and Chen Zheng, *'Wutuobang' Ji: 1959 Nian Lushan Zhi Xia,* Beijing, Zhongguo Xinwen, Nov. 1988), "Sea Burial" (Qian Gang, "Haizang", *Jiefangjun wenyi,* 1, 1989), and *White Snow, Red Blood* (Zhang Zhenglong, *Xue bai xue hong,* Beijing, Jiefangjun, Aug. 1989). As Su Xiaokang pointed out, it was because problem-centered reportage literature emerged and caused a sensational effect that fiction lost the popularity in China that it had enjoyed earlier. This was something unavoidable; something not to be decided by literature itself (Su Xiaokang et al., "1988: a dialog on reportage literature", *Huacheng,* 6:10, 1988). See also "shanghen wenxue" (scar literature), and "yi wenti wei zhongxinde baogao wenxue" (problem-centered reportage literature).

红
hong
(red)

In the CCP lexicon, "hong" means "revolutionary", "socialist-minded", or "loyal to the Party". Hence "hongweibing" (Red Guards), "hongse kongbu" (Red Terror—as seen during the GPCR), "you hong you zhuan" (both red and expert, or, both socialist-minded and professionally proficient), "hongqi" (red flag—revolutionary banner), "hongse zhengquan" (revolutionary regime), "hongse jiangshan" (revolutionary regime), etc. As acknowledged in the GPCR, there were "five categories of revolutionary people" (hongwulei)—workers, poor and lower-middle peasants, revolutionary cadres, revolutionary armymen, and revolutionary martyrs. Their children were described as "genzheng miaohong" (good roots and shoots—revolutionary offspring). During the 1960s and 1970s when the CCP attacked the alleged "revisionist line" of the CPSU, there was a popular saying: "weixing shangtian, hongqi luodi" (Satellites have been launched while the red flag has fallen)—meaning that the Soviet Union has changed its colors though it has achieved much in science and technology. During the first few years after the end of the GPCR, the *People's Daily* was active in correcting the Party's past mistakes and thus very popular. In contrast, the magazine *Red Flag* was conservative and unpopular. Hence the new saying: "renmin shangtian, hongqi luodi". Though literally, "renmin" refers to "Renmin Ribao" *(the People's Daily)* and "hongqi" refers to "Hongqi Zazhi" *(Red Flag),* there was a strong implication—"The people have risen while the red flag has fallen".

In contrast to "hong", the Chinese character "bai" (white) means "reactionary", as in "baijun" (the White Army, that is, the KMT army), "baiqu" (areas under KMT rule), and "baise kongbu" (the "White Terror", that is, the brutality and persecution by the KMT to the Communists. The brutality and persecution during the GPCR were also damned as "White Terror", though they were hailed as "Red Terror" by their makers and their supporters at the time (today "Red Terror" is also used ironically, or implying a negation of the GPCR). "White" also implies "apolitical" as in "baizhuan" (apolitical specialization).

Interestingly, in the CCP lexicon, not only "bai" but also "hei" (black) can be used as the antithesis of "hong". "Hei" means "wicked, sinister, reactionary, anti-Party, anti-people, and anti-socialism, or, counter-revolutionary". Hence "heisilei" (four kinds of black elements—landlords, rich peasants, counter-revolutionaries and bad elements, people singled out for attack in the early days of the Communist regime); "heiwulei" (five kinds of black elements—"heisilei" plus Rightists, people singled out for attack since after the 1957 anti-Rightist campaign); "heijiulei" (nine kinds of black elements—"heiwulei" plus traitors, enemy agents, capitalist-roaders and bourgeois intellectuals, people singled out for attack during the GPCR); "heibang" (reactionary gang, that is, a gang consisting of any of the nine kinds of black elements); "heihui" (black meetings, that is, meetings organized and attended by the "reactionary gang" or the "nine kinds of black elements"); "heicailiao" (black material, for instance, documents concocted at black meetings); and "heishou" (black hands—vicious persons manipulating somebody or an event from behind the scenes).

While the political implication of the Chinese character "hei" remains the same today, some derivative terms are no longer used. Take "heiwulei" for example. On 5 April 1978, the PCC decided to "uncap" (tuomao) the Rightists. In accordance with the PCC's decision of 11 January 1979, the label for landlords, rich peasants, counter-revolutionaries, and bad elements was invalidated.

红黑之战
hong hei zhi zhan
(war between the Red and the Black)

See "hong" (red), "liang ge wen'ge lun" ("two Cultural Revolutions" theory), and "wen'ge" (Cultural Revolution).

红八月
hong bayue
(Red August of 1966)

See "hongse kongbu" (Red Terror).

红宝书
hongbaoshu
(treasured red books)

During the GPCR, the four volumes of the *Selected Works of Mao Zedong* were reverently called the "treasured red books", for they recorded the "brilliant Mao Zedong Thought". See "Mao Zedong sixiang" (Mao Zedong Thought).

红代会
hongdaihui
(congress of Red Guards)

See "hongweibing" (Red Guards).

红旗
hongqi
(red banner)

See "hong" (red) and "shijian shi jianyan zhenlide weiyi biaozhun" (practice is the sole criterion for testing truth).

红色江山
hongse jiangshan
(revolutionary regime)

See "hong" (red).

红色经济沙皇
hongse jingji shahuang
(red economic Tsar)

See "jingji shahuang" (economic "Tsar").

红色恐怖
hongse kongbu
(Red Terror)

Soon after the start of the GPCR, inspired by Mao's support, Beijing's Red Guards undertook "revolutionary actions" not only at school but also in society at large. Their slogans were: "It is right to rebel", "Sweep away all monsters and demons", and "Do away with the four olds and cultivate the four news" (see "po sijiu, li sixin"). The brutality reached a high tide in August 1966, which was proudly described as "Red August" (hong bayue). The Red Guards declared that they were making a "Red Terror" and that this was absolutely necessary for the defense of their "Red state power" (hongse jiangshan). According to incomplete statistics, during the period of one month and in Beijing alone, more than 33,000 families were subjected to house searches and confiscation of their property, and more than 1,700 people were beaten to death. Most notorious in the "Red Terror" of August were the Red Guards from the secondary schools attached to Beijing University, Qinghua University, and Beijing Teachers University, the "August First" Secondary School and the 101st Secondary School, all of which were aristocratic schools for children of cadres in the Party and the army.

Beijing Red Guards' "revolutionary actions" quickly became an example for Red Guards all over the country. Indeed, during the GPCR, "hongse kongbu" represented the epitome of the reality at the time. That was a period when tens of millions of people lost control of their fate, when many were tragically persecuted to death in the name of the revolution. The brutality, horror and misery can never be forgotten. In cultural circles, for instance, Deng Tuo, a famous essayist and former director/Editor-in-Chief of the *People's Daily,* was the first victim on the eve of the forthncoming political hurricane. Lao She, a novelist and playwright of international fame, was vice-chairman of the CWA. He left home to be publicly humiliated on a summer day of 1966 and never returned; how he died remains a mystery. After Luo Guangbin, one of the two co-authors of *Red Crag,* a best-seller in the early 1960s, was killed in the thick of the chaos, pictures of his corpse with his skull split into two were widely circulated as evidence of the charge that he had "alienated himself from the people". Tian Han, vice-chairman of the ACF and chairman of the Chinese Dramatists Association, died in prison, bearing the slanderous name of traitor. When public humiliation was more than he could stand, the highly-acclaimed translator Fu Lei committed suicide together with his loyal wife. Zheng Junli, one of the leading film directors in contemporary China, died as the result of a brutal arrest arranged directly by Jiang Qing, only because he knew too much about Jiang's career as a third-rate film star in Shanghai during the 1930s. Ba Ren, a respectable veteran writer and literary theorist, went mad after a long period of persecution and he died in misery. Zhou Xinfang, an outstanding performer who was vice-chairman of the Chinese Dramatists Association and president of the Shanghai Beijing Opera Company, finally reached a breaking point after suffering from humiliation and torture, and he took his own life... These are but a few well-known cases in cultural circles. Other such tragedies are too numerous to number. Moreover, it should be pointed out that, in the extreme zealotry incited by the "modern superstition" (xiandai mixin), few people thought those attacked had been wronged. Very often, even those persecuted were convinced that they were sinners and deserved such humiliation and punishment. That itself was an even more horrifying tragedy. That is why, after the GPCR, many Chinese vowed to draw lessons from the experience and to prevent it from happening again. Ba Jin, for instance, fell into this category. Very sincerely he offered the following testament:

"What other authors in the world in the entire course of history have undergone something so terrifying and ridiculous, so bizarre and agonizing? Practically not a single Chinese author was able to avoid becoming involved. People put on shows, made fools of themselves, were hurt, and even took their own lives. Those who survived, however, learned many important lessons. When I look back at what I said and did, I have great difficulty comprehending it all. I seemed to have been hypnotized into becoming so stupid and naive that cruelty and absurdity came to appear right and proper. I said to myself: If I don't reach some conclusions about those ten years of hardship and suffering, and clarify for myself what actually happened by undergoing a thorough self-examination, then perhaps some day, if the situation suddenly changed again, I might be hypnotized again and for no reason at all turn into another person. What a terrifying thought! That is a debt which lies heavily on my soul: the sooner I pay it back the better. It is as if a whip were lashing at my mind, as if the clock had been turned back fifty years, I hear the words 'Write! Write!' being repeated over and over, as if someone were shouting in my ear" (Ba Jin, "My Life and Literature", *CL*, 1:129, Spring 1984).

Unfortunately, up to the present, no great work has been written by Chinese writers about the historical truth of the GPCR. Serious GPCR studies remain yet to be carried out. See also "wen'ge" (Cultural Revolution) and "wuchanjieji zhuanzheng" (dictatorship of the proletariat).

红色企业家
hongse qiyejia
(red entrepreneurs)

See "hongse zibenjia" (red capitalist).

红色政权
hongse zhengquan
(revolutionary regime)

See "hong" (red).

红色资本家
hongse zibenjia
(red capitalist)

The so-called "red capitalists" refer specifically to those who were owners of private enterprises but supported the CCP even before it seized political power on the mainland. During the Mao period, though sometimes given official positions, they were on the whole in a state of depression. It was Deng's reform and open-door program that reactivated them and enabled them (including their children and grandchildren) to have much bigger business than before.

The most famous among them are Wang Guangying and Rong Yiren. Wang Guangying is brother of Wang Guangmei, the widow of the late PRC President Liu Shaoqi. He was vice-chairman of the Chinese Association for the Founding of a Democratic Nation, vice-chairman of the CPPCC, vice-chairman of the NPC Standing Committee, and honorary chairman of the Executive Committee of the All-China Federation of Industry and Commerce. He was also appointed to the position of board chairman and general manager of the Everbright Group Ltd. and the Everbright Industry Company. Rong Yiren was PRC vice-president from March 1993 till March 1998 when he was replaced by Hu Jintao at the 9th NPC. From 1979 to 1993, Rong headed the China International Trust and Investment Corporation, the biggest state-owned investment company, with an outpost in Hong Kong. In 1999, Rong reportedly ranked first on the list of fifty richest businessmen in mainland China, with assets of over one billion U.S. dollars.

With the growth of private ownership in present-day China, a new generation who may well be called "red capitalists" is emerging. But they do not want to be called "capitalists" or "red capitalists". Instead, they call themselves "red entrepreneurs" (hongse qiyejia). This is also the title the Party confers on them. See also "jingji gaige" (economic reform).

红卫兵
hongweibing
(Red Guards)

On 29 May 1966, the first Red Guard organization was set up at the secondary school attached to Qinghua University in Beijing. (The name "hongweibing" was reportedly first suggested by Zhang Chengzhi, then a student at the school, who is now a well-known fiction writer advocating "Islamic socialism".) This was quickly followed by students at a few other schools in the capital. On 28 July, they sent Mao a letter, together with two "big-character posters" (dazibao) entitled "On the Eternal Spirit of the Proletarian Revolutionary Rebellion" ("Lun wuchanjieji geming zaofan jingshen wansui") and "More on the Eternal Spirit of the Proletarian Revolutionary Rebellion" ("Zailun wuchanjieji geming zaofan jingshen wansui"). Just three days later, on 1 August, Mao answered them and gave them his support. This greatly encouraged these young people, and "Red Guard" organizations (their name "hongweibing" was often preceded by "Mao Zedong sixiang"—"Mao Zedong Thought" or by "Mao Zedong zhuyi"—"Mao Zedong-ism") were set up one after another.

On 18 August 1966, Mao first reviewed the Red Guards from Beijing and other places in the country (by the end of the year, Mao had reviewed thirteen million Red Guards on eight occasions). Responding to Mao's call to bombard the "bourgeois headquarters" and carry on the GPCR through to the end, Red Guards traveled all over the country to exchange "revolutionary experiences" and engage in what they thought to be revolutionary activities—to do away with the "four olds" and cultivate the "four news" and to struggle against alleged "capitalist-roaders" at various levels of the Party and government organizations.

On 2 September 1966, the authorities issued the "Red Guard Organization Regulations", which laid out the principles, nature, tasks, conditions, organizational discipline, badge, and entrance procedures for the Red Guards. Following these regulations, congresses of Red Guards ("hongweibing daibiao dahui", or "hongdaihui" for short) were formed all over the country. The first among them was the Congress of Red Guards of Universities and Colleges in Beijing, which was set up on 22 February 1967. However, not many acted strictly in accordance with the "Regulations", especially in the later days of the GPCR.

After the "January Revolution" of 1967 (see "yiyue geming"), Red Guards of various places were involved in "power seizure" struggles, which developed into a "full-scale civil war", as Mao later described it (see "wengong wuwei"). Armed conflicts between different factions took place almost everywhere in China in 1967 and 1968. The situation became so chaotic that in many places "military control" (junguan) had to be called in (see "sanzhi liangjun"). In the last few months of 1968 when most of students were sent to the countryside to receive what was called "re-education" (zai jiaoyu) from the poor and lower-middle peasants, the Red Guard movement drew to an end. Red Guard organizations were officially abolished on 19 August 1978 in a government document.

It is generally admitted that the Red Guards were a horrible, destructive force during the GPCR. However, as some scholars suggest, the Red Guard movement, like the GPCR, is a complicated issue and merits analysis. One can differentiate two major currents in the movement (see, for instance, Yin Hongbiao of Beijing University, "hongweibing yundongde liang da chaoliu"—"The Two Major Currents in the Red Guard Movement", *ES*, 26-38, Oct. 1992). The first Red Guards were organized to rebel against the "anti-Party and anti-socialist sinister line in educational circles", inspired by Mao's instructions. They were fanatical followers of the "lineage theory" (xuetong lun). Indeed, as many have pointed out, the Red Guards would not have emerged had it not been for this theory. Similar to the saying "Dragons beget dragons, phoenixes beget phoenixes, and those begotten by rats are good at digging holes", the theory claimed that "one will be a true man if his father is a hero, while reactionaries bear only bastards" ("Laozi yingxiong er haohan, laozi fandong er hundan"). That is why many—they called themselves "veteran Red Guards" (lao hongweibing)—later joined the notorious "Capital Red Guards United Action Committee" (see "liandong"). Because their parents were Party officials or army officers (some were very high-ranking), they considered themselves "born red" (zi lai hong), as "natural revolutionary successors" (dangrande geming jiebanren), and posed as masters of the world. Therefore, when engaging in what they called "Red Terror" (hongse kongbu) and cruelly persecuting "niuguisheshen"—class enemies of all descriptions—they also had another slogan: "Only Leftists can enjoy the right to rebel; no Rightists are allowed to change our regime" ("Zhizhun zuopai zaofan, buzhun youpai fantian"). Thus their actions can be seen as the "princes' clique's" first attempt to obtain power (see "taizidang"). Later, for a time, they did have to taste bitterness after their parents were marginalized from their posts (kaobianzhan) or toppled as "capitalist-roaders". But they again enjoyed privileges when their parents were restored to their positions (many of them doubled their efforts to expand their vested interests after being restored to power, as a "lesson" they drew from the GPCR or as "compensation" for their losses and suffering).

Another major current in the Red Guard movement appeared in October 1966. In response to the call from Mao's "proletarian revolutionary headquarters" to criticize and repudiate the "bourgeois reactionary line" (zichanjieji fandong luxian), new Red Guard organizations suddenly mushroomed all over the country. These were different from the "veteran Red Guards". First, calling themselves "rebel Red Guards" (hongweibing zaofanpai), or simply "rebels", they regarded the struggle against "capitalist-roaders" as their "general orientation" (da fangxiang) in the GPCR. In their opinion, "capitalist-roaders" were the "newborn bourgeois elements", who would restore capitalism without changing the name of the Communist Party. Therefore, the contradiction between them and the revolutionaries was the principal contradiction in the socialist period. Moreover, by that time, the Red Guards were no longer only secondary school students. Playing a leading role were students of higher education, who were much more knowledgeable and capable of influencing public opinion. Encouraged by the slogan "let the masses liberate themselves" (rang qunzhong ziji jiefang ziji), which was very popular at the time, many people with a family background not so "red", or who had simply been treated by the Party as "questionable", also organized themselves and established their own Red Guard organizations. Their purpose was to oppose the "natural revolutionary successors" and their parents—bureaucrats in the Communist regime. Indeed, these "rebel Red Guards" may well be described as "Black Guards" (heiweibing). In this sense, the GPCR was also a "war between the Red and the Black" (hong hei zhi zhan) in the entire society.

Needless to say, like the "veteran Red Guards", many of the "rebel Red Guards" were involved in illegal or criminal activities, poisoned by Mao's "struggle philosophy". In some cases, even worse, they were misled by their "bad leaders" (huai toutou), who were careerists with no scruples. The GPCR cultivated a great number of young people who engaged in "beating, smashing, and looting" (da za qiang), and who were so ferocious that, as the saying goes, they had "horns on their heads and spikes on their backs" (toushang sheng jiao, shenshang zhang ci).

Both the "veteran Red Guards" and the "rebel Red Guards" were finally rejected by Mao, though at different times and for different reasons. The former did not understand that Mao had set the "capitalist-roaders" as the major target for his attack, thus quickly turning them into obstacles for Mao's revolution. The latter at first did help Mao and his faction by attacking alleged "capitalist-roaders" of various levels, but they later became increasingly uncontrollable, so much so that Mao had to put an end to their movement. Significantly, after the GPCR, the CCP authorities' treatment towards these two kinds of Red Guards also differed. The "veteran Red Guards" were simply regarded as "anti-GPCR" heroes. Many of them were selected into the "third echelon" (disan-tidui) and then became officials at various levels. Today, some of them engage in commercial activities as company managers or directors, making huge profits from their power or their personal connections. Many of the former rebels, however, have not been so lucky. Some have become dissidents, thus rebelling in a different way. In a sense, as China observers assert, the "war between the Red and the Black" continues today. See also "wen'ge" (Cultural Revolution).

红卫兵代表大会
hongweibing daibiao dahui
(congress of Red Guards)

See "hongweibing" (Red Guards).

红卫兵心态
hongweibing xintai
(Red Guard mentality)

In 1986, when responding to the young critic Liu Xiaobo's criticism, Li Zehou accused Liu of possessing what Li described as a "Red Guard mentality". One of its manifestations was, by "negating all", trying to establish oneself as the "No. 1 authority under heaven" (laozi tianxia diyi), and as the only one holding the truth. This was something like those Red Guards inspired by the slogan "Suspect all, overthrow all" (huaiyi yiqie, dadao yiqie). Li said that he did not totally negate the Red Guards and the Red Guard movement in the GPCR. Even the GPCR itself deserved careful analysis. See also "huaiyi yiqie, dadao yiqie" (suspect all, overthrow all).

红卫兵造反派
hongweibing zaofanpai
(rebel Red Guards)

See "hongweibing" (Red Guards).

红卫兵运动的两大潮流
hongweibing yundongde liang da chaoliu
(two major currents in Red Guard movement)

See "hongweibing" (Red Guards).

红五类
hongwulei
(five categories of revolutionary people)

See "hong" (red).

红线
hongxian
(red line)

See "dangde jiaoyu fangzhen" (the Party's educational policy) and "hong" (red).

红小兵
hongxiaobing
(red little soldiers)

During the GPCR, organizations of "Red Little Soldiers" were set up among pupils in primary schools all over the country, which followed a circular concerning the GPCR in primary schools issued by the PCC on 4 February 1967.

宏观调控
hongguan tiaokong
(macro adjustment and control)

See "jingji shahuang" (economic "Tsar") and "jingji gaige" (economic reform).

後邓时代
hou Deng shidai
(late-Deng period)

The period from the June 4th Incident in 1989 up to the death of Deng Xiaoping on 19 February 1997 is generally referred to as the "late-Deng period". During this period, although Deng's influence in the CCP and government policy-making gradually decreased, he still is credited with two remarkable achievements. The first was his powerful support for Jiang Zemin, who was chosen to replace Zhao Ziyang as CCP general secretary after the June 4th Incident. The second was the great influence after his early 1992 "Southern tour", which led to the approval of a socialist market economy at the CCP's 14th National Congress.

Jiang Zemin, during his nearly 8 years as Party leader, tended to vacillate now to the left and now to the right, as he moved to consolidate his position and placate various feuding factions in the hierarchy. Nevertheless, he still showed to the world that he was ready for the post-Deng era (Deng hou shidai). On 30 January 1995, he raised an "eight-point proposal" concerning the re-unification of Taiwan and Chinese mainland. On 27 April 1995, he succeeded in bringing about the fall of Chen Xitong, a CCP Politburo member and secretary of the Beijing Municipal Party Committee. See also "Deng hou shidai" (post-Deng era).

後儒学
hou Ruxue
(post-Confucianism)

See "ruxue disanqi" (Confucianism in its third stage of development).

後儒学时代
hou ruxue shidai
(post-Confucian era)

See "ruxue disanqi" (Confucianism in its third stage of development).

後十条
hou shitiao
(Latter Ten Articles)

See "shejiao" (socialist education movement).

後现代主义
hou xiandaizhuyi
(post-modernism)

See "cuowei" (malposition).

後殖民文化
houzhimin wenhua
(post-colonial culture)

See "zhimin wenhua" (colonial culture).

後殖民心态
houzhimin xintai
(post-colonial mentality)

See "zhimin wenhua" (colonial culture) and "minzuzhuyi" (nationalism).

胡风案件
Hu Feng anjian
(Hu Feng case)

Hu Feng was an eminent literary theorist and close friend of Lu Xun. His literary views had been controversial ever since the period of the "Left-Wing Writers League" of the 1930s. On 22 July 1954, refusing to accept the criticism levelled against him, he presented to the PCC his "Report Concerning the Last Few Years' Literary and Art Situation" ("Guanyu jinianlai wenyi shijian qingkuangde baogao", also called "Sanshiwanyanshu"—"The 300,000-word statement"—because of its length, *WYB*, Supplement 1 & 2, 1955). It might well be called a systematic refutation of Mao's *Yan'an Talks*. After taking this step, Hu's fate was sealed.

The attack started in February 1955. Mao first invented the notion of a "Hu Feng Anti-Party Clique" and then developed it into a "Hu Feng Counter-Revolutionary Clique", launching a nationwide campaign to root out counter-revolutionaries. On 13 May, 24 May, and 10 June, the *People's Daily* published three selections from Hu's private correspondence, with prefaces and notes written personally by Mao accusing Hu of counter-revolutionary activities. The campaign thus escalated. Hu Feng was arrested on 18 May. In 1965, after ten years under arrest, he was sentenced to 14 years' imprisonment. In May 1969, when he asked to be released because he had completed his term, he was given a life sentence. Driven to despair, he became mentally deranged.

Hu Feng won his freedom on 15 January 1979. An old, partly-disabled man of seventy-nine, he reappeared in 1981, and then died on 8 June 1985. An official memorial ceremony was held in Beijing on 15 January 1986, half a year after his death. Interestingly, he was rehabilitated by the CCP on three occasions in September 1980, 1985, and June 1988. According to the 1980 Party document concerning Hu Feng's rehabilitation, over 2,100 people were involved in the case, and among the 93 arrested, 78 were convicted as "Hu Feng Clique" members.

华侨
huaqiao
(overseas Chinese; Chinese sojourners)

See "haiwai huaren" (overseas Chinese).

华人
huaren
(overseas Chinese; people of Chinese origin)

See "haiwai huaren" (overseas Chinese).

华裔
huayi
(foreign citizen of Chinese origin)

See "haiwai huaren" (overseas Chinese).

画圈圈
hua quanquan
(make "circles")

As a general practice in mainland China, an official would make a circle around his name on the first page of any document sent to him, so as to show that he had read it. Hence the term "make circles" used to satirize bureaucrats.

划成分
hua chengfen
(determine an individual's class status)

See "jiating chengfen" (family origin; class status of one's family).

划清界线
hua qing jiexian
(draw a clear line of demarcation)

In political campaigns, when someone was found questionable (for example, convicted as a Rightist in the 1957 anti-Rightist campaign), other people were required to draw a clear line of demarcation between that person and themselves. In the case of husband and wife, divorce was one way to show the demarcation. See "jieji douzheng" (class struggle).

坏头头
huai toutou
(bad leader)

See "hongweibing" (Red Guards).

怀疑一切
huaiyi yiqie
(suspect all)

See "huaiyi yiqie, dadao yiqie" (suspect all, overthrow all).

怀疑一切，打倒一切
huaiyi yiqie, dadao yiqie
(suspect all, overthrow all)

Soon after the GPCR started, the Red Guards, influenced by Mao's "struggle philosophy", suggested that everything, and everyone, must be subjected to a careful and thoroughgoing examination in light of Marxism-Leninism-Mao Zedong Thought. It came to be accepted that those in power were no good and could not be trusted, and therefore should be overthrown. The slogan "suspect all", said to be a slogan favored and used by Marx, spread all over the country. The authorities, that is, those from the so-called "Chairman Mao proletarian revolutionary headquarters", found this very dangerous. Obviously, "suspect all" would be followed by "negate all" and "overthrow all", and their people would be affected indiscrimately. They thus changed the slogan to "suspect all, overthrow all" or "suspect all, negate all" (yigai huaiyi, yigai fouding) and ended it, labeling it as "'Left' in form but Right in essence" (xing zuo shi you), a manifestation of an "anarchist trend of thought" (wuzhengfuzhuyi sichao). Furthermore, an article carried by the *People's Daily* on 28 April 1969 asserted that the slogan had been put forward by Liu Shaoqi and his clique in an attempt to turn the spearhead of the struggle against other Party leaders. After Liu Shaoqi was toppled, his clique and agents continued their tricks, making use of the slogan so as to sabotage the GPCR.

On 25 October 1980, when talking with some leading figures from the PCC, Deng said: "In appraising the 'Cultural Revolution', he (Mao) said that its mistakes amounted to only 30 percent and its achievements to 70 percent. And when he referred to the 30 percent of mistakes, he meant 'overthrowing all' and waging a 'full-scale civil war'. How can anyone reconcile this with the idea of 70 percent achievements?" *(SWD,* p. 287). See also "wen'ge" (Cultural Revolution).

还我长城
huan wo changcheng
(give me back my Great Wall)

See "changcheng" (Great Wall, i.e., the PLA).

环境决定论
huanjing jueding lun
(theory of the environment as the decisive factor)

See "wenxue duixiang zhutixing" (subjectivity of the object of literature).

皇甫平事件
Huang Fu Ping shijian
(Huang Fu Ping incident)

See "bu zhenglun lun" ("no debate" theory).

皇权
huangquan
(imperial power)

See "Deng hou shidai" (post-Deng era).

黄河文明
Huanghe wenming
(Yellow River civilization)

See "huangtu wenming" (yellow earth civilization) and "*Heshang* shijian" (*River Elegy* Incident).

黄祸论
huanghuo lun
(theory of "yellow peril")

See "dong xi wenming chongtu lun" (theory of the clash between the Eastern and the Western civilizations).

黄色文明
huangse wenming
(yellow civilization)

See "huangtu wenming" (yellow earth civilization) and "*Heshang* shijian" (*River Elegy* Incident).

黄土文明
huangtu wenming
(yellow earth civilization)

In the ideological trend of Westernization of the 1980s, some intellectuals regarded Chinese civilization as a "yellow earth civilization", the "Yellow River civilization" (Huanghe wenming), or simply a "yellow civilization" (huangse wenming), in contrast to the "blue civilization" (weilanse wenming) or the "oceanic civilization" (haiyang wenming) of the West. Quite a number of works of literature and art, such as the film *Yellow Earth (Huangtudi),* touched on the issue of the "yellow earth civilization", but it was *River Elegy (Heshang),* a television political commentary series, which was broadcast on Beijing's Central Television Station beginning on 11 June 1988, that gave rise to much controversy.

According to a general understanding, *Heshang*, the Chinese title of the series, means the "premature death" of the Yellow River. It implies that Chinese culture was cut off too soon, and not allowed to achieve a healthy development. But the authors of this work seem to have cherished some more profound and bitter ideas. As Su Xiaokang, one of its two general editors, revealed, they thought that a culture with the characteristics of a "Yellow River civilization" should have long ago died and been renewed. The fact that it had survived, with all its old burdens, was why it was now suffering such torments (See Su Xiaokang et al., "1988: A Dialog on Reportage Literature", *Huacheng,* 6:23, 1988). The message was clear: the Chinese people should not go on blindly singing the praise of, and vainly taking pride in, this culture. It concludes that Chinese culture is "in decline". It was in this sense that the authors of *River Elegy* enthusiastically hailed the reform and open-door policy. But they demanded even more. Up to the present, in their opinion, the reform had done little more than sprinkle a few drops of water from the deep blue-coloured oceanic civilization over the parched yellow earth.

However, as Li Zehou pointed out, the backwardness of China today should not be simply ascribed to its cultural problems. Moreover, *River Elegy*'s unfavorable treatment of traditional Chinese culture, which constituted an "intellectual backlash against the culture as a whole" and led to the conclusion that it was "in decline", was unacceptable to many scholars, both at home and abroad. In the hot debate that followed, some found untenable a theory of "geographical environments as a decisive factor" (dili huanjing jueding lun) which regarded Chinese civilization as a predestined backward and bad "yellow earth civilization" in contrast to a predestined advanced and good "oceanic civilization" of the West. See also "*Heshang* shijian" (*River Elegy* Incident) and "wenhua re" (culture craze).

回到国学
huidao guoxue
(return to Chinese traditional learning)

See "guoxue" (Chinese traditional learning) and "xin baoshouzhuyi" (neo-conservatism).

活学活用
huo xue huo yong
(study and apply in a creative way)

See "tuchu zhengzhi" (giving prominence to politics).

火箭式干部
huojianshi ganbu
(rocket cadres)

See "taijie lun" ("staircase" theory).

基本路线一百年不动摇
jiben luxian yibainian budongyao
(unwaveringly adhere to the basic line for one hundred years)

See "shehuizhuyi chuji jieduan lun" (theory of the primary stage of socialism) and "dangde jiben luxian" (the Party's basic line).

基本法
jibenfa
(Basic Law)

The Basic Law refers to the Basic Law of the Hong Kong Special Administrative Region of the PRC. After many years of negotiation, the final text of the Basic Law was released in February 1990. On 4 April 1990, the 3rd Session of the 7th NPC adopted and promulgated the Law. The next day, the British Foreign Office issued a statement, affirming that the Basic Law was an acceptable law, which basically embodied the spirit of the Sino-British Joint Declaration signed on 19 December 1984 by the heads of the two governments.

According to the Law, Hong Kong will exercise the "one country, two systems", "Hong Kong residents governing Hong Kong", and "a high degree of autonomy". The HKSAR will enjoy executive, legislative, and independent judicial power, including final adjudication, which had formerly rested with the Judicial Committee of the Privy Council in London during British rule.

机构改革
jigou gaige
(reform of administrative structures)

As early as the period of the War of Resistance Against Japanese Aggression, "jingbing jianzheng" (better troops and simpler administration) was suggested to the CCP leadership by Li Dingming, one of the "enlightened gentry" in the Communist-controlled Shanxi area. The suggestion, which mainly meant streamlining administrative structures (jingjian jigou), enjoyed Mao's support. In fact, Mao made it a slogan for the whole Party. It led to the "five objectives of simplification, unification, efficiency, economy, and opposition to bureaucracy" promoted by Mao at the time (*SWM*, 3, p. 115). After the founding of the PRC, Mao did not forget this task. During the GPCR, the revolutionary committees (the organs of power at the time) at various levels demanded that overlapping administrative structures be done away with in order to set up a "revolutionized leading group capable of integrating with the masses" (*RMRB*, 11 July 1968).

When Deng came into power, however, he found that the problem had become even worse. On 13 January 1982, at a meeting of the PCC Politburo concerning the streamlining of central organizations, Deng stated: "Streamlining organizations constitutes a revolution" (jingjian jigou shi yi chang geming). He said, seriously: "If we fail to carry out this revolution, if we let the present overstaffed and overlapping Party and state organizations stay as they are—without clearly defined duties and with many incompetent, irresponsible, lethargic, under-educated and inefficient staff members—we ourselves will not feel satisfied and we will not have the support of the lower cadres, much less of the people" *(SWD,* p. 374).

In March 1998, Zhu Rongji (b. 1928) , elected premier at the 9th NPC, promised to prune the world's largest public service. Within three years, the 40 ministries and commissions in the central government were to be reduced to 29 and their 80,000 working staff cut in half. Local governments at various levels would also follow suit. Zhu dovetailed quite nicely with the liberal agenda in 1998. The idea of "small government, large society" (xiaozhengfu, dashehui) was given much publicity in the country, taking advantage of the commemoration of the tenth anniversary of the Hainan Special Economic Zone (China's largest zone founded on 13 April 1988). Its alleged successful experience was held as a model for other local leaders. Reform of the administrative structure was regarded as a breakthrough point in the political reform.

Before Zhu Rongji's pledge, streamlining administrative structures had been carried out on six occasions in different periods after the founding of the PRC in 1949. Unfortunately, it was never successful. The cycle of "streamlining—expanding—streamlining again—expanding again" (jingjian—pengzhang—zai jingjian—zai pengzhang) did not end. Official Chinese government statistics show that China had one "public servant" for every 600 citizens in 1951. By 1994 the proportion was 1:30, and in a country with a population of 1.2 billion. It is certain that Zhou, like his predecessors, will face strong resistance from within. It is not easy for governments to make changes to themselves.

As China observers have noted, the key to its success lies in changing the functions of government—China's current government was designed to administer a "command economy" that no longer exists, and officialdom is not only too big but also too corrupt. There must be a true distinction between the functions of the Party and those of the government (dang zheng fen jia) and between government functions and enterprise management (zheng qi fenli). Furthermore, a distinction must also be made between the functions of the government and those of the society (zheng she fenkai). The government must give up those functions which it cannot perform well or should not perform at all. Officials must respond to the needs of citizens and not merely to orders from above. This will require genuine elections, a strong legal system, and respect for individual rights.

With their theory of "small government, large society", or a "limited government" theory (youxian zhengfu lun), "liberal" (ziyoupai) thinkers want government control of the society and of the people to be weakened, which will allow for the building of a civil society ("gongmin shehui" or "minjian shehui") with a great number of non-government organizations. However, this will not be feasible without a change of China's present political system. See also "ziyouzhuyi" (liberalism) and "zhengzhi gaige" (political reform).

急用先学
ji yong xian xue
(study first what must be urgently applied)

See "tuchu zhengzhi" (giving prominence to politics).

极权主义
jiquanzhuyi
(totalitarianism)

See "yi fa zhi guo" (ruling the nation by law).

极右
jiyou
(ultra-Right)
See "you" (Right).

极左
jizuo
(ultra-Left)
See "you" (Right).

集束手榴弹
jishu shouliudan
(a handful of grenades)
See "wangbuzhaode hudie" (a butterfly difficult to catch) and "yishiliude Zhongguo dailiren" (Chinese agent of the stream-of-consciousness).

集体所有制
jiti suoyouzhi
(collective ownership)
See "quanmin suoyouzhi" (ownership by the whole people), "jingji gaige" (economic reform), and "jiejue gongyouzhi xingshi shi you yici sixiang jiefang" (solving the issue of public ownership forms is another emancipation of the mind).

集体无意识
jiti wuyishi
(collective unconscious)
See "fansi" (reflection) and "wenhua re" (culture craze).

几刀切
jidaoqie
(several cuts)
See "zhengzhi biaozhun diyi, yishu biaozhun dier" (political criteria first artistic criteria second).

计划经济
jihua jingji
(planned economy)
See "jingji gaige" (economic reform).

计划经济为主，市场调节为辅
jihua jingji wei zhu, shichang tiaojie wei fu

(mainly exercising the planned economy while making market regulation subsidiary)

See "jingji gaige" (economic reform).

计划经济与市场经济相结合
jihua jingji yu shichang jingji xiang jiehe
(a combination of the planned economy and the market economy)

See "jingji gaige" (economic reform).

计划生育
jihua shengyu
(family planning)

See "yitaihua" (single-child policy) and "xin renkou lun" (new theory of population).

计划与市场内在统一的体制
jihua yu shichang neizai tongyide tizhi
(a system of inherent unity of planning and market)

See "jingji gaige" (economic reform).

纪实小说
jishi xiaoshuo
(factual literature)

This term emerged in the mid-1980s to describe such works as Liu Xinwu's "Zooming In on 19 May 1985" ("5.19 chang jingtou", *RMWX,* 7:4-28, 1985, reprinted in Wu Liang and Cheng Depei, ed., *Xin xiaoshuo zai 1985 nian—New Fiction in 1985,* Shanghai, Shanghai Shehui Kexueyuan, 1986, pp. 526-48; trans. in *Black Walls and Other Stories*, Hong Kong, Research Center for Translation, Chinese University of Hong Kong, pp. 147-76) and "Bus Aria" ("Gonggong qiche yongtangtiao", *RMWX,* 12, 1985, reprinted in *Xin xiaoshuo zai 1985 nian,* pp. 549-82; trans. in *CL,* 4:81-114, Winter 1986, and *Black Walls and Other Stories*, pp. 15-60). Thereafter, works of this kind mushroomed, so much so that critics claimed that a new popular genre had appeared.

Quite a number of these works were controversial, including Ai Bei's *Too Difficult to Call Father (Jiao fuqing taichenzhong,* Taipei, Yuanshen, May 1994), which implies that Ai Bei is Premier Zhou Enlai's illegitimate daughter. Authors of this literary genre claim that their works are based on facts, only that they are presented with techniques of fiction. Those who do not favor this genre argue that no such thing exists that simultaneously shares the merits of reportage literature and fiction. The fictitious components in the so-called "jishi xiaoshuo" indicate that their authors write about real events and real people in a false way. This is an example of unhealthy tendencies in literary circles (see, for example, Ma Zhenfang, "Xiaoshuo, xugao, jishi wenxue: 'jishi xiaoshuo' zhini"—"A Query of 'Factual Literature'", *WYB,* 21 Oct. 1999). See also "xinshiqi wenxue" (literature of the new period) and "xinshiqi wenxuede duoyuan fazhan" (pluralistic development of the literature of the new period).

"纪要"
"jiyao"
("Summary")

Short for "Lin Biao tongzhi weituo Jiang Qing tongzhi zhaokaide budui wenyi gongzuo zuotanhui jiyao" (Summary of the Forum on the Work in Literature and Art in the Armed Forces with Which Comrade Lin Biao Entrusted Comrade Jiang Qing).

With the backing of Mao's two instructions given respectively in 1963 and 1964, which clearly showed Mao's distrust of literary and art circles (see "dui wenyijiede liang ge zhiming daji"—two telling blows to literary and art circles), Jiang met Lin Biao in Suzhou towards the end of January 1966. Lin then entrusted Jiang to convene a forum on the literary situation in the armed forces, which was to be held in Shanghai 2 to 20 February 1966. In order to enhance Jiang Qing's status, before the forum participants left for Shanghai, Lin gave them instructions to listen to her advice. During the forum, Jiang invited Zhang Chunqiao to speak to the participants and entrusted him with the drafting of the "Forum Summary", which was revised by Chen Boda (1904-1989) after the forum.

Significantly, Mao also carefully revised the "Summary" (in fifteen places). On 22 March 1966, an ecstatic Lin Biao sent the document to members of the CMC Standing Committee and asked them to pay close attention to it. In his letter, he declared: "The 'Summary' is an excellent document, which has repeatedly been gone over by the comrades attending the forum and has personally been examined and revised by the chairman three times. It applies Mao Zedong's thought to answer many important questions concerning the cultural revolution in the period of socialism. It is of both extremely great practical and far-reaching historic significance" (Lin Biao, "Lin Biao tongzhi gei zhonggong zhongyang junweide xin"—"Comrade Lin Piao's Letter to Members of the CMC Standing Committee", *RMRB*, 29 May 1967; trans. in *CL*, 9:21-22, 1967). On 30 March 1966, the CMC approved the "Summary" and sent it to the PCC for final confirmation. On 10 April 1966, while holding a meeting criticizing Peng Zhen for his alleged "ten major errors" in the document "Outline Report on the Current Academic Discussion", the PCC Secretariat issued the "Summary" to the whole Party. When it was first published in the *People's Daily* on 29 May 1967 (by this time the document had been revised more than twenty times without explanation), the GPCR was in full swing.

In the "Summary", there was a vital phrase to describe the literary situation during the first seventeen years of the PRC: "dictatorship of a sinister line". Obviously, intending to overthrow PRC President Liu Shaoqi and what was called the "bourgeois headquarters" headed by him, its producers asserted that, since the founding of new China, literary and art circles had been "under the dictatorship of a sinister anti-Party and anti-socialist line, diametrically opposed to Chairman Mao's thought". They charged that there had been eight "sinister literary theories" as typical expressions of the "sinister line in literature and art" in the past seventeen years—"writing about reality" ("xie zhenshi" lun), "the broad path of realism" ("xianshizhuyi guangkuode daolu" lun), "the deepening of realism" ("xianshizhuyi shenhua" lun), opposition to "subject-matter as the decisive factor" (fan "ticai jueding" lun), "middle characters" ("zhongjian renwu" lun), opposition to "the smell of gunpowder" (fan "huoyao wei" lun), "the spirit of the age as the merging of various trends" ("shidai jingshen huihe" lun), and "discarding the classics and rebelling against orthodoxy" ("lijingpandao" lun). They further defined the line as a "combination of bourgeois ideas on literature and art, modern revisionist ideas on literature and art and what is known as the literature and art of the 1930s (in the KMT areas of China)". This assessment constituted one of the major arguments in support of the GPCR. Later, with Mao's support, Lin Biao, Jiang Qing, and their people extended the "dictatorship of a sinister line" theory to the fields of education, publishing, physical culture, public security, and the Party's organizational, propaganda, and United Front work, as well as to other fields of Party and government work, so as to make the GPCR appear to be all the more necessary. Indeed, the GPCR began with a "breakthrough" on the "front" of literature and art. During the ten-year turmoil from 1966 to 1976, almost all established literature and art were maltreated. Catastrophe descended on hundreds of thousands of men and women—writers and artists were prominent victims from the very start.

Because the "Forum Summary" was treated as a directive from Mao, for quite a long time post-Mao critics were reluctant to touch this Party document, though they still tried to rescind the charges listed in it. After the 3rd Plenum of the 11th PCC in December 1978, the Party formally declared that the criticism of the work in literature and art contained in Mao's two written instructions of 1963 and 1964 did not tally with the actual situation, and that this criticism was later used in Jiang Qing's February 1966 "Summary" in such a way as to have the most serious consequences. Even then the "Summary" was not openly attacked and things were still very confused. Illustrative was the controversy over "Liu Shaoqi's counter-revolutionary revisionist line in literature and art", which had been coined during the GPCR so as to verify the correctness of "Chairman Mao's revolutionary line in literature and art". By the end of 1978, many still maintained that, although the "sinister line dictatorship" theory should be overthrown, the fact that there had been a "sinister line in literature and art" during "the seventeen years" could not be denied. Those who did not agree argued that there had been no such thing as "Liu Shaoqi's counter-revolutionary revisionist line in literature and art", the reason being that Liu as president of state had seldom concerned himself with cultural matters and possessed no literary theories with which to develop a line on cultural matters. This was obviously a weak or even ridiculous argument. It was at the 17 August 1979 forum jointly sponsored by the editorial boards of the *Literary Gazette* and the *Literary Review* that a call was issued to eliminate the "pernicious influence" of the document. Literary and art circles throughout the country promptly responded to the call.

By the end of the 1980s, it was generally accepted that the "Summary", the 1966 CCP document providing major arguments in support of the GPCR, could be regarded as a new version of Mao's 1942 *Talks at the Yan'an Forum on Literature and Art* developed in the socialist period. After 1956 when the "three great transformations" (san da gaizao) were completed and the period of "socialist construction" began, a major concern for Mao was how to create "socialist literature and art". He was increasingly disappointed with the situation in literary and art circles under the leadership of Zhou Yang and his colleagues. That was why he ruthlessly issued the two instructions in 1963 and 1964. As a direct result of the two instructions, the "Summary" appeared. To Mao's delight, it answered many important issues concerning "socialist literature and art". Like the *Yan'an Talks,* the "Summary" was indeed of great importance, not only in the fields of literature and art, but also in political-ideological fields. It was in the making of the "Summary" that Mao, Lin Biao, and Jiang Qing succeeded in forming a "Holy Alliance"—in other words, the "Summary" was evidence of their conspiring, on the basis of which the GPCR was made possible. See also "wen'ge wenyi" (GPCR literature and art) and "wenyi wei zhengzhi fuwu" (literature and art serve politics).

"纪要"是社会主义时期的"讲话"

"jiyao" shi shehuizhuyi shiqide "jianghua" (the "Summary" is the "Yan'an Talks" in the socialist period)

See "jiyao" ("Summary").

继续解放思想，同时注意社会效果

jixu jiefang sixiang, tongshi zhuyi shehui xiaoguo (continue to emancipate the mind while taking social effect into consideration)

See "jiefang sixiang shi yin, shehui xiaoguo shi guo" (emancipation of the mind is the cause and social effect is the the result).

家庭出身

jiating chushen (family origin; class status of one's family)

The term "chushen" may refer to one's class status (one's previous experience or occupation) or the class status of one's family. In order to avoid confusion, the term "jiating chushen" (family origin or family background) is used, which refers to the class (social) status of one's family before one has obtained an independent economic status. Similarly, "chengfen" may refer to one's class status or the class status of one's family. To avoid confusion, the phrase "geren chengfen" is used to mean one's class status, which is determined by the nature of one's main source of income during a certain period. See also "xuetong lun" (lineage theory) and "jieji luxian" (class line).

加强党的领导，改善党的领导

jiaqiang dangde lingdao, gaishan dangde lingdao (strengthen and improve Party leadership)

After the founding of the Communist regime, the slogan "Strengthen Party leadership" was continually repeated.

After the GPCR, even CCP leaders themselves admitted that the existing Party leadership system was problematic, as had been revealed during the GPCR. A new slogan then was issued: "Strengthen and improve Party leadership". What it means is: to improve Party leadership is to strengthen it. Or: only by strengthening Party leadership can it be improved. But to most Chinese people, the phrase "jiaqiang dangde lingdao" (strengthen Party leadership) is frightening. An example is provided, for instance, by Zhao Dan, a distinguished and respected film star. In what was later known as the "Zhao Dan Testament" published two days before he died, he wrote that even those who were loyal to the cause of the Party and worked indefatigably would feel apprehensive (a conditioned response) about this phrase, because from their past experiences of political movements, they knew that on each occasion this kind of "strengthening" had meant an upheaval, wanton interference, and even "all-round dictatorship" (quanmian zhuanzheng). He hoped that there would be no more such "strengthening" in the future (Zhao Dan, "Guande tai juti, wenyi mei xiwang"—"Watched Too Closely, Literature and Art Have No Hope", *RMRB,* 8 Oct. 1980; trans. in *CL,* 1:107-11, 1981).

Later, the slogan was altered thus: "Uphold and improve Party leadership" (jianchi dangde lingdao, gaishan dangde lingdao), and up to the present this is used in all official documents (for instance, in the documents of the 15th CCP National Congress). Perhaps there has been only one exception—in the *People's Daily* editorial of 1 July 1980 in commemoration of the founding of the Party. In revising the editorial of the Party's mouthpiece, Hu Jiwei, then its director, argued with Hu Qiaomu (who was then in charge of Party propaganda work) on the order of the two phrases, "jianchi dangde lingdao" (uphold Party leadership) and "gaishan dangde lingdao" (improve Party leadership). Hu Jiwei insisted that the latter should be placed first, on the grounds that only *improved* Party leadership should be, and can be, upheld. This, according to Hu, was approved by Hu Yaobang, then PCC general secretary. As a result, written into the editorial was the following sentence: "Only on the premise of improving Party leadership can it be upheld." (See Hu Jiwei's article in Hong Kong's *Open* magazine, Jan. 1998, and his book *Cong Hua Guofeng Xiatai Dao Hu Yaobang Xiatai—Down Falls of Communist Tycoons: From Hua Guofeng to Hu Yaobang*, Hong Kong, Mingjing, Nov. 1997.) See also "dangde lingdao" (Party leadership), "zhengzhi gaige" (political reform), and "wuchanjieji zhuanzheng" (dictatorship of the proletariat).

夹着尾巴做人
jiazhe weiba zuo ren
(be modest and prudent)

See "qiao weiba" (get stuck-up).

假左真右
jia zuo zhen you
(pseudo-Left but genuinely Right)

See "you" (Right).

价格双轨制
jiage shuangguizhi
(dual price system)

The "dual price system" began in 1985, and was considered an expedient but necessary measure during the period of "economic mode transition" (jingji zhuanxingqi).

In a planned economy, the prices of goods are fixed by the government, while in a market economy the prices are determined by the market. In China, a particular product may have two prices: the so-called "planned price" regulated by the government and the market price. Beijing's reforms provided for the implementation of both price systems, where state-run enterprises may purchase at the planned price while private businesses buy at the market price. However, this legitimization of the difference between the "planned price" and "market price" opened the door for the creation of a "power economy". In order to buy products, especially those goods in short supply controlled by the government, at the lower "planned price", a purchaser must go through a series of government red-tape. Those who are able to cut through this red-tape and obtain goods at a planned price are generally those who have political power or have "guanxi" (personal connections). They make tremendous profits by then selling the goods on the market at market prices. In her 1997 well-known book *The Pitfalls of China*, He Qinglian reports that in 1988 alone, the difference in these two prices amounted to one hundred billion Chinese dollars, 70 percent of which fell into private pockets. The "dual price system" greatly helped those having power or connections to begin their "previous accumulation" (yuanshi jilei). See also "jingji gaige" (economic reform) and "yuanshi jilei" (previous accumulation).

坚持党的领导，改善党的领导
jianchi dangde lingdao, gaishan dangde lingdao
(uphold and improve Party leadership)

See "jiaqiang dangde lingdao, gaishan dangde lingdao" (strengthen and improve Party leadership).

"坚硬的稀粥"事件
"jianyingde xizhou" shijian
("Solid Rice Gruel" incident)

See "wangbuzhaode hudie" (a butterfly difficult to catch).

简体字
jiantizi
(simplified Chinese characters)

See "wenzi gaige" (reform of written Chinese).

江八条
Jiang batiao
(Jiang Zemin's eight-point proposal)

In a speech on 30 January 1995, Jiang Zemin, general secretary of the CCP and president of the PRC, issued an eight-point proposal concerning the re-unification of Taiwan and Chinese mainland. As earlier, he emphasized the "one China" principle, highly vigilant of the movement for "Taiwan independence" (Tai du) or "independent Taiwan" (du Tai). There was, however, something new in his proposal. In his sixth point, Jiang advanced for the first time that Chinese culture should be an important foundation for a peaceful re-unification. Jiang also raised the slogan "Chinese do not fight Chinese". See also "Taiwan wenti" (Taiwan issue).

江核心
Jiang hexin
(Jiang Zemin as the core of Party leadership)

See "dangde lingdao" (Party leadership).

江泽民时代
Jiang Zemin shidai
(Jiang Zemin era)

See "Deng hou shidai" (post-Deng era), "jiang zhengzhi" (talk politics), and "Deng Xiaoping lilun" (Deng Xiaoping Theory).

讲政治

jiang zhengzhi
(talk politics)

In the second half of 1995, Jiang Zemin launched a "talk politics" campaign. He made known his idea in a speech on 27 September 1995 at the 5th Plenum of the 14th PCC. (The relevant part was published in the *People's Daily* on 17 January 1996 under the title of "Leading Cadres Must Talk Politics"—"Lingdao ganbu yidingyao jiang zhengzhi".)

Jiangists stressed that the campaign was in no way a retreat from the economic reforms. China critics, however, felt Maoist overtones in the campaign: the Great Helmsman had insisted that all things remain subordinate to political ideology. This was a reminder of how Left ideology embodied in Mao Zedong Thought still held a certain allure. In addition, ultra-Leftists, such as octogenarian Deng Liqun, took the opportunity to denounce what they called the "bourgeois liberalization" of contemporary society and to maintain a power base within the ruling Party.

Whatever the case, the campaign was perceived as vitally important to the establishment and consolidation of Jiang Zemin's leadership. For instance, Zhang Mannian, CMC vice-chairman, fully understood this. He made it clear that in the military "talk politics" meant fundamentally to guarantee the absolute leadership of the Party over the military. Whatever the circumstances, the army must unswervingly be in keeping with the Party Center (yu zhongyang baochi yizhi), vindicate its authority, and listen to its orders with Jiang as its core.

As China critics emphasized, politics does not mean political trickery (quanshu). Essentially, it refers to the political system. "Talk politics" should lead to talking about "rule by law" and further to talking about "political reform". Relevant to the present situation in China it should lead to the establishment of a political system in which law possesses authoritativeness and power is restricted. This is an important condition for a healthy market economy and for a healthy spiritual civilization as well.

In 1995, Jiang Zemin failed to go so far. Those sympathizing with him say perhaps he needed time to get out of the shadow of Deng and other Party elders. Later, in his eulogy to Deng on 25 February 1997, he mentioned political reform for the first time in recent years. On 29 May 1997, to a large number of high-ranking Party-state officials at a graduation ceremony at the Central Party School, Jiang delivered his most liberal and unequivocally reformist oration, in which he forcefully attacked the Left ideology and impressively elucidated what he thought about political reform.

On 29 July 1997, Xing Bensi, editor-in-chief of *Seek Truth* magazine and vice-president of the Central Party School, interpreted Jiang's "talking politics" thus: "The fundamental difference between the new socialist view and the traditional view of socialism lies in that the former gives prominence to the economy, while the latter to politics. This is a fundamental change in the socialist view... 'Talking politics', as I understand it, is not to emphasize politics from a theoretical angle, from an angle with fundamental significance. If so, that would be another big retrogression" (Si Ren, "Chongfen renshi chuji jieduan, jianjue fang 'zuo'"—"Fully Understanding the 'Primary Stage' and Resolutely Defending Against the 'Left'", *Zhongguo jingji shibao,* 29 July 1997).

In recent years, with help from Party theorists, "talk politics" has developed into a "three-stresses" (sanjiang) drive in the whole Party, especially among Party leaders at various levels. The "three stresses" refer to study, politics, and healthy trends (jiang xuexi, jiang zhengzhi, jiang zhengqi). "Stress study" means that the whole Party should earnestly study Deng Xiaoping Theory and Jiang Zemin's viewpoints; "stress politics", as said above, mainly requires being in keeping with the Party Center; and "stress healthy trends" means fighting against corruption and setting up a starting point to serve the people wholeheartedly. In 1999 a nationwide mvoement of Party spirit and conduct education was carried out among leaders at and above county level, which focused on the "three stresses".

On 11 March 2000, in his closing speech to the CPPCC, Chairman Li Ruihuan praised Deng's idea about "stressing coordination, quality, and benefit" (jiangxietiao, jiang zhiliang, jiang xiaoyi) in economic construction. This is another "three stresses". See also "zhengzhi gaige" (political reform) and "jingji gaige" (economic reform).

讲协调，讲质量，讲效益
jiangxietiao, jiang zhiliang, jiang xiaoyi
(stress coordination, quality, and benefit)

See "jiang zhengzhi" (talk politics).

讲学习，讲政治，讲正气
jiang xuexi, jiang zhengzhi, jiang zhengqi
(stress study, politics, and healthy trends)

See "jiang zhengzhi" (talk politics).

交心
jiaoxin
(tender one's heart)

See "xiang dang jiaoxin" (tender one's heart to the Party).

交心运动
jiaoxin yundong
(heart-tendering movement)

See "xiang dang jiaoxin" (tender one's heart to the Party).

教条主义
jiaotiaozhuyi
(dogmatism)

See "xiuzhengzhuyi" (revisionism).

教育必须为无产阶级政治服务，必须同生产劳动相结合
jiaoyu bixu wei wuchanjieji zhengzhi fuwu, bixu tong shengchan laodong xiang jiehe
(education must serve proletarian politics and be combined with productive labor)

See "dangde jiaoyu fangzhen" (the Party's educational policy).

教育要革命
jiaoyu yao geming
(revolution must be carried out in education)

See "dangde jiaoyu fangzhen" (the Party's educational policy).

教育要面向现代化，面向世界，面向未来
jiaoyu yao mianxiang xiandaihua, mianxiang shijie, mianxiang weilai
(education must be modernization-oriented, world-oriented, and future-oriented)

See "dangde jiaoyu fangzhen" (the Party's educational policy).

揭盖子
jie gaizi
(remove the lid)

"To remove the lid" means to expose the truth of a situation. Before the "lid" is removed, contradictions of various kinds are either overlooked or covered up, either intentionally or unintentionally. Very often "to remove the lid" means to expose bad things from their dark veil. Hence to "remove the lid of class struggle" (jie jieji douzhengde gaizi) was simply a mobilization order to ferret out class enemies. The term was often used in political campaigns in the past.

揭阶级斗争的盖子
jie jieji douzhengde gaizi
(remove the lid of class struggle)

See "jie gaizi" (remove the lid).

揭思想盖子
jie sixiang gaizi
(remove the ideological cover)

See "sixiang baofu" (mental burdens) and "sixiang gaizao" (ideological remolding).

阶级报复
jieji baofu
(class reprisal)

"Class reprisal" refers to acts of retaliation taken by members of the overthrown classes on members, especially the offspring, of the revolutionary classes. In the Mao period, this was a frightening charge. As some have pointed out, in a sense the GPCR was a class reprisal on a large, national scale; but it was undertaken by the oppressed, consciously or not so consciously, on the bureaucrats of the regime. See also "wen'ge" (Cultural Revolution) and "liang ge wen'ge lun" ("two Cultural Revolutions" theory).

阶级标签主义
jieji biaoqianzhuyi

(class labelism)

See "jieji fuhao xue" (semiotic of classes).

阶级斗争
jieji douzheng
(class struggle)

According to Mao's teaching, in a class society (jieji shehui), everyone is born with the brand of a class (jieji laoyin) due to different class origins (jieji chushen). People are distinguished by different class instincts (jieji benneng), class natures (jieji benzhi), class feelings (jieji ganqing), and class stands (jieji lichang). Class contradictions (jieji maodun) will not be resolved until a stage of revolutionary violence in which one class overthows another is reached. It is in the struggle against the bourgeoisie that the proletariat was transformed from a "class in itself" (zizai jieji) into a "class for itself" (ziwei jieji), that is, it became mature, possessed a clear-cut class consciousness (jieji jiaowu), formed its revolutionary theory, set up its political party, and understood its class mission (jieji shiming) in history. For the success of the revolutionary cause, Communists must oppose class compromise (jieji tiaohe). They should never forget class struggle, especially its new features and trends (jieji douzheng xin tezheng xin dongxiang). They should always have class vigilance (jieji jingti), make class analysis (jieji fenxi), and take strict precautions against the sabotage and subversive activities of class enemies (jieji diren). They must adhere to class line (jieji luxian), according to which they must form class ranks (jieji duiwu) and class alignment (jieji zhenxian). They should pay special attention to those alien class elements (jieji yiji fenzi) who have wormed their way into the revolutionary ranks.

There has been class struggle ever since classes appeared in human society, and the history of social development is one of class struggle. Mao asserted: "Classes struggle, some classes triumph, others are eliminated. Such is history, such is the history of civilization for thousands of years" ("Cast Away Illusions, Prepare for Struggle", *SWM,* 4, p. 428).

In a socialist society, class struggle still exists everywhere and at all times. It has three basic forms—displaying itself in the economic field (economic struggle), the ideological field (ideological struggle), and the political field (political struggle). Economic struggle and ideological struggle must submit to the requirement of political struggle. The protracted nature of class struggle in socialist society is expressed as follows: "Throughout the historical period of proletarisan revolution and proletairan dictatorship, throughout the historical period of transition from capitalism to communism (which will last scores of years or even longer), there is class struggle between the proletariat and the bourgeoisie and a struggle between the socialist road and the capitalist road" ("The Communiqué of the 10th Plenum of the 8th PCC", *RMRB,* 29 Sept. 1962). At a PCC work conference held from 11 to 28 February 1963, Mao summed up his experience as follows: "Once class struggle is stressed, every problem will be solved" (jieji douzheng yizhua jiuling). The state is none other than a machine for the oppression of one class by another. During the GPCR, Mao established the doctrine of "continuing the revolution under the dictatorship of the proletariat" (wuchanjieji zhuanzhengxiade jixu geming) on the basis of the broadening of the scope of class struggle (jieji douzheng kuodahua).

The class struggle theory and its practice brought a lot of suffering to the Chinese people in the Mao period. Now, interestingly, after two decades of Deng's reform during which class consciousness and class struggle have almost become something of the past, some are suddenly aware that there might be a new problem.

They find a cruel fact in today's China: while ordinary people, especially those having been laid-off, still have to live in difficult circumstances, a new class, the so-called bureaucratic-bourgeoisie (guanliao zichanjieji), has come into being in the process of the economic reform and has been profiting the most from the reform. See also "wuchanjieji zhuanzheng" (dictatorship of the proletariat).

阶级斗争扩大化
jieji douzheng kuodahua
(broadening of the scope of class struggle)

See "jieji douzheng" (class struggle).

阶级斗争三种基本形式
jieji douzheng sanzhong jiben xingshi
(three basic forms of class struggle)

See "jieji douzheng" (class struggle).

阶级斗争是纲，其余都是目
jieji douzheng shi gang, qiyu doushi mu
(class struggle is the key link, and everything else hinges on it)

See "jieji douzheng" (class struggle), "anding tuanjie" (stability and unity), "yi sanxiang zhishi wei gang" (taking the three instructions as the key link), and "pi Deng, fanji youqing fan'anfeng" (campaign to criticize Deng Xiaoping and counter the Right deviationist trend to reverse correct verdicts).

阶级斗争熄灭论
jieji douzheng ximie lun
(theory of "the dying out of class struggle")

See "hei liu lun" (six sinister theories).

阶级斗争新动向
jieji douzheng xin dongxiang
(new trends of class struggle)

According to Mao's teaching about class struggle, people should heighten their vigilance, pay constant attention to the "new trends of class struggle", and take initiatives and launch attacks upon the class enemy. During the Mao period, a characteristic of the "new trends of class struggle" was said to be "lachuqu, dajinlai"—the class enemy, while dragging Party and government cadres into his camp, sneaks into the revolutionary ranks. See also "jieji douzheng" (class struggle) and "san da geming yundong" (three great revolutionary movements).

阶级斗争一抓就灵
jieji douzheng yizhua jiuling
(once class struggle is stressed, every problem will be solved)

See "jieji douzheng" (class struggle).

阶级分化
jieji fenhua
(class polarization)

See "jieji douzheng" (class struggle) and "pi Deng wanyanshu" (anti-Deng 10,000-character petitions).

阶级分析
jieji fenxi
(class analysis)

Class analysis was a basic method Mao employed for half a century to make his revolution. It was formed in his mind from early on. In his March 1926 article "Analysis of the Classes in Chinese Society", Mao raised what he insisted was "a question of first importance for the revolution"—to distinguish real friends from real enemies in order to unite with real friends and to attack real enemies. That needs "class analysis", he told his followers. And he set an example himself. In the article, he made a general analysis of the economic position of the various classes in Chinese society and of their respective attitudes towards revolution.

According to Mao's teaching, a Marxist must make use of the class struggle viewpoint and the class analysis method to observe life in society and analyze social problems. The Marxist method of class analysis is the "most thoroughgoing" method for analyzing social phenomena because it reveals the "material cause of all mankind's historical behavior". Today, as critics noted, the old-line Leftists and "neo-Leftists" employ this method to attack the CCP's current reform and open-door program, as in an anti-Deng petition entitled "Issues Concerning National Security" ("Yingxiang woguo guojia anquande ruogan yinsu"), which began to circulate in the winter of 1995. See also "jieji douzheng" (class struggle), "jieji luxian" (class line), and "pi Deng wanyanshu" (anti-Deng 10,000-character petitions).

阶级符号学
jieji fuhao xue
(semiotic of class)

When characters' living individuality is replaced by an abstract class nature, according to post-Mao critics, literature will no longer be "a study of man" but only a "semiotic of class". Hence the loss of the "subjectivity of the object of literature". This phenonemon can be seen in many works of "revolutionary literature" of the past. At that time, Chinese writers and artists had to face "class labelism" (jieji biaoqianzhuyi). A habitual practice in literary criticism was to put a class label on everything, calling one thing bourgeoisie and another proletariat. This was like taking men as the personification of classes and as possessing only class character. See also "wenxue duixiang zhutixing" (subjectivity of the object of literature).

阶级教育
jieji jiaoyu
(class education)

Class education was an important part of political education in the Mao period. It aimed at heightening the people's "proletarian consciousness". According to Mao's doctrine, proletarian consciousness comes from a correct understanding of the law of social development and the law of class struggle. Only when one understands the great significance and bright future of the revolutionary cause, understands the principle of classes and class struggle, and knows which is the leading class of the revolution, who is one's enemy, who is one's friend, whom to rely on, whom to unite with, and whom to overthrow, only then will one be able to acquire a clear political orientation, distinguish between the people and their enemy, and thus foster revolutionary self-awareness and initiative.

During the GPCR, besides class education, there was also "education in the two-line struggle" or "education in the proletarian revolutionary line" (luxian jiaoyu). People were urged to fight for "Chairman Mao's proletarian revolutionary line" and against "Liu Shaoqi's counter-revolutionary revisionist line". "Siding on the wrong line" (zhan cuo dui) was of course a serious political mistake. See also "jieji douzheng" (class struggle) and "jieji luxian" (class line).

阶级烙印
jieji laoyin
(the brand of a class)

See "xuetong lun" (lineage theory) and "jieji douzheng" (class struggle).

阶级路线
jieji luxian
(class line)

According to Mao's teaching, different people belong to different classes and represent the interests of these classes. The CCP's class line means that the class interests (jieji liyi) of the proletariat and its allies must be considered in determining general and specific revolutionary policies and in launching revolutionary action. This must be adhered to—relying resolutely on the most revolutionary class, uniting with those classes that can be united with, and isolating the reactionary exploiting class. In Party building, class purity (jieji chunjiexing) and the nature of class line as the vanguard of the proletariat must be strictly adhered to. Therefore, in the recruitment of Party members and selection of cadres, attention must be paid to applicants' or candidates' class status (chengfen), history, background, level of class consciousness (jieji juewu), and experience in class struggle.

The classification of "zhongnong" (middle peasants) in the Mao period can be cited to show how much Mao's doctrine about class, class struggle, and class line influenced government policy. In the document "Resolution on Class Status Differentiation" issued by the Government Administration Council (re-named the State Council in 1954) for the Land Reform in the early 1950s, there was already a detailed description of "middle peasants", differentiating them from "poor peasants" (pinnong), "rich peasants" (funong), and "landlords" (dizhu). Later, the differentiation was further detailed. In July and September 1955 Mao time and again advocated his new idea: 1. Marking middle peasants from before the Land Reform as "old middle peasants" (laozhongnong) and those from poor to middle peasant status after the Land Reform as "new middle peasants" (xinzhongnong). 2. According to their living conditions, middle peasants were divided into "upper middle peasants" (shangzhongnong, also called "fuyu zhongnong"—rich middle peasants) and "lower middle peasants" (xiazhongnong). Hence more terms: "old upper middle peasants" (laoshangzhongnong), "old lower middle peasants" (laoxiazhongnong), "new upper middle peasants" (xinshangzhongnong), and "new lower middle peasants" (xinxiazhongnong). In the CCP's enactment of class struggle, these different categories of "middle peasants" were said to have different attitudes towards socialist revolution, and therefore should be treated differently. While "upper middle peasants" were often subject to harassment, the revolution relied on "lower middle peasants" and "poor peasants". See also "xuetong lun" (lineage theory) and "jieji douzheng" (class struggle).

阶级调和
jieji tiaohe
(class compromise)

Class compromise was a common label in political-literary campaigns during the Mao period. In the 1964-66 criticism campaign and later in the GPCR, many works, such as the films *City Under Siege* (Bai Ren and Lin Nong, *Binglinchengxia*, Changchun Film Studio, 1964), *An Independent Brigade* (Lu Zhuguo and Wang Yan, *Duli Dadui*, *Dianying wenxue*, 4, 1963, Changchun Film Studio, 1964), the novels *Struggles in an Old Town* (Li Yingru, *Yehuo Chunfeng Dou Gucheng*, *Shouhuo*, 6, 1958, August 1st Film Studio, 1963), *Morning in Shanghai* (Zhou Erfu, *Shanghaide Caocheng*, *Shouhuo*, 2, 1958), and the local opera of Shanxi province (Jinju) *Come to Peach Peak Village Three Times* (Creation Group of the Cultural Bureau, Shanxi Province, *San Shang Taofeng*, 1974), were attacked as "negating revolutionary armed struggle", "opposing violent revolution", "preaching class compromise", and "obscuring the demarcation line between revolution and counter-revolution". See also "renxing lun" (theory of human nature) and "jieji douzheng" (class struggle).

阶级异己分子
jieji yiji fenzi
(alien class elements)

See "jieji douzheng" (class struggle).

阶级性和天性具有内在结合的关系
jiejixing he tianxing juyou neizai jiehede guanxi
(class character and innate nature are related by internal integration)

See "gongtong renxing" (common human nature).

节育
jieyu
(birth control)

See "yitaihua" (single-child policy) and "xin renkou lun" (new theory of population).

解放思想
jiefang sixiang

(emancipating the mind)

"Emancipating the mind" was first raised by Mao Zedong in the Yan'an Rectification Movement in the early 1940s. This led to criticism and repudiation of all "Left" or "Right" mistakes committed by previous CCP leaders from the founding of the Party in 1921 until the establishment of Mao Zedong Thought as the guiding ideology for the whole Party at the 7th CCP National Congress in 1945.

In the criticism movement after the end of the GPCR, people strongly felt the serious consequences of the "Left" influence and asked for "emancipating the mind". Deng Xiaoping made a quick response. In his 13 December 1978 speech at the closing session of the Central Work Conference (which made preparations for the epoch-making 3rd Plenum of the 11th PCC), Deng specifically announced: "The emancipation of minds is a current political issue of vital importance" ("Emancipate the Mind, Seek Truth from Facts and Unite as One in Looking to the Future"— "Jiefang sixiang, shishiqiushi, tuanjie yizhi xiangqiankan", *SWD,* p. 152). The entire speech, in fact, mainly focused on one question, namely, as he said, "how to emancipate our minds, use our heads, seek truth from facts and unite as one in looking to the future" (ibid.). In order to promote the "emancipation of minds", Deng sought help from "home-grown policies" (tuzhengce). He said: "We are opposed to 'home-grown policies' that violated the fundamental principles of those laid down by the Central Committee, but there are also 'home-grown policies' that are truly grounded in reality and supported by the masses. Yet such correct policies are still often denounced for their 'not conforming to the unified standards'" (ibid., p. 153). Furthermore, Deng raised the thesis that "Democracy is a major condition for emancipating the mind" (Minzhu shi jiefang sixiangde zhongyao tiaojian).

Deng Xiaoping added a new significance to the term "emancipating the mind". He was waging a struggle against the "two whatevers" view ("liang ge fanshi", as expressed in the statement, "We will resolutely uphold whatever policy decisions Chairman Mao made, and unswervingly follow whatever instructions Chairman Mao gave"), held by Hua Guofeng, CCP chairman, and his faction. Deng emphasized that practice should be the sole criterion for testing truth, which indicated, very clearly, that not all of what Mao had said was correct.

Later, according to post-Deng critics, Jiang Zemin's 29 May 1997 speech at the Central Party School and the 15th CCP National Congress in the following September brought about another, more substantial, emancipation of people's minds, which was characterized by breaking through the mental obstacles on the issues of public and private ownership. This time its significance could be seen in the establishment of the Jiang Zemin era, the new core of Party leadership.

Accompanying the term "emancipating the mind" is the term "thought-emancipation movement" (sixiang jiefang yundong). According to Zhou Yang in his speech at the symposium commemorating the 60th anniversary of the May 4th Movement convened by CASS in May 1979, there were three thought-emancipation movements in modern Chinese history: the May 4th Movement of 1919, the 1941-42 Yan'an Rectification Movement, and the thought-emancipation movement since the 1978 3rd Plenum of the 11th PCC, which was characterized by the elimination of "modern superstition" (see Zhou Yang, "Three Great Thought-Emancipation Movements", *RMRB,* 7 May 1979).

In 1997, the "three thought-emancipation movements" referred to: the destruction of "modern superstition" brought about by the debate at the end of the 1970s and the beginning of the 1980s on whether "practice is the sole criterion for testing truth"; the legitimatization of the market economy which became possible after Deng Xiaoping's "Southern tour" in early 1992; and the breaking through the mental obstacles on the issues of public and private ownerships, which was introduced in Jiang Zemin's 29 May 1997 speech at the Central Party School (see Li Junru, "The Third Thought Emancipation: Breaking Through the Mental Obstacle on the Ownership Issues", *Zhongguo jingji shibao,* 12 Aug. 1997).

Another interpretation was: the 1978 3rd Plenum of the 11th PCC, which eliminated Mao's concept of "taking class struggle as the key link", marked the first thought-emancipation; the establishment of a "socialist market economy" at the 14th CCP National Congess the second; and third was the breakthrough on the ownership issue at the 15th CCP National Congress. A detailed description was provided in the 1998 popular book entitled *Crossing Swords: Three Thought Emancipations in Contemporary China* (Ma Licheng and Ling Zhijun, *Jiaofeng—Dangdai San Ci Sixiang Jiefang Shilu,* Beijing, Jinri Zhongguo, Jan. 1998). The book is part of a 28-volume series called *China's Problems (Zhongguo Wenti Baogao Congshu).* The general adviser is Liu Ji, former vice president of CASS and a member of Jiang Zemin's think-tank.

CCP theorists enthusiastically hailed the "three thought-emancipation movements". But the interpretations of these movements are controversial. Some simply deny the concept of "three thought-emancipation movements". It is argued that the 13th CCP National Congress had already decided to build a market economy in China, which meant that a solution (though perhaps preliminary) had been worked out for issues concerning "capitalist or socialist nature" and "public or private ownership". The 15th Party Congress admirably reiterated this solution, but it is an exaggeration to say that it marked another "thought-emancipation movement". (Reportedly Zhao Ziyang, the disgraced CCP general secretary, shares this opinion—see, for instance, *Open* magazine, Sept. 1998.) More forcefully, it is argued that all these were part of the undertaking to break through Maoist shackles in the economic field as initiated by Deng. If there is to be another such movement, it is said, it should be in the field of political reform.

Fundamentally, it is further asked: Why should there be successive "thought-emancipation movements"? Why should each movement be initiated by CCP leaders, and be to their benefit? Does this mean that people can enjoy "thought-emancipation" only when it is allowed by the leadership? If Deng's assertion about democracy as a major condition for emancipating the mind is correct, does it mean that there are problems with democracy and the problems remain unsolved? This is reminiscent of a remark by Liang Qichao, a Chinese thinker at the beginning of the 20th century: "There will be no thought-emancipation without freedom of speech" (Meiyou yanlun ziyou, jiumeiyou sixiang jiefang). Indeed, if there is freedom of speech, if people can think freely all the time and publish what they think without fear of being persecuted, there is no need to have any "thought-emancipation movement". See also "liang ge fanshi" (two whatevers), "shijian shi jianyan zhenlide weiyi biaozhun" (practice is the sole criterion for testing truth), and "jiejue gongyouzhi xingshi shi you yici sixiang jiefang" (solving the issue of public ownership forms is another emancipation of the mind).

解放思想是当前一个重大政治问题
jiefang sixiang shi dangqian yige zhongda zhengzhi wenti (emancipation of minds is a current political issue of vital importance)

See "jiefang sixiang" (emancipating the mind).

解放思想是因，社会效果是果
jiefang sixiang shi yin, shehui xiaoguo shi guo (emancipation of the mind is the cause and social effect is the result)

"Emancipating the mind" was a strong voice towards the end of the 1970s. This caused panic among the conservatives. They appealed: "Continue to emancipate the mind while taking social effect into consideration". But this was found to be a specious argument. As the critic Shen Minte pointed out, when speaking of literary works under attack: "This formulation fails to express accurately the relationship between the emancipation of the mind and the issue of social effect. It probably will make people wrongly think there could exist works that have no good social effect and yet are emancipatory in thought, and that therefore the emancipation of the mind must be restricted or even rectified from the angle of taking social effect into consideration. Thus it reverses the relationship. While hampering the emancipation of the mind with an invisible trammel, the formulation will in the end prevent literary creation from achieving its due social effect" (Shen Minte, "Jiefang sixiang, zhenshixing, shehui xiaoguo: dui yixie liuxingde tifade sisuo"—"Emancipation of the Mind, Truthfulness, and Social Effect: Thoughts upon Some Popular Formulations", *Anhui Wenyi*, 5, 1980, extracted and reprinted in *XHYB, WZB*, 8:149, 1980).

Supported by evidence, Shen completely rejected the conservatives' appeal. Moreover, he asserted that he had discovered a "rule": "It is exactly the emancipation of the mind that has enabled literary creation to achieve its unprecedented positive social effect. We have further been furnished with experience—only when we continue to emancipate our minds, can literary creation achieve newer and greater social effect. Emancipation of the mind is the cause and social effect is the result!" (ibid., p. 150). See also "jiefang sixiang" (emancipating the mind) and "shehui xiaoguo lun" (social effect theory).

解放艺术生产力
jiefang yishu shengchanli (liberate artistic productivity)

See "wenhua lingdao yao genshang gaige kaifangde xin xingshi" (the cultural leadership must keep abreast of the new situation of reform and the open door).

解决公有制形式是又一次思想解放
jiejue gongyouzhi xingshi shi you yici sixiang jiefang (solving the issue of public ownership forms was another emancipation of the mind)

Before the September 1997 15th National Congress of the CCP, the official propaganda had already claimed that solving the issue of public ownership forms was a key in the current reform of the economic system. At the Congress, Jiang Zemin gave a full explanation to this key issue. The public sector, he said, includes not only the state- and collectively-owned sectors, but also the state- and collectively-owned elements in the sector of mixed ownership. Public ownership can and should take diversified forms. All management methods and organizational forms that mirror the laws governing socialized production may be utilized boldly. He urged the country to seek various forms for materializing public ownership that can greatly promote the growth of the productive forces. The joint stock system, he said, is a form of capital organization of modern enterprises, which is favorable for separating ownership from management and raising the efficiency of the operation of enterprises and capital. It can be used both under capitalism and under socialism.

"We cannot say in general terms that the joint stock system is public or private," Jiang said, "for the key lies in who holds the controlling share. If the state or a collective holds the controlling share, it obviously shows the characteristics of public ownership, which is favorable to expanding the area of control by public capital and enhancing the dominant role of public ownership." He told the Congress that there were a large number of diverse forms of joint stock partnerships in the urban and rural areas. They were new things arising in the process of reform, and should be given support and guidance.

Besides, Jiang pointed out, the non-public sector is an important component part of China's socialist market economy. As before, the non-public sector comprising the self-employed and private businesses should be encouraged and guided to facilitate their sound development. This is of great importance to satisfy the diverse needs of the people and to promote the development of the national economy. He noted the necessity to improve the legal system concerning property and to protect the legitimate rights and interests of, and fair competition among, all types of enterprises and at the same time to exercise supervision and control over them according to the law.

At the Congress, it was decided to undertake a large-scale, strategic restructuring of China's 118,000 industrial state enterprises. Among them, 512 of the largest enterprises (accounting for roughly half of state assets) would remain entirely state-owned. The rest would survive however they could—by issuing shares privately or by exchanges, merging, forming joint ventures, or dismissing workers.

It was confirmed that diversified forms for materializing public ownership include: solely state-funded companies, collective enterprises (such as township and village enterprises), joint-stock systems (an economic form that follows a principle of voluntary participation, autonomous management, and assumption of sole responsibility for profits, losses, and risks), joint-stock partnership systems (a new type of collective economic system and a new form of public ownership, under which all employees become shareholders), social fund ownership economies (a kind of social security fund ownership, where assets neither belong to the state, nor to the enterprise collectively, nor to individuals, but to members of the society concerned), entrusted management (enterprise owners entrusting legal entities or individuals to manage their properties with remuneration), and property management responsibility systems (which clearly define enterprise and management targets for property value preservation and increment, profit growth rates and rewards and penalties for managers during a set term as stipulated in the responsibility contract between the state and the enterprises).

In 1997, according to the State Information Center, the state-owned sector maintained its leading status amid the development of various economic sectors. However, its share in the national economy has declined on an annual basis.

Accomplishing this restructuring without the taboo of "privatization" (siyouhua) did require some rhetorical acrobatics. As reformist economists themselves admitted, in exploring various forms for materializing public ownership, existing but outdated concepts must first be changed. It should be understood that all enterprise organization systems and forms in the world, such as corporate, contract, leasing, entrusted, and proxy management, mergers, purchasing, auctions, and joint stock, are simply means to an end, and can be adopted under both private and public ownerships. Forms of capital circulation, incorporation, purchasing, merger, auction, and bankruptcy are also means and methods of allocating resources, which can be used under both capitalism and socialism. Practice, they argued, proves that exercising diversified forms of public ownership will not only not harm, but will help consolidate and expand the public economy. So now most of China's economists seem to agree: Public ownership does not amount to state ownership; it has various forms, and the joint stock system should be included as one such form.

To economists in the West, this means China has signaled its willingness to relinquish state ownership, one of the "last bastions of socialism". Those in China prefer to call this another "emancipation of the mind", or the "third thought-emancipation movement", which is characterized by breaking through the "mental obstacles" on the public ownership issue.

In concrete operation, the reform of state-owned enterprises is difficult and complicated. Their problems are too big and too many; and the consequences the reform will bring about may be something the Party is not yet ready to see. The 4th Plenum of the 15th PCC discussed issues concerning "the reform and development of state-owned enterprises". In the decision adopted on 22 September 1999, it announced that in the reform privatization should be avoided and Party leadership must be strengthened. See also "gufenzhi gaizao" (joint stock system reform), "jiefang sixiang" (emancipating the mind), and "jingji gaige" (economic reform).

戒急用忍
jie ji yong ren
("go slow, be patient" policy)

See "Taiwan wenti" (Taiwan issue).

金权政治
jin quan zhengzhi
(money-power politics)

See "fan fubai" (anti-corruption).

禁区
jinqu
(forbidden area)

For a long time under the cultural autocracy, there were quite a number of "forbidden areas", i.e., those highly sensitive and dangerous topics in various fields which few people dared to enter and those who did were tragically destroyed. After the 1976 downfall of the Gang of Four, Chinese writers and intellectuals one by one opened the door of the "forbidden areas", such as socialist tragedy, common human nature, and humanism.

Today in China, comparatively speaking, the term "forbidden area" is not so significant as before. See also "renxing lun" (theory of human nature).

近代
jindai
(recent times; modern times)

Recent times in Chinese history refers to the period from the Opium War in 1840 to the May 4th Movement in 1919, after which modern times (xiandai) begins. Many historians, however, regard "jindai" as part of modern times.

京剧革命
jingju geming
(revolution in Beijing opera)

See "wen'ge wenyi" (GPCR literature and art).

经济动物
jingji dongwu
(economic animals)

See "zhengzhi dongwu" (political animals).

经济多样化需要文化多样化
jingji duoyanghua xuyao wenhua duoyanghua
(the multiplicity of economic sectors requires the multiplicity of culture)

With the theory of the "primary stage of socialism", which was put forward at the 13th CCP National Congress in October 1987, some argued that the history of the PRC, as well as the history of Chinese literature since 1949, would have to be rewritten. More apparent was its effect on current social-cultural life. Minister of Culture Wang Meng stated that the principal contradiction in the cultural field in China today was between civilization and ignorance, which determined that culture in the primary stage of socialism must be enlightened and constructive and that cultural construction would be time-consuming and protracted (Wang Meng, "Woguo shehuizhuyi chuji jieduande wenhua chuyi"—"My Humble Opinion Concerning Culture in the Primary Stage of Socialism", *Jiushi,* 1, 1989, reprinted in *XHWZ,* 3:153-157, 1989). Since the primary stage of socialism justifies the existence of multi-economic sectors and the promotion of a commodity economy and free competiton, in which a small portion of people might first get rich, the multiplicity of economic sectors, as it was argued by many critics, inevitably requires the multiplicity of culture. For instance, "popular literature" (tongsu wenxue) with entertainment as its primary purpose, "social literature" (shehui wenxue), including "reportage literature", with reforming society as its noble mission, and "pure literature" (chun wenxue) or "explorative literature" (tansuo wenxue), with literature itself as its aim, should all have an equal right to develop. This meant that writers would have more room in their artistic creations. On the other hand, the actual practice of the "primary stage of socialism" had already introduced a number of new social issues, because it could be abused, especially by those in power, by engaging in corruption. For writers with a sense of social and historical mission, literature needed to "be involved in" life or people's souls. See also "shehuizhuyi chuji jieduan lun" (theory of the primary stage of socialism).

经济发展，个人自由，社会正义，政治民主
jingji fazhan, geren ziyou, shehui zhengyi, zhengzhi minzhu
(economic development, individual freedom,

social justice, and political democracy)

See "gaobie geming" (farewell to revolution).

经济改革
jingji gaige
(economic reform)

For several decades after the founding of the PRC in 1949, China, following the model of the Soviet Union, exercised a "planned economy" (jihua jingji), or more correctly, a "centrally planned economy" (zhongyang jihua jingji) or a "controlled economy of public ownership" (gongyouzhide kongzhi jingji). After the GPCR, some economists began to examine this policy. At the 1978 3rd Plenum of the 11th PCC, Deng's reform and open-door program was announced. At the 12th CCP National Congress held in September 1982, a new principle was approved: "Mainly exercising the planned economy while making market regulation subsidiary" (jihua jingji wei zhu, shichang tiaojie wei fu). At the October 1987 13th CCP National Congress, Zhao Ziyang confirmed the "combination of the planned economy and the market economy" (jihua jingji yu shichang jingji xiang jiehe). He wanted to have a "system of inherent unity of planning and market" (jihuo yu shichang neizai tongyide tizhi), in which the state adjusts the market, and the market guides the enterprises" (guojia tiaojie shichang, shichang yindao qiye).

In fact, on 26 November 1979 when meeting American and Canadian guests, Deng already clearly stated that "socialism can also have a market economy" (Ma Licheng and Ling Zhijun, *Crossing Swords: Three Thought Emancipations in Contemporary China,* p. 182). This was the first time for a CCP leader to approve market economy. But a really crucial change took place only after Deng's early 1992 tour to China's southern provinces, where he gave a series of talks calling for a more vigorous policy of reform, the open door, and economic activation. In October 1992, the 14th CCP National Congress passed a resolution that stated that a market economy would be built in China—which was called a "socialist market economy" (shehuizhuyi shichang jingji). Though still modified by the epithet "socialist", it was generally regarded as a new economic mode, essentially distinct from the traditional "socialist planned economy". In his 1992 "Southern tour" talks, Deng explained: "The planned economy does not amount to socialism; capitalism also needs planning. Similarly, the market economy does not mean capitalism; there is also a market in socialism. Planning and market are both economic measures." Thus Deng solved a big issue. In traditional CCP doctrine the two concepts "market" and "socialism" are incompatible. But Deng was in a position to link them together. As early as 1984, he said that there had been confusion in the past in the understanding of the question of what was Marxism and what was socialism ("Deng Xiaoping on Socialism with Chinese Characteristics", *Liaowang,* 34, 1984). He turned "socialism with Chinese characteristics" into "market socialism" (shichang shehuizhuyi), as China observers called.

After Deng's death, the reform, or, as some describe, "economic liberalization" (jingji ziyouhua), continued. At the September 1997 CCP 15th National Congress, the issue of public ownership forms, a key issue in the current reform of economic systems, was theoretically, and officially, solved. It was agreed that public ownership does not amount to state ownership; there are diversified forms to carry out public ownership, and a joint stock system should be counted as one of them. To Western economists, this signaled the Party's willingness to relinquish state ownership of industry, one of the "last bastions of socialism". Those in China call this another "emancipation of the mind", or, more exactly, the "third thought-emancipation movement", which is characterized by breaking through the "mental obstacles" to the public ownership issue (see, for instance, He Jiangtao, "Disan ci sixiang jiefang: chongpo xing 'gong' xing 'si' de sixiang yihuo"—"The Third Thought Emancipation: Breaking Through the Mental Obstacle on the Ownership Issue", *Zhongguo jingji shibao,* 12 Aug. 1997).

Achievements of the economic reform in the past two decades can be strongly felt by everyone. The economy has developed at record speeds. It is predicted that the Chinese economy will be the largest in the world before the year 2020, even if its growth slows from the average of 9 percent since 1979 to the 7 percent now forecast for the years ahead. Such profound changes have not only taken place in the economic field. The traditional Chinese civilization is in the process of being pounded by many new things emerging with the promotion of the market economy, such as a commodity consciousness (shangpin yishi), a marketing consciousness (shichang yishi), and a trend of people engaging in commercial activities (xiahai). A subtle but profound change can be seen in the people's way of thinking, in their sense of values, and in economics, culture, and social life at large. Within a broader historical perspective, this can be called a quiet revolution. It is unlikely it can be reversed. A country with one of the most ancient civilizations in the world is single-mindedly and rapidly modernizing.

At the same time, a number of problems have emerged. One of them is the role of power, which has been seriously corrupted, in the country's distribution of resources.

In the past twenty years, during the transition from a planned economy to a market economy, what can be called a "power economy" (quanli jingji) quickly expanded. A power economy involves the use of power, especially political power rather than the market, to control or influence the economy. It is a bureaucrat economy, a tool used by those in power at various levels or those close to power to directly involve themselves in or to indirectly influence economic activities. Such involvement is characterized by economic privileges, obtained unfairly, which affect the distribution of resources and capital. A power economy is also distinctive in terms of its economic mechanisms, under which a network of bureaucratic relationships is responsible for the movement of a substantial amount of capital and resources.

In the environment of a power economy, "power capital" (quanli ziben), the integration of power and capital, runs rampant. In the past two decades, by taking advantage of the dual price system, the "development zone" craze of the early 1990s, the joint stock system reform, etc., those in power or close to power unceasingly turned their power into capital, so that social wealth rapidly fell into their private pockets. That was their "previous accumulation" (yuanshi jilei), as a result of which their capital amounted to not less than thirty thousand billion Chinese dollars (as provided in 1998 by Yang Fan, a research fellow at the Economics Institute, CASS). A privileged bureaucratic stratum has thus come into being.

The disastrous consequences of a power economy are apparent. Corruption is now wide spread. The power economy, as pointed out above, is a major source of the corruption. Naturally, it also leads to tremendous losses for state properties. Once unchecked power is involved in business activities, power owners will do all they can to win the rights to state property. According to May 1998 statistics provided by the State Statistical Bureau, in the five years from 1993 to 1997, over 355 billion Chinese dollars of state assets and capital disappeared, of which over 250 billion went abroad. Other sources maintain that the rate of China's state-property losses totals about 30 billion U.S. dollars per year.

The power economy has brought about serious social problems, such as social unrest caused by disparities between the rich and the poor, degeneration of social morality, and subversion of the country's laws and regulations. The polarization of society is sharply felt. The power economy creates millionaires through corruption. These millionaires gain wealth overnight with little investment, forcing tens of millions of hardworking people and those out of work to live in a state of relative or absolute poverty. This has greatly intensified conflicts of interests in society. Social justice has become a serious problem which few could foresee when the economic reform started.

The ultimate goal of economic reform is to establish an orderly market economy that does not allow for unfair competition. However, a power economy, which resorts to non-economic measures to protect special interests and unfair competition, is by nature in conflict with a market economy. It presents great obstacles to a complete economic reform. But how did it emerge at the time that the state was implementing the reform and open-door program aimed at establishing a market economy?

To answer this question one has to trace the roots of China's power economy. Since the founding of the regime, the weight of the Party has been heavier than that of the law. It is easy for an unrestricted and unchecked political entity to evolve into a dictatorship. Moreover, there has been no separation of the Party from the government nor of the government from economic enterprises. Those who have unlimited political power have access to enormous economic/financial resources unavailable to ordinary citizens. Finally, since Deng's reform started twenty years ago, a merchandise economy has developed, and the merchandise economy makes political power into a merchandise that can be put into circulation. As a result, a power economy and corruption are inevitable.

From the very beginning, as many have pointed out, China's reform program should have included a reform of the old and undemocratic political system that allows for an unfair economic system and creates enormous room for the emergence and development of a power economy and corruption. Unfortunately, the economic reform has not been accompanied by political reform. No effective mechanism has been set up to curb corruption in economic activities. The Chinese central authorities have initiated several anti-corruption campaigns, but so far have had little success.

Now there is a complicated situation in post-Deng politics. On the one hand, as analyzed above, the power economy has become part of the establishment. To a certain degree it has strengthened the Party's control over the nation's economy, creating more obstacles for China's democratization movement. On the other, in the macro-environment of the power economy, there have appeared many regional centers of bureaucrat capital, big and small, throughout the country. A big problem for the Party Center is the rising influence or even centrifugal force of the provincial economy. What is dubbed the "duchy economy" (zhuhou jingji) has weakened, and will probably continue to weaken, the center's hold. The central authorities definitely do not want to see their rigid central power first collapse in the economic field.

The abuse of money and power was not intended to be a result of the reform. There is a danger that the problems accumulated in the past twenty years may work together to shake the foundation of the regime. Therefore, it is expected that the current Party leadership with Jiang Zemin as the core will do something to check the power economy and corruption.

Economists suggest examining the reform strategy, which was initially designed to proceed from easy to difficult, from superficial to profound, from the periphery of the institution to the inside. It was hoped that this strategy would avoid contradictions and the reform would easily be accepted by various social sectors. Of course, of vital importance to the Party was not to damage its leadership and its vested interests. However, when the reform entered into a "deepwater area", it was found that all those problems carefully avoided in previous stages had accumulated and become serious unavoidable social contradictions.

Thus, social justice and a healthy market economy are the focus of discussions today. In the propaganda wave of July to August 1997 in preparation for the forthcoming 15th CCP National Congress, Wu Jinglian, a prominent economist at the State Council Development Research Center (who is part of Zhu Rongji's think-tank) raised a new thesis that "the basic characteristic of socialism is social justice plus a market economy" (shehuizhuyi jiben tezheng shi shehui gongzheng jia shichang jingji). Or, as liberal economists put it: "Without justice, there will be no market economy" (meiyou gongzheng, bian meiyou shichang jingji). Many farsighted scholars shared the view that "man should be at the center of development" (fazhan shi yi ren wei zhongxinde fazhan). Development, as defined by international standards, is the sum total of various factors, including economic growth, political democracy, development of science and technology, change of cultural values, transition of the social mode, and ecological balance and protection.

Fundamentally, there must be a serious, substantial political reform. In *Ideas and Problems of China*, political scientist Liu Junning argues that without rights and freedoms for citizens, and without limited government, a market economy will only be a "pie in the sky". Li Shenzhi, a former CASS vice-president who is dubbed as a liberal patriarch, clearly pointed out that China's implementation of political reform will determine the ultimate success or failure of the economic reform ("Yeyao tuidong zhengzhi gaige"—"Also Promote Political Reform", *Gaige,* Jan. 1998). Some even warned: If there is no reform for democracy and rule by law, so that power must withdraw from the market, an economic-political crisis could break out within a few years, thus seriously affecting the global economy. See also "zhengzhi gaige" (political reform), "fan fubai" (anti-corruption), and "yi fa zhi guo" (ruling the nation by law).

经济基础
jingji jichu
(economic base)

In Marxist doctrine, the economic base (the lower structure) of a society—the basic manner of production in a given social system—determines the superstructure (shangcengjianzhu) of that particular society. The superstructure refers to the social, political, and cultural organs which exist above the economic base. The superstructure is divided into two parts. One is the social and political superstructure, which includes the state, the political parties, the government, the law and various organs, associations, and organizations. The other is the superstructure in the realm of ideology, i.e., the supreme superstructure, which comprises religion, ethics, literature, arts, etc. The ideological superstructure reflects, and is determined by, the social and political superstructure.

As Marxism holds, economics is the base and politics is the concentrated expression of economics (jingji shi jichu, zhengzhi zeshi jingjide jizhong biaoxian). Marxism also maintains that politics cannot but have precedence over economics (zhengzhi tong jingji xiangbi buneng bu zhan shouwei). Politics, including political ideologies, political systems, and political institutions, most directly express the economic basis. In particular, state power, the core of the superstructure, is the first ideological force governing human beings. In a society where classes have not yet been eliminated, political struggle will exert a strong influence on all aspects of ideology and on social life, including economic activities, at large. See also "jingji gaige" (economic reform), "zhengzhi" (political reform), and "wenyi wei zhengzhi fuwu" (literature and art serve politics).

经济沙皇
jingji shahuang
(economic "Tsar")

"Economic Tsar" (or "red economic Tsar"—"hongse jingji shahuang") is a nickname for Zhu Rongji (b. 1928) soon after his appointment in 1991 as vice-premier in charge of national economic work. Zhu does not like this nickname, as he indicated at a press conference on 19 March 1998, the last day of the 9th NPC, where he was elected premier of the State Council (replacing Li Peng who became NPC chairman after his second five-year term as premier had ended). At the press conference, Zhu also announced his dislike for his other nickname "China's Gorbachev", which is perhaps a praise but may imply a political message even more dangerous than the title "economic Tsar".

Zhu has still other nicknames. During the period from 1988 to 1991 when working in Shanghai as the mayor and then also the Party boss of this city, he earned the name "one-chop Zhu" because of his brisk, no-nonsense approach, his keenness to achieve quick decisions, and his hatred for bureaucratic processes. Most importantly, he was praised by Deng Xiaoping personally as "one of the few cadres who really understands how the economy works". One of his masterpieces was the 1996 "soft landing" (ruan zhuolu)—Chinese economists use this aviation term to refer to the success of the government's macro-economic control which began in mid-1993 under Zhu's auspices.

In that year, China's economy faced a host of outstanding problems, such as excessive growth in fixed asset investment, chaos in the financial sector, excessive issuance of banknotes, and damaging price hikes. The retail price index rose 13 percent, followed by a further rise of 21.7 percent in 1994. (Some ascribed these to the influence or abuse of Deng's 1992 talks during his "Southern tour".) Zhu oversaw an austerity program. His policy of "macro adjustment and control" (hongguan tiaokong) was carried out throughout the country (for this purpose, he found it necessary that he take over as governor of the Chinese People's Bank). For a time, in both the adjustment and the control of total supply and demand in the society, and in other important economic activities, strict executive measures were adopted by the central government. It is said that the policy met with great obstacles. By the end of 1996, however, the Chinese government announced that the policy of "macro adjustment and control" had succeeded and a "soft landing" had been realized. According to Premier Li Peng's "Report on the Work of the Government" delivered at the 5th Session of the 8th NPC on 1 March 1997, in 1996 prices rose 6.1 percent, an 8.7 percentage-point decline compared with 1995. The gross domestic product (GDP) reached over 6,770 billion yuan, an increase of 9.7 percent over the previous year, calculated in terms of comparable prices. Not only had the above-noted problems been resolved, but the economy had continued its rapid growth.

These were still problems: inflationary pressures remained, the quality of economic growth was poor, the agricultural foundation was fragile, state-owned enterprises faced difficulties, and capital construction was excessive. Any carelessness, as it was warned, would create fresh problems in the macro-economic environment. But many agreed that "Boss Zhu" ("Zhu Laoban"—Zhu Rongji's another nickname) appeared to have achieved what had appeared to be impossible earlier: steady, strong economic growth accompanied by ever-lower inflation. Not even China's most optimistic economic forecasters saw this coming. Zhu thus won support from the Party elders and even the military. On 17 March 1998, at the 9th NPC, Zhu's success was finally rewarded: he was elected premier (with 2,890 delegates endorsing his appointment, while 29 opposed and 31 abstained). The incoming premier was widely acclaimed as the right person for the job at the right time—also at a crucial time: China would be attempting to salvage its state-owned sector, bail out its debt-laden banks, and cut its public service, and against the backdrop of the Asian economic meltdown.

At the press conference on 19 March 1998, characterized by his decisiveness and no-nonsense approach, Zhu announced his administrative program to the public. This was summed up as "one ensure, three putting things into place, and five reforms" (yi ge quebao, san ge daowei, wu xiang gaige). By "one ensure", Zhu meant that facing various challenges against the backdrop of the Asian financial crisis, China would ensure an 8 percent increase in its GDP, with inflation lower than 3 percent and no devaluation of its RMB. The "three putting things into place" meant: within three years, most state-owned enterprises would be rescued from their current difficult situation, China's banking system would be thoroughly reformed, and central and local government institutions would be re-organized. The "five reforms" were reforms or further reforms in the circulation system of grain, the investment and financing system, the housing system, the medical care system and the fiscal and tax systems.

Zhu Rongji told the world at the press: "Even if a mine field or the abyss should lie before me, I will march straight ahead without looking back." Zhou's determination to carry out his program of "one ensure, three putting things into place, and five reforms" impressed the Chinese people strongly and favorably. But this newly-elected premier and ex-bourgeois Rightist (Zhu was convicted as "Rightist" in 1958) had to face many difficulties, which were generated chiefly because of China's present politico-economic system. One year later, he found some of the goals set in the program could not be achieved. Ironically, China was now facing a new problem different from the problem in the period 1993 to 1996—this time it was deflation (tonghuo shousuo) instead of inflation (tonghuo pengzhang). The government had to adopt a number of measures to stimulate economic growth, such as expanding domestic demand, implementing a proactive financial policy, and increasing capital spending.

Vital problems were those in political reform and economic reform. One such was the universal corruption in today's China. At another press conference in March 2000, Zhu said he hoped that after he stepped down he would be remembered as an "upright official" (qingguan) who had done something substantially good. It was likely that he was such an official. But as premier of the State Council, he was expected to be able to lead a clean, open, efficient, and democratic government. There was a story about one hundred coffins—Zhu was reported to have said that one hundred coffins should be ready, ninety-nine for corrupt officials and one for him. It was true that "Ironfaced Zhu" ("Zhu Tiemian", a nickname given to Zhu by Hong Kong people) was ruthless to corrupt officials, but it was doubtful that his anti-corruption drive would really succeed within the framework of China's present political system. See also "fan fubai" (anti-corruption), "zhengzhi gaige" (political reform), and "jingji gaige" (economic reform).

经济是基础，政治则是经济的集中表现
jingji shi jichu, zhengzhi zeshi jingjide jizhong biaoxian
(economics is the base and politics the concentrated expression of economics)

See "jingji jichu" (economic base).

经济特区
jingji tequ
(special economic zone)

On 15 July 1979 the PCC and the State Council agreed in principle that Guangdong and Fujian provinces could set up zones where goods would be processed for export (chukou jiagong qu). On 16 May 1980 the designation was assigned to Guangdong's Shenzhen, Zhuhai, and Shantou, and Fujian's Xiamen. At the 15th Session of the 5th NPC held 21 to 26 August 1980, this was confirmed for Guangdong, and the "special economic zones" was officially legitimized. On 10 December 1980 Xiamen's "special economic zone" was confirmed by the State Council. In the above-mentioned zones, which rely on both socialist economics and capitalist economics, a special administrative policy of the open door was implemented in order to lure foreign capital and introduce foreign technology and advanced business management techniques. On 24 April 1984, in a speech about the special economic zones and opening more cities to the outside world, Deng Xiaoping announced that the zones are windows of technology, knowledge of management, and China's foreign policy. They have a historical task as a "window for reform" (gaigede chuangkou).

From the very beginning Deng was an enthusiastic architect of the special economic zones. In his 1984 inspection tour to Shenzhen, Zhuhai, and Xiamen, he told his Party colleagues that his policy of setting up special economic zones had been proved correct and they should be further implemented. In 1992, he again visited Shenzhen and Zhuhai, where he gave his famous instructions to more vigorously carry out the reforms. Under the guidance of Deng's ideas about reform and the open door, in 1984 14 coastal cities were chosen as open areas to the outside world: Tianjin, Shanghai, Dalian, Qinhuangdao, Yantai, Qingdao, Lianyungang, Nantong, Ningbo, Wenzhou, Fuzhou, Guangzhou, Zhanjiang, and Beihai. In 1988, Hainan Island, originally part of Guangdong, became a separate province, to be administered as a special economic zone. In 1990, a special administration was established in the Pudong District of Shanghai, following Deng's instructions about building a few more Hong Kongs in the inland.

The great economic achievements of the special economic zones have been recognized throughout the world. Shenzhen, for example, can well be counted as the most rapidly developed city in the world during the 1980s. However, the special economic zones have always been controversial. As is well known, the zones enjoy preferential treatment granted by the central government. Hence the following accusations: "Special economic zone means special privilege" (tequ jiushi tequan) and "Special economic zone means capitalism" (tequ jiushi zibenzhuyi). A recent appeal was: "Special economic zones should enjoy no more preferential treatment".

In December 1995, when accompanying Cuban President Castro in a visit to Shenzhen, Jiang Zemin reiterated the "three no-change" (san ge bubian) policy of the central government towards the special economic zones. They are: no change in the central government's determination to develop the special economic zones, no change in the basic policies towards these zones, and no change in the role of the zones in China's reform, open-door, and modernization program. See also "tequ bu te" (special economic zones should enjoy no more preferential treatment) and "zhuhou jingji" (duchy economy).

经济现代化
jingji xiandaihua
(modernization of economy)

See "si ge xiandaihua" (four modernizations).

经济异化
jingji yihua
(economic alienation)

See "shehuizhuyi yihua lun" (theory of socialist alienation).

经济自由化
jingji ziyouhua
(economic liberalization)

See "ziyouhua" (liberalization) and "jingji gaige" (economic reform).

经济自由化优先于政治民主化
jingji ziyouhua youxianyu zhengzhi minzhuhua
(economic liberalization is prior to political democratization)

See "xin quanweizhuyi lunzheng" (neo-authoritarianism debate).

经济上反左，政治上反右
jingjishang fanzuo, zhengzhishang fanyou
(oppose Left ideology in the economic field and Right ideology in the political field)

See "liang tiao zhanxiande douzheng" (struggle on two fronts).

经济主义歪风
jingjizhuyi waifeng
(evil wind of economism)

In the last few months of 1966, taking advantage of the GPCR, workers in various parts of the country demanded better economic treatment. They formed nationwide mass organizations for their struggle. The authorities condemned this as an "evil wind of economism", for which the so-called capitalist-roaders were held responsible. They were accused of "making use of the trick of economic bribery to corrupt the revolutionary will of the masses" (*RMRB*, 16 Jan. 1967). See also "wen'ge" (Cultural Revolution).

经商热
jingshang re
(business fever)

From the early 1990s, especially after Deng Xiaoping's early 1992 tour of China's southern provinces, where he gave a series of talks calling for a more vigorous policy of reform, the open door, and economic activation, a second business fever erupted in the country. This can be described, though somewhat exaggeratedly, by the popular saying: "One billion people, 900 million businessmen, and another 100 million waiting in line" (shiyi renmin jiuyi shang, haiyou yiyi dengzhaoshang). Even many professionals and officials quit their jobs and "jumped into the sea of business" (xiahai—to engage in commercial activities). Private profiteering (sidao) and official profiteering (guandao) accompanied this business fever.

There was a controversy over whether or not the business fever was normal. Some found the phenomenon positive, for it showed that commercialism and the concept of a commodity economy had been accepted. Others, however, argued that it reflected an opportunistic money-hungry psychology which took advantage of Deng's reform and open-door policies.

精兵简政
jingbing jianzheng
(better troops and simpler administration)

See "jigou gaige" (reform of administrative structures).

精简机构
jingjian jigou
(streamline administrative structures)

See "jigou gaige" (reform of administrative structures).

精简机构是一场革命
jingjian jigou shi yi chang geming
(streamlining organizations constitutes a revolution)

See "jigou gaige" (reform of administrative structures).

精神包袱
jingshen baofu
(spiritual burden)

See "sixiang gaizao" (ideological remolding).

精神变物质
jingshen bian wuzhi
(turning spiritual strength into material strength)

See "zhua geming, cu shengchan" (take charge of the revolution, promote production) and "jingshen yuanzidan" (spiritual atom bomb).

精神贵族
jingshen guizu
(spiritual aristocrats)

See "Zhou Yang beiju" (tragedy of Zhou Yang).

精神文明
jingshen wenming

(spiritual civilization)

See "liang ge wenming" (two civilizations).

精神污染
jingshen wuran
(spiritual pollution)

In the last months of 1983, the CCP launched a campaign to eliminate the so-called spiritual pollution.

"Spiritual pollution", according to Deng Liqun, then director of the PCC Propaganda Department, could be classified into four categories: 1. obscene, barbaric, and reactionary things; 2. some base phenomena included in artistic performances; 3. the seeking of personal enjoyment, individualism, anarchism and liberalism; and 4. the expression of views in articles and speeches violating the socialist system. Many felt that the fourth category was the most important, because it mainly referred to humanism and the theory of socialist alienation as advocated by people like Zhou Yang and Wang Ruoshui. See also "qingwu yundong" (campaign to eliminate spiritual pollution).

精神原子弹
jingshen yuanzidan
(spiritual atom bomb)

A well-known metaphor for Mao Zedong Thought, it is derived from a statement by Lin Biao: "Mao Zedong Thought, once mastered by the broad masses, will turn into an inexhaustible force, a spiritual atom bomb unrivalled in power" *(RMRB*, 1 Jan. 1968). See also "Mao Zedong sixiang" (Mao Zedong Thought) and "tuchu zhengzhi" (giving prominence to politics).

精神主体性
jingshen zhutixing
(spiritual subjectivity)

See "wenxue zhutixing" (subjectivity of literature).

精英文化
jingying wenhua
(*elite* culture)

See "wenhua re" (culture craze) and "ziyouhua" (liberalization).

揪辫子
jiu bianzi
(to capitalize on people's vulnerable points)

See "sanbu zhengce" ("three don'ts" policy).

揪军内一小撮
jiu junnei yixiaocuo
(ferret out a handful of capitalist-roaders in the army)

See "changcheng" (Great Wall, i.e., the PLA) and "eryue niliu" (adverse February current).

九个指头和一个指头
jiu ge zhitou he yi ge zhitou
(nine fingers and one finger)

See "dashidafei wenti" (major issues of principle).

九评
jiu ping
(nine critiques)

See "xiuzhengzhuyi" (revisionism).

九三学社
Jiusan Xueshe
(September 3rd Academy)

See "minzhu dangpai" (democratic parties).

九一三事件
jiuyisan shijian
(September 13th Incident)

See "Lin Biao shijian" (Lin Biao Incident) and "Lin Jiang fan'geming jituan" (Lin Biao and Jiang Qing counter-revolutionary cliques).

开发区热
kaifaqu re
("development zone" craze)

From 1987 to 1992, especially after Deng's "Southern tour" in early 1992, a "development zone craze" spread throughout the country. Besides foreign investment, millions and millions of public funds were invested in real estate in the development zones. A direct result was a huge increase in the number of these zones. According to official statistics of March 1993, there were more than 6,000 zones at or above the county level, occupyig an area of 15,000 square kilometres, larger than the total area of all cities in China at that time (13.400 square kilometres). Another direct result was that the price of land in these zones rose dramatically, at a rate several times or even more than ten times within a few years. In mid-1993, Zhu Rongji, then vice-premier, oversaw an austerity program, which was called a policy of "macro-economic control" (hongguan tiaokong). This ended the "craze". By that time, however, many of those making investments with their power had already reaped huge profits for themselves. By conservative estimates, during the "craze" period the state lost over 10 billion Chinese dollars per year in the profits from land resources.

The unprecedented "development zone craze" is unlikely to occur again in China. It is compared to the "enclosure of the 18th century" in Britain, as in He Qinglian's book *The Pitfalls of China*. It represented a large-scale plunder of state land resources by bigwigs who colluded with officials or who were officials themselves at various levels of Party and government departments. (Because of this fact, some argue that the "enclosure of the 18th century" in Britain and the "development zone craze" in China in the 1990s were different by nature.) In the history of "previous accumulation" in contemporary China, there were the following several stages of crazes: individual business craze (including contracted farming), company establishing craze (stimulated by the dual price system), craze in the joint stock system reform, and finally the development zone craze. Among them, He Qinglian points out, the latter was the most "brilliant" and "charming" in previous accumulation myths. It easily produced a batch of billionaires, whereas the others only produced millionaires.

Some see the "enclosure of the 1990s" as a typical case of a "second previous accumulation" (de'er ci yuanshi jilei) in contemporary China. A "socialist previous accumulation" took place during the first few years following the 1949 Communist takeover of Chinese mainland. See also "yuanshi jilei" (previous accumulation) and "jingji gaige" (economic reform).

开放的社会主义现实主义体系
kaifangde shehuizhuyi xianshizhuyi tixi
(an open system of socialist realism)

See "shehuizhuyi xianshizhuyi" (socialist realism).

开後门
kaihoumen
(open the back door)

See "zou houmen" (get in by the back door).

开天窗
kaitianchuang
(open the windows of the sky)

"Kaitianchuang"—"opening the windows of the sky" or "putting in a skylight"—means leaving a blank in a publication to show that something has been censored. This was formerly a tactic employed by the Communists to embarrass and protest against the KMT regime. After the founding of the PRC, no one dared to use such a tactic again until 1987 when the editorial board of the *Literary Review* was ordered to remove an article originally featured in the journal's January 1987 issue. It was an ordinary literary essay entitled "A Layman's View of Fiction" ("Men wai yi xiaoshuo", *WXPL,* 1:11-14, 10, 1987), but its author Liu Binyan was considered by the top authorities as politically questionable in the ongoing "anti-bourgeois liberalization campaign". (Liu Binyan, together with the famous astrophysicist Fang Lizhi and the veteran writer Wang Ruowang, was expelled from the CCP at the very beginning of the 1987 campaign.) In protest, the journal's chief editor Liu Zaifu resigned (as did his deputy chief editor He Xilai). They took a clear-cut stand: their names would not be printed in the journal if it had to carry an article critical of Liu Binyan. Liu Zaifu became the first person openly to refuse to be involved in the accusations aginst Liu Binyan. Because of his stand, the *Literary Review* succeeded in avoiding carrying anything critical of Liu Binyan during the 1987 campaign.

Another "opening the windows of the sky" incident occurred during the pro-democracy movement of 1989, this time taking place in the CCP-led *Wenhui Daily* of Hong Kong. When the news was released that the PLA had killed demonstrating students in Beijing, the newspaper left a blank on its front page in the place usually devoted to its editorial. In its stead, there were printed four big Chinese characters—"tong xin ji shou" (with bitter abhorrence). See also "fandui zichanjieji ziyouhua yundong" (anti-bourgeois liberalization campaign) and "bajiu minyun" (1989 pro-democracy movement).

砍红旗
kan hongqi
(chop down the red banner)

See "hong" (red) and "shijian shi jianyan zhenlide weiyi biaozhun" (practice is the sole criterion for testing truth).

砍旗
kan qi
(chop down the banner)

The "banner" refers to the "red banner" or the "banner of Mao Zedong Thought. See "shijian shi jianyan zhenlide weiyi biaozhun" (practice is the sole criterion for testing truth).

抗日民族统一战线
kang Ri minzu tongyi zhanxian
(national anti-Japanese united front)

See "tongzhan" (united front).

靠边站
kaobianzhan
(to be set aside)

Though already used in the CCP's earlier cadre examination campaigns, the term appeared frequently in the GPCR, when many leading cadres were "set aside" from their posts or, even worse, toppled as "capitalist-roaders" by the "revolutionary rebels". Most of these cadres were later restored to their former positions.

科教兴国
ke jiao xing guo
(revitalize China through science and education)

From 26 to 30 May 1995, for the third time in more than forty years of China's Communist regime, a National Conference on Science was held in Beijing, with six thousand people in attendance. At the first conference held in 1956, Mao Zedong put forward the slogan: "Strive to develop science" (xiang kexue jinjun). At the second conference held in March 1978, Deng Xiaoping stressed the view that "Science and technology are part of the productive forces" (kexue jishu shi shengchanli) and he declared that "Intellectuals are part of the working class itself" (zhishifenzi shi gongrenjiejide yibufen). Currently, Jiang Zemin has advanced a new slogan: "Revitalize China through science and education."

At a press conference on 19 March 1998, the last day of the 9th NPC, the newly elected premier of the State Council, Zhu Rongji, echoed Jiang's slogan. He emphasized that revitalizing China through science and education will be the most important task for his government. This idea of strategic significance, he said, had been raised by President Jiang Zemin on several occasions but had not yet been seriously implemented. The reason was: the government lacked money—money had been spent on unwieldy government institutions at various levels and on many wasteful, duplicate constuction projects carried out with blind instructions from these institutions. This must be stopped, Zhu declared. Zhu also confirmed that a leading group to implement the task, with himself as leader and Vice Premier Li Lanqing as deputy leader, had been set up.

As many have pointed out, if the country is expected to be revitalized through science and education, then science and education must first be revitalized by the country (guo xing ke jiao). And this must be done immediately. At present, China ranks very low in the world in terms of intellectuals' average income and in funds to support education. In 1995, for example, educational funding was only 2.4 percent of the GNP. See also "ershinianlai zuiju yingxianglide shi ge kouhao" (ten most influential slogans in the past two decades).

科学技术是第一生产力
kexue jishu shi diyi shengchanli (science and technology are the first important productive forces)

See "kexue jishu shi shengchanli" (science and technology are part of the productive forces) and "ershinianlai zuiju yingxianglide shi ge kouhao" (ten most influential slogans in the past two decades).

科学技术是生产力
kexue jishu shi shengchanli (science and technology are part of the productive forces)

The view that "Science and technology are part of the productive forces" was long considered controversial in CCP doctrine. During the GPCR it was regarded as "reactionary".

Deng voiced his support for the view in 1975, but it was weak and short lived. He was accused of preaching the theory of "productivity as the sole factor determining social life" (weishengchanlilun), or "productivity fetishism" (shengchanli baiwujiao). In March 1978, Deng found an occasion to reiterate his support. In his speech at the opening ceremony of the National Conference on Science, he devoted much time to this issue. The basic factors in the productive forces, he explained, are the means of production and labor power. Throughout history, the means of production have always been linked with a given type of science and technology, and, likewise, labor power has always meant labor power armed with a certain degree of knowledge of science and technology. People often say that man is the most active productive force. "Man" here, Deng said, refers to people who possess a certain amount of scientific knowledge, experience in production, and skill in the use of tools to create material wealth. Deng also quoted Marx as saying that expansion of the use of machinery in production requires the conscious application of natural science and that science is among the productive forces (*SWD*, pp. 102-4).

Later, Deng further developed his views in this respect, which can be described as "Marxist scientism" (Makesizhuyide kexuezhuyi). On 12 September 1988, he said: "Marx expounded that science and technology were part of the productive forces, which was very correct. Judging from today, however, that is not enough. Perhaps they should be regarded as the first important productive forces" (Deng Xiaoping, "Kexue jishu shi diyi shengchanli"—"Science and Technology Are the First Important Productive Forces", in *Deng Xiaoping Wenxuan, Disanjuan—Selected Works of Deng Xiaoping,* 3, Beijing, Renmin, Oct. 1993). He reiterated this idea on several occasions, especially during his "Southern tour" in early 1992. CCP theorists hailed this thesis—"Science and technology are the first important productive forces"—as Deng's initiative in the history of Marxist development, which is of important significance as a guiding thought in China's current modernization drive. See also "xin shehuizhuyi guan" (new socialist view).

块块领导
kuaikuai lingdao
(regional geographical leadership)

See "tiaotiao lingdao" (vertical leadership).

框框
kuangkuang
(conventions)

"Kuangkuang" or "tiaotiao kuangkuang" refers derogatorily to such conventions as "old conventions" (lao kuangkuang) and "new conventions" (xin kuangkuang), "home-grown conventions" (tu kuangkuang), and "foreign conventions" (yang kuangkuang). They can come from book knowledge, older generations' experiences, authorities' opinions, regulations, or systems—anything that is conservative and has become an obstacle to progress. People are asked to break free from conventions (dapo kuangkuang) so that they can blaze new trails in their work.

扩大共识，增加信任，减少分歧，共创未来
kuoda gongshi, zengjia xinren, jianshao fenqi, gongchuang weilai
(expanding common ground, increasing trust, reducing differences, and building the future together)

See "weidu Zhongguo" (containment against China).

麒麟文化
Kylin wenhua
(Kylin Culture)

Following the unprecedented 10,000-strong Falungong protest in Beijing on 25 April 1999, the Chinese authorities have become alarmed by the popularity of such "qigong" spiritual groups, which stem from teachings on traditional Chinese breathing and meditation exercises. Falun Gong was banned as an "illegal organization" on 22 July 1999 and announced to be an "evil religion" on 25 October 1999. On 30 October 1999, the 12th Session of the NPC Standing Committee adopted a resolution concerning the banning of heretic cult organizations, prevention measures against them, and punishment for cult activities. According to this resolution, other organizations similar to the already banned Falun Gong were treated likewise. Among them was Zhong Gong (its full name is "Zhonghua Yangsheng Yizhi Gong"). Within half a year, 600 of its leaders were arrested, 3,000 of its legally registered industrial enterprises were shut down, and nine Zhong Gong books were banned, including: *Kylin Culture: A Transcript of the 1993-1998 Central Chinese Broadcasting Station's Special Program, Zhang Hongbao and His System of Kylin Culture, A Guide to Zhang Hongbao's Kylin Philosophy, Zhong Gong's Advanced Methods*, and *China's Kylin Gong Paintings.*

Founded in 1987 by Zhang Hongbao, Zhong Gong, like Falun Gong, is popular, reportedly having several million learners in twenty provinces; but it has a longer history and more elaborate organizational structure, and seems more politically conscious—it is guided by the so-called Kylin Culture, a set of philosophical-political-religious beliefs founded by Zhang Hongbao.

Zhang began studying Marxist classical works in 1969, and became a full-time official in charge of a local CCP committee's learning section in 1974. After more than twenty years of research, to his surprise, he discovered a conclusion completely opposite to his original intention. He found what he said was a "self-contradiction" in the Marxist system. On the basis of traditional Chinese philosophies and his criticism and repudiation of Marxism, he has created what he calls the "Kylin Culture" or "Kylin philosophy".

In his system is the "spirit-matter dialectics" (xin wu bianzhengfa), which challenges Marxist materialism. It maintains that spirit and matter are both objective existence, the only difference between them is that one is recessive or vacant existence and the other is dominant or real existence. They can transform mutually under certain conditions. There is no question of which is primary or which is secondary. Zhang published his "spirit-matter dialectics" in 1987 in the first Zhong Gong teaching material.

In 1992, on the basis of the theory of Yin and Yang, a traditional Chinese philosophy, Zhang put forward the "law of motion between things' Yin-Yang properties" (shiwu yingyang shuxingjiande yundong guilü) as one of what he said the eight basic laws of the universe. According to this law, everything not only can divide into two, but more important is that both divided parts have the properties of Yin or Yang in their own system and are subject to the law of Yin-Yang motion. Things conforming to this law will thrive and prosper; otherwise they will come to their doom. Yin and Yang are interdependent. This is what Zhang meant by the "law of Yin and Yang as each other's roots" (Yin Yang hugen). He applied this law to social system and asserted that the Marxist property right theory and political goal of "thoroughly eliminating private ownership", as raised in the "Manifesto of the Communist Party", is wrong and inevitably brings disasters to mankind.

In 1993, Zhang Hongbao published his "law of promotion-restriction-inhibition-transformation in the Five Elements" (wuxing shengke zhihualü), which derives from the traditional Chinese theory of the "Five Elements". According to this theory, all things in the universe, while coming into being as the result of the Yin-Yang interaction, can be summed up as five natures: earth, metal, water, wood, and fire (tu jin shui mu huo). There are relations of promotion and restriction of one another in the five elements. If the law of promotion is applied, there will appear a situation full of vitality, in which the new supersedes the old continuously without end; and when the law of restriction is followed, there will be failure and decline. Moreover, there is the restriction in the promotion and the promotion in the restriction.

For the CCP authorities, the vital problem of Zhang's law is, in explaining a Chinese philosophy of several thousand years ago about "restricting to balance" (zhiheng), he attacks the "irrationality" of totalitarian power structure in China. In contrast, he praises U.S. government structure of tripartite division of legislature, administration, and judiciary as implementing the principle "of the people, by the people, and for the people" and making the country strong and stable. Zhang also advocates supervision of public opinion and participation of religions on the basis of mutual restriction of governmental structures, so that a pentagon balancing stable structure is formed.

In addition, Zhang Hongbao found the official moral movement of "five stresses, four points of beauty, and three loves" (wujiang, simei, sanre'ai) to be "formalistic". Instead, he advanced in 1988 what he called "eight virtues and eight calls" (bade banian), a set of new norms of behavior and moral criteria, for Chinese to follow. He emphasized that his accorded with Chinese national conditions and folk customs.

Zhang Hongbao's "Kylin Culture" is obviously a challenge to Marxism and CCP's one-party rule. In view of the fact that Zhong Gong has drawn a large following of staunch believers throughout China and has a highly organized structure, the CCP authorities have reason to believe that this organization, if unchecked, will probably develop to become an opposition party.

In China's history there were a number of uprisings by religious organizations or under the cloak of religion. The largest and most famous among them was the Taiping Revolution under the leadership of Hong Xiuquan (1814-1864), which led to the establishment of the Taiping Heavenly Kingdom (1851-1864). All Chinese rulers definitely always bear this in mind. See also "Falun Gong" (Law Wheel Cultivation), "wujiang, simei, sanre'ai" (five stresses, four points of beauty, and three loves), and "chi butong zhengjianzhe" (dissidents).

拉出去，打进来
la chuqu, da jinlai
(pulling out, sneaking in)

This was a saying during the Mao period, referring to the class enemy's tactics—dragging Party and government cadres into his camp and sneaking into the revolutionary ranks. See "jieji douzheng" (class struggle) and "san da geming yundong" (three great revolutionary movements).

拉关系
la guanxi
(try to establish a relationship with someone; cotton up to)

See "zou houmen" (get in through the back door).

拉後腿
la houtui
(pull back the leg)

When one tries to influence someone else with his/her backward thoughts, Figuratively, it is referred to as "la houtui" or "che houtui". To pull back the leg of a person means to hinder the person from making progress or, more seriously, from making revolution.

来自右面的修正主义
laizi youmiande xiuzhengzhuyi
(Rightist revisionism)

See "xiuzhengzhuyi" (revisionism) and "you" (Right).

来自'左'面的修正主义
laizi 'zuo'miande xiuzhengzhuyi
('Leftist' revisionism)

See "xiuzhengzhuyi" (revisionism) and "you" (Right).

老红卫兵
lao hongweibing
(veteran Red Guards)

See "hongweibing" (Red Guards).

老九不能走
laojiu buneng zou
(we cannot do without number nine)

See "choulaojiu" (stinking number nine).

老三件
lao san jian
(former three most sought-after articles)

In the 1960s, for a Chinese family in the big cities, a watch, a bicycle, and a sewing machine were the "three most sought-after articles". To possess all three was considered a mark of a successful family. In the 1980s, a color television set, a refrigerator, and a washing machine were called the "new three most sought-after articles" (xinsanjian), in contrast to the "former three most sought-after articles" of the 1960s. In early 1996, as statistics showed, 96.7% of the families in Beijing had a refrigerator, 98.5% had a color television set, and 93.2% had a washing machine. Now families in the big cities are striving to own a computer, a private car, and a house—the "three super articles" (chaoji sandajian).

老三篇
laosanpian
(three frequently-read articles)

See "tuchu zhengzhi" (giving prominence to politics).

老五篇
laowupian
(five frequently-read articles)

See "tuchu zhengzhi" (giving prominence to politics).

老子党
laozi dang
(patriarchal party)

See "xiuzhengzhuyi" (revisionism).

老子英雄儿好汉，老子反动儿混蛋
laozi yingxiong er haohan, laozi fandong er hundan
(one will be a true man if his father is a hero, while reactionaries bear only bastards)

This was originally an antithetical couplet posted by Red Guards of the secondary school attached to the Beijing Aviation Institute on 29 July 1966. Its author was Tan Lifu, son of a Party elder (Tan is now deputy curator of the Beijing Library in charge of daily affairs). The couplet was considered a typical presentation of the "lineage theory", which was popular during the GPCR. See "xuetong lun" (lineage theory), "hongweibing" (Red Guards), and "sixiang gaizao" (ideological remolding).

劳动分工
laodong fengong
(division of labor)

See "zhongshen zhi" (life-tenure system) and "zichanjieji faquan" (bourgeois rights).

劳动改造
laodong gaizao
(reform through labor)

Under China's Communist regime, everyone was required to reform one's ideology; a major method of doing so was through manual labor. Hence the rise of a system of cadre participation in collective productive labor. Students were also required to do manual labor inside and/or outside schools.

The term also refers to a form of punishment for prisoners or alleged criminals who are waiting to be tried and sentenced, as stipulated in the "PRC Regulations Regarding Reform through Labor" ("Zhonghua Renmin Gongheguo Laodong Gaizao Tiaoli"), promulgated on 6 September 1954 by the Central Government. In accordance with the nature and degree of their crimes, prisoners are sent to jails under different supervision and management, where they are forced to engage in a certain amount of manual labor. They are supposed to reform themselves through forced labor and change themselves into new men. At the same time, of course, they are cheap forces of production. When used in this sense, the term is usually abbreviated as "laogai".

Another term related to "laogai" is "laodong jiaoyang", or "laojiao" for short (re-education through labor). In August 1957, the State Council promulgated its "Decision Regarding the Issue of Re-education through Labor" ("Guanyu Laodong Jiaoyang Wentide Jueding"). "Laojiao" was stipulated as another form of punishment, but for criminals guilty of small offences or for juvenile delinquents. In the Mao period, this punishment could be inflicted upon those called "historical counter-revolutionaries" (lishi fan'geming) who had once worked for the KMT or other enemy regimes or even on those who did not accept their work assignments.

People receiving re-education through labor were given somewhat better treatment than those serving a sentence. However, because they were not serving a sentence, there was no time limit to this form of punishment. (Later it was defined to mean a period not in excess of three years, with a one-year extension if necessary.) Also, many were forced to labor without having been properly tried in court—even one's leader was empowered to send his subordinates to "laojiao".

Hu Yaobang opposed this at a forum jointly sponsored in March 1981 by public security, procuratorial, and judicial departments. It was expected that this form of punishment, especially its name "laodong jiaoyang", would be changed. In 1983 both the "laogai" and "laojiao" institutions were transferred from the police to the Ministry of Justice. By 1985 re-education through labor was no longer part of the reform through labor penal system. See also "sixiang gaizao" (ideological remolding).

劳动教养
laodong jiaoyang
(re-education through labor)

See "laodong gaizao" (reform through labor).

劳动异化
laodong yihua
(labor alienation)

See "yihua laodong" (alienated labor) and "shehuizhuyi yihualun" (theory of socialist alienation).

劳改
laogai
(reform through labor)

See "laodong gaizao" (reform through labor).

劳教
laojiao
(re-education through labor)

See "laodong gaizao" (reform through labor).

雷锋精神
Lei Feng jingshen
(Lei Feng spirit)

Lei Feng was a PLA soldier who died on duty on 15 August 1962, at the age of twenty-two. In his short life, he was said to have done a lot of good deeds and to have been extremely loyal to Mao and the Party. After his death, the Lei Feng spirit was promoted by the CCP, describing a spirit of "fearing neither hardship nor death" (yibupa si, erbupa ku) and selfless devotion to others, consistency in words and actions, devotion to one's occupation, struggle despite personal risk, heroic fortitude, painstaking study, arduous work, and unity and fraternity. Most importantly, the Lei Feng spirit was characterized by a strong proletarian class consciousness (class love and class hatred), being a "docile tool" (xunfu gongju) of the Party, and a complete and unswerving loyalty to Mao and Mao's thought.

On 2 March 1963, the journal *China Youth* published Mao's inscription "Learn from Comrade Lei Feng" (Xiang Lei Feng tongzhi xuexi), and a nationwide "learn from Lei Feng" movement was then carried out. Supported by a mass media blitz, Lei Feng was made to be a "perfect man" (wanren), and has been regarded as such ever since. He is said to be one of the ten most important figures in mainland China in the twentieth century, standing with the three cores of Party leadership Mao Zedong (1893-1976), Deng Xiaoping (1904-1997), and Jiang Zemin (b. 1926); three Party elders Zhou Enlai (1898-1976), Liu Shaoqi (1898-1969), and Zhu De (1886-1976); revolutionary pioneer Sun Yat-sen (1866-1925); Sun Yat-sen's wife and late PRC vice president Soong Qingling (1893-1981); and leading writer Lu Xun (1881-1936). Lei Feng has become a symbol in Party culture.

The name of Lei Feng was even involved in inner-Party struggles. In 1975, as an example of the negative consequences of the GPCR, Deng said: "Uncle Lei Feng isn't around anymore." For this remark, he was attacked and vilified by those later known as the Gang of Four. In 1977, when recalling this episode, Deng noted that he had merely been stating the truth. That was "only what the masses were saying—I didn't invent the expression" *(SWD*, p. 97).

Against the background of the "decline of morality" (daode huapo) in today's China, Lei Feng is all the more a brilliant moral example for people to follow (as in the popular documentary movie, *Days without Lei Feng)*. In this sense, "learn from Lei Feng" activities may have reason to continue, especially among the young. But, as scholars have pointed out, the "learn from Lei Feng" movement initiated by Mao was not only a movement of moral education; it was also a religious movement and a political movement. Mao and his Party always emphasized the power of example, which is a Confucian tradition, and were good at identifying proper models for emulation in their various ideological remolding and Communist education movements, in struggles for their political goals. Lei Feng was such, and a most important, model, and thus became a tool for class struggle, for the cultivation of servility, and for the personality cult of Mao, which developed into a "modern superstition" on the eve of the GPCR. See also "sixiang gaizao" (ideological remolding) and "tuchu zhengzhi" (giving prominence to politics).

冷战
lengzhan
(Cold War)

See "lengzhanhou shidaide xin diguozhuyi" (neo-imperialism in the post-Cold War era).

冷战思维
lengzhan siwei
(Cold War mentality)

See "lengzhanhou shidaide xin diguozhuyi" (neo-imperialism in the post-Cold War era).

冷战後时代的新帝国主义
lengzhanhou shidaide xin diguozhuyi
(neo-imperialism in the post-Cold War era)

After the end of World War II in 1945 there appeared two antagonistic camps in the world: one was the capitalist camp headed by the United States, the other was the socialist camp headed by the Soviet Union. The United States and the Soviet Union, as later described by Beijing, were two "superpowers" (chaoji daguo). Confrontations and conflicts between them were called the Cold War, as distinct from a war in which weapons are used.

At that time, U.S. global strategy was shaped around the concept of "containment" (weidu) against the Soviet Union. But the relationship between China and the U.S. was also tense. Actually, the two measured their strength with each other on several occasions, as in the Korean War and the Vietnam War. One can recall the so-called "four-point statement" on China's policy towards the United States (Zhongguo dui Mei zhengce si ju hua). In an interview on 10 April 1966 (given to Ejaz Husain, correspondent of the Pakistan paper *Dawn),* PRC Premier Zhou Enlai made the following points: 1. China will not take the initiative to provoke war with the United States; 2. The Chinese mean what they say; 3. China is prepared; and 4. Once war breaks out, there will be no boundaries *(RMRB,* 10 May 1966).

In the early 1990s, a series of dramatic changes took place in the Soviet Union and Eastern Europe, which led to the end of their Communist regimes (the Soviet Union disintegrated on 26 December 1991). The United States became the only superpower in the world; the foundation for the Cold War thus ceased to exist. Thereafter, Sino-U.S. relations were characterized by fluctuation and fragility.

In late October 1997, Jiang Zemin paid a state visit to the U.S. An important task on his trip was to convince Washington and the American people that China was willing to forge a "strategic partnership" (zhanlüe huoban guanxi) with the U.S. Jiang seemed to have fulfilled this task, and he was very proud of it. Flush with his success in the just concluded 15th CCP National Congress, where he claimed credit for promoting bolder economic reform, he gained from his summit with President Clinton what he could not from domestic politics: international stature. The next year, from 25 June to 3 July 1998, U.S. President Bill Clinton paid a 9-day state visit to China. This was described as a new development in the "Sino-U.S. strategic partnership", another important step since Jiang's 1997 U.S. visit.

Significantly, while seeking to establish "strategic partnership" with the U.S., China is still suspicious of the U.S. As early as September 1991, Deng Xiaoping used the phrase "xin lengzhan" (a new cold war) to describe the Sino-U.S. conflicts, and the phrase has often since been repeated in the Chinese press. In May 1999, after the U.S.-led NATO bombing of the Chinese Embassy in Belgrade, a new upsurge of anti-U.S. sentiment spread throughout China. Chinese leaders could not believe the explanation that the embassy attack had been "unintentional and a tragic error". Moreover, they condemned the notion of "human rights over sovereignty" (renquan gaoyu zhuquan) or "humanitarian intervention" (rendaozhuyi ganyu). (The NATO claimed that it was "not fighting for land, but for values" in Kosovo.) On 25 August 1999, at the Bishkek summit of China, Russia and three Central Asian countries, Kyrgyzstan, Kazakhstan, and Tajikistan, Chinese President Jiang Zemin said that even though the Cold War ended ten years ago, the world is far from peaceful. He pointed to the emergence of what he called "neo-interventionism" (xin ganshezhuyi)—the trend of interfering in other countries' internal affairs under the pretext of "protecting human rights". Jiang stressed that it is a new form of hegemony and power politics (qiangquan zhengzhi), which greatly ruins the existing, and long established, rule for international relations.

There is a logic at work here: The core of American strategy in the twenty-first century is to build a perfect and multi-level economic and security mechanism by the year 2015, forming a new international community under its leadership. This will be a unilateral world centered around U.S. hegemony. China will not be a partner in this configuration. Instead, it will be a barrier to U.S. exercise of hegemonism, or a threat to U.S. Pacific and Atlantic strategy (or "Eurasian strategy". See, for instance, *Grand Chessboard* by Zbigniew Brzezinski, former U.S. National Security Adviser to U.S. President Jimmy Carter). The U.S. has thus created a China threat theory. China's stand on the Kosovo crisis was evidence of such a threat. Consequently, U.S.

missiles attacked the Chinese Embassy. This was a warning and also an exploration, a signal that the U.S. is speeding up the pace of its strategy of containing China. It is an essential part of its new strategy, although it came a little earlier than expected.

China referred to U.S. actions as "neo-imperialism in the post-Cold War era". U.S.-led NATO raids on Yugoslavia, in the name of "humanitarianism", were condemned as "out-and-out imperialist action". The only "difference" between the new and the traditional imperialists was said to be that gunboat policies have been replaced by missile attacks, capital and industrial exports by hi-tech exports, and direct plunder by forcefully opening-up another country's market.

China's strategists maintain that a Cold War mentality (lengzhan siwei) still lingers among the imperialists in the world. U.S.-led NATO military intervention in Yugoslavia, NATO's New Strategy for the twenty-first century, the New Japan-U.S. Defense Co-operation Guidelines, and the start of the U.S. "Post Star War" plan—all these demonstrate to the hilt the hegemonic intentions of the United States. The multi-polar structure is unbalanced. There have been new assessments on the overall structure of the world today. Though peace and development are current themes, China's strategists warn that one should still be on the look-out for neo-imperialism.

As part of China's global strategy, Jiang Zemin and his Russian counterpart President Boris Yeltsin signed on 10 December 1999 a communiqué urging all nations to join a "balanced, multi-polar world order". China and Russia were determined to develop their "cooperative strategic partnership" ("zhanlüe xiezuo huoban guanxi", which was established by Jiang Zemin and Yeltsin in April 1996). According to certain Western observers, the two countries have forged a "united front" to resist the post-Cold War dominance of the U.S. and its Western allies in a move reminiscent of their embrace in the 1950s as both sought to become Communist superpowers. This was an important event in international affairs at the end of the twentieth century.

Many doubt this "united front". But they predict that the "two poles pattern" (liangji geju)—which originally refers to the international situation during the Cold War, whereby the two confronting superpowers, the United States and the Soviet Union, constituted the two poles in the world—will be seen again during the first several decades of the twenty-first century. This time international struggles will unfold chiefly between China and the United States. See also "weidu Zhongguo" (containment against China).

离经叛道论
lijingpandao lun
(theory of "discarding the classics and rebelling against orthodoxy")

This was one of the "eight sinister theories" singled out for attack in the 1966 Party document the "Summary". If one traces those criticisms during and before the GPCR, Xia Yan, then vice minister of culture, can be said to be responsible for this theory. In his speech delivered on 21 July 1959 at a national conference attended by directors of feature film studios, he said: "Films today are all about the same old 'revolutionary classics' and 'war orthodoxy'. Apart from these, there is nothing. No new varieties will ever develop if we go on in this way. Let my words today mark a departure from the 'classics' and 'orthodoxy'". Actually, the speech represented a disagreement about the over-emphasis on the description of struggles. See also "jiyao" ("Summary") and "fan 'ticai jueding' lun" (theory of opposition to "subject-matter as the decisive factor").

李一哲事件
Li Yizhe shijian
(Li Yizhe incident)

In November 1974, Li Zhengtian (a painting student), Chen Yiyang (an educated youth), and Wang Xizhe (a worker), sharing the pen-name "Li Yizhe", wrote and published a lengthy article entitled "Socialist Democracy and the Legal System" ("Guanyu shehuizhuyi minzhu yu fazhi") in the form of a "big-character poster" posted on building walls in a Guangzhou central business district (the corner of Beijing Road and Section 5 of Zhongshan Road). Though fiercely attacked by the authorities, the authors did not yield. Instead, they responded with a number of eloquent big-character posters. In April 1977, all three men were arrested.

On 6 February 1979, the CCP Guangdong Provincial Committee convened a mass rally, where the three poster authors, together with their supporters, were declared rehabilitated. Two years later, however, Wang Xizhe was rearrested and sentenced to 14 years in prison on a charge of "counter-revolutionary propaganda and agitation". He was released on parole in 1993.

In September 1996, Wang once again (this time together with Liu Xiaobo, a scholar and prominent dissident) triggered the authorities' reprisals, for publishing the statement "Opinions Regarding Important Issues Facing Our Country: An October 10th Statement to Both the Kuomintang and the Chinese Communist Party" ("Shuangshi shengming", reprinted in *Beijing zhi chun,* Nov. 1996). In this statement, Wang and Liu called for the impeachment of Chinese President Jiang Zemin. One month later, Wang Xizhe escaped to Hong Kong and then sought asylum in the United States. See also "chi butong zhengjianzhe" (dissidents).

理解万岁
lijie wansui
(Long live understanding)

See "ershinianlai zuiju yingxianglide shi ge kouhao" (ten most influential slogans in the past two decades).

理性民族主义
lixing minzuzhuyi
(rational nationalism)

See "minzuzhuyi" (nationalism).

立场决定论
lichang jueding lun
(theory of class stand as the decisive factor)

See "sixiang gaizao" (ideological remolding).

历史背景的真实
lishi beijingde zhenshi
(truthfulness of the historical background)

See "shehuizhuyi xianshizhuyi" (socialist realism).

历史发展阶段超越论
lishi fazhan jieduan chaoyue lun
(theory of skipping over stage of historical development)

See "lishi fazhan jieduan buke chaoyue lun" (theory of the impossibility of skipping over stage of historical development).

历史发展阶段不可超越论
lishi fazhan jieduan buke chaoyue lun
(theory of the impossibility of skipping over stage of historical development)

Plekhanov (1856-1918), known as the "Father of Russian Marxism", firmly advocated the theory of the impossibility of skipping over any necessary stage of historical development, which negates any premature seizure of political power. He felt that any undue haste in trying to bring about socialism would lead to the most serious kind of economic disaster. This theory was confirmed as Marxist in the 1980s by most of the CCP leaders and theoreticians, as a lesson drawn from the bitter experience in the Mao period. Zhao Ziyang was one of them. At the 13th National Congress of the CCP held in October 1987, Zhao, with Deng's support, formally put forth the "theory of the primary stage of socialism" (shehuizhuyi chuji jieduan lun) as the Party's new "foothold" (lizudian) for China's current policies. Zhao also found support from *River Elegy,* a 1988 popular though controversial television political commentary series. This work makes it clear that the doubts entertained by Plekhanov have been taken up by history. It is not history that has to give way; those who try to transcend history are ultimately unable to escape punishment, as can be seen from what has happened in the Soviet Union, China, and the East European bloc. Now, one by one, they all have had to embark upon the path of reform.

Significantly, just like many other CCP leaders, before the establishment of the Communist regime Mao had also vigorously supported the theory of the impossibility of skipping over any necessary stage of historical development. For instance, during the CCP 7th National Congress (held in Yan'an from 23 April to 11 June 1945), Mao specifically explained that China must undergo the stage of capitalism. He sternly criticized the Populist view within the CCP that China could enter a socialist society directly from feudal economy. Hence the joke that Mao was a first "capitalist-roader" within the Party. Of course, Mao later (roughly in 1956) drastically changed his mind.

But, fundamentally, not everyone agrees with the theory of the "necessary stages of historical development" (lishi fazhan biran jieduan). For example, when Jiang Zemin echoed Zhao Ziyang's "theory of the primary stage of socialism" at the 1997 CCP's 15th National Congress, Cui Zhiyuan, a "neo-Leftist" scholar, asserted that this was precisely a "limitation" of the Congress. According to him, the "primary stage" theory fails to get rid of the monistic and Stalinist thinking mode about the "necessary stages of historical development" (Cui Zhiyuan, "Zhonggong shiwudade lilun chuangxin yu juxian"—"The 15th CCP National Congress: Theoretical Innovations and Limitations", *Zhongguo yu shijie,* Jan. 1998). See also *"Heshang* shijian" *(River Elegy* Incident), "shehuizhuyi chuji jieduan lun" (theory of the primary stage of socialism), "xin shehuizhuyi guan" (new socialist view), and "xinzuopai" (neo-Leftists).

历史反革命
lishi fan'geming
(historical counter-revolutionary)

See "zhengzhi wenti" (political issue) and "laodong gaizao" (reform through labor).

历史反思
lishi fansi
(historical reflections)

See "yi wenti wei zhongxinde baogao wenxue" (problem-centered reportage literature) and "fansi" (reflection).

历史角色的互换
lishi jiaosede huhuan
(an interchange of historical roles)

In 1986, as a reflection of the 1919 May 4th Movement, Li Zehou presented his views about what he called "the double variation of enlightenment and salvation". According to Li, in the "double variation", there appeared an interesting and significant phenomenon of an "interchange of historical roles" (see Li Zehou, "Qimeng yu jiuwangde shuangchong bianzou: 'wusi' huixiang zhi yi"—"A Double Variation of Enlightenment and Salvation: A Recollection of the 'May 4th Movement'", *Zouxiang weilai*, 1, Aug. 1986). Later, during the 1989 pro-democracy movement, Liu Zaifu also joined in the discussion. His article, "Lost and Regained: The Spirit of Enlightenment of May 4th Literature" ("Wusi wenxue qimeng jingshende shiluo yu huigui"), was published in the *Literary Gazette* in two parts on 22 and 29 April 1989 respectively. A revised version was also carried in the *People's Daily* on 25 April 1989 under the title "Two Historic Breakthroughs: From the May 4th Movement of New Culture to the 'Consciousness of Modern Culture' in the New Period" ("Liangci lishixingde tupo: cong 'wusi' xinwenhua yundong dao xinshiqide 'xiandai wenhua yishi'").

During the period of the May 4th Movement, the theme of which was enlightenment (which found expression in the "New Culture Movement" at that time), Chinese intellectuals, as the first recipients of the humanistic spirit of the West, played a vanguard role not only in cultural but also in political fields. Later, especially after Mao delivered his *Yan'an Talks* in 1942, this role was gradually weakened and even negated. Ironically, an interchange of historical roles took place: intellectuals, originally enlighteners, became objects to be enlightened and remolded, and peasants were in turn to give intellectuals their "re-education". During the process of the interchange, the spirit of enlightenment and the consciousness of self characteristic of the intellectuals (which at the time were only at an embryonic stage) were lost.

There were many complicated reasons for this. Historically, in the several decades after the May 4th Movement, especially during the War of Resistance against Japan (1937-1945), the greatest danger China faced was the fall of the nation. In such a situation, enlightenment, as seen during the period of the May 4th Movement, gave way to salvation, which became an urgent and overriding task for the whole country. In the fulfillment of this task, intellectuals, with their ideological education, found themselves not equal to workers, peasants, and soldiers, who made many more sacrifices and played a much more important role.

Inherently and fundamentally, perhaps one can say there was no soil at that time for the individuality, consciousness of self, and independent spirit, which were born during the "May 4th" period, to grow. Without a strong material foundation—a social form of free competition and commercial exchange—the tragic fate of the spirit of enlightenment was inevitable. In 1989, it was precisely because of Deng Xiaoping's policy of reform that some changes were possible. One achievement of the economic reform in the past decade or more was the emergence and development of a private sector. A diversified economy leads to a diversified culture; and a diversified culture leads to diversified politics. That is why in a sense the 1989 pro-democracy movement can be seen as an outcome of the ten years of reform.

The "interchange of historical roles" is an important theme in the study of modern and contemporary Chinese intellectuals. A few years later, Liu and Li were still obsessed with it, as seen in their 1995 book *Farewell to Revolution: Looking Back upon China of the Twentieth Century.* As they point out, the two occurrences—the decline of the "New Culture Movement" and the appearance of a "National Salvation Movement"—not only meant that enlightenment was replaced by salvation, but, more importantly, the change harbingered a coming alliance of an "ideological-cultural hegemony" and a "political hegemony" *(Farewell to Revolution,* p. 206). As history has already revealed, this alliance dominated and reorganized modern Chinese society.

历史唯物主义
lishi weiwuzhuyi
(historical materialism)

See "bianzheng weiwuzhuyi" (dialectical materialism).

历史唯心主义
lishi weixinzhuyi
(historical idealism)

See "bianzheng weiwuzhuyi" (dialectical materialism).

历史问题
lishi wenti
(historical issue)

See "zhengzhi wenti" (political issue).

利用小说反党是一大发明
liyong xiaoshuo fandang shi yida faming
(use of the novel for anti-Party activities is quite an invention)

On 24 September 1962, at the 10th Plenum of the 8th PCC, Mao Zedong issued his well-known call: "Never forget class struggle." In the same speech, he also warned: "Isn't it now much in vogue to write stories? The use of the novel for anti-Party activities is quite an invention. To overthrow political power, it is always necessary, first of all, to create public opinion, to do work in the ideological sphere. This is true for the revolutionary class as well as for the counter-revolutionary class." (The statement was originally written by Kang Sheng, which Mao read out during his speech.)

Here Mao was referring to *Liu Zhidan*, a 1962 novel written about Liu Zhidan (1903-1936), a local hero and Communist leader in the Shanxi-Gansu revolutionary base area before Mao and his men arrived in 1935 after completing the Long March. The first part of the second volume was published in installments in the *Workers' Daily* from 28 July to 4 August 1962. Soon afterwards Li Jiantong, its author, was framed and persecuted in a case which involved more than ten thousand people. In 1979 the verdict was reversed.

利用，限制，改造
liyong, xianzhi, gaizao
(using, restricting, and transforming)

"Using, restricting, and transforming" characterized CCP policy towards China's capitalist industry and commerce during the 1950s. Mao first touched on the issue of using and restricting private capital in his report to the March 1949 2nd Plenum of the 7th PCC. After the PRC was founded, a national policy was formulated, which was finalized in the Tenth Article of the PRC Constitution adopted at the First NPC on 20 September 1954. Its text reads as follows: "The policy of the state towards capitalist industry and commerce is to use, restrict, and transform them. Through control exercised by organs of state administration, leadership by the state sector of the economy, and supervision by the masses of workers, the state makes use of the positive aspects of capitalist industry and commerce which are beneficial to national welfare and the people's livelihood, restricts their negative aspects which are detrimental to national welfare and the people's livelihood, and encourages and guides their transformation into various forms of state-capitalist economy, gradually replacing capitalist ownership with ownership by the whole people" *(RMRB,* 21 Sept. 1954). The wording of "liyong, xianzhi, gaizou" was suggested by Li Weihan, director of the PCC United Front Department. Li was thus highly praised by Mao.

It is interesting to compare this policy with those policies carried out in the current economic reform.

联俄，联共，扶助农工
lian E, lian Gong, fuzhu nong gong
(allying Russians and Communists and assisting peasants and workers)

See "sanminzhuyi" (Three Principles of the People).

联动
liandong
(Capital Red Guards United Action Committee)

"Liandong" ("United Action") is an abbreviation for "Shoudu hongweibing lianhe xingdong weiyuanhui" (Capital Red Guards United Action Committee). It was set up in Beijing on 5 December 1966. About the same time, similar organizations were set up in other places, such as the "Three-character Soldiers" (Sanzibing) in Wuhan, the "Black Character Soldiers" (Heizibing) in Jinan, and the "Red Descendants" (Honghoudai) in Shenyang.

By this time, many "United Action" members' parents or relatives had been overthrown as "capitalist-roaders" (zouzipai—those in power within the Party taking the capitalist road). Against this background, the purpose of this organization was self-explanatory. In the early days of the GPCR, these Red Guards, because their parents or relatives were high-ranking Party officials or army officers, considered themselves as "natural revolutionary successors" and posed as masters of the world. When engaging in what they called "Red Terror" and cruelly persecuting "niuguisheshen"—class enemies of all descriptions—they made it clear: "Only Leftists can enjoy the right to rebel; no Rightists are allowed to change our regime". Then all of a sudden, they fell from paradise to hell and had to taste bitterness, which they never before had experienced. Naturally, they turned to oppose the Central GPCR Group as they thought it was Jiang Qing and her colleagues who had caused their misfortune.

On New Year's Day 1967, this Red Guard organization was declared by the authorities to be "counter-revolutionary", and quite a number of its members were arrested. By the summer of 1968, it had completely disintegrated, even though a few months earlier, on 22 April 1968, all its arrested members had been released following instructions from Mao.

In retrospect, some assert that the "Capital Red Guards United Action Committee" was good because it was suppressed by the authorities of the time, accused of opposing the GPCR. Others, however, argue that it is incorrect to come to this conclusion. An understanding of this organization provides insights into the GPCR. See also "hongweibing" (Red Guards).

联合舰队
lianhe jiandui
(United Task Fleet)

See "Lin Biao shijian" (Lin Biao Incident).

两次历史性飞跃
liang ci lishixing feiyue
(two historic leaps)

There have been "two historic leaps" in the more than 60 years of CCP history, as put forth by Zhao Ziyang in his report to the 1987 13th National Congress of the CCP—"Advancing Along the Road of Socialism with Chinese Characteristics" (*HQ*, 21:4, 24, 1987). They were the victory of the "new democratic revolution" in 1949 and the opening up of the "new stage of socialist construction" after the 3rd Plenum of the 11th PCC in December 1978. As Zhao noted, the first was marked by Mao's leadership, and the second by Deng's leadership. Zhao also described the "striking contrast" between the 20 years (not counting the 10 years of the GPCR) before the 3rd Plenum and the 9 years after it, in favor of Deng's leadership.

At the September 1997 CCP 15th National Congress, Jiang Zemin echoed the theory of the "two historic leaps", though his description was somewhat different. The integration of Marxism-Leninism with China's reality (Ma-Liezhuyi yu Zhongguo shijian xiangjiehe), he said, has experienced two historic leaps, resulting in two great theories. The result of the first leap was the theoretical principles concerning the revolution and construction in China and a summary of the experience therein, both of which have been proved "correct" by practice. With Mao Zedong as its principal founder, the CCP calls it Mao Zedong Thought. The result of the second leap was the theory of building socialism with Chinese characteristics. With Deng Xiaoping as its principal founder, the CCP calls it Deng Xiaoping Theory. Jiang stated that these two great theories represent the crystallization of the practical experience and collective wisdom of the Party and the people.

The integration of Marxism-Leninism with China's reality means Sinicized Marxism. Most of today's Chinese theorists agree with the concept of the "two historic leaps" in CCP history of Sinicized Marxism, but their appraisals of Mao Zedong Thought and of Deng Xiaoping Theory may differ from one another and from Party leaders'. See also "fan chuantong" (anti-tradition), "Mao Zedong sixiang" (Mao Zedong Thought), and "Deng Xiaoping lilun" (Deng Xiaoping Theory).

两大阵营
liang da zhenying
(two camps)

See "yibiandao" (lean to one side) and "lengzhanhou shidaide xin diguozhuyi" (neo-imperialism in the post-Cold War era).

两代诗人
liang dai shiren
(two generations of poets)

The term "two generations of poets" was first used in 1979. The first generation referred to those established poets before the GPCR, and the second generation consisted of those young poets emerging after the GPCR, especially the "misty" poets (menglong shiren).

There was a nationwide debate in the early 1980s about the problems of the "two generations of poets" and "misty poetry" (menglongshi). The debate was formally ignited after Gong Liu's article "A New Task—On Comrade Gu Cheng's Poems" ("Xinde keti—cong Gu Cheng tongzhide jishou shi tanqi", *Xingxing,* 1, Oct. 1979) was reprinted together with an editor's note in the January 1980 issue of the *Literary Gazette*. Gong Liu, a famous poet, raised what he saw as a "new task": Poets of the older generation must try as hard as possible to understand the new generation. The April 1980 Nanning Forum on Contemporary Poetry was the first public discussion of this topic, and Gu Cheng, the young poet discussed in Gong Liu's article, became the central controversial figure.

When so many people began discussing this young poet and the obscurity and eccentricity of his poetry, Gu Gong, Gu Cheng's father, who was a rather accomplished poet in his own right, could not hold back and felt compelled to join in the discussion. In his 1980 article, "Two Generations: About the 'Incomprehensibility' of Poetry" ("Liangdairen—cong shide 'budong' tanqi'", *SK,* 10:49-51, 1980), he recalled emotionally how his son began composing poems at the age of eight and how as the child grew up he had found his son's poems more and more difficult to understand. He said that he had tried to guide this young man but it seemed that he and his contemporaries were bit by bit losing ground. This veteran poet believed he was facing "the soul, the pursuit, and the poetry of a new generation". As to how Gu Cheng formed his style, thinking, and aesthetic sense, the father testified that his son had neither inherited the tradition of the "Crescent School" (xinyuepai) that emerged after the May 4th Movement, nor was he influenced by modernism in the West. Like most of his generation, Gu Cheng had grown up in a cultural desert. He had never read before, and seldom read even now, works of symbolism, futurism, expressionism, stream-of-consciousness, the theater of the absurd, etc. "He is not performing imitation", the father affirmed, not without a sort of satisfaction, "not looking for yesterday's or a foreign Crescent School. He is truly taking a road of his own".

Gu Gong admitted, nevertheless, that there did exist some similarity between Gu Cheng's poems and those written by modernists in foreign countries and, for a period of the past, in China. He advocated probing how modernism had come into existence, how the "lost generation", the "beat generation", and the "angry generation" had appeared in the West after the first and second world wars, and whether there was anything similar to those historical phenomena in China after the ten years of turbulence and damage. "If there is", he asked in the tone of a confident theorist: "then why is it surprising and frightening that there have appeared in today's China the 'exploring generation' (tansuode yidai), the 'bewildered generation' (panghuangde yidai), and the 'pragmatic generation' (qiushide yidai)? And what is strange or abnormal if they have begun displaying and unburdening themselves with ways of thinking and observing, and consequently with ways of artistic (including poetic) expression historically formed and characteristic of their own generation?" See also "menglongshi" (misty poetry) and "menglongshi lilunde san ci jueqi" ("three rises" in the theory of misty poetry).

两个凡是
liang ge fanshi
(two whatevers)

Upholding or opposing the "two whatevers" was the focus of the struggle between the Deng Xiaoping faction and the faction of CCP Chairman Hua Guofeng in 1977-1978.

The "two whatevers" refer to the statement, "We will resolutely uphold whatever policy decisions Chairman Mao made, and unswervingly follow whatever instructions Chairman Mao gave", contained in the 7 February 1977 joint editorial of the *People's Daily, Red Flag,* and the *Liberation Army Daily* under the title "Study the Documents Well and Grasp the Key Link" (Xue hao wenjian zhuazhu gang). In fact, as early as 26 October 1976, when talking with officials in charge of the PCC Propaganda Department, Hua Guofeng put forward his "two whatevers" view for the first time. Later, he reiterated it on several occasions. These statements were regarded as his resistance to popular demand at the time for Deng Xiaoping's return to power and a rehabilitation of the "Tiananmen Incident" of 5 April 1976.

Ye Jianying was the first person to oppose the "two whatevers" view, as indicated in his speech at the PCC work conference held in mid-March 1977. As to Deng himself, naturally, he all the more strongly sensed the problem. On 10 April 1977, in a letter to Hua Guofeng, Ye Jianying, and the PCC, Deng suggested the following concept: "genuine Mao Zedong Thought taken as an integral whole", implying that not every word of Mao should be followed. Then, on 24 May 1977 (soon after Hua Guofeng once again vowed to stick to the "two whatevers"), Deng explicitly pointed out that the "two whatevers" were at odds with Marxism and thus unacceptable. In a talk with Wang Zhen and Deng Liqun, then two of his close friends, he said: "If this principle were correct, there could be no justification for my rehabilitation, nor could there be any for the statement that the activities of the masses at Tiananmen Square in 1976 were reasonable" ("The 'Two Whatevers' Do Not Accord with Marxism", *SWD,* p. 51).

Related to the "two whatevers" issue was the 1978 debate over the criterion of truth. The debate led to Deng's victory at the 3rd Plenum of the 11th PCC held in December 1978, which marked the decline of Hua Guofeng and his faction who were accused of committing the mistake of sticking to the "two whatevers".

However, as Ling Zhijun and Ma Licheng, the authors of *Five Voices in Present China* point out, the "two whatevers" as a principle should be said to be a creation of the whole Party, or, to be more exact, of Mao himself (p. 123). See also "shijian shi jianyan zhenlide weiyi biaozhun" (practice is the sole criterion for testing truth) and "yingming lingxiu" (wise leader).

两个估计
liang ge guji
(two appraisals)

From April to July 1971, a national conference on education was held in Beijing. On 13 August 1971, the "Summary of the National Conference on Educational Work" ("Quanguo jiaoyu gongzuo huiyi jiyao") was published. The "two appraisals" were put forward in the document, which had been approved by Mao. The first appraisal was: During the seventeen years prior to the start of the GPCR (1949 to 1966), the bourgeoisie had exercised dictatorship over the proletariat in the educational sphere, that is, there was a "dictatorship by the proponents of a sinister line". The second appraisal was: the world outlook of the vast majority of intellectuals was basically bourgeois, that is, they were bourgeois intellectuals. The "two appraisals" served as a good excuse for the persecution of intellectuals. However, since the appraisals had been approved by Mao, they were not touched for a long time after the downfall of the Gang of Four. On 19 September 1977, Deng Xiaoping gave a talk to the leaders of the Ministry of Education, expressing his different view about the "two appraisals". Following Deng's talk, the Ministry of Education, in the name of a criticism group, published an article which repudiated the "two appraisals" and attributed them to the Gang of Four. ("Jiaoyu zhanxianshangde yichang dabianlun"—"A Great Debate on the Educational Front", *HQ,* 12, 1977; *RMRB,* 18 Nov. 1977). On 19 March 1979, a rescission of the "two appraisals" was finally endorsed in a written directive of the PCC. See also "dangde jiaoyu fangzhen" (the Party's educational policy).

两个基本点
liang ge jiben dian
(two basic points)

See "zhengzhi gaige" (political reform), "jingji gaige" (economic reform), and "Deng Xiaoping lilun" (Deng Xiaoping Theory).

两个口号之争
liang ge kouhao zhi zheng
(debate over two slogans)

See "sanshiniandai wenyi yundong" (literature and art movement of the 1930s).

两个文革论
liang ge wen'ge lun
("two Cultural Revolutions" theory)

The "two Cultural Revolutions" theory gave rise to another controversy on the nature of the GPCR. One of those promoting the theory is, for instance, Zheng Yi, a dissident writer now living in exile in the United States (see his "Autobiography, Party Three", *JN,* Aug. 1992, pp. 94-99).

Proponents of the theory admit the GPCR was an unavoidable, natural end-result of Mao's ever-worsening ultra-Left line, but while Mao and his followers were making their ultra-Left "revolution", millions of people were also waging a "revolution" of their own. They not only made use of the official slogan "Let the masses liberate themselves" (Rang qunzhong ziji jiefang ziji), but they also created their own slogan: "Kick aside Party committees to make revolution" (Tikai dangwei nao geming). In actuality, they were engaging in a rebellion against the tyranny of the Communist regime. Indeed, the revolution can be said, in a sense, to be a "war between the Red and the Black" in the whole society. For the "Reds", it might well have been a "class reprisal" (jieji baofu) on a large, national scale, one made by the oppressed, consciously or not, on their oppressors. That is why there were so many people at the time rising up in rebellion and so many so-called "capitalist-roaders" were toppled. Understandably, the "Blacks" called themselves "revolutionary rebels" (geming zaofanpai). They even claimed that they were "defending Chairman Mao". They appeared so sincere in the exciting revolutionary atmosphere that even they themselves were convinced, at least for a while, by their own high-sounding declarations. (This does not mean that their real intention passed entirely unnoticed. A warning was always there, as expressed in a slogan raised by those from the "hongwulei" families: "Only Leftists can enjoy the right to rebel; no Rightists are allowed to change our regime"—"Zhizhun zuopai zaofan, buzhun youpai fantian".)

In the chaos of the time, these "revolutionary rebels" thought they could change their lives, both materially and politically. As it turned out, they did not succeed. Their revolution ended in multiple tragedies. When they joined in struggling against those alleged "capitalist-roaders", they thought they were making use of the opportunity Mao gave them. But for Mao (and his colleagues), they were merely a tool in his strategy of political struggle. Unfortunately, many of them were willing to play such a role (some thought otherwise at the time, but they were too few in number). Their ideology was guided by Mao Zedong Thought. They could not avoid the "modern superstition (xiandai mixin), at least for a period of time. In many cases, they were misled by a handful of "bad leaders" (huai toutou), who were careerists with no scruples. Poisoned by Mao's "struggle philosophy" (douzheng zhexue), they became involved in illegal or criminal activities. It was inevitable that they would eventually be oppressed again when they realized the situation. In fact, this occurred by the 9th CCP National Congress of April 1969, at which the Mao Zedong-Lin Biao leadership system was established. The Congress can be regarded as the end of the GPCR, according to proponents of the "two Cultural Revolutions" theory (some even argue that the GPCR lasted only two years, from August 1966 to August 1968, indicating the rise and decline of the rebels). See also "wen'ge" (Cultural Revolution).

两个文明
liang ge wenming
(two civilizations)

The two civilizations refer to the "socialist spiritual civilization" (shehuizhuyi jingshen wenming) and the "socialist material civilization" (shehuizhuyi wuzhi wenming).

In his report, "Open Up All-Roundly a New Phase of Socialist Modern Construction", delivered at the September 1982 12th CCP National Congress, Hu Yaobang emphasized that, while enhancing the socialist material civilization, a socialist spiritual civilization must also be built. The relationship between the two is very close. The building of a material civilization is the necessary foundation for a socialist spiritual civilization (that is why economic construction is the center of

Party work). As to the latter, it not only exerts a massive impetus on the former, it also ensures that the former will develop in the right direction. The two are interdependent and have mutual goals.

At the Congress, a call was issued to cultivate "socialist citizens" with lofty ideals, moral integrity, a good education, and a strong sense of discipline ("si you"—you lixiang, you daode, you jiaoyu, you jilü). Deng played an important role in the "si you" formulation. In April 1983, when meeting an Indian Communist Party delegation, he said that the "si you" are the essence of a "spiritual civilization". In his speech on 7 March 1985 at the National Conference on Science and Technology, he expressed the view that of the "si you", lofty ideals and a strong sense of discipline are the most important.

On 28 September 1986, the 6th Plenum of the 12th PCC passed a resolution concerning the building of a socialist spiritual civilization. As stipulated, Marxism-Leninism-Mao Zedong Thought is the guiding foundation, and the civilization must be built by combining the promotion of socialist modernization, the carrying out of the reform and open-door policy, and the upholding of the "four cardinal principles".

From 7 to 10 October 1996, the 6th Plenum of the 14th PCC was held in Beijing. It was devoted exclusively to the issue of building a socialist spiritual civilization, and adopted a seven-part "Decision of the PCC Regarding Important Issues on Promoting Socialist Ethical and Cultural Progress". The repeated emphasis on the building precisely indicated the problem. As the "Decision" admitted, ideological education and ethical and cultural progress were being neglected by the leadership in some sectors. Some problems were quite serious. The Plenum called once again for the cultivation of "si you" socialist citizens.

As always emphasized, the Party should pay close attention to both civilizations (liang ge wenming yiqi zhua), or, figuratively, "liangshou zhua, liangshou douyao ying" (grasp firmly with both hands). The right hand takes charge of reform and the open door, which means to build material civilization, while the left hand upholds the "four cardinal principles", which means to build spiritual civilization. Very often, however, the case is that "yishou ying, yishou ruan" (one hand is tough, while the other soft). Even worse, the two hands fight against each other, as the inner-Party struggles show: sometimes the Right, sometimes the Left, gets the upper hand. Indeed, reform and the open door not only aim at building material civilization, and spiritual civilization cannot be built on the "four cardinal principles".

When addressing the 15th CCP National Congress, Jiang Zemin for the first time used the concept of a "socialist culture with Chinese characteristics" (you Zhongguo tese shehuizhuyi wenhua) instead of a "socialist spiritual civilization". Building a socialist culture with Chinese characteristics means taking Marxism as the guide, aiming at training "si you" people, and developing a national, scientific, and popular socialist culture geared to the needs of modernization, of the world, and of the future. As Jiang elaborated, the Party also strives for the building of a "socialist economy with Chinese characteristics" (you Zhongguo tese shehuizhuyi jingji) and the building of "socialist politics with Chinese characteristics" (you Zhongguo tese shehuizhuyi zhengzhi). The "three buildings" constitute the basic program of the Party for the primary stage of socialism. This was hailed by Jiang's supporters as being of great significance. See also "gongchanzhuyi shi shehuizhuyi jingshen wenmingde hexin" (Communist ideology is the core of a socialist spiritual civilization) and "shehuizhuyi chuji jieduan lun" (theory of the primary stage of socialism).

两个文明一起抓
liang ge wenming yiqi zhua
(pay close attention to the two civilizations)

See "liang ge wenming" (two civilizations).

两个中国
liang ge Zhongguo
(two Chinas)

See "Taiwan wenti" (Taiwan issue).

两类不同性质的矛盾
liang lei butong xingzhide maodun
(two kinds of contradiction with different natures)

In his 1957 speech "On the Correct Handling of Contradictions among the People", Mao Zedong called for a differentiation between the two kinds of contradiction with different natures—contradictions among the people and contradictions between the people and their enemies, and he put forth the thesis of the correct handling of contradictions among the people. See "zhengque chuli renmin neibu maodun" (correctly handling contradictions among the people).

两条路线的斗争
liang tiao luxiande douzheng
(struggle between two lines)

The concept of a "struggle between two lines" was first put forth by Wang Ming (1904-1974), then a CCP leader, in October 1930 in his political program entitled "The Two Lines" ("Liang tiao luxian", which was published in Moscow in 1932 under the title *Struggle for a More Bolshevized CCP—Wei Zhonggong Genjia Buershiweikehua Er Douzheng*).

As Mao summed up in his talks with local Party, government, and military leaders during his inspection tour in the southern part of China from 14 August to 12 September 1971, in CCP history there had been ten major struggles between what he called "the two lines". They were: 1. the struggle with Chen Duxiu's "Right opportunism" in and around 1927; 2. the 1927 struggle with Qu Qiubai, who opposed Mao's theory about peasant revolution; 3. the struggle with Li Lisan's "putschism" in the latter half of 1930; 4. the struggle from 1930 to 1931 with Luo Zhanglong, who set up an alternative Party Center; 5. the struggle with Wang Ming's "dogmatism" from January 1931 to January 1935; 6. the struggle with Zhang Guotao's "splittism", which intensified from June to September 1935; 7. the struggle in 1954 with the "anti-Party coalition" of Gao Gang and Rao Shushi; 8. the 1959 struggle with the "Peng Dehuai Anti-Party Clique"; 9. the struggle with the "counter-revolutionary revisionist clique" headed by Liu Shaoqi from November 1965 to 1967; and 10. the struggle with Lin Biao at the 1970 2nd Plenum of the 9th PCC (which later became the struggle with the "Lin Biao Counter-revolutionary Armed Coup Clique" that ended with the "September 13th Incident" of 1971). In all these struggles, naturally, Mao's "revolutionary line" was always considered correct.

On 22 June 1981, when mentioning Mao's errors during the Cultural Revolution in his speech during the preparatory meeting for the 6th Plenum of the 11th PCC, Deng Xiaoping said that he and his colleagues had decided not to refer to the above-mentioned struggles by the formulations "struggle between two lines" and "error of Party line". He stated that these formulations had been used "inaccurately, indiscriminately, and too often" *(SWD,* p. 293). In the future, he said, "so far as inner-Party struggles are concerned, we should judge their nature and the errors involved in each on their own merits. We should make their content clear and, in principle, should no longer present them as 'struggles between two lines'" (ibid., p. 294).

两条战线的斗争
liang tiao zhanxiande douzheng
(struggle on two fronts)

When Deng Xiaoping became the Party's paramount leader following the 1978 3rd Plenum of the 11th PCC, he faced a dilemma. On the one hand, he was aware that without reform, CCP rule would come to an end. On the other hand, he was haunted by the fear that reform could also possibly lead to the end of his Party—it would prove the fallacy of the Party's achievements and of the doctrines upon which it had exercised its leadership. In the politics of power, Deng had to deal with two forces within the Party which differed over solving problems left over from the GPCR—one advocated pulling the Party back to the "seventeen years" period in which the Party and its leader enjoyed supreme authority; the other advocated trying to save the Party by something new. Deng decided it was best to employ a strategy of political trickery, to maintain a balance so as to avoid extremes that might spin out of control, such that occurred during the GPCR.

Deng used the term "struggle on two fronts" to describe the general direction of his policies. He emphasized repeatedly that ideological struggles should be waged on "two fronts", that is, when the "Left" trend was rampant, stress should be put on opposing the "Left" trend; and when the Right ideology was dominant, an anti-Rightist struggle should be carried out. He even associated the two-front struggle with the "emancipation of the mind". In March 1981, Deng underlined "the danger of the Right ideological tendency", for he deemed that it had been underestimated by some Party people. He said: "Emancipation of the mind, too, means opposing both 'Left' and Right ideologies. The call by the Third Plenary Session of the Eleventh Central Committee for emancipating our minds was directed at the 'two whatevers', and the emphasis was on correcting 'Left' errors. Later a Right deviation emerged that must, of course, also be corrected" ("On Opposing Wrong Ideological Tendencies, Mar. 27, 1981", *SWD,* p. 356).

Some described the general direction of Deng's policies as a "middle course". But it was a zigzag course. With his principle of a "two-front" struggle, Deng always placed himself in a "correct" position. No matter whether the policy in question was repression or relaxation, and no matter how often and how abruptly he changed his policy, Deng found it easy to justify himself. Indeed, Deng's "two-front" struggles made the cycles of repression and relaxation inevitable and indispensable.

Actually, to wage ideological struggles on "two fronts" was not Deng Xiaoping's invention. It represented the long tradition of the CCP; and Mao Zedong had also resorted to it after he had been established as Party leader. This tactic enabled Mao to enjoy a "perpetually correct" position.

But Deng still made his own contribution. China critics maintain that he had a "dual tactic"—to adhere to the "four cardinal principles" on the one hand, and, on the other, to carry out the policies of reform and the open door (yishou zhua si ge jianchi, yishou zhua gaige kaifang). More specifically, he opposed Left ideology in the economic field and Right ideology in the political field (jingjishang fanzuo, zhengzhishang fanyou). See also "zhengzhi gaige" (political reform) and "jingji gaige" (economic reform).

两种改革观
liang zhong gaige guan
(two opposing views about reform)

See "xin shehuizhuyi guan" (new socialist view).

两岸关系是特殊的国与国的关系
liang'an guanxi shi teshude guo yu guode guanxi
(the cross-Straits relationship is a special state-to-state relationship)

See "Taiwan wenti" (Taiwan issue).

两报一刊
liangbao yikan
(two newspapers and one journal)

See "xinwen ziyou wenti" (issue of press freedom) and "Liu Zaifu shijian" (Liu Zaifu incident).

两参一改三结合
liangcan yigai sanjiehe
(two participations, one change, and three combinations)

See "An'gang xianfa" ("Charter of the Anshan Iron and Steel Company").

两点论
liangdianlun
("two points" theory)

The "two points" theory, or the doctrine that everything has two aspects, was said to be in accordance with Marxist law that states "One divides into two". As it goes, all things have their positive and negative aspects as well as their principal and secondary aspects. While paying attention to the main tendency, people should take note of the other tendency which might be hidden. They must fully recognize and lay a firm hold on the principal aspect and, at the same time, one by one solve the problems arising from the non-principal aspect. They should see the negative as well as the positive aspects of things. And they should see the problems that have already emerged and also allow for problems which have not yet been perceived but which may possibly emerge in the future.

Accordingly, people were asked to discard the "one point" theory (yidianlun), a popular expression referring to metaphysics and one-sidedness. See also "yi fen wei er" (one divides into two).

两分法
liangfenfa

(the application of the law
that "one divides into two")

See "yi fen wei er" (one divides into two).

兩国论
liangguo lun
("two states" theory)

See "Taiwan wenti" (Taiwan issue).

兩极格局
liangji geju
("two poles" pattern)

See "san ge shijie lun" ("three worlds" theory), "lengzhanhou shidaide xin diguozhuyi" (neo-imperialism in the post-Cold War era), and "weidu Zhongguo" (containment against China).

兩结合创作方法
liangjiehe chuangzuo fangfa
("two-in-one combination" creative method)

This refers to Mao's idea about the combination of revolutionary realism and revolutionary romanticism as the creative method for proletarian literature and art. See "shehuizhuyi xianshizhuyi" (socialist realism).

兩年文革
liangnian wen'ge
(two-year Cultural Revolution)

This is the argument that the GPCR only lasted two years, from August 1966 to August 1968, marked by the rise and decline of the rebels. See "wen'ge" (Cultural Revolution) and "liang ge wen'ge lun" ("two Cultural Revolutions" theory).

兩手抓, 兩手都要硬
liangshou zhua, liangshou douyao ying
(grasp firmly with both hands)

See "liang ge wenming" (two civilizations).

兩条腿走路
liangtiaotui zoulu
(walk on two legs)

This is a metaphor for a thinking and working method. In his 1956 speech "On the Ten Major Relationships" ("Lun shi da guanxi", *RMRB*, 27 May 1958; reprinted in *MZXJ*, 5, pp. 267-88) at the Enlarged Meeting of the PCC Politburo, Mao raised the principle of "walking on two legs". As he asserted, the principle embraces the relationship of the interpermeation of opposites, of "being one and the other at the same time", and the unity of opposites. It is alien to the metaphysical formula of "being one or the other". Accordingly, Mao suggested "five simultaneous developments" (wu ge bingju) in economic construction. They are: to develop industry and agriculture simultaneously; develop heavy industry and light industry simultaneously while giving priority to heavy industry; simultaneously develop national industries and local industries, develop large, medium-sized, and small enterprises, and use both modern and indigenous methods of production.

The principle of "walking on two legs" has generally been accepted by the Party. For instance, in May 1977, when talking about how to improve education, Deng said: "We must walk on two legs, that is, we must raise the standards of education at the same time as we make it available to more and more people" ("Respect Knowledge, Respect Trained Personnel", *SWD,* p. 53). Significantly, many describe the reform initiated by Deng, which tries to deal with economic issues without carrying out a true political reform, as "walking on one leg" (yitiaotui zoulu). See also "shi'er da guanxi" (twelve major relationships), "jingji gaige" (economic reform), and "zhengzhi gaige" (political reform).

林彪事件
Lin Biao shijian
(Lin Biao Incident)

The Lin Biao Incident has not yet been fully revealed. One description is as follows:

At the 2nd Plenum of the 9th PCC held at Lushan from 23 August to 6 September 1970, Lin Biao once again advocated his "theory of innate genius" (see "tiancai lun"). This time, however, he was blocked. On 31 August, seeing through Lin's trick, Mao Zedong wrote a statement entitled "A Point of View of Mine" ("Wode yidian yijian"), regarding the "theory of innate genius" as "idealist". Reportedly, Lin ostensibly urged Mao to accept the post of president of state, but in reality he wanted it for himself. Using political trickery, Mao focused his ire on Chen Boda, Lin's chief follower and one of the five members of the Politburo Standing Committee, completely disgracing him overnight. The event, of course, marked the beginning of the decline of Lin Biao, though he still kept his posts.

It is said that in February 1971, burning with a strong desire to seize supreme power and aware that Mao no longer trusted him, Lin Biao, along with his wife Ye Qun (then a Politburo member), began to take measures to stage an armed coup. In March, their son Lin Liguo (then deputy director of the Office of the Air Force Headquarters and deputy director of the Military Operations Department) held a secret meeting in Shanghai with his diehard followers in the Air Force Headquarters, that is, key members of the so-called "United Task Fleet" (lianhe jiandui) under his leadership, and an armed coup plan entitled "571 Project Minutes" ("wuqiyi gongcheng jiyao", "wuqiyi" is the homophonic of "armed uprising") was drafted. On 31 March, another secret meeting was held in Shanghai, and a command group was set up as a first step to implement the coup.

In August 1971, though unaware of the armed coup plan, Mao decided that the 3rd Plenum of the 9th PCC was to be held before National Day on 1 October to settle the Lin Biao issue. Mao left Beijing on 14 August and began an inspection tour in the South, where he had a number of talks with local Party, government, and military leaders, giving them a cue about the issue ("dazhaohu" or "chuifeng"). On 5 September, upon receiving the news of Mao's talks, Lin Biao decided to speed up the coup activities. On 8 September, he issued the following order: "Act according to the orders of Comrades Liguo and Yuchi." (Liguo refers to Lin Liguo and Yuchi refers to Zhou Yuchi, a leader of the planned coup, who was deputy director of the Office of the Air Force Headquarters.) They planned to assassinate Mao during his inspection tour.

On 11 September, however, Mao suddenly changed his route, and, after successfully foiling several attempts by his enemies, he arrived safely in Beijing in the early evening of the next day.

By that time, Lin Biao and his people realized that they had lost momentum. They first planned to flee to Guangzhou where they hoped to set up an alternate power center and engage in a north-south pincers attack on Mao in tandem with the Soviet Union. However, when they were informed that Premier Zhou Enlai was investigating the circumstances, Lin Biao, with his wife, son, and some others, had to hastily flee for the Soviet Union late at night on 12 September. In the early morning of the next day, at three o'clock, their chartered plane, a trident 256, crashed while flying over Wenduerkai, Mongolia, and they all were killed. The remaining participants in the coup attempt were subsequently arrested. In the winter of 1980, together with the "Jiang Qing Counter-revolutionary Clique", the "Lin Biao Counter-revolutionary Clique" were brought to a public trial.

It is generally accepted that the Lin Biao Incident represented the failure of the GPCR, both in theory and in practice, and marked a turning point from its upsurge to its decline. The incident also ended the myth of Mao being absolutely correct within his Party.

According to the above description (and others), Lin Biao is officially remembered as one of the great villains in modern China. But there are also alternative explanations. One is provided in the book *The Tragedy of Lin Biao: Riding the Tiger During the Cultural Revolution 1966-1971* (Frederick C. Teiwes and Warren Sun, Univ. of Hawaii Press, 1997), which argues that Lin possessed neither the ability nor the intention to usurp the chairman's power. See also "Lin Jiang fan'geming jituan" (Lin Biao and Jiang Qing counter-revolutionary cliques) and "wen'ge" (Cultural Revolution).

林江反革命集团
Lin Jiang fan'geming jituan (Lin Biao and Jiang Qing counter-revolutionary cliques)

In the latter part of September 1980, the Ministry of Public Security completed its investigation of the "Lin Biao and Jiang Qing Counter-revolutionary Cliques" and sent the case to a special procuratorial court in the Supreme People's Procuratorate for investigation and prosecution. On 5 November 1980, a series of "public trials" began to be held in a special court in the Supreme People's Court. On 25 January 1981 the court made the following decision concerning the sixteen major offenders of the two "counter-revolutionary cliques" headed respectively by Lin Biao and Jiang Qing:

Lin Biao (former CCP vice-chairman, PRC vice-premier, and defense minister) deceased and exempt from prosecution; Jiang Qing (former CCP Politburo member) sentenced to death with two years' reprieve and forced labor, which was later commuted to life imprisonment. On 14 May 1991, Jiang committed suicide; Kang Sheng (former member of the CCP Politburo Standing Committee) deceased and exempt from prosecution; Zhang Chunqiao (former member of the CCP Politburo Standing Committee) sentenced to death with two years' reprieve and forced labor, which was later commuted to life imprisonment; Yao Wenyuan (former CCP Politburo member) sentenced to 20 years' imprisonment and released in October 1996; Wang Hongwen (former CCP vice-chairman) sentenced to life imprisonment, died of hepatitis in prison on 3 August 1992; Chen Boda (former member of the CCP Politburo Standing Committee) sentenced to 18 years' imprisonment, died of myocardial infarction on 20 September 1989; Xie Fuzhi (former CCP Politburo member, PRC vice-premier, and public security minister) deceased and exempt from prosecution; Ye Qun (former CCP Politburo member, director of the Lin Biao Office) deceased and exempt from prosecution; Huang Yongsheng (former CCP Politburo member and chief of the General Staff) sentenced to 18 years' imprisonment; Wu Faxian (former CCP Politburo member, deputy chief of the General Staff and commander of the Air Force) sentenced to 17 years' imprisonment; Li Zuopeng (former CCP Politburo member, deputy chief of the General Staff and first political commissar of the Navy) sentenced to 17 years' imprisonment; Qiu Huizuo (former CCP Politburo member, deputy chief of the General Staff and director of the PLA General Logistics Department) sentenced to 16 years' imprisonment; Lin Liguo (former deputy director of the Office of the Air Force Headquarters and deputy director of the Military Operations Department of the Air Force) deceased and exempt from prosecution; Jiang Tengjiao (former political commissar of the Air Force in the Nanjing Military Area Command) sentenced to 18 years' imprisonment; and Zhou Yuchi (former deputy director of the Office of the Air Force Headquarters) deceased and exempt from prosecution. See also "Lin Biao shijian" (Lin Biao Incident) and "sirenbang" (Gang of Four).

领导出思想，群众出生活，作家出技巧
lingdao chu sixiang, qunzhong chu shenghuo, zuojia chu jiqiao
(thoughts from the leaders, life experience from the masses, and artistry from the writers)

See "sanjiehe" (three-in-one combination).

领导核心
lingdao hexin
(core of Party leadership)

See "dangde lingdao" (Party leadership).

领导就是服务
lingdao jiushi fuwu
(leadership means service)

A much propagandized slogan, it was first elucidated by Gao Zhanxiang, then a secretary of the CCP Hebei Provincial Committee in charge of ideological and cultural work (presently the CCP group secretary of the China Federation of Literary and Art Circles). "Leadership Means Service" was the title of an article he published in the *Hebei Daily (Hebei ribao)* on 19 November 1984. Deng Xiaoping publicly quoted it in his speech delivered at the National Conference on Education on 19 May 1985 ("Zai quanguo jiaoyu gongzuo huiyishangde jianghua"—"Speech at the National Conference of Education", *RMRB,* 20 May 1985). See also "sanbu zhengce" ("three don'ts" policy).

灵魂的拷问
linghunde kaowen
(interrogation of the soul)

In their self-reflection, some Chinese writers came to understand the seriousness of the reform of their own characters. Fundamentally, the reform of society is a precondition for the reform of man as a whole. Nevertheless, in a specific social structure, man, when not being a slave of necessity, can exercise his own choice, and the choice is subject not only to the rationale of his conceptions but also to the will of his character. In order to reform society, therefore, people must at the same time reform themselves—not only change their former conceptions but also transform their characters. A well-known case is the self-analysis, or self-repentance, of Ba Jin, as expressed in his *Random Thoughts* (*Suixiang ji*, Beijing, Sanlian, 1987), a collection of essays written after his rehabilitation following the downfall of the Gang of Four. In the 1988 discussion on Hu Feng, who was eventually regarded as the first theorist in the Left-Wing literary circle with an independent consciousness, China's intellectuals had a chance for further self-reflection. Many were aware that they really needed a serious "interrogation of the soul". As a theoretical treatise, Liu Zaifu's article, "Lost and Regained: The Spirit of Enlightenment of May 4th Literature", which was published on the eve of the 1989 "May Tempest", was a significant achievement.

Interrogation of the soul is a difficult and painful process. China's intellectuals and writers feel this all the more sharply when they struggle to rid themselves of their "prisons of the mind" (xinyu). In a private conversation in May 1996, Xu Chi, a veteran poet and scholar, bitterly confessed that he could not speak the truth of today, and nor could Ba Jin. (See Hong Yang, *Xu Chide di'er ci qingchun—The Second Youth of Xu Chi,* Wuhan, Central China Normal University Press, 1997, pp. 241-42.) See also "sixiang gaizao" (ideological remolding) and "ziwo biaoxian" (expression of the subjective ego).

灵魂深处爆发革命
linghun shenchu baofa geming
(a revolution breaks out in the depths of the soul)

See "dousi pixiu" (fighting one's self, criticizing and repudiating revisionism).

溜派
liupai
(movers)

See "fengpai" (tune-changers).

刘宾雁现象
Liu Binyan xianxiang
(Liu Binyan phenomenon)

As the first advocate in China of the idea that literature should "be involved in life" (ganyu shenghuo), Liu Binyan published his well-known works "At the Bridge Construction Site" and "The Confidential News of This Newspaper" in the mid-fifties, pungently exposing and criticizing the bureaucracy in real life. As a result, Liu paid dearly; he was labeled a "bourgeois Rightist" and cruelly persecuted for over twenty years. However, he did not change his ideas. His first important work after rehabilitation in 1979 was a piece of powerful exposé entitled "Between Man and Monster" ("Ren yao zhijian", *RMWX,* 9, 1979, reprinted in *QN,* 119, Dec. 1979, and *XWY*, *Reportage literature,* pp. 242-270; trans. in Lee Yee, ed., *The New Realism,* pp. 195-243, and in Perry Link, ed., *People or Monsters?* Bloomington,

Indiana University Press, 1983, pp. 11-68). To Liu Binyan, "involvement in life", for the most part, meant involvement in politics—writers should also function as public procurators and judges. More significantly, Liu did not merely expose the evils of local bigwigs and denounce corrupt officials; he was committed to helping those who had been wronged by the authorities. A sophisticated and indomitable reporter, one who had undergone so many hardships, Liu simply could not stand by in the face of social unfairness and crimes. That was why he was highly respected in China in those years, regarded as a symbol of "China's conscience" (Zhongguode liangxin). This "Liu Binyan phenonemon" expressed a Chinese cultural tradition—a universal identification of "intuitive knowledge" (liangzhi) and a worship of "social conscience".

Liu Binyan was also described as cherishing a "second type of loyalty" (di'erzhong zhongcheng). In 1985, Liu Binyan published a piece of reportage literature entitled "The Second Type of Loyalty" ("Di'erzhong zhongcheng", *Kaituo*, inaugural issue, 1985). He highly praised his protagonist, whose loyalty to the CCP never changed, even after suffering many hardships and persecution. On the other hand, the protagonist was very critical of what he deemed to be the mistakes of the Party and its leader, which was the very reason for his political persecution. Liu concluded that his protagonist possessed a second type of loyalty, and this loyalty should be treasured by the Party. Interestingly, many people identified Liu Binyan with the protagonist.

Like many other Chinese intellectuals who built, as Bai Hua described, a "prison of the mind" (xinyu) for themselves, Liu Binyan nurtured his own obsessive ideal picture of Marxism-Leninism and the CCP. The uprightness, loyalty, and indignation presented in his works were all firmly based on his faith in Marxist-Leninist theory. He tried his best to help the régime, of which he was a part. Only after the Beijing massacre of 4 June 1989 was Liu forced to take another road. The massacre destroyed his last illusions about the Party. He confessed: "I thought I was not a dissident, but the development of the situation inside China has more and more made a dissident of me; I did not want to live in exile, now it seems, however, that the increasing possibility is that I will be banished" (Lee Yee, "Zhongguo Faxisi jiao Riben geng canku: fang Liu Binyan"—"Chinese Fascists Are More Cruel than the Japanese: An Interview with Liu Binyan", *JN,* 234:30, July 1989). If it is correct to say that the June 4th Incident greatly altered the course of life of some China's writers and intellectuals, Liu Binyan's case is typical in this regard.

After the June 4th Incident of 1989, Liu Binyan had to live in exile in the United States. See also "ganyu shenghuo" (be involved in life), "sixiang gaizao" (ideological remolding), and "chi butong zhengjianzhe" (dissidents).

刘少奇反革命修正主义路线
Liu Shaoqi fan'geming xiuzhengzhuyi luxian
(Liu Shaoqi's counter-revolutionary revisionist line)

See "wen'ge" (Cultural Revolution), "luxian douzheng lun" ("line struggle" theory), and "xiuzhengzhuyi" (revisionism).

刘少奇反革命修正主义文艺路线
Liu Shaoqi fan'geming xiuzhengzhuyi wenyi luxian
(Liu Shaoqi's counter-revolutionary revisionist line in literature and art)

See "jiyao" ("Summary") and "xiuzhengzhuyi" (revisionism).

刘再复事件
Liu Zaifu shijian
(Liu Zaifu Incident)

In mid-April 1986, the authoritative *Red Flag* carried a significant article entitled "Problems Concerning Methodology in the Study of Literature and Art", openly attacking an important literary figure by name. This was a rare case of such an attack on an individual, a method that had become unfashionable since the 4th Congress of the CWA (held at the end of 1984). The author of the article was Chen Yong, an advisor to the Policy Research Office under the Secretariat of the PCC. The target was Liu Zaifu, director of the Literature Institute of CASS. The seriousness of the charge can be seen in the following passage in Chen's article:

"Only under the guidance of Marxist ideology, or on its basis, can the renewal of literary concepts have a correct orientation. Now there are obviously a small number of people who, in the name of "developing" Marxism or "renewing literary concepts", discard and even denounce Marxist principles. This is not a minor matter. It has a bearing on the destiny of Marxism and socialist literature and art in China."

To celebrate the publication of Chen's article, the editorial board of *Red Flag* sponsored a special forum. Personally presided over by Xiong Fu, editor-in-chief of this Party theoretical journal, the forum was attended mainly by Chen's supporters. Cheers permeated throughout the meeting, for the participants were sure that this represented a victory for Chinese Marxists who had been denied a forum for their views for too long.

On the other hand, the publication was a shock to many in literary and academic circles. As reported by the Hong Kong based *Ta-kung Daily,* they felt a "whiff" of the "two newspapers and one journal" (liangbao yikan), that is, of the *People's Daily, Red Flag,* and the *Liberation Army Daily,* during the GPCR. In a clearly discernible attempt to draw attention from overseas public opinion, Liu Xinwu focused on Chen's article when he was interviewed by Lee Yee, chief editor of *The Nineties,* during his April visit to Hong Kong. Sensing the unusual background of the attack, Liu Xinwu predicted that it could become a "political incident".

Though Liu Zaifu was targeted, he was, as observers have pointed out, but a small object in a big (albeit hidden) plan. It was noted that Chen Yong's article included an attack upon the so-called "reactionary" theory of "productivity as the sole factor determining social life" (weishengchanlilun), which conveyed a message definitely far beyond the literary sphere. Chen Yong, or rather the supervisors of the *Red Flag* editors, were apparently making oblique accusations against those in power who were in favor of carrying out reform in China, taking advantage of certain mistakes in economic policies during 1985 which had led to an excessive increase in the country's productivity and the occurrence of some undesirable side effects. This was reminiscent of the 1975-76 attack on Deng Xiaoping launched by those later known as the Gang of Four, and inevitably attracted the attention of some figures in the hierarchy—Propaganda director Zhu Houze, General Secretary Hu Yaobang, and Premier Zhao Ziyang. On 12 May 1986 a commentary in the *People's Daily* declared that academic exploration should be supported and the blazing of new trails in art encouraged. The following statement was in striking contrast to Chen Yong's judgment:

"In the field of literary theory, some people have absorbed the fruits of modern scientific research and new views in literary theory abroad. As a result, a new atmosphere has emerged in our literary theoretical research in which many new topics have been tackled. All this is gratifying."

On 19 May, the *People's Daily* carried another commentary, appealing for a better environment and atmosphere for literary explorations and initiative. *Red*

Flag's publication of Chen Yong's article was obliquely criticized as simplistic "massive criticism and repudiation" commonly used in the ten years of chaos.

The political scales had turned. Contrary to the expectations of Chen Yong and his superiors, the would-be political incident was aborted. Unlike Chen Yong, who found support among only a handful of people (like critics Cheng Daixi, Hou Minze, and Zheng Bonong, and novelist Yao Xueyin), Liu Zaifu enjoyed wide support both at home and abroad, as he noted in a July 1986 interview with a reporter of the *Hua Sheng Daily*:

"Since *Red Flag* published Chen Yong's article, everyday I receive many phone calls and letters extending warm support. Some writers and scholars abroad have also written to me to show their concern. I know many people overseas have been paying a good deal of attention to what has been going on with me. I am deeply touched" (*Hua Sheng Daily*, 11 July 1986).

After the June 4th Incident of 1989, Liu Zaifu had to live in exile in the United States. But that is another story. See also "sankuan" (generosity, tolerance, and relaxation), "ziyouhua" (liberalization), and "gaobie geming" (farewell to revolution).

留学生文学
liuxuesheng wenxue
(literature of overseas students)

See "yimin wenxue" (diaspora literature).

流放文学
liufang wenxue
(exile literature)

See "yimin wenxue" (diaspora literature).

六条标准
liutiao biaozhun
(six criteria)

These refer to the criteria put forth by Mao on 27 February 1957, in his speech "On the Correct Handling of Contradictions among the People" delivered at the 11th meeting (enlarged) of the Supreme State Council. See "zhengque chuli renmin neibu maodun" (correctly handling contradictions among the people), "si xiang jiben yuanze" (four cardinal principles), and "Deng Xiaoping lilun" (Deng Xiaoping Theory).

六四惨案
liusi can'an
(June 4th massacre)

See "bajiu minyun" (1989 pro-democracy movement).

六四反革命暴乱
liusi fan'geming baoluan
(June 4th counter-revolutionary rebellion)

See "bajiu minyun" (1989 pro-democracy movement) and "ziyouhua" (liberalization).

六四风波
liusi fengbo
(June 4th disturbance)

See "bajiu minyun" (1989 pro-democracy movement).

六四政治风波
liusi zhengzhi fengbo
(June 4th political disturbance)

See "bajiu minyun" (1989 pro-democracy movement).

六四情结
liusi qingjie
(June 4th complex)

See "bajiu minyun" (1989 pro-democracy movement).

六四事件
liusi shijian
(June 4th Incident)

See "bajiu minyun" (1989 pro-democracy movement).

龙生龙，凤生凤，老鼠的儿子会打洞
long sheng long, feng sheng feng, laoshude erzi hui dadong
(dragons beget dragons, phoenixes beget phoenixes, and those begotten by rats are good at digging holes)

See "xuetong lun" (lineage theory) and "hongweibing" (Red Guards).

庐山会议
Lushan huiyi
(Lushan conference)

This usually refers to the enlarged conference of the CCP Politburo held 2 July to 1 August 1959 and the 8th Plenum of 8th PCC held 2 to 16 August 1959—both were held at Lushan, where the central theme was to trump up charges against and denounce the Peng Dehuai "anti-Party clique". The Lushan conference may also refer to the 2nd Plenum of the 9th PCC held at Lushan 23 August to 6 September 1970, where Mao successfully carried out his plot against Lin Biao's military faction by criticizing the so-called "innate genius" theory (tiancai lun) and the "view about heroes creating history" (yingxiong shiguan) advocated by Lin Biao and Chen Boda. This led to Chen's disgrace and Lin's decline. See "Peng Dehuai shijian" (Peng Dehuai Incident) and "tiancai lun" ("innate genius" theory).

鲁迅文学奖
Lu Xun wenxue jiang
(Lu Xun literary prize)

See "Mao Dun wenxue jiang" (Mao Dun literary prize).

路线斗争论
luxian douzheng lun
("line struggle" theory)

Before Hua Guofeng stepped down, the official description of the nature of the GPCR was a "line struggle" (see "luxian douzheng"). There were two "line struggles" during the GPCR—the first was the struggle with the "counter-revolutionary revisionist clique" headed by Liu Shaoqi from November 1965 to 1967 and the second was the struggle with Lin Biao at the 1970 2nd Plenum of the 9th PCC (which later became the struggle with the "Lin Biao Counter-revolutionary Armed Coup Clique" that ended with the "September 13th Incident" of 1971). In these struggles, it was said, Mao's "proletarian revolutionary line" (wuchanjieji geming luxian) won a "great victory". See also "wen'ge" (Cultural Revolution) and "liang tiao luxiande douzheng" (struggle between two lines).

路线教育
luxian jiaoyu
(education in two-line struggle)

See "jieji jiaoyu" (class education).

路线是个纲，纲举目张
luxian shi ge gang, gang ju mu zhang
(the line is the key link; once it is grasped, everything falls into place)

The 2nd Plenum of the 9th PCC (held at Lushan from 23 August to 6 September 1970) marked the beginning of the decline of Lin Biao. In August 1971, Mao decided that the 3rd Plenum of the 9th PCC was to be held before National Day on 1 October to settle the Lin Biao issue. Then Mao made an inspection tour in the South from 14 August to 12 September, where he had a number of talks with local Party, government, and military leaders. Mao told them: "The line is the key link; once it is grasped, everything falls into place", implying that there was a "line struggle" (luxian douzheng) between him and Lin Biao.

Mao's statement, which was often quoted during the GPCR, is self-evident. It urged people to keep to Mao's "revolutionary line" and required that everything must be done under guidance of his line. Mao also had another concept: "Taking class struggle as the key link" (yi jieji douzheng wei gang). The two do not contradict each other, because in CCP terminology, inner-Party struggle is class struggle in society reflected within the Party, and "line struggle" is the highest form of inner-Party struggle. See "Lin Biao shijian" (Lin Biao Incident), "liang tiao luxiande douzheng" (struggle between two lines) and "jieji douzheng" (class struggle).

路线先行
luxian xianxing

(proceeding from the political line)

See "wenyi shi jieji douzhengde gongju" (literature and art are tools of class struggle) and "liang tiao luxiande douzheng" (struggle between two lines).

轮流坐庄
lunliu zuozhuang
(rotating the leadership)

"Rotating the leadership" means that the CCP and other political parties should compete against one another in elections for the leadership. This very brave idea was raised by Huang Xinping, a history teacher at a secondary school in Tianjin city. The *Tianjin Daily* carried it on 27 May 1957. Under fierce attack when "beating back bourgeois Rightists" began, this obscure teacher still sincerely adhered to his view. He published a long defense in the same newspaper on 23 June, not knowing that his was the very "teaching material by negative example" that the Party needed.

During the 1957 anti-Rightist campaign, "rotating the leadership" was linked to Zhang Bojun (1896-1969), an important figure who was then PRC transport minister, vice-chairman of the CPPCC, chairman of the Chinese Peasants and Workers Democratic Party (Zhongguo Nonggong Minzhudang), and vice-chairman of the Chinese Democracy Alliance (Zhongguo Minzhu Tongmeng). His remarks about a "political design academy" (zhengzhi shejiyuan) were interpreted as making a demand for "rotating the leadership". See also "zhengzhi shejiyuan" (political design academy).

马丁事件
Ma Ding shijian
(Ma Ding incident)

On 2 November 1985, an article entitled "The Ten Big Changes in China's Economics" ("Zhongguo jingjixue yanjiude shi da zhuanbian") was published in Beijing's *Workers' Daily*. The author, Song Longxiang, using the pen name "Ma Ding", was a young teacher at Nanjing University. The article, after being reprinted in magazines and newspapers both at home and abroad, caught the attention of both conservatives and reformists in the CCP. The conservatives found it to be a model of "bourgeois liberalization" and they planned to launch a large-scale attack on it, lending political overtones to the affair. But the storm ended after a few months. Their opponents, enjoying Deng Xiaoping's support, finally succeeded in blocking their attack. For the storm over Ma Ding's article, see Hou Sihuo, "The 'Ma Ding Incident' Arouses Public Indignation" ("'Ma Ding shijian' yin qi gongfen"), and Lu Jiang, "The Inside Story of the 'Ma Ding Incident'" ("'Ma Ding shijian' de lailongqumai"), both in *Guangjiao jing*, 164:15-17, 164:22-27, May 1986. An English translation (with omissions) of Ma Ding's article can be found in *BR*, 9 Dec. 1985. See also "ziyouhua" (liberalization) and "jingji gaige" (economic reform).

马克思主义不是无产阶级的世界观
Makesizhuyi bushi wuchanjiejide shijieguan
(Marxism is not the world outlook of the proletariat)

See "shijieguan" (world outlook).

马克思主义发展史上第三个伟大的里程碑
Makesizhuyi fazhanshishang disan ge weidade lichengbei (the third great milestone in the history of Marxist development)

See "wuchanjieji zhuanzheng" (dictatorship of the proletariat).

马克思主义关于人的哲学
Makesizhuyi guanyu rende zhexue (Marxist philosophy about man)

See "bianzheng weiwuzhuyi" (dialectical materialism) and "rendaozhuyi luzheng" (humanism debate).

马克思主义家族
Makesizhuyi jiazu (the Marxist family)

See "zhengtong Makesizhuyi zhengzai zou xiang siwang" (orthodox Marxism is heading for death).

马克思主义没有完整的文艺理论体系
Makesizhuyi meiyou wanzhengde wenyi lilun tixi (a complete system of literary theory did not exist in Marxism)

In 1980, Liu Mengxi, a literary critic, first expressed the view that a complete system of Marxist literary theory did not exist. (See his "Guanyu fazhan Makesizhuyi wenyixuede ji dian yijian"—"A Few Suggestions Concerning the Development of Marxist Study of Literature and Art", *WXPL,* 1, 1980, reprinted in *XHYB, WZB,* 3:155-58, 1980.) Liu did nothing more than note the plain fact that, unlike Marxist socio-economic theory, Marxist literary thought had evolved from fragmentary and ambiguous writings. However, panic immediately struck the literary-theoretical circles, and Liu was criticized for being "indiscreet". (See the column "Xuexi he fazhan Makesizhuyi wenyi lilun"—"Study and Develop Marxist Literary Theory", *Wenyi yanjiu*, 3, 1980, the relevant report in *GMRB,* 20 Aug. 1980, and Wei Li, "Makesizhuyi jingdian zuojiade wenyi lilun tixi he wenyi kexuede fazhan"—"The System of Literary and Art Theory Built by Classical Marxists and the Development of Literary and Art Science", *WXPL,* 5, Sept. 1980.) The term Liu used in his article was "Makesizhuyi wenyixue"—"Marxist study of literature and art". Facing fierce attacks after the publication of this article, Liu defended himself by emphasizing the difference between the two terms "Marxist literary theory" and "Marxist study of literature and art".

In a few years' time, Liu's view was almost unanimously accepted. In fact, the construction of a "new, systematic Marxist literary theory" was a central topic at the annual forum of the National Society of Mao Zedong Literary Thought and at the academic symposium on the transformation of literary concepts, both of which were held at Dunhuang, Gansu province, in August 1987.

马克思主义人道主义
Makesizhuyi rendaozhuyi
(Marxist humanism)

See "shehuizhuyi rendaozhuyi" (socialist humanism) and "rendaozhuyide Makesizhuyi" (humanistic Marxism).

马克思主义儒家化
Makesizhuyi rujiahua
(Confucianized Marxism)

See "fan chuantong" (anti-tradition), "sixiang gaizao" (ideological remolding), "Mao Zedong sixiang" (Mao Zedong Thought), and "Deng Xiaoping lilun" (Deng Xiaoping Theory).

马克思主义是发展的学说
Makesizhuyi shi fazhande xueshuo
(Marxism is a theory ever in development)

See "Zhou Yang beiju" (tragedy of Zhou Yang) and "zhengtong Makesizhuyi zhengzai zou xiang siwang" (orthodox Marxism is heading for death).

马克思主义是一门开放的科学
Makesizhuyi shi yimen kaifangde kexue
(Marxism is an open science)

See "wenhua lingdao yao genshang gaige kaifangde xin xingshi" (the cultural leadership must keep abreast of the new situation of reform and the open door) and "zhengtong Makesizhuyi zhengzai zou xiang siwang" (orthodox Marxism is heading for death).

马克思主义首先必须发展，然後才谈得上坚持
Makesizhuyi shouxian bixu fazhan, ranhou caitandeshang jianchi
(only by developing Marxism can one uphold it)

See "rendaozhuyide Makesizhuyi" (humanistic Marxism) and "zhengtong Makesizhuyi zhengzai zou xiang siwang" (orthodox Marxism is heading for death).

马克思主义现代化
Makesizhuyi xiandaihua
(modernized Marxism)

See "zhengtong Makesizhuyi zhengzai zou xiang siwang" (orthodox Marxism is heading for death).

马克思主义现代主义
Makesizhuyi xiandaizhuyi
(Marxist modernism)

See "xiandai re" (quest for modernism).

马克思主义只是人类思想发展史中的一个学派
Makesizhuyi zhishi renlei sixiang fazhanshizhongde yige xuepai (Marxism is only one school in the history of thought)

See "rendaozhuyi lunzheng" (humanism debate) and "zhengtong Makesizhuyi zhengzai zou xiang siwang" (orthodox Marxism is heading for death).

马克思主义中国化
Makesizhuyi Zhongguohua (Sinicized Marxism)

See "fan chuantong" (anti-tradition), "sixiang gaizao" (ideological remolding), "Mao Zedong sixiang" (Mao Zedong Thought), and "Deng Xiaoping lilun" (Deng Xiaoping Theory).

马克思主义最後的图腾
Makesizhuyi zuihoude tuteng (the "last totem" of Marxism)

See "zhengtong Makesizhuyi zhengzai zou xiang siwang" (orthodox Marxism is heading for death).

马克思主义的科学主义
Makesizhuyide kexuezhuyi (Marxist scientism)

See "kexue jishu shi shengchanli" (science and technology are part of the productive forces) and "xin shehuizhuyi guan" (new socialist view).

马列主义老太太
Ma-Liezhuyi laotaitai (Madam Marxism)

This refers to Qin Bo, wife of a vice-minister, in Shen Rong's novelette "At Middle Age", who is styled as "Madam Marxism". See "shehuizhuyi tiaojianxia rende yihua" (man's alienation under the condition of socialism).

马列主义与中国实践相结合的两次历史性飞跃
Ma-Liezhuyi yu Zhongguo shijian xiangjiehede liang ci lishixing feiyue (two historic leaps in the integration of Marxism-Leninism with China's reality)

See "liang ci lishixing feiyue" (two historic leaps).

猫论
mao lun

("cat" theory)

See "buguan baimao heimao, zhuazhao laoshu jiushi haomao" (no matter whether it is white or black, it is a good cat that catches mice).

茅盾文学奖
Mao Dun wenxue jiang
(Mao Dun literary prize)

The Mao Dun literary prize, named after Mao Dun (1896-1981), the late chairman of the CWA, is the first most coveted prize in the Chinese literary world. Beginning in 1982, it has been awarded to Chinese novels every three years. Today, besides the Mao Dun literary prize, there are a number of literary prizes in China. The most important among them is the Lu Xun literary prize (Lu Xun wenxue jiang).

矛盾的普遍性与绝对性
maodunde pubianxing yu jueduixing
(the universality and absoluteness of contradiction)

See "yi fen wei er" (one divides into two).

毛式资本主义
Mao shi zibenzhuyi
(capitalism in Mao Zedong style)

See "xinzuopai" (neo-Leftists).

毛泽东悲剧
Mao Zedong beiju
(tragedy of Mao Zedong)

See "Mao Zedong re" (Mao Zedong craze).

毛泽东搞下放，邓小平搞下海，江泽民搞下岗
Mao Zedong gao xiafang, Deng Xiaoping gao xiahai, Jiang Zemin gao xiagang
(Mao Zedong was keen on transferring cadres to lower levels; Deng Xiaoping asked people to jump into the sea of business; and Jiang Zemin resorts to massive lay-offs)

See "xiafang" (transfer to a lower level), "xiahai" (jumping into the sea of business), and "xiagang" (leaving one's post).

毛泽东理想主义外化论
Mao Zedong lixiangzhuyi waihua lun
(theory of the exteriorization of Mao's idealism)

Some scholars find that the "power struggle" theory is insufficient to explain the GPCR. For several decades after the "Zunyi Conference" which was held on the way of the 1935 Long March, they maintain, Mao's position in the whole Party remained unshakable. Liu Shaoqi did not have the ambition to challenge Mao's authority, neither did he have the ability or enough support to do so. In their 1995 book *Farewell to Revolution: Looking Back upon China of the Twentieth Century,* Li Zehou and Liu Zaifu write that Mao Zedong, with his strong Utopian ideals, regarded the GPCR as an experiment for future human society. In other words, the GPCR was an "exteriorization" of Mao's idealism. This included Mao's fight against bureaucratism. Some believe that Mao had long harbored a distrust of his Party machine run by Liu Shaoqi and his colleagues. They argue that had there not been so many intellecutals in 1956-57 voicing their dissident opinions about how to run the country (which Mao had not expected), instead of the anti-Rightist campaign, something like the GPCR would have taken place at that time (see Li Zhisui, *Mao Zedong Siren Yisheng Huiyilu—The Private Life of Chairman Mao,* Taipei, China Times, 1994, p. 195). Mao's tragedy was that he was too obsessed with his ideological system and his war-time experience. He carried everything to extremes and, as a result, disaster was unavoidable (Li Zehou and Liu Zaifu, ibid., pp. 108-115).

The GPCR was definitely an "exteriorization" of Mao's thinking; no one can deny the utmost importance of his personal role in it. Other scholars, however, look at the matter from a more negative perspective. They tend to ignore the high-sounding statements as to why the GPCR was necessary, such as "combating and preventing revisionism" (fan xiu fang xiu), "opposing bureaucracy", and "overcoming the dark side in the nation's political life". Rather, they emphasize that the GPCR was "an unavoitable end result of Mao's ever-worsening ultra-Left line" (Mao Zedong jizuo luxian buduan ehuade biran chanwu), which began with the founding of the PRC. In the ideological-cultural fields, this line first displayed itself in the movements carried out among intellectuals during the first few years of Mao's reign, such as the criticism and repudiation of the film *The Life of Wu Xun,* the campaign against Hu Shi's "reactionary ideological system", the criticism and repudiation of the book *Researches into "A Dream of Red Mansions",* the ideological remolding movement, the struggle against the Hu Feng Counter-Revolutionary Clique, and the struggle against the bourgeois Rightists. In this sense, the GPCR not only lasted ten years; it lasted as long as thirty years (sanshinian wen'ge)—after the victory of his armed revolution in Chinese mainland, Mao directly launched his cultural revolution.

Some try to trace and analyze the dark side in Mao's psychology, which they find problematic and even sinister. Mao was keen on rebelling against the established order, but this can be seen as a means to gain the upper hand over others. Another example is his actions in the International Communist Movement in the 1960s—which betrayed that he wanted to be its leader. Mao is said to have been a shifty person, a double-dealer. The GPCR was a stage upon which Mao, the number one protagonist, fully displayed his political trickery, which he played more skillfully than any Chinese emperors. Even worse, persecution was part of his character. The GPCR was a large-scale persecution of China's intellectuals. Mao's hostility towards them was characteristic of emperors in feudal China, and also was derived from his vindictive mentality—he had been looked down upon when he was young and obscure.

In any case, one may say that the GPCR would not have occurred had it not been for Mao Zedong (meiyou Mao Zedong jiu buhui you wenhua dageming). But this will involve issues of necessity (biranxing) and contingency (ouranxing) in the development of history. See also "wen'ge" (Cultural Revolution) and "Mao Zedong sixiang" (Mao Zedong Thought).

毛泽东热
Mao Zedong re
(Mao Zedong craze)

In the 1990s, there was intense popular interest in Mao Zedong. At the time of the centenary of his birth in December 1993, the celebrations reached a high tide. Two years later, there were commemorations for the 60th anniversary of the end of Mao's Long March. In 1996, twenty years after the end of the GPCR, nostalgically, theater and opera from the GPCR period became popular. In 1999, when the Party celebrated the 50th anniversary of the founding of the PRC, the continuity of the Communist regime was emphasized, and Mao was remembered as a great leader in modern Chinese history. "Neo-Maoists" (also called "neo-Leftists") became active in their support for the old guard. They felt that only Mao's legacy (wrapped in neo-Marxism) could save the country.

Since Mao's demise in 1976, great changes have taken place in China. Now the country is quite a different place from the rigid, communal society Mao sought to construct. And yet, as a Hong Kong based magazine observed, in a country where the focus on economic efficiency is displacing the Maoist mania for equality, the Great Helmsman's personal popularity has risen beyond even what he might have imagined. The memories of Mao today seem more positive—and incongruent. The awesome ghost of Mao lives on.

A reason for this phenomenon, according to China observers, is a reaction, or an expression of grievances, against the current universal corruption in the Party and society. It can also be seen as the attempt by the Leftists to make use of the dissatisfaction among those who face political, social, and cultural problems arising from the process of reform. (An example was the long article by a critic under the pen name Shanju Sanren, "Wei Mao Zedong bianhu: Jian tan Deng Xiaopingde lishi zeren ji benlai mianmu"—"In Defense of Mao Zedong: Also on Deng Xiaoping's Historical Responsibility and His True Colors", published on the Internet in 1999.) Mao might be imperial, ruthless, sexually outrageous, and responsible for a number of national disasters, but these do not impress those who did not experience the Mao period, especially, Mao's GPCR. Instead, they find Mao was not corrupt in the capitalist sense of that word in the 1990s. This helps explain why the craze is most popular among the young. A comprehensive and profound appraisal of Mao and Mao's disastrous GPCR has yet to be undertaken. The tragedy of Mao Zedong (Mao Zedong beiju) has been written into important Party documents, such as the 1981 "Resolution on Certain Questions in the History of Our Party since the Founding of the PRC". People realize that when it came to revolution and conflict, Mao was in his element. They also realize the problem, or the ultimate absurdity, of Mao was that he was unable, or unwilling, to stop being a revolutionary and that he craved revolution so much that he eventually launched a revolution against his own revolutionary party. Even this was not enough. As a result, the nation's collective memory of Mao the revolutionary or, more positively, the revolutionary hero, has etched itself deeply into the Chinese psyche. For some years in the future, some predict, it is unlikely that anything can really displace this. See also "xinzuopai" (neo-Leftists) and "si xiang jiben yuanze" (four cardinal principles).

毛泽东神话
Mao Zedong shenhua
(myth of Mao Zedong)

See "Lin Biao shijian" (Lin Biao Incident), "Mao Zedong re" (Mao Zedong craze), and "Mao Zedong sixiang" (Mao Zedong Thought).

毛泽东思想
Mao Zedong sixiang
(Mao Zedong Thought)

The concept of "Mao Zedong Thought" was first raised by Wang Jiaxiang, then CMC vice-chairman, in his article, "The Chinese Communist Party and the Road of Chinese National Liberation" ("Zhongguo Gongchandang yu Zhongguo minzu jiefangde daolu"), published in Yan'an's *Liberation Daily* on 8 July 1943. Mao Zedong Thought—the term "Maoism" has never been officially used—was said to represent the Sinification (Zhongguohua), or the nationalization (minzuhua), of the original European form of "scientific socialism" (kexue shehuizhuyi). At the CCP's 7th National Congress held in Yan'an from 23 April to 11 June 1945, Mao Zedong Thought, which was defined by Liu Shaoqi as "Comrade Mao Zedong's theory and policies concerning Chinese history and society and the Chinese revolution", was officially stipulated as the Party's guiding ideology. From then on, all Party leaders became its enthusiastic supporters, and more or less involved in the promotion of the personality cult of Mao. But many, such as Liu Shaoqi, Lin Biao, Chen Boda, and Kang Sheng, still fell into disfavor.

Mao Zedong Thought is of course most embodied in Mao's own works. During Mao's life, four volumes of the *Selected Works of Mao Zedong (Mao Zedong Xuanji)* were published—respectively in October 1951, April 1952, April 1953, and September 1960. After his death, the 5th volume was published in April 1977. However, many articles in these volumes were not written by Mao personally. In June 1995, a joint report was presented to the PCC Secretariat by the PCC Party Literature Study Society, the PCC Research Office of CCP History, and the PCC Central Party School regarding the authenticity of their authorship. According to the report, among the 160 or more articles in the first four volumes only 12 were written by Mao personally and 13 were revised mainly by him; all the rest were products of other Party leaders, or of Mao's secretaries, or of the PCC Office. This is even true of those important and well-known works, for example, "On Practice" ("Shijian lun", July 1937) and "On Contradiction" ("Maodun lun", August 1937) which in fact had been drafted by Zhou Enlai, Lin Boqu, Wang Jiaxiang, Kang Sheng, and Chen Boda; the major writers of "On the People's Democratic Dictatorship" ("Lun renmin minzhu zhuanzheng", 30 June 1949) were Chen Boda, Ai Siqi, and Deng Liqun. The copyright issue was also raised by Hu Qiaomu in early January 1992 when he was seriously ill. He claimed that the famous poem "Snow" ("Xinyuanchun: Xue") and the "three frequently-read articles"—"The Foolish Old Man Who Removed the Mountain" ("Yugong yi shan"), "In Memory of Dr Norman Bethune" ("Jinian Bai Qiuen"), and "Serve the People" ("Wei renmin fuwu")—were all based on his ideas.

The worship of Mao Zedong Thought or, more correctly, the personality cult of Mao, reached an apex during the GPCR. Mao Zedong Thought was hailed as the highest peak of Marxism-Leninism. The widespread personality cult of Mao was carried to such extremes that it became a kind of "modern superstition" (xiandai mixin). The four volumes of the *Selected Works of Mao Zedong* were called with great reverence the "treasured red books" (hongbaoshu), for they recorded the "brilliant Mao Zedong Thought". A large-scale unprecedented "little red book" movement (xiaohongshu yundong) took place throughout the country.

Most Party historians ascribe this movement to Lin Biao. As early as 1960, Lin Biao, then CCP vice-chairman and PRC minister of national defense, launched a Mao worship movement in the army based on Lin's slogan: "Study Chairman Mao's works, follow his teachings, act according to his instructions, and be his good soldiers". In order to truly grasp Mao Zedong Thought, Lin stated, one must repeatedly study many of Chairman Mao's basic concepts, while some of his aphorisms must be memorized, repeatedly studied and repeatedly applied. Lin demanded that the *Liberation Army Daily* should, in accord with the specific situation of the time, regularly publish quotations by Chairman Mao for study by cadres and soldiers. From then on, a great number of these "aphorisms" were carried in the paper. In May 1964, the PLA General Political Department, after supplementing, selecting, and editing these "aphorisms", published *Quotations from Chairman Mao*—what was dubbed the "little red book". The book, which is divided into 33 sections, with a total of 422 quotations, became a "must" for everyone in mainland China during the GPCR. With various editions in many languages, its circulation reached fantastic proportions. Only from 1966 to 1968, 740 million copies of the Chinese version were distributed.

In recent years, some historians have argued that the "little red book" movement was not Lin Biao's invention. Originally, the publication of *Quotations from Chairman Mao* came from a suggestion advanced by Zhou Enlai. But this argument is not important. Most tragic and most ridiculous was the fact that the Chinese people had to suffer from this "modern superstition" for more than ten years.

After the GPCR, Deng Xiaoping, himself a GPCR victim, established a new example to treat Mao Zedong Thought. He repeated time and again statements like the following: "It is no exaggeration to say that were it not for Chairman Mao there would be no New China. Mao Zedong Thought has nurtured our whole generation... Without Mao Zedong Thought, the Communist Party of China would not exist today, and that is no exaggeration either. Mao Zedong Thought will forever remain the greatest intellectual treasure of our Party, our army and our people" *(SWD,* p. 160). At the same time he raised an alternative opinion. In a letter of 10 April 1977 to Hua Guofeng, CCP chairman, and Ye Jianying, CCP vice-chairman, and to the PCC, Deng Xiaoping expressed his idea about "genuine Mao Zedong Thought taken as an integral whole". On 21 July 1977, at the 3rd Plenum of the 10th PCC, Deng further advanced the concept of a "Mao Zedong Thought System" (Mao Zedong sixiang tixi). He emphasized that Mao Zedong Thought should be correctly and comprehensively understood as a system and not just according to some fragmentary phrases or isolated sentences quoted from Mao's writings or speeches.

Deng's view helped establish a new authority to explain Mao. One year later, this was a powerful weapon in opposing the "two whatevers" view held by Hua Guofeng and his faction. On 30 March 1979, Deng Xiaoping put forth his "four cardinal principles", one of which was to "uphold Marxism-Leninism and Mao Zedong Thought". On 27 June 1981, under Deng's supervision, the 6th Plenum of the 11th PCC passed an important document "Resolution on Certain Questions in the History of Our Party since the Founding of the PRC", which defined the "living soul" of Mao Zedong Thought as its stand, viewpoint, and method. The essence of these was summed up as "seeking truth from facts" (shishi qiu shi), the "mass line" (qunzhong luxian), and "independence and self-reliance" (duli zizhu, zili gengsheng). For Deng, Mao Zedong Thought was a "crystallization of wisdom" collectively created by the whole Party (hence the meaninglessness of the authorship authenticity issue). In upholding his "Mao Zedong Thought", which did not amount to the thought of Mao Zedong the individual, Deng established himself in an unassailable position. He was able to do whatever he wanted, including things Mao absolutely opposed or could not think of doing during his life-time.

Today, the "theoretical basis" guiding the thinking of the CCP and the Chinese nation is said to be Marxism-Leninism, Mao Zedong Thought, and Deng Xiaoping Theory. This is stipulated in the CCP Constitution and the PRC Constitution. But to many Chinese, this stipulation does not carry great weight. Again, this may be due to Deng. Perhaps even Deng himself could not fully understand the serious consequences brought about by the 1978 debate about practice as the sole criterion in testing truth, in which he played a key role, and his victory over the "whateverists" faction. Indeed, since then, iconoclasm towards Mao and all other long-held revolutionary leaders, as well as towards Mao Zedong Thought, has become inevitable. See also "tuchu zhengzhi" (giving prominence to politics), "liang ge fanshi" (two whatevers), "sixiang jiben yuanze" (four cardinal principles), and "Deng Xiaoping lilun" (Deng Xiaoping Theory).

毛泽东思想大学校
Mao Zedong sixiang da xuexiao
(a great school of Mao Zedong Thought)

See "wuqi zhishi" (May 7 directive).

毛泽东思想挂帅
Mao Zedong sixiang guashuai
(putting Mao Zedong Thought in command)

See "tuchu zhengzhi" (giving prominence to politics).

毛泽东思想儒家化
Mao Zedong sixiang rujiahua
(Confucianized Mao Zedong Thought)

See "fan chuantong" (anti-tradition), "sixiang gaizao" (ideological remolding), and "Mao Zedong sixiang" (Mao Zedong Thought).

毛泽东思想体系
Mao Zedong sixiang tixi
(Mao Zedong Thought system)

See "Mao Zedong sixiang" (Mao Zedong Thought).

毛主席无产阶级革命路线
Mao zhuxi wuchanjieji geming luxian
(Chairman Mao's proletarian revolutionary line)

See "wen'ge" (Cultural Revolution), "luxian douzheng lun" ("line struggle" theory), and "liang tiao luxiande douzheng" (struggle between two lines).

"毛主席语录"
"Mao zhuxi yulu"
(Quotations from Chairman Mao)

See "Mao Zedong sixiang" (Mao Zedong Thought).

没有邓小平的邓小平路线
meiyou Deng Xiaopingde Deng Xiaoping luxian
(a Deng Xiaoping line without Deng Xiaoping)

See "Deng Xiaoping lilun" (Deng Xiaoping Theory).

没有调查就没有发言权
meiyou diaocha jiumeiyou fayan quan
(no investigation, no right to speak)

See "xiuzhengzhuyi" (revisionism).

没有发展便没有真正的稳定
meiyou fazhan bian meiyou zhenzhengde wending
(without development there will no true stability)

See "fazhan caishi ying daoli" (development is the most essential criterion).

没有公正便没有市场经济
meiyou gongzheng, bian meiyou shichang jingji
(without justice, there will be no market economy)

See "jingji gaige" (economic reform).

没有共产党就没有新中国
meiyou gongchandang jiumeiyou xin Zhongguo
(were it not for the Communist Party there would be no New China)

See "dangde lingdao" (Party leadership).

没有良心的经济学
meiyou liangxinde jingjixue
(no heart economics)

For two decades China's reform has mainly been carried out in the economic field, based on "with Chinese characteristics" and different from the reform in the former Soviet Union and the Eastern European countries. The strategy was to proceed from easy to difficult, from superficial to profound, from the periphery of the institution to the inside. It was anticipated that in this way contradictions could be avoided and the reform easily accepted by various sectors of society. Of vital importance to the Party was not to damage its leadership and its interests. However, when the reform entered into the "deepwater area", all those problems that had carefully been avoided in the previous stages had accumulated and become serious social contradictions that were absolutely unavoidable.

This reform strategy is certainly problematic. It can be called a "pure economic theory", that is, a study of a pure economic structure. It proceeds as if there were no political cells in China's economic structure and there were only an evolution from one economic structure to another. As many have pointed out, however, China's planned economic system is itself a product of the political structure. The planned economy "comes dripping from head to foot, from every pore, with politics" (following the tone of Marx's description of capital).

Indeed, the heart of economics is political economy. Economics without touching on political problems can well be called "no heart economics", especially against the background of China's current situation. An urgent task now, according to China's liberal economists, is to set up political economy for China during the "mode transition" period (zhuanxing). It will study the whole course of resource allocation during the period and all the factors deciding or affecting the forms of this allocation. It will expose the nature of the change in the man-material relationship in the social transition. Importantly, it will deal with issues left over from the old planned system. At the moment, there are a series of issues of vital importance to the reform, such as the role of power, which has seriously been corrupted, in the distribution of the country's resources. One cannot understand China's current economic problems if one avoids these issues. See also "jingji gaige" (economic reform).

没有毛泽东就不会有文化大革命
meiyou Mao Zedong jiu buhui you wenhua dageming
(the GPCR would not have occurred had it not been for Mao Zedong)

See "Mao Zedong lixiangzhuyi waihua lun" (theory of the exteriorization of Mao's idealism).

没有毛泽东思想就没有中国共产党
meiyou Mao Zedong sixiang jiumeiyou Zhongguo gongchandang
(without Mao Zedong Thought, the CCP would not exist)

See "Mao Zedong sixiang" (Mao Zedong Thought).

没有毛主席就没有新中国
meiyou Mao zhuxi jiumeiyou xin Zhongguo
(were it not for Chairman Mao there would be no New China)

See "Mao Zedong sixiang" (Mao Zedong Thought).

没有民主就没有社会主义
meiyou minzhu jiumeiyou shehuizhuyi
(without democracy there will be no socialism)

See "minzhu jizhongzhi" (democratic centralism).

没有民主就没有现代化
meiyou minzhu, jiumeiyou xiandaihua
(without democracy there will be no modernization)

See "yao minzhu haishi yao xinde ducai" (democracy or neo-dictatorship).

没有人民性就没有党性
meiyou renminxing jiumeiyou dangxing
(there will be no party spirit without affinity to the people)

See "renminxing he dangxingde maodun" (contradiction between Party spirit and affinity to the people).

没有社会主义人道主义，就没有社会主义
meiyou shehuizhuyi rendaozhuyi,
jiumeiyou shehuizhuyi
(without socialist humanism,
there will be no socialism)

See "shehuizhuyi rendaozhuyi" (socialist humanism).

没有稳定，甚么事也干不成
meiyou wending, shenmeshi yeganbucheng
(without stability, nothing can be achieved)

See "wending yadao yiqie" (the need for stability overwhelms everything else) and "shehuizhuyi chuji jieduan lun" (theory of the primary stage of socialism).

没有血统论就没有红卫兵
meiyou xuetonglun jiumeiyou hongweibing
(the Red Guards would not have emerged
had it not been for the lineage theory)

See "xuetong lun" (lineage theory).

没有言论自由，就没有思想解放
meiyou yanlun ziyou, jiumeiyou sixiang jiefang
(without freedom of speech there
will be no thought-emancipation)

See "jiefang sixiang" (emancipating the mind).

没有眼泪，就没有深邃的文学
meiyou yanlei, jiumeiyou shensuide wenxue
(without tears there will be no profound literature)

See "zuojia zhutixing" (writer's subjectivity).

没有勇气，就没有突破；
没有突破，就没有文学
meiyou yongqi, jiumeiyou tupo;
meiyou tupo, jiumeiyou wenxue
(no courage, no breakthrough;
no breakthrough, no literature)

In his speech at the 1979 4th Congress of Chinese Writers and Artists, Bai Hua pointed out that contemporary Chinese literature and art had played an important role in making a cocoon to confine the Chinese people. Now, like silkworms nibbling away at their cocoons, they had to painstakingly rid themselves of "blind faith", to get some fresh air and sunshine and find a place to live and develop. He thereby appealed for courage. He stated: "No courage, no breakthrough; no breakthrough, no literature!" (Bai Hua, "Meiyou tupo jiumeiyou wenxue"—"No Breakthrough, No Literature", *RMRB*, 13 Nov. 1979; trans. in *CL*, 4:95-101, 1980).

His (coauthor Peng Ning) 1979 film script "Unrequited Love" (adapted into a film by the Changchun Film Studio in 1980 under the title *Sun and Man)*, was certainly a work of courage, but it was fiercely attacked by the authorities in 1981. Significantly, the event, known as the "Bai Hua Incident", finally led to the Party launching its 1981 campaign against "bourgeois liberalization". See also "Bai Hua shijian" (Bai Hua Incident).

没有正确的政治观点，就等于没有灵魂
meiyou zhengquede zhengzhi guandian, jiudengyu meiyou linghun (not to have a correct political point of view is like having no soul)

See "tuchu zhengzhi" (giving prominence to politics).

没有政治改革经济改革不会成功
meiyou zhengzhi gaige jingji gaige buhui chenggong (without political reforms economic reforms will not succeed)

See "zhengzhi gaige" (political reform) and "jingji gaige" (economic reform).

没有自来红，只有改造红
meiyou zi lai hong; zhiyou gaizao hong (no one is born red; one becomes red only through ideological remolding)

The "lineage theory" (xuetong lun) was popular during the GPCR, but even earlier it had influenced many children from the so-called good families (that is, "hongwulei"—workers, poor and lower-middle peasants, revolutionary cadres, revolutionary armymen, and revolutionary martyrs). They felt they were a cut above the others and acted arrogantly, regarding themselves as "natural revolutionary successors". The authorities in the educational departments found this "born red" (zi lai hong) thinking harmful. They promoted the idea that "No one is born red; one becomes red only through ideological remolding".

Today in China, where "money" has begun to outweigh "power", teaching about "red" and "ideological remolding" seems irrelevant to the young people. See also "hong" (red) and "hongweibing" (Red Guards).

美国对台三不政策
Meiguo dui Tai sanbu zhengce (U.S. "three-nos" Taiwan policy)

On 30 June 1998, during his nine-day state visit to China (from 25 June to 3 July 1998), U.S. President Bill Clinton flatly and explicitly declared that the United States would not support the creation of two Chinas, the independence of Taiwan, or

Taiwan's re-entry into the United Nations—what are commonly called the "three nos" demanded by Beijing concerning Taiwan.

In a meeting with Shanghai community leaders, Mr. Clinton said his summit with President Jiang Zemin on 27 June had given him the chance to iron out "misunderstandings". He said: "I had a chance to reiterate our Taiwan policy which is that we don't support independence for Taiwan, or 'two Chinas' or 'one Taiwan, one China'. And we don't believe Taiwan should be a member in any organization for which statehood is a requirement." Mr. Clinton added that this U.S. policy had been "consistent". Reportedly, Taiwan had been informed of this "three nos" policy as early as 1994.

President Clinton did go further than any of his predecessors in publicly opposing the independence of Taiwan. That was why his remarks prompted a sharp reaction from Taipei and a warm welcome from Beijing. Clinton emphasized that there was no departure from established U.S. policy—while a secure and democratic Taiwan is in America's interest, an independent Taiwan is not. But observers pointed out that with his approval of building a "constructive, strategic partnership" with mainland China, the United States changed its strategic policy on the Taiwan issue from "peace but no reunification" (he er butong) to "peace but no independence" (he er budu). See also "weidu Zhongguo" (containment against China).

朦朧後
menglong hou
(post-misty poetry)

The term "post-misty poetry" was first used at the middle of the 1980s. At that time, the "misty poetry" had already changed. Many "misties" had tried not to repeat themselves. On the other hand, others also did not simply repeat the "misty" experiment either. The "misties" were subjected to various challenges; many other modernist poetic schools emerged; and the period of what was dubbed the "post-misty poetry" began. In October 1986, "A Grand Exhibition of Modernistic Poems in the 1986 Chinese Poetic World", divided into three parts, was published in the *Poetry Gazette* and the *Shenzhen Youth Herald.* Xu Jingya, as the poetry editor, made the following statement: "Wide-ranging explorations in the New Poetry since 'May 4th' are spreading all over China. Everywhere poets have stood up demanding serious recognition from the public and society. The authorities, however, are unable to understand and accept the reality of the great experiments in poetry. Therefore, with the emergence of as many as 2,000 local poetic organizations, the *Shenzhen Youth Herald* and the *Poetry Gazette* have organized a 'grand exhibition', unprecedented in the history of modernistic poetry in mainland China" *(Shenzhen qingnian bao,* 24 Oct. 1986).

Many of these schools differed from misty poetry. The latter tried to eliminate political control; its key tone was "emancipation of man", though presented with a kind of obscurity in social consciousness. The former, termed as the "post-misty" or the "third generation", aimed at the "emancipaton of poetry". They declared that any non-poetic function was not their responsibility. They deliberately sought cultural obscurity. Perhaps it can be claimed that these schools were genuinely modernist, while Bei Dao and his contemporaries only made use of the form of modernism. Indeed, these "post-misty" modernistic poets sought to bring about a "third wave".

Some claimed at the time that the age of Bei Dao and Shu Ting had passed. But this may be an exaggeration. As Gao Ertai, a veteran critic, said in 1986, in view of the present situation in China, the times still needed Bei Dao and Shu Ting (Gao Ertai, "Dangdai wenyide zhuxuanlu"—"The Major Melody of Contemporary Literature and Art", *WYB*, 15 Nov. 1986). Significantly, as it has turned out, it seems that thus far no one has surpassed them. See also "menglongshi" (misty poetry).

朦胧诗
menglongshi
(misty poetry)

Poetry is really a sensitive field. Whenever a new ideological trend rises in society, it often finds expression first in poetry. As in the early twentieth century, modernism appeared first in poetry in the post-Mao era. A group of precocious and nonconformist young people, brought up during the GPCR, appeared on the scene, writing poems tinged with what could be called a modernist tendency. At first these poems were only circulated among friends, or published in such unofficial magazines as the *Today*, or just kept by their authors. Then in March 1979, a breakthrough took place. "The Answer", a poem by Bei Dao, was published in *Poetry*, the most prestigious national journal devoted to poetic writings ("Huida", *SK,* 3:46, 1979; trans. in Stephen Soong and John Minford, eds., *Trees on the Mountain,* Hong Kong, Chinese University Press, 1984, pp. 59-60, in Michael S. Duke, ed., *Contemporary Chinese Literature: An Anthology of Post-Mao Fiction and Poetry,* New York, M. E. Sharpe, 1985, p. 41, and in Pang Bingjun & John Minford, with Seán Golden, eds., *100 Modern Chinese Poems,* Hong Kong, Shangwu, 1987, pp. 238-41). This was a significant event. In 1980, further efforts were made by this journal. It organized a short seminar for some of these young poets. In its 4th issue of the year, it carried a column of maiden works by seventeen young poets. Yan Chen, the editor-in-chief, heartily praised these works in his preface, claiming that they "explored new subject matter, new methods of expression and new styles, bringing a new 'flavour' into the poetic arena" *(SK,* 4:3, 1980). Then in its 8th, 10th and 11th issues of 1980, more space was devoted to the young poets. At the same time, many local literary journals began to compete with one another to publish their creations. *Anhui Literature,* for instance, after carrying thirty new poets' works in October 1979, further published in January 1980 four poems, selected from among those widely read by young people. Readers and critics continued to witness the emergence of more and more of these poems, poems that were dubbed disparagingly by some as "menglongshi". (Zhang Ming, himself also a poet, first used the term "menglong" in his critical article "The 'Mist' That Makes One Brood"—"Ling ren qimende 'menglong'", *SK,* 8:53-54, 1980.)

The first members of this school included Bei Dao, Shu Ting, Gu Cheng, Yang Lian and Jiang He. Within a few years, their ranks expanded, as a number of young people joined, such as Xu Jingya, Wang Xiaoni, Gao Falin, Fu Tianlin, Li Gang, and Chen Suoju. As their creations shocked the Chinese poetic world, a prolonged debate began at the Nanning Forum on Contemporary Poetry in April 1980. The publication of three essays by Xie Mian, Sun Shaozhen, and Xu Jingya, in 1980, 1981, and 1983 respectively, marked what was called the "three resurgences" (san ci jueqi) in the theory of "misty poetry". At the same time, there was a progressive escalation of the political criticism of this genre and its theory. A large scale and highly visible attack was launched at the Chongqing Forum on Poetry held 4 to 9 October 1983, three weeks before the announcement of the Party's decision to "eliminate spiritual pollution".

Labeled as "spiritual pollutants" during the 1983 purge, "modernist tendencies", such as those represented by "misty poetry" and its theory, faced severe criticism. Party critics resorted to extremes because they had reached the conclusion that the debate on modernism was not simply about methods and styles. Instead, it concerned the "overall road" literature and art should take. In their view, the current modernist tendencies were discarding the very principles of "socialist literature". That was why Zang Kejia, the former editor-in-chief of *Poetry,* stood in the forefront of the struggle to "eliminate spiritual pollution", carrying out what he called the "three defenses" (see "san ge baowei"). Ke Yan, secretary of the CWA, even declared that history would "throw away" those "misties" who "broke with socialist poetry" (Ke Yan, "Guanyu shide duihua"—"A talk about poetry", *SK,* 12:62, 1983).

Despite the attacks and the attempt at suppression, "misty poetry" did not seem to die out. On the contrary, as Xie Mian announced in March 1985, it was alive and well (Xie Mian, "Tamen cunzai bingqie shengzhang"—"They exist and grow", *Shenzhen qingnian bao*, 21 Mar. 1985). Though at this stage "misty poetry" still remained a controversial topic among China's literary circles, on the whole the discussion was of another nature. For instance, Liu Xiaobo, a political-literary critic, was one of those very critical of "misty poetry". Admittedly, "misty poetry" did not yield to external political pressure, but Liu stressed that it was the political pressure on it that made it well known, not only in China but also abroad. Due to some internal factors among the "misty" poets themselves, Liu continued, "misty poetry" in fact had already stopped developing by 1980, and from then on the "misty" poets achieved little (Liu Xiaobo, "Zai lun xinshiqi wenxue mianlin weiji"—"More on the Crisis of the New Period Literature", *Baijia,* 1:12-16, 1988). As Xie Mian saw it, however, a "total transfer" had appeared in the thinking of the "misty" poets—they had been changing their focus "from the past to the future" (Xie Mian, "Zhuiqiude licheng"—"The Course of the Pursuit", *Wenyi zhengming,* 2:9, 1986). The subjective ego was not their ultimate goal. After having attained it, they tried to find the epoch that the subjective ego belongs to, and the sense of mission belonging to that epoch. Some poets like Jiang He, for example, selected history and the people as his theme. They were pondering the character and fate of the Chinese nation, its yesterday, today, and tomorrow. Quite a number of their works demonstrated a more modernistic flavour, resorting more to abstraction, detachment, and symbols. Some like Yang Lian were making efforts to absorb and blend together Western modernistic art and traditional Chinese culture. They did try not to repeat themselves.

Now it is almost two decades since the prolonged debate on "misty poetry" in the first half of the 1980s. "Misty poetry", together with the debate, has already become history. Over time, there were new cycles of repression and relaxation (which seem to have been built into the contemporary Chinese political system itself). In 1987 there was another campaign against "bourgeois liberalization". Furthermore, in 1989, the June 4th Incident took place, which shocked the entire world. In the following purges, modernism and all other demonstrations of the so-called "bourgeois liberalization" in literature and art were naturally once again targets for attack. A number of "misties", including Bei Dao, Gu Cheng, Yang Lian, and Jiang He, went into exile. Significantly, even so, the historical truth remained. According to an investigation carried out in 1998 by *Poetry* magazine among its readers, modernistic poems and poems of the 1980s are highly praised by the public in today's China. Shu Ting eye-catchingly ranked first on the list of the fifty most popular Chinese poets in the last one hundred years, preceding these veteran poets such as Ai Qing (second), Zang Kejia (third), He Jingzhi (seventh), Ke Yan (eighth), Guo Moruo (fifteenth), and Tian Jian (forty-first). Gu Cheng, who in 1993 committed suicide after killing his wife, also placed eleventh. The list may be controversial. (For the investigation and the list, see *SK,* 9:4-8, 1998). For instance, perhaps for political reasons, Bei Dao failed to get what he deserved. Nevertheless, there was a message in this. From a long-term point of view, political attack can never kill an artistic life. "Misty poetry" and the so-called "rise" theory have won their due place in the history of contemporary Chinese literature. See also "menglongshi lilunde san ci jueqi" ("three rises" in the theory of misty poetry), "xinshiqi wenxue" (literature of the new period), and "xinshiqi wenxuede duoyuan fazhan" (pluralistic development of the literature of the new period).

蒙胧诗理论的三次崛起
menglongshi lilunde san ci jueqi
("three rises" in the theory of misty poetry)

At the Nanning Forum on Contemporary Poetry held in April 1980, a debate began on "misty" creations, which at the time shocked the Chinese poetic world. The debate later proved to be a prolonged one. While this new poetic genre was suspected and criticized, especially by official critics and poets of the older generation, many others raised their voices enthusiastically in its defense.

The first cheer for misty poetry was given by Xie Mian in May 1980 when he published his essay "Before the New Rise" ("Zai xinde jueqi mianqian", *GMRB,* 7 May 1980). From the very start, this Beijing University professor pointed to what he called an "undeniable fact"—that the New Poetry was facing a challenge from a group of young people. This situation, as he saw it, was reminiscent of the New Poetry movement during the "May 4th" period. Because of the early initiatives during the first decade of the period, there emerged a great variety of schools and styles. However, Xie claimed, this did not happen again for as long as half a century. The road for the New Poetry during the sixty years had not grown broader; on the contrary it became narrower. Currently, it is hoped that the New Poetry will restore its relations with world poetry, and a number of poets have begun broader explorations. He said that this was absolutely right and also very encouraging.

In another essay, Xie Mian said that divergence of opinion was vast and multiple. Issues for debate included: whether the New Poetry had met any setbacks in the last thirty years, causing its road, which had originally been broad, to become narrower and narrower; whether the New Poetry had to have a "basis" (that of "classical poetry + folk songs"), and an "-ism" (that is, "realism"), or whether it should possess a larger perspective and make use of wide-ranging methods of artistic expression; and whether one should admit that at the moment the New Poetry was facing a new and very hopeful upturn, and whether one should subject it to a scientific appraisal (Xie Mian, "Shiqule pingjing yihou"—"After Losing Equanimity", *SK,* 12:9, 1980).

In his defense for misty poetry, Xie Mian pointed out the fact that a whole generation of youth had been brought up during the ten years of calamity. As a result, they were always on guard against life, fearing that they might again be cheated. This was almost like a neurosis. As in Bei Dao's "The Answer", their answer to life was four words—"I do not believe". Because of their constant political vigilance, or because they were unclear about the disease of the era, they tended to express themselves in indefinite language and images. Their lines often wove confused, blurred thoughts and complicated, contradictory feelings. This is why some of their poems remained obscure. Moreover, in the abnormal psyche created by the abnormal era, some of these poets resorted to abnormal ways to express themselves, thus producing a sort of poetry that possibly appeared "eccentric", both ideologically and artistically. Xie said: "Perhaps there are some people who will not like to see it come into being, but it is, after all, a reasonable child of an unreasonable era" (Xie Mian, *SK,* 12:9, 1980). He further testified: "It is not all disasters that Pandora's box holds. It also hides hope—the best thing for human beings. But the box was closed after the disasters were released. The task today is to challenge the holy order of Zeus, 'the father of all gods', and to release the 'hope' from the bottom of the box" (Xie Mian, *SK,* 12:10, 1980).

The second cheer for misty poetry was given by Sun Shaozhen. He saw the rise of misty poetry as the rise of a "new aesthetic principle", as he explained in his March 1981 article "A New Aesthetic Principle Is Rising" ("Xinde meixue yuanze zai jueqi", *SK,* 3:55-58, 1981). Sun was fiercely attacked as a result, and the publication of this article was sarcastically dubbed the "second rise" in the theory of misty poetry. (See "xinde meixue yuanze zai jueqi"—a new aesthetic principle is rising).

Ironically, the attack only resulted in increasing the influence of the "rise" theory as advocated by critics like Xie Mian and Sun Shaozhen. At the beginning of 1983, Xu Jingya also joined in with his long treatise "A Body of Rising Poetry—On the Modernist Tendencies of Chinese Poetry" ("Jueqide shiqun—Ping woguo shigede xiandai qingxiang" *Dangdai Wenyi Sichao,* 1:14-27, 55, 1983, extracts trans. in Stephen Soong and John Minford, eds., *Trees on the Mountain,* pp. 59-65).

When talking about the "new tendencies" of the Chinese New Poetry as a natural end-result of its internal contradictions, Xu Jingya pointed out that such vast social turbulence as the GPCR and such extreme distortion of so many souls in the turbulence inevitably formed a strong force to break the restraints in the soul, thereby giving rise to a literary revolution. Poetry, as the most intimate friend of human nature and the most direct link between an individual soul and the external world, inevitably underwent a radical transformation. It is such "boasting poems", "ossified poems", and "slogan-like poems that cover-up and deceive" that have pushed the art of the New Poetry to the transform-or-die limit. Now a thorough change has taken place concerning the artistic appreciation of a whole generation. This is a self-negation of the New Poetry—an inevitable negation in literature accompanying the negation in society (Xu Jingya, *Dangdai Wenyi Sichao,* 1:24, 1983).

Furthermore, Xu Jingya believed in the long run the new tendencies, as can be seen in misty poetry, will become the mainstream of Chinese poetry. It will take a long time though, during which orthodox poetry and modernist poetry will coexist. He also believed at the moment it is possible for the new poets to form schools. In the past thirty years people almost lost hope of having different schools and styles and they did not understand that there must be some prerequisites before they are formed. According to Xu, these prerequisites are: 1. A unique social outlook which can even be disharmonious with the concerted keynote of society. To poetry, this means multiple ways and angles of experience. 2. A unique artistic stand which even dares to deny the "eternal answer", and opens up new poetic realms. 3. Social protection of special aesthetic interests and appreciative ideals in literature (Xu Jingya, *Dangdai Wenyi Sichao,* 1:26, 1983).

Since Xu Jingya himself was one of the young misties, he was very familiar with their creative situation. Many of his arguments had the support of rich material. On the other hand, however, as a young poet he tended to let himself be overcome by his fervor, and thereby he failed to make his points with sufficient clarity. He was brave, but sometimes his bravery was accompanied by cursoriness. Besides, since his dissertation dealt with such a number of complicated issues, it could be expected that defects occurred in some places. But the orthodox critics and theorists simply could not tolerate this academic thesis because of what they asserted to be its "political mistakes"—it was regarded as the "reactionary high tide" of the "three rises" in the theory of misty poetry. Criticism came almost at the same time as its publication, at the Lanzhou Forum convened on 7 January 1983.

Among the attackers was Cheng Daixi, a critic who had been officially praised for his earlier attack on Sun Shaozhen's "A New Aesthetic Principle Is Rising".

Cheng wrote Xu an open letter, in which he called Xu's article "a manifesto of bourgeois modernist poetry" and "a manifesto of bourgeois liberalization" (Cheng Daixi, "Gei Xu Jingya de gongkai xin"—"An Open Letter to Xu Jingya", *SK,* 11:41, 1983). He alleged that the "unique social outlook" advanced by Xu (as one of the prerequisites for the forming of new poetic schools) was in essence a "political idea", an "ideological kernel" of a new style and school that Xu was trying to establish. Accordingly, he said, the "keynote of society" as disharmonious with (here "disharmonious with" was interpreted by Cheng as "contradictory and antagonistic to") what Xu called the "unique social outlook" must also be a "political idea", and "not an ordinary but a fundamental" one. Then he asserted that Xu's "unique social outlook" implied a disbelief in the life of the past, and that what Xu meant by "the past" was not only the ten-year GPCR but also "the social life of more than thirty years since the founding of the PRC". Finally, making use of Xu's praise on young poets for "shaking a series of pillars of poetic theory which they had never questioned before" (Xu Jingya, "A Body of Rising Poetry", *Dangdai Wenyi Sichao,* 1:16, 1983), Cheng Daixi said: "The pillar of our poetic theory is none other than Marxism. How can you say you are not talking about political ideas, but only about poetry and art, when you have even shaken Marxism?" (Cheng Daixi, "An Open Letter to Xu Jingya", *SK,* 11:42, 1983).

In the 1983 wave of criticism of "misty poetry" and the so-called "rise" theory, Zang Kejia, a veteran poet who was a former editor-in-chief of *Poetry* and then a consultant to the CWA, gave a number of militant interviews for publication in newspapers, enthusiastically supporting the campaign to "eliminate spiritual pollution". Conspicuously, he alleged: "As far as theory is concerned, the poetic front at present is facing a situation in which 'three defenses' are needed—defense of Left-wing literature since the 'May 4th' period, defense of the tradition of realism, and defense of the leadership of the Party" *(SK,* 12:47, 1983).

A general and intensive attack was launched at the Chongqing Forum on Poetry (held in Chongqing city, Sichuan province, 4 to 9 October 1983). The thirty or more participants included Zhu Ziqi, member of the CWA Standing Secretariat, and Ke Yan, CWA secretary. Though absent from the Forum, Zheng Bonong, a Party critic, presented a keynote written speech, which might be called a comprehensive political attack. According to Zheng, what "rise" theorists had raised were not minor issues. How to treat the sixty-year-old revolutionary tradition of the New Poetry? How to regard the direction of the New Poetry in its future development? Whether it should discard its tradition since the May 4th Movement and take the road of Western modernism, or carry on and improve the tradition and take the road of a socialist literature and art with Chinese characteristics? All these had a bearing on the vital issues of whether poetry should adhere to the orientation of serving the people and socialism and whether it still bears the name of socialist literature and art. What is more, Zheng said, these were not only issues involving the poetic realm. The poetic wave promoted by the "rise" theorists had in fact exerted influence on all literary and art fields (Zheng Bonong, "Zai 'jueqi'de shenglang mianqian: Dui yi zhong wenyi sichaode pouxi"—"An Analysis of a Literary Trend", *SK,* 12:38, 1983).

Zheng Bonong accused the "rise" theory, allegedly characterized by two principles of "expression of the subjective ego" and "anti-rationalism", of advocating "the world outlook and art perspective of modernism in the West". Expression of the subjective ego, Zheng emphasized, was raised as a slogan "antagonistic to the expression of life and the people" and was "a sort of barefaced solipsist philosophy" (Zheng Bonong, *SK,* 12:36-45, 1983). As to "anti-rationalism", he regarded it as the "philosophical foundation" of Chinese modernism in fiction, drama, and painting, and also of misty poetry and its theory, which was "in opposition to the Marxist world outlook" (Zheng Bonong, op. cit.). In the opinion of Ke Yan, the "rise" theorists placed the subjective ego above "the motherland, the people, and even the universe". Posing as heroes against the "god-making movement" (zao shen yundong) of the past, she continued, they eventually tried to "deify themselves in the disguise of opposing the deification of others" (Ke Yan, "Guanyu shide duihua"—"A Talk about Poetry", *SK,* 12:46-56, 62, 1983). Xu Jingya was most fiercely attacked. His article was described as the "high tide" of the "three rises" of the theory of misty poetry.

According to the *Poetry* editor's note preceding a report on the Chongqing Forum, the Forum was "a militant clarion worthy of attention in the poetic circle" *(SK,* 12:33, 1983). In fact, in the 1983 campaign to eliminate "spiritual pollution", criticism of the so-called "three rises" in poetic theory was not only carried out in poetic circles but also in other circles. Besides *Poetry* publishing one critique after another, similar attacks were also launched in *Literary Gazette, Literary Review,* the *Guangming Daily,* and many other journals and newspapers throughout the country. The "three rises" were also targeted by Zhu Muzhi, minister of culture, when he talked about "spiritual pollutants" in culture and art (*RMRB,* 2 Nov. 1983). See also "menglongshi" (misty poetry) and "ziwo biaoxian" (expression of the subjective ego).

朦胧诗论争
menglongshi lunzheng
(debate on misty poetry)

See "menglongshi" (misty poetry) and "menglongshi lilunde san ci jueqi" ("three rises" in the theory of misty poetry).

棉里藏针，行正思圆
mianli cang zhen, xing zheng si yuan
(He is like a needle wrapped in cotton. His mind is round and his actions are square)

Early in the GPCR, Deng Xiaoping was overthrown as the second biggest "capitalist-roader" in China. After the 1971 Lin Biao incident, Mao decided to reinstate a number of disgraced officials, following Premier Zhou's advice. Among them, Deng was the most important. When Mao brought Deng back to Beijing in 1973, he lauded his prodigal lieutenant with two succinct and meaningful Chinese phrases: "mianli cang zhen, xing zheng si yuan" (He is like a needle wrapped in cotton. His mind is round and his actions are square). One year later, when talking with Wang Hongwen and Zhou Enlai in Changsha, Hunan province, on 23 December 1974, Mao evaluated Deng as "the kind of able person it is hard to come by" (rencai nande).

On 8 August 1977, after his second comeback after being overthrown another time in early 1976, Deng spoke of the Changsha episode as an example of Mao valuing able people *(SWD,* p. 63).

面对面批判
mian dui mian pipan
("face-to-face" criticism)

See "douzhenghui" (public accusation meeting).

民办刊物
minban kanwu
(unofficial magazines)

See "Beijing zhi chun" (Beijing Spring).

民间社会
minjian shehui
(civil society)

See "danwei" (unit) and "wenhua re" (culture craze).

民权主义
minquanzhuyi
(principle of people's rights)

See "sanminzhuyi" (Three Principles of the People).

民生主义
minshengzhuyi
(principle of people's livelihood)

See "sanminzhuyi" (Three Principles of the People).

民主比自由更重要
minzhu bi ziyou geng zhongyao
(democracy is more important than freedom)

See "xinzuopai" (neo-Leftists).

民主党派
minzhu dangpai
(democratic parties)

Today in mainland China, besides the CCP, there are eight legal political parties. They are: 1. the Chinese Nationalist Party Revolutionary Committee (Zhongguo Guomindang Geming Weiyuanhui, founded on 1 January 1948); 2. the Chinese Democracy Alliance (Zhongguo Minzhu Tongmeng, founded in 1941); 3. the Chinese Association for the Founding of a Democratic Nation (Zhongguo Minzhu Jianguohui, founded in Chongqing in August 1945): 4. the Chinese Democracy Promotion Association (Zhongguo Minzhu Cujinhui, founded in Shanghai in December 1945): 5. the Chinese Peasants and Workers Democratic Party (Zhongguo Nonggong Minzhudang, assumed its name in February 1947); 6. the Chinese Public Devotion Party (Zhongguo Zhigongdang, assumed its name in October 1925); 7. the September 3rd Academy (Jiu San Xueshe, assumed its name on 3 September 1945); and 8. the Taiwan Democratic Self-government League (Taiwan Minzhu Zizhi Tongmeng, founded in November 1947). By far the Chinese Democracy Alliance is the largest of the eight, with a membership of about 150,000 in 1994.

These parties had all come into existence before the CCP's 1949 take-over of the mainland. Historically, they opposed the KMT dictatorship and supported the CCP in its fight for a democratic China. That is why they have traditionally been called "democratic parties", and their leaders and members are called "democratic personages" (minzhu renshi). The term "democratic" was also intended to show the tolerance of CCP leaders toward the bourgeoisie for their "united front" (tongyi zhanxian) purposes. It is no secret that there were CCP members in these parties and some even held leading positions.

The eight democratic parties did help the CCP in its prolonged struggle for political power in the country. Mao recognized this; he highly praised the "united front" as one of his "three magic weapons" (san da fabao). After the founding of the PRC, naturally, the situation changed somewhat, but it was still important to have these "non-Communist parties". Their nature was stipulated as follows: Under the CCP leadership, the democratic parties, representing and linked with a definite class and social stratum, are strategic political organizations that struggle for the common political aim of constructing socialism in China.

On 25 April 1956, in his speech "On the Ten Major Relationships" *(MZXJ,* 5, pp. 267-88) at the Enlarged Meeting of the PCC Politburo, Mao for the first time put forth the phrase "long-term co-existence and mutual supervision" (changqi gongcun, huxiang jiandu) as a basic principle of the relationship between the CCP and the eight democratic parties. The principle was confirmed at the 8th CCP National Congress held in September 1956. In his speech "On the Correct Handling of Contradictions among the People" delivered on 27 February 1957 at the 11th Meeting (enlarged) of the Supreme State Council, Mao further elucidated this principle. The eight democratic parties could be allowed to enjoy this CCP policy as long as their nature and function remained unchanged. Most importantly, they must of their own free will accept the CCP leadership and take the socialist road. In order that they not forget this, during the 1957 anti-Rightist campaign, many of their leaders and members were labelled as "bourgeois Rightists". After that, they lost their vitality, and were regarded as "political flower vases" (zhengzhi huaping). During the GPCR, they had to completely stop all their activities.

After the GPCR, with the help of the CCP, the eight parties gradually resumed their former position. Of course, they still had to maintain their stipulated nature and function. In his 16 January 1980 speech "The Present Situation and the Tasks before Us", Deng Xiaoping specifically declared that no multi-partism (duodangzhi) would be allowed in China. China's democratic parties were not oppositions—they had to recognize the CCP leadership *(SWD,* p. 253).

According to a CCP document issued late in 1989, there should be more consultation between the CCP and the democratic parties, and more posts in the government and in the NPC would be opened to their members. Henceforth the eight democratic parties were to be referred to as "parties participating in government affairs" (canzheng dang). In 1993, the roles of the democratic parties were written into the PRC Constitution. Now the principle of the relationship between the CCP and the eight democratic parties has been developed into what is called "a system of multiparty cooperation and political consultation led by the Communist Party" (gongchandang lingdaoxiade duo dang hezuo ji zhengzhi xieshangzhi). According to Party theorists, this is a "new type" of relationship between political parties, not only an important political achievement in the building of socialism with Chinese characteristics but also a new experiment in the history of the international socialist movement (guoji shehuizhuyi yundong). It is also said to be a "brilliant product" of the combination of the basic Marxist-Leninist principles in the united front work with the concrete conditions in China.

The CCP authorities stress that the system has already successfully been put into practice throughout the country, as an answer to the increasing demand for political reform. It is believed, however, that the demand may be much greater than the Party anticipates. Some people in the eight parties would certainly like to dispose of their status as "political flower vases", but they must wait for an opportune time. See also "dangde lingdao" (Party leadership) and "wuchanjieji zhuanzheng" (dictatorship of the proletariat).

民主基础上的集中，集中指导下的民主
minzhu jichushangde jizhong, jizhong zhidaoxiade minzhu (centralism on the basis of democracy and democracy under the guidance of centralism)

See "minzhu jizhongzhi" (democratic centralism).

民主集中制
minzhu jizhongzhi (democratic centralism)

"Democratic centralism" is stipulated in the CCP Constitution and the PRC Constitution as the organizational principle of the Party and the state. A fundamental system in China's political life, it is the application of the Party's "mass line" (qunzhong luxian). It is also called "the proletarian system of democratic centralism" (wuchanjieji minzhu jizhongzhi).

Mao first used the term in 1928 *(SWM,* 1, p. 91). In 1937 he elaborated on it as the organizational form of the government he envisioned *(SWM,* 2, pp. 56-57). In his speech "On Coalition Government" ("Lun lianhe zhengfu") delivered at the CCP's 7th National Congress on 24 April 1945, Mao found a succinct expression for this idea: "Centralism on the basis of democracy and democracy under the guidance of centralism" (minzhu jichushangde jizhong, jizhong zhidaoxiade minzhu) *(SWM,* 3, p. 280). These two phrases were then written into the Party Constitution.

Accompanying "democratic centralism" is the concept of "socialist democracy" (shehuizhuyi minzhu). This was elaborated on in the 1981 Party document "Resolution on Certain Questions in the History of Our Party since the Founding of the PRC". It is said that one of the fundamental tasks of the socialist revolution is to gradually build a socialist political system with a high degree of democracy. The failure to stress this task since the founding of the PRC was an important reason why the bitter experience of the GPCR took place. From then on, almost all the CCP documents have not failed to repeat this sentence: There will be no socialism without democracy (Meiyou minzhu jiumeiyou shehuizhuyi). But up to the present, as many agree, democracy is still a big issue to be solved.

Some critics asserted that the root of the problem is "democratic centralism", on the basis of which "socialist democracy" is formed. "Socialist democracy" is also called "people's democracy" (renmin minzhu) or "proletarian democracy" (wuchanjieji minzhu). It is stipulated that socialist democracy is the basis of the proletarian dictatorship and the latter guarantees the former. Today, the term "proletarian democracy" is used less often. But the thesis still remains valid: "Socialist democracy is a democracy under the guidance of centralism" (Shehuizhuyi minzhu shi jizhong zhidaoxiade minzhu).

First, critics find Mao's view about democracy fundamentally wrong. In their opinion, democracy is both the means and the end (minzhu jiishi shouduan youshi mudi)—or the "unity of the means and the end" (shouduan yu mudide tongyi)—but chiefly the end. However, Mao asserted (as in his "On the Correct Handling of

Contradictions among the People") that democracy is only the means and not the end (minzhu zhishi shouduan er bushi mudi). According to Mao's calculation, democracy is a matter of style. It simply means: "Let others talk" (rang ren shuohua) or "Allow people to speak good and bad words". In addition, this must be under the condition of so-called "centralized guidance", as pointed out by Hu Jiwei, former director and chief editor of the *People's Daily* and former vice chairman of the NPC Standing Committee (who was ousted right after the 1989 June 4th Incident because of his appeal to the NPC for a peaceful solution to the crisis). In a 1998 article, Hu said, "democracy under centralized guidance" means that outside democracy there is something called "centralized guidance" to which democracy must be subject. Thus what Mao meant by "democratic centralism" is self-evident. In fact, rule of "democratic centralism" is: "individuals are subordinate to the organizations they belong to, the minority is subordinate to the majority, lower authorities are subordinate to higher authorities, and the whole Party is subordinate to the Party Center" (geren fucong jiti, shaoshu fucong duoshu, xiaji fucong shangji, quandang fucong zhongyang). What one sees is a tight power net: the whole country is subject to the Party's absolute rule and the whole Party is subject to the rule of a few leaders, and very often one leader at the very top. This system, critics observed, is highly effective only if the leaders at the top never make obvious mistakes, or people in the system have no sensitivity to mistakes. Unfortunately, neither scenario is possible by human nature.

Indeed, critics said, democracy in its true sense cannot be achieved if "democratic centralism", which is based on the Chinese tradition of "rule by individuals" (renzhi) and on Lenin's idea about the building of a proletarian party, remains valid as the fundamental system of the Party and state. See also "qunzhong luxian" (mass line) and "wuchanjieji zhuanzheng" (dictatorship of the proletariat).

民主既是手段又是目的
minzhu jishi shouduan youshi mudi
(democracy is both the means and the end)

See "minzhu jizhongzhi" (democratic centralism).

民主女神
minzhu nüsheng
(Goddess of Democracy)

On 30 May 1989, during the pro-democracy movement, a statue of the "Goddess of Democracy" was set up in Tiananmen Square by the student demonstrators to show their desire for democracy. The statue was smashed on the early morning of 4 June 1989 when the movement was suppressed by the authorities with violence.

The erection of the "Goddess of Democracy", as people have pointed out, showed the strong influence of Western thought on the 1989 pro-democracy movement. See also "bajiu minyun" (1989 pro-democracy movement).

民主人士
minzhu renshi
(democratic personages)

Like "democratic parties" (minzhu dangpai), this is a term formed in the history of the so-called "new democratic revolution" from the May 4th Movement of 1919 to the founding of the PRC in 1949. "Democratic personages" refer to those "patriotic personages of democratic parties or no particular party who at one time patronized the CCP in its fight against the KMT and for a democratic China, and supported the 'people's democratic dictatorship' with positive action". See also "minzhu dangpai" (democratic parties).

民主是解放思想的重要条件
minzhu shi jiefang sixiangde zhongyao tiaojian
(democracy is a major condition
for emancipating the mind)

See "jiefang sixiang" (emancipating the mind).

民主是手段与目的的统一
minzhu shi shouduan yu mudide tongyi
(democracy is the unity of the means and the end)

See "minzhu jizhongzhi" (democratic centralism).

民主只是手段而不是目的
minzhu zhishi shouduan er bushi mudi
(democracy is only the means and not the end)

See "minzhu jizhongzhi" (democratic centralism).

民主的和平
minzhude heping
(democratic peace)

See "weidu Zhongguo" (containment against China).

民主墙
minzhuqiang
(Democracy Wall)

The term "minzhuqiang" first appeared in May 1957 when Beijing University students put up their big-character posters on a campus wall, so as to respond to Mao's call to help the Party in its ongoing rectification movement. The posters, taking many forms, such as cartoons, poems, and satirical essays, soon became, or were regarded as, attacks on CCP current policies and even its basic principles. This liberal phase proved to be very short-lived, followed by the anti-Rightist campaign.

The term "minzhuqiang" appeared again in a pro-democracy and human rights movement that spontaneously erupted in Beijing in September 1978. It began with a protest against the banning of the Beijing-based youth magazine *Chinese Youth (Zhongguo Qingnian)*. On 11 September 1978, this pre-GPCR magazine resumed publication, carrying articles to justify the so-called "Tiananmen counter-revolutionary incident". This was regarded as a serious political incident, and the ban came from Wang Dongxing, CCP vice-chairman in charge of propaganda. Staff members of the magazine, however, refused to obey. In protest, they posted the magazine, page by page, on a wall in Xidan district. Immediately, many people followed this action. A great number of big-character posters were posted to express opinions and grievances against earlier miscarriages of justice. There were also suggestions concerning issues of freedom, democracy, and legal system. The wall soon became known as "Xidan Democracy Wall" (Xidan minzhuqiang) or "Democracy Wall", attracting a lot of people everyday during the exciting period of what was later called the "Beijing Spring". See also "fan youpai yundong" (anti-Rightist campaign) and "Beijing zhi chun" (Beijing Spring).

民族斗争说到底是一个阶级斗争问题
minzu douzheng shuodaodi shi yige jieji douzheng wenti (national struggle in the final analysis is a matter of class struggle)

On 8 August 1963, Mao issued a document entitled "Statement Supporting the American Negroes in Their Just Struggle Against Racial Discrimination by U.S. Imperialism". Mao said in the statement: "In the final analysis, national struggle is a matter of class struggle. Among the whites in the United States it is only the reactionary ruling circles who oppress the black people. They can in no way represent the workers, farmers, revolutionary intellectuals and other enlightened persons who comprise the overwhelming majority of the white people" (in *People of the World, Unite and Defeat the U.S. Aggressors and All Their Lackeys*, FLP, pp. 3-4). See also "minzuzhuyi" (nationalism).

民族分裂主义
minzu fenliezhuyi (national separatism)

See "minzuzhuyi" (nationalism).

民族革命战争的大众文学
minzu geming zhanzhengde dazhong wenxue (popular literature of the national revolutionary war)

See "sanshiniandai wenyi yundong" (literature and art movement of the 1930s).

民族化
minzuhua (nationalization)

See "dazhonghua" (popularization).

民族化是社会主义文艺的必由之路
minzuhua shi shehuizhuyi wenyide bi you zhi lu (nationalization is the only road for socialist literature and art)

See "dazhonghua" (popularization).

民族主义
minzuzhuyi (nationalism)

According to CCP doctrine, Communists should uphold what they call "proletarian internationalism" (wuchanjieji guojizhuyi), and should always draw a clear line of demarcation with bourgeois nationalism (zichanjieji minzuzhuyi). Domestically, nationalism sometimes appears as "big nationality chauvinism" (daminzuzhuyi) or "Han chauvinism" (da-Hanzuzhuyi), and sometimes as "local nationalism" (difang minzuzhuyi). "Big nationality chauvinism" is characterized by: despising and looking down upon the national minorities, disrespecting their language, customs, habits, and religious belief, negating their right to administer their internal affairs, and so on. The characteristics of "local nationalism" are conservatism and anti-foreignism, hostility to other nationalities and advocacy of "national separatism" (minzu fenliezhuyi).

In international relations, Communists regard nationalism as a product of a capitalist system, as the view of the bourgeois class on nations and its general policy in dealing with national issues. Sometimes nationalism appears as "big-nation chauvinism" (daguo shawenzhuyi) and sometimes as "parochial nationalism" (xia'ai minzuzhuyi). CCP doctrine stresses that the bourgeoisie tends to cover up class struggle with national struggle (yi minzu douzheng yan'gai jieji douzheng). In response, a Marxist should hold the view that national struggle is, in the final analysis, a matter of class struggle (minzu douzheng shuodaodi shi jieji douzheng wenti). But in some cases, CCP doctrine also states that nationalism is of a certain progressive nature—for example, in the national movements during the period when capitalism is on the rise, and in the movements for national liberation and independence waged by colonial or semi-colonial people.

In fact, as scholars point out, one of the important factors leading to the CCP's 1949 victory in taking over the mainland was its success in mobilizing the masses by appealing to nationalism. The Communist revolution was rooted in patriotic sentiment; it was as much a response to imperialism as it was to feudalism. The people rallied around the Communist defiance of the "no dogs or Chinese" attitude of the Western powers, and they sought to reclaim the country. Towards the end of the 1970s, when the Party began to shift the focus of its work to economic construction, nationalism was also a means of national mobilization. It was often said at that time: "A closed door leads to backwardness; and backwardness proves vulnerable to attack" (fengbi jiuyao luohou; luohou jiuyao aida). But the implementation of the reform and open-door program, which focused on economic construction, inevitably increased China's foreign relations. Many of the institutional frameworks and values of the West were brought into China. At that time, the slogan "Learn from the West" was acceptable. More concretely, there was also another slogan: "Be articulate with international norms" (yu guoji jiegui). Zhao Ziyang's strategic thinking about "merging into international circles" (rongru guoji daxunhuan) seemed to be accepted by many within and outside the Party, when it was put forward in 1987. Against this background, nationalism quickly faded. Instead, cosmopolitanism (shijiezhuyi) became popular.

Interestingly, in the 1990s, nationalism has been revived, after so many great changes have taken place in the country. Now subject to attack is the so-called "post-colonial mentality" (houzhimin xintai), or broadly speaking, the Western-centric beliefs, which are said to have seeped into China during the twenty years of the reform process. There was an appeal to "cultural nationalism" (wenhua minzuzhuyi) to resist the "cultural hegemonism" (wenhua baquanzhuyi) of Western imperialism (a more recent term for "Western-centrism"—xifang zhongxinzhuyi). Popular topics include the superiority of Chinese culture, Asian values, and the "Chinese century" (Zhongguo shiji). Correspondingly, another group of topics include: extreme U.S.-style individualism, Washington's hegemonism on the world stage, U.S.

"demonization" of China and "containment" policy. A survey, conducted in December 1995 by the China National Promotion Society of Guangdong, showed that over 85 percent of urban residents are willing to give their lives for the country if necessary. Another survey among young people conducted in September 1995 by the *China Youth Daily* indicated that 87.1 percent of the respondents regard the United States as the most unfriendly country to China. There is a "China can say no" mentality, which, for instance, found expression in the 400-plus-page book *China Can Say No—Political and Emotional Choices in the Post-Cold War Age (Zhongguo keyi shuo bu—Lengzhanhou shidaide zhengzhi yu qinggan jueze,* Beijing, Zhonghua Gongshang, 1996) and *China's Renaissance and the Future of the World (Zhonghua fuxing yu shijie weilai),* a compendium of essays by the much talked about scholar He Xin.

It is noted that the ideological trend of nationalism started after the June 4th Incident of 1989 and followed the unprecedented changes in the East European bloc and the Soviet Union. On the one hand, out of political reasons, many pro-democracy (or pro-"radicalism of the 1980s") intellectuals were silenced or fled abroad. The political tragedy turned out to be another historical starting point for the self-examination of China's intellectuals in the 1990s. On the other hand, many were worried that if China were to initiate the political reform promoted by the West, it would share a fate similar to that of Russia. Coincidentally, from 1994 to 1995, arguments supporting a "contain China" policy flourished in the United States. This lent credence to their fears. Chinese intellectual suspicion of the West deepened after Samuel P. Huntington published his theory about a clash between Eastern and Western civilizations. The rise in intellectual nationalism also had a societal explanation. Many of those promoting nationalism, such as the five co-authors of *China Can Say No,* had never traveled to the West and were quite narrow-minded. What was equally true was that some of them did have an experience abroad, only it was an unpleasant one. Feelings of discrimination triggered their pride, and their pride in turn manifested itself in the form of nationalistic statements.

As for the CCP leadership, in view of the post-1989 critical situation in China, it was natural that nationalism be called upon because of its pragmatic political value. (Reportedly, the first strategic recommendation made by Wang Huning, a Fudan professor of political science and now Jiang Zemin's strategist, upon filling his new position in Beijing, was: Nationalism is a useful tool in state building.) From a long-term point of view, more fundamentally, national/state interests are at work here. Now China eagerly wishes to speed up its modernization, with a deeply held cultural conviction that it must regain its ranking in world history. And it now possesses a more solid foundation to realize this dream. To achieve its goal, China will find the existing world order in many ways unreasonable, or harmful to its interests. It will try its best to change the order. In doing so, in many cases, and for a long time, nationalism will be needed by Beijing leaders. Moreover, from the angle of China being a Party-state, nationalism is a necessary supplement to Mao's Sinicized Marxism-Leninism. In view of the collapse of traditional Communist thought, nationalism is all the more a convenient tool to resist "peaceful evolution". It is indeed like a stone that can kill two birds. Besides, if it is right to say that nationalism is an objective existence in any nation and at any time, the rise of nationalism is only a universal phenomenon in today's world, to fill the vacuum left over at the end of the Cold War that was characterized by politico-ideological antagonism.

But all this can be called patriotism (the CCP leaders always stress that what they uphold is patriotism and not nationalism). There is some confusion there, especially in the context of international relations. Indeed, it is still difficult to define nationalism precisely, though it is now over two hundred years since the concept of nationalism originated in Western Europe in the late eighteenth century. Like the terms "democracy" and "liberty," the definition of nationalism changes with time, and it has been re-defined and re-interpreted many times. Some scholars advised that there was no need at all to deny nationalism. They suggested a differentiation between nationalism as a means and nationalism as a goal. While the latter is harmful, even to the nation's self-interests, the former plays some positive role. Some advocated what they called "rational nationalism" (lixing minzuzhuyi), an "ideal type" of nationalism, as an "effective prescription" to deal with the "China threat" theory and the call to contain China. Moreover, they believed nationalism, in its rationalization process, can help promote freedom and democracy. However, some others—mainly those called contemporary Chinese liberal thinkers—thought otherwise. They warned that nationalism is on the whole a "monster" difficult to control. It will bring about negative and even disastrous consequences, evolving into "parochial nationalism", xenophobia, or "irrational nationalism" (feilixing minzuzhuyi). And this can easily occur. An example was the irrational sentiments expressed in the book *China Can Say No.* They also pointed out that nationalism is very often the hotbed of a dictatorship (minzuzhuyi wangwang shi ducaizhede wenchuang). In view of the irrational nationalism existing in China, they suggested it would be better for the Chinese people to discard and transcend nationalism and to adopt human rights, freedom, and democracy—common standards shared by the world—as their own standards to build the country. Or, to put it this way, China should on its own initiative join in the world's mainstream civilization, play an active role, and help create what can be called "global values" (quanqiu jiazhi) shared by all nations of the world. After all, in today's world "globalization" (quanqiuhua) is gaining momentum.

Despite the controversies, nationalism already displayed itself as a force with great appeal. It emerged with the rise of neo-conservatism, the chief ideological trend of the 1990s, and played an important role in its formation and development. In May 1999, particularly, a storm of nationalism spread all over the country after the NATO bombing of the Chinese Embassy in Belgrade. "Neo-imperialism" (xin diguozhuyi) became a label for the United States. U.S.-led NATO raids on Yugoslavia were condemned as "out-and-out imperialist actions" in the name of "humanitarianism". Some slogans from the Mao period, such as "Maintain independence and keep the initiative in our own hands" (duli zizhu) and "Be self-reliant" (zili gengsheng) were revived. As a result, once again, "China Can Say No" became the strongest voice of the time.

During the first several decades of the twenty-first century, international struggles will probably unfold chiefly between China and the United States. It is no secret that certain forces in the United States have found a new archrival in China. They even regard China as the third "evil empire" following fascist Germany and the Soviet Union, thus justifying the confrontation between the two countries—it is one between democracy and Communism. It will be impossible for China to resist democracy with Communist ideology (the collapse of the Soviet Union has proved this). But China can resist U.S. hegemonism with nationalism. Scholars predict that from a long-term point of view, by upholding nationalism China may get the upper hand in this confrontation (see Ding Xueliang, "Zhongguo minzuzhuyi duikang Mei baquanzhuyi"—"China's nationalism v. U.S. hegemonism", *Mingbao,* Jan. 2000, p. 42). On the other hand, if radical nationalism (probably allied with neo-Maoism) will become China's leading ideological force in the coming one or two decades, which is not impossible, this is certainly not good news to the world or to China. See also "xin baoshouzhuyi" (neo-conservatism), "lengzhanhou shidaide xin diguozhuyi" (neo-imperialism in the post-Cold War era), and "weidu Zhongguo" (containment against China).

民族主义往往是独裁者的温床
minzuzhuyi wangwang shi ducaizhede wenchuang
(nationalism is very often the hotbed of dictatorship)

See "minzuzhuyi" (nationalism).

摸着石头过河
mozhe shitou guo he
(cross the river by feeling the stones)

"Crossing the river by feeling the stones" is a popular saying among Chinese people. Chen Yun cited it in his speech delivered at a PCC work conference on 16 December 1980 ("Jingji xingshi yu jingyan jiaoxun"—"The Economic Situation and Our Experience and Lessons", in *Chen Yun Wenxuan, 1956-1985—Selected Works of Chen Yun, 1956-1985,* Beijing, Renmin, 1995, p. 251). In October 1984, when meeting participants at a forum on Chinese-foreign economic cooperation, Deng Xiaoping also used the phrase. What he meant was that, in carrying out reform and the open-door policies in building socialism with Chinese characteristics, there was no reliable model to go by, and people had to advance step-by-step by summing up the situation from their experience, both positive and negative.

Like his "cat" theory (mao lun) and "no debate" theory (bu zhenglun lun), the theory of "crossing the river by feeling the stones" was also of great significance. Deng Xiaoping, dubbed the "general architect" of China's reform, did not seem to trust any ready-made blueprint or "guiding principles". While Mao ruled the country with a set of doctrines, Deng believed practice was the sole criterion for testing truth. This was regarded as Deng's best contribution. See also "Deng Xiaoping lilun" (Deng Xiaoping Theory).

陌生化
moshenghua
(defamiliarization)

"Defamiliarization" is a term in literary theory. Xie Mian used it in his defense of "misty poetry" in the debate of the early 1980s. According to Xie, it was an artistic characteristic of these newly emerging poems. Compared with the alarm and repercussions their ideological content aroused, the impact of their art was even stronger. The catching of momentary experience, delicate conveyance of the subconscious, the wide-ranging employment of synesthesia, the audacious and undecorated display of feelings, ingenious association of thoughts, unexpected images, strange and witty language, jumping and free rhythm—all these techniques were freely used by the young poets in a way they thought best, though sometimes as experiments. To many Chinese readers, the result was a sort of "defamiliarization". On this point, Xie Mian, as an enthusiastic defender, refuted the criticism of these poems as being "all hard to understand". He believed the critics were too attached to old things and thus had a bias against the new. "Mid-Autumn Night", a poem by Shu Ting, was taken as an example ("Zhongqiu ye", *Rongshu,* 2, 1980, reprinted in Bi Hua and Yang Ling, eds., *Jueqide shiqun—A Body of Rising Poetry,* Hong Kong, Dangdai Wenxue Yanjiushe, 1984, pp. 11-12). Its rich and somewhat gloomy implications are hidden in its drifting images, and rumination is required if one wants to discover its beauty, a beauty that is not easily discerned. With a contemptuous air, Xie compared it with lines from political poetry in the past. His message was: poems like Shu Ting's "Mid-Autumn Night" require some time to be understood and appreciated. See also "menglongshi" (misty poetry) and "menglongshi lilunde san ci jueqi" ("three rises" in the theory of misty poetry).

幕後老板
muhou laoban
(behind-the-scenes boss)

The term, very often derogatory, refers to the person who pulls strings behind the scenes. Deng Xiaoping, for instance, was once described as the behind-the-scenes boss in the 1976 Tiananmen Incident.

南巡
nanxun
(Southern tour)

This refers to Deng Xiaoping's tour to China's southern provinces from 18 January to 21 February 1992. See "Deng Xiaoping lilun" (Deng Xiaoping Theory).

南巡讲话
nanxun jianghua
(talks during the Southern tour)

See "Deng Xiaoping lilun" (Deng Xiaoping Theory).

内乱论
neiluan lun
("civil strife" theory)

During 1980-81 when the draft of the "Resolution on Certain Questions in the History of Our Party since the Founding of the PRC" was in the process of being written, Deng Xiaoping gave instructions that the GPCR, though "an error of particular gravity, one affecting the overall situation", should be written about in "broad outline" only. When the document was passed at the 6th Plenum of the 11th PCC in June 1981, the GPCR was described as a "civil strife", one that was started mistakenly by the Party leader and utilized by counter-revolutionary cliques, bringing serious disasters to the Party, the state, and the people of the whole country. On the one hand, the CCP authorities had to negate the GPCR, whose destructive and disastrous consequences were felt by all. Besides, without the negation, many Party leaders, including Deng himself, would not have been able to find grounds for rehabilitation, still less to carry out their new policies for reform. On the other hand, however, they had to emphasize that during the GPCR years, neither Chinese socialist society nor the CCP had changed its nature, and that the "mistakes" of Mao were those of "a great revolutionary, a great Marxist". See also "wen'ge" (Cultural Revolution).

内伤
neishang

(invisible injury)

See "renxing fuguide jilu" (record of the resuscitation of human nature).

内在自由
neizai ziyou
(interior freedom)

See "chuangzuo ziyou" (creative freedom).

能官能民
neng guan neng min
(be able to serve as an official and remain as one of the common people)

See "xiafang" (transfer to a lower level).

能上能下
neng shang neng xia
(be able to work at both higher and lower levels)

See "xiafang" (transfer to a lower level).

你办事，我放心
ni banshi, wo fangcxin
(with you in charge, I am at ease)

See "yingming lingxiu" (wise leader) and "an jiding fangzhen ban" (act according to the principles laid down).

逆反心理
nifan xinli
(converse psychology)

As a conspicuous social phenomenon, the converse psychology can be seen in many Chinese. If the authorities say that something was bad, they think it might be good. And vice versa. In cases concerning works of literature and art, this was especially true. Many officially attacked works in the 1980s, such as "Unrequited Love", a film script by Bai Hua, "Between Man and Monster", a piece of reportage literature by Liu Binyan, "What If I Really Were", a spoken drama by Sha Yexin and his colleagues, and *Humanity!*, a novel by Dai Houying, turned out to be well received by the readership. A recent case was *Shanghai Baby (Shanghai Baobei*, Shenyang, Chunfeng wenyi, Sep. 1999), a novel by Wei Hui, a young woman writer in Shanghai. It was banned in May 2000 and immediately became popular. Hence a saying in China: If you want to rise to fame, just produce a controversial work. Or: Let the PCC propaganda director become your salesman. See also "shehui xiaoguo lun" (social effect theory) and "yi wenti wei zhongxinde baogao wenxue" (problem-centered reportage literature).

鸟笼经济
niaolong jingji

("bird cage" economics)

On 2 December 1982, during his meeting with Shanghai representatives attending the 5th Session of the 5th NPC, Chen Yun said, when talking about economic construction: "Economic activation and market adjustment should be allowed to function only within the permission of the plan, and not overstep the guidance of planning." Drawing an analogy with a bird and its cage, he continued: "The bird must not be held tightly in the hand or it will die; it should fly, but only within the cage; without a cage, it will just fly away. If we say that the bird is an activated economy, then the cage is none other than state planning" *(Chen Yun Wenxuan,* 1956-1985, p. 287). The term "bird cage economics" vividly summarizes Chen's idea about Chinese socialist economy, which was obviously at odds with Deng Xiaoping's concept of a market economy. See also "jingji gaige" (economic reform) and "Deng Xiaoping lilun" (Deng Xiaoping Theory).

宁左勿右
ning zuo wu you
(rather be Leftist than Rightist)

See "you" (Right).

牛鬼蛇神
niuguisheshen
(monsters and demons)

Refers to class enemies of all descriptions. See "hengsao yiqie niuguisheshen" (sweep away all monsters and demons).

农村包围城市
nongcun baowei chengshi
(surrounding the cities by the countryside)

See "renmin zhanzheng" (people's war).

农村社会主义教育运动
nongcun shehuizhuyi jiaoyu yundong
(socialist education movement in the rural areas)

See "shejiao" (socialist education movement).

农业合作社
nongye hezuoshe
(agricultural cooperative)

See "renmin gongshe" (People's Commune).

农业学大寨
nongye xue Dazhai
(in agriculture, learn from Dazhai)

Dazhai was a "production brigade" in Shanxi province. It was set up by Mao in February 1964 as a "national model in agriculture".

The Dazhai model was repudiated in the early 1980s. Its "Leftist" practices included "cutting off capitalist tails" (ge zibenzhuyi weiba)—restricting private plots of land (ziliudi), sideline businesses, and periodic village markets.

Dazhai's first leader was Chen Yonggui, who was appointed PRC vice-premier in 1975 and dramatically lost his job in 1980. He died in March 1986. See also "tuchu zhengzhi" (giving prominence to politics).

诺贝尔奖综合症
nuobei'erjiang zonghezheng
(Nobel Prize syndrome)

At the end of each recent year, what can be called a "Nobel Prize syndrome" would afflict some people in China's literary circles. They were at first hopeful, and then they became disappointed and even turned angry and presumptuous, as the dream of a Chinese writer being awarded a Nobel Prize in literature was once again shattered. To a certain degree, this is understandable because there is no universal standard for literature, nor is there any convincing reason that no Chinese writer is qualified to win the prize. The syndrome will continue until a Chinese gets the prize—they attach too much importance to the prize.

This "Nobel Prize syndrome" has also infected some Chinese economists. Their argument for a Chinese economist (or more than one) to be awarded the prize was: as China is on a unique path of economic development and will become an economic superpower soon in the twenty-first century, a Chinese economist should be awarded for China's economic miracle and for his part in creating new economic theories.

排队
paidui
(queuing up)

See "fanyou renqunde difang, douyou zuo, zhong, you" (wherever there are masses of people, they are invariably divided into the Left, the middle, and the Right).

彷徨的一代
panghuangde yidai
(bewildered generation)

See "liangdai shiren" (two generations of poets).

炮打司令部
paoda silingbu
(bombard the headquarters)

On 5 August 1966, during the 11th Plenum of the 8th PCC, Mao Zedong unexpectedly put up a "big-character poster" which he had personally written under the eye-catching title "Bombard the Headquarters" ("Paoda silingbu"), accusing (though without directly naming) Liu Shaoqi, then PRC president and the CCP vice-chairman in charge of the PCC's routine duties, of suppressing the GPCR. Two days later, the poster was printed and circulated at the Plenum, which immediately became a battlefield where Liu was subject to attack. Then, the next day, the "CCP Central Committee's Decision on the GPCR" (the "Sixteen Articles") was passed. The Party document stated: The major target in the GPCR is "those in power within the Party taking the capitalist road". From then on, "Bombard the bourgeois headquarters" became a most popular slogan during the GPCR. See also "shiliutiao" (Sixteen Articles) and "wen'ge" (Cultural Revolution).

裴多菲俱乐部
peiduofei Juluobu
(Petofi Club)

The Petofi Club ws a well-known intellectual body in Hungary in the 1950s. The artists and intellectuals of the Petofi were pioneers in the 1956 Hungarian Incident.

After the 1962 10th Plenum of the 8th PCC, Mao gave a series of talks and instructions concerning Party work in literature and art, dealing telling blows to China's literary and art circles. In an instruction of 27 June 1964, Mao severely criticized literary officials for not having carried out Party policies. Mao said: "They have acted as high and mighty bureaucrats, have not gone to the workers, peasants and soldiers and have not reflected the socialist revolution and socialist construction. In recent years, they have slid right down to the brink of revisionism. Unless they remold themselves in real earnest, at some future date they are bound to become groups like the Hungarian Petofi Club."

After its 3rd Plenum in December 1978, the 11th PCC formally declared that Mao's criticism did not tally with the actual situation.

配套意识
peitao yishi
("complete set" in terms of ideology)

When Liu Zaifu's theory of the subjectivity of literature was attacked by Chen Yong, Liu Xinwu was the first to reveal the attack to overseas readers, obviously in the hope that more people would be concerned about the affair and give Liu Zaifu their support. This was a clear-cut stand. He claimed that China absolutely needed humanism. It seemed to him that Marxism, which should not be an ossified system but should be something flexible that could play a role in Chinese society, would be erroneous if it did not contain humanism. After all, he said, humanism could be found in Marxism. Logically, he found what Liu Zaifu was striving for to be exactly what present-day China needed, or what the current reforms in China needed. He opined that the reason why "wind" was so often stirred up (gua feng) in the country, which resulted in vacillation of policy and popular loss of confidence, was that there was no "complete set" in terms of ideology to justify the economic reforms being carried out in China. He said: "Reform, in the final analysis, aims at developing productivity and making China rich, in other words, enabling the Chinese people to lead a better life and enjoy a higher civilization. Therefore, it is absolutely in conformity with reform for literature to present humanism, to advocate respect and understanding of man, human dignity and human value, such as the subjectivity of literature and the theory about characterization as put forth by Liu Zaifu" ("Liu Xinwu on the Liu Zaifu Incident and Literary Trends in Today's China", *JN,* 197:80, June 1986).

As observers noted, building a "complete set" in terms of ideology means to reform Marxism in a systematic way. See also "Liu Zaifu shijian" (Liu Zaifu Incident).

彭德怀事件
Peng Dehuai shijian

(Peng Dehuai Incident)

In July 1959, an enlarged conference of the CCP Politburo was held at Lushan, Jiangxi province. Peng Dehuai, then a Politburo member and minister of national defense, gave two talks at the group discussion held successively on the 3rd and the 4th of the month. On 14 July, he further wrote a letter to Mao Zedong personally. Peng took aim at the grandiloquence and exaggeration of the "three red banners" (san mian hongqi) promoted by Mao, and criticized other shortcomings and mistakes, such as the loss and waste of manpower, material resources, and finances. To him, the "General Line" was "Left adventurism". The "Great Leap Forward" was compared to a "fraudulent fire, no more than a high fever". As to the People's Communes, he charged that they had been set up prematurely and were made a mess of. All this, in his opinion, was an expression of "petty bourgeois fanaticism" (xiaozichanjieji kuangrexing). In addition, he warned, "If it weren't for the good Chinese workers and peasants, there would have been a Hungarian Incident long ago and allied Soviet troops would have been called in."

This acid criticism had Mao beside himself with indignant rage. He found it necessary to beat off Peng's "attack", even at the cost of changing the tone of the conference, which had been set to check the "Left" mistakes made in the past year.

On 16 July Mao had Peng's letter printed and distributed to the conference participants. He told Liu Shaoqi, Zhou Enlai, and Zhu De, three members of the Politburo Standing Committee, that the nature of the letter should be discussed.

On 23 July Mao made a speech at the conference, fiercely attacking Peng.

On 24 July Peng was forced to make a self-criticism.

On 27 July Liu Shaoqi conveyed Mao's "important instruction" concerning the so-called "anti-Party clique" headed by Peng Dehuai (other members were Huang Kecheng, then member of the PCC Secretariat and chief of the PLA General Staff, Zhang Wentian, then alternate member of the Politburo and vice-minister of foreign affairs, and Zhou Xiaozhou, then alternate member of the PCC and first secretary of the CCP Hunan Provincial Committee, who were found to share Peng's opinion).

On 29 July Mao announced an urgent decision of the Politburo Standing Committee that the 8th Plenum of 8th PCC was to be held at Lushan from 2 to 16 August 1959. Peng and his supporters understood that their "mistake" had been regarded as a vital one from the perspective of the Party's political line struggle.

At the 8th Plenum of 8th PCC, the "clique" were accused of opposing Chairman Mao and the Party in a planned and organized way and with a sinister ambition. After the Plenum, which passed a resolution on the alleged "anti-Party clique", Lin Biao took over Peng's job in charge of the CMC routine duties. An "anti-Right deviation" campaign (fan youqing yundong) was carried out in the whole country. The Party's "Left" mistakes became even worse. Finally, a nationwide economic setback occurred in 1960 and lasted for three years.

The case of Peng Dehuai was redressed at the 1978 3rd Plenum of the 11th PCC, but he had already been persecuted to death in the GPCR (on 29 November 1974).

批倒批臭
pi dao pi chou
(to make someone overthrown and discredited by mass criticism)

See "dapipan" (mass criticism).

批邓，反击右倾翻案风 pi Deng, fanji youqing fan'anfeng (campaign to criticize Deng Xiaoping and counter the "Right deviationist trend to reverse correct verdicts")

In 1973, Deng Xiaoping returned to power after having been overthrown as the "second biggest capitalist-roader" in the early days of the GPCR. He fully enjoyed the support of Premier Zhou Enlai. When Zhou fell seriously ill in January 1975, Deng took over Zhou's duties. As vice-chairman of the CCP and the CMC and PRC first vice-premier, he avidly set about to carry out Zhou's "four modernizations" policy by launching an all-out reshuffling of economic, military, educational, and technological departments, and by reinstating older cadres purged during the GPCR. Adroitly, he linked together Mao's three instructions concerning promoting stability and unity, studying the theory of the proletarian dictatorship, and boosting the national economy. On 4 July 1975, in a speech to members of the fourth class for theoretical study organized by the PCC, Deng said: "These three instructions, being related to one another, form an organic whole and none of them should be left out. They form the key link in our work for the present period" (SWD, p. 23). Thus a new concept was advanced—"taking the three instructions as the key link" (yi sanxiang zhishi wei gang). On 7 October 1975, under Deng's auspices, a document to elucidate his idea was drafted by the Political Research Office of the State Council—"On the General Program for All Work of the Party and the Nation" ("Lun quandang quanguo ge xiang gongzuode zonggang"). Obviously, Deng was resisting the then dominant view of "taking class struggle as the key link". This was an important measure by Deng to block and rectify the mistakes of the GPCR. Deng also directed the drafting of two other documents with a similar purpose—"The Report Outline Concerning the Work in the Chinese Academy of Sciences" ("Kexueyuan gongzuo huibao tigang") and "Several Issues in Speeding Up Industrial Development" ("Guanyu jiakuai gongye fazhande ruogan wenti").

Deng's measures unavoidably led to a serious conflict with what was later dubbed the "Gang of Four", the vested interests of the GPCR. Mao, for his part, was also unable to bring himself to accept Deng's harsh criticism and systematic correction of mistakes made during the GPCR (though he agreed to make some readjustments to the Party's policies). During the several months from October 1975 to January 1976, Mao gave a series of talks concerning the Deng issue. On 20 November 1975, Mao suggested that a Politburo meeting be held so as to achieve a consensus of opinion about the GPCR and that Deng Xiaoping be placed in charge of drafting a resolution, which would consider the GPCR as consisting of thirty percent shortcomings and seventy percent achievements. But Deng refused to perform this task. Thereafter, Mao's suspicion and resentment increased. Finally, in the last month of 1975, Mao launched the last campaign of his life—a campaign to criticize Deng Xiaoping and to counter the so-called "Right deviationist trend to reverse correct verdicts", which was said to be sparked by Deng. In the campaign, the above-said three documents were attacked as "three big poisonous weeds" (san zhu daducao).

In the 1976 New Year's Day joint editorial of the *People's Daily*, *Red Flag,* and the *Liberation Army Daily*, a new directive of Mao's was published: "Stability and unity is not to give up class struggle. Class struggle is the key link, and everything else hinges on it." Mao asked his Party to "take class struggle as the key link" (yi jieji douzheng wei gang).

On 5 February 1976, at a meeting convened by the Party Center, another "supreme directive" was released: "You're making the socialist revolution, and yet you don't know where the bourgeoisie is. It is right in the Communist Party—those in power taking the capitalist road. The capitalist-roaders are still on the capitalist road." Obviously, Deng was referred to as a capitalist-roader who is still on the capitalist road.

On 5 April 1976, the so-called "Tiananmen Counter-Revolutionary Incident" took place. Deng Xiaoping was dismissed from all his posts inside and outside the Party, accused of being the behind-the-scenes instigator of the incident. Deng was labeled an "incorrigible capitalist-roader" (si bu gaihuide zouzipai). It was implied that the late Premier Zhou Enlai, Deng's former supporter, was also a "capitalist-roader".

In July 1977, the 3rd Plenum of the 10th PCC adopted a resolution restoring Deng to all his former posts. In December 1978, the 3rd Plenum of the 11th PCC decided to annul those documents related to the campaign to "criticize Deng Xiaoping and counter the Right deviationist trend to reverse correct verdicts", and formally announced Deng's rehabilitation. See also "siwu yundong" (April 5th Movement) and "wen'ge" (Cultural Revolution).

批邓运动
pi Deng yundong
(campaign to criticize Deng Xiaoping)

See "pi Deng, fanji youqing fan'anfeng" (campaign to criticize Deng Xiaoping and counter the Right deviationist trend to reverse correct verdicts).

批邓万言书
pi Deng wanyanshu
(anti-Deng 10,000-character petitions)

In 1995, an anonymous article, entitled "Issues Concerning National Security" ("Yingxiang woguo guojia anquande ruogan yinsu"), was circulated among Party and government officials. People call it "anti-Deng 10,000-character petition".

With "national security" as its theme, the document provides an analysis of what it asserts to be the key factors affecting China's security for the next ten years. These factors are: the ownership structure, class relations, social ideology, and the state of the ruling party. The author (or authors) obviously had grasped the essence of things—these are all issues of vital importance in light of current Chinese politics.

Its arguments are tantamount to an overall negation of Deng's reform and open-door policy. It states that since 1992, that is, since Deng's "Southern tour" early in that year, "bourgeois liberalization" has come to the fore. It warns of a "new threat" resulting from the reforms, which includes money worship among the people and an insidious increase in private entrepreneurship. The seriousness of the matter is: the private ownership economy re-appearing in China may become a backing for the "newborn bourgeoisie" to raise political demands. "When conditions are not yet ripe, the bourgeois class only participates in internal struggles of the Party... Once conditions are ripe, it will take over the whole Party, with the support and coordination of the international bourgeois class. A direct and overt bourgeois dictatorship will replace the proletarian dictatorship," the document predicts, employing time-honored Communist locutions.

The author feels extremely anxious about the fate of the CCP. One of the problems is that many local leaders only know reform and the open-door policy and have completely forgotten to uphold the "four cardinal principles"—the Party's "two basic points" have already become one basic point. Advice, or rather, a warning, the author gives to the PCC "leading collective of the third generation" is: "Hostile forces at home and abroad" may attempt to rehabilitate the 1989 pro-democracy movement, making a breakthrough point in the offensive against the Communist Party leadership and the proletarian dictatorship. The leading collective must show that they are capable of resisting the offensive. Otherwise, there is no point of talking about the future.

Deng Liqun explained that the document was not written by him but by a man called Li Yanming. It is generally believed, nevertheless, that its backer was "Little Deng" himself (a nickname for the former Party ideologue, used to distinguish him from his illustrious rival Deng Xiaoping). At least it had enjoyed his influence. Though not the first such effort from someone now considered little more than a gadfly, attacks like this cannot be dismissed because they appeal to those who have been left behind in the nation's uneven rush towards prosperity. In fact, within two years after "Issues Concerning National Security" was released, three other similar documents appeared, all very aggressively.

The second one is "National Security: A Preliminary Inquiry into Internal and External Situations and Major Threats in the Next One or Two Decades" ("Weilai yi er shi nian woguo guojia anquande neiwai xingzhi ji zhuyao weixiede chubu tantao", which was under the name of "Wei Ming" when reprinted in *Zhongguo yu shijie,* December 1997). It circulated in the late summer or early autumn of 1995. Like the first "petition", it still discusses issues of national security. But the focus of its concern is the international situation after the disintegration of the Soviet Union and the radical changes in the East European bloc. It emphasizes that since 1992, that is, since Deng's "Southern tour" early in that year, bourgeois liberalization has been running wild and a "peaceful evolution" has been taking place within the CCP. This document actually negates Deng's reform and open-door policy, though there are some remarks praising Deng Xiaoping Theory.

The third of its kind is a 23,000-character polemic entitled "Theoretical Issues and Policies in the Upholding of the Position of Public Ownership" ("Guanyu jianchi gongyouzhi zhuti diweide ruogan lilun he zhengce wenti"). Aimed at influencing the upcoming 15th National Congress of the CCP, the release of the document was well timed; it began being circulated in early 1997 immediately before Deng's death.

By exposing the evils of private ownership, which increased rapidly in a favorable situation during the previous few years, it stresses the need to keep public ownership paramount, quoting the view of Marx and Engels in their "Manifesto of the Communist Party" that the issue of ownership is a basic issue in the socialist movement. Its warning is: Once public ownership is no longer paramount, a serious class polarization (jieji fenhua) will take place, the Communist Party will lose the economic foundation for its rule, the nature of state power will change, and the socialist spiritual pillar will collapse.

The fourth "petition" is entitled "The Development and Characteristics of Bourgeois Liberalization since 1992" ("1992 nian yilai zichanjieji ziyouhuade dongtai he tedian"). Beginning to circulate in early 1997, this is a collection of 39 people's "bourgeois liberalization" remarks, similar to those during the GPCR, where "reactionary remarks of capitalist-roaders" were listed for mass criticism and repudiation. According to this petition, since 1992 Party committees at various levels failed to criticize bourgeois liberalization so that it had come to the fore. There are 6 categories of these "bourgeois liberalization" remarks: 1. negating socialism and advocating capitalism; 2. demanding abandoning and dispelling Marxism; 3. attacking Party leadership and the people's democratic dictatorship; 4. negating the history of the Chinese revolution; 5. opposing Mao's principles for proletarian literature and art; and 6. maintaining that a bourgeois class be cultivated. See also "xin shehuizhuyi guan" (new socialist view) and "Deng Xiaopig lilu" (Deng Xiaoping Theory).

批林批孔运动
pi Lin pi Kong yundong
(campaign to criticize Lin Biao and Confucius)

In March 1973, during a PCC work meeting, Mao Zedong first suggested that Confucius should be included in the criticism in the campaign condemning the "Lin Biao Counter-revolutionary Clique". In his opinion, Lin Biao, like the KMT, had respected Confucianism and opposed Legalism (zun Kong fan Fa). On 18 January 1974, Mao endorsed the national issuance of the document "Lin Biao and the Doctrines of Confucius and Mencius" ("Lin Biao yu Kong Meng zhi dao"), which Jiang Qing was in charge of compiling, and a large-scale campaign to criticize Lin Biao and Confucius unfolded.

In the campaign, Jiang Qing and her supporters set off a wave of "appraising the Legalists and criticizing the Confucianists" (ping fa pi ru), actually directing their spearhead at Zhou Enlai, the premier, at the moment their substantial obstacle on their way to achieve supreme Party and state power. However, when finding it difficult to launch a second GPCR and overthrow Zhou Enlai, Mao decided instead to criticize Jiang Qing and check her ambition. The campaign then lost momentum. See also "wen'ge" (Cultural Revolution).

批判电影"武训传"
pipan dianying *Wu Xun Zhuan*
(criticism of the film *The Life of Wu Xun*)

Not long after the founding of the PRC, Mao personally launched an attack on the film *The Life of Wu Xun,* which was the first major politico-ideological campaign in the Chinese Communist regime. *The Life of Wu Xun,* directed by Sun Yu and completed at the end of 1950, tells how Wu Xun (1838-1896), originally a beggar, ran free schools for the poor. Mao personally wrote an editorial for the 20 May 1951 *People's Daily*, entitled "Give Serious Attention to the Discussion of the Film *The Life of Wu Xun*" ("Yingdang zhongshi dianying 'Wu Xun zhuan' de taolun"). He fiercely attacked the film and similar writings about Wu Xun, as well as the writers and Party cadres involved. Following Mao's call, a wave of criticism immediately appeared in May, June, and July. Up to the end of August, more than one hundred critical articles were carried in the *People's Daily*, more than thirty in the *Guangming Daily*, and over one hundred in Shanghai's *Wenhui Daily*. From then on, political criticism became popular in the PRC literary arena.

Thirty-four years later, according to a report in the 6 September 1985 *People's Daily*, Politburo member Hu Qiaomu admitted that the criticism "cannot be said to be even basically correct". See also "sixiang gaizao" (ideological remolding).

批判胡适反动思想体系运动
pipan Hu Shi fandong sixiang tixi yundong
(campaign against Hu Shi's reactionary ideological system)

Hu Shi (1891-1962) was an important scholar and public figure in modern Chinese history. In 1954 and 1955, there was a campaign against his "reactionary ideological system". Following the decision jointly made on 2 December 1954 by the Chinese Academy of Sciences and the Presidium of the CWA, nine groups were set up to take charge of the criticism and repudiation of his "reactionary pragmatism" and "bourgeois idealism" in the fields of politics, philosophy, history, literature, education, and the natural sciences. Using the negative example of the "thought of Hu Shi" as its main focus, an ideological remolding movement among intellectuals concurrently unfolded throughout the country. For several decades, this representative of the liberalism movement in China of the 1930s and 1940s was condemned as a "lackey" of U.S. imperialism and the KMT reactionaries.

Significantly, a re-appraisal of Hu Shi took place in the 1990s, in the trend of reconfirming the value of liberalism and individualism among ideological-cultural circles in mainland China. See also "sixiang gaizao" (ideological remolding) and "ziyouzhuyi" (liberalism).

批判现实主义
pipan xianshizhuyi
(critical realism)

See "shehuizhuyi xianshizhuyi" (socialist realism).

批判俞平伯"红楼梦"研究中的资产阶级唯心主义观点
pipan Yu Pingbo *Honglou Meng* yanjiu-zhongde zichanjieji weixinzhuyi guandian
(criticism of Yu Pingbo's bourgeois idealist view in his research on *A Dream of Red Mansions*)

A famous professor at Beijing University, Yu Pingbo (1900-1990) had his book *Research on A Dream of Red Mansions (Honglou Meng Yanjiu, Honglou Meng* is the greatest classical Chinese novel) published in September 1952. Two years later, Li Xifan and Lan Ling, two young graduates of Shandong University, published two articles successively criticizing Yu's book for using a bourgeois idealist point of view and bourgeois methods of textual research. In his letter of 16 October 1954 to the Politburo members and other concerned persons, Mao hailed the two articles as "the first serious fire in over thirty years on the erroneous views of a so-called authoritative writer in the field of study of *A Dream of Red Mansions*". Then, a campaign to criticize Yu Pingbo was carried out in ideological-cultural circles. Furthermore, Mao turned the criticism into a nationwide struggle against the "Hu Shi School of bourgeois idealism". From October to December, the Presidium of the ACF and the CWA held eight criticism meetings in accordance with Mao's instructives.

Yu Pingbo was rehabilitated after the GPCR. Very sadly, however, before his death, he was convinced that all his studies of *A Dream of Red Mansions,* the fruit of a lifetime's painstaking labor, were of no value. See also "sixiang gaizao" (ideological remolding) and "dapipan" (mass criticism).

批判资产阶级反动路线
pipan zichanjieji fandong luxian
(criticism of the bourgeois reactionary line)

The term "bourgeois reactionary line" first appeared in an editorial in the 13th 1966 issue of *Red Flag* ("Zai Mao Zedong Sixiangde dalushang qianjin"—"Advancing on the Road of Mao Zedong Thought", *HQ,* 13, 2 Oct. 1966). This term, reportedly first coined by Guan Feng, a member of the Central GPCR Group, surprised many, including Premier Zhou Enlai when he heard the editorial broadcast on 3 October 1966 (Wang Li, *Xianchang lishi: Wenhua dageming jishi—Chronicles of the Cultural Revolution,* Hong Kong, Oxford University Press, 1993, p. 67). Criticism and repudiation of the "bourgeois reactionary line" was the central agenda of a PCC work conference held in Beijing from 9 to 28 October 1966, which was presided over by Mao personally.

At the conference, Chen Boda elaborated on the concept of a "bourgeois reactionary line". In his speech entitled "The Two Lines in the Great Proletarian Cultural Revolution" ("Wuchanjieji wenhua da gemingzhongde liang tiao luxian"), he asserted that there was a fierce "two line" struggle during the GPCR. One of the lines was Mao's line that allowed the masses of the people to educate and liberate themselves. The other was the bourgeois reactionary line that suppressed revolutionary people. Lin Biao further accused Liu Shaoqi and Deng Xiaoping of carrying out the bourgeois reactionary line. With Mao's approval, the two speeches were promulgated to the whole country.

In light of Mao's strategic plan for the GPCR, the conference was of vital importance. At that time, after the "Red August" terror carried out by "veteran Red Guards", the "general orientation" (da fangxiang) of the GPCR became confused. The major target for attack shifted to those so-called "monsters and demons" (class enemies of all descriptions) in society and not the "capitalist-roaders" that Mao had originally targeted.

After the conference, in response to the call from Mao's "proletarian revolutionary headquarters" to criticize and repudiate the "bourgeois reactionary line", new Red Guard organizations and other "rebel" organizations mushroomed all over the country. The upsurge redirected its spearhead at the alleged capitalist-roaders. For the rebels, there were two very useful slogans. One was "Let the masses educate themselves; Let the masses liberate themselves", which they adopted from the conference. The other was "Fight to the death in defending Chairman Mao's proletarian revolutionary line" (shisi baowei Mao Zhuxide wuchanjieji geming luxian), with which they justified their rebellion.

批文买卖
piwen maimai
(trade of bureaucratic red tape, trade permits, quotas, and documents that give a company legal sanction)

From the very first day of the Chinese Communist regime, there has been no separation of the Party from the government nor the government from economic enterprises. Party officials are essential for the existence and operation of a company as they provide access to trade permits and quotas, business certificates, government documents, etc. that are invaluable in China's bureaucratic infrastructure. Since the reform program started twenty years ago, a merchandise economy has developed in China, whereby political power is also a merchandise that can be put in circulation. Now exchanges of a particular political power with money, commodities, services, or other types of political power are so common that almost all ordinary businesses participate in such exchanges. One such case is the "piwen" trade, which the Party Center has tried hard to check. For some years bureaucratic red tape and documents that give a company legal sanction, trade permits, or quotas were prosperously sold on the market. The emergence of these types of special "merchandise", all closely associated with power, have severely disturbed the nation's economic order and created unprecedented opportunities for corruption. This is an evil practice in the "power economy". See also "jingji gaige" (economic reform).

皮之不存，毛将焉附
pi zhi bu cun, mao jiang yan fu
(with the skin gone, to what can the hair attach itself?)

See "zhishifenzi wenti" (issue of intellectuals).

痞子文化
pizi wenhua
(riffraff culture)

See "renwen jingshen lunzheng" ("humanistic spirit" debate).

痞子文学
pizi wenxue
(riffraff literature)

See "renwen jingshen lunzheng" ("humanistic spirit" debate).

贫下中农最高法庭
pinxiazhongnong zuigao fating
(poor and lower-middle peasants supreme court)

See "sileifenzi" (four kinds of elements).

贫穷不是社会主义
pinqiong bushi shehuizhuyi
(socialism is not equal to poverty)

As early as 1978, Deng surprisingly announced that a new Party policy would allow a portion of people to get rich first ("Emancipate the Mind, Seek Truth from Facts and Unite as One in Looking to the Future", *SWD*, pp.163-64). On 16 January 1980, at a meeting attended by high-ranking officials, Deng told his listeners that he was opposed to what he described as "absurd, reactionary concepts" touted by Lin Biao and the Gang of Four, such as "impoverished socialism", "transition in poverty to a higher stage" ("qiong guodu", that is, practicing communism without rich material foundation to meet people's needs) and "making revolution in poverty" ("The Present Situation and the Tasks before Us", *SWD*, pp. 247-48). On 30 June 1984, in a talk about building socialism with Chinese characteristics, Deng further developed his view. He asserted: "The fundamental task of socialism is to develop productivity" ("Deng Xiaoping on Socialism with Chinese Characteristics" ("Deng Xiaoping tan shenme shi you Zhongguo tesede shehuizhuyi", *Liaowang*, 34, 1984).

At a meeting on poverty alleviation co-sponsored by the PCC and the State Council in September 1996, Jiang Zemin quoted Deng saying: "Socialism is not equal to poverty". He said that poverty is by no means socialism, nor is it that a part of the people get rich while others are still in poverty. "It is too embarrassing to see," he continued, "that there will remain several millions of Chinese people short of food and clothing by the end of this century when the New China will have been founded for five decades" *(BR*, 24-30 Mar. 1997, p. 17).

During the 1978 to 1995 period, China's per-capita GNP index grew threefold. However, economic development in different regions was uneven. The majority of the poverty-stricken people are highly concentrated in central and western rural areas where natural conditions are harsh for living and production. At the meeting, several measures were highlighted to speed up poverty alleviation efforts, which included a strategic shift from mere relief to economic development. See also "ershinianlai zuiju yingxianglide shi ge kouhao" (ten most influential slogans in the past two decades).

评法批儒
ping fa pi ru
(appraisal of the Legalists and criticism of the Confucianists)

See "ru fa douzheng" (struggle between the Confucian and Legalist schools).

评"水浒"运动
ping *Shuihu* yundong
(criticism movement of *Water Margin*)

On 14 August 1975, in a talk with Ms. Lu Di, a teacher of Chinese Literature at Beijing University, Mao Zedong recalled what he had said about the Chinese classical novel *Water Margin* at an enlarged meeting of the Politburo in 1973. According to Lu, Mao had said: "The merit of the book *Water Margin* lies precisely in its portrayal of capitulation. It serves as teaching material by negative example to help all the people recognize capitulation." Mao also said: "*Water Margin* is critical of corrupt officials only, but not of the emperor. It excludes Chao Gai from the 108 people. Song Jiang promotes capitulationism, practices revisionism, changes Chao Gai's Assembly Hall of the Righteous (Juyi Tang) to the Hall of the Loyal and Righteous (Zhongyi Tang), and accepts the offer of amnesty and enlistment. Song Jiang's struggle against Gao Qiu is a struggle waged by one faction against another within the landlord class. As soon as he surrenders, Song Jiang goes to fight Fang La."

When this comment was officially published on 4 September 1975 as a "supreme directive", it came as a surprise to many. Later, under the direction of Yao Wenyuan, Jiang Qing, and others, criticism of *Water Margin* quickly became an overriding political movement, with almost everyone in China taking part.

平反
pingfan
(rehabilitation; reversal of verdicts)

See "pingfan weiyuanhui" (rehabilitation committee).

平反委员会
pingfan weiyuanhui
(rehabilitation committee)

On 21 May 1957, at a meeting organized by the PCC United Front Department, Luo Longji (1896-1965), then PRC minister of forestry, member of the CPPCC Standing Committee, and vice-chairman of the Chinese Democracy Alliance, suggested setting up what was later called "rehabilitation committees" from the central to the local levels. As he explained, the setting up of these organizations, which should consist of CCP members as well as of non-Party personages, would encourage people to air their opinions to help the Party in its on-going rectification drive. People would rid themselves of the habitual thinking about the "trilogy of loosening up, tightening up, and punishing" (fang shou zheng sanbuqu) formed from their experience of the past campaigns. Luo was sure that these organizations, when set up, would certainly help bring about a reversal of unjust verdicts of the past and the future *(Guangming Daily,* 23 May 1957).

Not long thereafter, Luo Longji's "rehabilitation committee", together with Chu Anping's remark that "the Party is the entire world" (dangtianxia) and Zhang Bojun's "political design academy" (zhengzhi shejiyuan), were condemned as the "three major reactionary theories" of China's Rightists.

"Pingfan", originally a judicial term used in the classical work *Han Shu (History of the Western Han Dynasty),* became a well-known phrase in contemporary China. There were so many political movements and social turbulences, in which so many cases were decided improperly or incorrectly; thus rehabilitations and reversal of verdicts were quite familiar to people. From 1977 to 1978, for example, cases of over 2 million "capitalist-roaders" and over 550,000 Rightists were corrected. Unfortunately, Luo Longji, labeled by Mao as an "absolutely unrepentant Rightist", was not among them. He then became an "uncapped Rightist" (tuomao youpai). This took place more than two decades after his death in misery. See also "fan youpai yundong" (anti-Rightist campaign).

破四旧，立四新
po sijiu, li sixin
(do away with the "four olds" and cultivate the "four news")

The two concepts—the "four olds" (old ideas, old culture, old customs, and old habits) of all the exploiting classes and the proletarian "four news" (new ideas, new culture, new customs, and new habits)—were first raised in a *People's Daily* editorial on 1 June 1966, under the title "Sweep Away All Monsters and Demons". In the August 1966 CCP document concerning the GPCR, the Chinese people were asked to carry out a nationwide movement to do away with the "four olds" of the bourgeois and exploiting classes and to cultivate the proletarian and socialist "four news". The Red Guards responded with a furious and unprecedented assault on the nation's heritage.

破字当头，立在其中
pozi dangtou, li zai qizhong
(destruction comes first, and in the course of it there is construction)

See "bu po bu li" (without destruction there is no construction).

普遍人权
pubian renquan
(universal nature of human rights)

See "renquan wenti" (human rights issue).

普遍人性
pubian renxing
(universal human nature)

See "gongtong renxing" (common human nature) and "rendaozhuyi lunzheng" (humanism debate).

普及与提高相结合
puji yu tigao xiangjiehe
(combination of popularization and raising of standards)

See "dazhonghua" (popularization).

普通话
putonghua
(modern standard Chinese)

See "wenzi gaige" (reform of written Chinese).

七大极左刊物
qi da jizuo kanwu
(seven ultra-Left publications)

In the early 1990s, there were seven publications in Beijing regarded by some people as "ultra-Left". Except for *Seeking Truth (Qiushi),* which started publication in 1988 after the close of *Red Flag,* the former "theoretical organ" of the PCC, they were all new magazines established following the June 4th Incident of 1989: *Midstream (Zhongliu), Ideological Trends of the Contemporary Age (Dangdai Sichao), Literary Theory and Criticism (Wenyi Lilun Yu Piping), In Quest of the Truth (Zhenlide Zhuiqiu), The Front (Zhendi),* and *On the Theoretical Front of Tertiary Education (Gaoxiao Lilun Zhanxian).* It was said that Deng Liqun, former member of the CCP Secretariat, was their general backer.

七分天灾，三分人祸
qifen tianzai, sanfen renhuo
(a disaster 30% man-made and 70% the result of natural causes)

See "dayuejin" (Great Leap Forward) and "qiqianren dahui" (7,000-person meeting).

七千人大会
qiqianren dahui
(7,000-person meeting)

The "7,000-person meeting" refers to the enlarged work conference convened by the PCC in Beijing from 11 January to 7 February 1962, at a time when China was drained by serious economic setbacks and the worst famine in its history. Unprecedented in CCP history, there were over 7,000 participants at the meeting. They were leading members of the PCC and its sub-bureaus; leading members of Party committees of the various provinces, municipalities, autonomous regions, prefectures, and counties; leading members of major factories, mines, and other large enterprises; and leading members of army units. Liu Shaoqi, CCP vice-chairman and PRC president, delivered a report on behalf of the PCC, analyzing the major mistakes the Party had made since the 1958 Great Leap Forward, and promising rehabilitation for those who had been wrongly treated in the 1959-60 "anti-Right deviation" campaign. With respect to the 1959-61 famine, Liu admitted with great courage that it was probably 70% man-made and 30% the result of natural causes (sanfen tianzai, qifen renhuo). Unlike many others, Lin Biao continued his excessive eulogy to Mao at the conference, as seen in his speech made on 29 January.

On 30 January, for the first time as Party chairman, Mao made a public self-criticism. In his speech, he expressed his appreciation for Lin Biao's help. But when Mao described the disaster as "30% man-made and 70% the result of natural causes" (qifen tianzai, sanfen renhuo), Liu Shaoqi corrected him.

At the "7,000-person meeting", Liu sowed the seeds of his misfortune, though for a time after the conference his power and prestige seemed to increase.

启蒙与救亡的双重变奏
qimeng yu jiuwangde shuangchong bianzou
(a double variation of enlightenment and salvation)

See "lishi jiaosede huhuan" (an interchange of historical roles).

企业下放
qiye xiafang
(putting an enterprise under a lower administrative level)

See "xiafang" (transfer to a lower level).

气功
qigong
(qigong)

See "Falun Gong" (Law Wheel Cultivation) and "Kylin wenhua" (Kylin Culture).

千万不要忘记阶级斗争
qianwan buyao wangji jieji douzheng
(never forget class struggle)

From the latter half of 1962, a new, strong "Left" trend re-emerged. On 24 September 1962, at the 10th Plenum of the 8th PCC, Mao Zedong issued the call: "Never forget class struggle." This was a signal that he was conceiving a new political struggle or, to be more exact, a new power struggle. From then on, indeed, the political situation became more and more tense, ending in the outbreak of the GPCR. See also "jieji douzheng" (class struggle).

前十条
qian shitiao
(Former Ten Articles)

See "shejiao" (socialist education movement).

枪打出头鸟
qiang da chutouniao
(shooting the outstanding bird)

See "fan youpai yundong" (anti-Rightist campaign).

枪杆子和笔杆子
qiangganzi he biganzi
(the gun and the pen)

On 7 August 1927, the PCC held an urgent meeting in Hankou, Hubei province, chiefly to rectify what was dubbed as the "Right-capitulationist line" of Chen Duxiu, who was then CCP general secretary. At the meeting (which is also called the "August 7th Meeting"), Mao raised for the first time the issue of seizing political power by armed struggle. The exact wording of the thesis "Political power grows out of the barrel of a gun" (qianganzi limian chu zhengquan), however, was found in Mao's speech entitled "Problems of War and Strategy" ("Zhanzheng he zhanlüe wenti"), delivered at the 6th Plenum of the 6th PCC on 6 November 1938. From the class struggle experience in the period of imperialism, he said, only with the power of guns could the working class and other laboring people defeat the armed bourgeois and landlord classes. In this sense, one can say, only through the barrel of a gun could the whole world be reformed. Mao noted that "Political power grows out of the barrel of a gun" was a truth that every Communist Party member must recognize.

Of equal importance was that, when stating what he believed to be the "truth" about the barrel of a gun, Mao warned at the same time: "Our principle is that the Party commands the gun, and the gun must never be allowed to command the Party" (*SWM,* 2, p. 224). This principle has remained unchanged from the period of CCP's armed struggle up to the present. Party branch is established in every company. At the top the Party has the Central Military Commission (CMC), controlled by the man called Party leader, Mao Zedong, Deng Xiaoping, and now Jiang Zemin. As the highest military command, the CMC exercises tight control over the Chinese armed forces. (The state also has a central military commission, which, while not so powerful, is also controlled by the Party.)

Mao's assertion about political power growing out of the barrel of a gun was proved by the success of the Communist revolution in mainland China. But the success did not entirely rely on "qiangganzi" (the gun). Mao also paid great attention to "biganzi" (the pen, or a metaphor for "effective writers"), that is, his Party propaganda machine, including "revolutionary literature". Mao found the service the "revolutionary literature" had rendered to his Party so remarkable that he simply regarded it as a "front" and an "army", and he never concealed his pride when he mentioned it. As Lin Biao summed up: The gun and the pen are the two things to rely on in making revolution (qiangganzi biganzi, gan geming kao zhe liangganze).

When the civil war was over and the PRC was founded under Mao's leadership, it was only logical that Mao would find the role of the "pen" even more important. Mao always demanded that writers be "engineers of the human soul" (zuojia shi renlei linghun gongchengshi). On the one hand, according to the principle of "socialist realism", literature and art, which should be subordinate to and in the service of Party politics, was a tool to unite and educate the people and expose and attack the enemy, so as to promote the socialist revolution and construction. On the other, the Party must always be highly vigilant against any possible "anti-Party and anti-socialism" ideas and activities on the part of writers and artists. "The overthrown bourgeoisie will attempt by any means to corrupt the masses and restore capitalism, using literature and art as the hotbed", Mao warned his Party. This helps explain why, after the founding of the PRC, Mao initiated so many political movements to remold China's intellectuals—he wanted them always to remain under strict control of the Party. His other principle was: the Party commands the pen.

It has now been shown that Mao's ambitious "ideological remolding" (sixiang gaizao) plan was a failure. Though the Party still controls the state's propaganda machine, the machine does not work as well as before. As to the "gun", this is a different matter. Because of historical reasons, the major one of course being that the CCP seized state power by armed struggle, many Chinese have become used to the *status quo* that China's army is strictly under CCP leadership. To the Party authorities, this leadership is of course of vital importance. In March 1997, the 5th Session of the 8th NPC passed the "National Defense Law", which conspicuously legalized the Party leadership over all state armed forces.

Different opinions, however, have also begun to be heard in recent years. In the spring of 1998, for instance, there was a theory about "limited government" (youxian zhengfu) upheld by "liberal" thinkers (ziyoupai sixiangjia). They not only asked for a separation of the CCP from government functions. As a further step, radical but natural, they also demanded that the CCP should be separated from army functions, so that the army would be controlled by the state and not by a certain political party.

枪杆子里面出政权
qiangganzi limian chu zhengquan
(political power grows out of the barrel of a gun)

See "qiangganzi he biganzi" (the gun and the pen).

枪杆子笔杆子，干革命靠这两杆子
qiangganzi biganzi, gan geming kao zhe liangganzi
(the gun and the pen are the two things to rely on in making revolution)

See "qiangganzi he biganzi" (the gun and the pen).

强中央，弱地方
qiang zhongyang, ruo difang
(strengthening the central government while weakening the local authorities)

See "zhuhou jingji" (duchy economy).

强权政治
qiangquan zhengzhi
(power politics)

See "lengzhanhou shidaide xin diguozhuyi" (neo-imperialism in the post-Cold War era) and "weidu Zhongguo" (containment against China).

翘尾巴
qiao weiba

(get stuck-up)

The Chinese character "qiao" means "stick up", and "weiba" "the tail". So the phrase "qiao weiba" figuratively describes those people who get stuck-up like a dog who sticks up its tail and is not obedient to its master. Mao and his Party cadres used this phrase to describe China's intellectuals. In their eyes, people with knowledge very often stick up their "tails" and that is why they had to be remolded by the Party and learn how to "tuck their tails between their legs" (jiazhe weiba zuo ren) *(MZXJ*, 5, p. 454). See also "zhishifenzi wenti" (issue of intellectuals), "sixiang gaizao" (ideological remolding), and "fan youpai yundong" (anti-Rightist campaign).

秦城监狱
qincheng jianyu
(Qincheng Prison)

Qincheng Prison, located in a Beijing's northwestern suburb about 70 kilometers from the city, began construction in 1958 (then Luo Ruiqing was the minister of public security). Its main building was completed in early 1960. At first it was mainly used to lock up war criminals. Later many of its prisoners were originally important CCP figures, such as members of the "Liu Shaoqi clique", the "Lin Biao clique", and the "Jiang Qing clique". After the June 4th Incident of 1989, a number of student leaders and their supporters (that is, the "black hands") were also locked up there.

清政治，清经济，清组织，清思想
qing zhengzhi, qing jingji, qing zuzhi, qing sixiang
(clean things up in the fields of politics, economy, organization, and ideology)

See "shejiao" (socialist education movement).

清污运动
qingwu yundong
(campaign to eliminate spiritual pollution)

"Qingwu yundong" is an abbreviation of "qingchu jingshen wuran yundong".

Some Party leaders, especially those in charge of ideological-cultural matters, were long dissatisfied with the situation in the ideological-cultural fields in the first few years of the 1980s. The publication in the *People's Daily* on 16 March 1983 of Zhou Yang's long treatise, entitled "An Inquiry into Some Theoretical Problems of Marxism" ("Guanyu Makesizhuyide jige lilun wentide tantao")—the highlight of the 1980-83 wave of humanism—led to the intervention by high-level authorities.

The treatise was originally a key speech delivered by Zhou Yang on 7 March 1983, the first day of the conference marking the centenary of Marx's death held under the auspices of these leading bodies: the PCC Propaganda Department, CASS, the Central Party School, and the Education Ministry. In four parts, with 17,000 Chinese characters, Zhou Yang discussed a series of theoretical problems, most conspicuously, Marxist humanism and socialist alienation.

Hu Qiaomu was the first person to criticize the article. He relayed to Zhou Yang his opinion on the tenth of the month, though in a polite and even ambiguous way. Another key person in this matter was Deng Liqun, then director of the PCC Propaganda Department and member of the PCC Secretariat. In an "important speech" reported in the *Guangming Daily* two days after the centenary conference of Marx's death, Deng Liqun told another commemorative symposium that the issues of human nature, humanism, and alienation were academic and theoretical matters which could be debated. He seemed to agree that differing opinions could be expressed and mutual criticisms carried out, but in actuality he wanted to have the views held by people like Zhou Yang criticized and repudiated. Indeed, his meaning soon became apparent. In a speech made at the Central Party School four months before the 2nd Plenum of the 12th PCC held in October 1983, Deng Liqun fiercely attacked "spiritual pollution" (jingshen wuran), the first time he referred to the term. Shortly before the Plenum, on 8 October, a front-page article in the *Guangming Daily* called attention to Marxist criteria in intellectual matters. This newspaper also carried another article a week later, criticizing the idea of "socialist alienation" (Li Yanming, "'Shehuizhuyi yihua' bushi Makesizhuyi guandian"—"'Socialist Alienation' Is Not a Marxist View", *GMRB*, 15 Oct. 1983). The call to uphold the "four cardinal principles" and the "struggle on two fronts" was revived in an article in the mid-October issue of *Red Flag* (Zhang Decheng, "Jianchi sixiang jiben yuanze he liang tiao zhanxian douzheng"—"Uphold the Four Cardinal Principles and the Struggle on Two Fronts", *HQ*, 20:31-34, 1983). It argued that bourgeois liberalization preached "humanistic Marxism" and slandered the Party and government leadership as a privileged bureaucratic stratum and therefore should be repudiated. Then, at the 2nd Plenum of the 12th PCC, which on its orginal agenda was to adopt a resolution about Party rectification, a decision against spiritual pollution was made. On 12 October, Deng Xiaoping delivered a speech at the Plenum, entitled "An Urgent Task of the Party on the Organizational and Ideological Fronts" ("Dang zai zuzhi zhanxian he sixiang zhanxianshangde poqie renwu"). He warned that the ideological front must not bring about spiritual pollution.

Peng Zhen, a Politburo member and president of the Standing Committee of the NPC, revealed the decision of the 2nd Plenum. As reported in the 24 October *People's Daily*, he had told non-Party personages at a forum the previous day that there existed in recent years serious spiritual pollution on the ideological and the literary and art "fronts", which was "a vital issue concerning the future of our Party, country, and nation". According to Peng, the two resolutions of the Plenum were "to rectify the Party" and "to eliminate spiritual pollution". On the same and following days, this Party organ also carried first the summary and then the full text of a speech delivered by Wang Zhen, another Politburo member, to participants of the inaugural meeting of the Chinese Scientific Socialism Society and of the 4th National Forum on the Teaching of Scientific Socialism held by the CCP's party schools. In a severe tone, Wang accused "some people" of "having constantly been preaching so-called 'socialist alienation'". Those views of theirs, he emphasized, "are completely antagonistic to Marxist scientific socialism. Essentially, they propagate a sentiment of no-confidence towards socialism, the Communist cause, and the Chinese Communist Party".

Here Wang Zhen was expressing the crux of the matter. It is obvious why a campaign to eliminate "spiritual pollution" could suddenly break out at a time when the "four modernizations" program was the center of all work of the whole Party and the whole nation, at a time when any interference in the form of a political movement would be harmful to the program, as had been proved in the past. Indeed, the ideological trend of propagating a humanistic conception of the world and history and the theory of socialist alienation as seen in 1980-83 was not just an academic, theoretical issue. The "humanistic tide" and the "alienation craze" in literary-ideological fields were not to be underestimated. Because they had become so widespread, the PCC was forced to take action. It was of vital political significance that the so-called basic Marxist principles be adhered to and the CCP-led revolutionary practice be understood, as expected by the Party. The root of the problem was a fear that the existing system could be destroyed.

Politically, the campaign to "eliminate spiritual pollution" was a power struggle, with the newly elected CCP General Secretary Hu Yaobang as the real target of attack. Conservative Deng Liqun, then a member of the PCC Secretariat, attempted to replace Hu Yaobang as CCP general secretary. Deng Liqun enjoyed the help of some important Party figures, especially Chen Yun, a Party elder, and Hu Qiaomu, the number one Party ideologue. However, the campaign, somewhat like a "palace coup" (gongting zhengbian), turned out to be short-lived, and was dubbed by intellectuals in Beijing as the "One Hundred Day Cultural Revolution" (baire wen'ge). It was aborted early by Hu Yaobang and Premier Zhao Ziyang. For various political reasons, the two eventually won the support of Deng Xiaoping. In January 1984, Hu Qiaomu published an article entitled "On Problems Concerning Humanism and Alienation" to bring an end to the campaign in a somewhat hasty way.

On 26 November 1986, in a speech to Shanghai officials, Hu Yaobang said that it was wrong to criticize Zhou Yang at the 2nd Plenum of the 12th PCC. This was perhaps the last time Hu expressed his disapproval of the campaign to "eliminate spiritual pollution". Not long thereafter, on 16 January 1987, Hu stepped down. See also "shehuizhuyi yihualun" (theory of socialist alienation) and "rendaozhuyi lunzheng" (humanism debate), and "fandui zichanjieji ziyouhua yundong" (anti-bourgeois liberalization campaign).

清除精神污染
qingchu jingshen wuran
(eliminate spiritual pollution)

See "qingwu yundong" (campaign to eliminate spiritual pollution).

清官戏
qingguan xi
(theatrical works about honest and upright officials in feudal times)

During the GPCR, theatrical works about honest and upright officials in feudal times were fiercely attacked. Soon after the GPCR, however, these works became popular again, and such officials as Hai Rui in *Hai Rui Dismissed from Office* and Xie Yaohuan in *Xie Yaohua* were lauded. Love and admiration for these officials is part of Chinese cultural tradition, and thus difficult to eliminate. See "renxing lun" (theory of human nature).

清算四人帮三大战役
qingsuan sirenbang san da zhanyi
(three battles to settle accounts with the Gang of Four)

See "sirenbang" (Gang of Four).

清谈
qingtan

(idle talk)

Traditionally, Chinese intellectuals tended to limit themselves to "idle talk". They hesitated when they were required to act. This was pointed out in the discussions in the 1980s about Chinese intellectuals. See "zhishifenzi wenti" (issue of intellectuals) and "sixiang gaizao" (ideological remolding).

穷过渡
qiong guodu
(transition in poverty to a higher stage)

See "pinqiong bushi shehuizhuyi" (socialism is not equal to poverty).

穷则思变
qiong ze si bian
(poverty gives rise to a desire for change)

See "dayuejin" (Great Leap Forward).

求实的一代
qiushide yidai
(pragmatic generation)

See "liangdai shiren" (two generations of poets).

曲线爱国
quxian aiguo
(love the nation by a devious path)

See "shijie dachuanlian" (a great trend of going abroad).

曲线救国
quxian jiuguo
(save the nation by a devious path)

See "shijie dachuanlian" (a great trend of going abroad).

取经
qujing
(learn from someone else's experience)

"Qujing", originally referring to Buddhist monks going on a pilgrimage for the Buddhist scriptures, is used to refer to "learning from someone else's experience". People are encouraged to go to "advanced units" ("xianjin danwei", such as the Dazai People's Commune and the Daqing oil enterprise in the Mao period) or advanced regions (such as special economic zones in the Deng period) to learn advanced experiences.

The largest-scale "qujing" in CCP history occurred during the GPCR. After Mao received the Red Guards for the first time on 18 August 1966, there appeared the so-called massive exchange of revolutionary experiences (geming dachuanlian) on a nationwide scale. Red Guards traveled all over the country in the name of "qujing". In the international Communist movement, "qujing" was also a common practice. Pol

Pot, as the leader of the Khmer Rouge, went to Beijing to learn Maoism at least three times in 1965, 1968, and 1970. In the 1950s, Chinese went to the USSR to learn experiences in building socialism.

Today, "qujing" activities continue to be popular in daily life. The practice, as before, can be abused. In the name of "qujing", some travel at home or abroad and spend time sightseeing at public expense, that is, with their "danwei" (the units where they work—either government departments, factories, or schools) responsible for the expenses. According to the circular issued on 1 March 1999 by the Central Commission for Discipline Inspection, in 1998, 438,200 people from different Party and government departments and state-owned enterprises traveled abroad or to Hong Kong in the name of "qujing", and the costs were over 2.2 billion U.S. dollars. See also "geming dachuanlian" (massive exchange of revolutionary experiences).

权大过法
quan da guo fa
(power is greater than the law)

See "yi fa zhi guo" (ruling the nation by law).

权力斗争论
quanli douzheng lun
("power struggle" theory)

Many scholars inside and outside of China regard the GPCR as a "power struggle".

As early as the end of 1953, according to Deng Xiaoping, Mao proposed that the work of the PCC be divided into a "front line" and a "second line" *(SWD,* p. 278). Mao thought of withdrawing to the "second line" ("tui ju erxian", that is, not to be in direct charge of Party and state affairs). In 1956, Mao told other Party leaders again that he intended to resign his position as PRC president, so that he could concentrate his attention on the strategy of remolding China. The real reason, as those for the "power struggle" theory assert, was that Mao wanted to test his colleagues' loyalty. Very soon the result came out: at the 8th CCP National Congress held in Beijing in September 1956, a new political line was adopted which emphasized economic construction, obviously at odds with Mao's idea about class struggle. Both Liu Shaoqi, CCP vice-chairman, and Deng Xiaoping, CCP general secretary, opposed "personality cult" and advocated "collective leadership". In the new Party Constitution, which Deng had supervised in its revision, Mao Zedong Thought was no longer regarded as the guidance for all Party work. A position without much power—CCP honorary chairmanship—was designed for Mao. (The 8th CCP National Congress is said to be a turning point after which Mao no longer trusted his two major colleagues Liu and Deng. Some, such as Lin Ke, Mao's private secretary from the autumn of 1954 to July 1966, think otherwise. According to him, all the resolutions adopted at the congress precisely followed Mao's suggestions. See Lin Ke, Xu Tao, and Wu Xujun, *Lishide Zhenshi—The True Life of Mao Zedong,* Hong Kong, Liwen, 1995, pp. 40-54.)

In December 1958, following the 6th Plenum of the 8th PCC (held in Wuchang from 28 November to 10 December 1958), Mao began to withdraw to the "second line". In April of the next year, Liu Shaoqi formally took over the state presidentship. By the mid-1960s, Liu's prestige in the Party had reached a peak. Finally, Mao sought to change the situation. His strategic plan was first to overthrow the CCP Beijing Municipal Committee and then to bombard Liu's "bourgeois headquarters".

Within just a few months, with the help of Red Guards, Mao easily toppled Liu Shaoqi and a great number of his followers, allegedly for being "capitalist-roaders". Mao was so pleased with the outcome that at the end of 1966, he joyfully declared that 1967 would see a decisive victory for "struggle, criticism, and reform"—the tasks set for the GPCR. As it turned out, however, 1967 instead witnessed an "all-round civil war" throughout the country. Later, the situation became even more complicated: a series of power struggles occurred among Mao, Lin Biao, Zhou Enlai, the Gang of Four, Deng Xiaoping, and Hua Guofeng. See also "dou pi gai" (struggle, criticism, and reform), "quanmian neizhan" (full-scale civil war), and "wen'ge" (Cultural Revolution).

权力经济
quanli jingji
(power economy)

See "jingji gaige" (economic reform).

权力下放
quanli xiafang
(transfer power to a lower level)

See "xiafang" (transfer to a lower level).

权力异化
quanli yihua
(alienated power)

See "zhengzhi yihua" (political alienation) and "zhengtong Makesizhuyi zhengzai zou xiang siwang" (orthodox Marxism is heading for death).

权力资本
quanli ziben
(power capital)

See "guanliao ziben" (bureaucrat-capital) and "jingji gaige" (economic reform).

权力资本化
quanli zibenhua
(power capitalization)

See "guanliao ziben" (bureaucrat-capital) and "jingji gaige" (economic reform).

全方位的彻底开放
quanfangweide chedi kaifang
(complete and thorough opening to the world)

See "quanpan xihua" (wholesale Westernization).

全方位的全球化
quanfangweide quanqiuhua
(complete and thorough globalization)

See "quanqiuhua" (globalization).

全国第一张马列主义大字报
quanguo diyi zhang Maliezhuyi dazibao
(first Marxist-Leninist big-character poster in the whole country)

On 25 May 1966, Nie Yuanzi, secretary of the CCP General Branch of the Philosophy Department, Beijing University, together with six people (a deputy secretary, a recent transfer to a post outside the universty, and four teachers in the department) put up a big-character poster on the campus of the university. The poster accused Song Shuo, Lu Ping, and Peng Peiyun, leaders of the CCP Beijing University Committee and the University Department of the CCP Beijing Municipal Committee, of suppressing the Cultural Revolution. Cao Yi'ou, Kang Sheng's wife, then leading an investigation group at the university, supported the writing of the poster. After it was put up, a hot debate ensued. Kang Sheng promptly reported this to Mao, who at the time was staying in Hangzhou. Mao received news of the poster mid-day on 1 June and immediately asked Kang Sheng and Chen Boda to have it broadcast by the Central People's Broadcasting Station. After it was broadcast that evening and published in the *People's Daily* the next day, together with a commentator's article, it was called a "brilliant example" to be followed by students of tertiary education throughout the country.

The poster was a magic weapon in Mao's strategy, with which, he said, "This reactionary bastion of Beijing University will be broken". He called it the "first Marxist-Leninist big-character poster in the whole country", a "Declaration of the Beijing Commune of the 1960s" (ershishiji liushiniandai Beijing Gongshe xuanyan). Mao saw it having more significance than the Paris Commune. On 5 August 1966, during the 11th Plenum of the 8th PCC, Mao's big-character poster entitled "Bombard the Headquarters" ("paoda silingbu") praised Nie's poster once again.

During the GPCR, Nie Yuanzi was one of the most well-known Red Guard leaders. In 1978, she was arrested and then, in 1983, sentenced to seventeen years' imprisonment.

全国都要学习解放军
quanguo douyao xuexi jiefangjun
(the whole nation should learn from the Liberation Army)

See "tuchu zhengzhi" (giving prominence to politics).

全国人大
quanguo renda
(National People's Congress)

See "xiangpi tuzhang" (rubber stamp).

全国人民代表大会
quanguo Renmin Daibiao Dahui
(National People's Congress)

See "xiangpi tuzhang" (rubber stamp).

全国山河一片红
quanguo shanhe yipian hong
(the whole country is red)

See "yiyue geming" (January Revolution).

全国一盘棋
quanguo yipanqi
(coordinate all the activities of the nation as in a chess game)

See "difangzhuyi" (localism).

全局观点
quanju guandian
(an overall point of view)

See "difangzhuyi" (localism).

全面接触
quanmian jiechu
(comprehensive engagement)

See "weidu Zhongguo" (containment against China).

全面内战
quanmian neizhan
(full-scale civil war)

A policy for the GPCR, as stipulated in the "Sixteen Articles", was: "In carrying out debates, it is necessary to struggle by reasoning, not by coercion or force" (yao wendou, buyao wudou). To struggle by reasoning meant exposing and criticizing, revealing the "reactionary words and deeds of all ghosts and monsters", and using such negative examples as teaching materials to educate the masses and the young generation. Common forms of struggling by reasoning were the use of big-character posters and great debates to expose arguments. A *People's Daily* editorial of 5 September 1966 explained: "Struggle by coercion or force can only touch the skin but not the soul. It cannot fully expose to the masses the ugly features of ghosts and monsters and cannot eradicate their reactionary poison."

However, as the GPCR unfolded, the situation changed. First, coercion or force was used in struggles against alleged capitalist-roaders and other "ghosts and monsters". Then strifes occurred among rival Red Guard and other mass organizations. With the announcement of the slogan "Attack in letters, defend with arms" (wengong wuwei), armed struggles rapidly led to a "full-scale civil war" (as it was later called by Mao) throughout the country. As a result, there were frequent bloody clashes.

This began with Shanghai's "January Revolution" (yiyue geming) of 1967. After the Central authorities appealed to "all proletarian revolutionary groups" to unite in seizing power from "a handful of capitalist-roaders", a struggle to seize power took place all over the country. Consequently, factional strife—what was dubbed "bourgeois factionalism" (zichanjieji paixing)—became increasingly violent, for each "proletarian revolutionary group" regarded itself as the only representative of "Chairman Mao's proletarian revolutionary line" and each group insisted that it had exclusive final say about new power organs. The so-called bourgeois factionalism stubbornly displayed itself in various fields, even a few years after the 1976 downfall of the Gang of Four, but it was the most vicious and damaging during the armed strifes of 1967 and 1968.

In this regard, Jiang Qing was accused of spreading the slogan "Attack in letters, defend with arms". In the first half of 1967, violent conflicts among mass organizations began to take place in quite a number of places. In these conflicts, the slogan "Attack in letters, defend with arms" first appeared in Henan province. On 22 July 1967, when receiving representatives from the "February 7th Commune", a Henan mass organization, Jiang Qing approved the slogan. "Attack in letters", she explained, meant exposing enemies and arousing the masses by using reason, and "defend with arms" meant that after the enemy resorted to arms, the revolutionary mass organizations too had to take up arms to protect themselves. This was published the next day in Shanghai's *Wenhui Daily*. On 5 September 1967, Jiang Qing once again referred to this slogan when receiving representatives from the mass organizations of Anhui province. Four days later, a notice was issued by the PCC General Office, asking the whole nation to study Jiang's "Talk of 5 September". Thereafter, all over the country, headquarters of "combat teams" were set up in sucession by conflicting mass organizations to "attack in letters, defend with arms". Armed clashes rapidly esculated, leading to the 1967-68 chaotic situation of "full-scale civil war". (The February 1979 short story "Maples"—"Feng"—by Zheng Yi, published after the downfall of the Gang of Four, detailed the sad truth about this civil war for the first time.)

In his talk with the American journalist Edgar Snow on 10 December 1970, Mao publicly used the phrase "full-scale civil war". On 30 April 1974, in a conversation with Hua Guofeng, Wang Hongwen, Zhang Chunqiao, Jiang Qing, Yao Wenyuan, and Wang Hairong, Mao admitted that the GPCR should be assessed as "70 percent achievements and 30 percent mistakes". The 30 percent mistakes referred to the "overthrowing all" and waging a "full-scale civil war". In fact, it was Mao himself who had first come up with the phrase. In a speech on 26 December 1966, Mao loudly announced: "Congratulations on the unfolding of a full-scale civil war!" (Wen Yu, *Zhongguo "Zuo" Huo—China's "Left" Disasters,* Beijing, Zhaohua, Feb. 1993, p. 429).

In view of the nature of the GPCR, which was guided by Mao's struggle philosophy, "struggling by reasoning and not by coercion or force" to "full-scale civil war" can be seen as a natural progression. During the GPCR, according to official statistics, 20 million people were killed, 100 million people persecuted, and 800 billion Chinese dollars lost (Ma Licheng and Ling Zhijun, *Crossing Swords: Three Thought Emancipations in Contemporary China,* p. 9). See also "wen'ge" (Cultural Revolution).

全面专政
quanmian zhuanzheng
(all-around dictatorship)

See "wuchanjieji zhuanzheng" (dictatorship of the proletariat).

全民党
quanmin dang
(a party of the entire people)

See "xiuzhengzhuyi" (revisionism).

全民国家
quanmin guojia
(a state of the entire people)

See "xiuzhengzhuyi" (revisionism).

全民皆兵
quanmin jie bing
(make everyone a soldier)

See "renmin zhanzheng" (people's war).

全民炼钢
quanmin liangang
(make steel by the whole people)

See "dayuejin" (Great Leap Forward).

全民所有制
quanmin suoyouzhi
(ownership by the whole people)

In traditional CCP doctrine, "ownership by the whole people" or "socialist ownership by the whole people" (shehuizhuyi quanmin suoyouzhi) means "state ownership" (guojia suoyouzhi) or "socialist state ownership" (shehuizhuyi guoyouzhi). It is the most important form of "socialist ownership" (shehuizhuyi suoyouzhi) or "socialist public ownership" (shehuizhuyi gongyouzhi). Another important form is "collective ownership" (jiti suoyouzhi) or "socialist collective ownership" (shehuizhuyi jiti suoyouzhi).

According to this doctrine, all enterprises with state property as a foundation, such as state-run factories, mines, railways, and farms, fall into the category of "ownership by the whole people". State-run enterprises are the property of the whole nation such that their means of production, finished products, and labor input by the staff and workers are publicly owned. Both the means of production and the finished products of enterprises under ownership by the whole people may be distributed in a unified and rational manner directly by the state, which represents the whole people, in accordance with the needs of the national economy. State-run enterprises are directly subordinate to the state, which is responsible for planning their activities and mapping out their basic work guidelines. This kind of ownership, traditional CCP doctrine asserts, comes into being and develops by means of socialist nationalization (shehuizhuyi guoyouhua) and socialist construction under the condition of proletarian dictatorship. It is an advanced form of socialist public ownership and plays a leading role in the national economy. Therefore, the system of collective ownership will develop step by step into a system of ownership by the whole people, the key to which lies in "the development of the productive forces and the heightening of the masses' consciousness".

During the course of two decades of reform, many of the above notions have changed. In 1997, Yu Guangyuan, an eminent economist, even pointed out that in economic reality there is no such thing as "ownership by the whole people". State ownership, he said, does not mean "ownership by the whole people", which is simply a man-made and false concept. As Yu appealed, this issue should now be solved (Ma Licheng and Ling Zhijun, *Crossing Swords,* p. 418). See also "jiejue gongyouzhi xingshi shi you yici sixiang jiefang" (solving the issue of public ownership forms is another emancipation of the mind).

全民文艺
quanmin wenyi
(literature and art of the whole people)

See "Zhou Yang beiju" (tragedy of Zhou Yang) and "wenyi wei zhengzhi fuwu" (literature and art serve politics).

全盘西化
quanpan xihua
(wholesale Westernization)

"Wholesale Westernization", a term first used in 1929 by Hu Shi in an English article for the *Chinese Christian Year-Book,* has always been controversial among China's intellectuals. The term cannot be treated strictly according to its literal meaning because it is a ridiculous demand (or a ridiculous fear by those who oppose the term), since there is no way it can occur. In fact, when suggesting "wholesale Westernization" as a national goal, Hu Shi explained that one can well spare no efforts to emphasize Westernization because the intrinsic inertia of Chinese culture will certainly at least halve the efforts.

After Mao there appeared resurrection of Westernism in mainland China. To resist this trend, from time to time the authorities accused those who were critical of certain Party policies and who called for a more thorough reform of advocating wholesale Westernization. For example, in the 1987 anti-bourgeois liberalization campaign, Fang Lizhi was expelled from the CCP, accused of preaching "wholesale Westernization", in spite of his statement that what he advocated was, in his own words, a policy of "complete and thorough opening" (quanfangweide chedi kaifang) to the world. Another well-known case was the *"River Elegy* Incident" in 1988 and 1989. See also "fandui zichanjieji ziyouhua yundong" (anti-bourgeois liberalization campaign) and *"Heshang* shijian" *(River Elegy* Incident).

全球价值
quanqiu jiazhi
(global values)

See "quanqiuhua" (globalization).

全球化
quanqiuhua

(globalization)

The globalization theory began to be popular in the West in the early 1990s. By the mid-1990s it already became a hot topic in China. This fact was interpreted by China's liberal thinkers to be of symbolic significance—globalization, as an irreversible trend, will certainly influence China's historical course. On a number of occasions in 1998 and 1999, General Secretary Jiang Zemin and Premier Zhu Rongji also talked about globalization and how to adapt China to this new situation. Under their auspices, China came to an agreement with the United States on 15 November 1999 concerning China entering the World Trade Organization.

Up to the present, during five hundred years, there have been four globalization waves. The first occurred after Columbus discovered the New Continent at the end of the fifteenth century, resulting in the spread of European civilization. The second began about the middle of the nineteenth century when Western big powers (lieqiang) forced the doors of Asian countries. The third was promoted by the new world pattern after the end of the Second World War. China did not have much to do with these three waves. Now is the fourth globalization wave, which is said to be one in its true and full sense, characterized by market globalization as its aim and information globalization as its motive force. Chinese leaders have come to the decision that China should take part in this globalization. This is in fact a natural end result of China's reform and open-door program which began in 1978. The benefits are apparent, especially in its bringing to China the most needed capital and advanced technology, so as to speed up China's modernization. This is why "Be articulate with international norms" (yu guoji jiegui), one of the most influential slogans in the last twenty years, is said to be a natural and inevitable choice of a nation constantly striving to become stronger and more prosperous in an age of globalization.

But globalization is a double-edged sword. China, as a developing country, will have to face a number of challenges. Neo-Leftists warn: Globalization, as far as China is concerned, means Westernization, or, even worse, Americanization. It is capitalist globalization. It will lead to capitalist restoration in China, placing the whole country under the control of transnational corporations. As they announce, they cannot accept a world led and controlled by financial and political oligarchies. Social justice and political democracy must also be practiced in economic fields. They try to find a different, unique road for China. Wang Hui, editor-in-chief of *Reading,* asks: Is it possible to have a modern society generated in a historical form which departs from capitalism, or, to follow a modernization course which can reflect upon modernity? Like other neo-Leftists, his answer is Mao's legacy. Judging from the conception of history and values, Wang Hui asserts, Mao's socialist thought is a modernity theory which opposes capitalist modernity. (See, for example, Wang Hui, "Dangdai Zhongguo sixiang zhuangkuang yu xiandaixing wenti"—"The State of Contemporary Chinese Thought and Modernity", *Tianya,* 5, 1997; Han Yuhai, "Quanqiuhua, haishi zibenzhuyihua?"—"Globalization or Merely Capitalism?", *ES,* 131-35, Apr. 1999; and Wang Xiaodong, Fang Ning, and Song Qiang, *Quanqiuhua Yinyingxiade Zhongguo Zhi Lu—China's Way Under the Shadow of Globalization,* Beijing, Zhongguo shehui kexue, 1999.)

One can see an alliance of neo-Maoism and radical nationalism in the last year of the twentieth century, in their common resistance to the influence of globalization in China. Indeed, there are a number of difficult issues. Market globalization requires information globalization, and information globalization requires freedom of the press, publication, and education. Furthermore, there must be globalization in legal system, democracy, and political behavior. Thus to "be articulate with international norms" is not only an orientation, or a requirement, for technical, scientific, and economic matters; it means that China's present legal system, political system, and many related concepts should also be reformed.

China's liberal thinkers favor such a "complete and thorough globalization" (quanfangweide quanqiuhua). They promote the concept of "global values" (quanqiu jiazhi). It may seem strange that this concept was raised in the upsurge of nationalism as an ideological trend in China in the 1990s. However, on the other hand, this can be seen as both natural and necessary. The trend of nationalism involves the criticism and repudiation of so-called "Western values" (xifang jiazhi). It accompanies the advocacy of theories of "Asian values" (Yazhou jiazhi), "the superiority of Chinese culture", or "the superiority of Eastern culture". Now once again the Chinese face this question: Should China enter into and mix together with the world's mainstream civilization? This is a critical question because China at the moment is undergoing a transition of social mode and must decide what system it will adopt.

In view of the irrational nationalism (feilixing minzuzhuyi) existing in China, liberals suggest that the Chinese people discard and transcend nationalism and adopt human rights, freedom, and democracy—common standards shared by the world—as their own standards in building the country. This means China should on its initiative join in the world's mainstream civilization, play an active role, and help create what can be called "global values" shared by all nations in the world. The world's mainstream civilization, after a development of several hundred years, has accumulated rich human experience and wisdom. It is wrong, therefore, to reject these on the grounds of a nation's individuality. Admittedly, there are drawbacks and evils in Western values. It is because of this that "global values" should be established on the basis of increased exchanges among all nations. According to these liberals, there is no alternative. After all, it is obvious that in today's world globalization is gaining momentum. Under the prevailing circumstances, China cannot, and should not, embark on its own road to modernization. They believe that liberalism, now rejuvenating in the country, will bring freedom to China and bring a free China to a world of globalization.

Some scholars emphasize the closeness between the concept of "globalization" and the Chinese concept "datong" (Great Harmony or Great Unity). Traditionally, with regard to social reform, Chinese intellectuals regarded the ultimate aim to be the achievement of "datong" in the world, which became an important part of Confucian thought from the Han dynasty (202 B.C.—220 A.D.) onwards. As has been pointed out, this traditional Confucian ultimate concern (zhongji guanhuai) allowed most intellectuals to accept the Marxist doctrine of communism without much difficulty during the various self-remolding movements after the CCP's 1949 takeover of the mainland. Since the beginning of the 1990s, with the revival of Confucianism, the concept of "datong" has reappeared. Significantly, it is found that Confucianism can be interpreted as compatible with Western concepts of liberty and democracy. Moreover, globalization, as a general trend in today's world, can be seen to be predicated on and directed by the Confucian ideal of "datong" in the world or as its logical outcome. According to these scholars, traditional Chinese cultural values may not only unify China but also become the mainstream of world culture in the twenty-first century. It is in this sense that the twenty-first century is regarded as the "Chinese century".

Not all are so optimistic and agree with these scholars—their school can be called "Confucian liberalism" (rujia ziyouzhuyi). But it is noted that many Chinese intellectuals are trying their best to advocate globalization. They do so also out of certain fears. As early as 1993, Li Shenzhi, former CASS vice president, stated: "China possesses rich resources for nationalism. If it takes on the road of nationalism and chauvinism, this, in my opinion, should never be considered as China's good fortune" (Li Shenzhi, "Issues of China's Modernization: From the Angle of Globalization"—"Cong quanqiuhua guandian kan Zhongguo xiandaihua wenti", speech of 18 December 1993 at the forum "Re-estimating the Theme of China's Modernization", held by the *Strategy and Management* magazine office).

It is difficult to establish "global values". Globalization will be a prolonged, painstaking course, and its realization requires efforts by all countries in the world. It is still early to say that the challenge of globalization has once and for all replaced the Cold War. One should not be surprised if there is any adverse current. As far as China is concerned, it is not impossible if the alliance of radical nationalism and neo-Maoism will become the country's leading ideological force in the coming one or two decades. And this is certainly not good news to the world as well as China, as liberals warned. See also "ziyouzhuyi" (liberalism), "xinzuopai" (neo-Leftists), and "minzuzhuyi" (nationalism).

全球化就是美国化
quanqiuhua jiushi Meiguohua
(globalization means Americanization)

See "quanqiuhua" (globalization).

全心全意为人民服务
quanxin quanyi wei renmin fuwu
(serve the people wholeheartedly)

On 8 September 1944, at a memorial meeting for Zhang Side, a soldier in the Eighth Route Army, Mao praised the soldier's spirit of serving the people wholeheartedly. In his 24 April 1945 article entitled "On Coalition Government", Mao wrote: "Our point of departure is to serve the people wholeheartedly and never for a moment divorce ourselves from the masses, to proceed in all cases from the interests of the people and not from one's self-interest or from the interests of a small group, and to identify our responsibility to the people with our responsibility to the leading organs of the Party" *(SWM,* 3, p. 315). From then on, "Serve the people" was an important slogan among the CCP and the CCP-led army. After the 1949 Communist takeover, the slogan became familiar to every Chinese in the mainland. In a talk on 16 June 1964, Mao suggested five requirements for "successors of the proletarian revolutionary cause". The second requirement is "serving the majority of the people". (These five requirements were cited in both the CCP constitution passed at the Party's 1969 9th National Congress and the CCP constitution passed at the 1973 10th National Congress.)

Not a few Party and government officials pay lip-service to the slogan "Serve the people". Essentially, "the people", as pointed out by scholars, is an "illusory collective" (xuhuande jiti). Moreover, those in power can use the slogan to justify a certain policy that may harm many people's interests. Nevertheless, when facing the universal corruption in the Party and society today, many Chinese recall Mao's words. That is why Jiang Zemin said at the 15th CCP National Congress: "The fight against corruption is a grave political struggle vital to the very existence of the Party and the state." There is no denying the fact that a current and more attractive slogan is: "Serve the money" (wei jinqian fuwu), which sarcastically follows the tone of "serve the people". See also "fan fubai" (anti-corruption).

群众斗争
qunzhong douzheng
(mass struggle)

See "qunzhong luxian" (mass line).

群众观点
qunzhong guandian
(mass viewpoint)

See "qunzhong luxian" (mass line).

群众路线
qunzhong luxian
(mass line)

"The masses are the real heroes" ("qunzhong shi zhenzhengde yingxiong", first seen in "Preface and Postscript to Rural Surveys, March and April 1941", *SWM,* 3, p. 12) is a well-known statement by Mao, in light of which Mao made his "mass line". According to the "Resolution on Certain Questions in the History of Our Party since the Founding of the PRC" passed on 27 June 1981 at the 6th Plenum of the 11th PCC, the "living soul" of Mao Zedong Thought was defined as its stand, viewpoint, and method, and the "mass line" was one of the three basic principles embodying the essence of these.

In June 1943, in the document "Several Issues Regarding Methods of Leadership" ("Guanyu lingdao fangfade ruogan wenti") written for the PCC, Mao used the phrase "from the masses, to the masses" (cong qunzhongzhong lai, dao qunzhongzhong qu) to describe his "mass line". In November 1943, Mao used the term "mass viewpoint" (qunzhong guandian) in his speech entitled "Get Organized" ("Zuzhi qilai"). Later, on a number of occasions, such as in the document "Sixty Articles of Working Methods (Draft)" which he wrote for the PCC in January 1958, Mao elucidated his idea about "mass viewpoint" and "mass line". He said: "In all the practical work of our Party, all correct leadership is necessarily 'from the masses, to the masses'. Such is the Marxist theory of knowledge" *(RMRB,* 5 Apr. 1956). This working method was called the "mass line". Accordingly, a "mass viewpoint" was required, which proceeded from the highest interest of the masses. A "mass viewpoint" meant serving the people wholeheartedly, trusting in the creativity of the masses, relying on the masses in all matters, trusting in the abilities of the masses to liberate themselves, and learning from the masses. Furthermore, in light of the "mass line", the Party found it necessary to carry out once and again "mass movements" ("qunzhong yundong", movements in which the broad masses of people participated), or, rather, "mobilization of the masses of people" (yundong qunzhong), in its struggles for the success of what it called the "socialist revolution" and "socialist construction".

In the mass movements carried out by the Party, especially the political movements, "mass struggles" (yunzhong douzheng) were the chief method. This was also true in matters of literature and art. In his work report delivered at the 1979 4th National Congress of Chinese Writers and Artists, the first congress after the end of the GPCR, Zhou Yang admitted that class struggle had been carried out on a much wider scale than was actually called for and the two kinds of contradictions were confused. Consequently, criticisms of ideology and of literary and artistic ideas were handled as if they were political movements and the method of mass struggle was used to handle problems belonging to the spiritual sphere. Zhou Yang said that facts had proved that it was extremely harmful to try to solve ideological issues with administrative measures and mass struggle. For instance, he said, during the 1957 anti-Rightist movement, a large number of writers and artists suffered, including some talented, enterprising writers and artists who had had the courage to explore fresh areas. They were wrongly accused, and their views on literature and art as well as their works were wrongly criticized.

Mao's "mass struggle" in light of his "mass line" did work well during war time, helping him finally to seize state power. But he was so obsessed with it that he continued using it in all fields throughout the country after the founding of his regime, thus once and again bringing disasters to the Chinese people. See also "minzhu jizhongzhi" (democratic centralism).

群众落後论
qunzhong luohou lun
(the theory that "the masses are backward")

See "hei liu lun" (six sinister theories).

群众是真正的英雄
qunzhong shi zhenzhengde yingxiong
(the masses are the real heroes)

See "qunzhong luxian" (mass line) and "tiancai lun" ("innate genius" theory).

群众运动
qunzhong yundong
(mass movement)

See "qunzhong luxian" (mass line).

群众专政
qunzhong zhuanzheng
(dictatorship of the masses)

According to Wang Li, a former member of the Central GPCR Group, Mao first used the term "dictatorship of the masses" in his 4 August 1967 letter to Jiang Qing. In the letter Mao said: "One of the most important issues to be solved in the Cultural Revolution is the dictatorship of the masses" (Wang Li, *Chronicles of the Cultural Revolution*, pp. 90-91). Three days later, on 7 August 1967, Xie Fuzhi made a speech calling Red Guards and other revolutionary people to "smash public security organs, procuratorial organs, and people's courts" (za lan gong jian fa), obviously a response to Mao's view about the "dictatorship of the masses". See also "wuchanjieji zhuanzheng" (dictatorship of the proletariat).

让群众自己解放自己
rang qunzhong ziji jiefang ziji
(let the masses liberate themselves)

See "hongweibing" (Red Guards) and "qunzhong luxian" (mass line).

让人说话
rang ren shuohua
(let others speak)

See "minzhu jizhongzhi" (democratic centralism).

让文学是文学
rang wenxue shi wenxue
(let literature be literature)

Since the downfall of the Gang of Four in 1976, along with the great changes in politico-social life, from time to time there appeared works dealing with politico-social problems and arousing huge reactions from the readership. They were called "explosive" writings (baozhaxing zuopin), such as "Unrequited Love", a film script by Bai Hua and Peng Ning, and "Between Man and Monster", a piece of reportage literature by Liu Binyan.

These works should be natural, and even unavoidable when society is at a historical turning point. But some writers, in their pursuit of art, thought otherwise. As early as 1983, at a forum at Chicago University, Wang Anyi, then a young writer, complained of the "excessive" interest overseas in those "explosive" works. In a literary sense, she stated, these were not very good works, for they had a "non-literary effect", and this was not a normal, good phenomenon. Like others, Wang was disgusted with the politicization of literature (wenxue zhengzhihua), a long-standing problem in modern and contemporary Chinese literature.

Once the shackle of the "tool theory" had been smashed, contemporary Chinese writers and artists wanted literature to return to its own true nature. From the mid-1980s on, this desire gradually became a conscious and conscientious pursuit on the part of a great number of writers and critics. They tried to make literature more artistic, with its own aesthetic. They not only wanted to rid literature of its subordinate position to politics, but also, as Zheng Wanlong said, to "discover and complete 'transcendence' in the relationship between life and art" ("Xiaoshuode neizai liliang"—"The Inherent Power of Fiction", *Xiandai zuojia,* 4, 1984). Various literary experiments appeared. Two seemingly contradictory phenomena—the search for "roots" (xungen re) and the quest for "modernism" (xiandai re)—co-existed. Some even wanted to make the two extremes meet: the classical taste of the Orient and the modern taste of the West, or, furthermore, to achieve a transcendence of both. (See, for instance, Chen Sihe, "Zhongguo wenxue fazhanzhongde xiandaizhuyi"—"Modernism in the Development of Chinese Literature", *SHWX,* 7, 1985; Song Yaoliang, "Yishiliu wenxue dongfanghua guocheng"—"The Process of Orientalization of the Stream of Consciousness", *WXPL,* 1:33-40, 1986; Zhou Ping, "Xinshiqi wenxuezhongde xiandaizhuyi jianjin"—"The Gradual Advance of Modernism in Literature of the New Period", *WXPL,* 1:28-34, 1987; Ren Hongyuan, "Dui xifang xiandaizhuyi yu dongfang gudian shixuede shuangchong chaoyue"—"Dual Transcendence of Western Modernism and Classical Eastern Poetics", *WXPL,* 5:119-26, 1988; Wang Ning, "Zhongguo dangdai wenxuezhongde Fuluoyidezhuyi bianti"—"A Variety of Freudianism in Contemporary Chinese Literature", *RMWX,* 2:106-12, 1989; Zhao Mei, "Xianfeng xiaoshuode zizu yu fufan"—"Self-Sufficiency and Superficiality of Vanguard Novels", *WXPL,* 1:31-39, 1989; Zhu Dake et al., "Baowei xianfeng wenxue"—"Defending Vanguard Literature", *SHWX,* 5:76-80, 1989; Hu Heqing, "Lun Acheng, Ma Yuan, and Zhang Wei: Daojia wenhua zhihuide yange"—"On Acheng, Ma Yuan and Zhang Wei: The Evolution of the Ingenuity of Taoist Culture", *WXPL,* 2:71-80, 1989; Wang Wei, "Fan guifande xiaoshuo shiyan"—"Experiments of Anti-Standard Stories", *SHWX,* 5:71-75,1989; Wang Meng and Wang Gan, "Wenxuede nixiangxing: fanwenhua, fanchonggao, fanwenming"—"Converse Character of Literature: Anti-Culture, Anti-Loftiness, and Anti-Civilization", *SHWX*, 5:66-70, 1989; and Li Jiefei, "Xinshiqi xiaoshuode liang ge jieduan ji qi bijiao"—"Two Phases of the Novels in the New Period and a Comparison between Them", *WXPL*, 3:78-86, 1989, and "Ping Zhongguo wenxuede minzu yishi"—"A Review of 'National Consciousness' in Chinese Literature", *SHWX*, 1:74-80, 1989). See also "xinshiqi wenxue" (literature of the new period) and "xinshiqi wenxuede duoyuan fazhan" (pluralistic development of the literature of the new period).

让一部分人先富起来
rang yibufen ren xian fu qilai
(allow a proportion of the people to get rich first)

See "facai guangrong" (to get rich is glorious).

仁及天下
ren ji tianxia
(benevolence for the people of the world)

A basic idea of Liu Zaifu's "subjectivity of literature" is what he calls the two "strategic transfers", occurring respectively in literary creation and literary study. In literary creation, the reflection of the "outer world" is replaced by the presentation of the "inner universe". The thesis, "Literature is the study of man", is further elucidated as a study of the soul, of human character, and of spiritual subjectivity. In literary study, accordingly, research accentuates the understanding of writers' specific states of mind, specific ways of thinking, and feelings characteristic to each of them. Liu also suggests that critics, in their critical activities, should achieve self-actualization. In short, writers and critics should not only present and study man; more important is to project their inner worlds, to project love, fraternity, or, in other words, "benevolence for the people of the world" (Theoretical Department, Literature Institute, CASS, "Ziyoude taolun, shenrude tansuo: guanyu Liu Zaifu 'Lun wenxuede zhutixing' yiwende taolun"—"A Discussion of Liu Zaifu's Article "On the Subjectivity of Literature", *WXPL*, 3:4, May 1986).

In the first half of the 1980s, "love" did become a central theme of both literature and philosophical study. Liu and his contemporaries (many of whom were survivors of earlier persecutions) fully committed themselves to promoting love. Another most enthusiastic preacher, for instance, was Liu Xinwu, a pioneer of "scar literature" (see "shanghen wenxue"). Working in concert with Liu Zaifu, he raised the concept of "sufficient love" (Liu Xinwu, "Guanyu wenxue benxingde sikao"—"Thoughts on the True Nature of Literature", *WXPL*, 4:25-37, 141, 1985). He suggested that excellent literature is not only a genuine study of man but also "a study of sufficient love". Liu Xinwu's view was regarded as a turning point away from the revolutionary literature of the past. Critics (including Wang Ruoshui), however, found Liu Zaifu's and Liu Xinwu's lauding of "love" to be pre-Marxist, and thus questionable. See also "rendaozhuyi lunzheng" (humanism debate).

人多好办事
ren duo hao banshi
(the more people, the more achievements)

See "xin renkou lun" (new theory of population) and "yitaihua" (single-child policy).

人还没死，作品已经死了
ren hai mei si, zuopin yijing sile (the author is alive, but his works are already dead)

At a discussion meeting held soon after the 1979 4th Congress of Writers and Artists (by the editorial board of *Literary Gazette* and the Film Research Office of the Literature and Art Institute under the Ministry of Culture), five prominent writers, Bai Hua, Li Zhun, Ye Nan, Liang Xin, and Zhang Tianmin, boldly and forcefully expressed their views on the relationship between politics and arts. As they summed up sarcastically, Chinese writers had been forced to eulogize in the past thirty years all politically erroneous practices, such as "arbitrary and impracticable directions" (xia zhihui), "proneness to boasting and exaggeration" (fukua feng), "the Communistic trend" (gongchan feng), and "anti-Right-deviation" (fan youqing). In works supposed to reflect socialist construction, almost without exception, class struggle was deliberately fabricated and contradictions among the people distorted to become like contradictions between enemies. What they actually propagated was nothing but "imprudence before victory", "violations of objective laws", and "wrong estimations of situations at home and abroad". For a long time, the Party leader was described as the "saviour" of the world. In the mammoth god-making movement during the GPCR, this practice reached its zenith.

The meeting participants compared the "conspiratorial literature" of the Gang of Four with the formulistic and stereotyped writings of the seventeen years. Though politically distinct from each other, they still had quite a lot in common, such as a false description of life and confusion about right and wrong and about the fundamental and the incidental—both being advocated by some people in power for their political interests. Eventually, serving politics meant serving certain current political needs, certain political lines and policies, and certain politicians or leading figures. Zhang Tianmin asked: "Since the founding of the PRC, our writers have written a great number of such works. There have always been works written to go with the Party's 'central tasks'. How many of them, however, have a reasonably long artistic life?" ("'Wenyide shehui gongneng': wu ren tan"—"A Five-Person Discussion of the 'Social Function of Literature and Art'", *WYB,* 1, Jan. 1980, reprinted in *XHYB, WZB,* 3:175, 1980). Li Zhun said, bitterly: "The author is alive, but his works are already dead. Sometimes, what is written early in the year will die by the end of the same year" (ibid., p. 172). See also "wenyi wei zhengzhi fuwu" (literature and art serve politics).

人是马克思主义的出发点
ren shi Makesizhuyide chufadian (man is the starting point of Marxism)

"Man is the starting point of Marxism" was a popular thesis in China in the early 1980s. Wang Ruoshi and a number of other philosophers advocated it, as in their 1981 book *Man Is the Starting Point of Marxism* (Wang Ruoshui et al., *Ren Shi Makesizhuyide Chufadian: Renxing, Rendaozhuyi Wenti Lunji,* Beijing, Renmin, 1981). Hu Qiaomu found it so serious a problem—it seemed to be agreed by almost everyone among China's philosophical-cultural circles—that he fully discussed it in his January 1984 article "On Problems Concerning Humanism and Alienation".

With Marx's assertion—"The human essence is no abstraction inherent in each single individual. In its reality is the ensemble of social relations"—Hu points out that the starting point of Marxism is human society, the social relations (first of all production relations) of human beings. The claim that "Man is the starting point of

Marxism", therefore, is a typical thesis that obscures the distinction between Marxism and bourgeois humanism and between historical materialism and historical idealism. As for the historical formula "human—inhuman—human", which generalizes human history as the history of human nature's alienation and resuscitation, Hu accuses it of being a typical idealistic humanistic conception of history. In summary, he says, humanism as an outlook on the world and on history is fundamentally antagonistic to the historical materialism of Marxism. Humanism cannot explain Marxism, or supplement, rectify, or develop it. On the contrary, only Marxism can explain the historical sources and historical functions of humanism, point out its historical limitations, and put an end to the era it represented in the development of the conceptions of human history.

In Hu's opinion, many of his opponents' discussions about "man is the goal", "human value", and "human dignity" are "abstract", and such abstract discussions cannot help people to realize the goal, the value, and the dignity, no matter how sincere those participating in the discussions may be, or how good their motives may be. Anyone who is enthusiastic about this sort of discussion, he warns, will fall into Utopian socialism of a certain kind, and this historical idealistic fantasy, different from Utopian socialism of the past that once played a progressive role, can only function negatively today. Hu points out that socialism first emphasizes the values of the people and only in the values of the people can the values of each individual be discussed. Moreover, he continues, in the relationship between each individual and society, human value should consist of two aspects: respect and satisfaction of an individual by society and the individual's responsibility and contribution to society. The same holds true, Hu says, for the issue "man is the goal": Only in realizing that "the people are the goal" can the goal of each individual be discussed. In addition, in order to realize man's goal, man cannot but be made into a means. This does not necessarily mean the loss of human dignity and honor, nor necessarily anguish and sacrifice. As Hu sees it, the principle of socialism should be the unity of the goal and the means, of social interests and personal interests, of enjoyment and labor, of rights and duties, and of freedom and discipline.

Hu Qiaomu's views about the starting point of Marxism, though seemingly powerful, did not convince everyone, particularly, his chief opponent Wang Ruoshui. In the spring of 1984, not long after the publication of Hu's treatise, Wang Ruoshui reiterated his view in an article entitled "My View on Problems of Humanism" ("Wo dui rendaozhuyi wentide kanfa", in *WRB*, pp. 239-74). The article, which could not be published until 1986, was nothing short of a serious counter-attack to Hu Qiaomu's views. In the second part of his article, Wang Ruoshui discusses the starting point of Marxism. He says that it is quite strange that Hu Qiaomu should have raised in his long thesis the issue of what is the motive force propelling human society forward, and should have emphasized it as one of the cores and essences of the debate. In actuality, the debate over humanism which had been going on for three years in Chinese ideological circles did not center around this issue. Strictly speaking, moreover, this issue does not concern humanism. Nevertheless, since Hu attacks the thesis, "Man is the starting point of Marxism", Wang finds it necessary to declare that what he means by "man" is man in reality, in society, and not abstract man at all—all of which is very clear in his article. In fact, Hu is not only opposed to regarding abstract man as the starting point of Marxism (which is absolutely correct and on which there is no divergence of opinion whatsoever). He is also opposed to regarding man in reality as the starting point of Marxism, and this is in diametrical contradiction to the relevant remarks by Marx himself. Are the two theses, "starting from man in reality" and "starting from human society", mutually exclusive? According to the Marxist point of view, Wang says, there is no contradiction at all between them. See also "rendaozhuyi lunzheng" (humanism debate).

人是目的，人是中心
ren shi mudi, ren shi zhongxin
(man is the aim, man is the center)

As early as November 1979, in literary circles, Liu Binyan put forth the maxim "Man is the aim, man is the center". He argued that one reason why class struggle in China persisted for so long over such a wide area without being checked, and why the legal system and democracy were unsound for so long without anyone thinking it unusual, was that the Chinese had not rid themselves of their feudal attitudes about man's status and about personal relationships. In order to justify himself, Liu quoted Lenin as having said that, after the capitalist countries of Western Europe had undergone their socialist revolution, there would still be a problem of "making up for missed lessons" (buke) within democracy. Liu argued that in China, with its several thousand years of feudal history, where productivity, the cultural level, and democratic traditions were underdeveloped, the job of "making up for missed lessons" would undoubtedly involve a much greater effort. He believed, therefore, that in this historical task, contemporary Chinese literature and art had a huge potential. To destroy the various obstacles in the path of life and in people's traditional attitudes, to enable the Chinese people to have their due dignity and rights in the various spheres of life, to stand up like masters, to take up the task of the Four Modernizations like heroes, taking the initiative with happiness in their hearts—all this, in Liu's opinion, was the contemporary task of literary workers, and it was "the most vital topic in this age". (See Liu Binyan, "Ren shi mudi, ren shi zhongxin"—"Man Is the Aim, Man Is the Center", *WXPL,* 6:10-15, 1979, reprinted in *WYLZJ,* pp. 158-69; trans. in Howard Goldblatt, ed., *Chinese Literature for the 1980s*, New York, M.E. Sharpe, 1982, pp. 121-31.) See also "rendaozhuyi lunzheng" (humanism debate), "ren shi Makesizhuyide chufadian" (man is the starting point of Marxism), and "shehuizhuyi rendaozhuyi" (socialist humanism).

人有多大胆，地有多大产
ren you duo da dan, di you duo da chan
(the bolder the man is, the higher yields the fields will turn out)

See "dayuejin" (Great Leap Forward).

人才难得
rencai nande
(it is hard to come by an able person)

See "mianli cang zhen, xing zheng si yuan" (He is like a needle wrapped in cotton. His mind is round and his actions are square).

人大
Renda
(National People's Congress)

See "xiangpi tuzhang" (rubber stamp).

人道的马克思主义
rendaode Makesizhuyi
(humanistic Marxism)

See "rendaozhuyide Makesizhuyi" (humanistic Marxism) and "shehuizhuyi rendaozhuyi" (socialist humanism).

人道主义干预
rendaozhuyi ganyu
(humanitarian intervention)

See "lengzhanhou shidaide xin diguozhuyi" (neo-imperialism in the post-Cold War era), "renquan wenti" (human rights issue), and "weidu Zhongguo" (containment against China).

人道主义论争
rendaozhuyi lunzheng
(humanism debate)

Humanism was always a target of attack after Mao gave his *Yan'an Talks* in 1942. The CCP rejected humanism on the grounds that Marx criticized and repudiated it when he became mature in his later years. More relevant for the CCP was their political considerations in actual struggles. The CCP found humanism on the one hand contradictory to its doctrines about class and class struggle and on the other hand compatible with liberty, equality, human rights, individualism, etc., which it opposed as "bourgeois". That was why it treated humanism mainly as a political issue and not merely as an issue of pure ideology. Indeed, typically during the Mao period, each time a political campaign was carried out, there would be a massive criticism of humanism (attacked as "bourgeois humanism") within ideological-literary circles. The larger the scale of the campaign was, the more fierce the criticism would become. As the scale of political campaigns expanded, criticism of humanism escalated. Humanism was simply a "forbidden zone", which few people dared to enter; whoever strayed into this zone would be tragically destroyed.

After the ten-year nightmare of the GPCR, during which what was dubbed the "brutal feudal-fascist dictatorship" was carried out, many Chinese suddenly found themselves responding to "humanism" as something splendid, and not as a term of opprobrium, which it had always been in the past. With the change in the general atmosphere of political life, China's intellectuals enthusiastically committed themselves to criticism of the ultra-Left ideology, to approval of humanism, to the introduction of mainstream concepts of value from the West, and to the designing of reform modes. First, in the literary field there was, as critics asserted, a "humanistic tide in literature" (rendaozhiyide wenxue chaoliu); more and more literary works were concerned with the fate of man. Not only were writers enlightened by their own experiences, they were also inspired by discussions among theorists and philosophers. Popular terms and theses included "re-discovery of man" (rende chongxin faxian) and "Man is the aim, man is the center" (ren shi mudi, ren shi zhongxin). There was a demand for a re-appraisal of humanism (as in the inaugural issue of *Foreign Literature Studies* in April 1979). The relationship between Marxist philosophy and humanism began to be explored directly in the early months of 1980. In the three years from 1980 to 1982, according to statistics provided in the *People's Daily* of 11 January 1983, 422 articles were published in 294 newspapers and magazines (for some influential titles, see "rendaozhuyide Makesizhuyi"—

humanistic Marxism). Authors writing about humanism or Marxist-humanism in Eastern Europe and other countries were seriously read and discussed. What is more, with the affirmation of humanism, people began to deal with the problem of alienation. The theory of socialist alienation was raised in the early 1980s by Zhou Yang, then deputy director of the PCC Propaganda Department, and Wang Ruoshui, then deputy editor-in-chief of the *People's Daily*, adding fuel to the fire. Around 1983, "man" was the central topic in every field of social and human sciences. As Wang Ruoshui declared: "A spectre is haunting the Chinese intellectual world—the spectre of humanism" (Wang Ruoshui, "Wei rendaozhuyi bianhu"—"A Defense of Humanism", *WHB*, 17 Jan. 1983). This statement, following the tone and pattern of the first sentence in the Chinese translation of the *Manifesto of the Communist Party,* struck a sympathetic chord among many Chinese intellectuals. As to why the issue of "man" aroused such a strong public interest and became such a influential social phenomenon, it was, as Wang Ruoshui explained, "not merely a reaction to the ten-year civil strife, but in addition a reflection of the demand created during the New Period to build a socialist society with a high degree of civilization and democracy" (ibid.). China's intellectuals regarded these discussions as a new enlightenment movement, a resumption of the May 4th enlightenment spirit, and they regarded it as their historical mission.

Though the political situation had changed quite a lot after the downfall of the Gang of Four, tackling issues of humanism (and alienation) proved to be still highly risky undertakings. In the last months of 1983, following the resolution of the 2nd Plenum of the 12th PCC, a campaign was carried out to "eliminate spiritual pollution" (qingchu jingshen wuran). Wang Ruoshui and his close ally Zhou Yang, together with their defense of humanism and their theory of "socialist alienation", were primary targets of the campaign. A great number of literary works were accused of preaching "bourgeois humanism", "human nature above classes", and "socialist alienation". The high tide of criticism was the publication of "On Problems Concerning Humanism and Alienation" ("Guanyu rendaozhuyi he yihua wenti", *RMRB*, 27 Jan. 1984; reprinted in *HQ,* 2:2-28, 1984; in book form by Beijing, Renmin, Jan. 1984; revised in *WYLZJ,* pp. 50-102) by Politburo and Secretariat member Hu Qiaomu, the No. 1 Party ideologue.

Hu's article was drafted by a writing group consisting of members from eight bodies: CASS, Beijing University, Chinese People's University, the Central Party School, *Red Flag* Editorial Board, *Guangming Daily* Editorial Board, the PCC Bureau of Compilation and Translation, and the PCC Office in Charge of Party Documents. The text underwent four major revisions over the course of three months. Certainly much energy was expended in its writing, and Hu was very proud of the final product (in a poem he called it "a sharp sword escaping from the scabbard"). As expected, no sooner was the article published in the *People's Daily* on 27 January 1984 was it hailed by official organizations throughout the country. A celebratory forum, for instance, was held at the Central Party School the next day. Hu's article was highly praised for having made it clear "what was Marxism and what was not". At the very outset, Hu's admirers said, the article grasps "the core and the essence" of the debate in recent years about humanism and alienation, because it starts by pointing out that the debate had a bearing on how to regard human history and the development of socialist society, and on how to observe and explain things: "Marxist historical materialism" or "abstract humanistic historical idealism". Hu's description of "alienation" was regarded as remarkable—on the one hand as a basic category, a basic law, a theory, and a methodology and on the other hand as a concept to describe certain phenomena in a given period. Of even greater significance, they said, was his division of the two meanings of humanism: one as a world-historical outlook, which is fundamentally opposite to Marxism, and the other as an ethical principle and moral norm, which can be accepted when reformed into "socialist humanism". Yang Xianzhen, advisor and former president of the Central Party School, opined that Hu Qiaomu expounded on the issue of humanism "clearly" in the way that he excluded abstract humanism from the Marxist conception of the world and history and cataloged socialist humanism in the realm of ethics. Han Shuying, deputy president of the school, even called the division a "theoretical breakthrough".

Thereafter, the exciting atmosphere in which everyone was discussing humanism and alienation died down. However, those so-called "humanistic Marxists" or "Marxist humanists" were more insistent on defending their belief. In 1986 a new tide appeared. Hu Qiaomu, and a series of orthodox views, were openly challenged.

Hu Qiaomu's opponents, first of all, accused him of confusing the different meanings of humanism in its narrow sense and in its broad sense. Hu was said to have deliberately distorted their application of humanism, so that it seemed as if they insisted that Marxism and various pre-Marxist humanisms were one and the same thing. Hu also confused the key concept of "man"—he ignored the complex and dynamic meaning of "man" as a philosophical term and failed to pay attention to the context in which his opponents used this term. He indiscriminately interpreted "man" as "an individual" or as "an abstract man" and then subjected it to criticism and repudiation. Hu was also said to have confused other spheres of study. Take the concept of "freedom". Admittedly, it means man's legal rights when used politically, while referring to the essence of man's existence as a philosophical term. Whenever his opponents mentioned "freedom", however, Hu interpreted it as the rejection of discipline, as ultra-individualism or anarchism, or as bourgeois liberalization. In addition, Hu used the formulation "the people are the goal" instead of "man is the goal" regardless of the fact that the former is a political thesis, and the latter is philosophical. Even if "people" is here used to mean "collective" and "man" is meant as "individual", the problem still exists. For one thing, a random interpretation of "man" as "individual" does not conform to Marx's original meaning. For another, "the people" here is an "illusory collective" (xuhuande jiti) that demands sacrifice of every individual.

Basic issues raised by Hu's opponents include:

Wang Ruoshui finds it quite strange that in his long thesis Hu Qiaomu should have raised the issue of what is the motive force propelling human society forward, and should have emphasized it as one of the cores and essences of the debate. In actuality, Wang points out, the debate over humanism in the past few years did not center around this. Strictly speaking, moreover, this issue is not related to humanism. Nevertheless, since Hu attacks his thesis, "Man is the starting point of Marxism", Wang points out that what he means by "man" is "man in reality". Are the two theses, "starting from man in reality" and "starting from human society", mutually exclusive? According to the Marxist point of view, Wang says, there is no contradiction at all between them ("My View on Problems of Humanism", in *WRB*, pp. 239-74). As to "the motive force propelling human society forward", the aesthete Gao Ertai refutes Hu Qiaomu's assertion that "the development of productivity, the contradiction between productivity and production relations, and the class struggle which expresses the above-said contradiction in class society, are the motive force of the development of history" ("On Problems Concerning Humanism and Alienation", *WYLZJ*, p. 55). Instead, Gao says, one should agree that the motive force is man's practice, the practice that first reforms nature and second society (Gao Ertai, "Rendaozhuyi: Dangdai zhenglunde beiwanglu"—"Humanism: A Memorandum on a Contemporary Debate", *Sichuan shida xuebao,* 4, 1986, extracted and reprinted in *XHWZ,* 10:25-33, 1986).

Many find Hu's division of the "two meanings of humanism" untenable. According to the critic Feng Chuan, Marx's idea of human nature is a conception of history and not merely of ethics (Feng Chuan, "Makesi suo lijiede renxing"—"Human Nature As Understood by Marx", *Da shidai*, 1, 1995). Sun Yuecai, a research fellow at the Philosophy Institute, Shanghai Academy of Social Sciences, holds that the unity between Marxism and humanism should be affirmed from a world-historical outlook. In his opinion, Marxism is infiltrated with humanism—he finds the wording "shentou" ("is infiltrated with") to be better than "baokuo" ("includes", as used by Zhou Yang). Sun directly criticizes Hu Qiaomu, and demands a public discussion of Hu's article "On Problems". (Sun Yuecai's article, "Issues of Humanism and Alienation and the 'Double Hundred' Policy: Hu Qiaomu Revisited"—"Rendaozhuyi, yihua wenti yu baijiazhengming: Cong du Hu Qiaomu", was published in an internal journal. See Wang Ruoshui, *Behind Hu Yaobang's Stepdown*, HK, Mingjing, 1997.) Wang Ruoshui also refutes this in his article "My View on Problems of Humanism", which was written in the spring of 1984 but could not be published until 1986.

Some saw it as somewhat of a change for those who had originally opposed humanism to recognize "socialist humanism". However, as Gao Ertai sees it, such a change does not exist. Furthermore, to treat socialist humanism as some ethical, moral norms in conformity with certain social relationships, as Hu Qiaomu does in his "On Problems", is not only not an original idea but also a retreat to a pre-Marxist, abstract humanism. Gao explicitly points out that "socialist humanism" means "Marxist humanism". Logically, socialist humanism is a world outlook as well as a conception of history (Gao Ertai, "A Memorandum). Wang Ruoshui, making use of the fact that the CCP is committed to the policy of reform, stresses that raising the issue of human value or socialist humanism is compatible with the needs of reform. On this point, Wang accuses Hu Qiaomu of reducing the significance of socialist humanism when he describes it as merely a collection of ethical, moral norms, and of failing to make a clean break with some bourgeois and petty-bourgeois humanists already criticized by Marx, one of whose major errors was precisely to "describe social problems as moral problems" (Wang Ruoshui, "Guanyu 'geming rendaozhuyi'"—"On 'Revolutionary Humanism'", *Workers' Daily*, Jan. 1985, reprinted in *WRB*, pp. 234-38).

Is man the means or the goal? What is human value? Both sides in the debate agreed with the thesis that man is the unity of the means and the goal, but their explanations and conclusions were different. The crux of the divergence lies in their different views about value. According to Gao Ertai, what is called the collective outlook about value (as held by Hu) confines the development of the individual in the name of the "collective" and makes individuality (gexing) conform to generality (gongxing). Gao advocates, therefore, the humanistic outlook on value which holds that the progress of the collective and the emancipation of the individual are interdependent and that generality should be enriched and developed by means of an all-around development of individuality and creativity (Gao Ertai, "A Memorandom").

If all this is rather theoretical and general, Wang Ruoshui tries to link his discussion with contemporary Chinese reality as much as possible when discussing the problems of socialist humanism and human value. The difference here between the two sides in the debate is very practical indeed. Hu Qiaomu, though agreeing with the term "socialist humanism", views it only as a collection of moral norms, which people have long been familiar with. As for Wang and those sharing Wang's view, however, they are not satisfied with this. They want to further discuss human nature; they want to discuss human feelings, happiness, freedom, dignity, rights, value, and emancipation. This, according to Hu, all amounts to propagating "abstract human nature, abstract human value, individualism, and a humanist conception of the world and history", something he condemns as "an erroneous ideological trend" which "distrusts Marxism-Leninism-Mao Zedong Thought, socialism, and the Party leadership" (Hu Qiaomu, "On Problems"). This outright condemnation helps to explain why such a dead silence prevailed in intellectual circles in China for some time after Hu's article was published.

When discussing humanism, one cannot evade the concept of alienation. In fact, during the first few years of the 1980s, alienation, or, to be more exact, socialist alienation, was a hot topic. Since Deng Xiaoping had warned at the 2nd Plenum of the 12th PCC that a discussion of socialist alienation would lead to a loss of confidence in socialism and in the Party leadership—and he banned the discussion from "an overall strategic consideration"—for a time no one in China's intellectual circles dared to openly touch on the problem of alienation again. A few years later, however, the ban ended. In 1986, Li Keming, president of South China Normal University, specifically pointed out that Marxist philosophy should deal with the alienation theory (Li Keming, "Makesizhuyi zhexue yao yanjiu yihua lilun"—"Marxist Philosophy Should Deal with the Alienation Theory", *Guangzhou Ribao,* 18 Dec. 1986). In early 1989, Gao Ertai published a long dissertation on the alienation issue in an article entitled "On the Concept of Alienation" ("Lun yihua gainian"), which Wang Ruoshui claimed was the most profound and comprehensive elucidation to appear thus far in China on alienation. In 1988 and early 1989, Wang Ruoshui himself also published three articles in two short-lived magazines *Reading Circles (Shulin) and Neo-enlightenment (Xin Qimeng),* further developing his view: "The Personality Cult and Alienation in the Ideological Realm" ("Geren chongbai he sixiang yihua"); "On Man's Essence and Social Relations" ("Lun rende benzhi yu shehui guanxi"); and "Does Alienation Not Exist in a Socialist Society?" ("Shehuizhuyi shehui meiyou yihua ma?").

The humanism debate, beginning soon after the 1976 downfall of the Gang of Four, lasted for about a decade in the 1980s. It was first ended by the 1983 campaign to eliminate "spiritual pollution", then by the 1987 campaign to oppose "bourgeois liberalization", and finally by the June 4th Incident of 1989. While the prolonged debate continued off and on, China was undergoing great changes, especially in its economic-social life. Orthodox Marxism has now obviously lost its former influence among the people. The momentum for "humanistic Marxism" or "Marxist humanism" has also been arrested. Nevertheless, China's intellectuals still remember the debate. Occasionally, some remarks indicate that the truth remains on the side of Zhou Yang and Wang Ruoshui, for example, in an article by a scholar with the pen-name "Chang Niansi" in 1995 (see Chang Niansi, "Lao lei zongheng hua Qiaomu"—"In Memory of Hu Qiaomu", *Dushu,* Dec. 1995). See also other entries concerning humanism.

人道主义是文学的灵魂
rendaozhuyi shi wenxuede linghun
(humanism is the soul of literature)

As a result of the "humanistic tide" in the first few years of the 1980s, the thesis that "humanism is the soul of literature" seemed to be deeply rooted among many Chinese writers and critics. The 1983 campaign to "eliminate spiritual pollution" ended the discussion only for a short time. From 1985 on, articles in its defense once again were openly published. Li Guiren, for instance, managed to publish his 1982 MA dissertation "Humanism: The Soul of Literature", in which he stated: "The aim of socialist literature, in the final analysis, is to help people realize the noble ideal of humanizing society. On this point, which is a matter of the most fundamental significance, socialist literature is basically compatible with, and not substantially different from, those traditional progressive literatures" (Li Guiren, "Rendaozhuyi: wenxuede linghun"—"Humanism: The Soul of Literature", *Wenxuejia,* 2:9, 1985). Dai Houying, a controversial woman writer, also spoke out. She wrote: "Without humanism, genuine literary creation and literary study cannot be carried out, just like an originally fresh and vigorous life abruptly deprived of its soul—all becomes deadly still, confused, and hard to understand" (Dai Houying, "I Built My Hut in a Zone of Human Habitation; I Write My Ideas and Feelings with My Hands", *WXPL,* 1:61, Jan. 1986). See also "rendaozhuyi lunzheng" (humanism debate) and "rendaozhuyi shi xinshiqi wenxuede zhuliu" (humanism is the mainstream in the literature of the new period).

人道主义是新时期文学的主流
rendaozhuyi shi xinshiqi wenxuede zhuliu (humanism is the mainstream in the literature of the new period)

In the 1920s and 1930s, many Chinese intellectuals, such as Hu Shi, regarded the May 4th New Culture Movement as a Chinese renaissance (Zhongguo wenyifuxing). In the discussion of humanism in the early 1980s, many talked about Chinese renaissance again.

Indeed, in the early 1980s, in the fields of literature and art, a great number of works concerned with the fate of man were produced. This, critics asserted, was a "humanistic tide in literature" (rendaozhuyide wenxue chaoliu), a tide in which a depiction of "man" sharply and profoundly monopolized literary themes. In their view, the "brilliance" of human nature and humanism could be found in almost all influential works at the time. Not only were writers enlightened by their own experience, they were also inspired by relevant discussions among theorists and philosophers. The relationship between Marxist philosophy and humanism, for example, began to be directly explored in the early 1980s.

There was agreement that the era, in a profound sense, made possible the emergence of the "re-discovery of man" (rende chongxin faxian). As Yu Jianzhang, a literary critic, said, the current humanistic tide in literature, from its inception to the development of some of its distinctive artistic characteristics, was produced by "the present era", which made literary creation change so dramatically in such a short period of time. But it was not just in the past few years. Historically, one could also trace back to those "ten years", the "seventeen years", and the sixty years since the May 4th Movement. The forming of the tide, in short, should be regarded as a "product of historical transformation". In the upsurge, many theorists and critics were intoxicated with the humanistic tide and saw in it a Chinese renaissance. They simply could not hold back their optimism and excitement. Yu Jianzhang announced: "The Chinese nation will undergo an era of re-vitalization with this transformation. This era will herald the socialist 'Renaissance' of the Chinese nation in the twentieth century" (see Yu Jianzhang, "On the Trend of Humanism among Contemporary Literary Works: A Review of Literary Creations of the Past Three Years", *WXPL,* 1, 1981, reprinted in *WYLZJ,* pp. 179-203).

While the term "Chinese renaissance" was controversial, many agreed with the thesis that "Humanism is the mainstream in the literature of the first ten years of the new period". Significantly, as director of the Literature Institute of CASS, Liu Zaifu declared his approval. Before several hundred participants (many of them important cultural figures) at the September 1986 "Conference on Chinese Literature in the Ten-Year New Period", where Liu was a major speaker, he mainly discussed this thesis. He said that the course of the development of the "new period literaure" was a replacement of the concept of "taking class struggle as the key link" by socialist humanism. Taking class struggle as the key link meant that everything must be sacrificed for a certain concept and that man was the tool of class struggle, while socialist humanism held that all social activities, including those of class struggle, should have man as their purpose, aiming at man's emancipation. It was through a call for human nature, human feelings, and humanism, for human dignity and human value, that a number of works achieved their moving effect. Thus Liu found an axis—the re-discovery of man—around which the new period literaure developed.

There were three stages: the first stage was characterized by the "scar literature" represented by Liu Xinwu's "Class Teacher"; the second stage was marked by a more conscientious appeal for human dignity and human value; and the third was the stage of the so-called "deepening of humanism". Recently, Liu Zaifu asserted, the ideological trend of humanism had developed even further, with a "modern consciousness compounded of socialist humanism" (shehuizhuyi rendaozhuyide xiandai yishi) presented in a more manifest way. Liu explained as follows:

First, man was viewed as man, that is, as living, genuine man and not as perfect, super man. This led to a series of changes in the description of characters: from monochrome to polychrome; from heroic to ordinary; from legendary heroes to individuals found in day-to-day life; and from tool-like characters to those with their own subjectivity. It also led to a greater internal freedom on the part of writers.

Second, more concern was shown for man as an individual, and more respect given to the value of man's individual subjectivity. That is to say, man was no longer treated merely as an entity rationalized by society and the collective he belonged to, or stipulated by his specific social relations. It was acknowledged in the new period literature that all individuals were equally important, having their own particularities and defiant of any replacement.

Related to respect for man's individuality is respect for man's spirituality. The spiritual world of each and every individual is rich and complicated and absolutely distinct from others. Man's problem is not simply a problem of survival. His success in obtaining a position in the material world does not mean that he has found a home for his spirit. He still may be confronted with perplexity, solitude, and sorrow. This was also acknowledged in the new period literature.

Liu Zaifu eloquently stated that humanism was the main trend in the new period literature. He had to admit, however, that it was at the time still extremely difficult for the concept of humanism to be universally accepted. It was his estimation that the conflict between the concept of socialist humanism and that of "class struggle as the key link" would be the most fundamental cultural collision in the literary arena of the twentieth century, and the conflict would perhaps continue into the twenty-first century (Liu Zaifu, "Lun xinshiqi wenxuede zhuchao"—"On the Mainstream of Literature in the New Period", *WHB*, 8, 10 Sept. and 7 Oct. 1986, reprinted in *XHWZ*, 11:141-49, 1986). See also "rendaozhuyi lunzheng" (humanism debate).

人道主义是一种价值观念
rendaozhuyi shi yi zhong jiazhi guannian
(humanism is a concept of value)

See "rendaozhuyide liang ge hanyi" (two meanings of humanism).

人道主义的两个含义
rendaozhuyide liang ge hanyi

(two meanings of humanism)

The division of the "two meanings of humanism" was devised by Hu Qiaomu in 1983. It was once highly praised by China's ideological officials as a "theoretical breakthrough". Hu's division was: humanism as a world-historical outlook that is fundamentally opposite to Marxism, while humanism as an ethical principle and moral norm that can be accepted when reformed into "socialist humanism" (Hu Qiaomu, "On Problems Concerning Humanism and Alienation").

Many found the division untenable. The following is Wang Ruoshui's refutation:

What humanism must answer, Wang expounds, is not "Which comes first, matter or spirit", but "Whether human value takes precedence". In essence, humanism is a concept of value (rendaozhuyi shi yi zhong jiazhii guannian), and this is included in its interpretation of the world. Its task is to appraise, and not to explain, the history of human society. When Hu Qiaomu discusses humanism as a world-historical outlook, however, he excludes the outlook of value; and when he speaks of ethics and morality as another meaning of humanism, he reduces the outlook of value. No wonder Hu sees little of any kind of humanism in history that can be inherited, for the very kernel and the very value of humanism fall beyond his field of vision. At this point, Wang emphasizes: "Besides a scientific explanation of the world, we also need an appropriate judgment of value concerning the world. Therefore, we need humanism as well as materialism. Both are world outlooks" (Wang Ruoshui, "My View on Problems of Humanism").

Wang then sets out to prove the fallacy of Hu's allegation that humanism as a world outlook is "idealistic". Logically, Wang says, the opposite of humanism is anti-humanism and not materialism, and the opposite of materialism is idealism and not humanism. A humanist, of course, like others, has to answer, conscientiously or not, such a question as "Which comes first, matter or spirit". In order to explain human value and how a man achieves his value, a humanist also has to explain man's position, role, destiny, and future in the world. This, beyond a pure outlook of value, touches upon the question of the origin of the world, thus unavoidably facing the choice between materialism and idealism. The basic principle of humanism, however, is not necessarily related to idealism, neither does it necessarily conflict with materialism. Historical facts show that either before or after the coming into being of Marxism, there was both materialistic humanism as well as idealistic humanism. Furthermore, Wang points out, no one can reach the conclusion that nothing can be inherited from a world-historical outlook that is idealistic and unable to explain the history of human society scientifically. In social outlook, there is a relationship of critical inheritance between Marxism and various kinds of humanism prior to it.

Different from Hu Qiaomu's view that humanism, as a world-historical outlook, explains history in terms of abstract human nature (that is, in Hu's terms, the "historical idealism of bourgeois humanism", or, the "historical idealism of the theory of abstract human nature"), Wang Ruoshui emphasizes that the theory of human nature and humanism, though related to each other, are not the same thing. To explain history in terms of abstract human nature is of course an idealistic conception of history, but it is not necessarily related to humanism. Indeed, humanism needs an ideological foundation, but the foundation can be idealistic or materialistic; it can be an interpretation of history in terms of abstract human nature, or a materialistic or scientific interpretation of history. To Wang Ruoshui, what should be made clear is the basic principle of humanism and its different forms in different periods. No matter how different socialist humanism is from those prior to it, they must have something in common since they are all classified as humanism; that essence is: "Man, the value of man, takes precedence" (Wang Ruoshui, "My View on Problems of Humanism"). See also "rendaozhuyi lunzheng" (humanism debate).

人道主义的马克思主义
rendaozhuyide Makesizhuyi
(humanistic Marxism)

Among the foreign ideological trends introduced to mainland China in the first few years after the end of the GPCR, a great quantity were various explanations of Marxism. Neo-Marxism (xin Makesizhuyi) and Marxology (Makesixue) in the West immediately attracted the attention of ideological-philosophical circles. The following important writers were introduced: Georg Lukács, Antonio Gramci, Kark Jorsch, Leszek Kolakowski, Nicos Poulantzas, Alvin Gouldner, Ralph Miliband, Ernst Bloch, Henry Lefebvre, Rudolf Bahro, David McLellan, Tom Bottomore, Louis Althusser, Robert Tucker, S. Avineri, Lucio Colletti, Enrich Fromm, Pere Jean-Yvez Calvez, Pierre Bigo, Maximilien Rubel, I. M. Bochénski, D. Bell, Heinrich Popitz, István Mészáros, Karl Popper and E. Thier. There were fierce debates about books that formerly had been banned, such as *Critique of Dialectical Reason* (J. P. Sartre), *A Philosophy of Man—Marxism and Existentialism* (Adam Schaff), *Adventures of the Dialectic* (Maurice Merleau-Ponty), *Geschichte des Marxismus* (Predrag Vranicki), *The Marxists* (C. Wright Mills), *Marxism and Humanism* (R. Garaudy), and *Revisionism* (L. Labedz).

This was very natural. Those setbacks, confusions, and tribulations the Chinese people had undergone in the past several decades had all taken place in the name of Marxism. There was a search for the shortcomings in the Marxism that had guided them. And the people could feel a resonance with the writers they read, most of whom recognized that humanism and the concept of alienation occupied an important place in Marxist theory.

Thereafter, also very naturally, there was a wave of humanistic Marxism, with slogans such as "Marxism in development" (fazhanzhongde Makesizhuyi) and "Only by developing Marxism can one uphold it" (Makesizhuyi shouxian bixu fazhan, ranhou cai tandeshang jianchi). From the end of 1979 to the first half of 1983, over five hundred articles were published on the issues of humanism and alienation (according to statistics provided by the Philosophy Institute of CASS and the Chinese People's University in Beijing). Influential articles included: Wang Ruoshui's "On the Concept of 'Alienation'—From Hegel to Marx" ("Guanyu 'yihua'de gainian—cong Heige'er dao Makesi", *Waiguo zhexue yanjiu jikan,* 1:1-34, 1978), Zhu Guangqian's "Problems Concerning Human Nature, Humanism, Human Touch, and a Common Sense of Beauty" ("Guanyu renxing, rendaozhuyi, renqingwei he gongtongmei wenti", *Wenyi yanjiu,* 3, 1979, extracted and reprinted in *XHYB, WZB,* 2:168-70, 1980), Wang Ruoshui's "Discussing the Alienation Question" ("Tantan yihua wenti", *Xinwen zhanxian,* 8:8-11, 1980, reprinted in *WRB*, pp. 186-99; trans. in David A. Kelly, ed. and trans., "Writings on Humanism, Alienation and Philosophy", *Chinese Studies in Philosophy,* vol. xvi, 3:25-38, Spring 1985), Ru Xin's "Is Humanism Just Revisionism?—A Re-understanding of Humanism" ("Rendaozhuyi jiushi xiuzhengzhuyi ma?—dui rendaozhuyide zai renshi", *RMRB,* 15 Aug. 1980) and Zhou Yang's "An Inquiry into Some Theoretical Problems of Marxism" ("Guanyu Makesizhuyide jige lilun wentide tantao", *RMRB*, 16 Mar. 1983).

Discussed repeatedly in these articles, as summed up by Ding Xueliang, a scholar advocating "humanistic Marxism" in the early and mid 1980s, were six major themes: 1. acknowledging a "common human nature" (see "gongtong renxing"—"common human nature") and questioning the long-standing, orthodox view that treated human nature simply as a human being's class character; 2. emphasizing man is the goal and not merely a means and that the essence of humanism is to treat man as man; 3. asserting that the concept of alienation played an important role in the founding of Marxism and that Marx never relinquished the theory and methodology of alienation; 4. acknowledging that alienation still exists in a socialist society and finds expression in political, ideological, and economic fields; 5. confirming that there were many mistakes in socialist practice during the Mao period, which resulted in serious consequences, and that the fundamental reason for this was that people failed to understand that socialism must accept the principle of humanism; and 6. emphasizing that the significance of acknowledging the value of humanism lies not only in criticizing and repudiating the mistakes of the past but more importantly in finding a correct direction for socialist construction today and in the future (Ding Xueliang, "The Influence of Neo-Marxism in Mainland China"—"Xin Makesizhuyi dui Zhongguo daludе yingxiang", in Chen Kuide, ed., *Changes in Contemporary Culture in Mainland China—Zhongguo dalu dangdai wenhua bianqian,* Taipei, Guiguan, 1991, pp. 115-44).

Compared with the humanistic trend in Eastern Europe in the last several decades, the trend in China at that time was not very critical of the CCP authorities. Chinese scholars, obviously, tried cautiously not to negate the old Marx with the young Marx, not to negate Marx's historical materialism and Communist doctrine with his theory of humanism, and not to negate Engels with Marx. They explained that socialist alienation could be overcome with reform of the present institutional structure. They even emphasized that in the Deng Xiaoping period progress had actually been made in overcoming alienation. Nevertheless, the trend was considered intolerable by the Party. A campaign to eliminate the so-called "spiritual pollution"—primarily humanism and the theory of socialist alienation—was launched directly after the 2nd Plenum of the 12th PCC held in October 1983. Finally, in January 1984, Hu Qiaomu, the number one Party ideologue, published an article entitled "On Problems Concerning Humanism and Alienation", in an attempt to refute theoretically the humanistic trend which was becoming stronger and stronger at that time. See also "qingwu yundong" (campaign to eliminate spiritual pollution) and "shehuizhuyi rendaozhuyi" (socialist humanism).

人道主义的文学潮流
rendaozhiyide wenxue chaoliu
(humanistic tide in literature)

See "rendaozhuyi lunzheng" (humanism debate) and "rendaozhuyi shi xinshiqi wenxuede zhuliu" (humanism is the mainstream in the literature of the new period).

人道主义的幽灵
rendaozhuyide youling
(spectre of humanism)

See "rendaozhuyi lunzheng" (humanism debate).

人的本质的还原效应
rende benzhide huanyuan xiaoying
(restoration effect of man's essence)

See "yishu jieshouzhede zhutixing" (subjectivity of art receptor).

人的重新发现
rende chongxin faxian
(re-discovery of man)

The "re-discovery of man", referring to the once "exiled" human nature and humanism being called back by social practice, was a popular term among China's ideological-cultural circles during the humanism discussion of the early 1980s. As He Xilai, a critic who later became a deputy director of the Literature Institute of CASS, explained, after a lengthy period of suppression, all these—human dignity, human value, human rights, human nature, human feelings, and humanism—had almost disappeared from the scope of theoretical research or artistic creation. Then they were rediscovered, forming new tidal current. In his view, the "re-discovery of man" was simply the "first and most important characteristic" of the literary tidal current in the "new period", which gave expression to "the content of the literary transformation and its development" (He Xilai, "Rende chongxin faxian"—"The Re-Discovery of Man", *Hong yan,* 3, 1980). Indeed, as critics agreed, it was because of the "re-discovery of man" that Chinese literature flourished and became popular after the downfall of the Gang of Four.

Full of pride and enthusiasm, Li Yihong, another critic, stated the following in early 1981:

"Issues of human nature and humanism were a forbidden area. However, once the door sealed up by God is opened by Man's practice, a huge energy will be released and rich spiritual deposits will be shining. In all the spheres of social practice, from material life to spiritual life, a fire will erupt, destroying all that is rotten, simultaneously with noises rousing the deaf and awakening the unhearing, so as to celebrate the beginning of a new historical period. This will be a re-discovery of man, a re-discovery under new historical conditions.

The sun of God has set. It is certain that the sun of Man will be rising. It was by Man's power that God's sun was raised, but the rising of Man's sun cannot rely on God. To create a truly magnificent sunrise, we must rely entirely on ourselves" (Li Yihong, "Rende taiyang biran shengqi"—"The Sun of Man Will Certainly Rise", *DS,* 2, 1981).

This statement vividly reveals what China's intellectuals were thinking at the time. See also "rendaozhuyi lunzheng" (humanism debate).

人的非人化
rende feirenhua
(inhumanization of man)

See "rende renhua(humanization of man), "shehuizhuyi tiaojianxia rende yihua" (man's alienation under the condition of socialism), and "rendaozhuyi lunzheng" (humanism debate).

人的价值
rende jiazhi
(human value)

The term "human value" was for a long time taboo in China. In the 1983 campaign to eliminate "spiritual pollution", Hu Qiaomu accused people of "persisting in raising the issue of human value one-sidedly from personal desires" ("On Problems Concerning Humanism and Alienation"). This charge, however, was rejected by many scholars, though not all of them did so openly at that time. One of the bravest to do so was Wang Ruoshui. In his 1985 article "On Revolutionary

Humanism", he points out that, if socialist humanism is genuinely accepted, the affirmation of human value, which is the core or the basic principle of humanism, should be unquestionable. As to why the term "human value" has become so popular in recent years among intellectuals and young people, the crux of the matter at present, Wang says, "is not that excessively high and impracticable demands have been made of socialism, but that many problems of immediate concern to the masses, which were reasonably raised and could have been solved if they had properly been dealt with, have been ignored and forgotten by the bureaucrats. Should those bureaucrats not be criticized for treating 'human value' with indifference? Besides, there are a small number of people who, relying on their special privileges, grab ill-gotten wealth and indulge themselves in creature comforts. They will naturally deny anything like 'human value'...." (Wang Ruoshui, *WRB*, p. 269).

In his long and seemingly exhaustive treatment of socialist humanism, Hu Qiaomu, disappointingly, failed to mention that a socialist society, for its part, should strive to gradually create favorable factors so that everyone can achieve a higher human value and make more contributions to society; nor did he mention the necessity to reform the institutional structure in China in order to do away with various malpractices existing in society. These were all pointed out by Wang Ruoshui. Making use of the fact that the CCP was committed to the policy of reform, Wang stressed that raising the issue of human value or socialist humanism was compatible with the needs of reform, which could well be regarded as a "revolution", inevitably bringing about a change in the concept of value (Wang Ruoshui, *WRB*, p. 273).

In July 1986, Wang Ruoshui published "On the Marxist Philosophy of Man", further developing his idea about human value ("Guanyu Makesizhuyide rende zhexue", *WHB*, 17 and 18 July 1986, reprinted in *WXZTX*, pp. 359-79). In his opinion, it is not enough for one to know the common principle of materialism that "matter comes first". One not only needs to understand the world but also needs to understand man; and the understanding should be carried out not only in the relationship between matter and spirit but also in the relationship between subject and object. What is more, man is the subject that reforms the world as well as the subject that understands it. Asserting that Marx sees the world as man's world, taking nature, society, and man as a whole, Wang emphasizes that the actual world is not only an object but also a subject, a world with man and not one without man.

Wang defended "self-actualization" (ziwo shixian), then a controversial concept held stubbornly by many writers, artists, and scholars. According to Marxism, Wang explained, there are three levels of human needs: to survive, to enjoy, and to develop (which is similar to Maslow's order, though the latter was still regarded by some as heretic at the time). By "develop", Marxism means to demonstrate one's vitality, to tap one's potential and to achieve one's ego. Since Marx focuses not on "matter" but on "man", not on "enjoyment" but on "creation" (which is itself a kind of enjoyment), Wang argued, the basic principle of communism should be "an all-round and free development of man", which is more illustrative of true Communism than the generally propagandized wording—"from each according to his ability; to each according to his needs". The all-round development of man means that man totally and freely exploits his potentialities and achieves self-actualization. It is wrong, therefore, to regard self-actualization as individualism or selfishness (Wang Ruoshui, *WXZTX*, pp. 359-61). See also "rendaozhuyide liang ge hanyi" (two meanings of humanism) and "rendaozhuyi lunzheng" (humanism debate).

人的价值第一
rende jiazhi diyi
(human value takes precedence)

See "rendaozhuyide liang ge hanyi" (two meanings of humanism) and "rende jiazhi" (human value).

人的能动性与受动性
rende nengdongxing yu shoudongxing
(man's activity and passivity)

See "wenxue zhutixing" (subjectivity of literature).

人的人化
rende renhua
(humanization of man)

In the humanism wave of the early 1980s, there was a view that all progressive literature and art, as far as aesthetic essence is concerned, is "humanistic". By truthfully describing human beings and their life, such literature and art succeeds in influencing people's thinking and feelings with artistic images, thus playing a role in helping to complete the process from "inhumanization of man" to "humanization of man". See also "shehuizhuyi tiaojianxia rende yihua" (man's alienation under the condition of socialism) and "rendaozhuyi lunzheng" (humanism debate).

人的异化
rende yihua
(man's alienation)

See "shehuizhuyi tiaojianxia rende yihua" (man's alienation under the condition of socialism) and "rendaozhuyi lunzheng" (humanism debate).

人的因素第一，政治工作第一，思想工作第一，活的思想第一
rende yinsu diyi, zhengzhi gongzuo diyi, sixiang gongzuo diyi, huode sixiang diyi
(first place must be given to man, to political work, to ideological work, and to living ideas)

See "tuchu zhengzhi" (giving prominence to politics).

人的主体性
rende zhutixing
(man's subjectivity)

See "wenxue zhutixing" (subjectivity of literature).

人的主体性的失落
rende zhutixingde shiluo
(loss of man's subjectivity)

See "wenxue zhutixing" (subjectivity of literature) and "wenxue duixiang zhutixing" (subjectivity of the object of literature).

人类灵魂工程师
renlei linghun gongchengshi
(engineers of the human soul)

See "qiangganzi he biganzi" (the gun and the pen) and "wangbuzhaode hudie" (a butterfly difficult to catch).

人类之爱
renlei zhi ai
(human love)

See "renxing lun" (theory of human nature).

人民
renmin
(people)

See "zhengque chuli renmin neibu maodun" (correctly handling contradictions among the people).

人民公社
renmin gongshe
(People's Commune)

At the "Chengdu conference", a CCP Politburo's work conference held in March 1958, Mao proposed a plan to combine the agricultural cooperatives (rural production organizations set up in the early 1950s after the "tugai yundong"—Land Reform Movement). Mao's proposal was adopted. No sooner had the conference been concluded was the plan carried out by enthusiastic cadres in various places. In May, the first People's Commune—the "Chaya People's Commune" was set up in Suiping county, Henan province. On 9 August, after listening to a report made by the Shandong Provincial Party Committee during an inspection tour of the province, Mao confirmed the name as invented by the Henan locals for the new combined organization. He said: "People's Communes are fine. The good point about the People's Commune is that it combines industry, agriculture, commerce, education, and military affairs, and makes the task of leadership much easier" (*RMRB*, 13 Aug. 1958). Then, at the enlarged meeting of the CCP Politburu held at Beidaihe from 17 to 30 August 1958, a resolution concerning the establishment of People's Communes in the countryside was passed. Within two months, over 99 percent of farm households in over 740,000 cooperatives throughout the country were reorganized into 26,000 People's Communes.

As part of Mao's "Three Red Banners" (san mian hongqi) campaign, the People's Communes were set up according to the principles of "large in size and collective in nature" (yi da er gong), "integrating government administration with commune management" (zheng she heyi), and "five positions in one body" (wuwei yiti, that is, a structure which puts agriculture, industry, commerce, education and military affairs together for unified leadership and management). However, after twenty years this practice was proved to be unsuccessful. Mao's idea was never accepted by the majority of China's farmers. Finally, in the winter of 1979, they proclaimed the necessity of liberating productivity from the antiquated organizational system of the People's

Commune. With their demand that land be returned to its owners, abolishing the communes, dividing up the fields, and going at it alone could be seen everywhere. In June 1981, in the "Resolution on Certain Questions in the History of Our Party since the Founding of the PRC", Mao's "Three Red Banners" campaign was considered to be "indiscreet". The 1982 PRC Constitution formally ended the all-comprehensive People's Communes and reestablished township as the basic rural administrative unit. The People's Communes gradually disappeared (12,702 People's Communes were disbanded in 1983, 39,838 in 1984, and the final 249 in 1985). The effort to end the People's Communes, an ambitious pioneering undertaking by Mao, was dubbed, ironically, the "second rural revolution" (di'er ci nongcun geming). What is left to history is a record of the total defeat of a "Kingdom of Great Harmony" (datong wangguo). See also "san mian hongqi" (Three Red Banners).

人民公社好
renmin gongshe hao
(People's Communes are fine)

See "renmin gongshe" (People's Commune).

人民利益高于一切
renmin liyi gaoyu yiqie
(the interests of the people are supreme)

"The interests of the people are supreme" is a popular slogan in the Communist regime. In the trend of the 1990s among China's ideological-cultural circles to reconfirm the value of liberalism (ziyouzhuyi) and individualism, the concept of "the people" was said to have been abused (by those in power), so as to strangle individual interests. If individual interests are denied, scholars argued, the interests of the people will come to nothing. See also "zhengque chuli renmin neibu maodun" (correctly handling contradictions among the people).

人民民主
renmin minzhu
(people's democracy)

See "minzhu jizhongzhi" (democratic centralism).

人民民主独裁
renmin minzhu ducai
(people's democratic dictatorship)

See "wuchanjieji zhuanzheng" (dictatorship of the proletariat).

人民民主统一战线
renmin minzhu tongyi zhanxian
(united front of people's democracy)

See "tongzhan" (united front).

人民民主专政
renmin minzhu zhuanzheng
(people's democratic dictatorship)

See "wuchanjieji zhuanzheng" (dictatorship of the proletariat) and "minzhu jizhongzhi" (democratic centralism).

人民内部矛盾
renmin neibu maodun
(contradictions among the people)

See "zhengque chuli renmin neibu maodun" (correctly handling contradictions among the people).

人民上天，红旗落地
renmin shangtian, hongqi luodi
(the people have risen while the red flag has fallen)

See "hong" (red).

人民是目的
renmin shi mudi
(the people are the goal)

See "ren shi Makesizhuyide chufadian" (man is the starting point of Marxism) and "rendaozhuyi lunzheng" (humanism debate).

人民战争
renmin zhanzheng
(people's war)

The concept of "people's war" was first raised by Mao in his speech "On Coalition Government" ("Lun lianhe zhengfu") delivered at the CCP's 7th National Congress on 24 April 1945 (*SWM*, 3, p. 263). As an important part of Mao Zedong Thought in military affairs, the principle of "people's war" is: to mobilize and rely on the broad masses of the people to wage a war in order to resist class oppression or to achieve national independence. It is waged by combining main military forces with regional military forces, regular armies with guerrilla armies and militias, the armed masses with the unarmed masses. Another key point is to establish bases in the countryside, where the enemy is relatively weak, so that regular and irregular troops, standard war and guerrilla war, armed struggle and other forms of struggle are organized to seize political power in a form of warfare whereby cities are surrounded by the countryside. The central idea of "people's war" is to arm the entire population and turn the entire population into a military force. Its strategy and tactics are: "You fight your battle, I fight mine. Continue to fight if we are sure of victory; retreat if we cannot win" (ni da nide, wo da wode; dadeying jiuda, dabuying jiuzou).

"People's war" was said to be the magic weapon with which the revolutionary peoples would defeat "imperialism and all its lackeys". Mao always maintained this idea. On 29 September 1958, Mao put forth the call: "We must also organize contingents of the people's militia on a big scale" (*RMRB,* 1 Oct. 1958). Thereafter, the task of the Party was to "make everyone a soldier" (quanmin jie bing). With the People's Commune as the unit, the people were organized into the people's militia, grouping workers, peasants, merchants, students, and soldiers together to make everyone a soldier.

On 3 September 1965, Lin Biao raised Mao's idea to a new level in an article published in the *People's Daily* in memory of the twentieth anniversary of the victory of the Chinese Anti-Japanese War. Under the eye-catching title "Long Live the Victory of People's War!" ("Renmin zhanzheng shengli wansui!"), the article explained that today's world revolution also involved "surrounding the cities by the countryside" (nongcun baowei chengshi). What Lin Biao meant by the "countryside" of the world was Asia, Africa, and Latin America, and the "cities" were those developed countries of North America and Europe. He called on all the oppressed nations and peoples to rise up in a united-front struggle against their enemies so as to win victory for world revolution.

After the open split between the CCP and the CPSU in the early 1960s, Beijing began to regard itself as the "center of world revolution", as the spokesman of the oppressed nations in the world (the "third world", as later termed). This was the starting point of Lin's idea about "people's war". In his speech of 20 March 1967 at a meeting attended by cadres including and above the level of army commander, Lin Biao systematically expounded on the theory of the center of world revolution. The ambition of Lin Biao and his colleagues was further revealed in an unpublished speech Lin made before the 1969 9th CCP National Congress when he was at the peak of his power. After analyzing the rise and fall of world civilizations and imperialist countries like Spain, Britain, the United States, and the Soviet Union, Lin Biao predicted that China, as the center of world revolution and armed with Mao Zedong Thought, would become the number one super power with worldwide influence. See also "shijie geming" (world revolution).

人民性和党性的矛盾
renminxing he dangxingde maodun
(contradiction between Party spirit and affinity to the people)

This "heretical" proposition that shocked many CCP leaders was advanced by Hu Jiwei, then editor-in-chief of the *People's Daily*, in a September 1979 speech at the CCP Central Party School. According to CCP doctrine, the Party represents the interests of the people. Therefore, there is a unity between Party spirit (which means the loyalty to the CCP) and affinity to the people (renminxing he dangxingde tongyi). But Hu argued that the Party could make mistakes. And in such a case, the Party should not be said to be great; and a Party member would probably have to face a crucial choice between Party discipline and his responsibility towards the people. A good Party member, Hu said, should listen to his "intuitive knowledge" (liangzhi) and give first place to his responsibility towards the people. Fundamentally, "there will be no Party spirit without affinity to the people" (Meiyou renminxing jiumeiyou dangxing), if the Party truly represents the interests of the people. He suggested that Party members should strengthen their Party spirit by strengthening their affinity to the people.

Hu Jiwei raised this proposition after long consideration of his own experience. Before the Cultural Revolution, he said, he had been very obedient and thus he was often praised by his superiors. As it turned out, however, most of what he had done according to the Party's instructions was wrong. After the Cultural Revolution, Hu no longer followed the Party blindly. Instead, he relied on his own judgment. In many cases, he proved to be right, but he was also often criticized by the Party.

Hu's close colleague Wang Ruoshui (then deputy editor-in-chief of the *People's Daily)* held a similar view. Wang thus raised the following question: as an organizational principle, the rule for democratic centralism stipulates that the minority is subordinate to the majority, lower authorities are subordinate to higher authorities, and the whole Party is subordinate to the Party Center; now to whom should the Party Center be subordinate? (Wang Ruoshui, *Behind Hu Yaobang's Stepdown,* HK, Mingjing, 1997).

人民性和党性的统一
renminxing he dangxingde tongyi
(unity between Party spirit and affinity to the people)

See "renminxing he dangxingde maodun" (contradiction between Party spirit and affinity to the people).

人情
renqing
(human feelings)

See "renxing lun" (theory of human nature).

人权高于主权
renquan gaoyu zhuquan
(human rights are higher than sovereignty)

See "renquan wenti" (human rights issue), "weidu Zhongguo" (containment against China), and "lengzhanhou shidaide xin diguozhuyi" (neo-imperialism in the post-Cold War era).

人权问题
renquan wenti
(human rights issue)

Human rights refer to personal freedoms and other democratic rights. The United Nations drew up its "Universal Declaration on Human Rights" in 1948, which maintains human rights are universal—all human beings have the same aspirations and a right to live in prosperity and happiness, no matter where they live. In June 1993, the United Nations held the World Conference on Human Rights in Vienna; 171 countries (of the UN's 185 member countries), together with 248 non-government organizations, adopted the Vienna Declaration and Program of Action. The Conference emphasized that the "Universal Declaration on Human Rights, which constitutes a common standard of achievement for all people and all nations, is a source of inspiration and has been the basis for the United Nations to make advances in standard-setting". The conference participants also reaffirmed their commitment to fulfill their obligations to promote universal respect for and observance and protection of all human rights and fundamental freedoms.

In Communist doctrine, the struggle for human rights is not included in the basic program of the proletariat. Regarding the extermination of classes and private ownership as its main task, the proletariat claims that its true emancipation will be achieved only by waging a proletarian revolution and founding a proletarian political power, in which private ownership will be exterminated, public ownership set up, and social productivity developed. For a long time during the Chinese Communist regime, the term "human rights" was considered taboo. In the mid-1980s, "human rights" were still regarded as having "a clear class nature" and not being universal. As the record shows, anyone challenging the authorities on the human rights issue would be severely punished.

On 2 November 1991, the Information Office of the PRC State Council promulgated a White Paper under the title "Human Rights in China" ("Zhongguode renquan zhuangkuang"), which consists of ten chapters plus an introduction. For the first time in mainland China, the human rights issue was openly and systematically discussed. This was regarded as progress by the CCP authorities, though the White Paper still conspicuously underlines opposition to all "bourgeois views" on human rights.

Chinese official statements now seem to have affirmed the universal nature of human rights ("pubian renquan" or "renquande pubianxing"), but on occasion the authorities also challenge the universality. They stress "Chinese values" (Zhongguo jiazhiguan), and differences of "guoqing" (national characteristics) and "wenhua" (culture) between China and the West. The 1991 White Paper states: "Owing to tremendous differences in historical background, social system, cultural tradition and economic development, countries differ in their understanding and practice of human rights." Thus the authorities argue that Western standards of human rights do not apply to China.

The 1991 document recalls: "To eat their fill and dress warmly were the fundamental demands of the Chinese people who had long suffered cold and hunger." The Chinese government praises itself, for it has achieved much in meeting these fundamental demands. It declares: "The right to subsistence is the most fundamental human right" (shengcunquan shi zuigenbende renquan). According to its standards, the human rights situation in China is very good, characterized by what it proudly calls "extensiveness" (guangfanxing), "fairness" (gongpingxing), and "authenticity" (zhenshixing), and this is because they are guaranteed by China's social system and law.

However, China critics observe, it is precisely because the present social and legal systems in China are unsound and need to be improved (which has been admitted by the Chinese authorities) that the conclusion provided by the White Paper and other documents is open to suspicion. They further argue that there are human rights problems under the one-party dictatorship in China today, which determines that the Party rights (dang quan) of the CCP are dominant. A number of scholars, at home and abroad, have tried to solve these problems. In 1994, Yan Jiaqi, together with other scholars, presented a document entitled "Human Rights in China: 99 Articles" ("Zhongguo renquan jiushijiutiao") to the 1994 Conference on Human Rights in China (held at the Asia Institute, University of California, Berkeley, U.S., sponsored by the Foundation for China in the 21st Century). In the mainland, it seems that more and more scholars are daring to touch upon this sensitive subject and openly speak out on this issue. For instance, in his January 1998 article "Also Promote Political Reform" ("Yeyao tuidong zhengzhi gaige", *Gaige,* Jan. 1998), Li Shenzhi, former CASS vice-president, asked the authorities to adopt the international standard immediately. These scholars held that the four freedoms—freedoms of speech, of religion, from fear, and from want—should not be separated, and that freedom of speech is the most important human right (yanlun ziyou quan shi zuizhongyaode renquan). They question the apparent trade-off—freedom in exchange for food—and ask whether people must in fact choose between these two miserable states of affairs. The sad truth, they point out, is that an authoritarian regime can practice political repression and starve the poor at the same time (as shown in the studies of Amartya Sen).

The Chinese authorities find it difficult to accept any criticism from dissidents. Even more, they cannot tolerate "imperialists", who, under the pretext of "protecting human rights", interfere in China's internal affairs, support dissidents, and carry out subversive activities. The 1991 White Paper argues that "the human rights issue falls by and large within the sovereignty of each state". This was reiterated in the second White Paper "The Progress of Human Rights in China" issued 1995 and the third White Paper "The 50 Years' Development of Human Rights in China" issued in 2000. The Chinese authorities oppose "some countries' hegemonic acts of using a double standard for the human rights (renquande shuangchong biaozhun) of other countries". The attempt of the West to apply universal standards of human rights to China is considered "disguised cultural imperialism" (weizhuangde wenhua diguozhuyi) and an attempt to obstruct China's development. Beijing condemns the U.S. notion: "Human rights are higher than sovereignty" (Renquan gaoyu zhuquan). It clearly states: "Sovereignty is more important than human rights" (zhuquan chongyu renquan).

In fact, the human rights issue has been a long-standing thorn in Sino-U.S. relations. For instance, when on 30 January 1997 the U.S. State Department released its *Country Report on Human Rights Practices for 1996*, which once again attacked at length China's human rights abuses, the Chinese government responded immediately, waging a tit-for-tat struggle. On 5 March 1997 the *People's Daily* published a lengthy article entitled "A Look at the U.S. Human Rights Record" (Ren Yanshi, "Qingkan Meiguode renquan jilu"). According to this article, the United States today has a very poor human rights record. Its problems include: 1. constitutional protection below international standards; 2. moneybag democracy; 3. a land of terror; 4. poverty, hunger, and homeless issues; 5. deep-rooted racial discrimination; 6. a deplorable state of women and children; and 7. human rights violations against other nations. A recent exchange of attacks occurred after the U.S.-led NATO bombing of the Chinese Embassy in Belgrade on 7 May 1999.

On the whole, the American public is very critical of the Chinese government with respect to the human rights issue. However, there is a current trend that the United States should adopt a mild, or flexible, attitude towards China, one of the reasons being American commercial interests in the vast Chinese market. "Today China's economic power," former President Richard M. Nixon observed in 1994, "makes U.S. lectures about human rights imprudent. Within a decade it will make them irrelevant. Within two decades it will make them laughable" (*Beyond Peace,* NY, Random House, 1994, pp. 127-28). The complexity of the matter can be seen in the Clinton Administration's China policy. On 13 March 1998, after Beijing indicated that it was preparing to sign the United Nation's International Covenant on Civil and Political Rights (it was signed on 5 October 1998), the White House immediately announced that it had withdrawn its support for the annual attack on China since the 1989 Beijing massacre at the United Nations Human Rights Commission in Geneva. This was certainly a reward to China in preparation for President Clinton's scheduled late June visit to Beijing. During his 9-day state visit (from 25 June to 3 July 1998), one of the important achievements was President Clinton's 27 June joint press conference with Chinese President Jiang Zemin, in which the issues of human rights and the Tiananmen Square crackdown were debated. The live broadcast was hailed as a breakthrough in China. Some overconfident observers even predicted that this could be the first step towards improvements in human rights and possibly a reversal of the decision on the June 4th crackdown. They asserted that the change in U.S. attitude marked the beginning of a new period in which the human rights issue was no longer of primary importance in Western dealings with China.

Since China has signed the UN Covenant on Civil and Political Rights, one has reason to hope that the human rights situation in China will gradually improve. One should also expect that for a fairly long period of time, the human rights issue would remain a focus in the Sino-U.S. conflicts. In 2000, for example, the United States resumed its attack on China at the 56th Session of the United Nations Human Rights Commission.

人权的普遍性
renquande pubianxing
(universal nature of human rights)

See "renquan wenti" (human rights issue).

人权的双重标准
renquande shuangchong biaozhun
(double standard for human rights)

See "renquan wenti" (human rights issue).

人人都是批判家
renren doushi pipanjia
(everyone is a critic)

See "dapipan" (mass criticism).

人人为我，我为人人
renren wei wo, wo wei renren
(all for one and one for all)

This was a popular slogan in 1958, the year of the Great Leap Forward, when CCP leaders thought communism was just around the corner. According to a *People's Daily* editorial on 15 March 1958, the slogan indicated "the fundamental relationship between the working class and the whole laboring people" and should be "the creed of the working class". Later, however, Mao found it to be problematic.

人文精神论争
renwen jingshen lunzheng
("humanistic spirit" debate)

The issue of a "crisis of the humanistic spirit in literature" was first raised in 1993 by the Shanghai-based critic Wang Xiaoming and his colleagues, as in their article "Literature and the Crisis of the Humanistic Spirit" (Wang Xiaoming et al., "Kuangyeshangde feixu: wenxue he renwen jingshen weiji", *SHWX*, 6, 1993). An active response appeared in 1994 in a number of magazines and newspapers, such as *Reading (Dushu), the Wenhui Daily, The Orient (Dongfang), and Modernity and Tradition (Xiandai Yu Chuantong).* Criticism of Wang Meng for his support of Wang Shuo's works appeared in the 6th issue in 1994 of *Contending in Literature and Art (Wenyi Zhengming).* A debate on the "humanistic spirit" occurred among China's literary circles.

The debate did somewhat originate from the controversy over Wang Shuo's works, which had already lasted for several years.

Wang Shuo, born in Nanjing in 1958, began publishing works in 1978, two years after graduating from secondary school. In 1988, he shocked China's literary and art circles with his four novelettes—"The Unrestrained Young Men" ("Wanzhu"), "Emerging from the Sea" ("Fuchu haimian"), "Half Is Fire, Half Is Sea Water" (Yiban shi huoyan, yiban shi haishui"), and "Rubber Man" (Xiangpi ren")—all filmed at the same time. His other well-known works include *A Game of Heartbeats (Wande Jiushi Xintiao), Never Take Me as a Human Being (Qianwan Bieba Wo Dang Ren),* and *I Am Your Dad (Wo Shi Ni Baba).* In the few years from 1989 to 1991, Wang Shuo was very popular in China. After 1992, his popularity declined. In 1994, the 36-year-old writer established a film-making company. He said that being a writer for too long robs one of vitality. (Wang Shuo resumed writing in 1999. His works can be found on the Internet under his name.)

The "Wang Shuo phenomenon" was a hot topic in the mid-1990s. On the one hand, in those few years Wang's works enjoyed a large readership, so much so that there was a Wang Shuo craze. No other contemporary writer could compare with him in terms of popularity. On the other hand, however, some writers and critics, to say nothing of those ossified cultural officials, found his works unworthy of praise. Even worse, they derogatorily dubbed them "riffraff literature" (pizi wenxue) because many of his characters were ill-behaved or even anti-social. Wang Shuo was considered to have deconstructed the seriousness of both politics and literature. Some took exception to him also because in his works he ridiculed intellectuals. Zhang Chengzhi, a Huizu writer, Zhang Wei, a writer in Shandong province, and Wang Xiaoming were among those who were very critical of such "riffraff literature". They appealed for the return to a "humanistic spirit" in literature. What they meant by a "humanistic spirit" was the need in one's innermost being for "truth, goodness, and beauty" (zhen shan mei), for an ultimate value (zhongji jiazhi), and unremitting efforts to obtain it (see, for instance, Wang Xiaoming et al., "Literature and the Crisis of the Humanistic Spirit").

Wang Shuo's most enthusiastic defender was Wang Meng. Wang Shuo and his like, Wang Meng asserted, bitterly detested the pseudo-morality and pseudo-sublimity seen in society and in literature. They deliberately resorted to a way (one that might be astonishing but safe) of belittling and even insulting themselves—and literature as well—so as to present the actual state of affairs, something like the situation implied in the fable of the "emperor's new clothes". Wang Meng even doubted whether those who attacked the "riffraff literature" really understood Wang Shuo. He felt that a "humanistic spirit" should be of a pluralistic nature, all-embracing and tolerant (Wang Meng, "Renwen jingshen wenti ougan"—"Accidental Thoughts about the Humanistic Spirit", *Dongfang,* May 1994).

In March and June 1995, Professor Xie Mian and literary critic Hong Zicheng successively chaired two forums of the "Beijing University Critics Weekend", which discussed the "ideal and spirit of literature". Currently, in Xie's opinion, China's writers refused to bear responsibility and they even upheld shallowness and vulgarity. As a result, the eternal value of a humanistic spirit in literature was disappearing. Hong Zicheng further accused "some key figures in the literary arena" (Wang Meng was obviously first among them) of promoting "riffraff culture" (pizi wenhua) in the name of advocating "pluralism".

Wang Meng, writer Chen Jiangong, and critic Li Hui responded in the form of a dialog published successively in three issues of the prestigious magazine *Reading* from June to August 1995. According to their observations, the condemnation of the so-called "riffaff literature" only showed the confusion and impotence of some *literati* before the wave of the market economy. Furthermore, they said, one was upholding a pseudo-humanistic spirit if one disdained the people's desire and effort for a better material life.

It was a natural development that there appeared in 1995 a debate on a "humanistic spirit". After the 1989 June 4th Incident, the so-called "*élite* culture" (jingying wenhua) of the 1980s, as a social phenomenon, had come to an end. Instead, there appeared a flourish of what can be called "popular culture" ("dazhong wenhua" or "tongshu wenhua"). Politically, this occurred at that time as an aftermath to the incident. Quite a number of intellectuals—dubbed "cultural *élite*" who had been very active in the 1980s' "intense search for culture" (wenhua re)—were more or less involved in the "May Tempest" of 1989. Now, in the post-incident criticism and crackdown, they were attacked as the "*élite* of the turmoil" (dongluan jingying). Some were arrested, others were forced to hide or flee abroad, and others stopped writing.

Another reason, perhaps more fundamental, can be found in the changes in the economic system. After the policies of reform and open door had been carried out for ten years, the original strict and devastating planned economy was step-by-step giving way to a vigorous and fruitful market economy. Multiple economic sectors came into being. There also appeared a multiplicity of culture, as it was required by the multiplicity of economic sectors. As one can see, the old Chinese civilization was being pounded away by many new things emerging with the promotion of the market economy, such as a commodity economy, a marketing consciousness, and the trend of "jumping into the sea of business". A subtle but profound change was taking place in the people's way of thinking, in their sense of value, and in economic, cultural, and social life at large. Against this background there did appear some negative phenomena, to which intellectuals expressed their opposition. To appeal for a humanistic spirit was of course correct and relevant. However, they needed to support the current social reform. In fact, the wave was irresistible. What was ironic was that in the autumn of 1995 there were two bestsellers in Beijing—one was Zhang Chengzhi's *Unassisted Thought (Wuyuande Sixiang,* Beijing, Huayi, 1995), and the other was Zhang Wei's *A Worried and Indignant Return Journey (Youfende Guitu,* Beijing, Huayi, 1995)—the two books, as part of the "resistance against surrender" series, severely attacked "commercial culture" (shangye wenhua) and Wang Shuo's works, but both became popular commodities themselves.

Outside China, some scholars were also involved in the discussion. In Li Zehou's opinion, Wang Shuo's fiction, which was part of popular culture, posited a great force of deconstruction (jiegou) upon the ossified ideology. An intellectual should not look down upon this kind of popular culture in inferior contrast to the "*élite* culture" *(Farewell to Revolution: Looking Back upon China of the Twentieth Century,* p. 61). But he also asked: What is to be done after "deconstruction"? (ibid., p. 241). Liu Zaifu shared Li's opinion. He said that there was something missing in Wang Shuo's works, that is, the necessary "humanistic solicitude" (renwen guanhuai) (ibid.). On another occasion, Liu more specifically expressed his concern. According to him, Wang Shuo's riffraff literature aims at deconstructing ideological dogmas, and the fiction of Yu Hua and Su Tong aims at deconstructing history and Man. While deconstructing outmoded ideology, their works, dubbed "neo-fiction" (xinxiaoshuo) or "vanguard fiction" (xianfeng xiaoshuo) or "experimental fiction" (shiyan xiaoshuo), have also deconstructed those universal ethical principles which hold a society together. Anything of significance has been deconstructed. The humanistic principle has thus become a target for mockery. This is very dangerous. See also "wenhua re" (culture craze), "jingji duoyanghua xuyao wenhua duoyanghua" (the multiplicity of economic sectors requires the multiplicity of culture), "jingshang re" (business fever), and "jingji gaige" (economic reform).

人物性格的二重组合
renwu xinggede erchong zuhe
(dual combination in characterization)

See "erchong zuhe yuanli" (principle of the dual combination in characterization).

人性复归的记录
renxing fuguide jilu
(record of the resuscitation of human nature)

See "ershishiji bashiniandai zichanjieji rendaozhuyi xuanyan" (the declaration of bourgeois humanism in the 1980s) and "rendaozhuyi lunzheng" (humanism debate).

人性论
renxing lun
(theory of human nature)

In modern and contemporary Chinese literary criticism, not only is the term "bourgeois humanism" often employed, but also the term "theory of human nature". Whenever a massive criticism of humanism was carried out, it was the "theory of human nature" that bore the brunt, since it was considered to be the core of "bourgeois humanism". Chinese writers and artists never forgot the warning: The demand that literature and art should express human feelings and human nature reveals a bourgeois view of literature and art, a reactionary ideology with which the bourgeoisie on the literary front opposes proletarian revolutionary literature and the Marxist theory of class literature and art in the era of the proletarian revolution.

One can list three major campaigns of this type from the founding of the PRC to the end of the GPCR. The first took place from 1957 to 1960, during which time a number of articles were criticized, such as "On Human Feelings" by Ba Ren, "On Human Feelings and Human Nature" by Wang Shuming ("Lun renqing yu renxing", *Xin gang,* 7:49-57, 1957), and "On 'Literature Is a Study of Man'" by Qian Gurong ("Lun 'wenxue shi renxue'", *Wenyi yuebao,* 5, 1957; trans. in Nieh Hualing, ed., *Literature of the Hundred Flowers,* v. 1, pp. 181-98). Literary works subject to attack included Yang Lüfang's spoken drama *The Cuckoo Sings Again* ("Buguniao you jiaole", *Juben,* 1, 1957; trans. in Edward M. Gunn, ed., *Twentieth-Century Chinese Drama: An Anthology*, pp. 277-323) and short stories "Love" by Li Weilun ("Aiqing", *RMWX,* 9, 1956), "On the Precipice" ("Zai xuanya shang") by Deng Youmei and "Red Beans" by Zong Pu ("Hongdou", *RMWX,* 7, 1957, reprinted in *Duanpian xiaoshuoxuan, 1949-1979, 3*, Beijing, Renmin Wenxue, 1979, pp. 98-130; trans. in W. J. E. Jenner, ed., *Fragrant Weeds*, pp. 195-228). The second lasted from 1964 to 1966, when a great number of works were reproached. The list of disgraced films included: *Early Spring (Zaochun Eryue*, Xie Tieli, Beijing Film Studio, 1964), *Two Actresses (Wutai Jiemei,* Xie Jin et al., Tianma Film Studio, 1965), *A Nightless City (Bu Ye Cheng*, Tang Xiaodan and Ke Ling, Jiangnan Film Studio, 1957), *Lin Family Shop* (*Linjia Puzi,* Xia Yan, Beijing Film Studio, 1959), *Story of a Village* (*Bei Guo Jiang Nan,* Yang Hansheng, Haiyan Film Studio, 1963), *City Under Siege (Binglinchengxia)* and *Red Sun* (*Hong Ri,* Qu Baiyin, Tianma Film

Studio, 1963). Disgraced works in other genres included the novels Morning in *Shanghai (Shanghaide Zaocheng)* by Zhou Erfu, *Three-Family Lane* (*San Jia Xiang,* Zuojia, 1961), and *Bitter Struggles (Ku Dou,* Zuojia, 1963) both by Ouyang Shan; the short stories "Snow in March" by Xiao Ping ("Sanyue xue", in *Sanyue xue,* Zuojia, 1958, also in *Duanpian xiaoshuo xuan 1949-1979, 2,* pp. 394-428), and "Party Fee" by Wang Yuanjian ("Dang fei", in *Dang fei,* Gongren, 1956, also in *Duanpian xiaoshuo xuan 1949-1979, 2,* pp. 34-44), and theatrical works *Hai Rui Dismissed from Office (Hai Rui Baguan)* by Wu Han, *Xie Yaohuan* by Tian Han *(Xie Yaohuan, Juben,* 7-8, 1961) and *Li Huiniang* by Meng Chao *(Li Huiniang, Juben,* 7-8, 1961). Then the third massive criticism took place in 1971. Newspapers and other publications throughout the country, almost without exception, carried articles one after another, repeating the allegation that the "theory of human nature" was the theoretical basis of the "revisionist line" in "the seventeen years" prior to the GPCR. Not only were many individuals who had not been criticized before now criticized, but those who had already been attacked were attacked again. A number of issues were involved, with the following as the four major focuses: 1. "bourgeois universal love and human touch"; 2. "the bourgeois individualistic view of happiness"; 3. "class compromise"; and 4. "pacifism".

Take the attack on Ba Ren's idea about "renqing" (human feelings, human sympathy, sensibilities) or "renqingwei" (human touch, human interest) as concrete manifestations of human nature. At the end of 1956, because, as Ba Ren himself said, he thought there was "too much politics and too little human feelings" in Chinese films and other literary genres, and also because he was so inspired by the Double Hundred policy which had just been proposed by Mao, he wrote his essay "On Human Feelings" ("Lun renqing", *Xin gang,* 1, 1957; trans. in Nieh Hualing, ed., *Literature of the Hundred Flowers,* v. 1, pp. 199-203). It was the first fairly profound exposition of the problem of human nature in Chinese academic circles. Unfortunately, not long after its publication, it was fiercely attacked. Yao Wenyuan, then a young Shanghai critic, charged that Ba's theory showed "no difference from the revisionist theory advertised by international modern revisionists in the service of the interests of imperialism". He went so far as to accuse Ba Ren of being a "revisionist" and a "class enemy", with a purpose of "serving the political aim of the bourgeoisie against socialism" (Yao Wenyuan, "Pipan Ba Ren de 'renxing lun'"—"A Criticism of Ba Ren's 'Human Nature Theory'", *WYB,* 2:39, 1960). After being cruelly persecuted for a long time, Ba Ren, a diplomat-turned-literary-theorist who was dedicated to a more humane literature in China, lost his mind and died miserably in July 1972. Ba Ren's case ended tragically.

In the early 1980s, with humanism, or, more correctly, the revitalization of humanism, being the main trend among China's literary-ideological circles, the so-called "theory of human nature" was rehabilitated. In fact, along with the restoration of realism in literary creation at that time, alienation and the resuscitation of human nature became basic themes in literature. A number of writers, with courage and insight, subtly delineated various forces of alienation emerging in the "socialist" period, especially during the GPCR. Three kinds of alienation of human nature were most written about: human beings persecuted as "niuguisheshen" (that is, class enemies of all descriptions who became "contemptible wretches" under the dictatorship of the proletariat), human beings degenerating into "beasts" (such as those Red Guards who cruelly persecuted their victims), and Mao worshipped as "god" in the "modern superstition" movement.

In the eyes of alienation critics, it was because their works presented or exposed alienation under socialist conditions that they were highly praised. Since these critics regarded human history as that of human nature subjected to constant alienation and resuscitation, the two most basic forms in the development of human nature, they believed to describe man in literature meant to present alienation and the resuscitation of human nature in the very complexity of social life. They asserted that the revelation of the phenomenon of alienation had brought a "profundity" to literarture reflecting social life and that the theme of man had thereby begun to be endowed with a "rational color". Fully convinced of their literary stand, alienation critics tried to provide contemporary Chinese literature with a historical duty. It seemed to them that literary creation, while continuously guarding against and overcoming its self-alienation, should give expression to human nature alienation (occurring both in the past and in present-day life), and to human nature resuscitation in its struggle to overcome alienation. It should furthermore probe the causes of alienation and determine a possible and practical way for human nature to be resuscitated in a given historical period, so as to push people, in their real life, forward constantly from the alienation of human nature to its resuscitation. See also "rendaozhuyi lunzheng" (humanism debate) and "gongtong renxing" (common human nature).

人性异化和复归
renxing yihua he fugui
(alienation and resuscitation of human nature)

See "renxing lun" (theory of human nature) and "rendaozhuyi lunzheng" (humanism debate).

人治
renzhi
(rule by individuals)

See "yi fa zhi guo" (ruling the nation by law).

人质政治
renzhi zhengzhi
(hostage politik)

See "chi butong zhengjianzhe" (dissidents).

融入国际大循环
rongru guoji daxunhuan
(merging into international circles)

See "minzuzhuyi" (nationalism) and "quanqiuhua" (globalization).

儒道释文化小说
ru dao shi wenhua xiaoshuo
(fiction of Confucian, Taoist and Buddhist cultures)

See "xungen re" (intense search for "roots").

儒法斗争
ru fa douzheng

(struggle between the Confucian and Legalist schools)

The Confucian and the Legalist schools first appeared in the Spring and Autumn and Warring States Period (770-221 B.C.). From then on, during every dynasty, there were debates about which of the two schools of thought should be adopted as the guiding thought to rule the country. Mao Zedong considered himself of the Legalist school, comparing himself to Ying Zheng, the first emperor of the Qin dynasty, during whose reign the first large-scale suppression of intellectuals—the "burning books and burying scholars alive" events (fen shu keng ru)—took place (the burning of the books took place in 213 B.C., and in the next year some 460 scholars were buried alive).

After Mao's appointed successor Lin Biao was killed on 13 September 1971, following an unsuccessful coup d'état in which Lin had attempted to kill Mao, Mao said that Lin Biao, like the KMT, had respected Confucianism and opposed Legalism and that the struggle between Mao and Lin was one between the Confucian and the Legalist schools. A campaign to criticize the combined target of Lin Biao and Confucius (pi Lin pi Kong) was launched, involving an "appraisal of the Legalists and criticism of the Confucianists" (ping fa pi ru). With help from Jiang Qing and her colleagues, a theory that regarded the whole of Chinese history in the main as a history of a "struggle between the Confucian and Legalist schools" became popular. In light of this theory, which was hardly considered tenable from an academic point of view, Liu Dajie (1904-1977), a Shanghai professor of Chinese literature, rewrote the entire history of Chinese literature in the new edition of his book *History of the Development of Chinese Literature*, which was published in Shanghai in 1976. See also "pi Lin pi Kong yundong" (campaign to criticize Lin Biao and Confucius).

儒家文化圈
rujia wenhua quan
(Confucian cultural ring)

See "ruxue disanqi" (Confucianism in its third stage of development).

儒家自由主义
rujia ziyouzhuyi
(Confucian liberalism)

See "quanqiuhua" (globalization), "ziyouzhuyi" (liberalism), and "ruxue disanqi" (Confucianism in its third stage of development).

儒家化的马克思主义
rujiahuade Makesizhuyi
(Confucianized Marxism)

See "fan chuantong" (anti-tradition) and "sixiang gaizao" (ideological remolding).

儒学第三期
ruxue disanqi
(Confucianism in its third stage of development)

Those making efforts for a new development of Confucianism in modern times are called "neo-Confucianists" (xin rujia). They were quite active more than half a century ago, such as He Lin, Liang Shuming, Xiong Shili, Feng Youlan, and Zhang Junmai. Liang Shuming asserted that the revival of Confucian culture was the destiny of the world as well as China in his book *Eastern and Western Cultures and Their Philosophies (Dong Xi Wenhua Jiqi Zhexue).* According to He Ling, Confucianism was the national philosophy (minzu zhexue); the revival of Confucianism meant national revival. In the 1950s, though Confucian study was suppressed in mainland China, it was continued in Taiwan, Hong Kong, and some places overseas, by scholars like Qian Mu, Tang Junyi, Xu Fuguan, Fang Dongmei, and Mou Zongsan, and then Liu Shuxian and Du Weiming. An important event in 1958 was the publication of "A Manifesto to the World on Chinese Culture" ("Wei Zhongguo wenhua jinggao shijie renshi xuanyan") by Mou Zongsan, Tang Junyi, Xu Fuguan, and Zhang Junmai.

After the implementation of the CCP's new policy of reform and the open door following the 1978 3rd Plenum of the 11th PCC, Confucian scholars, given the favorable environment, began to discuss how Confucianism could be revived. Advocates included Tang Yijie, Chen Lai (both of Beijing University), and Jiang Qing (Shenzhen Administration Institute). These scholars were convinced that Confucian culture is valuable, and possesses great vitality. This was confirmed by the economic successes of the East Asian areas, in Japan, and in Asia's so-called "four little dragons" (Singapore, Taiwan, Hong Kong, and South Korea), which can be regarded as a "Confucian cultural ring" (rujia wenhua quan). As an open system, they asserted, Confucian culture could be creatively transformed into a new modern culture. CCP authorities also joined in promoting study of Confucianism, expecting it to help reinforce the guiding thought of Marxism-Leninism-Mao Zedong Thought.

What neo-Confucianists advocate is called "xin ruxue" (neo-Confucianism). But this term can be confusing, which was first used by Feng Youlan to refer to "Song Ming lixue"—the Confucian philosophy of the Song and Ming dynasties (see Feng Youlan, "Why China Has No Science", *The International Journal of Ethics,* No. 32, 1922, pp. 237-63). The term "post-Confucianism" (hou ruxue), first used by Sinologists in the West in the early 1980s, may be more accurate than "neo-Confucianism". These Sinologists increasingly appreciated the value of Confucianism (a contrast to Joseph R. Levenson's declaration at the end of 1960 that Confucianism would be found only in museum). In his article "The Post-Confucian Challenge" *(The Economist,* 9 Feb. 1980), Roderick MacFarquhar opined that, as shown by the fact that Japan, South Korea, Singapore, Hong Kong, and Taiwan were all able to realize their economic takeoff because they shared the long cultural tradition of Confucianism, the role of Confucianism in the economic development in East Asia is not less important than that of Christianity in the capitalist development of the West. Responding to the post-industrial era in the West, he said, a post-Confucian era would emerge in the East. He even predicted that post-Confucianism would one day in the future regain its prominent position in world civilization.

Similar to "post-Confucianism" is the term "Confucianism in its third stage of development". This concept has been raised on the grounds that present-day Confucianism implies a new stage of Confucian development with a global significance. As to its previous stages, some regard Confucianism before the Qin dynasty and during the two Han dynasties, represented by Confucius and Mencius, as its first stage of development. The second stage refers to the Confucianism during the Song, Yuan, Ming and Qing dynasties, as represented by Zhu Xi and Wang Yangming. More broadly, many agree that the establishment of Confucianism as the mainstream of Chinese culture marks its first stage of development, and its next stage is marked by its spread over China and its absorption into the spiritual civilization of East Asia.

Harvard Professor Du Weiming has much confidence in a "third-stage Confucianism", as can be seen in his 1986 article entitled "The Perspectives of Confucianism in Its Third Stage of Development" ("Ruxue disanqi fazhande qianjing wenti", *Mingbao yuekan*, Mar. 1986). Of course, he said, whether it will come into being is yet to be decided by whether Confucian thinkers in various places will be able to solve the problems brought on by Western modernization and whether they will be able to present some unique ideas to help human beings extricate themselves from their current woeful predicaments. However, some other scholars took exception to Du's suggestion. They questioned the imagined global application of "Confucianism in its third stage of development". They argued that if anything can solve global problems, it may not be Confucianism but something else which can be more easily accepted and applied globally. It was irrelevant, they said, to talk about Chinese culture apart from world culture, just as one could not discuss Chinese politics without the background of international relations. Du Weiming was obviously opposed to talking about Chinese culture as counterposed to other cultures, but they still felt concern about the possible harmful consequences caused by advocacy of a "third-stage Confucianism". For example, they said, people, such as Professor Huntington of Harvard University, were spreading the theory of a clash between Eastern and Western civilizations (dong xi wenming chongtu lun). What's more, these scholars worried about using Confucianism for political purposes. They denounced what they called "political Confucianism" (zhengzhi rujia), with the theory of "Asian values" (Yazhou jiazhi lun) as its core. See also "wenhua Zhongguo" (cultural China), "dong xi wenming chongtu lun" (theory of the clash between the Eastern and the Western civilizations), and "quanqiuhua" (globalization).

入党作官论
ru dang zuo guan lun
(theory of "entering the Party in order to be an official")

See "hei liu lun" (six sinister theories).

软着陆
ruan zhuolu
(soft landing)

See "jingji shahuang" (economic "Tsar") and "jingji gaige" (economic reform).

三次思想解放运动
san ci sixiang jiefang yundong
(three thought-emancipation movements)

See "jiefang sixiang" (emancipating the mind).

三大差别
san da chabie
(three major distinctions)

This refers to the distinctions between workers and peasants, between cities and the countryside, and between manual and mental labor, a reality in today's China. In the discussion of alienation in the early 1980s, it was asserted that, besides other factors, the three major distinctions were also causing alienation under the condition of socialism. See also "zichanjieji faquan" (bourgeois rights).

三大法宝
san da fabao
(three magic weapons)

With the May 4th Movement of 1919 came the spread of Marxism in China. On 1 July 1921, the CCP was founded in Shanghai, and in less than three decades it seized political power on the mainland. According to Mao, it was the "three magic weapons", namely, the united front, armed struggle, and Party building, that enabled the CCP to defeat its enemy in what is called the "new democratic revolution". As early as 1939, in his "Foreword" (written on 4 October 1939) to *The Communist,* a PCC organization magazine, Mao suggested the "three magic weapons" for victory over the enemy. As to the interrelationship among the three, he wrote: "The united front and armed struggle are the two fundamental weapons for defeating the enemy. The united front is intended to carry out armed struggle, and the Party is the heroic warrior that, grasping the two weapons of the united front and armed struggle, charges and shatters enemy positions." The strategy of the "three magic weapons" can be summed up in one sentence: To mobilize the broad masses to the best of the Party's ability in order to attack their enemy in as concentrated and effective a manner as possible.

三大改造
san da gaizao
(three great transformations)

See "guodu shiqi zongluxian" (general line for the transitional period).

三大革命运动
san da geming yundong
(three great revolutionary movements)

On 9 May 1963, in a note on a document, which was entitled "The Seven Well-Written Documents of Zhejiang province Concerning Cadres' Participation in Physical Labor", Mao wrote: "Class struggle, the struggle for production, and scientific experimentation are the three great revolutionary movements to build a powerful socialist country. These movements are a sure guarantee that Communists will be free from bureaucracy and immune from revisionism and dogmatism, and will forever remain invincible. They are a reliable guarantee that the proletariat will be able to unite with the broad working masses and realize a democratic dictatorship. If, in the absence of these movements, the landlords, rich peasants, counter-revolutionaries, bad elements, and monsters were all allowed to crawl out, while our cadres were to shut their eyes to all this and in many cases fail even to differentiate between the enemy and ourselves but were to collaborate with the enemy and were corrupted, divided, and demoralized by him, if our cadres were thus pulled out or the enemy were able to sneak in, and if many of our workers, peasants, and intellectuals were left defenseless against both the soft and the hard tactics of the enemy, then it would not take long, perhaps only several years or a decade, or several decades at most, before a counter-revolutionary restoration on a national scale inevitably would occur, the Marxist-Leninist party would undoubtedly become a revisionist party or a fascist party, and the whole of China would change its color."

In 1964, Mao's above statement was written into the last of the "nine critiques": "On Khrushchev's Phoney Communism and Its Historical Lessons for the World" ("Guanyu Heluxiaofude jia gongchanzhuyi jiqi zai shijie lishishangde jiaoxun", *RMRB*, 14 July 1964). At the time, a fierce polemic was going on between the CCP and the CPSU (Zhong Su dalunzhan).

Mao's "three movements" thesis were said to be a remedy for the shortcoming of Marxism which only recognized class struggle as the motive force for the development of society—class struggle waged by slaves against slave owners, by peasants against feudal lords, and by workers against capitalists. Of course, Mao would never treat the three movements on an equal footing; the above-quoted statement is in fact mainly a warning about how complicated and grim class struggle will be. This is why it was written into the "ninth critique"—Khrushchev was considered to have betrayed Marxist doctrine about class struggle and proletarian dictatorship. Some years later, Mao simply asserted: "Class struggle is the key link, and everything else hinges on it" (Jieji douzheng shi gang, qiyu doushi mu). See also "xiuzhengzhuyi" (revisionism) and "anding tuanjie" (stability and unity).

三大纪律，八项注意
san da jilü, ba xiang zhuyi
(Three Main Rules of Discipline and Eight Points for Attention)

These were first drawn up by Mao Zedong and other leaders for the Chinese Workers' and Peasants' Red Army during the Second Revolutionary Civil War (1927-37). They varied slightly in content at different times and in different army units. In October 1944, the General Headquarters of the Chinese People's Liberation Army issued a standard version as follows:

The Three Main Rules of Discipline are: 1. Obey orders in all your actions; 2. Do not take a single needle or piece of thread from the masses; 3. Turn in everything captured.

The Eight Points for Attention are: 1. Speak politely; 2. Pay fairly for what you buy; 3. Return everything you borrow; 4. Pay for anything you damage; 5. Do not hit or swear at people; 6. Do not damage crops; 7. Do not take liberties with women; 8. Do not ill-treat captives.

三大作风
san da zuofeng
(three important styles of work)

In his political report, "On Coalition Government" ("Lun lianhe zhengfu"), delivered on 24 April 1945 at the 7th National Congress of the CCP, Mao said that his Party, armed with the ideological weapon of Marxism-Leninism, had formed three important styles of work—integrating theory with practice, forging close links with the masses, and practising self-criticism.

三个保卫
san ge baowei

(three defenses)

See "menglongshi lilunde san ci jueqi" ("three rises" in the theory of misty poetry).

三个不变
san ge bubian
("three no-changes" policy)

See "jingji tequ" (special economic zone).

三个不提
san ge buti
(three "don't mentions")

See "xiuzhengzhuyi" (revisionism).

三个代表
san ge daibiao
(three represents)

See "dangde lingdao" (Party leadership).

三个反思
san ge fansi
(three reflections)

See "fansi" (reflection).

三个坚持
san ge jianchi
(three upholds)

After Jiang Zemin's 29 May 1997 speech at the Central Party School, the phrase "three upholds" frequently appeared in China's official media. The "three upholds" are: upholding the basic line in the primary stage of socialism, upholding economic construction as the center of all Party work, and upholding the principle of the "three favorables".

It is said that great achievements had been made since the Party leadership adhered to the "three upholds". In welcoming the 15th National Congress of the CCP held in Beijing in September 1997, there was a nationwide propaganda upsurge about the "three upholds". See also "shehuizhuyi chuji jieduan lun" (theory of the primary stage of socialism), "zhengzhi gaige" (political reform), and "jingji gaige" (economic reform).

三个面向
san ge mianxiang
(three orientations)

See "dangde jiaoyu fangzhen" (the Party's educational policy).

三个世界论
san ge shijie lun
("three worlds" theory)

On 22 February 1974, when meeting President Kaunda of Zambia, Mao put forward his view on differentiating the three worlds. That was his well-known theory of "three worlds". The "first world", in his opinion, consisted of the two superpowers, the United States and the Soviet Union, which had the strongest military and economic power and practiced hegemonism in the world. The "third world" referred to the developing countries in Asia, Africa, Latin America, and other regions. And the developed countries between the first and third worlds belonged to the "second world". China considered itself to be part of the "third world". In unfolding its campaign for an international united front, China energetically targeted members of the "third world" to be its partners. In fact, it often acted as the spokesman for the "third world".

By the mid-1980s, the Chinese authorities found the "three worlds" theory outdated and at odds with the current situation in the world. In his speech before the U.S. Foreign Relations Committee on 20 September 1988, Qian Qichen (b. 1928), then China's foreign minister, suggested that the world was heading towards "multipolarity" (duojihua). According to the theory of "multipolarity", there were at least five polars in the world: the United States, Japan, Europe, the Soviet Union and China. By mid-1997, a new theory was devised, as revealed in "The 1996-97 International Situation: Analysis Report" ("1996-97 nian guoji xingshi fenxi baogao"), a authoritative paper released by the China Strategy and Management Society in Beijing. It asserted that the pattern of "multipolarity" in the post-Cold War era revealed itself in one superpower (the U.S.) plus a number of powers. This pattern, it predicted, will remain unchanged for 30 to 40 years, similar to the duration of the "two poles pattern" (liangji geju) during the Cold War period. But some scholars think otherwise. According to them, the "two poles pattern" will be seen again during the first several decades of the twenty-first century. This time international struggles will unfold chiefly between China and the United States. See also "lengzhanhou shidaide xin diguozhuyi" (neo-imperialism in the post-Cold War era) and "weidu Zhongguo" (containment against China).

三个统一
san ge tongyi
(three-unities)

This refers to "the unity of politics and art, the unity of content and form, and the unity of revolutionary political content and the highest possible perfection of artistic form". Mao demanded that China's writers and artists aim to achieve the "three-unities" in their works. See "zhengzhi biaozhun diyi, yishu biaozhun di'er" (political criteria first, artistic criteria second).

三个有利于
san ge youliyu
(three favorables)

The criterion of the "three favorables", raised by Deng Xiaoping during his "Southern tour" in early 1992, was dubbed the new "cat" theory (xin mao lun). See "Deng Xiaoping lilun" (Deng Xiaoping Theory).

三面红旗
san mian hongqi
(Three Red Banners)

The disastrous 1958 "Three Red Banners" were the "Great Leap Forward", the "People's Commune", and the "General Line for Socialist Construction", which were hailed during the Mao period as a great victory for Mao Zedong Thought. In the 1959-60 anti-Right-deviation campaign directly after the 1959 "Lushan Conference", at which Peng Dehuai, then a Politburo member and minister of national defense, was disgraced, anyone who did not support the "three red banners" was attacked.

In the "Resolution on Certain Questions in the History of Our Party since the Founding of the PRC", adopted on 27 June 1981 by the 6th Plenum of the 11th PCC, Mao's "Three Red Banners" campaign was considered to be "indiscreet". See also "dayuejin" (Great Leap Forward), "renmin gongshe" (People's Commune), and "shehuizhuyi jianshe zongluxian" (General Line for Socialist Construction).

三条识别党内走资派的根本标准
san tiao shibie dangnei zouzipaide genben biaozhun
(three fundamental criteria for identifying capitalist-roaders within the Party)

After his "October 6th coup" of 1976, Hua Guofeng, CCP chairman, still adhered to the struggle against "capitalist-roaders". He stipulated the "three do's and three don'ts" (sanyao sanbuyao)—(1) practice Marxism-Leninism and not revisionism; (2) unite and don't split; (3) be open and aboveboard and don't become involved in intrigues and conspiracies—as the three "fundamental criteria for identifying capitalist-roaders within the Party". The "three do's and three don'ts" were formulated by Mao in his talks with leading cadres of various localities during his inspection tour to South China between 14 August and 12 September 1971. At that time they were directed against the conspiratorial activities of Lin Biao and his followers.

三株大毒草
san zhu daducao
(three big poisonous weeds)

See "pi Deng, fanji youqing fan'anfeng" (campaign to criticize Deng Xiaoping and counter the Right deviationist trend to reverse correct verdicts).

三座大山
san zuo dashan
(three big mountains)

In their struggle to seize power, the CCP declared that its goal was to liberate the Chinese people from the oppression of the "three big mountains"—a metaphor for imperialism, feudalism, and bureaucrat-capitalism.

In 1987 Peng Zhen, a Party elder, used the term in the campaign against "bourgeois liberalization". When receiving about fifty "veteran literary and art fighters of the Yan'an period", he made a reference to the "three big mountains", as if those then alleged to be "engaging in bourgeois liberalization" would bring the Chinese people back to those miserable days when they were oppressed by imperialism, feudalism, and bureaucrat-capitalism.

三八作风
san-ba zuofeng
("three-eight" work style)

In the early 1960s, people of all walks of life were asked to learn from the PLA, and a movement of the "three-eight" work style was launched throughout the country. See "tuchu zhengzhi" (giving prominence to politics).

三不政策
sanbu zhengce
("three don'ts" policy)

China's writers and artists ironically described their rude treatment by Party's cultural officials as "wuzi dengke" ("five 'honorable' treatments"). The "five 'honorable' treatments" are: "entrapping" (she taozi), "seizing upon trivial mistakes" (jiu bianzi), "investigating one's past" (jie dizi), "labeling" (dai maozi), and "bludgeoning" (da gunzi). Since in Chinese each of the five phrases contains the character "zi", they have come to be known as the "wuzi". But originally, "wuzi dengke" means that all five children (wuzi) have honorably passed the imperial examination (dengke).

In order to reduce the worry of writers and artists, the Party formulated a "three don'ts" policy—which are: "not to capitalize on people's vulnerable points, not to stick on ideological or political labels, and not to adopt organizational measures" (bu jiu bianzi, bu dai maozi, bu da gunzi). When necessary, CCP leaders would promise to carry out the "three don'ts" policy. For instance, in his 1961 "Talk at the Forum on the Party's Work in Literature and Art and the Conference on the Creation of Feature Films", Premier Zhou Enlai said when speaking of those "Left" critics: "They set a frame (ding kuangkuang) and restrict everything to remain within it. If what others say or do doesn't fit the frame, they will attach labels, such as 'human nature theory', 'human love', and 'undue leniency'. They first capitalize on people's vulnerable points, then stick on ideological or political labels, and finally adopt organizational measures. But all this is done according to a subjective frame, to a definition that is erroneous and violates Marxism-Leninism. People thus labeled also have to analyze their ideological roots" (Zhou Enlai, "Zai wenyi gongzuo zuotanhui he gushipian chuangzuo huiyishangde jianghua", *HQ,* 3:4, 1979). The late premier agreed with writers and artists that there was "a sort of pressure", under which people had "misgivings", and he promised that this should not be allowed to continue. The message contained in Zhou's speech was definitely very encouraging to Chinese writers and artists. In 1979 when Zhou's speech was published for the first time (18 years after Zhou had delivered it), they were moved again. Hu Yaobang made a similar promise at the 1980 Script Writing Forum. Again the promise was well received by his listeners.

However, in 1986, in a more favorable political atmosphere, Shao Yanxiang, a famous poet, publicly challenged the "three don'ts" promise, finding it far from satisfactory. He put the case quite eloquently:

"Let me ask: who is able to pick on citizens within the Party and outside, put labels on them, and beat them with a big stick? Nobody without power can do it; and power is linked to a certain leading position. If it is admitted that 'Leadership means service' and cadres are public servants, then who has ever bestowed upon the servants, that is, the public servants of the people, the power to treat the objects of their service, that is, the masters of the country, by 'picking on them, putting labels on them, and beating them with a big stick'? Is this not, obviously, an unlawful practice that goes by an 'illegal law'? If this should not have happened, we should think of ways to put an end to it by means of law, discipline, and regulations. The democratic rights of a citizen must be earnestly protected by law, and the encroachments on citizens' rights must be punished. As such, a simple promise of the 'three don'ts' has truly proved much too abstract and weak" (Shao Yanxiang, "Shuo 'sanbu'"—"On the 'Three Don'ts'", *RMRB,* 24 June 1986).

三从四德
sancong side
(three obediences and four virtues)

See "banbiantian" (other half of the sky).

三反分子
sanfan fenzi
(three-anti elements)

The "three-anti" refer to "anti-Party, anti-people, and anti-socialism". (Sometimes, they refer to "anti-Party, anti-socialism, and anti-Mao Zedong Thought") In the numerous political campaigns of the past, quite a number of people were convicted as "anti-Party, anti-people, and anti-socialist elements". See also "fan youpai yundong" (anti-Rightist campaign).

三反运动
sanfan yundong
(campaign against the three evils)

This refers to the campaign against corruption, waste, and bureaucracy, which was conducted from the end of 1951 to October 1952 in government departments, army units, and state-owned enterprises.

三分天灾，七分人祸
sanfen tianzai, qifen renhuo
(a disaster 70% man-made and 30% the result of natural causes)

See "dayuejin" (Great Leap Forward) and "qiqianren dahui" (7,000-person meeting).

三纲五常
san'gang wuchang
(three cardinal guides and five constant virtues)

See "banbiantian" (other half of the sky).

三高
sangao
(three highs)

See "Zhou Yang beiju" (tragedy of Zhou Yang).

三和两全
sanhe liangquan
(three "peacefuls" and two "entires")

See "xiuzhengzhuyi" (revisionism).

三和一少
sanhe yishao
(three "milds" and one "less")

The three "milds" are "mild to imperialism, mild to modern revisionism, and mild to all the reactionaries in the world" (here "he" means "heqi"—"mild". It can also be an abbreviation for "heping"—"peaceful", as in the above entry), and the one "less" refers to "less support to the national liberation struggles in the world". See also "sanzi yibao" (three freedoms and one contract).

三害
sanhai
(three evils)

See "fan youpai yundong" (anti-Rightist campaign) and "sanfan yundong" (campaign against the "three evils").

三好
sanhao
(three goods)

On 30 June 1953, when meeting the presidium of the 2nd National Congress of the New Democratic Youth League of China, Mao congratulated the youth in their "good health, good study, and good work" (shenti hao, xuexi hao, gongzuo hao). In response to Mao's greeting, the Congress decided that the orientation of the League's work be to help youth to realize the "three goods". Thereafter, a movement of "three-good" students was launched in all schools throughout the country. This was followed by various other "three-good" movements, such as "three-good" commune members, "three-good" cadres, "three-good" workshops, "three-good" League branches, "three-good" communes, and "three-good" units, each having different content of "three goods".

During the first few years of the 1960s, there were various "five-good" movements, one of which was the movement of "five-good" soldiers. They were guided by the principle of "giving prominence to politics" (tuchu zhengzhi). See also "tuchu zhengzhi" (giving prominence to politics).

三好干部
sanhao ganbu
("three-good" cadres)

In the 1950s "three-good" movement, "three-good" cadres referred mainly to rural cadres who were good in labor, in uniting with the masses, and in implementing Party policies. Today in Jiang Zemin's anti-corruption drive, this term is sarcastically used, referring to Party and government officials who have committed economic crimes but are "good" in admitting guilt, in informing against others, and in returning illicit money and other bribes or paying compensation for them (taidu hao, jiefa hao, tuipei hao). See also "sanhao" (three goods) and "fan fubai" (anti-corruption).

三好学生
sanhao xuesheng
("three-good" students)

See "sanhao" (three goods).

三家村
sanjiacun
(three-family village)

In October 1961, Wu Han (historian, then vice-Mayor of Beijing), Deng Tuo (then secretary of the CCP Beijing Municipal Committee, former director and editor-in-chief of the *People's Daily),* and Liao Mosha (then secretary of the CCP Beijing Municipal Committee), began publishing their "Notes from Three-Family Village", essays in serial form, in *Frontline (Qianxian),* which, edited by Deng Tuo, was a theoretical organ of the CCP Beijing Municipal Committee. Under the collective penname "Wu Nanxing" ("Wu" for Wu Han, "Nan" for Nancun, i.e., Deng Tuo, and "Xing" for Fanxing, i.e., Liao Mosha), the series continued through July 1964, bringing the number of pieces to a total of 67. At the same time, Deng Tuo also published 153 essays in the column "Mt. Yan Evening Talks" ("Yanshan yehua") in the *Beijing Evening News* from March 1961 to September 1962. These articles mostly included critiques of current Party policies and satires of Party leaders. At the beginning of the GPCR the three authors were denounced as the "three-family village black inn", and they were cruelly persecuted; Deng Tuo and Wu Han ultimately committed suicide.

三讲
sanjiang
(three stresses)

See "jiang zhengzhi" (talk politics).

三结合
sanjiehe
(three-in-one combination)

The term "three-in-one combination" refers to a work method with regard to organizational form. It can be applied in different cases. The "revolutionary committees" (geming weiyuanhui) at various levels established during the GPCR, for example, were composed of representatives from government and Party cadres, mass organizations, and the army—a "three-in-one" form. The term was also used in literary and art fields. It was said that, under the "brilliant leadership" of the Party, there was no need for writers to make independent explorations; all they needed to do was listen to the Party. Hence the "three-in-one" formula for artistic creation—"thoughts from leaders, life experience from the masses, and artistry from writers"—which, though quite popular during the GPCR, was of course not first inspired by the Gang of Four.

三宽
sankuan
(generosity, tolerance, and relaxation)

"Sankuan" is a shorthand way of referring to "generosity (kuan hou), tolerance (kuan rong), and relaxation (kuan song)". Since in Chinese each of these three expressions contains the character "kuan", they have come to be known as the "san kuan" (three "kuan"s). In 1986, the most authoritative interpretation of the party's principles and policies for ideological-cultural affairs was "sankuan". Zhu Houze, then director of the PCC Propaganda Department, explained it on the basis of the ideas of Hu Yaobang and Hu Qili: "Sankuan puts to us the following questions: whether a tolerant attitude can be adopted towards ideological points of view not in conformity with our own; whether those comrades holding different opinions should be more generously treated; and whether the whole atmosphere or environment should be made more relaxed and flexible. An object made entirely of steel breaks easily, and is unable to withstand a clash. In social life, however, clashes can occur at any time, and in any sphere" (Zhu Houze, "Guanyu sixiang wenhua wentide jidian sikao"—"Some Thoughts on Ideological-Cultural Questions", *Zhongguo wenhua bao*, 23 July 1986).

To the delight of Hu Yaobang and his followers, the concept of "sankuan" immediately became very popular throughout the country. This was indeed the best public opinion to have before the 6th Plenum of the 12th PCC to be held in September. Hu was convinced that a relaxed political situation was vital for any resolution in favor of political reform, which was supposed to be the major item on the agenda of the Plenum. He also knew very well that, if they could get the upper hand over the conservatives at the forthcoming Party meeting and make the Party move a step forward to reform the political structure, his power would be strengthened. He would even be able to play the role of Deng Xiaoping, at least initially. One can say, indeed, that the putting forward and the implementation of the "sankuan" policy were of great significance in the overall strategy of Hu Yaobang and his faction. It showed their confidence and ambitions.

As a symbol of the "sankuan" policy and its implementation, Wang Meng was appointed minister of culture in 1986. Once he accepted the job as cultural minister, he tried to promote what he thought to be good for Chinese literature and art, making use of his influence and power. On the one hand, the CCP authorities found him to be the right person for the job. On the other hand, as "something of an artistic dissident", he actually served as an inspiration to many who wanted to see moves toward liberalization in China.

At that time, there certainly was a growing trend for liberalization. There was a general feeling of disgust with ossified and outdated theories. This made Party ideologues and professed Marxists very uneasy, for example, veteran writer Yao Xueyin (1910-1999). He referred to the "abnormal phenomena" whereby many Party newspapers and journals carried "non-Marxist" theoretical articles and "anti-realistic" literary works, while articles propagating "Marxist" literary theory and literature adhering to "revolutionary realism" were becoming increasingly unpublishable. Furthermore, he said: "The 'non-class' slogans of 'relaxation', 'tolerance', and 'generosity', as consistently applied by certain persons even in the face of this complex turbulence, are employed precisely by those 'theorists' characterized by their class nature. There was no 'relaxation', 'tolerance', or 'generosity' in their treatment of Marxists. To the broad masses of Communist Party intellectuals, this reality was undeniably grim" (Yao Xueyin, "Jicheng he fayang zuguo wenxueshide guanghui chuantong"—"Inherit and Promote the Brilliant Tradition of Chinese Literary History", *HQ*, 8:7, Apr. 1987).

Interestingly, the liberalization then rejected the "sankuan" policy. Fang Lizhi made the following comment: "Relaxation means only a certain size of space, as if the length of the rope with which you are bound was originally one metre and then it was extended to five metres, so that you could have a little more room for movement" ("Fang Lizhi's Speech at Tongji University", in *FLW*, p. 52). What Fang meant is clear; "minzhuhua" (democratization) was needed.

But the "sankuan" policy soon disappeared. Hu Yaobang was forced to step down at the beginning of 1987 as the highest-level victim of the Party's anti-bourgeois liberalization campaign. Hu Qili, Zhu Houze, and Wang Meng, one after another, had to leave their posts. The "sankuan" policy was accused of encouraging liberalization in literary and ideological circles. See also "ziyouhua" (liberalization) and "zhengzhi gaige" (political reform).

三宽政策的象征
sankuan zhengcede xiangzheng
(symbol of the "sankuan" policy)

See "sankuan" (generosity, tolerance, and relaxation) and "wangbuzhaode hudie" (a butterfly difficult to catch).

三老四严
sanlao siyan
(three honests and four stricts)

See "gongye xue Daqing" (in industry, learn from Daqing).

三论
sanlun
(three theories)

See "fangfalun nian" (a year of methodology).

三民主义
sanminzhuyi
(Three Principles of the People)

The "Three Principles of the People" were put forward by Dr. Sun Yat-sen (1866-1925), who has been canonized and worshipped by both the KMT and the CCP as a national cult figure. The Three Principles are: the Principle of People's Rights (minquanzhuyi), the Principle of People's Livelihood (minshengzhuyi), and the Principle of Nationalism (minzuzhuyi). People often compare them to Lincoln's well-known expression of a government "of the people, by the people, and for the people", as Sun did when he put them forward.

Sun presumably conceived these ideas in the last few years of the nineteenth century. After 1905 Sun and his comrades propagated them in *Minbao (the People's Report)*, the organ of their "Tongmenghua" (Revolutionary Alliance). He systematized his Three Principles around 1919 in Shanghai, but the only draft was destroyed during the coup d'état of Chen Jiongming in 1922. The actual text available today comes from his lecture notes, written in vernacular style, in 1924 when he reorganized the KMT in Guangzhou.

Notably, the Three Principles have been controversial since they were raised. The CCP emphasizes the Three Principles of 1924 when Sun agreed to carry out the "three new policies" of "allying Russians and Communists and assisting peasants and workers" (lian E, lian Gong, fuzhu nong gong). It also argues that Marxism-Leninism-Mao Zedong Thought is much better than the Three Principles. The KMT, however, emphasizes what it sees as the original idea of Sun, and propagates it as the guiding principle for the reconstruction of China as a modern democracy. In fact, it has canonized Sun as the source of its political legitimacy since 1925. Those most critical of the Three Principles treat them as part of a Soviet-style propaganda machine which set out not only to exploit political ignorance and complacency, but also to foster the nationalistic pride of the Chinese masses so that they could be betrayed later on by a one-party dictatorial government.

In the recent two decades, the KMT on Taiwan has suggested that the "Three Principles of the People" should be the guideline for the reunification of China. This was rejected by Deng Xiaoping as "unrealistic". See also "Taiwan wenti" (Taiwan issue).

三名
sanming
(three famous)

See "Zhou Yang beiju" (tragedy of Zhou Yang).

三年文革
sannian wen'ge
(three-year Cultural Revolution)

This theory argues that the GPCR lasted for only three years, from May 1966 to April 1969, marked by the rise of rebels and their decline. By the 9th CCP National Congress held in Beijing in April 1969, at which the Mao Zedong-Lin Biao leadership system was established, the rebels had been suppressed and lost power. This marked the end of the GPCR, according to the "two Cultural Revolutions" theory. See "wen'ge" (Cultural Revolution) and "liang ge wen'ge lun" ("two Cultural Revolutions" theory).

三批运动
sanpi yundong
(three-refutation movement)

See "dapipan" (mass criticism).

三七开
sanqikai
(a 70-30 ratio assessment)

See "chedi fouding wen'ge" (complete negation of the GPCR).

三起三落
sanqi sanluo
(three rises and three falls)

This refers to the three setbacks and three rises in Deng Xiaoping's political career.

Deng was among the earliest CCP members and vigorous activists. Following the decision of the CCP emergency meeting of 7 August 1927, which he attended, Deng launched armed uprisings and founded Red Army units and revolutionary bases. But in February 1933, soon after he arrived at the Central Base to support Mao's line, Deng was sacked as Party general secretary by mostly Russian-trained "Left" leaders who advocated revolution in cities. This was the first setback Deng suffered in his political career.

After the 1935 Zunyi Meeting during the Long March, which established Mao's leadership, Deng step by step became a major Party leader. Before the GPCR, he was PRC vice-premier, PCC general secretary, and member of the Standing Committee of the PCC Politburo. He was then denounced and stripped of all his posts, suffering another serious setback.

After Lin Biao's attempt to stage a coup d'etat was smashed, Deng returned to work, serving in 1975 as PCC vice-chairman, PRC vice-premier, CMC vice-chairman, and chief of the PLA General Staff, in charge of day-to-day affairs of the Party, state, and army. The next year, however, he suffered his third setback—he was accused of whipping up a "Right deviationist wind to reverse previous verdicts" and he was again deprived of all his posts.

After the downfall of the Gang of Four on 6 October 1976, China faced a critical historical juncture. On 10 April 1977, Deng wrote a letter to Hua Guofeng, CCP chairman, noting that he supported the Party Center headed by Hua and that he would never reverse the verdicts of the GPCR. In May 1977, due to a strong demand from his supporters inside and outside the Party, Deng was restored to his former posts. At the 3rd Plenum of the 10th PCC held in July, his restoration was officially confirmed. At the 1978 3rd Plenum of the 11th PCC, Deng's position was further established. He became China's paramount leader until his death on 19 February 1997.

三权分立
sanquanfenli
(tripartite division of legislature, administration, and judiciary)

The CCP leadership is always sensitive to any arguments for independent executive, judicial, and legislative branches, claiming it does not tally with China's current "national characteristics" (guoqing). In a talk to some leading officials on 30 December 1986, which was issued in early January 1987 as PCC No. 1 (1987) Document guiding the then "anti-bourgeois liberalization" campaign, Deng Xiaoping issued a clear-cut statement: No bourgeois democracy, such as a tripartite division of the legislature, administration, and judiciary, should be accepted.

In the opinion of China's dissidents, such a tripartite division is important, especially in view of the current widespread corruption in the Party and the government departments under the present one-party dictatorship. They argue that a tripartite division, though originating in the West, should not be regarded as a Western model or an American model, for it has been adopted in many countries not only in the West but also in the East. It has its shortcomings and can be abused, but so far no other system has been found to be better. See also "fandui zichanjieji ziyouhua yundong" (anti-bourgeois liberalization campaign) and "zhengzhi gaige" (political reform).

三十年文革
sanshinian wen'ge
(thirty-year Cultural Revolution)

See "Mao Zedong lixiangzhuyi waihua lun" (theory of the exteriorization of Mao's idealism).

三十年代文艺
sanshiniandai wenyi
(literature and art of the 1930s)

See "sanshiniandai wenyi yundong" (literature and art movement of the 1930s).

三十年代文艺运动
sanshiniandai wenyi yundong
(literature and art movement of the 1930s)

This refers to the literature and art movement of the Left during the 1930s in the KMT areas of China. It is also called the "Left-wing movement in literature and art" (zuoyi wenyi yundong) of the 1930s.

One of the most significant events in the movement was the founding of the CCP-led "Left-Wing Writers League" (Zuoyi Zuojia Lianmeng) in Shanghai on 2 March 1930, with the prominent support of the two important writers Lun Xun and Mao Dun. The founding is highly praised in the Party-approved history of modern Chinese literature. During the League's existence (1930-1936) and for few years thereafter, a great many men of letters came under the influence of the CCP, and through their creative activities they helped convince millions of Chinese people that the CCP was the only hope to cure the ills of the country.

But because of factional strifes and other issues, the movement has been open to controversy. In the 1966 Party document "Summary of the Forum on the Work in Literature and Art in the Armed Forces with Which Comrade Lin Biao Entrusted Comrade Jiang Qing" ("Lin Biao tongzhi weituo Jiang Qing tongzhi zhaokaide budui wenyi gongzuo zuotanhui jiyao") and other documents during the GPCR, what is known as the "literature and art of the 1930s" (sanshiniandai wenyi), i.e., the literature and art of the Left during the 1930s in the KMT areas of China, was condemned as a foundation for the so-called "sinister anti-Party and anti-socialist line", which had exercised dictatorship in literary and art circles since the founding of PRC.

"National defense literature" (guofang wenxue) bore the brunt of the attack. "National defense literature" was propagated in early 1936 by Zhou Yang, who was at that time assigned by the CCP to lead the movement, and other CCP cultural leaders in Shanghai, in view of the serious on-going Japanese aggression. Lu Xun did not agree with the slogan. Instead, in June 1936, he put forth another slogan: "popular literature of the national revolutionary war" (minzu geming zhanzhengde dazhong wenxue). He pointed out that far from abandoning its responsibility of class leadership, revolutionary literature aimed to increase and expand its responsibility. He also held that within the national united front, there should also be criticism of bourgeois literature. A debate ensued over these two slogans (liang ge kouhao zhi zheng) among the Left-wing writers at the time.

When revising the "Summary" in 1966, Chen Boda said that "national defense literature" was a "bourgeois slogan". During the GPCR, the so-called "Zhou Yang clique" was fiercely attacked as followers of "Wang Ming's Right capitulationist line" (Wang Ming was CCP leader for four years from January 1931). In addition, Liu Shaoqi was not only branded as "the general back-stage boss of the revisionist sinister line in literature and art of the 1960s", but also as "the active supporter and patron of the bourgeois slogan of 'national defense literature' as early as the 1930s" *(RMRB,* 16 Sept. 1967). In contrast, Lu Xun was highly praised for his emphasis on the leading responsibility of proletarian cultural thinking on the cultural united front: he represented a proletarian line in literature and art, and his slogan—"popular literature on the national revolutionary war"—was regarded as a proletarian slogan.

The slogan of "national defense literature" continued to be attacked in 1977, but this time it was Jiang Qing who bore the brunt of the attack. She was accused of having played various parts in "national defense dramas" and "national defense films" before leaving Shanghai for Yan'an in 1937. Two works she had been involved in were singled out: the film *Bloodshed on Wolf Mountain (Langshan diexue ji)* and the modern drama *Sai Jinhua (Sai Jinhua)*. But very soon, with the rehabilitation of Zhou Yang, the slogan of "national defense literature" was rehabilitated.

In the 1980 discussion of the relationship between the arts and politics, the historical background of the slogan "Literature and art are subordinate to and serve politics" was traced to the Left-wing movement of the 1930s. Indeed, Chinese literature and art was always closely related to politics. The name "Left-wing" in itself embodied a political concept. In his speech at the 1980 Script Writing Forum, by which time the Party had decided to drop the slogan, Zhou Yang said that he and many others advocated the slogan for several decades and it did play a role in the CCP-led revolution. Although the slogan was no longer used, that did not mean that it was wrong. On the whole, according to Zhou, it "played a positive role while at the same time it had some negative side effects" (Zhou Yang, "Emancipate the Mind, Truthfully Present Our Times", *WYB,* 4:9, 1981). See also "jiyao" ("Summary") and "wenyi wei zhengzhi fuwu" (literature and art serve politics).

三十三人公开信
sanshisan ren gongkaixin
(open letter from thirty-three intellectuals)

On 13 February 1989, an open letter to the NPC Standing Committee and the PCC was signed by 33 intellectuals in mainland China. In the letter they stated that they had felt deep concern when they learned of the open letter sent by Fang Lizhi to Deng Xiaoping on 6 January 1989. They stated that it was their opinion that, in the year that marked the 40th anniversary of the founding of the PRC and the 70th anniversary of the May 4th Movement, a declaration of a general amnesty, and especially the release of Wei Jingsheng and other political prisoners, would create an atmosphere of reconciliation that would be beneficial to the reform. At the same time, it would be in harmony with the general current of respect for human rights which was steadily increasing throughout the entire world. This was the first time that Chinese intellectuals, despite their past persecution, had taken direct and joint action under the Communist régime.

In addition to the poet Bei Dao, its initiator, signatories included Bing Xin, a veteran woman writer; Su Shaozhi, a dissident Marxist theoretician; Wang Ruoshui, a dissident Marxist theoretician; Wu Zuguang, a veteran dramatist and member of the CPPCC; Jin Guantao, a historian; Shao Yanxiang, a poet and council member of the CWA; Niu Han, a veteran poet and editor; Lao Mu, a young poet and editor of *Literary Gazette*; Li Tuo, a writer and deputy editor-in-chief of *Beijing Literature*; Zhang Jie, a woman writer and council member of the CWA; Zong Pu, a woman writer; Wu Zuxiang, a veteran writer and professor at Beijing University; Tang Yijie, a professor at Beijing University and president of the Chinese Culture Institute; Yue Daiyun, director of the Comparative Literature Institute of Beijing University; Huang Ziping, a young literary critic and lecturer at Beijing University; Yan Wenjing, a veteran writer and former editor-in-chief of *People's Literature*; Feng Yidai, a veteran writer and translator; Xiao Qian, a veteran writer and member of the Standing Committee of the CPPCC; Su Xiaokang, a writer and reporter for the *People's Daily*; Li Zehou, a researcher at the Philosophy Institute of CASS; and Bao Zunxin, a researcher at the History Institute of CASS. See also "bajiu minyun" (1989 pro-democracy movement).

三十万言书
sanshiwan yan shu
(300,000-word statement)

This refers to a 300,000 word report about literature and art presented by Hu Feng to the PCC. See "Hu Feng anjian" (Hu Feng case).

三通四流
santong siliu
(three opening-ups and four exchanges)

On 1 January 1979, the "Letter to Our Taiwan Compatriots" ("Gao Taiwan tongbao shu") was signed by the NPC Standing Committee. The CCP authorities, in an active intensification of its "united front" work directed toward Taiwan, first proposed "opening up transportation and postal communications", "scholarly exchanges" and "economic exchanges". These proposals were later systematized as the "three opening-ups" (which refer to "opening up postal communications, transportation, and trade relations") and "four exchanges" (which refer to "economic, scientific, cultural, and athletic" exchanges), as in Premier Hua Guofeng's government work report delivered to the 2nd Session of the 5th NPC on 18 June 1979. Similar proposals were later repeatedly raised in the "Nine Principles of Ye Jianying" (Ye jiutiao) of 30 September 1981, the "Six Principles of Deng Xiaoping" (Deng liutiao) of 26 June 1983, and the "Eight Principles of Jiang Zemin" (Jiang batiao) of 20 January 1995.

Initially, the Taiwan government responded with a "three no's" policy of no contact, no negotiation, and no compromise (bu jiechu, bu tanpan, bu tuoxie) with the mainland. In 1981 it started to shift away from this policy. In May 1986 the first negotiations took place between representatives of the two sides over the return of a Taiwan plane that had been hijacked to the mainland. Then, on 2 November 1987, a big step was taken by the Taiwan government— it officially dropped its ban on travel to the mainland.

In February 1991 Taiwan created the Straits Exchange Foundation ("Haixia Jiaoliu Jijinhui"), and then the mainland founded its Association for Relations Across the Taiwan Straits ("Haixia Liang'an Guanxi Xiehui") in December 1991, so that the two sides could communicate with each other. The first meeting was held in Singapore in April 1993, with subsequent meetings occurring on the mainland and in Taiwan. In 1996 both sides agreed that a form of direct-trade could be arranged. On 19 April 1997, the Chinese container ship "Sheng Da" (registered in St. Vincent) docked in Kaohsiung harbor. This was the first ship in almost five decades to carry freight as part of a regularly scheduled service directly from the mainland to Taiwan. Step by step, the "three opening-ups" and "four exchanges" have on the whole been realized. See also "Taiwan wenti" (Taiwan issue).

三同
santong
(three togethers)

See "san tuoli" (three divorced).

三突出
santuchu
(three prominences)

See "wen'ge wenyi" (GPCR literature and art).

三脱离
santuoli
(three divorced)

In the Mao period, China's intellectuals were attacked as "three divorced"—divorced from politics, reality, and labor, as a result of the long-term influence of the so-called "poisons of feudalism, bourgeois ideology, and revisionism" (feng, zi, xiu). Therefore, they had to be ideologically transformed under the guidance of Mao Zedong Thought. One common method was to send them to factories and the countryside to take part in manual labor and to receive "reeducation" (zai jiaoyu) from workers and poor and lower-middle peasants. In the countryside, they had to practice the "three-togethers" (santong), that is, to have the same meals, to live in the same house, and to labor together with poor and lower-middle peasants (tong chi, tong zhu, tong laodong). Later, another two-togethers were added—together to study Mao Zedong Thought and together to criticize feudalism, bourgeois ideology, and revisionism (tong xuexi, tong pipan)—and the "three-togethers" became the "five-togethers" (wutong). See also "dangde jiaoyu fangzhen" (the Party's educational policy).

三无小说
sanwu xiaoshuo
(fiction with no plot, no characterization, and no creation of typical characters in typical circumstances)

See "wangbuzhaode hudie" (a butterfly difficult to catch) and "shehuizhuyi xianshizhuyi" (socialist realism).

三线
sanxian
(third line)

The term "third line" refers to the vast strategic rear regions of China. Proceeding from the need to prepare for the possibility of war, in the early 1960s Mao and the PCC proposed that the different regions of China be classified into the first, the second, and the third lines according to their respective strategic importance. The "third line" regions were usually poor and backward, without an industrial foundation. Hence, the Party demanded that the whole country support "third line" construction (sanxian jianshe). This strategic principle, obviously at odds with the reform and open-door program, has long been abandoned.

三线建设
sanxian jianshe
(third-line construction)

See "sanxian" (third line).

三信危机
sanxin weiji
(crises of faith, confidence, and trust)

After the end of the GPCR, many agreed that, among people in society and even within the Party, there were crises of faith (xinyang) in Marxist-Leninist and Maoist doctrines, of confidence (xinxin) in the "four modernizations", and of trust (xinren) in the CCP. Although quite prevalent at the time, the argument was flatly rejected by Hu Yaobang in his 1980 "Speech at the Forum on Script Writing". If there was ever a crisis, he said, it could only have been before the Gang of Four was smashed. Thereafter, the Party was saved and this meant that the crisis had passed. In this regard, Hu earnestly asked writers and artists first of all to build up "five correct treatments" (wu ge zhengque duidai) in their minds, that is, the "correct treatment" of the CCP, Chinese society, the working people in China, the Chinese PLA, and Mao Zedong Thought. These, he said, were originally issues of correctly distinguishing and handling two kinds of contradictions with different natures.

Hu admitted that the consequences of the "three crises" could still be found everywhere, and that the Party had indeed suffered a loss of prestige. Hu guaranteed that within a few years, by taking measures such as carrying out rectification, the Party would not only restore its prestige but also raise it to a higher level than previously. This promise, if tested with what actually happened in later years, was empty. But one can believe Hu might have been very sincere when making the promise, as a Party leader who was on the rise and full of self-confidence at the time.

As scholars point out, since Chinese communism and Mao Zedong Thought are strongly attached with politico-religious characteristics, it is only natural that many Chinese were disillusioned after having experienced the Cultural Revolution. In recent years, their crisis of faith has worsened, against the background of universal corruption in the Party and in society. This helps explain why the "Law Wheel Cultivation" is so popular. See "Falun Gong" (Law Wheel Cultivation) and "shijian shi jianyan zhenlide weiyi biaozhun" (practice is the sole criterion for testing truth).

三要三不要
sanyao sanbuyao
(three do's and three don'ts)

See "santiao shibie dangnei zuozipaide genben biaozhun" (three fundamental criteria for identifying capitalist-roaders within the Party).

三支两军
sanzhi liangjun

(three supports and two militaries)

These refer to the tasks given to the Army during the GPCR. The "three supports" were supports to industry, agriculture, and the broad masses of the Left. The "two militaries" referred to military control (enforced in chaotic places and those vital units such as public security offices, courts, procuratorates, newspaper offices, radio stations, banks, warehouses, and departments of civil aviation and sea transportation) and political and military training (given to secondary and tertiary school students). In carrying out these tasks, the PLA greatly increased its influence in local politics.

After the GPCR, "three supports and two militaries" were open to controversy. Deng's conclusion was: one must say two things. First, at that time, it was correct for the army to go to the civilian units and deal with the situations there, which were otherwise uncontrollable. So the "three supports and two militaries" proved useful. But second, they also did great harm to the army, for in their wake they brought many bad things that greatly detracted from the army's prestige. Among others things, they were responsible for much of the factionalism (paixing) and some "Left" notions and practices *(SWD,* p. 358). See also "wen'ge" (Cultural Revolution).

三忠于

sanzhongyu

(three loyals)

See "xiandai mixin" (modern superstition) and "tuchu zhengzhi" (giving prominence to politics).

三资企业

sanzi qiye

(three types of foreign capital involved enterprises)

These refer to enterprises based solely on foreign investment, Chinese-foreign joint ventures, and Chinese-foreign joint management ventures, which are products of Deng's reform and open-door policies. On 1 July 1979, these types of enterprises were confirmed in a law passed at the 2nd Session of the 5th NPC.

三自爱国运动

sanzi aiguo yundong

(three-self patriotic movement)

The "three-self" refers to the "self-rule, self-maintenance, and self-promotion of missionary work" within Christian churches in China.

On 16 April 1951, the Religious Affairs Department under the Cultural and Educational Ministry held a meeting in Beijing concerning the treatment of religious bodies that received U.S. subsidies. After the meeting, the organization "China Christian Committee for Resisting the U.S. and Aiding Korea and for the Promotion of the Three-Self Reform Campaign" was set up, and the "three-self" patriotic movement was launched throughout the country.

三自一包

sanzi yibao

(three freedoms and one contract)

These refer to the rural policy initiated by Liu Shaoqi and his supporters in 1961-62, years of economic disaster, to establish "more farming plots for private use, more free markets, more enterprises with sole responsibility for their own profits or losses, and fixing output quotas on a household basis".

An embryonic form of the policy was first raised at the 9th Plenum of the 8th PCC (held from 14 to 18 January 1961) to reduce the confusion and damages brought about by the 1958 "Three Red Banners" movement. The policy was clarified in the document entitled "Several Policy Issues Concerning the People's Communes in the Rural Areas: A Suggestion" (Guanyu nongcun renmin gongshe ruogan zhengce wentide yijian"). Deng Zihui, director of the PCC Rural Work Department, presented this report to the PCC on 24 May 1962, in line with the spirit of the Plenum. The policy was confirmed at the 10th Plenum of the 8th PCC on 27 September 1962.

Mao Zedong, however, disagreed with the policy (though he did not prevent it from being approved). On 9 and 29 February 1964, in his talks with foreign guests, Mao criticized Wang Jiaxiang, director of the PCC Liaison Department, for his view of three "milds" and one "less", as well as Deng Zihui, for his rural policy. Mao also said that there were quite a number of Party officials, from the top level to the bottom, who were engaged in revisionism, and that the "sanhe yishao" policy, which abandoned class struggle, was their guiding principle for international work, while the "sanzi yibao" policy, which aimed at undermining the socialist system, was their guiding principle for domestic work. As it turned out, these policies were fiercely attacked during the GPCR as evidence of the crimes committed by Liu Shaoqi and his followers.

In the 1980s, under Deng Xiaoping's reform program, "sanzi yibao" gradually developed into various forms of a "responsibility system for agricultural production" (nongye shengchan zerenzhi). See also "sanhe yishao" ("three "milds" and one "less") and "xiuzhengzhuyi" (revisionism).

三种人
sanzhongren
(three kinds of people)

See "disan tidui" (third echelon) and "hongweibing" (Red Guards).

杀鸡儆猴
shaji jinghou
(to kill the chicken to frighten the monkey)

This is an old Chinese phrase which means to punish one person as a warning to others. Very often, especially during the Mao period, one intellectual would be singled out and treated like a "chicken killed to frighten the monkey". There are many such examples, for instance, Wang Shiwei, who was fiercely attacked in the 1941-42 Yan'an Rectification Movement. Another was the case of Bai Hua, whose controversial work "Unrequited Love" was attacked in 1981 as an example of "bourgeois liberalization". See also "Bai Hua shijian" (Bai Hua Incident), "baolu wenxue" (exposure literature), and "ziyouhua" (liberalization).

山头主义
shantouzhuyi
(mountain-stronghold mentality)

See "difangzhuyi" (localism).

伤痕文学
shanghen wenxue
(scar literature)

The 1976 downfall of the Gang of Four was an important event in contemporary Chinese politics, and it also proved to be a turning point for contemporary Chinese literature: it gave birth to a new literature. In its early stage, it was referred to as "shanghen wenxue" ("scar literature", also translated as "literature of the wounded" or "wound literature). A new genre in the history of socialist literature in China, scar literature takes its name from a short story "The Scar" ("Shanghen", *WHB,* 11 August 1978), a maiden work by Lu Xinhua, a first-year student of the Fudan University in Shanghai. Its first representative work, however, is Liu Xinwu's "Class Teacher" ("Ban zhuren", *RMWX,* 11, 1977). Growing from the political movement developing throughout the country to settle accounts with the two "counter-revolutionary cliques" of Lin Biao and the Gang of Four, the theme of these works was ideologically unimpeachable. Very much in conformity with Party propaganda at that time, the works exposed and denounced the crimes of Lin Biao, the Gang, and their accomplices. But for some people, these works, involving such sensitive issues as the dark side of society and the "socialist tragedy" (shehuizhuyi beiju), violated long-established principles of socialist literature and art, thus constituting a kind of threat. It was only natural that there were continued debates. The literature was called "exposure literature" (baolu wenxue), a term with frightening overtones for Chinese, recalling memories of writers attacked in 1942 and 1957, whose tragic fates were well known. For a period of time, there was a regular pattern: writers took a risk by submitting their first manuscripts; several critics, and a substantial number of readers, stood up to defend them; and then almost always controversy would follow. For an age at a turning point, this was not at all surprising. Even after December 1978 when the "two whatevers" were criticized, this phenomenon continued. Understandably, the "Left" ideology, which had dominated the Party for such a long time, could not be simply annulled with a single criticism or decision.

Nevertheless, the debate was conducted in the shifting political climate of the post-GPCR years. Scar literature enjoyed great support from a large readership. Finally, at the 4th Congress of the CWA convened at the end of 1984 and the beginning of 1985, the genre was formally praised for the first time. In his report to the Congress, Zhang Guangnian, vice-chairman of the Association, highly praised "scar literature" for its solemn and stirring color, which complemented its theme, and for the resonance it found in the hearts of hundreds of millions of people. He delivered a "historical verdict" on it:

"Scar literature, in my mind, is a literature that, along with the development of the 'new period literature', bravely and uncompromisingly took the lead in thoroughly negating the GPCR, a literature that, by complying with the wishes of the Party and the people, actively plunged into the movement to emancipate the mind and helped to fulfill the task of the times to bring order out of chaos.... We must, with a Marxist historical perspective, fully appreciate the role 'scar literature' played in creating a new way through difficulties for the development of socialist literature in the new historical period" (Zhang Guangnian, "Xinshiqi shehuizhuyi wenxue zai kuobu qianjin" (Socialist Literature of the New Period Is Striding Ahead", *RMWX,* 1:6, 1985).

Thus, eventually the term "scar literature" was used positively and the value of this literature was officially confirmed. If it is right to say that literature is a product of its age, this was never more true than with scar literature. Its coming into being coincided exactly with the discussion of "practice as the sole criterion for testing truth", which was going on throughout the country in the latter half of 1978, and with the historic 3rd Plenum of the 11th PCC, which was held at the end of the year. But this was more than mere coincidence. There was a historical inevitability. As Zhou Yang pointed out, scar literature was "an outcome of the current movement to emancipate the mind" and "in turn gave fresh impetus to this movement" (Zhou Yang, "Jiwangkailai, fanrong shehuizhuyi xinshiqide wenyi"—"Be Both Successors and Pioneers, Bring Literature and Art into Flower in the New Period of Socialism", *WYB*, 11-12:14, 1979). In the words of Hu Yaobang, then director of the PCC Propaganda Department, it "reflected the characteristics of our times" (Hu Yaobang, "Speech at the Forum on Script Writing", *HQ*, 20, 1981, reprinted in *WYLZJ*, p. 25). As for the hundreds of millions of ordinary people, it was very natural that they would sincerely welcome these works, even though they were rough artistically. Indeed, with blood and tears, scar literature recorded all the absurdities and evils of a unique era of darkness in modern Chinese history, an era the Chinese people never want to be repeated. See also "xinshiqi wenxue" (literature of the new period), "xinshiqi wenxuede duoyuan fazhan" (pluralistic development of the literature of the new period), and "wenyi wei zhengzhi fuwu" (literature and art serve politics).

商品生产
shangpin shengchan
(commodity production)

See "zichanjieji faquan" (bourgeois rights).

商业文化
shangye wenhua
(commercial culture)

See "xinshiqi wenxue" (literature of the new period) and "renwen jingshen lunzheng" ("humanistic spirit" debate).

上，管，改
shang, guan, gai
(attendance, management, and reform)

In his "July 21st Directive" of 1968, Mao said: "Students should be selected from among workers and peasants with practical experience, and they should return to production after a few years of study." In 1975, when institutions of tertiary education re-opened and began to admit students selected from among workers, peasants, and soldiers (gong nong bing xueyuan), the authorities urged students to plunge themselves actively into the class struggle on the educational front. They were reminded that they shouldered a "glorious task" of attending and managing universities and using Marxism-Leninism-Mao Zedong Thought to reform universities, to reform the old educational system and the old principles and methods of teaching.

上有政策，下有对策
shang you zhengce, xia you duice
(policy above, counter-policy below)

As admitted in a commentary in the *People's Daily* on 5 February 1985, the phenomenon described in a very popular saying: "Policy above, counter-policy below; you have your policy, I have my counter-policy" was common in mainland China. When a policy came down, there were people who tried to counter it for their own interests by taking advantage of its loopholes. Quite a number of cadres at various levels also adopted this recalcitrant attitude and practice when they found a certain policy of the Party Center (dang zhongyang) not in accord with their demands.

上层建筑
shangceng jianzhu
(superstructure)

See "jingji jichu" (economic base) and "wenyi wei zhengzhi fuwu" (literature and art serve politics).

上帝制造佳酿，魔鬼制造酒鬼
shangdi zhizao jianiang, mogui zhizao jiugui
(God makes wine, and the devil makes drunkards)

If in the 1980 "social effect" debate people did not yet fully expound upon their views on the social effect of literature and art in terms of theory, things were different afterwards. In 1982, for instance, Wu Minguang, a critic, dealt with the issue with regard to the following three aspects: the practice of artistic appreciation on the part of readers, the interrelations of various social factors, and the characteristics of literature and art (see his "Guanyu wenyi shehui zuoyongde tantao"—"Inquiries into the Social Effect of Literature and Art", *SHWX,* 11, 1982, extracted and reprinted in *XHWZ,* 1:153-154, 1983). More significantly, a few years later the writer Zhang Xianliang went so far as to announce openly that he did not think he should be held responsible if any of his works were found to have exerted a bad effect. His statement read as follows: "I welcome criticisms of my works. But this does not mean that I feel, in terms of ideology, there is any particular thing in my works which should be criticized. Otherwise, I would not have had them published. However, if by any chance these works 'could exert bad effects among young people who read them', I personally do not at all hold myself responsible for this. As a proverb in the West goes: God makes wine, and the Devil makes drunkards." (Zhang Xianliang, "Qing mai *Zhang Xianliang Zixuanji*"—"Please Buy *Selected Works of Zhang Xianliang*", *WHB*, 12 May 1986). See also "shehui xiaoguo lun" (social effect theory).

上海帮
Shanghai bang
(Shanghai gang)

The term "Shanghai gang" was first used by Mao at a Politburo meeting on 17 July 1974, when he warned Jiang Qing, Wang Hongwen, Zhang Chunqiao, and Yao Wenyuan against forming a gang of four.

The term began to be used again a few years after Jiang Zemin became Party general secretary in 1989, especially by Jiang's political opponents, such as Chen Xitong, then a CCP Politburo member and Beijing Party secretary. As a most powerful and most recalcitrant "duke", Chen was reported to have gone so far as to have accused Jiang of organizing a "Shanghai gang" (which meant that Jiang promoted his loyal Shanghai subordinates and transferred them to Beijing as leaders of various central Party and government departments). Jiang flatly rejected this accusation. For one thing, he said, he is not a native of Shanghai. See also "Deng hou shidai" (post-Deng era).

上海人民公社
Shanghai renmin gongshe
(Shanghai People's Commune)

See "yiyue geming" (January Revolution).

上头刮小风，下面下大雨
shangtou gua xiaofeng, xiamian xia dayu
(just a little wind from the higher-ups and their subordinates will turn it into a torrential rain)

This very often proved to be true in China. For instance, after the 1980 Script Writing Forum, the disguised bans on the three controversial scripts—"What If I Really Were", "In the Unwritten Records", and "A Woman Thief"—in turn gave some ideologically-rigid and heavy-handed people an excuse to continue their arbitrary meddling in literature and art. There were cases of political threats or unreasonable interference in various areas. Like "just a little wind from the higher-ups and their subordinates will turn it into a torrential rain", many writers and artists felt that the Forum should not have set the precedent of disguised bans. See also "shehui xiaoguo lun" (social effect theory).

少干预，少介入
shao ganyu, shao jieru
(less interference, less involvement)

"Less interference, less involvement" was said to be Zhao Ziyang's idea during his administration as Party general secretary, concerning Party leadership over literature and art.

After a number of postponements, the 5th National Congress of Chinese Writers and Artists was held from 8 to 11 November 1988. Hu Qili, on behalf of the PCC, publicized the idea, which was the key spirit in the Party document to be discussed at the Congress—"Some Suggestions from the PCC on How to Promote the Further Enrichment of Literature and Art". However, many participants were disappointed with the Congress. Symptomatic of the conflicts, strikingly, the Congress could not provide a report such as the one Zhou Yang had delivered at the previous congress, because opinions regarding the appraisal of literature and art in the past nine years were so divergent. More profoundly, having experienced the dramatic turn of events in 1987, many Chinese was haunted by a sense of depression and loss. Various contradictions had arisen in society, as well as in literary and art circles.

In 1991, two years after Zhao Ziyang stepped down, a new Party policy concerning literary and artistic creation was adopted, which actually ran counter to the idea of "less interference, less involvement"—the idea was attacked as one of Zhao's political mistakes.

少宣传个人
shao xuanchuan geren

(less publicity about individuals)

See "geren chongbai" (personality cult).

社共文化
she gong wenhua
(socialist-communist culture)

See "sixiang gaizao" (ideological remolding).

社会达尔文主义
shehui daerwenzhuyi
(social Darwinism)

See "zichanjieji rendaozhuyi shehuiguan" (bourgeois humanistic outlook on society).

社会帝国主义
shehui diguozhuyi
(social-imperialism)

See "xiuzhengzhuyi" (revisionism).

社会文明提高的一个标志
shehui wenming tigaode yi ge biaozhi
(a sign of the enhancement of social civilization)

See "ziwo biaoxian" (expression of the subjective ego).

社会文学
shehui wenxue
(social literature)

See "jingji duoyanghua xuyao wenhua duoyanghua" (the multiplicity of economic sectors requires the multiplicity of culture).

社会效果论
shehui xiaoguo lun
(social effect theory)

No one denies that literature and art have a social impact. However, it is very difficult and controversial to judge the social effect a specific work may exert or has exerted. This is specially the case when the work in question deals with sensitive political-social problems, and when it is not a mediocre production, because in such cases the reaction will be very strong and from a large readership, and judgments on it made by different people often differ strikingly. This was the situation China faced in the later months of 1979 and the following year, when a heated debate occurred about such works as "What If I Really Were" (also entitled "Impostor"), "In the Unwritten Records", and "A Woman Thief".

The debate was even brought into the 4th Congress of Chinese Writers and Artists. As no resolution could be reached when the Congress concluded, a special forum for the discussion—dubbed the Forum on Script Writing—was convened from

23 January to 13 February 1980. The authorities wanted to bring a conclusion to the debate. The "social effect" theory was created.

As a Chinese cultural tradition, the role of literature and art tended to be excessively exaggerated in China. This was strengthened by Communist ideology, such as the principle of socialist realism (shehuizhuyi xianshizhuyi). Interestingly, many writers found this unacceptable. Obviously it was not because they did not value their labor, but rather because they feared that they would be held responsible for any alleged bad social effect from their work. They knew that exaggeration could lead to suspicion. Sometimes, the suspicion was inclusive, as during the Mao period. Writers were also very careful in responding to the Party demand that writers possess a sense of social responsibility (shehui zerengan). One might encounter political troubles if one really had a high degree of this sense of social responsibility and devoted oneself to the fight against social evils such as bureaucracy and corruption. This was because what authorities actually meant by a "sense of social responsibility", first of all, was that a writer should write about the "excellent situation" and the "heroic images" of the proletariat and the Party, like Jiang Qing had required during the GPCR.

Against this background, writers reacted strongly to the "social effect" theory. Only two days after the close of the Script Writing Forum, where writers were reminded of the "social effect" of their works, Ba Jin explicitly expressed his disagreement with those who always imagined literary works would "go crashing around" like an elephant in a china shop (Ba Jin, "Zaitan tansuo"—"More on Explorations", in *Tansuo Ji—Explorations,* Hong Kong, Sanlian Shudian, 1982, p. 41). A literary work, he testified, cannot lead its readers by the nose, even if its art reaches the acme of perfection. The brains of the readers are not blank pieces of paper on which anyone can write anything. The reader has a sense of judgment as to whom to listen to. If literature has any influence on people, it is usually what people call an "imperceptible influence" (qianyimohuade zuoyong), and it must be chewed and digested like food before it is accepted. It has to pass through three tests: the reader's social education, home education, and school education. Therefore, Ba Jin believed he must raise his voice against what he called the "unfairness" of "making a literary work responsible for absolutely every evil" (ibid.).

It is true that many were disgusted with the "social effect" theory raised at the Forum. This ran quite counter to the desire of the authorities.

Take Sha Yexin, the chief co-author of the *de facto* banned work, "What If I Really Were". In June 1980, his new work *Mayor Chen Yi* (*Chen Yi shizhang*, *Juben,* 5:2-39, 1980, reprinted in *XWY, Scripts*, pp. 423-65) was acclaimed nationwide as a new model. But he would have rather preferred that people appreciated his previous controversial play. He denied the charge that "What If I Really Were" would have a "negative social effect" as some had charged. He believed "it is not art that has 'exaggerated' life; life is always more 'exaggerated' than art" (*Shanghai xiju,* 6:5, 1980). He even challenged his critics: "No one has the right to enforce a final judgment on the effect of a certain work in the name of the whole of society. Let practice be the impartial judge. History itself is just, and I am sure that in the end history will find the most reasonable and acceptable conclusion to the debate over 'The Impostor'" (ibid).

Sha Yexin did not wait idly for history to pass a judgment on his ill-fated work. He further questioned the social effect of the Forum on Script Writing itself. In an article he published in *Literary Gazette* in October 1980, he issued the following statement:

1. The original intention of the "social effect" theory raised at the Forum might be very good; but the disguised bans on the scripts made people relate these two

issues together and even think the "social effect" theory was the theoretical basis for the disguised bans. Consequently, the social effect brought about by the theory was very bad. This really warrants careful consideration.

2. The Forum should not at any rate have set the precedent of disguised bans. After the Forum, the disguised bans of the scripts in turn gave some ideologically-rigid and heavy-handed people an excuse to continue their arbitrary meddling in literature and art.

3. Because the three works in trouble all touched on current social problems with the aim of being involved in life, the disguised bans, naturally, frightened other similar works. After the Forum, in fact, few writers dared to write about similar subject matters and many of them turned to those with a greater "safety coefficient" (anquan xishu), hence the lack of due poignancy of facing reality and being involved in life characteristic of the true art of spoken drama.

4. To be involved in life not only refers to exposure of the ugliness in life; it also is meant to praise the bright side of society. Notably, though at present such works are vigorously advocated, this genre is not common. This also has something to do with the covert bans of the scripts and the suppression of other works of exposure. Really, who would like to praise the virtue of a person who prohibited people from criticizing his shortcomings? (Sha Yexin, "Che 'dan'"—"Chatter", *WYLZJ*, pp. 107-8).

Sarcastically, Sha Yexin said that the consequences mentioned above were "beyond people's expectations". To some Party authorities, as one can also see, Sha's critical remarks about the Forum of Script Writing itself were quite unexpected. See also "wenyi wei zhengzhi fuwu" (literature and art serve politics).

社会制度
shehui zhidu
(social system)

See "zhidu" (social system).

社会主义悲剧
shehuizhuyi beiju
(socialist tragedy)

No new breakthrough occurred after Liu Xinwu's "Class Teacher" until August 1978 when the story "The Scar" was published. It is noteworthy that it took so long and that it was a maiden work by a young university student that was ended up being called a breakthrough. More significantly, no sooner had it appeared did a debate ensue, and the crux of the matter in the debate was: Can tragedies exist in the socialist period, and should literature reflect them if they do?

It was unquestionable that the answer was affirmative. In fact, these issues had been favorably discussed before the GPCR. In the spring of 1962, during a conversation with playwrights, Zhou Enlai explicitly stated that, in addition to "legitimate" theater (zhengju), satirical drama, comedy, and tragedy were also valid. But the reality of the situation was very different. For a long time after the founding of the PRC, especially during the GPCR, the orthodox and only view was that the age of tragedy was gone forever. Moreover, to write tragedy would violate the principle that socialist literature should concentrate on promoting the brighter side of life and society. Since art was supposed to illustrate the struggles between the people and their enemies, between socialism and capitalism or revisionism, how could it but end in victory for the "true revolutionaries"? And what could inspire the people more than such a happy, glorious ending? Thus, since it was out of the question that there were any tragedies to be written in the socialist period, no tragedies were possible in socialist literature.

Since things were so confused, Xiang Tong, a critic, felt it necessary to explain from the very beginning why tragedies still could be generated in socialist society. According to Xiang, this was because first there still existed in socialist society "classes and class contradictions, and acute struggles between the proletariat and the bourgeoisie, between the socialist road and the capitalist road". Second, tragedies might occur in the "contradictions and struggles among the people". The last factor causing tragedies could be "vestiges of the ideology of the exploiting classes in the old society" and "old traditions and forces of habit of various kinds". The "lineage theory" (xuetong lun) of like begetting like was identified by Xiang Tong as one of these (Xiang Tong, "Wenyi yaobuyao fanying shehuizhuyi shiqide beiju: cong 'Shanghen' tanqi"—"Should Literature and Art Reflect the Tragedies of the Socialist Period? Beginning with 'The Scar'", *GMRB*, 3 Nov. 1978).

Wang Xiyan, a writer and critic, developed Xiang Tong's view. He explicitly pointed out that, besides the existence of class contradictions (which he admitted to be a major cause of tragedy), the following should not be ignored: defects in certain links of the system; big or small mistakes of the principles, policies, and measurements of the Party and the government; various deviations made by cadres in carrying out policies; and contradictions and struggles among the people. Wang's view, as such, seemed to have gone too far. His opponents insisted that the socialist system itself would no longer bring about tragedies to individuals, the collective, or the whole society. They emphasized that tragedies in socialist society were merely the "vicious results of the opportunist line pushed by conspirators and ambitionists in the Party". Facts, however, spoke louder than words, and these orthodox remarks did not seem to enjoy their earlier unquestionable appeal.

At that time, the "new period literature" was still in an early stage. Though "scar literature" brought about the first awakening of the spirit of tragedy, the great majority of authors still viewed literature in terms of "exposure" and "eulogy". Their works tended to go to extremes and were strongly affected by utilitarianism, which had been promoted by Mao in his *Yan'an Talks*. Later, the literary creation of tragedy underwent several other stages of development. The extremes of "exposure" and "eulogy" gradually disappeared. As one of the most outstanding features of the "new period literature", a great number of tragedies of a sort never before seen were produced. Important works that were either simple tragedies, or somewhat tinged with a tragic color, or expressed a sort of deliberate transcendence of tragic mentality, included: "A Legend of the Tianyun Mountains", "Li Shunda Builds a House" (Gao Xiaosheng, "Li Shunda zao wu", *Yuhua*, 7, 1979; trans. in Lee Yee, ed., *The New Realism*, pp. 31-55), "Love Must Not Be Forgotten" (Zhang Jie, "Ai, shi buneng wangjide", *Beijing wenyi*, 11, 1979; trans. in Zhang Jie, *Love Must Not Be Forgotten*, Beijing, Chinese Literature, 1987, pp. 1-15, and Perry Link, ed., *Roses and Thorns: The Second Blooming of the Hundred Flowers*, Berkeley and Los Angeles, Univ. of California Press, 1984, pp. 245-60), "Soul and Flesh" (Zhang Xianliang, "Ling yu rou", *Sufang*, 9, 1980; trans. in *Prize-winning Stories from China 1980-1981*, Beijing, FLP, 1985, pp. 58-92), "At Middle Age" (Shen Rong, "Ren dao zhongnian"), *Humanity!* (Dai Houying, *Ren a, ren!)* "When the Evening Glow Disappears" (Li Ping, "Wanxia xiaoshide shihou", *SY*, 1:77-137, 1981, reprinted in book form, Beijing, Zhongguo Qingnian, 1981; Part 4 trans. by Daniel Bryant in Michael S. Duke, ed. with introductions, *Contemporary Chinese Literature: An Anthology of Post-Mao Fiction and Poetry*, pp. 59-79), "Life" (Lu Yao, "Rensheng", *Shouhuo*, 3, 1982), "Wreaths at the Foot of the High Mountains", "A

Land of Wonder and Mystery" (Liang Xiaosheng, "Zheshi yipian shenqide tudi", *Beifang wenxue,* 8, 1982; trans. in *CL,* 5:5-34, 1983), "The Lure of the Sea" (Deng Gang, "Mirende hai", *SHWX,* 15, 1983; trans. in *CL,* 1:5-37, Spring 1984), "There Will Be a Storm Tonight" (Liang Xiaosheng, "Jinye you baofengxue", *Qingchun,* 1, 1983, reprinted in *1983 zhongpian xiaoshuo xuan, 2—A Selection of 1983 Novelettes, 2,* Beijing, Renmin Wenxue, 1984, pp. 394-549), *The Soul of the River* (Jiao Jian, *He hun,* Beijing, Shiyue Wenyi, 1987), "The Nineteen Tombs in the Mountains" (Li Cunbao, "Shan zhong, na shijiu zuo fenying", *Kunlun,* 6, 1984), "Chess Master" (Acheng, "Qiwang", *SHWX,* 7, 1984; trans. in *CL,* 2:84-131, Summer 1985, and in Bonnie S. McDougall, trans., *Three Kings: Three Stories from Today's China,* London, Collins Harvill, 1990), "You Have No Other Choice" (Liu Suola, "Ni bie wu xuanze", *RMWX,* 3:4-29, 1985), "The Wild Forest" (Kong Jiesheng, "Dalin wang", *SY,* 6, 1984, reprinted in *Zhongpian xiaoshuo xuankan—Selected Novelettes,* 1:5-55, 1985) and "Xiaobao Village" (Wang Anyi, "Xiaobao zhuang", *Zhongguo zuojia,* 2, 1985, reprinted in *Zhongpian xiaoshuo xuankan,* 6:81-109, 1986).

A better understanding of tragedy seemed to have informed contemporary Chinese literature. Engels' statement on the "tragic conflict between the inexorable demands of history and the practical impossibility of their fulfillment" as a guiding principle for tragedy began to be questioned, though in the previous 1978-79 discussion about tragedy, this classical Marxist explanation did help to widen the people's perspective. Neither were they any longer satisfied with Lu Xun's thesis that "tragedy takes the valued things in life and destroys them for people to see", which was often quoted in 1980 articles as a basic characteristic of tragedy. When Liu Zaifu's "theory of dual combination in characterization" was published, it became accepted that the profundity of tragedy lies not so much in the conflict between man and his external world as in the self-contradiction of his internal world. Liu's idea enabled people to pursue the profound aesthetics of tragedy and the transcendence of tragic mentality. The lack of a mentality of repentance (chanhui yishi) in Chinese literature was also noted. All this originated in the immature work "The Scar": the discussion about it, which lasted for more than half a year, became more significant when seen in this light. History shows that the establishment of the concept of "socialist tragedy", though somewhat ambiguous at the stage of "The Scar" debate, was a major breakthrough in contemporary Chinese literary theory. See also "wenyi wei zhengzhi fuwu" (literature and art serve politics) and "shehuizhuyi xianshizhuyi" (socialist realism).

社会主义初级阶段论
shehuizhuyi chuji jieduan lun
(theory of the primary stage of socialism)

The wording the "primary stage of socialism" first appeared in a talk on the necessity of commodity production given by Mao Zedong at a meeting held in Zhengzhou in November 1958 (in which Mao used "chuqi" instead of "chuji", but the two Chinese phrases share the same meaning). Unfortunately, Mao did not at that time or in the future discuss it in detail. After many years, in an article carried in the *People's Daily* on 5 May 1978, entitled "Putting into Effect the Socialist Principle of 'Distribution According to Work'" ("Guanche zhixing anlaofenpeide shehuizhuyi yuanze"), it was pointed out that today's China was not yet at the first stage of Communist society as conceived by Marx. This means that China was not yet a socialist society in its full sense (Marx regarded socialist society as the first or lower stage of Communist society). It was said that the article was written at Deng

Xiaoping's suggestion, so as to criticize and repudiate "Left" theory and practice. Then the term the "primary stage of socialism" appeared in the "Resolution on Certain Questions in the History of Our Party since the Founding of the PRC" adopted at the 6th Plenum of the 11th PCC on 27 June 1981. One year later, in his political report to the 12th Party Congress on 1 September 1982, Hu Yaobang also mentioned the phrase. But in neither case was the significance of the phrase fully understood. It was even omitted in such an important document as "The Decision About the Reform of the Economic Structure" (adopted at the 3rd Plenum of the 12th PCC on 20 October 1984). Not until the "Resolution Concerning the Guiding Principle in Building Socialist Spiritual Civilization" was passed at the 6th Plenum of the 12th PCC on 28 September 1986 was the theory of the "primary stage of socialism" for the first time employed in defense of policies relating to the existence of multi-economic sectors and the promotion of a commodity economy and free competiton, thereby a proportion of the people might get rich first.

Acting CCP General Secretary Zhao Ziyang and his political secretary Bao Tong took a great leap forward in 1987. On 21 March, Bao Tong drafted a letter for Zhao to Deng, suggesting that the report to the coming 13th CCP National Congress be based on the theory of the "primary stage of socialism". Zhao succeeded in obtaining Deng's agreement. On 25 October, Zhao expounded upon the theory in his report at the Congress. The theory, which was quite liberal, was adopted as Party's new "foothold" (lizudian) for China's current policies. It was justified by two newly confirmed "Marxist" viewpoints: "only on a high degree of commercialization and socialization of production can socialism be built", and "productivity is the ultimate determinant in the development of any society". The Party's basic line for the "primary stage of socialism" was expressed as "one center, two basic points" (yi ge zhongxin, liang ge jibendian). The "one center" means that economic construction is the center of all Party work; the "two basic points" are: on the one hand upholding reform and the open-door policy, and on the other upholding the "four cardinal principles".

Of great significance was that, ten years later, Jiang Zemin, as CCP general secretary, PRC president and CMC chairman, reiterated the theory of the "primary stage of socialism" (though without mentioning Zhao's name). This first occurred in his speech delivered on 29 May 1997 at the Central Party School, a speech generally regarded as an important statement in Jiang's era. On 12 September 1997, in his report at the CCP's 15th National Congress, Jiang Zemin further raised his basic line and program for the "primary stage".

According to Jiang, since the 3rd Plenum of the 11th PCC, the Party has correctly analyzed China's conditions and formulated the scientific thesis that China is still in the primary stage of socialism. The primary stage of socialism is an "undeveloped stage"; it will take at least a century to complete this historical process. The fundamental task of socialism is to develop the productive forces. During the primary stage, Jiang noted, it is all the more necessary to give first priority to concentrating on the development of the productive forces.

During the stage, Jiang said, the principal contradiction in society in China is the one between the growing material and cultural needs of the people and the backwardness of production. This principal contradiction will remain throughout the process of the primary stage of development and in all social activities. Hence China is destined to make economic development the central task of the entire Party and the whole country and to make sure that all other work is subordinate and serves this task.

Focusing on the fundamental task of developing the productive forces, China should take reform as the motive force for promoting all work in the building of socialism with Chinese characteristics. Furthermore, Jiang emphasized that it is of the utmost importance to balance reform, development, and stability and to maintain a stable political environment and public order. "Without stability, nothing can be achieved," he said.

Jiang Zemin also elaborated on three points to build a socialist economy, politics, and culture with Chinese characteristics in the primary stage of socialism. Building a socialist economy with Chinese characteristics means developing a market economy under socialism and constantly emancipating and developing the productive forces. Building socialist politics with Chinese characteristics means managing state affairs according to law and developing socialist democracy under the CCP leadership and with the people as the masters of the country. Building a socialist culture with Chinese characteristics means taking Marxism as the guide, aiming at training people so that they have high ideals, moral integrity, a good education, and a strong sense of discipline, and developing a national, scientific, and popular socialist culture geared to the needs of modernization, of the world, and of the future. The aforementioned basic targets of building a socialist economy, politics, and culture with Chinese characteristics and the basic policies are well integrated and inseparable. They constitute the basic program of the Party for the primary stage of socialism.

Now most of the CCP theorists seem to agree that the primary stage of socialism is the "most decisive national characteristic" (zuidade guoqing) in today's China. The term "socialism with Chinese characteristics", while having strong nationalistic sentiment, suggests that true socialism would take a long time to achieve. To understand this, as a *People's Daily* article said, is not at all easy. It took thirty years of tutuous and bitter experience. The theory is said to be a "golden key to a miracle" ("Zuidade guoqing: shehuizhuyi chuji jieduan"—"The Most Decisive National Characteristic: The Primary Stage of Socialism", *RMRB*, 5 Aug. 1997). However, there is another view, as held by those dubbed "neo-Leftists" (xinzuopai), that completely negates the "primary stage" theory. According to them, this theory fails to get rid of the monistic and Stalinist thinking mode about the "necessary stages of historical development" (lishi fazhan biran jieduan) (Cui Zhiyuan, "Zhonggong shiwudade lilun chuangxin yu juxian"—"The 15th CCP National Congress: Theoretical Innovations and Limitations", *Zhongguo yu shijie*, Jan. 1998). See also "xin shehuizhuyi guan" (new socialist view).

社会主义初级阶段是最大的国情
shehuizhuyi chuji jieduan shi zuidade guoqing
(the primary stage of socialism is the most decisive national characteristic)

See "shehuizhuyi chuji jieduan lun" (theory of the primary stage of socialism).

社会主义初级阶段的社会主要矛盾
shehuizhuyi chuji jieduande shehui zhuyao maodun
(the principal contradiction in society during the primary stage of socialism)

In his report of 12 September 1997 at the CCP's 15th National Congress, Jiang Zemin reiterated that China is still in the primary stage of socialism. During this stage, the principal contradiction in society in China is between the growing material and cultural needs of the people and the backwardness of production. This principal contradiction will remain throughout this stage and in all activities of society.

To determine the principal contradiction in society is of vital importance in China. Mao said in his article "On Contradiction": "If in any process there are a number of contradictions, one of them must be the principal contradiction playing the leading and decisive role, while the rest occupy a secondary and subordinate position. Therefore, in studying any complex process in which there are two or more contradictions, we must devote every effort to finding its principal contradiction. Once this principal contradiction is grasped, all problems can be readily solved" *(SWM,* 1, p. 332).

One of Mao's well-known views in this regard is: "Changes in society are due chiefly to the development of the internal contradictions in society, that is, the contradiction between the productive forces and the relations of production, the contradiction between classes and the contradiction between the old and the new; it is the development of these contradictions that pushes society forward and gives the impetus for the supersession of the old society by the new" *(SWM,* 1, p. 314). Mao asserted that the principal contradiction in the entire historical period of socialism is that between socialism and capitalism, between the proletariat and the bourgeoisie.

As far as the whole society is concerned, of course only the CCP authorities are entitled to make such a stipulation. With regard to a certain field, the leader in the field sometimes may offer his/her opinion. Wang Meng, former minister of culture, was one of the few who did so. Soon after Zhao Ziyang declared at the 13th CCP National Congress that the theory of the "primary stage of socialism" was the Party's basic line, Wang Meng adroitly stated that the principal contradiction in the cultural field was not that between socialism and feudalism or between socialism and capitalism, the resolution of which required endless struggles, but that between "civilization and ignorance". This kind of contradiction, Wang said, determines that culture in the primary stage of socialism must be of the nature of enlightenment and constructiveness and that cultural construction will be time-consuming and protracted (Wang Meng, "My Humble Opinion Concerning Culture in the Primary Stage of Socialism", *Jiushi,* 1, 1989, reprinted in *XHWZ,* 3:153-157, 1989). See also "shehuizhuyi chuji jieduan lun" (theory of the primary stage of socialism).

社会主义大家庭论
shehuizhuyi dajiating lun
(theory of the "socialist community")

After Soviet troops invaded Czechoslovakia on 20 August 1968, the CCP leadership condemned the Soviet Union as expansionist and aggressive, a "social-imperialist" country (shehui diguozhuyi)—"imperialism bearing the banner of socialism". The CPSU leaders were accused of resorting to the theory of the "socialist community" and the theory of "limited sovereignty" (youxian zhuquan lun). With these two theories, they justified interference in the domestic affairs of other countries in what they called the "socialist community". They claimed that the interests of the whole "socialist community" represented a "higher sovereignty" and the sovereignty of any single country in the community was "limited". On the one hand, they would not allow any intervention from outside the "socialist community"; on the other, they could trample on any of these countries' sovereignty on the pretext of mutual support in the community. See also "xiuzhengzhuyi" (revisionism).

社会主义法制国家
shehuizhuyi fazhi guojia
(country with a socialist legal system)

See "yi fa zhi guo" (ruling the nation by law).

社会主义法治国家
shehuizhuyi fazhi guojia
(socialist country ruled by law)

See "yi fa zhi guo" (ruling the nation by law).

社会主义改革观
shehuizhuyi gaigeguan
(socialist view about reform)

See "xin shehuizhuyi guan" (new socialist view).

社会主义公有制
shehuizhuyi gongyouzhi
(socialist public ownership)

See "quanmin suoyouzhi" (ownership by the whole people), "jingji gaige" (economic reform), and "jiejue gongyouzhi xingshi shi you yici sixiang jiefang" (solving the issue of public ownership forms is another emancipation of the mind).

社会主义国有化
shehuizhuyi guoyouhua
(socialist nationalization)

See "quanmin suoyouzhi" (ownership by the whole people), "jingji gaige" (economic reform), and "jiejue gongyouzhi xingshi shi you yici sixiang jiefang" (solving the issue of public ownership forms is another emancipation of the mind).

社会主义国有制
shehuizhuyi guoyouzhi
(socialist state ownership)

See "quanmin suoyouzhi" (ownership by the whole people), "jingji gaige" (economic reform), and "jiejue gongyouzhi xingshi shi you yici sixiang jiefang" (solving the issue of public ownership forms is another emancipation of the mind).

社会主义基本特征是社会公正加市场经济
shehuizhuyi jiben tezheng shi
shehui gongzheng jia shichang jingji
(the basic characteristic of socialism
is social justice plus a market economy)

See "xin shehuizhuyi guan" (new socialist view) and "jingji gaige" (economic reform).

社会主义积累
shehuizhuyi jilei
(socialist accumulation)

See "yuanshi jilei" (previous accumulation).

社会主义就是和谐
shehuizhuyi jiushi hexie
(socialism means harmony)

See "xin shehuizhuyi guan" (new socialist view).

社会主义集体所有制
shehuizhuyi jiti suoyouzhi
(socialist collective ownership)

See "quanmin suoyouzhi" (ownership by the whole people), "jingji gaige" (economic reform), and "jiejue gongyouzhi xingshi shi you yici sixiang jiefang" (solving the issue of public ownership forms is another emancipation of the mind).

社会主义建设总路线
shehuizhuyi jianshe zongluxian
(General Line for Socialist Construction)

At the 2nd Plenum of the 8th PCC (held from 5 to 22 May 1958), following Mao's proposal, the "General Line for Socialist Construction" was officially confirmed. The "General Line" was marked by the slogan "Go all out, aim high, and achieve greater, faster, better, and more economical results in building socialism" (according to Li Zhisui in his *Private Life of Chairman Mao,* Mao used the slogan as early as the end of 1955 and the beginning of 1956).

The basic points of the "General Line" were as follows: 1. "to mobilize all positive factors and correctly handle contradictions among the people; 2. to consolidate and develop socialist ownership, i.e., ownership by the whole people and collective ownership, and consolidate the proletarian dictatorship and proletarian international solidarity; 3. to carry out the technical revolution and cultural revolution step by step, while completing the socialist revolution on the economic, political, and ideological fronts; 4. to develop industry and agriculture simultaneously while giving priority to heavy industry; 5. with centralized leadership, overall planning, proper division of labor and coordination, to develop national and local industries and large, small, and medium-sized enterprises simultaneously; and 6. by means of all this to build our country, in the shortest possible time, into a great socialist country with modern industry, modern agriculture, and modern science and culture" *(RMRB,* 27 May 1958).

The "General Line", together with the "Great Leap Forward" and the "People's Commune", were collectively referred to as the "Three Red Banners". See also "shehuizhuyi chuji jieduan lun" (theory of the primary stage of socialism).

社会主义教育运动
shehuizhuyi jiaoyu yundong
(socialist education movement)

See "shejiao" (socialist education movement).

社会主义精神文明
shehuizhuyi jingshen wenming
(socialist spiritual civilization)

See "liang ge wenming" (two civilizations).

社会主义免费午餐
shehuizhuyi mianfei wucan
(socialist free lunch)

See "gufenzhi gaizao" (joint stock system reform).

社会主义民主
shehuizhuyi minzhu
(socialist democracy)

See "minzhu jizhongzhi" (democratic centralism).

社会主义民主是集中指导下的民主
shehuizhuyi minzhu shi jizhong zhidaoxiade minzhu
(socialist democracy is democracy under the guidance of centralism)

See "minzhu jizhongzhi" (democratic centralism).

社会主义民主是无产阶级专政的基础，无产阶级专政是社会主义民主的保障
shehuizhuyi minzhu shi wuchanjieji zhuanzhengde jichu, wuchanjieji zhuanzheng shi shehuizhuyi minzhude baozhang
(socialist democracy is the basis of the proletarian dictatorship, and the latter is the guarantee of the former)

See "minzhu jizhongzhi" (democratic centralism) and "wuchanjieji zhuanzheng" (dictatorship of the proletariat).

社会主义能够救中国
shehuizhuyi nenggou jiu Zhongguo
(socialism can save China)

See "zhiyou shehuizhuyi caineng jiu Zhongguo" (only socialism can save China).

社会主义全民所有制
shehuizhuyi quanmin suoyouzhi
(socialist ownership by the whole people)

See "quanmin suoyouzhi" (ownership by the whole people), "jingji gaige" (economic reform), and "jiejue gongyouzhi xingshi shi you yici sixiang jiefang" (solving the issue of public ownership forms is another emancipation of the mind).

社会主义人道主义
shehuizhuyi rendaozhuyi
(socialist humanism)

For a long time in China's Communist regime, any positive use of the concept of "socialist humanism" was unthinkable. A typical refutation was: humanism is fraudulent; when modified by "socialist", it is doubly fraudulent (One of those holding this view was Xing Bensi, as seen in his book *Humanism in the History of European Philosophy—Ouzhou Zhexueshishangde Rendaozhuyi).*

In the humanism debate of the early 1980s, "socialist humanism" was a controversial term. Zhou Yang, then consultant to the PCC Propaganda Department and chairman of the ACF, asserted that there must be something called "socialist humanism" or "Marxist humanism" (Zhou Yang, "An Inquiry into Some Theoretical Problems of Marxism", *RMRB,* 16 Mar. 1983). Among prominent philosophers and critics advocating a similar view were Ru Xin, vice-president of CASS, Wang Ruoshui, deputy editor-in-chief of the *People's Daily,* Wang Yuanhua, a leader of the CWA Shanghai Branch, Xue Dezhen, deputy editor-in-chief of the People's Publishing House, Zhu Guangqian, senior professor at Beijing University, and Ruan Ming, a teacher at the CCP Central Party School. With what they asserted to have been proved by social practice, they reached the following conclusion: Without socialist humanism there would not be socialism, but only "modern superstition" and "feudal-fascist dictatorship" as seen during the GPCR. Wang Ruoshui listed four concrete requirements for "socialist humanism":

—firmly abandoning the "total dictatorship" and cruel struggles of the ten-year civil strife; abandoning the personality cult which deifies one man and degrades the people; upholding the equality of every person before the truth and the law and the sanctity of personal freedom and dignity;

—opposing feudal concepts of ranks and privilege, capitalist money worship and the making of people into commodities or mere instruments; demanding that a human being genuinely be seen as a human being, and assessing an individual's worth on the basis of what he is in himself and not on the basis of origins, position, or wealth;

—recognizing man as the goal, not only of socialist production but of all work; establishing and developing a new type social relationship of mutual respect, mutual loving care, mutual help, and friendly co-operation which embodies socialist spiritual civilization; opposing callous bureaucracy, and extreme individualism which harms others for self-benefit;

—stressing the human factor in socialist construction; giving full play to the spirit of self-directedness and creativity of the working people; stressing education, the nurturing of talent and the all-round development of man.... (See Wang Ruoshui, "A Defense of Humanism", *WHB*, 17 Jan. 1983; David A. Kelly, ed. and trans., "Writings on Humanism, Alienation and Philosophy", *Chinese Studies in Philosophy,* vol. xvi, 3:87-88, Spring 1985).

In the 1983 campaign to eliminate spiritual pollution, Zhou Yang and Wang Ruoshui were fiercely attacked. Hu Qiaomu, the No. 1 Party ideologue, dominated China's ideological-theoretical circles. In his January 1984 article "On Problems Concerning Humanism and Alienation", he wrote that a Communist is opposed to the abstract propaganda of humanism and the humanistic idealist conception of history, but is not sweepingly opposed to humanism in all senses. What he demands is to give humanism a "Marxist analysis", criticizing bourgeois humanism and propagating and practicing "socialist humanism". By socialist humanism, Hu means an "ethical principle" with a Marxist interpretation of the world and history as its basis. On the one hand, it is the development of "revolutionary humanism" (geming rendaozhuyi). On the other, it is inferior to Communist morality, which is the highest moral standard for contemporary people.

But many found Hu's view unconvincing. As Gao Ertai, an aesthete, said, it seems a great change that those who originally opposed humanism now recognize socialist humanism, but such a change does not exist in its true sense. Furthermore, to treat socialist humanism as some ethical, moral norms in conformity with certain social relationships is not only not an original idea but also a retreat to something like pre-Marxist, abstract humanism. Gao explicitly pointed out that "socialist humanism" means "Marxist humanism" and that there should not be any doubt about it. Logically, socialist humanism is a world outlook as well as a conception of history (Gao Ertai, "Humanism: A Memorandum on a Contemporary Debate", *Sichuan shida xuebao,* 4, 1986, extracted and reprinted in *XHWZ,* 10:25-33, 1986). See also "qingwu yundong" (campaign to eliminate spiritual pollution) and "rendaozhuyi lunzheng" (humanism debate).

社会主义人道主义是双重的欺骗
shehuizhuyi rendaozhuyi shi shuangchongde qipian
(socialist humanism is doubly fraudulent)

See "shehuizhuyi rendaozhuyi" (socialist humanism) and "rendaozhuyi lunzheng" (humanism debate).

社会主义人道主义的现代意识
shehuizhuyi rendaozhuyide xiandai yishi
(modern mentality of socialist humanism)

See "rendaozhuyi shi xinshiqiwenxuede zhuliu" (humanism is the mainstream in the literature of the new period) and "rendaozhuyi lunzheng" (humanism debate).

社会主义时期的遵义会议
shehuizhuyi shiqide Zunyi huiyi
(Zunyi Conference of the socialist period)

See "Zunyi Huiyi" (Zunyi Conference) and "di'er ci geming" (second revolution).

社会主义市场经济
shehuizhuyi shichang jingji
(socialist market economy)

See "jingji gaige" (economic reform).

社会主义所有制
shehuizhuyi suoyouzhi
(socialist ownership)

See "quanmin suoyouzhi" (ownership by the whole people), "jingji gaige" (economic reform), and "jiejue gongyouzhi xingshi shi you yici sixiang jiefang" (solving the issue of public ownership forms is another emancipation of the mind).

社会主义条件下人的异化
shehuizhuyi tiaojianxia rende yihua
(man's alienation under the condition of socialism)

In the humanism wave of the early 1980s, "man's alienation", especially, "man's alienation under the condition of socialism", or "man's alienation in a socialist society", was frequently discussed. In literary circles, it was generally accepted that a writer with humanistic responsibility would be aware of, and thereby would present, man's alienation of every sort in society. In fact, there were a great number of stories that exposed and denounced the anti-humanistic social realities during the GPCR, in which the writers highlighted various tragedies of man's alienation. For instance, the spiritual world of Xie Huimin (in "The Class Teacher"), herself a pure and honest girl, is controlled by something diametrically contradictory to her nature. Wang Xiaohua (in "The Scar") loves her mother, but there is a force pushing her to another extreme. Bai Hui (in Feng Jicai, "Puhuade qilu"—"A Wrong Road Paved with Flowers", *Shouhuo,* 2, 1979, reprinted in *Feng Jicai ji—Works of Feng Jicai,* Fuzhou, Haixia Wenyi, 1986, pp. 1-129) is a girl with a gentle disposition, but she goes so far as to join others in beating a friend's mother to death. All this shows how human nature has been negated by inhuman nature. A typical phenomenon in the GPCR was "modern superstition". He Yuzhong, an old miner (in Da Li, "Qiancheng"—"Piety", *SHWX,* 1:23-31, 1980), and Jin Bu, a county Party secretary (in Gong Liu, "Chang gengzu"—"Intestinal Obstruction", *SHWX,* 10:15-25, 1979), are characters who have been alienated in this way. Alienation, in this case as a psychological phenomenon, takes place in the depths of their thoughts, which results in self-negation. Another also often quoted work is Zong Pu's "What Am I", a modernist description of how a couple commits suicide after having undergone all sorts of humiliation during the GPCR. As described in the above-mentioned works and many others, there were three kinds of alienation of human nature: human beings persecuted as "niuguisheshen" (that is, class enemies of all descriptions who became "contemptible wretches" under the dictatorship of the proletariat), human beings degenerating into "beasts" (such as those Red Guards who cruelly persecuted their victims), and Mao worshipped as "god" in the "modern superstition" movement. Quite a number of writers treated the upheaval of the GPCR as an extreme form of man's alienation, or "the inhumanization of man" (rende feirenhua).

Government and Party officials, who should be "public servants of the people" (gongpu), become the people's lords and masters (laoye)—this was a form of "socialist alienation", and a major danger to socialist society, according to the "alienation critics" in the early 1980s. There are plenty of examples. They include Ji Shen, a wicked Party official in Jiang Zilong's short story "Manager Qiao Assumes Office", the general who indulges in pleasure in Ye Wenfu's political poem "General, You Can't Do Such Things!", and Qin Bo, wife of a vice-minister who is styled as "Madam Marxism" in Shen Rong's novelette "At Middle Age". They are all corrupted by feudal autocracy, bureaucracy, and special privileges, and become alienated as the people's lords and masters. Their common characteristic is described as "both the products of a certain alienation force and also its incarnations".

In this regard, a work many critics have discussed is Wang Meng's 1980 novelette "The Butterfly" ("Hudie", *SY,* 4:4-37, 1980, reprinted in *XWY, Novelettes,*

1, pp. 313-51; trans. in *CL,* 1:3-55, 1981). Zhang Siyuan, the protagonist, reveals the alienation of human nature. It is the people, critic Zhang Ren said, who welcome Zhang—at the time a young "veteran revolutionary"—to the city with flowers and praise. However, ignoring the demand that Party cadres ought to be public servants, Zhang estranges himself from the people when he becomes the municipal Party secretary. "Power has made his character alienated" (Zhang Ren, "Lun Wang Meng de xiaoshuo"—"On Wang Meng's Fiction", *Xinwenxue luncong,* 2:84, 1982). Another critic, Yu Jianzhang, saw in it a description of the negation or alienation of human feeling—in this case, the sense of responsibility of a revolutionary (Yu Jianzhang, "Lun dangdai wenxue chuangzuozhongde rendaozhuyi chaoliu: dui sannian wenxue chuangzuode huigu yu sikao"—"On the Trend of Humanism among Contemporary Literary Works: A Review of Literary Creations of the Past Three Years", *WXPL,* 1, 1981, reprinted in *WYLZJ,* p. 186). According to the writer and critic Li Tuo, "Butterfly" describes the internal contradiction and agony of the protagonist, who feels a sort of personality division that causes him anguish day and night. Readers may ask: Why can a Communist be pushed by a certain force to become lord and master? Is it a form of man's alienation under the condition of socialism? And how can this alienation be overcome? (Li Tuo, "Dianying yinggai xiang wenxue xue xie shenme"—"What Should Film Learn from Literature", *Dianying juzuo,* 5:64, 1982). The critic He Xilai pointed out that, the protagonist, respectively as Old Zhang and Vice-Minister Zhang, has a dual nature. It is not created by the flaw in his personality but by the era and the social environment. This is a manifestation of human nature's alienation in one and the same person, which still exists under the "new social condition" (He Xilai, "Gongpu he zhuren zhijian: lun xinshiqi wenxuede yi ge chaoliu"—"Between Public Servant and Master: On a Trend in the New Period Literature", *SY,* 1:218, 1981). For this reason, he said, Wang Meng should be praised for his "exceptional insight", his accurate expression of "both the historical mechanism and psychological process of this alienation" (ibid.).

Having experienced the ten-year nightmare of the GPCR, many Chinese intellectuals came closer to humanism; and from humanism they found that they had to deal with the problem of alienation. Wang Meng was no exception. "Man's alienation under the condition of socialism" is indeed an important issue in humanistic Marxism. Due to political reasons, however, its exploration ended with the 1983 campaign against "spiritual pollution". See also "yihua wenxue" (alienated literature; literature of alienation), "shehuizhuyi yihua lun" (theory of socialist alienation), and "qingwu yundong" (campaign to eliminate spiritual pollution).

社会主义为文艺服务，文艺为人民服务
shehuizhuyi wei wenyi fuwu, wenyi wei renmin fuwu
(socialism serves literature and art, and literature and art serve the people)

See "wenyi wei zhengzhi fuwu" (literature and art serve politics).

社会主义文化大革命
shehuizhuyi wenhua dageming
(Great Socialist Cultural Revolution)

See "wen'ge" (Cultural Revolution).

社会主义文艺的根本任务
shehuizhuyi wenyide genben renwu
(fundamental task for socialist literature and art)

It was said that "to create heroic characters of workers, peasants and soldiers is the fundamental task for socialist literature and art". Though the idea was advocated most vigorously by the Gang of Four during the GPCR, its roots are found in Mao's 1942 *Yan'an Talks*. See "wenyi wei zhengzhi fuwu" (literature and art serve politics).

社会主义物质文明
shehuizhuyi wuzhi wenming
(socialist material civilization)

See "liang ge wenming" (two civilizations) and "gongchanzhuyi shi shehuizhuyi jingshen wenmingde hexin" (Communist ideology is the core of socialist spiritual civilization).

社会主义现实主义
shehuizhuyi xianshizhuyi
(socialist realism)

Realism is the objective representation of contemporary social reality. It claims to be all-inclusive in subject matter and aims to be objective in method, even though this objectivity is hardly ever achieved in practice. Realism is didactic, moralistic, reformist. Without always realizing the difference between description and prescription it tries to reconcile the two in the concept of 'type'. In some writers, but not all, realism becomes historistic: it grasps social reality as dynamic evolution (René Wellek, *Concepts of Criticism*, New Haven, Yale University Press, 1963, pp. 252-53).

Marxist critics highly praise the achievements of critical realism (pipan xianshizhuyi), which became the leading literary trend in Europe at the beginning of the nineteenth century. But they emphasize at the same time that critical realism should be applied to capitalism, while in a socialist society, writers should adopt socialist realism. The principle of socialist realism calls for a truthful, historically concrete representation of reality in its revolutionary development, taken in combination with the task of the ideological transformation and education of the working people in the spirit of socialism. It was formally put forward and adopted at the 1934 First USSR Writers Congress as the basic principle for literary creation and criticism in the Soviet Union. In 1954 when the second congress was held, the principle about education in the spirit of socialism was deleted. In the 1970s, most Soviet writers and artists agreed that socialist realism should be treated as an open system—"a historically open system of artistic styles" (this was attacked as revisionist at that time by China's Party critics).

As early as November 1933, Zhou Yang introduced the theory of socialist realism into China for the first time (Zhou Yang, "Guanyu 'shehuizhuyide xianshizhuyi yu gemingde langmanzhuyi'"—"On Socialist Realism and Revolutionary Romanticism", in *Zhou Yang Wenji, 1—Works of Zhou Yang,* 1, Beijing, Renmin wenxue, 1984, pp. 101-17). Thereafter, in view of the nature of the revolution the CCP was then making, CCP-led writers began to use the term "revolutionary realism" (geming xianshizhuyi), which in essence is the same as socialist realism. At the 2nd Plenum of the 8th PCC held in May 1958, Mao Zedong put forward a new idea: "A combination of revolutionary realism and revolutionary romanticism should be adopted as the creative method for proletarian literature and art." (This was first revealed by Zhou Yang in his article "Xin min'ge kaituole shigede xin daolu"—"New Folk Songs Have Opened Up a New Path for Poetry", *HQ,* inaugural issue, 1958.) Mao's "two-in-one combination" (shuang jiehe) was regarded as a "development" of socialist realism, but many post-Mao critics argue that there was no essential difference between the two ideas.

One of the many issues concerning socialist realism is the issue of "typicalness" (dianxing). Chinese critics often quoted Engels' formulation in his letter to Margaret Harkness in April 1888: "Realism, to my mind, implies, besides truth of detail, the truthful reproduction of typical characters under typical circumstances." For a long time in the past, they took "typicalness" as only embodied in something that existed in plenty and universally. At the 1980 Script Writing Forum, Chen Huangmei, a critic and senior cultural leader, admitted that this is dogmatic and one-sided, and agreed that some individual, incidental phenomena may be typical as well. It is absolutely all right, therefore, for literature and art to reflect those incidental, individual events, phenomena, and persons. However, he warned, there is one thing a writer should remember: as far as typical circumstances are concerned, political and social typical circumstances in a certain country are an entirety, a coherent whole that shows the inexorable trend of history under given conditions. In particular, when a writer deals with something like the GPCR, during which contradictions were very intricate, he must pay close attention to the essential aspect of the given times, and make sure that the incidental, individual phenomena, events, and persons are all the products of the typical circumstances. Only when the essential aspect of the times is truly and fully reproduced, can the complex, and even incidental, individual events and phenomena in life be reflected correctly and deeply. In other words, only then can the internal relations and the source of things (their essence) be found. He declared:

"If the essential aspect of typical circumstances (dianxing huanjingde benzhi bufen) has not been reflected, then the individual, incidental persons and events will lose their typicalness. There is no truthfulness of typicalness without the truthfulness of the historical background. Typicalness must have the brand of the times" (Chen Huangmei, "Bawo shidai jingshen, tigao chuangzuo shuiping: zai juben chuangzuo zuotanhuishangde jianghua"—"Speech at the Script Writing Forum", *Dianying yishu,* 4, 1980, reprinted in *XWY, Theory,* 2, p. 905).

In light of the spirit of socialist realism, the key to describe the "essential aspect of typical circumstances", the "truthfulness of the historical background", or the "brand of the times" is: to "write about the developing trend" (xie fazhan qushi). The idea (which may have slightly different expressions) had long been raised as a basic Party demand on China's writers. In his 1980 "Speech at the Forum on Script Writing", which can be said to be another elucidation after Mao's *Yan'an Talks* on literature and art made by a CCP leader, Hu Yaobang raised it again.

Hu stated in his speech: "The essence of society is the inherent law of social development. In order to reflect it correctly, we should not only reflect the contradictions and struggles between the old and the new, but also their developing trend, the progressive force which holds sway in this new society of ours. It does not mean that backward, gloomy things should not be reflected. Those things, as long as they are representative, typical, should also be reflected. As far as literature and art as a whole are concerned, however, if backwardness and gloominess are reflected one-sidedly and constantly, I don't think it can be said that the essence of our society is reflected sufficiently and accurately. It is not in accord with the total reality of society" (Hu Yaobang, "Speech at the Forum on Script Writing", *Guangjiaojing,* 92:29, May 1980).

Therefore, Hu asked writers and artists to pay attention to the two following points: "First, isolated and local cases should not be exaggerated in a way that makes them seem to have universal and overall significance. Second, superficial and temporary things should not be described as essential, immutable, and ever-lasting. Otherwise, there will be no truthfulness in your work. This is because something can look as if it were true if judged from isolated and local cases or from details in daily life, but actually not be true if judged integrally, essentially, and with an overall perspective which takes the developing trend into consideration" (ibid., p. 35).

In the 1981 version of Hu's speech, the entire second passage was deleted. Instead, a new passage was added: "First, not everything incidental can be taken indiscriminately as artistic truthfulness, which should be the truthfulness of typicality, the truthfulness of the essence of things. Second, temporary things should not be described as immutable and ever-lasting. Moreover, dialectics in the development of history should be reflected" *(WYLZJ,* p. 24). In the first passage as quoted above, the phrase "as one aspect of the essence" was added at the end of the following sentence: "Those things, as long as they are representative, typical, should also be reflected" (ibid., p. 11).

Hu Yaobang's view about "writing about the developing trend", even revised, was found erroneous. Socialist realism was seriously questioned.

Many critics expressed their views about the relationship between "phenomenon" (xianxiang) and "essence" (benzhi). Zhou Jieren reached the conclusion: there is no such thing as pure, undisguised "essence" in the objective world. What is called "essence" is "the inherent contradiction of the phenomenon, and the position of each aspect of the contradiction in the unity of opposites" (Zhou Jieren, "Ta zai nali shizu?"—"Where Does it Slip?", *WYB,* 7, 1980, reprinted in *XHYB, WZB,* 9:148, 1980). Essence, therefore, exists only in objective phenomena. Any natural, social, or spiritual phenomenon, no matter what it is, is the demonstration of a certain kind of essence. Even false appearance, if it is acknowledged to be "a distorted reflection of essence", must also be regarded as "a prescription, an aspect, or a link of essence" (ibid.).

Since all phenomena in the world possess their own essence, Zhou Jieren said, it is not only meaningless but also inconceivable to set essence as the measure by which to choose source material. Furthermore, he pointed out that it is ridiculous to say, for example, that the GPCR, along with bureaucracy and special privileges of leading cadres at each level of the Party and state institutions, were neither the "mainstream" nor the "essence" of Chinese socialist society (ibid., p. 151).

Critics strongly rejected this formula: "There is only one kind of essence for a specific society, only one kind of typical circumstance for a specific age, and only one kind of typical character for a specific class" (yi ge shehui zhiyou yi zhong benzhi, yi ge shidai zhiyou yi zhong dianxing huanjing, yi ge jieji zhiyou yi zhong dianxing renwu). The formula, though sounding very absurd, had long been held as correct. Since defenders quoted, almost without exception, Engels' remark about typical characters in typical circumstances, Hu Dezhi said that Engels' remark was not an annotation of the "spirit of realism" (Hu Dezhi, "Renhe yitiao tongwang zhenlide tujing du bu yinggai hushi"—"None of the Roads to the Truth Should Be Neglected", *Meishu,* 7, 1980, reprinted in *XHYB,WZB,* 9:146-48, 1980). Peng Lixun, another critic, expressed his disagreement with the thesis that "Typical characters in typical circumstances are those who are representative of the major tendency of historical development and representative of a rather large category of people" (Peng Lixun, "Ruhe lijie 'dianxing huanjingzhongde dianxing renwu'"—"How to Understand 'Typical Characters in Typical Circumstances'", *WXPL,* 4, 1980, extracted and reprinted in *XHYB, WZB,* 9:142-43, 1980).

As critic Xu Junxi pointed out, there was a popular view in China which held that, at the time of the proletarian revolution and socialism, only the circumstances of active struggle were typical. As a result, works chiefly describing negative characters and exposing the dark side of society were virtually illegal in the country. But this view was completely wrong. Xu gave two reasons. 1. "Essence" (benzhi) is not the same as "mainstream" (zhuliu). A work that succeeds in reflecting the essence and laws of the times does not necessarily describe the mainstream of life. One such example is Lu Xun's *The True Story of A Q*. 2. Typical circumstances in a specific work are not a complete "epitome" (suoying) of an entire social life. A work will be of typical significance if it presents a certain essential aspect of life (such as Shen Rong's "At Middle Age"), and one should not require it to reflect all the essential features of society (Xu Junxi, "Yi zhong bixu pochude gongshi: zailun dianxing huanjing he dianxing renwu"—"A Formulation That Must Be Done Away With: More on Typical Circumstances and Typical Characters", *SHWX*, 8, 1981, reprinted in *WYLZJ*, pp. 630-32).

As to the demand that "negative characters" should be presented in "positive circumstances" (see Cheng Daixi, "Buneng ruci qingshuaide piping Engesi"—"Engels Should Not Be Criticized in Such an Indiscreet Way", *SHWX*, 4, 1981, reprinted in *WYLZJ*, pp. 625-26), Xu's answer was also quite eloquent. First, he said, if a writer tries to endow his characters and their circumstances with traits and contents of the times, he should not rely on a description of an external background of the times. Instead, this can be achieved only by the writer's profound understanding and truthful description of the "actual relationships" (xianshi guanxi) in that part of social life he is presenting. Second, in terms of artistic practice, it is untenable and very harmful to require every work to set its "negative characters" in "positive circumstances", regardless of the different situations and peculiarities in the relationships of characters and in the events described in a specific work. On the one hand, characters are the products of their circumstances and, on the other, the circumstances are the result of the characters' activities. "The two depend on each other for existence and are both cause and effect to each other" (Xu Junxi, *WYLZJ*, p. 634). Furthermore, in actual life, the relationships between people and their circumstances are intricate and volatile, and cannot abide by a stereotypical rule. Thus he suggested: "Negative characters in negative circumstances should also be presented" (xiaoji huanjingzhongde xiaoji renwu ye yinggai biaoxian). He asked: "Since negative characters in negative circumstances do exist in actual life, why should this not be presented in literature and art, which should be a truthful and diverse reflection of life?" (ibid., p. 635).

These theoretical inquiries by critics in 1980 and 1981 seriously challenged Engels' formulation about typical circumstances and typical characters and its traditional interpretation. They also rejected accusations against controversial works such as "In the Unwritten Records", "What If I Really Were", and "A Woman Thief", including the accusations made by Chen Huangmei and Hu Yaobang at the 1980 Script Writing Forum. Nevertheless, these inquiries, understandably, were not thoroughgoing. For instance, when discussing whether a literary work should be allowed to describe backward, gloomy things which are of typical significance, Xu Junxi gave a very weak answer to the charge that he had failed to mention that writers should reflect in their works "the developing trend" (fazhan qushi) of the contradictions and struggles between the old and the new, like Hu Yaobang in his Script Writing Forum speech (Cheng Daixi, *WYLZJ*, pp. 624-25). In his defense, Xu argued that he had already pointed out that writers should "truthfully and correctly reflect the inherent characteristics (guyou tezheng) and internal relationships (neizai lianxi) of things". So, he said, his meaning was similar to Hu Yaobang's (Xu Junxi, *WYLZJ*, p. 637). Obviously, here he was distorting Hu's meaning. When using the term "the developing trend", Hu Yaobang was referring to the principle of socialist realism: this calls for a truthful, historically concrete representation of "reality in its revolutionary development" taken in combination with the task of the ideological transformation and education of the working people in the spirit of socialism. Following the term "the developing trend", Hu inserted another phrase: "the progressive force which holds sway in this society of ours" (Hu Yaobang, "Speech at the Forum on Script Writing", *Guangjiaojing,* 92:29, May 1980). The meaning of these words is self-explanatory: when a writer is asked to write about "the developing trend", it means that he should write about "reality in its revolutionary development", i.e., "the progressive force which holds sway in this society of ours". Xu Junxi's argument about negative characters in negative circumstances proved that Hu Yaobang was wrong to make demands of literature and art in this way. But Xu could not further point out the fallacy of writing about "the developing trend" or "reality in its revolutionary development".

Nevertheless, the debate was significant. Admittedly, as early as the early 1980s, socialist realism had declined in China. Many writers no longer accepted it as their guiding principle. In this respect, Wang Meng took the lead. In 1980, he shocked the Chinese literary world with six newly published stories which caused a national debate. He did not seem to care when he was charged with being influenced by the theory that fiction could dispense with plot, characterization, and the creation of "typical characters in typical circumstances". If he failed to create typical characters in some of his works, this was because he already believed this demand of Engels' was not the be-all and end-all of literature. For a time, Wang Meng was regarded as a "Chinese agent" of the "stream-of-consciousness". Under his influence, a number of new genres in fiction writing appeared in succession.

Later, both in theory and in creative practice, socialist realism was subjected to more criticism and repudiation. Many came to understand that the crux of the matter about socialist realism does not lie in the creation of typical characters in typical circumstances but in the demand for this kind of creation and its success being decided by whether to write about "the developing trend", or "the progressive force that holds sway in this society of ours", or "reality in its revolutionary development". This demand certainly means that literature and art must serve politics. As Xia Zhongyi, a young critic, pointed out, "The phrase 'reality in its revolutionary development' means that the general trend of the whole world, including life, history, and society, has already been indicated by the leader. The mission of writers and artists is merely to 'diagram' these doctrines with realistic skills, so as to lure readers into a foolish loyalty to the present order, no matter whether this order conforms with intuitive knowledge or not" (Xia Zhongyi, "Lishi wu ke bihui"—"History Cannot Be Ignored", *WXPL,* 4:12, July 1989). See also "xinshiqi wenxuede duoyuan fazhan" (pluralistic development of the literature of the new period) and "wenyi wei zhengzhi fuwu" (literature and art serve politics).

社会主义新人
shehuizhuyi xin ren
(new socialist man)

"New socialist man" was a frequently used concept in the Mao period. (Sometimes, it was replaced by the similar term "new Communist man"—"gongchanzhuyi xin ren".) From the 1980s, people were increasingly reluctant to use it, though from time to time it still appeared in official documents. New socialist men and women refer to those who work hard for the interests of the people, defend the honor of the socialist motherland, and dedicate themselves to her future. Mao demanded that China's writers and artists portray and help foster the new socialist man. They were asked to portray features of the pioneers in the socialist revolution and construction, their revolutionary ideals and scientific approach, their lofty sentiments and creative ability, and their broad and realistic vision. Images of this new man would stimulate the enthusiasm of the masses for socialism and inspire their creative activities. Deng reiterated Mao's demand when he spoke to China's writers and artists at their 4th National Congress (held from 30 October to 16 November 1979). Later, in a speech delivered at a cadre meeting on 16 January 1980, when explaining why discarding the slogan that literature and art are subordinate to politics does not mean that they can be divorced from politics, Deng said: "The fostering of a new socialist man means politics." (*SWD*, p. 240).

社会主义新生事物
shehuizhuyi xinsheng shiwu
(newly emerging socialist things)

Like the term "new socialist man", "newly emerging socialist things" was also a frequently used term in the Mao period. People were urged to support and praise those things. The GPCR was hailed at that time for making possible many "lively and vigorous newly emerging socialist things". They included: the vigorous development of the mass movement to study Marxism-Leninism-Mao Zedong Thought, the birth of the revolutionary committee, the strengthening of a centralized Party leadership, the creation and popularization of model revolutionary theatrical works, the revolution in education, the rustication of educated young people, barefoot doctors and cooperative medical service for rural areas, the mass movement to study the historical experience of the struggle between Confucianism and Legalism and of class struggle as a whole, and the three-in-one combination of the old, the middle-aged, and the young in leading bodies at various levels. These things, which had been said to indicate progress in China's socialist cause, disappeared one after another after the GPCR. See also "wen'ge" (Cultural Revolution) and "xinzuopai" (neo-Leftists).

社会主义异化论
shehuizhuyi yihua lun
(theory of socialist alienation)

As early as the first half of the 1960s, the alienation issue came up in the PRC. But it was among a small circle, basically some CCP theorists, and the exploration ended during the GPCR before it had substantially developed. Nevertheless, it did have some achievements. Wang Ruoshui's 1978 essay "On the Concept of 'Alienation'" *(Waiguo zhexue yanjiu jikan,* 1:1-34, 1978), for example, was actually written in 1963-64. Also, at the May 1982 forum on Mao Zedong Thought in literature and art (jointly sponsored by the ACF and the Literature Institute of CASS), Zhou Yang said that he still adhered to the view he had raised in a speech he gave on 26 October 1963 to the Department of Philosophy and Social Sciences, Chinese Academy of Sciences. In the speech, entitled "Fighting Tasks of Workers in Philosophy and the Social Sciences" ("Zhexue shehui kexue gongzuozhede zhandao renwu", *RMRB,* 27 Dec. 1963), he said: "If alienation is explained according to a materialistic point of view; if it is understood in light of the dialectic law that 'one invariably divides into two' and that they will go to their own opposites... it should be admitted that alienation is a kind of phenomenon universal in the natural world, and in human society as well, and that its forms are varied" (Zhou Yang, "Yi yao jianchi, er yao fazhan"—"Firstly to Maintain, Secondly to Develop", *RMRB,* 23 June 1982).

But in the early 1980s, alienation, together with humanism in general, was propagated throughout the country with great *élan*. The exploration of human nature and humanism greatly promoted the exploration of alienation within political-philosophical circles. While a prolonged war between rival exegeses of the relevant works by Marx and Engels, especially by the young Marx, continued, those who accepted the alienation theory seemed to be competing with one another to make use of it to explore a variety of problems in different spheres. The concept of "alienation" had been largely neglected by the public since it was introduced into China several decades earlier. But then it suddenly became the main topic of discussion. There appeared an "alienation craze" (yihua re).

One of the new distinctions, and no doubt the most important one, in the explorations of the time can be seen in the following assertion by Wang Ruoshui: "As to the question of whether there is alienation in socialism... we should admit that practice has proved that there is. There is not only ideological alienation, but also political and even economic alienation" (Wang Ruoshui, "Tantan yihua wenti"—"Discussing the Alienation Question", *Xinwen zhanxian,* 8, 1980, reprinted in *WRB*, p. 189). Wang even explained the CCP's policies in light of alienation. According to him, the ideological, political, and organizational lines laid down by the Party since the 1978 3rd Plenum of its 11th Central Committee can all be understood to include the content of how to overcome alienation (Wang Ruoshui, "Wenyi yu rende yihua wenti"—"Literature and Art and the Problem of the Alienation of Man", *SHWX,* 9, 1980, reprinted in *WHB,* 25 Sept. 1980).

Wang's view, judging from numerous articles published from 1980 to 1983, undoubtedly enjoyed a lot of support. Other articles complemented Wang's work by exploring the differences between socialist alienation and capitalist alienation (see, for instance, Zhang Quanliang, "Shehuizhuyi yihua yu zibenzhuyi yihuade qubie"—"The Differences between Socialist Alienation and Capitalist Alienation", *Shehui kexue Jikan,* 3 1982). What was of great significance was Zhou Yang's response three years later. On the solemn occasion of the three-day conference marking the centenary of the death of Marx held under the auspices of CASS, the CCP Central Party School, and other leading bodies, he devoted much of his speech to an elucidation of alienation.

Zhou Yang first defined alienation: "Alienation appears when a subject in its process of development creates by its own activity something which is its opposite, and which then becomes an external, alien force, turning around to oppose or control the subject itself" (Zhou Yang, "An Inquiry into Some Theoretical Problems of Marxism", *RMRB,* 16 Mar. 1983).

He continued: "Acknowledging socialist humanism and opposing alienation are two aspects of one matter. Although socialism wipes out exploitation, which means it has overcome the most important form of alienation, and although socialism is greatly superior to capitalism, this does not mean that there is no alienation in socialism. We did many stupid things in the past in economic construction due to our lack of experience and understanding of socialist construction—a realm of necessity—and in the end we ate our own bitter fruit; this is alienation in the economic realm. Since democracy and the legal system are not on a sound basis, public servants of the people sometimes make indiscriminate use of the power conferred on them by the people and turn into the people's masters; this is alienation in the political realm, also called alienation of power. As for alienation in the ideological realm, the most typical example is the personality cult, which is similar in some aspects to the alienation of religion criticized by Feuerbach" (ibid.).

This is what is called the "theory of socialist alienation" which became a nationwide ideological trend. Theorists tried to analyse what they saw as the phenomena of alienation in socialist society, and trace the reasons why alienation can be generated under the condition of socialism. Socialist society, some explained, is a rudimentary stage of communism and inevitably still has some vestiges of the capitalist society from which it was born. In this stage, there exist commodity production, division of labor in society, and the "three great differences" (san da chabie) between workers and peasants, between cities and the countryside, and between manual and mental labor. Bourgeois rights also exist in the means of distribution. All this determines that equality in socialist society is only preliminary. What is more, China has not undergone the stage of capitalism, entering into a socialist society directly from a semi-colonial and semi-feudal society. As a result, there is a strong feudal influence, which forms a vast trammel confining the people, in terms of psychology, customs, morality, and tradition (Zhang Kuiliang et al., "Lun shehuizhuyi shehui rende jiazhi wenti"—"On the Problem of Human Value in Socialist Society", *Xuexi yu tansuo,* 1, 1982). Where the above analysis only concentrates on the issue of stages in society, many other critics began touching on the problems of China's socialist system itself. Critic Liu Ben, for instance, tried to explain what he called "the mystery of the present-day worship of power" (Liu Ben, "Quanli chongbai ji qi genyuan—tan xianshi shenghuozhongde yichong yihua xianxiang"—"Power Worship and Its Cause: A Discussion of the Phenomenon of Alienation in Actual Life", *Xueshu yuekan,* 6, 1981). First of all, he pointed out, the life-long cadre-post system (zhongshen zhi) naturally defines the division of labor as between administrators and workers, and makes possible the formation of special interests of a few administrators. Accordingly, this will lead to a separation of the ownership of the means of production and the right to control and to enjoy it, thus damaging socialist public ownership. Moreover, as a result of the long-standing practice that blurs the different functions of the Party and the government and intertwines political and economic powers together, there has appeared an excessive concentration of power in the hands of a few people.

While scholars were enthusiastically discussing alienation and humanism, a power struggle was developing at the top level of the CCP. Some Party figures wanted to topple the newly elected Party General Secretary Hu Yaobang. Most active were the two Party ideologues, Hu Qiaomu and Deng Liqun. They found they could kill two birds with one stone by attacking what they called "spiritual pollution" (jingshen wuran). At the 2nd Plenum of the 12th PCC held in October 1983, they succeeded in obtaining Deng Xiaoping's support. Deng demanded an end to the discussion of alienation from what he said "an overall strategic consideration" and he warned that the ideological front must not bring about "spiritual pollution". Then, a campaign to eliminate "spiritual pollution" followed. According to Wang Zhen, a Politburo member, the view of those "preaching so-called socialist alienation" was "completely antagonistic to Marxist scientific socialism" *(RMRB,* 25 Oct. 1983). Essentially, they were propagating "a sentiment of no-confidence in socialism, the Communist cause, and the Chinese Communist Party" (ibid.). Zhou Yang, the major victim, told Deng that Mao had agreed that alienation exists in socialist society. But Deng refuted him, saying that "this was the theoretical basis on which Mao launched the Cultural Revolution". (See Ruan Ming, *Hu Yaobang on the Historical Turning Point,* P. 9.) In the thick of the campaign, Zhou Yang had to make a "self-criticism", which was reported in the *People's Daily* on 6 November 1983. After this telling blow, he was never able to recover, and he died on 31 July 1989.

In January 1984, Hu Qiaomu published an article entitled "On Problems Concerning Humanism and Alienation" to bring an end to the campaign in a somewhat hasty way. Hu scathingly criticized and repudiated the theory of socialist alienation. After what he said was a careful examination of Marx's works, Hu believed, when Marx had matured, he had already rejected the theory and methodology of alienation, which he realized could not expose the essence of things, thereby affirming the sciences of dialectical materialism and historical materialism. Therefore, Hu asserted, Marxism refuted alienation as a basic category and a basic law, as a theory and a methodology, and used it only as a concept to describe certain phenomena (including some with regularity) during a given historical period. What is more, the application of the concept should strictly be confined to societies of antagonistic classes, in particular, capitalist society.

With this premise, Hu could easily find fault with Zhou Yang's and others' definition of alienation. Hu found it to be an "abstract formula" (chouxiang gongshi), which his opponents used to raise the issue of socialist alienation, thus lumping together socialist and capitalist societies in a completely erroneous way (Hu Qiaomu, "On Problems Concerning Humanism and Alienation", *RMRB*, 27 Jan. 1984).

Many, however, found Hu Qiaomu's arguments unconvincing. Wang Ruoshui, in particular, was one of them. Following the 1983 attack, Wang lost his post in the *People's Daily*. In the 1987 campaign against "bourgeois liberalization", he was forced to withdraw from the CCP. However, Wang continued his exploration of what he thought was the right track. In his study of the Marxist philosophy of man, he explained the two reactions in man's creative activity. One is that the object man has created in turn satisfies the need of man (the subject) and helps develop his potentials. This is the humanization of the object (duixiangde renhua). Another is that the object rids itself of control by the subject and becomes an alienated force against it. Obviously, he said, there is not only labor alienation, though it is no doubt the most important form of alienation. Anything that is created by man can become alienated—social relations, social organizations, superstructures, and ideologies. People often think Marxism opposes only exploitation. In actuality, Wang testified, Marxism "demands an elimination of all kinds of alienation"—exploitation is but a form of labor alienation—in order to "bring man's total emancipation" (Wang Ruoshui, "Guanyu Makesizhuyide rende zhexue"—"The Marxist Philosophy of Man", *WHB*, 17 and 18 July 1986, reprinted in *WXZTX*, p. 373). Wang directly refuted Deng Xiaoping, who had warned that a discussion of socialist alienation would lead to a loss of confidence in socialism and in Party leadership. He said: "Though Marx subjected the phenomenon of alienation to a profound exposure, he never deemed it abnormal and entirely negative. Alienation occurs with social progress" (ibid., p. 374). Furthermore, he asserted: "Alienation is the price of social progress. Moreover, during the process of alienation, conditions to eliminate it are also developed. Human beings will be able, and on a higher level, to restore their own subjectivity and be masters of their fates, ridding themselves of alienation in any form" (ibid.).

In 1988 and early 1989, Wang published three articles in two short-lived magazines *Reading Circles (Shulin)* and *Neo-enlightenment (Xin Qimeng),* further developing his alienation theory. They were: "Personality Cult and Alienation in the Ideological Realm"; "On Man's Essence and Social Relations"; and "Does Alienation Not Exist in a Socialist Society?" He said that the article about man's essence and social relations most clearly expressed his view.

Wang Ruoshui stated that the central idea of Marxism is alienation. Human beings, he said, have become controlled by what they have created and as a result have lost their human nature; the purpose of Marxism is to emancipate human beings from alienation so that they will be able to bring their potential into full play. Though this view is nothing new in the West, to many Communists in China, it greatly altered the revolutionary doctrine that had guided them in all their thoughts and actions for more than half a century.

As early as October 1983, Hu Qiaomu pointed out that Wang Ruoshui was propagating the alienation theory much more enthusiastically than the theories about class struggle, surplus value, and proletarian dictatorship. What he had done, however, did not help people believe in Marxism. Instead, he made them oppose socialism resolutely (see Wang Ruoshui, *Behind Hu Yaobang's Stepdown,* Hong Kong, Mingjing, 1997). The crux of the matter is: What is Marxism? And what is socialism? But whatever the case, Deng and his colleagues certainly did a right thing for the interests of their Party by banning the discussion of "socialist alienation". See also "rendaozhuyi lunzheng" (humanism debate), "qingwu yundong" (campaign to eliminate spiritual pollution), and "Zhou Yang beiju" (tragedy of Zhou Yang).

社会主义原始积累
shehuizhuyi yuanshi jilei
(socialist previous accumulation)

See "yuanshi jilei" (previous accumulation).

社会主义阵营
shehuizhuyi zhenying
(socialist camp)

See "lengzhanhou shidaide xin diguozhuyi" (neo-imperialism in the post-Cold War era) and "yibiandao" (lean to one side).

社会主义的根本任务是发展生产力
shehuizhuyide genben renwu shi fazhan shengchanli
(the fundamental task of socialism is to develop productivity)

See "xin shehuizhuyi guan" (new socialist view).

社教
shejiao
(socialist education movement)

The CCP carries out socialist education movements time and again. But the term "shejiao" usually refers to the nationwide socialist education movement carried out from the winter of 1962 to the beginning of the GPCR in May 1966, first mainly in the rural areas and then also in cities, especially in factories, mines, other enterprises, and schools. ("Shejiao", or "shejiao yundong", is an abbreviation for "nongcun shehuizhuyi jiaoyu yundong" or "shehuizhuyi jiaoyu yundong".) This movement is also known as the "siqing" (four clean-ups) or "siqing yundong" ("four clean-ups" movement).

In his opening speech at the 10th Plenum of the 8th PCC (held in Beijing from 24 to 27 September 1962), Mao Zedong told his Party: "Never forget class struggle." Following Mao's instructions, a socialist education movement was carried out in the countryside during the winter of 1962 and the spring of 1963. On 20 May 1963, a "Decision on Certain Problems in the Present Rural Work (Draft)" was drawn up under

Mao's personal leadership. The document, also called the "Ten Articles " ("Shitiao") or the "Former Ten Articles" ("Qian shitiao"), asserted that the socialist education movement was a struggle for "reorganizing revolutionary class ranks", one pertaining to "who will win out, Marxism or revisionism". It first raised the "four clean-ups" issue—to clean up account books, warehouses, assets, and work points among rural organizations.

In September 1963, within four months of the issuance of the "Ten Articles", the PCC, supervised by Liu Shaoqi, issued another Party document: "Provisions of Certain Concrete PCC Policies Concerning the Socialist Education Movement in the Rural Areas (Draft)", which is also called the "Latter Ten Articles" ("Hou shitiao"). Subsequently, the "Latter Ten Articles" was revised, based on the "Taoyuan experience" (Taoyuan jingyan), the experience of how to lead the movement summed up by Wang Guangmei, Liu's wife, during her "squatting at point" (dundian) from the end of 1963 to the end of 1964 in the Taoyuan village, Funing county, Hebei province. On 10 September 1964, the PCC promulgated the "Decision on Some Problems in Current Rural Work (Draft)", which is called the "Second Latter Ten Articles".

On 14 January 1965, the PCC issued another document: "Some Problems Currently Raised in the Rural Socialist Education Movement" ("Nongcun shehuizhuyi jiaoyu yundongzhong muqian tichude yixie wenti", also called the "Twenty-three Articles"—"Ershisan tiao"). Originally the minutes of the National Work Conference called by the PCC Politburo and presided over by Mao, it was issued as "Zhong Fa 65/026", to supersede the "Second Latter Ten Articles". The new document stated that from then on the socialist education movement in both rural and urban areas would be called the "four clean-ups" movement—it aimed at "cleaning things up in the fields of politics, economy, organization, and ideology" ("qing zhengzhi, qing jingji, qing zuzhi, qing sixiang", which were very different from the former "four clean-ups"). The document criticized the approach of "the contradictions between the four clean-ups and the four unclean-ups", as raised in Liu Shaoqi's "Second Latter Ten Articles", for the approach "did not explain the fundamental nature of the socialist education" and "did not indicate what kind of society in which the contradictions exist between the four clean-ups and the four unclean-ups". Specifically, the document pointed out that the major targets of attack in the movement were "those in power within the Party taking the capitalist road" (dangnei zou zibenzhuyi daolu dangquanpai). According to it, the capitalist-roaders stay behind the scenes in some cases or remain in the front in others, and they have supporters in the provinces and in the central Party and government departments. This was the first time the shocking concept of "capitalist-roader" had been officially advanced in a PCC document.

Notably, the movement underwent different guiding policies made respectively by Mao and Liu Shaoqi. Even at that time people could strongly feel their growing conflict. Soon after the GPCR, Liu was fiercely attacked for his role in the "four clean-ups" movement, accused of "covering up the nature of the struggle between the two classes and the two roads" and "attempting to wrest power from the proletariat".

After the start of the GPCR, as indicated in the communiqué of 11th Plenum of the 8th PCC adopted on 12 August 1966, Mao and his colleagues still planned to continue the "four clean-ups" movement. But this was obviously impossible. In fact, many verdicts brought in during the movement were reversed during the GPCR, mostly by the victims themselves, thus making the situation very complicated.

社教运动
shejiao yundong

(socialist education movement)

See "shejiao" (socialist education movement).

深化改革
shenhua gaige
(deepening of reform)

See "fazhan caishi ying daoli" (development is the most essential criterion) and "jingji gaige" (economic reform).

神道
shendao
(theocracy)

See "wanquan fouding rendaozhuyi jiu daozhi shendao he shoudao" (a total negation of humanism will lead to "theocracy" and "barbarism").

神秘的信仰主义
shenmide xinyangzhuyi
(mystic fideism)

This term was used derogatorily, as in the scathing attacks on a 1981 novelette "When the Evening Glow Disappears", a maiden work by Li Ping, a university student ("Wanxia xiaoshide shihou", *SY*, 1, 1981, reprinted in book form by Beijing, Zhongguo Qingnian, 1981; part 4 trans. by Daniel Bryant in Michael S. Duke, ed. with introductions, *Contemporary Chinese Literature: An Anthology of Post-Mao Fiction and Poetry*, pp. 59-79).

Divided into four chapters—"Spring", "Summer", 'Winter", and "Autumn"—the novelette relates the loss of love between Li Huaiping, a Red Guard and son of a victorious PLA officer, and Nan Shan, the granddaughter of a defeated KMT general. There are several very impressive passages: the unexpected meeting of the hero and the heroine and their transient affections, and their naive and happy days before the Cultural Revolution; Li's cruel treatment of Nan's family in the fierce Red Guard Movement; the miserable fate of Nan and her younger brother in the GPCR; and another unexpected meeting of the two former lovers on the top of Taishan Mountain after twelve years of separation and turmoil. Indeed, the story develops with a series of soul-stirring episodes, and it raises provoking philosophical issues, such as the law of history, the meaning of life, destiny and chance, fortune and misfortune in one's career, ideal and reality, good and evil, and religious beliefs and atheism. All this made it very popular, especially among university students, as soon as it appeared in early 1981.

If it is right to say that this novelette truthfully presents the spiritual state of some Chinese youth at the time (which must be one of the major reasons for its popularity), this very truthfulness about the wavering of their Marxist convictions, however, makes it a work destined to be attacked under the standards of the campaign to eliminate "spiritual pollution". In fact, as early as 1982, a Party critic named Lu Zhichao (who was later promoted to be CPPCC deputy secretary-general) observed that, through its hero and heroine's ponderings on the philosophy of life, this work resulted in advocating "mystic fideism", or, "a sort of delicate religious idealism" (Lu Zhichao, "Yige buke hushide zhandou renwu"—"A Fighting Task That Cannot Be Neglected", *GMRB*, 13 June 1982). This, in effect, meant negating "the observations of Marxist historical materialism on human history and on current social problems" (ibid.). Wei Jianlin, another Party critic who worked in the Research Office of the PCC Secretariat, emphasized that the work was not only advertising religious beliefs, but more seriously portraying "the natural end result of disillusionment with the socialist system" (Wei Jianlin, "Shehuizhuyi shijian he suowei 'shehuizhuyide yihua'"—"Socialist Practice and So-called "Socialist Alienation", *RMRB,* 13 Nov. 1983). The work was also criticized in the *People's Daily* for "regarding ugliness as beauty", praising "undeservedly" the hero and the heroine who explored the "true meaning of life" in religious doctrines (Deng Yizhong and Zhong Chengxiang, "Qingchu jingshen wuran, nuli biaoxian xinren"—"Eliminate Spiritual Pollution, Strive to Represent New-Type People", *RMRB,* 31 Oct. 1983). The author Li Ping was held responsible for the following alarming consequences: hindering people from building socialist spiritual civilization, distorting the reality of socialist China, and imposing on people serious spiritual pollution. This is why criticism of works like "When the Evening Glow Disappears" was raised (as by Lu Zhichao) as "a fighting task that cannot be neglected".

Quite strangely, Zhao Puchu, president of the Chinese National Buddhist Association, claimed that the author of the novelette did not really understand religions (see *RMRB*, 19 Nov. 1983). But it did not matter much whether Li Ping understood religions or not, and whether he was trying to advertise them or not. The value of the novelette lies in its truthful presentation of the spiritual state of some Chinese youth (the author himself included).

Later, in his self-criticism, Li Ping said: "The current overflowing of religious activities in many places is something I completely did not expect before. If I could have foreseen it, I probably would have written this story with another tone" (Li Ping, "Wo xie 'wanxia xiaoshide shihou' suo si suo xiang"—"My Thoughts in Writing "When the Evening Glow Disappears", *Qingnian wenxue,* 3:81, 1982). This confession of almost twenty years ago is full of meanings, especially against the background that religious and superstitious beliefs of all kinds (Falun Gong, for instance) have become even more popular in China today.

生产力拜物教
shengchanli baiwujiao
(productivity fetishism)

See "xin shehuizhuyi guan" (new socialist view).

生产力是任何社会发展的最终决定因素
shengchanli shi renhe shehui fazhande zuizhong jueding yinsu
(productivity is the ultimate determinant in the development of any society)

See "shehuizhuyi chuji jieduan lun" (theory of the primary stage of socialism) and "xin shehuizhuyi guan" (new socialist view).

生存权是最根本的人权
shengcunquan shi zuigenbende renquan
(the right to subsistence is the most fundamental human right)

See "renquan wenti" (human rights issue).

生活与艺术的矛盾
shenghuo yu yishude maodun
(contradiction between life and art)

See "chuangzuo ziyou" (creative freedom).

生活与艺术的统一
shenghuo yu yishude tongyi
(unity of life and art)

See "chuangzuo ziyou" (creative freedom).

胜利大逃亡
shengli dataowang
(triumphant fleeing from home)

See "shijie dachuanlian" (a great trend of going abroad).

圣旨
shengzhi
(imperial edict)

In feudal dynasties, evil ministers and eunuchs, when necessary, would provide their emperor with false information so as to influence his decisions which were issued in the form of imperil edicts. Then they would make use of the edict for their own interests. The term "shengzhi" is employed sarcastically today when a similar situation occurs.

十大关系
shi da guanxi
(ten major relationships)

This refers to Mao's 1956 "ten major relationships" in the socialist revolution and construction. See "shi'er da guanxi" (twelve major relationships).

十大元帅
shi da yuanshuai
(ten marshals)

In an order of 23 September 1955, Mao Zedong, then PRC president, conferred the military title of marshal on the following ten army officers: Zhu De, Peng Dehuai, Lin Biao, Liu Bocheng, He Long, Chen Yi, Luo Ronghuan, Xu Xiangqian, Nie Rongzhen, and Ye Jianying (*RMRB,* 24 September 1955).

The ten PLA marshals have all since deceased, and the title has not been conferred on others.

十次路线斗争
shici luxian douzheng

(ten "two-line" struggles)

See "liang tiao luxiande douzheng" (struggle between two lines).

十二大关系
shi'er da guanxi
(twelve major relationships)

On 28 September 1995, at the 5th Plenum of the 14th PCC, Jiang Zemin asked for a correct handling of what he advanced as the "twelve major relationships". He said: "The twelve relationships constitute major issues which concern the overall situation under the new situation of reform and development" (*BR*, 6-12 Nov. 1995, p.7). The twelve relationships include: 1. the relationship between reform, development, and stability; 2. the relationship between speech and efficiency; 3. the relationship between economic construction on the one hand and population, resources, and the environment on the other; 4. the relationship between primary, secondary, and tertiary industries; 5. the relationship between the eastern and western regions; 6. the relationship between market mechanisms and macro-control; 7. the relationship between the public economic sector and other economic sectors; 8. the relationship between the state, enterprises, and individuals in income distribution; 9. the relationship between opening up wider to the outside world and adhering to self-reliance; 10. the relationship between central authorities and local authorities; 11. the relationship between national defense building and economic development; and 12. the relationship between the promotion of material progress and ideological and cultural progress.

The "twelve major relationships" are regarded as Jiang's first systematic, though preliminary, elucidation of his ideas about running the country. There is no doubt that Jiang based these concepts on Mao's and Deng's ideas about building socialism in China.

It is interesting to compare Jiang's "twelve major relationships" with Mao's "ten major relationships" (shi da guanxi). On 25 April 1956, in a speech at an enlarged meeting of the Politburo, Mao Zedong expounded upon what he summed up as the "ten major relationships" in the socialist revolution and construction. They included those between: 1. heavy industry on the one hand and light industry and agriculture on the other; 2. coastal industry and inland industry; 3. economic construction and national defense construction; 4. the state, production units and individual producers; 5. central and local authorities; 6. the Han Chinese people and ethnic minorities; 7. Party and non-Party people; 8. revolution and counter-revolution; 9. right and wrong; and 10. China and foreign countries. As Mao himself said, it was out of his concern for a "fundamental principle" that he raised the issue of the "ten major relationships", and that concern was "to bring every positive factor at home and abroad into play to serve the socialist cause" (see Mao Zedong, "Lun shi da guanxi"—"On the Ten Major Relationships", in *MZXJ*, 5, pp. 267-88).

十二年工作纲要
shiernian gongzuo gangyao
(12-Year Work Program)

From the spring of 1956 to the first half of 1957, there was a short-lived renaissance of Chinese literature. This, and the liberation of thought that accompanied it, came as a logical consequence of the historical turning point when the CCP declared that the "three great transformations" (sanda gaizao) had been completed and the period of "socialist construction" had begun. The situation was

quite encouraging to many writers and intellectuals. A literary program for the period from 1956 to 1967 was approved at the CWA's second council meeting (enlarged) held in February 1956. The document optimistically predicted: "During the next twelve years, the contingent of writers in our country will be enlarged several times and a great number of works worthy of our people and the age will be produced. They will educate the people with the socialist spirit and help promote the complete victory of the socialist cause in China."

Unfortunately, in the next year the program ended with the beginning of the anti-Rightist campaign. In 1967, the year the program had been scheduled to complete a great development of literature and art, the GPCR was in full swing, bringing unprecedented disasters to Chinese people, writers and artists included.

十六条
shiliutiao
(Sixteen Articles)

On 8 August 1966, the "PCC Decision on the GPCR" was passed at the 11th Plenum of the 8th PCC. The "Decision" was referred to as the "Sixteen Articles" because it had sixteen articles. These articles were: 1. the classes in the socialist revolution; 2. the main trend and divergences; 3. fully arousing the masses with "dare to" take the lead; 4. letting the masses educate themselves in the movement; 5. firmly carrying out the Party's class line; 6. correctly handling contradictions among the people; 7. being vigilant against those who attack the revolutionary masses as counter-revolutionary; 8. cadre issues; 9. Cultural Revolution groups, committees, and congresses; 10. educational reform; 11. issues concerning criticism with naming in newspapers and journals; 12. policies regarding scientists, technicians, and ordinary working personnel; 13. the deployment as regards the integration with the urban and rural socialist education movement; 14. taking charge of the revolution and promoting production; 15. the armed forces; and 16. Mao Zedong Thought is the guide in the Great Proletarian Cultural Revolution.

The "Sixteen Articles" stated that the major target for attack in the GPCR was "those in power within the Party taking the capitalist road". See also "wen'ge" (Cultural Revolution).

十年浩劫
shinian haojie
(ten-year catastrophe)

A term for the GPCR. Another similar term is "shinian zainan" (the ten-year catastrophe). According to official statistics, as revealed in a speech by Marshal Ye Jianying shortly after the downfall of the Gang of Four, 100 million people fell victim to the GPCR; 20 million people died tragically; also 800 billion Chinese dollars were lost (Ma Licheng and Ling Zhijun, *Crossing Swords: Three Thought Emancipations in Contemporary China,* p. 9). See also "wen'ge" (Cultural Revolution).

十年文革
shinian wen'ge
(ten-year Cultural Revolution)

A term for the GPCR. See "wen'ge" (Cultural Revolution).

十年灾难
shinian zainan
(ten-year catastrophe)

See "shinian haojie" (ten-year catastrophe) and "wen'ge" (Cultural Revolution).

十七年
shiqinian
(seventeen years)

This refers to the seventeen years from the founding of the PRC in 1949 until the start of the GPCR in 1966. In the 1966 Party document "Summary of the Forum on the Work in Literature and Art in the Armed Forces with Which Comrade Lin Biao Entrusted Comrade Jiang Qing", there was a key phrase describing the literary situation during the first seventeen years of the PRC: "dictatorship of a sinister line" (heixian zhuanzheng). It was asserted that, since the founding of the PRC, literary and art circles had been "under the dictatorship of a sinister anti-Party and anti-socialist line, diametrically opposed to Chairman Mao's thought", and that line was a "combination of bourgeois ideas on literature and art, modern revisionist ideas on literature and art and what is known as the literature and art of the 1930s (in the KMT areas of China)". This assessment constituted one of the major arguments in support of the GPCR. Later, the "sinister line dictatorship" theory was extended to the fields of education, publishing, physical culture, public security, and the Party's organizational, propaganda, and united front work, as well as to other fields of Party and government work, so as to make the GPCR appear all the more necessary.

Because the assessment of the "seventeen years" was of vital importance, it was only natural that after the "October 6th coup" of 1976 the first thing the Party did was to refute the Gang of Four's "sinister line dictatorship" theory. It was emphasized that during the seventeen years "Chairman Mao's revolutionary line" had held sway and therefore the "general orientation" of literature and art was correct. It was described as follows:

"The seventeen-year history of literature and art was one that saw Chairman Mao's revolutionary line triumphing over the revisionist line, one of proletarian literature and art triumphing over bourgeois literature and art. Our Party persisted in promoting what is proletarian and liquidating what is bourgeois on the ideological and cultural fronts, and upheld the socialist revolution in the spheres of literature and art. Ever since the founding of the PRC, Chairman Mao launched and personally led the criticism and repudiation of the film *The Life of Wu Xun,* the criticism and repudiation of the book *Research into 'A Dream of Red Mansions'*, the struggle against the Hu Feng Counter-Revolutionary Clique, the struggle against the bourgeois Rightists, and the GPCR, each seriously deflating the bourgeoisie and significantly consolidating and strengthening the ideological fronts of the proletariat. Victories were achieved one after another in the two-line struggles, guaranteeing the dominant position of the proletariat in the fields of literature and art" (Criticism Group of the Ministry of Culture, "Yichang hanwei Mao zhuxi geming luxiande weida douzheng"—"A Great Struggle to Defend Chairman Mao's Revolutionary Line", *HQ,* 1:34-41, 1978).

A few years later, statements like this, instead of praising the "victories" of Mao's line, denounced Mao's mistakes. To the majority of Chinese writers and artists, what hurt most during the seventeen years was those political campaigns carried out one after another. Many writers and artists were victims of more than one campaign, and then they were persecuted during the GPCR. When the 4th National

Congress of Chinese Writers and Artists was held in 1979, a number were unable to attend. Some were dead; others had not yet been rehabilitated, though they had escaped death. Hu Feng, for example, was one such survivor. An old, partly-disabled man of seventy-nine, he reappeared in 1981. Several of his friends had passed away after being convicted of being members of the "Hu Feng Counter-Revolutionary Clique" in 1955. Other political victims did have the chance to be Congress participants, but each had his own sad story to tell. The Congress, naturally, became an occasion to condemn the wrongdoings of the "seventeen years" as well as of the GPCR. The self-criticism Zhou Yang made at the Congress was impressive, but it failed to satisfy every participant. Some found it be be an attempt to return to the theoretical position of the 1942-1966 period. Many people, needless to say, did not want to turn back. From bitter experience, they used the term "vicious circle" (exing xunhuan) to describe the politics of the "seventeen years". One of them was Wang Ruowang, a former Rightist who was not allowed to return to his position until March 1979. Wang believed the relationship between arts and politics had not been solved at the Congress. His estimation of the "seventeen years" was quite poignant:

"Those seventeen years were thus like a vicious circle. Every time a political movement would come along literature was the first victim. A bunch of 'hatchet men' were trained and because of this it is very, very difficult to eradicate ultra-Leftist influence. 'Leftist' forces had already laid their foundation, the 'gang of four' just led the tendency to its highest peak" (Kyna Rubin, "An Interview with Mr. Wang Ruowang", *China Quarterly,* 87:511-512, 1981). See also "jiyao" ("Summary").

十五年赶超英国
shiwunian ganchao yingguo
(catch up with and surpass Britain within 15 years)

From 2 to 21 November 1957, at the invitation of Khrushchev, CPSU first secretary, Mao was in Moscow to celebrate the 40th anniversary of the October Revolution. At the celebration gathering, Khrushchev advanced the ambitious goal that the USSR would not only catch up with but also surpass the United States within 15 years. Much encouraged, Mao declared at the conference of Communist workers parties on 18 November 1958 that China would catch up with and surpass Britain within 15 years. Two weeks later, Mao's declaration became a slogan shouted loudly throughout China.

In July 1957 Mao formed an estimation that China would catch up with the United States in 40 to 50 years (see his "1957 nian xiaji xingshi"—"The Situation in the Summer of 1957", *MZXJ,* 5, p. 463). See also "dayuejin" (Great Leap Forward).

时代精神汇合论
shidai jingshen huihe lun
(theory of the "spirit of the age as the merging of various ideologies")

As one of the "eight sinister theories" singled out for attack in the 1966 Party document the "Summary", the theory of "the spirit of the age as the merging of various trends" was raised by Zhou Gucheng, a famous scholar, in 1962.

In his article "On the Historical Position of Artistic Creation" ("Yishu chuangzuode lishi diwei", *Xin jianshe,* 12, 1962), Zhou revealed his thoughts on a series of major issues concerning artistic creation, which involved the spirit of the age. According to Zhou, the spirit of the age, which was formed with various ideologies merged during a given age, would always constitute a unified whole, but it might be reflected in diametrically opposed ways in different classes or different individuals. As it prevailed throughout the society as a whole, it was called the "spirit of the age"; as it was reflected in a specific work, it was called an "expression of genius". Zhou's view attracted a great deal of attention from scholars and students of artistic theory, aesthetics, and philosophy. Nearly one year later it was openly criticized by Yao Wenyuan, who classified the concept of "the spirit of the age" as "historical idealism divorced from class analysis" (Yao Wenyuan, "Lue lun shidai jingshen wenti"—"Briefly on the Issue of the Spirit of the Age", *GMRB,* 24 Sept. 1963). Then, eight months later, Yao launched his second attack, this time focusing on the philosophical grounds on which Zhou formed his view (see his "Ping Zhou Gucheng xianshengde maodunguan"—"On Mr. Zhou Gucheng's View on Contradiction", *GMRB,* 10 May 1964).

At that time, in the already strained political situation prior to the GPCR, almost no one dared openly to take Zhou's side. With the denunciation of Zhou's theory, a high-sounding aesthetic view became dominant in cultural circles, a view which included the following three main points: 1. Only the spirit of the revolutionary classes constitutes the spirit of the age, which later became the theoretical foundation for the Gang of Four's entire cultural policy. 2. Only positive heroes could directly embody the spirit of the age, while negative characters could serve merely to contrast the brightness. 3. Revolutionary literature and art must strive to create lofty and perfect images of proletarian heroes. Hence the later concocted principle of the "three prominences" and the theory of the "fundamental task".

If deprived of its seemingly complicated philosophical exposition, Zhou's theory was a denial of the view that the spirit of the age was merely that of revolution, as once claimed by some powerful people in China. This helped to explain why after the downfall of the Gang of Four the top authorities was still reluctant to redress the case. Even in early 1979, some people continued to consider the theory as "deviating from Marxism". Consequently, as Wang Tongsheng, a critic, complained, because the issue was not resolved, a thorough criticism of the "three prominences" principle was impossible, as the formation of the principle was the direct result of the denunciation of Zhou's theory. In fact, as he pointed out, more than two years after the Gang's downfall, the "three prominences" principle, the most influential and most harmful of the Gang of Four's erroneous views on culture, had not yet been subjected to the profound criticism it deserved. He considered this "a question worth pondering" (Wang Tongsheng, "'Shidai jingshen huihe' lun bian"—"In Defense of the Theory of the 'Spirit of the Age as the Merging of Various Trends'", *Xin wenxue luncong,* 2, 1979, extracted and reprinted in *XHYB, WZB,* 3:170, 1980). See also "jiyao" ("Summary").

时代的烙印
shidaide laoyin
(brand of the times)

See "shehuizhuyi xianshizhuyi" (socialist realism).

时间就是金钱
shijian jiushi jinqian
(time is money)

See "ershinianlai zuiju yingxianglide shi ge kouhao" (ten most influential slogans in the past two decades).

实践出真知
shijian chu zhenzhi
(genuine knowledge comes from practice)

See "xiuzhengzhuyi" (revisionism) and "shijian shi jianyan zhenlide weiyi biaozhun" (practice is the sole criterion for testing truth).

实践是检验真理的唯一标准
shijian shi jianyan zhenlide weiyi biaozhun
(practice is the sole criterion for testing truth)

In 1978, there was an important debate on the criterion for testing truth.

The debate was ignited by an article, first drafted by Hu Fuming, a teacher in the Philosophy Department of Nanjing University. Hu Yaobang, then director of the PCC Organization Department, found it very relevant and helpful to the struggle currently being waged with the "whateverists" ("fanshipai") headed by Hua Guofeng, CCP chairman. Under his supervision it was revised ten times by Yang Xiguang, Ma Peiwen, Wang Qianghua, (all from the *Guangming Daily*), and Wu Jiang and Sun Changjiang (from the CCP Central Party School). Then, Hu approved it and had it published in *Trends in Theoretical Fields,* a magazine run by the Central Party School, on 10 May 1978, and in the *Guangming Daily* the next day as a special commentator's article entitled "Practice Is the Sole Criterion for Testing Truth". On 12 May, the full text was reprinted in the *People's Daily* and the *Liberation Army Daily*.

As expected, the article evoked great repercussions. A nationwide discussion about the criterion of truth ensued. Also as expected, Hua Guofeng tried his best to reduce its influence. He instructed his men not to be involved in the discussion. Wang Dongxing, then CCP vice-chairman in charge of propaganda, attacked the article on several occasions. He was convinced that its authors were "chopping down the banner" (kan hongqi) of Mao Zedong Thought.

On 2 June 1978, Deng Xiaoping, in a speech delivered at a conference on PLA political work, voiced his full support for the views stated in the article. (Deng must agree that for fighting against the "two-whatevers" view, the thesis "Practice is the sole criterion for testing truth" is more powerful than his idea about "correctly and comprehensively understanding Mao Zedong Thought System".) The tables had been turned. On 24 June the *Liberation Army Daily* published an article, under the name of a special commentator, entitled "A Most Fundamental Principle of Marxism" ("Makesizhuyide yi ge zuijibende yuanze"), which was written by Wu Jiang. This was a favor from Luo Ruiqing, a friend of Deng Xiaoping and Hu Yaobang, who was at the time CMC general secretary. Then, from August to November, almost all local Party and army leaders, one after another, stood on Deng's side.

At the 3rd Plenum of the 11th PCC (held from 18 to 22 December 1978), a showdown took place between the two factions. As a result, the "whateverists" lost power and Deng's leadership was established. A call was issued to "emancipate the mind" (jiefang sixiang) and "seek truth from facts" (shishi qiu shi). This paved the way for Deng's reform and open-door program. (See, for instance, Yu Guangyuan, "Jinian zhenli biaozhun wenti taolun shizhounian"—"Tenth Anniversary of the Discussion of Problems Concerning the Criterion of Truth", *RMRB,* 6 May 1988; Tao Kai, Zhang Yide and Dai Qing, "Zouchu xiandai mixin: guanyu zhenli biaozhun wentide dabianlun"—"Farewell to Modern Superstition: A Great Debate over Problems Concerning Criterion of Truth", *Zhongshan,* 3, 1988; reprinted in book form by Hong Kong, Sanlian, 1989, and Ma Licheng and Ling Zhijun, *Crossing Swords: Three Thought Emancipations in Contemporary China*).

History has shown the significance of the publication of "Practice Is the Sole Criterion for Testing Truth" and the debate following it. To the CCP it was not merely a pure theoretical debate; it was also a power struggle. In official language, the debate served as "ideological preparation" for the 3rd Plenum of the 11th PCC. As it turned out, it brought about a "thought-emancipation" movement.

Academically, however, the tenability or the accuracy of the "practice" thesis, which stems from Mao's 1937 philosophical work *On Practice*, may be questionable. As scholars point out, man's practice, any activity of the subject functioning to the world (to the object), must be guided by a theory or an idea, no matter how rough it may be, and the theory of idea may be incorrect. So practice is not necessarily on the right track. It also needs to go by criteria. No predestined truth exists in practice itself. What is correct, therefore, is not that "practice is the sole criterion for testing truth" but that "people should prove the truth of their thinking in practice". Moreover, this proof should not be carried out only once. Very often, it should be repeated in different stages of social practice.

It should also be noted that any proof or test is done and judged by man. The vital problem of this thesis is that the judgement may be linked with power and power may mean truth. This has occurred many times in CCP history. For instance, every Party policy, when raised and promoted by Mao, was said to have been tested by practice as correct. So, fundamentally, without independent judgement and legal guarantees, the thesis about practice as the sole criterion for testing truth cannot automatically become a weapon to protect and develop truth. In the worst case, it can possibly become a tool of dictatorship.

Nevertheless, one should well recognize the *fait accompli* politico-social significance of the putting forth of the thesis and the ensuing debate on it in 1978. Indeed, since then, iconoclasm towards Mao and all other long-held revolutionary leaders has become inevitable. This includes many Party doctrines, such as those that earlier had cruelly decided the destiny of hundreds of millions of Chinese people. Deng himself highly praised the debate, saying that it was "really a debate about ideological line, about politics, about the future and the destiny of our Party and nation" *(SWD*, p. 154). He was correct. But its consequences may not be what Deng expected. See also "liang ge fanshi" (two whatevers), "ershinianlai zuiju yingxianglide shi ge kouhao" (ten most influential slogans in the past two decades), and "jiefang sixiang" (emancipating the mind).

实践主体性
shijian zhutixing
(experiential subjectivity)

See "wenxue zhutixing" (subjectivity of literature).

实践的唯人主义
shijiande weirenzhuyi
(humanism in practice)

See "zhengtongde Makesizhuyi zhengzai zou xiang miewang" (orthodox Marxism is heading for death).

实事求是
shishi qiu shi
(seek truth from facts)

According to the "Resolution on Certain Questions in the History of Our Party since the Founding of the PRC" passed on 27 June 1981 at the 6th Plenum of the 11th PCC, the "living soul" of Mao Zedong Thought was defined as its stand, viewpoint, and method, and "seeking truth from facts" was one of the three basic principles embodying their essence. The other two principles were the "mass line" (qunzhong luxian), and "independence and self-reliance" (duli zizhu, zili gengsheng). See also "shijieguan" (world outlook).

实现公有制的多种形式
shixian gongyouzhide duozhong xingshi
(diversified forms for materializing public ownership)

See "jiejue gongyouzhi xingshi shi you yici sixiang jiefang" (solving the issue of public ownership forms is another emancipation of the mind).

实现四个现代化是最大的政治
shixian si ge xiandaihua shi zuidade zhengzhi
(to achieve the "four modernizations" is the most important politics)

See "si ge xiandaihua" (four modernizations) and "wenyi wei zhengzhi fuwu" (literature and art serve politics).

实验小说
shiyan xiaoshuo
(experimental fiction)

See "xinshiqi wenxue" (literature of the new period).

使用自由
shiyong ziyou
(freedom exploitation)

See "chuangzuo ziyou" (creative freedom).

市场社会主义
shichang shehuizhuyi
(market socialism)

See "Deng Xiaoping lilun" (Deng Xiaoping Theory), "xin shehuizhuyi guan" (new socialist view), and "jingji gaige" (economic reform).

试点
shidian
(key-point experiment)

See "zhong shiyantian" (cultivating experimental farming plots).

试验田
shiyantian
(experimental farming plots)

See "zhong shiyantian" (cultivating experimental farming plots).

世界大串联
shijie dachuanlian
(a great trend of going abroad)

In the last few years of the 1980s, for various reasons, one of which was the loss of political faith and enthusiasm, a large number of Chinese students and professionals went abroad. The wave was so great that it was dubbed a "shijie dachuanlian"—"a great trend of going abroad". The term was reminiscent, but in a sarcastic sense, of the Red Guards who, encouraged by Mao's call to carry on the GPCR through to the end, traveled all over the country in the last few months of 1966 to exchange "revolutionary experiences" (geming dachuanlian) and engaged in what they thought to be revolutionary activities.

Another sarcastic term for this phenomenon was "dataowang"—"a great trend of fleeing from home". Bo Yang, a veteran Taiwan-based writer, said that the Chinese were a "run-away" nation (taopaode minzu). But what made these young students and professionals flee from home in the 1980s? One explanation, though not a profound one, is given in the work of reportage literature from whose title the term "shijie dachuanlian" is derived. Consisting of several poignant stories of young people, many of whom had great talent, who went abroad, this work was very well-known for a time in China. Readers might agree with the two young authors that there must be something wrong with the society (Hu Ping and Zhang Shengyou, "Shijie dachuanlian"—"Going Abroad: A Great Trend", *DD,* 1, 1988).

These disillusioned Chinese described their choice as "loving the nation (China) by a devious path" (quxian aiguo). Or, even more sarcastically, they said they were "saving the nation by a devious path" (quxian jiuguo—originally an accusation against the KMT by the CCP for its alleged policy of "capitulating to Japanese imperialists and fighting Chinese Communists" during the War of Resistance Against Japan).

Notably, there was still another term to describe the wave: "triumphant fleeing from home" (shengli dataowang), a term deriving from a German film about the Second World War. Later, however, the term was used specifically with reference to those leaving China with a lot of money who feared that they might get into trouble if they were to stay home. Many of them had been officials (or people close to power) and had reaped huge profits. It was reported that in the last twenty years China's foreign investments totalled about one hundred and sixty billion U.S. dollars, and much of the money had run off to private pockets for the "triumphant fleeing from home".

世界革命
shijie geming
(world revolution)

Internationalism (guojizhuyi), or proletarian internationalism (wuchanjieji guojizhuyi) in the CCP lexicon, is one of the guiding principles for the international Communist movement (guoji gongchanzhuyi yundong), that is, world revolution. Antagonistic to bourgeois nationalism and chauvinism, its basic spirit is embodied in the following two slogans: "All the proletarians in the world, unite!" put forth by

Marx and Engels, and "All the proletarians and the oppressed nations in the world, unite!" put forth by Lenin. According to proletarian internationalism, the interests of the proletarian struggle in a country must be subordinated to those in the world, and nations triumphing over the bourgeoisie domestically must make the biggest possible national sacrifice for overthrowing the international capital. The proletariat and other laboring people of all countries must support one another in their struggles against oppression and exploitation and for national emancipation and socialism. All Marxist-Leninist parties must uphold unity in the international Communist movement on the basis of Marxism-Leninism and proletarian internationalism. They must also educate the people in their countries with the spirit of proletarian internationalism combined with revolutionary patriotism (gemingde aiguozhuyi).

For a long time, especially during the GPCR, Beijing was very proud of its upholding proletarian internationalism. It regarded itself as the "center of world revolution", a replacement of Moscow. As declared by Mao and his colleagues, the CPSU had betrayed proletarian internationalism and the Soviet Union had changed its political color (bianse). They condemned Khrushchev, CPSU first secretary, as the "chief representative of modern revisionism". In order to save the international Communist movement, they put forth a 25-point proposal concerning what they regarded as the "General Line" for the movement and related questions of world revolution *(RMRB*, 17 June 1963).

Shouldering its responsibility of world revolution, Beijing became the spokesman for the "third world" (Mao claimed that "We have friends all over the world"). There were two frequently used slogans: "Oppose hegemonism" and "Down with imperialism, revisionism, and all reactionaries in various countries". (The somewhat academic statement, "Only by emancipating all mankind can the proletariat achieve its own final emancipation", was also often quoted, but "The working men have no country", a saying from the "Manifesto of the Communist Party", was rarely used.) According to China's strategists at that time, world revolution also involved "surrounding the cities by the countryside"—a strategic principle of "people's war". What was meant by the "countryside" of the world was Asia, Africa, and Latin America, and the "cities" were those developed countries of North America and Europe. Beijing called on all the oppressed nations and peoples to rise up in a united-front struggle against their enemies so as to win victory for world revolution.

For world revolution, or for Mao's desire to be the leader of world revolution, the Chinese people were forced to make great sacrifices. For instance, according to official sources, from the 1950s to 1978, China's military and economic aid to Vietnam exceeded 20 billion U.S. dollars. From 1965 to 1973, 320 thousand Chinese soldiers were sent to the Vietnam War. Among them 4,200 were wounded and 1, 100 killed *(Kaifang,* May 1999, pp. 34-36). According to Geng Biao, former ambassador to Albania, China's aid to this small country with a population of 2 million (which was praised by Mao's Party as a "bright socialist lamp in Europe") came to nearly 9 billion Chinese dollars *(Kaifang,* May 1999, p. 48). The Albanian Government asked China to help popularize television in the countryside, while in China at that time (1968), black-and-white television was rare even in big cities like Beijing and Shanghai.

After the decline of Maoism by the end of 1970s, slogans like the "center of world revolution" and "Down with imperialism, revisionism, and all reactionaries in the world" were dropped. Today, instead of "the international Communist movement", the official term is "the international socialist movement" (guoji shehuizhuyi yundong). The term "proletarian internationalism" has almost completely disappeared in Party documents. China's proletarian internationalist enthusiasm has been replaced by its nationalist aspiration for domestic economic development. This of course results from the change of the CCP's political line. (Some, such as Cao Siyuan, a prominent economist who has been dubbed as the "father of China's insolvent law", even predicted that the CCP would change its name to "Zhongguo Shehuidang"—the Chinese Socialist Party—before 2010.) In this regard Deng Xiaoping played an important role. In a talk with Party leaders on 3 March 1990 (at that time the East European bloc and the Soviet Union were undergoing unprecedented changes), Deng indicated that China would not carry out any ideological debate with Russians, no matter what changes would take place in the USSR (Ma Licheng and Ling Zhijun, *Crossing Swords,* p. 165). On 24 December 1990, Deng warned again, referring to the suggestion that China should shoulder the responsibility as the "center of world revolution". He said: "We should never act as a head. This is a fundamental national policy. We are not in a position to be such a head; we do not have sufficient strength. It is absolutely no good being the head, for this will lead to the loss of many initiatives" (ibid.).

The concept of "hegemonism", however, is still referred to. In international affairs, Mao claimed that China was not a superpower and that it firmly opposed hegemonism. (This is said to be an important part of Mao Zedong Thought.) For a time during the 1960s and the 1970s, Chinese leaders regarded hegemonism as the most essential characteristic of the foreign policy of the "two superpowers"—the United States and the Soviet Union. When the border war between China and Vietnam broke out in 1979, the Chinese leaders realized that a small country could also promote hegemonism (which, of course, was a local one). On 16 January 1980, in his speech "The Present Situation and the Tasks before Us", Deng stipulated that "opposing hegemonism and safeguarding world peace in dealing with international affairs" was one of China's three major tasks for the 1980s *(SWD,* pp. 224-25). China's anti-hegemonism stand was often reiterated, sometimes focusing on the United States and sometimes on the Soviet Union. After the Soviet Union disintegrated (it ceased to exist on 26 December 1991), the United States was the only superpower in the world and the major target in China's anti-hegemonism undertaking.

As part of its global strategy, China today makes efforts to ally itself with Russia, neutralize West Europe, and seek supports from the third world, so as to concentrate fire on U.S. hegemonism. Derived from the concept of "hegemonism" are a number of terms, such as the "cultural hegemony of Western imperialism" (xifang diguozhuyi wenhua baquan), "neo-imperialism in the post-Cold War era" (lengzhanhou shidaide xin diguozhuyi), and "neo-interventionism" (xin ganshezhuyi). Chinese leaders find nationalism, or patriotism as officially and tenably promoted, to be of great value in their struggle. Relevant slogans include: "Revitalize China" (zhenxing Zhonghua), "Sovereignty is supreme" (zhuquan zhishang), and "China can say no" (Zhongguo keyi shuo bu). These slogans help Beijing to cement internal forces against what it insists is the "international conspiracy" (guoji yinmou) of the West. See also "minzuzhuyi" (nationalism), "renmin zhanzheng" (people's war), "xiuzhengzhuyi" (revisionism), "lengzhanhou shidaide xin diguozhuyi" (neo-imperialism in the post-Cold War era), and "weidu Zhongguo" (containment against China).

世界革命中心
shijie geming zhongxin
(center of world revolution)

See "shijie geming" (world revolution).

世界革命中心论
shijie geming zhongxin lun
(theory of the world revolution center)

See "renmin zhanzheng" (people's war) and "shijie geming" (world revolution).

世界观
shijieguan
(world outlook)

The philosophical term "world outlook" ("shijieguan" or "yuzhouguan")—a general, fundamental view one takes towards the world (the sum total of all things in nature and in human society)—is familiar to Chinese people mainly because of its political implications.

According to CCP doctrine, there are various antitheses in terms of world outlook, such as those between materialistic and idealistic world outlooks or between dialectical and metaphysical world outlooks. The proletariat and its political party adopt a world outlook characterized by dialectical materialism and historical materialism. This is a Marxist world outlook, the only correct one, which is the theoretical weapon and scientific methodology wherewith the proletariat and its political party understand and remold the world.

In his article "Reform Our Study" ("Gaizao womende xuexi"), Mao re-interpreted an old Chinese maxim, "shishi qiu shi". "Shishi", he said, refers to all kinds of things of objective existence; the last character "shi" means the internal relations of objective things, i.e., their inherent law; and "qiu" means to explore *(MZXJ,* 3, 1968, p. 759). In Deng's words, "Marx and Engels propounded the ideological line of dialectical and historical materialism, a line which Comrade Mao Zedong summarized in the four Chinese characters 'Seeking truth from facts'" *(SWD,* p. 263). To seek truth from facts, one must proceed from reality in all things, link theory with practice, and hold practice to be the touchstone of truth. Deng regarded Mao's idea as "the basis of the proletarian world outlook as well as the ideological basis of Marxism" *(SWD,* p. 154).

In light of Mao's idea about class and class struggle, world outlook was an issue of vital importance. Different classes have different world outlooks; one's world outlook is decided by his class status. Class struggle in society, therefore, will find expression in one's world outlook. Mao made it clear and definite: "In every branch of learning there may be many schools and trends; in the matter of world outlook, however, today there are basically only two schools, the proletarian and the bourgeois. It is one or the other, either the proletarian or the bourgeois world outlook" *(MZXJ,* 5, p. 409). Mao also said: "The proletariat seeks to transform the world according to its own world outlook, and so does the bourgeoisie" (ibid.). The bourgeois world outlook was regarded as decadent, moribund, and reactionary, while the proletarian world outlook was said to be revolutionary, progressive, and correct.

In the fields of literature and art, world outlook was involved in a number of key issues. It was said that the truthfulness (zhenshixing) in a certain literary work is the product of how its author understands and epitomizes life, conditioned by his class status and his class's world outlook. There was the "theory of world outlook as the decisive factor" (shijieguan jueding lun), which asserts that writers' world outlook can decide everything in their creative activities. Another similar view was: No one can have creative or academic freedom if they do not possess a Marxist world outlook and have not mastered a Marxist method. Therefore, the Party demanded that writers must have a Communist world outlook before they begin to write (which Hu Feng described as one of the "five daggers"). Liu Binyan's theory of "being involved in life" (ganyu shenghuo) was said to be problematic, if it meant deviating from a Marxist world outlook and the guidance of the Party's correct line, principles, and policies, and exaggerating the dark side of society so as to make people lose confidence in life (Hu Yaobang, "Speech at the Forum on Script Writing"). In 1983, Party critics accused the theory of "misty poetry" of advocating the world outlook and art perspective of modernism in the West. (Thus its advocates committed a "political mistake".) In the humanism debate of the 1980s, world outlook was a key point. Gao Ertai pointed out that socialist humanism means Marxist humanism. Logically, socialist humanism is a world outlook as well as a conception of history (Gao Ertai, "A Memorandum). Hu Qiaomu asserted that humanism as a world-historical outlook is "idealistic", fundamentally opposite to Marxism (Hu Qiaomu, "On Problems Concerning Humanism and Alienation"). Wang Ruoshi, Zhou Yang, and many others, however, emphasized that the unity between Marxism and humanism should be affirmed from a world-historical outlook.

"Contradictions in one's world outlook", though a highly philosophical term, is also familiar to many Chinese. Particularly, it is employed in literary criticism (with Chinese characteristics). Mistakes can be attributed to contradictions in one's world outlook. An example was the September 1981 *Literary Gazette* critique, coauthored by Tang Yin and Tang Dacheng, two assistant chief editors of the gazette. In commenting on Bai Hua's problematic work "Unrequited Love", they ascribed Bai Hua's mistake to the contradiction in his world outlook ("On the Erroneous Tendency in 'Unrequited Love'"—"Lun 'Kulian' de cuowu qingxiang", *WYB*, 9, 1981, reprinted in *RMRB*, 7 Oct. 1981, and *WYLZJ*, pp. 139-52). Then in his self-criticism written on 25 November 1981, in the form of an open letter to the editorial boards of the *Liberation Army Daily* and the *Literary Gazette*, Bai Hua mainly talked about the "contradictions" in his world outlook.

During the Mao period, China's intellectuals were regarded as "bourgeois intellectuals" or as having a "bourgeois world outlook". They were strictly required to study Marxism-Leninism-Mao Zedong Thought and to remold their ideology so that their bourgeois world outlook would be gradually cast away and they would adopt a proletarian world outlook. For this purpose, a series of politico-ideological education movements were carried out over several decades, which proved to be a long and bitter experience. Moreover, Mao decided that most of China's intellectuals failed to be remolded well. Mao must have firmly believed that this was the best way to control and make use of China's intellectuals.

Deng Xiaoping resorted to another method. After his return to power, he rehabilitated most of those who had been disgraced in the past movements. In his speech at the opening ceremony of the National Conference on Science held in Beijing on 18 March 1978, Deng announced that China's intellectuals were already part of the working class *(SWD,* p. 105). According to him, the basic question as regards world outlook is whom one is to serve (shejieguande zhongyao biaoxian shi wei shui fuwu). Deng said, if a person loved the socialist motherland and was serving socialism and the workers, peasants, and soldiers of his own free will and accord, then he should be said to have begun acquiring a proletarian world outlook. In terms of political standards, he could not be considered "white" but should be called "red" (ibid., pp. 107-8). Deng's above elucidation greatly relieved China's intellectuals at that time.

But now it is said that Marxism is not the world outlook (or the ideology) of the proletariat. In 1992, when talking about Marxism, Li Zehou, an outstanding philosopher, made known this view which he had not dared to state earlier. Quoting

Lenin as saying that Marxism should be instilled from the outside into the workers, Li asserted that Marxism has nothing to do with the working class. It is the world outlook and ideology of certain intellectuals of recent times (see *Farewell to Revolution: Looking Back upon China of the Twentieth Century*, pp. 177-78).

More significantly, due to the two decades of reform, world outlook is no longer a political issue of vital importance to China's intellectuals. They may well refute Marx's "mistaking" the working class for the leading force of society. In light of China's profound social changes today, Mao's metaphor about "skin" and "hair" appears ridiculous. As many hold, it is a personal matter for one to have his own world outlook, and an intellectual's world outlook may be the most progressive. See also "rendaozhuyide liang ge hanyi" (two meanings of humanism), "sixiang gaizao" (ideological remolding), and "dangde jiaoyu fangzhen" (the Party's educational policy).

世界观决定论
shijieguan jueding lun
(theory of "world outlook as the decisive factor")

See "shijieguan" (world outlook) and "wenxue duixiang zhutixing" (subjectivity of the object of literature).

世界观的矛盾
shijieguande maodun
(contradictions in one's world outlook)

See "shijieguan" (world outlook).

世界观的重要表现是为谁服务
shijieguande zhongyao biaoxian shi wei shui fuwu
(the basic question as regards world outlook is whom one is to serve)

See "shijieguan" (world outlook).

世界主义
shijiezhuyi
(cosmopolitanism)

See "minzuzhuyi" (nationalism).

收
shou
("tightening up" policy)

See "fang" (loosening up).

兽道
shoudao
(barbarism)

See "wanquan fouding rendaozhuyi jiu daozhi shendao he shoudao" (a total negation of humanism will lead to "theocracy" and "barbarism").

抒人民之情
shu renmin zhi qing
(to convey the people's emotion)

See "ziwo biaoxian" (expression of the subjective ego).

双百方针
shuangbai fangzhen
(Double Hundred policy)

This is a shorthand way of referring to the policy of "Let a hundred flowers bloom and a hundred schools of thought contend" (baihuaqifang, baijiazhengming). Since in Chinese each of the two expressions begins with the character "bai" (hundred), they have come to be known as the "shuangbai", or the "double hundred".

According to Lu Dingyi (Director of the PCC Propaganda Department in the 1950s), Chen Boda first linked the two expressions together at a private discussion with Mao and Lu. On 25 and 28 April 1956, at an enlarged meeting of the Politburo, Mao suggested his Double Hundred policy, aimed at guiding and promoting science, culture, literature, and art. On 27 February 1957, Mao reaffirmed the policy in his speech, "On the Correct Handling of Contradictions among the People", delivered at the 11th meeting (enlarged) of the Supreme State Council. For a while, when the policy was being carried out, it did achieve its aim, at least to some extent. In a favorable situation, a number of fine works emerged, such as those reprinted in the 1979 anthology *Reblooming Flowers*, boldly exposing the dark side of social life, or truthfully presenting the characters' inner selves, or both. In the fields of literary criticism and literary theory, a number of critics tried to break out of the confines of dogmatism and explore new issues with unprecedented courage. But all this, unfortunately, was short-lived. As pointed out by many critics, Mao canceled the policy only a year after he raised it.

After the Double Hundred policy was put forward, however, many Chinese writers and intellectuals quoted from it from time to time, in the hopes that it would really be carried out some day. Ironically, to some people in power, this sincere wish is but an expression of "bourgeois liberalization", something that the Double Hundred policy must not bring about. In his speech at the 1981 Forum on Problems Arising on the Nation's Ideological Front, Hu Qiaomu specifically pointed out that the "Double Hundred" was not the only policy of the Party in ideological work. It could not be separated from the aim of the Party and all the Communists in the new historical period, nor could it be divorced from the Party's Marxist ideological line. Besides, the Party also had other policies, such as "weeding through the old to bring forth the new" (tuichenchuxin), "making the past serve the present" (gu wei jin yong), and "making foreign things serve China" (yang wei zhong yong). As often emphasized, Hu said, what deserved special attention was that the Double Hundred policy must be linked with the principle of establishing the guiding position of Marxism in all social, political, and ideological spheres, and with the principle of criticism and self-criticism (see Hu Qiaomu, "Dangqian sixiang zhanxiande ruogan wenti"—"Some Current Problems on the Ideological Front", *HQ,* 23:2-22, 1981, reprinted in *WYB,* 5:3-23, 1982; partially trans. in *BR,* 4:15-18, 25 Jan. 1982). See also "chuangzuo ziyou" (creative freedom).

双重领导
shuangchong lingdao
(dual leadership)

See "tiaotiao lingdao" (vertical leadership).

双为方针
shuangwei fangzhen
("double service" principle)

See "wenyi wei zhengzhi fuwu" (literature and art serve politics).

顺藤摸瓜
shun teng mo gua
(following the vine to get the melon)

See "fan youpai yundong" (anti-Rightist campaign).

思想包袱
sixiang baofu
(mental burdens)

"Sixiang baofu" was a term frequently used in political movements during the Mao period. Generally speaking, it referred to "erroneous" ideas of all kinds, anything weighing on one's mind, anything that stood in the way of "progress", the many "encumbrances" in one's mind. "Many things may become baggage, may become encumbrances, if we cling to them blindly and uncritically," Mao said *(SWM,* 3, p. 173). For example, "lack of achievement in work may breed pessimism and depression, while achievement may breed pride and arrogance". "Even age may become grounds for conceit" (ibid.).

In fact, any idea out of line with Party principles and policies and Mao Zedong Thought could be condemned as bourgeois, as erroneous or even criminal, and thus could become the most serious "sixiang baofu". In political movements, phrases like the following were often used: "fangxia baofu" or "fangxia sixiang baofu" ("to get rid of baggage", which means to free one's mind of encumbrances, rectify mistaken ideas and liberate one's mind), and "jie sixiang gaizi" ("to remove the ideological cover", which means to expose one's own or others' secrets, to confess one's alleged mistakes or crimes). There was also the term: "sixiang lanhan" ("ideological sluggards"), referring to those who do not bother to think profoundly enough to solve problems.

People were often asked "to get rid of the baggage" or "to remove the ideological cover". Their exposure of hidden secrets was so they could relieve themselves of their mental burdens and truly correct their mistakes. Sometimes, one would be highly praised, even set up as a fine example, after one "got rid of the baggage", especially when at the same time one could inform against others. Very often, unfortunately, one would still ultimately be punished because what one confessed would be used as criminal evidence against him. Sometimes, when one found the "sixiang baofu" in question too serious to confess, one would have no choice but to commit suicide. See also "sixiang gaizao" (ideological remolding).

思想改造
sixiang gaizao
(ideological remolding)

Soon after the 1949 Communist takeover of mainland China, Mao and his colleagues declared the remolding of China's intellectuals to be a task of vital importance. In his opening speech at the 3rd Plenum of the 1st National Committee of the CPPCC held in October 1951, Mao said: "Ideological remolding, primarily the ideological remolding of intellectuals of various types, is one of the important prerequisites for our country to thoroughly realize democratic reform in all respects and to achieve industrialization gradually" (*RMRB,* 24 Oct. 1951). Then, on 17 November 1951, the Standing Committee of the All-China Federation of Literary and Art Circles adopted a relevant decision about ideological remolding. In January 1952, the CPPCC launched a study movement for the ideological remolding of people from many walks of life. The movement spread throughout the country.

From then on, numerous political and remolding movements, big or small, were carried out one after another within China's intellectual circles. For most intellectuals, such movements ended up being bitter and never-ending nightmares. The "ideological remolding" could well be said to be an "ideological conquest". They had to accept the "self-remolding" (ziwo gaizao). And as the result of this "self-remolding", they were branded as "bourgeois intellectuals", humiliation could befall them at any time, and they had to accept the label and the humiliation willingly. Contemporary Chinese intellectuals seemed to have lost their moral courage (daode yongqide lunsan).

Traditionally, according to Liu Qingfeng, a historian-philosopher, there were three sources of moral courage for Chinese intellectuals: their own intuitive knowledge (liangzhi), their culture and knowledge gained through education, and their enthusiasm for a norm of social behavior. It was in these three aspects that their moral courage was destroyed by Sinicized Marxism (Zhongguohuade Makesizhuyi) promoted by Mao and his Party.

What shook Chinese intellectuals' moral courage most was the destruction of their sense of superiority in possessing culture and knowledge. In the ideological remolding movement, they were told that knowledge was of a class nature. It was by exploiting workers and peasants that they had been able to receive their education, and their knowledge, as the result of this education, served the reactionary, exploiting classes. When they were convinced of this view, their sense of superiority immediately dissipated. Many of them had thought they were patriotic and they supported the new regime and loved the Communist Party, but the question of "whom to serve" made them doubt whether they were moral. In addition, they found themselves unable to have recourse to their own intuitive knowledge—the theory of "human nature", subjected to most vigorous attacks from the very beginning of the movement, had been replaced by the theory of "class stand as the decisive factor" (lichang jueding lun), which was characterized by class struggle and class analysis.

It would be simplistic to say that Marxism, as an official ideology, succeeded in conquering Chinese intellectuals because it possessed an integral critical force over the traditional sources of their moral courage. For the majority of Chinese intellectuals to be willing to receive ideological remolding, Liu Qingfeng said, there were two important historical and cultural factors. One was that Marxism, after being introduced into China, had greatly altered the course of modern Chinese history. The victory of the widespread social revolution, the realization of national independence, and the honest and efficient administration in the early days of the new regime—all these easily made Chinese intellectuals convinced of Marxism and the CCP leadership. The other was that Marxism, in the course of spreading throughout China, had developed into Mao Zedong Thought—a Sinicized Marxism—which had integrated itself with traditional Chinese culture, sharing the same deep structure with tradition, especially in the concept of value. This official ideology, while criticizing and repudiating the traditional sources of moral courage, displayed itself in a new value system which Chinese intellectuals were very familiar with and which they easily accepted. In fact, the three traditional sources can be identified in the Sinicized Marxist system of value—expressed by different contents of course: the proletarian class stand stands for the moral sense and intuitive knowledge, the study of Marxism and Mao Zedong Thought stands for the study of Confucian and other ancient classics, and the good political record in the revolutionary cause stands for the vindication and enthusiasm of traditional norms of social behavior (Liu Qingfeng, "Shilun wen'geqian dangdai Zhongguo zhishifenzi daode yongqide lunsan"—"On the Loss of Moral Courage of Pre-Cultural Revolution Chinese Intellectuals", in Jin Guantao and Liu Qingfeng, *Xin Shiritan—New Decameron,* Hong Kong, Cosmos Books, 1990, pp. 251-87. For criticism of the views of Liu Qingfeng and Jin Guantao, see, for instance, Tan Shuangquan, "Ping suowei 'Mao Zedong sixiang rujiahua'"—"On the So-called 'Confucianized Mao Zedong Thought'", *Qiushi,* 23:24-29, 1 Dec. 1991).

Instead of the "Sinicized Marxist system of value", those taking exception to China's Communist regime also used some other terms. "Party culture" (dangwenhua), for instance, refers to the series of modes of thinking, the stand, viewpoints, logic, and methods which the Party impresses upon the people, so that they understand the world and deal with issues in the way the Party thinks correct. Mao Zedong Thought and Deng Xiaoping Theory are the main body of the Party culture; a new development is Jiang Zemin's "three-stresses" (sanjiang). The Party culture has produced a great number of terms and theses (most of them can be found in this book), which many Chinese use everyday without questioning their tenability or their credibility. This helps the stability of the Communist regime. Another term is "socialist-communist culture" (she gong wenhua). Su Wei, a former research fellow at CASS, pointed out that after the founding of the PRC, many Chinese intellectual found new ideological shackles. This was a result of being educated for years by a "socialist-communist culture", a culture based on "socialism" plus the proletarian dictatorship of the CCP. Su asserted that there were at least three mechanisms for this culture: lies, threats, and forgetfulness (see Lee Yee, "Chongxin miandui jiben wenti—fang Zhongguo zhishifenzi Su Wei"—"Re-facing the Basic Issues: An Interview with Su Wei, a Chinese Intellectual", *JN,* 238:76-82, Nov. 1989).

Under the influence of the "socialist-communist culture" or the "Party culture", everyone had a "spiritual burden" ("jingshen baofu" or "mental burden"—"sixiang baofu") of one kind or another. Everyone had self-doubts (ziwo huaiyi), and was always haunted by a fear of their being out of line with Party principles and policies. As to writers and artists, there was always the fear that their works may have exceeded a certain line of demarcation and had intruded into any of the many "forbidden zones" (jinqu). Many built, as Bai Hua described, a "prison of the mind" (xinyu) for themselves. A great writer must possess freedom—freedom of thinking and observation—but many of China's writers were deprived of this freedom. At first, it was taken away by external forces, by a set of political and cultural conventions; with the gradual effect of the influence of several decades, one eventually built a prison of the mind of one's own. Even worse, one might clearly realize this, but there was no way to escape it. Bai Hua confessed that he also had his prison of the mind. He had his own problems, such as a mechanical conception of history, mechanical ethics, a mechanical class viewpoint, and a mechanical collectivism. He knew that he could not possibly approach real life until he had completely conquered these (see Lee

Yee, "Bai Hua hai zhimi buwude kulian zuguo ma?"—"Does Bai Hua Still Stubbornly Love His Motherland?", *JN*, 216:84-92, Jan. 1988).

Most inconceivable of the "prison of the mind" was perhaps the so-called "original sin" consciousness (yuanzui yishi) of China's intellectuals during the Mao period. They had a sense of shame simply because of the idea inculcated by the Party that they, unlike workers and peasants, did not produce any material wealth for society. They were deeply tortured for not having the simple and pure way of thinking characteristic of workers and peasants, resulting from their education and the culture and knowledge they possessed.

The consciousness of the "original sin", deriving from Christian culture, is not part of Chinese cultural tradition. No doubt, influenced by Confucian norms and philosophy, such as the golden mean (zhongyong zhi dao), which is widespread in China, Chinese intellectuals generally tend towards self-restraint, by self-reflection (zixing), cruelly strangling their sense of freedom and initiative. Nevertheless, as a politico-moral sense and ideology, the consciousness of the "original sin" only took shape as the result of the "ideological remolding movement" carried out soon after the 1949 Communist takeover. Thereafter, similar movements erupted in succession. Most Chinese intellectuals gradually lost their moral courage. Correspondingly, their "original sin" consciousness became stronger and stronger.

This was really a great achievement by Mao. The intellectuals' role in society was thus greatly reduced, exactly as Mao wished. In literary and art creation, the consciousness of the "original sin" became the greatest psychological obstacle to writers' and artists' self-actualization. It made them easily accept Mao's slogan that literature and art are subordinate to, and in service of, politics. Since aesthetic pursuits had to be subservient to political concepts, writers and artists had to constantly change color to suit different political climates. They had to extinguish their creative individuality, which was often condemned as an evil revelation of their original sin (yuanzui xingzhide e). Of course, some could not be remolded by Mao Zedong Thought. But their number was few, and they had to pay dearly for their stubbornness. They were given various political labels, such as "bourgeois Rightist", "counter-revolutionary", and "anti-Party, anti-people, and anti-socialism", etc. Most sadly, they were not only condemned by Party cadres but also by their close colleagues.

That contemporary Chinese intellectuals lost their moral courage even long before the GPCR was a hotly-discussed topic in the late 1980s. In fact, with iconoclasm towards Mao and Mao's doctrine becoming dominant in China's intellectual circles after the 1978 debate about practice as the sole criterion for testing truth, all Mao's and his Party's efforts of several decades to remold China's intellectuals were by then merely a subject for academic research. Of course, there still were bitter, frightening, and clear memories. But Deng Xiaoping's reform and open-door program brought an end to the remolding efforts. Ironically, today China's intellectuals once again are facing the danger of losing their moral courage—this time mainly because of the lure of money due to the general corruption of society.

思想改造运动
sixiang gaizao yundong
(ideological remolding movement)

See "sixiang gaizao" (ideological remolding).

思想盖子
sixiang gaizi
(ideological cover)

See "sixiang baofu" (mental burdens) and "sixiang gaizao" (ideological remolding).

思想工作
sixiang gongzuo
(ideological work)

See "tanxin" (heart-to-heart talk) and "sixiang gaizao" (ideological remolding).

思想解放运动
sixiang jiefang yundong
(thought-emancipation movement)

See "Beijing zhi chun" (Beijing Spring) and "jiefang sixiang" (emancipating the mind).

思想懒汉
sixiang lanhan
(ideological sluggard)

One who does not bother to think profoundly enough or indulges in empty talk (qingtan) or stereotyped phrases is criticized as a "sixiang lanhan". Today the criticism is used to refer to an undesirable attitude towards work. In the Mao period, it often referred to one's attitude towards "ideological remolding". See also "sixiang baofu" (mental burdens) and "sixiang gaizao" (ideological remolding).

思想理论的改革
sixiang lilunde gaige
(theoretical-ideological reform)

See "fansi" (reflection).

思想内容可以成为一种美
sixiang neirong keyi changwei yi zhong mei
(ideological content can manifest itself as a kind of beauty)

This thesis was raised by Mai Tianshu, a writer of reportage literature, in 1988.

Mai and other writers of reportage literature realized, some quite reluctantly, that their works evoked a warm response from the readership mainly not as works of art but as demonstrations of the "intuitive knowledge of society" (shehui liangzhi). They argued that they did not neglect the literary, but their works needed to be judged by a new set of aesthetic criteria suitable for the new genre, and not by traditional criteria or by those criteria for fiction or other genres. At the July 1988 forum held in Guangdong, Mai Tianshu said:

"Society requires not only that a writer of reportage literature possess artistic techniques; more importantly, you must be a thinker and not a *literati* in the first place. It is very likely that this attribute characteristic of reportage literature writing will be the watershed between masterpieces and mediocre works and between great writers and those with limited ability" (Su Xiaokang et al., "1988: guanyu baogao wenxuede duihua"—"1988: A Dialog on Reportage Literature", *Huacheng,* 6:8, 1988).

One month later, during another forum held in Shanxi, Mai further asserted: "When profundity of thinking is universally demanded by the readership, the ideological content in a work of reportage literature will manifest itself as a kind of beauty—it will transform into literariness through means of literature" (Su Xiaokang et al., "Taihang yehua: baogao wenxue wuren tan"—"Reportage Literature: A Five-person Discussion", *GMRB*, 23 Sept. 1988).

This view of Mai's might be controversial, adding fuel to the existing debate about the form of problem-centered reportage literature. To the delight of Mai and his supporters, many readers and critics did come to acknowledge the artistic quality of this new genre, and agreed that this had become its essential attribute—to be courageously and resolutely involved in political struggles with keen insight and to promote in a direct way the reform of institutional structures in Chinese politics, economy, and culture. They further regarded this as the basic social role which works of this genre should play in contemporary China. (One of them, significantly, was Feng Mu, a veteran critic and cultural official. See his "Baogao wenxue mantan: cong Su Xiaokangde chuangzuo tanqi"—"Reportage Literature: Starting from Su Xiaokang's Works", *WYB*, 27 Aug. 1988. See also Qin Jin, "Zouchu kunjing: guanyu baogao wenxue pipingde sikao"—"Some Thoughts in Regard to the Criticism of Reportage Literature", *GMRB*, 18 Nov. 1988).

This might be too great a task for writers—it forced them to be veritable sociologists, thinkers, and statesmen, and with independent thinking and not yielding to power. Many of them were aware that they were running a risk which could bring them terrible disaster. As Su Xiaokang confessed, he felt a kind of "cruelty" from his readership. But he had no other choice: he had to go on, to strive for breakthroughs with a sense of social responsibility. "This is a challenge to my own conscience", he said. (See Ai Ni, "Longchaorende qiusuo: wenti baogao wenxue yantaohui gaishu"—"A Summary of the Symposium for Reportage Literature with Social Problems as Its Main Concern", *WXPL,* 3:68, 1988). See "yi wenti wei zhongxinde baogao wenxue" (problem-centered reportage literature).

思想文化霸权
sixiang wenhua baquan
(ideological-cultural hegemony)

See "lishi jiaosede huhuan" (an interchange of historical roles) and "dapipan" (mass criticism).

思想文化霸权与政治霸权的结盟
sixiang wenhua baquan yu zhengzhi baquande jiemeng
(an alliance of ideological-cultural hegemony and political hegemony)

See "lishi jiaosede huhuan" (an interchange of historical roles).

思想问题
sixiang wenti

(ideological problems)

See "tanxin" (heart-to-heart talk) and "sixiang gaizao" (ideological remolding).

思想异化
sixiang yihua
(ideological alienation)

Ideological alienation was, as held by alienation scholars like Zhou Yang and Wang Ruoshui, a phenomenon of socialist alienation, exemplified by the personality cult of Mao Zedong. Hu Qiaomu, however, while allowing that the cult was a malignancy developing out of natural admiration, found that even during the GPCR people's attitudes towards Mao were very complex and should not be placed on a par with religious beliefs. In his January 1984 article, "On Problems Concerning Humanism and Alienation", he wrote that the application of Feuerbach's ideas, except for presenting a frivolous caricature, could not account for the cause of the event at all; still less could it explain why the Party was able to bring order out of chaos so smoothly. See also "shehuizhuyi yihua lun" (theory of socialist alienation).

思想战线不要搞精神污染
sixiang zhanxian buyaogao jingshen wuran
(the ideological front must not bring about spiritual pollution)

On 12 October 1983 at the 2nd Plenum of the 12th PCC, which in its original agenda was going to adopt a resolution about Party rectification, Deng Xiaoping warned that the ideological front must not bring about "spiritual pollution". A relevant decision was made at the Plenum, which was followed by the campaign to "eliminate spiritual pollution" throughout the country. See "qingwu yundong" (campaign to eliminate spiritual pollution).

私倒
sidao
(private profiteering)

See "jingshang re" (business fever).

私有化
siyouhua
(privatization)

See "jiejue gongyouzhi xingshi shi you yici sixiang jiefang" (solving the issue of public ownership forms is another emancipation of the mind).

死不改悔的走资派
si bu gaihuide zouzipai
(incorrigible capitalist-roaders)

See "zou zibenzhuyi daolu dangquanpai" (those in power taking the capitalist road) and "pi Deng, fanji youqing fan'anfeng" (campaign to criticize Deng Xiaoping and counter the Right deviationist trend to reverse correct verdicts).

死人统治
siren tongzhi
(rule by the dead)

After the 1962 10th Plenum of the 8th PCC, Mao gave a series of talks and instructions concerning Party work in literature and art. On 12 December 1963, in an instruction to Peng Zhen and Liu Ren, then Party leaders in Beijing, he pointed out that "the 'dead' still dominate in many departments". See "dui wenyijiede liang ge zhiming daji" (two telling blows to literary and art circles).

四大家族
si da jiazu
(four notorious clans)

See "guanliao ziben" (bureaucrat-capital).

四二一现象
si er yi xianxiang
("four-two-one" phenomenon)

See "yitaihua" (single-child policy).

四个存在
si ge cunzai
(four existences)

During the Mao period, everyone, Party member in particular, was never to forget the "four existences" in the historical period of socialism. They were: 1. classes, class contradictions, and class struggle; 2. the struggle between the socialist road and the capitalist road; 3. the danger of capitalist restoration; and 4. the threat of subversion and aggression by imperialism and modern revisionism. See also "dangde jiben luxian" (the Party's basic line).

四个第一
si ge diyi
(four firsts)

See "tuchu zhengzhi" (giving prominence to politics).

四个第一好
si ge diyi hao
(the "four firsts" are great)

See "tuchu zhengzhi" (giving prominence to politics).

四个凡是
si ge fanshi
(four whatevers)

See "si xiang jiben yuanze" (four cardinal principles).

四个关系
si ge guanxi
(four relationships)

See "tuchu zhengzhi" (giving prominence to politics).

四个坚持
si ge jianchi
(four upholds)

See "si xiang jiben yuanze" (four cardinal principles).

四个念念不忘
si ge niannian buwang
(four never-forgets)

See "si xiang jiben yuanze" (four cardinal principles) and "tuchu zhengzhi" (giving prominence to politics).

四个伟大
si ge weida
(four greats)

In the latter half of 1966, Mao began to be addressed, first by Lin Biao, with the four titles "great leader, great teacher, great commander, and great helmsman" (weida lingxiu, weida daoshi, weida tongshuai, weida duoshou). During his talk with the American journalist Edgar Snow on 10 December 1970, Mao indicated that he was unhappy about these titles. If possible, he said, he would like to have only one—"teacher", because he originally had been a teacher. See also "Mao Zedong sixiang" (Mao Zedong Thought) and "tuchu zhengzhi" (giving prominence to politics).

四个现代化
si ge xiandaihua
(four modernizations)

The concept of the "four modernizations"—modernizations of agriculture, industry, science and technology, and national defense—was first advanced by Zhou Enlai on 29 January 1963 at a Shanghai meeting discussing work in science and technology. Then, in his report delivered on 21 December 1964 at the 1st Session of the 3rd NPC, Zhou declared that his government would accomplish, in a two-step plan, the "four modernizations" within not too long a period. On 13 January 1975, at the 1st Session of the 4th NPC, by that time China's economy had seriously been damaged by the GPCR chaos, the premier brought up for the last time before his death the issue again in his report on government work.

At the 11th CCP National Congress held in August 1977, the authorities reaffirmed the goal of accomplishing the "four modernizations" by the end of the twentieth century.

At the PCC Work Conference held November to December 1978, which made preparations for the 3rd Plenum of the 11th PCC, the Party announced that the nationwide mass movement to expose and criticize Lin Biao and the Gang of Four had ended. A decision was taken to advance the fundamental guiding principle to shift the focus of all Party work to the "four modernizations" (that is, to economic construction) and from "taking class struggle as the key link" (which the Party had upheld for several decades after the founding of the PRC). The decision was confirmed at the following historic 3rd Plenum of the 11th PCC. This was said to be a turning point in CCP history, and a great victory for Deng's line.

In conformity with his assertion that "the fundamental task of socialism is to develop productivity", Deng was obsessed with his idea about the "four modernizations". In his speech greeting the 1979 4th Congress of Writers and Artists, he told the participants that the overriding nationwide task was to work single-mindedly for the "four modernizations". At that time, a popular slogan was: To achieve the "four modernizations" is the most important politics (shixian si ge xiandaihua shi zuidade zhengzhi).

As many agree, however, the formulation of the "four modernizations" is problematic. Modernization means to modernize the whole society. So to list specifically the above four items only results in deleting many others. For instance, one can point out, modernization should also, and more fundamentally, be carried out in the fields such as politics, economics, culture, concepts, the way of life, and human relationships. In order to overcome the problem, Wei Jingsheng, then a radical activist of the Beijing Spring, suggested the "fifth modernization" in December 1978. He asserted that if the Chinese people want to realize the "four modernizations", they must first practice democracy and modernize China's social system. Wei thus regarded democracy as the fifth modernization, a necessary condition for the "four modernizations". Today, many scholars promote a new concept of "four modernizations"—modernizations of economy ("jingji xiandaihua", which includes the above four items promoted by CCP leaders), politics (zhengzhi xiandaihua), social system (zhidu xiandaihua), and ideology (yishixingtai xiandaihua). See also "zhengzhi gaige" (political reform) and "jingji gaige" (economic reform).

四个转移
si ge zhuanyi
(four shifts)

At the 1983 "National Economic Work Conference" held in Beijing, the "four shifts" were raised as a key issue having a bearing on national economic development. The "four shifts" were the shifts from foreign to domestic, from scientific research to production, from coastal regions to the inland, and from military industry to civil industry. See also "jingji gaige" (economic reform).

四条汉子
si tiao hanzi
(four fellows)

The "four fellows" was a derogatory term Lu Xun used to describe Zhou Yang, Xia Yan, Tian Han, and Yang Hansheng, four prominent writers and critics in the 1930s. It first appeared in his article entitled "In Reply to Xu Mouyong and on the Question of the United Front against Japan". The four people suffered a great deal during the GPCR (Tian Han ultimately committed suiside) partly because of this appellation, since Lu Xun was highly regarded by Mao as the greatest revolutionary writer and all of his judgements were considered correct. This remained unquestioned even for some time after the downfall of the Gang of Four. The article "An Out-and-Out Old-Time Capitulationist" ("Yi ge dididaodaode lao touxiangpai"), published in the 21 October

1976 issue of the *People's Daily*, was the first public (albeit oblique) attack on the Gang of Four, but its primary target was still the "four fellows" headed by Zhou Yang, who were described by the commentator as the chief culprits on whose behalf Di Ke (a pseudonym for Zhang Chunqiao in the 1930s) committed the crime of slandering Lu Xun. See also "sanshiniandai wenyi yundong" (literature and art movement of the 1930s).

四项基本原则
si xiang jiben yuanze
(four cardinal principles)

A long meeting called the Forum on Principles for Theoretical Work (lilun gongzuo wuxuhui) was held by the PCC in Beijing from 18 January to 3 April 1979 (adjourned for over one month during the Sino-Vietnam war, which began on 17 February and ended on 26 March 1979). Similar but shorter meetings were also held in Shanghai, Shandong, Fujian, Guangdong, Liaoning, Hunan, and Jiangsu. The Beijing meeting, which was divided into two sessions, began with a very encouraging speech by Hu Yaobang, newly appointed director of the PCC Propaganda Department. (Ruan Ming helped draft the speech. See his *Hu Yaobang on the Historical Turning Point,* pp. 34, 106-108.) The meeting, or most of the meeting, did make a theoretical breakthrough, marking the high tide of the first "thought-emancipation movement", where the Left line and theories were strongly criticized.

On 30 March 1979, dramatically, an abrupt change took place. Deng delivered a speech (which had been drafted by Hu Qiaomu) at the forum. In his speech, Deng put forward his "four cardinal principles"—keep to the socialist road, uphold the dictatorship of the proletariat, uphold the leadership of the Communist Party, and uphold Marxism-Leninism and Mao Zedong Thought—and demanded that the whole Party uphold them ideologically and politically. Deng's speech shocked the entire country, bringing the first "thought-emancipation movement" to an end.

The "four cardinal principles" greatly affected the course of China's politics for the next 20 years. It constituted part of Deng Xiaoping's line of "one center, two basic points". Obsessed with his theory of the "two basic points", Deng on the one hand upheld reform and the open-door policy and on the other he upheld the "four cardinal principles". He explicitly treated his political campaigns, such as those in 1983 and 1987 to eliminate "spiritual pollution" or to oppose "bourgeois liberalization", as "guarantees" for the successful implementation of his economic reforms. More specifically, critics said, his line opposed Left ideology in the economic field (with his reform and open-door policy) and Right ideology in the political field (with his "four cardinal principles").

Endowed with the force of law, the "four cardinal principles" were stipulated as the "political foundation for the unity of the whole Party" in the CCP Constitution adopted in September 1982 at the 12th CCP National Congress. They were also written into the preamble to the 4th Constitution of the People's Republic of China adopted on 4 December 1982 at the 5th Session of the 5th NPC (in both constitutions the "dictatorship of the proletariat" was changed to the "people's democratic dictatorship").

For a time after Deng first raised the "four cardinal principles", people hesitated to oppose them openly. Instead, one would try to re-interpret them. Noteworthy are the three articles by Li Honglin, then deputy director of the Theory Bureau of the CCP's Propaganda Department, published in the *People's Daily*, obviously with the help of Hu Jiwei and Wang Ruoshui, then respectively editor-in-chief and deputy editor-in-chief of the *People's Daily*. (The three articles are: "Women jianchi shenmeyangde shehuizhuyi"—"What Kind of Socialism Should We Adhere to?", "Women jianchi shenmeyangde wuchanjieji zhuanzheng"—"What Kind of Proletarian Dictatorship Should We Adhere to?" and "Women jianchi shenmeyangde dangde lingdao"—"What Kind of Party Leadership Should We Adhere to?", in *RMRB*, 9 May, 22 June, and 5 October 1979). Ten years later, though persecuted, Li still managed to publish the last of the series, "What Kind of Marxism Should We Adhere to?" ("Women jianchi shenmeyangde Makesizhuyi", *Makesizhuyi yanjiu,* 1, 1989, reprinted in *XHWZ,* 5:1-3, 1989).

With the lapse of time, more and more people have found the "four cardinal principles" simply unacceptable. Again, Li Honglin was one such case. In his book *A History of Chinese Thought, 1949-1989 (Zhongguo Sixiang Yundongshi, 1949-1989,* Hong Kong, Tiandi Tushu, 1999), Li finds the "four cardinal principles" to be a replacement of Hua Guofeng's "two whatevers" which Deng himself overthrew in 1978. He mockingly calls Deng's principles the "four whatevers" (si ge fanshi).

Deng himself emphasized that the core of the "four cardinal principles" was the upholding of Party leadership *(SWD,* p. 339). Some, however, thought otherwise. Hu Jiwei, for example, asserted that the core is upholding Mao Zedong Thought. The other three—Party leadership, the socialist road, and the dictatorship of the proletariat—are all the major contents of Mao Zedong Thought. The "four upholds", therefore, are essentially "one uphold" *(Downfalls of Communist Tycoons: From Hua Guofeng to Hu Yaobang,* Hong Kong, Mingjing, 1998).

Hu Jiwei wanted to point out the ideological and political continuity between Mao and Deng. Deng himself also emphasized that the "four cardinal principles", far from being new, had long been upheld by the CCP *(SWD,* p. 172). And that was why many compare them with the "six criteria" (liu tiao biaozhun) that Mao put forward on 27 February 1957, in his speech "On the Correct Handling of Contradictions among the People" delivered at the 11th meeting (enlarged) of the Supreme State Council. The "six criteria" are: (1) Words and deeds should help to unite, and not divide, the people of all China's nationalities. (2) They should be beneficial, and not harmful, to socialist transformation and socialist construction. (3) They should help to consolidate, and not undermine or weaken, the people's democratic dictatorship. (4) They should help to consolidate, and not undermine or weaken, democratic centralism. (5) They should help to strengthen, and not shake off or weaken, the leadership of the Communist Party. (6) They should be beneficial, and not harmful, to international socialist unity and the unity of the peace-loving people of the world *(MZXJ,* 5, p. 393).

Mao put forth the "six criteria" by which to judge what is a "xianghua" (fragrant flower) and what is a "ducao" (poisonous weed). Of these six criteria, Mao explained, the most important are the two about the socialist path and Party leadership. Mao no doubt did pioneering work in forming and raising his "six criteria". However, Deng's "four cardinal principles" seem more succinct, impressive, and forceful, while the "six criteria" are a bit too vague. Therefore, when one says that Deng's "four cardinal principles" were derived from Mao's "six criteria", one must add that Deng certainly kept and developed the essential of Mao Zedong Thought.

Some people also compare Deng's "four cardinal principles" to Lin Biao's "four never-forgets" (si ge niannian buwang). In his well-known speech of 18 May 1966, Lin Biao, who was described as Mao's "good student", talked in details about his "four never-forgets"—"never forget class struggle, never forget the dictatorship of the proletariat, never forget to give prominence to politics, and never forget to hold high the red banner of Mao Zedong Thought". In his opinion, the "four never-forgets" guarantee that proletarian political power will be everlasting and ever-victorious. (The "four never-forgets" were first published on the front page of the

People's Daily on 28 May 1966.) Poignantly, Hu Jiwei points out in his 1998 book *Downfalls of Communist Tycoons* that the "four cardinal principles" are a reproduction of the "four never-forgets".

From the above comparisons, one can see how some Chinese regard the "four cardinal principles". This can also be seen clearly and generally in the trend of so-called "bourgeois liberalization" (zichanjieji ziyouhua) in mainland China in the past two decades or more, a trend which is clearly troublesome to the CCP leadership. As the hardliners put it (and quite correctly), the "bourgeois liberalization" is the equivalent of negating the "four cardinal principles", thus there is always confrontation between the two. See also "wuchanjieji zhuanzheng" (dictatorship of the proletariat), "dangde lingdao" (Party leadership), "xin shehuizhuyi guan" (new socialist view), "zhengtong Makesizhuyi zhengzai zou xiang siwang" (orthodox Marxism is heading for death), and "ziyouhua" (liberalization).

四项基本原则是四个"凡是"
si xiang jiben yuanze shi si ge "fanshi"
(the "four cardinal principles" are the "four whatevers")

See "si xiang jiben yuanze" (four cardinal principles).

四项基本原则是四个"念念不忘"的翻版
si xiang jiben yuanze shi si ge
niannian buwangde fanban
(the "four cardinal principles" are a
reproduction of the "four never-forgets")

See "si xiang jiben yuanze" (four cardinal principles).

四项基本原则的核心是坚持党的领导
si xiang jiben yuanzede hexin
shi jianchi dangde lingdao
(the core of the "four cardinal principles"
is upholding Party leadership)

See "si xiang jiben yuanze" (four cardinal principles).

四项基本原则的核心是坚持毛泽东思想
si xiang jiben yuanzede hexin
shi jianchi Mao Zedong sixiang
(the core of the "four cardinal principles"
is upholding Mao Zedong Thought)

See "si xiang jiben yuanze" (four cardinal principles).

四大
sida
(four bigs)

"Sida" is an abbreviation for "daming, dafang, dazibao, dabianlun" (speaking out freely, airing one's views fully, writing big-character posters, and holding great debates). Since in Chinese each of these expressions contains the character "da", they have come to be known as "sida", or the "four bigs".

The "sida" first appeared in Shanghai and elsewhere in early 1957. At the PCC National Propaganda Conference held in March 1957, Mao highly praised them (some historians believe Mao was sincere at the time) as a good political practice in the ongoing Party rectification movement. Greatly encouraged, many people even more actively exposed bureaucrats in Party and government departments. However, before long, Mao suddenly turned the rectification movement into an anti-bourgeois Rightist campaign. Many innocent people who had been involved in the "sida" were convicted as "Rightists" and cruelly persecuted. Mao argued that this was not a "conspiracy" (yinmou) but an "overt trick" (yangmou), with which to discover a great number of "Rightists" who made use of the "sida" to engage in "anti-Party, anti-people, and anti-socialism" activities.

During the GPCR, the "sida" practice became very popular and was used widely, encouraged by the "PCC Decision on the GPCR" passed on 8 August 1966 at the 11th Plenum of the 8th PCC. At the 4th National People's Congress held from 13 to 17 January 1975 they were written into the Constitution (Article 45) as a legal form for the socialist revolution, and they were hailed as a "great creation by the masses of the people". In 1980, following Deng Xiaoping's order to suppress the Beijing Spring (Beijing zhi chun), the "sida" practice was banned and the provision was deleted from the Constitution. Deng said that this was done "not because we are against socialist democracy, but because practice over the years has shown that the *si da* are not a good method of promoting either stability or democracy" (*SWD*, pp. 261-62).

四害
sihai
(four pests)

The four Party leaders during the GPCR—Jiang Qing, Zhang Chunqiao, Wang Hongwen, and Yao Wenyuan—were condemned as the "Gang of Four" and the "four pests" after they were arrested on 6 October 1976 in the coup staged by Hua Guofeng and his supporters.

In a campaign in the mid-1950s, rats, sparrows, flies, and mosquitoes were singled out as the "four pests" to be eliminated. See "chu sihai" (eliminate the four pests) and "sirengang" (Gang of Four).

四好连队运动
sihao liandui yundong
(movement of a "four-good" company)

See "tuchu zhengzhi" (giving prominence to politics).

四旧
sijiu
(four olds)

See "po sijiu, li sixin" (do away with the "four olds" and cultivate the "four news").

四类分子
sileifenzi
(four kinds of elements)

Also called "heisilei" (see "hei"). The term, originating during Mao's land reform program (tudi gaige yundong) of the early 1950s, refers to landlords, rich peasants, counter-revolutionaries, and the catch-all category of "bad elements" (huaifenzi), people who were singled out for attack. After the 1957 anti-bourgeois Rightist campaign, "Rightists" were added to the list so that there was a new term "heiwulu" (the five kinds of black elements). During the GPCR, the categories increased to nine—landlords, rich peasants, counter-revolutionaries, bad elements, Rightists, traitors, enemy agents, capitalist-roaders, and bourgeois intellectuals ("heijiulei"—the nine kinds of black elements).

Frightening persecution of the four kinds of elements and their children took place in many rural areas during the GPCR, simply decided upon by the so-called "poor and lower-middle peasants supreme court" (pinxiazhongnong zuigao fating), an organization temporarily set up by a handful of people controlling the local areas. For example, in Lingling prefecture, Hunan province, according to investigations by some concerned official departments, those executed numbered 7,696; forced to commit suicide 1,397; and maimed 2,146. Among the counties in the prefecture, the most horrible persecutions occurred in Dao county. During the period of 13 August to 17 October 1967, those executed numbered 4,193, and forced to commit suicide 326. In many cases, all the members of a family were killed together. The oldest was 78 and the youngest only 10 days old. There were 826 people not yet of age (Wen Yu, *China's "Left" Disasters,* p. 444). Methods of executions included: 1. by gun; 2. by knife; 3. drowning; 4. by explosives; 5. being thrown into deep caves (generally preceded by knife-chopping); 6. burying alive; 7, by sticks or any stick-like things; 8. strangling or hanging; 9. burning or suffocating by smoke; and 10. being thrown onto the ground (mainly for those not yet of age).

Those deprived of their citizenship and living in permanent discrimination and humiliation suffered greatly. But Mao's tactic of dividing people into different categories and getting some, as the social foundation of his reign, to help repress others, did work in maintaining his Communist regime. This, of course, was a society in which human nature was completely distorted.

四清
siqing
(four clean-ups)

See "shejiao" (socialist education movement).

四清与四不清的矛盾
siqing yu sibuqingde maodun
(contradictions between the four clean-ups and the four unclean-ups)

See "shejiao" (socialist education movement).

四清运动
siqing yundong
("four clean-ups" movement)

See "shejiao" (socialist education movement).

四权
siquan
(four authorities)

See "banbiantian" (other half of the sky).

四人帮
sirenbang
(Gang of Four)

According to CCP documents, at a Politburo meeting on 17 July 1974, Mao first criticized Jiang Qing (then a Politburo member), Zhang Chunqiao (then a Politburo Standing Committee member), Yao Wenyuan (then a Politburo member) and Wang Hongwen (then a Politburo Standing Committee member and Party vice-chairman) for engaging in factional activities. On that occasion, Mao used the term "Shanghai gang". In December 1974, when Wang Hongwen went to Changsha, Hunan province, to report to Mao on Party work, Mao warned him against forming a "Gang of Four" with Jiang Qing, Zhang Chunqiao, and Yao Wenyuan. This was the first time Mao used the term.

Following Mao Zedong's death on 9 September 1976, the above four, known as the Gang of Four, were arrested on 6 October after Hua Guofeng staged a coup. From October 1976 until the end of 1978, orchestrated by the CCP, a nationwide mass movement to "settle accounts" with the Gang of Four (and also with Lin Biao) was carried out in three stages. (It should be noted that the expression the "Gang of Four" may also refer to the Gang of Four's political line rather than to the four members of the "Gang". The same is true with the term of "Lin Biao".) The main task of what was called the "first battle" was to expose and condemn the Gang's plot to "usurp Party and state power". The "second battle" centered on publicizing the Gang's "criminal history". Theoretical criticism of the Gang's "line" constituted the "third battle". At the 3rd Plenum of the 10th PCC (held from 16 to 21 July 1977), a resolution was passed concerning the "Anti-Party Clique of Wang Hongwen, Zhang Chunqiao, Jiang Qing, and Yao Wenyuan". In the winter of 1980, together with the "Lin Biao Counter-Revolutionary Clique", the "Jiang Qing Counter-Revolutionary Clique" was brought to a public trial.

The downfall of the "Gang of Four" was of tremendous significance in contemporary Chinese political life, marking the beginning of the "new period", so called by the post-Mao CCP leadership. Interestingly, with regard to the issue of the GPCR, the CCP leaders faced a dilemma: On the one hand, they had to negate the GPCR, whose destructive and disastrous consequences were felt by everyone. Without such a negation, many Party leaders, including Deng Xiaoping, would not have been rehabilitated, still less, their new policies for reform could not have been carried out. On the other hand, they had to emphasize that during the GPCR years, neither Chinese socialist society nor the CCP had changed its nature, and that Mao's "mistakes" were those of "a great revolutionary, a great Marxist". Whenever possible, a line of demarcation was drawn between Mao and the Gang. For instance, in the 1977 campaign against the Gang of Four, Mao's three 1975 directives concerning the film *The Pioneers* (Zhang Tianmin, *Chuangye,* Changchun Film Studio, directed by Yu Yanfu, 1975, script in *RMWX,* 8, 1976; trans. in *CL,* 1:9-63, 2:26-85, 1977), the publication of the *Complete Works of Lu Xun (Lu Xun quanji),* and the classical novel *Water Margin (Shuihu)* were revived. Party critics tried to justify the allegation that Mao had dealt the Gang of Four "three heavy blows". An article published in the *People's Daily* on 22 December 1980 strongly stated that Mao was certainly not a criminal though he made serious political mistakes in his remaining years.

The Party authorities were fully aware of the danger that one step further and the "Gang of Four" would become a "Gang of Five", with Mao Zedong as the number one "gangster". China critics argued, however, that it was an indisputable fact that without Mao's support, it simply would not have been possible for the Gang of Four to dominate Chinese politics during the latter part of the GPCR. In addition, Mao, in his last days, seemed to have concluded that Jiang Qing could be his successor, for only Jiang and her close colleagues were most likely to carry on the GPCR after his death. It may be merely a matter of time, they predict, that the term "Gang of Five", now already appearing in books such as Jung Chang's *Wild Swans: Three Daughters of China (Hong: Sandai Zhongguo Nürende Gushi,* Anchor Books/Double Day, Nov. 1992) will be openly used by the public. See also "Lin Jiang fan'geming jituan" (Lin Biao and Jiang Qing counter-revolutionary cliques) and "wen'ge" (Cultural Revolution).

四人帮文艺路线
sirenbang wenyi luxian
(the Gang of Four's "line" in literature and art)

See "wen'ge wenyi" (GPCR literature and art).

四五运动
siwu yundong
(April 5th Movement)

On 8 January 1976, Zhou Enlai died in Beijing. Thereafter, the Gang of Four and their supporters openly attacked the premier. An article entitled "We Must Keep On Fighting the Capitalist-roader As Long As He Is Still on the Capitalist Road" ("Zouzipai haizai zou, women jiuyao tong ta dou") published in Shanghai's *Wenhui Daily* on 25 March 1976 indicated that Zhou Enlai was a capitalist-roader who had helped Deng Xiaoping to return to power. This, together with other articles and various activities, greatly angered the people. From the end of March to the first few days of April, mass movements broke out in Beijing and many other cities to commemorate Zhou Enlai, to oppose what was later known as the "Gang of Four", and to express disapproval of the criticism of Deng Xiaoping, who had by the time already officially been described as an "unrepentant capitalist-roader".

These events, of course, aroused the hostility of the authorities. After an urgent meeting of the PCC Politburo held on 1 April, the authorities took measures to end all the mourning activities. However, the people's indignation became even stronger. The protest reached a climax on the Qingming Festival (a Chinese traditional day of remembrance for the dead, falling on 4 April in 1976), when several hundred thousand people from all walks of life congregated in Tiananmen Square, particularly at its center—the Monument to the People's Heroes—bringing wreaths and poems and delivering speeches in memory of the late premier and openly denouncing the ruling clique, a scene never before seen in PRC history. In the evening, another urgent meeting of the PCC Politburo was held, which reached the conclusion that they must take drastic measures to stop the protest. Suppression took place on the next day. At 9:30 PM, five battalions of PLA men, three thousand public security officers, and ten thousand militiamen came to "clean up" the Square. They finished their job before dawn.

The protest is known as the April 5th Movement (or the April 5th Incident). It was branded by the Politburo headed by Mao Zedong as the "Tiananmen Counter-revolutionary Incident" (Tiananmen fan'geming shijian). Deng Xiaoping was dismissed from all his posts inside and outside the Party, accused of being the behind-the-scenes instigator.

Though suppressed, the April 5th Movement simultaneously expressed what the Chinese people hated and what they wanted at that time, foretelling the downfall of the Gang of Four, which occurred on 6 October 1976, only a few months later. It also inspired the following "Beijing Spring" and other pro-democracy movements.

After the Gang of Four were toppled, there were calls for Deng to be rehabilitated, and for the assessment of the Tiananmen Incident to be reversed. Finally, in July 1977, the 3rd Plenum of the 10th PCC adopted a resolution restoring Deng to all his former posts. In December 1978, the 3rd Plenum of the 11th PCC annulled those documents related to the campaign to "criticize Deng Xiaoping and counter the Right deviationist trend to reverse correct verdicts" and to the 1976 Tiananmen incident. It formally announced Deng's rehabilitation and the reversal of the assessment of the incident. Thus this "Tiananmen counter-revolutionary incident"—which was the first Tiananmen incident in PRC history—became the "Tiananmen revolutionary incident". See also "pi Deng, fanji youqing fan'anfeng" (campaign to criticize Deng Xiaoping and counter the "Right deviationist trend to reverse correct verdicts).

四新
sixin
(four news)

See "po sijiu, li sixin" (do away with the "four olds" and cultivate the "four news").

四有
siyou
(four have's)

They refer to "having lofty ideals, moral integrity, a good education, and a strong sense of discipline" (you lixiang, you daode, you jiaoyu, you jilü). See "aiguozhuyi" (patriotism), "liang ge wenming" (two civilizations), and "wujiang, simei, sanre'ai" (five stresses, four points of beauty, and three loves).

四有，三讲，两不怕
siyou, sanjiang, liangbupa
(four have's, three stresses, and two defy's)

See "wujiang, simei, sanre'ai" (five stresses, four points of beauty, and three loves) and "liang ge wenming" (two civilizations).

随大溜
suidaliu
(follow the main current reluctantly)

This term derogatorily describes those who lack sufficient political enthusiasm and do not join a movement or an activity voluntarily and consciously, but simply recognize the general trend and join it reluctantly.

随着经济建设高潮的到来 必将出现文化建设的高潮
suizhe jingji jianshe gaochaode daolai bijiang chuxian wenhua jianshede gaochao (an upsurge in economic construction is bound to be followed by an upsurge of construction in the cultural sphere)

At the time of the founding of the PRC, Mao told the world: "The Chinese people have stood up!" He also predicted: "An upsurge in economic construction is bound to be followed by an upsurge of construction in the cultural sphere" ("The Chinese People Have Stood Up!" *SWM,* 5, p. 18). In 1979, in his speech greeting the 4th Congress of Writers and Artists, Deng Xiaoping echoed Mao's words ("Speech Greeting the Fourth Congress of Chinese Writers and Artists", *SWD,* pp. 206-7). In the second half of the 1990s, in view of the better economic situation in the country, there was an appeal that the Party and government pay more attention to cultural and educational undertakings. In his report to the 15th CCP National Congress, Jiang Zemin devoted a whole chapter to what he called "socialist culture with Chinese characteristics", juxtaposd with "socialist economy with Chinese characteristics" and "socialist politics with Chinese characteristics". See also "shehuizhuyi chuji jieduan lun" (theory of the primary stage of socialism).

台独
Tai du (Taiwan independence)

See "Taiwan wenti" (Taiwan issue).

台阶论
taijie lun ("staircase" theory)

The "staircase" theory means to promote cadres one step at a time. During the GPCR, some cadres were elevated so quickly that they were described sarcastically as "riding a helicopter" (zuo zhishengfeiji) or as "rocket cadres" (huojianshi ganbu) because they soared like a rocket or a helicopter. For example, Wang Hongwen was promoted by Mao from a Shanghai rebel leader to CCP vice chairman, and then Mao's successor after the fall of Lin Biao. Deng expressed his disapproval of this practice in 1975. But in 1980, when the Party Center was under Deng's control, he asked his colleagues to do away with the outdated concept of the "staircase" theory and not to pay merely lip-service to the necessity of promoting young and middle-aged cadres. "Exceptional candidates should be provided with a sort of light ladder so they can climb up more quickly, skipping some rungs", he said, when expounding on reform of the system of Party and state leadership *(SWD,* p. 306).

台湾地位未定论
Taiwan diwei weiding lun
(theory of the status of Taiwan being outstanding)

See "Taiwan wenti" (Taiwan issue).

台湾民主自治同盟
Taiwan Minzhu Zizhi Tongmeng
(Taiwan Democratic Self-government League)

See "minzhu dangpai" (democratic parties).

台湾问题
Taiwan wenti
(Taiwan issue)

In 1949 the PRC was founded in Beijing, following the Communist takeover of the mainland. At the same time, Chiang Kai-shek and his KMT supporters, after fleeing the mainland, continued their rule in Taiwan. In international politics there have since appeared a number of views on this issue, such as "two Chinas" (liang ge Zhongguo), "one China, one Taiwan" (yi Zhong yi Tai), and "the status of Taiwan is outstanding" (Taiwan diwei weiding). In the 16 December 1978 joint communiqué signed by PRC Premier Hua Guofeng and U.S. President Jimmy Carter regarding establishment of diplomatic relations on 1 January 1979, the United States recognized the PRC government as the sole legal government of China, with Taiwan as one of China's provinces. This, however, did not mean the end of the above-mentioned views as held by some political forces in the United States and other countries.

In view of the possibility of international interference, CCP authorities always strongly emphasize that the Taiwan issue is within the scope of Chinese internal affairs (Taiwan wenti shi Zhongguo neizheng wenti). The slogan "We are determined to liberate Taiwan" was repeated every year on the mainland. A change took place in January 1979 when Beijing conspicuously intensified its "united front" work directed at Taiwan. Of course, the CCP authorities did not give up their "historical task" of reunifying China. On the contrary, they decided to try something new to solve the Taiwan issue as quickly as possible (though it seemed that for a time they underestimated the difficulties).

On 1 January 1979, the NPC Standing Committee signed a "Letter to Our Taiwan Compatriots" ("Gao Taiwan tongbao shu"). During his U.S. visit the same month, Deng Xiaoping announced the end of the slogan about "liberating Taiwan". Deng announced that his Party and government would respect Taiwan's reality and current social system. On 30 September 1981, Ye Jianying, vice-chairman of the CCP and chairman of the NPC Standing Committee, put forth nine principles for a solution to the Taiwan issue. In January 1981, Deng Xiaoping advanced the issue of the reunification of Taiwan and the mainland as one of the "three issues for the 1980s" (bashiniandai san jian dashi). On 26 June 1983, when meeting Yang Liyu, a Chinese American academic, Deng raised his six principles for reunification ("Deng liutiao"). He made known his tentative plan of "one country, two systems" (yiguo liangzhi) for the first time. According to this plan, after reunification, Taiwan could enjoy a high degree of autonomy and retain its own armed forces, and its social and economic system, life styles, and foreign investment would not change. The peaceful reunification of the motherland, Deng said, had become a common language shared by both the CCP and the KMT. He made it clear that he opposed the idea of "complete autonomy" (wanquan zizhi) for Taiwan. He also found it "unrealistic" to reunite China with the "Three Principles of the People" (sanminzhuyi), as suggested by the KMT.

Jiang Zemin, CCP general secretary and PRC president, took a further step on 30 January 1995 when he announced an eight-point proposal concerning reunification (see "Jiang batiao"). At the 15th CCP National Congress, Jiang reiterated his eight-point proposal, especially the two basic principles of "peaceful reunification" and "one country, two systems". Beijing would not renounce the use of force, but "this is not directed against compatriots in Taiwan," Jiang said.

The situation developed further when Wang Daohan, Jiang's senior adviser and Beijing's top negotiator with Taiwan, announced a "new concept of 'one China'" (yi ge Zhongguo xin gainian). On 16 November 1997, he told his guest Xu Linong, president of Taiwan's New Alliance (Xin Tongmenghui), that while Beijing insists that talks be held under the precondition of "one China", that does not mean Taiwan must accept that "one China" is the People's Republic of China. Significantly, he declared that "one China" is the country after reunification as a result of the efforts jointly made by both sides of the Taiwan Straits. (However, Wang later revised this concept by adding a 86-Chinese character statement—see *Yazhou Zhoukan*, 25 Apr. 1999.) In an interview published in the *Times* on 18 October 1999, Jiang Zemin predicted that the reunification issue will be solved within the first half of the twenty-first century. CCP leaders have apparently realized that at least 80 percent of the people on Taiwan want to maintain the *status quo,* at least at this stage, rather than support a quick reunification with the mainland as was suggested in propaganda material in the past. They seem now to have more patience to deal with the issue and has complemented more pragmatic policies to broaden exchanges with the island. Of course, the premise is that Taiwan does not seek independence.

On the other side of the Taiwan Straits, for many years Chiang Kai-shek was dreaming of "launching a counterattack and recovering the lost mainland" (fangong dalu). He strongly held to the "one-China" view until his death in 1975. Since then the situation has become more complicated.

In the past 20 years, generally speaking, tensions have relaxed between the island and the mainland. At first, to the CCP authorities' proposals, such as "three opening-ups" ("santong", which refer to "opening up postal communications, transportation, and trade relations") and "four exchanges" ("siliu", which refer to "economic, scientific, cultural, and athletic" exchanges), the Taiwan government responded simply with a "three no's" policy of no contact, no negotiation, and no compromise with the mainland (bu jiechu, bu tanpan, bu tuoxie). In 1981 it started to shift away from this policy. In May 1986 the first negotiations took place between representatives of the two sides over the return of a Taiwan plane that had been hijacked to the mainland. Then, on 2 November 1987 a big step was taken by the Taiwan government—it officially dropped its ban on travel to the mainland.

In February 1991 Taiwan created the Straits Exchange Foundation (Haixia Jiaoliu Jijinhui), and then the mainland founded the Association for Relations Across the Taiwan Straits (Haixia Liang'an Guanxi Xiehui) in December 1991, so the two sides could communicate with each other. The first meeting was held in Singapore in April 1993, and subsequent meetings occurred on the mainland and Taiwan.

This, however, does not mean the road is straight for reunification. Based on the great tradition of Chinese culture, many people on Taiwan support reunification, but their approaches are different from one another. In December 1997, five scholars (Shen Junshan, Weng Songran, Ma Yingjiu, Chen Qinan, and Zhu Yunhan) proposed establishing a common organization to develop ties between the two sides of the Taiwan Straits, which could be called, for the time being, "Zhonghua Liang'an Lianhehui" (Chinese Cross-Straits Joint Council). Some believe Taiwan is different from Hong Kong, and they criticize Beijing's efforts to promote the "one country, two systems" initiative as "merely a unilateral wish". They consider the issue of democratization in the whole of China to be more important than the country's reunification. Aware of dangers of "Taiwan independence" (Tai du), they favor an "independent Taiwan" (du Tai). In this case, each of the two sides of the Taiwan Straits would respectively enjoy its own independent sovereign status, the two governments on the two sides would treat each other as equals—something that can be called "one country, two governments" (yiguo liangfu), and the *status quo* would remain as long as necessary. This would be similar to a commonwealth type of structure (lianbangzhi).

In Taiwan's multiparty system, different voices from different parties are now being heard. For the Democratic Progressive Party (Minzhu Jinbu Dang, abbreviated as "Minjindang" or "DPP", set up in 1986), Taiwan is a *de facto* sovereign state under threat from China. The DPP rejects unification with the mainland and seeks to protect Taiwan's sovereignty. The Taiwan Independence Party (Jianguo Dang), formed in October 1996 by a group of people breaking ranks from the DPP, is even more strongly in favor of "Taiwan independence". The New Party (Xin Dang), formed in 1994 as a result of a split with the KMT, maintains that both Taiwan and China, still divided by an unfinished civil war, should work towards reunification. The People First Party (Qinmin Dang), formed by James Soong after he lost the 18 March 2000 presidential election, also maintains a similar view. As to the KMT, generally speaking, it holds that Taiwan and China are two separate political entities and at the same time part of a greater Chinese nation. It promotes notions such as "the Republic of China in Taiwan" (zai Taiwande Zhonghua minguo) and "Taiwan and the mainland are two political entities on an equal footing". If the mainland becomes prosperous and democratic, Taiwan would reunite with it.

During a whole decade of the 1990s, Lee Teng-hui, (Li Denghui, b. 1923) controlled Taiwan's politics. On 8 April 1995, as chairman of the National Unification Council, he published his "six-point proposal" in response to Jiang Zemin. On 15 December 1997, his assistant Vice-President Lien Chan proposed a "sanbu sanyao" policy: "no independence, no reunification, and no confrontation" ("bu du, bu tong, bu duikang") and "exchanges, peace, and a win-win policy" ("yao jiaoliu, yao heping, yao shuangying"). As to "exchanges", there should first be "exchanges of information, thoughts, and culture" across the Taiwan Straits ("tong zixun, tong siwei, tong wenhua") as explained later by Chang Ching-yü, chairman of Taiwan's Mainland Affairs Committee. These should be conducted in accordance with the "go slow, be patient" (jie ji yong ren) policy of Lee Teng-hui.

In December 1998, in support of Ma Yingjiu's candidacy for Taipei mayor, Lee Teng-hui broached the concept of "the new Taiwanese" ("xin Taiwanren"), which refers to people living in Taiwan, no matter their origins, who are concerned about Taiwan and are willing to struggle for the island. In May 1999, Lee announced his "seven regions" theory for China (Zhongguo qikuailun). He asked CCP leaders to reject the "Greater China doctrine" (da Zhonghuazhuyi). Instead, China should be divided into seven economically competing regions: Taiwan, Tibet, Xinjiang, Mongolia, Northeastern China, Northern China, and Southern China. The separate regions should have different characteristics, and each should be managed and developed according to their respective needs (see Lee Teng-hui's book *Taiwan's Viewpoints—Taiwande Zhuzhang,* Taipei, Yuanliu, May 1999). On 9 July 1999, in an interview with the Voice of Germany radio, Lee Teng-hui raised his "two states" theory (liang guo lun), or "two states in one nation" (yi ge minzu, liang ge guojia) theory. According to this theory, since the Republic of China's constitutional reforms of 1991, the jurisdiction of the constitution has been confined to Taiwan, and it acknowledges the legality of the People's Republic of China to exercise its power of rule in mainland China. Legislators and National Assembly deputies have been elected from among the people of Taiwan, as have the president and vice president. Lee defined the cross-Straits relationship as a "special state-to-state" relationship (teshude guo yu guode guanxi), thus taking a big step away from the former notion of "two political entities on an equal footing".

A more complicated situation followed Taiwan's second direct "presidential" election (the CCP calls it "local leaders election") on 18 March 2000. CCP leaders closely watched every development of the events. On 21 February 2000, they released a White Paper, the second of its kind, under the title "The One-China Principle and the Taiwan Issue" ("Yige Zhongguode yuanze yu Taiwan wenti"). They made it very clear that the "one-China" principle is the foundation of peaceful reunification. Furthermore, for the first time, CCP leaders declared that if their counterparts in Taiwan refuse to take part in reunification talks on the basis of the "one-China" principle, they will have to resort to any means they think appropriate, including force, to achieve their aim. On 15 March 2000, Chinese Premier Zhu Rongji seriously warned the Taiwan people not to elect Chen Shui-bian of the Democratic Progressive Party, which is pro-Taiwan independence. But Chen was elected, by "vote of defiance". On 20 May 2000 Chen became Taiwan's tenth president.

This is said to be a quantum leap in Chinese politics. For the first time in five thousand years, a Chinese government was devolved from one political party/dynasty to another, not through revolution but peacefully, by the people's will. However, the breaking of the KMT's stranglehold on power, ironically, did not please the CCP. As pointed out by many, rather than the KMT candidate Lien Chan, Chen Shui-bian is the ideal successor of Lee Teng-hui (though Lee lost his KMT chairmanship on 24 March 2000, held responsible for the loss of his KMT state power). During the campaign Chen did promise that he would not formally seek independence, but at the same time he also reiterated his refusal to compromise on "Taiwan's sovereignty". In fact, Chen's supporters openly advocated independence, and hailed their victory as marking the beginning of the end of "four hundred years of domination of the island's original inhabitants by Chinese settlers".

CCP leaders have been highly suspicious of Taiwan politicians. In the past, one major reason was their perception of Lee Teng-hui. They were sure they fully understood Lee's "pragmatic diplomacy" (wushi waijiao). After Lee's June 1995 visit to the United States, the situation between the two sides of the Taiwan Straits became tense, reaching a peak before Taiwan's first direct presidential election on 23 March 1996. As to Lee's "two states" theory, CCP leaders regard it as absolutely unacceptable, an attempt at separatism. Tensions again flared when CCP authorities accused Lee of "playing with fire". Now since Chen Shui-bian has come to power, their suspicion is even greater. It is predicted that anything can happen.

The vast majority of the Chinese people cannot accept Taiwan independence. At the same time, they do not want to see a war break out again among the Chinese; such a war will be a great disaster to the Chinese nation. But while "peaceful reunification" and "one country, two systems" remain in its program, observers believe that Beijing will have to resort to force if anything like Taiwan independence were to occur. How this long-standing issue of vital importance will be solved remains unclear. This is a great concern not only of the two sides of the Taiwan Straits but also of many other countries in the world.

台湾问题是中国内政问题
Taiwan wenti shi Zhongguo neizheng wenti

(the Taiwan issue is a Chinese internal affair)

See "Taiwan wenti" (Taiwan issue).

太子党
taizidang
(princes' clique)

When speaking of the "princes' clique", people refer to elder statesmen's children who occupy key positions in the Party, the government, the army, and commercial circles (see, for instance, Ho Pin and Gao Xin, *CPC Princes —Zhonggong Taizidang,* Hong Kong, Mirror Books, 6th ed., 1995).

The princes' clique is not an actual organization, but the "princes" do have relations with one another. Of vital importance of course is their connections with high-ranking officials and even top party-state leaders who are CCP policy-makers. They enjoy special privileges and often have the upper hand over their competitors in commercial activities. Well-known among them in commercial circles are: Deng Zhifang (Deng Xiaoping's son), Deng Pufang (Deng Xiaoping's son), He Ping (Deng Xiaoping's son-in-law), Wu Jianchang (Deng Xiaoping's son-in-law), Ding Peng (daughter of Deng Xiaoping's younger brother), Wang Jun (son of Wang Zhen, late PRC vice-president), Wang Zhi (Wang Zhen's son), Ye Xuanning (son of Ye Jianying, late CCP vice-chairman), Ye Xuanlian (Ye Jianying's son), Rong Zhijian (son of Rong Yiren, PRC vice-president), Wu Keli (son of Wu Lanfu, former vice-premier), Chen Xiaojin (son of Chen Pixian, former NPC vice-chairman), Liang Dan (daughter-in-law of Ye Fei, former NPC vice-chairman), Xiao Yongding (son of Xiao Jinguang, former NPC vice-chairman), Chen Weili (daughter of Chen Yun, late CCP vice-chairman), Jiang Xiaoming (son of Qiao Shi, former member of the CCP Politburo Standing Committee and NPC chairman), Ren Kelei (son of Ren Zhongyi, former secretary of the CCP Guangdong Provincial Committee), and Zhang Xiaobin (son of Cui Yueli, former minister of public health).

Members of the princes' clique are frequently involved in scandals. In 1989, for example, a subsidiary of the Kanghua Company was ordered by the authorities to stop its business because of corruption. The Kanghua Company, which was established by Deng Pufang, was therefore dubbed "China's first official profiteer". On 13 February 1995, Zhou Beifang, then the chief executive of the Capital Iron and Steel Company in Hong Kong, was arrested in Beijing (in November 1996 Zhou was sentenced to death with two years' reprieve). The event was shocking because both Zhou Beifang and his father Zhou Guanwu (who was one day later dismissed from his post as the president of the Board of directors of the colossal Capital Iron and Steel Company) had enjoyed a close relationship with Deng's family.

At the CCP's 15th National Congress held in Beijing in September 1997, significantly, except for Deng Pufang and Xi Jinping (son of Xi Zhongxun, former NPC vice-chairman and member of the CCP Politburo and Secretariat) who were the last two elected alternate PCC members, no other "princes" joined the PCC. Politically, this was regarded as an important step for Jiang Zemin's consolidation of power, because generally the "princes" did not accept him as the "core" of the leadership of the third gerneration. In addition, many "princes" today are more keen to be involved in commercial activities and to make huge profits. See also "fan fubai" (anti-corruption).

太子党谋求权力的第一次尝试
taizidang mouqiu quanlide diyici changshi

(the princes' clique's first attempt to obtain power)

See "hongweibing" (Red Guards).

弹钢琴
tan gangqin
(the work method of "playing the piano")

Mao compared his method of leadership to playing the piano. In playing the piano all ten fingers are in motion; it won't do to move some fingers only and not others. But if all ten fingers press down at once, there is no melody. To produce good music, the ten fingers should move rhythmically and in coordination. A Party committee, Mao said, should follow the work method of "playing the piano" *(SWM,* 4, p. 379).

谈心
tanxin
(heart-to-heart talk)

As a method of ideological work (sixiang gongzuo), heart-to-heart talk between the leadership and the led and among comrades was said to be effective in helping solve "ideological problems" (sixiang wenti—problems arising from erroneous thinking). Heart-to-heart talk is usually between two persons. If more people are involved, that is a heart-to-heart meeting (tanxinhui). In either case, first of all, the ideological background of the person involved is presented and analyzed, and then through conversation, everyone freely pours out their thoughts. The person or persons having ideological problems will gradually be persuaded of what is right and what is wrong. See also "sixiang gaizao" (ideological remolding).

谈心会
tanxinhui
(heart-to-heart meeting)

See "tanxin" (heart-to-heart talk).

探求者
tanqiuzhe
(pursuers)

See "ganyu shenghuo" (be involved in life).

探索文学
tansuo wenxue
(explorative literature)

See "jingji duoyanghua xuyao wenhua duoyanghua" (the multiplicity of economic sectors requires the multiplicity of culture).

探索的一代
tansuode yidai
(exploring generation)

See "liangdai shiren" (two generations of poets).

糖衣炮弹
tangyi paodan
(sugarcoated bullets)

"Sugarcoated bullets" refers to the tactics employed by the "bourgeoisie" to corrode the revolutionary ranks, including bribery and sex-traps. A revolutionary must be on guard against the bourgeoisie's attack with sugarcoated bullets, Mao warned in his 5 March 1949 speech delivered at the 2nd Plenum of the 7th PCC, when the CCP was about to take over the country. Mao predicted: "There may be some Communists, who were not conquered by enemies with guns and were worthy of the name of heroes for standing up to these enemies, but who cannot withstand sugarcoated bullets; they will be defeated by sugarcoated bullets" (*SWM,* 4, p. 374). The prediction has been realized in today's China. See also "fan fubai" (anti-corruption).

桃园经验
Taoyuan jingyan
(Taoyuan experience)

See "shejiao" (socialist education movement).

特区不特
tequ bu te
(special economic zones should enjoy no more preferential treatment)

Special economic zones, after their establishment in the early 1980s, have developed rapidly, partly because they have enjoyed preferential treatment from the central government. But there have been appeals to end these treatments. For example, Hu An'gang, a key research fellow in the State Situation Analysis Group, CASS, discussed the "preferential treatment" issue for the first time in mid June 1994 when talking to a group of provincial leaders studying at the Central Party School. This was consistent with another of his appeals: "strengthen the central government while weakening the local authorities" (qiang zhongyang, ruo difang). He raised the issue because, he said, giving preferential treatment to the special economic zones implied discrimination against other provinces and districts. In October 1994, in a speech to Shanghai officials and scholars, Hu emphasized that there needed to be unified taxation and tax rates throughout the country.

Hu's view met with opposition, especially from local officials in the special economic zones, such as Li Youwei, top leader in Shenzhen city. In fact, Li Youwei personally counterattacked by publishing the text of an interview ("Fangtan lu") in the *Shenzhen Special Zone Daily* of 7 August 1995. He argued that the historical task of the zones as a "window for reform" (gaigede chuangkou) had not yet been completed and the central government should continue its support. He stated: The more you wish to develop the poor interior areas, the more you must first develop the special economic zones. In this way more funds and experience can be accumulated, so as the poor interior areas can achieve faster development. Finally, he claimed that any policy unfavorable to the development of the special economic zones violated Deng Xiaoping's view about reform and the open door.

The counterattack escalated with several articles carried successively within a few weeks in the mouthpiece of the CCP Shenzhen Committee. On 14 September 1995, obviously urged by the Central authorities, the Committee ordered an end to such articles. Even in the interests of Shenzhen and other special economic zones, observers said, the debate should stop, for it would only arouse more resentment from the poor interior areas. Now the Central authorities have promised that more attention will be paid to developing the poor interior areas, while preferential treatment will continue to be given to the special economic zones, at least for a period of time. See also "jingji tequ" (special economic zone) and "zhuhou jingji" (duchy economy).

特区就是特权
tequ jiushi tequan
(special economic zone means special privilege)

See "jingji tequ" (special economic zone), "zhuhou jingji" (duchy economy), and "tequ bu te" (special economic zones should enjoy no more preferential treatment).

特区就是资本主义
tequ jiushi zibenzhuyi
(special economic zone means capitalism)

See "jingji tequ" (special economic zone), "zhuhou jingji" (duchy economy), and "tequ bu te" (special economic zones should enjoy no more preferential treatment).

踢开党委闹革命
tikai dangwei nao geming
(kick aside Party committees to make revolution)

This was a well-known slogan raised by the rebels in the GPCR. See "liang ge wen'ge lun" ("two Cultural Revolutions" theory) and "wuchanjieji zhuanzheng" (dictatorship of the proletariat).

体制
tizhi
(institutional structure)

See "zhidu" (social system).

体制下放
tizhi xiafang
(organizational decentralization)

See "xiafang" (transfer to a lower level).

体制内的改革派
tizhineide gaigepai
(reformists within the establishment)

See "Beijing zhi chun" (Beijing Spring).

体制内的还原派
tizhineide huanyuanpai
(restoration faction within the establishment)

See "Beijing zhi chun" (Beijing Spring).

体制外的激进民主派
tizhiwaide jijin minzhupai
(radical democrats outside the establishment)

See "Beijing zhi chun" (Beijing Spring).

天安门
Tiananmen
(Tiananmen)

See "siwu yundong" (April 5th Movement) and "bajiu minyun" (1989 pro-democracy movement).

天安门惨案
Tiananmen can'an
(Tiananmen massacre)

See "bajiu minyun" (1989 pro-democracy movement).

天安门反革命事件
Tiananmen fan'geming shijian
(Tiananmen counter-revolutionary incident)

There were two Tiananmen counter-revolutionary incidents in PRC history.

The first incident, also called the April 5th Incident or the April 5th Movement, occurred around 1976 the Qingming Festival (which fell on 4 April). In December 1978, the 3rd Plenum of the 11th PCC formally announced Deng Xiaoping's rehabilitation and the reversal of the assessment of this incident. Thus the "Tiananmen counter-revolutionary incident" became the "Tiananmen revolutionary incident".

As part of the 1989 pro-democracy movement, there was another Tiananmen incident, which was suppressed with the massacre on 4 June 1989 by the CCP authorities and branded as the "Tiananmen Counter-revolutionary Incident".

On 19 September 1977, when speaking of the 1976 Tiananmen incident, Deng said: "In view of the very large numbers of people involved in the Tiananmen Incident, it definitely cannot be labeled counter-revolutionary" ("Setting Things Right in Education", *SWD*, p. 80). As many forcefully argue, Deng's statement can also well be applied to the 1989 incident. It is predicted that a reversal of its assessment will also take place some day in the future. See also "siwu yundong" (April 5th Movement) and "bajiu minyun" (1989 pro-democracy movement).

天安门革命事件
Tiananmen geming shijian
(Tiananmen revolutionary incident)

See "siwu yundong" (April 5th Movement).

天安门事件
Tiananmen shijian
(Tiananmen incident)

See "siwu yundong" (April 5th Movement) and "bajiu minyun" (1989 pro-democracy movement).

"天安门诗抄"出版事件
Tiananmen shichao chuban shijian
(incident concerning the publication of *Tiananmen Poems*)

During the first Tiananmen incident of 1976, a great number of poems were displayed in Tiananmen Square and recited in memory of the late Premier Zhou Enlai. They denouncd the ruling clique that later became known as the Gang of Four. Though most of these poems, which were written hurriedly by amateurs, had little artistic merit, they were full of intense feeling, expressing the people's hatred to the Gang and love of the premier. As part of the April 5th Movement, the Tiananmen poems were essentially a starting point for the literature and art of the so-called "new period", beginning with the later downfall of the Gang of Four.

After the movement was suppressed, a number of the poems displayed on the Square were secretly circulated among the people. No sooner had the Gang been toppled then did several editions of the poems appear. Their official publication, however, was delayed. This was because Mao Zedong had approved the Politburo's condemnation of the "Tiananmen Incident" as "counter-revolutionary". It was not until December 1978, when the Tiananmen Incident was declared to have been "revolutionary" by the 3rd Plenum of the 11th PCC, that the poems could be officially published. The calligraphic inscription on its title-page, ironically, was by Hua Guofeng, then Party chairman, who had opposed the "rehabilitation" of the Tiananmen Incident. This did not help Hua, though. In fact, the publication of the *Tiananmen Poems* was in itself one of the events that marked the political decline of this "successor" to Mao Zedong. As it turned out, Hua, after being criticized at the December 1978 Plenum, lost his Party chairmanship at the 6th Plenum of the 11th PCC in June 1981 and his Politburo membership at the 12th PCC in September 1982. See also "siwu yundong" (April 5th Movement) and "yingming lingxiu" (wise leader).

天才论
tiancai lun
("innate genius" theory)

Lin Biao first described Mao Zedong as an "innate genius" in his 18 May 1966 speech at an enlarged Politburo meeting. Immediately, the whole Party, the whole army, and the whole country echoed this idea, with feelings of great reverence. Furthermore, the communiqué of the 11th Plenum of the 8th PCC passed on 12 August 1966 confirmed Lin's theory.

Mao supported all of this. He obviously appreciated Lin's help to establish his "absolute authority" (juedui quanwei), though he later questioned the phrase. Lin Biao, of course, also cherished an ulterior ambition. In his speech of 23 August 1970 at the 2nd Plenum of the 9th PCC (held at Lushan from 23 August to 6 September 1970), he once again advocated the "theory of innate genius". According to CCP documents, Lin ostensibly urged Mao to accept the PRC presidentship, but in reality he wanted it for himself. This time, Mao decided to block Lin's trick. On 31 August, he wrote a statement entitled "A Point of View of Mine" ("Wode yidian yijian"), criticizing and repudiating the so-called "theory of innate genius" as "idealist". The theory, together with the derived "view about heroes creating history" (yingxiong shiguan) or an eclectic "view about heroes and slaves creating history together", became a common target for attack during the latter part of the Plenum.

Lin Biao fell into Mao's trap. Lin's speech was in fact an attack on Zhang Chunqiao, accusing him of causing opposition to Mao being regarded as an innate genius. Reportedly, Mao had read it, and only suggested that the attack be made without mentioning Zhang's name. As to whether the PRC presidency should be restored, Mao did not make known his opinion. Thus Mao, taking advantage of the contradiction between Lin's military faction and Zhang's faction of civil officials, successfully carried out his plot against Lin Biao, whom earlier he had personally chosen as his successor but whom he now wanted to get rid of. Out of strategic considerations, Mao could not directly attack Lin, who at the time still enjoyed very high prestige among the Party and the army. So Mao found a scapegoat. Chen Boda, then a member of the PCC Politburo Standing Committee and Lin's number one assistant in preaching the "theory of innate genius", was toppled.

This was merely an expedient measure. Thereafter, the rupture between Lin and Mao, the two so-called "closest comrades-in-arms", was almost inevitable. As it turned out, Lin Biao quickly fell, and died while trying to escape.

While the truth of the 1970 Lushan struggle has not yet fully revealed, Mao's political tricks are now no longer a secret. Mao's philosophical views as presented in his article "A Point of View of Mine" are also a topic for discussion. Officially, they are regarded as correct. Mao is said to have defended the "mass viewpoint" characteristic of historical materialism, for he not only opposed idealist apriorism but also eclecticism in his "Point of View". But many scholars approve the "view about heroes and slaves creating history together". They also poignantly point out that Mao opposed this view because he regarded himself, and his Party also regarded him, as the only leader (or representative) of the "slaves" (the people). This is why for several decades the more Mao advocated that "The masses are the real heroes", the more rampant the personality cult of Mao became. See also "Lin Biao shijian" (Lin Biao Incident) and "qunzhong luxian" (mass line).

天天读
tiantiandu
(reading Mao's works every day)

As part of the mass movement to show loyalty to Chairman Mao during the GPCR, everyone was assigned a definite amount of time every day to study Mao's works. See also "xiandai mixin" (modern superstition).

天下大乱达到天下大治
tianxia daluan dadao tianxia dazhi
(great disorder across the land leads to great order)

"Great disorder across the land leads to great order" was Mao's strategic principle to carry out the GPCR. In his letter to Jiang Qing dated 8 July 1966, he wrote that he wanted a revolution from below. In the great disorder across the land, those so-called "capitalist-roaders" would be revealed, attacked, and toppled. Then a new and genuine proletarian regime could be established and great order achieved. In the same letter, Mao also expressed his wish that a Great Cultural Revolution be carried out several times (wenhua dageming yao jinxing duoci)—"once every seven or eight years".

According to some authoritative historians, the 8 July 1966 letter was forged by Jiang Qing and Kang Sheng, obviously with Mao's approval, after the 1971 Lin Biao Incident. It served as evidence that early on Mao had suspected Lin's treachery. See also "wen'ge" (Cultural Revolution) and "yingming lingxiu" (wise leader).

条条框框
tiaotiao kuangkuang
(conventions)

See "kuangkuang" (conventions).

条条领导
tiaotiao lingdao
(vertical leadership)

"Vertical leadership" means to give policy and operational control by the "Center"—the Party Central Committee and the Central Government (its ministries and other national agencies)—to their local departments or branches at various levels in the country. A typical example is the case of the finance system. Following Zhu Rongji's decision, it is now one hundred percent controlled by the "Center", so as to restrain the so-called "duchy economy" (zhuhou jingji). In the past, many large state-owned enterprises and key institutions were directly controlled by the "Center". For instance, the Capital Iron and Steel Company of Beijing was managed by the Ministry of Metallurgical Industry, and Beijing University was under the direct leadership of the Ministry of Education.

In light of Deng's idea about reform of the political institutional structure, the general trend in China today is: the "Center" gives up part of its power (zhongyang fang quan) and local autonomy is increased. So many large enterprises and key institutions are now under "regional geographical leadership" (kuaikuai lingdao) by local authorities. For instance, the Capital Iron and Steel Company and Beijing University are now under the leadership of the Beijing municipal authorities.

As it was always emphasized in the past, those departments, enterprises, or institutions under "vertical leadership" are also subject to "regional geographical leadership", that is, "dual leadership" (shuangchong lingdao). When a contradiction occurs, the "vertical leadership" should submit to the "regional geographical leadership". Up to the present, China's institutional structure is still very complicated. Enterprises and institutions are often managed by the "Center" for vocational work, and by the local authorities for expenditure and personnel matters. "Dual leadership" also refers to the two leaderships, from the Party system and the government system. For instance, a new body was set up in June 1998—the PCC Finance Work Committee—which chiefly supervises personnel and other important matters in the national finance system but does not supervise vocational operations. This means that China's finance system is controlled by the Central Govenment headed by Zhu Rongji and by the Party Center Committee headed by Jiang Zemin. Similarly, another new body was set up on 9 July 1998—the PCC Large Enterprises Work Committee.

铁饭碗
tiefanwan
(iron rice bowl)

See "daguofan" (big cauldron canteen food).

铁老虎
tielaohu
(iron tiger)

See "zhilaohu" (paper tiger).

通灵宝玉
tongling baoyu
(stone of spiritual understanding)

When Jia Baoyu, the hero in *A Dream of Red Mansions (Honglou Meng*, also translated as *The Story of the Stone*), was born, he had a "stone of spiritual understanding" in his mouth. He always has to keep it with him. Whenever he lost it, he would immediately become stupid. In the 1980 discussion of the relationship between arts and politics, those people, who felt affection towards the old slogan that "Literature and art are subordinate to and serve politics", immediately felt stupefied upon hearing that the slogan would be dropped—in a trance like Jia Baoyu losing his "stone of spiritual understanding". They were completely baffled, not knowing where to turn. See also "wenyi wei zhengzhi fuwu" (literature and art serve politics).

通俗文学
tongsu wenxue
(popular literature)

See "jingji duoyanghua xuyao wenhua duoyanghua" (the multiplicity of economic sectors requires the multiplicity of culture).

通资讯，通思维，通文化
tong zixun, tong siwei, tong wenhua
(exchanges of information, thoughts, and culture)

See "Taiwan wenti" (Taiwan issue).

统一战线
tongyi zhanxian
(united front)

See "tongzhan" (united front) and "san da fabao" (three magic weapons).

统战
tongzhan
(united front)

"Tongzhan", an abbreviation for "tongyi zhanxian", means the united front organized by the CCP under a certain historical condition in the struggle against its major enemy and for the victory of the revolution and/or construction. The key point is to uphold CCP leadership by taking advantage of contradictions, winning over the majority, attacking the minority individually, and uniting with all the forces outside the Party that can be united. The united front is one of the Party's "three magic weapons" (san da fabao). The other two are "armed struggle" and "Party building".

During what is called the "first revolutionary civil war" period from 1924 to 1927, the united front was called a "revolutionary united front" (geming tongyi zhanxian), in which there was cooperation between the CCP and the KMT in their Northern Expedition (beifa) against China's local warlords. From 1937 to 1945, there was a "national anti-Japanese united front" (kang Ri minzu tongyi zhanxian), and a second cooperation between the CCP and the KMT was achieved in the War of Resistance against Japan. During what is called the "third revolutionary civil war" period from 1945 to 1949, in which the CCP defeated the KMT and founded the PRC, there was an "anti-U.S. and anti-Chiang Kai-shek united front" (fan Mei fan Chiang tongyi zhanxian). After the founding of the PRC in 1949, the CCP leadership established what was called a "united front of people's democracy" (renmin minzhu tongyi zhanxian), which virtually ended when the GPCR began in 1966. There is currently a "patriotic united front" (aiguo tongyi zhanxian) for the "new period" (since the 1976 downfall of the Gang of Four), which was first officially proposed in the "Resolution on Certain Questions in the History of Our Party since the Founding of the PRC", an important Party document passed at the 1981 6th Plenum of the 11th PCC. See also "san da fabao" (three magic weapons).

突出经济
tuchu jingji
(giving prominence to the economy)

See "xin shehuizhuyi guan" (new socialist view), "jingji gaige" (economic reform), and "tuchu zhengzhi" (giving prominence to politics).

突出政治
tuchu zhengzhi
(giving prominence to politics)

For a long time in China, politics was emphasized to a frightening degree. According to Mao, "Political work is the lifeblood of all economic work" ("zhengzhi gongzuo shi yiqie gongzuode shengmingxian", *MZXJ,* 5, p. 243). In his 1957 well-known speech "On the Correct Handling of Contradictions among the People", Mao said: "Not to have a correct political point of view is like having no soul" *(MZXJ,* 5, p. 385). Mao also initiated the concept of "putting politics in command" (zhengzhi guashuai). In the 1958 document "Sixty Articles of Working Methods (Draft)", he wrote: "Ideological and political work is the supreme commander as well as the soul." (See *Red Flag* editorial, "Zhengzhi shi tongshuai shi linghun"—"Politics Is the Supreme Commander as well as the Soul", *HQ,* 1, 1966.)

Lin Biao, as Mao's good pupil, vigorously developed Mao's idea. After replacing Peng Dehuai as minister of national defense following the 1959 Lushan Conference, he promoted a series of his principles for the army's political work, guided by his obsequious assertion that Mao Zedong Thought was the highest peak of Marxism-Leninism. He developed Mao's concept of "putting politics in command" by emphasizing that "giving prominence to politics means to place Mao Zedong Thought in command of all work".

At the enlarged CMC meeting held in Guangzhou in February 1960, Lin Biao first put forth the concept of the "three-eight" work style (san-ba zuofeng). He launched a "three-eight work style" movement, so as to carry forward the "fine tradition" of the army. The "three-eight" refers to three phrases and eight characters, summed up by Mao as the work style of his army. The three phrases are: a firm and correct political orientation, an industrious and simple style of work, and a flexible strategy and tactics. The eight characters are: Be united, alert, earnest, and lively. During the War of Resistance against Japan (1937-1945), the three phrases formed the educational policy of the Anti-Japanese Military and Political College in Yan'an, and the eight characters were the college's motto.

On 12 September 1960, at an enlarged meeting of the CMC Standing Committee, Lin Biao brought up the question of how to deal correctly with the "four relationships" (si ge guanxi) in the political work of the army—relationships between man and weapons, between political work and other work, between ideological work and other aspects of political work, and between living ideas and books. According to Lin, the principle for handling these four relationships was: first place must be given to man, to political work, to ideological work, and to living ideas (rende yinsu diyi, zhengzhi gongzuo diyi, sixiang gongzuo diyi, huode sixiang diyi). This was Lin Biao's well-known principle of the "four firsts" (si ge diyi).

In the resolution of the enlarged CMC meeting held in Beijing from 13 September to 20 October 1960, there appeared the following statement: "Study Chairman Mao's works, follow his teachings, act according to his instructions, and be his good soldiers".

In November 1960, Lin Biao launched a new movement of "five-good" soldiers (wuhao zhanshi yundong) in the army. PLA men were required to be good in political ideology, in military techniques, in the "three-eight" work style, in carrying out assigned tasks, and in physical training. (The movement of "five-good" soldiers was initiated in May 1958. At that time, the contents of the "five goods" were: study, work, taking care of arms and putting an end to accidents, carrying out production and practicing economy, and physical health.)

In January 1961, Lin Biao summed up a series of methods to study Mao's works. They were later written into his 16 December 1966 "Foreword to the Second Edition" of *Quotations from Chairman Mao Zedong,* and became a well-known passage to all Chinese. It reads as follows: In studying the works of Chairman Mao, one should have specific problems in mind (daizhe wenti xue), study and apply his works in a creative way (huo xue huo yong), combine study with application (xue yong jiehe), first study what must be urgently applied so as to get quick results (ji yong xian xue, li gan jian ying), and strive hard to apply what one is studying.

In 1961, Lin Biao launched the movement of a "four-good" company (sihao liandui yundong) as part of the political work he advocated in the army. The "four goods" were: good in political thoughts, good in the "three-eight" work style, good in military training, and good in the management of livelihood (zhengzhi sixiang hao, san-ba zuofeng hao, junshi xunlian hao, shenghuo guanli hao).

Under Lin's supervision, the 1965 New Year's Day editorial of the *Liberation Army Daily* first raised the concept of "giving prominence to politics". On 22 February 1965, the army mouthpiece published another editorial entitled "How to Give Prominence to Politics" (reprinted in *RMRB*, 23 Feb. 1965). It specifically stated: "Giving prominence to politics means to place Mao Zedong Thought in command of all work". Then on 18 March, 14 July, and 13 October 1965 there were three successive editorials on this subject furthermore. On 18 November 1965, Lin Biao summed up a five-point principle for "giving prominence to politics". The five points were: 1. Regard Chairman Mao's works as "supreme instructions" (zuigao zhishi) in all aspects of army work; creatively study them and particularly make the utmost effort to apply them; 2. Persist in the "four-firsts" and particularly make the utmost effort to grasp "living ideas" (huo sixiang); 3. Leading cadres must go to the basic units and give energetic leadership to the "outstanding companies" campaign; 4. Boldly promote really good commanders and soldiers to key posts of responsibility; and 5. Train hard and master the best techniques and close-range and night fighting tactics *(RMRB,* 25 Jan. 1966).

Lin Biao maintained that studying Mao's works was a short-cut for studying Marxism-Leninism. He promoted a "study Chairman Mao's works" movement in the army. On 18 September 1966, when meeting army cadres in Beijing, Lin asked to study the so-called "three frequently-read articles" (laosanpian). According to him, among Mao's works it was quite satisfactory to study well the following three articles—"The Foolish Old Man Who Removed the Mountain" ("Yugong yi shan"), "In Memory of Dr Norman Bethune" ("Jinian Bai Qiuen"), and "Serve the People" ("Wei renmin fuwu"). He called them "three frequently-read articles" which should be the basic material for the "daily reading of Mao's works" ("tiantiandu", a form of showing loyalty to Mao). Later, two articles by Mao—"On Rectifying Wrong Ideas in the Party" ("Guanyu jiuzheng dangneide cuowu sixiang") and "Oppose Liberalism" ("Fandui ziyouzhuyi")—were added, making up what was known as the "five frequently-read articles" (laowupian).

In Lin's opinion, in order to truly grasp Mao Zedong Thought, one must repeatedly study many of Chairman Mao's basic concepts, while some of his aphorisms must be memorized, repeatedly studied and repeatedly applied. In May 1964, under Lin's auspices, the PLA General Political Department published *Quotations from Chairman Mao*—what was dubbed the "little red book". The book, which is divided into 33 sections, with a total of 422 quotations, became a "must" for everyone during the GPCR. With various editions in many languages, its circulation reached fantastic proportions. Only from 1966 to 1968, 740 million copies of the Chinese version were distributed.

In his well-known speech of 18 May 1966, Lin Biao talked in details about his "four never-forgets" (si ge niannian buwang)—"never forget class struggle, never forget the dictatorship of the proletariat, never forget to give prominence to politics, and never forget to hold high the red banner of Mao Zedong Thought". In his opinion, the "four never-forgets" guarantee that proletarian political power will be everlasting and ever-victorious. (The "four never-forgets" were first published on the front page of the *People's Daily* on 28 May 1966.) In the latter half of 1966, Mao began to be addressed, first by Lin Biao, with the four titles "great leader, great teacher, great commander, and great helmsman" (weidade lingxiu, weidade daoshi, weidade tongshuai, weidade duoshou). The following statement by Lin was familiar to every Chinese: "One word from Chairman Mao is worth ten thousand from others. His every statement is truth. We must carry out those that we understand as well as those we don't."

Thus, with support from Lin Biao, the term "giving prominence to politics", together with a series of Lin's other ideas, such as "Politics is the first" (zhengzhi diyi) and "Politics pushes over and overwhelms everything else" (zhengzhi chongji yiqie, zhengzhi yadao yiqie), was widely applied to all work in all fields, not only in the army but also in the Party and government departments. All these slogans were frequently used during the GPCR. "Giving prominence to politics" led to the rampancy of the personality cult of Mao—the cult was carried out to such extremes that it was like a kind of "modern superstition" (xiandai mixin). Lin succeeded in launching a "god-making" movement on an unprecedented scale in modern China.

Mao highly appreciated Lin Biao's initiative. For instance, Mao praised Lin's principle of the "four firsts", saying: "The 'four firsts' are great. We did not think of anything like this before. This is really a creation." Following Mao's instructions, the *People's Daily* announced in its 1964 New Year's Day editorial that the whole nation should learn from the experience of the PLA in political work. Then, on 1 February 1964, the slogan "The whole nation should learn from the Liberation Army" was officially promoted in an editorial of the *People's Daily* ("Quanguo douyao xuexi jiefangjun"—"The Whole Nation Should Learn from the Liberation Army"). The editorial (in which the "four firsts" were made known to the public for the first time) emphasized that it was necessary to learn from the precious experience of the PLA, such as grasping political and ideological work in a big way, putting Mao Zedong Thought in command, persisting in the "four-firsts" and the "three-eight work style", setting up "four-good" companies, and strengthening basic-level construction.

Most significantly, there was an all-inclusive slogan: "In industry, learn from Daqing; in agriculture, learn from Dazhai. The whole nation should learn from the PLA; the PLA should learn from the people of the whole country" (Gongye xue Daqing, nongye xue Dazhai, quanguo xue renmin jiefangjun, jiefangjun xue quanguo renmin). This slogan, vigorously promoted in the 1972 New Year's Day editorial in the *People's Daily* and *Red Flag*, became a great call by Chairman Mao. With a system of principles and working methods about "giving prominence to politics", as embodied in this all-inclusive slogan, Mao seemed to be full of confidence in his way of ruling China. See also "Mao Zedong sixiang" (Mao Zedong Thought) and "xin shehuizhuyi guan" (new socialist view).

突出政治就是以毛泽东思想统帅一切工作
tuchu zhengzhi jiushi yi Mao Zedong sixiang tongshuai yiqie gongzuo
(giving prominence to politics means to place Mao Zedong Thought in command of all work)

See "tuchu zhengzhi" (giving prominence to politics).

突出政治五项原则
tuchu zhengzhi wu xiang yuanze
(five-point principle for "giving prominence to politics")

See "tuchu zhengzhi" (giving prominence to politics).

土政策
tuzhengce
(home-grown policies)

See "jiefang sixiang" (emancipating the mind).

团结、教育、改造知识分子
tuanjie, jiaoyu, gaizao zhishifenzi
(uniting with, educating, and remolding intellectuals)

See "zhishifenzi wenti" (issue of intellectuals).

团结－批评－团结
tuanjie—piping—tuanjie
(unity—criticism—unity)

As early as 1942, Mao raised the formula "unity—criticism—unity" to deal with issues of inner-Party struggle. In the mid-1950s when he put forth the concept of "contradictions among the people", he said that the "democratic method" of resolving this kind of contradiction was epitomized in the 1942 formula. "Unity—criticism—unity" means "starting from the desire for unity, resolving contradictions through criticism or struggle, and arriving at a new unity on a new basis". It also means "learning from past mistakes to avoid future ones and curing the sickness to save the patient" (cheng qian bi hou, zhi bing jiu ren). See "zhengque chuli renmin neibu maodun" (correctly handling contradictions among the people).

推陈出新
tuichenchuxin
(weeding through the old to bring forth the new)

"Weeding through the old to bring forth the new" was adopted by Mao in 1942 as a policy to reform opera. In October 1952, at the first national opera festival, Mao preceded it with another phrase "Let a hundred flowers bloom" (baihua qifang). Thus "Let a hundred flowers bloom and weed through the old to bring forth the new" became a new directive for opera reform. See also "shuangbai fangzhen" (Double Hundred policy).

退居二线
tui ju erxian
(withdraw to the "second line")

See "erxian" (second line) and "quanli douzheng lun" ("power struggle" theory).

退居书斋
tui ju shuzhai
(go back to studies)

See "xin baoshouzhuyi" (neo-conservatism).

脱帽右派
tuomao youpai
(uncapped Rightist)

A term for those whose Rightist labels have been removed. Politically, these people should have been treated in the same way as other citizens, but in the Mao period this was not necessarily the case. In reality, even if they were officially "uncapped", they were still politically discriminated against as "uncapped Rightists". Up to 1982, they continued to be called "corrected Rightists" (gaizheng youpai). What was frightening about this spiritual torture, as Liu Binyan testified, was that it kept you thinking all the time in your subconscious that you were a Rightist, a guilty person. Today, such political labels are already part of history. See also "fan youpai yundong" (anti-Rightist campaign).

外因通过内因起作用
waiyin tongguo neiyin qi zuoyong
(external causes become operative through internal causes)

See "bianzheng weiwuzhuyi" (dialectical materialism).

外在自由
waizai ziyou
(exterior freedom)

See "chuangzuo ziyou" (creative freedom).

完全否定人道主义就导致神道和兽道
wanquan fouding rendaozhuyi jiu daozhi shendao he shoudao
(total negation of humanism will lead to "theocracy" and "barbarism")

In the discussion of humanism in the early 1980s, humanism for the first time was no longer treated as a prerogative of the bourgeoisie. Synchronous with human history, critics argued, humanism emerges, exists, and develops, not only as an ideological trend but also as a kind of human strength. Prosperity as it exists in today's human society becomes possible, they said, because human beings, noble and full of dignity and strength, are always fighting for their rights and freedom and have already created material and spiritual conditions and standards for further development. Otherwise, human beings "would inevitably have vanished like certain kinds of animals" (Sun Zhepu, "Renxing, rendaozhuyi he wenxuede mingyun"—"Human Nature, Humanism and the Fate of Literature", *Shenyang shifan xueyuan xuebao*, 4:36, 1980). They justified humanism, for a total negation of humanism would lead to "theocracy" (shendao, that is, the personality cult of Mao) and "barbarism" (shoudao, that is, the ruthless struggles as seen in the innumerable political movements during the Mao's period), as Wang Ruoshui warned ("Literature and Art and the Problem of the Alienation of Man", *SHWX*, 9, 1980; *WHB*, 25 Sept. 1980). Their conclusion was—and it was said to have been reached on the basis of numerous bitter lessons: "Marxism should contain the principle of humanism. If not, it will probably lead to its opposite, turning into a deadly cold dogmatism that shows no concern for the people, or, even worse, into a new form of alienation that rules people" (Ru Xin, "Rendaozhuyi jiushi xiuzhengzhuyi ma? Dui rendaozhuyide zai renshi"—"Is Humanism Just Revisionism? A Re-understanding of Humanism", *RMRB*, 15 Aug. 1980). See also "rendaozhuyi lunzheng" (humanism debate).

万般皆下品，唯有读书高
wanban jie xiapin, weiyou dushu gao
(the most noble is to be a scholar; everything else is inferior)

See "Zhongguo shehui dui wenren min'gande chuantong" (traditional sensitivity of Chinese society towards literati), "dushu wuyong lun" ("futility of education" theory), and "dangde jiaoyu fangzhen" (the Party's educational policy).

王朔热
Wang Shuo re
(Wang Shuo craze)

See "renwen jingshen lunzheng" ("humanistic spirit" debate).

王朔现象
Wang Shuo xianxiang
(Wang Shuo phenomenon)

See "renwen jingshen lunzheng" ("humanistic spirit" debate).

网不着的蝴蝶
wangbuzhaode hudie
(a difficult-to-catch butterfly)

In 1980 Wang Meng (b. 1934) created a controversy over his literary innovations, beginning with his short story "Eyes of the Night" ("Yede yan", *GMRB*, 21 Oct. 1979; trans. in *CL,* 7:41-59, 1980, Lee Yee, ed., *The New Realism,* pp. 92-101, and Perry Link, ed., *Roses and Thorns,* pp. 43-55). When the story appeared in the autumn of 1979, not many people understood its significance. The literary world, however, was soon startled by a series of his works, similar in kind, coming out in succession: "The Bolshevik Salute" ("Buli", *DD,* 3:4-39, 1979; trans. by Wendy Larson, Seattle & London, University of Washington Press, 1989), "Voices of Spring" ("Chun zhi sheng", *RMWX,* 5:10-16, 1980; trans. in *CL,* 1:23-36, 1982), "Kite Streamers" ("Fengzheng piaodai", *Beijing wenyi,* 5:6-15, 1980; trans. in *CL,* 3:5-28, 1983, and *Best Chinese Stories, 1949-1989*, Beijing, Chinese Literature Press, 1989, pp. 150-67), "Dreams of the Sea" ("Haide meng", *SHWX,* 6:4-10, 1980), and "Butterfly" ("Hudie", *SY,* 4:4-37, 1980, reprinted in *XWY, Novelettes,* 1, pp. 313-51; trans. in *CL,* 1:3-55, 1981). They were indeed "a handful of grenades" (jishu shouliudan), as Wang Meng himself later described them when recalling the event (see He Xilai, "Xinlingde bodong yu yingtu: lun Wang Meng de chuangzuo"—"On Wang Meng's Creation", *Wenxue pinglun congkan,* 10, 1981, reprinted in *Wang Meng Zhuanji—Collected Essays on Wang Meng,* Guiyang, Guizhou Renmin, 1984, p. 160).

As soon as Wang Meng published "Eyes of the Night", there were protests: "How can fiction be written in this way?" When this and Wang's other five works of this kind were discussed in the *Beijing Evening News* in the summer of 1980, they were attacked for being too obscure and difficult, and for abandoning the masses of workers, peasants, and soldiers. Most hostile, perhaps, was a group of local writers from Hebei province who were influenced by the writer Sun Li and the poet Tian Jian. Among important critics, Yan Gang's judgment was ambivalent. On the one hand, he had to admit that "a new method of fiction writing" had emerged with the publication of Wang Meng's six works and that the "strong impact" of Wang's explorations and innovations on the form of fiction was "unprecedented in the history of contemporary fiction since the founding of the PRC". On the other, he regretted that Wang had been influenced by the theory that fiction could dispense with plot, characterization, and the creation of "typical characters in typical circumstances" (sanwu xiaoshuo). He told Wang that Engels' remarks on realism still remained "sound", and should not be "casually discarded" (Yan Gang, "Xiaoshuo chuxian xin xiefa"—"A New Method of Fiction Writing Has Emerged", *Beijing shiyuan xuebao,* 4, 1980, reprinted in *Wang Meng Zhuanji,* p. 189).

Nevertheless, as it turned out, with Wang Meng taking the lead, a number of new genres in fiction writing later appeared in succession. For a time in the early 1980s, Wang Meng was regarded as a "Chinese agent" of the "stream-of-consciousness". He was so popular that he was elected vice-chairman of the CWA at its 4th National Congress held 29 December 1984 to 5 January 1985.

Wang Meng compared himself to a "butterfly", always in its element, and said that critics would fail to catch him, no matter how hard they tried (see Liao Tianqi, "Deguo duzhede xindalu" Zhongguo dangdai wenxue"—"Contemporary Chinese Literature: The New Continent for German Readers", *JN,* 188:81, Sept. 1985). Liu Xinwu believed Wang possessed a sort of "temperamental superiority" (xingge youshi) and was able to gain the advantage in various situations, good at "quickly achieving a psychological equilibrium" (see Lee Yee, "Liu Xinwu tan Liu Zaifu shijian yu Zhongguo wenxue sichao"—"Liu Xinwu on the Liu Zaifu Incident and the Ideological Trend in Chinese Literature", *JN,* 197:77, June 1986). In 1986, this butterfly surprised many when he was appointed PRC's minister of culture, enjoying a meteoric rise to prominence on the national cultural scene. His appointment was regarded as a symbol of the "sankuan" policy. ("Sankuan", a shorthand way of referring to "generosity—kuanhou, tolerance—kuanrong, and relaxation—kuansong", was the most authoritative interpretation of the Party's principles and policies for ideological-cultural affairs in 1986.)

It was said that Wang Meng had been reluctant to accept the post, but was finally persuaded by top Party leaders such as Hu Yaobang. Politically, Hu Yaobang and Zhao Ziyang, then respectively CCP general secretary and PRC premier, were wise to choose Wang Meng. With his political conformity (Wang was a PCC member at that time), Wang definitely could enjoy their confidence. Indeed, Wang, benefiting from the policies of the "new period", supported Hu and Zhao and their "sankuan" policy.

Wang's appointment was indeed a strong evidence of the implementation of the "sankuan" policy: his creative activities had proved that he was a liberal artist, winning him fame and popularity both at home and abroad. As it turned out, this appointment was welcomed by the majority of Chinese writers and artists. After all, as Bai Hua said, after the 1983 campaign to eliminate "spiritual pollution", Wang Meng was almost the only person in literary and art circles who could hold a dialog with top CCP leaders (see Lee Yee, "Bai Hua hai zhimi buwude kulian zuguo ma?"—"Does Bai Hua Still Stubbornly Love His Motherland?", *JN,* 216:86, Jan. 1988).

Once Wang Meng accepted the job, he tried to promote what he thought to be good for Chinese literature and art, making use of his influence and power. On the one hand, the CCP authorities found him to be the right person for the job. On the other hand, as "something of an artistic dissident", he actually served as an inspiration to many who wanted to see moves toward liberalization in China.

After the June 4th Incident of 1989, as a result of the event, Wang Meng stepped down from his post as cultural minister. Thereafter, the "sankuan" policy was accused of encouraging liberalization in literary and ideological circles. Wang Meng also became a controversial figure.

In 1991 he began to be openly attacked. In January, the theoretical journal *Literary Theory and Criticism* carried Yan Zhaozhu's critique "On the Theory of the Plural Nature of Literature" ("Lun wenxue benzhi duoyuanlunde shizhi") in its first issue of 1991. According to this article, the theory of the plural nature of literature advocated by Wang Meng, as in such articles as "The Triplicity of Literature" ("Wenxue sanyuan", *WXPL,* 1:5-10, Jan. 1987) and "This Magic Pattern of Literature" (coauthor Wang Gan, "Wenxue zhege mofang",*WXPL,* 3:38-46, May 1989), should be held responsible for the great number of "bad" works emerging in the past few years. Furthermore, on 14 September 1991, the *Literary Gazette* carried a letter by a "reader" named Shen Ping fiercely attacking Wang Meng's prize-winning short story "Solid Rice Gruel" ("Jianyingde xizhou", *Zhongguo zuojia,* 2:4-12, 1989) in a way that was similar to a political frame-up. Wang Meng, refusing to give in, sued for libel. His action enjoyed great support from many in literary and art circles. This was called "'Solid Rice Gruel' incident" ("jianyingde xizhou" shijian).

In 1994, in an article published in *Literary Theory and Criticism*, which was considered by many to be one of the "seven ultra-Left publications" in Beijing at the time, Wang was sarcastically compared to a big butterfly in a dream—a good dream doomed to failure. The attack focused on the issue of writers as "engineers of the human soul" (renlei linghun gongchengshi). Mao always demanded that writers be engineers of the human soul. In his congratulatory message to the 1979 4th National Congress of Chinese Writers and Artists, Deng reiterated this idea *(SWD,* p. 204). Many Chinese writers, however, find the demand exorbitant, fearing that it may become an excuse for persecution of the abused. Wang Meng held a similar view. When speaking about a writer's social role at a forum held in Taipei on 24 December 1993, for the first time outside of the mainland, he revealed his views. Wang Meng was thus accused of openly opposing Deng's ideas in the sensitive place of Taiwan. The attack borrowed an ancient Chinese allegory of "golden millet dream" ("huangliang meng", a story of a poor scholar who dreamt that he had become a high official but awoke to find only the pot of millet still cooking on the fire). Everyone would understand its implication (see Jiang Chao, "Yizhen huangliang 'dahudie' meng"—"A Good Dream of the 'Big Butterfly'", *Wenyi lilun yu piping,* 3:29-31 & 26, May 1994).

In 1997, this former cultural minister was accused of being a "dissident within the Party" (dangnei chi butong zhengjianzhe), as in an article entitled "An Analysis of Wang Meng" (Gong Yizhou, "Wang Meng qi ren qi shi", *Zhongliu,* Jan. 1997). As the author recalled, Wang Meng openly supported the 1989 "counter-revolutionary rebellion". After the rebellion was quelled, Wang, on the excuse of being sick, refused to congratulate the Beijing martial law troops and to attend PCC's urgent conference concerning the rebellion. For several years, Wang spread a series of "reactionary remarks". If compared with Liu Binyan, the "dissident defecting to the West", Wang Meng can easily do what Liu wants but is unable to do. The author even hinted that Wang Meng has some difficult-to-explain ties with "foreign reactionary forces".

At that time when Wang Meng was dismissed from his post as cultural minister, people asked: Can this ex-bourgeois Rightist (Wang was convicted as "Rightist" in 1958) and self-styled difficult-to-catch butterfly continue to adapt successfully to the ever-changing circumstances in China? Up to the present the answer still seems to be affirmative. Wang Meng is really a unique figure. See also "sankuan" (generosity, tolerance, and relaxation) and "ziyouhua" (liberalization).

危机文学
weiji wenxue
(crisis literature)

In the winter of 1983 when "misty poetry" was under great political pressure, Wai-lim Yip, one of the leading modernist poets and critics writing in Taiwan in the 1960s, tried to explain why this genre—which he called "crisis literature"—was so fiercely attacked. Like many others, Yip also believed that misty poems were not difficult to understand. They were regarded as "incomprehensible", he said, because the meaning of the images presented in them were "uncertain" or "multiple". To Party critics, these images were thus suspicious and even potentially dangerous because their uncertain meaning might stimulate the readers' thinking and propel them in a direction the Party could not control. Second, this poetry presented a strong sense of self-awareness. Though it often dealt with the theme of "looking for a new China", the pursuit was carried out through "an individual" questioning of the *status quo,* presenting one's own doubts and fears. What the Party wanted, however, was that everything be directed by a "patriarchal consciousness" (that is, the Party). But the most vital reason why Party critics found misty poetry intolerable, as Yip saw it, was that: "They are probably not very clear about the exact referents of certain particular images in a poem, and they make this an excuse to attack misty poets; but they do fully understand the overall implication of the whole poem. Perhaps it is because they are so clear about this overall thrust that they are determined to carry out their criticism. If all the images are considered integrally, what they are referring to is not only the ten-year GPCR, but the whole political structure, the whole social system. This is apparently the major reason for the criticism" (Wai-lim Yip, "Weiji wenxuede lilu: Dalu menglongshide shengbian"—"The Logic of Crisis Literature: The Rise and Development of Misty Poetry in Mainland China", *JN,* 173:95, June 1984). See also "menglongshi" (misty poetry).

微调艺术
weitiao yishu
(art of "fine tuning")

Inspired by Hu Yaobang's 1985 anti-Left disposition, in December 1985 Gao Zhanxiang, Party secretary of Hebei province in charge of ideological and cultural work, raised the idea of "fine tuning" as an art of leadership ("Tantan wenyi gongzuode 'weitiao' yishu"—"The Art of 'Fine Tuning' in Work in the Literary Fields", *RMRB,* 2 Dec. 1985). According to Gao, the "fine tuning" was based on three premises. First, since the 1978 3rd Plenum, China had entered the best period of its history, a period in which there were stability and unity in politics and promise of economic prosperity. In the fields of literature and art, the Party's principles and policies had proved to be effective and did not need to be greatly altered. Second, cultural reform also needed to be carried out steadily. Too much encouragement would probably bring about a right-left-right swing. Third, work in literature and art had its own specific laws, and, therefore, Party leadership should be adroitly and reasonably exercised according to different circumstances and there should be no administrative decrees or arbitrary meddling. As to how to apply this "fine tuning", Gao Zhanxiang reiterated the idea he first put forth at a forum on literary criticism in Hebei province in April 1984, when the aftermath of the so-called elimination of "spiritual pollution" was still strongly felt. On that occasion he proposed that the major method in guiding cultural work should be to lay emphasis on "watering fine flowers" (guangai jiahua) and not on "wiping out loathsome weeds" (jianchu ecao), the latter being a policy carried out consistently since the founding of the PRC. He argued that, since artistic creation involved complex mental effort and meant taking new paths, it was only normal that shortcomings and mistakes could occur. Writers and artists, therefore, should be encouraged to go boldly ahead. Moreover, in his opinion, this shift of focus was in answer to the demand of the age and the desire of the people. It was also the concrete application of what he called the Party's "fine tradition" in ideological-political work which held that "praise is essential" (biaoyang wei zhu).

To adopt an appropriate measure at an opportune moment, with the aim of bringing about change little by little, Gao Zhanxiang claimed, is the basic way to apply the art of "fine tuning" to cultural endeavours. The sooner problems are identified the better, of course; but while some problems can be solved immediately, others should not. For example, when appraising a controversial literary work or a controversial literary view, a leader should first investigate and then exchange views with the author, and should not rush to conclusions imprudently. If a leader wants to raise new requirements for artistic creation, likewise, he should do it at a carefully chosen time. He should pay attention to all external conditions as well and proceed in an orderly and appropriate way, using earnest, down-to-earth, rigorous, and meticulous methods, so that the desired success can be achieved. Gao emphasized that to apply the art of "fine tuning" in cultural spheres requires that the leader have both high political and high artistic qualities. While unswervingly carrying out the principles and policies laid down by the Party Center, he should have an overall plan for cultural development that is feasible, and in conformity with local conditions. See also "sankuan" (generosity, tolerance, and relaxation).

围堵中国
weidu Zhongguo
(containment against China)

The father of "containment" was an American foreign-service officer named George F. Kennan. In 1946, he wrote a landmark memo that became the foundation for U.S. foreign policy over the next four decades. Indeed, from the end of the Second World War until the early 1990s, the global strategy of the United States was shaped around the concept of containment against the Soviet Union. It changed only after the drastic changes in the Soviet Union and Eastern Europe, which led to the end of the Cold War (lengzhan). Thereafter, the "China threat" theory arose. Some Americans designated China as the archrival of the United States and as a new target for containment. In 1993 the American public ranked China second only to Iran as the country that posed the greatest danger to their country (Samuel Huntington, *The Clash of Civilizations and the Remaking of World Order,* p. 224). *The Coming Conflict with China*, the title of a foreign policy book which predicts a difficult relationship, gained attention in Washington (Richard Bernstein and Ross H. Munro, Alfred A. Knopf, 1997).

China constitutes a threat to the United States and other countries, according to the advocates of this theory, in the following five ways. First, China, though in the process of building a market economy, remains a totalitarian Communist state, which is a source of evil. Second, China is a rapidly rising power, and thus will inevitably come into conflict with the existing international order dominated by the West. Third, China, with its low labor costs and introduction of high technology, is likely to dump its cheap products in the markets of the United States and other Western countries, thus posing an economic threat. Fourth, the new sources of conflicts after the end of the Cold War are different religions and civilizations rather than ideologies. The Confucian civilization represented by China poses a threat to the Western Christian civilization. Fifth, China's growing military power is becoming a cause of concern to its neighbors. The concern arises also from China's efforts to reunite with Taiwan.

Some further suggested that attention should be paid to the deep structure of Chinese culture, to the "collective unconscious" (jiti wuyishi) of a nation that has been humiliated by Western powers for too long and is now increasingly and rapidly becoming strong. Bill Jenner, an Australian National University Sinologist, notes that Chinese culture attaches enormous importance to revenge and the settling of scores. "Throughout this century," he said, "they have cultivated an awareness of cultural humiliation and this transcends generations" *(Sydney Morning Herald,* 30 Nov. 1996). A popular Chinese saying is illustrative: "It won't be too late for a gentleman to take revenge in ten years' time" (Junzi baochou, shinian buwan). The psychology of a well-armed and wealthy China that feels the resentment of colonial humiliation as keenly as if the Opium Wars had been lost only yesterday, therefore, is a worrying problem. In addition, the Chinese (mainly referring to the Han nationality) have yet to learn how to treat other people equally, because they lacked such experience in their history. Typically, they always manage to be a cut above the others, so as to show off their advantages, and when in adverse circumstances, they will wait with all the necessary servility. This can be seen in the mother-daughter-in-law relationship in traditional Chinese families. One can also study the psychology of upstarts (baofahu) who are now mushrooming throughout China.

So containing China is considered necessary before the world suddenly finds it is too late. According to an article entitled "Why We Must Contain China" carried in the 31 July 1995 U.S. edition of *Time*, a "rational" China policy should be based on the following two components: establishing or bolstering security ties with China's neighbors to contain its expansion, and supporting Chinese dissidents in their democracy activities, so that in the end democratization will take place in the country.

Many, however, hold a different view. They find the Chinese "victim mentality" (shouhai yishi) to be normal, formed deeply but naturally after repeated national crises for more than 100 years. It is noted that China has exhibited no expansionist tendencies over the past 500 years. And, at present, the regime in Beijing is far more preoccupied with managing the monumental forces unleashed at home by its economic reforms than with creating instability among its neighbors, much less exporting revolution. The so-called "China threat" is nothing but a pretext to contain China's development. Some, moreover, fear that the "China threat" theory could become a self-fulfilling prophecy—"If you think they are a threat, they will behave accordingly" *(Sydney Morning Herald,* ibid.). Another danger is that China may be boxed into a corner. William Overholt, author of the 1993 best-seller, *The Rise of China: How Economic Reform Is Creating a New Superpower,* warns that the world stands on the verge of a "second Cold War", which, however, is "totally gratuitous", partly because Washington "misreads" China as being dangerously aggressive. The conclusion is: The most practical response to China's growing strength is to help steer it onto peaceful and mutually beneficial paths. China's economic growth is already a spark plug for the entire region—and perhaps for the world.

Under the present international situation, containment against China can hardly be an open government policy. The Clinton Administration proposed an "engagement" policy towards China in September 1993. From then on, President Clinton has emphasized on several occasions that his China policy is not one of containment but rather one of "comprehensive engagement" (quanmian jiechu). As a senior State Department official put it, the "engagement" policy aims at three goals: seeking U.S. interests at all levels; building up mutual trust and reaching agreement wherever the two countries' interests coincide; and reducing differences through dialog.

China definitely wants to have a normal relationship with the United States and other countries in the West. In fact, as early as 1992, at a meeting with President Bill Clinton shortly after he took office, Chinese President Jiang Zemin proposed a 16-character principle of "increasing trust, reducing troubles, developing cooperation, and avoiding confrontation" (zengjia xinren, jianshao mafan, fazhan hezuo, bugao duikang), as China's policy to deal with the United States. In a news conference in Beijing on 7 March 1997, Vice-Premier and Foreign Minister Qian Qichen confirmed that, as far as the governmental policies of China and the United States were concerned, the two countries shared common ground and common interests. He announced that he was confident that China and the United States would see further growth rather than conflict in their relations. Later, in August 1997 when meeting U.S. National Security Adviser Sandy Berger, Jiang Zemin further developed his 16-character principle thus: "expanding common ground, increasing trust, reducing differences, and building the future together" (kuoda gongshi, zengjia xinren, jianshao fenqi, gongchuang weilai). The key was the last four characters, which implies building a "strategic partnership" (zhanlüe huoban guanxi) with the United States, as Jiang set for his task in his U.S. trip in late October 1997.

However, the situation was not so simple. To Chinese leaders, the Clinton Administration's proposal of an "engagement" policy was tantamount to admitting the failure of the sanctions the United States had imposed on China after the 1989 Tiananmen Incident and acknowledging China's international standing and legitimacy. Why the policy was adopted, as they understood, was that the United States needed China's co-operation on a number of regional and global issues and it also sought to influence China's domestic and foreign policy through engagement. After all, an "engagement" policy did not always mean a friendly policy.

Fundamentally, Chinese see "White superiority" (bairen youyue lun) at work in the West. As Harvard Professor Samuel Huntington admitted, "West vs. Rest" has become a dominant thinking pattern for many Westerners. This has amply been borne out in the case of China. It is, therefore, not very important whether the Americans actually have a document outlining their intentions to "contain China". More significant is the fact that the differences between China and the United States—on ideology, human-rights, democratization, family planning, value concepts and many other things—are becoming more and more open. As long as such differences exist, Americans will perceive the growth of Chinese economic and military power to be threatening. Such is the basis for the "contain-China" theory.

Sino-U.S. relations in the 1990s exhibited the following two features: fluctuation and fragility. In certain ways, Sino-U.S. clashes are to be expected. The latest clashes included U.S. clamours over Chinese efforts to steal U.S. military secrets and influence U.S. elections, the NATO bombing (on 7 May 1999) of the Chinese Embassy in Belgrade and China's strong public anti-U.S. sentiment thereafter. In the U.S., Clinton was accused of changing "virtually at the speed of light" his view of China from the "bloody butchers of Beijing" to America's "strategic partner". It is argued that China is not necessarily the most important country in Asia and that the U.S. should strengthen its relations with Japan, South Korea, and Taiwan as "a counterweight to China". Notably, in 1999, the American public ranked China the number one country likely to pose a danger. A "third way" concept appeared—America's China policy should be something between President Clinton's notion that China is a "strategic partner" and some Republicans' conviction that China is a "strategic adversary" (zhanlüe duishou) or an "enemy". Hence the new idea: "congagement" (weihe)—something between "containment" and "engagement", characterized by waving carrots and sticks at the same time. The task of Americans is to keep the pressure on, restraining China wherever necessary, engaging it whenever possible. Another suggestion is: "democratic peace" (minzhude heping)—make efforts to maintain peace by supporting freedom, democracy, and human rights.

Indeed, there are many issues between the two countries which are hard to resolve, and the very foundation supporting bilateral relations is unstable. Overall, it is predicted, Sino-U.S. relations will, as in the past few years, continue to be characterized by both challenges and opportunities, friction and cooperation, contention and compromise, tension and relaxation.

围和
weihe
(congagement)
See "weidu Zhongguo" (containment against China).

唯成分论
weichengfenlun
(theory of the unique importance of class origin)
See "xuetong lun" (lineage theory), "zhengque chuli renmin neibu maodun" (correctly handling contradictions among the people), and "jiating chengfen" (family origin; class status of one's family).

唯生产力论
weishengchanlilun
(theory of "productivity as the sole factor determining social life")
See "xin shehuizhuyi guan" (new socialist view).

唯物辩证法
weiwu bianzhengfa
(materialist dialectics)
See "bianzheng weiwuzhuyi" (dialectical materialism).

伟大领袖，伟大导师，伟大统帅，伟大舵手
weida lingxiu, weida daoshi, weida tongshuai, weida duoshou
(great leader, great teacher, great commander, and great helmsman)
See "si ge weida" (four greats) and "tuchu zhengzhi" (giving prominence to politics).

伪装的文化帝国主义
weizhuangde wenhua diguozhuyi
(disguised cultural imperialism)
See "renquan wenti" (human rights issue).

魏京生事件
Wei Jingsheng shijian
(Wei Jingsheng incident)
See "yao minzhu haishi yao xinde ducai" (democracy or neo-dictatorship).

为金钱服务
wei jinqian fuwu

(serve the money)

See "quanxin quanyi wei renmin fuwu" (serve the people wholeheartedly).

为人民服务
wei renmin fuwu
(serve the people)

See "quanxin quanyi wei renmin fuwu" (serve the people wholeheartedly).

为矢造的
wei shi zao di
(framing a target to attack)

This was a common practice in political campaigns. See also "dangdai lunzheng beiwanglu" (a memorandum on a contemporary debate).

为艺术而艺术
wei yishu er yishu
(art for art's sake)

"Art for art's sake" was condemned in Mao's *Yan'an Talks* as a bourgeois view of art, but today many Chinese writers and artists openly and proudly declare that art is the pursuit of their creative activities. Hence, the terms "pure art" (chun yishu) and "pure literature" (chun wenxue) are popular. One should note, however, that the official stand is that literature and art cannot be divorced from politics. See "wenyi buneng tuoli zhengzhi" (literature and art cannot be divorced from politics) and "wenyi wei zhengzhi fuwu" (literature and art serve politics).

卫星上天，红旗落地
weixing shangtian, hongqi luodi
(satellites have been launched while the red flag has fallen)

See "hong" (red) and "xiuzhengzhuyi" (revisionism).

卫星田
weixing tian
(satellite fields)

See "dayuejin" (Great Leap Forward).

蔚蓝色文明
weilanse wenming
(blue civilization)

See "huangtu wenming" (yellow earth civilization) and "*Heshang* shijian" *(River Elegy* Incident).

稳定压倒一切
wending yadao yiqie
(the need for stability

overwhelms everything else)

This thesis was first put forth by Deng Xiaoping on 26 February 1989 when meeting visiting U.S. President Bush. Of all issues in China, Deng said, the need for stability predominant. The CCP's ultimate aim was to develop socialist democracy, but it could not be done in a hurry; the country must maintain a stable situation.

At the time when Deng made the remark, the 1989 pro-democracy movement was just beginning. Several months later, the tragic June 4th Incident took place. On 4 June 1990, its first anniversary, the *People's Daily* published an editorial entitled "The Need for Stability Overwhelms Everything Else" ("Wending yadao yiqie"), which has since become a common political slogan. At the 15th CCP National Congress held in September 1997, Jiang Zemin echoed Deng's idea. He said: "Without stability, nothing can be achieved" (meiyou wending, shenmeshi yeganbucheng).

"The need for stability overwhelms everything else" is regarded as part of Deng's strategic thinking, a conclusion he made in light of China's modern history and the prevailing circumstances. (An interesting comparison is Deng's other thesis: Development is the most essential criterion—"fazhan caishi ying daoli"). Party leaders at various levels fully support it, obviously also out of their own interests. It seems that many Chinese also share the idea, which partly explains why neo-conservatism has become popular among China's ideological-cultural circles in the 1990s.

China's dissidents, however, worry about it being abused to suppress the demand for political reform. There are various kinds of stability, they argue, but true stability must be premised on social justice (wendingde qianti shi gongzheng). On this issue, Bao Tong, former PCC member and political secretary to Party chief Zhao Ziyang, said: "Only by restricting CCP power can stability be achieved." Bao revealed his views in an interview given to the Reuters reporter on 3 June 1998, soon after he resumed his citizen rights. (Bao was the highest Party official jailed for his role in the 1989 pro-democracy movement. He was secretly tried and sentenced to seven years in jail for leaking state secrets. Released in May 1996, he was held under house arrest for another two years.) In Bao Tong's opinion, the June 4th tragedy took place because there was no mechanism at that time to check CCP power, especially the power of paramount leader Deng Xiaoping. He warned that CCP power without restrictions would be a hard-to-predict factor affecting domestic stability and even world peace. See also "anding tuanjie" (stability and unity) and "chi butong zhengjianzhe" (dissidents).

稳定的前提是公正
wendingde qianti shi gongzheng
(stability must be premised on social justice)

See "wending yadao yiqie" (the need for stability overwhelms everything else).

文攻武卫
wengong wuwei
(attack in letters, defend with arms)

See "quanmian neizhan" (full-scale civil war).

文以载道
wen yi zai dao

(literature should transmit principles)

Zhou Dunyi (1017-1073) of the Song dynasty first put forth the thesis: "Literature should transmit principles". What is meant by "principles" is "self-cultivation" (xiu shen), "establishing one's family" (qijia), "serving one's country" (zhiguo), and "unifying the world" (ping tianxia); in other words, moral, philosophical, and political values; or in modern terms, the identity of ethics and politics.

The idea that "Literature should transmit principles" was generally accepted in the past as part of Chinese cultural tradition. Today, it is argued that it is not necessary that literature transmit principles. See "wenyi buneng tuoli zhengzhi" (literature and art cannot be divorced from politics) and "wenyi wei zhengzhi fuwu" (literature and art serve politics).

文斗
wendou
(struggle by reasoning)

See "quanmian neizhan" (full-scale civil war) and "wen'ge" (Cultural Revolution).

文革
wen'ge
(Cultural Revolution)

"Wen'ge", "Wenhua Geming", and "Wenhua Dageming" are all abbreviations of "Wuchanjieji Wenhua Dageming"—the Great Proletarian Cultural Revolution. Notably, before the August 1966 11th Plenum of the 8th PCC, at which the "Decision Regarding the GPCR" was passed, it was called the "Great Socialist Cultural Revolution" (Shehuizhuyi Wenhua Dageming).

The GPCR officially started with the issuance on 16 May 1966 of the "Circular of the Central Committee of the CCP" (that is, the "May 16th Circular", see "wuyiliu tongzhi") and ended with the arrest of the so-called Gang of Four on 6 October 1976. It can be divided into three stages.

The first stage lasted three years from May 1966 to April 1969. During that time, Mao Zedong, Lin Biao, and Jiang Qing co-operated in launching the revolution, by promoting a struggle to seize power (duoquan douzheng) throughout the country. Major events included:

In May 1966 the PCC Politburo held an enlarged meeting at which the "Outline Report on the Current Academic Discussion" (see "eryue tigang") was fiercely attacked and the "May 16th Circular" was passed. A new body, the Central GPCR Group, with Chen Boda as its director, Jiang Qing as its first deputy director, and Kang Sheng as its advisor, was set up directly under the Politburo Standing Committee. It replaced the dissolved "Group of Five in Charge of the Cultural Revolution" headed by Peng Zhen. The "May 16th Circular", implying that Liu Shaoqi was "China's Khrushchev", called on the whole Party and the whole nation to struggle against "leading bourgeois proponents" who had sneaked into the Party, the government, the military, and various cultural circles.

On 8 August 1966, the 11th Plenum of the 8th PCC passed a "Decision on the GPCR" (which was referred to as the "Sixteen Articles". See "shiliutiao"). The document stated that the major targets of attack in the GPCR were "those in power within the Party taking the capitalist road". Red Guards, encouraged by Mao's call to bombard the "bourgeois headquarters" and to carry out the GPCR through to the end, traveled all over the country to exchange what they called "revolutionary experiences". They engaged in what they considered revolutionary activities—doing away with the "four olds" and cultivating the "four news" (see "po sijiu, li sixin") and struggling against alleged "capitalist-roaders" at various levels of the party-state apparatus.

In January 1967, what was termed the "January Revolution" (see "yiyue geming") took place in Shanghai. A new organ of power—the "Shanghai People's Commune" (later renamed the "Shanghai Municipal Revolutionary Committee" according to Mao's advice)—was founded the next month. Thereafter, responding to Mao's call, "all proletarian revolutionary rebels" in the country were involved in seizing power from the alleged capitalist-roaders. The GPCR entered a "new phase".

The "new phase" was a phase of "full-scale civil war". Different factions of Red Guards and "rebels" did not unite in their power seizure struggle as Mao had expected. Instead, armed conflicts took place between them almost everywhere in 1967 and 1968 (see "wengong wuwei"). The situation became so serious that the Army had to be summoned in to help. Military control was enforced in chaotic places and vital units (see "sanzhi liangjun").

By 5 September 1968, "revolutionary committees" (geming weiyuanhui) had been set up in all 29 provinces and autonomous regions and the two cities of Beijing and Shanghai. From 1 to 24 April 1969, the CCP held its 9th National Congress in Beijing, at which Lin Biao, Mao's successor as stipulated in the newly revised CCP Constitution, hailed the "great victory" of Mao's theory of "continuing the revolution under the dictatorship of the proletariat".

The 9th CCP National Congress marked the beginning of the second stage of the GPCR, which saw a dramatic fall of Lin Biao from the apex of power into the abyss of disgrace and ruin within just two years.

This successor to Mao, after failing in his attempt to assume the post of PRC president at the 2nd Plenum of the 9th PCC (held at Lushan from 23 August to 6 September 1970), began in February 1971 to take measures to stage an armed coup. During the next month, under the leadership of his son Lin Liguo, an armed coup plan entitled "571 Project Minutes" was secretly made (see "wuqiyi gongcheng jiyao").

In August 1971, Mao decided that the 3rd Plenum of the 9th PCC was to be held before National Day on 1 October to settle the Lin Biao issue. On 14 August, Mao left Beijing and began an inspection tour to the southern part of China, where he held a number of talks with local Party, government, and military leaders, giving them a cue about the situation.

In the early evening of 12 September 1971, Mao, having successfully foiled several attempts by his enemies, arrived safely in Beijing. Lin Biao and his followers were shocked by this news and realized that they had lost momentum. They attempted to flee to the Soviet Union late that night, but were killed early the next morning, when their chartered plane crashed while flying over Wenduerkai, Mongolia (see "Lin Biao shijian").

After the "September 13th Incident" of 1971, with the support of Zhou Enlai, Deng Xiaoping and a number of veteran Party officials returned to power. At the same time, Mao found a new successor in Wang Hongwen, originally a leader of the Shanghai "rebels". Wang then became a vice-chairman of the CCP at its 10th National Congress held in August 1973.

The third stage of the GPCR was characterized by struggles between the Party elders and what later came to be known as the Gang of Four, that is, Jiang Qing, Mao's wife, and her colleagues Wang Hongwen, Zhang Chunqiao, and Yao Wenyuan (see "sirenbang").

Taking advantage of the campaign launched by Mao in March 1973 to criticize the combined target of Lin Biao and Confucius (see "pi Lin pi Kong"), the Gang of Four tried to overthrow Premier Zhou Enlai. After Zhou died on 8 January 1976, Deng Xiaoping became their major target. Deng stepped down following the so-called "Tiananmen Counter-Revolutionary Incident" of 5 April 1976 (see "siwu yundong"), which brought a high tide to the campaign to criticize Deng and counter the "Right deviationist trend to reverse correct verdicts", the last campaign of Mao's lifetime (see "pi Deng, fanji youqing fan'anfeng").

Mao died on 9 September 1976, after he had selected Hua Guofeng to be first vice chairman of the CCP and premier of the State Council. On 6 October, aware of the danger that he would probably be toppled by the Gang of Four, Hua Guofeng, allying with Ye Jianying, Wang Dongxing, and Li Xiannian, successfully staged a coup and arrested all of the Gang members. At the 11th CCP National Congress held in Beijing in August 1977, Hua Guofeng officially announced the end of the GPCR, which was marked by the downfall of the Gang of Four.

In the winter of 1980, the two "counter-revolutionary cliques" headed respectively by Jiang Qing and Lin Biao were brought to a public trial (see "Lin Jiang fan'geming jituan").

It has been over twenty years since the end of the GPCR, but quite a number of questions about it have not yet been answered satisfactorily. One of the major controversial issues is its nature. Major views include the "line struggle" theory, the "power struggle" theory, the "civil strife" theory, the theory of "the exteriorization of Mao's idealism", the theory of "an unavoitable end result of Mao's ever-worsening ultra-Left line", and the "two Cultural Revolutions" theory.

Perhaps any single theory cannot fully explain the GPCR. But one thing is certain: the GPCR was a catastrophe to the Chinese nation, a catastrophe that lasted as long as ten years, or, in Chinese words, "shinian zainan" or "shinian haojie". Compared with the 1957 anti-Rightist campaign, it was a bigger and more horrifying event in contemporary Chinese history. Ba Jin, the well-known novelist, saw it even in terms of the whole of mankind. (Ba Jin, "Wo he wenxue"—"My Life and Literature: An Address Delivered at the Cultural Lecture Series in Kyoto, Japan on 11 April 1980", in his *Tansuo Ji*, pp. 136-41; trans. by Don J. Cohn in *CL*, 1:126-129, Spring 1984). See also "chedi fouding wen'ge" (complete negation of the GPCR) and other relevant entries.

文革博物馆
wen'ge bowuguan
(Cultural Revolution museum)

In 1986, Ba Jin suggested building a "Cultural Revolution Museum". Of course, as Gong Liu, a prominent poet, pointed out, a museum such as the one proposed by Ba Jin, no matter how many Chinese supported him in the idea, and how sincerely and strongly they did so, could not actually be built even in the year 2000 for various reasons, mostly political. Later Ba Jin himself must have understood the difficulties to carry out his suggestion. He wrote in 1987, in his "Postscript" to the one-volume edition of *Random Thoughts (Suixiang Lu,* originally in five volumes), that he would like to take his book as a museum exposing the GPCR with words of truth.

Significantly, with the joint efforts of a number of Chinese scholars in America, an electronic museum of the GPCR has been built on the Internet at "http://www.cnd.org/CR/". A statement quoted from Ba Jin precedes the great quantity of data about the catastrophe: "'The tragedy of history must not be re-staged'—that should not be empty talk. In order to enable everyone to understand and remember clearly, the best way is to build a 'Cultural Revolution Museum'."

Recently, it has been suggested that the Chairman Mao Memorial Hall in Beijing be turned into a Cultural Revolution Museum. Of course, for obvious reasons, this is out of the realm of possibility for the Party leadership. See also "chedi fouding wen'ge" (complete negation of the GPCR).

文革三七开
wen'ge sanqikai
(a 70-30 ratio in the assessment of the GPCR)

See "chedi fouding wen'ge" (complete negation of the GPCR), "wen'ge" (Cultural Revolution), and "xinzuopai" (neo-Leftists).

文革是毛泽东极左路线不断恶化的必然产物
wen'ge shi Mao Zedong jizuo luxian buduan ehuade biran chanwu
(the GPCR was an unavoidable end result of Mao's ever-worsening ultra-Left line)

See "Mao Zedong lixiangzhuyi waihua lun" (theory of the exteriorization of Mao's idealism), "wen'ge" (Cultural Revolution), and "liang ge wen'ge lun" ("two Cultural Revolutions" theory).

文革突破口
wen'ge tupokou
(breakthrough point for the GPCR)

See "*Hai Rui Baguan* pipan" (the attack on *Hai Rui Dismissed from Office).*

文革文艺
wen'ge wenyi
(GPCR literature and art)

GPCR literature and art, generally speaking, can be represented by the eight so-called "model revolutionary dramas" (geming yangbanxi) or "model dramas" (yangbanxi): the Beijing operas *Shajia Creek (Shajiabang), Taking Tiger Mountain by Strategy (Zhiqu weihushan), Raid on the White Tiger Regiment (Qixi baihutuan), The Red Lantern (Hongdeng ji),* and *On the Docks (Haigang),* the symphonic work *Shajia Creek (Shajiabang),* and the ballets *Red Detachment of Women (Hongse niangzijun)* and *The White-haired Girl (Baimao nü).* Hence the saying "eight dramas for 800 million people" (bayi renmin ba chu xi) during the ten years of the GPCR.

Shajia Creek (originally called *Ludang huozhong—Sparks in the Reeds,* which grew out of a Shanghai opera with the same title), *Taking Tiger Mountain by Strategy, Raid on the White Tiger Regiment,* and *The Red Lantern* were first staged at the 1964 Festival of Beijing Operas on Contemporary Themes, at which Jiang Qing delivered the speech, "On the Revolution in Beijing Opera" ("Tan jingju geming", *HQ,* 6, 1967; trans. in *CL,* 8:118-24, 1967), to hail the event and confirm her contributions in it. *On the Docks* was adapted in the spring of 1965 by the Shanghai Beijing Opera Company from a Huaiju (a local opera in Jiangsu province) called *Morning at the Harbor (Haigangde zaochen). The White-haired Girl* was adapted by the Shanghai Dance Academy from an opera and also a film with the same title. Similarly, following Jiang Qing's instructions, the Chinese Ballet Troupe turned the film *Red Detachment of Women* into ballet form, and the Central Philharmonic Orchestra composed the symphonic work *Shajia Creek,* based on the Beijing opera of the same title.

GPCR literature and art, of course, included other works. (See, for instance, Yang Jian, *Wenhua Dagemingzhongde Dixia Wenxue—The Underground Literature During the Cultural Revolution,* Beijing, Zhaohua, Jan. 1993; and Wang Yao, ""Guanyu 'wen'ge wenxue'de shiyi yu yanjiu"—"GPCR Literature: Definition and Studies", *Wenyi lilun yanjiu,* May 1999, reprinted in *XHWZ,* 1:109-112, 2000.) An important genre was the so-called "conspiratorial literature and art" ("yinmou wenxue"). In February 1976, shortly after the death of Zhou Enlai, Jiang Qing and Zhang Chunqiao summoned the confidants they had planted in the Ministry of Culture to make arrangements for creating literary works with the theme of the struggle against capitalist-roaders. The slogan "writing about the struggle against capitalist-roaders" (xie yi zouzipai zuo douzheng) was formally put forward. Several such works had already been produced earlier in conformity with the Gang's plot to seize power. After the slogan was publicized, a major campaign was launched in film, drama, ballet, and other forms of literature and art. Soon the entire country was flooded with such works. Most instructive about how the Gang put their demand into effect was perhaps the making of the film *Counterattack (Fanji,* dir. Li Wenhua, Beijing Film Studio, 1976). A story about how a first secretary of a provincial Party committee restores "capitalism" as soon as he has resumed his original post, and then is counterattacked by the "revolutionary people", it was rushed out at an unprecedented speed.

Works about the struggle against capitalist-roaders were dubbed by post-Mao critics as "conspiratorial literature and art". It was noted that these works were actually a development of the "model revolutionary dramas", according to the "experiences" of which they were produced. Included in these experiences were the theory of the "fundamental task" (genben renwu lun) and the principle of the "three prominences" (santuchu).

The fundamental task of socialist literature and art in fact had long been stipulated by the Party, as embodied in the slogan "Literature and art serve workers, peasants, and soldiers, and the proletarian politics", which Mao had explained clearly in his 1942 *Yan'an Talks*. On the one hand, according to this theory, socialist literature and art must "praise virtue" (ge de)—the virtue of the Communist Party, its leader, and the workers, peasants, and soldiers, as well as the virtue of the socialist cause. On the other hand, they should expose the people's enemies, mainly capitalist-roaders during the GPCR.

In light of the "fundamental task", the principle of the "three prominences" was put forth during the GPCR. But post-Mao critics emphasized that Jiang Qing had long harbored the idea of the "three prominences". She was found, in her 1964 speech on "revolution in Beijing opera" (jingju geming), to have advocated that the fundamental purpose of all literature and art was to create positive, heroic characters, and this view was regarded as the "theoretical foundation" for the "three prominences". In 1965, when the Beijing opera *Guerrillas of the Plain* was being produced, she asked the artists concerned to reduce the importance of the other characters in the play so that Li Xiangyang, the hero, could enjoy the "greatest prominence". In 1968, following Jiang's instructions, Yu Huiyong, a teacher at the Shanghai Conservatory of Music (who later became minister of culture), first proposed the slogan of the "three prominences" when summing up the creative experiences of the "model revolutionary dramas". In 1969, Yao Wenyuan slightly revised it and inserted it into a *Red Flag* article he was examining. It read as follows:

"Among all characters give prominence to positive characters; among positive characters give prominence to heroic characters; among heroic characters give prominence to the principal heroic character." Thereafter the "three prominences" was no longer only "an important principle in portraying characters" as originally suggested; it was a mandatory principle for the "creation of proletarian literature and art". After the "Lin Biao Incident" of 13 September 1971, Jiang Qing seemingly restrained herself a bit. But she did not fail to enhance her prestige with such "model dramas". In 1972, in a Party document drawn up under the control of the Gang of Four, the "three prominences" were regarded as "the fundamental principle of proletarian literary and art creation". From 1972 to 1974, *Red Flag,* as the theoretical organ of the Party, together with other newspapers and journals, successively carried the full texts of those works and also a great number of articles which praised them. By administrative order, the "three prominences" principle was rigidly applied to all literary and artistic genres "with a high level of political consciousness in carrying out Chairman Mao's revolutionary line in literature and art". At that time, to deny the "three prominences" meant "to deny the GPCR and to restore capitalism".

When condemning the "three prominences" for following what was called Lin Biao's "theory of innate genius" (tiancai lun) and the "view about heroes creating history" (yingxiong shiguan), post-Mao critics had a lot to say. Quoting theorists of the Gang of Four as saying that the principal heroic character must be "lofty, great, and perfect" (gao da quan), and "always in a dominant position", with all the dispositions of plots and characters, inclusive of positive characters, serving his (or her) prominence, they raised two accusations. First, they claimed this was tantamount to reducing the masses of the people to a state of being controlled. The relationship between the hero and the people thus became that between the ruling and the ruled. Therefore, it was a "vicious vilification" of socialism and the proletarian dictatorship; it revealed the relationship in which the Gang of Four and their followers "enslaved and oppressed" the broad masses of the people. Second, such a portrayal meant that the principal heroic character did not need to be educated by the Party, and, instead, "stood above the Party"; this was a "negation of the centralized Party leadership".

Soon after the downfall of the Gang of Four, works about the struggle against "capitalist-roaders" were rigorously denounced. Jiang Qing and her colleagues' call for creating such works was treated seriously by post-Mao critics. It was said to be a component of the Gang's general plot, aiming at inciting people to rise up in counter-revolutionary revolts to seize power from veteran revolutionaries. (That was why these works were dubbed "conspiratorial literature and art".) The Gang of Four, it was claimed, had two related purposes in advocating such literature. On the one hand, they could voluntarily describe leading cadres of the Party, army, and government as "unrepentant capitalist-roaders" who must be overthrown, such as Du Wenjie in *Spring Shoot* (*Chun miao*, Shanghai Film Studio, dir. Xie Jin et al., 1975), Han Ling in *Counterattack,* Gao You in *Gala Celebrations* (*Shengdade jieri,* Shanghai Film Studio, dir. Chi Qun, 1976), and Deputy Director Xia in *The Cheerful Xiaoliang River* (*Huantengde Xiaolianghe,* Shanghai Film Studio, dir. Liu Qiong and Shen Yaoting, 1976). On the other hand, they could build up their own public image, posing as high-minded "leaders", "standard-bearers", or "heroes opposing capitalist-roaders".

While works about the struggle against "capitalist-roaders" were denounced, the Party cultural leaders' attitude towards "model dramas" remained somewhat unclear. In the 1977 attacks on Jiang Qing's "three prominences" principle, quite notably, the critics had to say something in defense of the "model dramas". Of course, the term "model dramas" was dropped and their original style—"revolutionary theatrical works on contemporary themes" (geming xiandai xi)—was restored. It was argued that the principle of the "three prominences" was simply at odds with the actual relationships of the characters in each of these works, which had been produced only under the guidance of Mao's idea about the "combination of revolutionary realism and revolutionary romanticism" (liang jiehe). Moreover, most of these works had already taken shape by the 1964 Festival of Beijing Operas on Contemporary Themes and at that time the "three prominences" had not yet been put forward. It was admitted that Jiang Qing and the company did have something to do with these works, but this was seen as a manifestation of the "acute struggle between the two lines".

There were some dissident opinions, primarily political. "Model drama phobia" (yangbanxi kongbu zheng) was a term invented by Deng Youmei and Liu Shaotang, two Beijing writers, to describe their reaction upon hearing "model dramas" (Deng Youmei and Liu Shaotang, "Womende yidian kanfa"—"Our View", *Beijing wanbao*, 30 Dec. 1980). In Wang Ruowang's words, "model dramas" were the "strongest voice of the times" (shidai zui qiang yin) during the GPCR, which could in an instant revive "all the terror, the bloodiness, destruction, conspiracies, and national retrogression" of that long-past but far-from-forgotten decade (Wang Ruowang, "Shidai 'zui qiang yin'"—"The 'Strongest Voice' of the Times", *Tuanjie bao,* 14 June 1986). Huang Shang, another veteran writer, said that there was simply no point in discussing whether the eight "model dramas" were excellent art or not. Any recollection of how they were forced into the ears of one billion people for ten years with "political violence" (zhengzhi baoli)—this was really unprecedented in history—was enough. Nevertheless, they should not sink into the limbo of oblivion. Huang suggested that the best place to keep them should be a "GPCR Museum", for which Ba Jin made a sincere appeal in 1986 (Huang Shang, "'Biaoshu'de xiaxiang"—"A Reverie", *RMRB*, 10 June 1986).

In the discussion of GPCR literature and art, a term was frequently used—the "Gang of Four's line in literature and art" (sirenbang wenyi luxian), which was coined by post-Mao critics to differentiate it from Mao's line.

In the spring of 1977, the so-called Gang of Four's "line" in literature and art began to come under attack. This came to a head in the latter part of May 1977, on the occasion of the thirty-fifth anniversary of the publication of Mao's *Yan'an Talks*. Since the political line of the Gang of Four was deemed at the time by the Party as "ultra-Right" (jiyou), the "Right" nature of their line in literature and art was said to lie in the fact that it tried to turn the literary and art cause of the Party into that of their counter-revolutionary clique, into a tool with which to create public opinion to help them usurp Party and state power. It was a "sinister line", a line which was "totally antagonistic" to Mao's "revolutionary line" and was "more rampant, more vicious" than Liu Shaoqi's "counter-revolutionary revisionist line". Later, when the political line of the Gang of Four was redeemed to be "ultra-Left" (jizuo), and when Liu Shaoqi was rehabilitated, the above description was altered accordingly.

But many denied the existence of such a line of the Gang of Four. If there was such a term, they argued, it essentially meant "Mao's line in literature and art during the GPCR", much embodied in the 1966 Party document "Summary of the Forum on the Work in Literature and Art in the Armed Forces with Which Comrade Lin Biao Entrusted Comrade Jiang Qing". This document was regarded as Mao's *Yan'an Talks* in the socialist period ("jiyao" shi shehuizhuyi shiqide "jianghua").

Judging by the standards of "socialist literature and art" as stipulated in Mao's line, "model dramas" can be part of the repertoire. The principles embodied in the "model dramas" were developed from Mao's ideas on literature and art, presenting themselves as an important component of Mao Zedong Thought in literature and art in the "socialist age" (Xia Zhongyi, "Lishi wu ke bihui"—"History Cannot Be Ignored", *WXPL,* 4:14-18, July 1989). Therefore, some Party leaders were reluctant to drop them. As to the Gang of Four's slogan "writing about the struggle against capitalist-roaders" and works produced under it, it was only natural that they were subject to fierce attack by the new authorities who arrested the Gang. It should be pointed out, however, that the so-called "conspiratorial literature and art" was also a correct application of the principle that literature and art must be subordinate to, and work in the service of, politics, as elucidated in Mao's *Yan'an Talks*. There was nothing strange that the Gang of Four were eager to make full use of literary and art forms and the slogan "writing about the struggle against capitalist-roaders". Of course, understandably, at that time no one dared to touch this vital issue.

As the "standard-bearer of the proletarian cultural revolution", Jiang Qing claimed that she should be held chiefly responsible for the "revolution in Beijing opera" and the eight "model revolutionary dramas". Post-Mao critics on the one hand belittled Jiang Qing's role in producing the "model dramas" and on the other underlined Mao's involvement. It was true, indeed, that Jiang Qing alone should not be held chiefly responsible for these works. They were essentially the products of Mao Zedong Thought in literature and art. That was why Jiang Qing was so confident when she declared: "Since the Paris Commune the proletariat has never succeeded in solving the problem of orientation in literature and art. Not until 1964, when we produced the model revolutionary dramas, was this accomplished" (Mass Criticism Group of the Philosophy and Social Sciences Department, Chinese Academy of Sciences, "Geming wenyi shi dangde shiye, bushi hangbangde shiye"—"Revolutionary Literature and Art Are a Party Cause and Not a Clique Cause", *HQ*, 4:39, Apr. 1977).

It is now more than two decades since the end of the GPCR, and "model dramas" still remain an interesting subject. One can recall that at the 1986 Spring Festival official gathering, which was televised live to the whole country, to the surprise of many, "model opera" arias headed the program. This caused a nationwide controversy. In 1988 the controversy over the "model dramas" occurred again. Significantly, the plays *The Red Lantern* and *Shajia Creek* were re-staged in December 1990, the first time since the 1976 downfall of the Gang of Four. Then the ballet *Red Detachment of Women* was re-staged in Beijing in May 1993. Today, several of the "model dramas" are staged time and again, their CD products sell well, and there seems to be a lasting craze for them. Politically, this gives expression to a complicated feeling, a GPCR complex, of some people, especially the young who have not experienced the GPCR. After all, "model drama phobia" is something of the past. Artistically, the "three prominences" as artistic techniques are on the whole not out of keeping with the spirit of traditional Chinese theater. The "model dramas" do reserve some refined traditional theatrical features loved by the Chinese. See also "jiyao" ("Summary"), "yihua wenxue" (alienated literature; literature of alienation), and "wenyi wei zhengzhi fuwu" (literature and art serve politics).

文革序幕
wen'ge xumu
(prelude to the GPCR)

See "*Hai Rui Baguan* pipan" (the attack on *Hai Rui Dismissed from Office*).

文革後文学
wen'gehou wenxue
(post-GPCR literature)

See "xinshiqi wenxue" (literature of the new period).

文革学
wen'gexue
(GPCR study)

It is over two decades since the GPCR ended, but many people are still puzzled, as they were years ago, by the following questions: How could Mao Zedong mobilize hundreds and millions of people to join in the GPCR with great enthusiasm or fanaticism? This was not only unprecedented in Chinese history but also exerted a tremendous impact on the entire world. What are the *real* reason(s) for its occurrence? What lessons have been learned by this complicated and disastrous experience of ten years?

Scholars have examined and tried to explain the GPCR from various perspectives: historical, political, sociological, economic, cultural, pedagogical, and psychological. Many books and articles have been published, with interesting arguments and analyses. Mistakes were also made, some quite preposterous if judged today. A whole generation of starry-eyed China-watchers had to apologize for their failure to grasp the dark truth of the GPCR. People still remember the acute academic embarrassment. (See, for example, Song Yongyi and Sun Dajin, *The Cultural Revolution: A Bibliography, 1966-1996,* Cambridge MA, Harvard Yenching Library, 1998.)

A new interest in studying the GPCR seems to be on the rise again. One can see the eagerness of scholars in mainland China to conduct some serious research of their own. Apparently, they are not satisfied with Deng Xiaoping's conclusion about the nature of the GPCR as a "civil strife" (as in the document "Resolution on Certain Questions in the History of Our Party since the Founding of the PRC" passed at the 6th Plenum of the 11th PCC in June 1981). In their opinion, "civil strife" is only a description of the phenonemon, and does not reveal its inherent, essential nature. Furthermore, they argue, since so many years have past, the GPCR should no longer be written about only in "broad outline" (cuxiantiao), as instructed by Deng. But this is a formidable task. For one thing, a great quantity of files remain secret. In addition, these scholars often find themselves at odds with the authorities, rendering their studies extremely difficult.

When Deng gave his conclusion, he was aware that this was an expedient measure. He said that he would rather let the next generations—who would be more clever—go ahead with the job. More important for him was to maintain stability, both in society and within the Party. He could not afford the damage that a thorough and comprehensive examination of the GPCR, with Mao most likely the number one target, would produce. Today the political situation is on the whole still the same. Since the post-Deng era has just begun and the new core of the Party leadership needs time to establish its authority, the slogan, "The need for stability overwhelms everything else", has immediate significance. Patience will be required, perhaps, if one wants to see some substantial achievements in China's "Wen'geology" (GPCR study). See also "wending yadao yiqie" (the need for stability overwhelms everything else) and "wen'ge" (Cultural Revolution).

文化霸权主义
wenhua baquanzhuyi
(cultural hegemonism)

See "xin baoshouzhuyi" (neo-conservatism) and "minzuzhuyi" (nationalism).

文化冲突
wenhua chongtu
(cultural clash)

See "fan chuantong" (anti-tradition).

文化大革命
wenhua dageming
(Great Cultural Revolution)

See "wen'ge" (Cultural Revolution).

文化大革命要进行多次
wenhua dageming yao jinxing duoci
(the Great Cultural Revolution must be repeatedly carried out)

See "tianxia daluan dadao tianxia dazhi" (great disorder across the land leads to great order), "wuchanjieji zhuanzheng" (dictatorship of the proletariat), and "xinzuopai" (neo-Leftists).

文化革命
wenhua geming
(Cultural Revolution)

As a proper noun, this is an abbreviation for "Wuchanjieji Wenhua Dageming" (Great Proletarian Cultural Revolution), referring to the Cultural Revolution which took place in mainland China from 1966 to 1976 (as officially described). See "wen'ge" (Cultural Revolution).

文化激进主义
wenhua jijinzhuyi
(cultural radicalism)

See "guoxue" (Chinese traditional learning), "wenhua re" (culture craze), and "xin baoshouzhuyi" (neo-conservatism).

文化精英
wenhua jingying
(cultural *elite*)

See "wenhua re" (culture craze) and "ziyouhua" (liberalization).

文化浪漫主义
wenhua langmanzhuyi
(cultural romanticism)

See "xinzuopai" (neo-Leftists).

文化领导要跟上改革开放的新形势
wenhua lingdao yao genshang

gaige kaifangde xin xingshi
(the cultural leadership must keep abreast of the new situation of reform and the open door)

In July 1986, as a vice-minister of culture in charge of day-to-day business, Gao Zhanxiang asked China's cultural leaders at various levels to "keep abreast of the new situation of reform and the open door". In the first place, he asked them to devote most of their energies to legislation and the perfection of policies on the basis of investigation and research. Making use of Deng Xiaoping's thesis that "the fundamental task of socialism is to develop productivity", Gao said: "In order to further liberate artistic productivity, we should step-by-step build up a set of scientifically ordered policies. This is a key issue bearing on whether China's culture and art can enjoy long-term steady and harmonious development." (Gao Zhanxiang, "Wenhua lingdao gongzuo yao shiying gaige kaifangde xin xingshi"—"The Cultural Leadership Must Keep Abreast of the New Situation of Reform and the Open Door", *RMRB*, 28 July 1986).

Second, cultural leaders should strengthen their sense of reform. They should protect and support reformers in the cultural sphere as economic leaders did in their sphere. As to how to carry out reform, Gao suggested that the focus at present should be placed on reform of the system of leading bodies, and on the management of art performance organizations, both of which were vital to artistic productivity.

Third, cultural leaders should enhance their sense of strategy. They should have a strategy that enables culture to develop harmoniously with the country's politics and economy. This ambitious vice-minister emphasized: "Marxism is an open science. In the situation of reform and the open door, a strategy for cultural development must be carried out under the guidance of the principle of reform and the open door. It should not only aim at present needs, but also cater to the future, the world, and modernization. In creating a cultural development strategy, therefore, we should not only consider the cultural causes at home but also exchanges with international culture. This will be beneficial to the early vitalization and prosperity of Chinese literature and art" (ibid.).

Finally, Gao Zhanxiang asked cultural leaders to strengthen their sense of service. With a spirit of devotion to the arts, they should set a fine example and do their jobs "actively, with initiative and creativity" (ibid.).

The above proposals were raised at a national meeting of directors of cultural departments and bureaux convened by the Ministry of Culture in July 1986, the first important gathering of China's cultural leaders since the appointment of Wang Meng as minister of culture. These proposals, perhaps high-sounding, indicated that the new cultural leaders did want to achieve something—they wanted, as they announced, to "strive for a long, steady development of literature and art in China" (this was their "strategic guiding thought"). Accordingly, one of their important tasks was, in Wang Meng's words, to understand and carry out "comprehensively and accurately" the Party and the government's principles and policies for literature and art in the new historical period ("An Interview with Wang Meng", *RMRB*, 13 July 1986).

文化民族主义
wenhua minzuzhuyi
(cultural nationalism)

See "xin baoshouzhuyi" (neo-conservatism) and "minzuzhuyi" (nationalism).

文化热
wenhua re
(culture craze)

After the end of the GPCR there was the so-called "political reflection" (zhengzhixing fansi). As a result, "scar literature", "reflection literature", and "reform literature" appeared in the literary field. As a development of the "political reflection", for several years from the latter half of 1984 there was a great mass fervor in what was called a "cultural reflection" (wenhuaxing fansi) or an "intense search for culture". A number of cultural issues, some very important, such as "tradition and modernization" and "China and the West", were hotly debated. By the end of 1986, the term "culture" was extremely popular in academic circles.

Some of the major events during the period were as follows:

The Chinese Culture Academy was founded by Tang Yijie, a professor at Beijing University.

A forum on the history of Chinese culture in recent times was held in Zhengzhou city, Henan province.

The first forum on a comparative study of Eastern-Western cultures was held in Shanghai, and then a center was set up there.

The first seminar on Chinese culture was held in Beijing, with a number of famous scholars at home and abroad participating.

The Institute of Confucius Study was founded in Beijing.

A culture study salon was founded in Wuhan city, Hubei province; similar organizations also appeared in Guangzhou, Xi'an, and Shanghai.

A discussion for coordination in the comparative study of Eastern-Western cultures was held in Shenzhen city, Guangdong province.

A seminar on traditional Chinese culture and modernization was held in Huangshi city, Hubei province.

Three discussions were held successively in Wuhan on the history of the Ming and the Qing dynasties.

The first international forum on Chinese culture was held in Shanghai, sponsored by Fudan University.

The editorial board of the "Culture: China and the World" series was established in Beijing, with Gan Yang as editor-in-chief and Yang Zhouhan, Li Zehou, and Pang Pu as advisors.

The second forum on a comparative study of Eastern-Western cultures was held in Hangzhou city, Zhejiang province.

At the same time, a number of other universities, academies of social sciences, as well as national and local magazines and newspapers were involved in the discussions.

Furthermore, several municipal governments, such as those of Shanghai and Guangzhou, showed great interest in their own local cultural development strategy. They sponsored a number of forums discussing their long-term plans for cultural development.

In literary circles, "root-seeking" literature (xungen wenxue) emerged. There were a number of outstanding works, both as a product and an expression of the intense search for cultural "roots" (xungen re), providing marvelous food for meditation in the people's "cultural reflection". Interestingly, in various literary experiments, two seemingly contradictory phenomena—the search for "roots" and the quest for "modernism" (xiandai re)—co-existed. Some even wanted to make the two extremes meet: the classical taste of the Orient and the modern taste of the West, or, furthermore, to achieve a transcendence of both.

The mass fervor was dubbed by some scholars as the "Second New Culture Movement" (di'er ci xinwenhua yundong), for it had something in common with the

"New Culture Movement" of the "May 4th" period. During the few years, various views and theories, both ancient and modern, Chinese and foreign, became popular on stage one by one, or, very often, all together, usually drawing attention from the audience. Again, like what happened during the "May 4th" period, an anti-tradition trend, together with the "ideological trend of Westernization" (xihua sichao), became the mainstream of the fervor. Of great significance was the general acceptance of "pluralism" (duoyuanzhuyi) or "pluralistic openness" (duoyuan kaifangxing) among China's academic circles, which later became a signboard for "academic freedom", "creative freedom", and "political freedom". The fervor, in fact, was part of the ideological trend of "liberalization". Many so-called "cultural *élite*" (wenhua jingying) made efforts to build up their *élite* culture (jingying wenhua). They tried to expand their own independent "public sphere" (gonggong kongjian) and set up a "civil society" (minjian shehui), something suspicious and unacceptable to the authorities. No wonder the fervor was suppressed during the 1987 anti-liberalization campaign. Though it re-emerged in the summer of 1988, most conspicuously with the *River Elegy (Heshang)*, a television political commentary series broadcast on national and local television stations, it was eventually stopped by the June 4th Incident of 1989. In the post-1989 criticism and repudiation campaign, many "cultural *élite*" were attacked as "*élite* of turmoil" (dongluan jingying) for their involvement in the "May Tempest" of 1989. See also "*Heshang* shijian" (*River Elegy* Incident), "xungen re" (intense search for "roots"), "xinshiqi wenxuede duoyuan fazhan" (pluralistic development of the literature of the new period), and "ziyouhua" (liberalization).

文化殖民主义
wenhua zhiminzhuyi
(cultural colonialism)

See "zhimin wenhua" (colonial culture) and "minzuzhuyi" (nationalism).

文化中国
wenhua Zhongguo
(cultural China)

From the mid-1980s on, "cultural China" has been a popular topic among Chinese scholars at home and abroad.

"Cultural China" refers to the "Greater China culture circle" (da Zhonghua wenhuaquan). According to Du Weiming, a scholar of Confucianism at Harvard University, the term "cultural China" can be explained by what he defines as its "three worlds": the first world consists of mainland China, Taiwan, Hong Kong, Macao, and Singapore; other Chinese communities all over the world constitute the second world; and all other people who have something to do with Chinese affairs constitute the third world (See Du Weiming, "'Wenhua Zhongguo' yu huayi zhishifenzide 'ziwo yishi'"—"'Cultural China' and Chinese Intellectuals' 'Consciousness of Self'", *Shijie ribao,* 22 Sept. 1991).

In addition to "cultural China", there are two other related concepts—"political China" (zhengzhi Zhongguo), i.e., the "Greater China political circle" (da Zhonghua zhengzhiquan), and "economic China" (jingji Zhongguo), i.e., the "Greater China economic circle" (da Zhonghua jingjiquan). Though the three concepts may co-exist, cultural studies not only infiltrate but also transcend politics and economics. Distinct from "political China" and "economic China", both of which reflect and are mainly interested in current realities, "cultural China" embodies a higher-level ideal.

"Cultural China" is relevant to the situation today because since ancient times, Chinese have tended to emphasize culture more than politics. Many scholars agree that Chinese culture of several thousand years should be solid ground on which mainland China and Taiwan can start a process of reunification. Significantly, this suggestion seems to have been accepted by political leaders on the two sides of the Taiwan Straits. In the sixth point of his eight-point proposal of 30 January 1995 concerning reunification, Jiang Zemin, CCP general secretary and PRC president, proposed for the first time that Chinese culture should be an important foundation for peaceful reunification. On 8 April 1995, Lee Teng-hui, as chairman of the National Unification Council, Republic of China, published his "six-point proposal" in response to Jiang. In its second point, Lee said that exchanges between the two sides of the Taiwan Straits should be strengthened on the basis of Chinese culture.

To questions such as "whither Chinese culture", "how to reconstruct Chinese culture", and "what should be the core of cultural China or Chinese culture identified and recognized by all", universally convincing answers are not simple. The difficulty of this question is that in mainland China today three major cultures—traditional Chinese culture, Marxist-Leninist culture (or revolutionary culture), and modern Western culture—coexist, clash, and coalesce. But many scholars have tried—and will certainly keep doing so—to provide some food for thought. For instance, Fu Weixun, a scholar of Chinese philosophy teaching in America, suggested "ten levels of the value of life" (Fu Weixun, *"Wenhua Zhongguo" yu Zhongguo wenhua—"Cultural China" and Chinese Culture,* Taipei, Dongda, 1988, p. 91). Some scholars are very optimistic about traditional Chinese cultural values chiefly characterized by Confucianism. They find them compatible with "nationalism", "egalitarianism", and "secularism", the three major modern concepts of value developed in the West since the Renaissance. Moreover, "globalization", as a general trend in today's world, can be seen to be predicated on and directed by the traditional Confucian ultimate concern (zhongji guanhuai), the Confucian ideal of "Great Harmony" (datong) in the world. According to such scholars, traditional Chinese cultural values may not only unify China but also become the mainstream of world culture in the twenty-first century. It is in this sense that the twenty-first century is regarded as the "Chinese century".

While this perspective seems inspiring, they warned, the road will be long and difficult. For the Chinese intellectuals in the mainland, Taiwan, and overseas, most relevant at the moment is to stop unnecessary arguments over "political identification" (zhengzhi rentong), a long-standing issue caused by past and current CCP-KMT struggles. They should make a joint effort to exploit the spiritual resources characteristic of the Chinese nation. See also "ruxue disanqi" (Confucianism in its third stage of development) and "Taiwan wenti" (Taiwan issue).

文化专制主义
wenhua zhuanzhizhuyi
(cultural autocracy)

This is a term used by post-Mao critics to describe the rule of the Lin Biao clique and the Gang of Four in cultural fields during the GPCR. Later, "cultural autocracy" was also regarded as a characteristic of Mao's regime. See "wuchanjieji zhuanzheng" (dictatorship of the proletariat).

文化性反思
wenhuaxing fansi
(cultural reflection)

See "wenhua re" (culture craze) and "fansi" (reflection).

文体年
wenti nian
(year of style)

1987 was said to be the "year of style" in mainland China. Literary criticism began to focus on the aesthetic form of literature. All aspects of literary creation—perspective of narration, structural form in the awareness of time and space, structure of literary language, artistic modes, and ways of expression—were enthusiastically researched and discussed. New features of literary criticism emerged. See also "fangfalun nian" (a year of methodology).

文学对现实的超越
wenxue dui xianshide chaoyue
(transcendence of literature over reality)

See "wenxue zhutixing" (subjectivity of literature).

文学对象主体性
wenxue duixiang zhutixing
(subjectivity of the object of literature)

The three most important components of the subjectivity of literature are: the subjectivity of the object of literature (characters in a literary work), of its creator (its author), and of its receptor (its reader or critic). The object of literature includes nature, history and society; but only man is its fundamental object. To affirm the subjectivity of the object means to affirm the position of man as the subject (zhuti diwei), and his image as such (zhuti xingxiang), in the structure of the literary object. Man as the referent in literature has a dual nature: to the writer, he is an objective existence which is to be known; whereas in relation to the environment (society) in which he lives, he is an existence as the subject that is capable of understanding his environment. A writer, therefore, should not treat his/her characters as either playthings or idols. Instead, he must see them as living, independent individuals who have a consciousness and values of their own, behaving according to their feelings and sense of logic.

There are three situations in which the subjectivity of the object of literature will be lost: 1. when the history of a character's internal development is written off because of the influence of the "theory of the environment as the decisive factor" (huanjing jueding lun); 2. when the living individuality of a character is replaced by abstract class nature, and literature is no longer a study of man but only a "semiotic of class" (jieji fuhao xue); and 3. when profound struggles within a character's soul are covered up by superficial outer conflicts. According to Liu Zaifu, who devised the above summation, all this is due, fundamentally, to the writer ignoring man's position and values, not acknowledging that "man is the goal" (Liu Zaifu, "On the Subjectivity of Literature", *WXPL,* 6:18, Nov. 1985).

If a writer fully respects the subjectivity of his referent, an "unexpected" effect will take place: the writer will be led by the characters he produces, even to the extent of their defying his own will. Liu Zaifu thus makes the following pronouncements: the more talented a writer is, the more he is powerless before his characters; the more inferior a writer is, the more he can control his characters; the more a work succeeds, the more its author is enslaved by his characters; and the more a work fails, the more its author can dispose of his characters.

Liu also adds that both the writer and the characters he creates are both active and passive. The whole process of creation is a dialectical movement of the activity and passivity of these two subjectivities. Hence, the more a writer is in an active state when engaged in creation, the more he is passive before his characters; the more the creator brings his own subjectivity into play, the more he is occupied by the subjectivity of his object.

In order to make what he calls the "reverse law" more convincing, Liu quotes François Mauriac (1885-1970), the French Nobel Prize winner, and Hegel. He feels quite satisfied with his discovery. As he says, the "reverse law" offers an explanation for eccentric, elusive characters as found in some famous literary works. The "theory of world outlook as the decisive factor" (shijieguan jueding lun)—a long-held irrefutable Marxist view that a writer's world outlook can decide everything in his creative activities—is found to be untenable.

Liu Zaifu complained that for a very long time contemporary Chinese literature generally suffered from the loss of subjectivity. It was high time, he proclaimed, to restore and affirm this subjectivity, and to explore how to realize it. He asked writers to return to their characters their subjectivity, their due position as a subject. But the philosopher Wang Ruoshui reminded Liu that the loss of man's subjectivity is not merely a literary issue. In the first place, it is an issue of reality. Therefore, essentially, it should not be expected to be solved with a literary means. When in reality man is enslaved by power, money, institutions, ideology, and habits, a writer's task is to describe this state of alienation as truthfully as possible. He should protest against it and call for an awakening of man's self-awareness so as to restore man's position in actual struggles (Wang Ruoshui, *Behind Hu Yaobang's Stepdown,* HK, Mingjing, 1997). See also "wenxue zhutixing" (subjectivity of literature).

文学对象主体性的失落
wenxue duixiang zhutixingde shiluo
(loss of the subjectivity of the object of literature)

See "wenxue duixiang zhutixing" (subjectivity of the object of literature).

文学规律论争
wenxue guilü lunzheng
(1986 debate on the law of literature)

One of the issues in the 1986 debate initiated by Chen Yong, a Party cultural official, was that of the extrinsic and intrinsic laws of literature.

When discussing trends in literary studies in recent years, Liu Zaifu underlined the following "shift" as a significant change: "A shift has taken place from extrinsic to intrinsic, that is, from the concentration on inspecting the extrinsic laws of literature to a deep-study of its intrinsic laws" (Liu Zaifu, "Expanding the Scope of Thinking in Literary Research", *WXZTX,* p. 5). In the past, Liu said, China's literary studies had focused on extrinsic laws, that is, on the relationships of literature to the economic base and to ideological forms in the superstructure, such as the relationships between literature and politics, between literature and social life, and between the writers' world outlook and their creative methods. In recent years, stress has shifted to intrinsic laws, such as the aesthetic features of literature, the interrelations of various key elements within literature as well as the modes of construction and laws of movement of the various literary genres. In short, it was a return to literature itself.

In his article—"Problems Concerning Methodology in the Study of Literature and Art"—published in the authoritative *Red Flag* in mid-April 1986, Chen Yong condemned Liu Zaifu's view on the extrinsic and intrinsic laws of literature. After quoting Liu's passage, Chen reminded people that, though Liu was not the first person to regard Marxist basic principles of literature and aesthetics as so-called "extrinsic laws", a statement such as Liu's, so point-blank and detailed, was rare. From the Marxist point of view, Chen noted, many of the relationships listed by Liu did in fact determine the nature, content, and direction of literature and art. Instead of being "extrinsic laws", they were "precisely the most fundamental and most profound intrinsic laws of literature and art" (Chen Yong, "Problems Concerning Methodology in the Study of Literature and Art", *WXZTX*, p. 127).

Since "extrinsic laws" and "intrinsic laws" of literature became an important theoretical issue with which Chen Yong formed his major arguments, critics began to focus on them. As they pointed out, Chen's assertion that the relationships between literature and the economic base, between literature and politics, and between literature and social life were Marxist "aesthetic principles", the "most fundamental and most profound intrinsic law of literature and art" revealed his ossification. It is general knowledge that, in the field of literary study, people divide extrinsic and intrinsic laws of literature into two categories of study and that different schools emphasize different directions, which is quite normal and even necessary. The study of both categories, of course, constitute the main theoretical structure of a book, such as *Theory of Literature* by René Wellek and Austin Warren. In this regard, Wang Chunyuan, a literary critic, explained: "Extrinsic laws" is not a derogatory term implying something contemptible. It is only a comparative term, to be taken together with "intrinsic laws". All these pairs—extrinsic and intrinsic laws, outward and inward relationships, and universal and specific laws—mean the same thing; they refer to the different relation, position, and function of one thing in a different system (see Wang Chunyuan, "Wenxuede waibu guilü he neibu guilü"—"The Extrinsic and Intrinsic Laws of Literature", *WYB*, 16 Aug. 1986).

Hong Yongping, a young master's student, tried to explain this in terms of semantics and logic. After elaborating on what are the intrinsic laws of literature and what are the extrinsic laws, Hong added that, on the one hand, there is no absolute dividing line, or impassable chasm, between intrinsic and extrinsic laws; in this case, a dialectical relationship of the unity of opposites applies. What is an inward relationship to one thing can be regarded as an outward relationship to another; what is regarded as an inward relationship in a big system can be an outward relationship in a small system. On the other hand, since all things have an essential formulation of their own, extrinsic laws cannot play the role of intrinsic laws, and an understanding of extrinsic laws cannot replace the discovery of intrinsic laws. Hong Yongping countered Chen Yong's allegation that his opponents talked about aesthetic traits without a "grasp of the socio-ideological attributes of literature", in a way that these traits were "separated" from the politico-economic conditions of a specific age, from actual life, and from what he asserted to be the basic concept that literature and art are a reflection of life. Hong accused Chen of deliberately leading the discussion into absurdity. He asked: Where can one find such a condition which is so pure with so many "separations"? And where can one obtain a "scientific explanation" of universal laws with "separation" from all those concrete traits, those specific laws? If the "separations" are not absolute but relative, he said, they are acceptable and tenable in terms of scientific methodology. One should know not only that all things are universally interrelated and in the process of movement, but also that they are distinct from one another and have their relative rest and isolation. Otherwise, "one will fail to grasp the specific forms of things and fall into relativism", Hong concluded (Hong Yongping, "Makesizhuyi yu wenyi guilü wenti"—"Marxism and the Laws of Literature and Art", *WXPL,* 4:4-11, July 1986).

Xu Junxi, a literary critic, said that, rather than the "replacement" theory (daiti shuo) proposed by Chen Yong as a way of solving problems concerning "intrinsic laws" of literature and art by historical materialism, he endorsed Liu Zaifu's "transfer" theory (zhuanyi shuo)—literary study undergoing a transfer from outwards to inwards and returning to literature itself. He concluded that Chen had actually done nothing to develop Marxist aesthetic theory (Xu Junxi, "Ye tan wenyide zhutixing he fangfalun"—"Also on Literary Subjectivity and Methodology", *WYB*, 21 June 1986, reprinted in *WXZTX,* pp. 219-26). Cheng Ma, another critic, held a similar view. He simply regarded Chen Yong's article as a symbol of the "end" of an outdated mode of literary criticism (Cheng Ma, "Yi zhong wenyi piping moshide zhongjie: yu Chen Yong tongzhi shangque"—"The End of a Mode of Literary Criticism: A Discussion with Comrade Chen Yong", *Wenlunbao*, 21 July 1986, reprinted in *WXZTX*, pp. 292-98). Sun Shaozhen listed three reasons why he concluded that Chen Yong had gone astray in his theoretical research (Sun Shaozhen, "Chen Yong tongzhi zai lilunshang wuru qitude san ge yuanyin"—"The Three ReasonsWhy Chen Yong Went Astray in His Theoretical Research", *Wenlunbao*, 21 Sept. 1986).

At the Yangzhou Forum on the Study of Literature and Art and Its Methodology held in April 1985, participants enthusiastically heralded what they called "a favorable turn" (da zhuanji) in the sphere of Chinese literary study. As Liu Zaifu summed up, the new trend displayed itself in six respects: 1. The emphasis in research had begun to shift from the extrinsic laws of literature to its intrinsic laws. 2. Literature had begun to be studied from many angles, such as aesthetics, psychology, ethics, history, and anthropology, and not only from the single angle of philosophical epistemology or of political class theory. 3. There had been a shift from micro-analysis (of isolated authors or works) to systematic macro-synthesis, so that the historico-philosophic sense had increased. 4. Narrowly confined research in the past had become open, constantly drawing nourishment from other countries' literary theories and from achievements in other disciplines, including the natural sciences. 5. Literature had begun to be regarded as a dynamic process, and the contingent factors in that process had begun to be emphasized. 6. Research not only involved literature; stress had begun to be laid on its creative subject (writer) and the subject of art receptor (reader, critic). (See Qian Jing, "Ji Yangzhou wenyixue yu fangfalun wenti xueshu taolunhui"—"A Comprehensive Account of the Yangzhou Forum on the Study of Literature and Art and Its Methodology", *WXPL,* 4:50, July 1985).

The 1986 debate on the law of literature served as an example of the "favorable turn" in the sphere of Chinese literary study. See also "shehuizhuyi xianshizhuyi" (socialist realism) and "xinshiqi wenxuede duoyuan fazhan" (pluralistic development of the literature of the new period).

文学批评家的三层超越
wenxue pipingjiade san ceng chaoyue
(three-level transcendence of literary critics)

See "yishu jieshouzhede zhutixing" (subjectivity of art receptor).

文学体现人的本质力量
wenxue tixian rende benzhi liliang (literature embodies man's essential force)

See "wenxue zhutixing" (subjectivity of literature).

文学向内转
wenxue xiang nei zhuan ("inward turning" of literature)

There were two 1986 and 1987 debates concerning the "inward turning" of literature and the nature of literature and its place in the superstructure, which resulted from Lu Shuyuan's two articles, "On the "Inward Turning" of the New Period Literature" ("Lun xinshiqi wenxuede 'xiang nei zhuan'", *WYB*, 8 Oct. 1986), and "Earth and Clouds" ("Dadi yu yunni", *WYB*, 11 July 1987). Respectively, they were in essence a continuation of the debate on Liu Zaifu's subjectivity theory. See "wenxue zhutixing" (subjectivity of literature).

文学研究应以人为思维中心
wenxue yanjiu ying yi ren wei siwei zhongxin (man should be the center of thinking in literary research)

See "wenxue zhutixing" (subjectivity of literature).

文学政治化
wenxue zhengzhihua (politicization of literature)

See "rang wenxue shi wenxue" (let literature be literature) and "xinshiqi wenxuede duoyuan fazhan" (pluralistic development of the literature of the new period).

文学主体性
wenxue zhutixing (subjectivity of literature)

Liu Zaifu suggested in July 1985 that a research system of literary theory and literary history be built with "man" as the center of thinking (Liu Zaifu, "Wenxue yanjiu ying yi ren wei siwei zhongxin"—"Man Should Be the Center of Thinking in Literary Research", *WYB*, 8 July 1985). In November 1985 and January 1986, his long treatise "On the Subjectivity of Literature" was published in two successive issues of *Literary Review*, of which he was the editor-in-chief ("Lun wenxuede zhutixing", *WXPL*, 6:11-26, Nov. 1985, and 1:3-20, Jan. 1986, reprinted in *WXZTX*, pp. 54-116). In this treatise, Liu Zaifu complains that for a very long time contemporary Chinese literature has suffered from a loss of subjectivity. It is high time, he proclaimed, to restore and affirm this subjectivity, and to explore how to realize it. That was why he discussed these issues—the subjectivity of the object of literature (characters in a literary work), of the creator (its author), and of the receptor (its reader or critic).

Man's subjectivity is Liu Zaifu's general theoretical premise in dealing with the subjectivity of literature. First Liu points out that man is the object as a kind of existence and at the same time the subject when in action, in his practice. Hence man's "dual attributes" of passivity (shoudongxing) and activity. Liu Zaifu thus explained: "As an objective entity, man manifests his passivity, that is, he is conditioned by certain natural and social relations. As a human being in action, he manifests his activity, that is, he acts and controls the outer world with his will, ability, and initiative. That we emphasize subjectivity means we emphasize man's activity, will, ability, and initiative, his strength, the position and value of the subjective structure in the movement of history" ("On the Subjectivity of Literature", *WXPL*, 6:11-12, 1985).

Man's subjectivity consists of experiential subjectivity (shijian zhutixing) and spiritual subjectivity (jingshen zhutixing). There are two basic points, accordingly, in emphasizing subjectivity in literary creation. First, man should be seen as man, as the subject of practice in the movement of history. He should be regarded as the master of history, and not simply as a thing, a cog, or a screw in the political or economic machine; nor is he to be considered as a link to be manipulated in the class chain. Second, stress should be placed on man's spiritual subjectivity, on the dynamic role, autonomy, and creativity of his spiritual world. History is a process of movement during which the outer universe of the objective world and the inner universe of man's spiritual being integrate with each other.

The subjectivity theory of literature, in short, affirms that literature embodies man's essential force (Wenxue tixian rende benzhi liliang), which, consequently, leads to the affirmation of the transcendence of literature over reality (wenxue dui xianshide chaoyue). In the history of modern Chinese literary theory, Hu Feng was one of the few theorists to advocate this idea openly, but he was tragically silenced. In the 1980s, Liu Zaifu, who continued on the path of Hu Feng's literary thought, exposed thirty-year historical mistake. Of course, as He Xilai, then deputy director of the Literature Institute of CASS, said, Liu's theory of the subjectivity of literature should not be simply considered the same as Hu Feng's "subjective fighting spirit" (zhuguan zhandou jingshen). Liu's theory shared with Hu's theory only a certain historical origin, which mainly displayed itself in the category of "creative subject". Hu was unclear about the other two categories of subjectivity expounded upon by Liu—"subjectivity of the object" and "subjectivity of the receptor". As a result of his painful reflection over the systematic deviation in the past several decades, Liu's theory was characterized by "profound historical meaning and contemporary consciousness" (He Xilai, "Duiyu dangqian woguo wenyi lilun fazhan taishide jidian renshi"—"My View on the Current Situation in Chinese Literary Theory", *Wenyi zhengming*, 4, 1986, extracted and reprinted in *XHWZ*, 10:150, 1986).

Thirty years ealier, Hu Feng's literary idea about the "subjective fighting spirit" had been severely attacked as "subjective idealism" (zhuguan weixinzhuyi)—a serious label indicating an anti-Marxist position. Now some people wished to cast Liu Zaifu in the same light. Fortunately, they failed, at least in 1986. In defense of Liu's theory on the subjectivity and the transcendence of literature, Yang Chunshi, a critic, argued vigorously that Liu's theory was not, as Chen Yong (Liu's chief opponent) alleged, "subjective idealism" marked by a "separation from social practice". On the contrary, it was an achievement obtained in light of the Marxist theory of practice. Marxist philosophy, as seen by Yang, is that of subjectivity on the basis of the theory of practice. It justifies man's essential force which forms and develops in social practice. Man's subjectivity (on the basis of practice), on the one hand, is restricted by the socio-historical conditions he has created and by his social relations. On the other hand, and more importantly, it can, with its inherent demand for freedom and with its practical ability, transcend the restriction and promote both the development of history and of itself. The Marxist philosophy of subjectivity and practice, therefore, as Yang noted, is also a philosophy of transcendence, in light of which historical materialism is formed. As a complement to Liu Zaifu's theory, Yang Chunshi proposed the thesis of what he called "sufficiency in subjectivity and in transcendence" (chongfen zhutixing he chongfen chaoyuexing), as the two essential characteristics of literature and art (see Yang Chunshi, "Lun wenyide chongfen zhutixing he chaoyuexing"—"Sufficiency in Subjectivity and in Transcendence for Literature and Art", *WXPL,* 4:19-24, July 1986).

In the opinion of He Xilai, the subjectivity of literature is a philosophical formulation of humanism in the field of literature (wenxue zhutixing shi rendaozhuyi zai wenxue lingyuzhongde zhexue biaoda). By raising the theory of the subjectivity of literature, Liu Zaifu carried on the theory expounded upon by Ba Ren and Qian Gurong, which had been criticized in the 1950s. Liu also developed the more recent meditations and introspections of Zhou Yang, Wang Ruoshui, and others over the problems of humanism. The key to changing literary concepts, He Xilai said, lies in a correct treatment of humanism. To stress respect of man in the relationship between literature and social life, to stress the respect of the writer in the relationship between literature and its creation, and to stress the respect of the receptor in the relationship between literature and its appreciation—all these are permeated with a humanistic spirit. An emphasis on benevolence in terms of the content of literature is also relevant (He Xilai, "My Views on the Current Situation in Chinese Literary Theory", *XHWZ,* 10:151, 1986).

Liu Zaifu, as he himself admitted, was much influenced by Li Zehou's "philosophy of subjectivity" (zhuti zhexue, as elucidated in Li's 1979 book *A Critique of the Critical Philosophy (Pipan Zhexuede Pipan*, Beijing, Renmin, 1979). The difference was that Liu stressed humanism, while Li tried to play it down. But neither Liu nor Li dealt with the concept of "alienation". Because of this, in Wang Ruoshui's opinion, their theories were somewhat out of line with reality (see Wang Ruoshui, *Behind Hu Yaobang's Stepdown*).

Nevertheless, as hailed by many critics in 1986, Liu's theory about the subjectivity of literature was a systematic challenge to Mao's 1942 *Yan'an Talks*, a breakthrough from the old system of literary theory and the fulcrum of a new one. Its vital significance can be seen in the following three aspects:

1. A big step forward on the right track, it emphasizes the thesis "Literature is the study of man", and enables people to better understand the intrinsic essence of literature.

2. While actively expanding the thesis "Literature is the study of man", it further opens up the thesis, greatly widening people's field of vision and tremendously promoting an adjustment and renewal of the basic frame of literary theory.

3. Since Liu Zaifu's theory grasps subjectivity, the crucial quality by virtue of which literature is called literature, it is certain that it will vigorously infiltrate all other spheres of the whole system of literary theory.

After the June 4th Incident of 1989, Liu Zaifu had to live in exile in the United States. His theory about the subjectivity of literature was subject to "mass criticism" (dapipan)—a political attack—with critical articles numbering nearly 100. Quoting Hegel's description about history, Liu found the attack to be a "farce" *(Farewell to Revolution,* p. 201). See also "zhuti zhexue" (philosophy of subjectivity) and other entries concerning the subjectivity of literature and humanism.

文学主体性是人道主义在文学领域中的哲学表达
wenxue zhutixing shi rendaozhuyi zai wenxue lingyuzhongde zhexue biaoda

(the subjectivity of literature is a philosophical formulation of humanism in the field of literature)

See "wenxue zhutixing" (subjectivity of literature).

文学的阶级性
wenxuede jiejixing
(class character of literature)

In the late 1920s, there was a debate between Lu Xun and Liang Shiqiu as to whether or not literature has a class character. Lu's essay, "The Class Character of Literature" ("Wenxuede jiejixing", *Yusi,* v. 4, 34, 1928, reprinted in *XWX,* 2, p. 175), fully expresses his view on this issue. During the Mao period, this was often cited in literary research.

In the 1979-81 "human nature" discussion, critics in favor of the concept of a "common human nature" tried to re-explain Lu Xun's essay. They asserted that it was a misunderstanding of Lu Xun if one reached the conclusion that he was of the opinion that human nature amounted to class character. When attacking Liang Shiqiu and others' views on human nature, Chen Jianyu, a critic, said, Lu Xun put forth many incisive ideas about the class character of literature and class content in human nature. But he did not deny the existence of a common human nature. On the contrary, he explicitly expressed his disapproval of any denial of a common human nature. Later, Ni Moyan, another critic, further suggested that Lu Xun, while admitting that human nature as expressed in a human being's dispositions, feelings, etc. bore a class character, did not forget to point out that class character was not the only element in human nature. There were non-class factors as well, which Lu Xun referred to as a "common human nature". In short, Ni held that Lu Xun considered human nature as the "integration of a human being's class and non-class (including innate) characters", and thereby his was a "comprehensive view of human nature", which was "in conformity with a Marxist theory of human nature" (Ni Moyan, "Xuexi Lu Xun guanyu renxingde lunshu"—"A Study of Lu Xun's Expositions of Human Nature", *WYB,* 20, 1981, reprinted in *XHWZ,* 12:156-61, 1981).

文学的三重意义
wenxuede san chong yiyi
(a three-layer meaning of literature)

During the humanism discussion in the first half of the 1980s, many writers and critics expounded upon what they understood to be literature's humanistic meaning. Dai Houying, the author of the controversial novel *Humanity!,* was one such person. After having been fiercely attacked in the 1983 campaign to "eliminate spiritual pollution, Dai, like many other writers, still firmly adhered to her stand on humanism. In an article explaining her literary views, published in the first month of 1986, she suggested a three-layer meaning of literature—literature truly worthy of its description as the "study of man". First, as she saw it, literature conveys the author's taste of life. Second, it is a human being's cry of agony, a symbol of depression. And, finally, the highest aim and purpose of literary creation is to strive for the perfection of man (Dai Houying, "Jie lu zai ren jing, wo shou xie wo xin"—"I Built My Hut in a Zone of Human Habitation; I Write My Ideas and Feelings with My Hands", *WXPL,* 1:61, Jan. 1986). See also "ershishiji bashiniandai zichanjieji rendaozhuyi xuanyan" (the declaration of bourgeois humanism in the 1980s) and "rendaozhuyi lunzheng" (humanism debate).

文学的外部规律和内部规律
wenxuede waibu guilü he neibu guilü
(extrinsic and intrinsic laws of literature)

See "wenxue guilü lunzheng" (1986 debate on the law of literature).

文艺八条
"wenyi batiao"
(Eight Articles on Work in Literature and Art)

At a forum on the Party's work in literature and art held from 1 to 28 June 1961 by the PCC Propaganda Department, participants discussed a document drafted by Zhou Yang and others entitled "Suggestions Concerning Current Work in Literature and Art" ("Guanyu dangqian wenxue yishu gongzuode yijian cao'an").

In December 1961, Lu Dingyi, then director of the Propaganda Department, revised the document and changed its ten articles to eight, hence name: "Wenyi Batiao"—"Eight Articles on Work in Literature and Art". In April 1962, the PCC Propaganda Department finalized the document, and circulated it among literary and art circles. This document was regarded asa measure to check the Party's "Left" mistakes in the fields of literature and art. See also "wenyi wei zhengzhi fuwu" (literature and art serve politics).

文艺不能脱离政治
wenyi buneng tuoli zhengzhi
(literature and art cannot be divorced from politics)

See "wenyi wei zhengzhi fuwu" (literature and art serve politics).

文艺不能有任何限制
wenyi buneng you renhe xianzhi
(literature and art must be free from any restriction)

See "Zhao Dan yizhu" (Zhao Dan testament) and "wenyi wei zhengzhi fuwu" (literature and art serve politics).

文艺不再从属政治
wenyi buzai congshu zhengzhi
(literature and art are no longer subordinate to politics)

See "wenyi wei zhengzhi fuwu" (literature and art serve politics).

文艺从属政治
wenyi congshu zhengzhi
(literature and art are subordinate to politics)

See "wenyi wei zhengzhi fuwu" (literature and art serve politics).

文艺立法
wenyi lifa
(legislation on literature and art)

See "chuangzuo ziyou" (creative freedom) and "wenyi wei zhengzhi fuwu" (literature and art serve politics).

文艺沙皇
wenyi shahuang
(the "Tsar" of Chinese literary and art circles)

See "Zhou Yang beiju" (tragedy of Zhou Yang).

文艺是阶级斗争的工具
wenyi shi jieji douzhengde gongju
(literature and art are tools of class struggle)

In April 1979, a month after the publication of Liu Binyan's article "On 'Writing about the Dark Side' and 'Being Involved in Life'", the long-held Marxist thesis that "Literature and art are tools of class struggle" began to be questioned—in *Shanghai Literature* in an article entitled "Redefine Literature and Art" written by the magazine's own commentators. The thesis had long been regarded as unquestionable, not only because it was endorsed by many Marxist theoreticians but also because it had been favored by such important writers as Maxim Gorky and Lu Xun. Indeed, any lack of faith in it would have inspired indignation in those who believed themselves to be Marxists, as it did, on this occasion. For example, there were two articles in opposition to the view in "Redefine literature and art" in the June 1979 issue of *Shanghai Literature*: "A Letter to the Commentators of *Shanghai Literature*" (Wang Dehou, "Gei *Shanghai Wenxue* pinglunyuande yifeng xin") and "'Literature and Art Are tools of Class Struggle': A Scientific Slogan" (Wu Shichang, "'Wenyi shi jieji douzhengde gongju' shi ge kexuede kouhao"). But the magazine, confident of its position, carried a number of supporting articles in its June and July issues, obviously hoping that its readers would be more convinced and disengage themselves from the "tool" theory.

In the discussion, many emphasized the "fact" that it was the Gang of Four who had most vigorously advocated that "Literature and art are tools of class struggle" as the basis of their literary theory, on which they developed a whole set of principles for literary and art creation, such as the "three prominences" (santuchu), "proceeding from the political line" (cong zhengzhi luxian chufa), and "theme taking the lead" (zhuti xianxing). With this theory, they brutally destroyed many artistic works, and even an entire cultural and art heritage, no matter whether it was Chinese or foreign, that they deemed unable to function as a "tool of class struggle". On the other hand, they recommended and protected mediocrity, so long as it met their need for class struggle, with the result that literature and art became a tool to "usurp Party and state power". Furthermore, critics pointed out, it was because the "tool" theory had not yet been subjected to due criticism that some writers and artists, while opposing the Gang politically, still imitated their models artistically.

These critics knew that "Literature and art are tools of class struggle" was simply another expression of Mao's idea about literature and art being subordinate to and serving politics, and that was what they opposed. See also "wenyi wei zhengzhi fuwu" (literature and art serve politics) and "shehuizhuyi xianshizhuyi" (socialist realism).

文艺是整部革命机器中的齿轮
wenyi shi zhengbu geming jiqizhongde chilun
(literature and art are cogs and wheels in the whole revolutionary machine)

In his 1942 *Talks at the Yan'an Forum on Literature and Art*, Mao attributed to Lenin the idea that literature and art should be cogs and wheels in the whole revolutionary machine. However, according to a new official translation of Lenin's article in question, "Party Organization and Party Publications" ("Dangde zuzhi yu dangde chubanwu"), published in the 22nd issue of *Red Flag* in 1982, what Lenin was referring to was not "literature" (wenxue) but "publications" (chuban wu). See "wenyi wei zhengzhi fuwu" (literature and art serve politics).

文艺为工农兵服务
wenyi wei gong nong bing fuwu
(literature and art serve workers, peasants, and soldiers)

See "wenyi wei zhengzhi fuwu" (literature and art serve politics).

文艺为人民服务，为社会主义服务
wenyi wei renmin fuwu, wei shehuizhuyi fuwu
(literature and art serve the people and socialism)

See "wenyi wei zhengzhi fuwu" (literature and art serve politics).

文艺为无产阶级政治服务
wenyi wei wuchanjieji zhengzhi fuwu
(literature and art serve proletarian politics)

See "wenyi wei zhengzhi fuwu" (literature and art serve politics).

文艺为政治服务
wenyi wei zhengzhi fuwu
(literature and art serve politics)

With efforts by Qu Qiubai, Deng Zhongxia, Yun Daiying, and other radical intellectuals, Marxist aesthetic thought was first introduced to China in 1923. Thereafter, it was widely propagated throughout the country, a country whose rich cultural heritage could not help it to deal with its present predicament. Later, in the 1930s, the theory that "Literature and art are subordinate to politics" (Wenyi congshu zhengzhi) arrived from the Soviet Union, and was immediately accepted by the CCP-led literary and art circles. As a logical result, after the founding of the PRC, there gradually appeared a thesis—and the thesis itself became a slogan—"Literature and art serve politics".

Interestingly, neither Marx, Engels, Lenin, nor Stalin had ever explicitly raised this slogan or thesis, which originated with Mao Zedong. As an important quotation from Mao, the following statement was published on 23 May 1967, on the 25th anniversary of Mao's *Yan'an Talks:* "Literature and art serve the workers, peasants, and soldiers, proletarian politics, and socialism" (*CL,* 1:4, 1968).

But Mao had conceived of the idea earlier. It can be traced back to 1940 when he wrote "On New Democracy", in which he had said: "As for the new culture, it is the ideological reflection of the new politics and the new economy which it sets out to serve."

Two years later, Mao delivered his *Yan'an Talks*. This work essentially deals with the relationship between literature and art on the one hand and politics on the other. It seemed to Mao that in the contemporary world all culture, literature, and art belong to definite classes and are geared to definite political lines. There is no such thing as art for art's sake, art that stands above classes, art that is detached from or independent of politics. He expounded upon why and how literature and art serve politics, though he did not use the phrase "serve politics". He regarded the arts as "cogs and wheels" in the "whole revolutionary machine". Therefore, in judging a work, political criteria should be put first.

Ever since before the founding of the PRC, because of the overwhelming authority of Mao's *Yan'an Talks* and Mao Zedong Thought at large, the idea of literature and art serving politics was accepted and reaffirmed in Party documents or theoretical articles. For a long time, no one in China's literary and art circles dared to challenge it openly or directly. But it did not mean that they did not do anything about it. In the early 1960s, for instance, a voice could be heard about the negative consequences of too rigid an application of the theory. In order to reduce writers' and artists' resentment, Zhou Enlai suggested what he called a "socialist orientation" (shehuizhuyi fangxiang) for literature and art: "Serve workers, peasants, and soldiers; the laboring people; and the masses of the people under the system of the proletarian dictatorship." (see Zhou Enlai, "Zai wenyi gongzuo zuotanhui he gushipian chuangzuo huiyishangde jianghua"—"Talk at the Forum on Party Work in Literature Art and the Conference on the Creation of Feature Films", *WYB*, 2, 1979, reprinted in *HQ*, 3:2-16, 1979; extracts trans. in *CL*, 6:83-95, 1979). Under Zhou's aegis, the Party document "Eight Articles on Literature and Art" was stipulated to include criticism of the over-simplification of literature and art's political function. The 23 May 1962 *People's Daily* editorial, "Serve the Broadest Masses of the People" ("Wei zui guangdade renmin qunzhong fuwu") even went so far as to produce a somewhat modified slogan, as conspicuously indicated in its title. Zhou Enlai and his supporters were trying to harmonize the two theses of "serving politics" and "serving the people". They did not forego the "serve politics" demand. But even so, from 1963 onwards, all their attempts were denied and attacked.

The slogan "Literature and art serve politics" was shouted most loudly during the GPCR years when the ultra-Left political line was dominant. It was clear that only by a change in the CCP's political line would bring about a change in the slogan. And also, since the relationship between arts and politics had been established by the highest leader of the CCP, any change would have to come from the top of the Party. After the downfall of the Gang of Four, such a change occurred when Deng Xiaoping returned to power at the 1978 3rd Plenum. To the delight of Chinese writers and artists, Deng's new political line adopted at the Plenum made possible a serious re-examination of this long-held Marxist slogan and its eventual rejection, which occurred not long after the 1979 4th National Congress of Chinese Writers and Artists.

As for Chinese writers and artists, the relationship between arts and politics was a key issue they had long been eager to see tackled, even if preliminarily. They began to challenge the slogan openly, encouraged by the current favorable political climate, and also inspired by the vitality of the "new period literature", which provided a striking contrast to the literary barrenness of the previous thirty years. Then, at the emotionally charged Congress (where there was a free and democratic atmosphere, something they had not experienced since 1949), they spent much time discussing the arts-politics relationship, carrying it to a high tide. After the close of the Congress, the discussion continued among literary and art circles on a much larger scale. Their repeated appeals finally were heard. Deng Xiaoping, after considering the whole matter very carefully, issued an important decision about China's literature and art at a meeting of cadres called by the PCC on 16 January 1980. He said: "We will drop the slogan that literature and art are subordinate to politics, because it is too easily used as a theoretical pretext for arbitrary intervention in literary and art work. Long practice has proved that this slogan has done more harm than good to the development of literature and art" *(SWD,* p. 240).

It was noted that Deng failed to mention his view about another slogan— "Literature and art serve politics". A few days later when Zhou Yang got a chance at the Forum on Script Writing (held in Beijing from 23 January to 13 February 1980), he revealed that the two slogans in fact were really two parts of one slogan and they would no longer be valid.

In his speech, entitled "Emancipate the Mind, Truthfully Present Our Times", ("Jiefang sixiang, zhenshide biaoxian womende shidai", *WYB,* 4:2-10, 1981), Zhou Yang expounded again on the relationship between arts and politics from what he believed to be a Marxist point of view, so as to make the change more impressive. As ideological forms which are subordinate to the economic base, he said, literature and art indeed often depend on politics as an intermediary because politics is the concentrated expression of the economy. But the economic base is the ultimate motive force that pushes literature and art forward. Politics, literature, and art belong to the superstructure, whose development is ultimately decided by the economic base. Quoting from Marx on the thesis that "The mode of production of material life conditions the social, political, and intellectual life process in general" (this is often cited from Marx's Preface to *A Critique of Political Economy*), Zhou Yang said that this basic definition of historical materialism given by Marx made it very clear that Marx (and also Engels) emphasized that the economic base plays a decisive role in the development of the history of society.

This discovery of historical materialism, according to Zhou Yang, brought about a great revolution in the social sciences and it was as important as the theory of surplus value. In order to propagate it, however, the decisive role of the economic base was unduly stressed to the point that some people even came to believe it played an exclusive role. It seemed as if the economic situation was cause, active by itself alone, and all else had only a passive effect. In this regard, Engels in his later years made a self-criticism, saying that both he and Marx, in emphasizing the decisive role of the economic base, neglected the roles of other factors: for example, the interaction between the economic base and the superstructure and among the various aspects of the superstructure as well as the relative independence of every aspect, ideology in particular, of the superstructure in its historical development.

As if it were a first revelation, Zhou Yang pointed out that, although Marx and Engels attached great importance to the enormous influence of politics upon literature and art, neither of them said that arts should be subordinate to politics. In fact, arts are not only influenced by politics, but also by other forms of ideology, such as philosophy, social ethics, and religion. There is a close relationship among the various aspects of the superstructure and they influence one another. At the same time, every form of ideology retains a relative independence in its historical development. The conclusion Zhou reached was that, if one oversimplifies and vulgarizes the very complicated relationships between the superstructure and the economic base as well as among the various aspects of the superstructure, one does not follow true materialism but goes in the opposite direction. Therefore, he found it a very good thing that the PCC had decided to dethrone the long-held slogan "Literature and art serve politics".

For many writers and artists, Zhou Yang's explanation was unnecessary. The end of the slogan was no doubt good news. It coincided with the first creative surge of the "new period" in 1979-80. For those who wanted to preserve the old slogan, however, Zhou Yang's was not a convincing argument. They pointed out that the independence of arts from politics is relative (with which Zhou Yang agreed). Furthermore, they noted, when the proletariat takes over power, the arts-politics relationship should be essentially different from before. Since the people have now already become "the masters of the country", politics is thus a people's politics as are literature and art. The "unity" of the arts-politics relationship, therefore, should greatly reduce the relative independence of literature and art. Besides, no one can deny that politics, including political ideology, political systems, and political institutions, most directly express the economic base. In particular, state power, the core of the superstructure, is the first ideological force governing human beings. In a society where classes have not yet perished, political struggle will exert a strong influence on social life and all aspects of ideology.

The above-said "unity" theory was nothing new and had proved in the past several decades to be very harmful to the development of genuine literature and art. But a view such as this was no doubt in conformity with orthodox Marxism, which was so far still officially held as correct. As an alternative, those who wanted to preserve the old slogan suggested that it would be all right if the concept of politics were appropriately enlarged. In fact, in Marxist language, the definition of politics is very broad and it can vary according to different environments, different times, and different interpreters. Significantly, CCP leaders seemed to follow this suggestion, and in a clear way. At the 1980 Forum on Script Writing, Zhou Yang told the participants that what the PCC had decided was to use "serving the people and socialism" to replace "serving politics" as a new general slogan for literature and art. The new slogan, which is dubbed the "double service" principle (shuangwei fangzhen), was later published in the 26 July 1980 *People's Daily* editorial entitled "Literature and Art Serve the People and Socialism" ("Wenyi wei renmin fuwu, wei shehuizhuyi fuwu").

Both Deng's and Zhou Yang's speeches delivered at the 1979 4th Congress of Writers and Artists had in fact already indicated that there is no essential difference between "serving politics" and "serving the people and socialism". Deng told the participants that the overriding nationwide task was to work singlemindedly for the "four modernizations" and that therefore the basic standard for judging writers and artists' works was whether they helped or hindered the effort to modernize *(SWD,* pp. 201-2). Accordingly, Zhou Yang urged that literature and art should answer the needs of socialist modernization. They should describe and reflect whatever is good for the modernization effort, whatever directly and indirectly inspires people to dedicate themselves to building socialism in China. The reason is, he said, to realize the four modernizations is at the present time the urgent demand and strong wish of the whole Chinese nation, entirely in keeping with the interests of the proletariat and the broad masses of the people, and is thus the "most important politics" (Zhou Yang, "Be Both Successors and Pioneers, Bring Literature and Art into Flower in the New Period of Socialism", *RMRB,* 20 Nov. 1979). Zhou Yang's statement can be interpreted in the following way: to serve politics, at the present time, means to serve the four modernizations, and to serve the four modernizations means to serve the people and socialism; or, the other way round, to serve the people and socialism means to serve the four modernizations and also means to serve politics. No wonder, therefore, Zhou Yang added in his speech at the 1980 Forum on Script Writing that the proposals put forth at the 1979 4th Congress—Chinese literature and art should help nurture a new generation of socialist-minded people, elevate the people's spiritual life, help improve and develop socialist society, and meet the public's growing needs for cultural life—could be considered as an elaboration of the new slogan.

Moreover, CCP leaders always stress that literature and art cannot be divorced from politics. When declaring the end of the slogan that literature and art are subordinate to politics, Deng said: "Of course this doesn't mean that they can be divorced from politics. That is impossible. Every progressive and revolutionary writer or artist has to take into account the social effects of his works and the interests of the people, the state and the Party. The fostering of a new socialist man means politics" (*SWD*, p. 240). In his speech greeting the 6th National Congress of Chinese Writers and Artists and the 5th National Congress of the CWA (both held in Beijing in December 1996), Jiang Zemin echoed Deng's view. He said that the practice of almost two decades had proved the "correctness" of the thesis that "Literature and art cannot be divorced from politics" (wenyi buneng tuoli zhengzhi). When a Party leader attaches so much weight to this thesis, the results are self-evident—he of course wants literature and art to continue serving his politics.

China's writers and artists are clear about there being no essential difference between the new and the old slogans, and the problem has not yet really been solved by replacing the old slogan with the new one. But they know what they want. In 1988, with respect to the relationship between politics and literature, Bai Hua described them as "beginning to go through the procedures of divorce" (Xu Jing, "Zhongguo zuojia fang fa de nan wang jingtou"—"Some Unforgettable Episodes during the Chinese Writers' French Visit", *JN,* 223:49, Aug. 1988). Liu Binyan modified this metaphor somewhat: "Literature and art do want to be divorced from politics. But politics is like an obstinate husband. He has no more love for you; but he deliberately refuses to start divorce proceedings, so as to keep you in a miserable state and always under his control" (ibid.). More significantly, in view of the "double service" principle being unsatisfactory, there has appeared a unique view which turns the new slogan "Literature and art serve the people and socialism" almost upside down. It is expressed as follows: "Socialism serves literature and art, and literature and art serve the people" (shehuizhuyi wei wenyi fuwu, wenyi wei renmin fuwu). This was advanced in 1995 by Sha Yexin, a well-known but sometimes controversial Shanghai-based playwright (see his *Jingshen Jiayuan—Spiritual Garden,* Shanghai, Shanghai Renmin, Jan. 1995). See also "shehuizhuyi xianshizhuyi" (socialist realism), "xinshiqi wenxue" (literature of the new period), and "xinshiqi wenxuede duoyuan fazhan" (pluralistic development of the literature of the new period).

文艺为最广大的人民群众服务 wenyi wei zui guangdade renmin qunzhong fuwu (literature and art serve the broadest masses of the people)

See "wenyi wei zhengzhi fuwu" (literature and art serve politics).

文艺与政治的关系本质上是文艺与人民的关系 wenyi yu zhengzhide guanxi benzhishang shi wenyi yu renminde guanxi (the relationship between arts and politics is in essence one between arts and the people)

See "xie zhenshi" (writing about reality) and "shehuizhuyi xianshizhuyi" (socialist realism).

文艺与政治关系的统一
wenyi yu zhengzhi guanxide tongyi
(the unity of the arts-politics relationship)

See "wenyi wei zhengzhi fuwu" (literature and art serve politics).

文艺与政治关系的相对独立性
wenyi yu zhengzhi guanxide xiangdui dulixing
(the relative independence of the arts-politics relationship)

See "wenyi wei zhengzhi fuwu" (literature and art serve politics).

文艺源于生活，低于生活
wenyi yuanyu shenghuo, diyu shenghuo
(literature and art have source in life and are on a lower plane than life)

See "zhengzhi biaozhun diyi, yishu biaozhun di'er" (political criteria first, artistic criteria second).

文艺源于生活，高于生活
wenyi yuanyu shenghuo, gaoyu shenghuo
(literature and art have source in life and are on a higher plane than life)

See "zhengzhi biaozhun diyi, yishu biaozhun di'er" (political criteria first, artistic criteria second).

文艺战线上的一场大辩论
wenyi zhanxianshangde yichang da bianlun
(a great debate on the literary and art front)

From 6 June through September 1957, together with three other cultural figures Chen Qixia, Feng Xuefeng, and Ai Qing, Ding Ling was scathingly criticized at successive enlarged meetings of the leading Party group of the CWA. Finally, at its 25th meeting (enlarged) on 16 September, Zhou Yang, on behalf of the Party, made a summation in his speech entitled "A Great Debate on the Front of Literature and Art" ("Wenyi zhanxianshangde yichang dabianlun", *RMRB*, 28 Feb. 1958), thus deciding the fate of Ding Ling and many other "bourgeois Rightists" in literary and art circles. Of course, there was no debate; it was a cruel political struggle, including a sectarian struggle, as Ding Ling pointed out many years later at the 1979 4th National Congress of Chinese Writers and Artists. See also "fan youpai yundong" (anti-Rightist campaign) and "wenyi wei zhengzhi fuwu" (literature and art serve politics).

文艺作品只起潜移默化的作用
wenyi zuopin zhi qi qianyimohuade zuoyong
(literature and art exert only an imperceptible influence)

See "shehui xiaoguo lun" (social effect theory).

文艺的无为而治
wenyide wuweierzhi
("governing by doing nothing that goes against nature" in literary and art fields)

In September 1979, Wang Ruowang, then an active Shanghai-based writer and critic (now living in exile in America as a dissident), expressed his wish that, in the fields of literature and art, the Party could "govern by doing nothing that goes against nature". The application of this ancient Taoist concept to modern Communist political life was no doubt very bold and even heretical. But Wang Ruowang could defend himself by denying that this was his invention. In fact, this idea can be traced to the 1962 talk by Chen Yi (1901-1972), then PRC vice premier. When speaking of how to exercise leadership, Chen said:

"It seems that there are many things that can be governed by doing nothing that goes against nature. If you insist on exercising leadership over everything, you will probably do a bad job; whereas, there are some things that may turn out to be better without your leadership. It should be understood that there is successful leadership and there is unsuccessful leadership. When you are sure that you can succeed, then go ahead; if you are not, you'd better let those who are experienced do it instead and just 'sit idly by and enjoy the fruits'." (Chen Yi, "Zai quanguo huaju, geju, ertongju chuangzuo zuotanhuishangde jianghua"—"Talk at the National Forum on the Writing of Spoken Drama, Opera, and Children's Plays", *WYB*, 7:7, 1979).

Moreover, Wang Ruowang tried to make sure that his words could not be interpreted as rejecting the Party leadership as a whole. He admitted that it was still necessary for cultural leaders to "make checks", the standards of which were the "four cardinal principles" and the Double Hundred policy. However, he did express his scorn for and rejection of those leaders who, standing high above the masses and indulging in arrogance, treated it as their prerogative to reprimand and punish. He even asserted: "Both in China and in other countries, in both modern and ancient times, there have been golden ages of literature and art, but none of them was formed by harsh and all-encompassing interference and administrative orders given by leading organs of the state" (Wang Ruowang, "Tan wenyide 'wuweierzhi'"—"On 'Governing by Doing Nothing That Goes against Nature' in Literature and Art", *HQ*, 9:47-48, 1979). See also "wenyi wei zhengzhi fuwu" (literature and art serve politics).

文艺的真实性与政治性的统一
wenyide zhenshixing yu zhengzhixingde tongyi
(identity of the truthfulness and political nature of literature and art)

See "xie zhenshi" (writing about reality).

文艺界牛鬼蛇神总後台
wenyijie niuguisheshen zonghoutai
(general backer of all "monsters and demons" in literary and art circles)

See "Zhou Yang beiju" (tragedy of Zhou Yang) and "wenyi wei zhengzhi fuwu" (literature and art serve politics).

文字改革
wenzi gaige
(reform of written Chinese)

The reform of written Chinese was first put forward by radical intellectuals during the New Culture Movement in the 1910s and 1920s. Mao Zedong, then a young man, seemed to have been much influenced by their proposals, and he was in favor of the reform thereafter. In 1940, he said: "Written Chinese must be reformed, given the requisite conditions" ("On New Democracy", *SWM,* 2, p. 382). After the PRC was founded, the reform was carried out step-by-step in accordance with Mao's instructions. A campaign was launched, following the establishment of the Association for the Reform of Written Chinese in Beijing on 10 October 1949. It was agreed that the new written Chinese was not only "the sole powerful tool for wiping out illiteracy" but also "a powerful tool for developing a new culture" *(RMRB,* 11 Oct. 1949). In December 1954, the Association was reorganized as the Committee for the Reform of Written Chinese. It had three main tasks (as stipulated in a report by Premier Zhou Enlai in January 1958): 1. To simplify the Chinese written language, that is, to simplify the number of strokes and words of the traditional Chinese written language, so as to facilitate the teaching, learning, and application of the language. (Three batches of simplified characters have so far been issued respectively in 1956, 1964, and 1977. The last batch was however withdrawn soon after its issuance because many characters were found unacceptable, simplified in an improper way.) 2. To popularize modern standard Chinese (putonghua) which takes the Beijing pronunciation as its standard and makes it the common language of the Han nationality. 3. To work out and put into effect a system of phonetic alphabets for the phonetic annotation of the Chinese language, and to promote the teaching and learning of modern standard Chinese.

After several decades of work supported by the government, there were remarkable achievements in the fulfillment of these tasks. Problems, however, still remain, a major one being that the achievements do not seem to be recognized by all Chinese—those in Taiwan in particular. See also "wenhua Zhongguo" (cultural China" and "Taiwan wenti" (Taiwan issue).

文字狱
wenzi yu
(literary inquisitions)

In Chinese history, "literary inquisitions" were common in the Ming and the Qing dynasties when many intellectuals lost their lives because of what they had written (which was often deliberately distorted). Misfortune could suddenly befall anyone who might be loyal to the emperors. It was therefore impossible to know whether one had committed a "crime" which one might subsequently be accused of having committed. Moreover, punishment could involve a great number of people, such as the "offender's" wife, parents, children, relatives, teachers, students, and friends. Sometimes the victims even included the publishers, salesmen, readers, and collectors of the works in question. After the GPCR, this was a popular topic among Chinese intellectuals because many of them had undergone similar experiences in the recent past.

问题小说
wenti xiaoshuo
(problem fiction)

When Liu Xinwu's short story "Class Teacher" was published, some people held that it went against the spirit of socialist literature, and labeled it "exposure literature". It was also called "problem fiction", on the grounds that it was wrong to raise problems since there was "no problem in our socialist country". For some people, the task of socialist literature was to praise socialism, to depict "advanced models", to extol the glorious deeds of the workers, peasants, and soldiers. The term "problem fiction" was also used by some other critics in a complimentary sense. They held that short stories should take the lead in discussing the problems existing in society. Liu Xinwu, nevertheless, did not seem satisfied with the term, regardless of the definition. See also "shanghen wenxue" (scar literature) and "xinshiqi wenxue" (literature of the new period).

无产阶级爱国主义
wuchanjieji aiguozhuyi
(proletarian patriotism)

See "aiguozhuyi" (patriotism) and "minzuzhuyi" (nationalism).

无产阶级革命功利主义
wuchanjieji geming gonglizhuyi
(proletarian revolutionary utilitarianism)

See "zhengzhi biaozhun diyi, yishu biaozhun di'er" (political criteria first, artistic criteria second) and "wenyi wei zhengzhi fuwu" (literature and art serve politics).

无产阶级革命事业接班人
wuchanjieji geming shiye jiebanren
(successors to the proletarian revolutionary cause)

See "geming jiebanren" (revolutionary successors) and "hongweibing" (Red Guards).

无产阶级革命事业接班人的五个条件
wuchanjieji geming shiye jiebanrende wu ge tiaojian
(five requirements for successors to the proletarian revolutionary cause)

See "geming jiebanren" (revolutionary successors) and "hongweibing" (Red Guards).

无产阶级革命造反派
wuchanjieji geming zaofanpai
(proletarian revolutionary rebels)

See "zaofan youli" (it is right to rebel).

无产阶级国际主义
wuchanjieji guojizhuyi
(proletarian internationalism)

See "shijie geming" (world revolution) and "aiguozhuyi" (patriotism).

无产阶级民主
wuchanjieji minzhu
(proletarian democracy)

See "minzhu jizhongzhi" (democratic centralism).

无产阶级民主集中制
wuchanjieji minzhu jizhongzhi
(proletarian system of democratic centralism)

See "minzhu jizhongzhi" (democratic centralism).

无产阶级司令部
wuchanjieji silingbu
(proletarian headquarters)

See "wen'ge" (Cultural Revolution) and "huaiyi yiqie, dadao yiqie" (suspect all, overthrow all).

无产阶级文化大革命
wuchanjieji wenhua dageming
(Great Proletarian Cultural Revolution)

See "wen'ge" (Cultural Revolution).

无产阶级文化革命旗手
wuchanjieji wenhua geming qishou
(standard-bearer of the proletarian cultural revolution)

In 1964, a rectification campaign was carried out in literary and art circles, following the two stern instructions Mao issued respectively in 1963 and 1964. Jiang Qing was especially adept at making use of this political climate, enjoying Mao's support as his wife. She made her début at the July 1964 Forum of Theatrical Workers Participating in the Festival of Beijing Operas on Contemporary Themes, in which she delivered a speech "On the Revolution in Beijing Opera". In November 1965, together with Zhang Chunqiao and Yao Wenyuan in Shanghai, she directed scathing fire at the re-written historical play *Hai Rui Dismissed from Office*, thus sounding the clarion call for the "Great Proletarian Cultural Revolution". In early 1966, Lin Biao brought her into the limelight, praising her as "full of ideas" and "very sharp politically and knowledgeable about art". Chen Boda even put her on a par with Dante of the Renaissance and Lu Xun of the May 4th Movement. He was the first to say that "the heroic standard-bearer is none other than Jiang Qing". Similarly, Zhang Chunqiao alleged that the "model revolutionary dramas personally nurtured by Jiang Qing have ushered in a new era for proletarian literature and art". And Yao Wenyuan agreed by acclaiming that Jiang's leadership in revolutionizing Beijing opera had "set a shining example for the revolution in literature and art". Thus, from the very beginning of the GPCR, Jiang Qing was promoted as its "standard-bearer".

On 6 October 1976, this "heroic standard-bearer" was arrested. Then, in January 1981, she was convicted of leading the now condemned GPCR. Her death sentence with a two-year reprieve and forced labor was later commuted to life imprisonment. On 14 May 1991, she committed suicide. See also "jiyao" ("Summary") and "wen'ge wenyi" (GPCR literature and art).

无产阶级只有解放全人类，才能最後解放自己
wuchanjieji zhiyou jiefang quanrenlei, caineng zuihou jiefang ziji
(only by emancipating all mankind can the proletariat achieve its own final emancipation)

See "shijie geming" (world revolution).

无产阶级专政
wuchanjieji zhuanzheng
(dictatorship of the proletariat)

Phenomena of class struggle were discovered long before Marx's time, but it was Marx who formed the doctrine of the dictatorship of the proletariat on the basis of the theory of class struggle. Mao developed Marxism, establishing the doctrine of "continuing the revolution under the dictatorship of the proletariat" (wuchanjieji zhuanzhengxiade jixu geming) and broadening the scope of class struggle (jieji douzheng kuodahua). The following ideas—"The fundamental question of revolution is political power", "Political power grows out of the barrel of a gun", and "Continuing the revolution under the dictatorship of the proletariat"—are the basic points in Mao's doctrine about state power.

Mao first described his dictatorship as the "people's democratic dictatorship" ("renmin minzhu zhuanzheng" or "renmin minzhu ducai"). In his well-known article "On the People's Democratic Dictatorship" ("Lun renmin minzhu zhuanzheng") published on 30 June 1949, Mao explained the concept. In the first PRC Constitution adopted in 1954, the "people's democratic dictatorship" was stipulated as the "state system" (guoti), which was expressed as follows: Under the leadership of the working class (through the CCP) and on the basis of an alliance of workers and peasants, the people's democratic dictatorship unites the whole nation to practice democracy among the people and to exercise dictatorship over their enemies. After the 1957 anti-Rightist campaign, with Mao's "ultra-Left" thought increasingly rampant and finally dominant in the whole Party, the term "people's democratic dictatorship" gradually disappeared, giving way to the term "dictatorship of the proletariat".

In his speech of 18 May 1966, Lin Biao, who was described as Mao's "good student", put forward the following thesis: "Political power is a power of suppression" (zhengquan jiushi zhenya zhi quan). It was hailed for a time as the most correct and most succinct summation of CCP theory about proletarian political power. During the GPCR, Mao called on his followers to overthrow the "bourgeois dictatorship" (zichanjieji zhuanzheng), which, he alleged, very obscurely, had been ruling his Communist regime. Mao's idea was developed into the thesis "Exercise an all-round dictatorship over the bourgeoisie" (dui zichanjieji shixing quanmiande zhuanzheng), which was first made public in an article published in the *People's Daily* on 6 November 1967. Entitled "Advancing Along the Road Opened Up by the October Socialist Revolution" ("Yanzhe shiyue shehuizhuyi geming kaipide daolu qianjin"), it was written in the name of the editorial boards of the *People's Daily*, *Red*

Flag, and the *Liberation Army Daily* to commemorate the 50th anniversary of the Soviet Union's October Revolution. Later, in a 1975 article, Zhang Chunqiao further expounded upon it as succinctly embodying the spirit and practice of the GPCR ("On Exercising an All-round Dictatorship over the Bourgeoisie"—"Lun dui zichanjiejide quanmian zhuanzheng", *HQ,* 4, 1975; *RMRB,* 1 Apr. 1975).

The "all-round dictatorship" thesis was considered to be an important component of the theory of "continuing the revolution under the dictatorship of the proletariat" when it was preliminarily formed in the 1966 Party document "May 16th Circular". One year later, the theory was first revealed to the public in an article to celebrate the first publication of the "May 16th Circular" in the *People's Daily* the previous day (Editorial Boards of the *People's Daily* and *Red Flag,* "Weidade lishi wenjian"—"A Document of Great Historic Significance", *RMRB,* 18 May 1967). In the article, which had been examined by Mao himself, the theory was praised as the "third great milestone in the history of Marxist development" (Makesizhuyi fazhanshishang disan ge weidade lichengbei).

On 6 November 1967, at the Beijing meeting to commemorate the 50th anniversary of the Soviet Union's October Revolution, Lin Biao enthusiastically and highly praised this theory. On the same day, in the article "Advancing Along the Road Opened Up by the October Socialist Revolution", the theory was summed up by six major points:

1. The Marxist-Leninist law of the unity of opposites must be employed in observing a socialist society;

2. During the historical period of socialism, there will still exist classes, class contradictions, class struggles, struggles between the two roads of socialism and capitalism, and the danger of capitalist restoration. In order to prevent the occurrence of a capitalist restoration and "peaceful evolution", the socialist revolution on the political and ideological fronts must be carried out through to the end;

3. The class struggle under the dictatorship of the proletariat is, in essence, still an issue of political power. The proletariat must exercise an all-round dictatorship over the bourgeoisie in the superstructure which includes all the cultural spheres;

4. The struggle between the two classes and the two roads in society will definitely find expression in the Party. The handful of those in power within the Party who take the capitalist road are bourgeois representative figures in the Party;

5. The most important form of continuing the revolution under the dictatorship of the proletariat is the great proletarian cultural revolution; and

6. The fundamental program of the great proletarian cultural revolution in the ideological sphere is "fighting one's self and criticizing and repudiating revisionism" (dousi pixiu).

At the CCP's 9th National Congress held in Beijing in April 1969, Mao's successor Lin Biao, as stipulated in the newly revised Party Constitution, hailed the "great victory" of Mao's theory of "continuing the revolution under the dictatorship of the proletariat" (see his "Report to the Ninth National Congress of the Communist Party of China", *RMRB,* 28 Apr. 1969; trans. in *CL,* 7:3-62, 1969).

This theory, regarded as the most comprehensive expression of Mao's idea about dictatorship, ultimately justified the GPCR. Or, conversely, the GPCR was an unprecedented practice of this theory.

After the end of the GPCR, Hua Guofeng still adhered to this theory, so as to show that he was Mao's true successor (see, for instance, his article "Carry the Continuing Revolution under the Dictatorship of the Proletariat Through to the End"—"Ba wuchanjieji zhuanzhengxiade jixu geming jinxing daodi", *RMRB,* 1 May 1977, *HQ,* 5:3-18, 1977). This, however, almost foreboded his failure. Suffice it to say that at that time the Chinese people used the term "feudal-fascist dictatorship" (fengjian faxisi zhuanzheng) to describe what they had experienced during the GPCR.

Notably, in May 1977, the *People's Daily* editors presented a report, obviously with a political purpose, which pointed out that Mao had never used the term "continuing the revolution under the dictatorship of the proletariat". Similarly, when the sentence "The proletariat must exercise an all-round dictatorship over the bourgeoisie in the superstructure which includes all the cultural spheres" was published in the 6 November 1967 article, it was printed in boldface, implying that it was a quotation from Mao. This was a fabrication of Chen Boda, then leader of the Central GPCR Group. Of course, since Mao had examined the article before it was published, it is correct to say that it enjoyed Mao's approval. (See Ling Zhijun and Ma Licheng, *Huhan: Dangjin Zhongguode Wu Zhong Shengyin—Five Voices in Present China,* Guangzhou, Guangzhou, Jan. 1999, pp. 113-14).

Two years later, Deng Xiaoping began to criticize the theory directly. He said: "Practice has proved that this formulation is wrong if it is construed—as it was when it was advanced—to mean 'seizing power from the capitalist-roaders', or making revolution by kicking aside the Party committees and toppling everything. As for making a new interpretation, that is something we can continue to study within the Party" *(SWD,* p. 190). Then in June 1981, when the 6th Plenum of the 11th PCC passed the "Resolution on Certain Questions in the History of Our Party since the Founding of the PRC" (*RMRB,* 30 June 1981), the theory of "continuing revolution under the dictatorship of the proletariat" was officially refuted. The resolution noted that the theory must be deleted from Mao Zedong Thought. It was determined to be preposterous, meaning that the CCP, as a ruling party that embodies the dictatorship of the proletariat, is to lead a revolution—and time and again—in which Party leaders at various levels and even the Party itself are targets of attack.

Deng, as CCP leader, of course could not abandon the dictatorship of the proletariat. On 30 March 1979 at a forum on the principles for Party theoretical work, Deng presented his well-known "four cardinal principles" (si xiang jiben yuanze), the second of which was "to uphold the dictatorship of the proletariat". He did not forget to explain, of course, that his had nothing in common with the "dictatorship" Lin Biao and the Gang of Four had exercised during the GPCR. One may note, interestingly, that when the "four cardinal principles" were written into the new CCP Constitution (adopted in September 1982 at the 12th CCP National Congress) and into the Preamble to the 4th PRC Constitution (adopted on 4 December 1982 at the 5th Session of the 5th NPC), the "dictatorship of the proletariat" was changed to the "people's democratic dictatorship".

As scholars have pointed out, a vital problem of the "dictatorship of the proletariat" is that it cannot prevent the occurrence of alienation in the ruling party and its leaders. Marx should be blamed for this. When he established his colossal ideological system, he evaded the issue of power alienation (quanli yihua)—which is as crucial as labor alienation (laodong yihua)—thus opening a broad road for autocracy to evolve into totalitarianism at its ultimate stage. That is why Marx has become the patron saint of all Communist tyrants (Zheng Yi, "Zuihoude tuteng: yuanjiaozhi Makesizhuyi qingsuan"—"The Last Totem: Squaring Fundamentalist Marxism", *Beijing zhi chun,* Jan. 1996).

Scholars find CCP's one-party dictatorship being exercised in today's China, no matter whether it is called the "dictatorship of the proletariat" or the "people's democratic dictatorship". They made an interesting historical comparison. "One doctrine, one party, and one leader" was a 1930s slogan used by the KMT under the leadership of Chiang Kai-shek (Jiang Jieshi, 1887-1975). What it meant was self-evident. At that time, Mao Zedong observed that the fatal problem of the KMT was its "one doctrine, one party, and one leader" policy, as in his 1940 articles "On New Democracy", "Ten Demands to the KMT", and "On New Democratic Constitutionalism". Today the fatal problem of the CCP is the same "one doctrine, one party, and one leader" policy. Hu Jiwei, former director and chief editor of the *People's Daily* and vice-chairman of the NPC Standing Committee, also shared this opinion. In an article written on 13 January 1998, he wrote that the KMT and the CCP had reversed their positions. After retreating to Taiwan, the KMT learned the lesson that its failure in China's civil war was the result of its totalitarian rule. The KMT started economic reform in the Chiang Kai-shek era and took the first steps towards political reform during Jiang Jingguo's (1910-1988) presidency. Mao Zedong, in contrast, completely changed after the CCP came to power in China. His actions brought many disasters to the country. For several decades, the Chinese people were living under the horror of three political charges: anti-Party, anti-socialism, and anti-Marxism-Leninism-Mao Zedong Thought, as a result of which many experienced extreme hardships, and others died tragically.

After Mao it was the Deng period; and now it is the Jiang Zemin period, but CCP's one-party dictatorship remains basically unchanged. Many Chinese hope to change such a dictatorship by peaceful means. In their recent appeals, they want to have a blueprint for an all-around political reform. This should include: making a law of political parties in which political parties, including the CCP, are subordinate to government power; keeping the army completely under the jurisdiction of the state; and holding direct elections.

There is a key question here: Can China be transformed into a democracy via one-party dictatorship? In the opinion of many Chinese dissidents, a one-class dictatorship will inevitably lead to a one-party dictatorship and then to a dictatorship by the individual. A multiparty system is the cornerstones of a constitutional democracy. Whether China becomes a constitutional democracy will largely depend on whether the Chinese people can establish a multiparty system and form true democratic parties representing the interests of different social strata. This view concludes that China cannot achieve democracy without the overthrow of the CCP's one-party dictatorship. Wang Ruowang a veteran dissident, even thus predicted: "Proletarian parties rose due to their opposition to tyranny and one-party dictatorship; they will perish with the one-party dictatorship of the Communist party and their own personal tyranny" ("Butong zhengjianzhede piping: Wang Ruowang tan zhengzhi gaige"—"Criticism from a Dissident: Wang Ruowang on Political Reform", *JN,* 227:65, Dec. 1988).

Some others think otherwise. At the New York press conference on 23 April 1998, Wang Dan, the recently released student leader of the 1989 pro-democracy movement, said that China could be transformed into a democracy via its one-party dictatorship. He based his conclusion on the grounds that the CCP could be transformed by being pushed forward by the trend of the times and the desire of the people. Wang was not alone. For example, Gan Yang, a Chinese politico-philosophical scholar, showed theoretically that it is possible to transform China into a democracy via various forms or stages of one-party rule (Gan Yang, "Build a Country with a United Constitutional Government Rooted in Individual Freedom and Rights"). His idea is based on Giovanni Sartori's theory of political parties: 1. China's transition from the Mao era to the Deng era can be seen as a transition from a one-party totalitarian polity to a one-party pragmatic polity; 2. The current Chinese system under Jiang Zemin, i.e., the nominal "multi-party cooperative system under the CCP leadership", is basically a pragmatic-hegemonic party polity; 3. The next feasible goal of China's political reform is a predominant party polity; and 4. In the long run when the predominant party polity becomes weak, a "single-party government" in a two-party system is still preferable to a multiparty coalition government.

Under China's current circumstances, Gan Yang suggested that the next feasible step that is key to establishing a constitutional democracy is to promote the transition from a pragmatic-hegemonic party polity to a predominant party polity. Such a transition will push the ruling party to become a electoral party or a parliamentary party. Simply put, a hegemonic party rules without an election, but a predominant party has absolute dominance in an election. If this transition can be achieved, it will mark the beginning of a new era of "electoral politics" or "parliamentary politics" in China. Although a predominant party polity is not a satisfactory conclusion, there is a consensus that it is a democratic system.

CCP leaders do not describe their rule as a one-party dictatorship. They claim that there exist eight "democratic parties" in China and all of them enjoy the CCP policy of "long-term co-existence and mutual supervision" (changqi gongcun, huxiang jiandu). What they claim being exercised in China (and exercised successfully) is a "multi-party cooperative system under the CCP leadership". This is a "new type" of relationship between political parties, which is not only an important political feature of the building of socialism with Chinese characteristics but also a new experiment in the history of the international socialist movement.

Regarding the one-party dictatorship issue, there was an episode (recorded in the autobiography of former CPSU General Secretary Mikhail Gorbachev) which may be of significance to CCP history. On the afternoon of 16 May 1989, when meeting Gorbachev, who was visiting China, Zhao Ziyang, CCP general secretary, asked the following rhetorical question: "Is it possible to exercise democracy and effectively eliminate corruption under the one-party system? If it is impossible, does it mean a multiparty system is imperative?" See also "zhengzhi gaige" (political reform).

无产阶级专政下的继续革命
wuchanjieji zhuanzhengxiade jixu geming
(continuing the revolution under the dictatorship of the proletariat)

See "wuchanjieji zhuanzheng" (dictatorship of the proletariat).

无政府主义思潮
wuzhengfuzhuyi sichao
(anarchist trend of thought)

See "huaiyi yiqie, dadao yiqie" (suspect all, overthrow all).

五把刀子
wu ba daozi
(five daggers)

In his "Report Concerning the Literary and Art Situation over the Last Few Years" (*WYB*, Supplement 1 & 2, 1955) presented to the PCC in July 1954, Hu Feng described the following five demands on writers made by the CCP authorities as "five daggers" sticking into their heads: 1. first of all writers must have a perfect and flawless Communist world outlook before they begin to write; 2. only the life of workers, peasants, and soldiers is considered to be real life; 3. one is allowed to write only after undertaking ideological remolding; 4. only certain old forms are considered acceptable national literary styles; and 5. only revolutionary struggles are treated as important subject-matter, and they must be presented as bright and forward-looking, not grim and depressing. On 20 January 1955, the PCC Propaganda Department called for a criticism of "Hu Feng Thought". In the concerned document, Hu Feng's ideas on literature and art were said to be "anti-Party and anti-people". See also "Hu Feng anjian" (Hu Feng case), "sixiang gaizao" (ideological remolding), and "wenyi wei zhengzhi fuwu" (literature and art serve politics).

五个并举
wu ge bingju
(five simultaneous developments)

See "liangtiaotui zoulu" (walk on two legs).

五个统一
wu ge tongyi
(five unifications)

See "zhuhou jingji" (duchy economy).

五个正确对待
wu ge zhengque duidai
(five correct treatments)

See "sanxin weiji" (crises of faith, confidence, and trust).

五爱
wu'ai
(five loves)

These are love for the motherland, the people, labor, science, and public property. Article 42 of the 1949 "Common Program" ("Gongtong Gangling") of the CPPCC stipulated that the "five loves" be put forth as a manifestation of the public spirit of the Chinese people (*RMRB,* 30 Sept. 1949). The Young Pioneers, a national organization for China's children, also adopted the "five loves" as its guiding spirit. Later, the "love of public property" was changed to "love of socialism". See also "aiguozhuyi" (patriotism).

五反运动
wufan yundong
(campaign against the "five evils")

The campaign against the "five evils"—bribery, tax evasion, theft of state property, cheating on government contracts, and stealing of economic information—was carried out in 1952 in capitalist industrial and commercial enterprises.

五好运动
wuhao yundong
("five-good" movement)

See "tuchu zhengzhi" (giving prominence to politics) and "sanhao" (three goods).

五好战士运动
wuhao zhanshi yundong
(movement of "five-good" soldiers)

See "tuchu zhengzhi" (giving prominence to politics).

五讲，四美，三热爱
wujiang, simei, sanre'ai
(five stresses, four points of beauty, and three loves)

On 25 February 1981, in response to the call of the PCC to build a "socialist spiritual civilization" (shehuizhuyi jingshen wenming), the All-China Federation of Trade Unions, the Central Committee of the Chinese Communist Youth League, the All-China Women's Federation, and six other organizations jointly issued the "Proposal for Unfolding Activities to Foster Socialist Decorum". They suggested activities to promote the "five stresses"—stresses on decorum (wenming), manners (limao), hygiene (weisheng), discipline (jilü), and morals (daode), and the "four points of beauty"—beautification of the mind (xinling), language (yuyan), behavior (xingwei), and the environment (huanjing). On 6 January 1983, the *People's Daily* published a commentary asking for a unity of the "five stresses" and the "four points of beauty" on the one hand and the "three loves" (love of the motherland, of socialism, and of the CCP) on the other. Thus, the ideological level of the former would be accordingly greatly elevated. On 30 March 1983, a "Central Committee in Charge of Activities of the Five Stresses, Four Points of Beauty, and Three Loves" was established in Beijing, with Wan Li, a CCP Politburo member, as its director.

Similarly, the army put forward the slogan of "four haves, three stresses, and two defy's" (siyou, sanjiang, liangbupa) in the February 1981 "Instructions on Strengthening the Youth Work in the Army", issued by the PLA General Political Department. The "four haves, three stresses, and two defy's" were: "to have lofty ideals, moral integrity, knowledge, and a strong physique; to stress appearance and bearing, manners, and sense of discipline; and to defy hardships and sacrifice". In January 1983, in keeping with the formulations in the documents of the CCP 12th National Congress on the building of a socialist civilization, the content of the slogan was revised to read as follows: "to have lofty ideals, moral integrity, general education, and sense of discipline; to stress appearance and bearing, manners, and hygiene; and to defy hardships and sacrifice".

五君子事件
wu junzi shijian
(five gentlemen incident)

See "chi butong zhengjianzhe" (dissidents) and "ziyouhua" (liberalization).

五篇哲学著作
wupian zhexue zhuzuo
(five philosophical works)

The five philosophical works refer to Mao's "On Practice" ("Shijian lun"), "On Contradiction" ("Maodun lun"), "Problems of Strategy in China's Revolutionary War" ("Zhongguo geming zhanzhengde zhanlüe wenti"), "Problems of Strategy in Guerrilla War Against Japan" ("Kang Ri youji zhanzhengde zhanlüe wenti"), and "On Protracted War" ("Lun chijiuzhan"). Chen Yun, a Party elder, suggested in 1981 that a study movement be promoted in the Party—mainly to study philosophy and these five philosophical works by Mao. As Chen recalled, when he came back to Yan'an from Moscow soon after the outbreak of the War of Resistance Against Japan (1937-45), Mao advised him on three occasions to study philosophy, emphasizing in particular the significance about "seeking truth from facts" (shishi jiu shi). As a result, Chen benefited greatly from the study.

Deng Xiaoping endorsed Chen's suggestion, as in his speech on 27 March 1981 to leaders of the PLA General Political Department, in which he called for opposing "wrong ideological tendencies" *(SWD,* pp. 356-59).

五七干校
wuqi ganxiao
(May 7 cadre schools)

See "wuqi zhishi" (May 7 directive).

五七指示
wuqi zhishi
(May 7 directive)

The "May 7 Directive" refers to a letter Mao wrote to Lin Biao on 7 May 1966, after examining the "Report on Further Developing Agricultural Production and Side-Occupations in the Armed Forces" submitted by the PLA General Logistics Department. Mao proposed in his letter a comprehensive plan for turning the whole country into what was understood to be "a great school of Mao Zedong Thought" (Mao Zedong sixiang da xuexiao), where all personnel, no matter whether they worked in the areas of agriculture, industry, the military, commerce, service professions, or Party and government organizations, must study politics, military affairs, and culture, and must take part in the criticism of the bourgeoisie, while also engaging in sideline work to supplement their regular professions. In this letter, which was later referred to as the "May 7 Directive", Mao asked students to carry out a revolution in education, so as to end what he said was the rule of schools by bourgeois intellectuals.

According to the "May 7 Directive", the first "May 7 cadre school" (wuqi ganxiao) was set up on 7 May 1968 in Liuhe, Qing'an county, Heilongjiang province. Since this school was highly appreciated by Mao, others soon mushroomed all over the country. A great number of cadres and intellectuals were sent to be "re-educated" by engaging in hard labor and living in deprived circumstances.

After the end of the GPCR, these schools gradually disappeared. A few years later, Mao's "May 7 Directive" was refuted as a "concentrated expression of the self-closed small-scale peasant consciousness". Sending cadres and intellectuals to "May 7 cadre school" was condemned as a form of political punishment.

五七一工程纪要
wuqiyi gongcheng jiyao
(571 Project Minutes)

This was allegedly an armed coup plan ("wuqiyi" is the homophone of "armed uprising") devised in Shanghai in March 1971 by Lin Liguo (Lin Biao's son who was then deputy director of the Office of Air Force Headquarters and deputy director of the Military Operations Department) and his diehard followers in the Air Force Headquarters, that is, key members of the so-called "United Task Fleet" (lianhe jiandui) under his leadership. The "Minutes" consisted of the following parts: The Necessity; The Basic Conditions; The Opportunity; The Strength; The Slogan and Guiding Principle; The Major Points in Implementation; The Policy and Tactics; and Security and Discipline. The "571 Project Minutes" have not been publicly released in mainland China, but in 1972 they were printed as an appendix to the PCC document under the file of "Zhong Fa (1972) No. 4".

The truth about the Lin Biao Incident is said to be unclear, as are the case about the "571 Project Minutes", which were part of the Incident. See also "Lin Biao shijian" (Lin Biao Incident).

五人帮
Wurenbang
(Gang of Five)

See "sirenbang" (Gang of Four) and "chedi fouding wen'ge" (complete negation of the GPCR).

五十年不变
wushinian bubian
(remain unchanged for fifty years)

See "yiguo liangzhi" (one country, two systems).

五四传统
wusi chuantong
(May 4th tradition)

On 4 May 1919, some three thousand Beijing students gathered in Tiananmen Square, protesting against the traitorous warlord government. The protest was responded to by people of all walks of life throughout the country, and developed into what was later called the May 4th Movement.

After the 1840-42 Opium War, China, which had always considered itself the Central Kingdom, gradually degenerated into a semi-feudal and semi-colonial country. The encroachment by foreign powers; the weak, incompetent, and corrupt administration of the Manchu Empire; the backwardness of the Chinese economy and of Chinese culture as contrasted strikingly with that of the modern West; the instability of society and the sufferings of the broad masses of the people—all these factors spurred Chinese intellectuals to come to the rescue of their country and their fellow countrymen. The May 4th Movement in 1919 (and the various revolutions and reform movements that preceeded and followed it) grew out of this situation.

The Movement was no doubt a great patriotic movement, characterized by a strong anti-imperialism and anti-feudalism sentiment. The CCP highly praises it, regarding it as marking the beginning of what is called the "New Democratic Revolution". In fact, ideologically, and even organizationally, the movement prepared for the founding of the CCP on 1 July 1921.

The May 4th Movement was the political expression of what is called the "New Culture Movement" which, as agreed by most historians, originated in the publication of the politico-cultural magazine *New Youth (Xin Qingnian).* Setting the feudal culture as its target of attack, the movement called for "Mr. Science and Mr. Democracy". In the sphere of literature and art, the new literature movement was born. Using new genres introduced from the West, a great number of writers and poets exposed the darkness of society, criticized evil, and expressed the desire of the people for a better life. A strong social consciousness, a clear awareness of the age, and a spirit of unequivocal love and hatred were characteristic of the critical, revolutionary temper of the May 4th literary tradition.

But the May 4th literary tradition, or the May 4th tradition at large, is a controversial issue. The May 4th Movement brought Marxism to China, and, at the same time, also introduced the ideological trend of Westernization (as characterized by the two banners of "democracy" and "science"). Some scholars, such as Lin Yusheng (professor of History at the University of Wisconsin) basically negate the May 4th Movement (see Lin Yusheng, *The Crisis of Chinese Consciousness: Radical Antitraditionalism in the May Fourth Era,* University of Wisconsin Press, 1979). For many Chinese, the May 4th Movement has not yet fulfilled its historical mission. Whenever they have a chance, they will evoke the "May 4th" spirit, first of all, its critical consciousness (pipan yishi), as can be seen in the 1989 pro-democracy movement. On 4 May 1989, on the 70th anniversary of the May 4th Movement, the "Autonomous Alliance of Beijing Students" (an organization of the demonstrators) announced a "May 4th Manifesto". It proclaimed: "Let us once more struggle and search together in the name of democracy, science, freedom, human rights, and the legal system." For the CCP as a ruling party, the critical consciousness of the "May 4th" can be very dangerous and must be suppressed. Jiang Zemin's 4 May 1998 speech at the grand celebration of Beijing University centennial *(Beijing daxue xuebao, shehui kexue ban,* 3:5-7, 1998) revealed the Party's vigilance. This was also a lesson the Party drew from the 1989 pro-democracy movement. See also "fan chuantong" (anti-tradition), "sixiang gaizao" (ideological remolding), "siwu yundong" (April 5th Movement), and "bajie minyun" (1989 pro-democracy movement).

五四文学传统
wusi wenxue chuantong
(May 4th literary tradition)

See "wusi chuantong" (May 4th tradition), "fan chuantong" (anti-tradition), and "shehuizhuyi xianshizhuyi" (socialist realism).

五四宣言
wusi xuanyan
(May 4th Manifesto)

See "bajiu minyun" (1989 pro-democracy movement).

五四运动
wusi yundong
(May 4th Movement)

See "wusi chuantong" (May 4th tradition).

五同
wutong
(five-togethers)

See "santuoli" (three divorced).

五位一体
wuwei yiti
(five positions in one body)

This refers to the structure of the People's Commune, which combined agriculture, industry, commerce, education and military affairs under unified leadership and management. See "renmin gongshe" (People's Commune).

五行生克制化律
wuxing shengke zhihualü
(law of promotion-restriction-inhibition-transformation in the Five Elements)

See "Kylin wenhua" (Kylin Culture).

五行学说
wuxing xueshuo
("Five Elements" theory)

See "Kylin wenhua" (Kylin Culture).

"五一六通知"
wuyiliu tongzhi
(May 16th Circular)

This refers to the document "Circular of the Central Committee of the CCP" ("Zhongguo Gongchandang Zhongyang Weiyuanhui tongzhi"), which was drafted under the supervision of Chen Boda. On 16 May 1966, after undergoing revision seven times by Mao, the CCP Politburo passed it and issued it to the whole Party as "Zhong Fa (66) 267". According to the "Circular", a new group in charge of the GPCR, with Chen Boda as its director, Jiang Qing as its first deputy director, and Kang Sheng as its advisor, was set up directly under the Politburo Standing Committee to replace the dissolved "Group of Five in Charge of the Cultural Revolution" headed by Peng Zhen. The "Outline Report on the Current Academic Discussion" ("eryue tigang"), a document made by the dissolved "Group of Five" and approved by the CCP's Politburo Standing Committee just three months earlier, was now fiercely attacked for containing "ten major errors". The "May 16th Circular", insinuating that Liu Shaoqi was "China's Khrushchev", called on the whole Party and the whole nation to struggle against leading bourgeois exponents who had sneaked into the Party, the government, the military, and various cultural circles.

The "May 16th Circular" was the programmatic document with which Mao started the GPCR. In fact, the next day when it was published in the *People's Daily* and other newspapers and broadcast by all the radio stations throughout the country, it became clear that a big storm was coming. 16 May 1966, the day of its issuance, is regarded as the formal beginning of the GPCR. See also "eryue tigang" ("February Outline Report") and "wen'ge" (Cultural Revolution).

五月风暴
wuyue fengbao
(May tempest)

See "bajiu minyun" (1989 pro-democracy movement) and "ziyouhua" (liberalization).

五只小风筝事件
wuzhi xiao fengzhen shijian
("five little kites" incident)

In 1981, Gao Xingjian, a prominent playwright and fiction writer, published his popular book *A Preliminary Discussion of Contemporary Narrative Techniques* (*Xiandai Xiaoshuo Jiqiao Chutan*, Guangzhou, Huacheng, 1981; extracts trans. in Stephen Soong and John Minford, eds., *Trees on the Mountain*, pp. 55-58). Though controversial, it was enthusiastically praised by Wang Meng, who published "A Letter to Gao Xingjian" ("Zhi Gao Xingjiande xin", *Xiaoshuo jie,* 2, 1982, reprinted in *WYLZJ,* pp. 557-61). Then, the editorial board of *Shanghai Literature* published the correspondence between Feng Jicai, Li Tuo, and Liu Xinwu, which discussed Gao's book and modernism at large ("Guanyu dangdai wenxue chuangzuo wentide tongxin"—"Letters Concerning Problems in Current Literary Creation", *SHWX,* 8:88-96, 1982, reprinted in *WYLZJ*, pp. 562-80). In his letter, Feng Jicai, a famous Tianjin writer (who was elected vice-chairman of the ACF at its 5th national congress in November 1988), compared Gao's book to a "little kite" in the open sky which brings joy to everyone. He even claimed that Chinese literature needed "modernism" (Feng Jicai, "Zhongguo wenxue xuyao 'xiandaipai'"—"Chinese Literature Needs 'Modernism'!" *SHWX,* 8, 1982). Gao's book and the letters of Wang Meng, Li Tuo, Liu Xinwu, and Feng Jicai were obviously unacceptable to some conservatives. They were dubbed "five little kites", and their publication was called the "five little kites" incident, which was held responsible for the "unhealthy trend" in the early 1980s, during which a number of writers and artists tried to observe, reflect, and comment on Chinese society with a social outlook and philosophical approach similar to that of some modernists in the West.

The event was of remarkable significance to the development of contemporary Chinese literature. With the joint effort of the five writers, modernist literature arrived in China advocating "the independence of the form" (xingshi duli), and no longer under the disguise of "realism in its broad sense" (guangyi xianshizhuyi), which had been necessary during the 1980 debate on Wang Meng's "stream-of-consciousness" fiction (yishiliu xiaoshuo). From then on, various experiments in the form appeared, such as "stream-of-consciousness", long sentences with no punctuation marks, space-time disorder (shi kong daocuo), mystic reality (mohuan xianshi), anti-plot (fan qingjie) and anti-motif (fan zhuti). See also "xinshiqi wenxuede duoyuan fazhan" (pluralistic development of the literature of the new period) and "yishiliude Zhongguo dailiren" (Chinese agent of the stream-of-consciousness).

五子登科
wuzi dengke
(five "honorable" treatments)

See "sanbu zhengce" ("three don'ts" policy).

武斗
wudou
(struggle by coercion or force)

See "quanmian neizhan" (full-scale civil war) and "wen'ge" (Cultural Revolution).

捂派
wupai
(cover-up faction)

See "fengpai" (tune-changers).

务实
wushi
(deal with concrete matters)

See "wuxu" (discuss principles or ideological guidelines).

务实会
wushi hui
(meetings to deal with concrete matters)

See "wuxu" (discuss principles or ideological guidelines).

务实外交
wushi waijiao
(pragmatic diplomacy)

See "Taiwan wenti" (Taiwan issue).

务虚
wuxu
(discuss principles or ideological guidelines)

Dealing with concrete matters relating to work, such as work quotas and business techniques, is called "wushi". Correspondingly, discussing principles, policies, theories, or ideological guidelines is called "wuxu", hence the terms "wushi hui" (meetings to discuss concrete matters) and "wuxu hui" (meetings to discuss principles or ideological guidelines). One of the most important "wuxu hui" after the downfall of the Gang of Four was the Forum on Principles for Theoretical Work (Lilun Gongzuo Wuxuhui) held by the PCC in Beijing from 18 January to 3 April 1979 (adjourned for over one month during the China-Vietnam war, which started on 17 February and ended on 26 March). See also "si xiang jiben yuanze" (four cardinal principles).

务虚会
wuxu hui
(meetings to discuss principles
or ideological guidelines)

See "wuxu" (discuss principles or ideological guidelines).

物质文明
wuzhi wenming
(material civilization)

See "liang ge wenmin" (two civilizations).

西单民主墙
Xidan minzhuqiang
(Xidan Democracy Wall)

See "minzhuqiang" (Democracy Wall) and "Beijing zhi chun" (Beijing Spring).

西方马克思学
xifang Makesixue
(Marxology in the West)

See "rendaozhuyide Makesizhuyi" (humanistic Marxism).

西方价值
xifang jiazhi
(Western values)

See "quanqiuhua" (globalization) and "minzuzhuyi" (nationalism).

西方中心主义
xifang zhongxinzhuyi
(Western-centrism)

See "xin baoshouzhuyi" (neo-conservatism) and "minzuzhuyi" (nationalism).

西化思潮
xihua sichao
(ideological trend of Westernization)

See "*Heshang* shijian" (*River Elegy* Incident) and "wenhua re" (culture craze).

西学
xixue
(Western learning)

See "xin baoshouzhuyi" (neo-conservatism).

希望工程
xiwang gongcheng
(Project Hope)

The birthplace of Project Hope is Taomugeda Primary School, Taomugeda village, Laiyuan county, Hebei province. On 30 October 1989, the China Youth and Children Development Fund provided aid to eleven dropouts at the school, in the name of Project Hope. During the 1990s, the project evolved into an extensive social campaign. The hearts of many Chinese people were touched by the desperate yearning to continue education for the several hundred thousand children who had to quit school each year because of poverty. Donators included individuals, enterprises, institutions, and government organizations. Liang Xiaosheng, a famous Beijing-based writer, made five donations. In Hong Kong and Taiwan, residents participated in the campaign which proceeded under the banner of "Sacrificing one day to save a life". Many world famous companies, such as Coca-Cola, Motorola, and Philips, also actively joined this public welfare program. By April 1997, the project had attracted donations of nearly 1,000 million Chinese yuan from both home and abroad. It helped more than 1.5 million dropouts in poverty-stricken areas return to school, and built over 3,600 Project Hope primary schools throughout the country.

Implementation of Project Hope has not only extensively promoted elementary education in poor areas, but has also taught people in these areas to overcome difficulties and escape poverty. The program has also opened channels to link poverty-stricken areas with other localities, enabling them to further socio-economic development.

On 28 April 1997, China's Trademark Bureau issued a trademark registration for the China Youth and Children Development Fund.

From the year 2000, according to the secretary of the Fund, Project Hope will no longer accept donations because by that time its aim will have already been achieved.

吸烟大国
xiyan daguo
(a big smoking nation)

According to the 1997 World Health Organization report, China is the world's largest tobacco producer whose output quadruples that of the second largest producer, the United States. As a result, it also leads in sales volume of tobacco and the number of people who smoke.

A 1997 survey shows that in China smokers at or above the age of 15 account for 37.62 percent of the total population of this age group, up 3.74 percentage points over 1984. This implies that China has a smoking population of 320 million, including 300 million men. On average, smokers begin using tobacco at age 20, three years earlier than that revealed in the 1984 survey. Thirteen years ago, men smoked 13 cigarettes per person a day; today they smoke 15 cigarettes per day.

The negative consequences of smoking are obvious. Data show that each year about 750,000 Chinese die of smoke-related illnesses, such as apoplexy, heart trouble, lung cancer, and respiratory tract disorders. These diseases are common causes of death in the country. Based on current trends, some 2 million Chinese will die annually due to tobacco by the year 2020. More worrying is the fact that 200 million of today's young Chinese under the age of 20 will likely become smokers, at least 50 million of whom will die at an early age because of tobacco use.

In August 1997, the 10th World Conference on Tobacco and Health was held in Beijing. The Chinese government understands that, as research results show, economic losses accruing from smoke-related unhealthy conditions far exceed the taxes and profits created by the tobacco industry. It has taken measures to control smoking. The situation, however, is still serious. It will take a long time to reduce the industry's share of overall national financial revenue.

瞎指挥
xia zhihui

(arbitrary and impractical directions)

See "dayuejin" (Great Leap Forward).

狭隘爱国主义
xia'ai aiguozhuyi
(parochial patriotism)

See "aiguozhuyi" (patriotism) and "minzuzhuyi" (nationalism).

狭隘民族主义
xia'ai minzuzhuyi
(parochial nationalism)

Some scholars point out that it is unnecessary to use the modifier "parochial", because nationalism itself is a narrow-minded ideology, which tends towards exclusivism in the slogan "The nation state is supreme" (minzu zhishang or Guojia zhishang). See also "aiguozhuyi" (patriotism) and "minzuzhuyi" (nationalism).

下放
xiafang
(transfer to a lower level)

"Xiafang" is an expression commonly used in mainland China during the Mao period. A cadre, for instance, should be able to work at both higher and lower levels (neng shang neng xia), and serve as an official and remain as one of the common people (neng guan neng min). Hence the practice of "ganbu xiafang" (transfer cadres to lower levels, especially to work at the grass-roots levels or to do manual labor in the countryside or in factories). Cadres sent to lower levels are called "xiafang ganbu".

Related terms include: "quanli xiafang" (transfer power to a lower level; decentralization of power), "tizhi xiafang" (organizational decentralization), and "qiye xiafang" (placing an enterprise at a lower administrative level). Sending educated urban youth to the countryside for re-education from the poor and lower-middle peasants, as occurred during the GPCR, was also a form of "xiafang". See also "xiagang" (leaving one's post).

下放干部
xiafang ganbu
(cadres sent to lower levels)

See "xiafang" (transfer to a lower level).

下岗
xiagang
(leaving one's post)

"Xiagang", literally meaning "leaving one's post", is a euphemistic expression for "being laid off".

In March 1997, all three of China's top leaders, Jiang Zemin, Li Peng, and Qiao Shi, used the annual session of the NPC currently underway in Beijing to call for urgent measures to rescue the country's hopelessly indebted state sector, which made up 70 percent of the total state sector and employed a large number of workers. There was a fear that these relics of Communist China's planned economy—with their cradle-to-grave job security, comprehensive staff welfare, outmoded products, and, in many cases, crippling debts—were a reservoir of potentially explosive political trouble. More than 6,200 state-sector enterprises had already declared bankruptcy in 1996, a staggering 261 percent rise over the previous year. Those still operating are shedding millions of workers (by the end of May 1997, 13 million workers had been laid off). Chinese officials reportedly admitted that about 54 million, or about 36 percent of the workers in the state-run sector, were surplus laborers. Of these, the government believed about 36 million would be redeployed, leaving about 20 million urban jobless by the turn of the century. A growing population of resentful urban unemployed could increase the dangers of unrest and pose a challenge to government authority.

The problem has proved very difficult to tackle. A thorough reform of the state-run sector is desirable, which includes privatization of much of the once sacrosanct backbone of China's Communist economy. But this may be a highly risky undertaking. In any case, the government must allow further massive lay-offs, while introducing an expensive comprehensive welfare system. Hence, a popular saying currently circulating in the country is: "Mao Zedong gao xiafang, Deng Xiaoping gao xiahai, Jiang Zemin gao xiagang" (Mao Zedong was keen on transferring cadres to lower levels; Deng Xiaoping asked people to jump into the sea of business; and Jiang Zemin resorts to massive lay-offs). According to some analysts, it is ironic that the Chinese leadership, while insisting that the outside world observe a "one-China" policy, has split the country into "two-Chinas" at home: the first China was created during 30 years of central planning and the second was created with Deng Xiaoping's market reforms. See also "jingji gaige" (economic reform).

下海
xiahai
(jumping into the sea of business)

See "jingshang re" (business fever) and "jingji gaige" (economic reform).

先锋小说
xianfeng xiaoshuo
(vanguard fiction)

See "xinshiqi wenxue" (literature of the new period) and "renwen jingshen lunzheng" ("humanistic spirit" debate).

现代
xiandai
(modern times)

See "jindai" (recent times).

现代迷信
xiandai mixin
(modern superstition)

The personality cult of Mao had existed for a long time even before the GPCR. During the GPCR the cult was carried out to such extremes that it was like a kind of "modern superstition". In CCP history, this was a "god-making movement" (zaoshen yundong).

There was the "three loyals" movement ("sanzhongyu yundong", which reportedly was first launched by the Red Guards of Beijing University). It aimed at urging people to "be forever loyal to Chairman Mao, to Mao Zedong Thought, and to Chairman Mao's proletarian revolutionary line". There were a number of practices (most of which had been created in the army). For instance, the authorities made it a rule at the time that all people, as a way of expressing allegiance to Mao, take part in performing what was called a "loyalty dance" (zhongziwu). All public meetings must begin with a three-part ritual of "yizhu erchang sandu": first greeting (the standard greetings were "May Chairman Mao live for tens of thousands of years" and "May Vice Commander Lin enjoy good health forever", both repeated twice), second singing (all attending the meeting then sing the song "Sailing the Seas Depends on the Helmsman"—"Dahai hangxing kao duoshou"), and third reading (all read Mao's quotations, selected by the chairperson in accordance with the theme of the meeting). Other forms of the superstition activities included wearing Mao badges, displaying "loyalty tablets" (zhongzi pai, i.e., tablets bearing the Chinese character "zhong"—"loyalty"—and Mao's picture, which was intended to take the place of the traditional ancestral tablets. People also held "loyalty tablets" during march-rally), reading Mao's works every day, (tiantiandu), and "requesting instructions from Chairman Mao in the morning" (zaoqingshi), and "reporting to Chairman Mao in the evening" (wanhuibao).

Later, on 12 June 1969, a CCP document was issued asking people to stress practical results and not outward forms in their expression of loyalty to Mao, but the personality cult of Mao Zedong was hardly restrained until after the end of the GPCR. See also "Mao Zedong sixiang" (Mao Zedong Thought), "shehuizhuyi yihua lun" (theory of socialist alienation), and "tuchu zhengzhi" (giving prominence to politics).

现代企业制度
xiandai qiye zhidu
(modern enterprise system)

See "gufenzhi gaizao" (joint stock system reform).

现代热
xiandai re
(quest for modernism)

Unlike humanism and similar issues in the art-politics relationship, modernism was never a bone of contention during the numerous political campaigns in the first thirty years of the PRC. This is not to say that modernism never existed in China. In the first two or three decades of the twentieth century, when modernism as a cultural phenomenon first came into existence in the West, its impact could already be felt in Chinese literature and art, especially in the realm of poetry. (Famous modernist poets include Dai Wangshu and Li Jinfa. Members of the *Xinyuepai*—the "Crescent School"—are sometimes also regarded as precursors of Chinese modernism.) But in Mao's China modernism was not tolerated. In fact, it was completely negated, as can be seen in the following entry from the 1965 edition of *The Chinese Dictionary (Ci Hai)*, which defined modernism as follows:

"A general name for various decadent schools and tendencies of bourgeois literature and art in the period of imperialism; characterized by a distortion of reality, undermining the established forms and basic laws of literature and art, and negating tradition and typicality; it preaches cosmopolitanism and other reactionary ideologies of various kinds."

Indeed, until the late 1970s, modernism in China was a dead cause. Since then, however, with the policies of the "four modernizations" and "open door" adopted by the CCP, changes quickly began to occur. Qian Xuesen, the leading Chinese nuclear physicist, even said to Chinese writers and artists: "The modernization of science and technology will undoubtedly bring about the modernization of literature and art" (Qian Xuesen, "Kexue jishu xiandaihua yiding yao daidong wenxue yishu xiandaihua"—"The Modernization of Science and Technology Will Definitely Bring About the Modernization of Literature and Art", *Kexue wenyi,* 2, 1980, reprinted in *XHYB, WZB,* 8:144-47, 1980). Modernization does not amount to modernism, of course. But within only a few years, modernist theory and literature from the West were introduced into China—a country awakened from a ten-year nightmare and undergoing a series of changes in many aspects of its social life. Modernism gradually became one of the most discussed topics, not only among scholars but also among artists and writers and readers.

After the downfall of the Gang of Four, Liu Mingjiu and his wife Zhu Hong were among the first to come into contact with modernism in the West. In 1978, Zhu's lengthy article "On the Theater of the Absurd" appeared in *World Literature*, a newly resumed journal devoted to foreign literature. In December 1978, at a national foreign literature conference held in Guangzhou, Liu gave a long lecture on "problems concerning the appraisal of modern and contemporary bourgeois literature in the West". Notable later events included the publication of the following books: Chen Kun's *A Study of Modernist Literary Theory in the West (Xifang Xiandaipai Wenxue Lilun Yanjiu,* Beijing, Beijing Daxue, 1981) published in 1981, which was dubbed the *Bible* for modernism in China at the time, Yuan Kejia's comprehensive compendium, *Selected Works of Foreign Modernism (Waiguo Xandaipai Zuopin Xuan,* Yuan Kejia, ed., Shanghai, Shanghai Wenyi, 1981, etc.), published from 1981 onwards, and Gao Xingjian's popular book, *A Preliminary Discussion of Contemporary Narrative Techniques,* published in 1981. By the eve of the 1983 campaign to "eliminate spiritual pollution" over four hundred articles and more than ten monographs on Western modernism had been published, many of which attempted to provide what they deemed to be a fair appraisal (see He Li's summary of the discussion on Western modernism and the direction of contemporary Chinese literature, *RMRB,* 13 Sept. 1983; trans. by Geremie Barmé, with introduction and annotations in *Trees on the Mountain,* pp. 44-54).

Of greater impact was the fact that a number of writers and artists emerged after 1979 who did try to observe, reflect, and comment on Chinese society with a social outlook and philosophical approach similar to that of some modernists in the West. Modernist techniques were quite apparent in a number of works of literature and art in mainland China. As Feng Jicai, a famous Tianjin writer, claimed, Chinese literature needed "modernism". Xu Chi, a veteran poet and scholar, found that there was a certain link between modernization and modernism. He called for a "Marxist modernism" (Xu Chi, "Xiandaihua yu xiandaipai"—"Modernization and Modernism", *Waiguo wenxue yanjiu,* 1, 1982, reprinted in *WYLZJ,* pp. 552-56. See also his *Wenyi He Xiandaihua—Arts and Modernization,* Chengdu, Sichuan Renmin, 1981). Xu Jingya, one of the young writers engaged in "misty poetry", thus declared:

"The transformation of Chinese society as a whole, during which several hundred million people are marching towards modernization, has determined that in China a modernist literature is bound to be generated that is in conformity with the situation.... Sooner or later, modernist tendencies will come into being. If not today, then tomorrow; if it does not start with this generation of youth, it will with the next. This is absolutely unquestionable" (Xu Jingya, "A Body of Rising Poetry: On the Modernist Tendencies of Chinese Poetry", *Dangdai Wenyi Sichao,* 1:25, 1983). See also "xinshiqi wenxuede duoyuan fazhan" (pluralistic development of the literature of the new period).

现代的世界是开放的世界
xiandaide shijie shi kaifangde shijie
(today's world is an open world)

On 30 June 1984, when meeting a Japanese delegation attending the second conference of Sino-Japanese nongovernmental personages, Deng discussed the present world: "Today's world is an open world", he said. In his opinion, all countries, capitalist or socialist, developed or developing, should open to the outside. China should link its economy with the international markets and world economy—its development is inseparable from the world. Later, on various occasions, Deng reiterated this idea.

On 25 February 1997, in his funeral eulogy to Deng's mourners in Beijing's Great Hall of the People, Jiang Zemin reminded his listeners of Deng's aphorism. He asked the people to do the following: soberly assess the development of the world; courageously meet the severe challenge; adhere to opening-up the fundamental national policy; develop an all-directional and multi-layer pattern of opening-up; strive to enhance the level of opening-up; extensively absorb and draw on all results of advanced civilization created by all countries in the world including developed capitalist countries; and actively participate in international economic and technological cooperation and competition.

The Chinese are now convinced by the lesson paid for with blood and tears over one hundred years: A closed-door leads to backwardness; and backwardness proves vulnerable to attack (fengbi jiuyao luohou; luohou jiuyao aida). This dates to the failure of the so-called "national policy" (guoce) of the Qing dynasty—the "closed-door policy" (biguan zhengce) or "closing the country to international intercourse" (biguan zi shou). The 1840-42 Opium Wars between Britain and China, one of whose humiliating consequences to China was the loss of Hong Kong, is a case in point. See also "quanqiuhua" (globalization) and "minzuzhuyi" (nationalism).

现代修正主义
xiandai xiuzhengzhuyi
(modern revisionism)

See "xiuzhengzhuyi" (revisionism).

现代主义
xiandaizhuyi
(modernism)

See "xiandai re" (quest for modernism) and "xinshiqi wenxuede duoyuan fazhan" (pluralistic development of the literature of the new period).

线式思维惯性
xianshi siwei guanxing
(mental inertia of linearity)

See "fansi" (reflection).

现实主义广阔道路论
xianshizhuyi guangkuo daolu lun
(theory of the "broad path of realism")

As one of the "eight sinister theories" singled out for attack in the 1966 Party document the "Summary", the theory of the "broad path of realism" was first presented by the literary critic Qin Zhaoyang (under the pseudonym "He Zhi") in his 1956 treatise "Realism—A Broad Path" ("Xianshizhuyi—guangkuode daolu", *RMWX,* 9, 1956); trans. in Nieh Hualing, ed., *Literature of the Hundred Flowers,* v.1, pp. 121-44). In Qin's view, the requirement about arts serving politics should be a long-term and general one, and writers and artists should not be so short-sighted as to use it as mere propaganda for current politics. He appealed for due account to be given to the characteristics of the arts. Indeed, Qin's article was the first forceful refutation of dogmatism in literary criticism and creation since 1949. With support and help from Qin, then a deputy editor-in-chief of *People's Literature,* Liu Binyan's "The Confidential News of This Newspaper" and Wang Meng's "A Young Newcomer to the Organization Department" ("Zuzhibu xinlaide qingnianren", *RMWX,* 9, 1956; trans. in Nieh Hualing, ed., *Literature of the Hundred Flowers,* v. 2, pp. 473-511, and in W. J. F. Jenner, ed., *Fragrant Weeds,* pp. 71-116) were published. The publication of Qin's article and Liu's and Wang's works were of great significance, arousing prompt and strong repercussions. (For an introduction to these two stories and Qin Zhaoyang's support, see, for instance, Merle Goldman, *Literary Dissent in Communist China,* Cambridge, Harvard University Press, 1967, pp. 178-80.) Qin Zhaoyang praised Liu Binyan for "opening up a new road of realism" of his own and at the same time setting an example to others. Qin himself, admittedly, of course also played a similar role.

Qin Zhaoyang began to be attacked just three months after the publication of his treatise. Yao Wenyuan accused him of being "'a megaphone' of international revisionism, an agent of imperialism in the realm of literature and art" (Yao Wenyuan, "Bo Qin Zhaoyang wei zichanjieji zhengzhi fuwude lilun"—"A Refutation of Qin Zhaoyang's Theory That Serves Bourgeois Politics", *Wenxue yanjiu,* 3:115, 1958). After 1978, quite a few critics tried to support Qin. However, the first article (Lu Yuan, "Zhenli jingdeqi suiyuede moxi"—"Truth Can Stand the Test of Time", *Guangxi ribao*, 2 Mar. 1979) in defense of his theory did not appear until March 1979. Even then there were people still holding that the general inclination of Qin's article was questionable, a "product of the influence of the ideological trend of international revisionism". (See Chen Shen, "Chong du 'xianshizhuyi: guangkuode daolu'"—"Re-reading 'Realism: A Broad Path'", *Yanhe,* 5, 1979.) See also "jiyao" ("Summary") and "shehuizhuyi xianshizhuyi" (socialist realism).

现实主义深化论
xianshizhuyi shenhua lun
(theory of the "deepening of realism")

See "zhongjian renwu lun" (theory of "middle characters") and "jiyao" ("Summary").

现实主义原则
xianshizhuyi yuanze
(principle of realism)

See "shehuizhuyi xianshizhuyi" (socialist realism).

现象与本质
xianxiang yu benzhi
(phenomenon and essence)

See "xie zhenshi" (writing about reality).

线性因果论
xianxing yinguo lun
(theory of linear causality)

See "fanyinglun shi wenxue yanjiude zhexue jichu" (the theory of reflection is the philosophical basis for literary study).

限制资产阶级法权
xianzhi zichanjieji faquan
(restraining bourgeois rights)

See "zichanjieji faquan" (bourgeois rights).

香风
xiangfeng
(fragrant breeze)

This term, or another similar term "bourgeois fragrant breeze" (zichanjieji xiangfeng), was used in the Mao period to describe the so-called bourgeois way of life, such as wearing fashionable dresses, using make-up, and having stylish hair-styles. Today all of this is normal and popular among urban women in China. The term has thus gradually disappeared.

香花
xianghua
(fragrant flower)

See "ducao" (poisonous weed).

香港学
Xianggang xue
(the study of Hong Kong)

The study of Hong Kong, focusing on its economy, is a new popular discipline in Chinese mainland in recent years. It also includes Hong Kong history, politics, culture, and society, and relations between Hong Kong and the mainland. See also "dongfang zhi zhu" (pearl of the Orient) and "gangren zhi gang" (Hong Kong residents governing Hong Kong).

向党交心
xiang dang jiaoxin
(tender one's heart to the Party)

Tendering one's heart to the Party used to be an unavoidable part of political life in China. For instance, in March 1958, following the 1957 anti-Rightist campaign, a so-called "heart-tendering movement" (jiaoxin yundong) was carried out, mainly among intellectuals and students of tertiary education. People were asked to conduct "five laying-bares" before the Party: 1. lay bare their understanding of the CCP; 2. lay bare their understanding of socialism; 3. lay bare their words, thinking and activities during the 1957 "great airing of views" (daming dafang) period; 4. lay bare their being influenced by Rightists; and 5. lay bare the change in their thinking after the anti-Rightist campaign.

When discussing Wang Meng's 1979 novellete "Bolshevik Salute" ("Buli"), Leo Ou-fan Lee found that, with his protagonist's rehabilitation and his final "Bolshevik salute" to Hua Guofeng, Ye Jianying, and Deng Xiaoping, Wang Meng did try to convey his gratitude and praise for the Party—"to tender his heart to the Party" (Leo Ou-fan Lee, "The Politics of Technique: Perspectives of Literary Dissidence in Contemporary Chinese Fiction", in Jeffrey C. Kinkley, ed., *After Mao: Chinese Literature and Society 1978-1982*, Cambridge, Harvard University Press, 1985, p. 170). But the term "tender one's heart to the Party" became somewhat outdated after the downfall of the Gang of Four. It was later conspicuously used on the back cover of the 1996 book *An Intimate Talk with the General Secretary (Yu Zongshuji Tanxin,* Beijing, Zhongguo shehui kexue, Oct. 1996). It said that the purpose of the book was "to tender their (the authors') heart to the leader of the third generation". See also "sixiang gaizao" (ideological remolding) and "zhishifenzi wenti" (issue of intellectuals).

向共产党领导和无产阶级专政进攻的突破口
xiang gongchandang lingdao he wuchanjieji zhuanzheng jin'gongde tupokou
(a breakthrough point in the offensive against the Communist Party leadership and the proletarian dictatorship)

See "pi Deng wanyanshu" (anti-Deng 10,000-character petitions) and "wuchanjieji zhuanzheng" (dictatorship of the proletariat).

向科学进军
xiang kexue jinjun
(strive to develop science)

See "ke jiao xing guo" (revitalize China through science and education).

向新民歌学习
xiang xin min'ge xuexi
(learn from new folk songs)

See "dazhonghua" (popularization).

向前看
xiang qian kan
(look to the future)

"Looking forward" was a political slogan vigorously advocated by the CCP after the end of the GPCR. The slogan helped people to rid themselves of the nightmare of the past ten years. More profoundly, it helped lure people away from probing into the matter of why the GPCR occurred, which would further damage their faith in Mao and the CCP. In particular, Deng Xiaoping asked people to "look forward" in his speech, "Emancipate the Mind, Seek Truth from Facts and Unite as One in Looking to the Future", delivered at the closing session of the Central Work Conference of the CCP on 13 December 1978 (*SWD,* pp. 151-65). He emphasized that a revolutionary must look forward.

Coincidentally, the pronunciation of the Chinese character "qian" can also be understood as "money". The phrase "xiang qian kan" thus may mean "looking to the future" or "looking towards money". Interestingly, today in mainland China, people, in looking to the future, do look towards money. Or, because they look towards money, they look to the future—the reform and open-door policy provide a bright future to make money. However, because of the current tendency in society to try to make money, a number of social problems have also appeared. Most serious is the corruption of the Party itself, as many have pointed out. See "jingji gaige" (economic reform), "fan fubai" (anti-corruption), and "fazhan caishi ying daoli" (development is the most essential criterion).

向钱看
xiang qian kan
(look towards money)

See "xiang qian kan" (look to the future) and "jingji gaige" (economic reform).

向後看文艺
xiang hou kan wenyi
(backward-looking literature)

In April 1979, just after Deng Xiaoping put forth his "four cardinal principles", Huang Ansi, an influential figure who for a long time had held leading propaganda and cultural posts in Guangdong province, published six successive essays in two Guangzhou-based newspapers, *South Daily* and *Guangzhou Daily*. In one of these essays, entitled "Look Forward, Literature and Art!" ("Xiang qian kan na! wenyi",*Guangzhou ribao,* 15 Apr. 1979). Huang came up with three categories of literary works produced in the past three years with the theme of exposing the Gang of Four. One category described "heroic characters bravely resisting the Gang", such as "Where Silence Prevails" (Zong Fuxian, "Yu wu sheng chu", *XHYB*, *WZB,* 1:94-111, 1979, reprinted in *Shanghen*, Hong Kong, Sanlian shudian, 1978, pp. 321-84; trans. and retitled *When All Sounds Are Hushed* in *CL,* 4:3-56, 1979, and retitled *In a Land of Silence* in Edward M. Gunn, ed., *Twentieth-Century Chinese Drama: An Anthology,* pp. 409-47); another discussed "social problems emerging under the Gang's disastrous influence", like "The Class Teacher"; and the third category described "personal suffering caused by the Gang's persecution". All these works, according to Huang, should be regarded as "backward-looking literature". While admitting that works about resistance to the Gang could arouse indignation among readers, and that those raising social problems could help make people think, Huang particularly resented the third group. He believed that "in describing personal deaths, ruined families, vicissitudes of life or twists and turns in love", it was hard to avoid "sentimental appeal" and, therefore, these works should be held responsible for readers feeling that "fate was elusive and the future uncertain". Instead, Huang Ansi advocated what he called "forward-looking literature" (xiang qian kan wenyi), that is, a literature that "directly reflects subject matter about the 'four modernizations'".

Many critics questioned Huang Ansi's categories. They could not see why works which exposed personal deaths, family ruin, vicissitudes of life, or tribulations in love caused by the Gang could be considered not to reflect social problems, and could be classified as unable to arouse readers' indignation against the Gang. As to the division of "forward-looking literature" and "backward-looking literature", they pointed out that it was a mechanical application of the political concept of "looking forward" to literary and art creation and subject matter, and it certainly violated literary laws. See also "wenyi wei zhengzhi fuwu" (literature and art serve politics).

向前看文艺
xiang qian kan wenyi
(forward-looking literature)

See "xiang hou kan wenyi" (backward-looking literature).

橡皮图章
xiangpi tuzhang
(rubber stamp)

According to the PRC Constitution, the National People's Congress ("Quanguo Renmin Daibiao Dahui" or "Quanguo Renda" for short) is the "highest organ of state power", "the sole organ exercising the legislative power of the state". Its power includes amending the PRC Constitution, enacting and amending laws, electing and dismissing the PRC president and vice-president, deciding on, or dismissing, the premier and other members of the State Council, and examining and approving the premier's report, the budget, and other major government reports. But for many years, as is well-known, all important decisions were made by the Party Center (dangzhongyang), and very often by the one person who was called the Leader, or the "core of the Party leadership". Hence a very poignant saying circulated among the people: "The Party Center writes plays, the State Council puts them on, the NPC makes comments, and the CPPCC functions as an audience" (dangzhongyang bianxi, guowuyuan yanxi, renda pingxi, zhengxie kanxi).

The situation has somewhat changed in recent years. Qiao Shi, former chairman of the NPC, is credited for Beijing's halting steps towards a meaningful legal system. It was reported that he also advocated a "measured view" of the June 4th Incident of 1989. At the September 1997 CCP's 15th National Congress, Qiao lost his position on the Politburo Standing Committee and all other posts within the Party. Then, in March 1998, he stepped down from the NPC chairmanship. Nevertheless, his successor Li Peng seemed to continue the job of making the "rubber stamp" harder, though Li did not impress people when he was premier of the State Council.

There is no denying the fact that fundamentally, the NPC is still not yet worthy of the name. A crucial issue, as often raised by the public, is: to whom the NPC deputies should hold themselves responsible, the Party or the people. But China watchers predict that with the continuation of the reforms, it will be more difficult for the NPC to be only a "rubber stamp". When the practice of appointing official candidates for the People's Congress is challenged at county, prefecture, provincial, and national levels, the voting behavior of these representatives will be more independent. When NPC representatives are freely elected, the NPC will be able to compete with, or even replace, the CCP Politburo as China's "supreme authority". These will be major steps toward democratization in China. See also "zhengzhi gaige" (political reform).

消极环境中的消极人物也应该表现
xiaoji huanjingzhongde xiaoji renwu ye yinggai biaoxian
(negative characters in negative circumstances should also be presented)

See "shehuizhuyi xianshizhuyi" (socialist realism) and "wenyi wei zhengzhi fuwu" (literature and art serve politics).

逍遥派
xiaoyaopai
(bystanders)

See "zaofan youli" (it is right to rebel).

小报
xiaobao
(small-sized newspapers)

See "xinwen ziyou wenti" (issue of press freedom).

小传统
xiaochuantong
(petit tradition)

See "fan chuantong" (anti-tradition) and "sixiang gaizao" (ideological remolding).

小道消息
xiaodao xiaoxi
(information from obscure sources)

See "xinwen ziyou wenti" (issue of press freedom).

小红书
xiaohongshu
(little red book)

This refers to *Quotations from Chairman Mao*. See "Mao Zedong sixiang" (Mao Zedong Thought).

小红书运动
xiaohongshu yundong
("little red book" movement)

See "Mao Zedong sixiang" (Mao Zedong Thought).

小皇帝
xiaohuangdi
(little emperors)

See "yitaihua" (single-child policy).

小脚女人
xiaojiao nuren
(women with bound feet)

On 31 July 1955, at a conference of secretaries of provincial, municipal, and autonomous region Party committees, Mao delivered a report on the questions of agricultural cooperation. In his opinion, a new upsurge in the socialist mass movement was imminent throughout the countryside, but his Party had failed to see it. He said: "Some of our comrades are tottering along like a woman with bound feet and constantly complaining, 'You're going too fast.' Excessive criticism, inappropriate complaints, endless anxiety, and the raising of countless taboos—they believe this is the proper way to guide the socialist mass movement in the rural areas" *(RMRB,* 17 Oct. 1955).

Because of the fear of becoming a "woman with bound feet", local leaders had to follow Mao's advice. Cases of impetuous and rash advance, of attempts to exceed real possiblitities, increased. On 20 June 1956, in light of the overwhelming view of the Politburo, the *People's Daily* published an editorial entitled "Oppose Both Conservation and Impetuosity". It aimed at opposing rash advance (fan maojin). Accordingly, various localities put stress on solving those problems. This, however, did not please Mao. In his speech at the 3rd Plenum (enlarged) of the 8th PCC held in the autumn of 1957, he began to criticize the 1956 effort to oppose rash advance. At the Nanning meeting of January 1958 and the Chengdu meeting of March 1958, Mao subjected it to further severe criticism—by that time Mao had already devised his ambitious "Great Leap Forward". See also "dayuejin" (Great Leap Forward).

小节
xiaojie
(small matters)

See "dajie" (political integrity).

小金库
xiaojinku
(small treasury)

In mainland China, many government offices and state-owned units have their own "small treasury", in which they deposit money from the illegal collection of fees and funds. This of course is a form of corruption, and a cause of enormous damage to the state. In 1995 the central authorities carried out a nationwide investigation campaign to try to check it. In the first two months (by the end of June) of the inspection monitored by the Ministry of Finance, according to the *People's Daily,* "small treasury" funds totalled 1.47 billion Chinese dollars in 1.15 million enterprises across the country—1.067 billion Chinese dollars in local enterprises and 403 million Chinese dollars in central enterprises. See also "fan fubai" (anti-corruption).

小蜜
xiaomi
(sweetheart; secretary-turned mistress)

See "dakuan" (upstarts).

小气候
xiaoqihou
(micro-climate)

On 9 June 1989, a few days after the June 4th Incident, Deng Xiaoping made the following remark, referring to the 1989 "May Tempest": "The storm was bound to break out sooner or later. This was a matter that had been determined by the international macro-climate and the micro-climate in China. It was bound to happen and was independent of man's will" (*RMRB*, *HWB*, 28 June 1989).

By the "macro-climate" Deng meant the international political situation, and by the "micro-climate" he meant the domestic political situation in mainland China. As pointed out in an article in *Liaowang* magazine published on 4 September 1989, the eight characteristics of the "micro-climate" included advocating "bourgeois" democracy, freedom and human rights, and political pluralism.

With respect to this remark, China critics observed, Deng was certainly correct. Democracy was a general trend occurring throughout the world. Great changes had taken place in the Soviet Union and the East European bloc. For ten years or more, many Chinese, with a sense of historical responsibility, had made efforts to promote the trend in China; and eventually, the "micro-climate", China's own democratic trend, took shape. From the series of politico-cultural events taking place during the so-called "new period", one can see that the changes were profound—the 1989 "May Tempest" was indeed the culmination of this trend and its inevitable result. See also "bajiu minyun" (1989 pro-democracy movement) and "ziyouhua" (liberalization).

小政府，大社会
xiaozhengfu, dashehui
(small government, large society)

See "yi fa zhi guo" (ruling the nation by law).

小资产阶级知识分子
xiaozichanjieji zhishifenzi
(petty bourgeois intellectuals)

See "zhishifenzi wenti" (issue of intellectuals).

效率就是生命
xiaolü jiushi shengming
(efficiency is life)

See "ershinianlai zuiju yingxianglide shi ge kouhao" (ten most influential slogans in the past two decades).

写发展趋势
xie fazhan qushi
(write about the developing trend)

See "shehuizhuyi xianshizhuyi" (socialist realism) and "wenyi wei zhengzhi fuwu" (literature and art serve politics).

写十三年
xie shisannian
(write about the "thirteen years")

See "daxie shisannian" (go all out to write about the "thirteen years").

写阴暗面
xie yin'anmian
(write about the dark side)

See "ganyu shenghuo" (be involved in life).

写与走资派作斗争
xie yu zouzipai zuo douzheng
(write about the struggle against capitalist-roaders)

See "wen'ge wenyi" (GPCR literature and art).

写真实
xie zhenshi
(writing about reality)

"Writing about reality" was one of the eight "sinister theories" in the 1966 Party document the "Summary". This should be of no surprise in view of the fact that for a long time the following view held sway in Chinese literary and art circles:

"The truthfulness in a certain literary work is the product of how its author understands and epitomizes life, conditioned by his class status and his class's world outlook. It is not, therefore, something in its natural form, but a kind of ideology with a clear-cut class nature. What the proletariat believes to be true the biased bourgeoisie may turn a blind eye to, adopting a policy of non-recognition; whereas in the eyes of the proletariat, what the bourgeoisie considers to be true is exactly a distortion of real life. On these issues of whether something is true or not, typical or not, profound or not, different classes have different views and different standards of their own" (Chu Lan, "Ba shenghuozhongde maodun he douzheng dianxinghua"—"On the Typification of Contradictions and Struggles in Real Life", *RMRB*, 14 Oct. 1974).

That "writing about reality" was one of the eight "sinister theories" should be of no surprise also because Hu Feng, convicted personally by Mao of heading the so-called "Hu Feng Counter-revolutionary Clique", was held chiefly responsible for the theory. Another "reactionary" thesis put forth by Hu Feng in the early 1950s was that a good writer should bring his "subjective fighting spirit" (zhuguan zhandou jingshen) into full play. This literary view was regarded as a political view and had been subject to fierce attacks more than ten years ealier (see, for instance, *Hu Feng Wenyi Sixiang Pipan Lunwen Huiji—A Collection of Essays Critical of Hu Feng's Literary Thought,* Beijing, Zuojia, 1955). Now one of the charges against the "writing about reality" theory was that it meant a "self-expansion" (ziwo kuozhang) of the "subjective fighting spirit" in people like Hu Feng.

By mid-1978, almost two years after the downfall of the Gang of Four, "writing about reality" was still regarded as wrong, and critics were quite proud because they could argue that they had long preceded the Gang of Four in attacking it. A major obstacle in its rehabilitation obviously was that Hu Feng had been a major figure in initiating the thesis. Later there was some change as Stalin was found also to have been in favor of it. However, since Hu Feng had been convicted by Mao and since his case had not yet been reversed, even those less conservative critics had to condemn Hu Feng and declare that there was a line of demarcation between Hu and themselves on the issue of "writing about reality". Liu Mengxi, for instance, said that Hu Feng did advocate the slogan of "writing about reality", but what he meant by "writing about reality" was writing about the backwardness of society which could never be overcome, and about people's "wounds under spiritual enslavement" (Liu Mengxi, "Geming xianshizhuyi shi liangjiehe chuangzuo fangfade jichu: ping 'Sirenbang' dui 'xianshizhuyi shenhua lun' de pipan"—"Revolutionary Realism Is the Foundation of the 'Two-in-One Combination' Creative Method: On the 'Gang of Four's' Criticism of the 'Theory of the Deepening of Realism'", *WXPL,* 6:42-50, 1978, extracted and reprinted in *XHYB, WZB,* 2:201-05, 1979). With this "shop sign", Liu emphasized, Hu had been engaged in exposing the darkness of socialism and in anti-Party activities. A special guest commentator of the *Literary Gazette*, under the premise that Hu Feng's "writing about reality" meant the "self-expansion" of the "subjective fighting spirit" of people like himself, concluded, quite astonishingly: Hu Feng, Lin Biao, and the Gang of Four "reached a consensus in this regard" ("Wenyi wei shixian si ge xiandaihua fuwu"—"Literature and Art Serve the Striving to Realize the Four Modernizations", *WYB,* 2:23, 1979). In any case, as Liu Mengxi emphasized, Hu's view about "writing about reality", though already subjected to criticism in the past, had to continue to be criticized in the future (Liu Mengxi, "Geming xianshizhuyi", p. 203).

Later, with the increasing emancipation of the people's minds, all these criticisms became ridiculous. The theory about "writing about reality", together with Hu's view about the "subjective fighting spirit", was finally rehabilitated. An official statement was issued in the work report delivered at the 1979 4th National Congress of Chinese Writers and Artists by the 72-year old ACF vice-chairman Zhou Yang. For the first time, he announced: It is not the relationship between arts and politics but that between arts and the life of the people which is fundamental and plays a decisive role. Literature and art are reflections of social life, with the integrity of life as their object. They start from and go back to life, exerting a tremendous influence on life. With this as a starting point, Zhou Yang asked writers to place themselves at all times in the thick of life, to be faithful to life, and to write about what they know well, what they are interested in, what they react to most deeply, and what they have given a great deal of thought to. Writers, in Zhou's opinion, rather than basing their writings on specific contemporary policies, should observe, portray, and evaluate life against a broad historical background.

Zhou Yang said: "The relationship between arts and politics is in essence that between arts and the people" (Zhou Yang, "Be Both Successors and Pioneers, Bring Literature and Art into Flower in the New Period of Socialism", *WYB,* 11-12:8-26, 1979 and *RMRB,* 20 Nov. 1979). He made it clear that by politics he meant politics of classes, politics of the masses, not that of a few politicians, still less that of a handful of careerists and conspirators. Socialist literature and art, he explained, on the one hand, when reflecting the life of the people and their needs and interests, cannot be dissociated from politics but are closely connected with it. On the other hand, so long as they truthfully reflect the people's needs and interests, they will have a tremendous influence on politics. "It is precisely in this sense," he said, "that we speak of the identity of the truthfulness and political nature of literature and art" (ibid.).

Zhou emphasized the prime importance of reality in literary and art creation. He asserted: "Truthfulness is the lifeblood of art. Without truthfulness, a creative work can have no ideological or artistic value" (ibid.). He officially rehabilitated the theories of the "broad road of realism" (xianshizhuyi guangkuo daolu), "writing about reality", and "writing about middle characters" (xie zhongjian renwu). He assured his audience that these old issues, which were raised in the early and mid-fifties and early sixties, were all academic questions that could be freely discussed, and it was wrong to oppose them by a simplistic and sweeping identification with bourgeois or revisionist thinking in literature and art. With "truthfulness" as a premise, Zhou Yang also saw "praising" (gesong) and "exposing" (baolu) not as incompatible but as two aspects of the same question.

But the problem was not fundamentally settled. In 1980, there were people still disagreeing with the thesis "writing about reality", as can be seen in the article, "Investigations of the Thesis of 'Writing about Reality'", published in the 4th issue of *Red Flag* in 1980 (Li Yuming and Han Zhijun, "Dui 'xie zhenshi' shuode zhiyi", *HQ,* 4:39-43, 48, 1980). Another article, under the title of "How to Understand 'Writing about Reality'", in *Red Flag*, though not totally against the thesis, raised some points of view which were specious and more harmful (Lu Guishan, "Zenyang lijie 'xie zhenshi'", *HQ,* 9:45-48, 1980). The article, classifying phenomena (xianxiang) into various categories according to whether or not they reflected the essence of things and to what degree, tried to show China's writers a way to choose source material which possessed "essence" (benzhi), so that their works would "reflect some essential aspects of revolution" (ibid., p. 46).

Because of the unsettled problem concerning "writing about reality", great divergencies of opinion arose in the 1980 debate on works like "In the Unwritten Records", "What If I Really Were", and "A Woman Thief". The "logic" employed by those attacking these works, as Ma Debo, a critic, summed up, was often as follows: 1. The phenomena reflected in these works do exist in life, but they are unrealistic; 2. They are unrealistic because they are not typical; 3. They are not typical because they fail to reflect the essence of things; and 4. They fail to reflect the essence of things because these phenomena do not belong to the mainstream of life (see Ma Debo, "Maotou, jiaodian he qingxiang—guanyu 'Zai shehuide dang'an li' ji qi pinglun"—"On 'In the Unwritten Records' and Criticisms of It", *WYB,* 11:51, 1980).

In fact, these views, preposterous as they are, had been dominating Chinese literary and art circles for a long time. Zhou Jieren, another critic, had tried to tackle them. He concentrated on clarifying the relationship between "phenomenon" and "essence". He concluded: There is no such thing as pure, undisguised "essence" in the objective world. What is called "essence" is "the inherent contradiction of the phenomenon, and the position of each aspect of the contradiction in the unity of opposites". Essence, therefore, exists only in objective phenomena. Any natural, social, or spiritual phenomenon, no matter what it is, is the demonstration of a certain kind of essence. Even false appearance, if it is acknowledged to be "a distorted reflection of essence", must also be regarded as "a prescription, an aspect, or a link of essence" (Zhou Jieren, "Ta zai nali shizu?"—"Where Does it Slip?", *WYB,* 7, 1980, reprinted in *XHYB, WZB,* 9:148-51, 1980).

Since all phenomena in the world possess their own essence, Zhou Jieren said, it is not only meaningless but also inconceivable to set essence as a measure by which to choose source material. Furthermore, Zhou pointed out, when the author of "How to Understand 'Writing about Reality'" categorized phenomena, he was actually, though perhaps unconsciously, regarding "essence" as a favor bestowed upon objective phenomena by human beings' brains. This was of course incorrect.

As Zhou Jieren said, people like the author of the *Red Flag* article often announced plausibly that the essence of Chinese socialist society was "brightness". When dealing with Lin Biao and the Gang of Four, they would argue that Lin Biao and the Gang of Four were particular social phenomena and not the essence of society. They would even go so far as to say that the GPCR, along with the bureaucracy and the special privileges of leading cadres at each level of the Party and state institutions, were neither the "mainstream" nor the "essence" of Chinese socialist society. "What a ridiculous and terrible view it is!" Zhou exclaimed (ibid., p. 151). See also "shehuizhuyi xianshizhuyi" (socialist realism), "wenxue zhutixing" (subjectivity of literature), "jiyao" ("Summary"), and "wenyi wei zhengzhi fuwu" (literature and art serve politics).

写真实论
xie zhenshi lun
(theory of "writing about reality")

See "xie zhenshi" (writing about reality).

新保守主义
xin baoshouzhuyi
(neo-conservatism)

The concept "neo-conservatism" was advanced in December 1990 by Xiao Gongqin, a professor at Shanghai Teachers University, at a forum held by the Ideology and Theory Department of the *China Youth Daily*. Typically, the forum was named "Traditional Chinese Culture and Socialist Modernization". (One can see from the following discussion the difference between China's neo-conservatism in the early 1990s and neo-conservatism or conservatism as understood in the West, which is generally considered to be an integral part of the great tradition of liberalism.)

China of the 1980s was somewhat like Europe during the Renaissance. In those years, a great number of books, ancient and modern, Chinese and foreign, were first published or re-printed; various schools and trends of thought were formed or introduced from abroad; and many talented young people emerged, one by one or group by group, shocking the ideological-cultural circles with their unique, and often controversial, views. Once again it was confirmed that knowledge is of value, thoughts possess meaning, and man should be respected. For a few years from the latter half of 1984, there was a great mass fervor in "cultural reflection" (wenhuaxing fansi) and an "intense search for culture" (wenhua re). The role of what was dubbed the "*élite* culture" (jingying wenhua), characterized by an independent critical spirit, a sense of angst (youhuan yishi), and a sense of social-political participation was conspicuous. The mainstream of this culture strongly displayed itself in favor of the so-called "Westernization".

The June 4th Incident of 1989 suddenly put an end to this trend, now dubbed the "radicalism of the 1980s". For political reason, those still maintaining their pro-democracy (or pro-radicalism, as termed by neo-conservstism proponents) stands were silenced or fled abroad. The political tragedy turned out to serve as another historical starting point for the "self-examination" by China's intellectuals in the 1990s. It was concluded that the eagerness of the 1980s' intellectuals for quick success and instant benefits, their keenness for "Western learning" (xixue), had led to the rise of the 1980s' radicalism. And this was the cultural cause for the historical bitter fruit people tasted in 1989. Criticism of the "intense search for culture" and the cultural spirit of the 1980s became dominant, enjoying support from the authorities. There was an atmosphere of self-repentance and self-reproach. Popular slogans included: "anti-radicalism" (fan jijinzhuyi), "go back to studies" (tui ju shuzhai), and "return to Chinese traditional learning" (huidao guoxue). Masters of Chinese traditional learning, such as Chen Yinke, Zhang Taiyan, Liang Shuming, Gu Xiegang, Wang Guowei, Du Yaquan, and Zhang Jumai were often cited. There was also an identification with popular culture. This was natural since the *élite* status or responsibility among the cultural-ideological circles was spurned. Neo-conservatism in the cultural field apparently displayed itself in a return to traditionalism (chuantongzhuyi).

Under the circumstances at home and abroad, China's neo-conservatism developed rapidly, not only in the cultural field. It became a strong ideological trend dominating both intellectual and government circles throughout the 1990s. No doubt, it presented itself as a miscellaneous collection of schools or factions, with numerous and jumbled views and theories. Those in favor of it, nevertheless, described it thus: Neo-conservatism stresses positivism, gradualism, and rationalism, and opposes any anti-order, anti-society, and anti-culture actions characteristic of irrationalism. It holds that China's modernization should be realized by making full use of the rational factors in the national tradition and in the existing establishment. In the political-economic fields, it seeks a strengthening of the state's central authority, for a new centralization on the basis of a modern economic system. In the ideological-cultural fields, neo-conservatism promotes a creative transformation of the traditional culture. An organic integration of socialism, traditional Chinese culture, patriotism, and various modern rational spirits, it serves as a spiritual resource for the building of China's modernization. Its defenders even claim that neo-conservatism is a sign of the maturity of China in the 1990s (xin baoshouzhuyi shi jiushiniandai Zhongguo zou xiang chengshude biaozhi).

One may not agree with the claim, but, perhaps, one can say that the emergence of neo-conservatism in China of the 1990s was natural and even reasonable. Symbolic was the proposition "farewell to revolution" (gaobie geming) as put forward by Li Zehou, a well-known philosopher and aesthete, and Liu Zaifu, former director of the Literature Institute of CASS, in their 1995 book *Farewell to Revolution: Looking Back upon China of the Twentieth Century*. They find that revolution—either of the Left or of the Right—tragically affected the fate of China and decided its features throughout the 20th century. And now it is time to bid it farewell. They suggest an order for "gradual reform": 1. economic development; 2. individual freedom; 3. social justice; and 4. political democracy. And all these presuppose social stability (p. 55).

Advocates of neo-conservatism share the thesis "The need for stability overwhelms everything else" (wending yadao yiqie), which is regarded as part of Deng's strategic thinking, a conclusion made in light of China's modern history and the prevailing circumstances. But the following deduction certainly does not avoid controversy: China's reform presupposes economic development, economic development presupposes social stability, and social stability presupposes the strengthening of the Party and government authority.

Significantly, this is a key point in the controversy between neo-conservatism and liberalism. In the opinion of the liberals, the key issue in China is not how to further strengthen the government's power. The Chinese government is one of only a handful in the world that enjoys unlimited power. Its power (essentially the power of the Party) penetrates every corner of Chinese society. Most of the difficulties in the economy are caused by improper government intervention. Therefore, liberals advocate the concept of "small government, large society" (xiaozhengfu, dashehui). Their goal is to limit governmental power through political reform, eventually creating a limited, responsive, and fair government based on popular consent. This should be a major criterion for a successful modernization program.

Controversy has also arisen from the arguments of "neo-Maoism", or "neo-Leftists", which is regarded by some as a school of neo-conservatism. Cui Zhiyuan, a Chinese scholar now teaching in America, is regarded as one of the major advocates of the school. According to his neo-Marxist interpretation, the "People's Commune" was a form of villagers' self-government; the 1958 "Great Leap Forward" was a harbinger of the present thriving of the "township and village enterprises" (which were set up and collectively owned by villagers and townships); the "Charter of the Anshan Iron and Steel Company" ("An'gang Xianfa") was a Chinese example of Fordist economic democracy; and the GPCR was a praiseworthy experiment about how to restrain powerholders and to eliminate social injustice. "Neo-Leftists" hope to restore the role of Mao Zedong and to systematize what they call "the rational factors of the Cultural Revolution". They not only negate the immediate need for liberalism in China, but also reject its ultimate value. In their eyes, only Mao's legacy (wrapped in neo-Marxism) can save China. They ignore the fact that under Mao China was a totalitarian society similar to the Soviet Union under Stalin.

In the fields of politics and economics, neo-authoritarianism is said to be an early, though not regular, stage of neo-conservatism. The June 4th Incident of 1989 offered a historical opportunity for the transformation from neo-authoritarianism to neo-conservatism. Notably, many who now advocate "neo-conservatism" are those who supported "neo-authoritarianism" in the 1980s. An important figure in the transformation is Xiao Gongqin. The most visible symbol, however, is He Xin, a controversial CASS scholar. His role in the transformation was conspicuous and unique. Interestingly, He Xin disdained neo-authoritarianism. He also refused the title of neo-conservative. He preferred to be a spokesman of nationalism.

Significantly, both neo-authoritarianism and neo-conservatism favor a centralized state power (zhongyang jiquan), as does nationalism, especially when it is employed in modernization, as a cure-all guiding ideology. As early as 1991, Chen Yuan (son of CCP elder Chen Yun) announced his view about "vigorously enhancing the central government's authority and actual strength, and re-creating a system of macro adjustment and control" ("Woguo jingjide shenceng wenti he xuanze"—"Deep-level Issues of China's Economy and Its Choices", *Zhongguo qingnian bao,* 2 Jan. 1991). The book by Wang Shaoguang and Hu An'gang, *A Report on China's National Capability (Zhongguo Guojia Nengli Baogao),* can be said to be a systematic elucidation of Chen Yuan's view. Furthermore, for several years Hu An'gang has repeatedly preached the following idea: "strengthening the central government while weakening the local authorities" (qiang zhongyang, ruo difang). These people can be called "nationalists" (guojiazhuyizhe) who support and practice the theory favoring the supremacy of the state (guojiazhishang).

In China, both the confrontation and transformation of radicalism and conservatism share nationalism as their foundation. This can be seen in the emergence of neo-conservatism after the June 4th Incident of 1989. After Deng's 1992 "Southern tour" when China's reform entered a new round, neo-conservatism also entered a new period of rapid development. A distinguishing feature in this period was the popularity of not only neo-conservatism but also of nationalism and the combination of nationalism with neo-conservatism. Now both neo-conservatism and nationalism see themselves as products of optimism, and not of pessimism as they were seen shortly after the June 4th Incident. What can be called "cultural nationalism" (wenhua minzuzhuyi) has also emerged. First there was resentment against Chinese studies with Western methodology and Western stands. Then this developed into criticism and repudiation of the so-called "Western values" (xifang jiazhi). "Cultural nationalism" was used to resist "Western-centrism" (xifang zhongxinzhuyi), or, as more recently termed, the "cultural hegemony of Western imperialism" (xifang diguozhuyi wenhua baquan). Correspondingly, "Asian values", "the superiority of Chinese culture", or "the superiority of Eastern culture" were advocated. The 21th century was called the Chinese century. Many believed that the rejuvenation of Chinese culture (in the sense of world history) would be forthcoming. Thus, ironically, neo-conservatism could possibly evolve into neo-radicalism (again, with nationalism as the foundation), as some critics have pointed out. See also "wenhua re" (culture craze), "xin quanweizhuyi lunzheng" (neo-authoritarianism debate), "minzuzhuyi" (nationalism), "xinzuopai" (neo-Leftists), and "ziyouzhuyi" (liberalism).

新保守主义是九十年代中国走向成熟的标志
xin baoshouzhuyi shi jiushiniandai Zhongguo zouxiang chengshude biaozhi (neo-conservatism marked China of the 1990s heading for maturity)

See "xin baoshouzhuyi" (neo-conservatism).

新长征
xin changzheng (new Long March)

Soon after the "October 6th coup" of 1976, the term "new Long March" appeared. Hua Guofeng used it to describe his great mission. In fact, as CCP chairman and PRC premier, he was hailed at that time as the "wise leader" (yingming lingxiu) who would lead the Chinese people into the twenty-first century in a so-called "new Long March". The term continued to be used by other leaders, such as Deng Xiaoping (for instance, in his 13 December 1978 speech at the closing session of the Central Work Conference which made preparations for the epoch-making 3rd Plenum of the 11th PCC) and Jiang Zemin (for instance, in his 29 May 1997 speech at the Central Party School). See also "yingming lingxiu" (wise leader).

新传统
xin chuantong (new tradition)

See "fan chuantong" (anti-tradition) and "sixiang gaizao" (ideological remolding).

新凡是派
xin fanshipai (new whateverists)

After the "whateverists" headed by former CCP Chairman Hua Guofeng were toppled, anyone holding views similar to those of Hua was dubbed a "new whateverist". See "fanshipai" (whateverists) and "chongpo lun" (theory of breakthrough).

新共产党宣言
xin gongchandang xuanyan
(new manifesto of the Communist Party)

See "xiuzhengzhuyi" (revisionism).

新帝国主义
xin diguozhuyi
(neo-imperialism)

See "lengzhanhou shidaide xin diguozhuyi" (neo-imperialism in the post-Cold War era) and "weidu Zhongguo" (containment against China).

新干涉主义
xin ganshezhuyi
(neo-interventionism)

See "lengzhanhou shidaide xin diguozhuyi" (neo-imperialism in the post-Cold War era) and "weidu Zhongguo" (containment against China).

新海外文学
xin haiwai wenxue
(new overseas literature)

See "yimin wenxue" (diaspora literature).

新冷战
xin lengzhan
(a new Cold War)

See "lengzhanhou shidaide xin diguozhuyi" (neo-imperialism in the post-Cold War era) and "weidu Zhongguo" (containment against China).

新马克思主义
xin Makesizhuyi
(neo-Marxism)

See "rendaozhuyide Makesizhuyi" (humanistic Marxism).

新猫论
xin mao lun
(new "cat" theory)

See "san ge youliyu" (three favorables).

新毛泽东主义
xin Mao Zedong zhuyi
(neo-Maoism)

See "xinzuopai" (neo-Leftists).

新民主主义革命
xin minzhuzhuyi geming
(new democratic revolution)

See "disan liliang" (third force).

新民族主义
xin minzuzhuyi
(neo-nationalism)

See "xinzuopai" (neo-Leftists) and "minzuzhuyi" (nationalism).

新启蒙沙龙
xin qimeng shalong
(neo-enlightenment salon)

See "xin qimeng yundong" (neo-enlightenment movement).

新启蒙运动
xin qimeng yundong
(neo-enlightenment movement)

Some scholars suggest that the neo-enlightenment movement began in 1984, marked by such cultural events as the publication of the first of the *Towards the Future* series, the founding of the Chinese Culture Institute (with Tang Yijie, professor at Beijing University, as its president), and the popularity of *Reading* magazine, many of whose writers were controversial scholars of the younger generation (Xu Jilin, "Qimengde mingyun: ershi nian lai de Zhongguo xixiangjie"—"The Fate of Enlightenment: Chinese Intelligentsia during the Past Two Decades", *ES,* 4-13, Dec. 1998).

In the few previous years there had been a "thought-emancipation" movement, which was basically an official movement pushed by the Deng Xiaoping-Hu Yaobang faction, aimed at overthrowing the "two whatevers" and those "whateverists" headed by Party Chairman Hua Guofeng. But the significance of the movement turned out to be much greater than Deng had expected. As a natural development, criticism of the ultra-Left ideology led to an approval of humanism. Within the establishment, for a time, humanistic Marxism seemed to be the only panacea for the much damaged Party. Outside the establishment, China's intellectuals enthusiastically committed themselves to introducing those mainstream concepts of value in the West, and to designing reform modes based on their pursuit of cultural modernity. They regarded their historical mission as a movement of "neo-enlightenment", a resumption of the May 4th enlightenment spirit.

On the part of the Party authorities, there was strong suspicion against such "enlightenment". Step by step, as it turned out, those intellectuals found themselves very much at odds with the regime. For instance, at a "neo-enlightenment salon" held by Su Shaozhi, Fang Lizhi, and others on 28 January 1989 at Beijing's "Capital

Entertainment Room" with over one hundred participants, Fang explicitly called on the participants to adopt a critical attitude towards the current state of affairs. After analyzing the political situation in which he said there was a very heavy atmosphere of hostility, Fang told his listeners that the time had come for China's intellectuals to take action.

The June 4th Incident of 1989 put an end to the "neo-enlightenment" movement. After the Incident, China's intellectuals underwent a period of bitter self-reflection. (According to Li Shenzhi, this was not self-reflection but rather a kind of fear. See Li Shenzhi and He Jiadong, *Zhongguode Daolu—The Road China Takes,* Guagzhou, Nanfang Ribao, Jan. 2000.) See also "qimeng yu jiuwangde shuangchong bianzou" (a double variation of enlightenment and salvation), "wenhua re" (culture craze), and "ziyouzhuyi" (liberalism).

新权威主义论争
xin quanweizhuyi lunzheng
(neo-authoritarianism debate)

"Neo-authoritarianism" was first mentioned in 1986. An important event to mark this was Beijing University teacher Zhang Bingjiu' advocacy of a combination of centralization of state power and a market economy in a speech at the CCP Central Party School. The term "authoritarianism" was modified by "neo" because in modern Chinese history there had already been three debates on authoritarianism, taking place respectively in the period from the Revolution of 1911 to the May 4th Movement of 1919, the period from the end of the 1920s to the mid-1930s, and the period around the victory of the War of Resistance Against Japan.

From the last few months of 1988 to the first few months of 1989, there appeared a high tide in the debate on the desirability for neo-authoritarianism. People hotly debated this issue at seminars and in journals and newspapers. The *People's Daily,* an organ of the CCP, also devoted a special column to it. (For the debated, see, for instance, Liu Jun and Li Lin, ed., *Xin Quanweizhuyi: Dui Gaige Lilun Ganglingde Lunzheng—Neo-Authoritarianism: A Debate on the Theory of Reform,* Beijing, Beijing Jingji Xueyuan, Apr. 1989, and the articles concerned in *XHWZ,* 4:1-9; 6:14-24, 1989.) The background was a series of problems, such as the reversion to a high birth rate, cultural and educational crises, agricultural collapse, and industrial imbalances, together with the failure of the "price reform" in the summer of 1988. Economic reform had to slow down, and in some fields reversals occurred. Political reform became all the more remote. At the same time, corruption in the Party and government was becoming more serious. Social injustices led to the people's resentment; complaints were heard everywhere. It seemed that the country was haunted by a sense of depression and loss, or by a "reform fatigue symptom" (gaige pilaozheng).

In view of this situation, some turned to authoritarianism. Their basic point was: the establishment of a market economy was a premise of democracy, and only the "new authority" (obviously referring to Zhao Ziyang, then CCP general secretary, or someone of his type as his successor) could bring it about. The public was said not to yet have the political ability to exercise their democratic rights. Democracy, therefore, needed to be postponed until a market economy had been fully established by the "new authority". The masses, for their part, should fully support the "new authority" and vest him with enough power. Hence the tenability of their thesis "Freedom precedes democracy" (ziyou xianyu minzhu), or, to be more exact, economic liberalization is prior to political democratization (jingji ziyouhua youxianyu zhengzhi minzhuhua). Indeed, those in favor of neo-authoritarianism enthusiastically embraced the powerful "new authorities". At a seminar held in September 1988 by the *New Observer* magazine and other organizations, Dai Qing, a famous woman writer, asserted that the reform in China needed political "strong men", similar to those in some East and Southeast Asian countries in the past several decades. On the same occasion, Wu Jiaxiang, a Beijing-based economist, advanced the hypothesis that in order to modernize, a nation with the weight of tradition needed to undergo a dual process of a centralization of power at the top and the development of individual freedom at the bottom.

Among the "neo-authoritarianism" advocates, there was a difference between the so-called "northern school" (beipai) represented by Zhang Bingjiu and Wu Jiaxiang and the so-called "southern school" (nanpai) represented by Xiao Gongqin. Both had difficulties promoting their ideas. Since Zhao Ziyang seemed to support neo-authoritarianism, his political opponents naturally opposed it. As to many Chinese who remembered the Mao period, they instead advocated a sound social mechanism that could revise mistakes in its functioning process rather than a "good emperor" who controlled their fate. It was said that the ultimate goal of neo-authoritarianism was modernization and a democratic system, though during the course of the process it had to resort to monopolized power. Those who opposed it did not believe in this "necessary scourge" (biyaode huohai), and they were convinced that this was not merely a question of means—means, very often, betrays the goal. In actuality, for a developing country, a crucial lesson is: while asking the people to go all out for economic development, the authoritarian authorities tend to suppress the people's demands for an increasing voice in politics (but the demands will inevitably emerge with social mobilization and economic growth). Indeed, the vital problem of neo-authoritarianism is that the so-called "new authority" it advocates is still of an old type, "traditional" or "charismatic", its establishment relying on leaders and *élite* but not on the people's involvement and supervision. It is not a "legal-rational" authority.

Nevertheless, the "neo-authoritarianism" debate was of great significance—both a natural result of the ten years' economic reform and an attempt to make a breakthrough in face of the reform's predicament. It was the first initiative by intellectuals in the field of politics in forty years. Some held that, if it had not been stopped by the June 4th Incident of 1989, it would have brought about a new and perhaps profound political enlightenment. Ironically, the failure of the 1989 pro-democracy movement not only led to the downfall of the "neo-authoritarianism" supporter Zhao Ziyang, but also to a strengthening of the authoritarian mentality on the part of the new top CCP leaders. The incident offered a historical opportunity for the transformation from neo-authoritarianism to neo-conservatism. See also "xin baoshouzhuyi" (neo-conservatism).

新人口论
xin renkou lun
(new theory of population)

Ma Yanchu (1882-1982), former president of Beijing University, was well-known for his insistence on his belief in his theory of population.

In 1953, 1954, and 1955, Ma Yanchu carried out a population investigation in Zhejiang province (his native place). Aware of the danger of the high natural rate of China's population growth which had already exceeded the critical point of 2 percent, he suggested that a reasonable population policy, the key being family planning (jihua shengyu), be carried out. In July 1955, he presented his idea to the 2nd Session of the 1st NPC, as a motion entitled "Population Control and Scientific Research"

("Kongzhi renkou yu kexue yanjiu"). Thereafter, he further developed his idea, which he styled as a "new theory of population", so as to differentiate it from that of Malthus. On 2 March 1957 at a meeting of the Supreme State Council, Ma revealed his "new theory of population". Mao was present at the meeting, and expressed appreciation for Ma's speech. In fact, it was because of Mao's encouragement that Ma presented his theory at the 4th Session of the 1st NPC on 3 July 1957, and published it in the 5 July 1957 issue of the *People's Daily*.

Unfortunately, Ma Yanchu did not understand that his view was fundamentally at odds with Mao's ideas. On 27 May 1958, the *People's Daily* published Mao's later well-known statement: "In addition to the leadership of the Party, a decisive factor is our population of 600 million. More people mean a greater ferment of ideas, more enthusiasm, and more energy. Never before have the masses of the people been so inspired, so militant, and so daring as at present" ("Jieshao yi ge hezuoshe"—"Introducing a Co-operative", *RMRB*, 27 May 1958). A specious argument, "the more people, the more achievements" (ren duo hao banshi), was accepted by the Party as absolutely unquestionable.

In April 1958, Ma was criticized as the "Malthus of China". During the second half of 1958, a massive attack was launched upon him, with more than 200 critical articles published in the nation's major newspapers and magazines. Facing the huge political pressure, Ma did not yield. He even published his defense. This greatly angered the Party leaders. In March 1960, Ma was dismissed as president of Beida.

It was not until July 1979 that he was rehabilitated by the authorities. They admitted that, as facts had shown, Ma's "new theory of population" was correct. Unfortunately, within the period of twenty years, China's population crisis had already reached crisis proportions. See also "yitaihua" (single-child policy).

新儒家
xin rujia
(neo-Confucianists; neo-Confucianism)

See "ruxue disanqi" (Confucianism in its third stage of development) and "ziyouzhuyi" (liberalism).

新儒学
xin ruxue
(neo-Confucianism)

See "ruxue disanqi" (Confucianism in its third stage of development) and "ziyouzhuyi" (liberalism).

新三件
xin san jian
(new three most sought-after articles)

See "lao san jian" (former three most sought-after articles).

新社会主义观
xin shehuizhuyi guan
(new socialist view)

"New socialist view" is a key term in the controversy about China's reform and open-door program.

The central point of Deng's view about socialism is: The fundamental task of socialism is to develop productivity (shehuizhuyide genben renwu shi fazhan shengchanli). On 30 June 1984, in a talk with visiting Japanese friends, Deng explained his idea about building socialism with Chinese characteristics. He said: "What is socialism? What is Marxism? In the past we were not entirely clear-headed in understanding this issue. Marxism most stresses developing productivity. The fundamental task in the socialist period is to develop productivity." This was the first time Deng put forth his view about the fundamental task of socialism, which was later revealed in an article entitled "Deng Xiaoping on Socialism with Chinese Characteristics" ("Deng Xiaoping tan shenme shi you Zhongguo tesede shehuizhuyi", *Liaowang,* 34, 1984). Two years later, another article published in the same Party magazine, "Deng Xiaoping on Reform, the Open Door, and Peaceful Development" ("Deng Xiaoping tan gaige, kaifang yu heping fazhan wenti", *Liaowang,* 44, 1986), indicated that Deng had long cherished this idea.

This is very true. At the 8th CCP National Congress held in September 1956, for example, Deng helped establish a new Party line which stressed economic construction. In 1975, after taking over Zhou Enlai's duties, Deng avidly set about to carry out Zhou's "four modernizations" policy. He supported the view that "Science and technology are part of the productive forces". In March 1978, Deng found another occasion to reiterate his support—at the National Conference on Science. Later, Deng further developed his views by confirming the thesis "Science and technology are the first important productive forces".

Under Deng's auspices, at the PCC Work Conference held November to December 1978, which made preparations for the 3rd Plenum of the 11th PCC, the Party announced that the focus of all Party work was to be shifted from "taking class struggle as the key link" to economic construction. Furthermore, the 13th CCP National Congress (held in October 1987) put forward the "theory of the primary stage of socialism" and stipulated it as Party's "foothold" for China's current policies. The theory was justified by two "Marxist" viewpoints. One was: "Only on a high degree of commercialization and socialization of production can socialism be built", and the other: "Productivity is the ultimate determinant in the development of any society".

In his talks during the famous "Southern tour" in early 1992, Deng most powerfully expounded upon his views about productivity and socialism. He urged that science and technology be vigorously developed. He raised the "three favorables"—favorable to developing the productive forces in the socialist society, to consolidating China's comprehensive national strength, and to raising the people's living standards. He asked the people to defend against the "Left". He spoke favorably about market economy. He declared: "Development is the most essential criterion".

Jiang Zemin, as Deng's successor, found that he must follow Deng's line. (Deng said during his "Southern tour": "Whoever does not engage reform must step down.") At the October 1992 14th CCP National Congress, a "socialist market economy" was approved. After Deng's death, on 29 May 1997, Jiang delivered an arguably most liberal and unequivocally reformist oration he had ever made. He declared that Deng Xiaoping Theory about building socialism with Chinese characteristics had become the "guiding ideology" of the CCP. He agreed that public ownership does not amount to state ownership—it can and should take diversified forms. Then, in the propaganda wave of July to August 1997 prior to the forthcoming 15th CCP National Congress, a number of noteworthy articles or interviews were published in China's official media, each trying to interpret Jiang's 29 May 1997 speech by stressing the "new socialist view".

Xing Bensi, editor-in-chief of *Seeking Truth* magazine and vice-president of the Central Party School, said: "The fundamental difference between the new socialist view and the traditional view of socialism lies in the fact that the former gives prominence to the economy, while the latter to politics. This is a fundamental change in the socialist view" ("Fully Understanding the 'Primary Stage' and Resolutely Defending Against the 'Left'", *Zhongguo jingji shibao,* 29 July 1997). He interpreted Jiang Zemin's 1995 "talking politics" demand thus: "'Talking politics', as I understand it, is not to emphasize politics from a theoretical angle, from an angle with fundamental significance. If so, that would be another big retrogression" (ibid.).

Wu Jinglian, a prominent economist at the State Council's Development Research Center (who is regarded as part of Zhu Rongji's think-tank), asserted, "the basic characteristic of socialism is social justice plus a market economy" ("Shehuizhuyi jiben tezheng shi shehui gongzheng + shichang jingji"—"The Basic Characteristic of Socialism Is Social Justice plus a Market Economy", *Zhongguo jingji shibao,* 5 Aug. 1997). Dong Fureng, who was dubbed a "liberal economist", suggested that state-owned enterprises should be reformed according to the requirements set by the socialist market economy. In his opinion, the socialist market economy is "socialism plus market efficiency" ("Anzhao shehuizhuyi shichang jingjide yaoqiu gaige guoqi"—"State-owned Enterprises Should Be Reformed According to the Requirements Set by the Socialist Market Economy", *Jingji cankao bao,* 5 Aug. 1997).

Li Junru, deputy director of the Theory Bureau of the CCP Propaganda Department, asserted that Jiang's 29 May 1997 speech had brought about a "third emancipation of the mind". And it was even a more substantial emancipation, which was characterized by breaking through the "mental obstacles" on the issues of public ownership and private ownership ("The Third Thought Emancipation: Breaking Through the Mental Obstacle on the Ownership Issues", *Zhongguo jingji shibao,* 12 Aug. 1997).

After these interpretations, the "new socialist view" became even more clear. However, as critics said, such a "new socialist view", characterized by the theory of developing productivity as the fundamental task of socialism, might be questionable if judged by an orthodox Marxist view. In 1975 and 1976, during the campaign to "criticize Deng Xiaoping and counter the Right deviationist trend to reverse correct verdicts", Deng was accused by those later known as the Gang of Four of preaching the so-called "reactionary" theory of "productivity as the sole factor determining social life" (weishengchanlilun), or "productivity fetishism" (shengchanli baiwujiao). During and after the Deng period, Deng's view was still a major target of attack, though attackers inside mainland China did not mention Deng's name.

In 1986, for example, in an article by Chen Yong, a stern message was conveyed in the following passages:

"The vulgar view that the economy is the sole factor determining social life was already severely criticized by Engels in his later years, who deemed it totally incompatible with historical materialism."

"At present, as we still can see, the view is in vogue that the development of capitalist productivity, including that of the natural sciences and technology, can determine everything else."

"Regarding productivity as the sole factor determining social life (including literature and art) is far inferior to the view criticized by Engels in his later years" (Chen Yong, *WXZTX*, pp. 134-35).

After the June 4th Incident of 1989, in view of the grave domestic and international situations (the changes in the East European bloc and the Soviet Union were unprecedented in the international Communist movement), the Party carried out a nationwide propaganda campaign, focusing on the theme that "only socialism can save China" (zhiyou shehuizhuyi caineng jiu Zhongguo), so as to save the Chinese people's confidence in socialism. The campaign betrayed certain forces within the Party stubbornly opposing Deng's reform and the open-door program and attempting to draw China back on the old track. For example, Wang Renzhi, director of the PCC Propaganda Department, questioned whether the reform was socialist or not (Wang Renzhi, "Guanyu fandui zichanjieji ziyouhua"—"On Opposing Bourgeois Liberalization", *RMRB,* 22 Feb. 1990). On 30 July 1990, an article carried in the *People's Daily* asked, obviously directing the spearhead at Deng: Who says socialism cannot be made clear? (Xu Zhengfang, "Shui shuo shehuizhuyi 'liang bu qing'"—"Who Says Socialism Cannot Be Made Clear".) The Beijing-based magazine *In Quest of the Truth* carried an article condemning what it said the "vulgar view about productivity" ("Yongsu shengchanli guandian shi shifen youhaide"—"The Vulgar View about Productivity Is Very Harmful", *Zhenlide Zhuiqiu,* 10, 1991). On 10 December 1991, an attack was launched in an article entitled "The Seven Issues in Establishing the Socialist View about Reform". By accusing what it said the "capitalist view about reform", the article questioned Deng's reform program on a number of issues ("Guanyu shuli shehuizhuyi gaigeguande qi ge wenti", see *Crossing Swords,* pp. 186-93).

In the 1995 "anti-Deng 10,000-character petition" (pi Deng wanyanshu) and several other similar articles circulating later, attacks focused on the "harmful consequences" of Deng's talks during his 1992 "Southern tour". In the spring of 1997, the Beijing-based magazine *Midstream* was published with an attack on a 1996 book, *An Intimate Talk with the General Secretary* (Zhang Xining et al.,*Yu Zongshuji Tanxin,* Beijing, Zhongguo shehui kexue, Oct. 1996). The book was accused of raising a "new socialist view" that is contradictory to Party resolutions (see Feng Baoxing, "*Yu Zongshuji Tanxin* shi yi ben shenmeyangde shu?"—"What Kind of Book Is *An Intimate Talk with the General Secretary?" Zhongliu,* 2, 1997). Liu Ji, then CASS vice president and alleged to be part of General Secretary Jiang Zemin's think-tank, was also attacked because he highly praised the book in his "preface".

Yang Deming, a State Council official, published a long article entitled "Review of the New Socialist View" ("Guanyu 'xin shehuizhuyi guan'de jidian pinglun", *Zhongguo yu shijie,* supplementary issue No.1, 15, Feb. 1998). This was the most comprehensive refutation of the "new socialist view" as interpreted by Wu Jinglian, Xing Bensi, Dong Fureng, and Li Junru. What they advocated, according to the author, is not a Marxist slogan, but a slogan of social-democrats and bourgeoisie in the West. It is a theoretical program which preaches privatization plus unrestrained freedom, and does not regard the elimination of exploitation and class polarization as a necessary condition for socialism.

In 1999, Fang Ning, a professor at Beijing Normal University, raised a new thesis: "Socialism means harmony" (shehuizhuyi jiushi hexie). In Fang's opinion, socialism, rather than satisfy the people's needs, aims at changing their needs. It must completely abandon the concept of "competition" (jingzheng), which is characteristic of capitalism. It is a pitfall for socialist countries if they concentrate on developing productivity so as to catch up with and even surpass developed capitalist countries in the West. This is impossible of attainment, Fang writes, if the existing global economic structure does not fundamentally change. Essentially, the historical mission of socialism is to change human beings' traditional modes of production, life, and thinking, and their social relations, so as to realize a harmony in society and between human beings and nature (see Fang Ning, "Shehuizhuyi shi yi zhong hexie"—"Socialism Means Harmony", *Zhongguo yu shijie,* Nov. 1999). Rather than revise Marxism from a "Right" perspective, the "harmony" theory is close to Mao's "Left" thinking in his remaining years. The new and old-line Leftists highly praised this "harmony" theory, according to which Deng's theory about productivity and socialism can be completely cast away. They said that "socialism means harmony" should be the slogan for a new round of socialist movement.

Xing Bensi has perhaps found a good argument to defend the "new socialist view". He suggested a "coordinate" theory (zuobiao shuo) in differentiating between Marxism and anti-Marxism. According to him, half of the Marxist fundamental tenets have become outdated (see his 1996 *People's Daily* article "Unswervingly Upholding Marxism"). "If we take those Marxist theories and points of view as our reference frame," he said, "then it is ourselves who will become targets for attack" ("Fully Understanding the 'Primary Stage' and Resolutely Defending Against the 'Left'", *Zhongguo jingji shibao,* 29 July 1997). Therefore, he suggested that when talking about Marxism today, one should "take Deng Xiaoping Theory as the reference frame" (yi Deng Xiaoping lilun zuo canzhaoxi) (ibid.).

As early as the Beijing Spring period, the Chinese people began to openly question the socialism that had been practiced in China for several decades under Mao's rule. During the 1980s, China's intellectuals further pondered the traditional Marxist doctrine of socialism. One of such intellectuals was Jin Guantao, then editor-in-chief of the *Towards the Future* series *(Zouxiang Weilai Congshu)* and chief consultant for the "Future Study Association of Beijing University". On 7 December 1988, at a symposium he had organized—"China's Future and the World", Jin asserted that "the socialist experimentation and its failure are two legacies of the human race in the twentieth century". In the new century, the Chinese people may find a better social system for themselves to live in, whatever name it will be given. See also "shehuizhuyi chuji jieduan lun" (theory of the primary stage of socialism), "Deng Xiaoping lilun" (Deng Xiaoping Theory), "zhengtong Makesizhuyi zhengzai zou xiang siwang" (orthodox Marxism is heading for death), "jingji gaige" (economic reform), and "zhengzhi gaige" (political reform).

新诗派形成的先决条件
xin shipai xingchengde xianjue tiaojian
(prerequisites for the forming of new poetic schools)

See "menglongshi lilunde san ci jueqi" ("three rises" in the theory of misty poetry).

新市民文学
xin shimin wenxue
(new citizens' literature)

The "new citizens' literature", as a new and noteworthy literary phenonemon, came into being with the new socioeconomic situation in China in the early 1990s. Works in this genre, such as those by Wang Shuo, a popular writer in Beijing, were quite popular among China's readers. See "renwen jingshen lunzheng" ("humanistic spirit" debate).

新台湾人
xin Taiwanren

(new Taiwanese)

See "Taiwan wenti" (Taiwan issue).

新文学理论的支撑点
xin wenxue lilunde zhichengdian
(fulcrum of a new literary theory)

See "wenxue zhutixing" (subjectivity of literature).

新血统论
xin xuetong lun
(neo-lineage theory)

See "xuetong lun" (lineage theory).

新自由主义
xin ziyouzhuyi
(neo-liberalism)

See "ziyouzhuyi" (liberalism).

新的课题
xinde keti
(a new task)

See "liangdai shiren" (two generations of poets).

新的美学原则在崛起
xinde meixue yuanze zai jueqi
(a new aesthetic principle is rising)

In his article "A New Aesthetic Principle Is Rising" published in March 1981, Sun Shaozhen did not precisely define what he called "a new aesthetic principle", but it can be deduced from his description of the emerging poets of the "Misty School".

First, these poets did not want to be clarions for the era, or to make contributions beyond their own emotional worlds. They even avoided writing about experiences, struggles, and toils with the spirit of selflessness which people were long familiar with. Unlike the tradition of eulogies in the 1950s, and the battle songs in the 1960s, they sought after the secrets of life already dissolved in the heart and mind, instead of directly glorifying life.

Second, as Sun saw it, if traditional aesthetic principles laid greater stress on the unanimity between sociology and aesthetics, then the young poets of the "Misty School" placed more emphasis on their differences. He further pointed out that it would be superficial if one regarded it only as a divergence of two aesthetic principles. Essentially, he asserted, it was a divergence of two criteria concerning human value. When an individual's status rises in society and his rights are gradually restored; when society, class, and the age gradually no longer function as a ruling force over the individual, then, Sun said, the individual's feelings in poetry, his sorrow and happiness, and his inner world, will naturally come to have a greater value. The resuscitation of human nature in society will certainly lead to its resuscitation in art.

It was of social value, Sun asserted, to reflect on this progress by means of art; but this value differed greatly from the "orthodox" one. Take Shu Ting for example. Her aesthetic conception was to search for harmony. Since this was not easily found in real life, she very often could not but sigh and reveal in her poems a sort of loneliness and weariness with the abnormality in the human relations. Sun saw this as "a kind of refraction of the age" and argued that Shu Ting's feeling was also a "typical" kind of feeling. Judging aesthetically, he explained, the beauty in man's heart is not necessarily only displayed in struggle as stipulated by orthodox aesthetic principles. Indeed, a struggle cannot be carried out when it is dissociated from unity, and contradictions may lead to harmony.

As the third part of his description of the "new aesthetic principle", Sun emphasized the place of the irrational in artistic creation. The young innovators (the "misties"), while striving to overcome the restraints of the old conventions, obviously intended to set up new ones. In order to do that, however, it is insufficient to rely only on one's "consciousness of self" (ziwo yishi), which means to rely only on concepts. One must at the same time spend quite a long time dealing with "involuntary", "spontaneous" subconsciousness, since convention is the unity of consciousness and subconsciousness. As Sun explained, conventional forces in art are very stubborn, much more stubborn than those in life. People guide their ideology and practice with a consciousness of self in life. Though this too requires a process to overcome the old consciousness of self with the new, it is in the realm of the rational and therefore simpler. In art, however, it is not only the rational that dominates; there are also feelings. Quoting Hippolyte Taine's (1828-1893) statement about the poet's temperament, Sun observed that art, since it is tinged with feelings, must possess the nature of "involuntariness" and "spontaneity", which sometimes even "prevails". Extended artistic praxis not only trains an artist's conscious but also his subconscious, thus enabling him, when his feelings have reached a saturation point, to function with a sort of "involuntary", "spontaneous" convention, amounting to a conditioned reflex (tiaojian fanshe). What Sun tried to explain here is the particularity of artistic creation, or, in other words, the place of the irrational in artistic creation.

In Sun's opinion, it was of great significance to give the irrational due place in artistic creation. It was on this point that he very much admired the courage of the young innovators of the "misty school" and what they had achieved.

Finally, Sun said, artistic innovation means to contradict artistic tradition, and to contradict artistic tradition in effect means to contradict artistic convention. He asked people not to underestimate Gu Cheng's statement about convention being the enemy of poetry (for Gu Cheng's statement, see his "Xue shi zhaji, 2"—"Notes in Poetry Study, Part Two", *Shanquan*, 1:51, 1983). At the same time, he pointed out that conventions, even outdated ones, are not merely the stagnant swamps that Gu Cheng described, but they also contain the achievements and experience of the past. Though facing the stubborn grip of artistic convention, the young challengers still cannot neglect the positive factors of tradition, or they will someday be punished by dialectics.

With full confidence, Sun declared that a new aesthetic conception was being discovered. Without the discovery, he added, the limitations of traditional art could not be broken and there would be no possibility for emancipation in art, with the result that art would always merely repeat itself like a pendulum.

Though Sun Shaozhen discussed in this article an "aesthetic principle", there was insufficient analysis of what he called works of "young innovators" from the perspective of aesthetics or poetics. Sun was too devoted to philosophical-sociological theories. This has to be regarded as a shortcoming in his article, which he later admitted was "not yet very mature and well-conceived in some aspects". However, his was certainly not a "muddled" article. It was quite ingenious of Sun to find in the current poetic wave the "upturn of a new aesthetic principle". Moreover, he made as his starting point in his discussion these very sensitive issues—human nature, human value, expression of the subjective ego, and humanism. It certainly required a lot of courage. See "menglongshi" (misty poetry) and "menglongshi lilunde san ci jueqi" ("three rises" in the theory of misty poetry).

新的社会主义历史时期
xinde shehuizhuyi lishi shiqi
(new historical period of socialism)

See "xinshiqi" (new period).

新侨会议
Xinqiao huiyi
(Xinqiao conference)

In 1961 and 1962, a force within the CCP was able to exploit the natural disasters which occurred during those years in many parts of China and the economic setbacks brought about by the "Left" mistakes on the part of Mao's leadership since the 1957 anti-Rightist campaign. In the fields of literature and art, a number of important meetings were held to check the Left influence and to reduce the damage to China's ideological-cultural circles. In June 1961, two meetings, the Forum on Party Work in Literature and Art and the Conference on the Creation of Feature Films, were held in Beijing's Xinqiao (New Overseas Chinese) Hotel, (hence the name the "Xinqiao conference"). Zhou Enlai's speech to the participants at these two conferences was regarded as very important in the history of Communist literature and art. It was a systematic criticism and repudiation of the "Left" policies in the cultural sphere. This explains why it could not be published until 1979, eighteen years after Zhou had delivered it.

In March 1962, a similar meeting—the Forum on the Writing of Spoken Drama, Opera, and Children's Theater—was held in Guangzhou (hence the name the "Guangzhou conference"). Before that, a preliminary meeting was convened by Zhou Enlai in Beijing on 17 February 1962, and attended by over one hundred Beijing playwrights. Zhou Enlai and Chen Yi, a Politburo member and vice premier, delivered speeches on these two occasions, conveying the same message as that at the Xinqiao conference. See also "wenyi wei zhengzhi fuwu" (literature and art serve politics).

新生中产阶级
xinsheng zhongchanjieji
(new-born middle class)

See "xinsheng zichanjieji" (new-born bourgeoisie).

新生资产阶级
xinsheng zichanjieji
(new-born bourgeoisie)

The most impressive turnaround after two decades of economic reform has been the rapid development of the non-state economy. The private sector in 1996 accounted for a remarkable 69.1 percent of China's GNP and was growing at a rate more than three times that of the state sector (as provided by the 1996 *Abstract of Chinese Statistics* released by the official State Statistical Bureau). Along with the expansion of the private sector has been the formation of a "bourgeois class" (some prefer to call it "zhongchanjieji"—a "middle class", a new term in China, so as to make it more tolerable in the ideological environment). According to 1995 official statistics, about 20 million people, that is, 2 percent of the total population of the country, could be classified into this new rich class. China watchers note its significance, against the background that before reform China was basically a two class society, with only a privileged party stratum and a working class.

Issues related to this new-born class in China have indeed aroused people's interest, such as its composition, social and political positions, economic status, education, culture, relations with other classes, role in China, and similarities and differences with counterparts in other countries. This class has tremendous and growing economic power that enables them to participate with real influence in China's social development and to impact China's market in real terms. Politically, the class is building up a coalition with some factions in the CCP out of mutual interests. This alliance is expanding the private sector, which in turn is creating a space in which many strict orders from the central government are ignored. The alliance also provides opportunity for popular participation in state affairs. For instance, there is much evidence that this new class is exerting an influence on the NPC, at least at the grass-roots level, by affecting local elections.

In addition, it is argued that, in China's situation today, it is better not to confuse the two terms "zichanjieji" (the bourgeois class) and "zhongchanjieji" (the middle class). While the middle class is composed of ordinary government officials, private businesspersons, and professionals, the new-born bourgeoisie include the bureaucrat-bourgeois class (about 15 million people), the compradore bourgeois class, capitalists owning big private companies, and the rogue bourgeois class (those controlling secret societies). A Chinese derogatory term for those in this new-born class is "baofahu" (upstarts or nouveaux riches). They are regarded as a product of China's much hated "power economy" (quanli jingji). Their "previous accumulation" (yuanshi jilei) is considered most brutal and vicious, as He Qinglian, a controversial woman economist, points out in her well-known book *The Pitfalls of China*. The rise of this class has contributed to the worsening of social injustices in contemporary China.

Orthodox Communists worry about the fate of the CCP. They see a "new threat" from this class (though at the moment it is perhaps still a "class in itself"—"zizai jieji"), resulting from Deng's reform. This constitutes the central theme in an anti-Deng petition, entitled "Issues Concerning National Security" ("Yingxiang woguo guojia anquande ruogan yinsu"), which was circulated in the winter of 1995 and the spring of 1996. "When conditions are not yet ripe," the document warns, "the bourgeois class only participates in internal struggles of the Party.... Once conditions are ripe, it will take over the whole Party, with the support and coordination of the international bourgeois class. A direct and overt bourgeois dictatorship will replace the proletarian dictatorship."

The petition's argument is in line with traditional CCP doctrine. In the Mao period, political campaigns were often carried out to attack what was called "new-born bourgeois elements" (xinsheng zichanjieji fenzi). These elements referred to "those degenerate elements in a socialist society who formerly belonged to the ranks of the working class or the petty bourgeoisie", or to "those former officials or working personnel of Party and government departments who have degenerated as a result of contamination and corrosion by bourgeois ideas and who have lost their proletarian stand". During the GPCR, the concept of the "new-born bourgeoisie" was often discussed. It was said that the bourgeoisie had three forms in history: following the "liberal bourgeoisie" and the "monopoly bourgeoisie", the bourgeoisie within a proletarian party was its "last form emerging in the process during which the whole class heads towards its doom". According to this theory, the CCP is now facing a threat with the development of a new-born bourgeoisie, the bourgeoisie within the Party in particular.

Is China's emerging bourgeois class a stabilizing factor or a factor deepening class contradictions? Is it a major force for China's democratization? Is it true that the behavior, thinking, and lifestyle of this class constitute the so-called "Chinese dream", something that is universally pursued? Or does its rise imply a worsening of social injustices in China? The answers to these questions have universal significance. One cannot truly understand China today without first understanding the emerging bourgeois class. See also "jieji douzheng" (class struggle), "fan fubai" (anti-corruption), and "pi Deng wanyanshu" (anti-Deng 10,000-character petitions).

新生资产阶级份子
xinsheng zichanjieji fenzi
(new-born bourgeois elements)

See "xinsheng zichanjieji" (new-born bourgeoisie).

新诗论争
xinshi lunzheng
(New Poetry debate)

Se "menglongshi lilunde san ci jueqi" ("three rises" in the theory of misty poetry).

新诗的自我否定
xinshide ziwo fouding
(self-negation of the New Poetry)

See "menglongshi lilunde san ci jueqi" ("three rises" in the theory of misty poetry).

新时期
xinshiqi
(new period)

After the successful "October 6th coup" of 1976, the new CCP leadership was established with Hua Guofeng as its core. The leadership advanced the concept of "xinde shehuizhuyi lishi shiqi" (new historical period of socialism), which commonly is abbreviated as "xinshiqi" (new period). It suggested that 1976 marked a "new period" in Chinese history. The general task for the "new period" was stipulated as follows: to firmly carry out the line of the 11th Party Congress, steadfastly continue the revolution under the dictatorship of the proletariat, deepen the three revolutionary movements of class struggle, the struggle for production and scientific experiment, and transform China into a great and powerful socialist country with modern agriculture, industry, national defense, and science and technology by the end of the century.

Such a general task clearly revealed what Hua Guofeng and his supporters meant by "new". Soon Hua was toppled and the above stipulation was cast aside. As China scholars agree, it was at the 1978 3rd Plenum of the 11th PCC that the "new period" was endowed with significant new meaning. Thereafter, the "new period" was characterized by Deng Xiaoping's reform and the open-door program and by the confrontation between the trend of so-called "bourgeois liberalization" and the "four cardinal principles". The confrontation led to the occurrence of the June 4th Incident of 1989, which marked the end of the "new period". See also "yingming lingxiu" (wise leader) and "ziyouhua" (liberalization).

新时期文学
xinshiqi wenxue
(literature of the new period)

The 1976 downfall of the Gang of Four was a turning point not only for contemporary Chinese politics but also for contemporary Chinese literature. It was the dawn of a "new period" (as noted by the authorities), and with it the birth of a new literature was inevitable, even if the criticism and repudiation of the Gang's literary policies had not been as thoroughgoing as some would have wished. In fact, as some literary theorists and critics suggest, the birth of the "new period literature" can be traced back to the poems posted in Tiananmen Square during the 1976 Qingming demonstration, though strictly speaking the "new period" began with the fall of the Gang of Four, which was half a year later (some even assert that it did not begin until the 1978 3rd Plenum of the 11th PCC). One can even argue that stories by Chen Jo-hsi (Chen Ruoxi) about the GPCR published in Hong Kong during the period from 1974 to 1976 marked the birth of the "scar literature" and, logically, of the new period literature itself, as the "scar literature" was the most conspicuous feature of the new period literature in its early stage.

Some critics find the term the "new period literature" ambiguous and even unscientific. Instead, they suggest another term—"post-GPCR literature" (wen'gehou wenxue)—to describe China's literature after the end of the GPCR. The reason is simple: this literature is closely related to the GPCR, which can be seen from its themes, characters, plots, and language. Also, the most important writers of the post-GPCR literature can be grouped into two categories—the first and the second generations. The first are those who suffered greatly during the GPCR, those ex-Rightists, such as Wang Meng, Liu Binyan, Lu Wenfu, Cong Weixi, Zhang Xianliang, Liu Shahe, and Bai Hua. The second are those who emerged from among the "educated youth" (zhiqing), those who had been Red Guards during the GPCR such as Zhang Chengzhi, Shu Ting, Jia Pingwa, Wang Anyi, Han Shaogong, Kong Jiesheng, Ye Xin, and Liang Xiaosheng.

Or it might be more correct to say that there are two threads in the development of the new period literature. One is the "scar literature" (shanghen wenxue)—"reform literature" (gaige wenxue)—reportage literature (baogao wenxue); the other is "misty poetry" (menglongshi)—"root-seeking" fiction (xungen xiaoshuo)—"experimental fiction" (shiyan xiaoshio). A characteristic of the first group is that, while critical of the status quo and the CCP regime, their basic system of values and concepts still supports the official ideology. In contrast, the three genres in the second group are of a rebellious nature. Though quite distinct from one another (and even contrary to one another in the case of misty poetry and "root-seeking" fiction) in their external forms, they share the same internal relations. In language, they present a challenge to the "central discourse" (zhongxin huayu) with a "periphery discourse" (bianyuan huayu). This view may be controversial, but it also seems to be shared by many, for instance, the literary theorist Li Tuo. (See "A Summary of the Forum of Chinese Writers Abroad"—"Haiwai Zhongguo zuojia taolunhui jiyao", *Jintian*, 1990).

For ten years the "post-GPCR literature" underwent a process of ridding itself of the influence of GPCR styles. Finally, a leap occurred in 1987 when works in the genre of "neo-fiction" (xinxiaoshuo) or "vanguard fiction" (xianfeng xiaoshuo) or "experimental fiction" began to be created by those who were dubbed the "third generation" writers, such as Wang Shuo, Yu Hua, Hong Feng, Su Tong, Liu Heng, Li Xiao, Ye Zhaoyan, Ge Fei and Sun Ganlu.

For the writers of "experimental fiction", literature is a kind of power, and no longer a vehicle of meaning. They are not seeking the lost world of meaning. Instead, they appreciate such a loss. With an extremely subjective imagination and a unique, vivid language, they make their works into a subversive force, rebelling against and deconstructing the regulations of the established orthodox culture, ideology, and narrative. As a result, man, history, and meaning have all been deconstructed (see Liu Zaifu, "From Monolog to Polyphony: The Literature of Forty Years in Mainland China"—"Cong dubaide shidai dao fudiaode shidai: dalu wenxue sishinian", *ES*, 100-111, Apr. 1994). No wonder from the very beginning, the "experimental fiction" gave rise to much controversy. (For some works of this kind, see, for instance, Wang Xiaoming, ed., *Zhongguo Xianfeng Xiaoshuo Jingxuan—A Selection of China's Vanguard Fiction,* Lanzhou, Gansu Renmin, Dec. 1993; and Li Tuo, ed., *Zhongguo Shiyan Xiaoshuo Xuan—A Selection of China's Experimental Fiction,* Hong Kong, Sanlian, Jan. 1995).

With the emergence of "experimental fiction", the "new period literature", or the "post-GPCR literature", came to an end, or, more correctly, developed into a new phase. See also "xinshiqi wenxuede duoyuan fazhan" (pluralistic development of the literature of the new period).

新时期文学的多元发展
xinshiqi wenxuede duoyuan fazhan (pluralistic development of the literature of the new period)

Those who are more sympathetic to the new period literature describe it as "a pluralistic development".

During a brief honeymoon after the end of the GPCR, literature and politics enjoyed each other's company. In fact, the coming of the "new period literature" was not the result of the development of literature itself. It was also brought about by a tremendous political force. More explicitly, it occurred after the downfall of the Gang of Four and the beginning of Deng Xiaoping's new era. Literature, in return, extended to the new political force its enthusiastic support in denouncing Lin Biao and the Gang of Four, in denying the GPCR, and in repudiating the "two-whatevers". As Perry Link, an American scholar, points out, at that time there was a "happy three-way convergence" between what writers wanted to say, what readers wanted to hear, and what Deng Xiaoping and his followers wished to see expressed (Perry Link, "The Limits of Cultural Reform in Deng Xiaoping's China", *Modern China,* v. 13, 2:121, Apr. 1987).

Soon, however, the two "partners" felt more and more dissatisfied with each other.

First, as a reasonable demand, as soon as the shackles of the "tool theory" had been smashed, literature wanted to return to its own true nature. After 1984-85, this desire gradually became a conscious and conscientious pursuit on the part of a great number of writers and critics. They tried to make literature more artistic, with an aesthetic of its own. They not only wanted to have literature rid itself of its subordinate position to politics, but also, as Zheng Wanlong said, to "discover and complete 'transcendence' in the relationship between life and art" (Liu Na, "Zai nixianxiangzhong xingjinde xinshiqi wenxue"—"The Advance of the New Period Literature among Adverse Phenomena", *WXPL,* 5:4, 1986). Various literary experiments appeared. Two seemingly contradictory phenomena—the search for "roots" (xungen re) and the quest for "modernism" (xiandai re)—co-existed. Some even wanted to make the two extremes meet: the classical taste of the Orient and the modern taste of the West, or, furthermore, to achieve a transcendence of both. In their artistic pursuits, these writers felt disgusted with the politicization of literature (wenxue zhengzhihua), a long-standing problem in modern and contemporary Chinese literature. Indeed, as early as 1983, at a forum at the University of Chicago, Wang Anyi, then a young writer, had complained of the "excessive" interest from overseas in "explosive" works like "Unrequited Love" and "Between Man and Monster". In a literary sense, she stated, those were not very good works, for they had a "non-literary effect" (see Xiao Ling, "Zhongguo zuojia chuangzuo jingyan tan"—"Chinese Writers on Creative Experience", *QN,* 170:86, Mar. 1984).

In contrast to the above trend that tried to avoid politics as much as possible, another trend tried to influence society and even to be involved in politics. This can be seen in works of the writers of reportage literature, such as Liu Binyan, Su Xiaokang, Mai Tianshu, Zhao Yu, Zu Wei, Li You, and Jia Lusheng; of poets such as Ye Wenfu and of fiction writers such as Liu Xinwu, Gao Xiaosheng, Bai Hua, Jiang Zilong, Zhang Jie, Zhang Xinxin, and Ke Yunlu. Many of these writers viewed the current literary situation with mixed feelings. On the one hand, they welcomed the above-discussed new aesthetic trend, the appearance of which was psychologically a natural reaction to the devastating demand that "literature and art serves politics". Moreover, the trend had produced a number of works with remarkable artistic value, for which their authors deserved congratulations. An unprecedented phenomenon at least since the founding of the PRC, the trend had certainly enriched the content of contemporary Chinese literature, endowing it with the possibility of polydirectional development. On the other hand, however, these writers found the new wave too big and too vigorous, and difficult to accept. Liu Binyan, for instance, earnestly reminded readers that the trend was more and more remote from reality and amounted to the authors shutting their eyes to problems of significance to the Chinese people. He argued that he was not opposed to writers' artistic pursuits, but he wanted people to understand fully that China was still a country where tens of millions of people suffered from cold and hunger and where human rights were often violated; that writers and artists should shoulder their historical responsibility (see Lee Yee, "Another Interview with Liu Binyan", *JN,* 220:30, May 1988).

The literature Liu Binyan and his supporters advocated was one which could function as a "judge" in both social life and politics. Liu believed that though literature had multiple functions, in any specific age, one specific function might be more important than others. In view of the literary situation in China at that time, Liu certainly had reasons to say this. In the "new period", the most welcomed and most influential works were no doubt those with a greater value in cognition. In fact, in the last few years of the 1980s, when some other genres of literature faced problems, reportage literature, which was devoted to social problems, was popular.

Perhaps, for some other writers and critics, especially those of the younger generation who were more rebellious, the two above trends were still undesirable. For instance, Liu Xiaobo, a young critic, explored the crisis of the new period literature (Liu Xiaobo, "Weiji! xinshiqi wenxue mianlin weiji"—"The New Period Literature Is Facing a Crisis", *Shenzhen qingnian bao*, 3 Oct. 1986; "Zai lun xinshiqi wenxue mianlin weiji"—"More on the Crisis of the New Period Literature", *Bai jia,* 1:12-26, Jan. 1988). Nevertheless, with each individual effort by writers of various styles, there appeared some new features in the new period literature which were noteworthy. First, there was a revival of humanism. Critical realism was again employed by many writers. Then, surpassing the "reflection" stage, various explorations and experiments became more common on the literary scene. Literature began to enjoy a pluralistic development. The long-held "socialist literature" gradually disintegrated. Many writers, not wanting to be a "tool" of the Party and regarding themselves as the most advanced social elements, expressed a spirit of enlightenment which was characteristic of the May 4th literature (For discussions of these, see, for instance, Yang Yi, "Dangjin xiaoshuode fengdu yu fazhan qianjing"—"Fiction in China: The Present Condition and Future", *WXPL,*5:20-32, Sept. 1986; Zhang Zhong, "The Transformation of Contemporary Chinese Literature", *CL,* 2:185-90, Summer 1987; Liu Xinwu, "Jin shi nian Zhongguo wenxuede ruogan texing"—"Some Characteristics of Chinese Literature in the Last Decade", *WXPL,* 1:5-12, Jan. 1988; Miao Junjie, "A Preliminary Study of Literary Schools in the New Era", *CL,* 4:175-86, Winter 1988; Liu Zaifu, "Jinshiniande Zhongguo wenxue jingshen he wenxue daolu"—"Chinese Literature in the Past Ten Years: Spirit and Direction", *RMWX,* 2:115-28, 1988; trans. by Stephen Fleming in *CL,* 3:151-77, Autumn 1989; Xie Mian, "Meiyou zhuchaode wenxue shidai"—"A Literary Period without a Mainstream, *Wenyi zhengming,* 3:4-13, 1988; Gao Shang, "Lun xinshiqi xiaoshuo chuangzuode shendu moshi"—"The Pattern of Depth for Fiction Writing in the New Period", *WXPL,* 4:61-69, July 1989; Li Ziyun, "Sound and Fury", *CL,* 1:181-86, Spring 1989; Wang Gan, "Surrealism and Factuality in Fiction", *CL,* 4:174-177, Winter 1989; Helen F. Siu, "Social Responsibility and Self-expression: Chinese Literature in the 1980s", *Modern Chinese Literature,* v. 5, 1:7-31, Spring 1989; and Liu Zaifu, "Two Historic Breakthroughs: From the May 4th Movement of New Culture to the 'Consciousness of Modern Culture' in the New Period", *RMRB*, 25 Apr. 1989.)

Indeed, developing alongside (and as part of) the general ideological trend of liberalization in society, the mainstream of the new period literature displayed itself as a reflection of social life in contemporary China, and particularly as a reflection of the Chinese people's (and the authors') aspirations. In turn, it influenced people (often unconsciously) in their pursuit of the truth, the good, and the beautiful, in their pursuit of modern consciousness, and also in their demands for democracy and freedom. Its social effect should not be underestimated.

新时期文学的两条线索
xinshiqi wenxuede liang tiao xiansuo
(two threads of the literature of the new period)

See "xinshiqi wenxue" (literature of the new period) and "xinshiqi wenxuede duoyuan fazhan" (pluralistic development of the literature of the new period).

新时期文学面临危机
xinshiqi wenxue mianlin weiji
(the new period literature faced a crisis)

At the September 1986 Symposium on Chinese Literature in the Ten-Year New Period, when Liu Zaifu, the host and major speaker, along with most participants, was intoxicated with what Liu considered to be the great achievements in contemporary Chinese literature since the downfall of the Gang of Four, Liu Xiaobo, then a young Ph.D. candidate at Beijing Normal University, issued a warning that the "new period literature" was in fact facing a "crisis". Dissatisfied with the comparison often made between literature in the "new period" and that in the GPCR, or with that in the seventeen years prior to the GPCR, he mockingly likened it to "having a poor meal especially prepared to recall past bitterness" (chi yiku fan), a common practice during the GPCR. Liu asserted that the "new period literature" was not a continuation of the "May 4th literature", but a poorly refurbished version of classical literature. He pointed out: As seen from the works by writers in the "new period", as well as by those in the 1920s and 1930s, the spirit which is characteristic of the Chinese people is "always looking to the past", and this is deplorable (Liu Xiaobo, "The New Period Literature Is Facing a Crisis", *Shenzhen qingnian bao*, 3 Oct. 1986). Liu Xiaobo admitted that the realities in contemporary China, the characteristics of Chinese life, have determined that it is hard for contemporary Chinese art to develop into a pure art, and that "literature as a vehicle for a significant message" (wen yi zai dao) is still the fate of his Chinese contemporaries. However, he argued, it is because the force of tradition is so strong that one must vigorously advocate a non-rational aesthetic view (ibid.).

At the beginning of 1988, having survived the 1987 campaign against "bourgeois liberalization", Liu Xiaobo, adhering to his stand, once again pondered the question of a "crisis". In a treatise entitled "More on the Crisis of the New Period Literature" ("Zai lun xinshiqi wenxue mianlin weiji", *Bai jia,* 1:12-26, Jan. 1988), he presented his views on "misty poetry", "root-seeking" literature, artistic form, and the non-rational. He found that "misty poetry" had already stopped developing as early as 1980. As to "root-seeking" literature, Liu asserted that it deserved to be criticized because it played the role of strengthening Chinese tradition from various perspectives. The artistic form was also said to be problematic. Many works were produced, in the main, with the rational, or social significance, taking the lead. If in the GPCR period, comparisons were made between classes and between the old and the new societies, now one could see comparisons between the good and the bad, between reform and anti-reform, between upright and corrupt officials, between ignorance and civilization, between humanity and barbarity, etc. Rich as they were, all these works could be reduced to two social modes: one "political" and the other "moral", and, very often, these two modes were interwoven in a single work (Liu Xiaobo, "More on the Crisis of the New Period Literature", *Bai jia,* 1:12-26, Jan. 1988). See also "xinshiqi wenxue" (literature of the new period) and "xinshiqi wenxuede duoyuan fazhan" (pluralistic development of the literature of the new period).

新时期早期报告文学的两大流派
xinshiqi zaoqi baogao wenxuede liang da liupai
(two main schools of reportage literature in the early stage of the new period)

After the downfall of the Gang of Four in 1976, reportage literature was very popular among Chinese readers, though it often faced obstacles because of political interference. In its first stage, there were two outstanding pieces arousing great repercussions: Xu Chi's 1978 "The Goldbach Conjecture" ("Gedebahe caixiang", *RMWX,* 1:53-68, 1978; trans. in *CL,* 11:78-91, 1978) and Liu Binyan's 1979 "Between Man and Monster".

"The Goldbach Conjecture", detailing the sorrowful experience of the accomplished mathematician Chen Jingrun, aroused a general concern in the society for the fate of intellectuals, a serious issue at that time. It can be classified as the first important work of "lobby literature" (Rudolf Wagner describes science-fantasy fiction as lobby literature in his "Lobby Literature: The Archeology and Present Functions of Science Fiction in China", in Jeffrey C. Kinkley, ed., *After Mao: Chinese Literature and Society 1978-1981*, pp. 17-62. Most representative of "lobby literature" in China are pieces of reportage literature as represented by "The Goldbach Conjecture"). As for "Between Man and Monster", it succeeded in drawing people's attention to the corruption within the CCP and to the serious problems in China's social and political systems, by exposing and analyzing the corruption of Wang Shouxin. The author of "The Goldbach Conjecture" was originally a poet. With the strong passion characteristic of a poet, he provides a moving and detailed description of the fate of his hero. Liu Binyan, on the other hand, was a professional reporter. He liked to probe the "why" of the typical events and people he was writing about; his writing is full of elaborate analyses and incisive expositions, with an intention to arouse people's vigilance. As a result, "Between Man and Monster", with the strength of logic, was more of a socio-political nature. Reportage literature in the "new period", as critics pointed out, was more or less developing along the two courses as represented by the above two works, and its achievements were apparent. See also "xinshiqi wenxue" (literature of the new period), "xinshiqi wenxuede duoyuan fazhan" (pluralistic development of the literature of the new period), and "wenyi wei zhengzhi fuwu" (literature and art serve politics).

新时期的总任务
xinshiqide zongrenwu
(general task for the new period)

See "xinshiqi" (new period), "yingming lingxiu" (wise leader), and "Deng xiaoping lilun" (Deng Xiaoping Theory).

新闻报导二八开
xinwen baodao erbakai
(a 80-20 ratio in news reports)

See "xinwen ziyou wenti" (issue of press freedom).

新闻封锁反效应
xinwen fengsuo fan xiaoying
(reverse effect of a news blockade)

See "xinwen ziyou wenti" (issue of press freedom) and "yi wenti wei zhongxinde baogao wenxue" (problem-centered reportage literature).

新闻立法
xinwen lifa
(legislation for journalism)

See "xinwen ziyou wenti" (issue of press freedom).

新闻是党的喉舌
xinwen shi dangde houshe
(journalism is the Party's mouthpiece)

See "xinwen ziyou wenti" (issue of press freedom).

新闻自由问题
xinwen ziyou wenti
(issue of press freedom)

On a number of occasions in the 1940s and 1950s, Mao talked about journalism's class nature and its Party spirit principle. He asserted that freedom of the press, as advocated by the bourgeoisie, was fraudulent. During his period, all newspapers, from the *People's Daily* controlled by the PCC (as its mouthpiece since August 1949) to local newspapers controlled by local CCP committees at various levels (provincial, municipal, prefectural, and county), were "dangbao" (Party newspapers), that is, Party's mouthpieces (dangde houshe). They aimed to explain and extol Party principles and policies, control and remold the people's thinking, and help standardize their behavior. Among China's press circles, everyone understood what "guided public opinion" (yulun daoxiang) meant. Freedom of speech (yanlun ziyou) was stipulated in the PRC Constitution, but no one dared to practice it. As an important feature of Party culture, "one and single public opinion" (yulun yilü) or, figuratively, arbitrary "one voice chamber" (yiyantang), fully displayed itself in China's journalism. Mao and his Party achieved all this easily because from the very beginning of the Communist regime the media became an integral part of government apparatus and were financed by the government.

Journalism as the Party's mouthpiece and tool of class struggle was most emphasized during the GPCR. Since many of the media were closed down, the roles of the *People's Daily*, the *Liberation Army Daily* (the mouthpiece of the CMC, formally beginning publication on 1 January 1956), and *Red Flag* (the PCC theoretical journal which began publication on 1 June 1958, and was renamed *Qiushi—Seeking Truth* in July 1988) were even more important and conspicuous. They were dubbed "liangbao yikan" (the two newspapers and one journal). Party decisions (usually stern, uncompromising messages concerning publication, explanation, and implementation of Mao's new directives) were often made known in the form of their joint editorials. Most important articles of "mass criticism" (dapipan) were usually first published by them.

During the GPCR almost all people were involved in the "sida" practice, i.e., to "speak out freely, air one's views fully, write big-character posters (dazibao), and hold great debates". Throughout the country, there were a great number of "xiaobao" (small-sized newspapers) run by Red Guard and other mass organizations. This was so-called "extensive democracy" (daminzhu) during the GPCR. Thanks to these "xiaobao" and other unofficial publications, some heterodox concepts and theories were widely spread. (See, for example, Song Yongyi and Sun Dajin, ed., *Wenhua Dage'ming He Tade Yiduan Sichao—Heterodox Thoughts During the Cultural Revolution,* Hong Kong, Tianyuan Shuwu, 1996.) But Mao's "extensive democracy" did not mean freedom of speech or press freedom in its modern legal sense. Mao made it clear that democracy was something used to deal with enemies (see, for instance, Li Shenzhi and He Jiadong, *Zhongguode Daolu—The Road China Takes,* Guagzhou, Nanfang Ribao, Jan. 2000). Red Guards' "xiaobao" were mainly tools conducted by Mao and his comrades to expose and attack alleged capitalist-roaders and counter-revolutionaries.

In the first few years after the end of the GPCR, Deng Xiaoping's faction encouraged people to express opinions and grievances against earlier miscarriages of justice. In Beijing such grievances were posted on a wall in Xidan district known as "Xidan Democracy Wall" or "Democracy Wall". During the exciting period of what was later called the "Beijing Spring", a pro-democracy movement rapidly expanded and spread to other cities. Towards the end of 1978 some of the poster-writers and democracy activists, in Beijing and in other cities, cooperated in publishing quite a number of unofficial magazines and journals. Famous among these in Beijing included *Siwu Luntan (April 5th Tribune,* edited by Xu Wenli and Liu Qing), *Tansuo (Exploration,* edited by Wei Jingsheng), *Beijing Zhi Chun (Beijing Spring,* edited by Wang Juntao), and *Jintian (Today,* edited by Bei Dao). The more radical activists were not only against a few "bad" Party and state leaders, but also against the entire Communist regime in China. They demanded emancipation of individuality, human rights, and democratic reform of the political structure. Naturally, all these publications were soon banned because they had gone too far away from what Deng expected.

During the GPCR and the few years after its end, a notable phenomenon was the popularity of "xiaodao xiaoxi" (a verbal transmission of news). People very often would rather believe information from obscure sources rather than news released through the official media. Information from obscure sources covered a wide variety of topics, ranging from national affairs to the personal lives of Party and government leaders at various levels. It might consist of groundless rumors or the hard truths that the authorities were trying to conceal. Passing around such information became a part of daily life at that time and people seemed to enjoy it.

Information from obscure sources found support among people in China because of the lack of transparency in the country's public and political affairs. In his speech of 13 December 1978, when referring to the popularity of "xiaodao xiaoxi", Deng pointed out, very correctly, that "this is a kind of punishment for the long-standing lack of political democracy" ("Emancipate the Mind, Seek Truth from Facts and Unite as One in Looking to the Future", *SWD,* p. 156).

In the Deng period, with the carrying out of reform and open-door program, many new concepts and new ways of thinking found expression in the media. A number of officially published newspapers and magazines were popular and influential, including *Shijie Jingji Daobao (World Economy Herald), Xin Qimeng (New Enlightenment), Sixiangjia (Thinker),* and *Shehui Bao (Society)* in Shanghai, *Shenzhen Qingnian Bao (Shenzhen Youth Daily), Shekou Tongxun Bao (Shekou News),* and *Tequ Gongren Bao (Special Economic Zone Workers Daily)* in Shenzhen, *Qingnian Luntan (Youth Forum)* in Wuhan, *Xibu Chenbao (West China Morning Post)* in Lanzhou, and *Xin Guancha (New Observer), Zouxiang Weilai (Toward the Future),* and *Jingjixue Zhoubao (Economics Weekly)* in Beijing. The *People's Daily* also impressed people favorably when supervised by Hu Jiwei, its director.

But Party leaders found it difficult to abandon the CCP principle of journalism as the Party's mouthpiece. Hu Yaobang, who was considered by many to be enlightened, was no exception. In his speech on journalism delivered on 8 February 1985 before the Secretariat of the PCC, he reaffirmed that all news media must be under strict Party control and serve current policies as the Party's mouthpiece. He proclaimed: "The bright side of socialism is the dominant one, at the same time there also exists a dark side.... In general, 80 percent of the newspaper should contain achievements, praise, and the bright side of things, while 20 percent should contain shortcomings, criticism, and the dark side of things." Hu stated that in presenting the dark side, it is important to pay attention to attitude: "A black outlook should be avoided" (see Hu Yaobang, "Guanyu dangde xinwen gongzuo"—"On Party Work in Journalism", *HQ,* 8, 1985, reprinted in *XHWZ,* 6:1-7, 1985).

To be fair, this conservative view of Hu Yaobang merely followed CCP tradition. Admittedly, Hu Yaobang gave Hu Jiwei much support in his work in the *People's Daily.* While Hu Jiwei lost his directorship in the 1983 "eliminating spiritual pollution" campaign, the real target of the campaign was Hu Yaobang (see, for instance, Wang Ruoshui, *Hu Yaobang xiataide beijing: Rendaozhuyi zai Zhongguode mingyun—Behind Hu Yaobang's Stepdown,* HK, Mingjing, 1997). The above-mentioned newspapers and magazines (except the *People's Daily)* were later all banned one after another, charged with "bourgeois liberalization"; Hu Yaobang was also forced to step down on 16 January 1987 on the grounds that he was too weak in opposing liberalization.

News blockade led to a "reversal effect" (xinwen fengsuo fan xiaoying). This, interestingly, helped an unprecedented flourishing of "problem-centered reportage literature" (yi wenti wei zhongxinde baogao wenxue), a genre between literature and journalism, so much so that 1988 was dubbed the year of the "reportage literature craze" (baogao wenxue re). Inspired both by the large number of social problems needed to be redressed and by the strong demand for this genre from a large readership, a number of journalists turned to writing of this genre. Several works caused great repercussions in society, such as "Going Abroad: A Great Trend" ("Shijie dachuanlian", *DD,* 1, 1988) by Hu Ping and Zhang Shengyou, "Migrants in Western China" ("Xibu zai yimin", *RMWX,* 5, 1988) by Mai Tianshu; *On the Altar of "Utopia"—1959 Summer in Lushan Mountain* (*Wutuobang' Ji: 1959 Nian Lushan Zhi Xia,* Beijing, Zhongguo Xinwen, Nov. 1988) by Su Xiaokang, Luo Shixu, and Chen Zheng; "Farewell to Modern Superstition: A Great Debate over Problems Concerning Criterion of Truth" ("Zouchu xiandai mixin: guanyu zhenli biaozhun wentide dabianlun", *Zhongshan,* 3, 1988) by Tao Kai, Zhang Yide and Dai Qing.

Mai Tianshu spoke out what other journalists thought when he confessed: "I feel that this is a very convenient way for me. You have pondered so much about China. If you put your thoughts into a thesis, few would read it. If you write them as fiction, people might say that it is made up. But when you employ the genre of reportage literature, you can spread your ideas and understandings in this very popular form. Under the present cultural conditions in China, this is the most convenient way of enlightenment" (Su Xiaokang et al., "1988: guanyu baogao wenxuede duihua"—"1988: A Dialog on Reportage Literature", *Huacheng,* 6:6, 1988). These journalists can be said to be followers of Liu Binyan. As far as reportage literature is concerned, Liu's maxim, "Be involved in life" (ganyu shenghuo), was no doubt relevant. Now, his ideas was carried forward by these journalists who were obviously trying to be involved in politics. The issue of democracy was the soul of Liu's reportage literature; now writers of this genre like Su Xiaokang and Dai Qing were dealing with this issue in a more daring fashion.

Significantly, by the last few years of the 1980s, editors and journalists all enthusiastically pushed and participated in reforms for China's media, with press freedom as their political pursuit. An example was Hu Jiwei, who tried to include press freedom in the press law when he was in charge of its drafting. (Hu later lost his job.) Their struggle came to a high tide during the 1989 pro-democracy movement, when they demonstrated in Beijing streets, carrying banners with the slogan "We want to speak the truth!"

The June 4th Incident put an end to this political struggle. Changes in China's media, however, did not stop. In the 1990s, media reform focused on how to make journalism in keeping with a market economy. An eye-catcher was the rapid growth of the market-oriented "xiaobao". According to a report by the official China News Agency in July 1992, "xiaobao" numbered 1,018 in 1992, 70.6 percent of the 1,442 newspapers published in that year. In addition, all "xiaobao" had a huge circulation. For instance, in 1990, the Shanghai-based *Newspapers and Magazines Digest (Baokan Wenzai)* enjoyed a circulation of two million and twenty thousand. In contrast, the *Liberation Daily,* the organ of the CCP Shanghai Municipal Committee, had a circulation of six hundred thousand.

The essential difference between "xiaobao" and "dangbao" is not their sizes—though "dangbao" are always big-sized newspapers (dabao). Most importantly, the appearance of "xiaobao" means the end of the monopoly of "dangbao". "Xiaobao" do not play the role of "Party's mouthpiece". Characterized by informativeness (zhishixing), interestingness (quweixing), and recreational nature (yulexing), they aim to serve society, to meet various needs of the people from all walks of life. This is why there are large variety of "xiaobao". "Dangbao" are published, so to speak, for Party and government officials, whereas "xiaobao" for common people (laobaixing). In most cases, therefore, one subscribes to "xiaobao" with one's own money, while subscriptions to "dangbao" are usually paid by the "danwei" with public money. For instance, in 1993, over 90 percent of the subscribers to evening papers (a kind of "xiaobao" numbering about 50 in the country in that year) were private, but private subscribers to the *People's Daily* were only 2.5 percent of its total subscribers. Readers of "dangbao" would spend some time reading "xiaobao", but not many readers of "xiaobao" would read "dangbao" as well. Hence the saying: "one country, two kinds of newspaper" (yiguo liangbao).

In the past, as tools of propaganda, the Party mainly considered the media's political benefit (zhengzhi xiaoyi). Today, most "xiaobao" assume sole responsibility for their profits or losses, and thus become commodities in society. In keen commercial competition, their editors and journalists must take economic benefit (jingji xiaoyi) into consideration and try their best to make their products attractive to readers. They themselves must be professionally proficient and no longer merely know how to please Party leaders. Another significant aspect is that "xiaobao" provide much space on their pages for freelance writers (ziyou zhuan'gao-ren), thus helping the development of this profession, which reappeared in China just a few years earlier after an absence of almost half a century.

Nevertheless, the flourishing of "xiaobao" and the marketization of the media still do not mean freedom of the press. "Xiaobao" do not concern themselves very much with politics. They help little in building the seriousness, accurateness, objectiveness, and justice of the press as the "fourth power". Instead, their contents and ways of operation (commercialization) can damage the taste of readers, editors, and journalists to serious journalism.

Corruption exists in journalism as well as in other fields. A major problem is "paid news-writing" (youchang xinwen). First appearing in the mid-1980s with what is called "commercial tide" (shang chao), this practice is now widespread, so much so that "no money no report" becomes the guideline for some reporters. This is common knowledge: If you pay, you can have something published to your advantage, no matter whether it is true to the facts or not; the more you pay, the more complimentary the news writing will be, and the greater the benefits. For building press ethics, a meeting was jointly held on 16 February 1998 by the PCC Propaganda Department, the Ministry for Broadcasting, Film, and Television, the Press and Publication Bureau, and the Chinese Journalists Association. As announced after the meeting, paid news-writing was banned. Press circles were asked to "distinguish" between those staff members assigned to engage in commercial activities and those assigned to professional work. But it is doubtful that these measures will succeed.

There is an appeal for legislation for journalism (xinwen lifa). A press law is strongly asked for, which will favor press freedom and will be strictly enforced and observed. Not only corruption of journalism itself should be checked. More importantly, journalists' rights must not be infringed and journalism's social functions must be strengthened. In October 1999, Premier Zhu Rongji wrote an inscription for the staff of the Central Television Station, wishing the media to be "supervisor as public opinion, mouthpiece of the masses, warner to the government, and path breaker of the reform" (yulun jiandu, qunzhong houshe, zhengfu jingjian, gaige jianbing). Indeed, journalism should have these functions, especially against the background that in China today corruption has become a serious problem. But first journalists should enjoy press freedom and be protected by law. Ironically, it is sixteen years since the drafting of press law began in 1984, and the law still has not been formulated. Obviously, most difficult is the issue of press freedom, which is also a major issue in an overall political reform.

However, those who are more optimistic believe that China's media will soon be dramatically changed. After China enters the World Trade Organization, its information industry, including publication and journalism, will be forced to open to foreign countries. China's domestic media will face an "innovation or demise" choice. High technology in information industry, which develops rapidly everyday, will make news blockade increasingly difficult. Take the Internet for example. According to official statistics, its subscribers in China numbered 16.9 million at the middle of 2000, sixteen times the figure at the end of 1995. It is predicted, very encouragingly, that the Internet will lead to China's next Cultural Revolution (guoji hulianwang jiang yinglai Zhongguo xia yi ge wenhua dageming). Of course, this time it will be a cultural revolution in its true sense. See also "zhengzhi gaige" (political reform) and "jingji gaige" (economic reform).

新闻的党性原则
xinwende dangxing yuanze
(journalism's Party spirit principle)

See "xinwen ziyou wenti" (issue of press freedom).

新闻的阶级性
xinwende jiejixing
(journalism's class nature)

See "xinwen ziyou wenti" (issue of press freedom).

新文学运动
xinwenxue yundong
(New Literature Movement)

See "wusi wenxue chuantong" (May 4th literary tradition).

新小说
xinxiaoshuo
(neo-fiction)

See "xinshiqi wenxue" (literature of the new period) and "renwen jingshen lunzheng" ("humanistic spirit" debate).

新月派
xinyuepai
(Crescent School)

A Chinese literary school during the 1920s and 1930s, its theory and practice was long regarded by Party critics as "bourgeois". During the "new period", it was reassessed, and its representatives became so popular that they were often cited by writers and critics. See also "liang dai shiren" (two generations of poets).

新左派
xinzuopai
(neo-Leftists)

Neo-Leftists, also called "neo-Maoists" (xin Mao pai), became active in the second half of the 1990s as a reaction to the general corruption in the Party and in society at large.

They vigorously appeal for social justice in China. They declare that social justice and political democracy must also be practiced in economic fields (see Han Yuhai, "Ziyouzhuyide lilun pinfa"—"The Poor Theory of Liberalism", *Yazhou yuekan,* 23 Jan. 2000). In their opinion, democracy is more important than freedom—under the conditions of a market economy, freedom very often means freedom to be slaves. They are convinced that many social evils currently rampant in China are introduced from the West, as a result of Deng's reform and open-door program, which they deem to be capitalist, revisionist, and reactionary. According to them, Deng's principle of "mainly defending against the Left" is essentially erroneous; corruption is an incurable disease caused by "taking economic construction as the center of all Party work", especially by establishing a market economy; and the theory of the "new age of peace and development" should also be held responsible for the Party's many erroneous judgments in handling international affairs. They assert that China has been involved in globalization and has already been harmed by it. As far as China is concerned, they point out, globalization means Westernization, or, even worse, Americanization. It will lead to capitalist restoration, placing China under the control of transnational corporations. They cannot accept a world led and controlled by financial and political oligarchies. (See Wang Hui, "Dangdai Zhongguo sixiang zhuangkuang yu xiandaixing wenti"—"The State of Contemporary Chinese Thought and Modernity", *Tianya,* 5, 1997; Han Yuhai, "Women shifou yao jieshou yige tongzhihua shijie?"—"Do We Need to Accept Uniformity in the World?", *ES,* 138-41, Aug. 1999; and Wang Xiaodong, Fang Ning, and Song Qiang, *Quanqiuhua Yinyingxiade Zhongguo Zhi Lu—China's Way Under the Shadow of Globalization,* Beijing, Zhongguo shehui kexue, 1999.)

At first, like old-line Leftists, neo-Leftists criticized Deng Xiaoping without naming. They even tried to make use of Deng's words to support their arguments. Now their attacks have escalated. Some of them simply regard Deng as the very "China's Khrushchev" Mao had asked people to be watchful against. Pledging to defend Mao's doctrine, they engage in exposing Deng's "true color" and finding out his "historical responsibility" for the problems in today's China. They absolutely cannot accept Deng Xiaoping Theory as the "guiding ideology" (zhidao sixiang) of the CCP in running the Party and the country. They find all these descriptions for the Theory untenable: "Marxism in modern China", "inheritance and development of Mao Zedong Thought", and a "new stage of development for Marxism in China". Neo-Leftists try to find a different, unique road for China. As Wang Hui, editor-in-chief of *Reading,* asks: Is it possible to have a modern society generated in a historical form which departs from capitalism, or, to follow a modernization course which can reflect on modernity?

They resort to Mao's legacy (often wrapped in neo-Marxism). For example, the so-called "Charter" of the Anshan Iron and Steel Company (a large state-run enterprise in Anshan city, Liaoning province), a policy for enterprises suggested by Mao in 1960, is highly praised by Cui Zhiyuan, a Chinese scholar now teaching in America. Interpreted in light of neo-Marxism, the "Charter" is seen to be a Chinese version of post-Fordism that advocates economic democracy (Cui Zhiyuan, "An'gang xianfa yu hou Futezhuyi"—"The Charter of the Anshan Iron and Steel Company and post-Fordism", *Zhongguo yu shijie,* Jan. 1997). Similarly, the "People's Commune" is a form of villagers' self-government, and the 1958 "Great Leap Forward" a harbinger of the present thriving of the "township and village enterprises". (Collectively owned by villagers and townships, these enterprises mushroomed after Deng's reform and open-door policies were carried out in 1978.)

In the opinion of the neo-Leftists, a "system innovation" (zhidu chuangxin) will be the cure for current social evils, and this can be achieved by absorbing "the rational factors of the Cultural Revolution" (see Cui Zhiyuan, "Mao Zedong 'wen'ge' lilunde deshi yu 'xiandaixing'de chongjian"—"The Success and Failure of Mao Zedong's Cultural Revolution Theory and the Rebuilding of Modernity", *Xianggang shehui kexue xuebao,* 7:49-74, Spring 1996). Mao is found to have tried "extensive democracy" (daminzhu) to solve the series of inner contradictions in the structure of China's "state socialism" (guojia shehuizhuyi), thus making a great contribution to the Marxist doctrine about socialism and state. The "sida" practice—"speak out freely, air one's views fully, write big-character posters, and hold great debates"—is said to have an immortal place in the history of the international socialist movement, similar to that of the 1789 Human Rights Declaration in history of world capitalism (Shi He, "Jinzhi yu pipan: chuli sixiang wenhua maodunde liang zhong butong celü"—"Prohibition or Criticism: Two Different Tactics in Handling Contradictions in Ideological-Cultural Fields", *Zhongguo yu shijie,* Feb. 2000). Neo-Leftists highly praise Mao's GPCR slogan "Take charge of the revolution, promote production" (zhua geming, cu shengchan). This idea, they say, truly embodies the socialist spirit, revealing the truth of "turning spiritual strength into material strength" (jingshen bian wuzhi). Mao's suggestion that the Cultural Revolution be carried out "once every seven or eight years" is also considered to be of foresight and sagacity, which can be systematized as nationwide direct election. In short, they find the GPCR to be a praiseworthy experiment about how to restrain power holders and to eliminate social injustice. They even ask for another GPCR in economic fields to be immediately carried out to "expropriate the expropriators".

As Wang Hui asserts, judging from the conception of history and values, Mao's socialist thought is a modernity theory which opposes capitalist modernity. In light of Mao's thought, a critic under the pen name "Xin Mao" (implying "neo-Maoist") strongly opposes the 1980s criticism of the planned economic system and of "daguofan" ("big cauldron canteen food", a colloquial reference to the egalitarian practices during the Mao period). He highly praises Mao's fight against the "economic man" (jingjiren) tendency. Today's reform is precisely guided by the concept of "economic man", Xin Mao warns. "If this is not changed, socialism will lose its last chance to exist in China" (Xin Mao, "Gaige yu jingjiren"—"Reform and Economic Man", *Zhongguo yu shijie,* May 1997). In 1999, furthermore, a new thesis, "Socialism means harmony" (shehuizhuyi jiushi hexie), was raised. According to Fang Ning, a professor at Beijing Normal University, socialism, rather than satisfy the people's needs, aims at changing their needs. It must completely abandon the concept of "competition" (jingzheng), which is characteristic of capitalism. Essentially, the historical mission of socialism is to change human beings' traditional modes of production, life, and thinking, and their social relations, so as to realize a harmony in society and between human beings and nature (see Fang Ning, "Shehuizhuyi shi yi zhong hexie"—"Socialism Means Harmony", *Zhongguo yu shijie,* Nov. 1999). Rather than revise Marxism from a "Right" perspective, the "harmony" theory is close to Mao's "Left" thinking in his remaining years, according to which Deng's theory about productivity and socialism can be completely cast away. No wonder "Socialism means harmony" has been hailed by neo-Leftists as a slogan for a new round of socialist movement.

The old-line Leftists or Maoists warmly welcome the neo-Leftists, though sometimes quite confused by their approaches and even their language. (Many of the neo-Leftists have been educated in the West and often employ novel terms from the latest Western schools.) Significantly, besides other things, they share a new model, "Nan Jie", a village in Henan province, first promoted in July 1994 by the Beijing-based magazine *Zhongliu (Midstream)*. The village is highly praised by Wei Wei, Cui Zhiyuan, Deng Yingtao, and other Leftists, as an experimental unit for Chinese communism. Like many other places in China today, joint ventures have been set up there; foreign investment and some foreign measures in business management (no doubt somewhat of a capitalist nature) have been accepted. However, the village authorities claim that they take the road of "all getting rich together" and not "some getting rich first". Most conspicuous is the fact that the village places itself under the guidance of Mao Zedong Thought. The villagers still follow many GPCR practices, hence the mocking description "capitalism in Mao Zedong style" (Mao shi zibenzhuyi).

1999 saw a debate between neo-Leftists and liberals, which was caused by a long article by Han Yuhai, "Behind the Posturing of Liberalism" ("Zai ziyouzhuyi zitaide beihou", *Tianya,* Sept. 1998). The debate focused on globalization, modernization, freedom, democracy, the market economy, social justice, and a number of other sensitive issues, including the U.S.-led NATO bombing of the Chinese Embassy in Belgrade. Liberal thinkers found it to be an exaggeration that China had been involved in globalization and already been harmed by it. In addition, they pointed out, what hinders China from progress is its inherent outdated institutional system and ideology, and this can be solved only by a deepening reform and further open-door program. As far as China is concerned, corruption is a "political cancer", with Chinese characteristics. It is a Chinese disease, a disease of "power economy". As to the issue of social injustice, one should agree that it had long existed in the Mao period, and at that time not only in the economic field, but also, and more frighteningly, in the political field.

Since many of the neo-Leftists did not have a GPCR experience, their evocation of "rational factors of the Cultural Revolution" was ridiculed by liberals as "cultural romanticism" (wenhua langmanzhuyi) or "political romanticism" (zhengzhi langmanzhuyi). Liberals further pointed out that the emergence of the neo-Leftists is in fact retribution for the CCP authorities' suppression of the GPCR studies, resulting in many Chinese failing to fully understand the dark truth of the GPCR.

Neo-Leftists can also be said to be neo-nationalists. Liu Kang, a Chinese scholar teaching in America, asserts that the big bourgeoisie in the United States spares no effort to demonize China because it does not want to see a powerful China emerging in the world. When discussing Sino-U.S. relationship, he strongly emphasizes class analysis and class struggle, an essential element of Mao Zedong Thought (see Liu Kang et al., *Yaomohua Zhonguode Beihou—Behind the Demonization of China,* Beijing, Zhongguo Shehui Kexue, Dec. 1996). In an April 1997 article, "Creating Peace for All Ages in the Future" ("Wei wanshi kai taiping"), published in the *Beijing Youth Daily,* Sheng Hong, another scholar, claims that Chinese culture can be used to save the world. His tone and approach are reminiscent of those high sounding words during the GPCR (such as "Liberate all oppressed mankind" and "The East wind is prevailing over the West wind".)

It is noted that the neo-Maoism and old-line Maoism have entered into alliance with radical nationalism. After the 7 May 1999 bombing of the Chinese Embassy in Belgrade, the neo-Leftists republished "The Two Fundamentally Opposed Policies of

Peaceful Co-existence" ("Liang zhong genben duilide heping gongchu zhengce", *RMRB,* 12 Dec. 1963), one of the "nine critiques" (liu ping) written under the supervision of Kang Sheng during the period of the CCP-CPSU polemics. At a forum held in Beijing on 10 October 1999 on *The Ten Years of Polemics (Shinian Lunzhan,* Beijing, Zhongyang Wenxian, 1999), a new book by Wu Lengxi (b. 1919), council chairman of the All-China Journalists Association, the struggle against "modern revisionism" by the CCP under Mao's leadership was highly praised. As liberals warned, it is not impossible if the alliance of radical nationalism and Maoism will once again become China's leading ideological force in the coming one or two decades. And this is certainly not good news to the world or China.

So far no scholar has accepted the title of "neo-Leftist". It was suggested that neo-Leftists and liberals should be regarded as "liberal Leftists" and "liberal Rightists". After the debate, it would be good if a "liberal intermediate section" could emerge. (Gan Yang made this suggestion on 29 September 1999 at a forum on China in the coming decade held by the University of Hong Kong.) It was also argued that both liberals and neo-Leftists had made a mistake in taking each other as opponents. Their common targets should be the state that monopolizes all important social resources, the government that has unlimited power, and the ideological system that controls the people's thinking. But as many others have pointed out, differences between neo-Leftists and liberals are apparent. Fundamentally, they differ from each other in the prescription they write out for the problems in today's China—deepening the reform and changing the present system or resorting to Mao's legacy and abolishing the present reform. See also "xin baoshouzhuyi" (neo-conservatism), "minzuzhuyi" (nationalism), and "ziyouzhuyi" (liberalism).

心物辩证法
xin wu bianzhengfa
(spirit-matter dialectics)

See "Kylin wenhua" (Kylin Culture).

心态小说
xintai xiaoshuo
(psychological fiction)

See "yishiliude Zhongguo dailiren" (Chinese agent of the stream-of-consciousness).

心性
xinxing
(mind nature)

See "Falun Gong" (Law Wheel Cultivation).

心狱
xinyu
(prison of the mind)

See "sixiang gaizao" (ideological remolding).

信任危机
xinren weiji
(crisis of trust)

See "sanxin weiji" (crises of faith, confidence, and trust).

信心危机
xinxin weiji
(crisis of confidence)

See "sanxin weiji" (crises of faith, confidence, and trust).

信仰危机
xinyang weiji
(crisis of faith)

See "sanxin weiji" (crises of faith, confidence, and trust).

兴，观，群，怨
xing, guan, qun, yuan
(agent of stimulation, way to judgment, means to communal spirit, and vehicle for one's aggrieved feeling)

This can be traced back more than 2000 years to Confucius, who stressed the didactic function of literature and art. According to Confucius, poetry, for instance, could serve one's father at home and one's sovereign abroad, through its multiple functions as an "agent of stimulation", as a "way to judgment", as a "means to communal spirit", and as a "vehicle for one's aggrieved feeling". These concepts were cited in the discussions concerning the multiple functions of literature and art.

兴无产阶级思想，灭资产阶级思想
xing wuchanjieji sixiang, mie zichanjieji sixiang
(foster proletarian ideas and eliminate bourgeois ideas)

The concept of "fostering proletarian ideas and eliminating bourgeois ideas" was first put forth by Deng Xiaoping in 1956, in a talk to cadres of the Chinese New Democratic Youth League (the Chinese Communist Youth League as renamed in May 1957).

In the 1957 rectification movement, the authorities were shocked by many opinions which expressed "anti-Party, anti-people, and anti-socialism" sentiments. Thereafter, they vigorously propagated the slogan "Foster proletarian ideas and eliminate bourgeois ideas", aiming to change people's thinking. In 1964, in an editorial in *Red Flag* entitled "A Great Revolution on the Cultural Front" ("Wenhua zhanxianshangde yi ge da geming", *HQ*, 12, 1964), the slogan was emphasized again. Its argument was: Alongside the development of the socialist revolution and construction in China, the socialist revolution in the politico-ideological spheres should be further carried out. Therefore, the task to "foster proletarian ideas and eliminate bourgeois ideas" is unavoidable.

After the GPCR, this slogan was generally considered to be "ultra-Left", resulting in disastrous consequences, as can be seen most clearly in the GPCR. But some Party figures thought otherwise. On 18 April 1980, the slogan was raised once again in CCP Chairman Hua Guofeng's speech at the PLA Political Work Conference.

(The speech was written under the auspices of Wei Guoqing, director of the PLA General Political Department.) This worried many others, such as Li Weihan, a Party elder. In May 1980, he told Deng that at the moment the Party's most important task in the ideological field was not to criticize bourgeois ideas but to eliminate the feudal influence. Deng seemed to have been persuaded by Li. In his speech to an enlarged meeting of the PCC Politburo on 18 August 1980, Deng discussed problems in the Party's organizational and working systems, including bureaucracy, over-concentration of power, patriarchal methods, life tenure in leading posts, and privileges of various kinds (*SWD,* p. 309). For the first time, he raised the issue of reform of the system of Party and state leadership.

Later, the political climate changed again. A new slogan was issued: "Oppose bourgeois liberalization."

兴无灭资
xingwumiezi
(foster proletarian ideas and eliminate bourgeois ideas)

"Xingwu miezi" is an abbreviation for "xing wuchanjieji sixiang, mie zichanjieji sixiang". See the preceding entry.

星火计划
xinghuo jihua
(Sparks Project)

In early 1986 the PRC State Council approved the "Sparks Project", a plan of the State Scientific and Technological Commission. The main idea of the plan was to use modern technology to "spark" the development of rural areas.

形左实右
xing zuo shi you
(Left in form but Right in essence)

See "you" (Right).

形象思维论
xingxiang siwei lun
(theory of "thinking in terms of images")

Thinking in terms of images and thinking in terms of logic are two different things. To form a system of theories, one relies on concepts, with which one can easily carry out logical thinking. Those engaged in arts are mainly involved in thinking in terms of images. Actually, thinking in terms of images is the particular law of art. If writers and artists do not pay attention to it, they will end up with generalization. This, however, was said to be a reactionary fallacy. On the eve of the GPCR, a Party critic named Zheng Jiqiao first launched an attack in his April 1966 article "The Marxist Theory of Knowledge Must Be Adhered to in the Fields of Literature and Art: A Criticism of 'Thinking in Terms of Images'" ("Wenyi lingyuli bixu jianchi Makesizhuyi renshilun: dui xingxiang siweide pipan", *HQ,* 5 1966). Later, Zheng further carried out his views and attacked Zhou Yang for having promoted the theory of "thinking in terms of images" in an effort to "turn literary and art circles into an independent kingdom over which the Marxist theory of knowledge cannot exercise control" *(RMRB,* 6 Aug. 1966).

Post-Mao critics approved the theory of "thinking in terms of images", but they built their argument on a letter written by Mao to Chen Yi, then vice premier, on 21 July 1965, in which Mao said that thinking in terms of images was necessary in poetry writing.

姓资姓社之争
xing "zi" xing "she" zhi zheng
(a debate over "capitalism" or "socialism")

See "bu zhenglun lun" ("no debate" theory).

修身，齐家，治国，平天下
xiushen, qijia, zhiguo, ping tianxia
(self-cultivation, establishing one's family, serving one's country, and unifying the world)

The ideas of "xiushen", "qijia", "zhiguo", and "ping tianxia", first discussed in *Liji: Daxue (The Book of Rites: The Great Learning),* one of the Confucian classics, became part of the traditional teaching for Chinese intellectuals. A Confucian ideal, it emphasized the significance of an individual's self-cultivation for the harmony of the family, the prosperity of the nation, and even for the peace of the world. In discussions of Chinese culture and a Confucian revival, such as "Confucianism in its third stage of development" (ruxue disanqi), this Confucian ideal or principle was often mentioned. See also "ruxue disanqi" (Confucianism in its third stage of development).

修正主义
xiuzhengzhuyi
(revisionism)

Revisionism is an important concept in traditional CCP doctrine.

Mao analyzed revisionism and dogmatism (jiaotiaozhuyi) in his speech at the CCP's National Conference on Propaganda Work on 12 March 1957. He said: "Both dogmatism and revisionism run counter to Marxism. Marxism must certainly advance; it must develop along with the development of practice and cannot stand still. It would become lifeless if it remained stagnant and stereotyped. However, the basic principles of Marxism must never be violated, or otherwise mistakes will be made. It is dogmatism to approach Marxism from a metaphysical point of view and to regard it as something rigid. It is revisionism to negate the basic principles of Marxism and to negate its universal truth. Revisionism is one form of bourgeois ideology. The revisionists deny the differences between socialism and capitalism, between the dictatorship of the proletariat and the dictatorship of the bourgeoisie. What they advocate is in fact not the socialist line but the capitalist line" *(MZXJ,* 5, pp. 417-18).

During the prolonged struggle for state power, Mao chiefly opposed dogmatism. In May 1930 he wrote an article entitled "Oppose Book Worship" ("Fandui benbenzhuyi", in *Maozhuxi Zhuzuo Xuandu—Selected Works of Chairman Mao,* Beijing, Zhongguo Qingnian, 1965, p. 14). "Book worship" means dogmatism. Mao held in contempt those (many of whom had been trained in the Soviet Union) who, in discussions within the Party, could not open their mouths without citing a book, as if whatever was written in a book was right. In this article, Mao advanced a well-known thesis: "No investigation, no right to speak" (meiyou diaocha jiumeiyou fayan quan). In his 1937 philosophical work *On Practice*, Mao emphasized the importance of practice. In his opinion, "Genuine knowledge comes from practice" (shijian chu zhenzhi). During the 1942 Yan'an rectification movement, Mao raised the slogan of "opposing stereotyped Party writing" (fandui dang bagu). The term "stereotyped Party writing" has since been used as a metaphor to ridicule dogmatism in the CCP.

In the first few years of his Communist regime, Mao still focused his efforts on dealing with dogmatism (in this regard Mao's major target was Stalin). An important contribution was his discussion "On the Ten Major Relationships", originally a speech delivered on 25 April 1956 at the Enlarged Meeting of the PCC Politburo ("Lun shi da guanxi", *RMRB*, 27 May 1958; reprinted in *MZXJ*, 5, pp. 267-88). But soon Mao made a sharp change. On 27 February 1957, in his well-known speech on the "correct handling of contradictions among the people", Mao said: "Revisionism, or Right opportunism, is a bourgeois trend of thought that is even more dangerous than dogmatism *(MZXJ*, 5, p. 392). According to Mao, the revisionists, the Right opportunists, pay lipservice to Marxism. When they attack "dogmatism", they are really attacking the quintessence of Marxism. They oppose or distort materialism and dialectics, oppose or try to weaken the people's democratic dictatorship and the leading role of the Communist Party, and oppose or try to weaken socialist transformation and socialist construction. After the basic victory of the socialist revolution in China, Mao said, there are still a number of people who vainly hope to restore the capitalist system and fight the working class on every front, including the ideological one. And their right-hand men in this struggle are the revisionists. Mao stressed, therefore, that criticism and repudiation of revisionism is an important task of the CCP on the ideological-theoretical front *(MZXJ*, 5, p. 418).

In addition to other considerations, Mao's change had much to do with the 1956 situation in the international Communist movement. Thereafter, for two decades until his death in 1976, Mao was preoccupied with his struggles against revisionism, both at home and abroad.

According to CCP doctrine, in the history of the international Communist movement, revisionism was a branch of "opportunism" which originated from social democratic parties in Western countries during the last decade of the 19th century. Eduard Bernstein (1850-1923), a leader of the German Social Democratic Party, first asked to revise Marxism, hence the term "revisionism" (and also the term "Bernsteinism"). Revisionism was accepted by Karl Kautsky (1854-1938), the leader of the Second International (which existed from 1889 to 1914). Kautsky asserted that capitalism can "growing peacefully into socialism" (heping zhangru shehuizhuyi). This view was accused of opposing the Marxist doctrine about class struggle and, especially, about the proletarian revolution and proletarian dictatorship. Bernstein, Kautsky, and their followers, were condemned as old-line revisionists and betrayers of the proletariat.

After the mid-1950s there appeared the issue of "modern revisionism". It first referred to the Yugoslav Communist Party under the leadership of Marshal Josip Broz Tito (1892-1980). Both documents—the "Declaration of the Meeting of Representatives of Communist and Workers' Parties of Socialist Countries held in Moscow in November 1957" *(RMRB*, 22 Nov. 1957) and the "Statement of the Meeting of Representatives of Communist and Workers' Parties of Various Countries held Moscow in December 1960" *(RMRB*, 6 Dec. 1960)—condemned Tito and his party followers as modern revisionists. After the open breach between the CCP and the CPSU in the early 1960s, a fierce polemic occurred between the two parties. The

CCP leadership was convinced that the Soviet Union had changed its political color (bianse) and that Khrushchev, CPSU first secretary, had become the "chief representative of modern revisionism".

On 14 June 1963, the PCC sent a letter in reply to the CPSU Central Committee, which was entitled "A Proposal Concerning the General Line of the International Communist Movement" ("Guanyu Guoji Gongchanzhuyi Yundong Zongluxiande Jianyi"). In view of the fact that "a number of major differences of principle exist in the international Communist movement", the letter put forth a 25-point proposal concerning what it regarded as the "General Line" for the movement and some related questions of principle *(RMRB,* 17 June 1963). On 14 July 1963, in an open letter to its organizations and members at all levels, the CPSU Central Committee revealed its long-standing contradictions with the CCP. In less than one year, from September 1963 to July 1964, the CCP, in the name of the editorial boards of the *People's Daily* and *Red Flag,* successively published nine critiques on the open letter:

"The Origin and Development of the Differences between the CPSU Leaders and Us" ("Sugong lingdao tong women fenqide youlai he fazhan", *RMRB,* 6 Sept. 1963);

"On the Yugoslavia Issue" ("Guanyu Nansilafu wenti", *RMRB,* 13 Sept. 1963);

"Is Yugoslavia a Socialist Country?" ("Nansilafu shi shehuizhuyi guojia ma?", *RMRB,* 26 Sept. 1963);

"An Apologist of the New Colonialism" ("Xin zhiminzhuyide bianhushi", *RMRB,* 22 Oct. 1963);

"The Two Lines on the Issue of War and Peace" ("Zai zhanzheng yu heping wentishangde liang tiao luxian", *RMRB,* 19 Nov. 1963);

"The Two Fundamentally Opposed Policies of Peaceful Co-existence" ("Liang zhong genben duilide heping gongchu zhengce", *RMRB,* 12 Dec. 1963);

"The CPSU Leaders Are Today's Biggest Splittists" ("Sugong lingdao shi dangdai zuidade fenliezhuyizhe", *RMRB,* 4 Feb. 1964);

"The Proletarian Revolution and Khrushchev's Revisionism" ("Wuchanjieji geming he Heluxiaofu xiuzhengzhuyi", *RMRB,* 31 Mar. 1964); and

"On Khrushchev's Phoney Communism and Its Historical Lessons for the World" ("Guanyu Heluxiaofude jia gongchanzhuyi jiqi zai shijie lishishangde jiaoxun", *RMRB,* 14 July 1964).

In the opinion of CCP theoreticians, the 22nd CPSU Congress "marked the systematization of revisionism which the CPSU leadership had developed step by step from the 20th CPSU Congress onward" *(RMRB,* 6 Sept. 1963). Khrushchev's modern revisionist line was summed up in four Chinese characters: "san he liang guan". They were said to have opened the way for "capitalist restoration" *(RMRB,* 14 July 1964).

"Sanhe" (three "peacefuls") referred to "peaceful coexistence" (heping gongchu), "peaceful competition" (heping jingsai), and "peaceful transition" (heping guodu).

In the opinion of CCP theoreticians at that time, the theory of "peaceful coexistence" was wrong because it failed to point out that the socialist countries and other countries with different social systems could not coexist in peace until the revolutionary forces and the peace-loving forces in the world united as one in waging a resolute and effective struggle against the aggressive forces of imperialism. Furthermore, they said, peaceful coexistence did not mean that socialist countries should give up their support for class struggle in capitalist countries and revolutionary struggles waged by the oppressed nations against imperialism.

"Peaceful transition" meant transition from capitalism to socialism in a peaceful way, hence another term with the same meaning: "growing peacefully into socialism". The idea was raised by Eduard Bernstein and Karl Kautsky in the late 19th century and the early 20th century. At the 20th CPSU National Congress held in

February 1956, Khrushchev gave it his approval on the grounds that the "fundamental change" in the world situation had made its realization possible. However, CCP theoreticians pointed out that the transition from capitalism to socialism must be achieved through proletarian revolution and the dictatorship of the proletariat, and not via the "parliamentary road" (yihui daolu) as Khrushchev and other old and new revisionists suggested.

"Peaceful competition" was also a slogan raised by Khrushchev at the 20th CPSU National Congress in February 1956. According to Khrushchev, peaceful competition between the socialist camp and the capitalist camp would favor the progressive and revolutionary forces in the world, and in the end the socialist camp would defeat the capitalist camp in the competition.

"Liangquan" (two "entires") meant that the CPSU leadership had been building the Soviet Union into "a state of the entire people" (quanmin guojia) and the CPSU into "a party of the entire people" (quanmin dang). Under the auspices of Khrushchev, the "Programme of the CPSU" stated: "As a result of the victory of socialism in the USSR and the consolidation of the unity of Soviet society, the Communist Party of the working class has become the vanguard of the Soviet people, a party of the entire people." It also said: "The dictatorship of the proletariat has ceased to be indispensable in the USSR. The state, which arose as a state of the dictatorship of the proletariat, has, in the new, contemporary stage, become a state of the entire people." These statements of course betrayed the Marxist-Leninist doctrines about class struggle and the proletarian dictatorship. In its 9th and last critique attacking Khrushchev and his CPSU, the PCC came to the conclusion that the two "entire people" theories were "modern revisionist fallacies". Khrushchev's "revisionist political line" had resulted in a "peaceful evolution" in the Soviet Union ("On Khrushchev's Phoney Communism and Its Historical Lessons for the World, *RMRB*, 14 July 1964).

The fierce polemic between the CCP and the CPSU (Zhong Su dalunzhan) constitutes an important chapter in the history of the relationship between the two parties and with the international Communist movement. Each of the nine critiques created a great sensation at that time. In the nine critiques, the CCP styled itself as the greatest standard-bearer in the international struggle against what it called "modern revisionism" with Khrushchev as its ring leader. Not long thereafter, Sino-Soviet relations greatly deteriorated. There were not only ideological divergencies, in which the CCP found the CPSU acting like a "patriarchal party" (laozi dang). After the Soviet troops invaded Czechoslovakia on 20 August 1968, the CCP leadership condemned the Soviet Union as expansionist and aggressive, a "social-imperialist" country (shehui diguozhuyi)—"imperialism bearing the banner of socialism". An armed border conflict between the PLA and the Soviet army occurred on the Zhenbao Island in March 1969. Reportedly, the Soviet leaders even planned to destroy China's nuclear strike capability with a massive surprise attack.

As a "lesson" drawn from Khrushchev's coming into power and his pushing of a "revisionist political line", Mao and his followers considered "peaceful evolution" to be the greatest danger faced by countries in the "socialist camp". Under Mao's leadership, the CCP carried out a nationwide socialist education movement (also called "siqing yundong"—the "four clean-ups" movement) from the winter of 1962 to the beginning of the GPCR in May 1966, first mainly in the rural areas and then also in cities, especially in factories, mines, other enterprises, and schools. At a central work conference held in 1964, Mao stated: "If revisionism appears in the Party Center, what are you going to do? It is possible that it will appear, and this is a great danger." When meeting a foreign Communist Party delegation on 10 April 1964, Mao even proposed that Marxists of foreign countries help the Chinese Marxists fight against the Chinese revisionists. Finally, in 1966, Mao launched the GPCR—Mao concluded that he had to wage a struggle of historic significance in "combating and preventing revisionism" (fan xiu fang xiu). The worry of "peaceful evolution", as Mao himself proclaimed, constituted the reason for the launching of the GPCR. The "May 16th Circular" of 1966, which marked the formal beginning of the GPCR, implied that Liu Shaoqi was "China's Khrushchev". It called on the whole Party and the whole nation to struggle against "leading bourgeois proponents" who had sneaked into the Party, the government, the military, and various cultural circles. At the 9th CCP National Congress held in April 1969, "Chairman Mao's revolutionary line" was hailed; it was considered to have achieved an all-round victory over "Liu Shaoqi's counter-revolutionary revisionist line".

Not long after the end of the GPCR, Liu Shaoqi was rehabilitated. The Party agreed that Mao had made a big mistake in judging China's domestic situation and launching the Cultural Revolution. But Mao was still a "great Marxist", whereas Lin Biao and the Gang of Four must be condemned. A new official view held that during the course of history, revisionism may have different faces. In addition to "Rightist revisionism" (laizi youmiande xiuzhengzhuyi), there is "'Leftist' revisionism" (laizi 'zuo'miande xiuzhengzhuyi), which distorts Marxism with revolutionary slogans and radical actions. Lin Biao and the Gang of Four were precisely representatives of "Rightist revisionism".

After the Deng period began, the term "revisionism" was quietly dropped. As to the issue of "peaceful evolution", it once again became a political focus after the June 4th Incident of 1989. On 5 June 1991, the *People's Daily* published an article calling on the Chinese people to oppose and prevent "peaceful evolution" (Duan Ruofei, "Jianchi renmin minzhu zhuanzheng, fandui he fangzhi 'heping yanbian'"—"Upholding the People's Democratic Dictatorship; Opposing and Preventing 'Peaceful Evolution'"). Opposing "peaceful evolution" also became a major point in General Secretary Jiang Zemin's speech on 1 July 1991 to mark the seventieth anniversary of the founding of the Party (which was hailed by the Leftists as the "New Manifesto of the Communist Party"). A differentiation was asked to make between two opposing views about reform and the open door—the socialist view and the capitalist view. It was asserted that "peaceful evolution" and "bourgeois liberalization" constituted an immediate threat to China's independence and sovereignty, and to its construction, reform, and open-door program. An "Anti-Peaceful Evolution Group" under the Politburo was reportedly set up with the aim of countering liberalization and any efforts for political pluralization. In view of the 1989 "political turmoil" in China and the unprecedented changes in the East European bloc and the Soviet Union (particularly the changes following the failure of the 19 August 1991 coup staged by the Soviet hardliners), for a time the CCP's major concern was how to prevent the outbreak of peaceful evolution in China.

This was ended by Deng Xiaoping's 1992 "Southern tour". Thereafter, "anti-peaceful evolution" no longer was an important item on the official propaganda agenda. Instead, the Party had to prevent the topic from being abused by the "Leftist" forces. Ouyang Shan, a Guangdong-based veteran writer, in an article published in the July 1994 issue of *Literary Theory and Criticism,* complained that the current situation, characterized by "three don't mentions" (san ge buti), was "even worse" than that before the June 4th Incident of 1989. Besides the two "don't mentions" (as advocated by Zhao Ziyang)—brushing aside "eliminating spiritual pollution" and "opposing bourgeois liberalization"—which led to the 1989 "turmoil", many people also supported another "don't mention"—brushing aside "opposing peaceful evolution". This sounded an alarm: the Chinese revolutionary régime was in danger. In a document beginning to circulate in the late summer or early autumn of 1995, entitled "National Security: A Preliminary Inquiry into Internal and External Situations and Major Threats in the Next One or Two Decades", a "peaceful evolution" was said to have been taking place within the CCP. The document was dubbed the "second anti-Deng petition".

But it seems that many Chinese welcome the trend of "peaceful evolution", which they understand to mean evolution towards democracy, freedom, and prosperity. As they argue, "peaceful evolution", instead of "violent evolution", is the only, and the best, way out for China. They also refer to what they call "another kind of peaceful evolution"—many children of high-ranking Party and government officials have settled down in Western countries, enjoying the bourgeois way of life as much as possible.

When looking back, one may remember that Marshal Tito was later highly praised by Mao and his CCP colleagues. He was given the heartiest of welcomes during his 1977 visit to China (Mao had died just one year earlier, and it was considered a pity that the two leaders, both said to be "great rebels", never met each other). In the 1980s, Khrushchev also began to enjoy a new (though unofficial) appraisal in China. He was admired for foresight, sagacity, and his many unique ideas.

As CCP general secretary, Deng Xiaoping played an important role during the 1963-1964 polemic between the CCP and the CPSU, supervising the writing of those nine critiques. If one compares his policies of reform and the open door in China today with Khrushchev's so-called revisionist policies in the Soviet Union at that time, it is clear that there was a serious historical misunderstanding. Ironically, Deng is now attacked by neo-Leftists and fundamentalist Leftists (old-line Leftists) as the very "China's Khrushchev" Mao had all the time asked people to be watchful against. But such an attack has already lost its earlier weight. "Revisionism" is no longer a frightening label. See also "shijie geming" (world revolution), "xin shehuizhuyi guan" (new socialist view), and "Deng Xiaoping lilun" (Deng Xiaoping Theory).

修正主义比教条主义更危险
xiuzhengzhuyi bi jiaotiaozhuyi geng weixian
(revisionism is even more dangerous than dogmatism)

See "xiuzhengzhuyi" (revisionism).

修正主义苗子
xiuzhengzhuyi miaozi
(shoots of revisionism)

See "dangde jiaoyu fangzhen" (the Party's educational policy) and "xiuzhengzhuyi" (revisionism).

虚幻的集体
xuhuande jiti
(illusory collective)

See "dangdai lunzheng beiwanglu" (a memorandum on a contemporary debate) and "ziyouzhuyi" (liberalism).

学用结合
xue yong jiehe
(combine study with application)

See "tuchu zhengzhi" (giving prominence to politics).

学术问题
xueshu wenti
(academic issue)

See "zhengzhi wenti yingdang ziyou taolun" (political issues should be freely discussed).

血统论
xuetong lun
(lineage theory)

The lineage theory serves privileged class or privileged stratum. In the Mao period, it was justified by the Party doctrine about class, class struggle, and the dictatorship of the proletariat, and became most deceitful and most harmful. It can be called the "neo-lineage theory" (xin xuetong lun), so as to be distinct from a similar theory in feudal society.

Mao said: "In a class society everyone lives as a member of a particular class, and every kind of thinking, without exception, is stamped with the brand of a class (jieji laoyin)" *(SWM,* 1, p. 296). Communists must oppose class compromise. They must adhere to class line, according to which class ranks and class alignment were formed, and special attention was paid to those alien class elements who had wormed their way into the revolutionary ranks. The Party policy was: 1. uphold the theory of the importance of class origin (youchengfenlun); 2. oppose the theory of the unique importance of class origin (weichengfenlun); and 3. lay stress on one's political behavior (zhong zai zhengzhi biaoxian). In reality, the second point was lip-service. As to "political behavior", it meant to be the "docile tool" of Party officials. Those without a good class status (geren chengfen) or a good family origin (jiating chushen) were deeply troubled by the issue of the so-called "class brand". They often felt that they were treated like "contemptible wretches".

The lineage theory was rampant during the GPCR. Many Red Guards followed it fanatically. As scholars point out, the Red Guards would not have emerged had it not been for the lineage theory (meiyou xuetonglun jiumeiyou hongweibing).

Take the first Red Guard organizations in Beijing for example. They were set up directly inspired by Mao's instructions to fight against the so-called "anti-Party and anti-socialist sinister line in educational circles". Because most of their parents were Party officials or army officers (some were very high-ranking), these Red Guards considered themselves "born red", to be "natural revolutionary successors", and posed as future masters of the world. They engaged in what they called "Red Terror" and cruelly persecuting "niuguisheshen"—class enemies of all descriptions. They declared: "Only Leftists can enjoy the right to rebel; no Rightists are allowed to change our regime". Furthermore, they claimed that "one will be a true man if his father is a hero, while reactionaries bear only bastards", similar to the old saying "Dragons beget dragons, phoenixes beget phoenixes, and those begotten by rats are good at digging holes".

But even during the GPCR, there were people who indomitably challenged the lineage theory. The most brave among them was Yu Luoke, a young man in Beijing. In October 1966 he wrote an article entitled "On Family Background" ("Chushen lun", *Zhongxue wen'ge bao*, 1967, reprinted in Hong Kong Chinese University

Student Union, ed., *Minzhu Zhonghua*, 1982, pp. 17-30. Today this article is highly prasied, regarded as "a human rights declaration in the dark years"). Thereafter, he also wrote a number of other articles further criticizing the lineage theory. In 1968, Yu Luoke was arrested. On 5 March 1970, he was executed, at the age of 27, a victim of this vicious theory.

After the end of the GPCR, the Chinese people got a chance to openly condemn the bitterly despised lineage theory (though it was regarded only as part of the Gang of Four's line or Lin Biao's line). The critic Chen Huangmei said that the theory brought various tragedies to innumerable families, thus becoming a "universal social problem" (Chen Huangmei, "Pian duan yi shen, qixiang yixin"—"New Achievements in Short Stories", *Shouhuo,* 1, 1979, reprinted in *XWY, Theory,* 2, p. 323).

In the 1978 debate over the short story "The Scar", many correctly pointed out that its most praiseworthy element was its exposure and reprobation of the lineage theory, which also explained why the work provoked such fierce reactions. Interestingly enough, it was in this regard that the denunciation in "The Scar" was not thoroughgoing enough. In the story, the unjust verdict on the mother was finally reversed, which changed the life of the protagonist Wang Xiaohua. However, as Xiang Tong, another critic, asked, if the mother had really been a traitor, what would Xiaohua's fate have been? This was indeed a thought-provoking question. In fact, Xiang Tong also pointed out that even after the Gang was toppled, in real life there were many officials who still stubbornly adhered to the lineage theory (Xiang Tong, "Should Literature and Art Reflect the Tragedies of the Socialist Period: Beginning with 'The Scar'", *GMRB,* 3 Nov. 1978).

Today, after twenty years of Deng's reform and open-door program, great changes have taken place in China's social structure, and the lineage theory based on Mao's doctrine about class struggle has lost its social foundation. In the past, élite selection was made according to the principle of lineage; now principles of assets and achievements also play a role. But there is an important phenomenon no one should overlook: in the transformation of political capital, economic capital, and cultural capital, a handful of people of the privileged stratum always reap most of the interests—which can be described as "inside transformation" (quannei zhuanhuan). During the process, ironically, workers and peasants, which make up 83 percent of China's total population and are stipulated in the Constitution as the leading and the second leading class, have in fact descended to the bottom of society. He Qinglian sounded an alarm for the seriousness of the class polarization in today's China in her March 2000 controversial article "A Total Analysis of the Evolution of China's Current Social Structure" ("Dangqian Zhongguo shehui jiegou yanbiande zongtixing fenxi", *Shuwu,* Mar. 2000). See also "hongweibing" (Red Guards), "taizidang" (princes' clique), and "jingji gaige" (economic reform).

驯服工具论
xunfu gongju lun
(theory of being "docile tools")

In his speech of July 1937 at the Yan'an Marxism-Leninism Institute, Liu Shaoqi explained in detail his view about "docile tools". (Liu's speech was later published as *Lun Gongchandangyuande Xiuyang—On the Self-Cultivation of Communists).* On 30 June 1958, Liu explained his view again in his speech summing up a discussion organized by the *Beijing Daily* on the personal aspirations of Communists. On the basis of this speech, an editorial was written, approved by Liu himself, and carried in *Beijing Daily* on 29 July 1958. Entitled "What Should Be the Aspirations of a Communist?" ("Gongchandangyuan yinggai you shenmoyangde zhiyuan?"), the editorial echoed Liu's view that one should "serve as a docile tool and a tool easy to control". All these became "teaching material by negative example" during the GPCR, when Liu was accused of promoting the so-called theory of being "docile tools", one of his "six sinister theories" (hei liu lun).

The attack was built on the argument that one should not be a tool of a revisionist party, of Liu Shaoqi's revisionist line. But to Chairman Mao and his "proletarian revolutionary headquarters" one must be one hundred percent obedient. In fact, traditionally, the CCP demanded that every individual be the Party's "docile tool" (in reality, the docile tool of Party officials, very often, one's superiors). Today, people no longer accept being "docile tools", nor do they accept the thesis that writers (or other professionals) who are Party members must first fulfill their duties as Party members, and only after that can they play the role of a writer (or other professional). This, in Liu Binyan's opinion, was mere nonsense (Lee Yee, "Another Interview with Liu Binyan", *JN,* 220:27, May 1988). Bai Hua's answer was: Writers should respect history and life. They should serve long-lasting history and not transient policies (Lee Yee, "Does Bai Hua Still Stubbornly Love His Motherland?" *JN,* 216:90, Jan. 1988). See also "hei liu lun" (six sinister theories).

寻根热
xungen re
(intense search for "roots")

The Hangzhou Forum of December 1984, held by *Shanghai Literature* and the Zhejiang Provincial Writers Association and attended by such writers as Han Shaogong, Wang Anyi, Li Tuo, Zheng Wanlong, Li Hangyu, and Acheng and such literary critics as Huang Ziping, Wu Liang, Cheng Depei, and Li Qingxi, was an important event for the "roots" school. (A second conference on the "root-seeking" literature was originally planned to be held in Shanghai in May 1989.) Thereafter, the "root-seeking" fiction (xungen xiaoshuo) became popular, reaching a peak in 1985 and the first few months of 1986. It consisted of the following types:

1. Fiction of Confucian, Taoist, and Buddhist cultures (ru dao shi wenhua xiaoshuo), as seen in the works of Wang Zengqi, Acheng, and He Liwei. Acheng's 1984 novelette "Chess Master" ("Qiwang", *SHWX,* 7, 1984) produced a strong reaction not only at home but also abroad.

2. Regional culture fiction (diyu wenhua xiaoshuo). This was the mainstream of the "root-seeking" fiction, represented by Han Shaogong, Jia Pingwa, Wang Anyi, Li Hangyu, Zheng Yi, Zheng Wanlong, Zhang Chengzhi, Tashi Dawa, and Zhang Wei. Inspired by ancient myths, folk customs and folk tales, they probed into the deep structure of Chinese cultural psychology. Some of their works can be considered to be modern classics, such as Han Shaogong's novelette "Papapa" ("Bababa", *RMWX,* 6:83-102, 1985; reprinted in Wu Liang and Cheng Depei, ed., *Xin Xiaoshuo Zai 1985 Nian—Neo-fiction in 1985,* Shanghai, Shanghai Shehui Kexueyuan, 1986, pp. 1-43).

3. The post-"root-seeking" fiction (hou xungen xiaoshuo), as represented by the works of Mo Yan, Ma Yuan, and Can Xue. The best known among them was Mo Yan's novelette "Red Sorghum" ("Hong gaoliang", *RMWX,* 3:4-36, 1986; reprinted in Xi Xi, ed., *Hong Gaoliang*, Taipei, Hongfan Shudian, 1987, pp. 143-250; dir. Zhang Yimou, Xi'an Film Studio, 1987). The "experimental fiction" (shiyan xiaoshuo), which became popular in 1988, was derived from this genre.

For statements by "roots" writers, see, for instance, "The Roots of Literature" (Han Shaogong, "Wenxuede gen", *Zuojia,* 4, 1985); "My Roots" (Zheng Wanlong, "Wode gen", *SHWX,* 5. 1985); "Sorting Out Our Roots" (Li Hangyu, "Liyili womende gen", *Zuojia,* 6, 1985); and "Culture Has Been Conditioning Human Beings" (Acheng, "Wenhua zhiyuezhe renlei", *WYB*, 6 July 1985). For comments on the "roots" school, see, for instance, "My View on Searching for 'Roots' in Literature" (Han Kang, "Wenxue xun 'gen' zhi wojian", *Furong,* 1, 1986, reprinted in *XHWZ,* 5:159-61, 1986); "Consciousness of the Search for Cultural Roots in Contemporary Literature" (Chen Sihe, "Dangdai wenxuezhongde wenhua xungen yishi", *WXPL,* 6:24-33, 1986); "In Search of the Root: Returning to the Things Themselves" (Li Qingxi, "Xungen: huidao shiwu benshen", *WXPL,* 4:14-23, 1988); "Concerning the Creative Works of Three Writers of the 'Roots' School" (Wang Xiaoming, "Bu xiangxinde he buyuan xiangxide—guanyu sanwei 'xungen' pai zuojiade chuangzuo", *WXPL,* 4:24-35, 1988); and "Roots Searchers: Primitive Tendency and Semi-primitivism" (Fang Keqiang, "Xungenzhe: yuanshi qingxiang yu ban yuanshizhuyi", *SHWX,* 3:64-69, 1989).

The achievements of "root-seeking" literature, which was both a product and an expression of the "intense search for culture" movement, were remarkable. Notably, the theory of "root-seeking" literature preceded its creative practice. This was rare in the history of modern and contemporary Chinese literature. See also "wenhua re" (culture craze) and "xinshiqi wenxuede duoyuan fazhan" (pluralistic development of the literature of the new period).

寻根文学
xungen wenxue
("root-seeking" literature)

See "xungen re" (intense search for "roots").

寻根小说
xungen xiaoshuo
("root-seeking" fiction)

See "xungen re" (intense search for "roots").

压制与放松的循环
yazhi yu fangsongde xunhuan
(cycles of repression and relaxation)

See "liang tiao zhanxiande douzheng" (struggle on two fronts) and "ziyouhua" (liberalization).

亚洲价值论
Yazhou jiazhi lun
(theory of "Asian values")

See "quanqiuhua" (globalization), "ruxue disanqi" (Confucianism in its third stage of development), "wenhua Zhongguo" (cultural China), and "minzuzhuyi" (nationalism).

亚洲四小龙
Yazhou si xiao long
(Asia's "four little dragons")

See "ruxue disanqi" (Confucianism in its third stage of development).

严打
yanda
("strike hard" campaign)

From time to time, based on needs, such as an increase in the crime rate or during periods of sensitivity, the Chinese authorities carry out a "strike hard" campaign. During such a campaign, many alleged criminals are tried and given severe sentences. China critics worry that these may involve miscarriages of justice. The human rights watchdog Amnesty International, for instance, accused China's legal system of failing to attain international standards which require careful legal procedures and safeguards for defendants in death penalty cases (more than 60 offences carry the death penalty in China). According to an Amnesty International report released on 25 August 1997, China executed more of its citizens in the previous year than all other countries combined. Chinese courts imposed the death penalty more than 6,100 times and there were 4,367 confirmed executions. This was almost double the 3,110 death sentences imposed and 2,190 executions in 1995, and the highest number of state-sanctioned killings since the campaign of mass executions of 1983.

In recent years, "strike hard" campaigns are not so often carried out as before.

言论自由
yanlun ziyou
(freedom of speech)

See "renquan wenti" (human rights issue) and "xinwen ziyou wenti" (issue of press freedom).

言论自由权是最重要的人权
yanlun ziyou quan shi zuizhongyaode renquan
(freedom of speech is the most important human right)

See "renquan wenti" (human rights issue).

洋为中用
yang wei Zhong yong
(make foreign things serve China)

See "shuangbai fangzhen" (Double Hundred policy).

阳谋
yangmou
(overt trick)

See "sida" (four bigs) and "fan youpai yundong" (anti-Rightist campaign).

样板戏
yangbanxi
(model dramas)

See "wen'ge wenyi" (GPCR literature and art).

样板戏恐怖症
yangbanxi kongbu zheng
(model drama phobia)

See "wen'ge wenyi" (GPCR literature and art).

要交流，要和平，要双赢
yao jiaoliu, yao heping, yao shuangying
(exchanges, peace, and a win-win policy)

See "Taiwan wenti" (Taiwan issue).

要警惕右，但主要是防止"左"
yao jingti you, dan zhuyao shi fangzhi "zuo"
(watch out for the Right, but mainly defend against the "Left")

See "you" (Right) and "Deng Xiaoping lilun" (Deng Xiaoping Theory).

要民主还是要新的独裁
yao minzhu haishi yao xinde ducai
(democracy or neo-dictatorship)

On 25 March 1979, Wei Jingsheng put up a big-character poster on Beijing's "Xidan Democracy Wall" as an extra issue of *Exploration (Tansuo, haowai)*, an unofficial Beijing-based journal he edited during the 1978-79 Beijing Spring period. In his article, entitled "Democracy or Neo-Dictatorship?" ("Yao minzhu haishi yao xinde ducai"), Wei raised an important question.

This was the time that the thought-emancipation movement was in full swing. Radical activists were demanding emancipation of individuality, human rights, and democratic reform of the political structure. In his article, Wei Jingsheng called on the people to beware of Deng Xiaoping becoming a dictator, at a time when Deng was hailed by many as a new savior (jiushizhu). Very astutely, Wei pointed out: "Deng Xiaoping's conduct has already demonstrated that he does not practice democracy. What he is upholding is no longer the people's interests: he is following the line of a dictator after having wormed his way into the people's confidence."

Wei Jingsheng, therefore, asked the people to withdraw support to Deng. "Without democracy," he said, "there will be no modernization" (ibid.). He explained: "To carry out reform of the social system, so as to set Chinese politics on the track of democracy—this is the premise for solving all social and economic problems in China today" (ibid.).

For this poster, Wei Jingsheng paid dearly. On 29 March 1979, just four days later, he was arrested. On 16 October 1979, he was sentenced to fifteen years' imprisonment on grounds of selling state secrets to foreigners and engaging in counter-revolutionary activities. The real reason, China critics argued, was his attack on Deng. Reportedly, Hu Yaobang was against Wei's arrest, but Deng was persuaded by Peng Zhen to give him a severe sentence.

During his years in prison, Wei did not forget the "democracy or neo-dictatorship" question. After he was released on 14 September 1993, he immediately resumed his activities for what he considered to be China's democratic cause. In April

1994, he suddenly disappeared. It was not until 21 November 1995 that Beijing announced his re-arrest. On 13 December 1995, he was charged with subversion, and sentenced to fourteen years' imprisonment. This case—the second Wei Jingsheng Incident—became the focus of international attention. On 16 November 1997, the Chinese authorities finally released Wei and sent him into exile in the United States for medical treatment.

Wei Jingsheng, the former Red Guard and Beijing Zoo electrician, was catapulted from obscurity in 1978 when he joined other ordinary Chinese in democracy activities. He then became the world's highest-profile political prisoner. He was awarded the 1996 Andrei Sakharov Human Rights Prize by the European Parliament, and has been nominated several times for the Nobel Peace Prize.

Some worried that since Wei was exiled from his country, he would not continue to have an influence on Chinese affairs (they also said, Wei had already done his share for China's struggle for democracy. After all he had suffered, he was entitled to choose survival). Many, however, thought otherwise. In any case, one thing was certain. Wei would, for the rest of his life, continue to commit himself to the cause he had set for himself almost two decades earlier when he put up his big-character poster "Democracy or Neo-Dictatorship".

Among Chinese dissidents, Wei's political courage, knowledge, and ability is generally acknowledged. But this does not mean that he is a figure beyond controversy. Again, his ill-fated poster was a question at issue. It was agreed that Wei's proposition reflected the people's hopes for democracy. It also gave expression to the people's worries: it was possible that Deng would become a new dictator. History proved Wei to be right. But some argued that Wei should not have put up the poster at that specific time. In the spring of 1979, they said, the reform and open-door program had just started, and Deng was measuring his strength vis-à-vis the anti-reform camp. What would be the result if one did not support him but instead attacked him at that crucial time? The answer was self-evident. In fact, Wei's poster served to be the very excuse the anti-reform force had been waiting for to suppress the pro-democratic forces in society and the reformists within the Party. When Deng gave his speech about the "four cardinal principles" on 30 March 1979 (the day after Wei's arrest), Wei's poster must have been one of the factors affecting his key tone. Deng's speech, in the first place, was an answer to the accusations against him from within the Party, a vindication that he had not gone astray from Party principles. Unfortunately, this speech abruptly put an end to the thought-emancipation movement that Deng had personally promoted (see, for instance, Li Honglin, *A History of Chinese Thought, 1949-1989,* Hong Kong, Mingbao, 1998).

It is possible that Wei Jingsheng had not done this, then someone else would have done a similar thing in that situation. But of course what is done cannot be undone; all this is now part of history. See also "Beijing zhi chun" (Beijing Spring) and "chi butong zhengjinzhe" (dissidents).

要文斗，不要武斗
yao wendou, buyao wudou
(struggle by reasoning, not by coercion or force)

See "quanmian neizhan" (full-scale civil war) and "wen'ge" (Cultural Revolution).

"野百合花"事件
"Ye baihehua" shijian

("Wild Lily" incident)

See "baolu wenxue" (exposure literature).

叶九条
Ye jiutiao
(Ye Jianying's nine principles)

On 30 September 1981, Ye Jianying, vice-chairman of the CCP and chairman of the NPC Standing Committee, advanced nine principles regarding Taiwan's return to the motherland and peaceful reunification. He suggested that the CCP and the KMT engage in reciprocal negotiations to enter into a "third era of cooperation". See also "Taiwan wenti" (Taiwan issue).

一不怕苦，二不怕死
yi bupa ku, er bupa si
(fear neither hardship nor death)

The slogan "Fear neither hardship nor death" was first raised in February 1966 when a movement was launched by the CCP to learn from Jiao Yulu, a Party secretary in Lankao county, Henan province, who devoted himself completely to his duty and finally died of liver cancer on 20 May 1964, leaving his plan to improve the life of his people unfulfilled. At the 1st Plenum of the 9th PCC held in April 1969, Mao said that he favored this slogan. The slogan then became a quotation from Mao, calling on the whole nation to fear neither hardship nor death.

A post-Mao fiction writer played a word game with the phrase, thus denigrating its significance. In his 1985 prize-winning novelette, "The Nineteen Tombs in the Mountains" ("Shanzhong, na shijiuzuo fenying", *Kunlun,* 6, 1984), army writer Li Cunbao altered Mao's quotation to "Better bear hardships and die" (yi pa buku, er pa busi), uttered by a PLA man in the story who was in a comatose state shortly before he died of hard labor.

一大二公
yi da er gong
(large in size and collective in nature)

See "renmin gongshe" (People's Commune).

一斗二批三改
yi dou er pi san gai
(one struggle, two criticisms, and three reforms)

See "dou pi gai" (struggle, criticism, and reform).

一分为二
yi fen wei er
(one divides into two)

The phrase "Yi fen wei er" (and similar terms "liangdianlun"—"the two points theory" and "liangfenfa"—"the application of the law of 'one dividing into two'") often appears in articles and daily conversations among Chinese. It means that everything has two aspects. For instance, when one asks to apply "one dividing into two" to those who have made mistakes, one means that those people should not be treated as totally bad or wrong. When applied to describing adverse circumstances, its meaning is similar to that of the proverb "every cloud has a silver lining".

But the phrase "Yi fen wei er" also may have political significance, as it was construed by Mao.

In his 1937 philosophical work *On Contradiction,* Mao made a comment on Marxist dialectics, which was summed up by Engels as consisting of three principles —the law of the unity of opposites, the law of mutual transformation of quantity and quality, and the law of the negation of negation. Mao asserted that of the three the law of the unity of opposites is the core, which is the fundamental law of the universe. In his 27 February 1957 speech "On the Correct Handling of Contradictions Among the People", Mao thus stated: "Marxist philosophy holds that the law of the unity of opposites is the fundamental law of the universe. This law operates universally, whether in the natural world, in human society, or in man's thinking. Between the opposites in a contradiction there is at once unity and struggle, and it is this that impels things to move and change. Contradictions exist everywhere, but they differ in accordance with the different nature of different things. In any given phenomenon or thing, the unity of opposites is conditional, temporary, and transitory, and hence relative, whereas the struggle of opposites is absolute" *(MZXJ,* 5, p. 372).

At the same time, Mao was trying to find an easy-to-understand expression for this law. In 1956, at the 2nd Plenum of the 8th PCC, he proposed two new theories, the "two points theory" and "one point theory" (yidianlun). He considered the former to be a popular expression of the dialectical relationship of the unity of opposites and the latter to be an expression of metaphysics and one-sidedness. He said that the "two points theory" would be valid for ten thousand years. In 1957, he found another easy-to-understand expression for his idea—"Yi fen wei er". He said: "'One divides into two', which is a universal phenomenon, is of dialectics" ("Dangnei tuanjiede bianzheng fangfa—"The Dialectics of the Party Unity", *MZXJ,* 5, p. 498). According to Mao, throughout the stages of a thing's development, there exists, from start to finish, a movement of opposites, that is, a movement of "one dividing into two". The struggle between opposites is omnipresent and continual, always existing whether they are simultaneously present or in a state of mutual transformation (in the latter case, the struggle manifests itself especially clearly). This is the universality and absoluteness of contradiction (maodunde pubianxing yu jueduixing).

Mao applied his idea of "one dividing into two" to class struggle (jieji douzheng). He emphasized that class struggle must be carried out repeatedly, even throughout the whole historical period of socialism. That was why so many political movements unfolded during his rule. Mao refused to acknowledge that things in the world were more complicated than the "two points" could solve and that social developments could be achieved in many ways.

The first challenge to this view came from Yang Xianzhen, an eminent CCP philosopher who was at the time a PCC member, president of the CCP Central Party School, and secretary of the school's Party committee. In November 1963, Yang put forth in his teaching material the thesis "two combine into one" (he er er yi), his own condensation of dialectics. Later, Ai Hengwu and Lin Qingshan, two teachers at the school, elaborated on Yang's idea in an article, "'One Divides into Two' and 'Two Combine into One'" ("Yi fen wei er" yu "He er er yi"), published in the *Guangming Daily* on 29 May 1964. Thereafter, the situation suddenly became serious. In July and August 1964, the *People's Daily* and *Red Flag* began to attack the view of "two combine into one". At the same time, a criticism campaign was carried out in China's philosophical-ideological circles. The view was said to be a revisionist concept diametrically opposed to the dialectic, Marxist concept "One divides into two", which had been personally put forth by Mao. As a result, Yang Xianzhen was dismissed from his posts in June 1965 and imprisoned in 1966.

In fact, quite some years ealier, Yang Xianzhen had already employed the concept of "two combine into one" in his explanation of Mao's 1937 philosophical work *On Contradiction*. In his opinion, Mao's thesis, "One divides into two", only serves as a method of observation. When dealing with issues, one must pay attention to the truth that "two combine into one", that is, to the inseparability, interdependence, and balance of opposites in things. The crucial point of "two combine into one" lies in its emphasis on the balance of opposites and the necessity of maintaining the balance. No wonder this kind of theory was criticized in 1964 for advocating "peaceful co-existence" (heping gongchu) and opposing "class struggle"; it was completely out of keeping with the times when the CCP leadership was engaging in fierce open polemics with Khrushchev and his colleagues in the CPSU and when Mao was thinking of launching a revolution to fight "China's Khrushchev" and his "revisionist" followers in the CCP.

When re-examining the 1964 campaign, post-Mao critics found the two theses, "One divides into two" and "Two combine into one", complementary to each other. Yang Xianzhen's premise was still the former, though he gave a little more emphasis to the "identity of thinking and being" (siwei yu cunzaide tongyixing). Furthermore, both theses were quite superficial, nothing more than skirting the relationship between contradiction and identity as had earlier been elucidated by Hegel (1770-1831). See also "jieji douzheng" (class struggle) and "douzheng chongbai" (struggle worship).

一个阶级只有一种典型人物
yi ge jieji zhiyou yi zhong dianxing renwu
(there is only one kind of typical character for a specific class)

See "shehuizhuyi xianshizhuyi" (socialist realism).

一个民族，两个国家
yi ge minzu, liang ge guojia
("two states in one nation" theory)

See "Taiwan wenti" (Taiwan issue).

一个确保，三个到位，五项改革
yi ge quebao, san ge daowei, wu xiang gaige
(one ensure, three putting things into place, and five reforms)

See "jingji shahuang" (economic "Tsar") and "jingji gaige" (economic reform).

一个社会只有一种本质
yi ge shehui zhiyou yi zhong benzhi
(there is only one kind of essence for a specific society)

See "shehuizhuyi xianshizhuyi" (socialist realism).

一个时代只有一种典型环境
yi ge shidai zhiyou yi zhong dianxing huanjing
(there is only one kind of typical
circumstance for a specific age)

See "shehuizhuyi xianshizhuyi" (socialist realism).

一个中国新概念
yi ge Zhongguo xin gainian
(a new concept of "one China")

See "Taiwan wenti" (Taiwan issue).

一个中国的原则是和平统一的基础
yi ge Zhongguode yuanze shi heping tongyide jichu
(the "one-China" principle is the
foundation of peaceful reunification)

See "Taiwan wenti" (Taiwan issue).

一个中心，两个基本点
yi ge zhongxin, liang ge jibendian
(one center, two basic points)

See "shehuizhuyi chuji jieduan lun" (theory of the primary stage of socialism), "si xiang jiben yuanze" (four cardinal principles), and "zhengzhi gaige" (political reform).

一个主义，一个党，一个领袖
yi ge zhuyi, yi ge dang, yi ge lingxiu
(one doctrine, one party, and one leader)

See "wuchanjieji zhuanzheng" (dictatorship of the proletariat).

一股就灵
yi gu jiu ling
(everything will be all right once
the joint stock system is adopted)

See "gufenzhi gaizao" (joint stock system reform).

一棍子打死
yi gunzi dasi
(finish off with a single blow)

"Yi gunzi dasi" literally means "to knock somebody down at one stroke, "to finish off with a single blow". It can be translated as "completely negate" or simply "bludgeon", as in the often quoted sentence: Instead of bludgeoning our erring comrades, we should not only see how they behave but give them help (yi kan er bang). This was said to be one of Mao's teachings, but his doctrine about class struggle often rendered it meaningless. See also "fang" (loosening up).

一看二帮
yi kan er bang
(observe and help)

See "yi gunzi dasi" (finish off with a single blow).

一怕不苦，二怕不死
yi pa buku, er pa busi
(better bear hardships and die)

See "yi bupa ku, er bupa si" (fear neither hardship nor death).

一盘散沙
yi pan sansha
(a heap of loose sand)

At a cadre meeting called by the PCC on 16 January 1980, Deng made the following remark: "China always used to be described as 'a heap of loose sand'. But when our Party came to power and rallied the whole country around it, the disunity resulting from the partitioning of the country by various forces was brought to an end" (*SWD,* p. 252). So he asked: "After all, what is the good of the multiparty system in capitalist countries?" (ibid.). See also "dangde lingdao" (Party leadership), "minzhu dangpai" (democratic parties), "wuchanjieji zhuanzheng" (dictatorship of the proletariat), "chi butong zhengjinzhe" (dissidents), "ziyouzhuyi" (liberalism), and "zhengzhi gaige" (political reform).

一穷二白
yi qiong er bai
(poverty and "blankness")

See "dayuejin" (Great Leap Forward).

一中一台
yi Zhong yi Tai
(one China, one Taiwan)

See "Taiwan wenti" (Taiwan issue).

一百年来三大历史巨变
yibainianlai san da lishi jubian
(three tremendous historic changes in the past century)

In his report delivered to the 15th CCP National Congress, Jiang Zemin reviewed the earth-shaking changes in China over the past century. In 1900 the Eight-Power Allied Forces occupied Beijing, subjecting the Chinese nation to great humiliation and bringing the country to the verge of subjugation. Jiang stated that in the year 2000, China would surely enjoy a fairly comfortable life on the basis of socialism and take big strides toward the goal of becoming prosperous and strong.

The past century, according to Jiang, has witnessed three tremendous historic changes on the road of advance of the Chinese people. The first change was represented by the Revolution of 1911, which overthrew the autocratic monarchy that had ruled China for thousands of years. Led by Sun Yat-sen, the revolution pioneered a true national and democratic revolution. The second change was marked by the founding of the PRC and the establishment of the socialist system. This was accomplished after the founding of the CCP and under the direction of the first generation of collective leadership with Mao Zedong at the core. The third change featured reform, the open door, and the endeavor to achieve socialist modernization. It was a new revolution initiated by the second generation of collective leadership with Deng Xiaoping at the core.

In Jiang's opinion, the conclusion drawn from these three changes is as follows: Only the CCP can lead the Chinese people to achieve victories of national independence, liberation, and socialism, pioneering the road of building socialism with Chinese characteristics, rejuvenating the nation, making the country prosperous and strong, and improving the people's well-being. See also "dangde lingdao" (Party leadership) and "zhengzhi gaige" (political reform).

一边倒
yibiandao
(lean to one side)

Mao first raised the concept of "leaning to one side" in his well-known article "On the People's Democratic Dictatorship" ("Lun renmin minzhu zhuanzheng", in *MZXJ,* 4, pp. 1473-86), released on 30 June 1949 in commemoration of the 28th anniversary of the CCP. He said that all Chinese without exception must lean to the side of imperialism or to the side of socialism and there was no third road. Under his leadership, China leaned to "one side", that is, taking the socialist road and allying with the Soviet Union. On 5 October 1949, a few days after the founding of the PRC, the Sino-Soviet Friendship Association (Zhong Su Youhao Xiehui) was founded among the Chinese people of all walks of life. On 14 February 1950, at the end of Mao's first visit to Moscow, a "Sino-Soviet Treaty of Friendship, Alliance, and Mutual Assistance" (Zhong Su Youhao Tongmeng Huzhu Tiaoyue) was signed, thus forming a military alliance and placing China as a "Soviet satellite". In the years that followed, in exchange, Soviet scientists, technicians, and military advisers, numbering more than 40,000, were sent to China. By 1954, the Soviet Union had agreed to help China build 156 production projects, as part of the PRC's first "Five Year Plan" (1953-57). It also began to assist China's nuclear development in 1955.

From 2 to 21 November 1957 Mao made his second visit to Moscow to celebrate the 40th anniversary of the October Revolution. In high spirits, Mao put forth the well-known thesis: "The East Wind is prevailing over the West Wind" (dongfeng yadao xifeng). That is to say, the forces of socialism have become overwhelmingly superior to the forces of imperialism, or, the "socialist camp" headed by the Soviet Union have overpowered the "capitalist camp" headed by the United States.

Among intellectuals and those called "democratic personages", and even among Party and government officials, not everyone agreed with the CCP's "leaning to one side" policy and the forming of the Sino-Soviet military alliance. During the 1957 anti-Rightist campaign, many of them were persecuted because they had questioned the policy.

The Sino-Soviet alliance began to disintegrate in 1958, when Mao launched his Great Leap Forward. In the early 1960s, China finally broke with the Soviet Union, thus ending the "leaning to one side" policy. On 3 April 1979, at the 7th Session of the 5th NPC, China announced that the "Sino-Soviet Treaty", which had long been dead, would not be prolonged.

According to Party files, Mao did not like Stalin (still less did he like Khrushchev). As a nationalist, Mao never agreed with Stalin's concept of "the two camps". (So in 1974 he put forth his "three worlds" theory.) The Korean War was an important event that tied China firmly to the "socialist camp". It is said that Mao decided to send troops to Korea with great hesitation, for he knew this would much affect China's future. In 1956, Mao tried to change the situation somewhat, one of his efforts, for instance, being the exploration of the "ten major relationships" (shi da guanxi) in the socialist revolution and construction. But it was too late; China had been deep in the Soviet mode characterized by Stalinism. Ironically, Mao even had to resort to Stalinism (as "a knife"—"yi ba daozi", *MZXJ*, 5, pp. 321-22) for the survival of his Communist regime. Mao's "independent" approach eventually resulted in the launching of the GPCR, bringing a great disaster to the Chinese nation. See also "xiuzhengzhuyi" (revisionism) and "zili gengsheng" (self-reliance).

一次革命论
yici geming lun
(theory of "a single revolution")

See "buduan geming" (uninterrupted revolution).

一旦公有制主导地位丧失，共产党就丧失执政的经济基础
yidan gongyouzhi zhudao diwei sanshi, gongchandang jiusanshi zhizhengde jingji jichu
(once public ownership is no longer paramount, the Communist Party will lose the economic foundation for its rule)

See "pi Deng wanyanshu" (anti-Deng 10,000-character petitions).

一党专政
yidangzhuanzheng
(one-party dictatorship)

See "zhengzhi gaige" (political reform), "minzhu dangpai" (democratic parties), "wuchanjieji zhuanzheng" (dictatorship of the proletariat), and "fan fubai" (anti-corruption).

一党专制
yidangzhuanzhi
(one-party autocracy)

See "zhengzhi gaige" (political reform), "minzhu dangpai" (democratic parties), "wuchanjieji zhuanzheng" (dictatorship of the proletariat), and "fan fubai" (anti-corruption).

一刀切
yidaoqie
(a single cut)

As a political term, this means oversimplification in drawing a demarcation line in making or carrying out a policy—which is done only in accord with a certain rigid principle without considering every different and complicated factor existing at the time. For instance, during the GPCR, the peasants' private plots of land (ziliudi), sideline businesses, and periodic village markets were condemned as "tails of capitalism" (zibenzhuyi weiba), and ordered to be abolished with "a single cut" (termed as "cut off capitalist tails"—"ge zibenzhuyi weiba"), so that they would take the socialist road wholeheartedly. This, naturally, gave rise to peasants' resentment.

The term "a single cut" was also often used to describe rigid, oversimplified literary criticism. See also "zhengzhi biaozhun diyi, yishu biaozhun dier" (political criteria first, artistic criteria second).

一点论
yidianlun
("one point" theory)

See "liangdian lun" ("two points" theory).

一定要解放台湾
yiding yao jiefang Taiwan
(we are determined to liberate Taiwan)

See "Taiwan wenti" (Taiwan issue).

一定的文学艺术是一定的政治和经济的反映
yidingde wenxue yishu shi yidingde zhengzhi he jingjide fanying
(a particular literature or art is the reflection of a particular economic and political system)

This thesis, which can be found in Mao's 1942 *Yan'an Talks*, was seriously questioned in the 1986 "subjectivity" debate. See "fanyinglun shi wenxue yanjiude zhexue jichu" (the theory of reflection is the philosophical basis for literary study).

一概怀疑，一概否定
yigai huaiyi, yigai fouding
(suspect all, negate all)

See "huaiyi yiqie, dadao yiqie" (suspect all, overthrow all).

一国比两制重要
yiguo bi liangzhi zhongyao
("one country" is more important than "two systems")

See "yiguo liangzhi" (one country, two systems).

一国多制
yiguo duozhi
(one country, several systems)

See "yiguo liangzhi" (one country, two systems).

一国两报
yiguo liangbao
(one country, two kinds of newspaper)

See "xinwen ziyou wenti" (issue of press freedom).

一国两府
yiguo liangfu
(one country, two governments)

See "Taiwan wenti" (Taiwan issue).

一国两制
yiguo liangzhi
(one country, two systems)

At the end of the 1950s Mao first advanced the idea that within the frame of one country each of the two sides of the Taiwan Straits could maintain its own social system, but Mao was not able to develop his idea, still less to put it in practice. It is generally accepted that the concept of "one country, two systems" and its actualization were a credit to Deng.

Deng conceived of the concept in January 1981 when suggesting that the re-unification of Taiwan and Chinese mainland was one of the "three issues for the 1980s" (bashiniandai sanjian dashi). When the Hong Kong issue was raised during the first China visit of Margaret Thatcher, then prime minister of the United Kingdom, in September 1982, Deng applied his idea to a new issue. It was, however, at his Beijing meetings with Hong Kong celebrities on 22 and 23 June 1984 that the wording of "yi ge guojia, liang zhong zhidu" was publicly revealed. When Deng met Margaret Thatcher again on 19 December 1984 to officially sign the joint statement of the Chinese and British governments, Deng abbreviated the term to "yiguo liangzhi".

The concept of "one country, two systems", when applied to the Hong Kong issue as a guiding principle, means that when Hong Kong was returned to Chinese sovereignty in 1997, its capitalist system, which was different from the socialist system in Chinese mainland, would remain unchanged for 50 years (wushinian bubian). Reportedly, it was after careful consideration for several years that Deng finally confirmed this principle (See *Fundamental Issues in Present-day China,* Beijing, FLP, 1987, pp. 48-52, 59-60, 93-96). This was not an easy decision. It indicated that the CCP leadership was willing to adopt a more realistic attitude towards the Hong Kong issue (and also towards the Taiwan issue).

On 1 July 1997, several months after Deng's death, Hong Kong was returned to China and became the Hong Kong Special Administrative Region of the People's Republic of China. The principle of "one country, two systems" was formally put into practice. The successful return was hailed by Chinese leaders as a great victory of Deng's "brilliant and unique" idea, an important component of Deng Xiaoping Theory.

In the first year after the return, ironically, Hong Kong's problems were not political as some had worried, but economic. Hong Kong had to ask for help from the Chinese central government to reduce its difficulties caused by the Asian financial crisis. With the lapse of time, however, political problems re-emerged. For instance, in 1999, there were differences in interpreting certain articles in the "Basic Law" ("Jibenfa"). The central authorities told Hong Kong politicians: "One country" is more important than "two systems" (yiguo bi liangzhi zhongyao). Some Hong Kong residents once again found themselves having no confidence in the promise of "no change for fifty years". At best, as a generally held view goes: As Hong Kong is reunited with China, it will change the mainland as much as China will change Hong Kong.

Beijing wants to make Hong Kong an example for Taiwan to follow, but the leaders in Taiwan found the concept of "one country, two systems" unacceptable, at least at present. Hong Kong, they argued, was a colony with no sovereignty, whereas since the end of the Second World War Taiwan has all the time been ruled effectively by the government of the Republic of China, a political entity on an equal footing with the mainland Communist government. As a replacement, some suggested "one country, two governments" (yiguo liangfu), or "one country, three systems" (yiguo sanzhi), or "one country, several systems" (yiguo duozhi). On 18 March 2000, Chen Shui-bian of the Democratic Progressive Party, which is pro-Taiwan independence, was elected Taiwan president. The application of "one country, two systems" in Taiwan became all the more remote. See also "Taiwan wenti" (Taiwan issue).

一国三制
yiguo sanzhi
(one country, three systems)

See "yiguo liangzhi" (one country, two systems).

一批二用
yipi eryong
(first subject intellectuals to criticism and then use them)

This phrase emerged after 1968 as a CCP policy towards China's intellectuals during the GPCR. As it suggested, on the one hand, the Party found it necessary to criticize and denounce the so-called "bourgeois intellectuals", and on the other, it was in the interest of the proletariat to make use of the intellectuals' services. See also "zhishifenzi wenti" (issue of intellectuals).

一手硬，一手软
yishou ying, yishou ruan
(one hand is tough, while the other soft)

See "liang ge wenming" (two civilizations).

一手抓四个坚持，一手抓改革开放
yishou zhua si ge jianchi, yishou zhua gaige kaifang
(to adhere to the "four cardinal principles" on the one hand, and, on the other, to carry out the policies of reform and the open door)

See "liang tiao zhanxiande douzheng" (struggle on two fronts), "zhengzhi gaige" (political reform), "jingji gaige" (economic reform), and "Deng Xiaoping lilun" (Deng Xiaoping Theory).

一胎化
yitaihua
(single-child policy)

The single-child policy, which means that a couple can have only one child, was first put forth by the central authorities in December 1979. It was legalized as national policy in the new Constitution passed at the 5th Session of the 5th NPC on 10 December 1982. Since then there has been a popular slogan: "Single-child families are fine" (zhi sheng yi ge hao). During pre-marital education (hunqian jiaoyu) couples should learn about "jieyu" (birth control) or "jihua shengyu" (family planning). Those who violate the single-child policy are punished, usually by fines and/or cancellation of promotions in their jobs.

In recent years, however, violations of this policy have increased. Some people, benefiting from the development of the multiplicity of economic sectors, are not afraid of the punishments. A major obstacle in implementing this population control measure is the traditional concept of "perpetuating the family name" (chuan zong jie dai). Some couples, especially those in the countryside or without much education, wish to have a male heir. If their first child is female, they will attempt by any means to have a second child. Some even kill female infants so that they are "legally eligible" to have a second child.

A side effect of the single-child policy is the "four-two-one" phenomenon (si er yi xianxiang)—the one child in the family is spoiled by the two parents and the four grandparents. Many parents look back sadly on their lost-childhood and are determined to make sure that their children will have better lives. They exhibit what psychologists call a "compensation syndrome". But the result is that there is a fear that the new generation will be the most self-centered in Chinese history and will thus destroy traditional Chinese ethics and morality. Scholars have sarcastically called these "little emperors" "China's real rulers". They ask: Is China's single-child policy creating a society of brats? See also "ershinianlai zuiju yingxianglide shi ge kouhao" (ten most influential slogans in the past two decades) and "xin renkou lun" (new theory of population).

一天等于二十年
yitian dengyu ershinian
(one day amounts to twenty years)

Karl Marx predicted that the proletarian revolution would usher in a great epoch during which people would be so full of energy and enthusiasm that they would make one day amount to twenty years. This saying was often quoted during the 1958 Great Leap Forward. See also "Great Leap Forward" (dayuejin).

一条腿走路
yitiaotui zoulu
(walking on one leg)

See "liangtiaotui zoulu" (walk on two legs).

一线
yixian
(front line)

See "erxian" (second line).

一言堂
yiyantang
(arbitrary "one voice chamber")

See "yi fa zhi guo" (ruling the nation by law) and "xinwen ziyou wenti" (issue of press freedom).

一元化领导
yiyuanhua lingdao
(centralized Party leadership)

See "dangde lingdao" (Party leadership) and "zhengzhi gaige" (political reform).

一月风暴
yiyue fengbao
(January Tempest of 1967)

See "yiyue geming" (January Revolution).

一月革命
yiyue geming
(January Revolution)

Not long after the start of the GPCR, most government and Party organizations were paralyzed, if not completely destroyed. In January 1967, the so-called "January Revolution" (also called the "January Tempest"—"yiyue fengbao") took place in Shanghai, when the rebels seized power from the local authorities.

On 4 January 1967, incited by Zhang Chunqiao and Yao Wenyuan who were then in Shanghai as investigators from the Central GPCR Group, the "Shanghai Workers' Revolutionary Uprising Headquarters", together with ten other mass organizations, issued an announcement to the people of the city—"Take Charge of the Revolution, Promote Production, and Thoroughly Destroy the New Counteroffensive of the Bourgeois Reactionary Line" ("Zhua geming, cu shengchan, chedi fensui zichanjieji fandong luxiande xinfanpu"). Two days later, a meeting of Shanghai's thirty-two mass organizations was held to struggle against Chen Pixian, Cao Diqiu, and other major Shanghai Party and government leaders. Two days later, Zhang Chunqiao, Yao Wenyuan, Wang Hongwen, and their followers set up a "forward command post to take charge of the revolution and to promote production", which issued a "ten-article urgent communiqué" on 9 January that ordered that the CCP Shanghai Municipal Committee, the Shanghai government, and the public security organs implement its decisions. On 11 January, under Mao's instructions, a congratulatory telegram was sent to them jointly from the CCP Central Committee, the State Council, the Central Military Commission, and the Central GPCR Group. What was later called the "January Revolution" was confirmed. On 5 February 1967, a new organ of power—the "Shanghai People's Commune"—was founded, which was hailed as "the new Paris Commune of the '60s in the twentieth century". (On 24 February 1967, according to Mao's instructions, the "Shanghai People's Commune" was renamed the "Shanghai Municipal Revolutionary Committee".)

Thereafter, the above-said four central authorities appealed to "all proletarian revolutionary groups" for unity in "seizing power from a handful of people in power within the Party who take the capitalist road". Responding to this appeal, a struggle to seize power took place all over the country. The GPCR entered a "new stage". By 5 September 1968, "revolutionary committees" had been set up in all 27 provinces and autonomous regions and in Beijing and Shanghai, two municipalities directly under the central government. Thus, as the *People's Daily* of 7 September 1968 hailed, "The whole country is red" (quanguo shanhe yipian hong).

In July 1979 when a revised constitution was passed at the 2nd Session of the 5th NPC, "revolutionary committees" were abolished and the former "people's govenments" were restored. On 27 June 1981, the 6th Plenum of the 11th PCC adopted the document entitled "Resolution on Certain Questions in the History of Our Party since the Founding of the PRC". The GPCR was officially negated and the January Revolution of 1967 was labeled a serious counter-revolutionary event. See also "quanmian neizhan" (full-scale civil war) and "wen'ge" (Cultural Revolution).

一祝二唱三读
yizhu erchang sandu
(first greeting, second singing, and third reading)

See "xiandai mixin" (modern superstition).

移民文学
yimin wenxue
(diaspora literature)

From the 1980s on, a great number of people emigrated from Chinese mainland, Taiwan, and Hong Kong. Especially after the June 4th Incident of 1989, about two hundred thousand students, writers, artists, and intellectuals from Chinese mainland remained overseas, forced to live in exile or reluctant to return home—unprecedented not only in Chinese but also in world history that so many *élite* became migrants. Among them were, for instance, writers of reportage literature Liu Binyan, Su Xiaokang, Li You, and Yuan Zhiming; novelists Zheng Yi, Ai Bei, Wang Ruowang, Zu Wei, Kong Jiesheng, Zhang Xinxin, Li Tuo, Lao Gui, Liu Suola, Wang Zhaojun, Gu Hua, and Acheng; dramatist and novelist Gao Xingjian; poets Bei Dao, Gu Cheng (deceased), Jiang He, Yang Lian, Yan Li, and Duo Duo; editors Ge Yang and Lao Mu; literary theorists Su Wei, Huang Ziping, and Liu Zaifu. Some of these people eventually returned to China, whereas others did not. In addition, in the 1990s others who were in China went abroad and did not return.

In the 1970s, from among Taiwan students studying in America emerged a few outstanding figures in the literary field, such as the writers Bai Xianyong, Nie Hualing, Yu Lihua, and Chen Ruoxi, poets Wai-lim Yip and Yu Guangchong, and critics Xia Zhiqing and Li Oufan. Now a number of literary figures have also been emerging from among the migrants from Chinese mainland. A new genre that can be called "diaspora literature" seems to have come into being. In its broad sense, "diaspora literature" refers to any literary works produced by overseas Chinese (huaqiao, huaren, or huayi), regardless of what language they use or of what subject matter they write about—whether about their receiving country or the land of their ancestors. Many of these works can be classified as "literature of overseas students" (liuxuesheng wenxue) because their authors are or have been students studying abroad. Some critics use the term "exile literature" (liufang wenxue) in view of the fact that the authors live in exile. Another term is "new overseas literature" (xin haiwai wenxue), which emphasizes artistic achievements of this genre (thus excluding memoirs, family histories, or anything like personal experience reports).

Hopefully, this new genre will help Chinese literature reach the outside world. Several works have already attracted a large readership in the West. In 1987, for instance, the publication of *Shanghai Shengsilian (Life and Death in Shanghai,* Penguin USA, May 1988), which describes some sad recollections of Zheng Nian (Nien Cheng), a GPCR survivor now living in America, caused a sensation. In 1991, Zhang Rong (Jung Chang), a woman lecturer at London University, published her maiden work *Hong: San Dai Zhongguo Nürende Gushi (Wild Swans: Three Daughters of China),* which immediately became a best-seller and won the NCR prize in the Britain. In 1992, *Hong Dujuan (Red Azalea: Life and Love in China,* Berkley Pub Group, June 1995), an autobiographical novel by Min Anqi (Anchee Min), a woman writer from Shanghai, was published in a number of languages and distributed in over eighty countries, winning the 1994 prize for the best new writers in the United States. There were two controversial works in 1994: *Jiao Fuqing Tai Chenzhong (Too Difficult to Call Father),* a novel by a woman writer Ai Bei, which implied that Premier Zhou Enlai had an illegitimate daughter, and *Mao Zedong Siren Yisheng Huiyilu (The Private Life of Chairman Mao: The Memoirs of Mao's Personal Physician,* Random House, Apr. 1996), memoirs of Li Zhisui, who was Mao's private doctor for about twenty years until Mao's death in 1976. In 1995, Wang Zhaojun's *Bai Lazhu (White Candle),* a novel about the cruel and disastrous "social experimentations" in the countryside in mainland China in the 1950s and 1960s, caused a strong reaction in American literary circles. In 1999, Ha Jin's novel *Dengdai (Waiting,* Pantheon Books, Sept. 1999), a story (set in China in the 1960s) of long-suffering love between a dutiful married doctor and an unmarried nurse, won the 1999 U.S. National Book Award for Fiction. In 2000, Chen Da published his maiden work *Shance (Colors of the Mountain,* Random House, Feb. 2000), a novel about the author's childhood and GPRC experience. Important works also include Gao Xingjian's *Lingshan (Soul Mountain,* Taipei, Lianjing, 1990; trans. by Mabel Lee, HarperCollins, June 2000). This novel describes the destruction of the self of the individual by the primitive human instinct for warmth and security. Conventional life resolves the problem of loneliness but brings with it many anxieties. This is the existential dilemma confronting the individual, in relationships with parents, partners, family, friends, and larger collective groups.

Perhaps great works of "diaspora literature" have not yet been produced (or not yet universally recognized), but there are certainly some good works, and the success of their authors is easy to understand. The clash between the Eastern and the Western cultures enriched their life experiences and developed their perspective in literary creation. Moreover, as Chinese who had been brought up on the one hand in a great cultural tradition and on the other in a historical period that was full of upheavals, changes, disasters, and hardships, their works often possessed a historical profundity, which had much appeal for readers. In addition, the authors obviously enjoyed unprecedented creative freedom that enabled them to pursue artistic truthfulness and eternalness.

以邓小平理论作参照系
yi Deng Xiaoping lilun zuo canzhaoxi
(take Deng Xiaoping Theory as the frame of reference)

See "xin shehuizhuyi guan" (new socialist view).

以法治国
yi fa zhi guo

(ruling the nation by law)

"Ruling the nation by law" is a term Jiang Zemin has used in recent years after first raising it at a PCC-run legal system forum on 9 February 1996. According to those who participated in drafting the report to be delivered by Jiang at the 15th CCP National Congress, Jiang personally made an important change in the report—the wording "build China into a country with a socialist legal system" (jianshe shehuizhuyi fazhi guojia) became "build China into a socialist country ruled by law" (jianshe shehuizhuyi fazhi guojia). These are two different meanings with the same pronunciation for "fazhi". The first means "legal system", while the second means "ruling by law" or "ruled by law". The change was hailed as a significant contribution by the "new core". Indeed, different from the past when there were no laws or regulations (wu fa ke yi), today's problem is that the laws and regulations (though they still need to be improved and complemented) fail to be enforced and strictly observed (you fa bu yi). Hence the immediate significance of stressing "ruling the nation by law".

In contrast to "ruling by law", there is the concept "ruling by individuals" (renzhi). Originating in the political thought of Confucianism, it has a long tradition in China. Relevant in Chinese society today, it is synonymous with autocracy, bureaucracy, feudal privileges, a patriarchal system, and the arbitrary "one voice chamber" (yiyantang). Wang Ruowang (a dissident writer and critic who now lives in exile in America) described it thus: "The lack of democracy within the Party and the system of arbitrary rule by one person has nurtured deformed administrative talents. It is a system in which power and hierarchy determine the pros and cons of any question. If you have power then truth is on your side. (According to the same principle, power is greater than the law and power can overthrow the law.) The leadership is eternally correct; no one is permitted to doubt it or to express differing views, otherwise they will be attacked for anti-Party crimes. Since the 3rd Plenum (in December 1978) this foul state of affairs has improved only marginally" ("Wang Ruowang yulu"—"Quotations from Wang Ruowang", *Shenzhen qingnian bao*, 30 Sept. 1986; in Geremie Barmé and John Minford, eds., *Seeds of Fire*, p. 361). Wang Ruowang made the statement in 1986, when demands for political reform were strong. He even challenged Deng directly: "Deng Xiaoping himself has said that our system of leadership encourages bureaucratism. I think he should add a line: 'And furthermore, it gives rise to personal arbitrariness in which only one person has a say'" (ibid., p. 362).

Also in 1986, in commemorating the thirtieth anniversary of the "Double Hundred" policy, Wang Ruoshui, a well-known philosopher, advised that it was not right to treat the "Double Hundred" only as Party policy. If it were, then people would think of it as a favor, which could be bestowed and also revoked at any time. In fact, as a policy of the Party, the "Double Hundred" was discarded by Mao himself the very year after it was published. Wang raised a very important issue: the CCP as a ruling party, should build up a legal system and conscientiously end the practice of the arbitrary "one voice chamber"; and the Chinese people should establish a concept of law in their minds and never yield to the practice of "ruling by individuals", nor should they praise this feudal tradition (Wang Ruoshui, "Shuangbai fangzhen he gongmin quanli"—"The Double Hundred Principle and the Rights of a Citizen), *Hua sheng bao,* 8 Aug. 1986).

As it is noted by many, "ruling by law" does not mean that everything will be all right; it can also be abused, if its premise in the sense of value—recognition of basic human rights—is ignored. Originally, "ruling by law" was the political view of ancient Chinese Legalists (fajia) about running a state. Han Fei (280 - 233 B.C.) established a complete theory of "ruling by law"—a combination of "fa", "shu", and "shi". "Fa" refers to policies and laws which embody the will of the ruling class; "shu" refers to various means and measures to judge officials in their appointments or dismissals, rewards, or punishments; and "shi" is the ruler's supreme position and authority. Obviously, the core of Han Fei's thoughts on governance is, in today's language, "totalitarianism" (jiquanzhuyi), using law to limit people's freedom instead of using it to balance the power of government. The Chinese people certainly find it unacceptable.

In the spring of 1998, a theory about "limited government", or "small government, large society", was openly proposed by the school of liberal thinkers. What is meant by "small government, large society" is that government functions should be reduced as much as possible such that many of them are carried out by enterprises, non-government organizations, and individuals in society. It was argued that the principle of "limited government" must be established if "ruling the nation by law" is to be genuinely practiced. In the other way around, it must be confirmed that the most important political function of "ruling by law" is to eliminate "unlimited government", and to establish and maintain a "limited government" that is subject to strict legal restrictions in its power, functions, and size.

Different from the "neo-conservatists", the liberals held that the key issue in China was not how to further strengthen the power of the government. The Chinese government was one of only a handful in the world that enjoyed unlimited power. Its power (essentially its power through the Party) penetrated every corner of Chinese society. The disastrous consequences of unlimited power was most clearly seen during the Mao period, when such events as the anti-Rightist campaign, the Great Leap Forward, and the GPCR were launched by it and the Chinese people paid an expensive price in these events. During the Deng period, there emerged a new issue: most of the difficulties besetting China's economy were caused by improper government intervention. Especially, a power economy has formed and caused serious social injustice. Therefore, the liberals asserted, the goal should be to limit governmental power through political reform, eventually creating a limited, responsive, and fair government based on popular consent. In this regard, they called for a separation of the Party from government functions and of enterprise management from government administration. As a further step, they advocated that the Party be separated from the military. They also asked for a distinction between the functions of government and those of society (zheng she fenkai).

In a "ruling by law" society, not only citizens but also the government, and first the government, must abide by the law. "Ruling by law" requires that all laws must not violate human rights and the Constitution. It refers to the theories and practice of modern politics as adopted today in many countries of the world, such as the advocacy of "Law is supreme" (falü zhishang), the promulgation and enforcement of a constitution, the tripartite division of the legislature, administration, and judiciary (san quan fen li), and the establishment of a legal system to protect civilians' rights of freedom. While some of these are still regarded by the Party as "bourgeois", it is likely that ultimately many will be acceptable. See also "zhengzhi gaige" (political reform) and "ziyouzhuyi" (liberalism).

以阶级斗争为纲
yi jieji douzheng wei gang
(taking class struggle as the key link)

"Taking class struggle as the key link" was a guiding principle in the Mao period. As a quotation from Mao it first appeared in the 1976 New Year's Day editorial in the *People's Daily*, *Red Flag*, and the *Liberation Army Daily*.

The concept of "taking class struggle as the key link", which actually means that everything must be sacrificed in the name of the revolution and that man is the tool of class struggle, was rejected by post-Mao critics as violating socialist humanism. They argued that all social activities, including class struggle, should have man as their purpose, aiming at man's emancipation. See also "pi Deng, fanji youqing fan'anfeng" (campaign to criticize Deng Xiaoping and counter the Right deviationist trend to reverse correct verdicts) and "shehuizhuyi rendaozhuyi" (socialist humanism).

以民族斗争掩盖阶级斗争
yi minzu douzheng yan'gai jieji douzheng
(cover up class struggle with national struggle)

See "minzuzhuyi" (nationalism).

以三项指示为纲
yi sanxiang zhishi wei gang
(taking the three instructions as the key link)

See "pi Deng, fanji youqing fan'anfeng" (campaign to criticize Deng Xiaoping and counter the Right deviationist trend to reverse correct verdicts).

以问题为中心的报告文学
yi wenti wei zhongxinde baogao wenxue
(problem-centered reportage literature)

In 1987 and 1988, although many other literary genres were stagnating, reportage literature, especially a new genre called "problem-centered reportage literature", was developing much more rapidly than before. There emerged a group of writers who produced a number of works that caused great repercussions in society. An example was the work by the two young writers Hu Ping and Zhang Shengyou entitled "Going Abroad: A Great Trend" ("Shijie dachuanlian", *DD,* 1, 1988), which consists of poignant stories about young Chinese, many of them with great talent, who emigrate abroad. The work was reprinted in book form after its publication in the magazine *Contemporary,* and one hundred thousand copies immediately sold out. For the competition under the theme of "China Tide", sponsored by ninety-nine magazines and newspapers in October 1987, nearly one thousand works were submitted. The whole literary arena was shocked by the popularity of this genre. Within half a year or more, several successive forums were held on it. Indeed, 1988 was the year of the "reportage literature craze" (baogao wenxue re).

New features of this genre appeared. At first, as in the past, one tended to write reportage literature using traditional methods similar to those also employed in fiction writing. In the last few years of the 1980s, however, a considerable number of pieces in this genre were more academic, and were written with a "macro", panoramic perspective; rather than focusing on one or a few characters, they were interested in reflecting, describing, and analyzing problems and events, very often, problems and events of great political and social weight.

These should not be regarded as merely changes in the form, or of artistic expression. In these changes, one can find a strong trend among Chinese writers and intellectuals to express their political demands. They wanted to make their own historical reflections (lishi fansi). This can be clearly seen in the following works: "Wang Shiwei and 'The Wild Lily'" (Dai Qing, "Wang Shiwei he 'Ye baihehua'",

Wenhui yuekan, 5:22-41, 1988), *On the Altar of "Utopia"—1959 Summer in Lushan Mountain* (Su Xiaokang, Luo Shixu, and Chen Zheng, *'Wutuobang' Ji: 1959 Nian Lushan Zhi Xia,* Beijing, Zhongguo Xinwen, Nov. 1988), "Sea Burial" (Qian Gang, "Haizang", *Jiefangjun wenyi,* 1, 1989), and *White Snow, Red Blood* (Zhang Zhenglong, *Xue Bai Xue Hong,* Beijing, Jiefangjun, Aug. 1989). They also wanted to reveal their own views or appraisals of sensitive (social or political) real issues which concerned all or a certain stratum of the people. Works in this catagory included: "A Vital Problem of China" (Zhao Yu, "Zhongguode yaohai", *Reliu,* 2, 1986, reprinted in *XHWZ,* 4:86-99, 1986), "A Memorandum of Freedom" (Su Xiaokang, "Ziyou beiwanglu", *Tianjin wenxue,* 9, 1987, reprinted in Su Xiaokang, *Ziyou Beiwanglu—A Memorandum of Freedom,* Hong Kong, Sanlian, 1989, pp. 36-81), "Going Abroad: A Great Trend", "Forest-destroyers, Wake Up!" (Xu Gang, "Famuzhe, xinglai", *Xin guancha,* 2, 1988), and "Migrants in Western China" (Mai Tianshu, "Xibu zai yimin", *RMWX,* 5, 1988, reprinted in *XHWZ,* 10:98-119, 1988). No longer succombing to the Party demand to produce enthusiastic praise, these authors wrote from the bottom of their hearts and with a sense of social responsibility. As a result, their works were often tinged with a cold, critical tone, which can be seen in many of the works submitted in the 1988 "China Tide" competition.

Indeed, after 1986, the critical, problem-centered reportage literature became the mainstream of this genre. Liu Binyan, its precursor and founder, had many young followers, many of whom achieved admirable successes. For instance, Mai Tianshu, one of those whom Liu Binyan most highly appreciated, won the first place in the "China Tide" competition with his "Migrants in Western China", an exposé of the appalling poverty and ignorance in Gansu province. 40-year-old Su Xiaokang, a former lecturer at Beijing Broadcasting College and a reporter for the *People's Daily,* was also praised by Liu Binyan. Many of his works embodied, and, at the same time, developed, Liu's ideas. Su began his career of writing reportage literature in 1983, and immediately won the third national prize for the genre with his "Buddha Carvings in the East" ("Dongfang fodiao", *RMWX,* 10:81-92, 1983). But this should not be considered an important work, if compared to his later works which were very different and of much greater significance. He concentrated more and more on two kinds of subject matter. One was involved in politics, where he emphasized the democratic spirit, pondering the defects in China's social and political systems and defending citizens' rights. In this category were "A Revelation of a Big Famine" ("Honghuang qishilu", *Zhongguo zuojia,* 2, 1986, reprinted in Su Xiaokang, *Ziyou Beiwanglu*, pp. 1-35), "A Memorandum of Freedom", and *On the Altar of "Utopia"—1959 Summer in Lushan Mountain*. Su also liked to write about serious issues of everyday concern, tending to probe them sociologically, which gave him an opportunity to promote a scientific spirit. These works included "Modern Marriage—Agonizing Thoughts" ("Yinyang da liebian: dui xiandai hunyinde tongku sikao", *Zhongguo zuojia,* 5, 1986) and "A Sacred Anxiety" (coauthor Zhang Min, "Shensheng yousi lu", *RMWX,* 9:4-22, 1987, reprinted in Su Xiaokang, *Ziyou Beiwanglu*, pp. 82-125).

As far as reportage literature is concerned, Liu Binyan's maxim, "Be involved in life", was no doubt relevant. Now, significantly, his followers carried forward his ideas. They were obviously trying to be involved in politics. The issue of democracy was the soul of Liu's reportage literature; now writers of this genre like Su Xiaokang were dealing with this issue in a more daring fashion.

Notably, many writers of reportage literature, such as Su Xiaokang, Dai Qing, Zhang Shengyou, and Mai Tianshu, either began life as journalists or were concurrently holding journalist positions. Since journalism in China is stipulated as a mouthpiece of the CCP and must serve the Party's current policies, they found it very difficult as journalists to tell the truth or to publish the results of their serious investigations. That was why they turned to writing reportage literature. After writing "Land and Local Despots", the first of his works of reportage literature ("Tudi yu huangdi", *Zhongguo zuojia,* 1, 1987), Mai Tianshu confessed: "I feel that this is a very convenient way for me. You have pondered so much about China. If you put your thoughts into a thesis, few would read it. If you write them as fiction, people might say that it is made up. But when you employ the genre of reportage literature, you can spread your ideas and understandings in this very popular form. Under the present cultural conditions in China, this is the most convenient way of enlightenment" (Su Xiaokang et al., "1988: guanyu baogao wenxuede duihua"—"1988: A Dialog on Reportage Literature", *Huacheng,* 6:6, 1988).

Mai Tianshu's remarks also help explain why so many writers of fiction also turned to writing reportage literature. In the late 1980s, as a result of the reform and open-door policy, great changes took place in China's economy and political and social life at large. Various contradictions became more and more apparent, and things became complicated. People also looked at the now complicated life with a complicated way of thinking. Some were haunted by a sense of depression or loss, and could hardly be sure what was good or bad, or what should or should not be done. They were seeking an outlet for their emotions, and, at the same time, if possible, a rational, reliable answer to their confusions. On the other hand, this was a news-making age, an age of information. With the market economy beginning to develop, conflicts and collisions between the old and new institutional structures became commonplace. Unexpected or astonishing things were taking place all the time. People were eager to obtain all kinds of information. If they could not get it in the newspapers, they turned to reportage literature. This phenomenon, which can be called a "reversal effect of the news blockade" (xinwen fengsuo fan xiaoying), greatly encouraged the writers. They were inspired both by the large number of social problems needed to be redressed and by the strong demand for this genre from a large readership.

So successful were their works that many became convinced: If a particular age can foster a rapid development of a particular literary genre to the point where it reaches its peak in terms of literary history, this was the age of problem-centered reportage literature. On the one hand, they understood that the boom of this genre, in the final analysis, was "the grief of the entire Chinese society" (Su Xiaokang et al., "1988: A Dialog on Reportage Literature", *Huacheng,* 6:9, 1988). Zhao Yu, a prominent writer, pointed out that, if society had been stable, if all parts of society had been able to run organically and efficiently, there would have been no context for this literary genre (ibid., p. 10). On the other hand, they felt proud that they were leading a contemporary trend. As Su Xiaokang said, it was because problem-centered reportage literature emerged and caused a "sensational effect" that fiction lost its earlier popularity in China, and this was something unavoidable, something not to be decided by literature itself (ibid., p. 12). He admitted that as far as he was concerned, he would rather write about the suicide of a nation in the genre of reportage literature than describe the suicide of an individual in the genre of fiction (ibid., p. 22).

One cannot be sure how many of these pieces will last as part of China's literary heritage, but the emergence of such reportage literature was certainly a contribution that should be recorded in the history of Chinese thought and literature. Some critics, such as He Xing'an of the *Literary Review*, were of the opinion that the significance of problem-centered reportage literature in China of the 1980s was so great that it should be written into the literary history not only of China but also of the world (see

Ai Ni, "Longchaorende qiusuo—wenti baogao wenxue yantaohui gaishu"—"A Summary of the Symposium for Reportage with Social Problems as Its Main Concern", *WXPL,* 3:64, 1988). Traditionally, Chinese intellectuals lacked an independent personality and strength, and were always subordinate to the authorities. Then they were urged to take a step forward from their purely academic research and concern for pure knowledge to political participation and intervention with a wider social perspective. Problem-centered reportage literature, as a literary form, thus contributed to the awakening of Chinese intellectuals. See also "xinshiqi wenxuede duoyuan fazhan" (pluralistic development of the literature of the new period).

以问题为中心的报告文学的时代
yi wenti wei zhongxinde baogao wenxuede shidai
(age of problem-centered reportage literature)

See "yi wenti wei zhongxinde baogao wenxue" (problem-centered reportage literature).

忆苦饭
yi ku fan
(meals to recall past bitterness)

See "yi ku si tian" (recall past sufferings and think about present happiness).

忆苦会
yi ku hui
(meetings to recall past bitterness)

See "yi ku si tian" (recall past sufferings and think about present happiness).

忆苦思甜
yi ku si tian
(recall past sufferings and think about present happiness)

The practice of "recalling past sufferings and thinking about present happiness" first appeared in a PLA education movement in the early 1960s. Various forms of this practice were suggested, such as holding meetings at which soldiers and officers told one another about past sufferings (yi hu hui) and ate poor meals especially prepared to recall past bitterness (yiku fan). Past sufferings referred to sufferings in the "old society" before the 1949 Communist takeover, and the present happiness of course referred to the happy lives Chairman Mao and the Party had provided for them. They were told that their happy lives would disappear and they would have to suffer once again (chi erbianku), if a "capitalist restoration" (zibenzhuyi fubi) were to take place. In this way, they were said to have greatly enhanced their "class consciousness".

During the GPCR, this practice was popularized all over the country.

异化
yihua
(alienation)

See "shehuizhuyi yihualun" (theory of socialist alienation).

异化分析法
yihua fenxi fa
(analytical method of alienation)

See "yihua wenxue" (alienated literature; literature of alienation).

异化劳动
yihua laodong
(alienated labor)

See "yihua wenxue" (alienated literature; literature of alienation) and "shehuizhuyi yihualun" (theory of socialist alienation).

异化批评法
yihua piping fa
(critical method of alienation)

See "yihua wenxue" (alienated literature; literature of alienation).

异化热
yihua re
(alienation craze)

See "shehuizhuyi yihua lun" (theory of socialist alienation).

异化是马克思主义的中心思想
yihua shi Makesizhuyide zhongxin sixiang
(the central idea of Marxism is alienation)

See "shehuizhuyi yihua lun" (theory of socialist alienation) and "rendaozhuyi lunzheng" (humanism debate).

异化是社会进步的代价
yihua shi shehui jinbude daijia
(alienation is the price of social progress)

See "shehuizhuyi yihua lun" (theory of socialist alienation) and "rendaozhuyi lunzheng" (humanism debate).

异化文学
yihua wenxue
(alienated literature; literature of alienation)

In the discussion of humanism and alienation in the early 1980s, the concept of "alienation" suddenly became an important topic among China's ideological-literary circles. It exerted a tangible influence on literature and art. The concept "yihua wenxue" was raised. As Wang Ruoshui warned, socialist literature and art could also become alienated. If a writer, for example, writes according to the "wind" (feng) blowing from above and to the "Left" formula, and does not make an effort to reflect truthfully on the people's lives, struggles, cries, sorrows, and happiness, then what he has written will be distorted, and that is "alienated" literature. According to Wang, there are three kinds of such literature. First, "god-making literature" (which describes Mao Zedong as something like a "god") and "conspiratorial literature" (which describes the struggle against "capitalist-roaders"), of the sort that appeared in great quantity during the GPCR, that looks down upon or is even hostile to the people. Second, literature that wrongly handles the relationship between arts and politics and is divorced from the people under the guidance of an erroneous political line, an erroneous leading method, and erroneous creative thought. And finally there is commercialized literature (shangye wenxue) (Wang Ruoshui, "Literature and Art and the Problem of the Alienation of Man", *SHWX,* 9, 1980, reprinted in *WHB,* 25 Sept. 1980).

The term "yihua wenxue" can also be used to refer to literature of alienation, especially literature describing "man's alienation under the condition of socialism" (shehuizhuyi tiaojianxia rende yihua). On the one hand, critics testified that the alienation described by contemporary Chinese writers could be found everywhere in daily life, and in the whole socialist stage. On the other hand, writers were inspired by the alienation discussion. Many works were devoted to the alienation of "public servants" becoming "lords and masters over the people" or of "genuine man" becoming "false man", the alienation of the times, the environment, the relationship between man and man, or the alienation of love or marriage. "Labor alienation" ("yihua laodong" or "laodong yihua") was also a popular theme. For instance, Gao Xiaosheng's short story "Chen Huansheng's Adventure in Town" documents how people live in alienation. The protagonist Chen Huansheng is an ordinary peasant. As an element of the laboring people, he should be respected in society. In reality, however, he is despised. "Li Shunda Builds a House", "A Rich Middle Peasant", "A Story Badly Edited", and "In the Village Street" all deal with similar problems. After reading these works, critics claimed that one should agree that Marx's thesis about alienated labor still has a certain practical significance in socialism.

Accordingly, a new literary theory and criticism method seemed to be emerging under the influence of the socialist alienation theory. In class society, it was said, everyone will undergo a certain kind of self-alienation (ziwo yihua), which brings about the complexity of their character, spirit, and ideology. If writers portray their characters according to what actually occurs in life, if they understand and give full expression to the truth that self-alienation in different people has different manifestations and that people's attitudes towards self-alienation differ from one another, they will be able to enhance their characters' typicality and ideological content. Why in contemporary Chinese literary creations were there so many false "lofty, great, and perfect" (gao da quan) styled characters, or "paper characters", and why could formulism and jargonism not be avoided in character portrayal—this was ascribed to the fact that writers and artists seldom studied and probed the "Marxist" view of alienation, still less made use of it to guide their creative praxes. Critics interested in analyzing and commenting upon literary works with the alienation theory as the "principle, measure, and standard" used the "analytical method of alienation" (yihua fenxi fa) or a "critical method of alienation" (yihua piping fa). As they argued, literary criticism in the past was confined to only one method, that is, the socialist critical method, or, as it was also called, the class analysis method or the method of Marxist literary criticism. In reality, however, even within Marxist literary criticism, there is more than one method. The analytical method of alienation, for instance, is one of them. See also "shehuizhuyi yihua lun" (theory of socialist alienation) and "rendaozhuyi lunzheng" (humanism debate).

异化随着社会进步而发生
yihua suizhao shehui jinbu er fasheng
(alienation occurs with social progress)

See "shehuizhuyi yihua lun" (theory of socialist alienation) and "rendaozhuyi lunzheng" (humanism debate).

异化论的抽象公式
yihualunde chouxiang gongshi
(an abstract formula of the alienation theory)

See "shehuizhuyi yihualun" (theory of socialist alienation) and "rendaozhuyi lunzheng" (humanism debate).

意识流东方化
yishiliu dongfanghua
(orientalization of the stream-of-consciousness)

See "yishiliude Zhongguo dailiren" (Chinese agent of the stream-of-consciousness).

意识流的中国代理人
yishiliude Zhongguo dailiren
(Chinese agent of the stream-of-consciousness)

In 1980, there was a controversy caused by Wang Meng's literary innovations, beginning with his short story "Eyes of the Night". When the story appeared in the autumn of 1979, not many people understood its significance. The literary world, however, was soon to be startled by what Wang himself described as "a handful of grenades"—a whole series of his works, similar in kind, which came out in succession—"The Bolshevik Salute", "Voices of Spring", "Kite Streamers", "Dreams of the Sea", and "Butterfly". Wang Meng was said to have discarded the "principle of realism" and employed the so-called stream-of-consciousness technique. In an open letter dated 9 December 1979, Wang Meng admitted that he had "deliberately" experimented with some new techniques (Wang Meng, "Guanyu 'yishiliu' de tongxin"—"An Open Letter on 'Stream-of-Consciousness'", *Yalu jiang,* 2:70-72, 1980, reprinted in *Wang Meng Zhuanji*, pp. 122-27; trans. by Michael S. Duke in *Moden Chinese Literature* v, 1, 1:25-28, Sept. 1984).

For a time in the early 1980s, Wang Meng was regarded as a "Chinese agent" of the "stream-of-consciousness". In a sense, he was, as Liu Xinwu put it, the first person to dare to "eat snails" (Liu Xinwu, "Ta zai chi woniu"—"He Is Eating Snails", *Beijing wanbao,* 8 July 1980). According to Feng Jicai, Wang Meng was a "Chinese modernist" (Feng Jicai, "Wang Meng zhaodaole ziji"—"Wang Meng Has Found Himself", *Wang Meng Zhuanji,* p. 329). In Leo Ou-fan Lee's words, he was "something of an artistic dissident" (Leo Ou-fan Lee, "The Politics of Technique: Perspectives of Literary Dissidence in Contemporary Chinese Fiction", in *After Mao,* p. 168). Wang Meng not only engaged in his own innovations but also encouraged others in their explorations. He enthusiastically praised *A Preliminary Discussion of Contemporary Narrative Techniques,* a controversial book by Gao Xingjian (Wang Meng, "Zhi Gao Xingjiande xin"—"A Letter to Gao Xingjian", *Xiaoshuo jie,* 2, 1982, reprinted in *WYLZJ,* pp. 557-61). He said that he understood those young writers who were enthusiastic about the "stream-of-consciousness", change of person and angle of view, the "absurd", or "distortion" (Wang Meng, "Qingtingzhe shenghuode shengxi"—"Listening to the Breathing of Life", *Wang Meng Zhuanji*, p. 101). It should be pointed out that in contemporary Chinese fiction writing, Wang Meng was not the first person to use the stream-of-consciousness technique. Before his "Eyes of the Night", Zong Pu had published her short story "Who Am I?" a Kafkaesque allegory about the GPCR ("Wo shi shui?", *Changchun*, 12, 1979, reprinted in *Zong Pu Xiaoshuo Sanwen Xuan—Selected Writings of Zong Pu*, Beijing, Beijing, 1981, pp. 130-39). One should also mention Zhao Zhenkai's "Waves", a novelette that was actually written in November 1974 and soon enjoyed quite a wide manuscript circulation, though its official publication was not until later (Zhao Zhenkai's "Waves"—"Bodong"—was first published in *Jintian*, 4:31-71; 5:113, 29-48; 6:21-56, Jun.-Oct. 1979, and then, officially, in *Changjiang wenxue congkan*, 1:21-76, Feb. 1981; trans. in Bonnie S. McDougall, ed., *Waves and Other Stories*, Hong Kong, Chinese University Press, 1985). But it was Wang Meng who did the most to remind people that the character-describing method employed previously was no longer sufficient—a remark by Engels that Wang Meng's defenders very often resorted to. With great skill, Wang Meng succeeded in making his writing attractive to the readers of fiction. Soon what had been taboo just a few years earlier suddenly became very popular. Editors of a number of literary journals confirmed that one-third to one-half of the submissions fell into the category of stream-of-consciousness. *Shanghai Literature* claimed that for a time in 1980 such works even constituted the majority of the manuscripts they received. Some authors declared that they were Wang Meng's followers.

With Wang's initiative, a new genre emerged—some critics called it "psychological fiction" (xintai xiaoshuo), another term for fiction of the stream-of-consciousness after "orientalization" (yishiliu dongfanghua). This genre focuses on describing a character's psychological behavior, the refraction of which presents society and life. Besides those mentioned above, works in this genre include Jin Fan's (the pen name for Jin Guantao and his wife Liu Qingfeng) "Open Love Letters" ("Gongkaide qingshu", *SY*, 1, 1980, reprinted in book form, Beijing, Beijing, 1981), Zhang Jie's "Love Must Not Be Forgotten", Shen Rong's "At Middle Age", and Dai Houying's *Humanity!*.

What is more, somewhat inspired by Wang Meng, writers like Liu Xinwu, Gao Xingjian, Feng Jicai, and Li Tuo later all went their own ways in their artistic experimentations. According to Philip Williams, an American critic of contemporary Chinese literature, Wang Meng's 1979-1980 championing of technical experimentation and literary craftsmanship challenged the widely held notion in China that it was a small step from reportage to serious fiction. In view of the inspiration and influence of Wang's innovation among Chinese writers, Philip Williams asserted that "the continued upgrading of modern Chinese fiction as an art may well depend more heavily upon the work of stylists like Wang Meng" (Philip Williams, "Stylistic Variety in a PRC Writer: Wang Meng's Fiction of the 1979-1980 Cultural Thaw", *Australian Journal of Chinese Affairs*, 11:76, Jan. 1984).

It would be wrong, however, to say that Wang Meng's works were simply "stream-of-consciousness" fiction. One can see the obvious difference between Wang Meng's fiction and that of the "stream-of-consciousness" in the West, and this seemed to have been generally accepted by most Chinese critics who preferred an "orientalization" of this technique. They did not go so far as William Tay, who found Wang Meng's works simply not in line with his definition of "stream-of-consciousness" on the grounds that in Wang's narratives "free association is not an ordering principle; neither does the interior monologue co-occur with free association" (William Tay, "Wang Meng, Stream-of-Consciousness, and the Controversy over Modernism", *Modern Chinese Literature*, v. 1, 1:14, 1984). Furthermore, despite

William Tay's argument to the contrary, they did not attempt to "separate the technique from the ideology" (ibid., pp. 14 and 17). No doubt, it was "a big leap forward in PRC literary criticism" that a sort of relaxation could be seen towards a modernist technique; but Chinese critics contended that "technique is not ideologically neutral" (ibid., p. 17, and Note 47). For them, it is pointless to discuss a certain "technique" without considering its ideological context. In fact, it was under the premise that the technique could not be separated from the ideology that they examined Wang Meng's works. The orientalization did not only occur to the stream-of-consciousness technique itself but also to the literary criticism applied to it, as can be seen in Song Yaoliang's 1986 article, "The Process of the Orientalization of the Stream of Consciousness" ("Yishiliu wenxue dongfanghua guocheng" *WXPL*, 1:33-40, Jan. 1986).

Wang Meng was not a formalist, nor an ordinary writer obsessed by some literary experiments. As he said, "Complex experience, thought, feeling, and life require complex artistic form" (Philip Williams, "Stylistic Variety", p. 39). That is to say, his unique artistic form was employed in the service of the thoughts and feelings he wanted to convey. See also "wangbuzhaode hudie" (a butterfly difficult to catch) and "xinshiqi wenxuede duoyuan fazhan" (pluralistic development of the literature of the new period).

意识形态现代化
yishixingtai xiandaihua
(modernization of ideology)

See "si ge xiandaihua" (four modernizations).

艺术标准第一，政治标准第二
yishu biaozhun diyi, zhengzhi biaozhun di'er
(artistic criteria first, political criteria second)

See "zhengzhi biaozhun diyi, yishu biaozhun di'er" (political criteria first, artistic criteria second).

艺术接受主体的还原原理
yishu jieshou zhutide huanyuan yuanli
(principle of the restoration of the subjectivity of art receptor)

See "yishu jieshouzhede zhutixing" (subjectivity of art receptor).

艺术接受者的主体性
yishu jieshouzhede zhutixing
(subjectivity of art receptor)

The subjectivity of art receptor is said to have been neglected by China's literary theorists during the Mao period. As a result, an artistic receptor was regarded as a passive reflector, like a mirror, and the process of artistic reception as merely a form of education. The overemphasis on the epistemological nature of artistic appreciation and on its ideological function inevitably caused a weakening, or, even worse, a loss of subjectivity of the art receptor. To critics who underline the subjectivity of literature, the basic meaning of the subjectivity of the art receptor is this: during the process of reception, an artistic reader brings his dynamic role in aesthetic creation into play and achieves a free and self-conscious human essence. As a result, he is revitalized as a free, complete, and self-conscious man. Actually, the whole process of artistic reception is that of the revitalization of human nature, the rediscovery and vindication of human dignity, value, and mission. This aesthetic effect is referred to by Liu Zaifu as "the restoration effect of man's essence" (rende benzhide huanyuan xiaoying). It can also be called "the principle of the restoration of the subjectivity of art receptor" (yishu jieshou zhutide huanyuan yuanli). Liu explains that, in actual life, one usually fails to achieve self-actualization, restrained by natural and social forces of various kinds. Very often, moreover, one is unaware of the loss of one's self, of one's subjectivity. Art, in this context, can exercise its function of restoration: when entering into the aesthetic state, one will immediately be revitalized and restored to one's consciousness as the subject, one will re-occupy one's free, self-conscious essence. In fact, people do achieve transcendence through aesthetic activities, so as to obtain what they cannot in actual life. "Thoroughgoing humanism, therefore, can only be realized in literature and art" (Liu Zaifu, "On the Subjectivity of Literature", *WXPL,* 1:6, 1986).

An art receptor realizing subjectivity means that he achieves self-actualization. More concretely, it includes: first, to turn constrained man into free man; second, to turn defective man into fulfilled man; and third, to turn man without a consciousness of self into man with a self-consciousness. The realization of subjectivity of the art receptor also relies on another mechanism—creativity on the part of the receptor. Only with a perfect aesthetic psychological structure can a reader bring his dynamic role in aesthetic re-creation into play. According to Liu, for a long time in China, the reader's aesthetic subjectivity was lost, because this aesthetic psychological structure was seriously damaged, distorted, and oversimplified.

For literary critics as high-grade artistic receptors, there is a three-level transcendence to achieve subjectivity:

First, like other readers, when appreciating an artistic work, a critic breaks out of the confines of the ideology in actual life and regains the position of man as the subject and his free essence.

Second, the critic should transcend the writer's ideology. On the basis of fully understanding the writer and his work, the critic arrives at his interpretation, with his own unique aesthetic view and aesthetic ideal. He becomes an aesthetic re-creator, discovering a value, a potential significance, in the work, which the writer himself may not have been aware of. He will enhance the writer's artistic experience into an abstract, theoretical form, which will in turn be absorbed by the writer.

Third, the critic should also possess the quality of self-transcendence. In his practice of literary criticism, by "assimilating" (tonghua) and "conforming" (shunying), the critic transcends his own ideology and achieves a transformation, or a re-creation, of his subjective structure. When he achieves a high level of self-actualization, his criticism will move from the realm of science into that of art.

When discussing the above points, Liu Zaifu considered it necessary to bring up the old issue of "understanding writers" (lijie zuojia), in view of the long-existing unsatisfactory situation in China. "Understanding writers", for the most part, means fully respecting the particularity of writers' labor and the specific laws of artistic creation ("On the Subjectivity of Literature", *WXPL,* 1:10, Jan. 1986). See also "wenxue zhutixing" (subjectivity of literature).

议会道路
yihui daolu

(parliamentary road)

See "xiuzhengzhuyi" (revisionism).

阴阳互根
Yin Yang hugen
(law of Yin and Yang as each other's roots)

See "Kylin wenhua" (Kylin Culture).

阴谋文艺
yinmou wenyi
(conspiratorial literature and art)

See "yihua wenxue" (alienated literature; literature of alienation), "xie yu zouzipai zuo douzheng" (writing about the struggle against capitalist-roaders), and "wenyi wei zhengzhi fuwu" (literature and art serve politics).

引火烧身
yin huo shao shen
(draw fire against oneself)

See "fan youpai yundong" (anti-Rightist campaign).

引蛇出洞
yin she chu dong
(lure the snake out of the pit)

See "fan youpai yundong" (anti-Rightist campaign).

英明领袖
yingming lingxiu
(wise leader)

Following the example of Mao who exclusively had the title of "great leader", Hua Guofeng was called the "wise leader" during the first few years after the 1976 downfall of the Gang of Four.

In his final year, Mao placed his hopes on Hua. On 21 and 28 January 1976, soon after Zhou Enlai died, Mao twice proposed that Hua be made acting premier in charge of the Center's daily activities. Then, on 5 April 1976, following the Tiananmen Incident, Mao appointed Hua to the positions of CCP first vice-chairman and PRC premier. On 30 April 1976, during a meeting with Mao, Hua Guofeng reaped another bumper political harvest. The Great Leader wrote three notes to his chosen successor: "Take it easy; don't worry" (Manman lai, buyao zhaoji), "Follow the principles of the past" (Zhao guoqu fangzhen ban), and "With you in charge, I am at ease" (Ni banshi, wo fangxin). The next month, Mao told concerned officials that Hua should be given publicity, so that the Chinese people would more appreciate their future leader.

But it was after Mao's death on 9 September 1976 that Hua obtained the title of "wise leader". This came after his successful coup d'état on 6 October 1976, during which he had the Gang of Four arrested in the name of the PCC Politburo, with the help of Ye Jianying (then CCP vice-chairman), Wang Dongxing (then a CCP

Politburo member), and Li Xiannian (then a CCP Politburo member and PRC vice-premier). On the next day, Hua Guofeng became CCP chairman, PRC premier, and CMC chairman, the first person in China's Communist regime concurrently holding these three top posts. By the end of the month, the title "wise leader" was invented in an editorial of the *Liberation Army Daily*. Hua was hailed all over the country as the "wise leader" who would lead the Chinese people into the twenty-first century in a so-called "new Long March" (xin changzheng).

The term "new Long March" symbolically described Hua's great mission. At that time, another term with the same significance was also used: "the new historical period of socialism" (xinde shehuizhuyi lishi shiqi), or, for short, "the new period" (xinshiqi). It suggested the start of a "new period" in China.

Hua Guofeng hoped to perform immortal feats as the wise leader. He expected a good beginning in 1977. Quoting a saying from Mao that "Great disorder across the land leads to great order", he predicted that 1977 would be a year of great order under his leadership, as in his speech of 25 December 1976 at the Second National Conference on Learning from Dazhai in Agriculture. In a tone of a wise leader, he said: "It is our belief that 1977 will be a year in which we shall smash the Gang of Four completely and go towards great order, a year of united struggle and triumphant advance" *(HQ,* 1, 1977, p. 40).

Unfortunately, Hua's wish did not come true. He was not the right leader for the Party at that time (though CCP historians argue that at first neither Deng Xiaoping nor Hu Yaobang intended to replace him). In 1977 Hua reached the culmination of his career and also the beginning of his decline.

On the very first day of 1977, he revealed his political program (as elucidated in the New Year's Day joint editorial of the *People's Daily, Red Flag,* and the *Liberation Army Daily,* "Advancing on the Crest of Victory"—"Chengsheng qianjin"), but this was none other than "grasping the key link in running the country" (zhua gang zhi guo). This meant that Hua still insisted on Mao's policy of "taking class struggle as the key link".

Hua was accused of putting forth the "two whatevers" (liang ge fanshi) principle. Succinctly, the principle was expressed in the following statement: "We will resolutely uphold whatever policy decisions Chairman Mao made, and unswervingly follow whatever instructions Chairman Mao gave", contained in the 7 February 1977 joint editorial of the *People's Daily, Red Flag,* and the *Liberation Army Daily* under the title of "Study the Documents Well and Grasp the Key Link" (Xue hao wenjian zhuazhu gang). In fact, as early as 26 October 1976, when talking with officials in charge of the PCC Propaganda Department, Hua had raised the "two whatevers" for the first time. Later, he reiterated this on several occasions. In addition to other purposes, his "two whatevers" principle indicated his resistance to the popular demand at the time for Deng Xiaoping's return to power and for a reversal of verdicts on the "Tiananmen Incident" of 5 April 1976.

In 1977, the "year of great order", a major political event was the CCP 11th National Congress held in Beijing from 12 to 18 August. In his political report to the Congress, Hua Guofeng reaffirmed the theories, policies, and slogans of the GPCR. The "general task" for his "new period" revealed what Hua and his supporters meant by "new". The task was stipulated as follows: to firmly carry out the line of the 11th Party Congress, steadfastly continue the revolution under the dictatorship of the proletariat, deepen the three revolutionary movements of class struggle, the struggle for production and scientific experimentation, and transform China into a great and powerful socialist country with modern agriculture, industry, national defense, and science and technology by the end of the century.

This was a serious issue, and Party elders had to respond with a rejection. On 30 September 1979, in his speech at the meeting in celebration of the 30th anniverary of the founding of the PRC, Marshal Ye Jianying formulated a new "general task": "Unite the people of all our nationalities and bring all positive forces into play so that we can work with one heart and one mind, go all out, aim high, and achieve greater, faster, better, and more economical results in building a modern, powerful, socialist country." Deng later declared that this "general task" formulation was "the first fairly comprehensive statement of our present general line" ("The Present Situation and the Tasks before Us", *SWD,* pp. 233-34).

Perhaps Hua Guofeng was not a capable politician. Or perhaps he possessed some moral excellence of Chinese tradition, and exercised vigilance against becoming a "Khrushchev-type" leader. But he went against the will of most Chinese people and the tide of the times. He hindered the process of "setting wrong things right" (boluanfanzheng) and thus also missed his golden chance.

As it turned out, upholding or opposing the "two whatevers" was the focus in the struggle between the Deng Xiaoping faction and the Hua Guofeng faction in 1977-78. At the 1978 Third Plenum of the 11th PCC, or to be more exact, on 13 December 1978 when making a self-criticism in his closing speech at the Central Work Conference which made preparations for the Plenum, Hua Guofeng began his downhill journey. At the 5th NPC session held in August and September 1980, Hua resigned as PRC premier and was replaced by Zhao Ziyang. From 10 November to 5 December 1980, the PCC Politburo held nine successive meetings to bring Hua under control. The "Circular on the PCC Politburo Meetings" listed Hua's "Left" and other alleged mistakes since his "October 6th coup" of 1976. The Party was also informed of the important personnel changes to take place at the forthcoming 6th Plenum of the 11th PCC. Then at the Plenum held in June 1981 Hua lost his two top posts—chairman of the PCC and chairman of the CMC (taken over by Hu Yaobang and Deng Xiaoping respectively). In September 1982, Hua lost his Politburo seat at the 12th PCC. He was finally and completely defeated by Deng Xiaoping, a man who had been toppled twice during the GPCR. See also "liang ge fanshi" (two whatevers) and "wen'ge" (Cultural Revolution).

英雄史观
yingxiong shiguan
(view about heroes creating history)

See "tiancai lun" ("innate genius" theory).

影射
yingshe
(attack by innuendo)

To "attack by innuendo", when referring to the Party, its leader, or the social system, was a serious accusation against an author.

This was the case when the 1981 Bai Hua Incident occurred. His (coauthor Peng Ning) film script "Unrequited Love" ("Kulian", *SY,* 3:140-71, 248, Sept. 1979, adapted into a film under the title of *Sun and Man* by the Changchun Film Studio in 1980) was accused of "attacking by innuendo" the Party, its leader, and socialist China.

This nearly occurred again when in the spring of 1983 Bai Hua published *The Wu King's Golden Lance and the Yue King's Sword (Wuwang Jin'ge Yuewang Jian, SY,* 2, 1983). It is a historical play sharing the same subject matter as *Revenge of the Yue*

King—a 1961 work coauthored by Cao Yu, a famous dramatist (Cao Yu, Mei Qian, and Yu Shizhi, *Dan jian Pian*, *RMWX*, 7, 1961). However, although both works deal with the war between the two states, Wu and Yue, during the Spring-Autumn Period, their themes are different. Unlike the Yue King in *Revenge of the Yue King*, in Bai Hua's play the King is a negative character, and the masses of the people are much more important than their rulers. This subject was so sensitive that soon after it was staged in Beijing, the *People's Daily* appealed that it should not be labeled as "attacking (Mao) by innuendo" on the grounds that the historical phenomenon it described bore some likeness to the present-day situation (*RMRB*, 10 May 1983). See also "Bai Hua shijian" (Bai Hua Incident) and "wenyi wei zhengzhi fuwu" (literature and art serve politics).

忧患意识
youhuan yishi
(sense of angst)

See "zuojia zhutixing" (writer's subjectivity).

游说文学
youshui wenxue
(lobby literature)

See "xinshiqi baogao wenxuede liang da liupai" (two main schools of reportage literature in the new period).

有理想，有道德，有教育，有纪律
you lixiang, you daode, you jiaoyu, you jilü
(have lofty ideals, moral integrity, good education, and a strong sense of discipline)

See "aiguozhuyi" (patriotism) and "shehuizhuyi chuji jieduan lun" (theory of the primary stage of socialism).

有权不用，过期作废
you quan buyong, guoqi zuofei
(if you don't use your power when you have it, you will be sorry when it expires)

A saying in China that satirizes those bureaucrats of various ranks who scramble for power and profit. See "fan fubai" (anti-corruption).

有中国特色社会主义
you Zhongguo tese shehuizhuyi
(socialism with Chinese characteristics)

See "Deng Xiaoping lilun" (Deng Xiaoping Theory) and "shehuizhuyi chuji jieduan lun" (theory of the primary stage of socialism).

有中国特色社会主义的经济
you Zhongguo tese shehuizhuyide jingji

(a socialist economy with Chinese characteristics)

See "shehuizhuyi chuji jieduan lun" (theory of the primary stage of socialism) and "jingji gaige" (economic reform).

有中国特色社会主义的文化
you Zhongguo tese shehuizhuyide wenhua
(socialist culture with Chinese characteristics)

See "shehuizhuyi chuji jieduan lun" (theory of the primary stage of socialism) and "liang ge wenming" (two civilizations).

有中国特色社会主义的政治
you Zhongguo tese shehuizhuyide zhengzhi
(socialist politics with Chinese characteristics)

See "shehuizhuyi chuji jieduan lun" (theory of the primary stage of socialism) and "zhengzhi gaige" (political reform).

有偿新闻
youchang xinwen
(paid news-writing)

See "xinwen ziyou wenti" (issue of press freedom) and "jingji gaige" (economic reform).

有成分论
youchengfenlun
(theory of the importance of class origin)

See "xuetong lun" (lineage theory) and "jiating chengfen" (family origin; class status of one's family).

有限政府论
youxian zhengfu lun
(limited government theory)

See "yi fa zhi guo" (ruling the nation by law), "ziyouzhuyi" (liberalism), and "zhengzhi gaige" (political reform).

有限主权论
youxian zhuquan lun
(theory of "limited sovereignty")

See "shehuizhuyi dajiating lun" (theory of the "socialist community").

又红又专
you hong you zhuan
(both red and expert)

In the "Sixty Articles of Working Methods (Draft)", a document Mao presented to the PCC on 31 January 1958, for the first time he used the terms "red" and "expert" to refer to "politics" and "profession". Thereafter a political-ideological education movement was carried out among students, intellectuals, and cadres. "Both red and expert", that is, "both socialist-minded and professionally proficient", became a slogan embodying the CCP's expectations.

As it turned out, few people were able to live up to the Party's expectations. And this could even be a reason for political punishment. Many people were vilified as "white and expert" (baizhuan), as "only expert and not red" (zhi zhuan bu hong), or as "shoots of revisionism" (xiuzhengzhuyi miaozi). For a long time, this slogan was a heavy burden on the people.

On 18 March 1978, Deng Xiaoping rectified this problem. At the opening ceremony of the National Conference on Science, he explained what was meant by "both red and expert" and what "reasonable standards" should be set for intellectuals. According to Deng, if a person loves the socialist motherland and is serving socialism and the workers, peasants, and soldiers of his own free will and accord, then it should be said that he has begun to acquire a proletarian world outlook. In terms of political standards, he could not be considered "white" but should be called "red". "Our scientific undertakings are an integral part of our socialist cause", Deng continued, "working devotedly for our socialist scientific enterprises and making contributions to them is, of course, a sign that one is expert; in a sense, it is also a sign that one is 'red'" ("Speech at the Opening Ceremony of the National Conference on Science", *SWD,* pp. 107-8). Two years later, this time mainly speaking of Party and government leaders, Deng said: "Being 'expert' does not necessarily mean one is 'red', but being 'red' means one must strive to be 'expert'. No matter what one's line of work, if he does not possess expertise, if he does not know his own job but issues arbitrary orders, harming the interests of the people and holding up production and construction, he cannot be considered 'red'" ("The Present Situation and the Tasks before Us", *SWD,* pp. 247-48). See also "hong" (red), "zhishifenzi wenti" (issue of intellectuals), and "dangde jiaoyu fangzhen" (the Party's educational policy).

右
you
(Right)

According to Mao in his 1937 philosophical work *On Practice (Shijian lun),* "ideology which lags behind reality and is unable to progress forward along with the objective conditions of change" is expressed as "Right". As for "ideology which transcends definite stages of development in the objective process and which has strayed from the practice of the majority of contemporaries and deviated from present reality", it is expressed as "Left" (zuo).

However, this is not so simple, when the concepts of "Right" and "Left" are given political significance. As Mao and his Party also held, "Left" means progressive and revolutionary, while "Right" means bourgeois and reactionary. In the Mao period, therefore, "anti-Right", or "anti-Right-deviation" (fan youqing), or "anti-Right opportunism" (fan youqing jihuizhuyi) was always a substantial part of political life. A dominant phenomenon was that a "Rightist" mistake could be of the nature of an antagonistic contradiction between the people and their enemy, while a "Left" mistake would be treated as belonging to the contradictions among the people, a mistake made by those with the best of intentions, who were in essence revolutionaries. To play it safe, many Party officials would rather make a "Left" mistake than to be regarded as possessing "Right-deviation" thinking (ning zuo wu you). In fact, they often resorted to strong-handed and excessive meaures and action in their struggles against "Right-deviation", and this was often the best route for their promotion. On the other hand, many innocent people fell victim to such political tactics.

In light of CCP doctrine, when "zuo" means something incorrect, it should have quotation marks attached, so as to differentiate it from the "correct" Leftist policies, principles, ideology or political line of the Party. The phrase "zuoqing" can mean something correct—Left-leaning, progressive, or inclined towards the revolution; or something incorrect—Left deviation, Left opportunism (zuoqing jihuizhuyi), or Left adventurism (zuoqing maoxianzhuyi). It is clear that "jizuo" (ultra-Left) must mean something incorrect and bad. Interestingly, however, many CCP leaders seemed reluctant to use this phrase. Immediately after the Lin Biao Incident of 13 September 1971, the Chinese people condemned Lin Biao and his supporters as ultra-Leftists. But Mao thought otherwise, and he banned any attempt to expose and criticize Lin's ultra-Leftist pernicious influence. Similarly, for a time after the fall of the Gang of Four, their political line was categorized by the Party leadership as "ultra-Right" (jiyou). In his speech at the Second National Learn-from-Dazhai Conference on 25 December 1976, Hua Guofeng, CCP chairman, asserted that the Gang of Four were "ultra-Rightists, out-and-out capitalist-roaders, and the most ferocious counter-revolutionaries", and they "could not have pursued a line farther to the Right!" Later, as a concession, they were described as "Left in form but Right in essence" (xing zuo shi you). With the convening of the 3rd Plenum of the 11th PCC in December 1978, the Party finally agreed that the political line of the Gang of Four (and of Lin Biao) was "ultra-Left", and not "ultra-Right", "Left in form but Right in essence", or "pseudo-Left but genuinely Right" (jia zuo zhen you).

The Chinese people know very well what "ultra-Left" means, having suffered a lot from the Party's "ultra-Left" or "Left" policies for several decades. To them, there is no question that the label of "ultra-Left" should be attached to the Gang of Four or to Lin Biao. This label is also suited to Mao, who cultivated both the Gang of Four and Lin Biao. But there is another issue China analysts (in particular, those supporting the "two Cultural Revolutions" theory) also want to point out: during the several so-called "anti-ultra-Left" (fan jizuo) campaigns carried out in and after the GPCR, those in power easily suppressed hundreds of thousands of their opponents who were accused of being "ultra-Left".

How to define revisionism and dogmatism, and conservatism and radicalism, is also an interesting subject. Briefly, it is dogmatism to approach Marxism from a metaphysical point of view and to regard it as something rigid, and it is revisionism to negate the basic principles of Marxism and to negate its universal truth. "Revisionism, or Right opportunism, is a bourgeois trend of thought that is even more dangerous than dogmatism" (*MZXJ,* 5, p. 392). Revisionism is one form of bourgeois ideology, but dogmatism is never regarded as bourgeois. While revisionism is regarded as "Rightist", it is never related to conservatism. In contrast, dogmatism may be conservative and at the same time (quite strangely but reasonably) "Leftist". Accordingly, radicalism, as an opposite to conservatism, is regarded as Left and necessary for the revolution before the Communist regime was founded. Thereafter, however, radicalism may be condemned as Rightist, liberal, revisionist, bourgeois, and reactionary. For example, during the 1978-79 Beijing Spring period, radical activists demanded emancipation of individuality, human rights, and democratic reform of China's political structure. In the self-examination wave of the 1990s, it was said that the eagerness of the 1980s' intellectuals for quick success and instant benefits in reform and the open door, their keenness for "Western learning"—these were termed as "bourgeois liberalization"—had led to the rise of the 1980s' radicalism. Similarly, the "neo-Leftist" or "neo-Maoist" school can be regarded as a school of "neo-conservatism" in the 1990s.

Notably, during the last few years of 1970s, after the political line of the Gang of Four (and of Lin Biao) had been stipulated to be "ultra-Left", the CCP authorities employed a new term "'Leftist' revisionism" (laizi 'zuo'miande xiuzhengzhuyi), in order to explain the problems of Mao's GPCR. It was said that during the course of history, revisionism may have different faces. Besides "Rightist revisionism" (laizi youmiande xiuzhengzhuyi), there is "'Leftist' revisionism", which distorts Marxism with revolutionary slogans and radical actions. Lin Biao and the Gang of Four were precisely representatives of "Rightist revisionism".

In addition, the terms "Right", "Left", "Right deviation", "Left deviation", "Right opportunism", and "Left opportunism" should mainly refer to a political party, or more precisely, to tendencies within the party, and to divergence from the current party line. However, in China they were often applied in the spheres of literature and art. The history of Chinese literature during the Mao period was part of the history of the internal struggles of the CCP. For a long time, "orthodox" literary critics regarded this as totally natural: inner-Party struggle is class struggle in society reflected within the Party, and literature and art are the "mirror", the "barometer", and the "tool" of class struggle. This explains why so many political campaigns involving writers and intellectuals were launched.

Throughout CCP history "Left" forces have predominated for most of the time and brought great disasters to the Party. Deng came to understand this in his remaining years. On his "Southern tour" in early 1992, where he gave a series of talks calling for a more vigorous reform and open-door policy, Deng abandoned his long-standing ambivalence about what he believed was more dangerous to his Party—threats from the political left or right. He said in Shenzhen: "Watch out for the Right, but mainly defend against the 'Left'." This thesis is regarded by many as a significant summation of CCP experience, both positive and negative, in the long history of Chinese revolution and construction. With this statement, Deng is said to have made an explicit, final break with China's Maoist past. Reformists claim that it should be taken as a guiding principle of strategic significance for the Party.

In the eyes of Maoists, Deng might be a Rightist. With Deng as an example, some China critics tend to divide CCP leaders into two categories—one consists of those who are considered to be Leftists, conservatives, and hawks; another Rightists, reformists and doves. But things are more complicated; this division is often misleading. In the first place, there is no such a clear-cut division. Deng (and many other leaders alike) had a dual nature. He was radical in his economic reform but conservative when facing demands for political reform. While a dove when he declared that China's intellectuals were already part of working class, he was a hawk when he ordered the army to gun down the demonstrating students in the June 4th Incident of 1989. One may remember the "two basic points" in Party line. Deng opposed "Left" ideology in the economic field with his reform and the open-door policy, while he opposed "Right" ideology in the political field with his "four cardinal principles". For Deng and other CCP leaders, the interests of the Party are supreme.

With reform and open-door program further carried out, one will more and more find it unsuitable to describe a certain figure as reformist or conservative—who may look like a reformist when dealing with some issues and is conservative with others, nor are the labels "Right" and "Left" suitable for someone who is defined even as a reformist or a conservative. It can be expected that the political significance of "Right" and "Left" will gradually weaken, since, due to Deng's initiatives, "giving prominence to politics" (tuchu zhengzhi) has been replaced by "giving prominence to the economy" (tuchu jingji) as the guiding principle to run the country. See also "liang tiao luxiande douzheng" (struggle between two lines), "fan youpai yundong" (anti-Rightist campaign), "tuchu zhengzhi" (giving prominence to politics), and "chi butong zhengjianzhe" (dissidents).

右派
youpai
(Rightists)

See "you" (Right) and "fan youpai yundong" (anti-Rightist campaign).

右派分子
youpai fenzi
(Rightists)

See "you" (Right) and "fan youpai yundong" (anti-Rightist campaign).

右倾
youqing
(Right deviation)

See "you" (Right).

右倾翻案风
youqing fan'an feng
(the Right deviationist trend
to reverse correct verdicts)

See "pi Deng, fanji youqing fan'anfeng" (campaign to criticize Deng Xiaoping and counter the Right deviationist trend to reverse correct verdicts) and "siwu yundong" (April 5th Movement).

右倾机会主义
youqing jihuizhuyi
(Right opportunism)

See "you" (Right) and "xiuzhengzhuyi" (revisionism).

余悸
yuji
(lingering fear)

See "anquan xishu" (safety coefficient).

舆论导向
yulun daoxiang
(guided public opinion)

See "xinwen ziyou wenti" (issue of press freedom).

舆论监督，群众喉舌，政府镜鉴，改革尖兵
yulun jiandu, qunzhong houshe,

zhengfu jingjian, gaige jianbing
(supervisor as public opinion, mouthpiece of the masses, warner to the government, and path breaker of the reform)

See "xinwen ziyou wenti" (issue of press freedom).

舆论一律
yulun yilü
(one single public opinion)

See "yi fa zhi guo" (ruling the nation by law) and "xinwen ziyou wenti" (issue of press freedom).

宇宙观
yuzhouguan
(world outlook)

See "shijieguan" (world outlook).

与国际接轨
yu guoji jiegui
(be articulate with international norms)

See "ershinianlai zuiju yingxianglide shi ge kouhao" (ten most influential slogans in the past two decades).

与人民保持一致
yu renmin baochi yizhi
(be in keeping with the people)

See "yu zhongyang baochi yizhi" (be in keeping with the Party Center).

与中央保持一致
yu zhongyang baochi yizhi
(be in keeping with the Party Center)

"Be in keeping with the Party Center" is a CCP political slogan, derived from its organizational principle "democratic centralism" (minzhu jizhongzhi). The rule for democratic centralism is: "individuals are subordinate to the organizations they belong to, the minority is subordinate to the majority, lower authorities are subordinate to higher authorities, and the whole Party is subordinate to the Party Center" (geren fucong jiti, shaoshu fucong duoshu, xiaji fucong shangji, quandang fucong zhongyang). This is a tight power net: the whole country is subject to the Party's absolute rule and the whole Party is subject to the rule of a few leaders, and very often one leader at the very top.

When Jiang Zemin launched a "talk politics" campaign in the second half of 1995, it was perceived by many as vital to the establishment and consolidation of his leadership. For instance, Zhang Mannian, then CMC vice-chairman, made it clear that to the military "talk politics" fundamentally meant to guarantee the absolute leadership of the Party over the military. Whatever the circumstances, he said, the army must unswervingly be in keeping with the Party Center, vindicate its authority, and listen to it orders with Jiang Zemin as its core.

Today in the national appeal for political reform, the demand "to be in keeping with the Party Center" is being questioned. Critics argue that people have the right not to be keeping with the Party Center. Furthermore, it is the people's responsibility to question the Party Center (or the Central Government) so as to keep the nation always on a correct track. Therefore, the correct expression should be: "Be in keeping with the people" (yu renmin baochi yizhi). The Party Center must always be in keeping with the people's wishes and interests. As to the army, it should belong to the state and not to a certain party. See also "minzhu jizhongzhi" (democratic centralism) and "jiang zhengzhi" (talk politics).

遇罗克事件
Yu Luoke shijian
(Yu Luoke Incident)

See "xuetong lun" (lineage theory).

预後不良
yuhoubuliang
(panic psychology of "doubtful prognosis")

See "anquan xishu" (safety coefficient).

预悸
yuji
(premonition)

See "anquan xishu" (safety coefficient).

原教旨马克思主义
yuanjiaozhi Makesizhuyi
(Fundamentalist Marxism)

See "zhengtong Makesizhuyi zhengzai zou xiang siwang" (orthodox Marxism is heading for death).

原始积累
yuanshi jilei
(previous accumulation)

China's economists of the 1990s differentiated "capitalist accumulation" (zibenzhuyi jilei) and "previous accumulation". The former was defined in a positive way as a transformation of "surplus value" (shengyu jiazhi) into capital by the mechanism of the market, while the latter was condemned as having nothing to do with the market but simply as a sort of banditry. It was argued that Marx did not regard the "previous accumulation" period as the "primary stage of capitalism". He did not even use the wording "capitalist previous accumulation". Instead, echoing the Scottish economist Adam Smith (1723-1790), Marx said that there was a "previous accumulation" before the "capitalist accumulation". However, perhaps out of a misunderstanding, "capitalist previous accumulation" became a popular term among official economists in the Soviet Union in the 1920s, and was then completely accepted by those Chinese pioneers who learned Marxism from the Russians.

Following the erroneous concept of "capitalist previous accumulation", Soviet economists also held that there should be a "socialist previous accumulation" before "socialist accumulation". This accumulation was carried out by the CPSU in the Soviet Union, in forms such as forced labor, a grain collection system, the forced exchange of unequal values, and forced collectivization. After the PRC was founded, similar things were also adopted in China. This kind of accumulation, while amassing society's vast wealth in the state treasury, brought great disasters to the country.

As liberal economists point out, not long ago another "previous accumulation" took place in China, simultaneously with the process of the "reform" program. This can be called the "second previous accumulation" (de'er ci yuanshi jilei), which was built on the condition of the "socialist previous accumulation". Certain people, with no effective supervision, easily transferred the wealth from the socialist state treasury, which they were in charge of, into their own pockets. This was another "miracle": from beginning to end this accumulation took little more than ten years at the highest speed in world history, and it was praised, because it was carried out in a peaceful way. In the opinion of liberal economists, those in the West who engaged in the "previous accumulation" several hundred years ago, though heartless and disgusting, are said to have completed a historical mission—they amassed scattered wealth in an agricultural society so as to help bring about the birth of an industrial society. However, today in China those who made great fortunes in their "second previous accumulation" cannot be said to have done anything positive. See also "jingji gaige" (economic reform).

原罪性质的恶
yuanzui xingzhide e
(an evil revelation of the original sin)

See "sixiang gaizao" (ideological remolding) and "zuojia zhutixing" (writer's subjectivity).

越位
yuewei
(offside)

See "cuowei" (malposition).

越位应用
yuewei yingyong
(offside application)

See "cuowei" (malposition).

运动群众
yundong qunzhong
(mobilize the masses of people)

See "qunzhong luxian" (mass line) and "wuchanjieji zhuanzheng" (dictatorship of the proletariat).

砸烂公检法
za lan gong jian fa
(smashing public security organs, procuratorial organs, and people's courts)

See "wuchanjieji zhuanzheng" (dictatorship of the proletariat).

再教育
zai jiaoyu
(re-education)

See "santuoli" (three divorced).

在普及的基础上提高
zai pujide jichushang tigao
(raising of standards on the basis of popularization)

See "dazhonghua" (popularization).

在台湾的中华民国
zai Taiwande Zhonghua minguo
(Republic of China on Taiwan)

See "Taiwan wenti" (Taiwan issue).

早请示，晚汇报
zao qingshi, wanhuibao
(requesting instructions in the morning and reporting in the evening)

See "xiandai mixin" (modern superstition).

造反有理
zaofan youli
(it is right to rebel)

In August 1966, as the GPCR was unfolding, the *People's Daily* re-published a passage from a speech Mao had delivered on 20 December 1939 at a Yan'an meeting to mark the sixtieth birthday of Stalin.The passage was: "In the final analysis, the innumerable truths of Marxism may be expressed in one sentence: 'It is right to rebel.'" From then on, the Red Guards regarded this sentence as a supreme directive from Mao. They then made it into a couplet: "Revolution is no crime; it is right to rebel" (Geming wuzui, zaofan youli), meant to justify all their so-called revolutionary actions. The authorities later changed the slogan "It is right to rebel" to: "It is right to rebel against reactionaries" *(RMRB,* 28 Apr. 1969).

Obviously inspired by Mao's statement, the term "zaofanpai" (rebels) was first used by the Red Guards in Beijing. They called themselves "hongweibing zaofanpai" (rebel Red Guards). Later, all those who were courageous enough to rebel against alleged "capitalist-roaders" styled themselves as "rebels". They even called themselves "revolutionary rebels" (geming zaofanpai), or "revolutionary proletarian rebels" (wuchanjieji geming zaofanpai). In contrast, those who defended alleged "capitalist-roaders", or what they thought to be correct Party leadership, were dubbed "royalists" (baohuangpai), though during the GPCR no one was willing to accept this contemptible appellation. As for those who neither rebelled against "capitalist-roaders" nor defended them, and instead were inactive during the GPCR, they were regarded as "bystanders" (xiaoyaopai). With the unfolding of the so-called power-seizing struggle starting in early 1967, bloody conflicts were widespread. Many came to abhor such evil, factional activities and kept away from them. So, the number of "bystanders" increased. See also "hongweibing" (Red Guards), "wen'ge" (Cultural Revolution), and "liang ge wen'ge lun" ("two Cultural Revolutions" theory).

造反派
zaofanpai
(rebels)

See "zaofan youli" (it is right to rebel).

造神运动
zaoshen yundong
(god-making movement)

See "xiandai mixin" (modern superstition) and "tuchu zhengzhi" (giving prominence to politics).

造神文艺
zaoshen wenyi
(god-making literature and art)

See "yihua wenxue" (alienated literature; literature of alienation).

增加信任，减少麻烦，发展合作，不搞对抗
zengjia xinren, jianshao mafan, fazhan hezuo, bugao duikang
(increasing trust, reducing troubles, developing cooperation, and avoiding confrontation)

See "weidu Zhongguo" (containment against China).

摘帽右派
zhaimao youpai
(uncapped Rightist)

See "tuomao youpai" (uncapped Rightist).

站错队
zhan cuo dui
(siding on the wrong line)

See "jieji jiaoyu" (class education).

站好最後一班崗
zhanhao zuihou yi ban gang
(continue working well until the last minute)

This is a requirement for those who are about to leave their jobs. For Party elders who are about to retire, it is a matter of whether or not to "maintain their revolutionary integrity in their later years" (baochi geming wanjie). The most important criterion is whether or not to "be in keeping with the Party Center" (yu zhongyang baochi yizhi), as stated in a document issued by the PCC Secretariat in May 1998 entitled "Veteran Comrades Should Continue Working Well Until the Last Minute For Socialist Modernization with Chinese Characteristics". See also "jiang zhengzhi" (talk politics).

战略对手
zhanlüe duishou
(strategic adversary)

See "weidu Zhongguo" (containment against China).

战略上藐视一切敌人, 战术上重视一切敌人
zhanlüeshang miaoshi yiqie diren, zhanshushang zhongshi yiqie diren
(strategically despise all our enemies, but tactically take them all seriously)

See "zhilaohu" (paper tiger).

章罗同盟
Zhang-Luo tongmeng
(Zhang Bojun and Luo Longji alliance)

See "fan youpai yundong" (anti-Rightist campaign).

赵丹遗嘱
Zhao Dan yizhu
(Zhao Dan testament)

In September 1980, making use of a letter submitted by two Beijing readers, the *People's Daily* began an open discussion about how to strengthen and improve Party leadership over literature and art. The most notable of the discussion participants, perhaps, was Zhao Dan, a distinguished and respected Chinese film star. Though seriously ill in the hospital, he closely followed this vital discussion, writing what was later known as the "Zhao Dan testament", under the uncompromising title "Watched Too Closely, Literature and Art Have No Hope". This was published in the *People's Daily* on 8 October 1980 ("Guande tai juti, wenyi mei xiwang", *RMRB*, 8 Oct. 1980; trans. in *CL*, 1:107-11, 1981). Two days later, Zhao Dan died, leaving behind his regrets, hopes, anger, concerns, and his anguish.

Indeed, the last words of this "king of Chinese film" were very poignant. He simply stated the concern he felt when he read the words "jiaqiang dangde lingdao" (strengthen Party leadership) in the "Editor's Note" of the *People's Daily*. He said that he knew that some artists who were loyal to the cause of the Party and worked indefatigably would feel apprehensive (a conditioned response) upon hearing these words, because from their past experiences of political movements, they knew that on each occasion this kind of "strengthening" had meant an upheaval, wanton interference, and even "all-around dictatorship". It was Zhao Dan's hope that there would be no more such "strengthening" in the future. The best thing for the Party to do, in his opinion, was to "firmly carry out the policy of letting a hundred flowers bloom and a hundred schools of thoughts contend'". That, he maintained, ought to be the meaning of "strengthening and improving".

Zhao Dan drew a parallel. If the Party exercises its leadership only over planning the national economy and implementing agricultural and industrial policies and there is no need for the Party to direct how to do the farming, how to make a stool, how to sew a pair of trousers, and how to cook a dish, then, in his opinion, there is no need for the Party to exercise its leadership over how to write an article or perform a drama. He recalled that the Gang of Four had been very rigid in their control of literature and art. They went so far as to dictate the belt of a performer or a patch on a coat. As a result, there were only eight operas for eight hundred million people. He considered this a grave warning. He appealed:

"Literature and art are the concern of artists and writers themselves. If the Party gives too specific a leadership to literature and art, then literature and art will stagnate" *(RMRB,* 8 Oct. 1980).

As further justification, Zhao Dan pointed out that people did not become writers because the Party asked them to. Neither Lu Xun nor Mao Dun were asked by the Party to become writers. It seemed to Zhao Dan that it was life and struggle—the progress of history—that gave rise to a certain culture and produced a generation of artists and theoreticians. The vigour of artists or writers, and their philosophical outlook, could not be determined by a party, a faction, an organization, or a party branch. As to the argument that the leaders in literary and art circles at different levels all professed to adhere to the Party's literary policies, maintaining the correct ideas guiding revolutionary literature and art, Zhao Dan said that this sounded as though all artists and writers were a "bunch of dull mediocrities" (ibid.). Otherwise why should so many cadres who knew little or nothing about the arts be invited to lead several million "proletarian literary and art workers", from the center to the local levels, in provinces, prefectures, counties, communes, factories, and mines?

Zhao Dan then affirmed that in literary and art history from ancient times, the worship of one school of thought and the ignoring of all others never led to a flourishing of the arts. To the questions of whether or not Chinese literary and art associations or groups should stipulate a certain ideology as the guiding principle and whether or not Chinese writers and artists should take a certain article as their guiding thought, Zhao Dan—who knew that he was dying and who declared that there was nothing for him to be afraid of—declared: "We had better not!" (ibid.).

From bitter experience, Zhao Dan concluded that artistic creation was highly individual. One could comment, criticize, encourage, or applaud, but one should not insist on having too rigid control. A good work can never be produced by many levels of scrutiny. A vital work has never been the result of censorship. "From a historical point of view", Zhao Dan stated, "literature and art must be free from any restriction" (ibid.). See also "wenyi wei zhengzhi fuwu" (literature and art serve politics) and "wuchanjieji zhuanzheng" (dictatorship of the proletariat).

照过去方针办
zhao guoqu fangzhen ban

(follow the principles of the past)
See "yingming lingxiu" (wise leader).

真善美
zhen shan mei
(truth, goodness, and beauty)
See "zhengzhi biaozhun diyi, yishu biaozhun di'er" (political criteria first, artistic criteria second).

真善忍
zhen shan ren
(truthfulness, compassion, forbearance)
See "Falun Gong" (Law Wheel Cultivation).

真理面前，人人平等
zhenli mianqian, renren pingdeng
(everyone is equal before the truth)
See "eryue tigang" ("February Outline Report").

真实是艺术的生命
zhenshi shi yishude shenming
(truthfulness is the lifeblood of art)
See "xie zhenshi" (writing about reality) and "wenyi wei zhengzhi fuwu" (literature and art serve politics).

震派
zhenpai
(shakers)
See "fengpai" (tune-changers).

振兴中华
zhenxing Zhonghua
(revitalize China)
See "shijie geming zhongxin" (center of world revolution).

正面教育
zhengmian jiaoyu
(education by positive examples)
See "fanmian jiaocai" (teaching material by negative example)

正面教员
zhengmian jiaoyuan

(positive teachers)

See "fanmian jiaocai" (teaching material by negative example)

正确处理人民内部矛盾
zhengque chuli renmin neibu maodun
(correctly handling contradictions among the people)

On 29 December 1956, the Editorial Department of the *People's Daily* published an article entitled "More on the Historical Experience of the Dictatorship of the Proletariat" (Zai lun wuchanjieji zhuanzhengde lishi jingyan"), as the response of the CCP to the Hungarian Incident which took place on 23 October 1956, or more directly, to Tito's speech of 11 November 1956. The term "contradictions among the people" was for the first time put forth in the article, which was based on the discussion at an enlarged meeting of the CCP Politburo, but it was mainly based on Mao's ideas.

In his speech delivered at the 11th meeting (enlarged) of the Supreme State Council on 27 February 1957, Mao further elaborated on "contradictions among the people" and other related concepts. He first discussed the concept of "the people". Like the concept of "the enemy", he said, it varied in content in different countries and in different periods of history in the same country. According to Mao, an historical experience of the dictatorship of the proletariat was correctly differentiating and handling the two types of contradictions—contradictions between the people and their enemies (di wo maodun) and those among the people. The second type was contradictions between this and that group of people, between this and that group of comrades within the Communist Party, between the government and the people in socialist countries, between socialist countries, between Communist parties, etc. After analyzing these various expressions of "contradictions among the people", Mao suggested ways to handle them correctly. At the same time, he also discussed the concept of "contradictions between the people and their enemies" and explained how these two kinds of contradictions could be transformed from one to the other.

Mao's speech was officially published on 19 June 1957, at a crucial moment during the anti-Rightist campaign. Entitled "On the Correct Handling of Contradictions among the People", it had been elaborately revised, so as to justify the on-going struggle (see "Guanyu zhengque chuli renmin neibu maodunde wenti", *MZXJ*, 5, p. 363-402).

"The Correct Handling" is considered a very important constituent part of Mao Zedong Thought, a "creative development" of Marxism-Leninism. Differentiating between the two types of contradictions in a socialist country and correctly handling contradictions among the people constitute the first of the six major points of the theory of "continuing the revolution under the dictatorship of the proletariat". A forceful elucidation was provided in an article of 6 November 1967 by the editorial boards of the *People's Daily*, *Red Flag*, and the *Liberation Army Daily* to commemorate the 50th anniversary of the Soviet Union's October Revolution. This article, entitled "Advancing Along the Road Opened Up by the October Socialist Revolution" ("Yanzhe shiyue shehuizhuyi geming kaipide daolu qianjin"), was examined by Mao personally. In his political report delivered at the 9th CCP National Congress in April 1969, Lin Biao pointed out that Mao's "Correct Handling" provided a theoretical foundation for the GPCR. In the Deng Xiaoping period, this work was still highly appreciated within the CCP, as in the 1981 document "Resolution on Certain Questions in the History of Our Party since the Founding of the PRC".

As many have pointed out, however, this work is full of problems. Mao used many concepts as he pleased, such as "renmin" (the people), "diren" (enemies), "duikangxing maodun" (antagonistic contradiction), "feiduikangxing maodun" (non-antagonistic contradiction), "xianghua" (fragrant flowers), "ducao" (poisonous weeds), "gongcun" (co-existence), and "jiandu" (supervision). A vital problem was that this work was not a statute book, but it was treated as being above the law because it came from Mao's mouth. Take the two concepts "renmin" and "diren" for example. Mao defined them as follows:

"At the present stage, the period of building socialism, the classes, strata, and social groups which favor, support, and work for the cause of socialist construction all come within the category of the people, while the social forces and groups which resist the socialist revolution and are hostile to or sabotage socialist construction are all enemies of the people."

One can ask: what can be regarded as "resisting the socialist revolution" or "hostile to or sabotaging socialist construction"? No strict demarcation was drawn here. When Mao gave his definition, he actually meant that if one does not belong to the people, one must be in the category of the people's enemies. Furthermore, Mao only talked about classes, strata, social groups, and social forces, and not about individuals. This easily led to the harmful "theory of the unique importance of class origin" (weichengfenlun), which was widespread during the Mao period. Finally, and most importantly, here Mao resorted to political and not legal criteria, presented by Mao himself and not made through a legislative process. Consequently, the only judges were the Party, the Party's committees at various levels, the Party's central committee, and Mao himself.

Therefore, one may well say that Mao's handling of "contradictions among the people" unavoidably led to a breach of the law, and "contradictions among the people" were easily handled as "contradictions between the people and their enemies". Lin Biao was right when he said that this work provided a theoretical foundation for the GPCR.

In his "Correct Handling", Mao said that the "democratic method" of resolving "contradictions among the people" was epitomized in the formula "unity—criticism—unity" (tuanjie—piping—tuanjie), which Mao had raised in the 1942 Yan'an Rectification Movement to deal with issues of inner-Party struggle. "Unity—criticism—unity" means "starting from the desire for unity, resolving contradictions through criticism or struggle, and arriving at a new unity on a new basis". It also means "learning from past mistakes to avoid future ones and curing the sickness to save the patient" (cheng qian bi hou, zhi bing jiu ren). Obviously, the formula "unity—criticism—unity" is irrelevant to economic issues, where the principal contradiction in society, and among the people, displays itself. In addition, this formula cannot really resolve political, social, and cultural problems either (most of them are "contradictions among the people"). A true solution of these contradictions relies on the building of a legal system, democracy, and exercise of human rights. Unfortunately, this was something beyond Mao. See also "wuchanjieji zhuanzheng" (dictatorship of the proletariat).

正统马克思主义正在走向死亡
zhengtong Makesizhuyi zhengzai zou xiang siwang (orthodox Marxism is heading for death)

In the discussion in the 1980s concerning Marxism, humanism, and alienation, even those posing as orthodox Marxists came to admit that Marxism should be developed. But they emphasized that one must first adhere to it and then develop it.

This, however, was rejected by many scholars. Li Zehou asserted that only by developing Marxism can one uphold it. Only in the process of development, he explained, can a concrete, objective, and scientific differentiation be made as to which are the basic principles of Marxism and which are not. If one only emphasizes "upholding" and makes it separate from social reality and from the people's social activities which are extremely rich, complicated, and ever changing and developing, then what one upholds, very probably, will precisely be those theories, viewpoints, and methods that do not conform to actual practice and that are erroneous. As a result, the "upholding" will become an obstacle to any development (Li Zehou, "Jianchi yu fazhan"—"Upholding and Developing", *Beijing wanbao,* 31 July 1986).

Li Zehou thus endowed the phrase "Marxism in development" (fanzhanzhongde Makesizhuyi) with new significance. In fact, during the "new period", many tried to "reform" or "modernize" Marxism. One suggestion was put forth by Jin Guantao, a prominent historian. He asserted: "A mixture of the ossified Marxist-Leninist dogmas and certain elements not worth praising in Chinese culture has already become an ideological burden. To have Marxism modernized (Makesizhuyi xiandaihua), the best of Western thought should be adopted with no reservations, and at the same time healthy things in Chinese tradition should be dug out" ("Zhishifenzi xianqi 'pi ma re'"—"A Fad of Criticizing Marxism among Intellectuals", *Yazhou zhoukan,* 3 Apr. 1988, p. 9).

Many other scholars and writers sincerely advocated "humanistic Marxism" or "Marxist humanism", in view of the widespread pernicious influence of China's long feudal tradition (which was said to be a cultural foundation for the GPCR). At the same time, they challenged the supremacy of Marxism-Leninism-Mao Zedong Thought. Under Mao's rule—"The theoretical base guiding our thinking is Marxism-Leninism"—Party ideologues were haunted by the following obsession: If both sides in a debate claim to be Marxists, one of them must be revisionist; and if one side in a debate is non-Marxist, then that side must be completely wrong. There is only one possibility: either "fragrant flower" or "poisonous weed". This was found to be preposterous. Wang Ruoshui said: "Not only is Mao Zedong Thought one school of Marxism-Leninism and Leninism one school of Marxism, Marxism also is only one school in the history of thought" ("Makesizhuyi he xuepai wenti"—"Marxism and the Question of Schools", *DS,* 9, 1986, reprinted in *XHWZ,* 11:19, 1986). Wang also pointed out that Marxism could neither end nor monopolize the truth; it was open to every truth, but it did not consider itself as all-inclusive. What is more, he said, one would be anti-Marxist if one were to think Marxism could last forever and never be surpassed and replaced (ibid.). Of course, in the eyes of those "Marxist fundamentalists" or "fundamentalist Marxists" (yuanjiaozhi Makesizhuyizhe), so called because they cling to a literal interpretation of the traditional beliefs of Marxism, in opposition to more modern teachings, Wang Ruoshui was no doubt advocating heretical beliefs.

The debate concerning Marxism, humanism, and alienation, beginning soon after the 1976 downfall of the Gang of Four, lasted about a decade in the 1980s. It was first ended by the 1983 campaign to eliminate "spiritual pollution", then by the 1987 campaign to oppose "bourgeois liberalization", and finally by the June 4th Incident of 1989. While the prolonged debate continued off and on, China was undergoing great changes, especially in its socioeconomic life (against the background of an increasingly influential market economy). Marxism has since obviously lost its original influence among the people. In an article written in October 1995, Wang Ruoshui came to the conclusion that "Orthodox Marxism is heading for death". This should be natural, he said, for things emerging in history are bound to vanish in history. Concretely speaking, Marxist economics has in the main been outdated; its communism is still an utopia. What Wang believed to still have "vitality" and to be "most valuable" was the Marxist philosophy about man, or its philosophical anthropology, or, as Wang called it, "shijiande weirenzhuyi"—"humanism in practice" (Wang Ruoshui, "Wode Makesizhuyi guan"—"My View on Marxism", *Beijing zhi chun,* Jan. 1996).

Significantly, Wang Ruoshui is not alone in his opinion, though not many people openly proclaim "Orthodox Marxism is heading for death". For instance, Xing Bensi, vice president of the Central Party School and editor-in-chief of *Seeking Truth* magazine (who was Wang's opponent in the humanism debate more than ten years earlier), admitted that half of the Marxist fundamental tenets have become outdated (see his "Jianchi Makesizhuyi budongyao"—"Unswervingly Upholding Marxism", *RMRB,* 6 June 1996). The outdatedness of Marxism is so serious a problem that Xing raised the "coordinate" (zuobiao) issue in differentiating between Marxism and anti-Marxism. He said, very frankly, that if they take those Marxist theories and points of view as their reference frame, they will find it difficult to justify what they have been doing and will become targets for attack. Therefore, he suggested that when talking about Marxism today, one should "take Deng Xiaoping Theory as the reference frame" ("Fully Understanding the 'Primary Stage' and Resolutely Defending Against the 'Left'", *Zhongguo jingji shibao,* 29 July 1997).

These people still call themselves Marxists. Many others rather regard themselves as "victims of Marxism", and want to overthrow what they call its "last totem" (Makesizhuyi zuihoude tuteng). Marxism itself, or "Fundamentalist Marxism" (yuanjiaozhi Makesizhuyi), they argue, is fundamentally erroneous. In an article written in October 1995, Zheng Yi, a dissident now living in exile in the United States, refuted a series of what he thought to be such errors. First, regarding the issue of human nature, Marx and Engels held that evils had nothing to do with human nature and that they appeared only after private ownership had come into being. On this "mistaken premise", they preached communism as the ideal society of human beings, where private ownership, and consequently all kinds of evils, are eliminated. In order to realize communism, they asserted that the dictatorship of the proletariat—the representative of goodness—is necessary. The second issue concerns the nature of history. Admittedly, history is merely the activities of human beings in pursuit of their aims. In Marx and Engels's theoretical system about communism, however, human beings became tools, and conscious tools at that, to realize the aim of history. The third issue concerns power alienation. Marx evaded the issue of power alienation—which is as crucial as labor alienation—thus opening a broad road for autocracy to evolve into totalitarianism at its ultimate stage. That is why Marx has become the patron saint of all Communist tyrants (Zheng Yi, "Zuihoude tuteng: yuanjiaozhi Makesizhuyi qingsuan"—"The Last Totem: Squaring Fundamentalist Marxism", *Beijing zhi chun,* Jan. 1996).

For twenty years, as Marxism critics observe, there has been a trend in China of the "Marxist family" (Makesizhuyi jiazu) retreating step-by-step to what they call "Fundamentalist Marxism". Soon after the end of the GPCR, there was an appeal made personally by Deng Xiaoping for a "correct and comprehensive" understanding of Mao Zedong Thought. Mao Zedong Thought itself was said to be good, but it had been distorted by people like Lin Biao and the Gang of Four. Later, a new view held that Mao Zedong Thought was no better than the universally cursed Stalinism, but Marxism-Leninism should not be negated. Soon it was said that Lenin also erroneously revised Marxism, and raised a number of untenable theories. Today even Marxism itself, or "Fundamentalist Marxism", is considered erroneous, and should be overthrown as the "last totem" of Marxism.

Critics of Marxism see these changes as a symbol of the "bankruptcy of Communist ideology". Of course, this is open to controversy. Human beings should have some high ideals for their society; communism as an ideal will not be forgotten. In fact, there are conscientious efforts by veteran and new-born Leftists to restore the legacy of Mao Zedong Thought, which is said to be a cure-all for China's, and perhaps the world's, problems today. See also "rendaozhuyi lunzheng" (humanism debate) and "rendaozhuyide Makesizhuyi" (humanistic Marxism).

政企分离
zheng qi fenli
(separating enterprise management from government administration)

See "jigou gaige" (reform of administrative structures), "yi fa zhi guo" (ruling the nation by law), and "jingji gaige" (economic reform).

政社分开
zheng she fenkai
(to make a distinction between the functions of government and those of society)

See "jigou gaige" (reform of administrative structures) and "zhengzhi gaige" (political reform).

政社合一
zheng she heyi
(integrating government administration with commune management)

See "renmin gongshe" (People's Commune).

政权就是镇压之权
zhengquan jiushi zhenya zhi quan
(political power is a power of suppression)

See "si xiang jiben yuanze" (four cardinal principles) and "wuchanjieji zhuanzheng" (dictatorship of the proletariat).

政协
zhengxie
(CPPCC)

The CPPCC is an abbreviation for the Chinese People's Political Consultative Conference (Zhongguo Renmin Zhengzhi Xieshang Huiyi).

Following a suggestion made by Mao on 1 May 1948, the Preparatory Committee of the New Political Consultative Conference met in Beijing from 15 to 19 June 1949. The Conference was modified by the adjective "new" so as to distinguish it from the previous political consultative conference convened in KMT-ruled Chongqing on 10 January 1946. It got its present name at its first plenum on 21 September 1949. A "Common Program" (Gongtong Gangling) was also adopted at the plenum.

The CPPCC, stipulated as a "CCP-led revolutionary united front organization", holds congresses every five years, coinciding with NPC congresses, together with yearly sessions. Delegates go through the motions of debate, knowing that their organization chiefly serves as a transmission belt for conveying CCP principles and policies to people like them—leading figures from among "democratic parties" and academic circles.

The current chairman is Li Ruihuan, a member of the CCP Politburo Standing Committee. Zhou Enlai, Deng Xiaoping, and Li Xiannian also once held this post. See also "xiangpi tuzhang" (rubber stamp) and "zhengzhi gaige" (political reform).

政治霸权
zhengzhi baquan
(political hegemony)

See "dapipan" (mass criticism) and "lishi jiaosede huhuan" (an interchange of historical roles).

政治标签
zhengzhi biaoqian
(political labels)

A most important feature of Mao's rule was sharp vigilance against the danger of "capitalist restoration". According to Mao, there were mainly two world outlooks: the proletarian world outlook and the bourgeois world outlook. He further asserted that in the socialist period the problem has not yet been solved as to who will triumph over whom—the proletariat or the bourgeoisie. He demanded, therefore, an ever-strengthening dictatorship of the proletariat over the bourgeoisie. In the numerous political-ideological campaigns in "the seventeen years", there were a great number of labels for the term "bourgeois". Among them were, for instance: "bourgeois universal love" (zichanjieji bo'ai), "bourgeois intellectuals" (zichanjieji zhishifenzi), "bourgeois Rightists" (zichanjieji youpai fenzi), "reactionary bourgeois academic authorities" (zichanjieji fandong xueshu quanwei), "the bourgeois way of life" (zichanjieji shenghuo fangshi), "bourgeois individualism" (zichanjieji gerenzhuyi), "the bourgeois individualistic view of happiness" (zichanjieji gerenzhuyi xingfuguan), "bourgeois humanism" (zichanjieji rendaozhuyi), "the bourgeois humanistic outlook on society" (zichanjieji rendaozhuyi shehuiguan), "historical idealism of bourgeois humanism" (zichanjieji rendaozhuyide weixinshiguan), "bourgeois human touch" (zichanjieji renqingwei), "bourgeois sentimentalism" (zichanjieji shangganzhuyi), "bourgeois undue leniency" (zichanjieji wenqingzhuyi), and "the bourgeois view of literature and art" (zichanjieji wenyiguan). During the GPCR, there were some new labels, such as "bourgeois factionalism" (zichanjieji paixing) and "the bourgeois reactionary line" (zichanjieji fandong luxian).

In the Deng Xiaoping period, many of these labels continued to be used. But there were some changes. For instance, in the 1987 campaign against "bourgeois liberalization", a number of literary works were accused of advocating a "bourgeois ultra-individualist view of value" (zichanjieji jiduan gerenzhuyi jiazhiguan). This was characterized by "self-existence", "self-awareness", and "self-affirmation". It was emphasized that equally erroneous were existentialism, social-Darwinism, Freudianism, and the Nietzschean philosophy of "superman", all popular concepts at that time. A label, rarely heard of during Mao's time, was "bourgeois liberalization" (zichanjieji ziyouhua). At the forum on "problems arising on the nation's ideological front" convened by the Propaganda Department of the PCC in early August 1981, Hu Qiaomu defined it all-inclusively.

As it turned out, during Deng's time and thereafter, the label of "bourgeois liberalization" was frequently used, as liberalization is something that the Party has always tried to suppress. See also "ziyouhua" (liberalization).

政治标准第一，艺术标准第二
zhengzhi biaozhun diyi, yishu biaozhun di'er (political criteria first, artistic criteria second)

As Mao Zedong stated in his 1942 *Yan'an Talks,* he and his Party were "proletarian revolutionary utilitarians" (wuchanjieji geming gonglizhuyizhe). Their purpose was, he said, "to ensure that literature and art fit well into the whole revolutionary machine as a component part, that they operate as powerful weapons for uniting and educating the people and for attacking and destroying the enemy, and that they help the people fight the enemy with one heart and one mind" *(SWM,* 3, p. 70). According with this utilitarianism, Mao put forth a well-known view—"political criteria first and artistic criteria second"—with respect to the treatment of literature and art. He stated: "There is the political criterion and there is the artistic criterion; what is the relationship between the two? Politics cannot be equated with art, nor can a general world outlook be equated with a method of artistic creation and criticism. We deny not onlv that there is an abstract and absolutely unchangeable political criterion, but also that there is an abstract and absolutely unchangeable artistic criterion; each class in every class society has its own political and artistic criteria. But all classes in all class societies invariably put the political criterion first and the artistic criterion second" (ibid., p. 88).

Consequently, Chinese literature and art during the Mao period were deeply involved in politics. Obsessed with his utilitarianism, Mao, and the Party under his leadership, expected too much of literature and art; and, in the end, the excessive political demands led to the destruction of the arts. Many in China's literary and art circles were affected by this disaster. It was true that for several decades no one dared to challenge Mao's criteria openly, but it did not mean that they did not have their own view. Those with more independent thinking, for instance, would advocate "truth, goodness, and beauty" (zhen shan mei) as a universally accepted set of three standards of judgement in literary criticism. For example, during the GPCR years, Liu Zaifu spent most of his time studying Lu Xun, with the result that as early as 1980 he had finished writing *The Aesthetic Thought of Lu Xun*, his first notable book. By echoing Lu Xun's promotion of these three standards, Liu was rejecting Mao's view.

Significantly, Hu Yaobang, as a high-ranking Party official, also joined in this rejection. In his speech delivered at the 1980 Script Writing Forum, he officially negated Mao's stipulation. When speaking of literary criticism, he figuratively called the dogmatic method used in the past "a single cut" (yidaoqie), which, in a simplistic way, regarded a work as either totally good or completely bad, or as either totally correct or completely wrong. He believed this was bound to lead to disaster. Instead of "a single cut", Hu advocated "several cuts" (jidaoqie). This was progress, though his metaphor is still problematic, for an artistic work simply should not be "cut" in any way.

Hu stated explicitly that he was not in favor of Mao's mechanically separating political criteria and artistic criteria and regarding the former as more important than the latter. Mao had asked for a "three-unity" in artistic works: "the unity of politics and art, the unity of content and form, the unity of revolutionary political content and the highest possible perfection of artistic form". In an excellent work, there must appear a high degree of unity of ideological content and artistic quality. Therefore, Hu held, "good literary criticism must give a profound and meticulous analysis in light of the unity of these two aspects". Hu promised that he would adopt a prudent policy when using the term "poisonous weeds" (ducao). It was not right to think that a work must be a "poisonous weed" if it could not be staged or published for the time being, and that it must therefore be totally weeded out. Defects in works of literature and art should not become an excuse to carry out political persecution against authors, Hu assured his listeners.

Interestingly, in early 1995, there appeared a more daring view about literary criticism: "Artistic criteria first, political criteria second" (yishu biaozhun diyi, zhengzhi biaozhun di'er). This was advanced by the Shanghai-based playwright Sha Yexin in his book *Spiritual Garden (Jingshen Jiayuan,* Shanghai, Shanghai Renmin, Jan. 1995). Together with this thesis, Sha Yexin also suggested two other controversial theses. One is "Socialism serves literature and art, and literature and art serve the people", which revises the official slogan "Literature and art serve the people and socialism". The other is "Literature and art have source in life and are on a lower plane than life" (wenyi yuanyu shenghuo, gaoyu shenghuo), which opposes Mao's idea in his *Yan'an Talks* that literature and art should be on a higher plane than life. They were attacked as "three reactionary slogans" (see "Ping san ju fandong kouhao"—"On Three Reactionary Slogans", *Zhongliu,* 6, 1996). See also "wenyi wei zhengzhi fuwu" (literature and art serve politics).

政治冲击一切，政治压倒一切
zhengzhi chongji yiqie, zhengzhi yadao yiqie
(politics pushes over and overwhelms everything else)

See "tuchu zhengzhi" (giving prominence to politics).

政治动物
zhengzhi dongwu
(political animals)

In the Mao period, politics occupied an important place in people's daily lives. One had to take into consideration what he or she said or did, no matter how private or unintentional it was. The political consequences of doing otherwise could be terrible. The price was much higher than most people were able to pay, hence the sarcastic saying that the Chinese people, because they were living in such a repressed political atmosphere and because they had undergone "political training" for so many years, had already become "political animals" (see, for instance, Gong Liu, "Xinshou xielai—guanyu 'Chensi' he 'Xianrenzhang'"—"About the Two Poems 'Meditation' and 'Cactus'", *SK,* 7:55, 1985).

Interestingly, after two decades of economic reforms, another extreme has now appeared. It is no secret that there is serious corruption in the Party and government. The "morality sliding-down" (daode huapo) is a common social phenomenon. There are "barbarians wearing modern materials"—upstarts with their four "belongings" (villa, mistress, limousine, and pet dog characteristic of a "dakuan" in the 1990s). Farsighted scholars warn the Chinese of the danger of becoming "economic animals" (jingji dongwu). See also "jieji douzheng" (class struggle), "fazhan caishi ying daoli" (development is the most essential criterion), and "jingji gaige" (economic reform).

政治改革
zhengzhi gaige
(political reform)

As early as 1980, Deng Xiaoping brought up the issue of political reform, a program of which was his 18 August 1980 speech "On the Reform of the System of Party and State Leadership". The PCC even accepted his proposals. But Deng soon retreated from his earlier stance, apparently influenced by a letter Hu Qiaomu wrote on 24 September 1980 concerning the "Poland Incident", which took place in July 1980. (Originally a letter to Hu Yaobang, Hu Qiaomu sent it to other Party and government leaders. For the letter and Ruan Ming's comment, see Ruan Ming, *Hu Yaobang on the Historical Turning Point,* pp. 49-54; 129-32. See also Li Honglin, *A History of Chinese Thought, 1949-1989*; and Yang Jiayue, "Hu Yaobang xiatai zhenxiangdabai"—"The Truth of Hu Yaobang's Stepdown", *Ming Pao Monthly,* 6:32-37, 1999). In his speech delivered at the Central Work Conference on 25 December 1980, Deng called for "criticizing and opposing the tendency to worship capitalism and to advocate bourgeois liberalization" (*SWD,* p. 350). The tone of this speech, entitled "Implement the Policy of Readjustment, Ensure Stability and Unity", was very different from that of his 18 August 1980 speech.

According to China critics, this conference marked a great setback of China's political reform. A principle was set: any reform must not harm the Party's stability and unity. Thereafter, the Party followed Deng's line of "one center, two basic points" (which was formally put forth at the CCP 13th National Congress). The "one center" means that economic construction is the center of all Party work; the "two basic points" are: on the one hand upholding reform and the open-door policy, and on the other upholding the "four cardinal principles". Obsessed with his "two basic points", critics said, Deng launched political campaigns in 1981, 1983, 1985, 1987, and 1989 to eliminate "spiritual pollution" or to oppose "bourgeois liberalization". He regarded them as a "guarantee" for the successful implementation of his economic reform. More specifically, he opposed Left ideology in the economic field with his reform and the open-door policy, while he opposed Right ideology in the political field with his "four cardinal principles".

Guided by Deng Xiaoping Theory, China's reform was carried out with "Chinese characteristics", obviously different from the reform in the former Soviet Union and Eastern Europe. The CCP authorities carefully skirted those difficult issues, issues of political reform which could damage Party leadership and its interests. On 9 November 1988, at a meeting with Japanese Prime Minister Nakasone, Deng said that there were three goals of the reform of the political institutional structure: 1. preserving the vitality of the Party and the state; 2. overcoming bureaucracy and increasing work efficiency; and 3. motivating the initiative of grass-roots units and the people. As Deng had anticipated, the CCP had not yet figured out how to embark on political reform. The reform of the political institutional structure will not be completed for at least ten years, and national elections are at least twenty or thirty years away. In his remaining years, Deng upheld his strategy of "socialism with Chinese characteristics". Fundamentally, it defines the base line for his blueprint of reform: in order to build a powerful, prosperous China, economic liberalization was necessary, but not to the point of eliminating the CCP's monopoly on power.

After Deng's death on 19 February 1997, Jiang Zemin seemed certain to continue this line. At the 15th National Congress held in September 1997, Jiang proposed bold measures, such as a joint stock system to privatize the sprawling state-sector industries. These measures, China observers said, implied that the Party was abandoning communism for the main. There were signs in recent years that the Party leadership had decided to deepen reforms and open China wider to the outside world. Jiang must have considered the following factors: setting up his authority as the new "core" of Party leadership, guaranteeing the interests of the ruling clique, finding measures to check the power economy and corruption, maintaining social stability, promoting economic development, and trying to enter the mainstream of world civilization. Like Deng, Jiang emphasized that China's political reform must be instituted under the strong leadership of the CCP. No challenge to the Party's monopoly on political power is to be tolerated. Officially, China's ultimate goal is full general elections, but the Party's firm control will remain essential until the 1.3 billion people are ready for the responsibility of democracy.

Yet, China critics maintain that democracy is not simply a dead destination; first of all it is a live process. People must have a chance to enjoy democracy in their practice of it, in their fight for its perfection. Moreover, the odds against achieving full modernization without losing political control are daunting. The Party's claim to legitimacy chiefly rests on its ability to deliver sustained economic growth and rising incomes. Once the people are better off, they will demand a say in their own governance. China will not be able to continue its long-term economic advances without modifying—or being forced to modify—its repressive political system. Logically, then, the more the Party wins in its reform drive, the more it loses in maintaining its power.

Indeed, having undergone much suffering during the Mao period, especially during the GPCR, the Chinese people cherish great expectations from political reform, so that they will enjoy more democracy and freedom. There have been several upsurges in this regard over the last two decades. First there was the 1978-1980 pro-democracy movement, marked by the short-lived "Beijing Spring". In 1986, on the 30th anniversary of the Double Hundred policy, the 20th anniversary of the issuing of the "May 16th Circular" by the PCC, and the 10th anniversary of the end of the GPCR, discussions on political reform once again became popular. The CCP authorities suppressed them in the 1987 anti-bourgeois liberalization campaign. Then the 1989 pro-democracy movement occurred. It developed vigorously and rapidly and reached a high tide within a short period of a half a year. Unfortunately, it ended in bloodshed, shocking the whole world.

The political environment in the 1990s was somewhat different from that in the 1980s. But calls for democratization to accompany the economic reforms were always heard. In early August 1997, for instance, in a letter to Jiang Zemin, Shang Dewen, a Beijing University economics professor, presented a proposal for a 25-year orderly transition towards full democracy. Wang Shan, the author of the controversial book *The Third Eye,* also warned that measures aimed at averting the collapse of the heavily indebted state sector, which employed about 100 million workers, would be insufficient without matching political reforms. A pluralistic political system, he suggested, would be better suited to absorb the social upheavals arising from China's shift to a market economy. On 20 November 1997, Fang Jue published a document entitled "China Needs a New Change" ("Zhongguo xuyao xinde zhuanbian"), which was regarded as a program of the so-called "democrats" (minzhupai). In addition, some influential, though controversial, books were published in succession, such as *Crossing Swords: Three Thought Emancipations in Contemporary China* (Jan. 1998), *The Pitfalls of Modernization* (He Qinglian, *Xiandaihuade Xianjing,* Beijing, Jinri Zhongguo, Jan. 1998, which is another edition of *The Pitfalls of China),* and *Political China: Facing the Era of Choosing a New Institutional Structure* by over thirty authors (Dong Yuyu and Shi Binhai, ed., *Zhengzhi Zhongguo: Mianxiang Xin Tizhi Xuanzede Shidai,* Beijing, Jinri Zhongguo, Aug. 1998). Liberalism was promoted in these two books: *Gu Zhun's Diary (Gu Zhun Riji,* Chen Minzhi and Ding Dong ed., Beijing, Jingji ribao, 1997) and *The Beida Tradition and Modern China—The Harbinger of Liberalism (Beida Chuantong Yu Jindai Zhongguo—Ziyouzhuyide*

Xiansheng, Beijing, Zhongguo renshi, 1998), published in 1997 and 1998 respectively.

There seemed to have been a consensus among many Chinese: the economic reform could not succeed without a political reform. As facts showed, because of the delay in political reform, the economic environment has been becoming worse. The universally detested power economy has quickly expanded into a huge monster. Corruption, unfair competition, cheating, and unfair distribution caused by political factors have become so serious that suspicion and resentment have affected the economic reform itself. The lack of a system of checks and balances is the worst shortcoming of the present political system. In his January 1998 article "Also Promote Political Reform" ("Yeyao tuidong zhengzhi gaige") on the 10th anniversary of the publication of *Reform* magazine, Li Shenzhi, former CASS vice-president, pointed out that China's implementation of political reform will clearly determine the ultimate success or failure of its economic reform. It is vigorously argued that a mere open door to the outside world is not enough, or even not genuine, without a "domestic opening" (duinei kaifang). Domestically, the door should also be open in all spheres: the economy, politics, society, culture, the media, freedom of speech, freedom of association, etc. Only by doing so can China make true progress.

When liberalism is applied to political issues, a reform of the political institutional structure will be insufficient—that was something from the 1980s, including some changes in the existing institutions, such as reform of the administrative structures, separating Party from government functions, putting into effect a civil service system, and the abolition of life tenure for leading posts. When the issues of the planned economy and ownership have basically been solved, people will make more demands for political reform, calling for a change in the "political spirit" and in the "mentality of political values". As Liu Junning, a CASS research fellow who has vigorously promoted liberalism in recent years, explained, among the two political spirits, the one marked by "the class struggle theory" should be forever cast away; and it is time to promote a "spirit of magnanimity" (Jiang Tiegang, "Cong zhengzhi tizhi gaige dao zhengzhi tizhi tupo: Fang Liu Junning boshi"—"An Interview with Dr. Liu Junning", *Qianshao,* Sept. 1998, pp. 35-36). China's liberal thinkers envisaged a situation where people with different political stands coexist peacefully, each enjoying an equal right to express their own views. This would be the best way to realize "stability and unity".

As an experiment to achieve these liberal ideals, Wang Youcai, a Zhejiang-based pro-democracy activist, and his comrades announced on 25 June 1998 that preparations was being made for the founding of what they named the China Democracy Party (Zhongguo Minzhudang). Taking advantage of U.S. President Clinton's China visit (on occasions such as this, the Chinese authorities usually act somewhat carefully), they attempted to register this first opposition party under the Chinese Communist regime. This put the CCP leadership to a crucial test. As it turned out, the Party was not yet ready for this landmark action. Wang Youcai and a number of other activists were arrested and sentenced to long-term imprisonment. In an interview with the German daily *Handelsblatt* on 23 November 1998, Li Peng, NPC chairman, ruled out any new political parties or organizations. In an apparent reference to the embryonic China Democracy Party, he said: "If it is designed to establish a multiparty system and to try to negate the leadership of the Communist Party, then it will not be allowed to exist" *(RMRB,* 1 Dec. 1998).

Nevertheless, as cycles of relaxation and repression, which seem to be a built-in mechanism of China's Communist regime, continue, the trend toward democracy in China—the natural end-result of true political reform—is irreversible. Some, such as Cao Siyuan, a prominent economist who has been dubbed as the "father of China's insolvent law", even predicted that the CCP will have to change its name to "Zhongguo Shehuidang" (the Chinese Socialist Party) before 2010. See also "dangde lingdao" (Party leadership) and "ziyouhua" (liberalization).

政治工作是一切经济工作的生命线
zhengzhi gongzuo shi yiqie jingji gongzuode shengmingxian
(political work is the lifeblood of all economic work)

See "tuchu zhengzhi" (giving prominence to politics).

政治挂帅
zhengzhi guashuai
(putting politics in command)

See "tuchu zhengzhi" (giving prominence to politics).

政治价值观念改革
zhengzhi jiazhi guannian gaige
(reform of the mentality of political values)

See "zhengzhi gaige" (political reform).

政治精神改革
zhengzhi jingshen gaige
(reform of the political spirit)

See "zhengzhi gaige" (political reform).

政治花瓶
zhengzhi huaping
(political flower vases)

See "minzhu dangpai" (democratic parties).

政治浪漫主义
zhengzhi langmanzhuyi
(political romanticism)

See "xinzuopai" (neo-Leftists).

政治认同
zhengzhi rentong
(political identification)

See "wenhua Zhongguo" (cultural China).

政治儒家
zhengzhi rujia
(political Confucianism)

See "ruxue disanqi" (Confucianism in its third stage of development).

政治润色
zhengzhi runse
(political polishing)

In order to make sure that their works could be easily published and that there would not be future trouble after their publication, Chinese writers were always concerned with political conformity. When their works were reprinted, even those published many years earlier, "political polishing" to be in conformity with the current political climate was a vital consideration. The result, unfortunately, was very often disastrous. Take Liu Qing (1916-1978), a veteran writer with rich creative experience. After the downfall of the Gang of Four but before the rehabilitation of Liu Shaoqi, Liu Qing was engaged in revising the first volume of his *Builders (Chuangye shi*, v. 1, *Yanhe,* 8-11, 1959; trans. by Sidney Shapiro, Beijing, FLP, 1964), a 1959 novel which can be said to be the fruit of his lifetime's painstaking labor. The amazing willpower with which he made the revisions cannot be forgotten, as at the time he was already on his deathbed as a result of many years of persecution. But still he could not exclude himself from those who went out of their way to curry favor. When the revised work came out in March 1978, readers found that there were several changes in the plot where the author had subjected the former head of state to denunciations, though those were very unlikely to have taken place at the time of the story.

There are many similar cases. In the first edition of the novel *The Song of Ouyang Hai (Ouyang Hai zhi ge*, *Jiefangjun wenyi,* 6, 1965, reprinted in book form, Beijing, Jiefangjun Wenyi, 1965; excerpts trans. by Sidney Shapiro in *CL,* 7:71-132, 8:30-96, 9:88-141, 10:75-103, 11:61-104, 1967), there was a description of how the hero Ouyang Hai eagerly and conscientiously studied Liu Shaoqi's *How to Be a Good Communist*. During the GPCR when Liu's book, which earlier had been regarded as one of the CCP classics, was fiercely attacked, Jin Jingmai, the author, distorted this episode into something which was unlikely to have happened: when the hero found the book of the not-yet-disgraced PRC president in a heap of waste paper, in a burst of hatred he threw it back into the rubbish heap in a huff.

When such "political polishing" occurred to a veteran writer, such as Ye Shengtao (1894-1988), it made people especially sad. Ye's *Schoolmaster Ni Huanzhi (Ni Huanzhi*, *Jiaoyu zazhi,* 1928, reprinted in book form by Beijing, Renmin Wenxue, 1953; trans. by A. C. Barnes, Beijing, FLP, 1958), a novel written in the late 1920s, is one of the excellent works appearing quite early in the history of Chinese new literature. Nearly thirty years later, in the early 1950s, in order to meet political needs, Ye Shengtao rewrote the entire plot after the twenty-fourth chapter, making his hero, who dies in grief after the failure of the "Great Revolution" in the original, plunge himself into the struggle of the masses of the people, thus beginning to take a "correct road". As a "May 4th" writer, Ye had long adopted a rigorous attitude toward realism, but now he broke with his earlier vow to give a truthful description of every character in his story. Fortunately, when the work was reprinted in the late 1970s, the original ending was restored. See also "wenyi wei zhengzhi fuwu" (literature and art serve politics).

政治设计院
zhengzhi shejiyuan
(political design academy)

A "political design academy", a very brave concept even by today's standards, was advanced in 1957 by Zhang Bojun (1896-1969), then PRC minister of transportation, CPPCC vice-chairman, chairman of the Chinese Peasants and Workers Democratic Party (Zhongguo Nonggong Minzhudang), and vice-chairman of the Chinese Democracy Alliance (Zhongguo Minzhu Tongmeng). At that time, following Mao's instructions, the CCP was engaged in a rectification movement, and the leaders of the "democratic parties" and other non-party "democratic personages" were often invited to meetings to air their suggestions and criticisms. It was at one such meeting on 21 May 1957, organized by the PCC United Front Department, that Zhang said: "At present there are many industrial design academies, but there is no such academy for political measures. In my opinion, the Political Consultative Conference, the National People's Congress, the various democratic parties, and the various people's organizations should be considered as four political design academies" *(RMRB*, 22 May 1957). Zhang hoped that these academies could play a greater role. "Basic political undertakings should be submitted to them for discussion before being implemented," he said (ibid.).

What Zhang Bojun meant was very clear. He did not want a special "political design academy" to be set up. Even if he had, there was nothing wrong. Wasn't Deng Xiaoping later regarded as "general designer" for reform? However, in the following anti-Rightist campaign, Zhang was convicted as a bourgeois Rightist. His remarks were interpreted as making a demand for "rotating the leadership" (lunliu zuozhuang). That was "attempting to draw state power away from the working class and from the leadership of its vanguard the CCP". Zhang's "political design academy", together with Luo Longji's suggestion about setting up a "rehabilitation committee" (pingfan weiyuanhui) and Chu Anping's remark that "the Party is the entire world" (dangtianxia), were condemned as the "three major reactionary theories" of China's Rightists. See also "fan youpai yundong" (anti-Rightist campaign).

政治思想好，三八作风好，军事训练好，生活管理好
zhengzhi sixiang hao, san-ba zuofeng hao, junshi xunlian hao, shenghuo guanli hao
(good in political thoughts, in the "three-eight" work style, in military training, and in the management of livelihood)

See "tuchu zhengzhi" (giving prominence to politics).

政治体制改革的三个设想目标
zhengzhi tizhi gaigede san ge shexiang mubiao
(three anticipated goals of the reform of the political institutional structure)

See "zhengzhi gaige" (political reform).

政治同经济相比不能不占首位
zhengzhi tong jingji xiangbi buneng bu zhan shouwei
(politics cannot but have precedence over economics)

See "jingji jichu" (economic base).

政治问题
zhengzhi wenti
(political issue)

A "zhengzhi wenti" is a "political issue", similar to a "xueshu wenti" (academic issue). Hence the thesis: Political issues should be freely discussed. But when the term is used in reference to someone, it means that the man/woman in question is politically unreliable. The same is true for the term "lishi wenti" (historical issue), which can mean a "question of a political nature in someone's history"—such a person can be a "historical counter-revolutioary (lishi fan'geming). Other terms include: "jingji wenti" (economic issue), "sixiang wenti" (ideological issue), and "daode wenti" (moral issue). See also "zhengzhi wenti yingdang ziyou taolun" (political issues should be freely discussed).

政治问题应当自由讨论
zhengzhi wenti yingdang ziyou taolun
(political issues should be freely discussed)

While academic issues were allowed to be freely discussed, political issues could not—for a long time this was CCP policy, and many Chinese intellectuals seemed to accept it. In 1979, Guo Luoji, a controversial scholar, first raised the view that political issues should also be discussed by the public (Guo Luoji, "Zhengzhi wenti shi keyi taolunde"—"Political Issues Can Be Discussed", *RMRB,* 14 Nov. 1979). In 1986, this issue came up again. Yu Haocheng, director of the Masses Publishing House, found the following to be a specious argument (which many had held before): the Double Hundred policy had not been feasible because academic issues were wrongly treated as political; everything would be fine if a line of demarcation were to be drawn between the two kinds of issues. Yu bluntly refuted this. For one thing, in reality it was very difficult to draw such a line; for another, if one agreed that the Double Hundred policy should be carried out on the premise of drawing such a line, it meant that only academic and not political issues could be discussed. According to Yu, however, the "Double Hundred" itself was based on the principle of "practising political democracy in the ideological-cultural spheres" and it should enjoy the "protection of the legal system" (Yu Haocheng, "Shuangbai fangzhen yu fazhi baozhang"—"The Double Hundred Principle and the Guarantee of the Legal System", *RMRB,* 30 May 1986).

Yu Haocheng's view was shared by many, one of whom was Li Chunguang, an anti-Gang of Four hero in 1975 and then deputy editor of *Literary Gazette.* Li found strong support in some of Engels' documents, particularly a 1892 letter in which he held that a journal could be established to criticize and oppose the Party's program, tactics, and specific measures. Li noted that this opinion of Engels had never been quoted or discussed, either in China or in the Soviet Union. In 1972, for instance, when this letter was collected in a book entitled *Marx and Engels on Publication,* the relevant passage was completely omitted. Did Engels make a mistake here? Li Chunguang's answer was no. He recalled such events as the 1955 "Hu Feng Counter-Revolutionary Clique" case, the 1957 conviction of several hundred thousand intellectuals, the 1958 "Great Leap Forward", the 1959 Peng Dehuai case, the 1966 "May 16th Circular", and the 1969 revision of the Party Constitution. If these vital political issues could have been discussed and criticized in the way that Engels had suggested, Li said, things would have been quite different (Li Chunguang, "Zhengzhi wenti yingdang ziyou taolun"—"Political Issues Should Be Freely Discussed", *Xin guancha,* 16, 1986, reprinted in *XHWZ,* 10:19, 1986).

Open support from the top Party leaders on this issue was given by Wan Li, then a CCP Politburo member and PRC vice premier. At a national forum on software science held in August 1986, Wan Li said: "The crux of the matter is not to separate academic issues from political issues, but to apply the 'Double Hundred' principle to issues of politics and policies as well" *(RMRB,* 15 Aug. 1986).

政治现代化
zhengzhi xiandaihua
(modernization of politics)

See "si ge xiandaihua" (four modernizations).

政治异化
zhengzhi yihua
(political alienation)

This is also called "quanli yihua" (alienated power). In his January 1984 article "On Problems Concerning Humanism and Alienation", Hu Qiaomu found the idea of political alienation or alienated power to be completely in violation of the Marxist theory of politics and state. On the one hand, he said, the proletarian dictatorship is a necessity for the transition to a classless society; on the other, any revolutionary party or regime wants not only democracy but also a concentration of power. To hold that alienated power is bound to take place where there exists power is nothing but anarchism. As Hu recalled, neither Marx nor Engels nor Lenin ever referred to any of the various sorts of adverse deviations, ideological trends, or factions they fought so hard all their lives as alienation in the working class movement. Hu also reminded his opponents that their ideas about political alienation were very similar to the theoretical grounds upon which the GPCR had been based and which they had bitterly abhored.

To many Chinese, the occurrence of "political alienation" was an indisputable fact, and Hu's argument was simply not worth refuting. See also "shehuizhuyi yihua lun" (theory of socialist alienation) and "zhengtong Makesizhuyi zhengzai zou xiang siwang" (orthodox Marxism is heading for death).

政治之癌
zhengzhi zhi ai
(political cancer)

See "fan fubai" (anti-corruption).

政治性反思
zhengzhixing fansi
(political reflection)

See "fansi" (reflection) and "wenhua re" (culture craze).

知青
zhiqing
(educated youth)

"Zhiqing" is an abbreviation for "zhishi qingnian".

On 12 December 1968, Mao published a statement, saying "It is very necessary for educated young people to go to the countryside to be re-educated (zai jiaoyu) by the poor and lower-middle peasants" *(RMRB,* 22 Dec. 1968). In accordance with Mao's instructions, Red Guards and other urban students were sent to the countryside (xiafang), where they settled down to live and work with the peasants and to receive a "re-education". All together they numbered over ten million.

By 1979, most of them had returned home, many with bitter and unforgettable stories. The large-scale "educated youth" movement, which lasted so many years, was unique even in the whole of human history. When some of these young people became writers, an "educated youth" literature was born. Well-known works include the novels *Those Years Wasted (Cuotuo Suiyue,* Beijing, Zhongguo Qingnian, June 1982) by Ye Xin, and *Bloody Twilight (Xuese Huanghun,* Beijing, Gongren, 1987) by Lao Gui, and the novelettes "There Will Be a Storm Tonight" by Liang Xiaosheng, "The Wild Forest" by Kong Jiesheng, and "Chess Master" by Acheng.

Today, after thirty years, the negative consequences of the "educated youth" movement is even more apparent. Many of these people, not young any more and without enough education, have faced, are facing, or will face the fate of "xiagang" (leaving their posts, that is, losing their jobs). This means that they have, or will have, to suffer again, even when many others have benefited from the reform and open-door program. A discussion of this problem was carried in the Hong Kong magazine *Twenty-first Century* in December 1999, entitled "From 'xiafang' to 'xiagang': 1968-1998" (Chen Yixin, "Cong xiafang dao xiagang 1968-1998", *ES,* 122-36, Dec. 1999). See also "xiagang" (leaving one's post).

知青文学
zhiqing wenxue
("educated youth" literature)

See "zhiqing" (educated youth).

知识青年
zhishi qingnian
(educated youth)

See "zhiqing" (educated youth).

知识越多越反动
zhishi yueduo yue fandong
(the more a person knows, the more reactionary he will become)

See "dangde jiaoyu fangzhen" (the Party's educational policy).

知识分子问题
zhishifenzi wenti
(issue of intellectuals)

In China, generally speaking, those having a comparatively higher level of culture are regarded as intellectuals.

Admittedly, intellectuals are most often characterized by their ability and courage to speak out the truth, even if it is critical of the present regime. But as studies have showed, there is a traditional vital weakness—the dependent character—of Chinese intellectuals. Mao and his Party fully understood this. In 1957, when speaking of the question of the intellectuals, Mao repeatedly used the idiom: "With the skin gone, to what can the hair attach itself?" ("pi zhi bu cun, mao jiang yan fu", derived from the section entitled "The Fourteenth Year of Duke Xigong" in the classical work *Zuo Zhuan*.). Mao metaphorically implied that, with the basic completion of the socialist transformation of the ownership of the means of production, the "skin", that is, the economic base of old China to which the intellectuals educated in the pre-Liberation years had attached themselves, was gone, and that now these intellectuals (the "hair") had no alternative but to attach themselves to the new "skin" of public ownership, that is, to the proletariat *(MZXJ,* 5, pp. 452-54, 487, 490). Since Mao was the leader of the CCP, and the CCP was the "vanguard" of the proletariat in China, his underlying meaning was apparent.

Mao did not look upon China's intellectuals as a class (jieji), but he found most of their family origins ("jiating chushen" or "chushen") and their individual class status ("geren chengfen" or "chengfen") to be problematic. Mao emphasized that they must be remolded to change their original world outlook, and he decided that most of them failed to be remolded well. Thus it was inevitable that China's intellectuals faced a miserable fate. During the Yan'an period and in the early years of the People's Republic, they were classified as "petty bourgeois intellectuals" (xiaozichanjieji zhishifenzi). Then as Mao sped up his "socialist revolution", they became "bourgeois intellectuals" (zichanjieji zhishifenzi) or "intellectuals possessing a bourgeois world outlook".

There was a Party policy concerning intellectuals, which boiled down to one phrase: "uniting with, educating, and remolding" intellectuals ("tuanjie, jiaoyu, gaizao", as raised in Premier Zhou Enlai's report at the "Conference on the Issue of Intellectuals" called by the PCC in January 1956). In accordance with this policy, numerous political campaigns were carried out and a great number of intellectuals were cruelly persecuted. In the 1957 anti-Rightist campaign, there were more than 550,000 "bourgeois Rightists", 11 percent of the five million intellectuals in the entire country at the time. Mao and his Party controlled China's intellectuals effectively—by controlling their means of livelihood, by brain-washing, and by "divide and rule" (Dong Yuesheng, "Zhongguode '1984': lun Zhongguo zhishifenzide ruanruoxing"—"China's '1984': On Chinese Intellectuals's Vital Weakness", *Kaifang,* May 1999, pp. 7-11).

During the GPCR, almost all intellectuals who had achieved certain accomplishments in their academic fields were criticized as "reactionary bourgeois academic authorities" (zichanjieji fandong xueshu quanwei). Intellectuals were slandered as the "stinking No. 9" (chou laojiu)—the ninth category after landlords, rich peasants, counter-revolutionaries, bad elements, Rightists, renegades, enemy agents, and capitalist-roaders.

After the end of the GPCR, Deng Xiaoping, himself a victim of the GPCR, was the first Party elder to speak for intellectuals. After his return to power, he adopted a series of new policies concerning intellectuals.

For example, on 24 May 1977, when meeting two leaders from the Party Center, Deng Xiaoping said: "We must create within the Party an atmosphere of respect for knowledge and respect for trained personnel (zunzhong zhishi, zunzhong rencai). The erroneous attitude of not respecting intellectuals must be opposed. All work, be it mental or manual, is labor" ("Respect Knowledge, Respect Trained Personnel", *SWD,* p. 54). In his speech at the opening ceremony of the National Conference on Science held in Beijing on 18 March 1978, Deng reiterated this view. Instead of carrying out the "uniting with, educating, and remolding intellectuals" policy, he announced that China's intellectuals were already part of the working class ("Speech at the Opening Ceremony of the National Conference on Science", *SWD,* p. 105). In his

"Congratulatory Message" to the 1979 4th Congress of Chinese Writers and Artists, Deng promised that China's writers and artists would be better treated. Under Deng's auspices, the Party rehabilitated most of those who had been disgraced in the various movements during the Mao period.

For some time there was still a fear that Deng's promise would not be kept. Moreover, there was an unforgettable bitter lesson: if you were promised something, it could certainly be taken away as well. Significantly, due to the two decades of reform, whether the promise is kept or not and the promise itself are no longer vital to China's intellectuals. This is mainly because their social status has risen as a result of their involvement and commitment to the reform and open-door programs. They have become much more independent. For instance, they can refute Marx's "mistaking" the working class for the leading force of society. In light of China's profound social changes today, Mao's 1957 metaphor about "skin" and "hair" appears ridiculous. China's intellectuals can point out that, instead of intellectuals attaching themselves to the proletariat, the fifty million workers in China at that time, who were poor in knowledge, should be educated by the five million intellectuals. The truth is most apparent today. With the increasing importance of knowledge and information as the most advanced social productivity, intellectuals are naturally the most advanced and thus the leading force in society, and their unique role and position will become even more important in the twenty-first century. See also "dangde jiaoyu fangzhen" (the Party's educational policy) and "sixiang gaizao" (ideological remolding).

知识分子是工人阶级的一部分
zhishifenzi shi gongrenjiejide yibufen
(intellectuals are part of the working class itself)

See "zhishifenzi wenti" (issue of intellectuals).

知识分子是社会的主导力量
zhishifenzi shi shehuide zhudao liliang
(intellectuals are the leading force in society)

See "zhishifenzi wenti" (issue of intellectuals).

知识分子是最先进的社会力量
zhishifenzi shi zuixianjinde shehui liliang
(intellectuals are the most advanced social force)

See "zhishifenzi wenti" (issue of intellectuals).

殖民文化
zhimin wenhua
(colonial culture)

In the upsurge of nationalism as an ideological trend in China in the 1990s, attacks were launched from time to time on what was regarded as "cultural colonialism" (wenhua zhiminzhuyi). People were urged to resist "colonial culture" or "post-colonial culture" (houzhimin wenhua), as in "Watch Out for Symptoms of Colonialism" (Zhao Yingyun, "Jingti zhiminzhuyide miaotou", *RMRB*, 23 Sept. 1995) and "Ten Questions Concerning Post-Colonial Culture as Seen in the Musical

Circle" ("Guanyu yuetan hou zhimin wenhuade shige wenti", *Wei Nin Fuwu Bao,* 8 Feb. 1996).

This issue became conspicuous when Jiang Zemin asked his Party to pay attention to the resurfacing of what he called the "dregs of colonial culture left over from the past" in his closing speech (on 10 October 1996) at the 6th Plenum of the 14th PCC. His criticism of "some Chinese" was as follows: "They believe all things foreign are good, worship foreign countries blindly and unduly underestimate the development of the motherland. Out of self-interest, some people even do not care about undermining national prestige and personal dignity, nor about harming state and national interests".

On 20 October 1996, a warning (obviously in response to Jiang's call) was issued in Shanghai's prestigious newspaper *Liberation Daily:* Watch out for the resurfacing of dregs of colonial culture (Xie Fangping, "Jingti 'zhimin wenhuade chenzha fuqi"—"Watch Out for the Resurfacing of Dregs of 'Colonial Culture'"). Interestingly, a few weeks later, a commentary was published on the front page of the same newspaper, which disputed the view of the previous article and found it to be too large of a political "cap" (Sima Xin, "Maozi taidale yidian"—"The Cap Is A Size of Too Big", *JFRB,* 14 Nov. 1996). Later, former Minister of Culture Wang Meng and others also expressed their disapproval of exaggerating some social phenomena with the label of "colonial culture".

In December 1996, General Secretary Jiang had another chance to express his view. In his speech greeting the 6th National Congress of Chinese Writers and Artists and the 5th National Congress of the CWA, he called for resistance to the corrosive influence of colonial culture. National independence, he said, means independence not only in the political and economic fields but also in the ideological-cultural fields. See also "aiguozhuyi" (patriotism) and "minzuzhuyi" (nationalism).

直通车
zhitongche
("through-train")

A "through-train" figuratively describes the arrangement for the Legislative Council of the British Hong Kong government to become the first Legislative Council of the Hong Kong Special Administrative Region (HKSAR) of the PRC after 1 July 1997. The possibility for such an arrangement ended when Chris Patten, the last Hong Kong Governor, advanced a "political package" in his 7 October 1992 administrative report, which included reforms for the election of the last Legislative Council. This allegedly led to the landslide victory of the Hong Kong democrats in the 1995 election. As Chinese leaders saw it, Britain's purpose in implementing Patten's political package was by no means to "step-up democracy" as it professed, but to retain maximum British influence on the authorities of the future HKSAR, so as to realize "a British administration even without a British presence". Accordingly, in 1994, the NPC decided that the term of the last British Hong Kong Legislative Council, Urban Council, Regional Council, and District Boards would end on 30 June 1997.

To avoid a legislative vacuum, the Preparatory Committee of the HKSAR established a Provisional Legislative Council (PLC). The 60-member PLC was elected by the 400 members of the Selection Committee of the first HKSAR government. Its term ran from 1 July 1997 to 30 June 1998. See also "yiguo liangzhi" (one country, two systems).

纸老虎
zhilaohu
(paper tiger)

This is a well-known metaphor Mao first used to describe "imperialism and all reactionaries" in an interview with Anna Louise Strong (1885-1970), an American journalist, in Yan'an in August 1946. Mao stated: "All reactionaries are paper tigers. In appearance, the reactionaries are terrifying, but in reality they are not so powerful. From a long-term point of view, it is not the reactionaries but the people who are really powerful" *(SWM,* 4, p. 100).

In his speech at the Moscow Meeting of Communist and Workers' Parties on 18 November 1957, Mao reiterated his "paper tiger" theory. "I have said that all the reputedly powerful reactionaries are merely paper tigers," Mao stated. "The reason is that they are divorced from the people. Look! Was not Hitler a paper tiger? Was Hitler not overthrown? I also said that the tsar of Russia, the emperor of China, and Japanese imperialism were all paper tigers. As we know, they were all overthrown. U.S. imperialism has not yet been overthrown and it has the atom bomb. I believe it also will be overthrown. It, too, is a paper tiger" *(MZXJ,* 5, p. 499).

With his "paper tiger" theory, Mao introduced a concept the CCP had developed over a long period for the struggle against the enemy: "Strategically we should despise all our enemies, but tactically we should take them all seriously" (zhanlüeshang miaoshi yiqie diren, zhanshushang zhongshi yiqie diren). This means, Mao said, "that we must despise the enemy with respect to the whole, and take him seriously with respect to each and every concrete question. If we do not despise the enemy with respect to the whole, we shall be committing the error of opportunism. Marx and Engels were only two individuals, and yet in those early days they already declared that capitalism would be overthrown throughout the world. But in dealing with concrete problems and particular enemies we shall be committing the error of adventurism unless we take them seriously. In war, battles can only be fought one by one and the enemy forces can only be destroyed one by one. Factories can only be built one by one. The peasants can only plough the land plot by plot. The same is even true of eating a meal. Strategically, we take the eating of a meal lightly—we know we can finish it. But actually we eat it mouthful by mouthful. It is impossible to swallow an entire banquet in one gulp. This is known as a piecemeal solution. In military parlance, it is called wiping out the enemy forces one by one" (ibid., p. 500).

On 1 December 1958, at a Politburo meeting (the Wuchang meeting), Mao again perfected his "paper tiger" theory, describing the "dialectical relationship" between a "paper tiger" and an "iron tiger" (tielaohu). He said: "Just as there is not a single thing in the world without a dual nature (this is the law of the unity of opposites), so imperialism and all reactionaries have a dual nature—they are real tigers and paper tigers at the same time. In past history, before they won state power and for some time afterwards, the slave-owning class, the feudal landlord class and the bourgeoisie were vigorous, revolutionary and progressive; they were real tigers. But with the lapse of time, because their opposites—the slave class, the peasant class and the proletariat—grew in strength step by step, struggled against them more and more fiercely, these ruling classes changed step by step into the reverse, changed into reactionaries, changed into backward people, changed into paper tigers. And eventually they were overthrown, or will be overthrown, by the people. The reactionary, backward, decaying classes retained this dual nature even in their last life-and-death struggles against the people. On the one hand, they were real tigers; they devoured people, devoured people by the millions and tens of millions. The cause of the people's struggle went through a period of difficulties and hardships, and along the path there were many twists and turns. To destroy the rule of imperialism, feudalism and bureaucrat-capitalism in China took the Chinese people more than a hundred years and cost them tens of millions of lives before the victory in 1949. Look! Were these not living tigers, iron tigers, real tigers? But in the end they changed into paper tigers, dead tigers, bean-curd tigers. These are historical facts. Have people not seen or heard about these facts? There have indeed been thousands and tens of thousands of them! Thousands and tens of thousands! Hence, imperialism and all reactionaries, looked at in essence, from a long-term point of view, from a strategic point of view, must be seen for what they are—paper tigers. On this we should build our strategic thinking. On the other hand, they are also living tigers, iron tigers, real tigers which can devour people. On this we should build our tactical thinking" *(SWM,* 4, pp. 98-99).

Many Chinese are familiar with these teachings by Mao. They apply them to almost everything, from learning a foreign language (in cases like this, the "enemy" refers to difficulties), fulfilling a production target, to international struggles or building socialism.

只打苍蝇，不打老虎
zhi da cangying, bu da laohu
(only swat flies but not hunt tigers)

See "da laohu" (big tigers) and "fan fubai" (anti-corruption).

只生一个好
zhi sheng yi ge hao
(single-child families are fine)

See "yitaihua" (single-child policy) and "ershinianlai zuiju yingxianglide shi ge kouhao" (ten most influential slogans in the past two decades).

只专不红
zhi zhuan bu hong
(only expert and not red)

See "dangde jiaoyu fangzhen" (the Party's educational policy).

只有社会主义才能救中国
zhiyou shehuizhuyi caineng jiu Zhongguo
(only socialism can save China)

See "xin shehuizhuyi guan" (new socialist view).

只有生产高度商品化和社会化，社会主义才能建成
zhiyou shengchan gaodu shangpinhua he shehuihua, shehuizhuyi caineng jiancheng
(only on a high degree of commercialization and socialization of production can socialism be built)

See "shehuizhuyi chuji jieduan lun" (theory of the primary stage of socialism).

只有限制共产党的权力才能取得稳定
zhiyou xianzhi Gongchandangde quanli caineng qude wending
(only by restricting CCP power can stability be achieved)

See "wending yadao yiqie" (the need for stability overwhelms everything else).

只准左派造反，不准右派翻天
zhizhun zuopai zaofan, buzhun youpai fantian
(only Leftists can enjoy the right to rebel; no Rightists are allowed to change our regime)

See "xuetong lun" (lineage theory) and "hongweibing" (Red Guards).

治国必先治党，治党务必从严
zhi guo bi xian zhi dang, zhi dang wubi cong yan
(the Party must strictly discipline itself before it can run the country well)

See "fan fubai" (anti-corruption).

制度
zhidu
(social system)

"Zhidu" can be used as an equivalent of "tizhi", which means certain institutional structures. For instance, "zhidu chuangxin", a phrase often appearing in the "neo-conservatism" articles of the 1990s, means "institutional innovation" when translated into English.

In many cases, however, "zhidu" is an abbreviation for "shehui zhidu", which refers to the whole social (particularly, political) system of a country. When used in this way, it must not be confused with the concept of "tizhi". As Party propagandists emphasized, China may make changes in its institutional structures as part of a political reform, but this will not involve a change in its social system—socialism. Party leaders from Mao Zedong to Deng Xiaoping and Jiang Zemin reiterated that "Only socialism can save China" (zhiyou shehuizhuyi caineng jiu Zhongguo).

Scholars in mainland China have to be very careful when dealing with these two differing concepts and very often they are put into difficult positions. One such case was that of Zhou Yang, the veteran theorist who put forward the theory of "socialist alienation" in the early 1980s. He was undoubtedly very brave in insisting on the existence of alienation in a socialist society. Only by admitting its existence can alienation be overcome, he said. At the same time, he claimed that it is perfectly possible to overcome alienation by working within the socialist system itself. The causes of alienation, he explained, lie not in the socialist system (zhidu) itself, but in problems of the institutional structure (tizhi) and elsewhere. See also "Zhou Yang beiju" (tragedy of Zhou Yang) and "xin shehuizhuyi guan" (new socialist view).

制度现代化
zhidu xiandaihua

(modernization of social system)

See "si ge xiandaihua" (four modernizations).

中俄战略协作伙伴关系
Zhong-E zhanlüe xiezuo huoban guanxi
(Sino-Russian cooperative strategic partnership)

See "lengzhanhou shidaide xin diguozhuyi" (neo-imperialism in the post-Cold War era) and "weidu Zhongguo" (containment against China).

中美战略伙伴关系
Zhong-Mei zhanlüe huoban guanxi
(Sino-U.S. strategic partnership)

See "lengzhanhou shidaide xin diguozhuyi" (neo-imperialism in the post-Cold War era) and "weidu Zhongguo" (containment against China).

中苏大论战
Zhong Su dalunzhan
(polemic between the CCP and the CPSU)

See "xiuzhengzhuyi" (revisionism).

中苏友好协会
Zhong Su Youhao Xiehui
(Sino-Soviet Friendship Association)

See "yibiandao" (lean to one side).

中苏友好同盟互助条约
Zhong Su Youhao Tongmeng Huzhu Tiaoyue
(Sino-Soviet Treaty of Friendship, Alliance and Mutual Assistance)

See "yibiandao" (lean to one side).

中外艺术习惯的矛盾
Zhong wai yishu xiguande maodun
(contradictions between Chinese artistic conventions and those of other nations)

The difficulties in dealing with the contradictions between Chinese artistic conventions and those of other nations have been noted by many.

In his article "A New Aesthetic Principle Is Rising" published in March 1981, Sun Shaozhen, while asking people not to underestimate Gu Cheng's statement about convention being the enemy of poetry, did not forget to add that here also lay the weak point in the aesthetic of the "misty" poets; conventions, even outdated ones, were not merely the stagnant swamps that Gu Cheng described—they also contained the achievements and experiences of the past. He further warned that, though facing the stubborn grip of artistic convention, the young challengers still could not neglect positive traditional factors, or they would someday be punished by dialectics.

However, as Sun also found out, the complexity of the matter was that the young poets did not in fact neglect their inheritance; but what they paid attention to was inheriting other nations' conventions. In this regard, Sun suggested, there was a historical lesson to be learned. Though in the history of New Poetry most schools had benefited by the stimulation of other nations' exotic arts in building up their own "originality", even their outstanding representatives failed to solve the contradictions between Chinese artistic conventions and those of other nations. These contradictions were so rooted that, when their intensification reached a certain degree, it led to a narrow nationalistic tendency. Nevertheless, Sun said, there was no need for pessimism, for the best among the young poets were not as some critics described them. They had the wisdom to know themselves. See also "menglongshi lilunde san ci jueqi" ("three rises" in the theory of misty poetry).

中产阶级
zhongchanjieji
(middle class)

See "xinsheng zichanjieji" (new-born bourgeoisie).

中国霸权
Zhongguo baquan
(Chinese hegemony)

See "ershiyishiji shi Zhongguorende shiji" (the twenty-first century will be the Chinese century).

中国对美政策四句话
Zhongguo dui Mei zhengce si ju hua
("four-point statement" on China's policy towards the United States)

See "lengzhanhou shidaide xin diguozhuyi" (neo-imperialism in the post-Cold War era) and "weidu Zhongguo" (containment against China).

中国封建社会的超稳定结构
Zhongguo fengjian shehuide chaowending jiegou
(ultra-stable structure of Chinese feudal society)

Why did Chinese feudal society last for more than two thousand years? An answer is provided by Jin Guantao and Liu Qingfeng: Chinese feudal society had an ultra-stable structure, a system possessing tremendous stability and at the same time displaying itself in a cycle of vibrations. On the one hand, in its long history, Chinese feudal society was not ossified or stagnant, but always in a process of change and development. On the other hand, however, the movement of the society was a vibration, in which disintegration and rehabilitation replaced each other repeatedly. Judging from the whole formation, the structure, though always changing, changed within an intrinsic frame and never developed into a new structure.

Jin Guantao and Liu Qingfeng conceived this idea in the early 1970s. In 1974 they wrote a draft of about seventy thousand Chinese characters. In 1979 their thesis, entitled "A Hypothesis on Chinese Feudal Society's Ultra-stable System"

("Zhongguo fengjian shehuide chaowending xitong jiashuo"), was completed. In the early 1980s the thesis was published in the *Journal of Guiyang Normal College* (1 & 2, 1980) under the new title "The Structure of Chinese Feudal Society—An Ultra-stable System" ("Zhongguo fengjian shehuide jiegou—yi ge chaowending xitong"). This work was reprinted in book form by the Hunan People's Publishing House in 1984. The book's title was: *Prosperity and Crisis: On the Ultra-stable Structure of Chinese Feudal Society (Xingsheng yu weiji—Lun Zhongguo fengjian shehuide chaowending jiegou).* During the ten years, Chinese society was undergoing sharp turns and rapid change. Against this background many Chinese, especially the young, were very much attracted by the novel, though controversial, view and methodology of the book. Those who agreed with the two authors found the history of Chinese feudal society to be a unique textbook in human life. As it showed, the coordination obtained by suppressing creativity led to ossification; after a short-term prosperity brought about by rigid control there was a long stagnation. It was the bureaucratic network organized on the basis of the small-scale peasant economy that caused so many upheavals by destructive power. The ideology strangling individuality for the harmony between individual, family, and state and between man and nature (though able to resist the multiplication of religions) inevitably became a conservative ideological system. This was a significant warning that was relevant to the current demand for reform.

In 1993, Jin Guantao and Liu Qingfeng once again discussed their "ultra-stable structure" ("Kaifangzhongde bianqian: Zailun Zhongguo shehui chaowending jiegou"—"Changes in the Open Door: More on the Ultra-stable System of Chinese Society", special issue by the Center of the Contemporary Chinese Culture, Chinese University of Hong Kong, 1993). Again, their theory was open to controversy. One of their opponents was Li Zehou, who found Jin Guantao and Liu Qingfeng mistake the history of human society for a history of structures or systems. "If history is indiscriminately explained by the structure theory, everything will become a necessity as asserted by fatalism. But can this be true?" Li asked *(Farewell to Revolution,* p. 38).

中国改革开放的总设计师
Zhongguo gaige kaifangde zong shejishi
(general architect of China's reform and open-door program)

See "Deng Xiaoping lilun" (Deng Xiaopin Theory).

中国共产主义的试点
Zhongguo gongchanzhuyide shidian
(an experimental unit for China's communism)

See "Mao shi zibenzhuyi" (capitalism in Mao Zedong style).

中国国民党革命委员会
Zhongguo Guomindang Geming Weiyuanhui
(Chinese Nationalist Party Revolutionary Committee)

See "minzhu dangpai" (democratic parties).

中国魂
Zhongguo hun
(soul of China)

On 15 April 1989, Hu Yaobang, disgraced former CCP general secretary, died. Before that, inspired by some intellectuals, students had adopted plans for large-scale events in commemoration of the 70th anniversary of the May 4th Movement, so as to show their displeasure with the current state of affairs. Hu's unexpected death was like "throwing a lighted match into a barrel of gunpowder". From 17 April on, the largest scale student demonstrations since 1949 broke out in Tiananmen Square. There were demands that the CCP authorities implement a democratic form of government and redress the wrongs done to Hu Yaobang. On the evening of 21 April, about sixty thousand students, at an all-night peaceful sit-in in Tiananmen Square, mourned Hu's death. Their mourning activities, in which Hu was highly praised as "the soul of China", were part of the 1989 pro-democracy movement. See also "bajiu minyun" (1989 pro-democracy movement).

中国价值观
Zhongguo jiazhiguan
(Chinese concept of values)

See "renquan wenti" (human rights issue).

中国可以说不
Zhongguo keyi shuo bu
(China can say no)

In May 1996, a 400-plus-page book, *China Can Say No—Political and Emotional Choices in the Post-Cold War Age (Zhongguo Keyi Shuo Bu—Lengzhanhou Shidaide Zhengzhi Yu Qinggan Jueze)* was published by the China Industry and Commerce Joint Publishing House. The 50,000 copies of the first edition sold out immediately; it quickly became the hottest title of the year, stirring passions both at home and abroad.

The five co-authors—Zhang Zangzang, Tang Zhengyu, Song Qiang, Qiao Bian, and Gu Qingsheng—were freelance writers, lecturers, or journalists, aged from 27 to 42. They admitted that they were not scholars of international politics and had never traveled to the West. Nor did they have any official affiliations. They wrote the book totally on their own initiative.

The work, which discusses Sino-U.S. and Sino-Japanese ties, represents the third such book following *The Japan That Can Say No* written by Japanese authors Akio Morita and Shintaro Ishhara, and *Asia Can Say No* by Malaysian Prime Minister Datuk Seri Mahathir Bin Mohammed. Despite failing to match the previous authors in terms of experience and prestige, the Chinese authors, each composing independent sections, clearly make their points in the book—a common thread is the path from infatuation to disillusionment in Chinese perceptions of America's values and political system. The polemic takes aim at Washington's "hegemonism" on the world stage, extreme U.S.-style individualism, and American "demonization" of China over issues such as arms proliferation, human rights, and family planning. The authors vehemently denounce the U.S.-led "containment" against China, with Japan a compliant partner in the endeavor.

The book succeeded, its authors stressed, because it unequivocally proclaimed the end of a "post-colonial mentality" (houzhimin xintai), or, broadly speaking, the Western-centric beliefs they claimed have enveloped the Chinese during the almost twenty years of the reform process. The book attacked this type of mentality and swept it aside.

A survey among young people conducted in September 1995 by the *China Youth Daily* indicated that 87.1 percent of the respondents regarded the United States as the most unfriendly country to China. The popularity of this book confirmed this rising sentiment.

It was also noted that the book aroused strong disapproval from many critics at home and abroad. An easy target was its radical wording and highly emotional conclusions. It could provoke parochial nationalism or, even worse, xenophobia. Some said that efforts should be made to promote mutual understanding between countries instead of saying "No" to each other. "Perhaps it is time for some people to try saying 'Yes'", they said. There was also a view suggesting that China could say "No" only after the Chinese people could say "No" to its government.

Interestingly, there was a change in the official attitude towards *China Can Say No*. Soon after its release, the authorities tacitly approved of the book. Official media even praised it as a "most welcome" book, "containing food for thought" and "fully expressing a popular view". Its authors were said to have "represented a new breed of Chinese intellectuals". Later, the book was reportedly criticized by the CCP Propaganda Department for being irresponsible. Its problems included "creating mental confusion among readers at home and abroad", "giving the impression that China's growing patriotism had become irrational" and "exerting a negative effect on the implementation of China's foreign policy".

China Can Say No was a symbol as well as a product of the rise of nationalism in China in the 1990s. By the end of 1996, a number of paralled titles with similar themes had been published.

China Can Still Say No (Zhongguo Haishi Neng Shuo Bu, Beijing, Zhongguo wenlian, Oct. 1996), the sequel to *China Can Say No*.

Why Is China Saying No (Peng Qian et al., *Zhongguo Weishenme Shuo Bu,* Beijing, Xin shijie, Oct. 1996). Written by three international relations and strategic studies experts at the Academy of Military Sciences and Beijing University, this book argues that U.S. foreign policy in the 1990s has moved decisively towards encircling China.

A Record of Confrontations Between China and the United States (Zhun Feng and Huang Zhaoyü, *Zhong Mei Jiaoliang Da Xiezhen,* Beijing, Zhongguo renshi, 1996). This covers milestones in Sino-U.S. relations ranging from the Korean War of the 1950s to the 1996 crisis in the Taiwan Straits, revealing that China has long said "No" to the United States.

How Can China Say No? by Zhang Xueli, a retired vice-principal of the Xi'an Railway Police Academy. In answer to the question posed by the title of the book, Zhang argues, less irascibly, that China can say "No" for the simple reason that it is now able to do so.

Containing China: Myth and Reality edited by Sun Geqin and others *(Ezhi Zhongguo: Shenhua Yu Xianshi,* Beijing, Zhongguo yanshi, Oct. 1996). This is the third volume in the *Global Challenges* series, following *A Portrait of the Sino-U.S. Contest* and *Whither Taiwan?* Written by experts at China's prestigious universities and research institutes (Sun Geqin as chief writer), this book is considered by some to be the most engaging, reasonable, and cogently argued, backed by prodigious amounts of data and documentation. The authors warn against hyperbole or exaggeration. They hope that the Chinese will adopt a proper perspective regarding their country's rise as a major regional and world power.

Behind the Demonization of China (Yaomohua Zhonguode Beihou, Beijing, Zhongguo shehui kexue, Dec. 1996). This book of 414 pages was written by Li

Xiguang, a reporter of the Xinhua News Agency, Liu Kang, a Chinese scholar teaching in America, and six others. All of them had visited the U.S. or were studying or working there, when they wrote this book. They found themselves duty-bound to tell the "truth" behind the "demonization" of China by U.S. media. Eye-catchingly, when discussing Sino-U.S. relationship, they strongly emphasized class analysis and class struggle.

China's Renaissance and the Future of the World (Zhonghua Fuxing Yu Shijie Weilai, Chengdu, Sichuan renmin, 1996), a compendium of essays by the controversial scholar He Xin. The book is said to be the most belligerent of all these works. He Xin criticizes all U.S. actions, displaying virtually no understanding of how domestic dynamics in the U.S. can influence foreign policy. In contrast, his arguments sometimes make the views of the authors of *China Can Say No* appear to be carefully considered.

The wave of these publications was certainly a notable social phenomenon. They were products of nationalism. "China Can Say No" will be the strongest voice resounding in the country, at least for a period of time. See also "minzuzhuyi" (nationalism) and "xinzuopai" (neo-Leftists).

中国可以通过一党制走向民主
Zhongguo keyi tongguo yidangzhi zouxiang minzhu (China can be transformed into a democracy via one-party rule)

See "wuchanjieji zhuanzheng" (dictatorship of the proletariat).

中国历史文化心理的一面镜子
Zhongguo lishi wenhua xinlide yimian jingzi (a mirror of Chinese historical cultural psychology)

See "fansi wenxue" (reflection litetrature) and "wenhua re" (culture craze).

中国民主促进会
Zhongguo Minzhu Cujinhui (Chinese Democracy Promotion Association)

See "minzhu dangpai" (democratic parties).

中国民主建国会
Zhongguo Minzhu Jianguohui (Chinese Association for the Founding of a Democratic Nation)

See "minzhu dangpai" (democratic parties).

中国民主同盟
Zhongguo Minzhu Tongmeng (Chinese Democracy Alliance)

See "minzhu dangpai" (democratic parties).

中国民主党
Zhongguo Minzhudang
(Chinese Democracy Party)

See "zhengzhi gaige" (political reform).

中国农工民主党
Zhongguo Nonggong Minzhudang
(Chinese Peasants and Workers Democratic Party)

See "minzhu dangpai" (democratic parties).

中国七块论
Zhongguo qikuailun
("seven regions" theory for China)

See "Taiwan wenti" (Taiwan issue).

中国人民政治协商会议
Zhongguo Renmin Zhengzhi Xieshang Huiyi
(Chinese People's Political Consultative Conference)

See "Zhengxie" (CPPCC).

中国社会对文人敏感的传统
Zhongguo shehui dui wenren min'gande chuantong
(traditional sensitivity of Chinese society towards literary men)

A common belief in traditional Chinese society was, as the old saying goes: "wanban jie xiapin, weiyou dushu gao" (The most noble is to be a scholar, whereas everything else is inferior). The social pecking order was accordingly: scholar (shi), farmer (nong), craftsman (gong), and businessman (shang). For many intellectuals, a successful career meant being a scholar who was selected by examination to appointment as an official. In fact, it was in this way that many officials were selected and appointed to office in various dynasties. Hence another facet of the matter: the sensitivity of society towards literature, literary undertakings, and literary men. People often showed great interest in the fortunes of literary men, both past and present. As for the rulers, their reactions were more often political than cultural. While trying to win over intellectuals with high positions and handsome salaries, Chinese rulers tended to suppress those who dissented. See also "zhishifenzi wenti" (issue of intellectuals) and "sixiang gaizao" (ideological remolding).

中国威胁论
Zhongguo weixie lun
("China threat" theory)

See "weidu Zhongguo" (containment against China).

中国文化优越论
Zhongguo wenhua youyue lun
(theory of the superiority of Chinese culture)

See "quanqiuhua" (globalization) and "minzuzhuyi" (nationalism).

中国文学缺乏忏悔意识
Zhongguo wenxue quefa chanhui yishi
(Chinese literature lacks a consciousness of repentance)

See "shehuizhuyi beiju" (socialist tragedy).

中国文学研究的大转机
Zhongguo wenxue yanjiude da zhuanji
(favorable turn for Chinese literary study)

See "wenxue guilü lunzheng" (1986 debate on the law of literature).

中国文艺复兴
Zhongguo wenyifuxing
(Chinese renaissance)

See "rendaozhuyi lunzheng" (humanism debate) and "rendaozhuyi shi xinshiqi wenxuede zhuliu" (humanism is the mainstream in the literature of the new period).

中国文艺批评的历史转折点
Zhongguo wenyi pipingde lishi zhuanzhedian
(a historical turning point in Chinese literary and art criticism)

In the last months of 1979 and the following year there was a heated debate focused around such works as "What If I Really Were" (also entitled "The Impostor"), "In the Unwritten Records", and "A Woman Thief".

The debate continued at the 4th Congress of Chinese Writers and Artists. As no resolution could be reached when the Congress was drawing to its close, Hu Yaobang, then director of the PCC Propaganda Department, and other cultural leaders decided that, since it was unsuitable to impose a conclusion by means of dispatching a document from the PCC, and since it was undesirable to extend the Congress, a special forum should be held some time in the near future. With considerable preparation, the proposed meeting—dubbed the Forum on Script Writing—was convened from 23 January to 13 February 1980, jointly sponsored by the Chinese Dramatists Association, the CWA, and the Chinese Film Association, and presided over by He Jingzhi, then deputy director of the PCC Propaganda Department.

The Forum thereby can be said to be a continuation of the 4th Congress of Chinese Writers and Artists. The Party authorities intended to solve the problem raised by the controversial works from two angles. On the one hand, they found it necessary to criticize the liberal tendency among writers and intellectuals so that they could control the situation. On the other hand, they were vigilant of any excessive demand made by "Left" forces which would damage their own interests. The spirit of the Forum found full expression in the long speech delivered by Hu Yaobang in the last two days, which brought the gathering to its climax.

The Forum was highly praised by some Chinese critics. As Zhu Zhai said: "If the 4th Congress of Chinese Writers and Artists is considered to have marked a historical turning point in Chinese literature and art as a whole, then the Forum on Script Writing can be said to be a historical turning point in Chinese literary and art criticism" ("Lishi zhuanzhezhongde wenxue piping: *Zhongguo xinwenyi daxi (1976-1982) lilun erji* daoyan"—"Literary Criticism at a Historical Turning-Point: An Introduction to *XWY, Theory* 2, *WXPL*, 4:15, July 1984).

Zhou Yang regarded the Forum as a "turning point" because it was the first time that a "correct atmosphere" surrounded literary criticism (ibid., p. 16). According to Chen Huangmei, another cultural official, the "Double Hundred" principle was carried out at the Forum, and all the participants, no matter whether they were Party leaders or literary critics or creative workers, discussed problems in current literary creation "equally, freely, and in an organized way" (Chen Huangmei, "Speech at the Script Writing Forum", *Dianying yishu*, 4, 1980, reprinted in *XWY, Theory* 2, p. 897).

As it turned out, however, not everyone wholeheartedly supported the Forum or Hu's speech. In fact, after the Forum, quite a number of articles with divergent views appeared. Some people, such as the editors and supporters of the *Report of the Age (Shidaide baogao)*, a newly-established journal, obviously were more critical of those controversial works. (On 15 March 1980, its inaugural issue published fierce attacks on "In the Unwritten Records".) Many writers and critics, on the other hand, feared that arbitrary attacks would re-appear based on the excuse of the "social effect", an issue raised at the Forum, and the past few years' hard-earned gains in the literary situation would be lost. As Bai Hua and Su Shuyang, two well-known writers, complained, the Script Writing Forum had a chilling effect on playwrights, and they were afraid of all high level meetings on literature (*China News Analysis*, 1205:6, 24 Apr. 1981). Sha Yexin, the chief author of "What If I Really Were", simply accused the Forum of setting a precedent of disguisedly banning theatrical works after the downfall of the Gang of Four, and he asserted that the social effect brought about by the "theory of social effect", consequently, was very bad (Sha Yexin, "Che 'dan'"—"Chatter", *WYB*, 10:7-11, 1980, reprinted in *WYLZJ*, pp. 103-08).

After one year's delay, Hu Yaobang's "Speech at the Forum on Script Writing" was published nationally, with elaborate alterations. Even then, however, what the Party authorities thought should be the due social effect of Hu's speech and the Forum was not achieved. What was called "wrong ideological tendencies"—Right in essence—became "rampant" among literary and art circles. This was a development that the CCP authorities had not expected. On an important occasion commemerating the centenary of the birth of Lu Xun on 25 September 1981, Hu Yaobang, chairman of the CCP, sternly expressed his dissatisfaction:

"While fully affirming the mainstream on the literary and art front, we have also pointed out that in the fields of literature and art there have existed as well certain unhealthy, negative features that are harmful to the people. In this regard, as you may remember, in the winter of 1979 and the spring of 1980, our Party issued a series of opinions and, after having had a number of cordial discussions with comrades from literary and art circles, further made many suggestions aiming at promoting literary and art prosperity. It is a pity, however, that comrades in literary and art circles have failed to pay sufficient attention to some of our Party's ideas that are of fundamental importance" (Hu Yaobang, "Zai Lu Xun dansheng yibai zhounian jinian dahuishangde jianghua"—"Speech at the Commemoration of the Centennary of the Birth of Lu Xun", *HQ*, 19:4, 1981).

Indeed, Hu Yaobang had reason to feel disappointed. He must have noted that speeches by Party leaders no longer enjoyed overwhelming authority like that enjoyed by Mao's *Yan'an Talks*. No one regarded Hu's speech at the 1980 Forum on Script Writing as a new *Bible* for literature and art in China. Even worse, the bad "social effect" of the Forum itself—Hu's speech included—was not forgotten. Spoken drama in China, after a flourish in the first few years subsequent to the downfall of the Gang of Four, was in a depressing state for the rest of the so-called "new period". It was at the 1980 Script Writing Forum that the very soul of spoken drama—its nimble and acute involvement in social problems—was castrated. See also "shehui xiaoguo lun" (social effect theory) and "wenyi wei zhengzhi fuwu" (literature and art serve politics).

中国要出问题，还是在共产党内部
Zhongguo yaochu wenti, haishi zai gongchandang neibu
(if any serious problems occur in China, they are likely to occur within the Communist Party)

See "Dangde lingdao" (Party leadership).

中国右派的三大反动理论
Zhongguo youpaide san da fandong lilun
(three major reactionary theories of China's Rightists)

See "zhengzhi shejiyuan" (political design academy), "pingfan weiyuanhui" (rehabilitation committee), and "dangtianxia" (the Party is the entire world).

中国知识分子的苦恋情结
Zhongguo zhishifenzide kulian qingjie
(the bitter love complex of Chinese intellectuals)

See "Bai Hua shijian" (Bai Hua incident) and "zhishifenzi wenti" (issue of intellectuals).

中国致公党
Zhongguo Zhigongdang
(Chinese Public Devotion Party)

See "minzhu dangpai" (democratic parties).

中国转型期的政治经济学
Zhongguo zhuanxingqide zhengzhi jingjixue
(political economy for China during the "mode transition" period)

See "meiyou liangxinde jingjixue" (no heart economics).

中国最後的皇帝
Zhongguo zuihoude huangdi
(China's last emperor)

See "bajiu minyun" (1989 pro-democracy movement).

中国作家应该关心的十个问题
Zhongguo zuojia yinggai guanxinde shige wenti
(ten problems Chinese writers should be concerned with)

In his speech at Nankai University, Tianjin on 21 November 1986, Liu Binyan listed what he deemed to be ten serious problems in China, which Chinese writers had no right to evade. These problems were: 1. the degeneration of a large number of Chinese people; 2. the lack of a sound legal system in many places; 3. many Chinese of ability found it difficult to live in China; 4. contempt of human values and suppression of human nature; 5. the cruel means of revolution; 6. difficulties to protect the good and subdue the bad; 7. why so many high-sounding slogans did not work; 8. what led to those tragedies like the Cultural Revolution; 9. why freedom was still treated by some in power as something terrible and intolerable; and 10. how to reflect on the change of the times (see "Liu Binyan's Speech at Nankai University", in *FLW*, pp. 115-20).

Later, Liu argued that he was not opposed to a writer's artistic pursuits, but he wanted to make it clear that as a Chinese writer, one must be concerned about the fate of the nation. He said: "China is after all China. It is a country where tens of millions of people suffer from cold and hunger and where human rights are often trodden on. It cannot be compared to Germany in the 1920s. Moreover, problems already solved in the France of the 1880s, the cradle of modernist trends, still remain unsolved in China today" (See Lee Yee, "Another Interview with Liu Binyan", *JN,* 220:30, May 1988).

中国的戈尔巴乔夫
Zhongguode Ge'erbaqiaofu
(China's Gorbachev)

See "jingji shahuang" (economic "Tsar").

中国的赫鲁晓夫
Zhongguode Heluxiaofu
(China's Khrushchev)

Not long after the beginning of the GPCR, Liu Shaoqi, PRC president, was overthrown as the "biggest capitalist-roader". He was dubbed "China's Khrushchev" (the insinuation was first made in the "May 16th Circular" of 1966 ("wuyiliu tongzhi"). He was also charged with being a "renegade", "hidden traitor", and "scab". On 12 November 1969, he died in Kaifeng city, Heman province, while still in prison. At the 5th Plenum of the 11th PCC held in February 1980, Liu Shaoqi was officially rehabilitated.

After Deng Xiaoping died on 19 February 1997, Leftists attacked him as the very "China's Khrushchev" Mao had asked the Chinese people to be vigilant against. See also "xiuzhengzhuyi" (revisionism) and "Deng Xiaoping lilun" (Deng Xiaoping Theory).

中国的崛起
Zhongguode jueqi
(the rise of China)

See "ershiyishiji shi Zhongguorende shiji" (the twenty-first century will be the Chinese century) and "weidu Zhongguo" (containment against China).

中国的良心
Zhongguode liangxin
(China's conscience)
See "Liu Binyan xianxiang" (Liu Binyan phenomenon).

中国化的马克思主义
Zhongguohuade Makesizhuyi
(Sinicized Marxism)
See "fan chuantong" (anti-tradition), "sixiang gaizao" (ideological remolding), "Mao Zedong sixiang" (Mao Zedong Thought), and "Deng Xiaoping lilun" (Deng Xiaoping Theory).

中国人的世纪
Zhongguorende shiji
(Chinese century)
See "ershiyishiji shi Zhongguorende shiji" (the twenty-first century will be the Chinese century).

中国人民政治协商会议
Zhongguo Renmin Zhengzhi Xieshang Huiyi
(Chinese People's Political Consultative Conference)
See "zhengxie" (CPPCC).

中华文化升值
Zhonghua wenhua shengzhi
(increasing value of Chinese culture)
A term often heard today accompanying the economic boom of China and other Asian countries and areas which are in varying degrees under the influence of Chinese culture. See "da Zhonghua" (Greater China).

中华民国在台湾
Zhonghua minguo zai Taiwan
(Republic of China on Taiwan)
See "Taiwan wenti" (Taiwan issue).

中间路线
zhongjian luxian
(middle road)
See "disan liliang" (third force).

中间人物论
zhongjian renwu lun
(theory of "middle characters")

This was one of the eight "sinister literary theories" singled out for attack in the 1966 Party document "Summary of the Forum on Work in Literature and Art in the Armed Forces". Shao Quanlin (1906-1971), a prominent literary theorist and a CCP cultural official, was held responsible for this theory. Another "sinister literary theory", "the deepening of realism" (xianshizhuyi shenhua lun), was also attributed to him.

As early as March 1961, Shao Quanlin focused on issues of realism. After Zhang Guangnian's treatise "On Problems of Subject Matter" ("Ticai wenti", *WYB,* 3 1961) was published, Shao told the staff members of *Literary Gazette* that another monograph on typicality should follow it, so as to advocate the diversity of characters in literary creation. At the August 1962 Dalian meeting—a forum on writing short stories on rural subjects—Shao, as Party secretary and vice-chairman of the CWA and the major organizer of the forum, further expounded upon his view. He was dissatisfied with the current neglect of "middle characters". He thus called for a "deepening of realism" (xianshizhuyi shenhua). Writers, he said, should not gloss over things and sidestep contradictions. They should write about the protractedness, the ardor, and the complexity of struggle. Since "contradictions were often concentrated in middle characters",writers should write about complex middle characters and "everyday" events. Shao claimed that only works of this nature would carry a high sense of reality.

Unfortunately, Shao was fiercely attacked in 1964 and persecuted to death during the GPCR. In 1978, the two theories were still considered to contain mistakes, while "possibly providing some rational suggestions" (Zhou Ke, "Bo luan fan zheng, kaizhan chuangzaoxingde wenxue yanjiu pinglun gongzuo"—"Bring Order Out of Chaos and Carry Out Creative Studies and Comments on Literature", *WXPL,* 3:7, 1978). Moreover, it was added that their mistakes "had already been criticized and repudiated by revolutionary literary and art circles before the Cultural Revolution" (ibid.). This did not change until after the 1979 4th National Congress of Chinese Writers and Artists. See also "jiyao" ("Summary").

中学
Zhongxue
(Chinese traditional learning)

See "guoxue" (Chinese traditional learning).

中央
Zhongyang
(Party Center)

In mainland China, "Zhongyang" (Center) generally refers to "dangzhongyang" (Party Center). The Party Center may refer to the CCP Central Committee, the Politburo, or the Politburo Standing Committee. It may also refer to the top Party policymakers, especially the person who is called the Leader, and not to a specific organization. See also "xiangpi tuzhang" (rubber stamp).

中央计划经济
zhongyang jihua jingji
(centrally planned economy)

See "jingji gaige" (economic reform).

中央文革
zhongyang wen'ge
(Central GPCR Group)

See "zhongyang wenhua geming xiaozu" (Central Group in Charge of the Cultural Revolution).

中央文革小组
zhongyang wen'ge xiaozu
(Central GPCR Group)

See "zhongyang wenhua geming xiaozu" (Central Group in Charge of the Cultural Revolution).

中央文化革命小组
zhongyang wenhua geming xiaozu
(Central Group in Charge of the Cultural Revolution)

"Zhongyang wenhua geming xiaozu" is called "zhongyang wen'ge xiaozu" or "zhongyang wen'ge" (Central GPCR Group) for short.

In mid-1964, on Mao's instructions, a "PCC Group in Charge of the Cultural Revolution" was set up, which was dubbed the "Group of Five" because it consisted of five people: Peng Zhen, its head, Lu Dingyi, deputy head, and Kang Sheng, Zhou Yang, and Wu Lengxi. The offices under the Group supervised the rectification movement unfolding among literary and art circles at the time. On 16 May 1966, the CCP Politburo "Circular" announced the dissolution of the "Group of Five" and the setting up of a new "Central Group in Charge of the Cultural Revolution" directly under the Politburo Standing Committee. The new body consisted of group leader Chen Boda; adviser Kang Sheng; first deputy leader Jiang Qing; deputy leaders Liu Zhijian and Zhang Chunqiao; and group members Wang Li, Guan Feng, Qi Benyu, Xie Tangzhong, Yin Da, Mu Xin, and Yao Wenyuan. (According to Li Zhisui, the author of the 1994-95 bestseller *The Private Life of Chairman Mao,* the list was first put forth by Lin Biao, which Mao approved, after adding Tao Zhu (1908-1969) to it as another adviser and Wang Renzhong (1917-1992) as another deputy leader. Other sources, however, assert that the list was mainly put forth by Jiang Qing. (See Wang Yi, "'Zhongyang Wen'ge Xiaozu' ji qi wenhua jiyin"—"'The Central Cultural Revolutionary Group' and Its Geneology", *ES,* 55-60, Dec. 1998).

On 8 August 1966, the "PCC Decision on the GPCR" (the "Sixteen Articles"), passed at the 11th Plenum of the 8th PCC, stipulated that the Central GPCR Group was an organ of power for the GPCR. On 30 August, the PCC announced that when Chen Boda was on sick leave or away from Beijing, Jiang Qing would be the acting leader of the Group. In January 1967, the PCC Secretariat stopped functioning. The next month the PCC Politburo also stopped functioning. Their jobs were all taken over by the Group.

After the 9th National Congress of the CCP, which was held in Beijing in April 1969, the Group was dissolved and its major figures (those having survived a series of cruel inner struggles) became members of the PCC Politburo or the Politburo Standing Committee. See also "eryue tigang" ("February Report Outline") "wuyiliu tongzhi" (May 16th Circular), and "shiliutiao" (Sixteen Articles).

中庸之道
zhongyong zhi dao
(doctrine of the mean)

While controversial, the Confucian philosophy of the golden mean is widespread in China and practiced by many Chinese in their daily lives. See "buke dui" (remedial teaching team).

终极关怀
zhongji guanhuai
(ultimate concern)

See "quanqiuhua" (globalization).

终身制
zhongshen zhi
(life-tenure system)

In the discussion of "alienation" in the early 1980s, it was pointed out that the existing life-tenure system for cadres was one of the reasons for the generation of alienation in China. As critics argued, China did not undergo the developmental stage of capitalism, entering into a socialist society directly from a semi-colonial and semi-feudal society. As a result, there was a strong feudal influence, which formed a vast trammel confining the people, in terms of their psychology, customs, morality, and tradition. This led to the establishment of the life-tenure system which contributed to what was called "the mystery of the present-day worship of power". The system naturally defined the division of labor as between administrators and workers, and made possible the formation of the special interests of the few administrators. Accordingly, this led to a separation of the ownership of the means of production and the right to control and enjoy it, thus damaging what was called "socialist public ownership", the foundation of CCP rule. Moreover, as a result of the long-standing practice that blurred the different functions of the Party and the government and confused political and economic powers, excessive power was concentrated in the hands of a few people.

At the 5th Plenum of the 11th PCC when the draft of the new CCP Constitution was being discussed, it was proposed that the life-tenure system be abolished and be replaced by a retirement system during the process of reform. See also "shehuizhuyi yihualun" (theory of socialist alienation).

忠君报国
zhongjun baoguo
(loyalty to one's sovereign and dedication to the service of one's country)

In feudal times, loyalty to one's sovereign and dedication to the service of one's country were nearly synonymous. After the GPCR, many Chinese intellectuals criticized this, linking it to the "modern superstition"—the personality cult of Mao. See "xiandai mixin" (modern superstition) and "shehuizhuyi yihualun" (theory of socialist alienation).

忠于生活，干预灵魂
zhongyu shenghuo, ganyu linghun
(be loyal to life and involved in the soul)

See "ganyu shenghuo" (be involved in life).

忠字牌
zhongzi pai
("loyalty" tablet)

See "xiandai mixin" (modern superstition).

忠字舞
zhongziwu
("loyalty" dance)

See "xiandai mixin" (modern superstition).

种试验田
zhong shiyantian
(cultivating experimental farming plots)

The term "experimental farming plots" was first officially used by the CCP Hubei Provincial Committee in a report submitted to the PCC on 29 November 1957. As a result of this report, which was about "cultivating experimental farming plots by cadres of various levels", on 14 February 1958 the PCC asked that the Hubei experience be popularized all over the country.

Cultivating an "experimental farming plot", in its direct sense, means cultivating a plot of farmland by new techniques so as to attain high yields. The Party asked leading cadres and functionaries to leave their offices, cast away their airs, and cultivate experimental farming plots together with the peasants, in order to overcome bureaucracy and subjectivism. Later, the term "experimental farming plots" was used in more a broad sense. It refers to "key-point experimentation" or "spot testing" (shidian). As an important method of leadership, leading cadres stay at selected grass-roots units ("dundian"—squatting at points) to help improve their work and gain firsthand experience to guide overall work. Hence another related term: "make a key-point experiment" (gao shidian). Today to cultivate an experimental farming plot simply means to try to create a model of one's own. This applies to all walks of life. For example, in 1980, Zhong Dianfei, a well-known film critic and director, used the term to refer to his desire to film the controversial script "A Woman Thief" (Nü zei). See also "anquan xishu" (safety coefficient).

重在政治表现
zhong zai zhengzhi biaoxian
(lay stress on one's political behavior)

See "xuetong lun" (lineage theory) and "jiating chengfen" (family origin; class status of one's family).

周扬理论探索的丰碑
Zhou Yang lilun tansuode fengbei
(a monument to Zhou Yang's theoretical inquiry)

See "Zhou Yang beiju" (tragedy of Zhou Yang), "shehuizhuyi yihua lun" (theory of socialist alienation), and "rendaozhuyi lunzheng" (humanism debate).

周扬三部曲
Zhou Yang sanbuqu
(Zhou Yang trilogy)

See "Zhou Yang beiju" (tragedy of Zhou Yang).

周扬悲剧
Zhou Yang beiju
(tragedy of Zhou Yang)

As a Marxist literary and philosophical critic, Zhou Yang's entire life (1908-1989) was closely connected with the CCP's cause in the fields of ideology, literature, and art. In 1930, when he returned from Japan at age 22, he was a Party representative among cultural circles. He then became the Party secretary in the League of the Left-Wing Writers. In the Yan'an years he was president of both the Lu Xun Art Institute and Yan'an University. When the PRC was founded in 1949, he was appointed PRC vice-minister of culture and deputy director of the PCC Propaganda Department, in charge of literature and art throughout the country. He was also vice-chairman of the ACF. Naturally, Zhou Yang was the supreme executor and supervisor of the numerous political movements carried out successively among literary and art circles. Under his leadership thousands of writers and artists were persecuted, hence he was called the "Tsar" of literary and art circles (wenyi shahuang) by China's writers and artists.

From the late 1950s on, Mao's suspicion of Zhou Yang increased. Mao's two fatal "instructions" in 1963 and 1964 were telling blows to Zhou Yang (also, no doubt, to all members of the ACF and its affiliated associations, which Zhou Yang controlled). He was further disgraced in the 1966 Party document "Summary of the Forum on Work in Literature and Art in the Armed Forces" ("Jiyao"), which Mao revised elaborately on three occasions. During the GPCR, he was dismissed from his high position and imprisoned, where for ten years he tasted all the bitterness he had inflicted on others. One of his alleged major crimes, ironically, was that he was the "general backer" of all the niuguisheshen—"monsters and demons", that is, class enemies of all descriptions—in the realms of literature and art. He was accused of having carried out the "three-famous" (sanming) principle which advocated that "famous writers, famous directors, and famous actors" should be well treated with the policy of "three-highs" (sangao)—high salaries, high royalties, and high awards. His "scheme" was said to bring about a "peaceful evolution" throughout the ranks of literary and art workers, which meant that he tried to turn literary and art workers into "spiritual aristocrats" (jingshen guizu) that stand above the masses. He was accused of opposing the correct orientation for literature and art—to serve the workers, peasants, and soldiers—as formulated by Mao, and advocating "literature and art of the whole people", which was regarded as "revisionist". One piece of evidence for this was his approval of the publication of the 23 May 1962 *People's Daily* editorial, "Serve the Broadest Masses of the People" ("Wei zui guangdade renmin qunzhong fuwu"). Since Zhou Yang was the leader of the Left-wing movement in literature and art in the 1930s, he and the so-called "Zhou Yang clique" were fiercely attacked as the followers of "Wang Ming's Right capitulationist line" (Wang Ming was CCP leader for four years in the early 1930s).

The most fierce fire came from Yao Wenyuan, a rising political star. In his 1967 article "On the Counter-Revolutionary Double-dealer Zhou Yang", Yao wrote, satirically: "There are certain people who like to write trilogies. In a broad sense, Zhou Yang played a three-part intrigue: frenzied attacks on the Party and Mao Zedong's thought; then a prompt but sham self-criticism or assumed enthusiasm to show that he was taking the correct side; then a large-scale revengeful counter-attack, and new attacks. Zhou Yang's history of being 'correct all along' is a history of a counter-revolutionary double-dealer" (Yao Wenyuan, "Ping fan geming liangmianpai Zhou Yang", *HQ,* 1, 1967; trans. in *CL,* 3:43, 1967).

After the GPCR, Zhou Yang underwent significant changes and finally became determined to break completely with his past Left views. In 1982, when discussing how to treat Marxism, Zhou Yang raised the issue of developing Marxism (Zhou Yang, "Yi yao jianchi, er yao fazhan"—"Upholding and Developing Marxism", *RMRB,* 23 June 1982). In his 1983 ill-fated speech "An Inquiry into Some Theoretical Problems of Marxism" (*RMRB,* 16 Mar. 1983), Zhou Yang further pointed out that Marxism is a theory ever in development and it does not accept any ultimate truth. This article marked the highlight of the 1980-83 wave of humanism, and was hailed as a monument to Zhou Yang's theoretical inquiry.

Drafted with the help of Wang Yuanhua (a literary critic, and once director of the Propaganda Department of the CCP Shanghai Municipal Committee), Gu Xiang (literary critic, then working at the Literature and Art Bureau of the PCC Propaganda Department), and Wang Ruoshui (philosopher, and deputy editor-in-chief of the *People's Daily*), "An Inquiry" was originally a major speech Zhou Yang delivered on 7 March 1983 at the conference marking the centenary of Marx's death held in Beijing under the auspices of the PCC Propaganda Department, CASS, the Central Party School, and the Education Ministry. It consists of four parts, of some 17,000 Chinese characters. In the first part Zhou Yang points out that Marxism is a theory ever in development which does not accept any ultimate truth. In the second part Zhou Yang asks the people to pay attention to issues concerning epistemology. One of the major weaknesses of the CCP, according to Zhou Yang, is its lack of Marxist theoretical preparations before it was founded and when it entered the period of socialist revolution and construction. The third part consists of cultural criticism. While complaining that both Stalin and Mao Zedong excluded the law of negation of negation, Zhou calls for a correct interpretation of the key Marxist concept of "sublimation" ("yangqi", deriving from the Hegelian expression "aufhebung"). The final part is devoted to a discussion of the relationship between Marxism and humanism, in which Zhou reveals the following points:

1. He reaffirms his break with his pre-GPCR view (that is, the orthodox view) that humanism is revisionism and incompatible with Marxism. He writes that the criticism of humanism in the past was to a great extent one-sided and even erroneous.

2. Echoing Wang Ruoshui's "A Defense of Humanism" of two months earlier, he writes that "man is the goal of all our work".

3. He also holds that Marxism includes, but is not subordinate to, humanism. This, he writes, is Marxist humanism, and only with this can bourgeois humanism be genuinely overcome.

4. Alienation, in his view, is not an idealistic but a dialectical concept, which Marx never abandoned. As explained clearly in his *Capital,* Marx developed the idea of "alienated labor", which was first put forth in his *Economic and Philosophic Manuscripts of 1884,* into the later theory of "surplus value" (shengyu jiazhi lun). The establishment of historical materialism and the theory of surplus value enabled Marx to place his humanistic idea on a more scientific basis. Communism, in which

man can develop freely and in an all-round way, is a mature thought which Marx formed on the basis of inheriting various humanist ideas occurring earlier in history.

5. Zhou believes recognition of socialist humanism and opposition to alienation are two sides of the same thing. Socialism is vastly superior to capitalism, but that does not mean that no alienation exists in socialist society. Like Wang Ruoshui, Zhou Yang lists phenomena of alienation in Chinese economic, political, and ideological realms.

6. Thoroughgoing materialists, Zhou writes, are not afraid to face reality: only by admitting its existence can alienation be overcome. As expected, Zhou emphasizes that it is perfectly possible for them to overcome alienation by working within the socialist system. The causes of alienation, he explains, lie not in the socialist system (zhidu) itself, but in problems of the institutional structure (tizhi) and elsewhere.

In view of Zhou Yang's special position, the question of how to treat this speech was controversial. Eventually, against Hu Qiaomu's wishes, it was soon published without any changes in the PCC mouthpiece, obviously with the help of Wang Ruoshui and Hu Jiwei (then director of the *People's Daily).* Naturally, there were great repercussions among ideological-cultural circles in China. Its publication also marked the beginning of interference from the top authorities. As its climax, at the 2nd Plenum of the 12th PCC held in October 1983, Deng Xiaoping banned any discussion of alienation from what he said "an overall strategic consideration" and warned that the ideological front-line must not bring about "spiritual pollution". After the Plenum, a campaign to "eliminate spiritual pollution" was carried out. Zhou Yang had to make a "self-criticism", which was reported to the whole country in the *People's Daily* on 6 November 1983. This proved to be a telling blow to Zhou Yang, even heavier than what he had suffered when jailed in Qincheng Prison during the GPCR. Not long thereafter, this veteran cultural figure, much disgraced, much hurt, fell ill, and was hospitalized. He never left his hospital bed until his death on 31 July 1989.

Many in China's ideological-literary circles remember Zhou Yang from his disgrace in the 1983 campaign. If the respect for him shown at the opening ceremony of the 4th Congress of the CWA on 29 December 1984 was their first moving demonstration, by 1986 he was openly defended. Zhou Yang's controversial article was praised as a treatise that comprehensively, systematically, and on the level of world outlook settled accounts with the "Left" ideological-political line that had lasted over thirty years, and also as "an ingenious Marxist work" giving theoretical justification to the various ongoing nationwide reforms. It was considered not only the peak of Zhou Yang's theoretical accomplishments, but also as a peak of works of real theoretical and academic value produced by China's ideological-literary circles in the past ten years.

As Gu Xiang (in 1986 he was deputy director of the Creation Research Office of the CWA) pointed out, this article and others written by Zhou Yang at that time voiced the "heartfelt wishes and aspirations of intellectuals in contemporary China" (Gu Xiang, "Dangdai zhishifenzide xinsheng"—"The Heartfelt Wishes and Aspirations of Intellectuals in Contemporary China", *WHB*, 18 Aug. 1986). The attack on his views on humanism and alienation ultimately turned out to be a monument to him, because he "had once again been tested, had gone through both mental and physical purgatory in his quest for the truth" (ibid.).

It is almost two decades now, but the "tragedy of Zhou Yang", those events taking place in the first few years of the 1980s concerning issues of humanism and alienation, still remain fresh in the people's memories. According to the authors of the 1999 book *Five Voices in Present China,* Zhou's tragedy lay not only in his sincerely admitting his past mistakes but also in his public disdain for autocracy and his democratic ideals (p. 407). "His reflection went beyond the limits of what the establishment could tolerate" (p. 409).

Wang Ruoshui, Zhou's comrade-in-arms during those years, recorded this episode in his 1997 book *Behind Hu Yaobang's Stepdown*. The book's last two lines read:

"Zhou Yang died on 31 July, no tolerance given to him all along.

The 1980s began in China with an appeal for humanism and ended with the 'June 4th' gunshots."

See also "shehuizhuyi yihua lun" (theory of socialist alienation) and "rendaozhuyi lunzheng" (humanism debate).

诸候经济
zhuhou jingji
(duchy economy)

The term "duchy economy" was used in 1990 by Chen Yuan, son of Party elder Chen Yun, who was then vice governor of the People's Bank of China. He Xin, the controversial scholar, was perhaps the first person who pointed out that a "duchy economy" exists in China (see his "Dangdai Zhongguo zhengzhi jingjide shenke weiji yu yuanyin"—"The Deep Crisis of Contemporary Chinese Politics and Economics", *Mingbao Yuekan*, Nov. 1988; and *Zhi Zhongnanhai Miza/Wei Zhongguo Shengbian—Letters only for Zhongnanhai & Arguments to Justify the Chinese Cause*, Hong Kong, Mingjing, Feb. 1997, p. 358).

With the policies of reform and the open door carried out since the early 1980s, China's strict central control system of the past was subjected to a radical change. A local autonomous system has developed to activate the economy. However, this also enables local governments to control local products and prices and to carry out monopoly systems that result in conflicts in economic operations between local areas. This economic system is reminiscent of the ancient Chinese feudal system in which princes owned and dominated feudal states and ran their states independently, hence the term "duchy economy".

Two characteristics of a "duchy economy" are trade blockade and the looting of others' resources. Today there are open "trade wars" between regions in mainland China.

It has been suggested that the problem of the "duchy economy" should be solved by establishing a sound and effective system under the central government. For that purpose, Hu An'gang, a scholar actively advocating "a strengthening of the central government while a weakening of the local authorities" (qiang zhongyang, ruo difang), proposed a "five-unification" (wu ge tongyi) solution: 1. there must be a unified market (tongyi shichang) within the country—protective tariffs by the local authorities on goods imported from other districts should be eliminated; 2. there must be unified taxation and tax rates—special economic zones should enjoy no longer preferential treatment (tequ bu te); 3. there must be a unified policy of "macro-adjustment and macro-control" (hongguan tiaokong) for the whole country; 4. there must be a unified system of social distribution; and 5. there must be unified public service standards (Hu An'gang, "Zhidu chuangxinde shidai"—"An Era for Creating New System", *Lianhe Zaobao*, Singapore, 11 June 1995). See also "guanliao ziben" (bureaucrat-capital) and "jingji gaige" (economic reform).

主观唯心主义
zhuguan weixinzhuyi

(subjective idealism)

See "wenxue zhutixing" (subjectivity of literature) and "xie zhenshi" (writing about reality).

主观战斗精神
zhuguan zhandou jingshen
(subjective fighting spirit)

See "xie zhenshi" (writing about reality).

主权重于人权
zhuquan chongyu renquan
(sovereignty is more important than human rights)

See "renquan wenti" (human rights issue) and "lengzhanhou shidaide xin diguozhuyi" (neo-imperialism in the post-Cold War era).

主权至上
zhuquan zhishang
(sovereignty is supreme)

See "shijie geming zhongxin" (center of world revolution).

主题先行
zhuti xianxing
(the theme takes the lead)

In an early refutation of Mao's idea about literature and art being subordinate to and serving politics, the theory of the "theme taking the lead" was said to have been vigorously advocated by the Gang of Four.

The theory was accused of being "idealist", for it demands that literary and artistic creation should start from a certain ideological-political line. Ignoring objective reality, it takes the relationship between art and the wish and will of a certain class as the first and most important fundamental relationship in literary and artistic creation. This contradicts the "materialist view" that the most important and fundamental relationship is that between art and life. A popular saying in the early years of the post-Mao period was: without truthfulness to life there can be no artistic vitality.

But as experience in literary and artistic creation has shown, many writers claim that very often the "theme" (which has nothing to do with "a certain ideological-political line") does take the lead. See also "wenyi shi jieji douzhengde gongju" (literature and art are tools of class struggle).

主体意识
zhuti yishi
(consciousness of being the subject)

See "ziwo yishi" (consciousness of self).

主体性哲学
zhutixing zhexue
(philosophy of subjectivity)

Soon after the end of the GPCR, Li Zehou published what he considered to be his most important work, *A Critique of the Critical Philosophy (Pipan zhexuede pipan,* Beijing, Renmin, 1979). It was the fruit of his study of the German philosopher Immanuel Kant (1724-1804) during the dark years of the GPCR. In it he tried to promote man's subjectivity (zhutixing) with the thought of the enlightenment since Kant. Then he published three successive books on Chinese thought in ancient, recent, and modern times in 1984, 1986 and 1988 respectively based on his "philosophy of subjectivity" to re-examine the history of Chinese thought. For a long time during the Chinese Communist regime, the dominant philosophy was dialectical materialism, whose basic thesis was the question of which is primary, matter (being) or spirit (consciousness). Now Li's "philosophy of subjectivity" brought the basic thesis of philosophy back to man, to man's fate, the meaning of life, and other relevant issues.

In the culture craze, a national fervor took place during the latter half of the 1980s, during which Li Zehou's influence in literary and art circles was great. For instance, inspired by his "philosophy of subjectivity" Liu Zaifu suggested in July 1985 that a research system of literary theory and literary history be built with "man" as the center of thinking, and he then further devised his theory of the "subjectivity of literature" (wenxue zhutixing) in November 1985.

But an emphasis on man's subjectivity, on man's dignity and value, on the thesis that man is the goal and the center, logically would weaken the "Party spirit" (dangxing), the demand of "being an obedient tool", the servility (nuxing), and furthermore the philosophical foundation of the entire Communist regime. No wonder after the June 4th Incident of 1989, the "philosophy of subjectivity" became one of the major targets for attack. However, according to Li Zehou, Marx's philosophy was in fact a philosophy of subjectivity. What those Party critics attacked was the quintessence of a crucial Marxist point *(Farewell to Revolution: Looking Back upon China of the Twentieth Century*, pp. 186-87). See also "wenxue zhutixing" (subjectivity of literature).

抓革命，促生产
zhua geming, cu shengchan
(take charge of the revolution, promote production)

This was formally raised in the "PCC Decision on the GPCR" passed on 8 August 1966 at the 11th Plenum of the 8th PCC. As the authorities explained, people must first take charge of the GPCR, and regard this as the motive force to enhance their political consciousness. Once they have enhanced their political consciousness, they can develop their activity and creativity and, therefore, promote production. This is what is called "turning spiritual strength into material strength" (jingshen bian wuzhi). Most post-Mao critics find this thesis untenable—a most forceful argument is that the GPCR led China's national economy to the verge of bankruptcy. Neo-Leftists, however, think otherwise. They argue that the failure of the GPCR was caused by many objective and subjective factors at that time, and it did not necessarily prove the incorrectness of the idea of "taking charge of the revolution to promote production". This idea of Mao, they say, truly embodies the socialist spirit. See also "wen'ge" (Cultural Revolution) and "xinzuopai" (neo-Leftists).

抓纲治国
zhua gang zhi guo
(grasping the key link to run the country)

This was the political program of Hua Guofeng, then concurrently holding three top posts of CCP chairman, PRC premier, and CMC chairman.

The term first appeared in the 1977 New Year's Day joint editorial of the *People's Daily, Red Flag,* and the *Liberation Army Daily,* "Advancing on the Crest of the Victory" ("Chengsheng qianjin"). It became the most widespread political slogan during the short period that Hua Guofeng was leader. What it meant was "grasping the key link of class struggle and bringing about great order across the land". At that time, all Chinese detested and rejected the chaotic situation left over by the GPCR and they naturally wished to have a "wise leader" who could bring about great order across the land. But this definitely could not be achieved by "taking class struggle as the key link", the long-standing principle during the Mao period. Unfortunately, Hua still insisted on Mao's principles and was obsessed by his "two whatevers" view, thus missing his opportunity. Very soon, therefore, in the power struggle following Mao's death Hua was sidelined, as Deng Xiaoping rose to the top. See also "yingming lingxiu" (wise leader).

抓两头，带中间
zhua liangtou, dai zhongjian
(grasp the two ends to bring along the middle)

The "two ends" refer to the advanced and the backward. In any situation there are these two ends, but the majority is in the middle. If a leader keeps watch over the most advanced and the most backward, he will bring along the majority in the middle. Another method as described in Mao's "Sixty Articles of Working Methods (Draft)" ("Gongzuo fangfa liushi tiao cao'an") is "to grasp the intermediate link to bring forward the two ends" (zhua zhongjian, cu liangtou). It is said that those in the middle embrace the two possibilities of being transformed to the advanced or to the backward. If the majority in the middle is grasped, it will be possible to make the advanced become even more advanced and the backward will catch up with the advanced. These were regarded as two dialectical methods of leadership that had been proved effective in practice.

抓中间，促两头
zhua zhongjian, cu liangtou
(grasp the intermediate link to bring forward the two ends)

See "zhua liangtou, dai zhongjian" (grasp the two ends to bring along the middle).

抓住百年不遇的历史机遇
zhuazhu bainian buyude lishi jiyu
(firmly seize the historical opportunity once in a century)

See "heping yu fazhan shi dangjin shijiede liang da zhuti" (peace and development are the two themes of today's world).

专职党务工作人员
zhuanzhi dangwu gongzuo renyuan
(full-time working personnel for Party affairs)

See "dangde lingdao" (Party leadership).

转型期
zhuanxingqi
(mode transition period)

See "meiyou liangxinde jingjixue" (no heart economics) and "jingji gaige" (economic reform).

转移说
zhuanyi shuo
("transfer" theory)

See "wenxue guilu lunzheng" (1986 debate on the law of literature).

涿州会议
Zhuozhou huiyi
(Zhuozhou conference)

From 6 to 12 April 1987, in the thick of the campaign against "bourgeois liberalization", an extraordinary forum, under the guise of soliciting contributions, was held in Zhuozhou city, Hebei province, sponsored by the literary departments of *Red Flag* and *Guangming Daily* and the editorial board of *Literary Theory and Criticism* (a newly established journal with Chen Yong as its editor-in-chief). The forum's keynote speakers were He Jingzhi and Xiong Fu. Lin Mohan, Liu Baiyu, Yao Xueyin, and Chen Yong also delivered speeches. They heralded the coming of what they called an "excellent situation" (dahao xingshi). As He Jingzhi put it, this was "the first time in the past several years that the flood of bourgeois liberalization had genuinely been checked". Or, as Xiong Fu described it, "a new macroclimate has appeared to oppose resolutely, healthily, and constantly the erroneous trend (towards bourgeois liberalization)". They called on their followers to "speak up without fear of being labeled as "ultra-Leftists" or as "elements keen on eliminating spiritual pollution."

Their activities were soon checked by Zhao Ziyang, CCP acting general secretary, and his followers. After Zhao was overthrown following the June 4th Incident of 1989, the Zhuozhou conference was cited as a glorious page in the struggle against "bourgeois liberalization". See also "ziyouhua" (liberalization).

资本主义复辟
zibenzhuyi fubi
(capitalist restoration)

See "dangde jiben luxian" (the Party's basic line) and "xiuzhengzhuyi" (revisionism).

资本主义改革观
zibenzhuyi gaigeguan

(capitalist view about reform)

See "xin shehuizhuyi guan" (new socialist view).

资本主义积累
zibenzhuyi jilei
(capitalist accumulation)

See "yuanshi jilei" (previous accumulation).

资本主义全球化
zibenzhuyi quanqiuhua
(capitalist globalization)

See "quanqiuhua" (globalization).

资本主义尾巴
zibenzhuyi weiba
(tails of capitalism)

See "yidaoqie" (a single cut).

资本主义阵营
zibenzhuyi zhenying
(capitalist camp)

See "lengzhanhou shidaide xin diguozhuyi" (neo-imperialism in the post-Cold War era) and "yibiandao" (lean to one side).

资产阶级博爱
zichanjieji bo'ai
(bourgeois universal love)

See "renxing lun" (theory of human nature) and "zhengzhi biaoqian" (political labels).

资产阶级法权
zichanjieji faquan
(bourgeois rights)

"Bourgeois rights" refers to certain citizens' rights in the means of distribution generated in capitalist private ownership, which are equal in form but unequal in fact. Previously existing in the overthrown capitalist regime, they still exist in the new socialist regime. Hence the issue of "bourgeois rights". Zhang Chunqiao, then director of the Propaganda Department of the CCP Shanghai Municipal Committee, first attracted Mao's attention in an article on this issue. Entitled "Breaking with the Idea of Bourgeois Rights" ("Pochu zichanjiejide faquan sixiang"), it was published on 15 September 1958 in the 6th issue of *Jiefang (Liberation)*, a newly established theoretical organ of the Shanghai Party Committee. Mao highly appreciated it, and had it reprinted in the *People's Daily* on 13 October 1958, with a favorable "Editor's Note" that he had personally written. Zhang's article, as its title indicated, advocated the abolition of "bourgeois rights" and the establishment of a "supply system" (gonggeizhi), a system of payment-in-kind similar to that practiced in the CCP-led army and other organizations from the Red Army period up to 1954.

In a nationwide movement to study the theory of the proletarian dictatorship starting in February 1975, "bourgeois rights" was a central topic. Zhang Chunqiao, now a powerful CCP Politburo Standing Committee member, published his much praised article "On Exercising an All-round Dictatorship over the Bourgeoisie" ("Lun dui zichanjiejide quanmian zhuanzheng", *HQ,* Apr. 1975). Yao Wenyuan also discussed this issue in his article "On the Social Foundation of the Lin Biao Clique" ("Lun Lin Biao jituande shehui jichu", *HQ,* Mar. 1975; *RMRB,* 1 Mar. 1975). They quoted a series of instructions recently given by Mao on restraining "bourgeois rights". One of them was: "Our country at present practices a commodity system, and the wage system is unequal too, there being the eight-grade wage system, etc. These can only be restrained under the dictatorship of the proletariat. It would be quite easy for people like Lin Biao to promote a capitalist system if they were to come to power."

The issue of "bourgeois rights" was also involved in the alienation discussion of the early 1980s. The existence of "bourgeois rights" was traced as one of the reasons why alienation could be generated under the condition of socialism. Socialist society, "alienation critics" explained, is the rudimentary stage of communism and inevitably still has some vestiges of the capitalist society from which it was born. In this stage, there exist commodity production, division of labor in society, and the three major distinctions between workers and peasants, between cities and the countryside, and between manual and mental labor. In the means of distribution, there are also bourgeois rights. All these provide soil for seeds of alienation. See also "shehuizhuyi yihualun" (theory of socialist alienation) and "wuchanjieji zhuanzheng" (dictatorship of the proletariat).

资产阶级反动路线
zichanjieji fandong luxian
(bourgeois reactionary line)

See "pipan zichanjieji fandong luxian" (criticism of the bourgeois reactionary line).

资产阶级反动学术权威
zichanjieji fandong xueshu quanwei
(reactionary bourgeois academic authorities)

See "dou pi gai" (struggle, criticism, and reform), "zhengzhi biaoqian" (political labels), and "zhishifenzi wenti" (issue of intellectuals).

资产阶级个人主义
zichanjieji gerenzhuyi
(bourgeois individualism)

See "ziyouzhuyi" (liberalism), "baizhuan" (white and expert), and "zhengzhi biaoqian" (political labels).

资产阶级个人主义幸福观
zichanjieji gerenzhuyi xingfuguan

(bourgeois individualistic view of happiness)

See "ziyouzhuyi" (liberalism), "renxing lun" (theory of human nature), and "zhengzhi biaoqian" (political labels).

资产阶级极端个人主义价值观
zichanjieji jiduan gerenzhuyi jiazhiguan
(bourgeois ultra-individualist view of value)

See "ziyouzhuyi" (liberalism) and "zhengzhi biaoqian" (political labels).

资产阶级就在共产党内
zichanjieji jiuzai gongchandangnei
(the bourgeoisie is right in the Communist Party)

From October 1975 to January 1976, Mao Zedong criticized Deng Xiaoping on a number of occasions, which led to the campaign to counter the so-called "Right deviationist trend to reverse correct verdicts" with Deng as the number one target. On 5 February 1976, at a meeting convened by the Party Center to launch the campaign, a new statement by Mao was released: "You're making the socialist revolution, and yet you don't know where the bourgeoisie is. It is right in the Communist Party—those in power taking the capitalist road. The capitalist-roaders are still on the capitalist road."

Mao's "supreme directive" was considered to be of great significance in the development of Marxist theory. Maoists claimed, in light of it, that the bourgeoisie had three forms in history: following the "liberal bourgeoisie" and the "monopoly bourgeoisie", the bourgeoisie within a proletarian party was its "last form emerging in the process during which the whole class heads towards its doom". In an article entitled "An Important Fighting Task" ("Yi xiang zhongyaode zhandao renwu") that the followers of the Gang of Four in the Ministry of Culture had commissioned just before their downfall, the "supreme directive" was highly praised as the theoretical basis for "writing about the struggle against capitalist-roaders". The Maoists suggested, accordingly, an "important fighting task" for Chinese writers—to analyse "how the new-born bourgeoisie, the bourgeoisie within the Party in particular, come into being, develop, and die", or in other words, to reflect on how "revolutionary people" wage a struggle against "capitalist-roaders". (They dared not publish the article even after revising the manuscript three times with instructions from Yao Wenyuan, because it was too straightforward.)

Indeed, the thesis that "the bourgeoisie is right in the Communist Party" served as an argument for Mao's theory of "continuing the revolution under the dictatorship of the proletariat". But at that time, many people, including Mao's supporters, still found it hard to believe that within the CCP, the vanguard of the proletariat, there could be a bourgeois class. Now, after twenty years, the old-line Maoists and the neo-Leftists claim that Mao's prediction was correct. Many Party secretaries have become company directors, making huge profits from the "power economy" (quanli jingji). See also "zou zibenzhuyi daolu dangquanpai" (those in power taking the capitalist road) and "wen'ge" (Cultural Revolution).

资产阶级民族主义
zichanjieji minzuzhuyi
(bourgeois nationalism)

See "minzuzhuyi" (nationalism) and "shijie geming" (world revolution).

资产阶级派性
zichanjieji paixing
(bourgeois factionalism)

See "quanmian neizhan" (full-scale civil war) and "zhengzhi biaoqian" (political labels).

资产阶级权利
zichanjieji quanli
(bourgeois rights)

For a time, "bourgeois rights" was translated as "zichanjieji quanli" and not as "zichanjieji faquan" because the term "faquan", which means "legal rights" or "rights obtained by law", was considered inappropriate. See "zichanjieji faquan" (bourgeois rights).

资产阶级人道主义
zichanjieji rendaozhuyi
(bourgeois humanism)

See "rendaozhuyi lunzheng" (humanism debate), "renxing lun" (theory of human nature), and "zhengzhi biaoqian" (political labels).

资产阶级人道主义社会观
zichanjieji rendaozhuyi shehuiguan
(bourgeois humanistic outlook on society)

This was a label used in China's political-literary campaigns. In the 1983 campaign to eliminate "spiritual pollution", for instance, a number of works were accused of being preoccupied with a bourgeois humanistic outlook on society, when trying to criticize the ten years of turbulence and to find new ideals for life and society. There were two "representative" works. One was "On the Same Horizon" ("Zai tongyi dipingxianshang", *Shouhuo*, 6, 1981, reprinted in *XXWY*, 4, pp. 7-65), a novelette by Zhang Xinxin, a young woman writer. The author was reproached for sympathizing with the two protagonists. Even worse, the two characters and their philosophy of life were said to be a reflection of the author's social outlook—the "abnormal" characters were the products of her "abnormal" social outlook. Zhang was thus accused of preaching "social Darwinism" (a popular sociological theory of the nineteenth century, regarded as "vulgar evolutionism", for it applies Darwin's "struggle for existence" principle to human society). The second was Dai Houying's novel *Humanity!*, a work that had already been attacked for several years. It was said that in answering the question of how to treat socialist reality in today's China, unlike "On the Same Horizon" which presented the "struggle for existence", *Humanity!* urged its readers "to love one another", a maxim that was nothing but outmoded "crazy talk". Though different, both answers were accused of promoting a bourgeois outlook and social ideals, and being divorced from the socialist orbit (see Zhang Ren and Yang Zhijie, "Cong 'A, ren....' dao *Ren a, ren!:* ping jinjinian wenxue chuangzuozhongde renxing, rendaozhuyi wenti"—"On human nature and humanism in recent years' literary works", *WXPL,* 2:6, 1984).

资产阶级人道主义的唯心史观
zichanjieji rendaozhuyide weixinshiguan
(historical idealism of bourgeois humanism)

See"rendaozhuyide liang ge hanyi" (two meanings of humanism) and "zhengzhi biaoqian" (political labels).

资产阶级人情味
zichanjieji renqingwei
(bourgeois human touch)

See "renxing lun" (theory of human nature) and "zhengzhi biaoqian" (political labels).

资产阶级伤感主义
zichanjieji shangganzhuyi
(bourgeois sentimentalism)

See "renxing lun" (theory of human nature) and "zhengzhi biaoqian" (political labels).

资产阶级温情主义
zichanjieji wenqingzhuyi
(bourgeois undue leniency)

A label often used in the political-literary campaigns of the Mao period. In considering an issue, sentimentalists would subject principle to their own emotions, and therefore could not maintain the firm standpoint of the masses or the interests of the revolution. In the name of proletarian political interests, as seen in those campaigns, emotive yearnings or expressions of respect and love for family members, relatives, or friends might be denounced as "bourgeois undue leniency". People were encouraged or even forced to attack one another, even parents and children, husbands and wives, or teachers and students. As post-Mao critics pointed out, this practice caused a perversion of normal flesh-and-blood relations and a degeneration of public morality. See also "renxing lun" (theory of human nature) and "jieji douzheng" (class struggle).

资产阶级文艺观
zichanjieji wenyiguan
(bourgeois view of literature and art)

A label often used in the political-literary campaigns during the Mao period. See "renxing lun" (theory of human nature).

资产阶级现代主义诗歌宣言
zichanjieji xiandaizhuyi shige xuanyan
(manifesto of bourgeois modernist poetry)

See "menglongshi lilunde san ci jueqi" ("three rises" in the theory of misty poetry).

资产阶级右派分子
zichanjieji youpai fenzi
(bourgeois Rightists)

This can also be abbreviated as "Rightists" ("youpai" or "youpai fenzi"). In the 1957 anti-Rightist campaign, which lasted about one year, more than 550,000 "bourgeois Rightists" were named, 11 percent of the five million intellectuals in the whole country at the time. By 1980 almost all of the former "Rightists" had been rehabilitated. Ironically, ex-Rightist Zhu Rongji (convicted in April 1958 and rehabilitated in September 1978) was elected premier of the PRC State Council at the March 1998 NPC meeting. Wang Meng, another ex-Rightist, became minister of culture in 1986. See "fan youpai yundong" (anti-Rightist campaign).

资产阶级在历史上的三种形态
zichanjieji zai lishishangde sanzhong xingtai
(three forms of the bourgeoisie in history)

See "zichanjieji jiuzai gongchandangnei" (the bourgeoisie is right in the Communist Party).

资产阶级知识分子
zichanjieji zhishifenzi
(bourgeois intellectuals)

See "zhishifenzi wenti" (issue of intellectuals).

资产阶级专政
zichanjieji zhuanzheng
(bourgeois dictatorship)

See "jiyao" ("Summary") and "wuchanjieji zhuanzheng" (dictatorship of the proletariat).

资产阶级自由化
zichanjieji ziyouhua
(bourgeois liberalization)

See "ziyouhua" (liberalization).

自来红
zi lai hong
(born red)

See "meiyou zi lai hong; zhiyou gaizao hong" (no one is born red; one becomes red only through ideological remolding).

自发势力
zifa shili
(spontaneous force)

This refers to the "blind capitalist tendency" among peasants, a tendency which has the potential of developing into capitalism. Any speculative and exploitative activities, which include "carrying out business undertakings", "giving loans", and "hoarding grain", were called a "spontaneous force". The term often appeared in Party documents during the Mao period, but it is obviously outdated in today's China.

自毁长城
zihui changcheng
(self-destruction of the Great Wall)

See "changcheng" (Great Wall, i.e., the PLA).

自力更生
zili gengsheng
(self-reliance)

Mao raised the slogan of "self-reliance" as early as 1945. He told his Party: "We stand for self-reliance. We hope for foreign aid but cannot be dependent on it; we depend on our own efforts, on the creative power of the whole army and the entire people" ("We Must Learn to Do Economic Work, January 10, 1945", *SWM,* 3, p. 241). On another occasion, Mao said: "On what basis should our policy rest? It should rest on our own strength, and that means regeneration through one's own efforts. We are not alone; all the countries and people in the world opposed to imperialism are our friends. Nevertheless, we stress regeneration through our own efforts. Relying on the forces we ourselves organize, we can defeat all Chinese and foreign reactionaries" ("The Situation and Our Policy After the Victory in the War of Resistance Against Japan, August 13, 1945", *SWM,* 4, p. 20). To strengthen the effect of his teaching, Mao told about an ancient Chinese fable called "The Foolish Old Man Who Removed the Mountains" ("The Foolish Old Man Who Removed the Mountains, June 11, 1945", *SWM,* 3, p. 322).

In 1960, China was isolated after the CCP fell out with the CPSU and the Soviet Union canceled all aid to China and recalled its experts. This severe blow came when China was facing unprecedented economic setbacks caused by the failure of Mao's "Great Leap Forward". In view of that situation, the Party vigorously propagandized a spirit of self-reliance, spreading the two phrases—"to be self-reliant" and "to struggle arduously" (jianku fendou) throughout the country. The Dazhai production brigade and the Daqing oil enterprise were designated by Mao as two "brilliant examples" in agriculture and industry respectively following the slogan "Be self-reliant, struggle arduously". Another important slogan was: "Maintain independence and keep the initiative in our own hands" (duli zizhu), which justified the CCP's defiance to the CPSU, the former "laodage" (elder brother), and thc ending of the "leaning to one side" policy.

According to the "Resolution on Certain Questions in the History of Our Party since the Founding of the PRC" passed on 27 June 1981 at the 6th Plenum of the 11th PCC, the "living soul" of Mao Zedong Thought was defined as its stand, viewpoint, and method, and "independence and self-reliance" were one of the three basic principles embodying their essence. (The other two principles were the "mass line" and "seeking truth from facts"). It is emphasized today that independence and self-reliance do not mean a "closed-door policy" (biguan zhengce), that is, "closing the country to international intercourse" (biguan zi shou). As Deng pointed out, "Today's world is an open world." China should link its economy with the international markets and world economy—its development is inseparable from the world. See also "yibiandao" (lean to one side), "minzuzhuyi" (nationalism), and "xiandaide shijie shi kaifangde shijie" (today's world is an open world).

自力更生，艰苦奋斗
zili gengsheng, jianku fendou
(be self-reliant and struggle arduously)

See "zili gengsheng" (self-reliance).

自为阶级
ziwei jieji
(class for itself)

See "jieji douzheng" (class struggle).

自我
ziwo
(subjective ego)

See "ziwo biaoxian" (expression of the subjective ego) and "zuojia zhutixing" (writer's subjectivity).

自我表现
ziwo biaoxian
(expression of the subjective ego)

One of the contributions of "misty poetry" (menglongshi) was that the "subjective ego" and an "expression of the subjective ego" could be openly and positively discussed among China's literary and art circles.

In 1980, when speaking of the established literature and art of the past that had gone under the name of socialist realism, the young poet Gu Cheng pointed out:

"The old kind of literature and art, poetry in particular, has always propagandized a non-self 'I', a 'I' that is self-denying and self-destructive. Before something that is claimed to be sacred, that 'I' is reduced to a grain of sand, a pebble, a cog, or a screw. In short, it is never a human being, a human being who can think, doubt, and possess all passions and desires. If you must say that it is a man, it is nothing more than a robot, a robot 'I'. This kind of 'I' may have a religious beauty of self-sacrifice, but, having eradicated his most concrete, individual being, he himself is bound to lose control and take the road of destruction" ("Qing tingting womende shengyin—qingnian shiren bitan"—"Please Listen to Us: Young Poets' Discussions", *Shi tansuo*, 1, Dec. 1980, reprinted in Bi Hua and Yang Ling, eds., *Jueqide shiqun*; Hong Kong, Dangdai Wenxue Yanjiushe, 1984, p. 143).

In Gu Cheng's opinion, what was considered incomprehensible was not the form, but mainly the content, of their poems, and this should be attributed to the diversity of ideological bases and pursuits. The solution to this problem, therefore, lay not inside, but outside, the poems. Then what was the real content of their poems? What was their newness? Gu Cheng said that it was none other than the emergence of a "subjective ego", a "subjective ego" that was characteristic of contemporary youth. In his article "A Body of Rising Poetry", Xu Jingya also pointed out that they advocate a subjective ego with a modern character and they look down upon the beauty embodied in religious self-abnegation as seen in traditional poetry. They firmly believe in human rights, human free will, and all just demands of a human being. The subjective ego in their poems possesses a strong sense of history and nation, and is characterized by universal human nature (Xu Jingya, *Dangdai Wenyi Sichao,* 1:18, 1983).

Sun Shaozhen, a critic supporting the "misty school", studied the "subjective ego" and the "expression of the subjective ego". As he noted in his 1981 article "A New Aesthetic Principle Is Rising" ("Xinde meixue yuanze zai jueqi", *SK,* 3:55-58, 1981), if the traditional aesthetic principle lays greater stress on the unanimity between sociology and aesthetics, then the innovators of the "misty school" lay more emphasis on their differences. He further pointed out that it would be superficial if one regarded it only as a divergence of two aesthetic principles. Essentially, he asserted, it is one between two criteria of human value. Under the pen of the young explorers, the criterion of human value has changed tremendously: No longer does it entirely depend on social-political criterion. In fact, though social-political ideas influence and, under certain conditions, even determine certain human ideologies and feelings, they cannot replace the latter, for the two have different connotations and are subject to different laws. The goal of politics, for instance, is unification, while human feeling (which is the goal of art) is pluralistic. There exists a contradiction between the utilitarianism of politics and the somewhat non-utilitarian nature of human feelings.

Consequently, as Sun pointed out, the young innovators were determined to bridge the man-made chasm between the "conveyance of the people's emotions" (shu renmin zhi qing) and the "expression of the subjective ego"—for a long time in the past, the former was highly praised, while the latter was denounced as rebelling against orthodoxy in poetic theory. In the innovators' opinion, since it is man as an individual who creates society, it is not right to deny the individual's interests for the sake of society; moreover, since it is man who creates society's spiritual civilization, then the spirit of the age, or of society, should not be counterposed as a force hostile to an individual's spirit. Therefore, the history of man's "alienation" should be re-examined, and the individual should enjoy a higher status in society. In addition, from the perspective of sociology, social value cannot be separated from the individual's spiritual value: what is important to the psyches of many individuals is also important to society and politics; it cannot be purely decided by temporary political demands. Sun insisted that when an individual's status rises in society and his rights are gradually restored; and when society, class, and the age gradually no longer function as a ruling force over the individual, then an individual's feeling in poetry, his sorrow and happiness, his inner world, will naturally come to have a greater value. Human nature's resuscitation in society will certainly lead to its resuscitation in art, and this is a "sign of the enhancement of social civilization", Sun declared (ibid.).

However, other critics disagreed. At the Chongqing Forum on Poetry (held in Chongqing city, Sichuan province, from 4 to 9 October 1983), Zheng Bonong, a Party critic, attacked the "rise" theory, characterized by its two principles of an "expression of the subjective ego" and "anti-rationalism" (fan lixing), of advocating "the world outlook and art perspective of modernism in the West". An "expression of the subjective ego", Zheng noted, was raised as a slogan "antagonistic to the expression of life and the people" and was "a sort of barefaced solipsist philosophy" (Zheng Bonong, "Zai 'jueqi'de shenglang mianqian: dui yi zhong wenyi sichaode pouxi"—"An Analysis of a Literary Trend", *SK,* 12:36-45, 1983). As Ke Yan, then CWA secretary, saw it, the "rise" theorists placed the subjective ego above "the motherland, the people, and even the universe", and, posing as heroes against the "god-making movement" (zao shen yundong) of the past, they eventually tried to "deify themselves in the disguise of opposing the deification of others" (Ke Yan, "Guanyu shide duihua"—"A Talk about Poetry", *SK,* 12:46-56, 62, 1983).

Significantly, having undergone the tests of the 1981-83 drives against "bourgeois liberalization" and "spiritual pollution", the concept of the "expression of the subjective ego" became all the more an attractive topic for research among China's literary and art circles. In July 1985, for instance, Sun Shaozhen published a more theoretical article, "On 'Three-dimensional' Images and Freedom in the Depth of a Writer's Heart" ("Xingxiangde sanwei jiegou he zuojiade neizai ziyou", *WXPL,* 4:10-25, 1985), defending his much-attacked view on this issue. Since the physiological activity of the human brain is still a "black box", Sun says, it is inevitable that a writer will probe others' psychological activities by self-exploration. A writer's exploration of life, therefore, will definitely be branded as his subjective ego. Expressions of the subjective ego, according to Sun, are perhaps an instinct, and, more importantly, a law governing artistic creation. Furthermore, Sun confirms the phenomenon noted by Sigmund Freud that by self-observation a writer tends to split his subjective ego into many part-egos and to personify the conflicting currents of his own mental life in several heroes (Sigmund Freud, "Creative Writer and Day-dreaming" in *The Complete Psychological Works of Sigmund Freud,* v. 9, London, Hogarth Press, 1959, p. 150).

The essence of life as presented through artistic images, therefore, does not entirely belong to life itself; simultaneously, it is also an expression of the essence of the writer's subjective ego. Of course, Sun adds, a writer cannot unconditionally distribute his own essence to his protagonists (in this sense, Freud's view is inaccurate). If no due consideration is given to the traits of the object, egocentricity will appear, and this will lead to a distorted art. If the opposite takes place, that is, if the subjective ego is suppressed, the two-dimensional structure of the image's embryo will likewise be damaged. "The dishonesty of the writer's subjective ego will certainly lead to the falsehood of the artistic images he has produced" (Sun Shaozhen, *WXPL,* 4:20, 1985).

By the mid-1980s, the concept of an "expression of the subjective ego" was quite accepted among China's literary and art circles as a law of artistic creation. For example, Yang Kuanghan, a critic who had fiercely attacked Xu Jingya, when making a general review of trends in poetic aesthetics in the "new period" in 1986, tried to adopt a fair attitude towards the "expression of the subjective ego" as seen in the works of "excellent young poets" such as Shu Ting, Bei Dao, and Jiang He. Eventually he agreed: "The Muses always seek after artistic conceptions in the world through the window of the poet's soul. A poet cannot provide evidence of essential strength in poetry if he fails to reveal, and further condense and sublimate, the total depth, the total content, the total emotions and desires, and the total infinitude of his individual inner world" (Yang Kuanghan, "Zhongguo xinshiqide shimei liuxiang"—"Trend of Poetic-Aesthetics in the New Period in China", *WXPL,* 3:19, 1986).

Indeed, as pointed out by speakers at the National Forum on the Theory of the New Poetry (held in Lanzhou from 26 to 30 August 1986), the most significant breakthrough in poetic theory for the last ten years was the re-affirmation of the "subjectivity of poetry", of the "self-actualization sought by poets through artistic creation". The essential nature, or the greatest pursuit, of human beings is to achieve free development, or self-actualization. Among the various ways to reach this self-actualization, there is the way of poetry, a sort of creative labor innate in human nature. Moreover, many participants at the Forum found this to be consistent with Marxism. The fundamental aim of Marxism, they said, is man's free development and self-actualization; what is called Communist society, in terms of Marx and Engels, is a kind of "association" where the free development of each is the premise of all. They claimed thus: "In this sense, Marxism might as well be poetic" *(XHWZ,* 2:140, 1987). Significantly, Marxism was used to promote modernist tendencies in poetry. As to the "misty school" itself, perhaps, it shared Liu Zaifu's view in this regard. When discussing misty poetry in his long 1988 essay about the spirit and direction of Chinese literature over the past ten years, Liu enthusiastically pointed out: "The rise of this New Group with their new set of predominant images, and the concomitant rise of the new aesthetic principles contained in their works, was a manifestation of a general awakening of basic human freedoms" (Liu Zaifu, "Jinshiniande Zhongguo wenxue jingshen he wenxue daolu"—"Chinese Literature in the Past Ten Years: Spirit and Direction", *RMWX,* 2:126, 1988; trans. by Stephen Fleming in *CL,* 3:171, Autumn 1989).

Nevertheless, while some theorists stressed "interior freedom" (neizai ziyou) and the "expression of the subjective ego" in artistic creation, and hailed what they deemed to be "the most significant breakthrough in poetic theory", others were more practical and sober. For example, fiction writer Dai Houying confessed in an article expounding on her literary views that, consciously or not, she still had to "disguise herself" when writing because of subjective and objective factors of various kinds. Therefore, she said, "Whenever I find people worried about writers 'expressing their subjective ego', I cannot help but laughing inside. They are just entertaining imaginary fears, and show an inadequate understanding of China and Chinese writers. The time, in fact, has not yet come to express the subjective ego sincerely and frankly. To reach that realm requires rigorous self-struggle" ("Jielu zai renjing, woshou xie woxin"—"I Built My Hut in a Zone of Human Habitation; I Write My Ideas and Feelings with My Hands", *WXPL,* 1:62, 1986). See also "chuangzuo ziyou" (creative freedom).

自我改造
ziwo gaizao
(self-remolding)

"Self-remolding" was a slogan during the Mao period. Everyone was required by the Party to carry out a self-remolding of their original ways of thinking and lives in accordance with Mao Zedong Thought and Marxism-Leninism. This was an especially stern and never-ending political task for China's intellectuals. See "sixiang gaizao" (ideological remolding).

自我怀疑
ziwo huaiyi
(self-doubt)

See "sixiang gaizao" (ideological remolding).

自我扩张
ziwo kuozhang
(self-expansion)

See "xie zhenshi" (writing about reality).

自我实现
ziwo shixian

(self-actualization)

A term first used by A. Maslow (1908-70), an American humanist psychologist. According to Maslow, there are five levels of basic human needs—physiological needs, the need for safety, the need for love, affection, and belongingness, the need for esteem, and the need for self-actualization (see his *Motivation and Personality*, Harper & Row, 1954, pp. 80-92). When first introduced to mainland China in the early 1980s, Maslow's view was regarded as heresy by the authorities. To many writers, artists, and literary critics, however, "self-actualization" was completely acceptable. Wang Ruoshui bravely defended it. Today "self-actualization" is the outlook on life of many young people. See "rendaozhuyide liang ge hanyi" (two meanings of humanism) and "rende jiazhi" (human value).

自我意识
ziwo yishi
(consciousness of self)

In the 1980s, the "consciousness of self", or the "consciousness as being the subject" (zhuti shizhi), was a major topic in literary studies. Many critics and writers regarded the "consciousness of self" as the highest form of imaginative thinking. They advocated an aesthetic view that held that the culmination of beauty could not be reached until the rational was subordinated to self-intuition. In the 1987 campaign against "bourgeois liberalization", this view was attacked as a negative phenomenon among ideological-literary circles. See also "xinde meixue yuanze zai jueqi" (a new aesthetic principle is rising), "yishu jieshouzhede zhutixing" (subjectivity of art receptor), and "ziyouzhuyi" (liberalism).

自我异化
ziwo yihua
(self-alienation)

See "yihua wenxue" (alienated literature; literature of alienation).

自省
zixing
(self-reflection)

See "zuojia zhutixing" (writer's subjectivity) and "sixiang gaizao" (ideological remolding).

自由恐惧症
ziyou kongjuzheng
(freedom-fearing disease)

See "chuangzuo ziyou" (creative freedom).

自由先于民主
ziyou xianyu minzhu
(freedom precedes democracy)

See "xin quanweizhuyi lunzheng" (neo-authoritarianism debate).

自由撰稿人
ziyou zhuan'gaoren
(freelance)

This concept in today's China refers to those not belonging to a certain "unit" (danwei), without a fixed salary, and earning their living mainly by writing.

For several decades after the New Culture Movement of the early twentieth century, freelance writers were active in China's cultural arena, many of whom became prominent writers, scholars, and publishers. Not long after the 1949 Communist takeover, privately operated cultural undertakings, including media and publishing, were banned. All people of letters, or cultural workers as they were then generally called, had to work at a certain "unit" controlled by the government. Since the Yan'an period of the 1940s, Mao was determined to remold China's intellectuals. After seizing state power, he finally obtained an effective social organizational form to deal with them.

Today, however, with the emergence of a market economy, even newspapers, magazines, and publishing houses, formerly ideological tools in service of politics, have gradually (though not completely) become economic elements directed by the market. As a result, writers are judged not according to what they are but by how much they are needed by the market. Once people of letters become aware of their market value, "units" are no longer so important. They now are free to engage in freelance work. (The market is vast. For example, there are more than two thousand newspapers in China today.)

This is evidence of China's intellectuals beginning to possess an independent consciousness, reinforced by the mottos: my value is determined by myself; my existence needs my proof; my fate should be in my hands; my future depends on my own efforts. See also "xinwen ziyou wenti" (issue of press freedom) and "jingji gaige" (economic reform).

自由的兩种含义
ziyoude liang zhong hanyi
(two meanings of freedom)

See "chuangzuo ziyou" (creative freedom).

自由化
ziyouhua
(liberalization)

The term "liberalization" was first used by Western journalists in the 1950s to describe the political change in the Soviet Union after the death of Stalin, in which there was increased freedom in literary-ideological circles and in social life as a whole. Perhaps because of this suspicious origin it was regarded as a derogatory term, equivalent to anti-Party and anti-socialism. This is why in China liberalization is always modified by the word "bourgeois". During the Mao period it was almost non-existent.

However, after the end of the GPCR, many Chinese became interested in liberalization, which displayed itself in cycles of relaxation and suppression. The first high tide was the "Beijing Spring". In the spirit of the April 5th Movement of 1976, a pro-democracy and human rights movement began spontaneously in Beijing in September 1978. Within the establishment, pro-democratic leanings also became an ideological trend.

This greatly worried Party ideologues such as Deng Liqun and Hu Qiaomu, and Party elders such as Chen Yun. Deng Xiaoping shared their opinions and put forth his "four cardinal principles" in March 1979. In his speech at the Central Work Conference on 25 December 1980, Deng raised the concept of "bourgeois liberalization" (zichanjieji ziyouhua). In August 1981, he launched the first "anti-bourgeois liberalization" campaign. At the forum on "problems arising on the nation's ideological front" convened in the same month by the PCC Propaganda Department, Hu Qiaomu delivered a speech entitled "Some Current Problems on the Ideological Front", which became the guiding document for the campaign. For the first time an all-inclusive definition of "bourgeois liberalization" was given:

"Characterized by vigorously propagating, advocating, and seeking after bourgeois freedom, it strives for bourgeois parliamentarism, the two-party system, and elections; bourgeois freedom of speech, publication, assembly, and association; bourgeois individualism and anarchism within a certain framework; the bourgeois profit-before-everything mentality and behavior; the bourgeois way of life and vulgar tastes; bourgeois moral and artistic norms; worship of the capitalist system and its manifestations, etc. These trends are 'introduced' or infiltrated into China's political, economic, social and cultural life, so as to, in principle, negate, oppose, and sabotage the Chinese socialist cause and the leadership of the Chinese Communist Party. The social nature of these ideological trends is to demand, consciously or unconsciously, a breaking away from the socialist orbit and the implementation of the so-called bourgeois free system in all political, economic, social, and cultural spheres" (Hu Qiaomu, *WYB,* 5:4, 1982).

To justify the campaign, Hu explained that the 6th Plenum of the 11th PCC marked the fulfillment of the historical task of rectifying the "Left" deviation in the Party's guiding ideology. The major problem at present, therefore, was "bourgeois liberalization in society (to some extent also within the Party) which violates the four cardinal principles" (ibid., p. 3). Hu identified a series of "mistaken" views in ideological circles. On the issue of the Double Hundred policy, he said, some people onesidedly emphasized it, erroneously regarding it as the sole principle in the Party's ideological work. It was their wish that with the Double Hundred policy, they could break into every "forbidden zone". He also denounced doubts whether the social system in China was genuine socialism, and whether the whole theory of Mao Zedong Thought was tenable. Hu found it necessary to refute the view which counterposed socialist democracy to Party leadership. As he noted, there were people who "wantonly exaggerated" negative aspects in Party work. Moreover, "certain individuals have simply gone so far as to indulge in slandering the Party, and for that purpose they have fabricated and spread 'theories' of one kind or another" (ibid., p. 12).

It seemed, however, that none of these "mistaken" views were eliminated. In the last months of 1983, following the October 1983 2nd Plenum of the 12th PCC, another campaign began. This time the slogan "Oppose bourgeois liberalization" was replaced by "Eliminate spiritual pollution".

In 1986, many people openly rejected this slogan. First of all, they said, it was wrong to treat "liberalization" as a derogatory term. Quoting Engels' statement that "A genuine freedom and equality means communism" and that a Communist society would be "an association in which the free development of each is the premise of the all", Li Chunguang, then editor of the *Literary Gazette*, asserted that socialism and communism were actually synonymous with true liberalization. In addition, memories of the past were evoked. This strengthened Li's case: Zhou Yang, Lu Dingyi, Liu Shaoqi, Deng Xiaoping, and many other important figures had all been attacked by their political opponents for "bourgeois liberalization". Conclusively,

Li claimed, the slogan of "opposing liberalization" or "opposing bourgeois liberalization", one of the major and most frequently used slogans in "mass criticism and repudiation" during the GPCR, belonged to an "out-and-out feudal autocracy", and it was high time to discard it (Li Chunguang, "Zhengzhi wenti yingdang ziyou taolun"—"Political Issues Should Be Freely Discussed", *Xin guancha,* 16, 1986, reprinted in *XHWZ,* 10:20, 1986).

Similar views were also popular in 1986. Indeed, never before had Chinese academic circles been so active, taking up so many issues that would not have been touched at all in the past. They were apparently encouraged by the widespread rumor that reform of the political structure would be the chief topic at the 6th Plenum of the 12th PCC, which was due to be held in September 1986. Furthermore, 1986 was the thirtieth anniversary of the Double Hundred policy, the twentieth anniversary of the "May 16th Circular", and the tenth anniversary of the end of the GPCR. Inspired by a sense of historical responsibility, many Chinese intellectuals openly discussed issues of democracy and freedom. They were deeply involved in the call for political reform, as if the time had finally arrived for some genuine progress in this regard.

In the eyes of the Party hardliners and their ideologues, this was exactly an expression of "bourgeois liberalization", and absolutely intolerable. In January 1987, the CCP Politburo announced a campaign against "bourgeois liberalization". A series of purges followed. Three prominent intellectuals, astrophysicist Fang Lizhi, journalist Liu Binyan, and writer Wang Ruowang, were expelled from the Party. Party General Secretary Hu Yaobang was dismissed.

All this was warmly welcomed by the old guard. For instance, on 20 and 24 March 1987, Xiong Fu, editor-in-chief of *Red Flag*, happily reviewed what he called the "anti-bourgeois liberalization struggle" of the past eight years. He described a course of "eight ups and downs". At that time, Xiong and his comrades thought they had won the struggle, and things would henceforth return to what they asserted was the "right track of Marxism-Leninism-Mao Zedong Thought".

The campaign appeared to be very fierce and threatening at first, but in the end it fizzled out, similar to previous campaigns. One of the reasons for this was the positive role played by Zhao Ziyang, Hu Yaobang's successor. A more compelling factor was the resistance on the part of dissidents, students, and intellectuals. Despite heavy political pressure, they did not retreat. Their demand for freedom and democracy finally culminated in what was called "the May Tempest" (wuyue fengbao) of 1989, an unprecedented event in contemporary Chinese history. Not only did they discuss theoretical concepts such as humanism, human dignity, and human rights; they took concrete action against the tyranny and corruption of the regime. Then, on 4 June 1989, the "Beijing Massacre" took place. The movement was suppressed. In a most tragic way, which shocked people all over the world, the incident proved the inevitability of a conflict between the CCP dictatorship and the ever-increasing need of China's intellectuals for freedom in their creative, academic, and political activities.

In the ten years since the June 4th Incident of 1989 opposition to "bourgeois liberalization" has continued to be a major task of the Party. At the 6th Plenum of the 14th PCC (held in Beijing from 7 to 10 October 1996), it was emphasized that the opposition should be carried out alongside with the whole process of the socialist modernization.

Liberalization, however, has not stopped, especially in economic areas. Ironically, economic liberalization has in fact been promoted by Deng's reform and open-door policy. As China critics have pointed out, this is genuine "bourgeois" liberalization—in the course of which what is called a newborn bourgeoisie has come into being and has been growing rapidly, leading China onto the capitalist road.

This is Deng's "socialism with Chinese characteristics": at its most fundamental it defines the base line of his blueprint for reforms: in order to build a powerful, prosperous China, economic liberalization is necessary, but it must not sweep away the Communist Party's monopoly on power. Jiang Zemin, the new "core" of the leadership of the third generation, seems certain to continue this line. Yet, China critics maintain that the odds against achieving full modernization without losing political control are daunting. In fact, in the spring of 1998, demands for political reform were once again heard. Many pro-democracy thinkers and activists called themselves "liberals". See also "ziyouzhuyi" (liberalism).

自由派
ziyoupai
(liberals)

See "ziyouzhuyi" (liberalism).

自由主义
ziyouzhuyi
(liberalism)

"Liberalism" was a familiar term to Chinese people during the Mao period. It was considered "a wrong tendency in the revolutionary ranks". The "perniciousness" of liberalism was very often a central focus of self-criticism. This was the result of Mao's teaching. In his 7 September 1937 article "Combat Liberalism" ("Fandui ziyouzhuyi", *MZXJ,* 2, pp. 330-32), Mao stated that liberalism manifests itself in as many as eleven ways. Mao said: "Liberalism rejects ideological struggle and stands for unprincipled peace, thus giving rise to a decadent, philistine attitude and bringing about political degeneration in certain units and individuals in the Party and the revolutionary organizations" (ibid., p. 331). Mao also said: "Liberalism is extremely harmful in a revolutionary collective. It is a corrosive which eats away unity, undermines cohesion, causes apathy and creates dissension. It robs the revolutionary ranks of compact organization and strict discipline, prevents policies from being carried through and alienates the Party organizations from the masses which the Party leads. It is an extremely bad tendency" (ibid., p. 332).

In the CCP, liberalism also refers to: 1. "a reactionary politico-ideological trend of the bourgeoisie from the early 19th century to the early 20th century, which, under signboards of individual freedom, essentially advocates exploitation and the freedom of competition"; and 2. "a reactionary economic theory of British and American bourgeois economists in the early 19th century that promotes the freedom of the bourgeoisie to carry out exploitation and plunder". But these two definitions, even though interpreted in a totally orthodox Communist doctrine, remained obscure to Chinese people during the Mao period, since there was no chance at all for them to touch any "reactionary" politico-ideological trend or theory.

In the 1930s and 1940s, liberalism (in its true sense) did hold currency among Chinese scholars, with Hu Shi as an outstanding representative. Beijing University, from its founding in 1898, was the cradle of China's liberalism. However, in the 1950s, soon after the 1949 Communist takeover, Hu Shi and other liberal figures were fiercely attacked as "lackeys of imperialists and other reactionaries". The ban on liberalism lasted for more than thirty years. At the end of the 1980s, liberalism was a topic in discussions about culture (but it was stopped following the June 4th Incident of 1989). Then, after the mid-1990s, liberalism was openly advocated by a number of liberal thinkers, including Li Shenzhi, former CASS vice-president (who is dubbed a liberal patriarch); Xu Youyu, a research fellow at the Philosophy Institute, CASS; Zhu Xueqin, professor of History at Shanghai University; Liu Junning, a research fellow at the Politics Institute, CASS; Xu Jilin, professor of History at Shanghai Normal University; and Wang Dingding, a research fellow at the Economics Institute, Beijing University. A first major event in the promotion was in November 1997, when the *South Weekend (Nanfang zhoumo,* a Guangzhou newspaper) devoted a whole page to marking the death of Isaiah Berlin. Then, the diary of Gu Zhun (1915-1974), an economist who was cruelly persecuted in the Mao period and died miserably in the GPCR, was published. In his preface, Li Shenzhi claimed that Gu Zhun pursued liberalism at the price of his life. In May 1998, in the book Liu Junning edited, *The Beida Tradition and Modern China—The Harbinger of Liberalism,* liberalism was highlighted as the tradition of Beijing University. Liberalism came together with nationalism, the theory favoring the supremacy of the state, the Frankfurt School, cultural conservatism, post-modernism, etc. As a rival ideological trend of those various schools, liberalism also served as a "stage" for them to perform.

Liberalism associates itself with the market economy. Since the door to the market economy has been opened, it is only natural for liberalism to re-emerge and exert its influence. In the economic field, scholars did not stop at a general approval of economic liberalism. They went further into the relationships of the market economy with the state system and the limits of its authority, and with law, morality, and public order. China's liberal economists were concerned about the problems brought about by the "power economy" (quanli jingji) in the period of the "economic mode transition". In her 1997 book *The Pitfalls of China*, He Qinglian convincingly exposed what she said was the most brutal and vicious "previous accumulation" (yuanshi jilei) or the "second previous accumulation" (de'er ci yuanshi jilei) in contemporary China. She compared the "development zone craze" (kaifaqu re) in the early 1990s to the "enclosure of the 18th century". The joint stock system reform, according to He Qinglian, was a "socialist free lunch", a large-scale plunder of state property carried out by "insiders" by the means of their power.

Liberals (ziyoupai) issued an urgent call for political reform, claiming that many of the problems in contemporary China were the result of the delay of liberalism over the last two decades. In early August 1997, Shang Dewen, a Beijing University professor, wrote a letter to Jiang Zemin proposing a 25-year orderly transition towards full democracy, including a directly elected parliament serving four-year terms, an independent judiciary, civilian control over the military, an expansion of local power, and a free press. The first step, according to Shang, was the need for a new constitution. In his January 1998 article, "Also Promote Political Reform" ("Yeyao tuidong zhengzhi gaige"), for the tenth anniversary of the publication of *Reform Magazine,* Li Shenzhi pointed out that China's implementation of political reform will clearly determine the ultimate success or failure of its economic reform. As to human rights, a very sensitive issue in China, Li asked the authorities to immediately adopt international standards. In the spring of 1998, liberal thinkers proposed the theory of "small government, large society" (xiaozhengfu, dashehui), or the "limited government" theory (youxian zhengfu lun). In their opinion, the key issue in China at the moment was not how to further strengthen the power of the government, as advocated by the "neo-conservatists" two years earlier, but how to limit government power. They not only called for a separation of the Party from government functions, they also demanded that the Party be separated from military functions.

The question remains of how to apply liberalism to political issues. The 1980s reform of the political institutional structure, which involved reform of administrative structures, separating the Party from government functions, establishing a civil service system, and the abolition of life tenure in leading posts, was insufficient. Now that issues in the planned economy and ownership have basically been solved, liberals are demanding a reform and change in the political spirit and in the concept of political value. As Liu Junning explained, there are two political spirits: one is characterized by the theory of class struggle, the other by magnanimity. China's liberal thinkers envisage a society where people with different political stands coexist peacefully, each enjoying an equal right to express their views. In this way "stability and unity" (anding tuanjie) will be realized.

In the rejuvenation of liberalism in China during the second half of the 1990s, scholars found it necessary to justify individualism (gerenzhuyi). Traditionally, Chinese people were asked to ignore the self. Mao's Sinicized Marxism made full use of this. In the CCP lexicon, individualism must be "bourgeois individualism". It is egoism, a censurable feeling or behavior of a person who puts his/her own private interests first. The Party, therefore, opposes individualism. One must be more concerned about the revolution than about oneself. One must relinquish one's personal interests, one's personal freedom, future, dignity, marriage, or even life to the needs of "the people", an "illusory collective" (xuhuande jiti) that demands sacrifice by every individual.

A deeper understanding of liberalism will unavoidably lead to a break with those ideas in China's new and old traditions which tend to suppress individuality. Individualism is now found to be a social theory. As contrasted with the theory favoring the supremacy of the state (guojiazhuyi), it favors free action and complete liberty of belief by individuals. The core of liberalism, liberals argue, is to confirm an individual's value and dignity and to respect and protect his/her rights and interests. State, society, or collective are all merely means or tools in the service of individual rights. Logically, individualism is the best resistance to autocracy (gerenzhuyi shi duikang zhuanzhide zuijia fangshi). Every right an individual wins back from a dictator will weaken the dictator's monopoly of rights. Any development of an individual's "consciousness of self" (ziwo yishi) will be a check on the dictator's megalomania. As a result, all dictators are opposed to individualism.

Liberalism in contemporary China should fight against the enslavement of man by the old system (referring to the Maoist social-political system), and, at the same time, it should criticize "labor alienation" (laodong yihua), which has been intensified after twenty years of Deng's reform program. It should, as Wang Dingding suggests, promote evolutionary universalism, dialog as shared logos, and communicative individualism (Wang Dingding, "Zhongguo jiushi niandai gaigede zhengzhi jingjixue wenti"—"The Political Economy Issues in China's Reform in the 1990s", *ES,* 23-29, June 1999).

Liberalism is part of the mainstream thought and culture of the West, whereas Confucian culture is part of Chinese tradition. Those who can be called "neo-Confucianists" (xin rujia) testify that Confucianism and liberalism, though two fundamentally different traditions, must have something in common, both as a crystallization of wisdom accumulated in the experience of human existence. Furthermore, they assert, once liberalism has taken root in China, it will be the result of its combining with Confucian tradition (referring to the acceptable tradition of Confucianism after its outdated, unacceptable compositions, such as institutional Confucianism, have been deleted). This is called "Confucian liberalism" (rujia ziyouzhuyi). The market economy built up on the basis of liberal economics will serve as an intermediary for such a combination.

On the one hand, one can find the continuity between liberalism in the 1990s and the 1980s ideological trends of neo-enlightenment and humanism (see Xu Youyu, "Ziyouzhuyi yu dangdai Zhongguo"—"Liberalism and Contemporary China",

Kaifang shidai, 43-51, May & June 1999). On the other hand, according to Liu Junning, the "coming on the stage" of liberalism constituted the biggest watershed between China's thinking public of the 1990s and that of the 1980s (Liu Junning, "Ziyouzhuyi: jiushiniandaide 'bu su zhi ke'"—"The 'unexpected guest' of the 1990s", *Nanfang zhoumo*, 29 May 1998). Many scholars have come to believe that liberalism has a universal value. It can be a political doctrine, an economic thinking, or a social philosophy. Moreover, it is a social-political system. It is also an attitude towards life. Only when the majority in society possess this attitude can this society be considered a modern society, and the country considered one ruled by law (fa zhi guojia).

China's liberals claim that the rejuvenation of liberalism (also called "neo-liberalism"—"xin ziyouzhuyi", though it seems that China's liberals prefer to keep the original name so as to stress its unchanged tradition) in today's China is a gradual but irresistible process. In spite of the fact that liberalism is being challenged in the West, Li Shenzhi is optimistic in his prediction that the rejuvenation of liberalism will bring freedom to China and bring a free China to a world of globalization. Ironically, in the first year of the twenty-first century, Li Shenzhi, Liu Junning, and some other liberal thinkers were attacked by the authorities. Liu even lost his job at the CASS. The road ahead of them certainly would not be straight. See also "ziyouhua" (liberalization), "minzuzhuyi" (nationalism), "xinzuopai" (neo-Leftists), "quanqiuhua" (globalization), and "Deng Xiaoping lilun" (Deng Xiaoping Theory).

自在阶级
zizai jieji
(class in itself)

See "jieji douzheng" (class struggle) and "xinsheng zichanjieji" (newborn bourgeoisie).

自尊，自信，自助
zizun, zixin, zizhu
(self-esteem, self-confidence, and self-reliance)

See "aiguozhuyi" (patriotism).

宗教式的克己
zongjiaoshide keji
(religious self-abnegation)

See "ziwo biaoxian" (expression of the subjective ego), "menglongshi lilunde san ci jueqi" ("three rises" in the theory of misty poetry), "xinde meixue yuanze zai jueqi" (a new aesthetic principle is rising), "wenyi wei zhengzhi fuwu" (literature and art serve politics), and "sixiang gaizao" (ideological remolding).

宗派主义
zongpaizhuyi
(sectarianism)

Sectarianism was a problem for the CCP. In the 1942 Yan'an rectification movement, Mao labeled subjectivist and sectarian tendencies as two targets for attack.

Admittedly, sectarianism was also a problem in Chinese literary and art circles. The famous woman writer Ding Ling, who suffered political persecution during the Mao period, tended to regard herself as a victim of factional strifes in literary and art circles, with Zhou Yang as her chief enemy. At the 1979 4th National Congress of Chinese Writers and Artists, Ding Ling noted that those who had been attacked by the Gang of Four were already rehabilitated and highly respected by the public, whereas the same treatment did not yet seem to have been given to those who were criticized, persecuted, and completely discredited in 1957. This seventy-six-year-old celebrated woman writer hoped that a formal apology could be publicly extended to Ai Qing, Feng Xuefeng, and herself. She said:

"It was sectarianism, another form of feudalism, in literary and art circles. It is impossible to look forward, to achieve the unification of the country, to achieve the hundred flowers blooming and the hundred schools of thought contending if sectarianism is not wiped out. For people like me it will be over, but we have the young who have a future and should not suffer the way we did" (Ding Ling, "Jiang yidian xinli hua"—"A Few Words from My Heart", *HQ,* 12:52, 1979). See also "difangzhuyi" (localism).

总路线
zongluxian
(General Line)

The CCP put forth one "general line" for the "transitional period" in 1953 and another one for socialist construction in 1958. During the so-called "new period" there were two different "general task" formulations put forth respectively by Hua Guofeng and Ye Jianying. See "guodu shiqi zongluxian" (general line for the transitional period), "shehuizhuyi jianshe zongluxian" (General Line for Socialist Construction) and "yingming lingxiu" (wise leader).

走後门
zou houmen
(get in through the back door)

To secure advantages through pull or influence (through secret and underhanded means), or as the popular saying goes, "zouhoumen"—to get in through the back door, is commonplace in China, whether in the fields of economics, social activities, or one's personal life, though this practice is condemned as a manifestation of "unhealthy tendencies" (buzheng zhi feng). To consent to the requests of those who seek to "get in through the back door" is expressed by the phrase "kaihoumen"—to open the back door. The consequences of "getting in through the back door" and "opening the back door" can be very damaging. According to the World Bank, roughly $10 billion in state assets has been sold through the back door over the past decade.

In the practice of "getting in through the back door", a key word is "guanxi" (personal connections). Today even foreigners understand the meaning of this Chinese term. In China, it indeed plays a part in the people's lives, especially in economic fields. When doing business, for example, if you have "guanxi", you enjoy a good relationship with someone who has certain power or influence and would like to help, you already have a good beginning and have won half the battle, or even more. The best "guanxi" is often provided by those from the so-called "princes' clique", those children of high-ranking officials who occupy key positions in state-operated industry and commerce, army enterprises, or private companies, both at home or abroad. Thus the rise of the saying (which sarcastically follows the tone of Deng Xiaoping about science and technology) that "guanxi" is part of the productive force, or even the first important productive force.

Other related terms included: "zou neixian" (seek someone's favor by approaching his family members, especially, wife, or confidant; use private influence to achieve one's end; go through private channels), "zou shangceng luxian" (use upper-level influence to achieve one's end), and "la guanxi" (try to establish a relationship with someone; cotton up to). See also "taizidang" (princes' clique) and "jingji gaige" (economic reform).

走内线
zou neixian
(use private influence to achieve one's end)

See "zou houmen" (get in through the back door).

走上层路线
zou shangceng luxian
(use upper-level influence to achieve one's end)

See "zou houmen" (get in through the back door).

走资本主义道路分子
zou zibenzhuyi daolu fenzi
(elements taking the capitalist road)

This term, obviously derived from the GPCR term "zou zibenzhuyi daolu dangquanpai" (those in power taking the capitalist road), was used in the 1987 campaign against "bourgeois liberalization". Fang Lizhi, Liu Binyan, and Wang Ruowang were attacked as "elements taking the capitalist road", in a series of articles published in *Red Flag*, the CCP mouthpiece, early in the year. See "fandui zichanjieji ziyouhua yundong" (anti-bourgeois liberalization campaign).

走资本主义道路当权派
zou zibenzhuyi daolu dangquanpai
(those in power taking the capitalist road)

This term, often abbreviated as "zouzipai" (capitalist-roaders), was frequently used during the GPCR.

This concept was first officially advanced in the document "Some Problems Currently Raised in the Rural Socialist Education Movement" ("Nongcun shehuizhuyi jiaoyu yundongzhong muqian tichude yixie wenti", that is, "The Twenty-three Articles"—"Ershisan tiao"), released by the PCC on 14 January 1965. The document stated that the major targets of attack in the "rural socialist education movement" unfolding at the time were "those in power within the Party taking the capitalist road"—those who did not follow the socialist road but carried out capitalist activities. "These capitalist-roaders," it said, "stay behind the scenes in some cases or remain in the front in others. Some of their supporters come from below and some from above. Those from below are people who have been labeled landlords, rich peasants, counter-revolutionaries, and other bad elements, as well as people who have not been marked as such through an oversight. Those from above are people opposing socialism in the communes, townships, counties, prefectures, or even the provinces and the central departments."

An unprecedented national struggle against the so-called "capitalist-roaders" took place during the GPCR. This struggle, with "great historical significance", was noted in the "May 16th Circular" of 1966 (its issuance marked the beginning of the GPCR), and was ratified in the "PCC Decision on the GPCR" (passed at the 11th Plenum of the 8th PCC on 8 August 1966). By 1967, with the GPCR developing fiercely, most government and Party organizations were paralyzed, if not completely destroyed. A great number of Party and government leaders at various levels had been overthrown as "capitalist-roaders", with Liu Shaoqi, PRC president and PCC vice-chairman, as the number one and Deng Xiaoping, PRC vice-premier and PCC general secretary, as the number two capitalist-roader.

In January 1967, the so-called "January Revolution" (yiyue geming) took place in Shanghai, when the rebels seized power of the local authorities and the "Shanghai Municipal Revolutionary Committee" was established. Thereafter, four central authorities—the CCP Central Committee, the State Council, the Central Military Commission, and the Central GPCR Group—appealed to "all proletarian revolutionary groups" for unity in "seizing power from a handful of people in power within the Party who take the capitalist road". Responding to this appeal, a struggle to seize power took place all over the country. The GPCR entered a "new stage". By 5 September 1968, "revolutionary committees" had been set up in all twenty-seven provinces and autonomous regions and Beijing and Shanghai. Thus, as the *People's Daily* of 7 September hailed, "The whole country is red" (Quanguo shanhe yipian hong).

But the GPCR was not yet over. Among the last several important events was the campaign Mao launched in 1976 to criticize Deng Xiaoping and to counter the so-called "Right deviationist trend to reverse correct verdicts". Mao finally agreed that Deng was an "incorrigible capitalist-roader" (si bu gaihuide zouzipai), judging from his performance over the previous two years (Deng had been brought back to power by Mao in 1973). On 5 February 1976, at a meeting convened by the Party Center to launch the campaign, a new "supreme directive" by Mao was released: "You're making a socialist revolution, and yet you don't know where the bourgeoisie is. It is right in the Communist Party—those in power taking the capitalist road. The capitalist-roaders are still on the capitalist road." In April 1976, Deng was once again toppled. It was also insinuated that the late Premier Zhou Enlai, Deng's former supporter, was a "capitalist-roader".

In the first few months after the downfall of the Gang of Four following the "October 6th coup" of 1976, the CCP authorities headed by Hua Guofeng called on the people to continue their struggle against "capitalist-roaders", criticizing Deng Xiaoping as an "incorrigible capitalist-roader". This, obviously, went against the will of most people in China at the time. The struggle was finally ended. By the end of 1978, all the "capitalist-roaders" had been rehabilitated, numbering over two million *(Five Voices in Present China,* 1999, p. 57).

But capitalist-roaders are still an issue in China today. When Mao's above-mentioned "supreme directive" was published, it was considered to be of great significance in the development of Marxist theory. Indeed, the thesis that "the bourgeoisie is right in the Communist Party" justified Mao's theory of "continuing the revolution under the dictatorship of the proletariat". Mao's most loyal followers thus claimed that the bourgeoisie had three forms in history: following the "liberal bourgeoisie" and the "monopoly bourgeoisie", the bourgeoisie within a proletarian party was its "last form emerging in the process during which the whole class heads towards its doom". But at that time, many still found it hard to believe that within the CCP, the vanguard of the proletariat, there could be a bourgeois class. Now, after twenty years, not only are the Maoists and "neo-Leftists" fully convinced by what they claim to be the correctness of Mao's statement (now a "brilliant prediction") but also many other Chinese have come to the conclusion that there must be something disastrously wrong with the CCP, as so many Party secretaries and their family members have become company directors, reaping huge profits from the "power economy". See also "shiliutiao" (Sixteen Articles), "wen'ge" (Cultural Revolution), "fan fubai" (anti-corruption), and "jingji gaige" (economic reform).

走资派
zouzipai
(capitalist-roaders)

See "zou zibenzhuyi daolu dangquanpai" (those in power taking the capitalist road).

走资派还在走
zouzipai haizaizou
(the capitalist-roaders are still on the capitalist road)

See "zou zibenzhuyi daolu dangquanpai" (those in power taking the capitalist road).

走过场
zouguochang
(perfunctory manner)

When carrying out a task, some officials only acted superficially, caring nothing about the effect, though abiding by the procedures. This was usually a way to resist political movements. These officials were accused of having a perfunctory manner and not working in a down-to-earth manner to carry out the movement in a deep-going and thorough way.

族阀资本主义
zufa zibenzhuyi
(nepotic capitalism)

See "guanliao ziben" (bureaucrat-capital) and "jingji gaige" (economic reform).

最高指示
zuigao zhishi
(supreme instructions)

On 18 November 1965, when summing up a five-point principle for "giving prominence to politics", Lin Biao referred to Mao's works as "supreme instructions". After the *People's Daily* published the slogan "Take Chairman Mao's works as the supreme instructions for all our work" on 22 January 1966, the term began to be used when referring to any of Mao's articles, words, or quotations. After the end of the GPCR, the term gradually disappeared. See also "tuchu zhengzhi" (giving prominence to politics).

尊孔反法
zun kong fan fa
(respecting Confucianism and opposing Legalism)

See "pi Lin pi Kong yundong" (campaign to criticize Lin Biao and Confucius).

尊重知识，尊重人才
zunzhong zhishi, zunzhong rencai
(respect knowledge, respect trained personnel)

See "zhishifenzi wenti" (issue of intellectuals).

遵义会议
Zunyi huiyi
(Zunyi conference)

The Zunyi Conference refers to the Enlarged Conference of the PCC Politburo held in January 1935 in Zunyi, Guizhou province. According to Party historians, the Conference had two achievements: 1. liquidating the third "Left" opportunist military line headed by Wang Ming and affirming Mao's military line; and 2. re-electing the CCP Secretariat and the Central Revolutionary Military Affairs Committee and affirming the new PCC leadership headed by Mao. It is regarded as very important in CCP history, for at a crucial moment during the Long March, it established Mao's leadership in the Party for the first time.

The phrase "Zunyi conference" was often used as a symbol to describe a certain important meeting. For instance, the 1978 3rd Plenum of the 11th PCC was said to be "the Zunyi Conference of the socialist period". The 4th Congress of the CWA (held from 29 December 1984 to 5 January 1985) was also hailed by Xia Yan, a prominent writer and senior cultural leader, and many other writers and artists, as something like the 1935 historic Zunyi Conference (However, not long after its closing, the 4th Congress of the CWA was accused of promoting "bourgeois liberalization"). Today, it seems that this symbol is not so common as before.

左
zuo
(Left)

See "you" (Right).

左倾
zuoqing
(Left deviation)

See "you" (Right).

左倾机会主义
zuoqing jihuizhuyi
(Left opportunism)

See "you" (Right).

左翼文艺运动
zuoyi wenyi yundong
(Left-wing movement in literature and art)

See "sanshiniandai wenyi yundong" (literature and art movement of the 1930s).

作党的驯服工具
zuo dangde xunfu gongju
(be the "docile tool" of the Party)

See "xunfu gongju lun" (theory of being "docile tool").

作家内在精神主体的运动规律
zuojia neizai jingshen zhutide yundong guilü
(law governing the motion of a writer's interior spiritual subject)

See "zuojia zhutixing" (writer's subjectivity).

作家是人类灵魂工程师
zuojia shi renlei linghun gongchengshi
(writers are engineers of the human soul)

See "qiangganzi he biganzi" (the gun and the pen) and "wangbuzhaode hudie" (a butterfly difficult to catch).

作家主体性
zuojia zhutixing
(writer's subjectivity)

A writer's subjectivity mainly refers to "the law governing the motion of a writer's interior spiritual subject". Borrowing the five classifications of basic human needs of A. Maslow, an American humanist psychologist, Liu Zaifu claims that the highest level of a writer's subjectivity is his self-actualization (ziwo shixian), that is, a full display of his spiritual world.

The interior universe of a writer, Liu says, is not a closed world. His self-actualization, consequently, does not mean only a small personal freedom achieved in a closed world or only a small emancipation of his own human nature. To achieve the strength as the subject, a writer must merge his whole heart and soul with the age and society, and offer all that is good in his spiritual world to society and the whole of mankind. In the final analysis, a writer's self-actualization is the spreading of love. The wider and more profound the love, the higher the level of his self-actualization. "Love knows no bounds, nor the level of (a writer's) self-actualization" (Liu Zaifu, "Lun wenxuede zhutixing"—"On the Subjectivity of Literature", *WXPL,* 6:22, Nov. 1985).

Consciously or not, Liu Zaifu asserts, all distinguished writers can achieve psychological sublimation from a desire to survive (the lowest level of basic human needs) to one for self-actualization. Hence the three distinctions of their creative practice: transcending the norm, (chaochangxing), transcending precedents (chaoqianxing), and self-transcendence (chaowoxing).

When discussing transcending the norm, Liu points out that as the result of various historical causes, Chinese intellectuals generally tend towards self-restraint,

by self-reflection (zixing), thus cruelly strangling their sense of freedom and initiative. This is the greatest psychological obstacle to self-actualization. Some writers are also affected by the Confucian philosophy of the golden mean (zhongyong zhi dao), which is widespread in China. Moreover, since the founding of the PRC, because literature was required to serve politics, aesthetic pursuits had to be subservient to political concepts. Accordingly, instead of reforming those traits that impede social progress, writers had to extinguish their creative individuality as a sort of original sin (yuanzui xingzhide e). As a result, they always had to change color to suit the different political climates.

Transcending precedents means acquiring a sense of historical perspective and foresight which transcends time and place. When applied to the literary field, it means that what is impossible for many politicians and economists is possible for writers who do not passively reflect on life but instead actively respond to it. As the subject, their response (zhuti ganying) enables them to assimilate things of the present and the past, Chinese and foreign, thus making a reproduction of genuine beauty possible.

"Self-transcendence", when applied to the literary field, means that writers do not yield to any idols in the outer world, nor do they look to themselves as their idol, so as to achieve, as the subject, a strength in terms of ideals, wisdom, morality, and will. That is why writers should be characterized by self-transcendence—artistic creation, psychologically speaking, moves from self-discovery (zi wo) to self-transcendence (chao wo), and finally to self-oblivion (wu wo).

In order to achieve subjectivity, writers must have a high sense of mission (in its broad sense), in addition to a sense of freedom. Throbbing with the pulse of the times and history, they must shoulder all troubles of the world and all burdens of history. Inevitably, therefore, this sense of mission will lead to a sense of angst (youhuan yishi). As Liu Zaifu asserts, the sense of mission in the broad sense, or the sense of angst in the broad sense, is the most essential mentality of all eminent writers, present or past, Chinese or foreign.

This sense of angst is in itself a kind of sense of historical mission because, when possessing it, writers will no longer see the world and the course of life blindly. The angst stems from their commitment, their pursuit of truth, goodness, and beauty, and their longing for a bright future. Even when the course of life seems satisfactory, they can envision potential dangers hiding in social progress. Liu Zaifu concludes: "Without tears, there will be no literature, at least no profound literature" ("On the Subjectivity of Literature", *WXPL,* 6:26, Nov. 1985).

The sense of angst was one of the characteristics of what was dubbed the *"élite* culture" (jingying wenhua) of the 1980s (other characteristics included an independent critical spirit and a sense of social-political participation). This shows the relevance of Liu's thesis. See also "wenxue zhutixing" (subjectivity of literature).

作家的社会责任感
zuojiade shehui zerengan
(a writer's sense of social responsibility)

See "shehui xiaoguo lun" (social effect theory) and "wenyi wei zhengzhi fuwu" (literature and art serve politics).

坐直升飞机
zuo zhishengfeiji
(riding a helicopter)

See "taijie lun" (the "staircase" theory).

坐标说
zuobiao shuo
("coordinate" theory)

See "xin shehuizhuyi guan" (new socialist view).

Glossary of Entries Listed Alphabetically in English

"back-to-back" criticism, 19
backward-looking literature, 530
bad leader, 184
Bai Hua incident, 11
barbarism, 423
Basic Law, 187
basic characteristic of socialism is social justice plus a market economy, the, 389
basic principle of communism is an all-round and free development of man, the, 148
basic program of the Party for the primary stage of socialism, the, 64
basic question as regards world outlook is whom one is to serve, the, 423
battle song of communism, a, 148
be able to serve as an official and remain as one of the common people, 289
be able to work at both higher and lower levels, 289
be articulate with international norms, 621
be at one with the Party, 144
be bravely involved in life and seriously probe into it, 50
be in keeping with the Party Center, 621
be in keeping with the people, 621
be involved in life, 133
be involved in politics, 134
be involved in the soul, 133
be loyal to life and involved in the soul, 667
be modest and prudent, 194
be self-reliant and struggle arduously, 683
be set aside, to, 222
be the "docile tool" of the Party, 700
beating, smashing, and looting, 46
begin with a mass criticism, to, 56
behind-the-scenes boss, 288
Beijing massacre, 17
Beijing Spring, 17
Beijingers can talk about anything, Cantonese can eat anything, Shanghainese can do anything, 19
benevolence for the people of the world, 324
better bear hardships and die, 590
better troops and simpler administration, 218
bewildered generation, 291
big cauldron canteen food, 51
big nationality chauvinism, 54
big smoking nation, a, 521
big tigers, 47
big-nation chauvinism, 51
big-sized newspaper, 49
"bird cage" economics, 289
birth control, 203
bitter love complex of Chinese intellectuals, the, 661
black, 170
black hands, 172
black materials, 171
black meetings, 171
blast of cold wind in spring, a, 44
bludgeon, to, 46
blue civilization, 471
bombard the headquarters, 291
born red, 681
both red and expert, 616
bourgeois dictatorship, 681
bourgeois factionalism, 679
bourgeois human touch, 680
bourgeois humanism, 679
bourgeois humanistic outlook on society, 679
bourgeois individualism, 677
bourgeois individualistic view of happiness, 678
bourgeois intellectuals, 681
bourgeois liberalization, 681
bourgeois nationalism, 678
bourgeois reactionary line, 677
bourgeois Rightists, 681
bourgeois rights, 676
bourgeois rights, 679
bourgeois sentimentalism, 680
bourgeois ultra-individualist view of value, 678
bourgeois undue leniency, 680
bourgeois universal love, 676
bourgeois view of literature and art, 680
bourgeoisie is right in the Communist Party, the, 678
brand of a class, the, 202
brand of the times, 414
breakthrough point for the GPCR, 476
breakthrough point in the offensive against the Communist Party leadership and the proletarian dictatorship, a, 529
broadening of the scope of class struggle, 200
bureaucrat-capital is the first stage rocket, 155
bureaucrat-capital, 154
bureaucrat-capitalism, 155
burning books and burying scholars alive, 128
business fever, 217
bystanders, 532

cadres sent to lower levels, 522
campaign against Hu Shi's reactionary ideological system, 297

campaign against the "five evils", 512
campaign against the three evils, 363
campaign to counter the "Right deviationist trend to reverse correct verdicts", 121
campaign to criticize Deng Xiaoping and counter the "Right deviationist trend to reverse correct verdicts", 294
campaign to criticize Deng Xiaoping, 295
campaign to criticize Lin Biao and Confucius, 297
campaign to eliminate spiritual pollution, 307
Capital Red Guards United Action Committee, 237
capitalism in Mao Zedong style, 261
capitalist accumulation, 676
capitalist camp, 676
capitalist globalization, 676
capitalist restoration, 675
capitalist view about reform, 676
capitalist-roaders, 698
capitalist-roaders are still on the capitalist road, the, 698
capitalize on people's vulnerable points, to, 219
"cat" theory, the, 261
catch up with and surpass Britain within 15 years, 413
center of world revolution, 420
Central GPCR Group, 665
Central GPCR Group, 665
Central Group in Charge of the Cultural Revolution, 665
central idea of Marxism is alienation, the, 606
centralism on the basis of democracy and democracy under the guidance of centralism, 280
centralized Party leadership, 71
centralized Party leadership, 597
centrally planned economy, 664
Chairman Mao's proletarian revolutionary line, 266
change from public servants of the people to their lords and masters, 145
change political color, 20
Charter of the Anshan Iron and Steel Company, 4
Chen Xitong Incident, 31
China can be transformed into a democracy via one-party rule, 657
China can say no, 655
"China threat" theory, 658
China's conscience, 663
China's Gorbachev, 662
China's Khrushchev, 662
China's last emperor, 661
Chinese agent of the stream-of-consciousness, 608
Chinese Association for the Founding of a Democratic Nation, 657
Chinese century, 663
Chinese concept of values, 655
Chinese Democracy Alliance, 657
Chinese Democracy Party, 658
Chinese Democracy Promotion Association, 657
Chinese hegemony, 653
Chinese literature lacks a consciousness of repentance, 659
Chinese Nationalist Party Revolutionary Committee, 654
Chinese Peasants and Workers Democratic Party, 658
Chinese People's Political Consultative Conference, 663
Chinese Public Devotion Party, 661
Chinese renaissance, 659
Chinese traditional learning craze, 159
Chinese traditional learning, 159
Chinese traditional learning, 664
Chongqing Forum on Poetry, 37
chop down the banner, 222
chop down the red banner, 222
civil society ruled by law, 145
civil society, 278
"civil strife" theory, 288
class analysis, 201
class character and innate nature are related by internal integration, 203
class character of literature, 494
class compromise, 203
class education, 201
class for itself, 683
class in itself, 694
class labelism, 199
class line, 202
class polarization, 201
class reprisal, 198
class struggle is the key link, and everything else hinges on it, 200
class struggle, 199
clean things up in the fields of politics, economy, organization, and ideology, 307

closed door leads to backwardness, and backwardness proves vulnerable to attack, a, 129
closed-door policy, 20
closing the country to international intercourse, 20
Cold War mentality, 230
Cold War, 230
collective ownership, 189
collective unconscious, 189
colonial culture, 647
combating and preventing revisionism, 114
combination of popularization and raising of standards, 303
combination of revolutionary realism and revolutionary romanticism, 141
combination of the planned economy and the market economy, a, 190
combine study with application, 579
commercial culture, 378
commodity production, 378
Common Program, 149
common human nature, 149
common psychological phenomena, 152
common sense of beauty, 149
Communist ideology is the core of socialist spiritual civilization, 148
Communist Party is the vanguard of the working class, the, 147
Communist wind, 148
complete and thorough globalization, 313
complete and thorough opening to the world, 312
complete negation of the GPCR, 29
"complete set" in terms of ideology, 292
complete system of literary theory did not exist in Marxism, a, 258
complex experiences, thoughts, feelings, and life require a complex artistic form, 130
comprehensive engagement, 314
Confucian cultural ring, 354
Confucian liberalism, 354
Confucianism in its third stage of development, 354
Confucianized Mao Zedong Thought, 266
Confucianized Marxism, 259
congagement, 470
congress of Red Guards, 175
consciousness of being the subject, 672
consciousness of repentance, 27
consciousness of self, 687
consciousness of the "original sin" of contemporary Chinese intellectuals, 63
conspiratorial literature and art, 612
containment against China, 467
contemporary Chinese literature, 63
continue to emancipate the mind while taking social effect into consideration, 193
continue working well until the last minute, 626
continuing the revolution under the dictatorship of the proletariat, 511
contradiction between life and art, 409
contradiction between Party spirit and affinity to the people, 344
contradictions among the people, 343
contradictions between Chinese artistic conventions and those of other nations, 652
contradictions between the four clean-ups and the four unclean-ups, 439
contradictions between the people and their enemy, 78
contradictions in one's world outlook, 423
controlled economy of public ownership, the, 146
conventions, 455
converse psychology, 289
convey the people's emotion, to, 424
coordinate all the activities of the nation as in a chess game, 314
"coordinate" theory, 702
core of Party leadership, 250
core of Party leadership, the, 71
core of the "four cardinal principles" is upholding Mao Zedong Thought, the, 437
core of the "four cardinal principles" is upholding Party leadership, the, 437
corrected Rightist, 132
correctly handling contradictions among the people, 629
corruption is favorable, 130
corruption is reasonable, 130
cosmopolitanism, 423
counter-revolutionary, 121
country with a socialist legal system, 389
cover up class struggle with national struggle, 602
cover-up faction, 519
CPPCC, 633
creation of typical characters, 40
creative freedom, 40
Crescent School, 566

do away with the "four olds" and cultivate the "four news", 302
doctrine of the mean, 666
dogmatism, 197
domestic opening, 96
Double Hundred policy, 424
"double service" principle, 425
double standard for human rights, 348
double variation of enlightenment and salvation, a, 304
dragons beget dragons, phoenixes beget phoenixes, and those begotten by rats are good at digging holes, 255
draw a clear line of demarcation, 184
draw fire against oneself, 612
dual combination in characterization, 351
dual leadership, 425
dual price system, 194
duchy economy, 671

East wind prevails over the West wind, the, 89
eccentric school of poetry, 153
economic alienation, 217
economic animals, 209
economic base, 213
economic development, individual freedom, social justice, and political democracy, 209
economic liberalization is prior to political democratization, 217
economic liberalization, 217
economic reform, 210
economic "Tsar", 214
economics is the base and politics the concentrated expression of economics, 215
"educated youth" literature, 645
educated youth, 644
education by negative example, 122
education by positive examples, 628
education in two-line struggle, 256
education must be modernization-oriented, world-oriented, and future-oriented, 198
education must serve proletarian politics and be combined with productive labor, 197
education of national characteristics, 158
efficiency is life, 534
Eight Articles on Work in Literature and Art, 495
eight dramas for 800 million people, 10
eight sinister theories, 170
eight virtues and eight calls, 6
elements taking the capitalist road, 696
eleven musts in the reform and open-door program, 131
eliminate spiritual pollution, 309
eliminate the four pests, 39
eliminate the seven pests, 39
emancipating the mind, 204
emancipation of minds is a current political issue of vital importance, 205
emancipation of the mind is the cause and social effect is the result, 206
enclosure of the 1990s, the, 99
engineers of the human soul, 341
equal stress on political integrity and professional competence, 73
"essence" is not the same as "mainstream", 20
everyone is a critic, 348
everyone is equal before the truth, 628
everything will be all right once the joint stock system is adopted, 589
evil revelation of the original sin, an, 623
evil wind of economism, 217
exchanges of information, thoughts, and culture, 456
exchanges, peace, and a win-win policy, 584
exercise an all-round dictatorship over the bourgeoisie, 95
exile literature, 254
expanding common ground, increasing trust, reducing differences, and building the future together, 224
experiential subjectivity, 416
experimental farming plots, 418
experimental fiction, 417
experimental unit for China's communism, an, 654
explorative literature, 449
exploring generation, 449
"explosive" writings, 17
exposure and eulogy, 16
exposure literature, 16
expression of the subjective ego, 683
extensive criticism of the theory of mechanical reflection, an, 93
extensive democracy, 53
extensiveness, fairness, and authenticity, 156
exterior freedom, 462
external causes become operative through internal causes, 462
extrinsic and intrinsic laws of literature, 495
élite culture, 219
élite of the turmoil, 89

four standards for selecting cadres, 135
four steps in bidding farewell to revolution, 137
four upholds, 433
four whatevers, 432
"four-point statement" on China's policy towards the United States, 653
"four-two-one" phenomenon, 432
fragrant breeze, 528
fragrant flower, 528
framing a target to attack, 471
free lance, 688
free meals for all, 32
freedom exploitation, 417
freedom of speech, 583
freedom of speech is the most important human right, 583
freedom precedes democracy, 687
freedom-fearing disease, 687
from each according to his ability, to each according to his needs, 142
from the masses, to the masses, 45
front line, 596
fulcrum of a new literary theory, 551
full-scale civil war, 314
full-time working personnel for Party affairs, 675
fundamental question of revolution is political power, the, 142
fundamental task for socialist literature and art, 396
fundamental task of socialism is to develop productivity, the, 405
Fundamentalist Marxism, 622
"futility of education" theory, 93

Gang of Five, 515
Gang of Four, 440
Gang of Four's "line" in literature and art, the, 441
general architect of China's reform and open-door program, 654
general backer of all "monsters and demons" in literary and art circles, 503
General Line, 695
General Line for Socialist Construction, 390
general line for the transitional period, 156
general line of the international Communist movement, 157
general task for the new period, 561
generosity, tolerance, and relaxation, 366
gentle breeze and a mild rain, a, 163
genuine knowledge comes from practice, 415
get in through the back door, 695
get rid of baggage, 128
get stuck-up, 307
give me back my Great Wall, 185
give previous notice, 46
give the irrational due place in artistic creation, 144
giving prominence to politics, 457
giving prominence to politics means to place Mao Zedong Thought in command of all work, 460
giving prominence to the economy, 457
global values, 317
globalization, 318
globalization means Americanization, 320
go against the tide, 107
go all out to write about the "thirteen years", 57
go back to studies, 461
"go slow, be patient" policy, 208
God makes wine, and the devil makes drunkards, 379
god-making literature and art, 625
god-making movement, 625
Goddess of Democracy, 281
going against the tide is a Marxist principle, 108
good in political thoughts, in the "three-eight" work style, in military training, and in the management of livelihood, 642
good persons making mistakes, 162
"governing by doing nothing that goes against nature" in literary and art fields, 503
GPCR literature and art, 476
GPCR study, 481
GPCR was an unavoidable end-result of Mao's ever-worsening ultra-Left line, the, 476
GPCR would not have occurred had it not been for Mao Zedong, the, 268
grand tradition, 49
grasp firmly with both hands, 247
grasp the intermediate link to bring forward the two ends, 674
grasp the two ends to bring along the middle, 674
grasping the key link to run the country, 674
Great Cultural Revolution, 482
Great Cultural Revolution must be repeatedly carried out, the, 482
Great Harmony, 56
Great Leap Forward, 57
Great Proletarian Cultural Revolution, 506

ideological remolding, 426
ideological sluggard, 429
ideological trend of Westernization, 520
ideological work, 429
ideological-cultural hegemony, 430
idle talk, 310
if any serious problems occur in China, they are likely to occur within the Communist Party, 661
if you don't use your power when you have it, you will be sorry when it expires, 615
illusory collective, 578
imperial edict, 409
imperial power, 185
imperialism, modern revisionism, and reactionaries, 78
in agriculture, learn from Dazhai, 290
in front of the shop the sheep's head dangles, but inside the shop one sells dog's meat, 153
in industry, learn from Daqing, 147
incident concerning the publication of *Tiananmen Poems*, 453
incorrigible capitalist-roaders, 431
increasing trust, reducing troubles, developing cooperation, and avoiding confrontation, 625
increasing value of Chinese culture, 663
independence and self-reliance, 93
independent kingdom, 92
independent Taiwan, 92
individual's class status, an, 32
individualism is the best resistance to autocracy, 144
individualism, 144
individuals are subordinate to the organizations they belong to, the minority is subordinate to the majority, lower authorities are subordinate to higher authorities, and the whole party is subordinate to the Party Center, 143
information from obscure sources, 532
inhumanization of man, 338
"innate genius" theory, the, 453
institutional structure, 451
integrating government administration with commune management, 633
intellectuals are part of the working class itself, 647
intellectuals are the leading force in society, 647
intellectuals are the most advanced social force, 647
intense search for "roots", 581
interchange of historical roles, an, 235
interests of the people are supreme, the, 342
interior freedom, 289
international Communist movement, 157
international socialist movement, 157
internationalism, 157
internet will lead to China's next Cultural Revolution, the, 157
interrogation of the soul, 250
invisible injury, 289
"inward turning" of literature, 491
iron rice bowl, 456
iron tiger, 456
irrational nationalism, 128
irrational, 128
issue of intellectuals, 645
issue of press freedom, 562
it is hard to come by an able person), 327
it is right to rebel, 624

January Revolution, 597
January Tempest of 1967, 597
Jiang Zemin as the core of Party leadership, 195
Jiang Zemin era, 195
Jiang Zemin's eight-point proposal, 195
joint stock system reform, 152
journalism is the Party's mouthpiece, 561
journalism's class nature, 566
journalism's Party spirit principle, 566
jumping into the sea of business, 523
June 4th complex, 255
June 4th counter-revolutionary rebellion, 254
June 4th disturbance, 255
June 4th Incident, 255
June 4th massacre, 254
June 4th political disturbance, 255
just a little wind from the higher-ups and their subordinates will turn it into a torrential rain, 380
justice is the more essential criterion, 146

key-point experiment, 417
kick aside Party committees to make revolution, 451
kill the chicken to frighten the monkey, to, 376
Kingdom of Great Harmony, 57
Kylin Culture, 224

labor alienation, 229
labor under surveillance, 156
landlords, rich peasants, counter-revolutionaries, bad elements, and Rightists, 84
large formation warfare, 49
large in size and collective in nature, 586
"last totem" of Marxism, the, 260
late-Deng period, 181
Latter Ten Articles, 182
launch a counterattack and recover the lost mainland, 121
launch satellites, 128
Law Wheel Cultivation, 103
law governing the motion of a writer's interior spiritual subject, 700
law is supreme, 106
law of promotion-restriction-inhibition-transformation in the Five Elements, 517
law of the unity of opposites is the fundamental law of the universe, the, 95
law of Yin and Yang as each other's roots, 612
lay stress on one's political behavior, 667
leadership means service, 250
lean to one side, 591
learn from new folk songs, 529
learn from someone else's experience, 310
learning from past mistakes to avoid future mistakes and curing the sickness to save the patient, 31
leaving one's post, 522
Left deviation, 699
Left in form but Right in essence, 572
Left opportunism, 699
Left, 699
Left-wing movement in literature and art, 700
"Leftist" revisionism, 227
legislation for journalism, 561
legislation on literature and art, 496
Lei Feng spirit, 229
less interference, less involvement, 380
less publicity about individuals, 381
let a hundred flowers bloom and a hundred schools of thought contend, 11
let a hundred flowers bloom and weed through the old to bring forth the new, 11
let literature be literature, 323
let others speak, 323
let the masses liberate themselves, 322
Li Yizhe incident, 233
liberalism, 691
liberalization, 688
liberals, 691
liberate artistic productivity, 206
life tenure system, 666
lifting a rock only to drop it on one's own feet, 15
limited government theory, 616
Lin Biao and Jiang Qing counter-revolutionary cliques, 249
Lin Biao Incident, 248
line is the key link; once it is grasped, everything falls into place, the, 256
"line struggle" theory, 256
lineage theory, 579
lingering fear, 620
literary inquisitions, 504
literature and art are cogs and wheels in the whole revolutionary machine, 497
literature and art are no longer subordinate to politics, 495
literature and art are subordinate to politics, 495
literature and art are tools of class struggle, 496
literature and art cannot be divorced from politics, 495
literature and art exert only an imperceptible influence, 502
literature and art have source in life and are on a higher plane than life, 502
literature and art have source in life and are on a lower plane than life, 502
literature and art movement of the 1930s, 370
literature and art must be free from any restriction, 495
literature and art of the 1930s, 370
literature and art of the whole people, 317
literature and art serve politics, 497
literature and art serve proletarian politics, 497
literature and art serve the broadest masses of the people, 501
literature and art serve the people and socialism, 497
literature and art serve workers, peasants, and soldiers, 497
literature embodies man's essential force, 491
literature of overseas students, 254
literature of the new period, 556
literature should transmit principles, 473
little emperors, 533
little red book, 532
"little red book" movement, 532
Liu Binyan phenomenon, 251
Liu Shaoqi's counter-revolutionary revisionist line in literature and art, 252

Liu Shaoqi's counter-revolutionary revisionist line, 252
Liu Zaifu incident, 253
lobby literature, 615
local hegemonism, 84
local nationalism, 84
localism, 84
lofty, great, and perfect, 135
Long live understanding, 233
long-term co-existence and mutual supervision, 28
look to the future, 530
look towards money, 530
loosening up, 127
loss of man's subjectivity, 340
loss of moral courage of contemporary Chinese intellectuals, the, 63
loss of the subjectivity of the object of literature, 488
love is supreme, 2
love the nation by a devious path, 310
"loyalty" dance, 667
"loyalty" tablet, 667
loyalty to one's sovereign and dedication to the service of one's country, 666
Lu Xun literary prize, 256
lure the snake out of the pit, 612
Lushan conference, 255

Ma Ding incident, 257
macro adjustment and control, 181
macro-climate, 56
Madam Marxism, 260
mainly exercising the planned economy while making market regulation subsidiary, 190
maintain independence and keep the initiative in our own hands, 92
maintain one's revolutionary integrity in one's later years, 15
major issues of principle, 56
make a distinction between the functions of government and those of society, to, 633
make a distinction between the functions of the Party and the government, to, 65
make a key-point experiment, 136
make "circles", 183
make everyone a soldier, 316
make foreign things serve China, 583
make known one's position, 21
make sb. overthrown and discredited by mass criticism, to, 293
make steel by the whole people, 316
make steel in a big way, 47
make the past serve the present, 153
malposition, 45
man is the aim, man is the center, 327
man is the starting point of Marxism, 325
man should be at the center of development, 106
man should be the center of thinking in literary research, 491
man's activity and passivity, 340
man's alienation under the condition of socialism, 394
man's alienation, 40
man's subjectivity, 340
manifesto of bourgeois modernist poetry, 680
Mao Dun literary prize, 261
Mao Zedong craze, 263
Mao Zedong Thought system, 266
Mao Zedong Thought, 264
Mao Zedong was keen on transferring cadres to lower levels; Deng Xiaoping asked people to jump into the sea of business; and Jiang Zemin resorts to massive lay-offs, 261
market socialism, 417
Marxism in development, 106
Marxism is a theory ever in development, 259
Marxism is an open science, 259
Marxism is not the world outlook of the proletariat, 257
Marxism is only one school in the history of thought, 260
Marxist family, the, 258
Marxist humanism, 259
Marxist modernism, 259
Marxist philosophy about man, 258
Marxist scientism, 260
Marxology in the West, 520
mass criticism, 54
mass line, 321
mass movement, 322
mass struggle, 321
mass viewpoint, 321
masses are the real heroes, the, 322
massive exchange of revolutionary experiences, 50
massive exchange of revolutionary experiences, 138
material civilization, 520
materialist dialectics, 470
May 4th literary tradition, 516
May 4th Manifesto, 516

new "cat" theory, 542
new citizens' literature, 550
new Cold War, a, 542
new Communist man, 148
new concept of "one China", a, 589
new democratic revolution, 543
new historical period of socialism, 553
new Long March, 541
new manifesto of the Communist Party, 542
new overseas literature, 542
new period literature faced a crisis, the, 559
new period, 555
new socialist man, 400
new socialist view, 546
new Taiwanese, 551
new Taiwanese, 561
new task, a, 551
new theory of population, 545
new three most sought-after articles, 546
new tradition, 541
new trends of class struggle, 200
new whateverists, 541
new-born bourgeois elements, 555
new-born bourgeoisie, 553
new-born middle class, 553
newly emerging socialist things, 401
nine critiques, 220
nine fingers and one finger, 220
nine kinds of black elements, 171
no contact, no negotiation, no compromise, 23
no courage, no breakthrough; no breakthrough, no literature, 269
"no debate" theory, 23
no distinction between the functions of the Party and the government, 65
no heart economics, 267
no independence, no reunification, and no confrontation, 22
no investigation, no right to speak, 267
no matter whether it is white or black, it is a good cat that catches mice, 24
no matter whether it is white or black, it is a good mouse if it can escape from the cat, 25
no matter whether it is yellow or black, it is a good cat if it catches mice, 25
no one is born red only through ideological remolding, 270
Nobel Prize syndrome, 291
non-Party personages, 72
Northern Expedition, 17
not to have a correct political point of view is like having no soul, 270
Not-Not-ism, 128
observe and help, 590
oceanic civilization, 162
official profiteers, 153
offside application, 623
offside, 623
once class struggle is stressed, every problem will be solved, 200
once public ownership is no longer paramount, the Communist Party will lose the economic foundation for its rule, 592
one center, two basic points, 589
one China, one Taiwan, 590
"one country" is more important than "two systems", 593
one country, several systems, 593
one country, three systems, 595
one country, two governments, 594
one country, two kinds of newspaper, 594
one country, two systems, 594
one day amounts to twenty years, 596
one divides into two, 586
one doctrine, one party, and one leader, 589
one ensure, three putting things into place, and five reforms, 588
one hand is tough, while the other soft, 595
one hundred day Cultural Revolution, 13
"one point" theory, 593
one single public opinion, 621
one struggle, two criticisms, and three reforms, 586
one will be a true man if his father is an hero, while reactionaries bear only bastards, 228
"one-China" principle is the foundation of peaceful reunification, the, 589
one-party autocracy, 592
one-party dictatorship, 592
only by developing Marxism can one uphold it, 259
only by emancipating all mankind can the proletariat achieve its own final emancipation, 507
only by restricting CCP power can stability be achieved, 651
only expert and not red, 650
only Leftists can enjoy the right to rebel Rightists are allowed to change our regime, 651
only on a high degree of commercialization

and socialization of production can socialism be built, 650
only socialism can save China, 650
only swat flies but not hunt tigers, 650
open letter from thirty-three intellectuals, 371
open system of socialist realism, an, 221
open the back door, 221
open the windows of the sky, 221
opening to the outside world, 96
oppose Left ideology in the economic field and Right ideology in the political field, 217
opposing book worship, 117
opposing bourgeois liberalization, 118
opposing bureaucracy is an important mission of socialist literature, 118
opposing rash advance, 113
opposing stereotyped Party writing, 118
organizational decentralization, 451
organize contingents of the people's militia on a big scale, 49
orientalization of the stream-of-consciousness, 608
orthodox Marxism is heading for death, 630
other half of the sky, 14
overall point of view, an, 314
overseas Chinese economic circle, 162
overseas Chinese, 160
overseas Chinese; Chinese sojourners, 183
overseas Chinese; people of Chinese origin, 183
overt trick, 583
ownership by the whole people, 316

pacifism, 165
paid news-writing, 616
panic psychology of "doubtful prognosis", 622
paper tiger, 649
Paris Commune, 10
parliamentary road, 612
parochial nationalism, 522
parochial patriotism, 522
particular literature or art is the reflection of a particular economic and political system, a, 593
parties participating in government affairs, 27
Party Center, 73
Party Center writes plays, whereas the State Council puts them on, the NPC makes comments, and the CPPCC functions as an audience, the, 73
Party commands the gun, the, 65
Party commands the pen, the, 65
Party culture, 73
Party is the entire world, the, 72
Party leadership, 67
Party must strictly discipline itself before it can run the country well, the, 651
Party newspaper, 65
Party should supervise itself, the, 64
party of the entire people, a, 316
Party's basic line for the entire historical period of socialism, the, 65
Party's basic line, the, 65
Party's educational policy, the, 66
Party's mouthpiece, the, 65
Party's three important styles of work, the, 71
patriarchal party, 227
patriotic education, 2
patriotic united front, 1
patriotism, 1
pay close attention to the two civilizations, 244
peace and development are the two themes of today's world, 164
peace but no independence, 163
peace but no reunification, 163
peaceful coexistence, 163
peaceful competition, 164
peaceful evolution, 164
peaceful transition, 164
pearl of the Orient, 88
Peng Dehuai Incident, 293
people are the goal, the, 343
people have risen while the red flag has fallen, the, 343
people in power within the Party taking the capitalist road, 72
People's Commune, 341
People's Communes are fine, 342
people's democracy, 342
people's democratic dictatorship, 342
people's democratic dictatorship, 343
people's war, 343
people, 341
perfunctory manner, 698
perpetuating the family name, 40
personal connections, 155
personality cult, 142
personality cult, 143
persons under surveillance, 19
persons under surveillance, 156
petit tradition, 532
Petofi Club, 292
petty bourgeois intellectuals, 534

phenomenon and essence, 528
phenomenon of diminishing creativity, 44
philosophy of subjectivity, 673
philosophy of the Communist Party is the philosophy of struggle, the, 147
"pinnacle" theory, 86
planned economy, 189
pluralistic development of the literature of the new period, 557
poisonous weed, 92
polemic between the CCP and the CPSU, 652
policy above, counter-policy below, 378
political alienation, 644
political animals, 636
political cancer, 644
political Confucianism, 640
political criteria first, artistic criteria second, 635
political declaration and program of action of the third generation leadership, 79
political design academy, 641
political economy for China during the "mode transition" period, 661
political flower vases, 640
political hegemony, 634
political identification, 640
political integrity, 51
political issue, 643
political issues should be freely discussed, 643
political labels, 634
political polishing, 641
political power grows out of the barrel of a gun, 306
political power is a power of suppression, 633
political reflection, 644
political reform, 637
political romanticism, 640
political work is the lifeblood of all economic work, 640
politicization of literature, 491
politics cannot but have precedence over economics, 642
politics pushes over and overwhelms everything else, 636
poor and lower-middle peasants supreme court, 300
popular culture, 59
popular literature of the national revolutionary war, 283
popular literature, 456
popularization, 59
positive teachers, 629
post-colonial culture, 182
post-colonial mentality, 182
post-Confucian era, 182
post-Confucianism, 182
post-Deng era, 73
post-GPCR literature, 480
post-misty poetry, 271
post-modernism, 182
poverty and "blankness", 590
poverty gives rise to a desire for change, 310
power capital, 312
power capitalization, 312
power economy, 312
power is greater than the law, 311
power politics, 306
"power struggle" theory, 311
practice is the sole criterion for testing truth, 415
pragmatic diplomacy, 519
pragmatic generation, 310
praise is essential, 21
praising virtue and lacking virtu, 137
prelude to the GPCR, 480
premonition, 622
prerequisites for the forming of new poetic schools, 550
prevent from spreading, 126
previous accumulation, 622
primary stage of socialism is the most decisive national characteristic, the, 387
princes' clique's first attempt to obtain power, the, 449
princes' clique, 448
principal contradiction in society during the primary stage of socialism, the, 387
principle of people's livelihood, 278
principle of people's rights, 278
principle of realism, 528
principle of the dual combination in characterization, 97
principle of the restoration of the subjectivity of art receptor, 610
prison of the mind, 570
private profiteering, 431
privatization, 431
pro-democracy movement of 1989, 6
problem fiction, 504
problem-centered reportage literature, 602
proceeding from the political line, 257
productivity fetishism, 408
productivity is the ultimate determinant in the development of any society, 408

Project Hope, 520
proletarian democracy, 506
proletarian headquarters, 506
proletarian internationalism, 505
proletarian patriotism, 505
proletarian revolutionary rebels, 505
proletarian revolutionary utilitarianism, 505
proletarian system of democratic centralism, 506
pseudo-Left but genuinely Right, 194
psychological fiction, 570
public accusation meeting, 90
public ownership can and should take diversified forms, 146
public ownership does not amount to state ownership, 145
public sphere, 144
pull back the leg, 29
pull back the leg, 226
pull up the white flag and hoist the red flag, 10
pulling out, sneaking in, 226
pure literature, 44
pursuers, 449
put on a rival show, 27
putting an enterprise under a lower administrative level, 304
putting Mao Zedong Thought in command, 266
putting politics in command, 640

qigong, 304
Qincheng Prison, 307
quest for modernism, 524
queuing up, 291
Quotations from Chairman Mao, 266

radical democrats outside the establishment, 452
raising of standards on the basis of popularization, 624
rather be Leftist than Rightist, 290
rational nationalism, 233
re-discovery of man, 338
re-education through labor, 229
re-education, 624
re-writing the literary history, 38
reactionary bourgeois academic authorities, 677
reactionary gang, 171
reactionary humanism, 117
reading Mao's works every day, 454
reasonable child of an unreasonable era, a, 22
rebel Red Guards, 181
rebels, 625
reblooming flowers, 37
recall past sufferings and think about present happiness, 605
recent times; modern times, 208
record of the resuscitation of human nature, 351
red, 174
Red August of 1966, 175
Red Guard mentality, 180
Red Guards would not have emerged had it not been for the lineage theory, the, 269
Red Guards, 178
Red Terror, 176
red banner, 175
red capitalist, 177
red economic Tsar, 176
red entrepreneurs, 177
red line, 181
red little soldiers, 181
reflect the essential aspect of typical circumstances, 124
reflection literature, 123
reflection, 122
reform fatigue symptoms, 131
reform is China's second revolution, 132
reform literature, 132
reform of administrative structures, 187
reform of the mentality of political values, 640
reform of the political spirit, 640
reform of the system of Party and state leadership, 64
reform of written Chinese, 504
reform through labor, 229
reformists within the establishment, 451
regional culture fiction, 85
regional geographical leadership, 224
rehabilitation, 301
rehabilitation committee, 301
relationship between arts and politics is in essence one between arts and the people, the, 501
relative independence of the arts-politics relationship, the, 502
religious self-abnegation, 694
remain unchanged for fifty years, 515
remedial teaching team, 26
remove the ideological cover, 198
remove the lid, 198

remove the lid of class struggle, 198
"replacement" theory, 60
reportage literature craze, 16
Republic of China on Taiwan, 663
requesting instructions in the morning and reporting in the evening, 624
resisting the cultural hegemony of the West, 118
respect knowledge, respect trained personnel, 699
respecting Confucianism and opposing Legalism, 699
restoration effect of man's essence, 337
restoration faction within the establishment, 452
restraining bourgeois rights, 528
return to Chinese traditional learning, 186
reverse effect of a news blockade, 561
reverse law, 98
revisionism, 573
revisionism is even more dangerous than dogmatism, 578
revitalize China through science and education, 222
revitalize China, 628
revitalize national science and education, 157
revolution breaks out in the depths of the soul, a, 251
revolution in Beijing opera, 209
revolution is no crime, 141
revolution must be carried out in education, 198
revolutionary committee, 141
revolutionary dual tactics, 142
revolutionary humanism, 140
revolutionary mass criticism, 139
revolutionary mass organizations, 140
revolutionary patriotism, 141
revolutionary realism, 141
revolutionary rebels, 141
revolutionary regime, 175
revolutionary successors, 139
revolutionary theatrical works on contemporary themes, 141
revolutionary united front, 140
riding a helicopter, 701
riffraff culture, 300
riffraff literature, 300
Right deviation, 620
Right deviationist trend to reverse correct verdicts, the, 620
Right opportunism, 620
right to subsistence is the most fundamental human right, the, 408
Right, 617
Rightist revisionism, 226
Rightists, 620
rise of China, the, 662
River Elegy craze, 165
River Elegy debate, 165
River Elegy Incident, 165
rocket cadres, 187
"root-seeking" fiction, 582
"root-seeking" literature, 582
rotating the leadership, 257
royalist faction, 16
rubber stamp, 531
rule by individuals, 353
rule by law, 106
rule by the dead, 432
ruling the nation by law, 600
rush through the job, 132

safety coefficient, 4
satellite fields, 471
satellites have been launched while the red flag has fallen, 471
save the nation by a devious path, 310
scar literature, 377
science and technology are part of the productive forces, 223
science and technology are the first important productive forces, 223
second Cold War, 78
second echelon, 79
second line, 101
second New Culture Movement, 79
second previous accumulation, 79
second revolution, 78
second rural revolution, 79
second type of loyalty, 79
second world, 79
sectarianism, 694
seek truth from facts, 417
self-actualization, 687
self-alienation, 687
self-cultivation, establishing one's family, serving one's country, and unifying the world, 573
self-destruction of the Great Wall, 682
self-doubt, 686
self-esteem, self-confidence, and self-reliance, 694

socialist tragedy, 383
socialist view about reform, 389
socialist-communist culture, 381
society of units, 61
soft landing, 356
"Solid Rice Gruel" incident, 195
solving the issue of public ownership forms was another emancipation of the mind, 206
soul of China, 655
sovereignty is more important than human rights, 672
sovereignty is supreme, 672
Sparks Project, 572
speaking out freely, airing one's views fully, writing big-character posters, and holding great debates, 54
special economic zone means capitalism, 451
special economic zone means special privilege, 451
special economic zone, 216
special economic zones should enjoy no more preferential treatment, 450
spectre of humanism, 337
speed of corruption has surpassed the growth of the GNP, the, 130
spirit of going against the tide, 108
spirit-matter dialectics, 570
spiritual aristocrats, 218
spiritual atom bomb, 219
spiritual burden, 218
spiritual civilization, 219
spiritual pollution, 219
spiritual subjectivity, 219
spontaneous force, 681
squat at point, 96
stability and unity, 3
stability and unity is not to give up class struggle, 3
stability must be premised on social justice, 472
"staircase" theory, 443
standard-bearer of the proletarian cultural revolution, 506
state adjusts the market, and the market guides the enterprises, the, 158
state of the entire people, a, 316
state ownership, 158
state socialism, 158
state system, 158
stereotyped Party writing, 64
stick on ideological/political labels, 60
stinking number nine, 38
stir up a "wind", to, 153
stone of spiritual understanding, 456
strategic adversary, 626
strategically despise all our enemies, but tactically take them all seriously, 626
streamline administrative structures, 218
streamlining organizations constitutes a revolution, 218
strengthen and improve Party leadership, 193
strengthening the central government while weakening the local authorities, 306
stress coordination, quality, and benefit, 197
stress study, politics, and healthy trends, 197
"strike hard" campaign, 583
strive to develop science, 529
struggle against bourgeois Rightists, 118
struggle against Rightists, 114
struggle between the Confucian and Legalist schools, 354
struggle between two lines, 244
struggle by coercion or force, 519
struggle by reasoning, 473
struggle by reasoning, not by coercion or force, 585
struggle on two fronts, 245
struggle philosophy, 91
struggle worship, 90
struggle, criticism, and reform, 89
students selected from among workers, peasants, and soldiers, 146
study and apply in a creative way, 186
study first what must be urgently applied, 188
study of Hong Kong, the, 528
study of sufficient love, 36
subjective ego, 683
subjective fighting spirit, 672
subjective idealism, 672
subjectivity of art receptor, 610
subjectivity of literature is a philosophical formulation of humanism in the field of literature, the, 494
subjectivity of literature, 491
subjectivity of the object of literature, 487
successors to the proletarian revolutionary cause, 505
suffer once again, 32
sufficiency in subjectivity and in transcendence, 36
sugarcoated bullets, 450
"Summary", 191

"Summary" is the "Yan'an Talks" in the socialist period, the, 193
superpower, 28
superstructure, 379
supervisor as public opinion, mouthpiece of the masses, warner to the government, and path breaker of the reform, 621
supplementary lessons; to make up for missed lessons, 26
supremacy of the state, 158
supreme instructions, 698
surrounding the cities by the countryside, 290
surveillance, 155
suspect all, 184
suspect all, negate all, 593
suspect all, overthrow all, 184
swat flies, to, 46
sweep away all monsters and demons, 173
sweetheart; secretary-turned mistress, 534
symbol of the "sankuan" policy, 367
System of Law Wheel, 103
system of inherent unity of planning and market, a, 190
system of law, 107
system of multiparty cooperation and political consultation led by the Communist Party, the, 147

tails of capitalism, 676
Taiwan Democratic Self-government League, 444
Taiwan independence, 443
Taiwan issue is a Chinese internal affair, the, 448
Taiwan issue, 444
take charge of the revolution, promote production, 673
take Deng Xiaoping Theory as the frame of reference, 599
take difficulties on oneself and make things easy for others, 10
take small losses for the sake of big gains, 32
taking class struggle as the key link, 601
taking the three instructions as the key link, 602
talk politics, 196
talks during the Southern tour, 288
Taoyuan experience, 450
teacher by negative example, 122
teaching material by negative example, 121
ten major relationships, 409
ten marshals, 409
ten most influential slogans in the past two decades, 98
ten problems Chinese writers should be concerned with, 662
ten "two-line" struggles, 410
ten-year catastrophe, 411
ten-year Cultural Revolution, 411
tendency for boasting and exaggeration, 130
tendency to be formulistic and abstract, the, 145
tender one's heart, 197
tender one's heart to the Party, 529
the bolder the man is, the higher yields the fields will turn out, 327
the more a person knows, the more reactionary he will become, 645
theatrical works about honest and upright officials in feudal times, 309
theme takes the lead, the, 672
theocracy, 407
theoretical-ideological reform, 429
theory of "a single revolution", 592
theory of "Asian values", 582
theory of being "docile tools", 580
theory of breakthrough, 36
theory of class stand as the decisive factor, 233
theory of "discarding the classics and rebelling against orthodoxy", 232
theory of "entering the Party in order to be an official", 356
theory of "geographical environments as a decisive factor", 85
theory of human nature, 351
theory of "inner-Party peace", 71
theory of "limited sovereignty", 616
theory of linear causality, 528
theory of "merging private and public interests", 144
theory of "middle characters", 663
theory of "multipolarity", 96
theory of opposition to "subject-matter as the decisive factor", 113
theory of opposition to the "smell of gunpowder", 112
theory of "productivity as the sole factor determining social life", 470
theory of reflection is the philosophical basis for literary study, the, 125
theory of skipping over stage of historical development, 234
theory of socialist alienation, 401
theory of the "broad path of realism", 527

theory of the clash between the Eastern and the Western civilizations, 86
theory of the coalescence of Eastern and Western civilizations, 88
theory of the "deepening of realism", 527
theory of the development of revolution by stages, 139
theory of "the dying out of class struggle", 200
theory of the environment as the decisive factor, 185
theory of the exteriorization of Mao's idealism, 261
theory of the importance of class origin, 616
theory of the impossibility of skipping over stage of historical development, 234
theory of the primary stage of socialism, 385
theory of the "socialist community", 388
theory of the "spirit of the age as the merging of various ideologies", 413
theory of the status of Taiwan being outstanding, 444
theory of the superiority of Chinese culture, 659
theory of the superiority of Eastern culture, 88
theory of the unique importance of class origin, 470
theory of the world revolution center, 421
theory of "thinking in terms of images", 572
theory of White superiority, 13
theory of "world outlook as the decisive factor", 423
theory of "writing about reality", 538
theory of "yellow peril", 185
theory that "the masses are backward", the, 322
there is only one kind of essence for a specific society, 588
there is only one kind of typical character for a specific class, 588
there is only one kind of typical circumstance for a specific age, 589
there will be no party spirit without affinity to the people, 268
third echelon, 81
third "eye", the, 82
third force, 80
third great milestone in the history of Marxist development, the, 258
third line, 373
third road, the, 82
third world, 80
third-line construction, 374
thirty-year Cultural Revolution, 370
thoroughgoing humanism can only be realized in literature and art, 30
those in power taking the capitalist road, 696
thought-emancipation movement, 429
thoughts from the leaders, life experience from the masses, and artistry from the writers, 250
Three Main Rules of Discipline and Eight Points for Attention, 358
Three Principles of the People, 367
Three Red Banners, 361
three anticipated goals of the reform of the political institutional structure, 642
three basic forms of class struggle, 200
three battles to settle accounts with the Gang of Four, 309
three big mountains, 361
three big poisonous weeds, 361
three cardinal guides and five constant virtues, 363
three defenses, 359
three divorced, 373
three do's and three don'ts, 374
three "don't mentions", 359
"three don'ts" policy, 362
three evils, 364
three famous, 368
three favorables, 360
three forms of the bourgeoisie in history, 681
three freedoms and one contract, 375
three frequently-read articles, 227
three fundamental criteria for identifying capitalist-roaders within the Party, 361
three goods, 364
three great revolutionary movements, 357
three great transformations, 357
three heavy blows to the Gang of Four, 94
three highs, 363
three honests and four stricts, 367
three important styles of work, 358
three kinds of people, 376
three loyals, 375
three magic weapons, 357
three major distinctions, 356
three major reactionary theories of China's Rightists, 661
three major tasks for the 1980s, 9
three "milds" and one "less", 364
"three no-changes" policy, 359
three obediences and four virtues, 363
three opening-ups and four exchanges, 372
three orientations, 359

three "peacefuls" and two "entires", 364
three prominences, 373
three reflections, 359
three represents, 359
three rises and three falls, 369
"three rises" in the theory of misty poetry, 274
three stresses, 365
three super articles, 28
three supports and two militarys, 375
three theories, 367
three thought-emancipation movements, 356
three togethers, 373
three tremendous historic changes in the past century, 590
three types of foreign capital involved enterprises, 375
three upholds, 359
"three worlds" theory, 360
three-anti elements, 363
"three-eight work" style, 362
three-family village, 365
"three-good" cadres, 364
"three-good" students, 365
three-hundred-thousand-word statement, 372
three-in-one combination, 365
three-layer meaning of literature, a, 494
three-level transcendence of literary critics, 490
three-refutation movement, 368
three-self patriotic movement, 375
three-unities, 360
three-year Cultural Revolution, 368
"through-train", 648
Tiananmen counter-revolutionary incident, 452
Tiananmen incident, 453
Tiananmen massacre, 452
Tiananmen revolutionary incident, 452
Tiananmen, 452
"tightening up" policy, 423
time is money, 414
to achieve the "four modernizations" is the most important politics, 417
to get rich is glorious, 105
today's world is an open world, 526
"tool" theory, 146
total negation of humanism will lead to "theocracy" and "barbarism", 462
totalitarianism, 188
trade of bureaucratic red tape, trade permits, quotas, and documents that give a company legal sanction, 299
traditional Chinese characters, 107
traditional sensitivity of Chinese society towards literary men, 658
tragedy of Mao Zedong, 261
tragedy of Zhou Yang, 668
transcendence of literature over reality, 487
transcending precedents, 29
transcending the norm, 28
transfer power to a lower level, 312
"transfer" theory, 675
transfer to a lower level, 522
transferring cadres to the lower levels, 135
transition in poverty to a higher stage, 310
treasured red books, 175
trilogy of loosening up, tightening up, and punishing, 127
tripartite division of legislature, administration, and judiciary, 369
triumphant fleeing from home, 409
truth, goodness, and beauty, 628
truthfulness is the lifeblood of art, 628
truthfulness of the historical background, 233
truthfulness, compassion, forbearance, 628
try to establish a relationship with sb; cotton up to, 226
"Tsar" of Chinese literary and art circles, the, 496
tune-changers, 129
turning spiritual strength into material strength, 218
twelve major relationships, 410
twelve-Year Work Program, 410
twenty-first century will be the Chinese century, the, 100
Twenty-three Articles, 98
two appraisals, 241
two basic points, 241
two camps, 239
two Chinas, 244
two civilizations, 242
two combine into one, 162
"two Cultural Revolutions" theory, 241
two generations of poets, 239
two historic leaps in the integration of Marxism-Leninism with China's reality, 260
two historic leaps, 238
two kinds of contradiction with different natures, 244
two legacies of the human race in the twentieth century, 99
two main schools of reportage literature in the early stage of the new period, 560

two major currents in Red Guard movement, 181
two meanings of freedom, 688
two meanings of humanism, 335
two newspapers and one journal, 246
two opposing views about reform, 246
two participations, one change, and three combinations, 246
"two points" theory, 246
"two poles" pattern, 247
"two states in one nation" theory, 588
"two states" theory, 247
two telling blows to literary and art circles, 94
two themes of today's world, 63
two threads of the literature of the new period, 559
two whatevers, 240
"two-in-one" combination creative method, 247
two-year Cultural Revolution, 247
typical characters in typical circumstances, 85
typical circumstances are not the "epitome" of an entire social life, 86

U.S. "three-nos" Taiwan policy, 270
ultimate concern, 666
ultra-Left, 189
ultra-Right, 189
ultra-stable structure of Chinese feudal society, 653
uncapped Rightist, 461
uncapped Rightist, 625
undue broadening of the scope of the anti-Rightist struggle, 114
undue broadening of the scope of the anti-Rightist struggle, 126
unearthed cultural relic, 39
unhealthy tendencies, 26
uninterrupted revolution, 25
unit, 147
United Task Fleet, 238
united front of people's democracy, 342
united front, 456
uniting with, educating, and remolding intellectuals, 460
unity between Party spirit and affinity to the people, 345
unity of life and art, 409
unity of patriotism and internationalism, 2
unity of patriotism and socialism, 2
unity of the arts-politics relationship, the, 502
unity—criticism—unity, 461
universal human nature, 303
universal nature of human rights, 302
universal nature of human rights, 348
universality and absoluteness of contradiction, the, 261
unofficial magazines, 278
unwaveringly adhere to the basic line for one hundred years, 187
uphold and improve Party leadership, 195
upholding activation of the economy as a domestic policy and the open door as a foreign policy, 95
upstarts, 52
upstarts, 57
upsurge in economic construction is bound to be followed by an upsurge of construction in the cultural sphere, an, 443
urban people's communes, 32
use of the novel for anti-Party activities is quite an invention, 236
use private influence to achieve one's end, 696
use upper-level influence to achieve one's end, 696
using, restricting, and transforming, 237

vanguard fiction, 523
vertical leadership, 455
veteran Red Guards, 227
vicious circle, 97
view about heroes creating history, 614
virtue-eulogists, 137
virtue-praising literature, 137

walk on two legs, 247
walking on one leg, 596
Wang Shuo craze, 463
Wang Shuo phenomenon, 463
war between the Red and the Black, 175
watch out for the Right, but mainly defend against the "Left", 584
watched too closely, literature and art have no hope, 155
waving the "red flag" to oppose the red flag, 47
we are determined to liberate Taiwan, 593
we cannot do without number nine, 227
weeding through the old to bring forth the new, 461
Wei Jingsheng incident, 470
were it not for Chairman Mao there would be no New China, 268

were it not for the Communist Party there would be no New China, 267
Western learning, 520
Western values, 520
Western-centrism, 520
wherever there are masses of people, they are invariably divided into the Left, the middle, and the Right, 107
white, 13
white and expert, 14
white terror, 13
whole country is red, the, 314
whole nation should learn from the Liberation Army, the, 313
wholesale Westernization, 317
"Wild Lily" incident, 586
wind, 129
window for reform, 132
wise leader, 612
with the skin gone, to what can the hair attach itself?, 300
with you in charge, I am at ease, 289
withdraw to the "second line", 461
without democracy there will be no modernization, 268
without democracy there will be no socialism, 268
without destruction there is no construction, 23
without development there will no true stability, 267
without freedom of speech there will be no thought-emancipation, 269
without justice, there will be no market economy, 267
without Mao Zedong Thought, the CCP would not exist, 268
without political reforms economic reforms will not succeed, 270
without socialist humanism, there will be no socialism, 269
without stability, nothing can be achieved, 269
without tears there will be no profound literature, 269
women hold up half the sky, 131
women with bound feet, 533
work method of "playing the piano", the, 449
working class must exercise leadership in everything, the, 146
working men have no country, the, 146
world outlook, 421
world revolution, 418
worst famine, the, 47
writing about reality, 535
write about the dark side, 535
write about the developing trend, 535
write about the struggle against capitalist-roaders, 535
write about the "thirteen years", 535
writer's sense of social responsibility, a, 701
writer's subjectivity, 700
writers are engineers of the human soul, 700
writers of the third generation, 80

Xidan Democracy Wall, 520
Xinqiao conference, 553

Ye Jianying's nine principles, 586
year of concepts, 155
year of great order, 59
year of methodology, 126
year of style, 487
Yellow River civilization, 185
yellow civilization, 185
yellow earth civilization, 186
Yu Luoke incident, 622

Zhang Bojun and Luo Longji alliance, 626
Zhao Dan testament, 626
Zhou Yang trilogy, 668
Zhuozhou conference, 675
zones where goods are processed for export, 39
Zunyi conference, 699
Zunyi conference of the socialist period, 393